Who's Who
in Biblical
Studies and
Archaeology

Who's Who
in Biblical Studies and Archaeology

Second Edition
1993

Biblical Archaeology Society

About the
Biblical Archaeology Society

The **Biblical Archaeology Society (BAS)**, publisher of this
volume, is also the publisher of **Biblical Archaeology
Review** and **Bible Review**, the largest circulation
magazines in their fields.

A nondenominational, charitable organization created
in 1974, the **Biblical Archaeology Society** supports the
preservation of excavated archaeological sites, conducts
travel/study programs, awards biennial citations to the
best publications in the field (**BAS** Publication Awards),
publishes major slide sets (Biblical Archaeology, Jerusalem
Archaeology, New Testament Archaeology, Egypt-Sinai-Negev,
Galilee Archaeology, Archaeology and Religion, Mesopotamia)
and books, and distributes replicas of important archaeological
finds often otherwise unavailable.

Introduction

The Biblical Archaeology Society is pleased to present to the profession and to the reference world the second edition of *Who's Who in Biblical Studies and Archaeology*, a compilation of women and men of superior achievement and status who are devoting their professional lives to helping the world better understand the Bible.

The first edition appeared in 1986. We hoped to publish the second edition two years later. That we did not will come as no surprise in the world of archaeology and the Bible. Things always take longer than we think they will. The delay, however, allows us to ruminate briefly on the burgeoning interest in our field, not only in academia, but among the public at large. In looking at the first edition of this work, I noticed that the abbreviation listing did not include **Bible Review**. It barely existed at that time. Today it has over 50,000 subscribers. **Biblical Archaeology Review** has over 200,000 subscribers. Over 7,000 scholars now attend the annual joint meeting of the Society of Biblical Literature, the American Academy of Religion and the American Schools of Oriental Research. And, finally, as I write, a new international organization, the Association of Bible Teachers, has been formed for teachers of Bible in high schools, religious schools, adult education groups and other informal non-university settings.

For all of these people, this volume will be an indispensable resource. It will also be useful to students, foundations, universities and colleges, governments and journalists.

The first edition of this book included around 1,500 listings. This edition contains almost 2,000, some indication of the growth of the field.

In most cases the individuals whose biographies are included here have themselves provided the data. If selected for publication, a pre-proof copy of the sketch was sent to the biographee for review before putting it into final form. The corrected sketch was then sent to the printer to become part of history.

In some few cases, we have had to obtain the material from other sources. We have taken every precaution to be accurate. But we know that in some instances, inevitably, we have failed. Please let us know of any errors, so they can be corrected in future editions.

Anyone who notices an omitted name that should have been included—whether it be yourself or someone else—please send us such individual's name and address so it can be included in subsequent editions. Our address is 3000 Connecticut Avenue, N.W., Suite 300, Washington, D.C. 20008.

In addition to the listings, this volume also includes two indexes, one that lists biographees by geographical location and a second that lists them by areas of specialization.

It is my pleasant duty to acknowledge the contribution of Carol Andrews, Ilana Berenbaum, Hillary Black, Robin Cather, Cynthia Chason, Thomas DePaul, Marissa Feinsilver, Katie Goldstein, Priscilla Huff, Tina Kent, Jonathan Laden, Simone Ledeen, Kathy Long, Margaret Owen, Emily Piper, Barak Weinstein and Susi White in collecting the data. Most especially I acknowledge the thoroughness of Laurie Andrews, the diligence of Judy Horowitz and Sean O'Brien, and the dedication of project manager Judy Wohlberg and publisher Susan Laden. Their combined commitment turned the data into this book.

Hershel Shanks   Biblical Archaeology Society
President   Washington, D.C.
September 1993

Contents

Abbreviations

PUBLICATIONS AND PROFESSIONAL ORGANIZATIONS

AAJR	American Academy for Jewish Research
AAR	American Academy of Religion
AAS	American Archaeological Society
AASOR	*Annual of the ASOR*
AB	Anchor Bible
ABD	*Anchor Bible Dictionary*
ACOR	American Center for Oriental Research
AH	Academy of Homiletics
AIA	Archaeological Institute of America
AJS	Association for Jewish Studies
ANRW	*Aufstieg und Niedergang der römische Welt*
AOS	American Oriental Society
APA	American Philological Association
ASOR	American Schools of Oriental Research
ASSR	American Society for the Study of Religion
ATANT	Abhandlungen zur Theologie des Alten und Neuen Testaments
ATR	*Anglican Theological Review*
AUSS	*Andrews University Seminary Studies*
BA	*Biblical Archaeologist*
BAR	*Biblical Archaeology Review*
BAS	Biblical Archaeology Society
BASOR	*Bulletin of the American Schools of Oriental Research*
BASORSup	BASOR Supplemental Series
BETL	Bibliotheca ephemeridum theologicarum lovaniensium
BHT	*Beiträge zur historischen Theologie*
BI	*Biblical Illustrator*
BIA	British Institute of Archaeology
BJRL	*Bulletin of the John Rylands Library*
BR	*Bible Review*
BS	*Bibliotheca Sacra*
BSA	British School of Archaeology
BT	*Bible Translator*
BTB	*Biblical Theology Bulletin*
BZ	*Biblische Zeitschrift*
BZAW	Beihefte zur Zeitschrift für die alttestamentliche Wissenschaft
BZNW	Beihefte zur Zeitschrift für die neutestamentliche Wissenschaft

CAH	*Cambridge Ancient History*
CAS	Catholic Archaeological Society
CBA	Catholic Biblical Association
CBQ	*Catholic Biblical Quarterly*
CSBR	Chicago Society for Biblical Research
CSBS	Canadian Society for Biblical Studies
CSSR	Canadian Society for the Study of Religion
CTSA	Catholic Theological Society of America
EAEHL	*Encyclopedia of Archaeological Excavations in the Holy Land*
EJ	*Encyclopaedia Judaica*
EQ	*Evangelical Quarterly*
EstBib	*Estudios biblicos*
EstEcl	*Estudios eclesiásticos*
ET	*Evangelische Theologie*
ETL	*Ephemerides theologicae lovanienses*
ETR	*Etudes théologiques et religieuses*
ETS	Evangelical Theological Society
ExpTim	*Expository Times*
FRLANT	Forschungen zur Religion und Literatur des Alten und Neuen Testaments
HAR	*Hebrew Annual Review*
HDR	Harvard Dissertations in Religion
HSM	Harvard Semitic Monographs
HSS	Harvard Semitic Studies
HTR	*Harvard Theological Review*
HTS	*Harvard Theological Studies*
HUCA	*Hebrew Union College Annual*
IACS	International Association for Coptic Studies
IBR	Institute for Biblical Research
IDB	*Interpreter's Dictionary of the Bible*
IEJ	*Israel Exploration Journal*
IES	Israel Exploration Society
IOSCS	International Organization for Septuagint and Cognate Studies
IOSOT	International Organization for the Study of the Old Testament
ISBE	*International Standard Bible Encyclopedia*
ISBR	Israel Society for Biblical Research
JAAR	*Journal of the American Academy of Religion*
JANES	*Journal of the Ancient Near Eastern Society*
JAOS	*Journal of the American Oriental Society*
JBL	*Journal of Biblical Literature*
JCS	*Journal of Cuneiform Studies*
JEH	*Journal of Ecclesiastical History*
JES	*Journal of Ecumenical Studies*
JETS	*Journal of the Evangelical Theological Society*
JJS	*Journal of Jewish Studies*
JNES	*Journal of Near Eastern Studies*
JNSL	*Journal of Northwest Semitic Languages*
JQR	*Jewish Quarterly Review*
JR	*Journal of Religion*

JSJ	*Journal for the Study of Judaism*
JSNT	*Journal for the Study of the New Testament*
JSNTSup	JSNT Supplemental Series
JSOT	*Journal for the Study of the Old Testament*
JSOTSup	JSOT Supplemental Series
JSP	*Journal for the Study of the Pseudepigrapha*
JSPSup	JSP Supplemental Series
JSS	*Journal of Semitic Studies*
JTS	*Journal of Theological Studies*
NABI	National Association of Biblical Instructors
NABPR	National Association of Baptist Professors of Religion
NAPH	National Association of Professors of Hebrew
NAPS	North American Patristic Society
NEAS	Near Eastern Archaeological Society
NEH	National Endowment for the Humanities
NRT	*La nouvelle revue théologique*
NT	*Novum Testamentum*
NTS	*New Testament Studies*
NTSUP	Novum Testamentum Supplemental Series
OS	*Oudtestamentische Studiën*
PEF	Palestine Exploration Fund
PEQ	*Palestine Exploration Quarterly*
PES	Palestine Exploration Society
RA	*Revue d'assyriologie et d'archéologie orientale*
RB	*Revue biblique*
RivB	*Rivista biblica*
RPh	*Revue de Philologie*
RQ	*Revue de Qumran*
RSR	*Recherches de science religieuse*
RSRev	*Religious Studies Review*
RTL	*Revue théologique de Louvain*
SANT	Studien zum Alten und Neuen Testaments
SBL	Society of Biblical Literature
SBLSBS	SBL Sources for Biblical Studies
SBLSCS	SBL Septuagint and Cognate Studies
SBR	Society for Biblical Research
SBS	Society of Biblical Studies
SC	*Second Century*
SEA	*Svensk exegetisk arsbok*
SJT	*Scottish Journal of Theology*
SNTC	Studiorum Novi Testamenti Coventus
SNTS	Studiorum Novi Testamenti Societas
SOTS	Society for Old Testament Study
SST	Society for the Study of Theology
SUNT	Studien zur Umwelt des Neuen Testament
TB	*Tyndale Bulletin*
ThHK	*Theologischer Handkommentar zum Neuen Testament mit Text und Paraphrase*
TLZ	*Theologische Literaturzeitung*

TR	*Theologische Rundschau*
TZ	*Theologische Zeitschrift*
UF	*Ugarit-Forschungen*
VC	*Vigiliae Christianae*
VT	*Vetus Testamentum*
VTSup	VT Supplemental Series
WMANT	Wissenschaftliche Monographien zum Alten und Neuen Testaments
WTJ	*Wesleyan Theological Journal*
WTS	Wesleyan Theological Society
WUJS	World Union of Jewish Studies
WUNT	Wissenschaftliche Untersuchungen zum Neuen Testament
ZA	*Zeitschrift für Assyriologie*
ZAW	*Zeitschrift für die alttestamentliche Wissenschaft*
ZDPV	*Zeitschrift des deutschen Palästina-Vereins*
ZNW	*Zeitschrift für die Neutestamentliche Wissenschaft*
ZTK	*Zeitschrift für Theologie und Kirche*

GENERAL ABBREVIATIONS

AB	Alberta	coll.	college
acad.	academy, academic	com.	committee
adj.	adjunct	comm.	commentary
admn.	administrator	commn.	commission
adv.	advisory	conf.	conference
affil.	affiliated, affiliation	cons.	consultant
AL, Ala.	Alabama	contb.	contributor
Amer.	America	coord.	coordinator
anc.	ancient	coun.	council
ann.	annual	crit.	criticism, critical
anthrop.	anthropology	CT, Conn.	Connecticut
antiq.	antiquity	ct.	court
apptd.	appointed	ctr.	center
AR, Ark.	Arkansas	cur.	curator
arch.	archaeology, archaeologist	curr.	curriculum
assn.	association	d.	daughter
assoc.	associate	DC, D.C.	District of Columbia
asst.	assistant	DE, Del.	Delaware
auth.	author	dec.	deceased
aux.	auxiliary	dept.	department
awd.	award	dict.	dictionary
AZ, Ariz.	Arizona	dip.	diploma
b.	born	dir.	director
Bapt.	Baptist	diss.	dissertation
BC	British Columbia	disting.	distinguished
bd.	board	div.	divinity, division
bibl.	biblical	doc.	doctoral, doctorate
bldg.	building	Dr.	Doctor
Brit.	British	E	east
bull.	bulletin	east.	eastern
bur.	bureau	eccles.	ecclesiastical
CA, Calif.	California	ed.	edition, editor
Cath.	Catholic	educ.	education
cen.	central	ency.	encyclopedia
cert.	certificate, certification	evang.	evangelical
ch.	church	exam.	examination
chap.	chapter	excvn.	excavation
chmn.	chairman	exec.	executive
civ.	civilization	expdn.	expedition
class.	classical, classics	fac.	faculty
CO, Colo.	Colorado	fedn.	federation

fellow.	fellowship	**MT, Mont.**	Montana
fgn.	foreign	**mus.**	museum
FL, Fla.	Florida	**N**	north
found.	foundation	**natl.**	national
GA, Ga.	Georgia	**NB**	New Brunswick
gen.	general	**NC, N.C.**	North Carolina
geog.	geography, geographic	**ND, N.Dak.**	North Dakota
grad.	graduate	**NE**	northeast, northeastern
habil.	habilitation	**NE, Nebr.**	Nebraska
HI	Hawaii	**NF**	Newfoundland
hist.	history, historic, historian	**NH, N.H.**	New Hampshire
hon.	honorary	**NJ, N.J.**	New Jersey
hum.	humanities	**NM, N.Mex.**	New Mexico
IA	Iowa	**north.**	northern
ID	Idaho	**NS**	Nova Scotia
IL, Ill.	Illinois	**NT**	New Testament
IN, Ind.	Indiana	**NV, Nev.**	Nevada
inst.	institute	**NW**	northwest, northwestern
instr.	instructor	**NY, N.Y.**	New York
intl.	international	**OH**	Ohio
intro.	introduction	**OK, Okla.**	Oklahoma
jour.	journal	**ON**	Ontario
jr.	junior	**OR, Oreg.**	Oregon
KS, Kans.	Kansas	**ord.**	ordination
KY, Ky.	Kentucky	**orgn.**	organization
LA, La.	Louisiana	**OT**	Old Testament
lang.	language	**PA, Pa.**	Pennsylvania
lbrn.	librarian	**phil.**	philosophy, philosophical
lect.	lecture, lecturer	**philol.**	philology, philological
lib.	library	**PO**	Post Office
lic.	license, licentia	**pont.**	pontifical
lit.	literature	**PR, P.R.**	Puerto Rico
Luth.	Lutheran	**prelim.**	preliminary
m.	married	**pres.**	president
MA, Mass.	Massachusetts	**Presbyn.**	Presbyterian
mag.	magazine	**prin.**	principal
Man.	Manitoba	**proc.**	proceedings
MD, Md.	Maryland	**prof.**	professor
ME	Maine	**prog.**	program
mem.	member	**prov.**	provincial
Meth.	Methodist	**publ.**	publisher, publication
MI, Mich.	Michigan	**quar.**	quarterly
midW	midwest, midwestern	**Que.**	Quebec
min.	minister	**ref.**	reference
MN, Minn.	Minnesota	**reg.**	region
MO, Mo.	Missouri	**relig.**	religion
mon.	monograph	**rep.**	representative
MS, Miss.	Mississippi	**res.**	research

Rev.	Reverend
rev.	review, revised
RI, R.I.	Rhode Island
S	south
SC, S.C.	South Carolina
sch.	school
schol.	scholar
sci.	science
SD, S.Dak.	South Dakota
SE	southeast, southeastern
sec.	secretary
sect.	section
sem.	seminary
ser.	series
SK	Saskatchewan
soc.	society
south.	southern
sr.	senior
St.	saint
stand.	standard
stud.	studies
sup.	supplement
supr.	supervisor
SW	southwest, southwestern
tchr.	teacher
theol.	theology
TN, Tenn.	Tennessee
trans.	translated
TX, Tex.	Texas
U.	university
U.P.	university press
UT	Utah
VA, Va.	Virginia
ver.	version
vis.	visiting
vol.	volume
V.P.	vice president
VT, Vt.	Vermont
W	west
WA, Wash.	Washington
west.	western
WI, Wis.	Wisconsin
WV, W.Va.	West Virginia
WY, Wyo.	Wyoming
YK	Yukon Territory

Biographies

AAGESON, James W., b. Havre, MT, November 24, 1947, s. of Eugene & Laura, m. Julie Kristine, chil: Erin Kristine; Anne Elizabeth; Megan Kathleen. Educ: Pacific Luth. U., BA 1970; Luther NW Theol. Sem., MDiv 1976; Union Theol. Sem., ThM 1977; Oxford U., England, PhD 1984. Emp: 1977-80, 1984-85 Parish Pastor; Concordia Coll., 1985-91 Asst. Prof., 1992- Assoc. Prof., NT. Spec: New Testament. Pub: *Written Also for Our Sake: Paul and the Art of Biblical Interpretation* (1993); "Typology, Correspondence, and the Application of Scripture in Romans 9-11" *JSNT* (1987); "Scripture and Structure in the Development of the Argument in Romans 9-11" *CBQ* (1986); and others. Mem: SBL; CBA; MidW Jewish Stud. Assn. Rec: Travel, photography, basketball. Addr: (o) Concordia College, Dept. of Religion, Moorhead, MN 56562 218-299-3435; (h) 606 S 6th St., Moorhead, MN 56560 218-233-7374.

ABEGG, Martin G., Jr., b. Peoria, IL, March 6, 1950, s. of Martin G. & Barbara C., m. Susan H., chil: Stephanie Marie; Jennifer Mae. Educ: Bradley U., BS 1972; NW Bapt. Sem., MDiv 1983; Hebrew Union Coll.-Jewish Inst. of Relig., MPhil 1990, PhD 1993. Emp: NW Bapt. Sem., 1982-84 Instr.; Comprehensive Aramaic Lexicon, 1988-91 Res. Fellow; U. of Cincinnati, 1990-91 Adj. Prof.; Grace Theol. Sem., 1992- Assoc. Prof., OT. Spec: Hebrew Bible, Semitic Languages, Texts and Epigraphy, Apocrypha and Post-biblical Studies. Pub: *A Preliminary Edition of the Unpublished Dead Sea Scrolls*, co-auth., vol. 1-2 (BAS, 1991-1992); "The Fragmentary Remains of 11QTorah (Temple Scroll): 11QT^b, 11QT^c, and 4QparaTorah" *HUCA* 67. Mem: NAPH; SBL. Rec: Backpacking & camping, technical rock climbing, gardening. Addr: (o) 200 Seminary Dr., Winona Lake, IN 46590 219-372-5100; (h) 2701 Jean St., Winona Lake, IN 46590 219-267-4967.

ABRAHAMSEN, Valerie A., b. Norwood, MA, October 5, 1954, d. of Frederick Henry & Ruth Eleanor (Pierce). Educ: U. of S.C., BA (magna cum laude) 1975; Harvard Div. Sch., MTS 1979, ThD 1986. Spec: Archaeology, New Testament. Pub: "Pagan Funerary Practices in Northern Greece During the Early Christian Era" *Macedonian Stud.* 6/1 (1989); "Christianity and the Rock Reliefs at Philippi" *BA* 51/1 (1988); and others. Awd: Harvard Div. Sch., Pfeiffer Fellow. 1979, 1980. Mem: SBL 1978-; AIA 1990-. Rec: Music, photography. Addr: (h) 90 Bacon St. #5, Waltham, MA 02154 617-899-2727.

ACKERMAN, James, b. Berwyn, IL, August 19, 1956. Educ: Northwestern U., BA 1955; Union Theol. Sem., MDiv 1959; Harvard U., ThD, OT 1966. Emp: Stillman Coll., 1962-66 Instr. of Relig.; Conn. Coll., 1966-69 Asst. Prof., 1969-76 Assoc. Prof.; Ind. U., 1976- Prof. of Relig., 1977- Assc. Dean of Arts & Sci. Spec: New Testament. Pub: *An Introduction to New Testament Literature*, co-auth. (Abingdon, 1978); *The Bible as/in Literature* (Scott-Foresman, 1976); *Biblical Images in Literature* (1975); "Prophecy and Warfare in Early Israel: A Study of the Deborah-Barak Story" *BASOR* (1975); *The Bible in Literature Series: Literature Interpretation of Biblical Narratives*, 5 vols., co-ed. (Abingdon, 1974); *Teaching the Old Testament in English Classes* (Ind. U., 1973); "The Rabbinic Interpretation of Psalm 82 and the Gospel of John" *HTS* (1966); and others. Mem: SBL; Colloquium OT Res.; AAR; ASOR. Addr: (o) Indiana U., Dept. of Religious Studies, Sycamore Hall 230, Bloomington, IN 47405 812-855-3555.

ADAM, Andrew K. M., b. Boston, MA, September 10, 1957, s. of Donald G. & Nancy Tuttle, m. Margaret (Bamforth), chil: Nathaniel Emerson; Josiah Pennington. Educ: Bowdoin

Coll., BA 1979; Yale Div. Sch., MDiv 1986, STM 1987; Duke U., PhD 1991. Emp: Eckerd Coll., 1990- Asst. Prof., Relig. Stud. Spec: New Testament. Pub: "The Future of Our Allusions" in *SBL 1992 Seminar Papers* (1992); "The Sign of Jonah: A Fish-Eye View" *Semeia* 51 (1991); "Biblical Theology and the Problem of Modernity: Von Wrederstrasse zu Sackgasse" *Horizons in Bibl. Theol.* 12/1 (1990). Awd: James B. Duke Fellow 1987-89; Episcopal Ch. Found. Fellow 1987-90. Mem: SBL; CBA. Rec: Post-structuralist theory, basketball, James Joyce, computer typography. Addr: (o) Eckerd College/LTR, 4200 54th Ave. S, St. Petersburg, FL 33711 813-864-8277; (h) 3775 40th Ln. S, #76-G, St. Petersburg, FL 33711 813-867-2064.

ADAMO, David T., b. Irunda-Isanlu, Nigeria, January 5, 1949, s. of Atesogun & Osayomi. Educ: South. Meth. U., MTh 1980; Indiana Christian U., Rel.D 1983; Baylor U., PhD, OT 1986. Emp: Titcome Coll., Nigeria, 1977-78 Instr. of Econ. & Relig.; Paul Quinn Coll., 1983-86, Prof.; Delta State U., 1987- Prof. Spec: Archaeology, Hebrew Bible. Pub: "The Question of Africa and Genesis 2:10-14" *Jour. of Relig. Thought;* "The African Queen: An Examination of I Kings 10:1-13" *Jour. of Arabic & Relig. Stud.* (1990); "Understanding Genesis Creation Account in An African Background" *Carribean Jour. of Relig. Stud.* 10/2 (Sept. 1989); "The African Wife of Moses" *African Theol. Jour.* 18/3 (1989); "The Problem of Translating the Hebrew Old Testament Book Titles into Yoruba Language of Nigeria" *BT* (1984); and others. Mem: AAR; SBL; ASOR; Amer. Missiological Soc.; NAPH. Rec: Soccer. Addr: (o) Delta State University, Dept. of Religion, Abraka, Delta State, Nigeria 054-66009.

ADAMS, Douglas G., b. De Kalb, IL, April 12, 1945, s. of Glenn & Harriet, m. Margo Alice. Educ: Duke U., BA 1967; Pacific Sch. of Relig., MA 1970, MDiv 1970; Grad. Theol. Union, ThD 1974. Emp: U. of Mont., 1975-76 Asst. Prof.; Pacific Sch. Relig., 1976- Prof.; Grad. Theol. Union, 1977- Doctoral Faculty, 1980-82 Chmn.; U. Houston, 1986 Vis. Prof.; West. Wash. U., 1980 NEH Lect. Spec: Hebrew Bible, New Testament. Pub: "Theological Expressions Through Visual Arts Forms" in *Art, Creativity and the Sacred* (Crossroads, 1984); "Biblical Criteria in Dance: Dance as Prophetic Form" *Relig. & Dance* (Natl. Dance. Assoc., 1982); "Meaning with the Arts" *Studia Mystica* (1978); and others. Awd: 3rd Intl. Cong. on Relig., Architecture and the Arts, 1973 Overseas Fellow; Smithsonian Post-Doc. Fellow 1974-75. Mem: AAR 1974-; Soc. for the Arts, Relig. & Contemporary Culture 1985-; N Amer. Acad. of Liturgy 1976-. Addr: (o) Pacific School of Religion, 1798 Scenic Ave., Berkeley, CA 94709 415-848-0528; (h) 6226 Bernhard, Richmond, CA 94805 415-237-2878.

ADAMS, William J., Jr., b. Cincinnati, OH, May 14, 1938, s. of William J. & Eleanor (Burley), m.

Florence Ann (Yokom), chil: Cynthia; Beth Ann; W. Jared; Thomas. Educ: Brigham Young U., BS 1964; Hebrew Union Coll., MA 1971; U. of Utah, PhD 1987. Emp: Brigham Young U., 1970-73 Instr., Semitic Lang.; Davis & Elkins Coll., 1973-80 Lect.; U. of Utah, 1980- Assoc. Lect. Excv: Tell-Qarqur, Syria, 1984 Epigrapher. Spec: Hebrew Bible, Semitic Languages, Texts and Epigraphy. Pub: "Diachronic Development of Narrative and Exhortation Discourse Structures in Hebrew Epigraphical Sources" in *SBL Seminar Papers* (1984); *The Code of Hammurabi: A Structured Approach to the Akkadian Language* (U. of Utah, 1981); *Authenticating and Deciphering Inscriptions* (Soc. for Early Hist. Arch., 1978); "A Computer Generated Technique for Dating Biblical Passages," co-auth. *Hebrew Computational Linguistics* 11 (1977); "Archaeological and Cryptological Analyses of the Manti Inscriptions," co-auth. *Utah Hist. Quar.* 44 (1976); and others. Awd: Hebrew Union Coll., Dr. David Lefkowitz Interfaith Fellow. 1966-68; U. of Utah, Grad. Res. Fellow. 1982-83; Intl. Biographical Ctr., England, Intl. Man of the Year 1992. Mem: NAPH 1970-; Soc. for Early Hist. Arch. 1973-; SBL 1978-. Rec: Archery, rifle, backpacking. Addr: (h) 1412 Sudbury Ave., Salt Lake City, UT 84093 801-566-7658.

ADAMSON, James B., b. Scotland, August 1, 1924, s. of James & Isabella, m. Jean M.M., chil: Fiona B.; Jennifer B.; Wendy S. Educ: Edinburgh U., Scotland, MA, BD; Cambridge U., England, PhD. Emp: St. Cuthberts Parish Ch., Scotland; Wilson Parish Ch., Scotland; First Presbyn. Ch., Santa Rosa, Calif. Spec: New Testament. Pub: *James: The Man and His Message* (Eerdmans, 1989); *The Epistle of James*, New Intl. Comm. of the NT (1977). Mem: SNTS 1954-. Rec: Golf, fishing, tennis. Addr: (h) 1808 Calavaras Dr., Santa Rosa, CA 95405 707-527-5480.

ADLER, Stephen J., b. Philadelphia, PA, February 17, 1941, s. of Sol & Rhoda, m. Ruth (Ziff), chil: Jay; Eitan; Noam; Chanan; Shmuel. Educ: Cornell U., BS 1962; Columbia U., School of Law, JD 1965. Emp: Natl. Labor Court of Israel, Judge, Deputy Pres.; *Labor Law Ann. Jour.,* 1991-92 Ed. Spec: Archaeology. Pub: "The Temple Mount in Court" *BAR* 17/5 (1991); and others. Mem: Israel Numismatic Soc. 1980-; Amer. Numismatic Soc. 1981-; Brit. Numismatic Soc. 1981-. Rec: Archaeology, anc. ceramic oil lamps, Hebrew Bible. Addr: (o) National Labor Court, PO Box 1328, Jerusalem 91013, Israel 02-829235; (h) Plugat HaKotel 11/5, Jerusalem 97500, Israel 02-281257.

AEJMELAEUS, Anneli P. M., b. Mikkeli, Finland, September 18, 1948, d. of Aimo & Ester Halonen, m. Lars Aejmelaeus, chil: Laura; Sylva. Educ: U. of Helsinki, BD 1972, DD 1983. Emp: Acad. of Finland, 1981-90 Younger Schol.; U. of Helsinki, 1983- Docent, OT Exegesis; U. of Gottingen, 1991- Prof., OT. Spec: Hebrew Bible.

Pub: "Translation Technique and the Intention of the Translator" *SCS* 31 (1991); "What Can We Know about the Hebrew *Vorlage* of the Septuagint?" *ZAW* 99 (1987); "Function and Interpretation of *ki* in Biblical Hebrew" *JBL* 105 (1986); *The Traditional Prayer in the Psalms*, BZAW 167 (1986); "ÓTI *causale* in Septuagintal Greek" in *La Septuaginta en la investigacion le contemporanea* (Biblia Poliglota Matritense, 1985); "*Participium coniunctum* as a Criterion of Translation Technique" *VT* 32 (1982); *Parataxis in the Septuagint: A Study of the Renderings of the Hebrew Coordinate Clauses in the Greek Pentateuch*, Annales Acad. Sci. Fennicae B Diss. 31 (1982); and others. Mem: SBL 1984-; IOSCS 1974-; Finnish Exegetical Soc. 1982-; Acad. Sci. Fennica 1992-. Rec: Picking berries and mushrooms, cross-country skiing. Addr: (o) Theologicum, Platz der Goettinger, Sieben 2, D3400 Goettinger, Germany 49-551-397153; (h) Oraskatu 3 C 26, SF-05880 Hyvinkaa 8, Finland 358-14-89280.

AEJMELAEUS, Lars J. T., b. Kauhajoki, Finland, July 21, 1945, s. of Lars & Salme, m. Anneli, chil: Laura; Sylva. Educ: U. of Helsinki, BD 1969, DD 1980. Emp: U. of Helsinki, 1980- Prof. NT Exegetics. Spec: New Testament. Pub: *Streit und Versohnung. Das Problem der Zusammensetzung des 2. Korintherbriefes* (1987); *Die Rezeption der Paulusbriefe in der Miletrede (Apg 20:18-35)*, Annales Acad. Scientiarum Fennicae B/232 (1987); *Wachen vor dem Ende. Die traditionsgeschichtlichen Wurzeln von 1. Thess 5:1-11 und Luk 21:34-36* (1985); and others. Awd: World Coun. of Ch. Fellow. 1975-77. Mem: SNTS 1982-; Finnish Exegetical Soc., V.P. 1985-. Addr: (o) Dept. of Exegetics, Neitsytpolku 1 B, SF-00140 Helsinki 14, Finland; (h) Oraskatu 3 C 26, SF-05880 Hyvinkaa 8, Finland.

AGUIRRE, Rafael, b. Bilbao, Spain, September 29, 1941, s. of Fidencio & Amalia. Educ: Gregoriana U., Rome, Lic. Theol. 1966; Pont. Bibl. Inst., Rome, Lic. 1971; Ecole Biblique, Jerusalem, Eleve Titulaire 1972; U. de Salamanca, ThD 1977; U. de Barcelona, Lic. Filologie Semitica 1975. Emp: U. de Deusto, Catedratico, Bibl. Stud.; *EstBib*, 1989- Ed. Spec: New Testament. Pub: *Evangelios Sinópticos y Hechos de los Apóstoles*, co-auth. (1992); "Pedro en el evangelio de Mateo" *EstBib* 47 *(1989); La Iglesia de Jerusalén* (1989); "La evolución de la iglesia primitiva a la luz de los códigos domésticos" in *Simposio Biblico Espanol* II (1987); *Del Movimiento de Jesus a la Iglesia cristiana* (1987); "La mujer en el cristianismo primitivo" *Iglesia Viva* (1986); "El método sociológico en los estudios biblicos" *EstEcl* 60 (1985); "La casa como estructura base del cristianismo primitivo" *EstEcl* 59 (1984); *Exégesis de Mateo 27,51b-53: Para una teologia de la muerte de Jesus en el evangelio de Mateo* (1980); and others. Mem: SNTS; Assn. Bibl. Espanola, Pres. 1989-. Addr: (h) Barraincura 16, 5, 48009 Bilbao, Spain 94-423-2488.

AHITUV, Shmuel, b. Tel Aviv, Israel, February 6, 1935, s. of Avigdor & Leah (Rosenbaum), m. Erella, chil: Hadas; Ilan. Educ: Hebrew U., BA 1960, MA 1967, PhD 1979. Emp: Bialik Inst., 1962-1982 Ed., *The Hebrew Biblical Ency. (Ency. Miqra'it)*, 1982- Gen. Ed., Ency. Miqra'it Lib. Ser.; Hebrew U., 1974-1984 Lect.; Ben Gurion U., 1984- Assoc. Prof., Coord. of Bibl. Stud.; *Mikra Leyisrael*, 1985- Ed. Spec: Hebrew Bible, Semitic Languages, Texts and Epigraphy, Egyptology. Pub: "The Lost District" *Eretz-Israel* 24 (1993); *Handbook of Ancient Hebrew Inscriptions* (Bialik Inst./IES, 1992); *Biblical Israel: State and People*, co-ed. (Magness/IES, 1992); "The Laws of the Cities of Refuge" *Shnaton* 10 (1990); *The Early Biblical Period: Historical Studies*, co-ed. (IES, 1986); *Canaanite Toponyms in Ancient Egyptian Documents* (Magness/Brill, 1984); "The Lebanon, Galilee and Bashan in Topographical List of Amenhotep III" *Eretz-Israel* 15 (1981); "Economic Factors in the Egyptian Conquest of Canaan" *IEJ* 28 (1978); "Two Ammonite Inscriptions" *Cathedra* 4 (1977); and others. Awd: Warburg Prize 1971; Friends of Hebrew U., England, Abe Sherman Found. & John Goodenday Trust, Awd. Mem: IES 1969-; WUJS 1971-. Addr: (o) Ben Gurion U. of the Negev, Dept. of Bible and Ancient Near East, Beer Sheva 84105, Israel 057-461092-3-4; (h) 38, Berlin, Jerusalem 92506, Israel 02-631542.

ALDEN, Robert L., b. Brockton, MA, December 10, 1937, s. of Allen & Lona (Simon), m. Mary Jane (Hauck), chil: John; Grace Ann. Educ: Westminster Theol. Sem., BD 1962; HUC-Jewish Inst. of Relig., PhD 1966. Emp: Denver Sem., 1966- Prof., OT. Spec: Hebrew Bible. Pub: *Proverbs: A Commentary of an Ancient Book of Timeless Advice* (Baker, 1983); *Psalms: Songs of Discipleship* (Moody, 1976); *Psalms: Songs of Dedication* (Moody, 1975); and others. Mem: ETS 1959-; SBL 1962-; NEAS 1971-; Cath. Bibl. Soc. 1971-. Rec: Mountain climbing, model railroading. Addr: (o) Denver Seminary, Box 10,000 University Park Station, Denver, CO 80250-0100 303-761-2482; (h) 3575 E Arapahoe Pl., Littleton, CO 80122 303-770-2298.

ALDERINK, Larry J., b. Holland, MI, August 2, 1940, s. of John & Hazel, m. Lynda, chil: Maria Lyn; Anna Marie. Educ: Calvin Theol. Sem., BD 1965; U. of Chicago. Div. Sch., MA 1967, PhD 1974. Emp: Luth. Sch. of Theol. at Chicago, 1968 Instr.; Elmhurst Coll., 1968-69 Instr.; Concordia Coll., 1969- Prof., Relig.; Hope Coll., 1980, 1985 Vis. Lect. Spec: New Testament. Pub: "Mythical and Cosmological Structure in the *Homeric Hymn to Demeter*" *Numen* 29 (1982); *Creation and Salvation in Ancient Orphism* (Scholars, 1981); and others. Awd: Bush Fellow 1984-85. Mem: AAR 1968-; SBL 1970-; Greco-Roman Relig. Group 1981-. Addr: (o) Concordia College, Dept. of Religion, Moorhead, MN 56562 218-299-3416; (h) 819 5th Ave. S, Moorhead, MN 56560 218-236-9962.

ALEXANDER, Patrick H., b. Arkadelphia, AR, June 10, 1952, s. of Jimmie D. & Martha H., m. Donna H., chil: Courtney. Educ: Central Bible Coll., BA; Gordon-Conwell Theol. Sem., MA. Emp: Hendrickson Publ., Sr. Acad. Ed.; *Dict. of Pentecostal and Charismatic Movements,* 1988- Assoc. Ed. Spec: New Testament. Pub: "The Literary Function of Mark 6:6b-13 and Its Message to Mark's Church" *Debarim* (1982-83). Mem: SBL 1983-; CBA 1987-. Rec: Fishing, reading, music. Addr: (o) 137 Summit St., Peabody, MA 01960 508-532-6546; (h) 29 Arbor St., Wenham, MA 01984 508-468-7482.

ALEXANDER, Ralph H., b. Tyler, TX, September 3, 1936, s. of Joe & Virginia, m. Myrna, chil: David; Christina; Jonathan. Educ: Dallas Theol. Sem., ThM 1963, ThD 1968. Emp: South. Bible Training Sch., 1962-65 Instr.; Wheaton Coll., 1966-72 Asst. Prof.; West. Bapt. Sem., 1972- Prof.; Bee Intl., Advanced Training Stud., Dir. Spec: Archaeology, Hebrew Bible, Semitic Languages, Texts and Epigraphy. Pub: *Theological Wordbook of the Old Testament,* contb. (Moody, 1986); *Commentary on Ezekiel* (Moody, 1976); and others. Awd: Hebrew U., Fulbright Grant 1964-65. Mem: ETS 1967-; ASOR 1968-; SBL 1968-; NEAS 1970-; AIA 1978-. Rec: Hiking, gardening. Addr: (o) Strehlgasse 13, A-1190 Vienna, Austria; (h) Donaustrasse 93, A-3421 Hoeflein, Austria.

ALLEN, Leslie C., b. Bristol, England, December 25, 1935, s. of Bert & Dorothy, m. Elizabeth, chil: Jeremy; Miriam. Educ: Cambridge U., MA 1960; London U., PhD 1967, DD 1991. Emp: London Bible Coll., England, 1960-83 Lect., Hebrew, Aramaic, Judaism; Fuller Theol. Sem., 1983- Prof., OT. Spec: Hebrew Bible. Pub: *Ezekiel 20-48* (Word, 1990); *1, 2 Chronicles* (Word, 1987); *Psalms 101-150* (Word, 1983); *The Greek Chronicles* (Brill, 1974); "More Cuckoos in the Hebrew Nest" *JTS* 24 (1973); and others. Mem: SOTS; Tyndale Fellow.; SBL; IBR. Rec: Gardening. Addr: (o) Fuller Theological Seminary, 135 N Oakland Ave., Pasadena, CA 91182 818-584-5241; (h) 1201 Beverly Way, Altadena, CA 91001 818-798-4250.

ALLISON, Dale C., b. Wichita, KS, November 25, 1955, s. of D. Clifford, m. Kristine. Educ: Wichita State U., BA, Relig. (summa cum laude) 1977; Duke U., Grad. Sch. of Relig., MA 1979, PhD 1982. Emp: U. of N.C., 1979 Res. Asst.; Duke U., 1979-82 Res. Asst.; *The Cambridge History of Judaism,* 1979- Ed. Asst.; Tex. Christian U., Dept. of Relig., 1982 Res. Assoc.; Friends U., 1989- Res. Fellow. Spec: New Testament. Pub: "The Interpretation of the Sermon on the Mount" *SJT* 44 (1991); *An International and Critical Commentary on the Gospel According to St. Matthew,* 3 vol., co-auth. (T & T Clark, 1988-1991); "The Eye is the Lamp of the Body" *NTS* 33 (1987); "The Structure of the Sermon on the Mount" *JBL* 103 (1987); "Jesus and the Covenant" *JSNT* 29

(1987); *The End of the Ages has Come: An Early Interpretation of the Passion and Resurrection of Jesus* (Fortress, 1985); and others. Awd: Phi Beta Kappa; Phi Kappa Phi. Mem: SBL; Soc. of Neoplatonic Stud. Rec: Golf, basketball. Addr: (o) Friends U., 2100 University, Wichita, KS 67213; (h) 1633 Porter, Wichita, KS 67203 316-262-6387.

ALLISON, Robert W., b. East Hartford, CT, July 25, 1943, s. of William B. & Edith M., m. Susan G., chil: William Arthur; Richard Gregory. Educ: Brown U., BA 1965; U. of Chicago, PhD 1975. Emp: U. of Chicago, 1974-80 Lect., Classics, Asst. Cur. of Manuscripts; Bates Coll., 1980- Assoc. Prof. of Relig. Excv: Gamala, 1985 Supr. Spec: Archaeology, Hebrew Bible, New Testament, Apocrypha and Post-biblical Studies. Pub: "Let Women Be Silent in the Churches (1 Cor 14, 33b-36): What Did Paul Really Say, and What Did it Mean?"*JSNT* 32 (1988); "The Oracular Style of the Cultic Proclamations of Antiochus I of Commagene" in *SBL 1976 Seminar Papers* (1976); *New Testament Manuscript Tradition.* Awd: Mt. Athos Greek Manuscripts Catalogue Project, NEH Res. Grant 1977-80, 1990-93; Dumbarton Oaks Byzantine Studies Ctr., Summer Fellow. 1984. Mem: SBL 1974-; CSBR 1974-; Byzantine Stud. Conference. Rec: Mountain climbing & hiking, carpentry and restoration, mustangs, model railroading. Addr: (o) Bates College, Dept. of Philosophy and Religion, Lewiston, ME 04240 207-786-6307; (h) RFD #1, Box 2390, Greene, ME 04236.

ALONSO-DIAZ, José, b. Asturias, Spain, March 28, 1914, s. of Ramon & Maria. Educ: Pont. Bibl. Inst., Rome, Jerusalem, Jesuitic Formation, Bibl. Formation 1946-49. Emp: Pont. U. Comillas, Madrid, 1949-84 Prof. of Bible, 1984- Prof. Emeritus. Spec: Hebrew Bible, New Testament, Apocrypha and Post-biblical Studies. Pub: *Literatura Apocaliptica* (PPC, 1977); *Commentaries on Mark, Esther, Daniel, James, Jude* (BAC, 1970); *Evangelio y Evangelistas* (Taurus Ediciones, 1967); and others. Mem: Intl. Pont. Bib. Commn., Rome 1972-84. Addr: (o) U. Pontificia Comillas, 28049 Madrid, Spain 734-16-50.

ALSUP, John E., b. Clovis, NM, April 22, 1941, s. of Charles Clark & Florence Evelyn (Conner), m. Carole Ann (Wright), chil: Daniel John. Educ: U. of the Pacific, BA 1963; Princeton Theol. Sem., MDiv 1966; U. Muenchen, ThD 1973. Emp: Austin Presbyn. Theol. Sem., 1975- D. Thomason Prof. of NT Stud. Spec: New Testament. Pub: *Comm. on the Book of Revelation,* co-trans. (Fortress, 1993); *Comm. on First Epistle of Peter,* trans. (Eerdmans, 1993); "Imagining the New: Feminism, Galatians 3:28, and the Current Interpretive Discussion" in *God's Steadfast Love,* Festschrift for Prescott Williams, Jr. (1990); "Resurrection and Historicity" *Austin*

Sem. Bull. 103/8 (1988); articles in *Harper's Bible Dict.* (1985); *Theology of the New Testament*, 2 vol., trans. (Eerdmans, 1981, 1982); *The Post-Resurrection Appearance Stories of the Gospel Tradition—A History-of-Tradition Analysis* (1975); and others. Mem: SNTS 1976-. Rec: Breeding, training of American quarter and Tennessee walking horses. Addr: (o) Austin Presbyterian Theological Seminary, 100 E 27th St., Austin, TX 78705 512-472-6736; (h) Rt. 2 Box 33, Georgetown, TX 78626 512-863-2040.

ALTER, Robert, b. New York City, NY, April 2, 1935, m. Carol (Cosman), chil: Miriam; Dan; Gabriel; Micha. Educ: Columbia Coll., (summa cum laude) 1957; Harvard U., MA 1958, PhD 1962. Emp: Columbia U., 1962-64 Instr., 1964-66 Asst. Prof.; U. of Calif., Berkeley, 1967-69 Assoc. Prof., 1969- Prof., Hebrew & Comparative Lit., 1970-72 Chmn., Dept. of Comparative Lit. Pub: *The Art of Biblical Poetry* (Basic, 1985); *The Art of Biblical Narrative* (Basic, 1981); and others. Awd: Guggenheim Fellow, 1957-58, 1978-79; NEH, Sr. Fellow 1972-73; Hebrew U., Inst. for Advanced Stud., Fellow 1982-83; Natl. Jewish Book Awd. for Jewish Thought 1982; Hebrew Union Coll, Los Angeles, DHL 1985. Mem: AJS.

ALTIZER, Thomas J. J., b. Cambridge, MA, September 28, 1927, s. of Jackson Duncan & Francis (Greetham), chil: John Jackson; Katharine Blake. Educ: U. of Chicago, AB 1948, AM 1951, PhD 1955. Emp: Wabash Coll., 1954-56 Asst. Prof., Relig.; Emory U., 1956-68 Assoc. Prof., Bible & Relig.; State U. of N.Y., 1968-Prof., English & Relig. Stud.; *Stud. in Relig.*, 1979-81 Ed. Spec: New Testament. Pub: *Genesis as Apocalypse* (Westminster/John Knox, 1991); and others. Addr: (o) State U. of New York, Religious Studies Dept., Stony Brook, NY 11794 516-246-7783; (h) 12 Laurel Path, Belle Terre, NY 11777 516-473-7285.

AMIET, Pierre J., b. Strasbourg, France, April 29, 1922, s. of Paul & Nelly (Bonnet), m. Francoise Ducrot, chil: Paul; Henriette; Elisabeth. Educ: Coll. Episc. Saint Etienne, Strasbourg, BA, Phil.; Ecole du Louvre, Dip. 1950; U. de Paris, Sorbonne, Lic. es-Letters 1953, PhD 1958. Emp: Ctr. Natl. de la Recherche Sci., 1949-65 Res.; Mus. d'Art et d'Hist. de Chambery, 1958-61 Keeper; Mus. du Louvre, Dept. de Antiq. Orientales, 1961-67 Conservateur, 1968-88 Conservateur en chef, 1988 Inspecteur General. Excv: Tell el Far'ah, Jordan, 1950-51, 1954. Spec: Archaeology, Mesopotamian Studies. Pub: "La naissance de l'ecriture ou la vraie Revolution" *RB* 97/4 (1990); *Suse: 6000 ans d'histoire* (1988); *L'age des Echanges inter-iraniens. 3500-1700 avant J.-C.* (1986); *La Glyptique mesopotamienne archaique* (1980); "Archaeological Discontinuity and Ethnic Duality in Elam" *Antiquity* 53 (1979); *L'Art antique du Proche Orient* (1977). Awd: Ordre National du Merite, Commandeur 1989;

"Biographie et Bibliographie de P. Amiet" in *Iranica Antiqua*, vol. 23 (1988); Mus. de France, Inspecteur Generale hon. 1988-; Ordre des Arts et Letters, Commandeur 1984; Legion d'honneur, chevalier 1974. Mem: Acad. de Savoie 1961-; Assn. des Anc. et Amis de l'Ecole Bibl. et Arch. 1972- Pres. Rec: Being a grandfather. Addr: (h) 20, rue Pierre Demours, 75017 Paris, France.

AMIRAN, Ruth, Excv: Canaanite Arad, 1987 Dir. Spec: Archaeology. Pub: "The Well at Arad," co-auth. *BAR* 13/2 (1987); *Pottery of the Holy Land*; *Ancient Arad*; and others. Addr: (h) 9 Alfasi St., Jerusalem, Israel 631-719.

ANATI, Emmanuel, b. Florence, Italy, s. of Ugo & Elsa (Castelnuovo), m. Ariela (Fradkin), chil: Daniel; Miriam. Educ: Hebrew U., Jerusalem, BA 1953, MA, Arch. 1955; Harvard U., AM, Anthrop. & Social Relations 1959; Sorbonne, Doc. es Lettres, Ethnology 1960. Emp: Harvard U., 1958-59 Fulbright Fellow; Hebrew U., Jerusalem, 1961-66 Res. Fellow; Tel Aviv U., 1964-68 Sr. Lect., 1968-72 Prof., Prehist.; Centro Camuno di Studi Preistorici, 1964- Exec. Dir.; U. of Lecce, 1980-Prof., Palaeo-Ethnology. Excv: Susita-Hippos, 1952; Negev Desert, 1952-54; Tell Abu-Hawam, 1952, 1956; Hazorea, 1956, 1960, 1967-68, 1970-71, 1979-80; Har Karkom, 1980-. Spec: Archaeology. Pub: *Le Radici Della Cultura* (Jaca, 1992); *The Mountain of God* (Rizzoli, 1986); "Has Mt. Sinai Been Found?" *BAR* 11/4 (1985); *Har Karkom: Montagna sacra nel deserto dell'Esodo* (Jaca, 1984); *Luine: Collina Sacra* (Edizioni del Centro, 1982); *I Camuni alle radici della civilta europea* (Jaca, 1980); and others. Addr: (o) Centro Camuno di Studi Preistorici, 25044 Capo Di Ponte (BS), Italy 33-364-42091.

ANDERSON, Bernhard W., b. Dover, MO. Educ: U. of the Pacific, BA 1936; Pacific Sch. of Relig., MA 1938, BD 1939; Yale U., PhD 1945; United Meth. Ch., Ord. 1939. Emp: Boston U. Sch. of Theol., Adj. Prof., OT; U. of N.C., Chapel Hill, 1948-50 James A. Gray Assoc. Prof. of Bible; Colgate-Rochester Div. Sch., 1950-54 Joseph B. Hoyt Prof. of OT; Drew U., Theol. Sch., 1954-63 Dean, 1954-63 Henry Anson Buttz Prof. of Bibl. Theol.; Princeton Theol. Sem., 1968-82 Prof., OT Theol., 1982-Prof. Emeritus. Excv: Tell Balata, Shechem, Co-orgn. Spec: Hebrew Bible. Pub: *The Books of the Bible*, 2 vol., ed. (Scribner, 1986); *Understanding the Old Testament* (Prentice-Hall, 1957, 1986); *The Eighth Century Prophets* (Fortress, 1978); and others. Awd: Pacific Sch. of Relig., DD 1960, STD 1961; Colgate U., DD 1965. Addr: (o) 13 Chipman Heights, Middlebury, VT 05753.

ANDERSON, Gary A., May 18, 1955, m. Lisa (Detlefs), chil: Christopher Michael; Matthew Tobias. Educ: Albion Coll., BA (summa cum laude) 1977; Duke Div. Sch., MDiv (magna cum laude) 1981; Harvard U., PhD, Hebrew Bible 1985. Emp: Mass. Inst. of Technology, 1983-84

Lect., Bibl. Stud.; Hebrew U., Jerusalem, Vis. Prof., Bible; U. of Va., 1985-90 Asst. Prof., 1990- Assoc. Prof., Hebrew Bible; *JBL*, 1990- Ed. Bd. Excv: Meiron Excvn. Project, 1981- Asst. Area Supr. Spec: Hebrew Bible. Pub: "Sacrifice" in *ABD* (1992); *Studies in the Cult and Priesthood of Ancient Israel*, JSOT Mon. Ser., co-ed. (Yale U.P., 1991); *A Time to Mourn and a Time to Dance: The Expression of Joy and Grief in Israelite Religion* (Penn. State, 1991); "The Interpretation of Genesis 1:1 in the Targums" *CBQ* 52 (1990); "The Expression of Joy as an Halakhic Problem in Rabbinic Sources" *JQR* 80 (1990); "Celibacy or Consummation in the Garden?: Reflections on Early Jewish and Christian Interpretations of the Garden of Eden" *HTR* 82 (1989); "The Cosmic Mountain: Eden and its Early Interpreters in Syriac Christianity" in *Genesis 1-3 in the History of Exegesis: Intrigue in the Garden* (Mellen, 1989); *Sacrifices and Offerings in Ancient Israel: Studies in the Social and Political Importance*, HSM (1988); and others. Awd: NEH Summer Grant 1988; Fulbright Res. Awd. 1988-89. Addr: (o) U. of Virginia, Dept. of Religious Studies, Cocke Hall, Charlottesville, VA 22903 804-924-6717; (h) 2412 Brook Rd., Charlottesville, VA 22901 804-978-1882.

ANDERSON, George W., b. Arbroath, Scotland, January 25, 1913, s. of George & Margaret Gordon (Wishart), m. Annie Phyllis (Walter), chil: Kenneth Walter; Margaret Joyce. Educ: St. Andrews U., Scotland, MA 1935; Cambridge U., England, BA 1937. Emp: Handsworth Coll., England, 1946-56 Tutor in OT; Birmingham U., England, 1946-56 Lect.; St. Andrews U., Scotland, 1956-58 Lect., OT Lit. & Theol.; Durham U., England, 1958-62 Prof., OT Stud.; Edinburgh U., Scotland, 1962-82 Prof., Hebrew. Spec: Hebrew Bible. Pub: "Sicut Cervus: Evidence in the Psalter of Private Devotion in Ancient Israel" *VT* (1980); *Tradition and Interpretation*, ed. (Oxford U.P., 1979); "Some Observations on the Old Testament Doctrine of the Remnant" *Glasgow U. Oriental Soc. Transactions* (1972); "Johannes Lindblom's Contribution to Biblical Studies" *Ann. of the Swedish Theol. Inst.* (1968); *The History and Religion of Israel* (Oxford U.P., 1966); *A Critical Introduction to the Old Testament* (Duckworth, 1959); and others. Awd: St. Andrews U., DD 1959; U. Lund, Sweden, Teol.D 1971; Fellow of the British Acad. 1972; Fellow of Royal Soc. at Edinburgh 1977; British Acad., Burkitt Medal for Bibl. Stud. 1982. Mem: SOTS 1945-; IOSOT 1950-, Pres. 1971-74. Rec: Reading, music. Addr: (h) 51 Fountainhall Rd., Edinburgh EH9 2LH, Scotland 031-667-2945.

ANDERSON, Hugh, b. Galston, Ayrshire, Scotland, May 18, 1920, s. of Hugh & Jeannie (Muir), m. Jean (Torbit), chil: Gordon; Kenneth; Nancy. Educ: Glasgow U., MA, Class. & Semitic Lang. 1940, BD, PhD 1950. Emp: Glasgow U., 1946-51 Lect., Hebrew & OT, 1954-57 A.B. Bruce Lect. in NT; Duke U., 1957-66 Prof., Bibl. Crit.; U. of Edinburgh,

1966-72 Prof., NT Lang., Lit., & Theol., Head of Dept.; Meredith Coll., 1985 Kenan Disting. Vis. Prof. of Relig.; Fla. South. Coll., 1986- Bishop E.J. Pendergrass Prof. of Relig. Spec: New Testament, Apocrypha and Post-biblical Studies. Pub: *The Gospel of Mark*, New Century Bible (Eerdmans, 1981); *Jesus* (Prentice-Hall, 1967); *Jesus and Christian Origins* (Oxford U.P., 1964); and others. Awd: U. of Glasgow, DD 1970; Fla. South. Coll., DD 1983. Mem: SNTS 1956-; Royal Soc. of Edinburgh, Fellow 1986-. Rec: Golf, gardening. Addr: (h) 5 Comiston Springs Ave., Edinburgh EH10 6NT, Scotland 031-447-1401.

ANDERSON, Janice Capel, b. New Orleans, LA, March 12, 1952, d. of Charles E. & June (Semple), m. Mark D. Anderson. Educ: Macalester Coll., BA, Relig. (summa cum laude) 1974; U. of Chicago, Div. Sch., MA, Div. 1975, PhD, Bible 1985. Emp: Macalester Coll., Dept. of Relig. Stud., 1977-78 Instr.; St. Olaf Coll., 1978-82 Instr.; U. of Idaho, 1985-90 Lect., 1990-93 Vis. Asst. Prof., 1993- Asst. Prof., Phil. Spec: New Testament. Pub: "Mapping Feminist Biblical Criticism: The American Scene, 1983-1990" in *Critical Review of Books in Religion* (1991); "Matthew: Sermon and Story" in *SBL 1988 Seminar Papers* (Scholars, 1988); "Mary's Difference: Gender and Patriarchy in the Birth Narratives" *JR* 67 (1987); "Double and Triple Stories, the Implied Reader and Redundancy in Matthew" *Semeia* 31 (1985); "Matthew: Gender and Reading" *Semeia* 28 (1983); *Mark and Method: New Approaches in Biblical Interpretation*, co-ed. (Fortress, 1992). Awd: M.F.J. Kagin Awd. 1972-73; Phi Beta Kappa 1973; U. of Chicago Div. Sch., Burchard Schol. 1974-77. Mem: SBL, V.P., Upper MidW reg. 1980-81; AAR; CBA. Rec: Hiking. Addr: (o) U. of Idaho, Dept. of Philosophy, Moscow, ID 83844-3016 208-885-6065; (h) 860 E Seventh St., Moscow, ID 83843 208-882-3907.

ANDERSON, Julian G., b. Minneapolis, MN, June 11, 1916, s. of Julius & Georgene (Gunderson), m. LaTona, chil: Duane; Diane; Leslie; Dale. Educ: Luther Coll., BA 1946; Luther Theol. Sem., BTh 1947; U. of Minn., MA 1951. Emp: U. of Minn., 1952-56 Instr.; Bethany Luth. Coll., Prof.; Bethany Luth. Sem., Prof. Spec: New Testament. Pub: *Jesus the Messiah, Acts and Letters* (Anderson, 1978); *The Story of Jesus the Messiah, Old Testament* (Anderson, 1977); *The Story of Jesus the Messiah, Four Gospels* (Anderson, 1977); and others. Addr: (h) 333 15th Ave. S, Naples, FL 33940 813-262-5592.

ANDERSON, Roger W., Jr., b. Centralia, Washington, December 1, 1948, s. of Roger W. & Elva V., m. Arletta J., chil: Brita C. Educ: Pacific Luth. U., BA 1971; Luth. Sch. of Theol., MDiv 1975; U. of Chicago, PhD 1985. Emp: Augustana Coll., 1978-79 Instr.; Loyola U., 1989 Instr.; United Theol. Coll., Zimbabwe, 1989-91 Lect.; U. of Zimbabwe, 1989-92 Lect.; Ill. Benedictine Coll., 1992- Lect. Excv: Tell el-Hesi,

1979- Area Supr., 1981- Bd. Mem., Joint Arch. Expdn. Spec: Archaeology, Hebrew Bible. Pub: "The Canon of the Bible: Present Understandings," "'To Your Descendants I Will Give This Land': Thoughts on the Promise of Land and; Rewriting the Bible" in *"Rewriting" the Bible: The Real Issues* (Mambo, 1993); "'And He Grasp Away Our Eye': A Note on II Sam. 20,6" *ZAW* 102 (1990); and others. Mem: SBL 1973-; ASOR 1975-; IES 1975-; CBA 1989-; CSBR 1989-. Rec: Racquetball, tennis, swimming. Addr: (o) Energy Systems Division, Bldg. 372, Argonne National Lab., 9700 S Cass Ave., Argonne, IL 60439 708-252-6406; (h) 1205 Natchez Trace Cir., Naperville, IL 60540 708-527-8960.

ANDREW, Maurice E., b. Auckland, New Zealand, January 28, 1932, s. of James & Eileen (Sansom), m. Gisela (Muller), chil: Teresa; Alexa; Christopher; Inge. Educ: U. of Otago, New Zealand, MA 1954, BD 1956; U. of Heidelberg, ThD 1959. Emp: Kirchliche Hochschule, Germany, 1963-65 Asst.; U. of Ibadan, Nigeria, 1965-68 Lect. in Relig. Stud.; Massey U., New Zealand, 1968-72 Sr. Lect. in German; U. of Otago, 1972-90 Sr. Lect. in Hebrew, 1978-80 Dean, Faculty of Theol.; Knox Coll., New Zealand, Theol. Hall, 1972-90 Prof. of OT Stud., 1985-90 Prin., 1990- Prof. Emeritus. Spec: Hebrew Bible. Pub: *Responsibility and Restoration: The Course of the Book of Ezekiel* (U. of Otago, 1985); *The Old Testament and New Zealand Theology* (U. of Otago, 1982); *The Ten Commandments in Recent Research*, co-auth. (SCM, 1967); and others. Mem: SOTS 1967-1990. Rec: Music, walking. Addr: (h) 127 Signal Hill Rd., Dunedin, New Zealand 473-8423.

ANNEN, Franz, b. Schwyz, Switzerland, March 16, 1942, s. of Franz & Maria (Huber). Educ: U. Gregoriana, Rome, Liz. Phil. 1964, Liz. Theol. 1968; Pont. Bibl. Inst., Rome, Liz. Bibelinst. 1970, Doc. 1974. Emp: Theol. Hochschule Chur, 1974-77 Asst. Prof., 1977- Ordentlicher Prof., NT; St. Luzi Chur, 1980-91 Regens des Priesterseminars. Spec: New Testament. Pub: "Ist der Teufel ausgetrieben? Das Neuen Testament und das Geheimnis des Bösen" in *Wie böse ist das Böse?* (1988); "Sie hielten fest am Brotbrechen (Apg 2,42)" in *Sonntag—der Kirche liebstes Sorgenkind* (1982); "Die Dämonenaustreibungen Jesu in den synoptischen Evangelien" *Theol. Berichte* 5 (1976); *Heil fur die Heiden: Zur Bedeutung und Geschichte der Tradition vom besessenen Gerasener (Mk 5,1-20 parr.)*, Frankfurter Theol. Stud. 20 (Knecht, 1976); and others. Mem: Kreis Katholischer Exegeten der Schweiz 1974-; SNTS 1978-; Schweizerische Theol. Gesellschaft 1978-; Schweizerische Gesellschaft fur Judaistische Forschung 1982-; Europaische Gesellschaft fur Katholische Theol. 1988-. Addr: (o) Seminar St. Luzi, Alte Schanfiggerstr. 7, CH-700 Chur, Switzerland 081-222012.

APOSTOLOS-CAPPADONA, Diane, b. Trenton, NJ, May 10, 1948, d. of William D. &

Stacia E., m. Joseph B. Educ: George Washington U., BA, Relig. 1970, MA, Relig. 1973, PhD 1988; Cath. U. of Amer., MA, Relig. & Culture 1978. Emp: Mt. Vernon Coll., 1980-85 Lect., Relig.; George Washington U., 1981-86 Lect., Relig.; Pacific Sch. of Relig., 1985- Adj., Christianity & Art; Georgetown U., 1985- Prof., Relig. & the Arts; Grad. Theol. Found., 1989- Teaching Fellow. Spec: Archaeology, New Testament, Apocrypha and Post-biblical Studies. Pub: "The Art of *Seeing*: Classical Paintings and *Ben-Hur*" in *Image and Likeness: Religious Visions in American Film Classics* (Paulist, 1992); "God in Culture: Images of God in Christian Art" *Dialogue and Alliance* 5/4 (1991-92); *Dance as Religious Studies*, ed. (Crossroad, 1990); *Art as Religious Studies*, ed. (Crossroad, 1987); *Art, Creativity and the Sacred: An Anthology in Religion and Art*, ed. (Crossroad, 1984); "Epiphany as Paradigm for the Visual Arts in Liturgy" *Modern Liturgy* 9/9 (1982); "Christ on the Cross: A Study in Image" *Liturgy* 23/5 (1978). Awd: Edward F. Albee Found., Fellow 1983; Soc. for the Arts, Relig. and Contemporary Culture, Fellow 1985; ACLS, Grant-in-Aid-of-Research 1989; AAR, Res. Grant 1990; NEH, Travel-to-Collections Grant 1990. Mem: Amer. Assn. of U. Women 1973-; AAR 1978-; Coll. Art Assn. 1979-; Coll. Theol. Soc. 1979-. Rec: Traveling, reading, visiting museums. Addr: (o) Georgetown U., Liberal Studies Program ICC 306, Washington, DC 20057.

ARAI, Sasagu, b. Omagari-shi, Akita-ken, May 6, 1930, s. of Genzaburo & Toshi, m. Eiko, chil: Keiko; Noriko. Educ: Tokyo U., BA 1954, MA 1956; U. in Erlangen, ThD 1962. Emp: Aoyama-Gakuin U., 1963-69 Asst. Prof.; Tokyo U., 1969-1977 Asst. Prof, 1977-91 Prof.; Ibaraki Christian Coll., 1991-92 Prof.; Keisen Jogakuen Coll., 1992- Pres.; *Seisho-Gaku-Ronshu*, 1982- Ed. Spec: New Testament, Apocrypha and Post-biblical Studies. Pub: "Stephanusrede—gelesen vom Standpunkt ihrer Leser" *Ann. of the Japanese Bibl. Inst.* 15 (1989); "Zum 'Tempelwort' Jesu in Apostelgeschichte 6.14" *NTS* 34 (1988); *Studies in the New Testament and Gnosticism* (Iwanami Shoten, 1986); *The Hidden Jesus—The Gospel According to Thomas* (Kodansha, 1984); "Individual- und Gemeindeethik bei Lukas" *Ann. of the Japanese Bibl. Inst.* 9 (1983); "Zum 'Simonianischen' in *AuthLog* und *Bronte*" in *Gnosis and Gnosticism* (Brill, 1981); "Simonianische Gnosis und die *Exegese über die Seele*" in *Gnosis and Gnosticism* (Brill, 1977); *Early Christianity and Gnosticism* (Iwanami Shoten, 1971); *Die Christologie des Evangelium Veritatis: Eine religionsgeschichtliche Untersuchung* (Brill, 1964); and others. Awd: Awd. of the Japan Acad. 1972. Mem: Japan Soc. of NT Stud. 1958-; Soc. of Hist. Stud. of Christianity 1958-; SNTS 1965-; Intl. Assn. of Patristic Stud. 1985-; IACS 1996-. Rec: Traveling. Addr: (o) Keisen Jogakuen College, 10-1 Minamino 2-Chome, Tama-shi, Tokyo 206, Japan 0423-76-8215; (h) 10-2-605 Keyakidaira, Miyamae-ku, Kawasaki-shi 216, Japan 044-888-4112.

ARANDA PEREZ, Gonzalo, b. Torralba de los Frailes, November 25, 1943, s. of Pedro & Dolores (Perez). Educ: U. de Navarra, Spain, ThD 1972; U. Complutense, Spain, PhD 1984. Emp: U. de Navarra, 1984-88 Adj. Prof., 1988- Prof., OT Exegesis, 1988- Dir., Sacred Scripture Dept.; *Scripta Theologica*, 1987- Redaction Com. Spec: Hebrew Bible, New Testament, Apocrypha and Post-biblical Studies. Pub: "El Apostal Pedro en la literatura gnóstica" *EstBib* 47 (1989); "La Versión sahidica de S. Mateo en Bodmer XIX y Morgan 569" *EstBib* 46 (1988); *El Evangelio de S. Marcos en copto sahidico* (CSIC, 1988); "El Magnificat" *EphMariol* 36 (1986); *El Evangelio de S. Mateo en copto sahidico* (CSIC, 1984); "Apocrifo de Jeremias sobre la cautividad de Babilonia" in *Apocrifos del Antiguo Testamento* (Cristiandad, 1982); "La Version Fayumica del Monasterio Blanco (Mc 8:2-4-9:12)" *Rivista degli Studi Orientali* (1979); and others. Mem: SNTS 1990-; IACS 1984-; Assn. Bibl. Espanola 1975-. Rec: Travel, art, mountains. Addr: (o) U. de Navarra, Facultad de Teologia, 31080 Pamplona, Spain 252700; (h) Iturrama, 39 3-B, 31007 Pamplona, Spain 260527.

ARBINO, Gary P., b. N. Hollywood, CA, January 16, 1960, s. of Pat & Cathie, m. Margaret. Educ: Humboldt State U., BA 1981; Golden Gate Bapt. Theol. Sem., MDiv 1989. Emp: Golden Gate Bapt. Theol. Sem., 1990- Television Studio Supr. & Engineer, 1991- Design Dir./Asst. Cur, Marian Eakins Arch. Collection, 1992- Adj. Prof. Excv: Tel Miqne/Ekron, Israel, 1992-93 Area Supr. Spec: Archaeology, Hebrew Bible. Awd: Broadman Sem. Awd., 1989. Mem: ASOR 1989-; SBL 1989-; Nat. Assn. of Prof. of Hebrew 1989-. Rec: Photography, videography, creative & dramatic arts. Addr: (o) G.G.B.T.S. #242, Mill Valley, CA 94941-3197 415-388-8080.

ARCHER, Gleason L., Jr., b. Norwell, MA, s. of Gleason & Elizabeth, m. Sandra (Larson), chil: Gleason, III; Jonathan; Heather; Laurel; Elizabeth. Educ: Harvard Coll., BA (summa cum laude) 1938; Harvard Grad. Sch., AM 1940, PhD 1944; Princeton Theol. Sem., BD 1945. Emp: Fuller Theol. Sem., 1948-65 Prof., Bibl. Lang.; Trinity Evang. Div. Sch., 1965-86 Prof. of OT & Semitics, 1986- Prof. Emeritus. Spec: Archaeology, Hebrew Bible, New Testament, Semitic Languages, Texts and Epigraphy, Egyptology. Pub: *Old Testament Quotations in the New Testament: A Complete Survey*, co-auth. (Moody, 1983); *Ency. of Bible Difficulties* (Zondervan, 1982); "A Reassessment of the Value of the *Septuagint* of I Samuel for Textual Emendation in the Light of the Qumran Fragments" in *Tradition and Testament: Essays in Honor of Charles Lee Feinberg* (Moody, 1981); "The Hebrew of Daniel Compared with the Qumran Sectarian Documents" in *The Law and the Prophets* (Presbyn. & Reformed, 1974); "The Aramaic of the 'Genesis Apocryphon' Compared with the Aramaic of Daniel" in *New Perspectives on the Old Testament* (Word, 1970); *A Survey of Old Testament Introduction*;

and others. Awd: Christian Res. Found. Awd. 1956. Mem: NABI 1954-; ETS, Pres. 1985-86; Intl. Coun. on Bibl. Inerrancy, 1977-; Rec. Numismatics, linguistics. Addr: (o) Trinity Evangelical Divinity School, Bannockburn, Deerfield, IL 60015 708-945-8800; (h) 812 Castlewood Ln., Deerfield, IL 60015 312-945-6053.

ARCHI, Alfonso, b. Pavia, Italy, December 28, 1940, s. of Gian Gualberto & Letizia (Zavagli), m. Stefania (Mazzoni). Educ: U. di Firenze, PhD 1964. Emp: Istituto per gli Studi Micenei ed Egeo-anatolici, CNR, 1966-80 Fellow; U. di Roma-La Sapienza, 1972- Prof., Hittitology. Spec: Anatolian Studies, Mesopotamian Studies. Pub: "Culture de l'olivier et production de l'huile a Ebla" in *Mél. P. Garelli* (1991); "Imar au IIIeme millenaire" *MARI* 6 (1990); "The Names of the Primeval Gods" *Orientalia* 59 (1990); "Harran in the 3rd Millennium B.C." *UF* 20 (1989); "Eine Anrufung der Sonnengottin von Arinna" in *Documentum Asiae Minoris Antiquae* (1988); *Testi Amministrativi: Archivi Reali de Ebla* vol. I (U. di Roma, 1985); *Circulation of Goods in Non-palatial Context in the Ancient Near East* (Edizione dell'Ateneo, 1984); *Keilschrifturkunden aus Boghazkoi,* Heft. 49, Akademie der Wissenschaft (1979); and others. Rec: Agriculture. Addr: (o) U. di Roma-La Sapienza, Dept. Scienze dell'Antichità, Via Palestro 63, I-00185 Roma, Italy 445-3672; (h) Via Chelini 9, I-00197 Roma, Italy 807-5726.

ARENS, Eduardo F., b. Dresden, Germany, January 18, 1943, s. of Eduardo & Anita (Kuckelkorn). Educ: St. Mary's U., BA 1965; U. Fribourg, STL 1973, STD, Bibl. Stud. 1976. Emp: Fac. of Theol., Lima, 1976-80 Asst. Prof.; Inst. Superior de Estudios Teologicos, Lima, 1977- Prof.; *Revista Teologica Limense*, 1977-79 Asst. Ed. Spec: New Testament. Pub: *Los Evangelios ayer y hoy* (Ed. Paulinas, 1989); *La violencia y el evangelio* (Ed. Paulinas, 1988); *Apocalipsis, revelación del fin del mundo?* (1988); *The Elthon-Sayings in the Synoptic Tradition* (Vandenhoeck & Ruprecht, 1976); and others. Mem: SNTS 1989-. Rec: Amateur radio, music. Addr: (o) Av. Conquistadores 1293, Lima 27, Peru 40-33-45.

ARMENTI, Joseph R., b. Neptune, NJ, September 11, 1950, s. of Rocco & Lucie, m. Maria. Educ: Villanova U., BA 1972; Dropsie U. for Hebrew & Cognate Learning, PhD 1982; Temple U. Sch. of Law, JD 1986. Emp: Dropsie U., 1974-80 Fellow. Spec: Hebrew Bible, Apocrypha and Post-biblical Studies. Pub: *Dimensions in the Human Religious Quest*, vol. I-IV (1986-1992); *Elements of Divine Power in the Old Testament* (1983); "On the Use of the Term 'Galileans' in the Writings of Josephus Flavius" *JQR* 72 (1981); *Wisdom and Knowledge*, ed. (Villanova U.P., 1976); *Transcendance and Immanence, Reconstruction in the Light of Process Thinking* (Abbey, 1972); and others. Awd: Dropsie U., Res. Fellow. 1974-80. Mem: SBL 1983-; AAR 1983-; St. Thomas Moore Soc.

1984-; Intl. Soc. for Neoplatonic Stud., Hellenic U. Club 1989. Rec: Golf, tennis, chess. Addr: (o) Suites 2001-2007, 125 S. 12th St., Philadelphia, PA 19107 609-869-9600; (h) 2730 N Kent Rd., Broomall, PA 19008 215-353-2841.

ARMERDING, Carl E., b. Boston, MA, April 30, 1936, s. of Howard & Grace (Horsey), chil: John C.; Jennifer R.; Geoffrey H.; Elizabeth G. Educ: Gordon Coll., AB 1957; Trinity Evang. Div. Sch., BD 1965; Brandeis U., PhD 1968. Emp: Wheaton Coll., 1969-70 Asst. Prof., OT; Regent Coll., 1970- Prof., OT, 1977-88 Pres.; Schloss Mittersill Study Ctr., 1992- Acad. Dir. Spec: Archaeology, Hebrew Bible, Mesopotamian Studies. Pub: "When the Spirit Came Mightily: The Spirituality of Israel's Charismatic Leaders" in *Alive to God: Studies in Spirituality* (1992); "Images for Today: Word from the Prophets" in *Studies in Old Testament Theology* (Word, 1992); "A Charismatic Theology of Judges" in *Gott lieben, und seine Gebote halten* (Brunnen Verlag, 1991); *Handbook of Biblical Prophecy*, ed. (Hendrickson, 1989); "The Meaning of Israel in Evangelical Thought" in *Evangelicals and Jews in Conversation* (Baker, 1987); *Obadiah, Nahum, Habakkuk*, co-auth., Expositions Bible Comm., Vol. 7 (Zondervan, 1985); *The Old Testament and Criticism* (Eerdmans, 1983); "Were David's Sons Really Priests?" in *Biblical and Patristic Interpretation* (Eerdmans, 1975). Mem: SBL 1965-, Pres., NW reg. 1975-76; ETS 1965-; NEAS 1965-; SOTS 1977-. Rec: Travel, hiking. Addr: (o) Schloss Mittersill, A5730 Mittersill, Austria 43-6562-4523.

ARNOLD, Bill T., b. Lancaster, KY, September 1, 1955, s. of Walter L. & Mildred Jean, m. Susan Virginia, chil: David Wesley; Jeremy Clark; Alexander Joseph. Educ: Asbury Coll., BA 1977; Asbury Theol. Sem., MDiv 1980; Hebrew Union Coll., PhD 1985. Emp: Wesley Bibl. Sem., 1985-91 Prof., OT; Ashland Theol. Sem., 1991- Assoc. Prof., OT. Spec: Hebrew Bible, Mesopotamian Studies, Semitic Languages, Texts and Epigraphy. Pub: "The Amalekite's Report of Saul's Death: Political Intrigue or Incompatible Sources?"*JETS* 32/3 (1989). Awd: Joseph & Helen Regenstein Found. Fellow. 1980-81; S.H. & Helen R. Scheuer Grad. Fellow. 1982-84; NEH Summer Stipend 1988. Mem: AOS; ETS; IBR; WTS. Addr: (o) Ashland Theological Seminary, 910 Center St., Ashland, OH 44805 419-289-5933; (h) 1320 Meadow Ln., Ashland, OH 44805 419-281-4121.

ARTZY, Michal, Educ: Brandeis U., PhD. Emp: U. of Haifa, Dept. of Maritime Civ. & Dept. of Arch., 1990- Sr. Lect. Excv: Tel Nami, 1986- Dir. Spec: Archaeology. Pub: "Akko and the Ships of the 'Sea Peoples'" in *Essays in Honour of M. Dothan* (1992); "Nami Land and Sea Project, 1989," *IEJ* 41 (1991); "Pomegranate Scepters and Incense Stand with Pomegranates Found in Priest's Grave" *BAR* 16/1 (1990); "On Soil Salinity in Southern Mesopotamia: A Defence of the Theory of Progressive Salinization," co-auth.

Geoarch. 3 (1988); "On Boats and 'Sea Peoples'" *BASOR* 266 (1987); *The Palestinian Bichrome Ware* (Brandeis U., 1972); and others. Addr: (o) U. of Haifa, Center for Maritime Studies, Mt. Carmel, Haifa 31999, Israel; (h) 38 Sderot Ha-Zvi, Haifa 34355, Israel 04-387-486.

ASHLEY, Timothy R., b. Wheaton, IL, June 2, 1947, s. of John & Dorotha (Ranard), m. Maxine (Clark). Educ: Amer. Bapt. Sem. of the West, MA 1972; U. of St. Andrews, St. Mary's Coll., Scotland, PhD 1976. Emp: Bapt. Ch., 1975-82 Minister; Iliff Sch. of Theol., 1979-80 Adj. Faculty; Acadia U., Div. Coll., 1982-87 Asst. Prof., 1987-92 Assoc. Prof., 1991- Vice Chmn. of Faculty of Theol., 1992- Prof., Bibl. Study. Spec: Hebrew Bible, Semitic Languages, Texts and Epigraphy. Pub: Articles in *Nelson's Illustrated Bible Dict.* (Nelson, 1986), *International Standard Bible Ency.* (Eerdmans, 1979). Mem: SBL 1974-; British Soc. OT Stud. 1983-; CSBS 1983-; IBR 1985-. Rec: Book collecting. Addr: (o) Acadia Divinity College, Wolfville, NS B0P 1X0, Canada 902-542-2285; (h) Box 1255 Wolfville, NS B0P 1X0, Canada 902-542-7003.

ATKINSON, Dewey F., b. Kenedy, TX, November 15, 1930, s. of Dewey & Rosa, m. Barbara (Harris), chil: Ruth; Jean; David. Educ: New Orleans Bapt. Theol. Sem., BD 1955, DTh 1958, MTh 1969. Emp: E Tex. Bapt. U., 1973-87 Prof., Dept. of Relig., 1987-91 V.P., Spiritual Affairs. Spec: Archaeology, Hebrew Bible. Pub: *God's Goodness* (Broadman, 1980); and others. Mem: New Orleans Bapt. Assn.; La. Bapt. Conv.; NABPR, V.P. 1981, Pres. 1982. Rec: Rotary club, fishing. Addr: (h) 806 Slone Dr., Marshall, TX 75670 214-938-7482.

ATTRIDGE, Harold W., b. New Bedford, MA, November 24, 1946, s. of Harold W. & Rita V. (Carroll), m. Janis, chil: Joshua; Rachel. Educ: Boston Coll., BA 1967; Cambridge, BA 1969; Harvard U., PhD 1975. Emp: Perkins Sch. of Theol., South. Meth. U., 1977-85 Assoc. Prof.; U. of Notre Dame, 1985- Prof., 1991- Dean, Coll. of Arts and Letters. Spec: New Testament, Apocrypha and Post-biblical Studies. Pub: "Let Us Strive to Enter That Rest: The Logic of Hebrews 4:1-11" *HTR* 73 (1980); "Thematic Development and Source Elaboration in John 7" *CBQ* 42 (1980); "The Original Text of Gos. Thom. Saying 30" *Bull. of the Amer. Soc. of Papyrologists* 16 (1979); *Nag Hammadi Codex I*, ed. (Brill, 1985); *The Apocalypse of Elijah*, co-auth.; *Philo of Byblos: The Phoenician History*, co-auth.; *The Epistle to the Hebrews*; and others. Awd: NEH, Summer Res. Stipend 1982; Guggengeim Fellow. 1983-84. Mem: SBL 1969-; CBA 1974-; APA 1976-; SNTS 1981-. Addr: (o) U. of Notre Dame, O'Shaughnessy 137, Notre Dame, IN 46556 219-631-6642; (h) 51141 Brenshire Ct., Granger, IN 46556 219-277-6483.

AUFRECHT, Walter E., Educ: U. of Toronto, Canada, PhD 1979. Emp: *Newsletter for*

Targumic & Cognate Stud., 1974-78 Ed.; U. of Lethbridge, Canada, 1981- Prof.; AASOR, 1989-90 Book Ed. Spec: Hebrew Bible, Semitic Languages, Texts and Epigraphy. Pub: A Corpus of Ammonite Inscriptions (Mellen, 1989); Studies in the Book of Job, ed. (Wilfred Laurier U.P., 1985); Targum Pseudo-Jonathan of the Pentateuch: Text and Concordance, co-auth. (Ktav, 1984); A Synoptic Concordance of Aramaic Inscriptions, co-auth. (Scholars/Bibl. Res. Assn., 1975). Awd: W.F. Albright Inst. of Arch. Res., Jerusalem, Ann. Prof. 1985-86. Mem: CSBS; SBL; ASOR; CBA; IES. Addr: (o) U. of Lethbridge, Lethbridge, AB T1K 3M4, Canada 403-329-2485.

AUNE, David E., b. Minneapolis, MN, November 8, 1939, s. of Edward & Anna, m. Mary, chil: Karl; Kristofer; Kurt; Karen. Educ: Wheaton Grad. Sch., MA 1963; U. of Minn., MA 1965; U. of Chicago, PhD 1970. Emp: St. Xavier Coll., 1968-1990 Prof., Relig. Stud.; U. of Trondheim, Norway, 1982-83 Fulbright Sr. Lect.; Loyola U. of Chicago, 1990-. Spec: New Testament. Pub: The New Testament in Its Literary Environment (Westminster, 1987); "The Influence of Imperial Court Ceremonial on the Apocalypse of John" Bibl. Res. 18 (1983); Prophecy in Early Christianity and the Ancient Mediterranean World (Eerdmans, 1983); The Cultic Setting of Realized Eschatology in Early Christianity (Brill, 1972); and others. Mem: SBL 1965-; CBA 1969-; CSBR 1969-; SNTS 1972-. Rec: Fishing. Addr: (o) Loyola U. of Chicago, Dept. of Theology, 6525 N Sheridan Rd., Chicago, IL 60626 312-508-2353; (h) 9410 S Hamilton, Chicago, IL 60620 312-445-2638.

AUNEAU, Joseph M., b. Cholet, France, June 3, 1936, s. of Gustave-Henri & Marie (Biziere). Educ: Petit Sem., BA, Phil. 1954; Grand Sem., France, BA, Theol. 1961; Inst. Cath., Paris, Lic. Theol. 1963; Pont. Bibl. Inst., Rome, Lic. Ecriture Sainte 1965. Emp: Grand Sem. de Coutances, 1965-71 Prof.; Grand Sem. de Caen, 1971-85 Prof.; Sem. Saint Sulpice, 1985- Prof. Spec: Hebrew Bible. Pub: Le sacerdoce dans la Bible, Cahiers Evangile 70 (Cerf, 1990); "I et II Chroniques, Esdras-Néhémie, Tobie, Judith, Baruch" in Les Psaumes et les autres Ecrits, ed. (Desclée, 1990); "Jérémie, II et III Isaie" in Les prophetes et les livres prophétiques, ed. (Desclée, 1985); "Marc" in Evangiles synoptiques et Actes des Apôtres (Desclée, 1981); and others. Mem: Assn. Cath. Francaise pour l'etude de la Bible 1965-; SBL 1965-. Rec: Walking. Addr: (o) Seminaire Saint Sulpice, 33 Rue General Leclerc, 92130 Issy-les-Moulineaux, France 16-1-46-621936.

AUS, Roger D., b. Jamestown, ND, September 26, 1940, s. of Adrian & Dagny, chil: Martin; Christopher; Jonathan. Educ: St. Olaf Coll., BA 1962; Luther Theol. Sem., BD 1967; Yale U., MA 1969, PhD 1971. Emp: Evang. Luthergemeinde, 1991- Pastor. Spec: New Testament. Pub: Barabbas and Esther (1992); Weihnachtsgeschichte, Barmherziger Samariter, Verlorener Sohn (1988); Water into Wine and the Beheading of John the Baptist (1988); "Luke 15:11-32 and R. Eliezer ben Hyrcanus's Rise to Fame" JBL 104 (1985); I-II Timothy, Titus, II Thessalonians, co-auth., Augsburg Comm. on the New Testament (Augsburg, 1984); "Three Pillars and Three Patriarchs: A Proposal Concerning Gal. 2:9" ZNW 70 (1979); "Paul's Travel Plans to Spain and the 'Full Number of the Gentiles' of Rom. XI 25" NT 21 (1979); "God's Plan and God's Power: Isaiah 66 and the Restraining Factors of 2 Thess. 2:6-7" JBL 96 (1977); "The Relevance of Isaiah 66:7 to Revelation 12 and 2 Thessalonians 1" ZNW 67 (1976); and others. Mem: JBL; SNTS. Addr: (o) Winterthurstr. 7, 1000 Berlin 51, Germany 030-496-5540.

AVALOS, Hector I., b. Nogales, Sonora, Mexico, October 8, 1958, s. of Magdalena, m. Lisa. Educ: U. of Ariz., BA 1982; Harvard Div. Sch., MTS 1985; Harvard U., PhD 1991. Emp: OT Abstracts, 1985- Abstractor; U. of N.C., 1991-93 Postdoc. Fellow. Spec: Hebrew Bible, Mesopotamian Studies. Pub: "The Comedic Function of the Enumerations of Officials and Instruments in Daniel 3" CBQ 53 (1991); "Exodus 22:9 and Akkadian Legal Formulae" JBL 109 (1990); "Deuro/deute and the Imperatives of hlk: New Criteria for the kaige Recension of Reigns" EstBib 47 (1989). Awd: Ford Found. Diss. Fellow. 1990-91; Memorial Found. for Jewish Culture, Doc. Fellow. 1990-91. Mem: SBL; AAR. Addr: (o) U. of North Carolina, Chapel Hill, Religious Studies Dept., Chapel Hill, NC 27514 919-962-5666; (h) 1521 E Franklin St. B-108, Chapel Hill, NC 27514 919-932-9592.

AVERY-PECK, Alan J., b. Chicago, IL, June 26, 1953, s. of Richard & Eileen (Peck), m. Lisa. Educ: U. of Ill., BA 1975; Brown U., PhD 1981. Emp: Dept. of Class. Lang., Tulane U., 1981- Assoc. Prof.. Spec: Semitic Languages, Texts and Epigraphy, Apocrypha and Post-biblical Studies. Pub: Mishnah's Division of Agriculture, The History and Theology of Sedar Zeraim, Brown Judaic Stud. (Scholars, 1985); "Yerushalmi's Commentary to Mishna Terumot: From Theology to Legal Code" in Studies in Liturgy, Exegesis and Talmudic Narrative, Approaches to Ancient Judaism vol. IV (Scholars, 1983); "Literature and Society: The Unfolding Conventions on Hillel," co-auth. Formative Judaism, Approaches to Ancient Judaism vol. III (Scholars, 1982); "Cases and Principles in Mishnah: A Study of Terumot Chapter Eight" in Text as Context in Early Judaism (Scholars, 1981); "Mishnah Terumot Before A.D. 70," "From Scripture to Mishnah Terumot" in Judaism: The Evidence of the Mishnah (Chicago U.P., 1981); The Priestly Gift in Mishnah, A Study of Tractate Terumot, Brown Judaic Stud. (Scholars, 1981); and others. Awd: Brown U. Fellow., 1977-78; Brown Center for Jewish Stud., Summer Res. Grant 1981. Mem: AAR 1977-; SBL 1977-; AJS 1977-. Addr: (o)

Tulane U., Newcomb Hall, New Orleans, LA 70118 504-486-0655; (h) 46 W Park Pl., New Orleans, LA 70124.

AVIRAM, Yosef, Emp: Israel Exploration Soc., Dir. Mem: ASOR; JBL. Addr: (o) Israel Exploration Society, PO Box 7041, Jerusalem 91070, Israel 227991; (h) Alfasi 15, Jerusalem, Israel 632376.

AVNI, Gideon Y., b. Jerusalem, April 23, 1957, s. of Haim & Esther, m. Orli, chil: Tiltan. Educ: Hebrew U., Jerusalem, BA 1984, MA 1992. Emp: Israel Dept. of Antiq. & Mus., 1985-88 Co-dir., Arch. Looting Prevention Unit; Israel Antiq. Authority, 1989- Jerusalem Dist. Arch. Excv: Kh. Hazzan, 1983-85 Co-dir.; Ramat Hanadiv, 1985-89 Area Supr. & Co-dir.; Beth Govrin Necropolis, 1986-90 Dir.; Har Oded, 1988-91 Co-dir.; Byzantine Necropolis, Jerusalem, 1989-91 Dir. Spec: Archaeology. Pub: *Archaeological Survey of Israel. Map of Har Sagi—The Negev Highlands* (1992); "Ancient Mosques in the Negev Highlands" *Atiqot* 20 (1992); "Christian Burial Caves from the Byzantine Period at Luzit" in *Christian Archaeology in the Holy Land* (1991); "The Jewish Necropolis of Beth Govrin" *Qadmoniot* (1988); and others. Mem: Byzantine Soc.; Israel Arch. Assn.; ICOMOS. Addr: (o) Israel Antiquities Authority, PO Box 586, Jerusalem 91004, Israel 972-2-292611; (h) 1/44 Givat Beit Hakerem, Jerusalem 92628, Israel 972-2-437435.

BAHAT, Dan, b. Lemberg, October 11, 1938, s. of Isaac & Rachel, m. Anath, chil: Joab; Amnon; Jonathan; Nadav. Educ: Hebrew U., Jerusalem, BA 1964, MA 1974, PhD 1992. Emp: Dept. of Antiq., Israel, 1963-91 District Arch., Jerusalem. Excv: Dan, 1966-71; Menahamiya, Shamir, Beth Shemesh, Beth Shean, 1966-74; The Western Wall Tunnels, 1985-; Ahdod; Arad; Masada. Pub: *Carta's Historical Atlas of Jerusalem* (1986); "Does the Holy Sepulchre Mark the Burial of Jesus?" *BAR* 12/3 (1986); "The Date of Dolmens near Kibbutz Shamir" *IEJ* 22; *The Illustrated Atlas of Jerusalem*, co-auth. (Simon & Shuster, 1983); "A propose de l'Eglise des 'Sept Douleurs'" *RB* 85 (1978); "A Synagogue Chancel Screen from Rehob" *IEJ* 23; "Roof Tile of Legio VI Ferrata" *IEJ* 24; and others. Mem: IES. Rec: Music, gardening, hikes. Addr: (o) Bar-Ilan U., Dept. of the Study of Israel, Ramat Gan, Israel 03-531-8350; (h) PO Box 738, Mevasseret Zion, Israel 02-345-567.

BAILEY, D. Waylon, b. Brantley, AL, August 16, 1948, s. of Donald & Margie Nell, m. Martha (Layton), chil: Anna; Emily. Educ: Samford U., AB 1970; New Orleans Bapt. Theol. Sem., ThM 1973, ThD 1976. Emp: New Orleans Bapt. Theol. Sem., 1978- Prof., OT & Hebrew, Chair, Div. of Bibl. Stud.; First Bapt. Ch., 1989- Sr. Pastor. Spec: Hebrew Bible. Pub: *Step by Step Through the Old Testament* (1991); *Biblical*

Hebrew Grammar, co-auth. (Insight, 1985); "Sackcloth and Ashes" *BI* (1984); *Disciple's Study Bible*, contb.; and others. Awd: New Orleans Bapt. Theol. Sem., Outstanding Grad. in Bibl. Stud. 1973. Mem: NAPH. Rec: Running, reading, flying. Addr: (o) New Orleans Baptist Theol. Sem., 3939 Gentilly Blvd., New Orleans, LA 70126 504-282-4455; (h) 18366 Hosmer Mill, Covington, LA 70433 504-892-8400.

BAILEY, Kenneth E., b. Bloomington, IL, November 24, 1930, s. of Ewing & Annette (Meader), m. Ethel (Milligan), chil: Sara; David. Educ: Pittsburgh Sem., MDiv 1955, MTh 1961; Concordia Sem., ThD 1972. Emp: Cairo Evang. Sem., Egypt, 1962-65 Instr., NT; Near East Sch. of Theol., Beirut, 1967-84 Prof., NT; Ecumenical Inst. for Theol. Res., Jerusalem, 1985- Res. Prof. of MidE NT Stud.; Princeton Sem., 1986 Alumni Lect.; and others. Spec: New Testament. Pub: *Finding the Lost: Cultural Keys to Luke 15* (Concordia, 1992); *The Prophecy of Amos* (Dar al-Thaqafa, 1981); *Through Peasant Eyes: More Lucan Parables, Their Culture and Style* (Eerdmans, 1980); *Poet and Peasant: A Literary-cultural Approach to the Parables in Luke* (Eerdmans, 1976); and others. Rec: Cabinetmaking, stamp collecting. Addr: (o) The Episcopal Church, Box 2075, Nicosia, Cyprus.

BAILEY, Robert E., b. Pittsburgh, PA, December 7, 1927, s. of Edson & Josephine (Turner), m. Annell (Gibson), chil: Robert, Jr.; Steven; Scott; Brian; Sharon; Karen; Cherlyn. Educ: U. of Dubuque, Theol. Sem., BD 1953, MDiv 1972; U. of Edinburgh, New Coll., PhD 1962. Emp: U. of Dubuque, 1956-65 Prof.; Park Coll., 1965-83 Prof.; Mo. South. State Coll., 1983-84 Asst. Prof.; Presbyn. Ch., 1985- Interim Pastor. Spec: New Testament, Apocrypha and Post-biblical Studies. Pub: "Is 'Sleep' the Proper Biblical Term for the Intermediate State?" *ZNW* 55 (1964); and others. Mem: AAR; SBL. Rec: Birds, golf, gardening. Addr: (o) Warrendale Presbyterian Church, 1040 Lomo Ave., St. Paul, MN 55103 612-489-6056; (h) 5521 10th Ave. S, Minneapolis, MN 55417 612-825-7534.

BAILEY, Wilma Ann, b. New Jersey, d. of Wilbur & Ann (Crawford). Educ: Hunter/Lehman Coll., BS; Assoc. Mennonite Bibl. Sem., MDiv 1979; Vanderbilt U., MA 1992. Emp: Messiah Coll., 1990- Asst. Prof., OT; Goshen Coll., 1981-85 Asst. Prof., Urban Min. Spec: Hebrew Bible. Pub: "Bathsheba: Seductress or Victim" *Gospel Herald* (1992); "Perjury," "Fringes," "Drunkenness" in *Mercer Dict. of the Bible* (1990); "Poetry in the Old Testament" *Evang. Visitor* (1990); "Look Forward in Faith: Hebrews" in *Adult Bible Study Guide* (1988). Mem: SBL 1988-; AAR 1988-; ASOR 1992-. Addr: (o) Messiah College, Grantham, PA 17027 717-766-2511.

BAIRD, J. Arthur, b. Boise, Idaho, June 17, 1922, s. of Jesse & Susanna, m. Mary Harriet, chil:

Andrew Arthur; Paul Chapman. Educ: Occidental Coll., BA 1944; San Francisco Theol. Sem., BD 1949; U. of Edinburgh, New Coll., PhD 1953. Emp: Community Presbyn. Ch., 1951-53 Pastor; Coll. of Wooster, 1954-85 Synod Prof. of Relig., 1985- Sr. Res. Schol., Prof. Emeritus; *The Computer Bible*, 1967- Ed. Spec: Archaeology, Hebrew Bible, New Testament. Pub: *A Comparative Analysis of the Gospel Genre* (Mellen, 1992); "The Holy Word" *NTS* (1988); "Content Analysis, Computers and the Scientific Method in Biblical Studies" *JBL* (1976); *A Critical Concordance to the Synoptic Gospels* (1968); *Audience Criticism and the Historical Jesus* (Westminster, 1967); and others. Awd: Phi Beta Kappa 1944. Mem: SBL 1954-; AAR 1954-; SNTS 1965-. Rec: Sailing, golf, travel, fly fishing. Addr: (o) College of Wooster, Wooster, OH 44691; (h) 1435 Gasche St., Wooster, OH 44691.

BAIRD, William R., b. Santa Cruz, CA, February 27, 1924, s. of William Robb & Martha (Watson), m. Shirley (Bauman), chil: Elisabeth (Parks); Eric Robb. Educ: NW Christian Coll., BTh 1946; U. of Oregon, BA 1947; Yale Div. Sch., BD 1950; Yale U., MA 1952, PhD 1955. Emp: Phillips U., 1952-56 Assoc. Prof., NT & Ch. Hist.; Lexington Theol. Sem., 1956-57 Prof., NT; Texas Christian U., Brite Div. Sch. 1967-92 Prof., NT; SBL Diss. Ser., 1980-84 Ed. Spec: New Testament. Pub: *History of New Testament Research* (Fortress, 1992); "Galatians" in *HBD* (Harper & Row, 1988); "Visions, Revelation and Ministry: Reflections on 2 Cor 12:1-5 and Gal 1:11-17" *JBL* 104 (1985); "Pauline Eschatological in Hermeneutical Perspective" *NTS* 17 (1971); *The Corinthian Church* (Abingdon, 1964); *Paul's Message and Mission* (Abingdon, 1960); and others. Awd: Phi Beta Kappa 1946; Yale Div. Sch., Tew Prize 1948; Yale U., Two Brothers Fellow. 1950-52. Mem: SBL, SW Reg. Pres. 1977-78; SNTS; Assn. of Disciples for Theological Discussion, Chair 1983-84. Rec: Music, photography. Addr: (h) 3824 Winifred Dr., Fort Worth, TX 76133 817-292-4479.

BAKER, David W., b. Toronto, Canada, February 22, 1950, s. of J. Weston & Mary, m. Morven (Ross), chil: Adam; Emily. Educ: Regent Coll., Dip. CS, MCS 1973; U. of London, MPhil 1976, PhD 1982. Emp: Bethel Coll., 1979-80 Asst. Prof., 1981-83 Min.; U. of the Witwatersrand, South Africa, 1983-85 Sr. Lect.; U. of Durban, South Africa, 1985- Assoc. Prof.; *Sources for Bibl. & Theol. Stud.*, 1985- Ed.; Ashland Theol. Sem., 1986- Prof.; *Bible Comm.*, 1992- Ed. Spec: Hebrew Bible, Semitic Languages, Texts and Epigraphy. Pub: *Obadiah, Nahum, Habakkuk, Zephaniah* (TOTC, 1989); "Leviticus 1-7 and the Punic Tarrifs" *ZAW* 99 (1987); "The Old Testament and Criticism" *Jour. of Theol. for South Africa* 40 (1984); "The Uniqueness of Mosaic Covenant" in *Proceedings of the Seventh South African Judaica Congress* (1984); articles in *ABD*; and others. Mem: Tyndale Fellow. 1974-; SBL 1977-; SOTS 1979-; IBR 1983-; CBA. Rec: Travel, Trivial Pursuit. Addr: (o) Ashland Theological Seminary, 910 Center St., Ashland, OH 44805 419-289-5177.

BAKIRTZIS, Charalambos, b. Thessaloniki, Greece, April 8, 1943, s. of Nikolaos & Olga (Fezoudis), m. Demetra (Papanikola), chil: Nikolaos; Olga-Maria. Educ: U. of Thessaloniki, BA 1967, MA 1973, PhD, History & Arch. 1984. Emp: Greek Arch. Service, Byzantine Antiquities, 1973-76; Epimelitis Thessaloniki, 1976-; U. of Ill., 1984-85 Vis. Schol.; U. of Thessaloniki, 1988- Asst. Prof., Byzantine & Greek Arch. Excv: Porto-Lago, 1980-82 Dir.; Abdera-Polystylon, 1982- Dir.; Synaxis-Maroneia 1985-90 Dir.; Amphipolis, 1990- Dir.; Ayios Georgios Peyia, Cyprus, 1991- Dir. Spec: Archaeology. Pub: *Synaxis*, co-auth. (1991); *Early Christian and Byzantine Thrace* (1989); *The Basilica of St. Demetrius* (Inst. for Balkan Stud., 1989); *Byzantina Tsoukaloloagena* (1989); "Des thermes romains et la basilique d'Acheiropoietos a Thessalonique" *Memoy Pelekanides* (1983); "New Observations on the Dome Inscription of St. Sophia" *Byzantina* 11 (1982); and others. Mem: Arch. Soc. of Athens; Hist. Soc. of Athens-Thessaloniki; Christian Arch. Soc. of Athens. Addr: (o) Ephoreia of Byzantine Antiquities, 14, odos Kyprou, 654 03 Kavala, Greece 51-224-716; (h) 47 odos Philippou, 54631 Thessaloniki,, Greece 31-287-250.

BALCH, David L., b. Pampa, TX, July 15, 1942, s. of Elmer & Claudine, chil: Alison; Christina; Justin. Educ: Abilene Christian U., BA 1964, MA 1966; Union Theol. Sem., BD 1969; Yale U., PhD 1974. Emp: Franklin & Marshall Coll., 1974-80 Asst. Prof., Relig. Stud.; Linfield Coll., 1980-83 Assoc. Prof., Chmn., Relig. Stud.; Princeton Theol. Sem., 1984 Vis. Prof., NT; Texas Christian U., Brite Div. Sch., 1983- Prof., NT. Spec: New Testament. Pub: *Social History of the Matthean Community: Cross-Disciplinary Approaches*, ed. (Fortress, 1991); *Greeks, Romans, and Christians: Essays in Honor of Abraham J. Malherbe*, ed. (Fortress, 1990); *The New Testament in its Social Environment*, co-auth. (Westminster, 1985); "Early Christian Criticism of Patriarchal Authority (1 Peter 2:11-3:12)" *Union Sem. Quar. Rev.* 39 (1984); "Two Apologetic Encomia: Dionysius on Rome and Josephus on the Jews" *JSJ* 13/1-2 (1982); *Let Wives Be Submissive: The Domestic Code in 1 Peter* (Scholars, 1981); "Backgrounds of I Cor. VII: Sayings of the Lord in Q; Moses as an Ascetic Theios Aner in II Cor. III" *NTS* 18 (1972); and others. Awd: Fulbright Grants, Tubingen, 1968-70, 1987-88; Ecumenical Inst., Tantur & Hebrew U., Rockefeller Stipend 1972-73. Rec: Tennis, backpacking, sailing. Addr: (o) Brite Divinity School, TCU, Ft. Worth, TX 76129 817-921-7582; (h) 2839 Merida, Ft. Worth, TX 76109 817-927-2582.

BALENTINE, Samuel E., b. Greenville, SC, August 12, 1950, s. of David, m. Betty, chil: David Graham; Lauren Ashley. Educ: SE Bapt. Theol. Sem., MDiv 1976; Oxford U., England, DPhil 1979. Emp: MidW Bapt. Theol. Sem., 1979-83 Asst. Prof., Hebrew & OT; SE Bapt. Theol. Sem., 1983- Assoc. Prof., Hebrew & OT;

Faith & Mission, 1983-85 Ed. Bd. Spec: Hebrew Bible, Semitic Languages, Texts and Epigraphy. Pub: *Prayer in the Hebrew Bible* (Fortress, 1993); "Enthroned on the Praises and Laments of Israel" *Princeton Seminary Bull.*, Sup. 2 (1992); "Prayers for Justice in the Old Testament: Theodicy and Theology" *CBQ* 51 (1989); "Prayer in the Wilderness Traditions: In Pursuit of Divine Justice" *HAR* 9 (1985); "The Prophet as Intercessor: A Reassessment" *JBL* 103 (1984); *The Hidden God* (Oxford, 1983); "A Description of the Semantic Field of Hebrew Words for 'Hide'" *VT* 30 (1980); and others. Awd: ATS, Theol. Schol. & Res. Awd. 1987-88; Alexander von Humboldt Fellow. 1987-88; Oxford U., Samuel E. Cox Awd. 1979. Mem: SBL; SOTS. Rec: Jogging, tennis, racquetball. Addr: (o) Southeastern Baptist Theological Seminary, 301 Stealey Hall, Wake Forest, NC 27587 919-556-3101; (h) 524 Robinson Dr., Wake Forest, NC 27587 919-556-6077.

BALTZER, Klaus, b. Hamburg, Germany, March 3, 1928, s. of Hans & Lotte (Barthelmes), m. Josepha C. (Brinkmann), chil: Jochen; Katrin E.; Anne C.; Dorothea L. Educ: U. Heidelberg, Promotion 1957, Habil. 1959. Emp: U. Heidelberg, 1958 Asst.; Kirchliche Hochschule Bethel/Bielefeld, 1963-68 Prof.; U. Muenchen, 1968- Prof.; Harvard Div. Sch., 1976 Vis. Prof. Spec: Hebrew Bible. Pub: "Stadt-Tyche oder Zion-Jerusalem? Die Auseinandersetzung mit den Goettern der Zeit bei Deuterojesaja" in *Alttestamentlicher Glaube und Biblische Theologie* (Kohlhammer, 1992); "Jerusalem in den Erzvaeter-Geschichten der Genesis? Traditionsgeschichtliche Erwaegungen zu Gen 14 und 22" in *Die Hebraeische Bibel und ihre zweifache Nachgeschichte* (Neukirchen, 1990); "Liberation from Debt Slavery After the Exile in Second Isaiah and Nehemia" in *Ancient Israelite Religion* (Fortress, 1987); *Die Biographie der Propheten* (Neukirchen, 1975); *The Covenant Formulary in Old Testament, Jewish and Early Christian Writings* (Fortress, 1971); "The Meaning of the Temple in the Lukan Writings" *HTR* 58 (1965); "Das Ende des Staates Juda und die Messias-Frage" in *Studien zur Theologie der alttestamentlichen Ueberlieferung* (Neukirchen, 1961); and others. Mem: SBL. Addr: (o) U. Munchen, Evangelisch-Theol. Fakultat, Schellingstr. 3, D-80799 Muenchen 40, Germany 089-2180-3479; (h) Bannzaunweg 21, D-82041 Deisenhofen, Germany 089-6132500.

BALZ, Horst, b. Leipzig, March 21, 1937, s. of Gerda & Adolf, m. Anneliese (Konig), chil: Christoph; Martin. Educ: U. Erlangen, Germany, ThD 1965; U. Kiel, Habil., NT 1969. Emp: U. Kiel, 1969-71 U. Tchr., 1972-73 Consistory; U. Bochum, 1974- Prof. Spec: New Testament. Pub: *Exegetisches Woerterbuch zum Neuen Testament*, 3 vol., ed. (1983); "Johanneische Theologie und Ethik im Licht der 'letzten Stunde'" in *Studien zum Text und zur Ethik des Neuen Testaments*, Festschrift H. Greeven (1986); "Eschatologie und Christologie" in *Das Wort und die Woerter*, Festschrift fur G. Friedrich (1973); "Anonymitaet

und Pseudepigraphie im Urchristentum" *ZTK* 66 (1969); "Furcht vor Gott? Uberlegungen zu einem vergessenen Motiv biblischer Theologie" *ET* 29 (1969); "Sexualitaet und christliche Existenz: Zum ethischen Problem der vorehelichen Geschlechtsbeziehung" *KuD* 14 (1968); and others. Mem: SNTS; Wissenschaftliche Gesellschaft fur Theol. Rec: Music, mountain climbing. Addr: (o) Ruhr-U. Bochum, Universitatsstrasse 150, Ev.-Theol. Fakultat, Gebaude GA 8, 147 Bochum, Germany 0234-700-3103; (h) Am Herrenbusch 46, 58456 Witten, Germany 02302-73784.

BANDSTRA, Barry L., b. Chicago, IL, April 5, 1951, s. of Arnold & Anjean, m. Debra Jean (Rosier), chil: Adam; Jonathan; Daniel. Educ: U. of Ill., BA 1972; Calvin Theol. Sem., BDiv 1975; Yale U., MA 1978, PhD 1982. Emp: Geneva Coll., 1978-82 Asst. Prof.; Calvin Theol. Sem., 1982-83 Vis. Prof.; Hope Coll., 1983-Assoc. Prof.; Harvard U., 1986- Mellon Faculty Fellow. Spec: Hebrew Bible, Semitic Languages, Texts and Epigraphy. Pub: *The Syntax of Particle* ky *in Biblical Hebrew and Ugaritic* (Yale U.P., 1982). Awd: Yale U., J.J. Obermann Fellow. 1977-78. Mem: SBL; IBR; CSBR. Rec: Raquetball. Addr: (o) Hope College, Holland, MI 49423 616-394-7752; (h) 6384 Blue Jay Ln., Holland, MI 49423 616-335-3345.

BANKS, Robert J., b. Wollahra, Australia, August 6, 1939, s. of John Charles & Evelyn Muriel, m. Julia (Lonsdale), chil: Mark; Simon. Educ: U. of Sydney, Australia, BA 1958; Australian Coll. of Theol., ThL 1961; U. of London, BD 1962, MTh 1965; U. of Cambridge, PhD 1969. Emp: Australian Natl. U., Res. Sch. of Social Sci., 1969-74 Res. Fellow, 1980-83 Vis. Fellow; Macquarie U., Australia, 1974-75 Lect., 1978-79 Sr. Lect.; ZADOK Centre, 1983-Assoc. Fellow; *Interchange*, 1975- Assoc. Ed.; Fuller Theol. Sem., 1989 Homer L. Goddard Prof. of Min. of Laity. Spec: Hebrew Bible, New Testament, Apocrypha and Post-biblical Studies. Pub: *Going to Church in the First Century* (Hexagon, 1980); "Rom. 7.25a: An Eschatological Thanksgiving" *Australian Bibl. Rev.* 26 (1978); and others. Mem: SNTS 1977-; Australian Hist. Soc. 1979-; Assn. for Christian Schol. 1982-; SBL 1989-; AAR 1990-. Rec: Walking, film. Addr: (h) 1080 E Rubio, Altadena, CA 91001 818-797-4549.

BARAG, Dan, Excv: Ein Gedi, ancient synagogue, Dir.; Khirbet Ghita'im, Roman-Byzantine cemetery. Spec: Archaeology. Pub: Articles in *The New Encyclopedia of Archaeological Excavations in the Holy Land* (IES/Carta, 1993); and others. Addr: (h) 3 Massavik St., Jerusalem 93106, Israel 664-041.

BARKAY, Gabriel, b. Budapest, Hungary, June 20, 1944, s. of Eliezer (Barkay-Breslauer) & Rachel (Ligeti), m. Rachel, chil: Elad; Naama. Educ: Hebrew U., BA 1967; Tel-Aviv U., PhD

1986. Emp: Tel-Aviv U., Inst. of Arch., 1970- Sr. Lect.; Amer. Inst. of Holy Land Stud., 1976- Tchr. Excv: Lachish, 1973-87 Area Supr.; Bashan, Southern Syria, 1973- Co-dir.; Ketef-Hinnom, Jerusalem, 1975, 1979-80, 1988-89 Dir.; Tumulus, 1983 Dir.; Ramat-Rachel, Israel, 1984 Dir. Spec: Archaeology, Semitic Languages, Texts and Epigraphy. Pub: "The Priestly Benediction on Silver Plaques from Ketef-Hinnom, Jerusalem" *Tel-Aviv* 19 (1992); *Introduction to the Archaeology of the Land of Israel: The Iron Age II-III* (Open U. of Israel, 1990); *Ketef Hinnom: Burial Treasures from Jerusalem* (Israel Mus., 1986); "The Garden Tomb: Was Jesus Buried Here?" *BAR* 12 (1986); "Jerusalem Tombs from the Days of the First Temple," co-auth., *BAR* 12 (1986); "Excavation in the Chapel of St. Vartan in the Holy Sepulchre," co-auth., *IEJ* 35 (1985); "A Group of Iron Age Scale Weights" *IEJ* 28 (1978); "Archaeological Survey in the Northern Bashan," co-auth., *IEJ* 24 (1974); and others. Awd: Yigal Allon Prize 1987. Mem: IES 1986-. Addr: (o) Tel Aviv U., Inst. of Archaeology, Ramat-Aviv, Tel-Aviv 69978, Israel 03-6409417; (h) Adam, 31a, Jerusalem 93782, Israel 02-715420.

BARKER, Kenneth L., b. Darfork, KY, August 13, 1931, s. of Herbert & Ruby (Wells), m. Isabelle, chil: Kenneth P.; Patricia L.; Ruth D.; David L. Educ: NW Coll., BA 1955; Dallas Theol. Sem., ThM 1960; Dropsie Coll. for Hebrew and Cognate Learning, PhD 1969. Emp: Trinity Evang. Div. Sch., 1966-68 Asst. Prof.; Dallas Theol. Sem., 1968-81 Prof., Chmn.; Capital Bible Sem., 1986-90 Acad. Dean; NIV Trans. Ctr., 1990- Exec. Dir. Spec: Archaeology, Hebrew Bible, Mesopotamian Studies, Semitic Languages, Texts and Epigraphy. Pub: "Proverbs 23:7—'To Think' or 'To Serve Food'?" *JANES* 19 (1989); *The NIV: The Making of a Contemporary Translation*, ed. (Zondervan, 1986); *The NIV Study Bible*, gen. ed. (Zondervan, 1985); "Zechariah" in *Expositor's Bible Comm.*, vol. 7 (Zondervan, 1985); "False Dichotomies Between the Testaments" *JETS* 25 (1982); "The Value of Ugaritic for Old Testament Studies" *BS* 133 (1976); and others. Awd: NW Coll., Disting. Alumnus 1988. Mem: SBL; NAPH; ETS, Pres. 1981; Intl. Bible Soc., Sr. V.P. 1981-86. Rec: Walking, ping-pong. Addr: (o) NIV Translation Center, Box 292307 Lewisville, TX 75029-2307 214-315-7288; (h) 1909 Hidden Trail Dr., Lewisville, TX 75067 214-315-7288.

BARNHART, Joe Edward, b. Knoxville, TN, November 1, 1931, s. of Clifford Edward & Irene Marie (Snyder), m. Mary Ann, chil: Ritschl Edward; Linda Jane. Educ: Carson-Newman Coll., BA 1953; South. Bapt. Theol. Sem., MDiv 1956; Boston U., PhD 1964. Emp: West. Carolina U., 1961-64 Instr.; U. of Redlands, 1964-66 Asst. Prof., Chair; U. of Calif., Riverside, 1965-66 Lect.; Parsons Coll., 1966-67 Assoc. Prof.; U. of N Tex., 1967- Prof. Spec: New Testament. Pub: Articles in *Mercer Dict. of the Bible* (Mercer U.P., 1990); "Text, Context and Epistemological Primitivism" *SJT* (1980); and others. Awd: Tex. Commn. for the Hum.,

grant 1976; U. of N Tex., Regents' Faculty Lect. Awd. 1992. Mem: AAR, Pres., SW reg. 1982-83; SW Commn. on Relig. Stud., Pres. 1985-86; N Tex. Phil. Soc., Pres. 1973-74; Soc. for the Sci. Study of Relig.; SBL. Rec: Hiking, theater. Addr: (o) U. of North Texas, Dept. of Philosophy & Religion Studies, Denton, TX 76203 817-565-2266; (h) 606 Headlee Ln., Denton, TX 76201-0853 817-387-3290.

BARR, David L., b. Belding, MI, April 24, 1942, s. of Frederick & H. Marie (Embody), m. Judith Kay (Dunlap), chil: Elizabeth Kay; Nathaniel David. Educ: Fort Wayne Bible Coll., BA, Bible & Theol. 1965; Fla. St. U., MA, Relig. 1969, PhD, Relig. 1974. Emp: Wright State U., 1975-80 Asst. Prof., 1980-86 Chair, Dept. of Relig., 1980-88 Assoc. Prof., 1987- Dir. of U. Honors Prog., 1988- Prof., Relig. Spec: New Testament. Pub: *New Testament Story: An Introduction* (Wadsworth, 1987); "The Apocalypse of John as an Oral Enactment" *Interpretation* 40/3 (1986); "Elephants and Holograms: From Metaphor to Methodology in the Study of John's Apocalypse" in *SBL 1986 Seminar Papers* (Scholars, 1986); "The Apocalypse as a Symbolic Transformation of the World: A Literary Study" *Interpretation* 38/1 (1984); "The Conventions of Classical Biography and the Genre of Luke-Acts" in *Luke-Acts: New Perspectives from the SBL Seminar*, co-auth. (Crossroad, 1983); "The Drama of Matthew's Gospel: A Reconsideration of its Structure and Purpose" *Theol. Digest* 24/4 (1977); *The Bible Reader's Guide*, co-auth. (Bruce, 1970); and others. Awd: Liberal Arts res. grant 1986; U. Res. Coun., grant 1985. Mem: SBL 1988; CBA; AAR; East. Great Lakes Bibl. Soc., VP 1984-85, Pres. 1985-86. Rec: Jogging, computers and related technology. Addr: (o) Wright State U., Honors Program, 179 Millett Hall, Dayton, OH 45435 513-873-2660; (h) 206 Cambria Dr., Dayton, OH 45440 513-429-9574.

BARRETT, C. Kingsley, b. Lancashire, England, May 4, 1917, s. of Fred & Clara (Seed), m. Margaret E. (Heap), chil: Anne Penelope; Charles Martin Richard. Educ: Pembroke Coll., Cambridge, BA 1938, MA 1942, BD 1948 DD 1957. Emp: Wesley Coll., Headingley, 1942-43 Asst. Tutor; Meth. Ch., 1943-45 Min.; Durham U., 1945-82 Prof.; *NT*, 1979- Chmn. of Ed. Bd. Spec: New Testament. Pub: "Paulus als Missionar und Theologe" *Zeitschrift für Theologie und Kirche* 86 (1989); *Freedom and Obligation* (SPCK, 1985); "What is New Testament Theology?" *Horizons in Bibl. Theol.* 3 (1981); *The Gospel According to St. John* (SPCK, 1955, 1978); *Jesus and the Gospel Tradition* (SPCK, 1967); "Christianity at Corinth" *BJRL* 46 (1964); *From First Adam to Last* (A & C Black, 1962); and others. Awd: British Acad., Fellow 1961; Burkitt Medal for Bibl. Stud. 1966; Hull U., DD 1970; Aberdeen U., DD 1972; Hamburg U., DTh 1981. Mem: SNTS 1947-, Pres. 1972-73; SOTS 1947-. Addr: (h) 22 Rosemount, Plawsworth Rd., Pity Me, Durham, DH1 5GA, England 091-386-1340.

BARRETT, J. Edward, b. Philadelphia, PA, December 18, 1932, s. of John E. & Edna Mae (Borlase), m. Suzanne (Lehr), chil: Jeanne Heather; Betsy Sue. Educ: Susquehanna U., BA 1955; Princeton Theol. Sem., BD 1958, ThM 1960; U. of St. Andrews, Scotland, PhD 1965. Emp: First Presbyn. Ch., 1958-62 Pastor; Muskingum Coll., 1964- Prof.; Tunghai U., Taiwan, 1971-72 Guest Prof. of Humanities; Chinese U. of Hong Kong, 1988-89 Guest Prof. Excv: Tell Aphek, 1974 Photo Asst. Spec: Archaeology, New Testament. Pub: "Can Scholars Take the Virgin Birth Seriously?" *BR* (1988); "God and Grace in Human Experience" *Amer. Jour. of Theol. & Phil.* (1981); "Piety and Patriotism-Secularism and Skepticism: The Dual Problem of Archaeological Bias" *BAR* (1981); and others. Mem: Amer. Assn. of U. Prof.; AAR. Rec: Sailing, tennis. Addr: (o) Muskingum College, New Concord, OH 43762 614-826-8366; (h) 102 Eastview Dr, New Concord, OH 43762 614-826-4143.

BARSTAD, Hans M., b. Asnes, Norway, June 7, 1947, s. of Sverre I. & Ester (Setervadet), m. Wenche (Roren), chil: Hans P.; Kristine O. Educ: U. of Oslo, MTh 1973, DTh 1982. Emp: Royal U. Lib., 1971- Sr. Acad. Lbrn.; Norwegian Res. Coun. for Sci. & Hum., 1976, 1978-79 Res. Fellow; Nordic Coun. of Min., 1981 Fellow; U. of Oslo, 1986- Prof., Chair of OT Theol. Spec: Hebrew Bible. Pub: *A Way in the Wilderness: The "Second Exodus" in the Message of Second Isaiah* (U. of Manchester, 1989); *The Religious Polemics of Amos* (Brill, 1984); *Veterotestamentica*, co-auth. (Universitetsforlaget, 1982); "The Historical-Critical Method and the Problem of Old Testament Theology" *Svensk Exegetisk Arsbok* 45 (1980); "HBL als Bezeichnung der fremden Gotter im A.T." *Studia Theologica* 32 (1978); "Festmahl und Ubersättigung: Der Sitz im Leben von RS 24.258" *Acta Orientalia* 39 (1978); "Der rasende zeus...Lukians 'De dea Syria,' Kap. 47" *Temenos* 12 (1976); and others. Mem: SBL; PEF; SOTS. Rec: House, garden. Addr: (o) U. of Oslo, Dept. of Biblical Studies, P.b. 1023, 0315, Oslo N-3, Norway 02-45-68-64; (h) Bregneveien 4, N-3300 Hokksund, Norway 03-75-30-16.

BARTCHY, S. Scott, b. Canton, OH, November 9, 1936, s. of Jacques Robert & Dorothy Elizabeth (Engle), m. Nancy L. (Breuer), chil: Beth; Christopher. Educ: Milligan Coll., BA 1958; Harvard U., MDiv 1963, PhD, Study of Relig. 1971. Emp: Inst. zur Erforschung des Urchristentums, Tuebingen, 1968-69, 1971-74, 1977-79 Dir.; Eberhard-Karls U., Germany, 1971-78 Lect., NT Exegesis, 1979-80, 1982, 1985, 1987 Guest Prof., Evang. Fac.; Emmanuel Sch. of Relig., 1974-77 Prof, Bibl. Hermeneutics; Westwood Christian Found., 1979-87 Resident NT Schol.; U. of Calif., Los Angeles, 1982- Adj. Assoc. Prof., Christian Origins & Early Ch. Hist. Spec: New Testament. Pub: "Paul's Letter to Philemon," "Philemon, Epistle to," "Slavery, Greco-Roman and NT" in *ABD* (Doubleday, 1992); "Table Fellowship" in *Dict. of Jesus and*

the Gospels (InterVarsity, 1992); "Community of Goods in Acts: Idealization or Social Reality?" in *The Future of Early Christianity: Essays in Honor Selbstverstaendnis im Urchristentum*" in *Die Bibel als politischer Buch* (Kohlhammer, 1982); and others. Awd: Staley Found., Disting. Christian Schol. 1974, 1976; U. of Calif., Los Angeles, Dept. of Hist. Disting. Teaching Awd. 1988-89, Disting. Lect. Awd. 1989. Mem: AAR 1965-; SBL 1965-; SNTS 1976-; IBR 1982-; CBA 1982-. Rec: Jazz pianist, running. Addr: (o) UCLA, Dept. of History, 405 Hilgard Ave., Los Angeles, CA 90024 310-825-4570; (h) 2260 N Cahuenga Blvd., Los Angeles, CA 90068 213-466-5649.

BARTH, Gerhard, b. Bad Homburg, December 31, 1927, s. of Emil. Educ: U. of Heidelberg, ThD 1955. Emp: Frankfurt am Main, 1955-63 Prof.; Mainz, 1968-70 Prof.; Sao Leopoldo, Brazil, 1964-67 Dozent, NT; Kirchliche Hochschule Wuppertal, 1970-90 Prof., NT. Spec: New Testament. Pub: *Der Tod Jesu Christi im Verstandnis des Neuen Testaments* (Neukirchen, 1992); "Pistis in hellenistischer Religiosität" *ZNW* 73 (1982); *Die Taufe in fruhchristlicher Zeit* (Neukirchen, 1981); "Art. Bergpredigt I" *Theol. Realenzyklopadie* 5 (1980); *A Primeira Epistola de Pedro* (Sao Leopoldo, 1967, 1979); *Der Brief an die Philipper*, Zurcher Bibelkommentare (1979); "Auseinandersetzungen um die Kirchenzucht im Umkreis des Matthausevangeliums" *ZNW* 69 (1978); "Glaube und Zweifel in den synoptischen Evangelien" *Zeitschrift fur Theol. & Kirche* 72 (1975); "Erwagungen zu 1.Kor 15,20-28" *ET*, (1970); and others. Mem: SNTS; Wissenschaft-liche Gesellschaft fur Theologie. Addr: (o) Kirchliche Hochschule Wuppertal, Germany; (h) 42369 Wuppertal, Ja der Krim 55, Germany 0202-46-604-90.

BARTH, Markus K., b. Safenwil, Switzerland, October 6, 1915, s. of Karl & Nelly (Hoffmann), m. Rose Marie (Oswald), chil: Peter; Anna; Ruth Lukas; Rose Marie. Educ: U. of Gottingen, Germany, ThD 1947. Emp: Evang. Reformed Ch., Switzerland, 1940-53 Parish Min.; U. of Dubuque, Presbyn. Theol. Sem., 1953-55 Vis. Prof., NT; U. of Chicago, Federated Theol. Fac., 1956-63 Assoc. Prof.; Pittsburgh Theol. Sem., 1963-72 Prof., NT; U. of Basel, Switzerland, 1973-85 Prof. Spec: New Testament. Pub: *Rediscovering the Lord's Supper* (1988); *Das Mahl des Herru* (Neukirchen, 1987); *Ephesians I-II*, Anchor Bible (1974); and others. Mem: SBL; SNTS. Rec: Hiking, history, music. Addr: (h) Inzlinger Str. 275, CH-4125-Riehen, Basel, Switzerland 061-67-08-80.

BARTLETT, John R., b. Manchester, U.K., March 13, 1937, s. of Ronald George & Kathleen Ruth (Atkins), m. Janet Ruth Stuart (Brown), chil: Penelope Ruth; Jessica Mary; Helen Elizabeth. Educ: Brasenose Coll., Oxford, BA 1959, MA 1962, MLitt 1962. Emp: Trinity Coll., Dublin, 1966-86 Lect. in Div., 1975-85 Fellow, *Hermathena*, 1976-88 Ed., 1979- Cur., Weingreen Mus. of Bibl. Antiq., 1986-92 Assoc.

Prof., Bibl. Stud.; Ch. of Ireland Theol. Coll., Dublin, 1989- Prin. Excv: Jerusalem, 1962, Site Supr.; Buseirah, 1973, 1974 Site Supr.; Moab survey, 1979, 1984. Spec: Archaeology, Hebrew Bible, New Testament, Apocrypha and Post-biblical Studies. Pub: *The Bible: Faith and Evidence* (Brit. Mus., 1991); *Edom and the Edomites* (Sheffield/PEF, 1990); "'Ezion-geber, which is near Elath on the shore of the Red Sea' (1 Kings ix.26)" *OS* 26 (1990); *Cities of the Biblical World: Jericho* (Lutterworth, 1982); "An Adversary Against Solomon, Hadad the Edomite" *ZAW* 88 (1976); *The First and Second Books of the Maccabees* (Cambridge U.P., 1973); "Sihon and Og, Kings of the Amorites" *VT* 20 (1970); "The Historical Reference of Numbers xxi.27-30"*PEQ* 101 (1969); "The Edomite king list of Genesis xxxvi.31-39 and 1 Chronicles i.43-50" *JTS* 16 (1965); and others. Mem: SOTS 1967-; Soc. of Antiquaries, London 1988-. Rec: Music, chess, walking. Addr: (o) Church of Ireland Theological College, Braemor Park, Dublin 14, Ireland 923506.

BARTNICKI, Roman, b. Rzadza, Poland, February 28, 1943, s. of Stefan & Cecylia. Educ: Cath. U., Lublin, Lic. Theol. 1969, ThD 1972; Pont. Bibl. Inst., Rome, Lic. Bibl. 1975; Cath. Theol. Acad., Warsaw, Habil. 1984. Emp: Metropolitalne Sem. Duchowne, Poland, 1975-Prof.; Cath. Theol. Acad., 1981- Prof. Spec: New Testament. Pub: *Ewangelie w analizie strukturalno-semiotycznej* (Cath. Theol. Acad., 1992); *Biblia w liturgii dni powszednich* (Cath. Theol. Acad., 1991); "Die Junger Jesu in Mt 9,35-11,1" *Collectanea Theologica* 58 (1988); *Uczén Jezusa jako glosiciel ewangelii. Tradycja i redakcja Mt. 9,35-11,1* (Cath. Theol. Acad., 1985); and others. Addr: (o) Akademia Teologii Katolickiej, 01 653 Warszawa, ul. Dewajtis 5, Poland 34-72-91; (h) ul. Ksiazeca 21, 00498 Warszawa, Poland 29-02-61.

BARTON, Bruce W., b. Ottumwa, IA, September 2, 1935, s. of Edith & Harold, m. Beverly, chil: Bric; Peter. Educ: San Diego State U., MA 1964. Emp: U. of Man., Canada, 1966-67 Lect.; Ohio State U., 1967-69 Chmn., Art; U. of Mont., 1969-83 Prof., Chmn., Art; Rockwell Intl., 1984- Supr., Graphic Art; *BA, BA Newsletter*, Design. Spec: Apocrypha and Post-biblical Studies. Pub: *The Tree at the Center of the World* (Ross-Erickson, 1980). Mem: AAR; Cath. Hist. Soc.; ASOR. Addr: (h) 2692 Riverside Dr., Costa Mesa, CA 92627 714-645-9031.

BARTON, John, b. London, England, June 17, 1948, s. of Bernard & Gwendolyn, m. Mary, chil: Katherine. Educ: Keble Coll., Oxford, BA 1969, MA 1972, D.Phil 1974, D.Litt 1988. Emp: Merton Coll., Oxford, 1973-74 Jr. Res. Fellow; St. Cross Coll., Oxford, 1974-91 Fellow, Lect., 1989-91 Reader; Oriel Coll., Oxford, 1991- Prof. Theol. Spec: Hebrew Bible. Pub: *People of the Book? The Authority of the Bible in Christianity* (SPCK, 1988); *Oracles of God: Perceptions of Ancient Prophecy in Israel after the Exile* (Darton, Longman & Todd/Oxford U.P., 1986); *Reading the Old Testament: Method in Biblical Study* (Darton, Longman & Todd/Fortress, 1984); "Gerhard von Rad on the World-View of Early Israel" *JTS* 35 (1984); "'The Law and the Prophets.' Who are the Prophets?" *OS* 23 (1984); "Ethics in Isaiah of Jerusalem" *JTS* 32 (1981); *Amos's Oracles Against the Nations* (Cambridge U.P., 1980); "Natural Law and Poetic Justice in the Old Testament" *JTS* 30 (1979); and others. Mem: SOTS 1975-. Addr: (o) Oriel College, Oxford OX1 4EW, England 0865-276537; (h) 11 Withington Court, Abingdon, Oxon OX14 3QA, England 0235-525925.

BARTON, Stephen C., b. Sydney, Australia, November 20, 1952, s. of George & Nancy, m. Fiona, chil: Anna; Thomas; Joseph; Miriam. Educ: Macquarie U., BA 1975; Lancaster U., MA 1978; King's Coll., London, PhD 1992. Emp: Salisbury & Wells Theol. Coll., 1984-88 Tutor, Bibl. Stud.; U. of Durham, 1988- Lect., NT, Dept. of Theol. Spec: New Testament. Pub: *The Spirituality of the Gospels* (SPCK, 1992); "The Communal Dimension of Earliest Christianity" *JTS* 43 (1992); "Community," "Ethos," "Mystery Cults" in *New Dict. of Biblical Interpretation* (SCM, 1990); "Paul's Sense of Place: An Anthropological Approach to Community Formation in Corinth" *NTS* 32 (1986). Mem: SST. Rec: Walking, playing piano, reading. Addr: (o) Abbey House, Dept. of Theology, Palace Green, Durham DH1 4QG, England 091-374-2059.

BASS, George F., b. Columbia, SC, December 9, 1932, s. of Robert D. & Virginia (Wauchope), m. Ann (Singletary), chil: Gordon; Alan. Educ: Johns Hopkins U., MA 1955; U. of Pa., PhD 1964. Emp: U. of Pa., 1964-73 Assoc. Prof.; Inst. of Nautical Arch., 1973-76 Pres.; Tex. A & M U., 1976- Disting. Prof.; *Arch., Natl. Geog. Res., Intl. Jour. of Nautical Arch., Amer. Jour. of Arch.*, Adv. Ed. Excv: Serce Limani, Turkey, 1977-79 Dir.; Kas, Turkey, 1984-85 Dir. Spec: Archaeology. Pub: "The Million Piece Glass Puzzle" *Arch.* 37 (1984); *Yassi Ada I: A Seventh-Century Byzantine Shipwreck* (Tex. A & M, 1982); "Cape Gelidonya and Bronze Age Maritime Trade" in *Orient and Occident*, Festschrift Cyrus Gordon (1973); "A Hoard of Trojan and Sumerian Jewelry" *Amer. Jour. of Arch.* 74 (1970); *Archaeology Under Water* (Thames & Hudson, 1966); and others. Awd: John Oliver La Gorce/Natl. Geog. Soc. Gold Medal 1979; Keith Muckelroy Memorial Awd., England 1984. Mem: AIA 1964-; Inst. of Nautical Arch. 1964-. Rec: Classical music. Addr: (o) Texas A&M U., Nautical Archaeology, College Station, TX 77843 409-845-6695; (h) 1600 Dominik Dr., College Station, TX 77840 409-693-6546.

BATEY, Richard A., b. Johnson City, TN, s. of Jackson Smith & Jessie (Alexander), m. Carolyn

T., chil: Evon; Richard; Kay. Educ: David Lipscomb U., BA 1955; Vanderbilt Div. Sch., MTh 1958; Vanderbilt U., PhD 1961. Emp: Harding Grad. Sch. of Relig., 1960-65 Asst. Prof., NT; U. of St. Andrews, St. Mary's Coll., Scotland, 1978 Vis. Prof.; Rhodes Coll., 1965- Prof. of Relig., Dir., Inst. for Bibl. Arch. Excv: Sepphoris, 1982-89 Asst. Dir. Spec: Archaeology, New Testament. Pub: "Jesus and the Forgotten City" *BAR* 18/3 (1992); *Jesus and the Forgotten City* (Baker, 1991); "Subsurface Interface Radar: Sepphoris, Israel, 1985" *Jour. of Field Arch.* Spring (1987); "Jesus and Theatre" *NTS* Oct. (1984); "Is Not This the Carpenter?" *NTS* 30 (1984); *New Testament Nuptial Imagery* (Brill, 1971, 1982); *Jesus and the Poor* (Harper & Row, 1972); *The Letter of Paul to the Romans* (Sweet, 1969); "Paul's Interaction with the Corinthians" *JBL* 84 (1965); and others. Awd: Fulbright Schol., 1963-64. Mem: SBL 1960-; SNTS 1970-. Rec: Golf. Addr: (o) Rhodes College, Memphis, TN 38112 901-726-3909; (h) 2020 Abergeldie Dr., Memphis, TN 38119 901-682-0824.

BATTO, Bernard F., b. Bandera, TX, January 16, 1941, s. of Raymond H. & Agatha Frances (Mazurek), m. Teresa Ann (Becker), chil: Rachel Ann; Nathan Frank; Amos Becker; Jeremiah Paul; Sarah Frances. Educ: Maryknoll Coll., BA 1963; Johns Hopkins U., PhD 1972. Emp: Mount St. Mary's Univ., 1971-75 Asst. Prof.; Willamette U., 1975-79 Asst. Prof.; U. of Dallas, 1979-86 Assoc. Prof.; DePauw U., 1987- Assoc. Prof.; *CBQ*, 1988-90 Assoc. Ed., 1990- OT Book Rev. Ed. Excv: Tell Halif (Lahav), 1980 Area Supr. Spec: Hebrew Bible, Mesopotamian Studies, Semitic Languages, Texts and Epigraphy. Pub: *Slaying the Dragon: Mythmaking in the Biblical Tradition* (Westminster/John Knox, 1992); *The Bible in Light of Cuneiform Literature*, co-ed., Scripture in Context IV (Mellen, 1991); "The Covenant of Peace: A Neglected Ancient Near Eastern Motif" *CBQ* 49 (1987); "The Sleeping God: An Ancient Near Eastern Motif of Divine Sovereignty" *Biblica* 68 (1987); "The Reed Sea: Requiescat in Pace" *JBL* 102 (1983); "Land Tenure and Women at Mari" *Jour. of the Economic and Social Hist. of the Orient* 23 (1980); *Studies on Women at Mari* (Johns Hopkins U.P., 1974); and others. Awd: NEH, Res. Grant 1975. Mem: CBA; SBL, V.P., SW reg. 1983-84, Pres., SW reg. 1985-86; AOS; ASOR. Rec: Photography, camping. Addr: (o) Depauw U., Dept. of Philosophy and Religion, Greencastle, IN 46135-2280 317-658-4716; (h) 636 E Seminary St., Greencastle, IN 46135 317-653-7411.

BAUCKHAM, Richard J., b. London, England, September 22, 1946, s. of John R. & Stephanie L. Educ: U. of Cambridge, BA 1969, MA 1972, PhD 1973. Emp: St. John's Coll., Cambridge, 1972-75 Fellow; U. of Leeds, 1976-77 Lect. in Theol.; U. of Manchester, 1977-87 Lect., 1987-92 Reader, hist. of Christian thought; U. of St. Andrews, 1992- Prof., NT Stud. Spec: New Testament, Apocrypha and Post-biblical Studies.

Pub: *The Theology of the Book of Revelation* (Cambridge U.P., 1993); "The Rich Man and Lazarus: The Parable and the Parallels" *NTS* 37 (1991); "Salome the Sister of Jesus, Salome the Disciple of Jesus, and the Secret Gospel of Mark" *NT* 33 (1991); "The Conflict of Justice and Mercy: Attitudes to the Damned in Apocalyptic Literature" *Apocrypha* 1 (1990); *Jude and the Relatives of Jesus in the Early Church* (T&T Clark, 1990); "Early Jewish Visions of Hell" *JTS* 41 (1990); "Pseudo-Apostolic Letters" *JBL* 107 (1988); *Moltmann: Messianic Theology in the Making* (Pickering, 1987); *Jude, 2 Peter*, Word Bibl. Comm. 50 (Word, 1983); and others. Mem: SNTS 1979-; SST 1980-; Assn. pour L'Etude de la Litterature Apocryphe Chretienne, 1986-; SBL 1992-. Rec: Novels, poetry, gardening, walking. Addr: (o) St. Mary's College, St. Andrews, Fife, KY16 9JU, Scotland 0334-76161; (h) 24 Kinkell Terrace, St. Andrews, Fife, KY16 8DS, Scotland.

BAUER, David R., b. Mansfield, OH, August 26, 1954, s. of Robert G. & Lois E. (Casto). Educ: Spring Arbor Coll., BA 1976; Asbury Theol. Sem., MDiv 1980; Union Theol. Sem., PhD 1985. Emp: Asbury Theol. Sem., 1979-80 Teaching Asst., NT Greek; Ashland Theol. Sem., 1980-81 Vis. Lect., NT; Va. Union U., Sch. of Theol., 1982-83 Vis. Prof., NT; Asbury Theol. Sem., 1984- Assoc. Prof.; Princeton Theol. Sem., 1989 Vis. Schol. Spec: New Testament. Pub: "The Major Characters in Matthew's Story: Their Function and Significance for the First Gospel" *Interpretation* 46 (1992); "Matthew" in *Asbury Bible Commentary* (Zondervan, 1992); "Son of David," "Son of God" in *Dict. of Jesus and the Gospels* (InterVarsity, 1992); "The Literary Function of the Genealogy in Matthew's Gospel" in *SBL 1990 Seminar Papers* (Scholars, 1990); "The Interpretation of Matthew's Gospel in the Twentieth Century" *ATLA Proc.* 42 (1988); *The Structure of Matthew's Gospel: A Study in Literary Design* (Almond, 1988); *Emmanuel— Studies in the Gospel of Matthew* (Light & Life, 1985). Awd: Amer. Bible Soc., Awd. for Excellence in Bible Stud. 1980. Mem: Wesleyan Theol. Soc. 1974-; SBL 1982-; CBA 1984-. Rec: Golf, tennis, photography. Addr: (o) Asbury Theological Seminary, Wilmore, KY 40390 606-858-3581; (h) 310 Maxey St., Wilmore, KY 40390 606-858-3480.

BAUMERT, Norbert, b. Penzig O/L, July 27, 1932, s. of Alfons & Johanna. Educ: Facultas Phil. Coll. S. Joh. Berchmans, Lic. Phil. 1958; Facultas Theol. St. Georgen, Frankfurt, Lic. Theol. 1962, Dr. Habil., NT 1982; Freie U. Berlin, PhD 1972. Emp: Fac. Theol. St. Georgen, Frankfut, 1980-85 Lect., NT, 1985- Prof., NT; *Filologia Neotestamentaria*, 1991- Adv. Bd. Spec: New Testament. Pub: *Antifeminismus bei Paulus? Einzelstudien*, FZB 68 (Echter, 1992); *Frau und Mann bei Paulus. Uberwindung eines Missverstaendnisses* (Echter, 1992); "Jesus Christus-Die endgultige Offenbarung Gottes. Biblische Sicht" in *Ist Christus der einzige Weg zum Heil?* (Nettetal, 1991); "'Charisma'-

Versuch einer Sprachregelung" *ThPh* 66 (1991); "Brueche im Paulinischen Satzbau?" *FN* IV (1991); "Zur 'Unterscheidung der Geister'" *ZKTh* 111 (1989); "Charisma und Amt bei Paulus" in *L'Apotre Paul*, BETL 73 (Peeters, 1986); *Ehelosigkeit und Ehe im Herrn. Eine Neuinterpretation von 1 Kor 7*, FZB 47 (Echter, 1984); *Taeglich sterben und auferstehen*, STANT 34 (Kosel, 1973); and others. Mem: Arbeitsgemeinschaft der deutschsprachigen katholischen Neutestamentler; SNTS 1987-. Addr: (o) Offenbacher Landstr. 224, D 60599 Frankfurt/M, Germany 069-6061317.

BAUMGARTEN, Joseph M., b. Vienna, Austria, September 7, 1928, m. Naomi (Rosenberg), chil: Rachel; Menachem; Judith; Philip; Debra; Minda. Educ: Brooklyn Coll., BA (summa cum laude) 1950; Mesitva Torah Vodaath, Rabbinical Ord. 1950; Johns Hopkins U., PhD 1954. Emp: Baltimore Hebrew Coll., 1953-54 Asst. Prof., 1954- Prof., Rabbinic Lit. & Inst.; U. of Maryland, 1962-63 Vis. Prof.; Towson State U., 1970-71 Vis. Prof., Relig. & Phil.; U. of the Negev, Israel, 1972-73; Hebrew U., Inst. of Advanced Study, 1986 Fellow. Spec: Hebrew Bible, Semitic Languages, Texts and Epigraphy, Apocrypha and Post-biblical Studies. Pub: "The Laws of the Damascus Document in Current Research" in *The Damascus Document Reconsidered* (1992); "4Q502, Marriage or Golden-Age Ritual?" *JJS* 34 (1983); "The 'Sons of Dawn' in CDC 13:14-15 and the Ban on Commerce Among the Essenes" *IEJ* 33 (1983); "Some Problems of the Jubilees Calendar in Current Research" *VT* 32 (1982); "The Pharisaic-Sadducean Controversies About Purity and the Qumran Texts" *JJS* 31 (1980); "The Heavenly Tribunal and the Personifiation of Sedeq in Jewish Apocalyptic" *ANRW* 19/1 (1979); *Studies in Qumran Law* (Brill, 1977); and others. Awd: William S. Raynor Fellow in Semitic Lang. 1952-53. Mem: AOS; SBL 1976-. Addr: (h) 3200 Labyrinth Rd., Baltimore, MD 21208 410-358-5164.

BAYER, Karel, b. Nachod, Czechoslovakia, May 8, 1931, s. of Vaclav & Karla, m. Vera. Educ: Charles U., Prague, MS 1954, PhD 1960, RNDr 1966. Emp: Czechoslovak Acad. of Sci., Prague, 1954-63 Res. Assoc.; Charles U., Prague, 1963-68 Assoc. Prof.; U. of Bonn, 1967-68 Vis. Prof.; U. of Wis.-Milwaukee, 1968-Assoc. Prof. Spec: Anatolian Studies, Hebrew Bible, New Testament. Mem: Assn. of Amer. Geog. 1971-; Amer. Geog. Soc. 1971-; Amer. Assn. for Adv. of Slavic Stud. 1981-; Soc. for Comparative Study of Civ. 1980-; AAR 1984-. Rec: Travel. Addr: (o) U. Wisconsin-Milwaukee, Dept. of Geography, PO Box 413, Milwaukee, WI 53201 414-229-4861; (h) 12929 N Colony Dr., Mequon, WI 53092 414-243-5626.

BEAGLEY, Alan J., b. Tatsfield, Surrey, U.K., September 3, 1940, s. of James & Ellen Millicent (Gambold), m. Jeanette Beagley-Koolhas, chil: Jonathan Andrew. Educ: U. of

Queensland, Australia, BA 1976, BD 1977; Fuller Theol. Sem., PhD 1983. Emp: U. of Queensland, 1984-86 Sr. Res. Asst., Relig. Stud.; Tainan Theol. Sem., 1988- Assoc. Prof., NT. Spec: New Testament. Pub: "The Exodus Motif in the Book of Revelation" *Tainan Theol. Rev.* Mar. (1991); "Computers and Biblical Studies" *Theol. & the Ch.* 18/1, 2 (1990); *The 'Sitz im Leben' of the Apocalypse with Particular Reference to the Role of the Church's Enemies*, BZNW 50 (de Gruyter, 1987). Mem: SBL 1980-. Rec: Music, amateur radio, travel. Addr: (o) Tainan Theological College & Seminary, 117 Tung Men Rd., Sec. 1, Tainan 701, Taiwan 886-6-238-9504; (h) 724 Bermuda Dr., Redlands, CA 92374 714-792-2722.

BEALL, Todd S., b. Greenwich, CT, February 24, 1952, s. of James Mandeville & Beverley (Pierce), m. Sharon J. (Pramschufer), chil: Jonathan Michael; Deborah Elizabeth. Educ: Princeton U., BA 1973; Capital Bible Sem., ThM (summa cum laude), Bibl. Stud. 1977; Cath. U. of Amer., PhD, Bibl. Stud. 1984. Emp: Capital Bible Sem., 1977- Prof., OT, 1990-Acting Acad. Dean; *Arch. & Bibl. Res.*, 1989-Cons. Ed. Spec: Archaeology, Hebrew Bible, Apocrypha and Post-biblical Studies. Pub: *Old Testament Parsing Guide (Job-Malachi)*, co-auth. (Moody, 1990); *Josephus' Description of the Essenes Illustrated by the Dead Sea Scrolls*, SNTS Mon. Ser. (Cambridge U.P., 1988); *Old Testament Parsing Guide (Genesis-Esther)*, co-auth. (Moody, 1986); and others. Awd: Capital Bible Sem., Acad. Schol. Awd. 1991. Mem: NAPH; ETS; SBL; Assn. for Bibl. Res. Rec: Computers, photography, chess, tennis, gardening. Addr: (o) Capital Bible Seminary, 6511 Princess Garden Pkwy., Lanham, MD 20706 301-552-1400; (h) 6328 Naval Ave., Lanham, MD 20706 301-577-6069.

BEASLEY-MURRAY, George R., b. London, England, October 10, 1916, s. of George & Kathleen (Beasley), m. Ruth, chil: Paul; Elizabeth; Stephen; Andrew. Educ: U. of London, BD 1941, MTh 1945, PhD 1952, DD 1963; Cambridge U., Jesus Coll., BA 1950, MA 1953, DD 1989. Emp: U. of London, Spurgeon Coll., 1950-56 Lect., 1958-73 Prin.; Intl. Theol. Sem., Zurich, 1956-58 Prof., Greek NT; South. Bapt. Theol. Sem., 1973-80 Prof., 1980-, Sr. Prof., NT Interpretation. Spec: New Testament. Pub: *John*, Word Bibl. Comm. (1987); "Second Thoughts on the Composition of Mark 13" *NTS* 29 (1983); "The Interpretation of Daniel 7" *CBQ* 45 (1983); *The Book of Revelation*, New Century Bible (1974); *Baptism in the New Testament* (Macmillan, 1966); "Demythologized Eschatology" *Theol. Today* 14 (1957); "The Two Messiahs in the Testaments of the Twelve Patriarchs" *JTS* 48 (1947); and others. Mem: SBL; SNTS; CBA. Rec: Music. Addr: (o) Southern Baptist Theological Seminary, 2825 Lexington Rd., Louisville, KY 40280; (h) 4 Holland Road Hove, E Sussex, BN3 1JJ, England (0273) 777-982.

BEATRICE, Pier Franco, b. Padova, Italy, June 29, 1948, s. of Alberto & Rachele (Zollo), m. Paola (Isaia), chil: Carlo; Filippo. Educ: U. of Padova, Degree in Class. Philol. 1970; Catholic U. of Milan, Doc., Hist. of Early Christianity & Anc. Christian Lit. 1978. Emp: U. of Padova, 1979- Prof., Anc. Christian Lit.; *Cristianesimo nella Storia,* 1982- Ed. Bd.; *Stud. Patavina,* 1985- Ed. Bd. Spec: New Testament, Apocrypha and Post-biblical Studies. Pub: *L'eredità delle origini. Saggi sul cristianesimo primitivo* (Marietti, 1992); *Storia della Chiesa antica* (Piemme, 1991); "Der Presbyter des Irenäus, Polykarp von Smyrna und der Brief an Diognet" in *Pleroma salus carnis* (Santiago de Compostela, 1990); "Une citation de l'Evangile de Matthieu dans l'Epitre de Barnabé" in *The New Testament in Early Christianity* (1989); "Le tuniche di pelle. Antiche letture di Gen. 3,21" in *La tradizione dell'Enkrateia* (1985); *La lavanda dei piedi. Contributo alla storia delle antiche liturgie cristiane* (Edizioni liturgiche, 1983); *Tradux peccati. Alle fonti della dottrina agostiniana del peccato originale* (Vita e Pensiero, 1978). Mem: SNTS 1983-; Intl. Assn. for Patristic Stud. 1982-; Int. Assn. for the Hist. of Relig. 1985-; NAPS 1992; Assn. pour l'Etude de la lit. apocryphe chrétienne 1992. Rec: Sports, music. Addr: (o) Dipartimento di Storia, Piazza Capitaniato, 3, 35139 Padova, Italy 049-662545; (h) Via Pietro Metastasio, 16, 35125 Padova, Italy 049-690802.

BEAVIS, MaryAnn L., b. Winnipeg, Canada, July 26, 1955, d. of Anne & Alvin. Educ: U. of Man., BEd 1978, MA 1981; U. of Notre Dame, MA 1984; Cambridge U., PhD 1987. Spec: New Testament. Pub: "Parable and Fable" *CBQ* 52 (1990); *Mark's Audience,* JSNTSup 33 (Sheffield, 1989); "Anti-Egyptian Polemic in the *Letter of Aristeas* 130-165 (The High Priest's Discourse)" *JSJ* 28 (1988); "Women as Models of Faith in Mark" *BTB* 18 (1988); "The Trial before the Sanhedrin (Mark 14:53-65, Reader Response, and Greco-Roman Readers)" *CBQ* 49 (1987). Awd: John O' Brien Fellow. in Theol. 1982-84; Social Sci. & Hum. Res. Coun. of Canada, Doc. Fellow. 1985-87; CBA, Mem. Stipend 1986-87. Mem: SBL; CBA; CSBS. Addr: (o) U. of Winnipeg, Institute of Urban Studies, Winnipeg, Man. R3B 2E9, Canada 204-786-9851; (h) 91-141 Donwood Dr., Winnipeg, Man. R2G 0V9, Canada 204-663-2892.

BECK, Astrid B., b. Germany, May 15, 1943, d. of Edmund Billes & Sigrid (Butze), chil: David C.; Stephen G.; Kathleen G. Educ: U. of Mich., MA 1974, PhD 1984. Emp: U. of Mich., 1984- Prog. Assoc., Stud. in Relig., Adj. Lect in Comparative Relig.; *ABD,* 1984- Co-ed. Pub: "Rachel," "Rebekah" in *ABD* (Doubleday, 1992). Mem: SBL. Addr: (o) U. of Michigan, Dept. of Religion, Ann Arbor, MI 48109-1092 313-764-4475.

BECK, Pirhiya, Addr: (o) Tel Aviv U., Institute of Archaeology, Ramat Aviv, Tel Aviv, Israel 6-409-703.

BECK, Robert R., b. Waterloo, IA, August 28, 1940, s. of Paul Clayton & Mildred Ann (Klein). Educ: Loras Coll., BA 1962; Aquinas Inst. of Theol., MA 1965; Ecole Biblique, Jerusalem, Cert. of Study 1978; Cath. U. of Amer., DMin, Scripture 1983. Emp: Aquinas Inst. of Theol., 1973-81 Instr.; Loras Coll., 1981- Prof. Spec: Hebrew Bible, New Testament. Pub: *A Bible Study Method for Use in Pastoral Settings* (U. Microfilms Intl., 1983); and others. Awd: Natl. Cath. Press Awd. 1982-83. Rec: Composing music, writing poetry, jazz piano. Addr: (o) Loras College, P.O. Box 9, Dubuque, IA 52001 319-588-7249.

BECKMAN, Gary M., b. Pittsburgh, PA, August 22, 1948, s. of Joseph & Leah, m. Karla (Taylor). Educ: Yale U., MPhil 1974, PhD 1977. Emp: Yale U., 1978- Assoc. Prof., Hittite Yale Babylonian Collection, Assoc. Cur.; *JCS,* 1991- Assoc. Ed. Spec: Anatolian Studies, Mesopotamian Studies. Pub: "Inheritance and Royal Succession Among the Hittites" in *H.G. Guterbock Anniversary Volume* (1986); "Proverbs and Proverbial Allusions in Hittite" *JNES* 45 (1986); *Hittite Fragments in American Collections,* co-auth. (Yale Babylonian Collection, 1986); *Hittite Birth Rituals* (1983); "Mesopotamians and Mesopotamian Learning at Hattusa" *JCS* 35 (1983); "The Anatolian Myth of Illuyanka" *JANES* 14 (1982); and others. Awd: Deutscher Akademischer Austauschdienst Fellow. 1975-77. Mem: AOS 1975-, Dir.-at-Large 1992-; Assn. Anc. Hist. 1978-. Addr: (o) Yale U., 326 Sterling Memorial Library, New Haven, CT 06520 203-432-1838.

BECKWITH, Francis J., b. New York, NY, November 3, 1960, s. of Harold Joseph & Elizabeth, m. Frankie Rozelle. Educ: U. of Nevada, BA 1983; Simon Greenleaf U., MA; Fordham U., MA, Phil. 1986, PhD, Phil. 1989. Emp: Fordham U., 1986-87 Teaching Fellow, Phil.; Clark County Community Coll., 1987-88 Instr.; U. of Nevada, 1987-89 Instr., 1989- Lect., Phil. Spec: New Testament. Pub: *The Mormon Concept of God: A Philosophical Analysis,* co-auth. (Mellen, 1991); and others. Mem: Soc. of Christian Phil. 1985-; EPS 1988-, Pres. 1992-93; APA 1985-. Rec: Basketball, jogging. Addr: (o) U. of Nevada, Philosophy Dept., Las Vegas, NV 89154 702-895-4038; (h) 3021 Nutwood St., Las Vegas, NV 89108 702-658-7900.

BEEGLE, Dewey M., b. Seattle, WA, January 17, 1919, s. of Burton Linton & Gladys Juliette (Smith), m. Marion (Butterworth), chil: Kathryn Nadine; Barbara Lee. Educ: Asbury Theol. Sem., MDiv (summa cum laude) 1948; Johns Hopkins U., PhD 1952. Emp: Bibl. Sem., N.Y., 1951-65 Assoc. Prof., Hebrew & OT; Wesley Theol. Sem., 1965-86 Prof., 1986- Prof. Emeritus, OT; Amer. Bible Soc., 1961- Trans. Com., Bd. of Trustees;

Roberts Wesleyan Coll., 1979 Staley Disting. Schol. Ser. Lect.; Smithsonian Inst., 1982 Lect. Excv: Tel Balatah, 1964 Square & Area Supr.; Tel Gezer, 1965 Square Supr.; Tel Hesban, 1968, 1973 Area Supr. Spec: Archaeology, Hebrew Bible, Semitic Languages, Texts and Epigraphy. Pub: "What Does the Bible Say? Translations Speak in Many Tongues" *BAR* 8/6 (1982); *Scripture, Tradition, and Infallibility* (Eerdmans, 1979); *Prophecy and Prediction* (Pettengill, 1979); "Moses" in *The New Ency. Brittanica* (1974); "Ligatures with *Waw* and *Yodh* in the Dead Sea Isaiah Scroll" *BASOR* 129 (1953); and others. Mem: SBL 1948-; AAR 1948-80; ASOR 1948; AOS; NAPH. Rec: Stamp collecting. Addr: (h) 2853 Ontario Rd., NW, Washington, DC 20009.

BEERS, V. Gilbert, b. Sidell, IL, May 6, 1928, s. of Ernest & Jean, m. Arlisle, chil: Kathleen; Douglas; Ronald; Janice; Cynthia. Educ: Wheaton Coll., AB, Bibl. Arch. 1950; North. Bapt. Theol. Sem., MRE 1953, MDiv 1954, ThM 1955, ThD 1960; Northwest. U., PhD 1963. Emp: North. Bapt. Theol. Sem., 1953-57 Assoc. Prof.; David C. Cook Publ. Company, 1957-67 Ed. Dir.; Books for Living, 1967- Pres.; *Christianity Today,* 1982-85 Ed. Spec: Archaeology, New Testament. Pub: *The Victor Handbook of Bible Knowledge,* contb. (Victor, 1981); *The Book of Life,* 24 vol., contb. (Zondervan, 1980). Addr: (h) Rt. 1, Box 321, Elgin, IL 60120 708-668-6000.

BEGG, Christopher T., b. Washington, DC, November 14, 1950, s. of George & Joan (Vessa). Educ: U. of Louvain, Belgium, PhB 1971, PhD 1979, STD 1980. Emp: Cath. U., 1982- Asst. Prof.; *CBQ,* 1983- Publ. Ed.; *OT Abstracts,* 1993- Gen. Ed. Spec: Hebrew Bible. Pub: "Unifying Factors in 2 Kings 1:2-17a" *JSOT* 32 (1985); "The Tables (Deut. X) and the Lawbook (Deut. XXXI)" *VT* 33 (1983); "'Seeking Yahweh' and the Purpose of Chronicles" *Louvain Stud.* 9 (1982); "'Bread, Wine, and Strong Drink' in Deut. 29:5a" *Bijdragen* 41 (1980); "The Literary Criticism of Deut. 4, 1-40: Contributions to a Continuing Discussion" *Ephemerides Theol. Lovanienses* 56 (1980); and others. Mem: CBA 1981-; SBL 1982-; WUJS 1984-. Addr: (h) Catholic U. of America, Washington, DC 20064 202-319-5667.

BEIT-ARIEH, Itzhaq, b. Lithuania, s. of Meir & Esther, m. Rachel, chil: Avivit. Educ: BA 1967, MA 1970, PhD 1977. Emp: Tel Aviv U., Inst. of Arch., Israel, 1970- Sr. Res. Assoc., Lect. Excv: Tel Beer-Sheba, 1969-76 Arch. Supr.; South. Sinai, 1971-82 Dir.; Tel 'Ira, 1979- Dir.; Horvat 'Uza, 1982- Co-dir.; Qitmit Sanctuary, 1984- Dir. Spec: Archaeology. Pub: "The Edomite Shrine at Horvat Qitmit in The Judean Negev: Preliminary Excavation Report" *Tel Aviv* 18 (1991); "The Ostracon of Ahiqam from Horvat 'Uza" *Tel Aviv* 13-14 (1986-87); "Serabit el-Khadim: New Metallurgical and Chronological Aspects" *Levant* 17 (1985); "New Evidence on the Relations

between Cannaan and Egypt During the Proto-Dynastic Period" *IEJ* 34 (1984); "An Early Bronze Age II Site near Sheikh 'Awad in Southern Sinai" *Tel Aviv* 8 (1981); *Qadmoniot Sinai,* contb. (1980); *The Desert, Past, Present, Future,* contb. (1977); and others. Mem: IES 1977-; Israel Survey Com. 1982-. Addr: (o) Tel Aviv U., Institute of Archaeology, Israel 03-6409323; (h) 10 Israeli St., Givatayim, Israel 03-6735506.

BEITZEL, Barry J., m. Carol. Educ: Bob Jones U., BA, MA; Dropsie U., PhD. Emp: Bob Jones U., Instr.; Faith Theol. Sem., Asst. Prof., OT; Calif. Grad. Sch. of Theol., Asst. Prof.; Trinity Evang. Div. Sch., 1976- Assoc. Acad. Dean, Prof. of OT & Semitic Lang. Spec: Hebrew Bible. Pub: "The Dead Sea—Background to the Bible" BR 3/3 (1987); *The Moody Atlas of Bible Lands* (Moody, 1985); "An Index to the Ugarit Passages in the *Ugaritic Textbook*" in *Orient and Occident: Essays Presented to Cyrus H. Gordon on the Occasion of his Sixty-fifth Birthday;* "From Harrān to Imar Along the Old Babylonian Itinerary: The Evidence from the Archives Royales de Mari" in *Biblical and Near Eastern Studies Presented to William Sanford LaSor;* "The Old Assyrian Trading System and Routes According the Geographical Notices Contained in the Royal Archives of Mari" in *Mari: The First Fifty Years;* "The Right of the Firstborn in the Old Testament" in *Festschrift for Gleason L. Archer;* "Zarephath," "Zur," "Tripolis," "Zobah," "Zemarite" in *ISBE.* Mem: ASOR; AOS, V.P.; MidW branch 1986-; ETS; NAPH. Addr: (o) Trinity Evangelical Divinity School, 2065 Half Day Rd., Deerfield, IL 60015 708-317-8084; (h) 34999 N Oak Knoll Cir., Gurnee, IL 60031.

BEKKEN, Per Jarle, b. Bergen, Norway, October 22, 1960, s. of Erna & Gunnar, m. Lise, chil: Erlend; Ida; Vegard. Educ: Free Faculty of Theol., Oslo, Cand. Theol. 1985. Emp: Res. Fellow 1988-92; Ansgar Theol. Sem., 1992- Assoc. Prof. Spec: New Testament. Pub: "Apropos jodedommens mangfold" *Tidsskrift for Teologi og Kirke* 3 (1988). Mem: Collegium Judaicum 1985-. Addr: (o) Ansgar Theological Seminary, Fr. Fransons Kei 4, Kristiansand, N4635, Norway 042-43900; (h) Vardasuegen 123, Kristiansand, N4638, Norway 042-40559.

BELLINGER, William H., Jr., b. Bennettsville, SC, December 28, 1949, s. of William & Lavicie W., m. Elizabeth Faye (Smith), chil: Gillian Kathleen; Charles Raymond. Educ: Furman U., BA 1972; SE Bapt. Theol. Sem., MDiv 1975; U. of Cambridge, England, PhD 1981. Emp: Bethel Theol. Sem., 1978-81 Asst. Prof.; SW Bapt. Theol. Sem., 1981-84 Asst. Prof.; Baylor U., 1984- Assoc. Prof., Dir. of Grad. Stud. Spec: Hebrew Bible, Semitic Languages, Texts and Epigraphy. Pub: "The Psalms and Acts: Reading and Rereading" in *With Steadfast Purpose: Essays on Acts in Honor of Henry Jackson Flanders, Jr.* (Baylor, 1990); *Psalms: Reading and Studying the Book of Praises* (Hendrickson,

1990); "Psalms of the Falsely Accused: A Reassessment" in *SBL Seminar Papers* (1986); "The Interpretation of Psalm 11" *Evang. Quar.* (1984); "'Let The Words of My Mouth...': Proclaiming the Psalms" *SW Jour. of Theol.* (1984); *Psalmody and Prophecy* (JSOT, 1984); and others. Mem: SBL 1978-; ASOR 1979-81; SOTS 1982-. Rec: Art, music, sports. Addr: (o) Baylor U., Religion Dept., PO Box 97284, Waco, TX 76798-7284 817-755-3735; (h) 9210 Acorn Dr., Waco, TX 76712 817-776-7525.

BELLINZONI, Arthur J., b. NY, February 21, 1936, s. of Arthur J. & Frances E. (Docherty). Educ: Princeton U., AB 1957; Harvard U., MA 1962, PhD 1963. Emp: Wells Coll., 1962- Prof., Relig. Spec: New Testament, Apocrypha and Post-biblical Studies. Pub: *The Influence of the Gospel of Saint Matthew on Christian Literature Before Saint Irenaeus*, 3 vol., ed., contb. (Mercer U.P., 1992); *The Two Source Hypothesis: A Critical Appraisal*, ed. (Mercer U.P., 1985); "Approaching the Synoptic Problem from the Second Century: A Prolegomenon" in *SBL Seminar Papers* (1976); *The Sayings of Jesus in the Writings of Justin Martyr* (Brill, 1967); *Intellectual Honesty and Religious Commitment*, co-ed. (Fortress, 1967); "History and Cult in the Gospel of John and in Ignatius of Antioch," trans., in *The Bultmann School of Biblical Interpretation: New Directions?* (1965); "The Source of the Agraphon in Justin Martyr's Dialogue with Trypho 47:5" *VC* 17 (1963). Mem: AAR; SBL; ASOR; SNTS. Rec: Travel, tennis, philanthropy. Addr: (o) Wells College, Aurora, NY 13026 315-364-3296; (h) Box 5, Main St., Aurora, NY 13026 315-364-8794.

BEN-DOV, Meir, Emp: Israel Ministry of Relig. Affairs, Israel Nature Reserve Authority, Arch. Advisor. Excv: Temple Mount, 1968 Field Dir. Spec: Archaeology. Pub: "Herod's Mighty Temple Mount" *BAR* 12/6 (1986); "Found After 1,400 Years—The Magnificent Nea" *BAR* 12/6 (1977); *In the Shadow of the Temple Mount* (1986); and others. Addr: (h) 20 Burla, Jerusalem, Israel 02-535-365.

BEN-TOR, Amnon, b. Jerusalem, November 26, 1935, s. of Jacob & Kathy, m. Daphna, chil: Anat; Tamar. Educ: Hebrew U., BA 1958, MA 1962, PhD (summa cum laude) 1968. Emp: Hebrew U., 1969-72 Lect., 1973-77 Sr. Lect, 1978-83 Assoc. Prof., 1984-87 Prof., Arch., 1988 Yigael Yadin Prof. of the Arch. of Eretz Israel, 1992- Head of Inst. of Arch.; Harvard U., 1974 Res. Fellow in Near East. Arch.; U. of Pa., 1979-80 Vis. Prof., Syro-Palestinian Arch.; Yale U, 1985, 1991 Vis. Prof., Arch.; Columbia U., 1985, 1991. Excv: Masada, 1963-65 Area Supr.; Arad, 1966-67 Area Supr.; Hazor, 1968 Area Supr., 1990 Dir.; Athienou, Cyrus, 1971-72 Co-dir.; Yoqne'am Reg. Project, 1977-88 Dir. Spec: Archaeology. Pub: *The Archaeology of Ancient Israel*, ed. (Yale U.P., 1992); "New Light on the Relations between Egypt and Southern Palestine during the Early

Bronze I" *BASOR* 281 (1991); "Byblos and Early Bronze I of Palestine" in *L'Urbanisation de la Palestine a l'Age du Bronze Ancien* (1989); *Hazor*, vol. III-IV, ed. (1989); "The Yoqne'am Regional Project: Tel-Qiri" *Qedem* 25 (1987); "Trade Relations of the Land of Canaan in the Early Bronze Age" *Jour. of the Economic & Social Hist. of the Orient* (1986); "A Stamp Seal of the Fourth Millennium B.C. from Gamla" *Eretz-Israel* 18 (1985); "Glyptic Art of Early Bronze Palestine" in *The Land of Israel* (1985); *Cylinder Seals of Third Millennium Palestine,* BASORSup 22 (1978); and others. Mem: IES Directory Com. 1986-; State of Israel Arch. Coun. 1987-. Rec: Hiking. Addr: (o) Hebrew U., Institute of Archaeology, Mount Scopus, Jerusalem, 91905, Israel 02-882-403/4; (h) 20 Mevo Ha-Ole St., Giv'at Oranim, Jerusalem, 93586, Israel 02-618-363.

BEN ZVI, Ehud, b. Loberia, Argentina, March 12, 1951, s. of Enrique N. & Herminia E. (Chervinsky), m. Perla Monica, chil: Amos; Naamah; Micha. Educ: Hebrew U., Jerusalem, BSc 1974; Open U., Ramat Aviv, BA 1985; Tel Aviv U., MA (summa cum laude) 1987; Emory U., PhD 1990. Emp: U. of Alberta, 1989- Asst. Prof. Spec: Hebrew Bible. Pub: "The List of the Levitical Cities" *JSOT* 54 (1992); "The Dialogue between Abraham and YHWH in Gen 18:23-32" *JSOT* 53 (1992); "The Account of the Reign of Manasseh in 2 Kgs. 21:1-18 and the Redactional History of the Book of Kings" *ZAW* (1991); "Once the Lamp has been Kindled . . . A Reconsideration of the Meaning of the MT *Nir* in 1 Kgs 11:36, 15:4, 2 Kgs 8:19, and 2 Chr 21:7" *Australian Bibl. Rev.* 39 (1991); "Isaiah 1:4-9, Isaiah, and the Events of 701 BCE in Judah: A Question of Premise and Evidence" *JSOT* 1 (1991); *A Historical-Critical Study of the Book of Zephaniah* (de Gruyter, 1991); "Who Wrote the Speech of Rabshakeh and When?" *JBL* 109 (1990); and others. Mem: SBL; AAR; NAPH; CSBS; Assn. for Res. in Relig. Stud. and Theol. Addr: (o) U. of Alberta, Religious Studies Dept., 11045 Saskatchewan Dr., Edmonton, AB T6G 2B4, Canada 403-492-7183; (h) 4412-115 St., Edmonton, AB T6J 1T7, Canada 403-437-1338.

BENJAMIN, Don C., Jr., b. Shreveport, LA, March 14, 1942, s. of Lt. Col. & Mrs. Don C. Educ: St. Bonaventure U., BA, Phil. 1964; Cath. U., MA, Semitic Lang. 1969; Claremont Grad. Sch., PhD, Relig. 1981. Emp: Mt. St. Mary's Coll., 1975-76 Lect., Theol.; Urban Retreat & Educ. Ctr., Los Angeles, 1976-78 Acting Dir.; Rice U., 1978-91 Lect., 1991-93 Schol. in Residence; U. of St. Thomas, Grad. Sch. of Theol. 1980-83 Lect.; U. of Houston, 1986 Scanlon Vis. Schol. Spec: Hebrew Bible, New Testament. Pub: "The Stubborn and the Fool" *BT* 29 (1991); "An Anthropology of Prophecy" *BTB* 21 (1991); "The Divine Assembly," co-auth., *BTB* 21 (1991); "Stories of Elijah" in *The Land of Carmel: A Festschrift for Joachim Smet on his 75th Birthday* (Inst. Carmelitanum, 1991); *Old Testament Parallels: Laws and Stories from the Ancient Near East*, co-auth. (Paulist, 1991); *Deuteronomy and*

City Life (U. Press of Amer., 1983); and others. Awd: Turner Found., Study Grant 1983-85. Mem: SBL; CBA; AIA; ASOR. Addr: (o) Rice U., Box 1892, Dept. of Religious Studies, Houston, TX 77251 713-527-8101; (h) 7637 Moline St., Houston, TX 77087 713-645-9035.

BENKO, Stephen, b. Budapest, Hungary, June 13, 1924, s. of Istavan & Vilma (Németh), m. Brigitta E., chil: Evelyn; Catherine; Stephen; Suzanne. Educ: Budapest Theol. Acad., Hungary, BD 1947; U. of Basel, Switzerland, PhD 1951. Emp: Temple U., 1955-59 Instr.; Conwell Sch. of Theol., 1960-68 Prof.; U. of Basel, Switzerland, 1967 Guest Lect.; Community Coll., Del County, 1968-69 Prof.; Calif. State U., 1969- Prof. Spec: New Testament. Pub: *Pagan Rome and the Early Christians* (Indiana U.P., 1984); "Magic and Early Christianity" in *SBL Seminar Papers* (1982); *The Catacombs and the Colosseum, The Roman Empire as the Setting of Primitive Christianity*, ed. (Judson, 1971, 1976); "Some Thoughts on the Fourth Eclogue" *Perspectives in Relig. Stud.* 2 (1975); *Protestants, Catholics and Mary* (Judson, 1968); and others. Mem: SBL; Friends of Anc. Hist. Addr: (o) California State U., Dept. of History, Fresno, CA 93740 209-2153; (h) 1822 Robin Ave., Sonoma, CA 95476 707-935-6926.

BENNETT, Boyce M., b. Brownwood, TX, July 19, 1928, s. of Boyce M. & Ruby (Kyle), chil: Rebecca Ann. Educ: Texas A&M U., BS 1949; Gen. Theol. Sem., MDiv 1953, ThD, OT 1969; Nashotah House, STM, OT 1963. Emp: St. Augustine's Episc. Ch., 1957-59 Vicar; Ch. of the Advocate, 1957-59 Curate; Grace Ch., 1959-63 Rector; Gen. Theol. Sem., 1963-67 Tutor & Fellow, 1968- Prof., 1980-91 Sub-Dean, Acad. Affairs; Albright Inst. of Arch., Jerusalem, 1967-68 James Allen Montgomery Fellow. Excv: Gezer, 1965 Digger; Gigal Surface Survey, 1967 Area Supr., rescue operation; Tel el-Hesi, 1973 Asst. Field Supr. Spec: Archaeology. Pub: *An Anatomy of Revelation* (Morehouse, 1990); *Bennett's Guide to the Bible* (Seabury, 1982); "Gilgal" in *ISBE* (1979); *Ency. of Bible Life* (Harper & Row, 1978); "The Search for Israelite Gilgal" *PEQ* (1972); and others. Mem: SBL 1964-; AAR 1964-. Addr: (o) 175 Ninth Ave., New York, NY 10011 212-633-1701.

BERGANT, Dianne, b. Milwaukee, WI, August 7, 1936, d. of Anton L. & Ann K. Educ: St. Louis U., MA 1970, PhD 1975. Emp: Marian Coll. of Fond du Lac, 1973-78 Lect.; Cath. Theol. Union, 1978- Prof.; *Bible Today*, 1979-86, 1990- Assoc. Ed., 1986-90 Ed.; *Collegeville Bible Comm. (OT)*, Ed. Spec: Hebrew Bible. Pub: "Women in the Bible" *Emmanuel* 91/3 (1985); "A Roman Catholic Paradigm" *JES* 20/4 (1983); *Introduction to the Bible* (Liturgical, 1985); *Job & Ecclesiastes* (Glazier, 1982); and others. Mem: CBA 1970-; SBL 1975-; CSBR 1979-. Rec: Sailing, music. Addr: (o) 5401 S Cornell Ave., Chicago, IL 60615 312-324-8000; (h) 6700 S Oglesby Ave., Chicago, IL 60649 312-684-0876.

BERGE, Kare, b. Bergen, March 24, 1951, m. Solveig W. Educ: Free Faculty of Theol., Oslo, Cand. Theol 1977; U. of Oslo, DrTheol 1985. Emp: Norwegian Teacher's Academy, 1985- Assoc. Prof. Spec: Hebrew Bible. Pub: *Die Zeit des Jahwisten*, BZAW (1990). Addr: (o) Norwegian Teacher's Academy, Amalie Skrams vei 3, N-5035 Bergen, Norway 05-325650; (h) Algroey, N-5368 Skalvik, Norway 05-333645.

BERGEN, Robert D., b. Lawrence, KS, May 18, 1954, s. of Delmar & Avis, m. Martha S., chil: Wesley. Educ: Hardin-Simmons U., BA 1976; SW Bapt. Theol. Sem., MDiv 1980, PhD 1986. Emp: U. of Tex. at Arlington, 1982- Adj. Asst. Prof., Linguistics; Summer Inst. of Linguistics, 1982- Tchr.; Hannibal-LaGrange Coll., 1986- Assoc. Prof. Spec: Hebrew Bible, Semitic Languages, Texts and Epigraphy. Pub: "Artificial Intelligence and the Future of Biblical Studies" *Jour. of Relig. & Theol. Info.* 1 (1993); "Text as a Guide to Authorial Intention" *JETS* 30 (1987); "The Role of Gen. 22:1-19 in the Abraham Cycle" *Criswell Theol. Rev.* 4 (1990); *Discourse Criticism* (Davar, 1981); *Verb Structural Profiles of the Narrative Framework of the Pentateuch* (Davar, 1984). Awd: Julius N. Olsen Medal 1976; Austin Awd., 1976; Gil Fewell Evang. Assn., Bibl. Res. Schol. 1981, 1982. Mem: ETS 1982-; SBL 1982-; NABPR 1988-; IBR 1992-. Rec: Computer programming. Addr: (o) Hannibal-LaGrange College, 2800 Palmrya Rd., MO 63401 314-221-3675.

BERGMEIER, Roland, b. Karlsruhe, Germany, February 7, 1941, s. of Wilhelm & Margarete, m. Ortrud, chil: Matthias. Educ: U. of Heidelberg, Theol. Exam. 1961, Grad. 1974. Emp: Protestant Reg. Ch. of Baden, 1967- Parson; Secondary Sch., 1968- Tchr., Scriptures. Spec: New Testament, Apocrypha and Post-biblical Studies. Pub: *Die Essenerberichte des Flavius Josephus* (Kok Pharos, 1993); "Die Erzhure und das Tier: Apk 12,18-13,18 and 17f." *ANRW* II 25/5 (1988); "Röm 7,7-25a (8,2): Der Mensch-das Gesetz-Gott-Paulus-die Exegese im Widerspruch?" *KuD* 31 (1985); "Koeniglosigkeit als nachvalentinianisches Heilspraedikat" *NT* 24 (1982); "Weisheit-Dike-Lichtjungfrau" *JSJ* 12 (1981); *Glaube als Gabe nach Johannes* (Kohlhammer, 1980); "Zur Fruehdatierung samaritanischer Theologumena" *JSJ* 5 (1975); and others. Mem: SNTS. Rec: Gardening. Addr: (h) Rulaenderweg 35, D-76356 Weingarten, Germany 07244-8897.

BERLIN, Adele, b. Philadelphia, PA, m. George, chil: Joseph; Miriam. Educ: U. of Pa., PhD 1976. Emp: U. of Md., 1979- Prof., Hebrew. Spec: Hebrew Bible, Mesopotamian Studies. Pub: *The Dynamics of Biblical Parallelism* (Ind. U.P., 1985); *Poetics and Interpretation of Biblical Narrative* (Almond, 1983); "Ethnopoetry and the Enmerkar Epics" *JAOS* 103 (1983); and others. Awd:

Guggenheim Fellow. 1986-87. Addr: (o) U. of Maryland, Hebrew & East Asian Language & Literature, College Park, MD 20742.

BEST, Ernest, b. Belfast, Ireland, May 23, 1917, s. of John & Louisa Elizabeth (Owen), m. Sarah E. (Kingston), chil: Sheila Elizabeth; Mary Louise. Educ: Queen's U., Ireland, BA 1938, MA 1939, BD 1942, PhD 1948. Emp: Austin Presbyn. Theol. Sem., 1955-57 Guest Prof.; *Bibl. Theol.*, 1962-71 Joint Ed.; U. of St. Andrews, Scotland, 1963-74 Sr. Lect.; U. Glasgow, Scotland, 1974-82 Prof., Div. & Bibl. Criticism, 1983- Prof. Emeritus; Knox Coll., New Zealand, 1983 Vis. Prof. Spec: New Testament. Pub: "Recent Continental New Testament Literature" *ExpTim* 93-104 (1981-92); *Mark: The Gospel as Story* (T & T Clark, 1983); *Following Jesus: Discipleship in the Gospel of Mark* (Sheffield, 1981); "Dead in Trespasses and Sins" *JSNT* 13 (1981); *From Text to Sermon* (T & T Clark, 1978); *1,2 Thessalonians* (Black, 1972; Hendrikson, 1978); "The Role of the Disciples in Mark" *NTS* 23 (1977); "1 Peter and the Gospel Tradition" *NTS* 16 (1969); and others. Mem: SNTS 1955-. Rec: Golf, vegetable growing. Addr: (h) 13 Newmill Gardens, St. Andrews, KY16 8RY, Scotland 0334-73315.

BETZ, Hans D., b. Lemgo, Germany, May 21, 1931, s. of Ludwig & Gertrude (Vietor), m. Christel (Wagner), chil: Martin; Ludwig; Arnold. Educ: U. of Mainz, Germany, ThD 1957, Habil. 1966. Emp: Claremont Grad. Sch., Sch. of Theol., 1963-78 Prof., NT; U. of Chicago, 1978- Prof., NT, 1985- Chmn., Dept. of NT & Early Christian Lit. Spec: New Testament. Pub: *Synoptische Studien* (Mohr, 1992); *The Greek Magical Papyri in Translation* (U. of Chicago, 1986, 1992); *Hellenismus und Urchristentum* (Mohr, 1990); *2 Corinthians 8 and 9* (Fortress, 1985); *Galatians* (Fortress, 1979); and others. Awd: Alexander von Humboldt Res. Awd. 1986. Mem: SBL 1963-; SNTS 1966-; CSBR 1978-; Wissenschaftliche Gesellschaft fuer Theol. 1984-. Rec: Travel, hiking, photography. Addr: (o) U. of Chicago, Swift Hall 228, 1025 E 58th St., Chicago, IL 60637 312-702-8228; (h) 5630 S Blackstone Ave., Chicago, IL 60637 312-684-4891.

BETZ, Otto W., b. Herrentierbach, Germany, June 8, 1917, s. of Wilhelm & Agnes, m. Isolde, chil: Cornelia; Dorothea; Martin; Matthias; Tsang Kuen Park. Educ: U. of Tubingen, Germany, Theol. 1952, Dr.Theol. 1959, Dr. Habil. 1961; Oberlin Grad. Sch. of Theol., STM. 1953. Emp: Oberlin, 1959 Haskell Lect.; Chicago Theol. Sem., 1962-67 Prof., NT; U. of Tubingen, 1968-83 Prof., NT; Arbeiten zum Neuen Testament und Judentum ser., Ed. Spec: New Testament, Apocrypha and Post-biblical Studies. Pub: *Was Wissen Wit Von Jesus?* (1991); *Jesus, der Herr der Kirche* (1990); *Jesus der Messias Israels* (1987); *Jesus und das Danielbuch* (1985); *Wie verstehen wir das Neue Testament* (Wuppertal, 1983); "Probleme des Prozesses Jesu" *ANRW* 25

(1982); and others. Mem: SBL 1962-; SNTS 1962-; Gesellschaft fur Wissenschafliche Theol. 1970-. Rec: Playing music. Addr: (o) Evang. Theologische Fakultaet, 12 Liebermeisterstrasse, 7400 Tubingen, Germany; (h) 11 Rappenberghalde, 7400 Tubingen, Germany 07071-43388.

BEUTLER, Johannes H., b. Hamburg, Germany, October 3, 1933, s. of Karl A. & Anneliese (Lisch). Educ: Pullach, Munich, Lic. Phil. 1958; Hoschule Sankt Georgen, Frankfurt, Lic. Theol. 1964; Pont. Bibl. Inst., Rome, Lic. Re. Bibl. 1967; Pont. U. Gregoriana, Rome, ThD 1972. Emp: Hochschule Sankt Georgen, Frankfurt, 1973- Prof., Theol. & NT. Spec: New Testament. Pub: *The Shepherd Discourse of John 10 and its Context* (Cambridge U.P., 1991); "Literarische Gattungen im Johannesevangelium" *ANRW* 25/3; "Greeks Come to See Jesus (John, 12,20)" *Biblica* 71 (1990); *Habt keine Angst: Die erste Johanneische Abschiedsrede (John 14),* Stuttgart Bible Stud. (Katholisches Bibelwerk, 1984); "Psalm 42/43 im Johannesevangelium" *NTS* 25 (1979); "Die 'Juden' und der Tod Jesu im Johannesevangelium" in *Exodus und Kreuz im oekumenischen Dialog zwischen Juden und Christen* (1978); "Glaube und Zeugnis im Johannesevangelium" *Bijdragen* 34 (1973); *Martyria: Traditionsgeschichtliche Untersuchungen zum Zeugnistema bei Johannes,* Frankfurt Theol. Stud. (Knecht, 1972); and others. Mem: SNTS 1975-; Pont. Bibl. Commn. 1993-. Rec: Chamber music (violin). Addr: (o) Offenbacher Landstr. 224, D-60599, Frankfurt a.M, Germany 069-60610.

BEYER, Bryan E., b. Rochester, MN, July 30, 1955, s. of Ronald C. & Irene L, m. Yvonne M., chil: Matthew; Sheri; Michaela. Educ: Colo. State U., BA 1976; Denver Conservative Bapt. Sem., MDiv 1980; Hebrew Union Coll., PhD 1985. Spec: Hebrew Bible, Mesopotamian Studies, Semitic Languages, Texts and Epigraphy. Pub: *Obadiah, Jonah,* co-auth. (Zondervan, 1988); and others. Mem: ETS 1983-; SBL 1983-; IBR 1989-; NAPH 1990-. Rec: Softball, fishing. Addr: (o) Columbia Bible College & Seminary, PO Box 3122, Columbia, SC 29230 803-754-4100; (h) 2431 Merrywood Rd., Columbia, SC 29210.

BIDDLE, Mark E., b. Fort Payne, AL, February 26, 1957, s. of Joseph William & Martha (Miller), m. Lucia (Kuykendall), chil: James William Colin; Arthur Joseph Graeme. Educ: Samford U., BA 1979; South. Bapt. Theol. Sem., MDiv 1982; Ruschlikon Bapt. Theol. Sem., Switzerland, ThM 1985; U. of Zurich, DTh 1988. Emp: Carson-Newman Coll., 1988- Asst. Prof., Relig. Spec: Hebrew Bible, Mesopotamian Studies, Semitic Languages, Texts and Epigraphy. Pub: "The Figure of Lady Jerusalem: Identification, Deification, and Personification of Cities in the Ancient Near East" in *The Canon in Comparative Perspective,* SIC 4 (Mellen, 1991); *History of Jeremiah 2:1-4:2,* ATANT 77 (TVZ, 1990); "The 'Endangered

Ancestress' and Blessing for the Nations" *JBL* 109 (1990); "The Literary Frame Surrounding Jeremiah 30:1-33:26" *ZAW* 100 (1988). Mem: SBL 1988-; NABPR 1988-. Rec: Classical and jazz piano, literature, gardening. Addr: (o) Carson-Newman College, Box 72040, Jefferson City, TN 37760 615-471-3243; (h) 823 E Ellis St., Jefferson City, TN 37760 615-475-5184.

BIEBERSTEIN, Klaus, b. Landshut, Bavaria, October 15, 1955, s. of Rainer & Elisabeth (Becker), m. Sabine. Educ: U. of Tuebingen, Dip. 1983, ThD 1992. Emp: U. of Tuebingen, 1985-87 Jr. Lect., OT; *Tuebingen Atlas of the Middle East,* 1983-85, 1987-91; U. of Fribourg, Switzerland, 1991- Jr. Lect., OT Stud. Excv: Survey of Ain al-Quderat, 1981-82; Hirbet ez-Zeraqon, Jordan 1984. Spec: Archaeology, Hebrew Bible. Pub: *Josua—Jordan—Jericho. Studien zu den Landnahmeerzaehlungen Josua 1-6* (U. of Tuebingen, 1992); *Tuebingen Atlas of the Middle East,* contb. (Reichert, 1992); "Die Porta Neopolitana, die Nea Maria und die Nea Sophia in der Neapolis von Jerusalem," co-auth., *ZDPV* 105 (1989); "St. Thomas Alemannorum oder St. Peter ad Vincula? Zur historischen Identifizierung einer neuentdeckten Kreuz-fahrerkirche in der Altstadt Jerusalems," co-auth., *ZDPV* 104 (1988); "St. Julian oder St. Johannes Evangelista? Zur historischen Identifizierung einer neuentdeckten Kreuzfahrerkirche in der Alstadt Jerusalems" *ZDPV* 103 (1987); and others. Rec: Prehist. of Cen. Europe, medieval hist., hist. of medieval architecture. Addr: (o) U. Miséricorde, Institut Biblique, CH 1700-Fribourg, Switzerland 0041-37-219387; (h) Grandes-Rames 10, CH-1700 Fribourg, Switzerland 0041-37-228568.

BIENKOWSKI, Piotr A., b. Wimbledon, London, October 22, 1957, s. of Mieczyslaw & Janina, m. Barbara A. (Chlebik), chil: Maximilian; Dominik. Educ: U. of Liverpool, BA 1980, PhD, Oriental Stud. 1985; U. of Lancaster, MPhil 1993. Emp: Merseyside County Mus., 1983-86 Asst. Keeper of Antiq.; *Levant,* 1985-92 Ed.; Natl. Mus. & Galleries on Merseyside, 1986- Cur. of Egyptian & Near East. Antiq.; Mon. in Mediterranean Arch., 1990- Ed. Bd.; *Jour. of Mediterranean Arch.,* 1993- Ed. Bd. Excv: Tell Nebi Mend, Syria, 1979 Site Supr.; Buseirah, Jordan, 1980 Site Supr.; Udhruh, Jordan, 1981 Site Supr., 1982 Asst. Dir.; Tawilan, Jordan, 1982 Sr. Site Supr.; Survey in Petra, Jordan, 1983, 1986 Dir. Spec: Archaeology. Pub: "The Beginning of the Iron Age in Southern Jordan: A Framework" in *Early Edom and Moab: The Beginning of the Iron Age in Southern Jordan,* Sheffield Arch. Mon., ed. (1992); "Changing Places: Architecture and Spatial Organisation of the Bedul in Petra," co-auth., *Levant 23* (1991); *Treasures from an Ancient Land: The Art of Jordan,* ed. (Sutton, 1991); "Umm el-Biyara, Tawilan and Buseirah in Retrospect" *Levant 22* (1990); "The Role of Hazor in the Late Bronze Age" *PEQ* (1987); *Jericho in the Late Bronze Age* (Aris & Phillips, 1986); *Egyptian Antiquities in the Liverpool Museum I: A List of the Provenanced Objects,* co-

auth. (Aris & Phillips, 1986); and others. Mem: Egypt Exploration Soc. 1983-; ASOR 1988-; PEF; BSA, Iraq 1989-; Brit. Assn. for Near East. Arch. 1991-. Rec: Class. music, piano playing, writing fiction, tennis. Addr: (o) Liverpool Museum, William Brown St., Liverpool L3 8EN, England 051-207-0001.

BIERINGER, Reimund, b. Homburg/Saar, Germany, May 2, 1957, s. of Guido J. & Alice K. Educ: Phil.-Theol. Hochschule St. Georgen, Frankfurt/Main, Philosophicum 1979; Catholic U. of Louvain, Belgium, MA, Relig. Stud. 1981, STL 1983, PhD, Relig. Stud. 1986, STD 1986. Emp: Roman Cath. Diocese of Speyer, Germany, 1988 Asst. Pastor; Cath. U. of Louvain, 1990 Asst. Prof. Spec: New Testament. Pub: "Paul's Divine Jealousy: The Apostle and His Communities in Relationship" *Louvain Stud.* 17 (1992); *Sharper than a Two-Edged Sword: Essays in Honor of Professor Dr. Jan Lambrecht, S.J.,* Louvain Stud. 17, co-ed. (1992); "Der 2. Korintherbrief in den neuesten Kommentaren" *ETL* 67 (1991); "Ein Dankleid für Gott: Unterrichtsentwurf für die Grundschule zum ersten Scöpfungsbericht (Gen 1,1-2,4a)" *Katechetische Bläer* 114 (1989); "2 Kor 5,19a und die Veröhnung der Welt" *ETL* 63 (1987); and others. Mem: SBL 1986-; Deutscher Katechetenverein 1986-. Rec: Biking, jogging, swimming, drawing, classical music, corresponding. Addr: (o) Ch. DeBeriotstraat 26, B-3000 Leuven, Belgium 00-3216283832; (h) Minderbroedersstraat 15, B-3000 Leuven, Belgium 00-3216204478.

BIERLING, Neal, b. The Hague, Netherlands, September 21, 1946, s. of Neal & Ann, m. Marilyn, chil: Joel; Rachel; Sara. Educ: U. of Mich., MA 1977. Emp: Chandler Christian Sch., 1977-84 Tchr.; Ada Christian Sch., 1984- Instr. Excv: Tel Gezer, 1972-73 Area Supr.; Tel Lachish, 1981 Area Supr.; Tel Miqne, 1984, 1986-87, 1990 Area Supr., 1992 Asst. Field Supr. Spec: Archaeology, Hebrew Bible, New Testament. Pub: *Giving Goliath His Due: New Archaeological Light on The Philistines* (Baker, 1992); *The House of Israel, the Day of the Lord,* contb. (Christian Sch. Intl., 1989); *A Light to the Gentiles* (Christian Sch. Intl., 1989); "The Trowel and the Bible" *Christian Educ. Jour.* Oct./Nov. (1981). Mem: SBL 1975-; ASOR 1975-. Rec: Traveling, motorcycling, camping. Addr: (o) Ada Christian School, 7192 Bradfield St. SE, Ada, MI 49301 616-676-1289; (h) 6941 Adaside Dr., Ada, MI 49301 616-676-2380.

BIETAK, Manfred F. K. W., b. Vienna, June 10, 1940, s. of Wilhelm & Ilse, m. Margarete, chil: Veronika; Verena Charlotte; Elisabeth. Educ: U. Vienna, PhD 1964. Emp: Austrian Arch. Inst. Cairo, 1971- Dir.; *Untersuchungen der Zweigstelle Kairo des Osterreichischen Arch. Inst.,* 1975- Ed.; U. Vienna, 1975 U.-Dozent, 1981 U.-Prof., 1986- Chmn., Inst. for Egyptology, 1989- Prof.; *Agypten & Levante,* 1990- Ed.; *Mitteilungen der Agyptischen Kommission,* 1990- Ed. Excv:

Sayala/Nubia, 1961-65 Site Supr., Field Dir.; Tell el-Dab'a, 1966-69, 1975- Dir.; Asasif, Thebes West/Luqsor, 1969-79 Dir. Spec: Archaeology, Egyptology. Pub: "Egypt and Cannan during the Middle Bronze Age" *BASOR* 281 (1991); *Tell el-Dab'a*, vol. II & V (1975, 1991); "Canaanites in the Eastern Nile Delta," "Comments on the Exodus" in *Egypt, Israel, Sinai* (1987); *Sayala*, vol. I, III, V, VIII, co-auth. (1963-1987); "Hyksos," "Schihor," "Tell el-Jahudija-Keramik" in *Lexikon der Agyptologie* (1980-1986); *Avaris and Piramesse* (1979, 1986); "Problems of Middle Bronze Age Chronology" in *AJA* 88 (1984); *Anch Hor*, vol. 1 & 2, co-auth. (1978, 1982); and others. Awd: Deutsches Arch. Inst., Fellow 1980; Inst. d'Egypte, Cairo, Fellow 1980; Austrian Acad. of Sci., Fellow 1981; Royal Swedish Acad. of Lit., Hist., & Antiq., Fgn. Fellow 1989. Mem: Osterreichische Gesellschaft fur Ur-und Fruhgeschichte 1958-; Osterreichische Anthrop. Gesellschaft 1959-; Egypt Exploration Soc. 1981-. Rec: Sleeping. Addr: (o) U. of Vienna, Institute for Egyptology, Frankgasse 1, A-1090, Vienna 42-43-00.

BIMSON, John J., b. Crewe, England, August 17, 1950, s. of Douglas & Marian, m. Maya, chil: James; Thomas. Educ: U. of Sheffield, England, PhD 1977. Emp: Tyndale House, Cambridge, 1977-79 Res. Asst.; *The Illustrated Bible Dict.*, 1979-80 Map Cons.; Trinity Coll., Bristol, England, 1981- Lect., OT & Bibl. Arch., 1983- Lbrn. Excv: Khirbet Nisya, 1986- Sq. Supr. Spec: Archaeology, Hebrew Bible. Pub: "Merenptah's Israel and Recent Theories of Israelite Origins" *JSOT* 49 (1991); "The Origins of Israel in Canaan: An Examination of Recent Theories" *Themelios* 15/1 (1989); *Travel Diary of the Holy Land* (Tring/Lion, 1989); *The World of the Old Testament* (Scripture Union, 1988); "Exodus and Conquest—Myth or History? Can Archaeology Provide the Answer?" *Jour. of the Anc. Chronology Forum* 2 (1988); "Redating the Exodus," co-auth. *BAR* 13/5 (1987); *New Bible Atlas*, contb. (InterVarsity, 1985); *Redating the Exodus and Conquest* (JSOT, 1978; Almond, 1981); "King Solmon's Mines? A Reassessment of Finds in the Arabah" *TB* 32 (1981). Mem: Tyndale Fellow. 1977-; SOTS 1983-. Rec: Ornithology, painting. Addr: (o) Trinity College, Stoke Hill, Bristol BS9 1JP, England 0272-682803; (h) 135 Maple Rd., Horfield, Bristol BS7 8RF, England 0272-246530.

BINDER, Hermann F., b. Halvelagen, Romania, December 25, 1911, s. of Michael & Josefine, m. Roswitha (Rether), chil: Gerhardt; Rolf; Erika; Hermann; Ingrid. Educ: Protestant Theol. Inst. Klausenburg, DTh 1949. Emp: Inst. Klausenburg, Cluj, 1950-55 Prof., NT; Inst. Hermannstadt, 1955-82 Prof., NT; Bischofsvikar der Evang. Kirche AB, 1962-78. Spec: New Testament. Pub: "Paulus und die Thessalonicherbriefe" in *The Thessalonian Correspondence* (Leuven U.P./Peeters, 1990); *Das Gleichnis von dem Richter und der Witwe, Lukas 18,1-8* (Neukirchener, 1988); "Erwaegungen zu Phil 2,6-7b" *ZNW* 78 (1987); "Von Markus zu den Grossevangelien" *TZ* (1984); "Das Geschenk der Geborgenheit" in *Bewaehrung und Erneuerung* (Klein, 1980); "Die angebliche Krankheit der Paulus" *TZ* 32 (1976); *Der Glaube bei Paulus* (EVA, 1968); and others. Mem: SNTS; Wissenschaftliche Gesellschaft fur Theol. Addr: (o) Str. G-ral Magheru 4, Sibiu, RO-2400, Romania 924-22850; (h) P-ta Grivita 17, Sibiu, RO-2400, Romania 924-11886.

BIOSMARD, Claude M. E., b. Seiches, France, December 14, 1916, s. of Armand & Marie (Collière). Educ: Convent Dominicain, St. Alban-Leysse, France, Lic. Theol. 1945; Ecole Biblique, Lic. Bibl. Sci. 1947. Emp: Ecole Biblique, 1948-50, 1953- Prof., NT; U. of Fribourg, Switzerland, 1950-53 Prof., NT. Spec: New Testament. Pub: *Synopsis Graeca Quattuor Evangeliorum*, co-auth. (1986); *Le texte Occidental des Actes: Reconstitution et Rehabilitation*, 2 vol., co-auth. (1984); *La vie des evangiles*, co-auth. (Cerf, 1980); *Synopse des quatre evangiles en Francais*, vol. 1-3, co-auth. (Cerf, 1965-1981); and others. Mem: SNTS; Assn. Cath. Francaise pour l'Etude de la Bible; Mitglieder des Wissenschaftlichen Beirats des Inst. fuer NT Textforschung. Addr: (h) Ecole Biblique & Archeologique Francaise, 6 Nablus Rd., PO Box 19053, Jerusalem, Israel 02-28-22-13.

BIRAN, Avraham, b. Israel, October 23, 1909, s. of Aharon & Naomi, m. Ruth (Frankel), chil: Aharon; Naomi; David. Educ: Johns Hopkins U., MA 1934, PhD 1935. Emp: Govt. of Palestine, 1937-48 Dist. Officer; Jerusalem, 1949-55 Dist. Commn., Govt. of Israel, 1955-58 Consul-Gen., 1958-61 Foreign Min., Dir. of Armistice Affairs, 1961-74; Dir., Antiq. & Museums; Atiqot, 1961-74 Ed.; Nelson Glueck Sch. of Bibl. Arch., 1974- Dir., Prof.; *Temples and High Places in Biblical Times*, 1981- Ed.; *IEJ*, Ed. Bd. Excv: Tel Halif, 1955 Dir.; Tel Dan, 1966-91 Dir.; Aroer, 1975- Dir.; Ira, 1979 Dir.; Deir es Sid, 1983 Dir. Spec: Archaeology, Hebrew Bible. Pub: *Tel Dan, 25 Years of Excavations* (1992); "The Triple Arched Gate of Laish at Tel Dan" *IEJ* (1984); "Aorer in the Negev" *Eretz-Israel* (1981); "The Stratigraphical Sequence at Tel Sippor" *IEJ* (1966); "The Israelite Tribe of Half-Manasseh" *JPOS* (1936); and others. Awd: Johns Hopkins U., Rainer Fellow. 1932-35; ASOR, Thayer Fellow. 1935-37; Israel Museum, Percia Schimmel Awd. 1984; HUC-Jewish Inst. of Relig., PhD 1992. Mem: IES, Chmn.; ICOMOS; Israel Govt. Names Com. Addr: (o) 13 King David St., Jerusalem 94101, Israel 02-203333; (h) 13 Marcus St., Jerusalem 92232, Israel 02-632564.

BIRCH, Bruce C., b. Wichita, KS, December 3, 1941, s. of Lauren E. & Marjory H., m. Susan (Halse), chil: Jeremy D.; Rebecca L. Educ: South. Meth. U., BD 1965; Yale U., MA 1967, MPhil 1968, PhD 1970. Emp: Yale Div. Sch., 1966-68 Asst. Lect.; Iowa Wesleyan Coll., 1968-70 Asst. Prof., Relig. & Phil.; Erskine Coll., 1970-71 Asst. Prof., Bible & Relig.; Wesley Theol. Sem., 1971- Prof., OT; Princeton Theol. Sem., 1988 Vis. Prof.

Spec: Hebrew Bible. Pub: *Let Justice Roll Down: The Old Testament, Ethics and Christian Life* (Westminster/John Knox, 1991); *Singing the Lord's Song: A Study of Isaiah 40-55* (Abingdon, 1989); *What Does the Lord Require?* (Westminster, 1985); "Biblical Hermeneutics in Recent Discussion: Old Testament" *RSRev* 10 (1984); *The Rise of the Israelite Monarchy* (Scholars, 1976); "The Choosing of Saul at Mizpah" *CBQ* 37 (1975). Mem: SBL, Pres., Chesapeake Bay reg. 1974-75. Rec: Tennis, science fiction. Addr: (o) Wesley Theological Seminary, 4500 Massachusetts Ave. NW, Washington, DC 20016 202-885-8673; (h) PO Box 183, Middletown, MD 21769 301-371-8810.

BIRD, Phyllis A., b. Urbana, IL, June 25, 1934, d. of Marion & Florence (Ralph). Educ: U. of Calif., AB 1956; Union Theol. Sem., BD 1964; Harvard Div. Sch., ThD 1972. Emp: Perkins Sch. of Theol., 1972-85 Assoc. Prof., OT; Garrett-Evang. Theol. Sem., 1985- Assoc. Prof., OT; *JBL*, 1974-77 Ed. Bd.; *HTR* 1975- Ed. Cons.; *VT*, Ed. Bd.; *Semeia*, 1993- Assoc. Ed.; Bibl. Interpretation Ser. (Brill), 1993- Adv. Bd. Excv: Heshbon, 1968 Area Supr. Spec: Hebrew Bible. Pub: "Women (OT)" in *ABD* (Doubleday, 1992); "Israelite Religion and the Face of Israel's Daughters: Reflections on Gender and Religious Definition" in *The Bible and the Politics of Exegesis* (1991); "'To Play the Harlot': An Inquiry into an Old Testament Metaphor" in *Gender and Difference* (1989); "The Harlot as Heroine in Biblical Texts: Narrative Art and Social Presupposition" *Semeia* 46 (1989); "The Place of Women in the Israelite Cult" in *Ancient Israelite Religion: Essays in Honor of Frank Moore Cross* (1987); *The Bible as the Church's Book* (Westminster, 1982); "Male and Female He Created Them: Genesis 1:27b in the Context of the Priestly Account of Creation" *HTR* 74 (1981); and others. Awd: U. of Calif., Phi Beta Kappa 1956. Mem: Bibl. Colloquim 1978-; ASOR; Albright Inst. for Arch. Res., Trustee 1977-83; SBL 1976-, V.P., SW reg. 1981-82, Pres., SW reg. 1983-84. Rec: Hiking, cooking, gardening. Addr: (o) Garrett-Evangelical Theological Seminary, 2121 Sheridan Rd., Evanston, IL 60201 708-866-3976.

BIRDSALL, J. Neville, b. Leicester, England, March 11, 1928, s. of Joseph Henry & Hilda (Hall), m. Irene (Adams), chil: Richard Neville; Alison Mary (Wightman); Jonathan Edward; Katherine Elisabeth (May). Emp: Bapt. Union of Great Britain & Ireland, 1951-56 Min.; U. of Leeds, 1956-60 Lect., Bibl. Stud.; U. of Birmingham, England, 1961-86 Prof., NT Stud. & Textual Crit., 1986- Prof. Emeritus; U. of Calif., Los Angeles, 1965-66 Vis. Assoc. Prof., Caucasian Lang.; U. of Oxford, 1979 Marjory Wardrop Lect. Spec: New Testament, Apocrypha and Post-biblical Studies. Pub: "Georgian Studies and the New Testament" *NTS* 29 (1983); "Rational Eclecticism and the Oldest Manuscripts" in *Studies in the Language and Text of the New Testament*, NTSup 44 (1976); "The Text and

Scholia of the Codex von der Goltz" in *Origeniana*, Quaderni de Vetera Christianorum 12 (1975); "Khanmeti Fragments of the Synoptic Gospels from MS.Vind.Georg.2" *Oriens Christianus* 55 (1971); "The Text of the Gospels in Photius" *JTS* 7 (1955); and others. Awd: U. of Oxford, Marjory Wardrop Schol. 1970-72; Royal Asiatic Soc., Fellow 1974. Mem: SNTS 1958-. Rec: Watching rugby football and cricket. Addr: (o) 75 Stanhope Rd. South, Darlington, County Durham DL3 7SF, England 0325 462 307.

BLACK, C. Clifton, b. High Point, NC, May 5, 1955, s. of Carl Clifton & Iris Rebecca (Hill), m. Harriet S. (Fesperman), chil: Caroline Elizabeth. Educ: Wake Forest U., BA (summa cum laude) 1977; U. of Bristol, England, MA 1980; Emory U., MDiv (summa cum laude) 1981; Duke U., PhD 1986. Emp: U. of Rochester, 1986-89 Asst. Prof., Relig.; Colgate Rochester Div. Sch., 1987-89 Vis. Prof.; South. Meth. U., Perkins Sch. of Theol., 1989- Asst. Prof., NT; AAR/SBL Ventures in Relig. Ser., 1989- Assoc. Ed.; JBL, Ed. Bd. 1993-. Spec: New Testament. Pub: *Persuasive Artistry: Studies in New Testament Rhetoric in Honor of George A. Kennedy*, JSNTSup 50, contb. (JSOT, 1991); *The Disciples According to Mark: Markan Redaction in Current Debate*, JSNTSup 27 (JSOT, 1989); "Rhetorical Criticism and Biblical Interpretation" *ExpTim* 100 (1989); "The Quest of Mark the Redactor: Why Has it Been Pursued, and What has it Taught Us?" *JSNT* 33 (1988); "The Rhetorical Form of the Hellenistic Jewish and Early Christian Sermon: A Response to Lawrence Wills" *HTR* 81 (1988); "The Johannine Epistles and the Question of Early Catholicism" *NT* 28 (1986); "Pauline Perspectives on Death in Romans 5-8" *JBL* 103 (1984); and others. Awd: Duke U., G.H. Kearns Fellow 1981-84; U. of Rochester, Mellon Fellow 1988. Mem: SBL; CBA 1984-; AAR 1986-. Rec: Reading, jogging, music. Addr: (o) Southern Methodist U., Perkins School of Theology, Dallas, TX 75275-0133 214-768-2082; (h) 1601 Idyllwild Ct., Plano, TX 75075-2124 214-867-5527.

BLACK, David Alan, b. Honolulu, HI, June 9, 1952, s. of John & Elvera (Arsu), m. Becky, chil: Nathan; Matthew. Educ: Talbot Sch. of Theol., MDiv, NT 1980; U. of Basel, Switzerland, DTh 1983. Emp: Biola U., 1976-85 Assoc. Prof., Bibl. Stud.; Grace Theol. Sem., 1985-90 Prof., NT; Lockman Found., 1990- Schol. in Residence. Spec: New Testament. Pub: *Linguistics and New Testament Interpretation*, ed. (Broadman, 1992); *Scribes and Scripture: New Testament Essays in Honor of J. Harold Greenlee*, ed. (Eisenbrauns, 1992); *New Testament Criticism and Interpretation*, co-ed. (Zondervan, 1991); "The Pauline Love Command: Structure, Style and Ethics in Romans 12:9-21" *Filologia NT* 2 (1989); "Conjectural Emendations in the Gospel of Matthew" *NT* 31 (1989); *Linguistics for Students of New Testament Greek* (Baker, 1988); "The Text of Mark 6.20" *NTS* 34 (1988); "New Testament Semitisms" *BT* 39 (1988); "A Note on 'the Weak' in 1 Corinthians 9:22" *Biblica* 64 (1983); and others. Mem: SBL; CBA; ETS; NEAS. Rec: Surfing, swimming, drawing. Addr: (o) 3590 Elm Ave., Suite B, Long Beach, CA 90807 213-595-5679; (h) 11849 Stamy Rd., La Mirada, CA 90638 213-947-7908.

BLACK, Matthew, b. Ayrshire, Scotland, September 3, 1908, s. of James & Helen (Currie), m. Ethel Mary (Hall), chil: James Harvey; Elizabeth Hall. Educ: U. of Glasgow, MA 1930, BD, OT 1934, DLitt 1944; U. Bonn, Germany, PhD 1937. Emp: U. of Aberdeen, 1939-42 Lect.; U. of Leeds, 1947-52 Lect., NT Lang. & Lit.; U. of Edinburgh, 1952-54 Prof., Bibl. Criticism & Antiq.; U. of St. Andrews, St. Mary's Coll., 1954-78 Prof. of Div. & Bibl. Criticism, Prin.; *NTS*, 1954-78 Ed.; Leiden Peshitta Project, 1968-80 Chmn. Spec: Hebrew Bible, New Testament, Semitic Languages, Texts and Epigraphy, Apocrypha and Post-biblical Studies. Pub: "Doxology of the *Pater Noster* with a Note on Matthew 6.13b" in *A Tribute to Geza Vermes,* JSOTSup 100 (Sheffield, 1990); "A Bibliography on I Enoch in the Eighties" *JSP* 5 (1989); *The Book of Enoch or I Enoch* (1985); "Second Thoughts IX: The Semitic Element in the New Testament" *ExpTim* 77 (1965-66); *The Scrolls and Christian Origins: Studies in the Jewish Background of the New Testament* (Scholars, 1961); "The Parables as Allegory" *BJRL* 42 (1959-60); "The Development of Aramaic Studies Since the Work of Kahle" in *In Memoriam Paul Kahle,* BZAW 103 (1968); *An Aramaic Approach to the Gospels and Acts* (Oxford, 1967); and others. Awd: U. of Glasgow, DD 1954; U. of Munster, DTheol 1960; Brit. Acad., Fellow 1955, Burkitt Medal for Bibl. Stud. 1962; Cambridge U., DD 1965; BAS, Pub. Awd. 1986. Mem: Natl. Bible Soc. of Scotland, Dir., Hon. V.P. 1962; SOTS, Pres. 1968; SNTS, Pres. 1971; Royal Soc. of Edinburgh, Fellow 1977; Royal Soc. of Uppsala, Hon. Mem. 1979. Rec: Golf. Addr: (h) St. Michael's, 40 Buchanan, Gardens, St. Andrews, Fife, KY16 9LX, Scotland.

BLAESER, Peter, b. Marl-Huels, July 28, 1910, s. of August & Maria (Feid). Educ: U. Muenster, Theol. Fakultaet, Promotion 1940. Emp: Phil.-Theol. Hochschule Oeventrop, 1941; Johann Adam Moehler Inst. fur Oekumenik, 1958 Geschaeftsfuehrer, 1981-84 Leitender Dir.; Phil.-Theol. Akademie/Fakultaet Paderborn, 1960 Lehrbeauftragter, 1965 Prof., Oekmenische Theol. Spec: Hebrew Bible, New Testament, Semitic Languages, Texts and Epigraphy, Apocrypha and Post-biblical Studies. Pub: *Ordination u. Kirchliches Amt.* (1976); *Amt u. Eucharistie* (1973); "Die Eucharistie im Neuen Testament u. in der reformatorischen Theologie" *Catholica* 18 (1964); and others. Mem: SNTS 1960-; Arbeitsgemeinschaft Christlicher Kirchen in Deutschland 1969-; Soc. Oecumenica 1979-. Addr: (h) Adolfkolpingstrasse 2, Paderborn, Germany.

BLAIR, Edward P., b. Woodburn, OR, December 23, 1910, s. of Oscar Newton & Bertha (Myers), m. Vivian (Krisel), chil: Phyllis Marie; Sharon Louise. Educ: Seattle Pacific Univ, BA 1931; New York Theol. Sem., STB 1934; Yale U., PhD 1939. Emp: Seattle Pacific U., 1939-41 Prof. of Bible, Dean, Sch. of Relig.; New York Theol. Sem., 1941-42 Prof.,OT Lang. & Lit.; Garrett Theol. Sem., 1942-75 Harry R. Kendall Prof. of NT Interpretation; *Bibl. Res.,* 1964-65 Ed. Excv: Anata, Palestine, 1936 Dir. Arch. Surroundings for W.F. Albright; Roman Jericho, 1951 Area Supr.; Tell er-Ras, 1966, 1968 Asst. Dir.; Ostia, Italy, 1965 Study Team of Mithraic Sanctuaries. Spec: Archaeology, Hebrew Bible, New Testament. Pub: *Abingdon Bible Handbook* (Abingdon, 1975); *The Illustrated Bible Handbook* (Abingdon, 1987); "The Dead Sea Scrolls" in *Interpreter's One-Volume Commentary on the Bible (1971); Illustrated Family Encyclopedia of the Living Bible,* co-ed., contb. (1967); *Deuteronomy/Joshua* (1964); "Soundings at Anata" *BASOR* (1936); and others. Awd: Yale, Jerusalem Two-Brothers Fellow 1935-36. Mem: SBL 1939-; CSBR; AAR. Rec: Golfing, organ playing. Addr: (h) 299 N Heather Dr., Camano Island, WA 98292 206-387-0464.

BLEDSTEIN, Adrien Janis, b. Los Angeles, CA, March 4, 1939, d. of Ada Rita Kallin (Steiner) & Sidney Janofsky, m. Burton J. Bledstein, chil: Noah J.; Hannah R. Educ: Coll. of Jewish Stud., Calif., Teaching Cert. 1958; U. of Calif. at Los Angeles, BA 1960. Emp: Dawn Schuman Inst. for Jewish Stud., 1985-90 Bible; The Reader's Acad., 1986-93 Dir.; Open U. for Adults, Jewish Community Ctr., 1986-93 Tchr., Bible & Anc. Near East. Lit.; K.A.M. Isaiah Israel Cong., 1967-93 Tchr., Bible & Anc. Near East. Lit. Spec: Hebrew Bible. Pub: "Was Eve Cursed? (or Did a Woman Write Genesis?)" *BR* 9/1 (1993); "Was *Habbirya* a Healing Ritual Performed by a Woman in King David's House?" *Bibl. Res.* 37 (1992); "Women's Humor in the Bible?" *Humanist Judaism* 19/3 (1991); "The Trials of Sarah" *Judaism* 30/4 (1981); "The Genesis of Humans: The Garden of Eden Revisited" *Judaism* 26/2 (1977); and others. Mem: AAR 1985-; SBL 1985-; Coalition of Feminist Theol. at Chicago Sem. 1987-; Natl. Coalition of Independent Schol. 1990-93; CSBR 1993-. Rec: Swimming. Addr: (o) 5459 S Hyde Park Blvd., Chicago, IL 60615-5806 312-324-6956.

BLEIBTREU, Erika S., b. Graz, Austria, March 2, 1940, d. of Gottfried & Ottilie. Educ: U. of Graz, PhD. 1964; U. of Vienna, Austria, Habil., Vorderasiatische Arch. 1978. Emp: *Wiener Zeitschrift fur die Kunde des Morgenlandes,* 1963-83 Ed.; Vienna U., 1964-74 Asst. Prof., 1976-87 Lect., 1990-92 Assoc. Prof.; Johann Wolfgang Goethe U., Germany, 1992- Prof., Anc. Near East. Arch. Spec: Mesopotamian Studies. Pub: "Five Ways to Conquer a City" *BAR* 16/3 (1990); "Layard's Drawings of Assyrian Palace Reliefs" in *Austen Henry Layard tra l'Oriente e Venezia* (1987); "Ackerbauern und Viehzüchter in Mesopotamien" *Beiträge zur Historischen Sozialkunde* 4 (1986); *Rollsiegel aus dem*

Vordeten Orient (1981); *Die Flora der neuassyrischen Reliefs* (1980); "Zur Problematik von 'Tierkapelle' und 'Tiersymposion' in der mesopotamischen Flachbildkunst" *Wiener Zeitschrift für die Kunde des Morgenlandes* 67 (1975); "Roll- und Stempelsiegel im Bernischen Historischen Museum" *Jahrbuch des Bernischen Historischen Museums* 51/52 (1971-72); and others. Mem: Deutsche Orient-Gesellschaft 1965-. Rec: Photography. Addr: (o) U. Wien, Institut fur Orientalistik, A-1010 Wien, Universitatstr. 7/V, Austria 222-401032595; (h) Am Leonhardsbrunn 16, D-6000 Frankfurt am Main 90, Germany.

BLENKINSOPP, Joseph, b. Durham, UK, chil: David; Martin. Educ: U. of London, BA, Hist. 1948; Bibl. Inst., Rome, LSS 1958; Oxford U., PhD 1967. Emp: Intl. Theol. Coll., England, 1958-62 Lect., Bibl. Stud.; Vanderbilt Div. Sch., 1968, 1978 Vis. Prof., OT; U. of Notre Dame, 1970- Prof., John A. O'Brien Chair of Bibl. Stud.; Ecumenical Inst., Israel, 1978 Rector; *JBL*, 1989-92 Ed. Bd.; *CBQ*, Ed. Bd.; *JSOT*, Ed. Bd. Excv: Capernaum, Greek Orthodox site, 1980-87 Coord. Spec: Archaeology, Hebrew Bible, Semitic Languages, Texts and Epigraphy. Pub: *The Pentateuch* (Doubleday/SCM, 1992); "The Social Context of the Outsider Woman in Proverbs 1-9" *Biblica* 72 (1991); "Temple and Society in Achemenid Judah" in *Second Temple Studies* (1991); *Ezekiel: A Commentary* (John Knox, 1990); "The Judge of All the Earth: Theodicy in the Midrash on Gen. 18:22-33" *JJS* 41 (1990); "A Jewish Sect of the Persian Period" *CBQ* 52 (1990); *Ezra-Nehemiah: A Commentary* (Westminster, 1988); "Second Isaiah: Prophet of Universalism?" *JSOT* 41 (1988); *A History of Prophecy in Israel* (Westminster/SPCK, 1983); and others. Mem: CBA, Pres. 1989; SBL; AAR; AJS; SOTS. Rec: Tennis, travel, talking. Addr: (o) U. of Notre Dame, Dept. of Theology, Notre Dame, IN 46556 219-631-7153.

BLEVINS, James L., b. Hot Coal, WV, August 25, 1936, s. of James & Lona, m. Maxine Ruth, chil: Jennifer; Cynthia; James III. Educ: Duke U., AB; East. Bapt. Sem., MDiv; SE Bapt. Sem., ThM; South. Bapt. Sem., PhD. Emp: Mars Hill Coll., 1969-76 Prof., Relig.; *Perspectives in Relig. Stud.*, 1975 Ed. Bd.; South. Bapt. Sem., 1976- Prof., NT; *Rev. & Expositor*, 1978-79 Ed. Bd. Spec: New Testament. Pub: *Mercer Dict. of the Bible*, contb. (Macon, 1991); *Biblical Monologues* (Broadman, 1990); *Revelation as Drama* (Broadman, 1983); *Revelation* (John Knox, 1983); "The Genre of Revelation" *Rev. & Expositor* Summer (1980); "Philippi" *BI* Spring (1980); *The Messianic Secret in Markan Studies* (U. Press, 1980); "The Christology of Mark" *Rev. & Expositor* Fall (1978); and others. Mem: SBL 1972-; SNTS 1986-; NABPR. Addr: (o) Southern Baptist Seminary, 2825 Lexington Rd., Louisville, KY 40280 502-897-4222; (h) 4412 Deepwood Dr., Louisville, KY 40241 502-228-3937.

BLOCK, Daniel I., b. Borden, SK, Canada, May 22, 1943, s. of Isaac & Ella, m. Ellen, chil: Jason;

Jonelle. Educ: Trinity Evang. Div. Sch., MA 1973; U. of Liverpool, England, PhD 1972. Emp: Winnipeg Bible Coll. & Theol. Sem., Canada 1973-78, 1980-83 Prof., OT; U. of Liverpool, England, 1978-80 Assoc. Prof., Hebrew; Bethel Theol. Sem., 1983-87 Assoc. Prof., 1987- Prof., Hebrew & OT. Spec: Hebrew Bible, Semitic Languages, Texts and Epigraphy. Pub: "Ezekiel's Boiling Cauldron: A Form Critical Solution to Ezekiel XXIV 1-14" *VT* 41 (1991); "Echo Narrative Technique in Hebrew Literature: A Study in Judges 19" *WTJ* 52 (1990); "The Prophet of the Spirit: The Use of RWH in the Book of Ezekiel" *JETS* 32 (1989); *The Gods of the Nations* (1988); "Text and Emotion: A Study in The 'Corruptions' in Ezekiel's Inaugural Vision" *CBQ* 50 (1988); "Gog and the Pouring Out of the Spirit: Reflections on Ezekiel XXXIX 21-29" *VT* 37 (1987). Mem: SBL; ETS; IBR. Rec: Gardening, carpentry. Addr: (o) Bethel Theological Seminary, St. Paul, MN 55112 612-638-6188; (h) 4294 Brigadoon Dr., Shoreview, MN 55126 612-483-1225.

BLOEDHORN, Hanswulf, b. Berlin, Germany, May 2, 1950. Educ: Free U., Berlin, PhD 1986. Emp: *Tuebingen Atlas of the Middle East*, 1982-90; Inst. Judaicum, 1982-86; Bibl. Arch. Inst., 1987-90; Troy-Project, 1991- Redactor, *Studia Troica*. Spec: Archaeology. Pub: *Tuebinger Atlas des Vorderen Orients*, contb. (1992); "Die Kapitelle der Synagoge von Kapernaum: Ihre zeitliche und stilistische Einordnung im Rahmen der Kapitellentwicklung in der Dekapolis und in Palaestina" in *Abhandlungen des Deutschen Palaestina-Vereins* 11 (1993); "Jerusalem: Vom Chalkolithikum bis zur Fruehzeit der osmanischen Herrschaft," co-auth., in *Tuebinger Atlas des Vorderen Orients*, Beiheft B 100 (1993); "Der alte und der neue 'Schurer'" *JSS* 35 (1990); and others. Addr: (o) Biblisch-Archaeologisches Institut, Liebermeister- Str. 14, D-72074 Tuebingen, Germany; (h) Eugen-Str. 18, D-72072 Tuebingen, Germany.

BLOMBERG, Craig L., b. Rock Island, IL, August 3, 1955, s. of John & Eleanor, m. Frances (Fulling), chil: Elizabeth Kristine; Rachel Katherine. Educ: Augustana Coll., BA (summa cum laude) 1977; Trinity Evang. Div. Sch., MA (magna cum laude) 1979; U. of Aberdeen, Scotland, PhD 1982. Emp: Palm Beach Atlantic Coll., 1982-85 Asst. Prof., Relig.; Tyndale House, Cambridge, 1985-86 Sr. Res. Fellow; Denver Sem., 1986- Assoc. Prof., NT; *Themelios*, 1988- N Amer. Book Rev. Ed. Spec: New Testament. Pub: *Matthew: New American Commentary* (Broadman, 1992); "The Liberation of Illegitimacy: Women and Rulers in Matthew 1-2" *BTB* 21 (1991); "Interpreting the Parables of Jesus: Where Are We and Where Do We Go From Here?" *CBQ* 53 (1991); "Marriage, Divorce, Remarriage and Celibacy: An Exegesis of Matthew 19:3-12" *Trinity Jour.* 11 (1990); *Interpreting the Parables* (Leicester & Downers Grove/InterVarsity, 1990); "New Testament

Genre Criticism for the 1990s" *Themelios* 15 (1990); "The Structure of 2 Corinthians 1-7" *CTR* 4 (1989); *The Historical Reliability of the Gospels* (1987); *The Miracles of Jesus*, Global Perspectives vol. 6, co-ed. (JSOT, 1986); and others. Awd: Tyndale House Sr. Res. Fellow. 1985-86. Mem: ETS 1978-; SBL 1980-; Tyndale Fellow. 1980-; IBR 1986-. Rec: Swimming, Piano, Travel, Lawn Care, Scrabble. Addr: (o) Denver Seminary, PO Box 10,000, Denver, CO 80250-0100 303-761-2482; (h) 7850 S Race St., Littleton, CO 80122 303-730-8827.

BOADT, Lawrence E., b. Los Angeles, CA, October 26, 1942, s. of A. Loren & Eleanor (Power). Educ: St. Paul's Coll., MA Relig. Stud. 1969; Cath. U. of Amer., Lic. Theol. 1971, MA, Semitic Lang. 1972; Pont. Bibl. Inst., Rome, Lic. in Scripture Stud. 1973, Doc. Bibl. Stud. 1976. Emp: Fordham U., 1974-76 Asst. Prof., Dept. of Theol.; Wash. Theol. Union, 1976- Assoc. Prof., Bibl. Stud. Spec: Hebrew Bible, Semitic Languages, Texts and Epigraphy. Pub: *Reading the Old Testament* (Paulist, 1985); *Jeremiah 26-52, Zephaniah, Habakkuk and Nahum* (Glazier, 1983); *Jeremiah 1-25* (Glazier, 1982); and others. Mem: ASOR; AAR; CBA; SBL. Addr: (o) Washington Theological Union, 9001 New Hampshire Ave., Silver Spring, MD 20910 301-439-0551; (h) St. Paul's College, 3014 4th St. NE, Washington, DC 20017 202-832-6262.

BOCCACCINI, Gabriele, b. Florence, Italy, March 24, 1958, s. of Walter & Maria Adelaide (Ghinozzi), m. Aloma (Bardi). Educ: U. of Florence, Laurea, Hist. of Early Christianity 1983; U. of Turin, PhD, Judaic Stud. 1991. Emp: U. of Turin, Dept. of Oriental Stud., 1987- Res.; *Henoch*, 1987-89 Ed. Bd.; Princeton Theol. Sem., 1989-90 Vis. Schol., Dept. of Bibl. Stud.; Waldensian Faculty of Theol., Rome, 1992 Vis. Prof.; U. of Mich., 1992- Vis. Assoc. Prof., Dept. of Near East. Stud. Spec: New Testament, Apocrypha and Post-biblical Studies. Pub: *Il medio giudaismo. Per una storia del pensiero giudaico tra il III sec. a.e.v. e il II sec. e.v.* (Marietti, 1993); *Portraits of Middle Judaism in Scholarship and Arts: A Multimedia Catalog from Flavius Josephus to 1991* (Zamorani, 1992); *Middle Judaism: Jewish Thought, 300 B.C.E. to 200 C.E.* (Fortress, 1991); "Middle Judaism and Its Contemporary Interpreters (1986-1992)" *Henoch* 15 (1993); "Jewish Apocalyptic Tradition: The Contribution of Italian Scholarship" in *Mysteries and Revelations* (Sheffield, 1991); "La Sapienza dello Pseudo-Aristea" in *Biblische und judaistische Studien* (Lang, 1990); "E' Daniele un testo apocalittico?" *Henoch* 9 (1987); "Origine del male, libertá dell'uomo e retribuzione nella Sapienza di Ben Sira" *Henoch* 8 (1986); "Il concetto di memoria in Filone Alessandrino" *Annali dell'Istituto di Filosofia di Firenze* 6 (1984); and others. Mem: Italian Coun. of Christians & Jews 1980-; Italian Soc. for Judaic Stud. 1986-; SBL 1991-. Rec: Classical music & opera. Addr: (o) U. of Michigan, Dept. of Near Eastern Studies, 3074 Frieze Bldg.,

Ann Arbor, MI 48109 313-763-0314; (h) Canto de' Nelli 10, 50123 Florence, Italy 55-291-477.

BOCK, Darrell L., b. Calgary, AB, Canada, December 8, 1953, s. of Bertram, m. Sally (Painter), chil: Elisa Lynne; Lara Ann; Stephen Gordon. Educ: U. of Texas, BA 1975; Dallas Theol. Sem., ThM 1979; U. of Aberdeen, Scotland, PhD 1983. Emp: Dallas Theol. Sem., 1982- Prof.; Trinity Fellow. Ch., 1984- Assoc. Pastor. Spec: New Testament. Pub: *Dispensationalism, Israel and the Church: The Search for Definition* (Zondervan, 1982); "Carefully Building on Precedent: Luke 1:1-4" *CTR* (1992); "The Son of Man in Luke 5:24" *BRB* 1 (1992); *Proclamation From Prophecy and Pattern, Lucan Old Testament Christology* (JSOT, 1987); "Jesus as Lord in Acts and the Gospel" *BS* Apr. (1986); "Evangelicals and the Use of the Old Testament in the New" *BS* July, Oct. (1985); and others. Awd: Dallas Theol. Sem., Fac. Senate 1983, 1985, Teaching Awd. 1987. Mem: ETS 1978-; Tyndale Soc. 1981-; SBL 1985-; IBR 1986-. Rec: Basketball, tennis, photography. Addr: (o) Dallas Theological Seminary, 3909 Swiss Ave., Dallas, TX 75204 214-841-3715; (h) 6478 Highgate, Dallas, TX 75214 214-696-3229.

BODINE, Walter R., b. Memphis, TN, February 4, 1938, s. of Walter A. & Elizabeth B., m. Betty S., chil: W. Ray, Jr.; Donald B.; Kenneth E.; Jon R.; Stephen P. Educ: Memphis State U., BA (magna cum laude) 1960; Dallas Theol. Sem., ThM 1966; Harvard U., PhD 1973. Emp: Crichton Coll., 1966-69 Instr.; Dallas Theol. Sem., 1975-1988 Assoc. Prof. Spec: Hebrew Bible, Semitic Languages, Texts and Epigraphy. Pub: *Linguistics and Biblical Hebrew*, ed. (Eisenbrauns, 1992); "Linguistics and Philology in the Study of Ancient Near Eastern Languages" in *Working with No Data: Semitic and Egyptian Studies Presented to Thomas O. Lambdin* (Eisenbrauns, 1987); "Kaige and Other Recensional Developments in the Greek Text of Judges" *Bull. of the IOSCS* 13 (1980); *The Greek Text of Judges: Recensional Developments*, HSM Ser. 25 (Scholars, 1980). Awd: Henry C. Thiessen Awd. in NT 1966; W.H. Griffith Thomas Schol. 1966; Harvard U., Grad. Sch. of Arts & Sci. Schol. 1972-74. Mem: ASOR; SBL 1975-; NAPH 1975-; Intl. Orgn. of Masoretic Stud. 1975-; AOS 1981-. Rec: Piano, swimming. Addr: (h) 5621 Tremont, Dallas, TX 75214 214-821-4076.

BOECHER, Otto, b. Worms, March 12, 1935, s. of Otto Karl & Anna Katharina (Lumm), m. Ortrud (Bauscher), chil: Hans-Georg; Wulf Otto; Urs Peter; Dorothea. Educ: U. Mainz, PhD, Hist. of Art 1958, ThD, NT 1963, ThD Habil., NT 1968. Emp: Evang. Ch., Wiesbaden, 1960-61 Curate, Selzen, 1962-64 Parson; U. Mainz, 1963-68 Asst. Prof., 1968-71 Lect., 1971-75, 1978 Prof.; Teachers' Coll. & U., Saarbruecken, 1975-78 Prof. Excv: Alte Synagoge, Worms 1956. Spec: New Testament. Pub: "Licht und Feuer" *TRE* 21 (1991); "Johannes der Taeufer"

TRE 17 (1988); "Matthaeusevangelium" in *Festschrift Wilhelm Pesch* (1988); *Kirche in Zeit und Endzeit: Aufsaetze zur Offb. des Johannes* (Neukirchen-Vluyn, 1983); *Christus Exorcista* (Kohlhammer, 1972); "Woelfe in Schafspelzen (Mt 7,15)" *Theol. Zts. Basel* 24 (1968); *Der johanneische Dualismus* (Gerd Mohn, 1965); *Die Alte Synagoge zu Worms* (Stadtbibliothek, 1960); and others. Awd: German Bishops' Conf., Bonifatius Medal 1978; Order of St. John, Knight's Cross, 1981. Mem: Der Herold 1985-; Humboldt-Gesellschaft 1978-; SNTS 1970-; Kommission fur die Geschichte der Juden in Hessen 1970-; Deutscher Hochschulverband 1968-. Rec: Genealogy, heraldry. Addr: (o) Johannes Gutenburg- Universitat, Fb. 02, Postfach 3980, Mainz D-55099, Germany 06131-39-2285; (h) Carl Zuckmayer Strasse 30, D-55127, Mainz 33, Germany 06131-47-6645.

BOLING, Robert G., b. Terre Haute, IN, November 24, 1930, s. of Lyman Francis & Helen (Groh), m. Jean (Gade), chil: Gail; Ruth; Martha. Educ: Ind. State U., BS 1952; McCormick Theol. Sem., MDiv 1956; Johns Hopkins U., PhD 1959. Emp: Coll. of Wooster, 1959-64 Assoc. Prof., Relig.; McCormick Theol. Sem., 1964- Prof., OT; *Bibl. Res.*, 1975- Ed. Excv: Tananir, 1968 Dir.; Madaba Plains Project, 1984 Assoc. Dir., Reg. Survey. Spec: Archaeology, Hebrew Bible, Semitic Languages, Texts and Epigraphy. Pub: *The Early Biblical Community in Transjordan* (Almond, 1988); *Biblical and Related Studies Presented to Samuel Iwry*, contb. (1985); *The Word of the Lord Shall Go Forth* (1983); *Joshua*, AB (Doubleday, 1982); "Excavations at Tananir, 1968" *ASORSup* 21 (1975); *Judges*, AB (Doubleday, 1975); "Bronze Age Buildings at the Shechem High Place" *BA* 32 (1969); "'Synonymous' Parallelism in the Psalms" *JSS* 5 (1960); and others. Awd: ASOR, Montgomery Fellow. 1968; Albright Inst., Ann. Prof. 1981; ACOR, Ann. Prof. 1984; NEH, Res. Grant 1984. Mem: ASOR; SBL; CSBR. Addr: (o) McCormick Theological Seminary, 5555 S Woodlawn Ave., Chicago, IL 60637 312-241-7800; (h) 858 W Belden Ave., Chicago, IL 60614 312-248-8088.

BONILLA-ACOSTA, Plutarco, b. Las Palmas de Gran Canaria, Spain, December 2, 1935, s. of Gregorio Bonilla & Matilde Acosta, m. Esperanza Rios, chil: Priscilla M.; Jonatan A.; Pablo E.; Daniel C. Educ: U. de la Laguna, BU 1953; Sem. Biblico Latinoamericano, Dipl. 1957; U. de Costa Rica, LPhil 1960; Princeton Theol. Sem., ThM 1962. Emp: U. de Costa Rica, 1962- Prof., Dir., Sch. of Phil.; Sem. Biblico Latinoamericano, 1965-80 Acad. Dean, Pres.; Latin Amer. Evang. Ctr. for Pastoral Stud., 1980-82 Dir., 1982-85 Coord., Bibl.-Theol. Formation; United Bible Soc., 1987- Trans. Adv.; *Traduccion de la Biblia*, 1991- Ed. Spec: New Testament. Pub: "Reina-Valera: una version de hoy o de ayer?" *Traduccion de la Biblia*

2/1 (1991); "Filosofia griega y tradición judeo-cristiana" *Reflexion Teológicas* 4 (1987); *Los Milagros Tambión son Parábolas* (Caribe, 1978); "El concepto paulino del logos" *Revista de Filosofia de la U. de Costa Rica* 5/17 (1965); and others. Awd: Costa Rican Phil. Soc., First Prize, Phil. Contest 1961; Costa Rica Min. of Educ. lit. contest, First Prize 1968; S Fla. Ctr. for Theol. Stud., DD 1992. Mem: Costa Rican Phil. Soc. 1965-, 1980-81 V.P.; Latin Amer. Theol. Frat. 1975-; Intl. Assn. for the Promotion of Christian Higher Educ. 1985-; SBL 1988-. Rec: Reading contemporary novels and science fiction, swimming, jogging. Addr: (o) Apartado 4900, 1000 San Jose, Costa Rica 506-25-11-75.

BOOMERSHINE, Thomas E., b. Dayton, OH, May 15, 1940, s. of Glenn G. & Garnet L., m. C. Jean, chil: Thomas G.; Michael G. Educ: Earlham Coll., BA 1962; Union Theol. Sem., BD 1966, STM (summa cum laude) 1969, PhD, NT 1974. Emp: New York Theol. Sem., 1972-79 Prof., Bibl. Stud.; United Theol. Sem., 1979- Prof., NT. Spec: New Testament. Pub: *Story Journey: An Invitation to the Gospel as Storytelling* (Abingdon, 1988); "Biblical Megatrends: Towards a Paradigm for the Bible in Electronic Media" in *SBL Seminar Papers* (Scholars, 1987); "Peter's Denial as Polemic or Confession: The Implications of Media Criticism for Biblical Hermeneutics" *Semeia* 25 (1987); "The Narrative Technique of Mark 16:8," "Mark 16:8 and the Apostolic Commission" *JBL* 100 (1981); and others. Mem: SBL; CBA; AAR; Network of Bibl. Storytellers; World Assn. of Christian Communicators. Rec: Organist, class. music, swimming. Addr: (o) United Theological Seminary, 1810 Harvard Blvd., Dayton, OH 45406 513-278-5817; (h) 2030 Harvard Blvd., Dayton, OH 45406 513-274-1273.

BORCHERT, Gerald L., b. Edmonton, AB, Canada, March 20, 1932, s. of Leo F. & Lillian V. (Bucholz), m. Doris A. (Cox), chil: Mark G.; Timothy W. Educ: U. of Alberta, BA 1955; East. Bapt. Theol. Sem., MDiv 1959; Princeton Theol. Sem., ThM 1961, PhD 1967. Emp: Princeton Theol. Sem., 1961-63 Lect., Greek; N Amer. Bapt. Sem., 1963-77 Prof., NT, Acad. V.P.; North. Bapt. Theol. Sem., 1977-80 Prof., NT, Dean; South. Bapt. Theol. Sem., 1980- T. Rupert Coleman Prof. of NT Interpretation. Spec: New Testament. Pub: "The Passover and the Narrative Cycles in John" in *Perspectives in John* (Mercer, 1992); articles in *Mercer Dict. of the Bible* (Mercer, 1991); *Assurance and Warning: Studies in 1 Corinthians, John and Hebrews* (Broadman, 1987); *Discovering Thessalonians* (Guideposts, 1986); *Paul and His Interpreters* (1985); and others. Mem: SBL; SNTS; Commn. on Bapt. Doctrine & Interchurch Cooperation for the Bapt. World Alliance, Chair 1990. Rec: Travel, photography, writing. Addr: (o) Southern Baptist Theological Seminary, 2825 Lexington Rd., Louisville, KY 40280 502-897-4699.

BORG, Marcus J., b. MN, March 11, 1942, d. of Glenn & Esther, m. Marianne (Wells), chil: Dane M.; Julie R. Educ: Oxford U., England, Dip. Theol. 1966, PhD 1972. Emp: Concordia Coll., 1966-69, 1972-74 Asst. Prof., Relig. Stud.; Carleton Coll., 1976-79 Asst. Prof.; Oreg. State U., 1979- Assoc. Prof., 1991- Disting. Prof. of Relig. & Culture; U. of Puget Sound, 1986-87 Chism Disting. Vis. Prof.; Pacific Sch. of Relig., 1989-91 Vis. Prof., NT. Spec: New Testament. Pub: *Jesus: A New Vision* (Harper & Row, 1987); *Conflict, Holiness and Politics in the Teaching of Jesus* (Mellen, 1984); *The Year of Luke* (Augsburg/Fortress, 1976); "A New Context for Interpreting Romans 13" *NTS* (1973); "The Currency of the Term 'Zealot'" *JTS* (1971); and others. Awd: Rockefeller Fellow. 1964-65; NEH Summer Seminar 1985. Mem: AAR; SBL. Addr: (o) Oregon State U., Religious Studies, Corvallis, OR 97331 503-737-2921; (h) 4137 SW Stephenson, Portland, OR 97219 503-246-8151.

BORGEN, Peder J., b. Lilleström, Norway, January 26, 1928, s. of Omar & Harda, m. Inger (Duesund), chil: Heidi; Ingunn. Educ: Drew U., PhD 1956; U. of Oslo, Norway, ThD 1966. Emp: Norwegian Res. Coun., 1958-62 Res. Fellow; Wesley Theol. Sem., 1962-66 Asst. Assoc. Prof; U. of Bergen, Norway, 1967-73 Asst. Prof., Relig. Stud.; U. of Trondheim, Norway, 1973-Sr. Prof., Relig. Stud., 1984-87 Provost; *NT*, Co-ed. Spec: New Testament, Apocrypha and Post-biblical Studies. Pub: *Philo, John and Paul* (Scholars, 1987); *Logos Was the True Light* (Tapir, 1983); *Paul Preaches Circumcision and Pleases Men* (Tapir, 1983); *Bread From Heaven* (Brill, 1965, 1981); and others. Mem: SBL 1955-; SNTS 1967-; Royal Norwegian Soc. for Sci. & Letters 1978-, V.P. 1990-; Royal Norwegian Acad. 1987-; Royal Acad. for Sci. & Letters, Uppsala 1985-. Rec: Travel. Addr: (o) U. of Trondheim, Dept. of Religious Studies, 7055 Dragvoll-Trondheim, Norway 07-596586; (h) Theodor Petersensvei 18B, 7049 Trondheim, Norway 07-940772.

BORING, M. Eugene, b. Maryville, TN, August 13, 1935, s. of Maynard, m. Karen Kay (Chapman), chil: Bonnie; Bradley; Beth. Educ: Johnson Bible Coll., BA, NT 1957; Christian Theol. Sem., BD, NT Semitics 1962; Butler U., MA, NT Semitics 1963; Vanderbilt U., PhD, NT Theol. 1969. Emp: Phillips U. Grad. Sem., 1966-69 Asst. Prof., 1969-73 Assoc. Prof., 1973-82 Prof., 1982-86 Darbeth Disting. Prof. of NT; Tex. Christian U., 1986-92 A.A. Bradford Prof. of Relig. Stud., Brite Div. Sch., 1992- Prof. of NT; *JBL*, 1983 Ed. Bd. Spec: New Testament. Pub: *The Continuing Voice of Jesus: Prophecy in Early Christianity* (Westminster/John Knox, 1991); "Prophecy in Early Christianity" in *ABD* (1991); "An Expostion of John 5" *Interpretation* (1991); "Mark 1:1-15 and the Beginning of the Gospel" *Semeia* (1991); *A Commentary in Interpretation: A Bible Commentary for Teaching and Preaching* (Westminster/John Knox, 1989); "The Language

of Universal Salvation in Paul" *JBL* (1986); *Truly Human/Truly Divine: Christological Language and the Gospel Form* (CBP, 1984); *Sayings of the Risen Jesus: Christian Prophecy in the Synoptic Tradition* (Cambridge U.P., 1982); and others. Awd: Lilly Fellow. 1963-64; Vanderbilt U., fellow. 1964-65. Mem: Assn. of Disciples for Theol. Discussion; SBL; SNTS; CBA. Rec: Running. Addr: (o) Texas Christian U., PO Box 30772, Fort Worth, TX 76129 817-921-7441; (h) 6616 Welch Ave., Fort Worth, TX 76133 817-294-4110.

BOROWSKI, Elie, b. Warsaw, Poland, May 27, 1913, s. of Hersz Wolf & Rajzl (Zonszajn), m. Batya. Educ: Coleggio Rabbinico Italiano-Firenze, Florence, Final Exam. Rabbino Maggiore 1935; Pont. Bibl. Inst., Cert., Cuneiform Texts & Bible, Semitic Epigraphy 1938; Ecole Des Hautes Etudes & Ecole Du Louvre, Eleve Titulaire, Cert. in Arch. Orientale 1939; U. of Geneva, Switzerland, MA 1944, PhD 1946. Emp: Mus. D'Art at d'Histoire, Geneva, 1943-44 Attache; Royal Ont. Mus. of Arch., Toronto, 1949-51 Lady Davis Fellow, Res. Assoc.; Bible Lands Mus., Jerusalem, 1986- Founder. Spec: Archaeology, Mesopotamian Studies. Pub: "Introduction to Kunst der Sarden" in *Praehistorische Staatssammlung* (1982); *Neighboring Civilizations*, Archaeologia Nr. 4, co-auth. (Israel Mus., 1965); "Siegel der Sammlung Layard" *Orientalia* 21 (1952); "Bronze Standard from Iran" *Arch.* 5 (1952); "Eine Hornerkrone aus Bronze" *Orientalia* 17 (1948); *Cylindres et Cachets Orientaux Conserves dans les Collections Suisses* (Artibus Asiae, 1947); "Le Cycle de Gilgamesh" *Genava* 22 (1944); and others. Addr: (o) Bible Lands Museum Jerusalem, 25 Granot St., Jerusalem 93706, Israel 972-2-611066; (h) 13 Diskin St., Jerusalem, Israel 972-2-669991.

BOROWSKI, Oded, b. Petakh Tikvah, Israel, August 26, 1939, s. of Meir-Shalom & Alina (Kleinman), m. Marcia (Weil), chil: Jonathan; Orly. Educ: Coll. of Jewish Stud., BHL 1968; U. of Mich., MA 1972, PhD 1979. Emp: U. of Michigan, 1971-75, Lect.; Emory U., 1977-Assoc. Prof.; *Lahav Res. Project Newsletter*, 1975-89 Co-ed.; Arch. Inst. of Amer. Lect. Ser., 1980-83 Lect.; *BAR*, 1983- Ed. Bd. Excv: Lahav reg., 1960-67 survey & salvage work; Tel Gezer, 1971 Staff, 1972-73 Area Supr.; Tel Dan, 1974 Area Supr.; Tel Halif, 1975-89 Core Staff, 1976-80, 1986-87, 1989, 1992 Field Supr., 1990 Co-dir., 1981, 1983, 1990, 1993 Field Res. Spec: Archaeology, Hebrew Bible. Pub: "The Iron Age Cemetary at Tel Halif" *Eretz-Israel* 23 (1992); "The Negev—The Southern Stage for Biblical History" *BR* 5/3 (1989); "The Sharon—Symbol of God's Abundance" *BR* 4/2 (1988); "The Biblical Identity of Tel Halif" *BA* 51 (1988); *Agriculture in Iron Age Israel* (Eisenbrauns, 1986); "Yadin Presents New Interpretation of Famous Lachish Letters" *BAR* 10/2 (1984); "The Identity of the Biblical Sir 'a" in *The Word of the Lord Shall Go Forth: Essays in Honor of David Noel Freedman* (Eisenbrauns, 1983); "Four Seasons of Excavations at Tel Halif/Lahav" *Qadmoniot* 15 (1981); and others. Awd: Ford Found. Grant 1972;

Zion Found. Grant 1972; NEH Grant 1982-84; AIAR, Annual Prof. 1988; Dorot Res. Prof. 1991-92. Mem: IES 1970-; ASOR 1973-; SBL 1973-. Rec: Hiking, camping, microcomputers. Addr: (o) Emory U., Dept. of Near Eastern & Judaic Languages & Literatures, Atlanta, GA 30322 404-727-7951; (h) 2350 Wineleas Rd., Decatur, GA 30033 404-633-4372.

BOROWSKY, Irvin J., b. Philadelphia, PA, November 23, 1924, s. of Emma (Rottenberg) & Samuel, m. Laurie (Wagman), chil: Scott; Gwen; Ned; Ted. Emp: N Amer. Publ. Company, Found. & Chmn.; Amer. Interfaith Inst., Found. & Chmn.; Anne Frank Inst. of Philadelphia, Pres.; *Explorations,* Publ. Spec: New Testament. Pub: *Jesus's Jewishness,* contb. (1992); *Jews and Christians,* contb. (1991); and others. Mem: AAR. Rec: Biking, tennis, travel. Addr: (o) American Interfaith Institute, 401 N Broad St., Philadelphia, PA 19108 215-238-5345; (h) 220 Society Hill Towers, 31 B, Philadelphia, PA 19106 215-574-0206.

BORSCH, Frederick H., b. Chicago, IL, September 13, 1935, s. of Reuben A. & Pearl H., m. Barbara S., chil: Benjamin; Matthew; Stuart. Educ: Princeton U., BA 1957; Oxford U., BA 1959, MA 1963; Gen. Theol. Sem., STB 1960; U. of Birmingham, England, PhD 1966. Emp: Gen. Theol. Sem., 1971-72 Prof., NT; Ch. Div. Sch. of the Pacific, 1972-81 Pres., Dean, Prof., NT; Princeton U., 1981-88 Dean of Chapel, Prof. of Relig.; Sch. of Theol. at Claremont, 1992 Colwell Lect.; Episc. Diocese of Los Angeles, 1988- Bishop. Spec: New Testament, Apocrypha and Post-biblical Studies. Pub: *Many Things in Parables* (Fortress, 1988); "Pentecost 1" in *Proclamation 3* (Fortress, 1985); "Waste and Grace: The Parable of the Sower" *Hist. Mag. of the Protestant Episc. Ch.* 53 (1984); *Power in Weakness* (Fortress, 1983); *God's Parable* (Westminster, 1976); *The Christian and Gnostic Son of Man* (SCM, 1971); "Who Has Ears" *Anglican Theol. Rev.* 52 (1970); and others. Awd: Keasbey Schol., 1957-59; Seabury-Western Theol. Sem, DD 1978; Ch. Div. Sch. of the Pacific, STD 1981; Berkeley Div. Sch., STD 1983; Gen. Theol. Sem., DD. Mem: AAR; SBL; SNTS; Exec. Coun. of the Episc. Ch.; Anglican Consultative Coun. Rec: Canoeing, tennis, racquetball. Addr: (o) Episcopal Diocese of Los Angeles, Box 2164, Los Angeles, CA 90051; (h) 2930 Corda Ln., Los Angeles, CA 90049.

BOSS, Edgar W., b. Lisle, IL, March 11, 1914, s. of Edward & Violet Cecilia, m. Ruth Lillian, chil: David; Janyce. Educ: North. Bapt. Sem., ThD 1948. Emp: Bapt. Ch., 1941-48 Pastor; North. Bapt. Sem., 1948-59 Fac., 1959-62 Acad. Dean, Collegiate Div.; Judson Coll., 1963-81 Acad. Dean, 1981-85 Prof. of Relig. Spec: New Testament. Mem: AAR; SBR; SBL; Amer. Bapt. Sch. & Coll. Admin. 1971-81, Pres. 1974-75. Rec: Camping, gardening. Addr: (h) 711 Grant Ave., Downers Grove, IL 60515 312-968-6749.

BOVON, Francois, b. Lausanne, Switzerland, March 13, 1938, s. of Andre & Helene (Mayor), chil: Pierre; Martin. Educ: U. de Lausanne, Faculty de Theol., Lic. 1961; U. de Bale, Doc. 1965. Emp: U. of Geneva, 1967-93 Prof., Theol.; Harvard Div. Sch., Frothingham Prof. 1993-. Spec: New Testament, Apocrypha and Post-biblical Studies. Pub: *Révélations et Ecritures. Recue* (Labor et Fides, 1993); *Das Evangelium nach Lukas (Lk 1, 1-9,50),* EKK 3,1 (Neukirchener/Benzinger, 1989); *Luke The Theologian: Thirty-Three Years of Research (1950-1983)* (Pickwick, 1987); *L'oeuvre de Luc: Etudes d'exegese et de theologie,* LeDiv 130 (1987); and others. Mem: SNTS; Assn. pour L'Etude de les lit. apocryphe, Pres. Rec: Sports. Addr: (o) Harvard U., The Divinity School, 45 Francis Ave., Cambridge, MA 02138.

BOWES, A. Wendell, b. San Francisco, CA, November 6, 1945, s. of Alpin P. & Betty J. (Smith), m. Virginia H. (Miller), chil: Heidi L.; Shelley M. Educ: NW Nazarene Coll., BA 1967; Nazarene Theol. Sem., MDiv 1970; Princeton Theol. Sem., ThM 1971; Ch. of the Nazarene, Ord. 1973; Dropsie Coll., PhD 1987. Emp: Ch. of the Nazarene, 1971-82 Pastor; NW Nazarene Coll., 1982- Prof., Head of Dept. of Relig., Coord. of Grad. Stud. in Relig. Excv: Madaba Plains Project, 1992 Student Supr., Square Supr. Spec: Archaeology, Hebrew Bible, Mesopotamian Studies, Semitic Languages, Texts and Epigraphy, Egyptology. Pub: *A Theological Study of Old Babylonian Personal Names* (1987); "The Basilomorphic Conception of Deity in Israel and Mesopotamia" in *The Biblical Canon in Comparative Perspective* (Mellen, 1991); and others. Mem: SBL; ASOR; NAPH. Rec: Gardening. Addr: (o) Northwest Nazarene College, Box 281, Nampa, ID 83686 208-467-8449; (h) 932 W Locust Ln., Nampa, ID 83686 208-466-6599.

BOWES, Paula J., b. Murnau, Germany, November 28, 1923, d. of Josef Haller & Anny (Jehle), m. James E. Bowes, chil: Christopher; Marie; Theresa; Peter; Catherine; Thomas; Margaret; Andrew; Patricia; Gregory; Robert; William; Elizabeth. Educ: Christian Theol. Sem., MAR 1971; HUC-Jewish Inst. of Relig., PhD 1979. Emp: St. Maur's Sem., 1975-76 Instr., OT; Ind. U. at Indianapolis, 1977-80 Instr., OT; Christian Theol. Sem., 1980-84 Instr., OT & Bibl. Lang.; Wesley Theol. Sem., Lay Resource Ctr., 1986, 1990 Instr., Hebrew; Pont. Bibl. Inst., Rome, 1987-88 Visiting Prof. Spec: Hebrew Bible. Pub: *Commentary on 1 and 2 Samuel* (Liturgical, 1985); "Women in the Hebrew Bible Syllabus" in *The Jewish Woman's Studies Guide* (Biblio, 1982); "The Structure of Job" *The Bible Today* (1982). Mem: CBA 1975-; SBL 1976-86. Addr: (h) 10947 Pleasant Walk Rd., Myersville, MD 21773 301-293-8966.

BOYD, Robert T., b. Charlotte, NC, December 8, 1914, s. of Robert & Frances, m. Peggy. Educ: Wash. Bible Coll., BA, Bibl. Educ. 1958. Emp: Clergyman, Ord. 1942; Wash. Bible Coll., 1960,

1964, 1970, 1978 G.A. Miles Lect.; Practical Bible Training Sch., 1984 M.L. Lowe Lect.; Antietam Bible Sem., 1984 Wm. Freed Lect. Excv: Dothan, 1954 Staff. Spec: Archaeology. Pub: *Boyd's Bible Handbook* (Harvest, 1983); *Pictorial Guide to Biblical Archaeology* (Harvest, 1969, 1981); and others. Awd: Indian Orthodox Ch., India, DD 1954; Antietam Bible Sem., DMin 1991. Rec: Travel, photography. Addr: (o) 1712 Academy St., Scranton, PA 18504 717-343-5996.

BRAENDLE, Rudolf, b. Aarau, Switzerland, August 25, 1939, s. of Ernst & Ida (Ruchti), m. Margrit (Lendenmann), chil: Martin; Andreas; Christian; Sabine. Educ: U. of Basel, 1961; U. of Goettingen, 1962; U. of Paris, 1964. Emp: U of Basel, 1978-85 Outside Lect., 1985- Prof., NT & Patristics. Spec: New Testament, Apocrypha and Post-biblical Studies. Pub: "Petrus und Paulus als nova sidera" *TZ* 48 (1992); *Franz Overbecks unerledigte Anfragen an das Christentum*, co-ed. (1988); "Christen und Juden in Antiochien in den Jahren 386/387: Ein Beitrag zur Geschichte altkirchlicher Judenfeindschaft" *Judaica* 43 (1987); "Theologie und Lebensgeschichte und Theologie: Ein Beitrag zur psychohistorischen Interpretation Augustins," co-auth. *TZ* 40 (1984); *Matt. 25,31-46 im Werk des Johannes Chrysostomos*, Beiträege zur Geschichte der Bibl. Exegese 22 (1979); "Jean Chrysostome— L'importance de Matth. 25,31-46 pour son ethique" *VC* 31 (1977); "Das Mysterium des christlichen Gottesdienstes: Anmerkungen zur Ethik des sogenannten Diognetbriefes" *SP* 13 (1975); *Die Ethik der 'Schrift an Diognet'*, ATANT 64 (1975); and others. Mem: Schweizerische Patristische Arbeitsgemeinschaft 1971-; Assn. Intl. d'etudes patristiques 1975-; SNTS 1984-. Rec: Rambling, cooking. Addr: (o) Theologisches Seminar, Nadelberg 10, CH-4051 Basel, Switzerland 061-267-29-04; (h) Feierabendstrasse 7, CH-4051 Basel, Switzerland 061-2818121.

BRAMS, Steven J., b. Concord, NH, November 28, 1940, s. of Nathan & Isabelle (Tryman), m. Eva, chil: Julie; Michael. Educ: Mass. Inst. of Tech., SB 1962; Northwest. U., PhD 1966. Emp: Inst. for Defense Analyses, 1965-67 Res. Assoc.; Syracuse U., 1967-69 Asst. Prof.; N.Y. U., 1969- Prof. Spec: Hebrew Bible. Pub: *Superior Beings: If They Exist, How Would We Know? Game-Theoretic Implications of Omniscience, Omnipotence, Immortality, and Incomprehensibility* (Springer-Verlag, 1983); *Biblical Games: A Strategic Analysis of Stories in the Old Testament* (MIT, 1980); and others. Awd: Natl. Sci. Found. Grants 1968-71, 1974-75, 1980-91; Ford Found. Grant 1984-85; Guggenheim Fellow. 1986-87; Sloan Found. Grants 1986-89; Amer. Assn. for the Advancement of Sci., Fellow 1992. Mem: Amer. Assn. for the Advancement of Sci.; Amer. Political Sci. Assn.; Intl. Stud. Assn.; Peace Sci. Soc.; Policy Stud. Orgn. Rec: Tennis, squash, ballet, opera. Addr: (o) New York U., Dept. of Politics, New York, NY 10003 212-998-

8510; (h) 4 Washington Sq. Village #17I, New York, NY 10012 212-260-4937.

BRASHLER, James A., b. Grand Rapids, MI, October 16, 1942, s. of Clarence & Wilma, m. Lenore (Vanden Bont), chil: Daniel John; Phyllis Cornelia. Educ: Calvin Coll., AB 1964; Calvin Theol. Sem., BD 1968; Claremont Grad. Sch., PhD 1977. Emp: Nag Hammadi Codices Trans. & Facsimile Ed. Project, 1970-83; Claremont Grad. Sch., 1973-83 Assoc. Dir., Inst. for Antiq. & Christianity; St. Mary's Sem. & U., 1984- Dean, Ecumenical Inst. Spec: New Testament, Apocrypha and Post-biblical Studies. Pub: "Nag Hammadi Codices Shed New Light on Early Christian History" *BAR* 10/1 (1984); and others. Awd: Woodrow Wilson Diss. Fellow. 1970. Mem: AAR 1970-; SBL 1970-. Rec: Gardening, choral music, cooking. Addr: (o) St. Mary's Seminary & U., 5400 Roland Ave., Baltimore, MD 21210 410-323-1463; (h) 812 Ridgeleigh Rd., Baltimore, MD 21212 410-337-8628.

BRATCHER, Robert G., b. Campos, Brazil, April 17, 1920, s. of Lewis M. & Artie P., m. June (Heaton), chil: Meredith L.; Priscilla Anne; Stephen J. Educ: South. Bapt. Theol. Sem., ThM 1944, ThD 1949. Emp: S Brazil Theol. Sem., Rio de Janeiro, 1950-54 Prof., NT, Dean; South. Bapt. Theol. Sem., 1954-55 Vis. Prof., NT; United Bible Soc., 1957- Trans. Cons. Spec: New Testament. Pub: *A Translator's Handbook on the Book of Psalms*, co-auth. (United Bible Soc., 1991); *A History of Bible Translations and the North American Contribution*, co-auth. (Scholars, 1991); *A Translator's Handbook on the Book of Joshua*, co-auth. (United Bible Soc., 1983); *A Translator's Handbook on the Gospel of Mark*, co-auth. (United Bible Soc., 1961); and others. Awd: Georgetown Coll., LittD 1968; Chicago Bibl. Soc., Gutenberg Awd. 1969. Mem: SBL. Addr: (h) 2 Spring Dell Ln., Chapel Hill, NC 27514 919-929-5018.

BRAWLEY, Robert L., b. Charlotte, NC, December 26, 1939, s. of John Gray & Mary Alice, m. Jane (Patrick), chil: Anna Patrick; Sara Frances. Educ: Erskine Theol. Sem., MDiv 1965; Luth. South. Theol. Sem., STM 1974; Princeton Theol. Sem., PhD 1978. Emp: Sem. Presbiteriano Asociado Reformado de Mexico, 1965-68 Instr.; Beaver Coll., 1978 Adj. Asst. Prof.; Memphis Theol. Sem., 1979-92 Prof.; McCormick Theol. Sem., 1992- Prof. Spec: New Testament. Pub: *Centering on God* (1990); *Luke-Acts and the Jews* (1987); *Luke-Acts*, contb. (1984). Mem: SBL 1976-. Rec: Oil painting, golf. Addr: (o) 5555 S Woodlawn Ave., Chicago, IL 60637 312-947-6300.

BREHM, H. Alan, b. McAllen, Tex., March 31, 1961, s. of Harold E. & Susan (Simonds), m. Gwen Lee, chil: Derek Alan; Michael Lee. Educ: Howard Payne U., BA (summa cum laude), Bible & Greek 1983; SW Bapt. Theol. Sem.,

MDiv 1986, PhD 1992. Emp: Vaughan Bapt. Ch., 1986-89 Pastor; SW Bapt. Theol. Sem., 1990-92 Adj. Tchr., NT Greek, 1992- Asst. Prof., NT. Spec: New Testament. Pub: "The Significance of the Summaries for Interpreting Acts" *SW Jour. of Theol.* Fall (1990). Awd: Eberhard-Karls-U., Fulbright Schol. 1989-90. Mem: SBL 1987-; IBR 1987-; AAR 1989-. Rec: Rose gardening, reading class. lit., water sports, camping. Addr: (o) Southwestern Baptist Theological Seminary, P.O. Box 22458, Fort Worth, TX 76122 817-923-1921; (h) 3000 Sixth Ave., Forth Worth, TX 76110 817-923-3008.

BRESLAUER, S. Daniel, b. San Francisco, CA, April 23, 1942, s. of Daniel & Lynette (Goldstone), m. Frances, chil: Don; Tamar. Educ: Hebrew Union Coll.-Jewish Inst. Relig., BHL 1965, MHL 1969; Brandeis U., MA 1970, PhD, Near East. Stud. 1974. Emp: Colgate U., 1971-75 Asst. Prof., Phil. & Relig.; U. of Nebr., 1975-76 Vis. Lect.; Princeton U., 1977-78 Vis. Lect.; U. of Kans., 1978-79 Assoc. Prof., 1980- Prof., Relig. Stud. Spec: Hebrew Bible. Pub: *Martin Buber on Myth* (Garland, 1990); "Scripture and Authority" *Perspectives on Relig. Stud.* 10 (1983); "Modernizing Biblical Religion" *Encounter* 38 (1977); and others. Mem: SBL; AAR; NAPH; MidW Jewish Stud. Assn., Pres. 1991-93. Addr: (o) U. of Kansas, Dept. of Religious Studies, 103 Smith Hall, Lawrence, KS 66045 913-864-4663; (h) 2404 Free State Ln., Lawrence, KS 66046.

BRETTLER, Marc Z., b. Brooklyn, NY, January 18, 1958, s. of Sidney & Miriam (Hershdorfer), m. Monica S. (Rosner), chil: Talya; Ezra. Educ: Brandeis U., BA 1978, MA 1978, PhD 1986. Emp: Wellesley Coll., 1982-83 Instr., Relig.; Yale U., 1984-86 Lect., Relig. Stud.; Brandeis U., 1988-92 Asst. Prof., 1992- Assoc. Prof., Near East. & Judaic Stud. Spec: Hebrew Bible. Pub: *Minhah le-Nahum: Biblical and Other Studies Presented to Nahum M. Sarna in Honour of his 70th Birthday,* JSOTSup 154, co-ed. (Sheffield, 1993); "Never the Twain Shall Meet? The Ehud Story as History and Literature" *HUCA* 62 (1991); "The Structure of 1 Kings 1-11" *JSOT* 49 (1991); *God is King: Understanding an Israelite Metaphor,* JSOTSup 76 (Sheffield, 1989); "The Book of Judges: Literature as Politics" *JBL* 108 (1989); "Ideology, History and Theology in 2 Kings XVII 7-23" *VT* 39 (1989); "The Promise of the Land of Israel to the Patriarchs" *Shnaton* 5-6 (1983); and others. Awd: Brandeis U., Michael L. Walzer Awd. for Excellence in Teaching 1991. Mem: SBL 1978-; AOS 1981-; AJS 1981-. Rec: Cross-country skiing, tennis, squash, origami. Addr: (o) Brandeis U., Dept. of Near Eastern Studies, Waltham, MA 02254 617-736-2968; (h) 62 Oak Cliff Rd., Newton, MA 02160 617-244-4952.

BRIGHT, John, b. Chattanooga, TN, September 25, 1908, s. of John & Elizabeth (Nall), m. Carrie Lena (McMullen), chil: Charles Crawford; Robert Nall. Educ: Presbyn. Coll., BA 1928; Union Theol. Sem., BD 1931, ThM 1933; Johns Hopkins U., PhD 1940. Emp: Presbyn. Ch., 1935-40 Pastor; Union Theol. Sem., 1940-75 Prof., Hebrew & OT Interpretation; U.S. Army, 1943-46 Chaplain. Excv: Tell Beit Mirsim, 1932 Staff; Bettin (Bethel), 1934 Staff. Spec: Hebrew Bible. Pub: *A History of Israel* (Westminster, 1981); *Covenant and Promise: The Prophetic Understanding of the Future in Pre-Exilic Israel* (Westminster, 1976); "The Apodictic Prohibition: Some Observations" *JBL* 92 (1974); "Jeremiah's Complaints: Liturgy or Expressions of Personal Distress" in *Proclamtion & Presence: Essays in Honour of C. Henton Davis* (SCM, 1970); *Jeremiah,* AB (Doubleday, 1965); "The Dare of Ezra's Mission to Jerusalem" in *Yehezkel Kaufman Jubilee Volume* (Magnes, 1960); "The Date of the Prose Sermons of Jeremiah" *JBL* 70 (1951); and others. Awd: Presbyn. Coll., 1947 DD; Davidson Coll., 1970 Dr. of Letters. Mem: SBL 1940-; AOS; The Bibl. Colloquium 1948-75. Rec: Reading, TV. Addr: (h) 1600 Westbrook Ave. Apt. 642, Richmond, VA 23227.

BRIGHTON, Louis A., b. Saskatoon, SK, Canada, October 30, 1927, s. of Louis F. & Helen E., m. Mary Belle (Williams), chil: Stephen Louis; Anne Louise; Christian Marie; Mary Helen Jeanette; Mark Andrew. Educ: Concordia Coll., BA 1950; Concordia Sem., MDiv 1952, STM 1964; St. Louis U., PhD 1991. Emp: Concordia Sem., 1974-91, Assoc. Prof., 1992- Prof., Exegetical Theol. Spec: Hebrew Bible, New Testament, Apocrypha and Post-biblical Studies. Pub: "The Book of Esther— Textual and Canonical Considerations" *Concordia Jour.* 13 (1987); "The Ordination of Women: A Twentieth-Century Gnostic Heresy?" *Concordia Jour.* 8 (1982); and others. Mem: SBL. Rec: Photography, travel. Addr: (o) Concordia Seminary, 801 DeMun Ave., St. Louis, MO 63105 314-721-5934; (h) 2541 Belmont Dr., Cape Town Village, High Ridge, MO 63049 314-677-2431.

BRIN, Gershon A., b. Tel Aviv, Israel, October 21, 1935, s. of Mendel & Tova, m. Dvora, chil: Ktsia; Amnon; Ayala; Shira. Educ: Tel Aviv U., BA, Bible, Hebrew Lang. & Lit. 1961, PhD, Bible 1971; Hebrew U., Jerusalem, MA, Bible 1965. Emp: Tel Aviv U., 1962-92 Assoc. Prof., 1979-82, 1989-90 Head, Dept. of the Bible. Spec: Hebrew Bible, Apocrypha and Post-biblical Studies. Pub: *Studies in the Biblical Exegesis of R. Joseph Qara* (Tel Aviv U., 1989); "Micah 2:12-13—A Textual and Ideological Study" *ZAW* 101 (1989); "Concerning Some Uses of the Bible in the Temple Scroll" *RQ* 48 (1987); *The Prophet in His Struggles* (Tel Aviv U., 1983); "R. Juda he-hasid—an Early Bible Exegete Rediscovered" *Immanuel* 12 (1981); "The Formulae 'From...and Onward/Upward' in the Bible" *JBL* 99 (1980); "The Firstling of Unclean Animals" *JQR* 68 (1977); *Studies in the Book of Ezekiel* (Hakibutz Hamenchad, 1975); and others. Awd: Samuel Young Awd. 1974-75; AAJR Awd. 1990, 1991. Mem: WUJS-; SBL; IOSOT. Addr: (o) Tel Aviv U., Dept. of Bible, Tel Aviv 69978, Israel 03-6409422; (h) 18 Blum St., Holon 58323, Israel 03-846185.

BRINKMAN, John A., b. Chicago, IL, July 4, 1934, s. of A. John & Alice C., m. Monique E. (Geschier), chil: Charles E. Educ: Loyola U., AB 1956, MA 1958; U. of Chicago, PhD 1962. Emp: U. of Chicago, Oriental Inst., 1964- Prof., 1969-72 Chmn., Oriental Inst., 1972-81 Dir., Oriental Inst. Tablet Collection, 1977- Cur., 1984- Charles H. Swift Disting. Service Prof., Dept. of Near East. Lang. & Civ.; *Chicago Assyrian Dict.*, 1977- Ed.; U. of Toronto, Royal Inscriptions of Mesopotamia Project, Babylonian Sect., 1979-91 Ed.-in-charge. Spec: Mesopotamian Studies. Pub: *Prelude to Empire* (1984); "Settlement Surveys and Documentary Evidence: Regional Variation and Secular Trend in Mesopotamian Demography" *JNES* 43 (1984); "Documentary Evidence for the Economic Base of Early Neo-Babylonian Society" *JCS* 35 (1983); "Notes on Arameans and Chaldeans in Southern Babylonia in the Early Seventh Century B.C." *Orientalia* 46 (1977); *Materials and Studies for Kassite History*, vol. 1 (Oriental Inst., 1976); *A Political History of Post-Kassite Babylonia, 1158-722 B.C.* (Pont. Bibl. Inst., 1968); and others. Awd: Amer. Coun. of Learned Soc., Fellow 1963-64; ASOR, Baghdad, Fellow 1968-69; NEH, Sr. Fellow 1973-74; Guggenheim Fellow 1984-85; Amer. Acad. of Arts & Sci., Fellow 1991-. Mem: AOS 1959-, MidW V.P. 1970-71, MidW Pres. 1971-72; ASOR 1962-; BIA, Ankara; BSA, Iraq; Deutsche Orient-Gesellschaft. Addr: (o) U. of Chicago, Oriental Institute, 1155 E 58th St., Chicago, IL 60637 312-702-9545; (h) 5535 S University Ave., Chicago, IL 60637 312-324-1526.

BRISCO, Thomas V., b. Hot Springs, AK, July 9, 1947, s. of Floyd & Mary, m. Judy, chil: Carole Renae; Brian Cooper. Educ: Ouachita Bapt. U., BA 1969; SW Bapt. Theol. Sem., MDiv 1974, PhD 1981. Emp: Ouachita Bapt. U., 1978-80 Instr.; SW Bapt. Theol. Sem., 1980- Assoc. Prof.; *SW Jour. of Theol.*, 1990- Assoc. Ed. Excv: Tel Batash (Timnah), Israel, 1981-84 Area Dir. Spec: Archaeology, Hebrew Bible, Egyptology. Pub: Articles in *Holman Bible Dict.* (1991), *ISBE* (Eerdmans, 1988); "The Sinai Peninsula and the Exodus" *SW Jour. of Theol.* (1977); and others. Mem: ASOR, V.P. 1982-83, Pres. 1983-84; NABPR, V.P., SW reg. 1991, Pres., SW reg. 1992. Rec: Fishing, hiking. Addr: (o) Southwest Baptist Theological Seminary, PO Box 22057, Fort Worth, TX 76122 817-923-1921; (h) 4359 Balboa, Ft. Worth, TX 76133 817-294-3355.

BRODIE, Thomas L., b. Crusheen, Ireland, November 3, 1940, s. of Bertram & Violet (MacMahon). Educ: Pont. U. of St. Thomas Aquinas, Rome, STL 1967, STD 1981; Pont.

Bibl. Commn., Vatican City, SSL 1972. Emp: Reg. Sem., Trinidad, 1968-72 Lect., Bibl. Stud.; Reg. Sem., Fla., 1976-80 Lect., OT; Grad Theol. Union, 1981 Lect., OT; Yale Div. Sch., 1981-84 Res. Fellow; Aquinas Inst., 1984-91 Prof., Bibl. Stud.. Spec: Hebrew Bible, New Testament. Pub: *The Quest for the Origin of John's Gospel. A Source Oriented Approach* (Oxford, 1993); "Greco-Roman Imitation of Texts as a Partial Guide to Luke's Use of Sources" in *Luke-Acts, New Perspectives from the SBL* (Crossroad, 1984); "Luke 7:36-50 as an Internalization of 2 Kings 4:1-37. A Study in Luke's Use of Rhetorical Imitation" *Biblica* (1983); "The Accusing and Stoning of Naboth" (1 Kings 21:8-13) as One Component of the Stephen Text (Acts 6:9-14, 7:58a)" *CBQ* (1983); "Jacob's Travail (Jer. 30:1-13) and Jacob's Struggle (Gen. 32:22-32): A Test Case for Measuring the Influence of the Book of Jeremiah on the Present Text of Genesis" *JSOT* (1981); *The Hebrew Method of Creative Rewriting as the Key to Unraveling the Sources of the Pentateuch* (1978); and others. Awd: Harvard U., NEH Fellowship 1982. Mem: SBL 1978-; CBA 1978-. Addr: (o) Cedara Theological Institute, P/B 6004, 3245 Hilton, South Africa 27-331-431232; (h) Las Casas Dominican House, Box 106, 3245 Hilton, South Africa.

BRODSKY, Harold, b. Brooklyn, NY, January 18, 1933, s. of Solomon & Mary, m. Naomi, chil: Jacob; Aaron; Joshua; Rebecca; Sarah. Educ: Brooklyn Coll., BS 1954; U. of Colo., MS 1960; U. of Wash., PhD 1966. Emp: U. of Md., Assoc. Prof., Dept. of Geog. Spec: Hebrew Bible. Pub: "The Jordan—Symbol of Spiritual Transition" *BR* 8/3 (1992); "Anti-Urbanism in the Bible" *Urbanism Past & Present* 17; "'An Enormous Horde Arrayed for Battle'—Locusts in the Book of Joel" *BR* 6/4 (1990); "Three Capitals in the Hills of Ephraim" *BR* 5/1 (1989); "The Shephelah—Guardian of Judea" *BR* 3/4 (1987). Mem: AAG, V.P.; BGG. Addr: (o) U. of Maryland, Dept. of Geography, College Park, MD 20742 301-405-4052; (h) 1411 Whittier St., NW, Washington, DC 20012 202-726-6335.

BROER, Ingo, b. Plauen. Educ: ThD 1970; Habil. 1972. Emp: Prof., Bibl. Theol. Spec: New Testament. Pub: "Die Juden im Urteil der Autoren des Neuen Testaments" *TG* 82 (1992); *Die Seligpreisungen der Bergpredigt: Studien zu ihrer Überlieferung und Interpretation*, BBB 61 (1986); "Die Parabel Jesu vom Verzicht auf das Prinzip von Leistung und Gegenleistung (Mt 18,23-35)" in *A Cause de l'Evangile: Melanges offerts a Dom J. Dupont*, LD 123 (1985); *Friede durch Gewaltverzicht?* (1984); *Freiheit vom Gesetz und Radikalisierung des Gesetzes: Ein Beitrag zur Theologie des Evangelisten Matthaeus*, SBS 98 (1980); "Die Gleichnisexegese und die neuere Literaturwissenschaft: Ein Diskussionsbeitrag zur Exegese von Mt 20,1-16" *Biblische Notizen* 5 (1978); *Die Urgemeinde und das Grab Jesu*, STANT 31 (1972); and others. Mem: SNTS. Addr: (o) U.

Gh Siegen, Postfach, 57068 Siegen, Germany 0271-7404521; (h) Klosterstr. 2, 57234 Wilnsdorf, Germany 0271-390497.

BRONNER, Leila L., b. Czechoslovakia, d. of Isaac & Rosa Amsel, m. Joseph, chil: Themey; Moshe; Esther. Educ: Hebrew U., Tchr. Cert. for Diaspora Educ. 1951; Witwatersrand U., BA 1955, MA 1959; Pretoria U., DLitt, NW Semitic Lang. 1964. Emp: Witwatersrand U., 1960-84 Prof. of Bible & Jewish Stud.; Hebrew Tchr. Coll., 1966-78 Sr. Lect.; Harvard U., 1984-85 Vis. Fellow; U. of South. Calif., Arch. Res. Collection, 1985-87 Vis. Schol.; U. of Judaism, 1987-90 Adj. Assoc. Prof., Bible & Hist. Spec: Hebrew Bible, Semitic Languages, Texts and Epigraphy, Apocrypha and Post-biblical Studies. Pub: "Biblical Prophetesses through Rabbinic Lenses" *Judaism* (1991); "The Changing Face of Woman from Bible to Talmud" *Shofar* 7 (1989); "Gynomorphic Imagery in the Bible" *Dor le Dor* 13 (1983/84); *Biblical Personalities and Archaeology* (Keter, 1974); *The Stories of Elijah and Elisha* (Brill, 1968); *Sects and Separatism during the Second Jewish Commonwealth* (Bloch, 1967); and others. Mem: AAR; SBL; AJS; NAPH; WUJS. Rec: Reading, chess, tennis. Addr: (h) 180 North Las Palmas Ave., Los Angeles, CA 90004 213-933-8026.

BROOKE, George J., b. Chichester, England, April 27, 1952, s. of Henry J.A. & Lesley M. (Noble), m. Rosemary Jane (Peacocke), chil: Peter G.; David J.; Rachel M. Educ: St. Peter's Coll., Oxford, MA 1978; Claremont Grad. Sch., PhD 1978. Emp: Salisbury & Wells Theol. Coll., England, 1978-84 Lect., NT Stud.; U. of Manchester, England, 1984- Lect., Intertestamental Lit.; London, 1992 Frankland-West Lect. Spec: Hebrew Bible, New Testament, Semitic Languages, Texts and Epigraphy, Apocrypha and Post-biblical Studies. Pub: *Women in the Biblical Tradition*, ed. (Mellen, 1992); *Septuagint, Scrolls and Cognate Writings*, co-ed. (Scholars, 1992); *Temple Scroll Studies*, ed. (JSOT, 1989); *Exegesis at Qumran: 4QFlorilegium in its Jewish Context* (JSOT, 1985); "Qumran Pesher: Towards the Redefinition of a Genre" *RQ* 10 (1981); "The Amos-Numbers Midrash and Messianic Expectation" *ZAW* 92 (1980); and others. Awd: Fulbright Schol. 1974; Ecumenical Inst., Jerusalem, Res. Schol. 1983; Annenberg Inst., Res. Fellow. 1992. Mem: SOTS 1978-; Brit. Assn. for Jewish Stud. 1986-. Rec: Sailing. Addr: (o) U. of Manchester, Dept. of Religions & Theology, M13 9PL, England 061-275-3609; (h) 45 Brookfield Ave., Poynton, Stockport, Cheshire, SK12 1JE, England 0625-872822.

BROOKS, Oscar S., b. Menlo, CA, December 24, 1928, s. of Charlie A. & Jessie A., m. Sarah (Rives), chil: Oscar; Philip II; Amanda. Educ: Carson-Newman Coll., BA 1949; South. Bapt. Theol. Sem., BD 1954, PhD 1959. Emp: Cumberland Coll., 1959-63 Prof., Relig.; William Jewell Coll., 1963-82 Prof., Relig.;

Perspectives, 1978-86 Ed. Bd.; Golden Gate Sem., 1982- Prof., NT. Spec: Archaeology, New Testament. Pub: "Matthew 28:16-20 and the Design of the First Gospel" *JSOT* 10 (1981); "A Contextual Interpretation of Galatians 3:27" *Bibl. Stud.* 3 (1978); "I Peter 3:21—The Clue to the Literary Structure of the Epistle" *NT* 16/4; and others. Awd: Johns Hopkins U., NEH grant 1977; Ind. U., NEH grant 1979, 1981; Cornell U., NEH grant 1992. Mem: ASOR; SBL. Rec: Photography, hiking. Addr: (o) Golden Gate Seminary, Mill Valley, CA 94941 415-388-8080; (h) 110 Chapel Dr., Mill Valley, CA 94941 415-388-5180.

BROOME, Edwin C., Jr., b. Mt. Vernon, NY, February 16, 1912, s. of Edwin C. & Grace R., m. Madelyn Kay, chil: Standish R.; Douglas; Jano. Educ: U. of Pa., BA 1933; Union Theol. Sem., BD 1936; Harvard Div. Sch., STM 1938; Brown U., PhD 1940. Emp: Colo. Coll., 1949-51 Prof., Relig.; Near East Found., 1956-59; Long Island U., Mitchel Coll., 1960-65 Provost; C.W. Post Coll., 1965-66 Prof., Relig.; Defense Lang. Inst., West Coast Branch, 1966-73 Dean. Spec: New Testament. Pub: "Dolmens of Palestine and Transjordan" *JBL* (1940); "Nebaioth, Nabayat and the Nabateans: The Linguistic Problem" *JSS* (1973). Mem: SBL 1936-; ASOR 1936-; AOS 1936-83. Rec: Camping. Addr: (h) 5920 Autumn Dr., McLean, VA 22101.

BROOTEN, Bernadette J., b. Coeur d'Alene, ID, January 29, 1951, d. of Kenneth Edward & Sadie Josephine (Assad). Educ: U. of Portland, BA (maxima cum laude) 1971; Harvard U., PhD 1982. Emp: Claremont Grad. Sch., 1980-84 Asst. Prof., Relig., Dir. of Res. in Women's Stud., Inst. for Antiq. & Christianity; U. of Tubingen, 1981 Vis. Instr., 1982-84 Res. Project Investigator; Hawaii Consortium for Theol. Educ., 1982 Instr.; Harvard Div. Sch., 1985-Assoc. Prof., Scripture & Interpretation; *Harvard Diss. in Relig.*, 1985- Co-ed. Spec: New Testament, Semitic Languages, Texts and Epigraphy, Apocrypha and Post-biblical Studies. Pub: "Iaēl prostatēs in the Jewish Donative Inscription from Aphrodisias" in *The Future of Early Christianity*, Festschrift for Helmut Koester (Fortress, 1991); "The Gender of Iael in the Jewish Inscription from Aphrodisias" in *Studies on the Hebrew Bible, Intertestamental Judaism, and Christian Origins* (U. Press of Amer., 1990); "Paul and the Law: How Complete was the Departure?" *Princeton Sem. Bull.*, Sup. Issue 1 (1990); "Response to 'Corinthian Veils and Gnostic Androgynes' by Dennis Ronald MacDonald" in *Images of the Feminine in Gnosticism* (1988); *Women Leaders in the Ancient Synagogue: Inscriptional Evidence and Background Issues*, Brown Judaic Stud. 36 (Scholars, 1982); and others. Awd: Harvard U., Sinclair Kennedy Traveling Fellow. 1977; Bunting Inst. of Radcliffe Coll., Fellow 1989; NEH Fellow. for U. Tchr. 1989; AAR, Res. Assistance Grant 1991; Amer. Assn. of U. Women, Fac. Career Enhancement Grant 1992.

Mem: AAR; SBL; CBA; SNTS; AJS. Addr: (o) Harvard Divinity School, 45 Francis Ave., Cambridge, MA 02138 617-495-0908.

BROSHI, Magen, Emp: Shrine of the Book Mus., Israel, 1965- Cur. Excv: Tel Megadim, 1967-69 Dir.; Mt. Zion, 1971-78 Dir. Spec: Archaeology. Pub: "The Gigantic Dimensions of the Visionary Temple in the Temple Scroll" *BAR* 13/6 (1987); "Beware the Wiles of the Wanton Woman" *BAR* 9/4 (1983); "Estimating the Population of Ancient Jerusalem" *BAR* 4/2 (1978); "Evidence of Earliest Christian Pilgrimage to the Holy Land Comes to Light in the Holy Sepulchre Church" *BAR* 3/4 (1977); and others. Addr: (o) Israel Museum, PO Box 71117, Jerusalem 91710, Israel 698-211.

BROWER, Kent E., b. Calgary, Canada, s. of Barry & Jean, m. Francine, chil: Deirdre; Derek. Educ: East. Nazarene Coll., MA 1969; U. of Manchester, PhD 1978. Emp: Brit. Isles Nazarene Coll., 1964-67 Lect., NT, 1985-86 Acting Acad. Dean, Lect., NT; Canadian Nazarene Coll., 1979-88 Assoc. Prof., Bibl. Lang. & Lit.; Nazarene Theol. Coll., Dean, Lect., NT. Spec: New Testament. Pub: "Elijah in the Markan Passion Narrative" *JSNT* (1983); "Seeing the Kingdom in Power: Mark 9:1" *JSNT* (1980); and others. Mem: SBL; CSBS; Wesleyan Theol. Soc., Tyndale Fellow. Rec: Hockey, golf. Addr: (h) The White House, Dene Rd., Didsbury, M2O 8GU, England.

BROWN, Cheryl A., b. Washington, DC, September 16, 1949, d. of Harry O. & Wilma F. Evans, m. Wesley Haddon Brown, chil: Julie Anne; Benjamin Joel. Educ: Oral Roberts U., BA (magna cum laude) 1972; Inst. of Holy Land Stud., MA 1977; U. of Calif., Berkeley, Grad. Theol. Union, PhD 1990. Emp: Oral Roberts U., 1972-76 Instr., Dept. of Theol.; Amer. Bapt. Ch., Intl. Min., 1976-84 Intl. Rep. in Jerusalem; U. of LaVerne, 1990- Adj. Asst. Prof., NT; Fuller Theol. Sem., 1990- Adj. Asst. Prof., Bibl. Stud. Spec: New Testament, Apocrypha and Post-biblical Studies. Pub: *No Longer Be Silent: First Century Jewish Portraits of Biblical Women* (Westminster/John Knox, 1992); and others. Mem: AAR; SBL; Amer. Bapt. Women in Min. Rec: Hiking, gardening, playing & listening to music. Addr: (h) 7600 Lucille Ave., Bakersfield, CA 93308 805-399-5229.

BROWN, Colin, b. Yorkshire, England, February 26, 1932, s. of Robert & Maud, m. Olive Margaret, chil: Verity (Dadd); Matthew; Stephanie (Harrison). Educ: U. of Liverpool, BA 1953; U. of London, BD 1958; U. of Nottingham, MA 1961; U. of Bristol, PhD 1970. Emp: Trinity Coll., Tyndale Hall, Bristol, 1961-78 Vice Prin.; U. of Bristol, 1961-72 Tchr.; Fuller Theol. Sem., 1978- Prof., 1988- Assoc. Dean, Ctr. Advanced Theol. Stud.; Episc. Ch., 1982- Assoc. Rector. Spec: New Testament. Pub: "The Unjust Steward:

A New Twist?" in *Worship, Theology and Ministry in the Early Church,* Festschrift for Ralph P. Martin (Sheffield, 1992); "Historical Jesus" in *Dict. of Jesus and the Gospels* (1992); "Trinity and Incarnation: In Search of Contemporary Orthodoxy" *Ex Auditu* 7 (1991); "The Gates of Hell: An Alternative Approach" in *SBL 1987 Seminar Papers* (1987); *Miracles and the Critical Mind* (Eerdmans, 1984); *The New International Dictionary of New Testament Theology,* ed. (Zondervan, 1978); "Person of Christ" in *ISBE*; and others. Awd: C. Davis Weyerhaeuser Awd. 1988. Mem: SBL; AAR. Rec: Gardening, house remodeling. Addr: (o) Fuller Theology Seminary, Pasadena, CA 91182 818-584-5243; (h) 1024 Beverly Way, Altadena, CA 91001 818-798-7180.

BROWN, John P., b. Hanover, NH, May 16, 1923, s. of Bancroft Huntington & Eleanor (Pairman), m. Dorothy Emily (Waymouth), chil: George Waymouth; Felicity Emily; Maryam Eleanor; David Pairman. Educ: Dartmouth Coll., BA 1944; Gen. Theol. Sem., STB 1952; Union Theol. Sem., ThD 1958. Emp: Hobart Coll., 1956-58 Instr., Class.; Amer. U. of Beirut, 1958-65 Assoc. Prof., Class.; Ch. Div. Sch. of the Pacific, 1965-68 Prof., NT; N Calif. Ecumenical Coun., 1976-83 Exec. Dir. Spec: Hebrew Bible, New Testament, Semitic Languages, Texts and Epigraphy. Pub: "The Ethnic Paradigm as a Pattern for Nominal Forms in Greek and Hebrew," co-auth. *Gen. Linguistics* 26 (1986); "The Ark of the Covenant and the Temple of Janus: The Magico-Military Numen of the State in Jerusalem and Rome" *BZ* 30 (1986); "Men of the Land and the God of Justice in Greece and Israel" *ZAW* 95 (1983); "Proverb-Book, Gold-Economy, Alphabet" *JBL* 100 (1981); "The Son of Man: 'This Fellow'" *Biblica* 58 (1977); "Literary Contexts of the Common Hebrew-Greek Vocabulary" *JSS* 13 (1968); *The Lebanon and Phoenicia* (Amer. U., 1966); and others. Rec: Peace education, anti-nuclear work. Addr: (h) 1630 Arch St., Berkeley, CA 94709 510-843-8719.

BROWN, Milton P., b. Bessemer, AL, June 5, 1928, s. of Milton Perry & Elaine H., m. Anne M. (Cochran), chil: Marie M.; George M. Educ: Birmingham South. Coll., BA 1950; Louisville Presbyn. Theol. Sem., BD 1954; Duke U., PhD 1959. Emp: Duke Div. Sch., 1955-58 Instr.; Washington & Lee U., 1958-60 Asst. Prof.; SW at Memphis, 1960-68 Assoc. Prof.; Rhodes Coll., 1968- Prof.; Union Theol. Coll., Belfast, 1980 Vis. Lect., NT. Spec: New Testament, Apocrypha and Post-biblical Studies. Pub: *To Hear the Word: Invitation to Serious Study of the Bible* (Mercer U.P., 1987); "Matthew as 'EIRENOPOIOS'" *Irish Bibl. Stud.* 4 (1982); *Studies in the History and Text of the New Testament,* contb. (Utah U.P., 1967); "Notes on the Language and Style of Pseudo-Ignatius" *JBL* 83 (1964); *The Authentic Writings of Ignatius: A Study of Linguistic Criteria* (Duke U.P., 1963); and others. Awd: Duke U., Andrew Patterson Fellow.; Gurney H. Kearns Fellow. 1955-58.

Mem: SBL 1956-. Rec: Tennis, photography, travel. Addr: (o) 2000 N Parkway, Memphis, TN 38100 901-726-3907; (h) 2725 Woodland Hills, Memphis, TN 38100 901-358-0265.

BROWN, Raymond E., b. New York, NY, May 22, 1928. Educ: Catholic U., BA 1948, MA 1949; St. Mary's Sem., STB 1951, STL 1953, STD 1955; Johns Hopkins U., PhD 1958; Pont. Bibl. Commn., Rome, SSB 1959, SSL 1963. Emp: ASOR, Jerusalem, 1959 Jordan Fellow, Dead Sea Scroll Concord.; St. Mary's Sem., 1959-71 Prof., Sacred Scripture; Union Theol. Sem., 1971-90 Auburn Disting. Prof. Emeritus of Bibl. Stud.; Pont. Bibl. Inst., Rome, Italy, 1973, 1988 Vis. Prof., NT; Columbia U., 1979-90 Adj. Prof., Relig. *CBQ, JBL, NTS* Ed. Bd. Spec: New Testament. Pub: *New Jerome Biblical Comm.* (Prentice-Hall, 1990); *Recent Discoveries and the Biblical World* (Glazier, 1983); *The Epistles of John* in *AB* (1982); and others. Awd: Cath. Press Book Awd.; Edgar J. Godspeed Awd.; BAS Publ. Awd., Best NT Comm. Mem: SBL, Pres. 1976-77; Bibl. Theologians; SNTS, Pres. 1986-87. Addr: (o) Union Theological Seminary, 3041 Broadway, New York, NY 10027 212-662-7100.

BROWN, Schuyler, b. New York, NY, August 21, 1930, s. of William Averell & Mary Alice, m. Margaret (Meredith). Educ: Harvard U., AB 1952; U. of Muenster, DTh 1969. Emp: Gen. Theol. Sem., 1973-78; U. of London, Heythrop Coll., 1978-80; U. of St. Michael's Coll., 1980-90 Assoc. Prof., 1990- Prof.; U. of Toronto, Ctr. for Relig. Stud., 1984- Mem.; *CBQ,* 1973-76 Assoc. Ed. Spec: New Testament, Egyptology. Pub: "Apostleship in the New Testament as an Historical and Theological Problem" *NTS* 30 (1984); *The Origins of Christianity: A Historical Introduction to the New Testament* (Oxford U.P., 1984); "Exegesis and Imagination" *Theol. Stud.* 41 (1980); "The Matthean Community and the Gentile Mission" *NT* 22 (1980); "Biblical Philology, Linguistics and the Problem of Method" *Heythrop Jour.* 20 (1979); *Apostasy and Perserverance in the Theology of Luke,* Analecta Biblica 36 (Pont. Bibl. Inst., 1969); and others. Mem: CSBS; CBA; SNTS. Rec: Piano. Addr: (o) 81 St. Mary St., Toronto, ON M5S IJ4, Canada 416-926-7140.

BROWNING, Daniel C., Jr., b. Albany, GA, October 26, 1956, s. of Daniel C. & Irene C., m. Felicia (Jernigan), chil: Sarah Elizabeth; Rachel Bethany. Educ: U. of Ala., Huntsville, BSE 1980; SW Bapt. Theol. Sem., MDiv 1984, PhD, Arch. & Bibl. Backgrounds 1988. Emp: SW Bapt. Theol. Sem., 1985-89 Teaching Fellow/Adj. in Bibl. Backgrounds; Tarrant County Jr. Coll., 1988-90 Instr., Relig.; William Carey Coll., 1990- Assoc. Prof., Relig. Excv: Tel Batash (Timnah), Israel, 1981 Staff Asst., 1983 Camp Manager, 1982-87 Lab Asst., Computer Prog., 1984-86 Area Supr.; Tel Qasile, Israel, 1991-92 Co-dir., Volunteer Group & Travel Prog.; Tel Beth Shean, Israel, 1993. Spec: Archaeology. Pub: "Land of Goshen" *BI* 19 (1993); Articles in *Holman Bible Dict.* (Holman, 1991); "Tirzah" *BI* 17 (1991); "Contracts, Deeds, and Their Containers" *BI* 16 (1990); "Computerizing Timnah Data" *ASOR Newsletter* 37 (1986); and others. Awd: ASOR, Endowment for Bibl. Res./Travel Grant 1984. Mem: ASOR 1982-; IES 1984-; SBL 1987-. Rec: Church work, travel, caving, electronics. Addr: (o) William Carey College, Hattiesburg, MS 39401 601-582-6156; (h) 120 Brycewood Circle, Hattiesburg, MS 39402 601-261-0243.

BROWNSON, James V., b. Hackensak, NJ, February 6, 1955, s. of William C., Jr. & Helen (Stewart), m. Kathryn (Mostrom), chil: Rachel K.; Anna C.; William J. Educ: U. of Mich., AB 1977; West. Theol. Sem., MDiv 1980; Princeton Theol. Sem., PhD 1989. Emp: Princeton Theol. Sem., 1984-88 Instr.; Calvin Coll., 1988-89 Asst. Prof., Relig.; West. Theol. Sem., 1989- Assoc. Prof., NT. Spec: New Testament. Pub: "The Virtuous Interpreter" *Perspectives* 6/9 (1991); "The Odes of Solomon and the Johannine Tradition" *JSP* 2 (1988); and others. Mem: SBL 1987-; CSBR 1991-. Rec: Raquetball, camping. Addr: (o) Western Theological Seminary, 86 E 12th St., Holland, MI 49423 616-392-8555; (h) 124 Orlando Ave., Holland, MI 49423 616-396-0465.

BUCHANAN, George W., b. Denison, IA, December 25, 1921, s. of George & Helen (Kral), m. I. Harlene (Bower), chil: George Wesley; Mary Colleen. Educ: Simpson Coll., BA 1947, LittD 1973; Garrett Theol. Sem., MDiv 1951; NW U., MA 1952; Drew U., PhD 1959. Emp: United Meth. Ch., 1944-59 Pastor; Wesley Theol. Sem., 1960- Prof., NT; *BAR,* Ed. Bd.; *Arts and Humanities Citation Index,* Adv. Bd. Spec: New Testament. Pub: *Typology and the Gospel* (U. Press of Amer., 1987); *Jesus, the King and His Kingdom* (Mercer U.P., 1984); "Worship, Feasts and Ceremonies in the Early Jewish-Christian Church" *NTS* 26 (1980); *Revelation and Redemption* (1978); *Letter To the Hebrews,* AB (Doubleday, 1972); *The Consequences of the Covenant* (Brill, 1970); "Midrashim Pre-Tannaites" *RB* (1965); and others. Awd: Horowitz Fellow 1957-58; Scheuer Fellow 1959-60; Notre Dame U., Rosenstiel Lec. 1975; Assn. of Theol. Sch., Fellow 1980-81; Claremont SBL-Fellow 1980-81. Mem: SBL, Pres., Mid-Atlantic Reg. 1965-66; SNTS; CBA; Amer. Assn. of U. Prof. Rec: Symphony performances, barbershop singing. Addr: (o) Wesley Theological Seminary, 4500 Massachusetts Ave., NW, Washington, DC 20016 202-885-8643; (h) 11404 Newport Mill Rd., Wheaton, MD 20902 301-942-4023.

BUCK, Erwin, b. Bessarabia, April 12, 1932, s. of Otto & Adeline, m. Gertrude (Freitag), chil: Sharon; Deborah; Darren. Educ: U. of SK, Canada, BA 1960; Luth. Faculty of Theol., Canada, BD 1963; Luth. Sch. of Theol., STM

1965, STD 1978. Emp: Luth. Sch. of Theol., 1963-66 Instr.; Inst. Judaicum Delitzschianum, Germany, 1967-69 Wissenschaftlicher Asst.; Luth. Theol. Sem., 1974- Prof., NT, 1988- Dean of Stud., 1991- Acting Pres. Spec: New Testament, Semitic Languages, Texts and Epigraphy, Apocrypha and Post-biblical Studies. Pub: "Healing in the New Testament" *Consensus* 17 (1991); "Christian Unity: The Perspective from Galatia" *Consensus* 4 (1978); articles in *Ency. Britannica* (1973); *A Complete Concordance to Flavius Josephus*, co-auth. (Brill, 1973); and others. Awd: Natl. Luth. Ed. Conf., Martin Luther Fellow. 1963-65. Mem: Franz Delitsch Gesellschaft 1968-; SBL 1980-. Rec: Music, gardening, farming. Addr: (o) Lutheran Theological Seminary, 114 Seminary Crescent, Saskatoon, SK S7N OX3, Canada 306-975-7004; (h) 331 Scissons Terr., Saskatoon, SK S7S 1C1, Canada 306-249-2167.

BUCK, Harry M., b. Enola, PA, November 18, 1921, s. of Harry & Edith, m. Esther (Gingrich), chil: David; Paul. Educ: United Theol. Sem., MDiv 1945; U. of Chicago, PhD 1954. Emp: Wellesley Coll., 1951-59 Asst. Prof.; Wilson Coll., 1959- Prof., Relig. Stud.; U. of Pa., 1967 Adj. Prof.; Shippensburg U., 1972 Adj. Prof.; *JAAR*, Ed.; Anima Publ., Exec. Ed. Spec: Hebrew Bible, New Testament. Pub: *People of the Lord: The History, Scriptures, and Faith of Ancient Israel* (Macmillan, 1966); "From History to Myth: A Comparative Study" *Jour. of Bible and Religion* 29 (1961); *The Johannine Lessons in the Greek Gospel Lectionary* (U. of Chicago, 1958); and others. Mem: AAR 1957-, Exec. Dir. 1958-72, Bd. of Dir. 1977; SBL 1956-; SNTS 1957-; East. Great Lakes Bibl. Assn. 1980. Addr: (o) Anima Publications, 1053 Wilson Ave., Chambersburg, PA 17201 717-267-0087.

BUCKLEY, Thomas W., b. Abington, MA, June 11, 1929, s. of Thomas H. & Helen L. (Moriarty). Educ: Harvard U., AB 1949; Fordham U., MA 1952; Cath. U. of Amer., STL 1958; Pont. Bibl. Inst., Rome, SSL 1960; U. St. Thomas Aquinas, Rome, STD 1962. Emp: Regis Coll., 1960-61 Lect., Theol.; St. John's Sem., 1963-81 Prof., NT Bibl. Greek; St. Paul's House of Stud., 1977-87 Lect., NT; St. Scholastica Priory, 1981-84 Lect., NT. Spec: New Testament. Pub: *Seventy Times Seven: Sin, Judgment, and Forgiveness in Matthew* (Liturgical, 1991); *Apostle to the Nations. The Life and Letters of St. Paul: A Biblical Course* (Daughters of St. Paul, 1981); *The Phrase 'Firstborn of Every Creature' (Colossians 1,15) in Light of its Jewish and Hellenistic Background* (Pont. Athenaeum Angelicum, 1962). Mem: CBA; SBL. Rec: Gardening, hiking. Addr: (o) PO Box 986, Essex, MA 01929 508-768-6284.

BULL, Robert J., Educ: Randolph-Macon Coll., BA 1943; Duke Div. Sch., BD 1946; Yale U., STM 1950, PhD 1956. Emp: Drew U., 1955-56 Instr., 1956-64 Asst. Prof., 1964-70 Assoc. Prof.,

1968- Dir. of Inst. for Arch. Res., 1970- Prof., Ch. Hist.; William Foxwell Albright Inst. of Arch. Res., Jerusalem, 1970-71 Dir., 1974-75 Ann. Prof.; Caesarea Maritima, Preliminary Reports, 1971- Gen. Ed. Excv: Tell Balatah, 1960, 1962, 1964 Area Supr.; Pella, 1966 Field Dir.; Tell er Ras, 1966, 1968, 1971 Dir.; Joint Expdn. to Khirbet Shema, 1970-72 Field Dir.; Joint Expdn. to Caesarea, 1971-74, 1976, 1978-79 Dir. Spec: Archaeology. Pub: *Fishers of Men: The Way of the Apostles*, co-auth. (Prentice-Hall, 1980); "Tell er Ras" in *EAEHL* vol. IV (Massada, 1978); "Two Tychai from Caesarea Maritima" in *SBL Seminar Papers* (1977); "An Archaeological Footnote to 'Our Fathers Worshipped on This Mountain,' John IV: 20" *NTS* 23 (1976); *The Joint Expedition to Caesarea Maritima, Preliminary Reports*, co-ed. (Scholars, 1975); "A Tripartite Sundial from Tell er Ras on Mount Gerizim" *BASOR* (1975); "An Archaeological Context for Understanding John 4:20" *BA* 38 (1975); *Tell er Ras, The Coins* (Smithsonian Inst., 1971); *Tell er Ras, The Pottery* (Smithsonian Inst., 1971); and others. Awd: Amer. Assn. of Theol. Sch. res. grant, 1959-60, 1966-67; Smithsonian Found., grant 1968-74; NEH/ASOR, res. grant 1980-81; Phi Beta Kappa. Mem: Amer. Soc. of Church Hist.; Intl. Patristic Congress; ASOR; AIA. Addr: (o) Drew U., 36 Madison Ave., NJ 07940 201-408-3537.

BULLARD, John M., b. Winston-Salem, NC, May 6, 1932, s. of Hoke Vogler & May (Moore). Educ: U. of N.C., AB 1953, AM 1955; Yale U., MDiv 1957, PhD 1962. Emp: Yale Div. Sch., 1957-61 Asst. Instr.; Wofford Coll., 1961- Albert C. Outler Prof. of Relig., Chmn., Dept. of Relig.; U. of N.C., 1966-67, 1974 Vis. Prof., Bibl. Lit.; Converse Coll., 1984 Vis. Prof., Comparative Relig. Excv: Tell Arad, 1965 Asst. Spec: Archaeology, Hebrew Bible, New Testament. Pub: Articles in *Interpreter's Dict. of Biblical Interpretation* (1992); "Psalm 139: Prayer in a Stillness" in *SBL Seminar Papers* II (1975). Awd: U. of London, NEH grant 1975; Harvard U., NEH sem. 1982; U. of Pa., NEH sem. 1986; Yale U., NEH Summer Sem. on Mesopotamia & the Bible 1987; Emory U., Dana Fellow 1989-90. Mem: SBL 1957-, Pres., South. Sect. 1967-68; AAR; S.C. Acad. of Relig. 1964-, Pres. 1974-75. Rec: Early keyboard music. Addr: (o) 227 Main Bldg., Wofford Coll., Spartanburg, SC 29307 803-597-4560; (h) 104 Hickman Ct., Hillbrook Forest, Spartanburg, SC 29307 803-582-8589.

BULLARD, Reuben G., b. Wheeling, WV, March 18, 1928, s. of Reuben & Vada (Bixler), m. Lynn (Maine), chil: Reuben, Jr.; Howard; Catherine; Suzanne. Educ: Cincinnati Bible Sem., ThB 1956, MA 1957; U. of Cincinnati, PhD, Geology/Arch. 1969. Emp: U. of Cincinnati, 1968- Lect.; Cincinnati Bible Coll., 1971- Prof.; Hist./Arch. Study Seminars, Egypt, Jordan, Israel, Turkey, Greece, Italy, Tunisia, Dir. Excv: Caesarea, 1981, Abila, Jordan, 1984-, Carthage, 1985 Cons. in Arch. Geology. Spec: Archaeology. Pub: "Sedimentary Environments in Lithologic Materials at Two Archaeological

Sites (Gezer & Carthage)" in *Archaeological Geology* (Yale U.P., 1985); "Further Excavations at Gezer, 1967-71," co-auth., *BA* 34 (1971); *Gezer II, HUCA*, co-auth.; and others. Mem: Geological Soc. of Amer. 1966-, Arch.-Geology Div. 1976-; ASOR 1966-; Soc. of Economic Geologists & Paleontologists 1967-76; NEAS 1971-, V.P. 1985-; AIA, Pres., Cincinnati Soc. 1975-79. Addr: (o) Cincinnati Bible College, 2700 Glenway, Cincinnati, OH 45204 513-244-8100; (h) Box 296, 5310 Madison Pike, Independence, KY 41051 606-356-2305.

BULS, Harold H., b. Garland, NE, January 4, 1920, s. of Herman & Theresa, m. Marjorie (Mann), chil: Jonathan; David; Barbara; Fredrik. Educ: Concordia Sem., St. Louis, BA 1945; U. of Chicago, MA 1958, PhD 1970. Emp: Alabama Conf., 1949-51 Teacher, Pastor; Immanuel Coll. & Sem., 1951-55 Prof.; St. John's Coll., 1956-69 Prof.; Concordia Theol. Sem., 1970- Prof. Spec: New Testament. Pub: "Luther's Translation of Colossians 2:12" *Concordia Theol. Quar.* 45 (1981); "Redaction Criticism and Its Implications (Mark and Luke)" *Springfielder* 36 (1973); Exegetical Notes, Gospel Texts & Epistle Texts Ser., contb. (Concordia Theol. Sem., 1980-1985); and others. Mem: SBL. Rec: Building projects. Addr: (o) Concordia Theological Seminary, 6600 N Clinton St., Ft. Wayne, IN 46825 219-481-2224; (h) 2202 Garden Park Dr., Ft. Wayne, IN 46825 219-483-6270.

BUNIMOVITZ, Shlomo, b. Tel-Aviv, Israel, November 20, 1952, s. of Haim & Genia, m. Shoshana, chil: Yonathan; N'ama. Educ: Tel Aviv U., BA 1977, MA 1983, PhD 1989. Emp: Tel Aviv U., 1978- Lect., Dept. of Arch. & Near East. Cultures; Bar-Ilan U., 1982- Lect., Dept. of Land of Israel Stud. Excv: Aphek-Antipatris, 1976-79 Staff Mem.; Sharon Plain Survey, 1976-79 Staff. Spec: Archaeology. Pub: "The Beginning of the Late Bronze Age in Palestine" *Eretz-Israel* 23 (1992); "Problems in the 'Ethnic' Identification of the Philistine Culture" *Tel Aviv* 17 (1990); "Cultural Processes and Socio-Political Change in the Central Hill Country in the Late Bronze-Iron I Transition" in *From Nomadism to Monarchy* (1990); "An Egyptian 'Governor's Residency' at Gezer?—Another Suggestion" *Tel Aviv* 15-16 (1988-89); "Glacis 10014 and Gezer's Late Bronze Age Fortifications" *Tel Aviv* 10 (1983); *Settlements, Population and Economy in Eretz-Israel in Antiquity* (Tel Aviv U., 1988); and others. Mem: Israel Assn. of Arch. Rec: Reading, touring, swimming. Addr: (o) Tel-Aviv U., Dept. of Arch. & Near Eastern Cultures, Ramat- Aviv, 69978 Tel-Aviv, Israel 03-6409703; (h) 39 Anatot St., Ganei-Zahala, Tel Aviv 69080, Israel 03-485089.

BURGE, Gary M., b. Covina, CA, April 28, 1952, s. of John T. & Shirlee E., m. Carol E. (Wright), chil: Ashley Elizabeth; Grace Elizabeth. Educ: Fuller Theol. Sem., MDiv 1978; U. of Aberdeen, King's Coll., Scotland, PhD 1983. Emp: King's Coll., 1981-87 Asst. Prof., NT, 1985-

87 Chair, Div. of Humanities; North Park Coll., 1987- Assoc. Prof, Chair, Dept. of Bibl. & Theol. Stud; Wheaton Coll. 1992- Assoc Prof., NT. Spec: New Testament. Pub: *Who Are God's People in the Middle East?* (Zondervan, 1993); *Interpreting the Fourth Gospel* (Baker, 1992); *The Anointed Community. The Holy Spirit in the Johannine Tradition* (Eerdman's, 1987); "John 7:53-8:11. The Woman Caught in Adultery" *JETS* 27 (1984); "'And Threw Them Thus on Paper': Recovering the Poetic Form of James 2:14-26" *Studia Biblica et Theologica* 7 (1977); and others. Mem: SBL; IBR; TFBR. Addr: (o) Wheaton College, Wheaton, IL 60187 708-752-5932.

BURGESS, Stanley M., b. Nagercoil, India, November 27, 1937, s. of John H. & Bernice F., m. Ruth Lenora (Vassar), chil: John B.; Stanley M.; Scott V.; Heidi; Justin. Educ: U. of Mich., BA 1957, MA 1959; U. of Mo.-Columbia, PhD 1971. Emp: Evang. Coll., 1959-76 Prof., Hist., 1965-68, 1971-76 Head, Dept. of Social Stud.; SW Mo. State U., 1976- Prof., 1981-85 Head, Dept. of Relig. Studies, 1977-82 Dir., Sponsored Res. Office. Spec: Apocrypha and Post-biblical Studies. Pub: *The Holy Spirit: Eastern Christian Traditions* (1989); *Dictionary of Pentecostal and Charismatic Movements*, co-ed. (1988); *The Spirit and the Church: Antiquity* (Hendrickson, 1984); and others. Awd: Andrew Mellon Found. Fellowship, 1989. Mem: AAR. Rec: Golf, stamp collecting, family trips. Addr: (o) Southwest Missouri State U., Dept. of Religious Studies, Springfield, MO 65804 417-836-5514; (h) Rt. 2, Box 307A, Strafford, MO 65757 417-833-0728.

BURKETT, Delbert R., b. Lamesa, TX, August 22, 1949, s. of Joe & Lorene. Educ: Abilene Christian U., BA 1971; Harvard Div. Sch., MTS 1973; Duke U., PhD 1989. Emp: West. Ky. U., 1989-90 Vis. Asst. Prof.; Appalachian State U., 1990-93 Lect. Spec: New Testament. Pub: *The Son of the Man in the Gospel of John*, JSNTSup (Sheffield, 1991); "Four Sahidic Songs to St. John the Evangelist" *Coptic Ch. Rev.* 9 (1988). Mem: SBL. Addr: (o) Appalachian State U., Dept. of Philosophy and Religion, Boone, NC 28607 704-262-2465; (h) 410 E. Howard St., Apt. 1, Boone, NC 28607 704-265-2337.

BURNETT, Fred W., b. Birmingham, AL, December 18, 1944, s. of Mr. & Mrs. A.F., m. Carol, chil: Brian; Kelli. Educ: Anderson Coll., BA 1967; Anderson Theol. Sem., MDiv (summa cum laude) 1970; Vanderbilt Div. Sch., D. of Min. 1973; Vanderbilt U., MA 1976, PhD 1979. Emp: Amer. Bapt. Sem., 1975-76 Instr.; Anderson Coll., 1976- Prof., NT Stud. & Class. Stud. Spec: Hebrew Bible, New Testament, Apocrypha and Post-biblical Studies. Pub: "Postmodern Biblical Exegesis: The Eve of Historical-Criticism" *Semeia* 51 (1990); "Prolegmenon to Reading Matthew's Eschatological Discourse: Redundancy and the Education of the Reader in Matthew" *Semeia* 31

(1985); "Philo on Immortality: A Thematic Study of Philo's Concept of *Palingenesia" CBQ* 46 (1983); *"Palingenesia* in Matthew 19:28: A Window on the Matthean Community?" *JSNT* 17 (1983); *The Testament of Jesus-Sophia: A Redaction-Critical Study of the Eschatological Discourse in Matthew* (U. Press of Amer., 1981); and others. Awd: Andrew W. Mellon Fac. Development Awd. 1981, 1985-87; AAR, Grant 1991; U. of Chicago Fellow. for Res. 1985, 1989. Mem: SBL 1977-; CBA 1981-; AAR 1984-. Rec: Jogging, basketball, travel. Addr: (o) Anderson College, Anderson, IN 46012-3462 317-641-4504; (h) 2601 Tamra Ln., Anderson, IN 46011 317-644-4064.

BUSS, Martin J., b. Shaoyang, Hunan, China, November 4, 1930, s. of Rudolph & Julie, chil: Samuel; Jonathan; Mary Aileen; Jeanne. Educ: Princeton Theol. Sem., BD 1954, ThM 1955; Yale U., PhD 1958. Emp: Macalester Coll., 1957-58 Vis. Asst. Prof.; Coe Coll., 1958-59 Vis. Instr.; Emory U., 1959- Prof.; *ZAW*, 1963- Staff; *JBL,* 1970-74 Assoc. Ed. Spec: Hebrew Bible. Pub: "Logic and Israelite Law" *Semeia* 45 (1989); "Selfhood and Biblical Eschatology" *ZAW* 100, Sup. (1988); "An Anthropological Perspective Upon Prophetic Call Narratives" *Semeia* 21 (1982); *Encounter with the Text,* ed. (Fortress/Scholars, 1979); "The Idea of Sitz im Leben-History and Critique" *ZAW* 90 (1978); *The Prophetic Word of Hosea: A Morphological Study* (Topelmann, 1969); "The Beginning of Human Life as an Ethical Problem" *JR* 47 (1967); and others. Awd: ACLS, Study Fellow. 1964-65. Mem: SBL 1957-; AAR 1958-77; WUJS 1974-. Addr: (o) Emory U., Dept. of Religion, Atlanta, GA 30322 404-727-7543; (h) 488 Burlington Rd. NE, #4, Atlanta, GA 30307 404-373-2017.

BYRNE, Brendan J., b. Melbourne, Australia, October 12, 1939, s. of Francis Patrick & Mary Alice (Flanagan). Educ: Melbourne U., BA 1966, MA 1972; Melbourne Coll. of Div., BD 1972; Oxford U., DPhil 1977. Emp: Jesuit Theol. Coll., Australia, 1977- Prof. of NT, 1986-88 Head, Dept. of Bibl. Lang. & Lit., 1992- Prin.; Cath. Theol. Coll., Australia, 1980-83 Vis. Lect.; Yarra Theol. Union, 1990- Vis. Lect.; *Pacifica,* 1989- Rev. Ed. Spec: New Testament, Apocrypha and Post-biblical Studies. Pub: *Lazarus: A Contemporary Reading of John II* (Liturgical, 1991); "Ministry and Community in 1 Corinthians" *Australian Bibl. Rev.* 35 (1987); *Reckoning with Romans* (Glazier, 1986); "The Faith of the Beloved Disciple and the Community in John 20" *JSNT* 23 (1985); "Living out the Righteousness of God" *CBQ* 43 (1981); *'Sons of God'—'Seed of Abraham': A Study of the Idea of Divine Sonship in Paul against the Jewish Background,* Analecta Biblica 83 (Pont. Bibl. Inst., 1979); and others. Mem: CBA, Australia, Pres. 1984; Fellow. for Bibl. Stud., Melbourne, Pres. 1987; SNTS; Pont. Bibl. Commn. 1990-. Rec: Reading, music, walking, cycling. Addr: (o) Jesuit Theological College,

175 Royal Parade, Parkville, Melbourne, 3052 Victoria, Australia 61-3-347-6366.

CAHILL, P. Joseph, b. Chicago, IL, October 29, 1923, s. of Peter & Ellen, m. Wanthong, chil: Peter; Mark. Educ: Xavier U., Litt.B. 1947; Loyola U., Lic.Phil. 1950, MA 1955, Lic.Theol. 1958; Gregorian U., STD 1960. Emp: Bellarmine Sch. of Theol., 1960-66 Asst. Prof.; *Ency. Britannica,* 1965- Cons.; Loyola U., 1966-67 Assoc. Dean; Notre Dame U., 1967-70 Vis. Prof.; U. of Alberta, 1970- Prof.; *Relig. Stud. & Theol.,* 1986- Ed. Spec: New Testament. Pub: "A Rustle in the Shadows" in *Religion from Different Perspectives* (Chaing Mai U.P., 1986); "The Unity of the Bible" *Biblica* 65/3 (1984); "Deciphering the Great Code" *Dalhousie Rev.* 63/3 (1983); *Dict. of Biblical Theology,* co-trans. (Seabury/Crossroad, 1973); *Eschatological Occurrence* (Gregorian U.P., 1960); and others. Mem: CBA 1960-; AAR 1960-; SBL 1960-; SNTS 1963-. Rec: Skiing, racquetball, music. Addr: (o) U. of Alberta, Religious Studies, Edmonton, AB T6C 2B4, Canada 403-492-2174; (h) 5730 Riverbend Rd. #216, Edmonton, AB T6H 4T4, Canada 403-434-9660.

CAIN, Clifford C., b. Zanesville, OH, February 15, 1950, s. of Clifford & Ethel (Bokelman), m. Louise (Lueckel), chil: Rachel; Zachary. Educ: Muskingum Coll., BA 1972; Princeton Theol. Sem., MDiv 1975; Vanderbilt U., D.Min 1981. Emp: Amer. Protestant Ch., The Hague, 1975-78 Assoc. Pastor; Muskingum Coll., 1978-81 Chaplain; Franklin Coll., 1981- Chaplain, Asst. Prof., 1987- Assoc. Prof. Spec: Hebrew Bible, New Testament. Pub: *Faith Faces the World* (1989); *The Intersection of Mind and Spirit,* contb. ed. (1985); "Omega: Some Reflections on the Meaning of Death and Afterlife" *Faith & Philosophy* (1984); "A Passionate God?" *St. Luke's Jour. of Theol.* (1981). Mem: AAR; SBL. Rec: Photography, music, Maya civ. Addr: (o) Franklin College, Franklin, IN 46131 317-738-8141; (h) 300 W Jefferson St., Franklin, IN 46131 317-736-5010.

CALLAN, Terrance D., b. Helena, MT, February 6, 1947, s. of Terrance D. & Mary P., m. Jane D., chil: Terrance D.; Anne K. Educ: Gonzaga U., BA 1969; Yale U., MPhil 1972, PhD 1976. Emp: Xavier U., 1975-80; Anthenaeum of Ohio, 1983- Prof. of Bibl. Stud., Dean; *Proc. of the East. Great Lakes & MidW Bibl. Soc.,* 1989- Ed. Spec: New Testament. Pub: "Pauline Midrash: The Exegetical Background of Gal 3:19b" *JBL* 99 (1980); "Ps 110:1 and the Origin of the Expectation that Jesus Will Come Again" *CBQ* 44 (1982); "Prophecy and Ecstasy in Greco-Roman Religion and in 1 Corinthians" *NT* 27 (1985); "The Preface of Luke-Acts and Historiography" *NTS* 31 (1985); "The Saying of Jesus in *Gos. Thom.* 22/2 *Clem.* 12/*Gos. Eg.* 5" *Jour. of Relig. Stud.* 16 (1989); *Forgetting the Root: The Emergence of Christianity From Judaism* (Paulist, 1986); *Psychological Perspectives on the Life of Paul: An Application of* the Methodology of Gerd Theissen (Mellen, 1990); and others. Awd: Woodrow Wilson Fellow 1969. Mem: SBL 1969-; CBA 1976-; East Great Lakes Bibl. Soc. 1979-, Pres. 1990. Rec: Reading, music, genealogy. Addr: (o) Athenaeum of Ohio, 6616 Beechmont Ave., Cincinnati, OH 45230 513-231-2223; (h) 7137 Wallace Ave., Cincinnati, OH 45243 513-793-3546.

CAMERON, Ron, Spec: New Testament. Pub: *The Other Gospels: Non-Canonical Gospel Texts,* ed. (Westminster, 1982); and others. Addr: (o) Wesleyan U., Dept. of Religion, 171 Church St., Middletown, CT 06459-0029.

CAMPBELL, Antony F., b. Christchurch, New Zealand, August 24, 1934, s. of William Orr & Laura (Loughnan). Educ: U. of Melbourne, BA 1963, MA 1972; Fac. of Theol., Lyon-Fourviere, STL 1968; Pont. Bibl. Inst., Rome, SSL 1970; Claremont Grad. Sch., PhD 1974. Emp: Jesuit Theol. Coll., 1974- Prof. of OT, 1975-85 Dean, 1986-91 Prin. Spec: Hebrew Bible. Pub: *Sources of the Pentateuch: Texts, Introductions, Annotations,* co-auth. (Fortress, 1993); *The Study Companion to Old Testament Literature: An Approach to the Writings of Pre-Exilic and Exilic Israel,* OT Stud. 2 (Glazier, 1989; Liturgical, 1992); "Past History and Present Text: The Clash of Classical and Post-Critical Approaches to Biblical Text" *Australian Bibl. Rev.* 39 (1991); "1 Samuel" in *The New Jerome Biblical Comm.* (Prentice-Hall, 1990); "The Reported Story: Midway Between Oral Performance and Literary Art" *Semeia* 46 (1989); *Of Prophets and Kings: A Late Ninth-Century Document (1 Samuel 1-2 Kings 10),* CBQ Mon. Ser. 17 (CBA, 1986); "Psalm 78: A Contribution to the Theology of Tenth Century Israel" *CBQ* 41 (1979); "Yahweh and the Ark: A Case Study in Narrative" *JBL* 98 (1979); *The Ark Narrative (1 Sam 4-6; 2 Sam 6): A Form-critical and Traditio-historical Study,* SBL Diss. Ser. 16 (Scholars, 1975); and others. Mem: CBA; CBA of Australia, Pres. 1975-76; Fellow. for Bibl. Stud.; SBL. Rec: Gardening, music, reading. Addr: (o) Jesuit Theological College, 175 Royal Parade, Parkville, VIC 3052, Australia 03-347-6366.

CAMPBELL, Edward F., b. New Haven, CT, January 5, 1932, s. of E. Fay & Edith M., m. Phyllis (Kletzien), chil: Thomas Edward; Sarah Ives. Educ: Yale U., BA 1953; McCormick Theol. Sem., BD 1956; Johns Hopkins U., PhD 1959. Emp: McCormick Theol. Sem., 1958- Francis A. McGaw Prof., OT; *BA*, 1959-75 Ed.; Harvard U., 1961 Asst. Prof.; St. George's Coll., Jerusalem, 1985, 1987, 1990 Vis. Prof.; SBL Mon. Ser., 1990-93 Sr. Ed. Excv: Tel Balatah, 1957-69 Core Staff, 1960- Treasurer, 1966-68 Field Dir.; Bab Edh-Dhra', 1965 Area Supr.; Tel el-Hesi, 1969-84 Project Adv. Spec: Archaeology, Hebrew Bible, Semitic Languages, Texts and Epigraphy. Pub: *Shechem II: Portrait of a Hill Country Vale* (1992); "Shechem" in *EAEHL* (1992); "William F. Albright and Historical Reconstruction" *BA* 42

(1979); "Jewish Shrines of the Hellenistic and Persian Periods" in *Symposia* (ASOR, 1979); *Ruth: New Translation with Introduction and Commentary* (Doubleday, 1975); "Moses and the Foundations of Israel" *Interpretation* 29 (1975); *BA Reader,* vol. 2-4, co-auth. (1964-84); *The Chronology of the Amarna Letters* (Johns Hopkins U.P., 1964); "The Amarna Letters and the Amarna Period" *BA* 22 (1960); and others. Awd: ASOR/Albright Inst., Jerusalem, Acting Dir. 1964, Ann. Prof. 1964-65. Mem: ASOR 1959-, Second V.P. 1974-81; SBL 1959-; Bibl. Colloquium 1960-; Albright Inst., Founding Pres. 1968-69; CBA 1975-. Rec: Hiking, ornithology, nature study, civil liberties, social justice. Addr: (o) McCormick Theological Seminary, 5555 S Woodlawn Ave, Chicago, IL 60637 312-947-6325; (h) 2535 Bennett Ave., Evanston, IL 60201 708-869-3979.

CAPES, David B., b. Atlanta, GA, December 16, 1955, s. of T.L. & Shirley, m. Cathy H., chil: David Bryan; Daniel Ryan; Jordan Michael. Educ: Mercer U., BA, Relig. 1978; SW Bapt. Theol. Sem., MDiv 1982, PhD 1990. Emp: Houston Bapt. U., 1990-92 Asst. Prof. Spec: New Testament. Pub: *Old Testament Yahweh Texts in Paul's Christology,* WUNT 2/47 (Mohr, 1992). Mem: SBL 1983-; IBR 1986-. Addr: (o) Houston Baptist U., 7502 Fondren Rd., Houston, TX 77074 713-774-7661; (h) 12319 Dorrance, Stafford, TX 77477 713-530-6802.

CARAGOUNIS, Chrys C., b. Greece, October 26, 1940, s. of Constantine & Maria, m. Sophie, chil: Rosanna; Yvonne-Marie; Vivian; Eva-Corina. Educ: London U., BDiv 1971; Uppsala U., DTh 1977. Emp: Uppsala U., 1972-86 Lect.; London Bible Coll., 1986-87 Sr. Lect.; Evang. Theol. Fac., 1987-90 Prof.; Lunds U., 1990- Assoc. Prof. Spec: New Testament. Pub: "The Kingdom of God/Kingdom of Heaven" in *Dict. of Jesus and the Gospels* (1992); "The Kingdom of God in John and the Synoptics: Realized or Potential Eschatology?" in *John and the Synoptics* (Louvain Colloquium, 1991); *Peter and the Rock,* BZNW 58 (de Gruyter, 1990); "L'Universalisme Moderne: Perspectives Bibliques sur la révélation de Dieu" *Hokhma* 45 (1990); *Nytestamentlig Syntax* (1990); "Greek Culture and Jewish Piety: The Clash and the Fourth Beast of Daniel 7" *ETL* 65 (1989); "Kingdom of God, Son of Man and Jesus' Self-understanding, 1-11" *TB* 40 (1989); *The Son of Man: Vision and Interpretation* (1986); and others. Mem: SNTS 1990-. Addr: (o) Lunds U., Dept. of Religious Studies, Allhelgona Kyrkogata 8, S-223 62 Lund, Sweden 46-46-105884; (h) Repslagarevagen 6, S-245 35 Staffanstorp, Sweden 46-46-253301.

CARDER, Muriel M., b. Woodford Green, England, November 1, 1922, d. of Carey Bradford Spurgeon & Elizabeth Frances (Keeley), m. W. Gordon Carder, chil: Gordon Kimberley; Karen Anne (Hunt). Educ: McMaster U., Canada, BA 1944, BD 1947;

Union Theol. Sem., STM (summa cum laude) 1958; Toronto Sch. of Theol., ThD 1969. Emp: Telugu Trans. Com. of United Bible Soc., 1961-76 Exegete; Ramapatnam Baptist Theol. Coll., India, 1967-69 Prof.; Andhra Christian Theol. Coll., India, 1969-76 Prof.; ON, Canada government, 1978- Chaplain; Intl. Greek NT Project. Spec: New Testament. Pub: "Is there a Caesarean Text of the Catholic Epistles?" *NTS* 16 (1969-70); "The Biblical Concept of Sin in Translation" *Indian Jour. of Theol.* 20/1-2 (1971). Awd: McMaster Div. Grad. Assn., Disting. Grad. Aw. 1988; McMaster Div. Coll., DD 1991. Mem: NT Soc. 1968-; Canadian Assn. for Pastoral Educ. 1977-. Rec: Badminton, pipe organ, gardening, calligraphy, canoeing. Addr: (o) Woodstock General Hospital, 270 Riddell St., Woodstock, ON N4S 6N6, Canada 519-421-4211; (h) 206 Bower Hill Rd., Woodstock, ON N4S 2N4, Canada 519-539-4922.

CARNAGEY, Glenn A., Sr., b. Hammond, IN, September 13, 1938, s. of Walter R. & Helen M. (Kiekenapp), m. Nan (Patton), chil: Glenn A., Jr.; Walter John. Educ: U. of Tex., BA 1960; Dallas Theol. Sem., ThM 1969; U. of Tulsa, MA 1978, PhD 1984. Emp: Tulsa Sem. of Bibl. Lang., 1974-89 Pres. & Prof., OT; SW Bapt. U., Kelley U. Coll., 1990-91 Adj. Prof., Bibl. Stud. & English; Cascade Sem. of Bibl. Lang., 1991- Prof., OT; *NEAS Bull.*, 1990- Ed. Excv: Abila of the Decapolis, Jordan, 1988 Asst. Area Supr., 1990- Area Supr., Supr. of Computer & D-base Operations, Ceramic Typologist. Spec: Archaeology. Pub: "The 1990 Abila Area AA Report" *NEAS Bull.* (1991); "Ebla and the Old Testament" *Lodestar Rev.* Apr. (1988). Awd: Dallas Theol. Sem., Rollin T. Chafer Awd. for Apologetics 1969. Mem: SBL 1978-; ASOR 1978-; NEAS 1988-. Rec: Computer applications to arch., skiing, downhill & mountain hiking, class. music, golf. Addr: (o) 206 Burwell St., Bremerton, WA 98312; (h) 1303 Corbet Dr., Bremerton, WA 98312 206-377-4175.

CARR, David M., b. Cleveland, OH, April 11, 1961, s. of John & Adrienne, m. Sharon, chil: Talia. Educ: Carleton Coll., BA 1980; Candler Sch. of Theol., MTS 1983; Claremont Grad. Sch., MA, PhD 1988. Emp: Sch. of Theol. at Claremont, 1986-88 Vis. Lect.; Meth. Theol. Sch. in Ohio, 1988- Assoc. Prof. Spec: Hebrew Bible, New Testament, Apocrypha and Post-biblical Studies. Pub: "Reaching for Unity in Isaiah" *JSOT* 57 (1993); *From D to Q: A Study of Early Jewish Interpretations of Solomon's Dream at Gibeon*, SBL Mon. Ser. 44 (Scholars, 1991); and others. Awd: Dempster Grad. Fellow. 1985-86, 1986-87. Mem: SBL 1986-; CBA 1989-. Rec: Banjo, bicycling, poetry. Addr: (o) Methodist Theological School in Ohio, 3081 Columbus Pike, PO Box 1204, Delaware, OH 43015; (h) 248 N Liberty St., Delaware, OH 43015.

CARRAS, George P., b. Turlock, CA, January 27, 1950, s. of Peter & Vivian, m. Elizabeth, chil: Peter Jonathan; Joel Alexander; Megan Elizabeth. Educ: U. of Calif., Berkeley, BA 1974; Manchester U., MA 1982; Oxford U., DPhil 1990. Emp: U. of Oxford, Mansfield Coll., 1983-90 Lect., NT, 1985-88 Coll. Dean; London U., 1987-88 Lect., NT; Gonzaga U., 1989-90 Vis. Prof., Relig. Stud.; U. of Calif., Berkeley, 1991-93 Post-doc. Fellow., Dept. of Near East. Stud. Spec: New Testament, Apocrypha and Post-biblical Studies. Pub: "Dependence or Common Tradition in Philo, Hypothetica viii.6.10-7.20 and Josephus, Contra Apionem 2.190-219" *Studia Philonica Ann.* 5 (1993); "Romans 2.1-29: A Dialogue on the Jewish Religion" *Biblica* 73 (1992); "Philo's Hypothetica—Josephus' Contra Apionem and the Question of Sources" in *SBL 1990 Seminar Papers* (Scholars, 1990); "Jewish Ethics & Gentile Converts: Some Remarks on 1 Thess. 4:3-8" in *The Thessalonian Correspondence* (Leuven U.P., 1990). Awd: Oxford U., Christ Church Coll., Res. Stipend 1980-82; Oxford U., Denyer & Johnson Fellow. 1981-83; Hall-Houghton Fellow. in Bibl. Stud. 1981-83. Mem: AAR 1983-; SBL 1983-; European Assn. of Jewish Stud. 1984-; Brit. Assn. of Jewish Stud. 1986-. Rec: Racquetball, golf, hiking, gardening, baroque music. Addr: (h) N 10708 Nelson Rd., Spokane, WA 99218 509-467-8690.

CARROLL, Robert P., b. Dublin, Ireland, January 18, 1941, s. of Thomas F. & Kathleen (Merrigan), m. Mary Anne Alice, chil: Fionn Tomas; Alice Louisa Ysabel; Saul Steve. Educ: Trinity Coll., Dublin U., BA 1962, MA 1967; U. of Edinburgh, PhD 1967. Emp: Glasgow U., 1968-69 Asst. Lect., Semitic Lang., 1969-81 Lect., 1981-86 Sr. Lect., OT Lang. & Lit., 1986-91 Reader, 1991- Prof., Bibl. Stud.; *JSOT*, 1990- Ed. Bd.; Cath. U.P. Bibl. Poetics Ser., 1992- Gen. Ed. Spec: Hebrew Bible, Semitic Languages, Texts and Epigraphy, Apocrypha and Post-biblical Studies. Pub: *The Bible as a Problem for Christianity* (Trinity, 1991); "Whose Prophet? Whose History? Whose Social Reality?" *JSOT* 48 (1990); *Jeremiah: A Commentary* (SCM/Westminster, 1986); "Theodicy and the Community: Text and Subtext of Jeremiah V 1-6" *OTS* 23 (1984); *From Chaos to Covenant* (SCM/Crossroad, 1981); *When Prophecy Failed* (SCM/Seabury, 1979); "The Sisyphean Task of Biblical Transformation" *SJT* 30 (1977); "Rebellion and Dissent in Ancient Israelite Society" *ZAW* 89 (1977); "Psalm LXXVIII: Vestiges of a Tribal Polemic" *VT* 21 (1971); and others. Mem: SOTS 1969-; SBL 1987-; European Soc. for Lit. & Relig. 1991-. Rec: Cinema, reading, daydreaming. Addr: (o) U. of Glasgow, Dept. of Biblical Studies, 4 The Square, Glasgow G12 8QQ, Scotland 041-339-8855; (h) 5 Marchmont Terrace, Glasgow G12 9LT, Scotland 041-339-0440.

CARTER, Warren C., b. Palmerston N, New Zealand, June 1, 1955, s. of Allan & Elaine, m. Janet Mary, chil: Emma; Rebekah. Educ: Victoria U. of Wellington, New Zealand, BA 1977; Christchurch Tchr. Coll., New Zealand, Tchr. Dip. 1978; Melbourne Coll. of Div., BD 1985, ThM

1987; Princeton Theol. Sem., PhD 1991. Emp: Kapiti Coll., New Zealand, 1979-81, Tchr.; New Zealand, 1981-86 Parish Min.; Princeton Theol. Sem., 1989 Vis. Instr., NT Greek; St. Paul Sch. of Theol., 1990-91 Instr., 1991- Asst. Prof., NT. Spec: New Testament. Pub: "The Crowds in Matthew's Gospel" *CBQ* 55 (1993); "Kernels and Narrative Blocks: The Structure of Matthew's Gospel" *CBQ* 54 (1992); "The Prologue and John's Gospel: Function, Symbol and the Definitive Word" *JSNT* 39 (1990); "The Earliest Christian Movement: Sectarian, Itinerant, or Liminal Existence?" *Koinonia* 1 (1989); "Rome (and Jerusalem): The Contingency of Romans 3:21-26" in *Irish Bibl. Stud.* 11 (1989); and others. Awd: U. of Auckland, New Zealand, Hebrew Lang. Awd. 1985; Princeton Theol. Sem., Doc. Fellow. 1986-90; Lilly Found., Fac. Development Grant 1992; ATS Globalization in Class. Theol. Disciplines Awd. 1992. Mem: SBL 1988-. Rec: Sports, music. Addr: (o) St. Paul School of Theology, 5123 Truman Rd., Kansas City, MO 64127 816-483-9604; (h) 6925 Barkley, Overland Park, KS 66204 913-831-1687.

CARTLEDGE, Tony W., b. Lincolnton, GA, December 5, 1951, s. of William C., Jr. & Hollie (Williamson), m. Jan (Rush), chil: Charles Russell; Bethany Rush. Educ: U. of Georgia, BSed (magna cum laude) 1973; SE Bapt. Theol. Sem., MDiv 1982; Duke U., PhD, OT & Semitic Stud. 1989. Emp: Baptist Church, 1979- Pastor; Appalachian State U., 1986-88 Lec., OT & NT; SE Bapt. Theol. Sem., 1987-89 Vis. Instr., OT. Spec: Hebrew Bible, Semitic Languages, Texts and Epigraphy. Pub: *Vows in the Hebrew Bible and the Ancient Near East*, JSOTSup 147 (JSOT, 1992); "Forgiveness," "Jonah," "Jonah, Book of" in *Mercer Dict. of the Bible* (Mercer U.P., 1990); "Were Nazirite Vows Unconditional?" *CBQ* 51 (1989); "Vow" in *International Standard Bible Ency.* (Eerdmans, 1988); "Conditional Vows in the Psalms of Lament: A New Approach to an Old Problem" in *The Listening Heart: Essays in Psalms and Wisdom in Honor of Roland E. Murphy, O. Carm.* (JSOT, 1987); and others. Mem: SBL 1986-; SBPR 1989-. Rec: Golf, reading, woodwork. Addr: (o) Woodhaven Baptist Church, 4000 Kildaire Farm Rd., Apex, NC 27502 919-362-0127.

CARVER, Frank G., b. Crookston, NE, May 27, 1928, s. of Frank Alonzo & Greeta (Gould), m. Betty Joan (Ireland), chil: Mark Erwin; Carol Denise (Monahan). Educ: Taylor U., BA 1950; Nazarene Theol. Sem., BD 1954; Princeton Theol. Sem., MTh 1958; U. of Edinburgh, Scotland, PhD 1964. Emp: Ch. of the Nazarene, 1954-59 Pastor; Pasadena/Point Loma Nazarene Coll., 1961- Prof. of Bibl. Theol. & Relig., 1967-82, 1991- Chmn., Dept. of Phil. & Relig., 1981- Dir.of Grad. Stud. in Relig. Spec: Hebrew Bible, New Testament. Pub: "The Quest for the Holy: The Darkness of God" *WTJ* (1988); "Biblical Foundations for the Secondness of Entire Sanctification" *WTJ* (1987); "The Second Epistle

of Paul to the Corinthians" in *Beacon Bible Comm.* (1968); and others. Mem: IBR; SBL; WTS, First V.P. 1985-86, Pres. 1986-87; ETS. Rec: Hiking. Addr: (o) Point Loma Nazarene College, 3900 Lomaland Dr., San Diego, CA 92106 619-221-2331; (h) 4037-95 Porte De Palmas, San Diego, CA 92122 619-457-5358.

CASEY, Philip M., b. Sunderland, England, October 18, 1942, s. of Philip Thomas & Florence, chil: Sian Elizabeth; Jonathan Mark Homer. Educ: U. of Durham, St. Chad's Coll., BA 1964, BA 1967, PhD 1977. Emp: U. of St. Andrews, 1977-79 Lect.; U. of Nottingham, 1979- Lect.; U. of Birmingham, 1985-86 Edward Cadbury Lect. Spec: Hebrew Bible, Apocrypha and Post-biblical Studies. Pub: *From Jewish Prophet to Gentile God. The Origins and Development of New Testament Christology* (Clarke/Westminster/John Knox, 1991); "Method in Our Madness, and Madness in Their Methods. Some Approaches to the Son of Man Problem in Recent Scholarship" *JSNT* 42 (1991); "Culture and Historicity: The Plucking of the Grain (Mark 2.23-28)" *NTS* 34 (1988); "General, Generic and Indefinite: The Use of the Term 'son of man' in Aramaic Sources and in the Teaching of Jesus" *JSNT* 29 (1987); "The Jackals and the Son of Man (Matt viii.20//Luke ix.58)" *JSNT* 23 (1985); *Son of Man. The Interpretation and Influence of Daniel 7* (SPCK, 1980); "Porphyry and the Origins of the Book of Daniel" *JTS* 27 (1976); and others. Mem: SNTS 1980-. Rec: Music, opera, ballet, drama, art. Addr: (o) U. of Nottingham, Dept. of Theology, University Park, Nottingham, NG7 2RD, England 0602-515859; (h) 100 Chaworth Rd., West Bridgford, Nottingham, NG2 7AD, England.

CASURELLA, Anthony, b. Chicago, IL, May 11, 1946, s. of Anthony & Anna Mildred, m. Sharon Marie, chil: Stephan Anthony; Joy Marie; Jonathan Paul; Alison Kathleen. Educ: Greenville Coll., BA 1968; Asbury Theol. Sem., MDiv 1971; U. of Durham, England, PhD 1981. Emp: Asbury Theol. Sem., Ky., 1971-72 Instr., Bibl. Lang.; Emmanuel Bible Coll., England, 1976-77 Lect., NT, 1977-87 Prin.; West. Evang. Sem., 1987- Prof., NT, Chair, Div. of Bibl. Lit. Spec: New Testament. Pub: *The Asbury Bible Comm.*, contb. (Zondervan, 1992); *The Johannine Paraclete in the Church Fathers: A Study in the History of Exeĝesis*, Beitrage zur Geschichte der bibl. Exegese 25 (Mohr/Siebeck, 1983); "The Paraclete in the Church Fathers" *Asbury Sem.* 34/3 (1979). Mem: Tyndale Fellow. 1976-; Evang. European Schol., Fellow 1977-87; SBL 1984-; SNTS 1985-; IBR 1987-. Rec: Photography, reading, walking/jogging, cycling. Addr: (o) Western Evangelical Seminary, PO Box 23939, Portland, OR 97281 503-639-0559; (h) 11353 SE 45th Ave., Milwaukie, OR 97222 503-598-4319.

CATCHPOLE, David R., b. Worthing, Sussex, England, May 1, 1938, m. Ann, chil: Helen;

Catherine. Educ: Queen's College, Oxford, BA, MA 1962; Pembroke Coll., Cambridge, PhD 1968. Emp: Clifton Theol. Coll., 1966-69 Lect.; U. of Lancaster, 1969-84 Sr. Lect.; U. of Exeter, 1984- Prof. Spec: New Testament. Pub: *The Quest for Q* (T & T Clark, 1992); "The Centurion's Faith and its Function in Q" in *F. Neirynck Festschrift* (Louvain U.P., 1992); "The Mission Charge in Q" *Semeia* 55 (1992); "The Beginning of Q: A Proposal" *NTS* (1992); "Temple Traditions in Q" in *E. Bammel Festschrift* (Academic, 1991); "Paul, James and the Apostolic Decree" *NTS* (1977); *The Trial of Jesus* (Brill, 1971); and others. Mem: SNTS 1976-. Rec: Philately, gardening, cricket. Addr: (o) U. of Exeter, Dept. of Theology, The Queen's Dr., Exeter EX4 4QH, England 264242.

CATE, Robert L., b. Nashville, TN, August 11, 1932, s. of George H. & Lucile (Cowherd), m. Dorothy (Wright), chil: Ruth; Robert L., Jr.; Fred H. Educ: Vanderbilt Univ., BE, 1953; South. Bapt. Theol. Sem., BD 1956, PhD 1960. Emp: 1959-74 Bapt. Pastor; Golden Gate Bapt. Theol. Sem., 1974-84 Prof., OT & Hebrew, 1984-91 Dean of Acad. Affairs; Okla. State U., 1991- Prof., Relig. Spec: Hebrew Bible, New Testament, Apocrypha and Post-biblical Studies. Pub: *A History of the New Testament and Its Times* (Broadman, 1991); *A History of the Bible Lands in the Interbiblical Period* (Broadman, 1989); "The Development of Monotheism" *BI* (1989); *An Introduction to the Old Testament and Its Study* (Broadman, 1987); "The Fear of the Lord in the Old Testament" *Theol. Educator* 35 (1987); *These Sought A Country: A History of Israel in Old Testament Times* (Broadman, 1985); "The Sheep Gate and the Pool of Bethesda" *BI* 1985; "Psalm 105: The Mighty Acts of God" *Theol. Educator* 29 (1984); and others. Mem: SBL; SOTS; NAPH; NABPR; IBR. Rec: Travel, reading. Addr: (o) Oklahoma State U., Dept. of Religion, 209 Hanner Hall, Stillwater, OK 74078 405-744-9232; (h) 1005 Woodcrest Dr., Stillwater, OK 74074 405372-8814.

CAULLEY, Thomas S., b. Eugene, OR, April 16, 1952, s. of James, m. Cherie (Zook), chil: Alisha; Justin. Educ: Puget Sound Coll. of the Bible, BA 1974; Fuller Theol. Sem., MA 1976; U. of Tubingen, Germany, ThD 1983. Emp: Puget Sound Coll. of the Bible, 1976-78 Instr.; Seattle Pacific U., 1976-78, 1982 Instr.; East. N Mex. U., 1983-88 Grad. Fac.; Manhattan Christian Coll., 1988- Assoc. Prof. Spec: New Testament. Pub: "The Holy Spirit" in *Baker Evangelical Dict. of Theology* (1984); "The False Teachers in 2nd Peter" *Studia Biblica* (1982); articles in *ABD;* and others. Mem: SBL; IBR. Rec: Racquetball, biking. Addr: (o) Manhattan Christian College, 1415 Anderson Ave., Manhattan, KS 66502 913-539-3571; (h) 3216 Highland Circle, Manhattan, KS 66502 913-537-8645.

CAVALLIN, Hans C. C., b. Ostersund, Sweden, November 14, 1938, d. of Sam & Inger. Educ: U. of Lund, Sweden, BD 1962,; Uppsala U., MTh 1969, DTh 1974. Emp: Ch. of Sweden, 1962-65

Parish Priest; Benedictine Monastery, 1970- Father Superior;´ U. of Uppsala, 1967- Prof.; *NTS,* 1966-88 Ed. Bd. Spec: New Testament, Apocrypha and Post-biblical Studies. Pub: *Manssamhallets forsvarare eller skapelsens?* (1982); "Tod und Auferstehung der Weisheitslehrer: Ein Beitrag zur Zeichnung des frame of reference Jesu" *Studien zum Neuen Testament und Seiner Umwelt* (1980); "The False Teachers of 2 Peter as Pseudo-Prophets" *NT* (1979); *Life After Death: Paul's Argument for the Resurrection of the Dead in I. Cor 15* vol. 1 (Gleerup, 1974); and others. Mem: SNTS. Rec: Skiing, prayer. Addr: (h) Ostanbacks Kloster S-733 96 Sala, Sweden 0224-25088.

CAZELLES, Henri, b. Paris, France, June 8, 1912, s. of Pierre & Clotilde. Educ: Dip. des Sci. Politiques 1932; Doc. en Droit 1935; ThD 1943; Lic. Sci. Bibl. 1950; l'Ecole Pratique Hautes Etudes, Sorbonne, Eleve titulaire. Emp: St. Sulpice, 1942-54 Seminiaire; *VT,* 1950-75 Ed. Bd.; Inst. Cath. de Paris, 1954-81 Prof.; *Supplement au Dict. de la Bible,* 1956-86 Ed. Bd.; l'Ecole Pratique des Hautes Etudes, 1973-80 Dir. Spec: Hebrew Bible, Mesopotamian Studies, Semitic Languages, Texts and Epigraphy, Egyptology. Pub: *La Bible et son Dieu* (1989); *Autour de l'Exode* (1987); *Alttestamentliche Christologie-Zur Geschichte der Messaisidee* (1983); *Naissance de l'Eglise, secte juive rejetee?* (1983); *Histoire politique d'Israel jusqu'a Alexandre* (1983); and others. Awd: Acad. royale de Belgique, Mem. Chevalier de la Legion d'Honneur. Mem: Soc. Asiatique; Soc. d'Egyptologie; Pont. Bibl. Commn.; SOTS; CBA. Rec: Landscape. Addr: (o) BOSEB, 21 Rue d'Assas, Paris 75006, France 42-22-21-80.

CERESKO, Anthony R., b. Detroit, MI, August 20, 1942, s. of Anthony & Mary (Tyrie). Educ: Niagara U., BA 1965; Catholic U., STB 1970, STL 1971; Pont. Bibl. Inst., SSL 1973, SSD 1981. Emp: Sts. Cyril & Methodius Sem., 1975-78 Instr.; St. Mary's Coll., 1975-78 Instr.; U. of St. Michael's Coll., Canada, 1978-91 Assoc. Prof.; St. Peter's Pont. Inst., India, 1991- Prof.; *CBQ,* 1984-91 Assoc. Ed. Spec: Hebrew Bible. Pub: "The ABC's of Wisdom in Psalm XXXIV" *VT* (1985); "A Rhetorical Analysis of David's Boast' (1 Samuel 17:34-37): Some Reflections on Method" *CBQ* (1985); "A Poetic Analysis of Psalm 105, with Attention to Its Use of Irony" *Biblica* (1983); *Job 29-31 in the Light of Northwest Semitic: A Translation and Philological Comm.* (Bibl. Inst., 1980); "The Function of Chiasmus in Hebrew Poetry" *CBQ* (1978); and others. Mem: CBA 1975-; SBL 1975-; ASOR 1979-. Rec: Walking, music. Addr: (o) St. Peter's Pontifical Institute, Malleswaram West P.O., 560 055 Bangalore, India.

CHADWICK, Jeffrey R., b. Ogden, UT, July 26, 1955, s. of Carl & Joyce (Rives), m. Kim, chil: Casandra; Daniel; David; Benjamin; Renee; Abigail. Educ: Weber St. Coll., BA 1978; Brigham Young U., MA, Near East. Stud. 1984;

U. of Utah, PhD, Arch./Anthrop. 1992. Emp: Roy LDS Sem., 1979-82 Instr., Anc. Scripture & Relig.; Ben Lomond LDS Sem., 1982-88 Instr., Anc. Scripture & Relig.; Bonneville LDS Sem., 1988-92 Instr., Anc. Scripture & Relig.; Jerusalem Ctr. for Near East. Stud., 1992- Prof., Near East. Stud. Spec: Archaeology, Hebrew Bible, New Testament. Pub: *The Holy Land: A Geographical, Historical and Archaeological Guide to the Land of the Bible*, co-auth. (HaMakor, 1990). Addr: (o) Brigham Young U., Ctr. for Near East. Stud., Mt. Scopus, Box 19604, Jerusalem, Israel 02-273181; (h) 16 Lehi St., Jerusalem, Israel 02-815940.

CHANEY, Marvin L., b. Horton, KS, November 13, 1940, s. of Irvin F. & Margaret (Faust), m. Rilla (McCubbins), chil: Anne Thayer; Nathania Lynn; Katharine Blythe. Educ: Phillips U., BA 1962; Harvard U., BD 1965, PhD 1976. Emp: San Francisco Theol. Sem., 1969-71 Instr., 1971-76 Asst. Prof., 1976-80 Assoc. Prof., OT, 1980- Nathaniel Gray Prof. of Hebrew; Exegesis & OT. Pub: "Debt Easement in Israelite History and Tradition" in *The Bible and the Politics of Exegesis: Essays in Honor of Norman K. Gottwald on his Sixty-Fifth Birthday* (Pilgrim, 1991); "Joshua" in *The Books of the Bible* vol. 1 (Scribner's, 1989); "Bitter Bounty: The Dynamics of Political Economy Critiqued by the Eighth Century Prophets" in *Reformed Faith & Economics* (U. Press of America, 1989); "Systemic Study of the Israelite Monarchy" *Semeia* 37 (1986); "Ancient Palestinian Peasant Movements and the Formation of Premonarchic Israel" in *Palestine in Transition: The Emergence of Ancient Israel* (Almond, 1983); and others. Awd: Assn. of Theol. Sch. in the United States & Canada, Grants 1977-78, 1991-92; Newhall Fellow. 1993. Mem: ASOR; AAR; Pacific Coast Theol. Soc.; SBL, Pres., Pacific Coast reg. 1990-91. Rec: Camping, jogging, cabinet making, needlepoint, travel. Addr: (o) San Francisco Theological Seminary, 2 Kensington Rd., San Anselmo, CA 94960 415-258-6578; (h) 116 Oak Springs Dr., San Anselmo, CA 94960 415-457-2048.

CHARLES, J. Daryl, b. Lancaster, PA, December 9, 1950, s. of J. Lester & Evaline (Hathaway), m. Rosemarie, chil: Melody Lee; Jesse Robin; Ian Alexander. Educ: West Chester State U., BS 1972; South. Calif. Coll., MA, Relig. Stud. 1986; Westminster Theol. Sem., PhD, Hermeneutics 1990. Emp: Ludenscheider Volkshochschule, Germany, 1981-83 Lang. Instr.; Chesapeake Theol. Sem., 1989- Lect., NT; Wilberforce Forum/Prison Fellow. Min., 1990- Colson Schol.-in-Residence. Spec: New Testament. Pub: *Literary Strategy in the Epistle of Jude* (Assoc. U., 1992); "The Greatest or the Least in the Kingdom? The Disciple's Relationship to the Law (Matt 5:17-20)" *TJ* 13/2 (1992); "Jude's Use of Pseudepigraphal Source-Material as Part of a Literary Strategy" *NTS* 37 (1991); "Literary Artifice in the Epistle of Jude" *ZNW* 82 (1991); "'Those' and 'These': The Use

of the Old Testament in the Epistle of Jude" *JSNT* 38 (1990); "Angels, Sonship and Birthright in the Epistle to the Hebrews" *JETS* 33/2 (1990); *The Unseen War*, co-trans. (CGM, 1977); and others. Mem: CSSR 1987-88; ETS 1988-; IBR 1990-; SBL 1990-. Rec: Sports, performing & creative arts, translation. Addr: (o) Wilberforce Forum, c/o Prison Fellowship Ministries, PO Box 17500, Washington, DC 20041 703-478-0100; (h) 10232 Wetherburn Rd., Ellicott City, MD 21042 410-461-9380.

CHARLESWORTH, James H., b. St. Petersburg, FL, May 30, 1940, s. of Arthur & Jean (Hamilton), m. Jerrie (Pittard), chil: Michelle; Eve; James, Jr. Educ: Duke Grad. Sch., PhD 1967. Emp: Duke U., 1969-84 Assoc. Prof., Dept. of Relig.; Intl. Ctr. on Christian Origins, Dir.; Princeton Theol Sem., 1984- George L. Collord Prof. of NT Lang. & Lit.; U. of Edinburgh, 1985 Gunning Lect.; *BR,* Ed. Bd. Excv: Balatah, 1968 Area Supr.; Turkey Expdn., 1983 Co-dir.; Sinai Expdn., 1985 Dir. Spec: New Testament, Semitic Languages, Texts and Epigraphy, Apocrypha and Post-biblical Studies. Pub: *Jesus and the Dead Sea Scrolls* (Doubleday, 1992); *Graphic Concordance to the Dead Sea Scrolls* (Mohr, 1991); *Jesus Within Judaism* (Doubleday, 1988); *The Old Testament Pseudepigrapha and the New Testament* (Cambridge U.P., 1985); *The Old Testament Pseudepigrapha*, vol. 1-2 (Doubleday, 1983, 1985); *The Pseudepigrapha and Modern Research* (Scholars, 1977, 1981); and others. Awd: Fulbright Fellow 1967; BAS Publ. Awd., Best Book on OT 1984, 1986. Mem: SBL; AAR; SNTS; ASOR; Found. on Christian Origins, Pres. Rec: Tennis, basketball. Addr: (o) Princeton Theological Seminary, Princeton, NJ 08540 609-497-7920; (h) 51 Ross Stevenson Cir., Princeton, NJ 08540 609-683-1422.

CHASE, Debra A., m. William J. Penhallurick. Educ: Dartmouth Coll., AB (summa cum laude) 1976; Harvard Div. Sch., MTS 1979; Harvard U., MA 1986, PhD 1993. Emp: Harvard U., 1982, 1985-87, Teaching Fellow. Excv: Numeira, Jordan, 1981, 1983 Field Supr.; Tell Es Sa'idiyyeh, Jordan, 1985 Field Supr. Spec: Archaeology, Hebrew Bible, Semitic Languages, Texts and Epigraphy. Pub: "Evidence of Disease in Ancient Near Eastern Texts: Leprosy in the Code of Hammurapi?" in *Human Paleopathologyy: Current Syntheses and Future Options* (Smithsonian Inst., 1991); "Ina Sitkuki Napisti: Starvation (Kwashiorkor-Marasmus) in Atra-Hasis" *JCS* 39 (1987); "A Note on an Inscription from Kuntillet 'Ajrud" *BASOR* 246 (1982); and others. Mem: AAR; ASOR; CBA; SBL. Addr: (h) 517 Fairfax Ave., Norfolk, VA 23507.

CHAVEZ, Daniel, b. Chicago, IL, April 19, 1929, s. of Ricardo & Ruth, m. Teresa, chil: Daniel; David (dec.); Duel. Educ: Spanish-Amer. Sem., AA 1948; South. Missionary Coll., BA 1950; Seventh Day Adventist Theol. Sem.,

MA 1955, BD 1956; Sch. of Theol., PhD 1960. Emp: Colegio de las Antillas, Cuba, 1951-61 Prof.; Antillian Coll., Puerto Rico, 1961-62 Dept. Head; U. de Montemorelos, Mexico, 1974-75 Prof.; Loma Linda U., 1978-84 Assoc. Prof. Spec: Hebrew Bible, New Testament, Semitic Languages, Texts and Epigraphy, Apocrypha and Post-biblical Studies. Pub: *El Padrenuestro* (1992); "El hombre mas ilustre de la historia" *The Good News* (1983); "La traduccion del Apocalipsis de Gregorio Lopez" *Revista de la UNAM* (1973); *El Salmo del Amor* (U. de Montemorelos, 1968). Mem: SBL. Addr: (h) 6620 Dorinda Dr., Riverside, CA 92503 714-354-8083.

CHERBONNIER, Edmond La Beaume, b. St. Louis, MO, February 11, 1918, s. of Edward & Adelaide, m. Phyllis (White), chil: Laurie; Camden. Educ: Harvard U., BA 1939; Union Theol. Sem., M.Div 1947; Cambridge U., England, MA 1952, BA 1958; Columbia U., PhD 1951; U. of Vermont, DD 1959. Emp: Vassar Coll., 1940-42 Asst. Prof.; Barnard Coll., 1951-55 Asst. Prof.; Union Theol. Sem., 1954-55 Lect.; Trinity Coll., 1955-83 Assoc. Prof. Pub: "The Logic of Biblical Anthropomorphism" *HTR* (1962); "Is There a Biblical Metaphysic?" *Theol. Today* (1959); "Mystical vs. Biblical Symbolism" in *The Christian Scholar* (1956); and others. Awd: Fiske Fellow. 1947. Mem: AAR; SBL; Royal Inst. of Phil., England. Rec: Tennis, skiing, music. Addr: (h) 843 Prospect Ave., West Hartford, CT 06105 203-233-7460.

CHERNICK, Michael L., b. Brooklyn, NY, December 8, 1943, s. of Samuel & Sara, m. Miriam, chil: Jeremy; Saul. Educ: Yeshiva Coll., BA 1965; Rabbi Isaac Elchanan Theol. Sem., Rabbinical Ord. 1969; Bernard Revel Grad. Sch., MA 1969, PhD 1978. Emp: HUC-Jewish Inst. of Relig., 1974-92 Prof., Rabbinic Lit. Spec: Apocrypha and Post-biblical Studies. Pub: "Internal Restraints of Gezerah Shawah's Application" *JQR* (1991); "Developments in the 'Mufneh' Requirements for Gezerah Shavah" in *Proceedings of the 10th World Congress of Jewish Studies* (1990); *Hermeneutical Studies in Talmudic and Midrashic Literatures* (Habermann Inst. for Lit. Res., 1984); "*Eesh* as Man and Adult in the Halakic Midrashim" *JQR* (1982); "The Development of Kelal Uferat Ukelal Hermeneutics" *Tarbiz* (1982); "Some Talmudic Responses to Christianity, 3-4 Century" *JES* (1980); and others. Mem: AJS; AAR; SBL; WUJS. Addr: (o) Hebrew Union College-Jewish Institute of Religion, Brookdale Center, 1 W 4th St., New York, NY 10012 212-674-5300; (h) 1599 Sussex Rd., Teaneck, NJ 07666 201-837-6157.

CHIAT, Marilyn J., b. Minneapolis, MN, August 3, 1932, d. of William Segal & Taube (Richman), m. Harvey J., chil: William; Penny Lynn. Educ: U. of Minn., BA 1969, MA 1972, PhD 1979. Emp: U. of Minn., 1981- Affil. Acad. Staff; Ctr. for the Documentation & Preservation

of Places of Worship, 1990- Co-dir. Spec: Archaeology, Apocrypha and Post-biblical Studies. Pub: "Using Archaeological Sources: The Synagogue and Church," co-auth., in *The Making of Jewish and Christian Worship* (Notre Dame U.P., 1991); *Handbook of Synagogue Architecture* (Scholars, 1982); "Ancient Synagogues in Eretz Israel" *Conservative Judaism* 35/1 (1981); "First Century Synagogue Architecture: A Comparative Study" in *Ancient Synagogues: The State of Research* (Scholars, 1981); "Synagogue Art and Architecture in Byzantine Beth She'an" *Jour. of Jewish Art* 7 (1980); and others. Awd: Hebrew Union Coll., Cincinnati, Lowenstein-Weiner Post-doc. Fellow. 1984. Mem: AIA, Pres., Minn. chap. 1979; Soc. of Arch. Hist., Pres., Minn. Soc. 1981-; AAR 1982-; North Amer. Acad. of Relig. 1991-. Rec: Hiking, biking, swimming, travel, reading. Addr: (o) Ctr. for Documentation & Preservation of Places of Worship, 100 N 6th St., Suite 531-B, Minneapolis, MN 55403 612-333-5365; (h) 3812 Drew Ave. South, Minneapolis, MN 55410 612-926-7936.

CHILTON, Bruce D., b. Roslyn, NY, September 27, 1949, s. of Bruce & Virginia, m. Odile (Sevault). Educ: Bard Coll., BA; General Theol. Sem., MDiv; Cambridge U., PhD. Emp: Sheffield U., 1976-85 Lect.; Yale Div. Sch., 1985- Assoc. Prof.; Bard Coll., 1987- Bernard Iddings Bell Prof. of Relig.; *JSNT,* 1978-85 Exec. Ed.; *Bull. for Bibl. Res.,* Ed.-in-Chief. Spec: Hebrew Bible, New Testament, Semitic Languages, Texts and Epigraphy, Apocrypha and Post-biblical Studies. Pub: *The Temple of Jesus* (Pa. State U.P., 1992); *Profiles of a Rabbi* (Scholars, 1989); "The Epitaph of Himerus from the Jewish Catacomb of the Via Applia" *JQR* (1989); *The Isaiah Targum* (1987); *Targumic Approaches to the Gospels* (U. Press of Amer., 1986); "A Comparative Study of Synoptic Development" *JBL* (1982); "Isaac and the Second Night" *Biblica* (1980); and others. Awd: Heinrich Hertz Schol. Mem: SNTS; SBL; European Assn. for Jewish Stud. Rec: French & German Theol. Addr: (o) Bard College, Annandale-on-Hudson, NY 12504 914-758-6822.

CHIU, Andrew M. J., b. Guangdong, China, February 4, 1929, s. of Shen Kurk & Shien Moi Mah, m. Sharon, chil: Mary; Mark; Mirium; Moses; Timothy; Lydia; Rose. Educ: Concordia Sem., STM 1967, ThD 1973. Emp: Concordia Theol. Sem., Hong Kong, 1973-76 Dean, 1977-88 Prof. & Pres.; Lutheran Church, Hong Kong Synod, 1969-82 Pres., 1967-71 Ed. of Lit. Dept.; *Asia Luth. News,* 1977-83 Ed.; Chinese Christian Lit. Coun., Hong Kong, Chinese Bible Comm., 1984- OT Ed.; Ecumenical Inst. for Theol. Res., Jerusalem, 1989-91 Resident Schol. Spec: Hebrew Bible. Pub: *Commentary on Genesis, Commentary on Exodus, Commentary on Deuteronomy* (Chinese Christian Lit. Coun., 1992); *Old Testament Introduction* (Chinese Christian Lit. Coun., 1986); "Natural Law, Decalogue and Gospel According to Luther and the Asian Context" in *The Gospel and Asian Traditions* (1979); and others. Mem: Christian Study Ctr. on Chinese Relig. & Culture, Hong Kong. Addr: (o) Kornhill Christian Church, Kornhill Plaza N, 1/F, 1 Kornhill Rd, Quarry Bay, Hong Kong; (h) 25 Hong Lee Rd., 14-A, Kowloon, Hong Kong 852-341-2640.

CHMIEL, Jerzy, b. Cracow, Poland, October 5, 1935, s. of Franciszek & Stefania (Fular). Educ: Gregorian U., ThD 1968; Bibl. Inst., Rome, Lic. Bibl. Stud. 1965; Pont. Acad. of Theol., Habil. 1975. Emp: Pont. Acad. of Theol., 1976- Asst. Prof., Bibl. Hermeneutics & Judaica,; Fac. of Theol., 1982-85 Vice Dean, 1985-91 Dean; *Ruch Biblijny i Liturgiczny,* 1982- Ed.-in-chief. Spec: Archaeology, Hebrew Bible, New Testament. Pub: *Studium Scripturae anima theologiae,* co-ed. (1990); "Das Inkulturationsproblem in heutiger Schriftauslegung" *Analecta Cracoviensia* 19 (1987); "Herméneutique" in *Dict. enc. de la Bible* (Brepols, 1987); "Agape als Grundbegriff des christlichen Ethos" *Analecta Cracoviensia* 14 (1982); "Quelques remarques sur la signification symbolique de la lumiére dans la littérature de l'Ancien Proche-Orient" *Folia Orientalia* 21 (1980); *The Interpretation of the Old Testament in the Apostolic Preaching About Christ's Resurrection* (1979); *Lumiére et charitéd'aprés la premiére épitre de Saint Jean* (1971); and others. Mem: Polish Theol. Soc., Cracow 1968-, Pres. 1978-87; Cath. U. Theol. Soc., Lublin 1976-; SNTS 1982-; Assn. Cath. Francaise pour l'Etude de la Bible 1989-. Addr: (h) Ul. Sw. Marka 10, PL 31-012 Cracow, Poland 22-56-94.

CHRISTENSEN, Duane L., b. Park Rapids, MN, s. of John & Elsie, m. Carol, chil: Beth Lynn (Welin); Sharon (Clark); Julie. Educ: Mass. Inst. of Technology, BS 1960; Calif. Bapt. Theol. Sem., MDiv 1963; Harvard U., ThD 1972. Emp: Bridgewater State Coll., 1969-78 Assoc. Prof.; Amer. Bapt. Sem. of the West, 1978- Prof.; Christian Witness Theol. Sem., 1991- Acting Dean. Excv: Tel Dor, 1985 Square Supr. Spec: Archaeology, Hebrew Bible. Pub: *Deuteronomy 1-11,* Word Bibl. Comm. 6A (Word, 1991); "The Identity of 'King So' in Egypt (2 Kings XVII 4)" *VT* 39 (1989); "Nahum" in *Harper's Bible Comm.* (Harper & Row, 1988); *Experiencing the Exodus,* ed. (Berkeley, 1988); "Narrative Poetics and the Interpretation of the Book of Jonah" in *Directions in Biblical Hebrew Poetry,* JSOTSup 40 (1987); "Prose and Poetry in the Bible: The Narrative Poetics of Deuteronomy 1:9-18" *ZAW* 97 (1985); "The March of Conquest in Isaiah 10:27c-34" *VT* 26 (1976); *Transformations of the War Oracle in Old Testament Prophecy: Studies in the Oracles Against the Nations,* Harvard Diss. in Relig. 3 (Scholars, 1975); and others. Awd: Mass. Inst. of Technology, Alfred P. Sloan Natl. Schol. 1957-60; Harvard U., NDFL Fellow in Modern Hebrew 1963-64, 1968-70; Zion Res. Found. Fellow. 1976; Assn. of Theol. Sch., res. grant 1980. Mem: ASOR; IOSOT; NEAS; ETS; SBL. Addr: (o) Christian

Witness Theol. Sem., 1525 Solano Ave., Berkeley, CA 94707 510-527-2716; (h) 845 Bodega Way, Rodeo, CA 94572 510-799-0858.

CHRISTOPHERSON, Kenneth E., b. Viborg, SD, July 7, 1926, s. of Harry A. & Clara (Bedin), m. Phyliss G. (Larson), chil: David; Dan; Jene; Bruce. Educ: Augustana Coll., BA 1946; Luther NW Theol. Sem., BTh 1950; U. of Minn., PhD 1972. Emp: Luth. Ch., 1950-58 Pastor; Pacific Luth. U., 1958-91 Prof. Pub: "Hallelujahs, Damnations, or Norway's Reformation as Lengthy Process" in *Church History* (1979); and others. Awd: Fulbright Schol. to Norway, 1955-56. Mem: AAR, Pres., Pacific NW Reg. 1984-85; Amer. Soc. of Ch. Hist.; Luther Acad for Schol. Rec: Skiing, mountain-climbing, photography. Addr: (h) 809 Tule Lake Rd. S, Tacoma, WA 98444 206-537-3328.

CIPRIANI, Settimio, b. Arezzo, Italy, April 24, 1919, s. of Cipriano & Giuseppa. Educ: Gregoriana U., Rome, ThD 1947; Bibl. Inst., Rome, Lic. Sacra Scriptura 1949. Emp: Pontificia Facolta Teologica Italia Meridionale, Napoli, Prof., NT; U. Lateranense, Rome, Prof., NT; Pontificia Fac. Teol. Italia Meridionale, Napoli, 1983-90 Rector; *Asprenas,* Dir. Spec: New Testament, Apocrypha and Post-biblical Studies. Pub: *Missione ed evangelizzazione negli Atti degli Apostoli* (1993); *Le Lettere di Paolo* (1991); *Le Lettere Pastorali* (1989); *La Preghiera Nel Nuovo Testamento* (1989); and others. Mem: SNTS; Assn. Bibl. Italiana; Colloquia Paulina Intl. Addr: (o) Viale Colli Aminei, 3, 80131-Napoli, Italy 081-741-3166; (h) Via Vergini, 51, 80137 Napoli, Italy 081-454811.

CLARK, Douglas R., b. Sussex, NJ, August 19, 1947, s. of Robert & Alice, m. Carmen L., chil: Robert LaVerne; Randall Loren. Educ: Walla Walla Coll., BA 1970; Andrews U., MDiv 1974; Vanderbilt U., MA 1984, PhD 1984. Emp: SW Adventist Coll., 1975-87 Assoc. Prof.; Walla Walla Coll., Sch. of Theol., 1987- Prof., 1990- Dean. Excv: Tell Hesban, Jordan, 1973, 1976 Square Supr.; Tell el-'Umeiri, Jordan, 1984, 1987, 1989, 1992 Field Supr.; Madaba Plains Project Consortium, 1987- Dir. Spec: Archaeology, Hebrew Bible. Pub: "Field B: The Western Defense System" in *Madaba Plains Project,* vol. 1 & 2 (Andrews U.P., 1989, 1992); "Madaba Plains Project: A Preliminary Report of the 1987 Season at Tell el-'Umeiri and Vicinity," co-auth., in BASORSup 26 (1990); "Madaba Plains Project: The 1987 Season at Tell el'Umeiri and Vicinity," co-auth., in *Ann. of the Dept. of Antiq. of Jordan* 23 (1989); and others. Awd: SW Adventist Coll., grants 1984, 1987; Walla Walla Coll., faculty res. grants 1989-91. Mem: SBL 1976-; Andrews Soc. for Relig. Stud. 1979-, Pres. 1985; Jewish Publ. Soc. of Amer. 1980-; ASOR 1987-; AIA 1988-, Pres., Walla Walla chap. 1990-. Rec: Flying, golf, reading. Addr: (o) Walla Walla College, School of Theology, College Place, WA 99324 509-527-

2194; (h) 1012 Highland Park Dr., College Place, WA 99324 509-525-6542.

CLARKE, Ernest George, b. Varna, ON, Canada, June 16, 1927, s. of Melvin E. & Eva M. (Epps), m. Ruth G. (Hunt), chil: E. Paul; Margaret J.; Patricia H.; David W. Educ: U. of Toronto, BA 1949; Victoria U., BD 1952; U. of Toronto, MA 1953; Leiden U., PhD 1962. Emp: Queen's U., Canada, 1956-61 Assoc. Prof.; U. of Toronto, 1961-92 Prof., 1992- Prof. Emeritus. Pub: "The Qere-Ketib of the Biblical Aramaic of Ezra and Daniel," co-auth. *VT* 36/4 (1986); *Targum Pseudo-Jonathan of the Pentateuch: Text and Concordance* (Ktav, 1985); "Reflections on Some Obscure Hebrew Words in the Biblical Job in the Light of XI Q Tg Job" in *Studies in Philology in Honour of Ronald James Williams* (1982); "Jacob's Dream at Bethel as Interpreted in the Targums and the New Testament" *Stud. in Relig.* 4/4 (1974); *The Wisdom of Solomon,* Cambridge English Bible Comm. (Cambridge U.P., 1973); "The Neofiti I Marginal Glosses and the Fragmentary Targum Witnesses to Gen 6-9" *VT* 22/3 (1972); "The Hebraic Spirit" *Canadian Jour. of Theol.* 21/3 (1966); *The Selected Questions of Isho bar Nun,* Studia Post Biblica 5 (Brill, 1962); and others. Mem: SBL; ASOR; CSBS; IOSOT; Intl. Assoc. for Targumic Stud. Rec: Bookbinding, gourmet cooking, gardening. Addr: (o) U. of Toronto, Dept. of Near Eastern Studies, Toronto, ON M5S 1A1, Canada 416-978-3184; (h) 171 Collier St., Toronto, ON M4W 1M2, Canada 416-964-2383.

CLEMENTS, Ronald E., b. London, England, May 27, 1929, s. of Cyril Clements & Elizabeth Cook, m. Valerie Winfred, chil: Gillian; Marian. Educ: Christ's Coll., Cambridge, BA 1956, MA 1960; U. of Sheffield, PhD 1960. Emp: U. of Edinburgh, 1960-67 Lect.; U. of Cambridge, 1967-83 Lect.; U. of Edinburgh, 1978 Croall Lect; U. of London, King's Coll. 1983-92 Prof., OT Stud. Spec: Hebrew Bible. Pub: *Jeremiah* (John Knox, 1988); "The Unity of the Book of Isaiah" *Interpretation* 36 (1982); "The Prophecies of Isaiah and the Fall of Jerusalem in 587 B.C." *VT* 30 (1980); *Isaiah and the Deliverance of Jerusalem,* JSOTSup 13 (1980); *Isaiah 1-39,* New Century Bible (Eerdmans, 1980); *Old Testament Theology. A Fresh Approach* (John Knox, 1978); "Baal-Berith of Shechem" *JSS* 13 (1968); and others. Awd: U. of Cambridge, DD 1979; Acadia U., Canada, DLitt 1982. Mem: SOTS 1956-; SBL 1988-. Rec: Photography, travel. Addr: (h) 8 Brookfield Rd., Coton, Cambridge CB3 7PT, England 0954-210593.

CLENDENEN, E. Ray, b. Dallas, TX, March 9, 1949, s. of Ewell & Bertha, m. Mary A., chil: Ann Kathleen; Jonathan Dean. Educ: Rice U., BA, Anthrop. 1971; Dallas Theol. Sem., ThM 1975; Dropsie U., MA 1982; U. of Tex., Arlington, PhD 1989. Emp: Rozetta Bapt. Ch., 1975-78 Pastor; Philadelphia Coll. of the Bible,

1979-82 Instr.; Criswell Coll., 1982-92 Prof. of Hebrew; *Jour. of Trans. & Textlinguistics,* 1989- Ed. Bd.; *New American Comm.,* 1992- Gen. Ed. Spec: Hebrew Bible. Pub: *Believer's Study Bible,* co-ed. (Thomas Nelson, 1991); "Discourse Strategies in Jer 10:1-16" *JBL* 106 (1987); "The Structure of Malachi: A Textlinguistic Approach" *Criswell Theol. Rev.* 4/1 (1987). Mem: ETS; SBL; IBR; Linguistic Soc. of Amer. Rec: Racquetball, fishing, canoeing. Addr: (o) Broadman Press, 127 Ninth Ave. North, Nashville, TN 37234 615-251-2400; (h) 1302 Parker Pl., Brentwood, TN 37027 615-661-6379.

CLINES, David J. A., b. Sydney, Australia, November 21, 1938, s. of Alfred W. & Ruby C., m. Heather A. (McKay), chil: Miriam J.; Jeremy M.S. Educ: U. of Sydney, BA 1960; St. John's Coll., Cambridge, BA 1963, MA 1967. Emp: U. of Sheffield, 1964- Prof., Bibl. Stud.; Fuller Theol. Sem., 1974-75 Vis. Prof., OT; *JSOT,* 1976- Ed.; Sheffield Acad. Press, 1986- Dir. Spec: Hebrew Bible. Pub: *What Does Eve Do to Help? And Other Readerly Questions to the Old Testament,* JSOTSup 94 (JSOT, 1991); *Job 1-20,* Word Bibl. Comm. 17 (Word, 1990); *Ezra, Nehemiah, Esther,* New Century Bible (Marshall, Morgan & Scott/Eerdmans, 1984); "In Search of the Indian Job" *VT* 33 (1983); "Nehemiah 10 as an Example of Early Biblical Exegesis" *JSOT* 21 (1980); "Story and Poem: The Old Testament as Literature and as Scripture" *Interpretation* 34 (1980); *The Theme of the Pentateuch* (JSOT, 1978); "Theme in Genesis 1-11" *CBQ* 38 (1976); and others. Mem: SOTS 1964-; SBL 1970-. Addr: (o) U. of Sheffield, Dept. of Biblical Studies, PO Box 595, Western Bank, Sheffield S10 2UJ, England 0742-824734; (h) 96 Ashland Rd., Sheffield S7 1RJ, England 0742-550562.

COATS, George W., b. Knox City, TX, August 13, 1936, s. of George & Bonnie (McClellan), chil: George; Charissa. Educ: McMurry Coll., BA 1958; South. Meth. U., BD 1961; Yale U., MA 1963, PhD 1966. Emp: Yale U., 1961-63 Teaching Fellow; McMurry Coll., 1965-68 Asst. Prof.; Lexington Theol. Sem., 1968- Prof., 1977 Fulbright Lect. Spec: Hebrew Bible. Pub: "Metanoia in Ancient Israel: Clues for Unity and Change" *Midstream* (1984); *Genesis: Forms of Old Testament Literature* (Eerdmans, 1983); "The Way of Obedience: Exegetical and Hermeneutical Perspectives on the Balaam Story" *Semia* (1982); *From Canaan to Egypt. Structural and Theological Context for the Joseph Story* (CBA, 1976); *Rebellion in the Wilderness* (Abingdon, 1968); and others. Awd: Fulbright Fellow 1976-77; Humboldt Fellow 1976-77. Mem: SBL; CBA; Inst. for Antiq. & Christianity; SOTS; CSBR. Rec: Swimming, hiking, camping. Addr: (h) 4707 Whispering Rock, Spring, TX 77388.

COCKERILL, Gareth L., b. Arlington, VA, July 13, 1944, s. of Welby Lee & Daisy Virginia,

m. Rosa (Bishop), chil: Allene Rose; Ginny Dora; Kathy Lee. Educ: Cen. Wesleyan Coll., BA 1966; Asbury Theol. Sem., MDiv 1969; Union Theol. Sem., ThM 1973, PhD 1976. Emp: Wesleyan Ch., 1969-72, 1976-79, 1981-84 Missionary; Wesley Bibl. Sem., 1979-81 Asst. Prof., Bibl. & Missiological Stud., 1984-85 Prof., Bibl. Stud., 1985-89 V.P. for Acad. Affairs, 1989- Prof., NT & Bibl. Theol. Spec: New Testament. Pub: Articles in *ABD* (1992); "Melchizedek or 'King of Righteousness'" *EQ* Oct. (1991); *The Wesley Bible: A Personal Study Bible for Holy Living*, NT ed. (Thomas Nelson, 1990); "Jesus and the Greatest Commandment in Mark 10:17-22: A Test Case for John Wesley's 'Theology of Love'" *The Asbury Sem.* (1985); "Heb. 1:1-14, I Clem. 36:1-6 and the High Priest Title" *JBL* 3 (1978). Awd: Assn. of Theol. Sch., Globalization in Theol. Educ. Grant 1990. Mem: SBL; IBR, Chmn., Deep South reg. 1990-91; ETS; Wesleyan Theol. Soc. Rec: Reading history, travel, languages. Addr: (o) Wesley Biblical Seminary, PO Box 9938, Jackson, MS 39286 601-957-1314; (h) 624 Berkshire St., Clinton, MS 39056 601-924-3263.

COETZEE, Johannes Christiaan, b. Potchefstroom, South Africa, May 2, 1936, s. of Johannes Christiaan & Johanna Aletta (van Rooy), m. Susanna (Coetsee), chil: Hendrika; Johannes Christiaan; Josef Adriaan; Aletta Johanna; Susanna Elisabeth Sophia. Educ: Potchefstroom U. for Christian Higher Educ., BA, Latin, Greek 1956, BTh 1960, MTh 1961, ThD, NT 1963. Emp: Potchefstroom U., 1957-59, 1961-63 Lect., 1971-73 Sr. Lect., 1974- Prof., NT & Bibl. Stud.; Gereformeerde Kerk, 1964-70 Min. Spec: New Testament, Apocrypha and Post-biblical Studies. Pub: "Satan en sy magte in die Nuwe Testament—besonderlik teenoor die Heilige Gees" in *Skrif en Kerk* (1987); "Jesus' Revelation in the *ego eimi* Saying in John 8 and 9" in *A South African Perspective on the New Testament: Essays Presented to Bruce Manning Metzger* (1986); "The Holy Spirit in 1 John" *Neotestamentica* 13 (1981); "Life (Eternal Life) in St. John's Writings and the Qumran Scrolls" *Neotestamentica* 6 (1972); "Christ and the Prince of this World in the Gospel and the Epistles of St. John" *Neotestamentica* 2 (1971); and others. Awd: Human Sci. Res. Coun. of South Africa, Financial Grants 1986-91. Mem: NT Soc. of South Africa 1964-; KOERS Soc. 1971-; South African Acad. for Sci. & Arts 1986-; SNTS 1986-. Rec: Golf, swimming, chess. Addr: (o) Potchefstroom U. for Christian Higher Education, Box 306, Potchefstroom 2520, South Africa 0148-23986; (h) 123 Molen St., Potchefstroom 2520, South Africa 0148-6190.

COGAN, Mordechai, b. Philadelphia, PA, December 24, 1939, s. of Jacob & Elizabeth. Educ: Gratz Coll., BHL 1960; U. of Pa., BA, Semitic Lang. 1961, PhD, Bibl. Stud. 1971. Emp: Gratz Coll., 1969-72 Asst. Prof.; Reconstructionist Rabbinical Coll., 1971-72 Lect.; Hebrew U., 1972-75, 1978-79, 1992- Prof.; Ben-Gurion U. of the

Negev, 1972-92 Prof. Spec: Hebrew Bible, Mesopotamian Studies. Pub: *Obadiah* (1992); "Chronology, Hebrew Bible" in *ABD* (Doubleday, 1992); *2 Kings* (1988); "The City That I Chose—The Deuteronomistic View of Jerusalem" *Tarbiz* 55 (1986/87); "...From the Peak of Amanah" *IEJ* 34 (1984); "Israel in Exile—The View of a Josianic Historian" *JBL* 97 (1978); *Imperialism and Religion: Assyria, Judah, and Israel in the Eighth and Seventh Centuries BCE*, SBL Mon. Ser. 19 (1974); and others. Mem: AOS; AJS; IES; ASOR. Rec: Hiking. Addr: (o) Hebrew U. of Jerusalem, Dept. of Jewish Hist., Jerusalem 91905, Israel 883-622; (h) 19 Shaked St., Omer 84965, Israel 460-735.

COHEN, Chaim, b. Brooklyn, NY, May 26, 1947, s. of Bernard & Selma, m. Sandra (Thal), chil: Yoav; Aliza. Educ: Jewish Theol. Sem., BHL 1969, MA 1972; Columbia U., PhD 1975. Emp: Jewish Theol. Sem., 1971-73 Preceptor; *JANES*, 1972-73 Assoc. Ed.; Tel Aviv U., 1973-80 Asst. Prof., Bible, 1973- Assoc. Prof., Overseas Div.; Menasseh District Coll., 1981-84 Asst. Prof.; Bar-Ilan U., 1983- Assoc. Prof., Hebrew Lang. Dept. Spec: Hebrew Bible, Mesopotamian Studies, Semitic Languages, Texts and Epigraphy. Pub: "Genesis 14:1-11—An Early Israelite Chronographic Source" in *The Biblical Canon in Comparative Perspective*, Scripture in Context IV (1991); "Jewish Medieval Commentary on the Book of Genesis and Modern Biblical Philology" *JQR* 81 (1990); "The 'Held Method' for Comparative Semitic Philology" *JANES* 19 (1989); *The Ugaritic Hippiatric Texts: A Critical Edition*, AOS Essays Ser. 9, co-auth. (AOS, 1983); "Neo-Assyrian Elements in the First Speech of the Biblical Rab-S-āqâ (II Kings 18:19-25, 27-35+ Isa. 36:4-10, 12-20)" *Israel; Oriental Stud.* 9 (1983); *Biblical Hapax Legomena in the Light of Akkadian and Ugaritic*, SBL Diss. Ser. 37 (Scholars, 1978); and others. Mem: AOS; SBL; IES; ASOR 1967-; ISBR 1970-. Rec: Bibl. cantillation, Jewish communal affairs. Addr: (o) Ben Gurion U., Hebrew Language & Literature Dept., New Campus, Beer-Sheva, Israel 057-461-132; (h) 6 Hagefen St., Omer 84965, Israel 057-460-292.

COHEN, Rudolph, Emp: Israel Antiquities Authority, Deputy Dir. Spec: Archaeology. Pub: "Solomon's Negev Defensive Line Contained Three Fewer Fortresses" *BAR* 12/4 (1986); "The Fortress King Solomon Built to Protect His Southern Border" *BAR* 11/3 (1985); "The Mysterious MB I People—Does the Exodus Tradition in the Bible Preserve the Memory of Their Entry into Canaan?" *BAR* 9/4 (1983); "The Marvelous Mosaics of Kissufim" *BAR* 6/1 (1980); and others. Addr: (h) 20 Neve Sha'anan, Jerusalem, Israel 528-634.

COHEN, Shaye J. D., m. Miriam S. May, chil: Zahava; Jonathan. Educ: Yeshiva Coll., BA, Class. 1970; Jewish Theol. Sem., MA, Judaica, Rabbinic Ord. 1974; Columbia U., MA, PhD, Anc. Hist. 1975. Emp: Jewish Theol. Sem.,

1974-91 Prof., Jewish Hist., 1981-85 Chmn. of Hist. Dept., 1982-86 Shenkman Assoc. Prof., 1986-91 Jack & Miriam Shenkman Prof. of Post-Bibl. Found. of West. Civ.; Columbia U., 1982 Vis. Assoc. Prof., Hist.; Brown U., 1991-Ungerleider Prof. of Judaic Stud. Spec: Hebrew Bible. Pub: "Judaism to the Mishnah: 135-220 C.E." in *Christianity and Rabbinic Judaism* (BAS, 1992); *From the Maccabees to the Mishnah*, Lib. of Early Christianity 7 (Westminster, 1987); "Was Timothy Jewish (Acts 16:1-3)? Patristic Exegesis, Rabbinic Law, and Matrilineal Descent" *JBL* 105 (1986); "Jews and Judaism in the Greco-Roman World" in *Early Judaism and its Modern Interpreters* (Scholars, 1986); "The Significance of Yavneh" *HUCA* 55 (1984); "Sosates the Jewish Homer" *HTR* 74 (1981); *Josephus in Galilee and Rome: His Vita and Development as a Historian*, Columbia Stud. in the Class. Tradition 8 (Brill, 1979); and others. Awd: Columbia U., Fac. Fellow & Whiting Fellow 1970-74; Jewish Theol. Sem., awd. in Talmud and schol. 1971-74; NEH, Summer Stipend 1985-86. Mem: AAJR; AAR; SBL; WUJS; AJS. Addr: (o) Brown U., Dept. of Judaic Studies, Box 1826, Providence, RI 02912 401-863-3911.

COHN, Robert L., b. IL, September 21, 1947, s. of Harold & Matilda, m. Renee (Levine), chil: Gideon; Michael; Jonathan. Educ: NW U., BA 1969; Stanford U., AM 1971, PhD 1974. Emp: Lafayette Coll., 1987- Assoc. Prof., Relig., Berman Schol. in Jewish Stud. Spec: Hebrew Bible. Pub: *The Shape of Sacred Space: Four Biblical Studies* (Scholars, 1981) "The Literary Logic of 1 Kings 17-19" *JBL* (1982); "Form and Perspective in 2 Kings 5" *VT* (1983); "Narrative Structure and Canonical Perspective in Genesis" *JSOT* (1983); "Literary Technique in the Jeroboam Narrative" *ZAW* (1985); "I Samuel" in *Harper's Bible Comm.* (1988); *Exploring the Hebrew Bible*, co-auth. (Prentice-Hall, 1988). Mem: SBL 1971-; AAR 1979-; CBA 1985-; AJS 1987-. Rec: Piano, jogging. Addr: (o) Lafayette College, Dept. of Religion, Easton, PA 18042 215-250-5182; (h) 1350 Doe Trail Rd., Allentown, PA 18104 215-398-2372.

COLE, Dan P., b. New York, NY, October 23, 1929, s. of Charles & Kathryn, m. Catharine (Crowding), chil: Jan; Barrie; Kim; Susan. Educ: Columbia U., BA 1950; Union Theol. Sem., BD 1953; Drew U., PhD 1965. Emp: Lawrence U., 1960-65 Assoc. Prof.; Lake Forest Coll., 1965-Prof., Relig. & Near East. Arch., 1970- Dir, Prog. in Greece & Turkey; *BAR*, Ed. Adv. Bd. Excv: Shechem, 1960, 1962, 1966 Staff; Gezer, 1966, 1968-71, 1973 Sr. Staff; Lahav, 1976-77, 1979-80, 1983 Assoc. Dir. Spec: Archaeology. Pub: BAS slide set/booklets, *Biblical Archaeology, Jerusalem Archaeology, New Testament Archaeology, Archaeology & Religion* (BAS, 1983-1991); "Hi-Tech Archaeology: Ground Penetrating Radar" *BAR* 14/1 (1988); "Corinth & Ephesus—Why Did Paul Spend Half His Journeys in These Cities?"

BR 4/6 (1988); *Shechem I: Middle Bronze Age II B Pottery* (ASOR, 1984); "How Water Tunnels Worked" *BAR* 6/2 (1980); and others. Addr: (o) Lake Forest College, Sheridan & College Rd., Lake Forest, IL 60045 708-234-2838.

COLE, R. Dennis, b. Daytona Beach, FL, November 24, 1950, s. of Carter & Peggy, m. Pamela, chil: Jennifer; Jessica; Elizabeth. Educ: West. Conservative Bapt. Sem., MDiv 1976, ThM 1978; New Orleans Bapt. Theol. Sem., ThD 1984. Emp: West. Conservative Bapt. Sem., 1976-78 Teaching Fellow, OT & Hebrew; New Orleans Bapt. Theol. Sem., 1981- Asst. Prof., 1992- Assoc. Prof., Bibl. Arch. Excv: Tel Batashi (Timnah), 1981-83, 1985 Field Supr.; Tel Qasile, 1991-92; Tel Beth Shean, 1992. Spec: Archaeology, Hebrew Bible, Semitic Languages, Texts and Epigraphy. Pub: "Jeremiah: Introduction and Commentary" in *New King James Study Bible* (Thomas Nelson, 1992). Mem: SBL 1981-; ASOR 1981-. Rec: Fishing, guitar. Addr: (o) New Orleans Baptist Theological Seminary, Box 62, 3939 Gentilly Blvd., New Orleans, LA 70126 504-282-4455; (h) 7204 Whitmore Pl., New Orleans, LA 70128 504-241-3713.

COLLIER, Gary D., b. Cloverdale, IN, August 31, 1950, s. of Albert & Trillis, m. Cheri, chil: Julie; Craig. Educ: Freed Hardeman Coll., AA 1970; David Lipscomb U., BA 1972; Harding Grad. Sch. of Relig., MDiv 1976; Fuller Theol. Sem., ThM 1991. Emp: Fuller Theol. Sem., 1981, 1989-90 Bibl. Lang. Fellow; Iliff Sch. of Theol., 1992- Adj. Spec: New Testament. Pub: "Bringing the Word to Life: Biblical Hermeneutics in Churches of Christ" *Christian Stud.* 11/1 (1990); "The Problem of Deuteronomy: The Problem of Perspective" *Restoration Quar.* 26/4 (1983). Awd: Gerald L. & Florence M. Schlessman Grad. Fellow., 1992-. Mem: SBL 1975-. Rec: Basketball, tennis, jogging. Addr: (h) 2295 E Iliff Ave. #208, Denver, CO 80210 303-733-8957.

COLLINS, Adela Y., b. USA, June 12, 1945, d. of Jesse Yarbro & Esperanza (Bejarano), m. John Collins, chil: Jesse; Sean; Aidan. Educ: Harvard U., MA 1972, PhD 1975. Emp: McCormick Theol. Sem., 1973-85 Prof.; *CBQ,* 1978-84 Assoc. Ed.; *JBL,* 1983-84 Assoc Ed.; *JR,* 1983- Bd. of Cons.; SBL Mon. Ser., 1985-90, Ed.; U. of Notre Dame, 1985-91 Prof. Excv: Caesarea Maritima, 1972 Asst. Supr., 1974 Supr. Spec: New Testament, Apocrypha and Post-biblical Studies. Pub: *The Beginning of the Gospel: Probings of Mark in Context* (Fortress, 1992); *Crisis and Catharsis: The Power of the Apocalypse* (Westminster, 1984); *The Apocalypse* (Glazier, 1979); *The Combat Myth in the Book of Revelation* (Scholars, 1976); and others. Awd: Fulbright Grad. Fellow. 1967; ATS Theol. Schol. & Res. Grant 1991. Mem: SBL 1971-; CBA 1971-; SNTS 1980-. Rec: Reading, piano. Addr: (o) U. of Chicago, Divinity School, Chicago, IL 60637 312-702-8265; (h) 1019 Brassie Ave., Flossmoor, IL 60422 708-799-5675.

COLLINS, John J., b. Tipperary, Ireland, February 2, 1946, s. of John & Margaret (Ryan), m. Adela (Yarbro), chil: Jesse; Sean; Aidan. Educ: University Coll., Dublin, BA 1967, MA 1969; Harvard U., PhD 1972. Emp: University Coll., Ireland, 1972-73 Lect.; St. Mary of the Lake Sem., 1973-78 Assoc. Prof.; De Paul U., 1978-85 Prof.; U. of Notre Dame, 1985-91 Prof.; U. of Chicago, 1991- Prof.; *HTR,* 1975-, *CBQ,* 1976-84, CBQ Mon. Ser., 1978- Ed. Bd.; *JBL,* 1989- Ed. Spec: Hebrew Bible, Apocrypha and Post-biblical Studies. Pub: *The Apocalyptic Imagination* (Crossroad, 1984); *Daniel, with an Introduction to Apocalyptic Literature* (Eerdmans, 1984); "Apocalyptic Eschatology as the Transcendence of Death" in *Visionaries and Their Apocalypses* (Fortress, 1983); *Between Athens and Jerusalem* (Crossroad, 1983); "The Historical Character of the Old Testament in Recent Biblical Theology" *CBQ* (1979); and others. Mem: SBL; CBA; CSBR. Addr: (o) U. of Chicago, Divinity School, Chicago, IL 60637; (h) 1019 Brassie, Flossmoor, IL 60422.

COLLINS, Oral E., b. Alton, NY, May 9, 1928, s. of Johnston H. & Thelma I. (Davis), m. Joyce I. (Towle), chil: Sandra Lynne; Rodney Johnston; Roger Gerald; Judith Anne; Paula Marie. Educ: Berkshire Christian Coll., BA 1950; Gordon-Conwell Theol. Sem., MDiv 1953; Brandeis U., MA 1966, PhD 1977. Emp: Berkshire Christian Coll., 1951-89 Prof. of Bibl. Stud., 1983-84 Admn. Coun. Chmn.; *Henceforth,* 1975-79 Assoc. Ed., 1979-80 Ed. Bd., 1985- Chmn., Ed. Bd.; Berkshire Inst. for Christian Stud., 1988- Prof. of Bible, Dir. of Bible Lands Travel Seminar; Advent Christian Gen. Conf. of Amer., Blessed Hope Sunday Sch. Quar. Ser., 1989- Ed.; Sem. of the East, 1990-91 Vis. Prof. Spec: Archaeology, Hebrew Bible, New Testament, Semitic Languages, Texts and Epigraphy, Apocrypha and Post-biblical Studies. Pub: "Premillennial Historicism" *Jour. of Hist. & Prophecy* (1987); *The Complete Biblical Library,* contb. (1985); *God's Prophetic Calendar,* co-auth. (Advent Christian Gen. Conference, 1983); *The Stem ZNH and Prostitution in the Hebrew Bible* (U. Microfilms, 1977); "Antichrist in the Book of Revelation" *Henceforth* Fall (1975); "Two Difficult Readings in Daniel 9:24: An Exercise in the Use of Source Texts in the Interpretation of Prophetic Passages" *Henceforth* Fall (1974); "Divorce in the New Testament" *Gordon Rev.* Summer (1964); and others. Mem: ETS 1954-; SBL 1970-; NEAS 1973-; IBR 1979-84; Assn. for Bibl. Res., 1982-. Rec: Travel, photography, genealogy. Addr: (o) 164 Stockbridge Rd., Lenox, MA 01240 413-637-0401.

COLLINS, Raymond F., b. Providence, RI, May 12, 1935, s. of Harold B. & Lillian Mabel (Monroe). Educ: Our Lady of Providence Sem., AA 1953; Cath. U. of Louvain, PhB 1955, STB 1959, MA, STL 1961, STD 1963. Emp: Our Lady of Providence Sem., 1962-66 Prof.; Pope John XXIII Natl. Sem., 1966-71 Prof.; Emmanuel Coll., 1968-71 Adj. Prof.; Cath. U. of Louvain, 1970- Prof., 1990- Chair, English Prog., Faculty of Theol.; *Louvain Stud.,* 1972- Ed.-in-chief. Spec: New Testament, Apocrypha and Post-biblical Studies. Pub: *Divorce in the New Testament* (Liturgical, 1992); *John and His Witness* (Liturgical, 1991); "God in the First Letter to the Thessalonians: Paul's Earliest Written Appreciation of *ho theos*" *Louvain Stud.* 16 (1991); *These Things Have Been Written* (Peeters, 1990; Eerdmans, 1991); "'The Gospel of Our Lord Jesus Christ' (2 Thes 1,8)" in *The Thessalonian Correspondence,* BETL 87 (Louvain U.P., 1990); *Letters that Paul Did Not Write: The Epistle to the Hebrews and the Pauline Pseudepigrapha* (Glazier, 1988); *Christian Morality: Biblical Foundations* (U. of Notre Dame, 1986); "A Propos the Integrity of 1 Thes" *ETL* (1979); "The Bible and Sexuality" *BTB* (1977); and others. Mem: AAR; ASOR; CBA; SNTS; SBL. Rec: Swimming, reading, travel. Addr: (o) Katholieke U. Leuven, Faculty of Theol., St. Michielsstraat 6, B-3000 Leuven, Belgium 32-16-283830; (h) Naamsestraat 100, B-3000 Leuven, Belgium 32-16-238435.

COMBRINK, Hans J. B., b. Lydenburg, South Africa, October 23, 1940, s. of Hans & Helena, m. Lucia (Antonites), chil: Hans; Alexander; Anna-Lucia; Helena. Educ: U. of Pretoria, South Africa, BA 1960, BD 1963, BA 1964; Free U., Amsterdam, ThD 1968. Emp: Dutch Reformed Ch., Pretoria 1968-70 Min.; Rand Afrikaans U., 1970-73 Head of Relig. Dept.; U. of Pretoria, 1974-75 Lect.; U. of Stellenbosch, 1976- Prof., Head of Dept. of NT, 1992 Dean, Faculty of Theol.; Cambridge, England, 1982 Tyndale NT Lect. Spec: New Testament. Pub: "Reference and Rhetoric in the Gospel of Matthew" *Scriptura* (1992); "The Gospel of Matthew in an African Context—In Dialogue with Chris Manus" *Scriptura* (1991); "Readings, Readers and Authors: An Orientation" *Neotestamentica* (1988); "Multiple Meaning and/or Multiple Interpretation of a Text" *Neotestamentica* (1984); "The Structure of the Gospel of Matthew" *Neotestamentica* (1983); *The Synoptic Gospels and Acts: Introduction and Theology* (Kerkboekhandel, 1983); *Die Ou Testament Vandag* (Dutch Reformed, 1979); *Structural Analysis of Acts 6:8-8:3* (Dutch Reformed, 1979); and others. Mem: NT Soc., South Africa; SBL; SNTS; Tyndale Fellow. Rec: Jogging, hiking, angling. Addr: (o) Theological Seminary, 171 Dorp St., Stellenbosch 7600, South Africa 2231-77-3255; (h) 1 Meerlust Ave., Stellenbosch 7600, South Africa 2231-83-3920.

CONNOLLY-WEINERT, Francis D., b. Philadelphia, Pa., September 27, 1941, s. of Philip Walter & Mary, m. Adele B. (McCollum), chil: James Bernard. Educ: St. Joseph's U., BS 1963; Maryknoll Sch. of Theol., MA 1967; Fordham U., PhD 1979. Emp: St. John's U., 1967-75, 1980- Assoc. Prof.; Coll. of St. Elizabeth, 1975-80 Assoc. Prof.; *Jour. of Theta Alpha Kappa,* 1980-88 Ed.; *NT Abstracts,* 1986- Abstractor. Spec: New Testament. Pub:

"Assessing Omissions as Redaction: Luke's Handling of the Charge Against Jesus as Detractor of the Temple" in *To Touch the Text: Festschrift in Honor of J. A. Fitzmyer* (Crossroad, 1990); "Luke, Stephen, and the Temple in Luke-Acts" *BTB* (1987); "The Multiple Meanings of Luke 2:49 and Their Significance" *BTB* (1983); "Luke, the Temple, and Jesus' Saying About Jerusalem's Abandoned House" *CBQ* (1982); "The Meaning of the Temple in Luke-Acts" *BTB* (1981); and others. Awd: St. John's U., Fac. Merit Awd. for Acad. Achievement 1990; NEH, Grant for Summer Study 1983. Mem: AAR, Pres., Mid Atlantic reg. 1986-90; Natl. Honor Soc. for Relig. Stud. & Theol., Pres. 1988-92. Rec: Poetry, opera, bowling. Addr: (o) St. John's U., Dept. of Religious Studies & Theology, Grand Central & Utopia Pkwy., Jamaica, NY 11439 718-990-6161; (h) 17 Wedgewood Dr., West Paterson, NJ 07424 201-812-8392.

CONRAD, Edgar W., b. Lancaster, PA, September 15, 1942, s. of Amos & Violet, m. Linda (Slonaker). Educ: Lebanon Valley Coll., BA 1964; United Theol. Sem., MDiv 1968; Princeton Theol. Sem., ThM 1969, PhD 1974. Emp: Princeton Theol. Sem., 1969-73 Teaching Fellow; Rutgers U., 1972-73 Intr.; LaSalle Coll., 1974-75 Asst. Prof.; U. of Queensland, Australia, 1977- Reader. Spec: Hebrew Bible. Pub: *Reading Isaiah* (Fortress, 1991); *Understanding the Word: Essays in Honor of Bernhard W. Anderson*, contb. (JSOT, 1985); *Perspectives on Language and Text: Essays in Honor of Francis I. Andersen*, contb. (Eisenbrauns, 1985); *Fear Not Warrior: A Study of 'al fīrā' Pericopes in the Hebrew Scriptures* (Scholars, 1975); and others. Awd: Bert V. Flinchbaugh Mem. Awd. 1968; U. of Rochester, Mellon Postdoc. Fellow. 1976. Mem: AAR; SBL; CBA; Australian Assn. for the Study of Relig.; Intl. Assn. for the Study of Relig. Rec: Golf, cooking. Addr: (o) U. of Queensland, Studies in Religion, Queensland 4072, Australia 07-365-2162; (h) 26 Depper St., St. Lucia, Queensland 4067, Australia 07-371-3683.

COOGAN, Michael D., b. Madison, WI, July 30, 1942, s. of Daniel & Daniel, m. Pamela (Hill), chil: Daniel; Elizabeth; Matthew. Educ: Fordham U., BA 1966; Harvard U., PhD 1971. Emp: Harvard Div. Sch., 1976-85 Assoc. Prof.; Wellesley Coll., 1986-89 Vis. Prof.; Stonehill Coll., 1985- Prof.; *CBQ*, 1991- Assoc. Ed. Excv: Tell El Hesi, 1970-75 Field Supr.; Idalion, 1974 Field Supr.; Wadi Tumilat, 1977 Assoc. Dir.; Numeira, 1979-83 Field Dir. Spec: Archaeology, Hebrew Bible, Semitic Languages, Texts and Epigraphy. Pub: "Joshua" in *The New Jerome Biblical Comm.* (Prentice-Hall, 1990); "Job's Children" in *Lingering over Words: Studies in Ancient Near Eastern Literature in Honor of William L. Moran*, HSS 37 (Scholars, 1990); "Archaeology and Biblical Studies: The Book of Joshua" in *The Hebrew Bible and Its Interpreters* (Eisenbrauns, 1990); "A Cemetery of the Persian Period" in *Tell el-Hesi: The Persian Period (Stratum V)*

(Eisenbrauns, 1989); "Of Cults and Cultures: Reflections on the Interpretation of Archaeological Evidence" *PEQ* 119 (1987); *Stories from Ancient Canaan* (Westminster, 1978); *West Semitic Personal Names in the Murašû Documents*, HSM 7 (Scholars, 1976); and others. Awd: NEH, Fellow. for Coll. Tchr. & Independent Schol. 1992-93. Mem: ASOR; AIA, V.P., Boston chap. 1982-83; Bibl. Colloquium, Pres. 1992; IES; SBL, Pres., New England reg. 1985-86. Addr: (o) Stonehill College., Dept. of Religious Studies, North Easton, MA 02357 508-230-1354; (h) 15 Whittemore St., Concord, MA 01742 508-369-0831.

COOK, Edward M., b. Travis AFB, CA, February 18, 1952, s. of Charles & Miriam, m. Laura (Ferguson), chil: Elizabeth; Tristan. Educ: U. of Tex., BA 1974; Fuller Theol. Sem., MDiv 1979; UCLA, PhD 1986. Emp: Fuller Theol. Sem., 1986-88 Adj. Instr., Bibl. Lang.; UCLA, 1987 Adj. Instr., Semitic Lang.; U. of Judaism, 1988 Instr., Bible; *MAARAV*, 1986-88 Managing Ed.; Hebrew Union Coll., 1988- Assoc. Res. Schol. Spec: Semitic Languages, Texts and Epigraphy. Pub: "An Aramaic Incantation Bowl from Khafaje" *BASOR* (1992); "Qumran Aramaic and Aramiac Dialectology" *Abr-Nahrain Sup.* (1992); *An Aramaic Bibliography*, vol. I, co-auth. (Johns Hopkins U.P., 1991); "The Orthography of Final Unstressed Long Vowels in Old and Imperial Aramaic" *MAARAV* (1990); *Sopher Mahir: Northwest Semitic Studies Presented to S. Segert*, ed. (Eisenbrauns, 1990); "In the Plain of the Wall" *JBL* 108 (1989); "Weights and Measures" in *ISBE* (1987); *Word Order in the Aramaic of Daniel* (Undena, 1986). Awd: Fuller Theol. Sem., William S. LaSor Awd. 1979. Mem: SBL 1981-; IBR 1991-. Rec: Basketball. Addr: (o) Hebrew Union College, 3101 Clifton Ave., Cincinnati, OH 45220 513-221-1875; (h) 8212 Indian Trail, Cincinnati, OH 45243 513-271-5155.

COOTE, Robert B., b. Wilmington, DE, m. Mary (Putney), chil: Marian; Margaret. Educ: Harvard U., AB 1966, BD 1969, PhD 1972. Emp: Northwestern U., Asst. Prof.; San Francisco Theol. Sem., Prof. Spec: Hebrew Bible, Semitic Languages, Texts and Epigraphy. Pub: *Elijah and Elisha in Socioliterary Perspective* (Scholars, 1992); *In the Beginning: Creation and the Priestly History* (Fortress, 1991); *In Defense of Revolution: The Elohist History* (Fortress, 1991); *Early Israel: A New Horizon* (Fortress, 1990); *Power, Politics, and the Making of the Bible: An Introduction* (Fortress, 1990). Mem: SBL 1973-; SOTS 1993-. Addr: (o) San Francisco Theological Seminary, San Anselmo, CA 94960 415-258-6571.

CORRINGTON, Gail P., b. Buffalo, NY, August 25, 1949, d. of Donald W. & Edith L. Educ: State U. of N.Y., BA (summa cum laude) 1971, MA, Class. 1973, MLS 1975; Drew U., MPhil 1981, PhD, Bibl. Stud., NT 1983. Emp: Drew U., 1981-83 Theol. Lbrn.; Penn State U., 1983-89 Asst.

Prof., Class &, Relig. Stud.; Harvard Div. Sch., 1988-89 Res. Assoc. & Vis. Lect. in NT; Coll. of William & Mary, 1989-90 Vis. Asst. Prof., Relig.; Rhodes Coll., 1990- Asst. Prof., Relig. Stud. Spec: N5Westminster/John Knox, 1992); "The Milk of Salvation: Redemption by the Mother in Late Antiquity and Early Christianity" *HTR* 83/2 (1990); "The Divine Woman: A Revision" *ATR* 70/3 (1988); *The Divine Man: His Origin and Function in Hellenistic Popular Religion* (Lang, 1986); "The Divine Woman? Propaganda and Power of Celibacy in the New Testament Apocrypha" *Helios* 13/2 (1986); "Power and the Man of Power in Hellenistic Popular Religion" *Helios* 13 (1986); and others. Awd: Phi Beta Kappa 1971; N.J. Coun. on the Hum., Jr. Schol. 1981. Mem: SBL 1985-; Soc. for the Culture & Relig. of the Anc. Mediterranean 1989-; SE Conf. for the Study of Relig. 1990-. Rec: Walking, racquetball, creative writing, choral singing. Addr: (o) Rhodes College, Religion Dept., 2000 N Parkway, Memphis, TN 38111 901-726-3935; (h) 664 S Belvedere Blvd., Memphis, TN 38104 901-726-4701.

CORSANI, Bruno, b. Naples, Italy, June 22, 1924. Emp: Union Theol. Sem., Buenos Aires, 1951-54 Prof., OT; Waldensian Ch. of Turin, Italy, 1955-62; Facolta Valdese di Teologia, Rome, 1962-92. Spec: New Testament. Pub: *Galati* (Marietti, 1990); *L'Apocalisse* (Claudiana, 1985); *I Miracoli di Gesu Nel Quarto Vangelo* (Paideia, 1983); *Introduzione al Nuovo Testamento,* vol. 1 & 2 (Claudiana, 1972, 1975). Mem: Assn. Bibl. Italiana 1962-; SNTS 1964-. Addr: (o) Facolta Valdese di Teologia, Via Pietro Cossa 42, 00193 Rome, Italy 6-321-0789.

COSBY, Michael R., b. Douglas, AZ, January 31, 1950, s. of Cecil M. & Gretchen L., m. E. Lynne N., chil: Allen M.; Evan P. Educ: West. Ky. U., MA 1980; Emory U., PhD 1985. Emp: Emory U., 1985 Instr.; Warner Pacific Coll., 1985- Assoc. Prof. Spec: Hebrew Bible, New Testament. Pub: "Paul's Persuasive Language in Romans 5" in *Persuasive Artistry,* JSNTSup (Sheffield, 1991); "The Rhetorical Composition of Hebrews 11" *JBL* 107 (1988); *The Rhetorical Composition and Function of Hebrews 11 in Light of Example Lists in Antiquity* (Mercer U.P., 1988); "Mark 14:51-52 and the Problem of Gospel Narrative" *Perspectives in Relig. Stud.* 11 (1984); and others. Mem: SBL 1983-; IBR 1991-. Rec: Swimming, cross-country skiing, hiking, backpacking. Addr: (o) Warner Pacific College, Dept. of Religion, 2219 SE 68th Ave., Portland, OR 97215 503-775-4366; (h) 7623 SE Woodward, Portland, OR 97206 503-775-5860.

COSGROVE, Charles H., b. Denver, CO, July 8, 1954, s. of Charles H. & Marjorie (Holtorf), m. Debbie (Fredericks), chil: Katherine Grace. Educ: Bethel Coll., BA 1976; Bethel Theol. Sem., MDiv 1979; Princeton Theol. Sem., PhD 1985. Emp: Princeton Theol. Sem., 1981-82 Teaching Fellow; North. Bapt. Sem., 1984-85

Vis. Instr., 1985-89 Asst. Prof., 1989- Assoc. Prof., NT. Spec: New Testament. Pub: *Faith and History: Essays in Honor of Paul W. Meyer,* co-ed., contb. (Scholars, 1990); "The Place Where Jesus Is: Allusions to Baptism and Eucharist in the Fourth Gospel" *NTS* 35 (1989); "Arguing Like a Mere Human Being: Gal 3:15-18 in Rhetorical Perspective" *NTS* 34 (1988); *The Cross and the Spirit: A Study in the Argument and Theology of Galatians* (Mercer U.P., 1988); "The Law Has Given Sarah No Children (Gal. 4:21-30)" *NT* 29 (1987); "Justification in Paul: A Linguistic and Theological Reflection" *JBL* 106 (1987); "What If Some Have Not Believed? The Occasion and Thrust of Romans 3:1-8" *ZNW* 78 (1987); and others. Awd: Princeton Theol. Sem., Fellow. 1979. Mem: SBL; AAR; CSBR; NABPR. Addr: (o) Northern Baptist Theological Seminary, 660 E Butterfield Rd., Lombard, IL 60148 708-620-2213; (h) 4230 Raymond Ave., Brookfield, IL 60513 708-387-7059.

COTHENET, Edouard, b. Bourges, France, July 25, 1924. Educ: Ecole Biblique, Jerusalem, Grad., Holy Scriptures 1956; DTh 1970. Emp: Inst. Catholique, Paris, 1965- Prof., *Sup. du Dictionnaire de la Bible,* 1981 Vice-dir., 1986 Co-dir.; *Dictionnaire des Religions,* 1983 Comm. of Redaction, Prof. Honoraire 1991. Spec: New Testament, Apocrypha and Post-biblical Studies. Pub: "L'arriere-plan vetero-testamentaire du IVe Evangile" in *Origine et Posterite de l'evangile de Jean* (Cerf, 1990); *Exegese et Liturgie* (Cerf, 1988); "Le Bapteme selon Saint Mattieu" in *Studien zum Neuen Testament und seiner Umwelt* (1984); *Les ecrits de Saint Jean,* co-auth. (Desclee, 1984); "Le realisme de l'esperance chretienne selon la Ie de Pierre" *NTS* (1981); *La Tradition johannique,* co-auth. (Desclee, 1977); "La Iere Epitre de Pierre: bilan de 35 ans de recherches," "Le Protevangile de Jacques: origine, genre et signification d'un premier midrash chretien sur la Nativite de Marie" *ANRW* II, 25; and others. Addr: (o) 3, rue Moliere, Fr. 18.000 Bourges, France 48-24-51-85.

COTTER, David W., b. Worcester, MA, March 14, 1952, s. of Paul B. & Mildred R. (Tierney). Educ: McGill U., Canada, BA 1974; St. John's U., MA 1977, MDiv 1979; Pont. Gregorian U., Rome, STL 1987, STD 1989. Emp: St. Anselm Coll., 1981-85 Instr., 1986- Asst. Prof.; *Studies in Hebrew Narrative,* Gen. Ed.; *Studies in Hebrew Poetry,* Gen. Ed. Spec: Hebrew Bible. Pub: *A Study of Job 4-5 in the Light of Contemporary Literary Theory* (Scholars, 1992). Mem: CBA 1985-; SBL 1991-; NAPH 1991-. Addr: (o) St. Anselm College, Dept. of Theology, 87 St. Anselm Dr., Manchester, NH 03102 641-7000; (h) St. Anselm Abbey, 87 St. Anselm Dr., Manchester, NH 03102 641-7000.

COTTON-PALTIEL, Hannah M., b. Jerusalem, Israel, August 28, 1946, d. of Gershon & Lena (Kalach), m. Ari M. Paltiel, chil: Tor; Yotham. Educ: Hebrew U., BA 1970, MA (summa cum laude) 1973; Oxford U., DPhil 1977. Emp: Hebrew U., Jerusalem, 1976-79 Instr., Anc. Hist. & Class., 1979-84 Lect., 1984- Sr. Lect.; U. of Calif., Berkeley, 1988 Vis. Assoc. Prof.; *Scripta Classica Israelica*, 1991- Ed. Pub: "The Guardianship of Jesus Son of Babatha: Roman and Local Law in the Province of Arabia" *Jour. of Roman Stud.* 83 (1993); "A Dedication from Dor to Gargilius Antiquus, Governor of Syria," co-auth. *IEJ* 41 (1991); "Fragments of a Declaration of Landed Property from the Province of Arabia" *Zeitschrift fuer Papyrologie und Epigraphik* 85 (1991); "Who Conquered Masada in 66 C.E. and Who Lived there Until the Fortress Fell?" *Zion* 55 (1990); "The Date of the Fall of Masada: The Evidence of the Masada Papyri" *Zeitschrift fur Papyrologie und Epigraphik* 78 (1989); *Masada: The Latin and Greek Documents*, co-auth. (IES/Hebrew U., 1989); *Documentary Letters of Recommendation in Latin from the Roman Empire*, Beitraege zur klassischen Philologie 132 (1981); and others. Awd: Friends of the Hebrew U. in England, Schol. 1973-76; Intl. Fedn. of U. Women in Geneva, Dorothy Leet Awd. 1974, Ida Smedlay Maclean Fellow 1975. Mem: Assn. for the Promotion of Class. Stud. in Israel 1982-. Rec: Hiking, dogs, reading, traveling. Addr: (o) Hebrew U. of Jerusalem, Dept. of Classics, Jerusalem 91905, Israel 02-883917; (h) 22 Sheshet Ha'yamim, PO Box 1678, Mevasseret Zion 90805, Israel 02-340378.

COUGHENOUR, Robert A., b. Youngwood, PA, November 28, 1931, m. Betty (Reed), chil: Reed; Mary Jo; John; Amy. Educ: Indiana U. of Pa., BS 1953; Pittsburgh Theol. Sem., MDiv 1960; Case West. Reserve U., MA 1967, PhD 1972. Emp: Westminster Coll., 1962-69 Asst. Prof., Relig.; Hope Coll., 1969-75 Prof., Bibl. Stud.; West. Theol. Sem., 1975-, 1982-86 Acad. Dean. Excv: Bethel, 1968 Pottery stud.; Tell Hesban, Jordan, 1976 Dir. of Educ.; Mugharat el-Wardeh, Jordan, 1976-78 Iron Mine Project. Dir.; Um el-Jimal, Jordan, 1981 Area Supr. Spec: Archaeology, Hebrew Bible, Apocrypha and Post-biblical Studies. Pub: Articles in *ISBE* (1985); "The Woe-Oracles in Ethiopic Enoch" *JSJ* 9 (1978); "The Exploration of Mugharat el-Wardeh and Abu Thawab, Jordan" *Ann. of the Dept. of Antiq. of Jordan* 21 (1976); and others. Awd: U. of Notre Dame, Rosentiel Fellow 1973; Hope Coll., Den Uyl Fellow 1973. Mem: SBL 1958-; ASOR 1960-; AAR 1962-; ACOR, Pres. of Trustees 1988-91. Addr: (o) Western Theological Seminary, Holland, MI 49423; (h) 13935 Ridgewood Dr., Holland, MI 49424.

COULOT, Claude, b. Seurre, France, September 5, 1944, s. of Robert & Renée (Broissiat). Educ: Fac. de Théol. Cath. de Strasbourg, Lic. Théol. 1973; Pont. Bibl. Inst., Rome, Lic. Sci. Bibl. 1976. Emp: Fac. de Théol. Cath. de Strasbourg, 1976-81 Asst. en Sci. Bibl., 1981-88 Maitre de Conf. en Sci. Bibl. du NT, 1989- Prof. Spec: New Testament. Pub: "La Nouvelle Alliance au pays de Damas" *Rev. des Sci. Relig.* 65 (1991); "Le témoignage de Jean-

Baptiste et la rencontre de Jésus et de ses premiers disciples (Jn 1,19-51): Approches diachroniques et synchronie" in *Origine et postérité de l'évangile de Jean*, Lediv 143 (1990); *Jésus et le disciple: Etude sur l'autorite messianique de Jesus*, Etudes Bibl. 8 (Gabalda, 1987); "L'investiture d'Elisée par Elie (1R 19,19-21)" *Rev. des Sci. Relig.* 57 (1983); "Recherches sur les récits bibliques de vocation" *Semiotique et Bible* 24 (1981); "Propositions pour une structuration du livre d'Amos au niveau rédactionnel" *Rev. des Sci. Relig.* 51 (1977); and others. Mem: SNTS; Assn. Cath. Francaise pour l'Etude de la Bible. Addr: (o) Palais U., Fac. de Théol. Cath 9, Place de l'Université, 67084 Strasbourg Cedex, France; (h) 1, rue Notre Dame, 67170 Hohatzenheim, France 88-51-27-24.

COUNTRYMAN, L. William, b. Oklahoma City, OK, October 21, 1941, s. of Louis & Bera Sue, m. Frances (Gray), chil: Sarah Holmes. Educ: U. of Chicago, AB 1962, MA 1974, PhD 1977; Gen. Theol. Sem., STB 1965. Emp: U. of Chicago., 1974-76 Lect.; SW Mo. State U., 1976-79 Asst. Prof.; Brite Div. Sch., 1976-83 Assoc. Prof.; Ch. Div. Sch. of the Pacific, 1983- Prof.; Haverford, 1979 Guest Lect. Spec: New Testament, Apocrypha and Post-biblical Studies. Pub: *The Language of Ordination* (Trinity, 1992); *The Mystical Way in the Fourth Gospel* (Fortress, 1987); "How Many Baskets Full? Mark 8:14-21 and the Value of Miracles in Mark" *CBQ* (1985); *Biblical Authority or Biblical Tyranny? Scripture and the Christian Pilgrimage* (Fortress, 1982); "Christian Equality and the Early Catholic Episcopate" *Anglican Theol. Rev.* (1981); *The Rich Christian in the Church of the Early Empire: Contradictions and Accommodations* (Mellen, 1980); and others. Mem: SBL 1964-; NAPS 1976-. Addr: (o) The Church Divinity School, 2451 Ridge Rd., Berkeley, CA 94709 510-204-0719; (h) 2215 Spaulding Ave., Berkeley, CA 94703 510-843-6083.

COURT, John M., b. Birmingham, England, July 5, 1943, s. of W.E. & D.M. (Mason), m. Kathleen (Chapman). Educ: U. of Durham, BA 1964, PhD 1973. Emp: U. of Kent at Canterbury, England, 1968- Chair, Bd. of Stud. in Theol.; Routledge Readings of the New Testament, 1992- Ser. Ed.; *NTS*, 1992- Ed. Bd. Spec: New Testament. Pub: *Myth and History in the Book of Revelation* (John Knox, 1979); "Paul and the Apocalyptic Pattern" in *Paul and Paulinism, Essays in Honour of C.K. Barrett* (SPCK, 1982); "Blessed Assurance: 1 John 3:19-22" *JTS* (1982); "Right and Left: The Implications for Matthew 25:31-46" *NTS* (1985); *The New Testament World*, co-auth. (Prentice-Hall, 1990); "Ariadne's Thread—An Essay in Deconstruction" *Theol.* (1991); and others. Mem: SNTS 1968-; PEF 1982-; SOTS 1984-. Rec: Gardening, photography. Addr: (o) U. of Kent at Canterbury, Keynes College, Kent, England 0227-764000; (h) 79A The Street Boughton Under Blean, Faversham, Kent, England 0227-751579.

COWE, S. Peter, b. Fraserburgh, Scotland, May 16, 1953, s. of Arthur & Adelaide (Duthie). Educ: U. of Aberdeen, MA, Class. 1975; U. of Oxford, Mansfield Coll., MA, Theol. 1983; Hebrew U., Jerusalem, PhD, Armenian Stud. 1983. Emp: Hebrew U., Jerusalem, 1983-84 Asst. Lect., Armenian Stud.; Columbia U., 1984-92 Asst. Prof., 1992- Assoc. Prof. Spec: Hebrew Bible. Pub: *The Armenian Version of Daniel* (Scholars, 1992); *Commentary on the Divine Liturgy by Xosrov Anjewac'i* (St. Vartan, 1991); "The Two Armenian Versions of Chronicles, Their Origin and Translation Technique" *Revue des etudes armeniennes* 22 (1990-91); "The Canticle of Azariah and its Two Armenian Versions" *Jour. of the Soc. for Armenian Stud.* 5 (1990-91); "Armenian Sidelights on Torah Study in 17th Century Poland" *JJS* 37 (1986); "The Armenian Version of Ruth and Its Textual Affinities" *La Septuaginta en la Investigacion Contemporanea* (1985); "The Typology of Armenian Biblical Manuscripts" *Revue des etudes armeniennes* 18 (1984). Mem: Soc. for Armenian Stud. 1979-; IOSCS 1979-; Assn. intl. des etudes armeniennes 1983-; AOS 1984-. Rec: Music, theatre. Addr: (o) Columbia U., Program in Armenian Studies, Kent Hall 500C, New York, NY 10027 212-854-5587; (h) 450 Riverside Dr., New York, NY 10027 212-663-9264.

COX, Claude E., b. Meaford, ON, September 23, 1947, s. of W. Ralph & Doris E. (Hindle), m. Elaine Frances (Webster), chil: Michael Webster; Jason Alexander. Educ: Abilene Christian U., BA (summa cum laude) 1969; Knox Coll., Toronto, MDiv 1972; Union Theol. Sem., Virginia, ThM 1973; U. of Toronto, MA 1974, PhD 1979. Emp: U. of Toronto, 1979-80 Lect.; Brandon U., 1980-84 Asst. Prof., 1982-84 Chair of Relig. Dept.; Wilfred Laurier U., 1988-. Spec: Hebrew Bible. Pub: *VII Congress of the IOSCS, Leuven, 1989,* SBLSCS 31 (Scholars, 1991); "Vocabulary for Wrongdoing and Forgiveness in the Greek Translations of Job" *Textus* 15 (1990); "A Review of Zeytunyan's Edition of Genesis from the Standpoint of Septuagint Criticism" *Rev. des Etudes Armeniennes* 21 (1988-89); "The Wrath of God Has Come to Me: Job's First Speech According to the Septuagint" *Stud. in Relig.* 16 (1987); *Hexaplaric Materials Preserved in the Armenian Version,* SBLSCS 21 (Scholars, 1986); *De Septuaginta: Studies in Honour of John William Wevers on his Sixty-fifth Birthday* (Benben, 1984); "Biblical Studies and the Armenian Bible, 1955-80" *RB* 89 (1982); *The Armenian Translation of Deuteronomy* (Scholars, 1981); and others. Awd: Canada Coun. Doc. Fellow. 1975-79; Canada-USSR Exchange Fellow. 1977-78. Mem: IOSCS 1973-; SBL 1975-; CSBS 1977-; Assn. Intl. des Etudes Armeniennes 1987-; Ontario Chaplains Assn. 1990-. Rec: Collecting old rock'n'roll records, family hist., reading. Addr: (o) Box 460, Barrie, ON L4M 4T7, Canada 705-722-7155; (h) 18 Roslyn Rd., Barrie, ON L4M 2X6, Canada 705-737-2272.

CRAIG, Kenneth M., Jr., b. Gastonia, NC, June 30, 1960, s. of Kenneth & Janette, m. Niki (Whitley), chil: Alexandra Maria; Luke McDuffie. Educ: Wake Forest U., BA 1982; South. Bapt. Theol. Sem., MDiv 1986, PhD 1989. Emp: *Paradigms,* 1985 Managing & Book Rev. Ed.; Simmons Coll., 1986 Instr.; South. Baptist Theol. Sem., 1986-87 Garrett Fellow, 1988-89 Instr.; Chowan Coll., 1989- Asst. Prof., E. Lee Oliver Chair of Bible & Religion. Spec: Hebrew Bible. Pub: *A Poetics of Jonah: Art in the Service of Ideology* (U. of S.C., 1993); "Jonah and the Reading Process" *JSOT* 47 (1990); "The Corrections of the Scribes" *Perspectives in Relig. Stud.* 17/2 (1990); and others. Awd: Israeli Study Grant 1987-88. Mem: SBL 1986-; NAPH 1986-. Rec: Fishing, tennis, basketball. Addr: (o) Chowan College, Dept. of Religion and Philosophy, Murfreesboro, NC 27855 919-398-4101; (h) 316 E High St., Murfreesboro, NC 27855 919-398-5267.

CRAIG, William L., b. Peoria, IL, August 23, 1949, s. of Mallory J. & Doris I., m. Jeanette L., chil: Charity Joy; William Mallory. Educ: Wheaton Coll., BA 1971; Trinity Evang. Div. Sch., MA (summa cum laude) 1975; U. of Birmingham, England, PhD 1977; U. of Munchen, Germany, DTh 1984. Emp: Trinity Evang. Div. Sch., 1980-86 Asst. Prof.; Westmont Coll., 1986- Assoc. Prof. Spec: New Testament. Pub: *Assessing the New Testament Evidence for the Historicity of the Resurrection of Jesus* (Mellen, 1989); "Paul's Dilemma in II Cor. v. 1-10: A 'Catch-22'?" *NTS* 34 (1988); *The Historical Argument for the Resurrection of Jesus during the Deist Controversy* (Mellen, 1985); "The Historicity of the Empty Tomb of Jesus" *NTS* 31 (1985); "The Guard at the Tomb" *NTS* 30 (1984); "The Bodily Resurrection of Jesus" in *Gospel Perspectives I* (JSOT, 1980); and others. Awd: Alexander von Humboldt Stiftung Fellow 1978-79. Mem: SBL 1979-; AAR 1979-. Addr: (h) Ave. des Rouges Gorges 8, 1950 Kraainem, Brussels, Belgium 322-731-7222.

CRANFIELD, Charles E. B., b. London, England, September 13, 1915, s. of Charles E. & Beatrice (Tubbs), m. Ruth E.G. (Bole), chil: Mary M.; Elisabeth F. Educ: Jesus Coll., Cambridge, BA 1936, MA 1941. Emp: U. of Durham, 1930-80 Prof., 1980- Prof. Emeritus.; *The International Critical Comm.,* Co-ed. Spec: New Testament. Pub: *Romans: A Shorter Commentary* (T & T Clark, 1985, 1991); "'The Works of the Law' in the Epistle to the Romans" *JSNT* 43 (1991); "The Resurrection of Jesus Christ" *ET* 101 (1989-90); *A Critical and Exegetical Commentary on the Epistle to the Romans* (T & T Clark, 1975, 1990); *The Gospel According to Saint Mark* (Cambridge U.P., 1959, 1989); "Some Reflections on the Subject of the Virgin Birth" *SJT* 41 (1988); "Thoughts on New Testament Eschatology" *SJT* 35 (1982); and others. Awd: Aberdeen U., DD 1980; British Acad., Fellow 1982-; Burkitt Medal for Bibl. Stud. 1989. Mem: SNTS. Rec: Walking. Addr: (h) 30 Western Hill, Durham City DH1 4RL, England 091-3843096.

CRENSHAW, James L., b. Sunset, SC, December 19, 1934, s. of B.D. & Bessie (Aiken), m. Juanita (Rhodes), chil: James Timothy; David Lee. Educ: Furman U., BA 1956; South. Bapt. Theol. Sem., BD 1960; Vanderbilt U., PhD 1964. Emp: Mercer U., 1965-69 Assoc. Prof.; Vanderbilt U. Div. Sch., 1970-87 Prof.; Duke U. Div. Sch., 1987- Prof.; SBL Mon. Ser., 1978-84 Ed.; *CBQ*, 1990- Ed. Bd.; *Hebrew Studies*, 1992- Ed. Bd. Spec: Hebrew Bible. Pub: *Old Testament Story and Faith* (Hendrickson, 1992); "Clanging Symbols" in *Justice and the Holy*, Fs. Walter Harrelson (1989); *Ecclesiastes* (Westminster/SCM, 1987); "The Expression *mi yodea'* in the Hebrew Bible" *VT* 36 (1986); "Education in Ancient Israel" *JBL* 104 (1985); "Wisdom and Authority: Sapiential Rhetoric and its Warrants" in VTSup 32 (1982); *Old Testament Wisdom* (John Knox/SCM, 1981); *Prophetic Conflict* (de Gruyter, 1971); "Method in Determining Wisdom Influence upon 'Historical' Literature" *JBL* 88 (1969); and others. Awd: Vanderbilt U., Fellow 1978; Guggenheim Fellow 1984-85; NEH Fellow 1990-91. Mem: SBL 1964; CBA; IOSOT; SOTS; Colloquium for Bibl. Res. Rec: Tennis, gardening. Addr: (o) Duke U., The Divinity School, Durham, NC 27706 919-660-3413; (h) 8 Beckford Place, Durham, NC 27705 919-383-4342.

CROATTO, Jose S., b. Cordoba, Argentina, March 19, 1930, s. of Jose & Dominga (Macor), m. Estela (Robirosa), chil: Juan; Maria. Educ: Pont. Bibl. Inst., Rome, Lic., Bibl. & Oriental Stud. 1957; Hebrew U., Jerusalem, Dip., Hebrew Lang. 1958. Emp: Inst. de Cultura Relig. Superior, Argentina, 1959-70 Prof., Hist. & Arch. of the Anc. Near East, Hebrew Lang.; Colegio Maximo, Argentina, 1962-72 Prof., OT & Hebrew; U. of Buenos Aires, 1964-73 Prof., Hist. & Phil. of Relig.; *Bibliografia Teologica Comentada*, 1975-77 First Dir.; ISEDET, 1977- Prof., OT & Hebrew Lang.; *Revista Bibl. Cuadernos de Teologia, Aula Orientalis*, Cons. Spec: Hebrew Bible, Semitic Languages, Texts and Epigraphy. Pub: *Mundo Biblico*, 3 vol. (ISEDET, 1992); *Métodos Exegéticos* (ISEDET, 1992); *Isaias 1-39* (La Aurora, 1989); *Crear y amar en libertad: Gn 2:4-3:24* (La Aurora, 1986); and others. Mem: Soc. Argentina de Prof. de Sagrada Escritura 1958-83; Concilium, Redaction Com. 1969-74. Addr: (o) ISEDET, Camacúa 282, 1406 Buenos Aires, Argentina 632-5039; (h) Estafeta N 2, 1665 Jose C. Paz, Pcia. de Buenos Aires, Argentina.

CROSS, Frank Moore, Jr., b. Ross, CA, July 13, 1921. Educ: Maryville Coll., 1942 AB; McCormick Theol. Sem., BD 1946; Johns Hopkins U., PhD, Semitic Lang. 1950. Emp: ASOR, Jerusalem, 1953-54 Ann. Prof.; Intl. Com. for Editing the Dead Sea Scrolls, 1953- Mem.; Harvard U., Dept. of Near East. Lang. & Civilizations, 1958-65 Chmn., 1958- Hancock Prof. of Hebrew & Other Oriental Lang.; Harvard Semitic Mus., 1958-61 Curator, 1974-87 Dir.; Hebrew Union Coll. Arch. Sch.,

Jerusalem, 1963-64 Dir.; Harvard Semitic Mon., 1968- Ed.; Harvard Semitic Stud., 1968- Ed., Chmn. of Ed. Com.; *BASOR*, 1969-91 Assoc. Ed., 1992 Cons. Ed.; Samaria Papyri from the Wadi ed-Daliyeh, Ed. Excv: Judaean Buqe'ah, 1955 Codir.; Carthage, 1975-80 Prin. Investigator. Spec: Archaeology, Semitic Languages, Texts and Epigraphy. Pub: "The Epic Traditions of Early Israel: Epic Narrative and the Reconstruction of Early Israelite Institutions" in *Poet and Historian: Essays in Literary and Historical Biblical Criticism* (Scholars, 1983); "Phoenicians in Sardinia: The Epigraphical Evidence" in *Studies in Sardinian Archeology* (U. of Mich., 1983); *Scrolls from the Wilderness of the Dead Sea* (Sch. of Theol. at Claremont, 1977); *Qumran and the History of the Biblical Text*, co-auth. (Harvard U.P., 1975); *Studies in Ancient Yahwistic Poetry*, co-auth. (Scholars, 1975); *Canaanite Myth and Hebrew Epic: Essays in the History of the Religion of Israel* (Harvard U.P., 1973); *Scrolls from Qumran Cave I*, co-ed. (Albright Inst. of Arch./Shrine of the Book, 1972); "The Development of the Jewish Scripts" in *The Bible and the Ancient Near East* (Doubleday, 1961); *The Ancient Library of Qumran and Modern Biblical Studies* (Anchor, 1961); *Early Hebrew Orthography*, co-auth. (AOS, 1952); and others. Awd: Harvard U., MA 1958; Maryville Coll., LittD 1968; Percia Schimmel Prize in Arch. 1980; SBL, W.F. Albright Awd. in Bibl. Schol. 1980; Hebrew U. of Jerusalem, PhD 1984; U. of Lethbridge, DSc 1990; U. of Madrid, Medalla de Honor de la U. Complutense 1991; Miami U., DHL 1992. Mem: Bibl. Colloquium, Pres. 1966-68; SBL, Pres. 1973-74; ASOR, Pres. 1974-76; Anc. Bibl. Manuscript Ctr., Trustee 1979-; IES. Addr: (o) Harvard U., Dept. of Near Eastern Languages, Cambridge, MA 02138.

CROTTY, Robert B., b. Melbourne, Australia, November 21, 1937, s. of Michael & Annie (Richardson), m. Marie, chil: Nicholas M.; Miriam. Educ: Angelicum U., Rome, STL 1964; Pont. Bibl. Inst., Rome, SSL 1966; U. of Melbourne, MA 1974; U. of Adelaide, Australia, PhD 1981. Emp: Yarra Theol. Union, Australia, 1967-72 Lect.; U. of Melbourne, 1972-74 Lect.; South Australia Coll. of Advanced Educ., 1975-91 Sr. Lect.; U. of South Australia, 1991- Assoc. Prof. Spec: Hebrew Bible, New Testament. Pub: "The Literary Structure of the Letter of James" *Australian Bibl. Rev.* (1992); "The Present State of Studies of Early Christianity" *Australian Relig. Stud. Rev.* (1989); "Qumran Studies Challenge to Consensus" *Relig. Traditions* (1984); "Changing Fashions in Biblical Interpretation" *Australian Bibl. Rev.* (1985); "Eschatological Ambiguity in Pre-Christian Judaism" *Colloquium* (1984); *Symbols, Signs and Sacraments* (Spectrum, 1983); *Good News in Mark* (Collins, 1975); and others. Mem: Australian & New Zealand Soc. for Theol. Stud. 1967-; Australian Assn. for the Study of Relig. 1975-, Pres. 1970-71. Addr: (o) U. of South Australia, Holbrooks Rd., Underdale, South Australia 5032, Australia 08-302-6436; (h) 15 Lloyd St., Hectorville, South Australia 5073, Australia 08-336-6765.

CROWN, Alan D., b. Leeds, England, September 28, 1932, s. of Abraham & Sarah (Addlestone), m. Sadie (Rose), chil: Ann Jacqueline (Lakos); Aviva Lesley (Rosenfeld). Educ: U. of Leeds, BA 1954, MA 1958; U. of Sydney, PhD 1966. Emp: Mount Scopus Coll., 1959-62 Tchr.; U. of Sydney, 1962-67 Lect., 1967-82 Sr. Lect., 1982-89 Assoc. Prof., 1990 Personal Chair; *Australian Jour. of Bibl. Arch.*, 1968-1975 Co-ed. Spec: Hebrew Bible, Semitic Languages, Texts and Epigraphy, Apocrypha and Post-biblical Studies. Pub: "The Abisha Scroll— 3,000 Years Old?" *BR* 7/5 (1991); *The Samaritans*, ed., contb. (Mohr, 1989); "Samaritan Bindings: A Chronological Survey with Reference to Nag Hammadi Techniques" *BJRL* 69/2 (1987); *A Bibliography of the Samaritans* (Scarecrow, 1984); "An Unpublished Fragment of a Samaritan Torah Scroll" *BJRL* 64/2 (1982); *Biblical Studies Today* (Chevalier, 1975); "Messengers and Scribes: the *sopher* and the *mazkir* in the Old Testament" *VT* 24 (1974); *Essays Presented to E.C.B. MacLaurin*, co-ed. (Devonshire, 1973); "The Fate of the Shapira Scroll" *RQ* 27 (1970); and others. Mem: Societe d'Etudes Samaritaines 1985-; SOTS; WUJS; PES. Addr: (o) U. of Sydney, Dept. of Semitic Studies, NSW 2006, Australia 61-2-6922188; (h) 1/24 Blaxland Rd., Bellevue Hill, NSW 2023, Australia 61-2-3652513.

CULLMANN, Oscar, b. Strasbourg, February 25, 1902, s. of Georges & Frederique (Mandel). Emp: U. Strasbourg, 1930-38, 1945-48 Prof.; U. Basel, 1938-72 Prof., 1968 Rector; Ecole des Hautes Etudes, 1949-72 Prof.; Fac. of Theol. Prot., 1951-68 Prof.; Sorbonne, 1953-63 Prof.; Inst. de France, 1972-. Spec: New Testament, Apocrypha and Post-biblical Studies. Pub: *La Priere dans le Nouveau Testament* (1992); *Einheit Durch Vielfalt* (Mohr, 1986); *Der Johanneisch e Kreis* (Mohr, 1975); *Christologie des Neuen Testaments* (Mohr, 1963); and others. Awd: U. of Lausanne, DTh 1944; U. of Manchester, DTh 1948; U. of Edinburgh, DTh 1951; U. of Lund, DTh 1953; Brit. Acad., Burkitt Medal 1956; U. of Basel, DPhil 1972; Commander Legion d'Honneur 1978. Mem: Brit. Acad. 1968-; Dutch Royal Acad. Sci. 1960-; Akademie Wissenschaften und Lit. Mainz 1957. Rec: Gardening. Addr: (o) 10A Birmannsgasse, CH-4055 Basel, Switzerland 61.261 15.66; (h) 20 Rue Ravignan, F-75018 Paris, France 1-4254-9912.

CULPEPPER, R. Alan, b. Little Rock, AR, March 2, 1946, s. of Hugo & Ruth, m. Jacquelyn (McClain), chil: Erin; Rodney. Educ: Baylor U., BA 1967; South. Bapt. Theol. Sem., MDiv 1970; Duke U., PhD 1974. Emp: Bapt. Ch., 1968-70 Pastor; South. Bapt. Theol. Sem., 1984-91 Assoc. Dean, Sch. of Theol., 1985-91 James Buchanan Harrison Prof., NT Interpretation; Vanderbilt Div. Sch., 1983 Vis. Prof.; *Rev. & Expositor*, 1982-91 Ed. Spec: New Testament. Pub: *Pentecost. Proclamation 3* (Fortress, 1986); *1, 2, 3 John* (John Knox, 1985); *Anatomy of the Fourth Gospel: A Study in Literary Design* (Fortress,

1983); and others. Mem: NABPR; SBL; SNTS. Rec: Boating, racquetball. Addr: (o) Baylor U., Dept. of Religion, Waco, TX 76798 817-755-3735; (h) 10004 Lost Oak Ridge, Waco, TX 76712 817-751-7145.

CULVER, Robert D., b. Yakima, WA, July 19, 1916, s. of Sinyeard C. & Emma (Mondor), m. Celeste (Knipmeyer), chil: Douglas J.; Keith E.; Loraine A. Educ: Heidelberg Coll., AB 1945; Grace Theol. Sem., BD 1945, ThM 1947, ThD 1952. Emp: Grace Theol. Sem., 1945-51 Prof.; Trinity Theol. Sem., 1951-54 Prof.; Wheaton Coll. & Grad. Sch., 1953-63 Assoc. Prof.; Northwestern Coll., 1963-64 Prof. Excv: Mt. of Olives, Jordan, 1962 Ann. Dir. Pub: *The Life of Christ* (Baker, 1977, 1981); *Daniel and the Latter Days* (Moody, 1954, 1977); and others. Mem: ASOR 1949-; ETS 1949-; SBL 1950-; NAPH. Addr: (h) Rte. 1, Box 166, Houston, MN 55943 507-864-7493.

CURRID, John D., b. Urbana, IL, August 3, 1951, s. of Raymond & Olive, m. Nancy, chil: Elizabeth; David. Educ: Barrington Coll., BA 1974; Gordon-Conwell Theol. Sem., MATS 1977; U. of Chicago, PhD 1986. Emp: Grove City Coll., 1980-93 Assoc. Prof.; Reformed Theol. Sem., 1993- Assoc. Prof., OT. Excv: Carthage, 1979; Tell el-Hesi, 1979; Lahav Grain Storage Project, 1985-. Spec: Archaeology. Pub: *Excavations at Manahat 1986-1988*, ed. (Israel Antiq. Auth., 1992); "Puzzling Public Buildings" *BAR* 18/1 (1992); "An Examination of the Egyptian Background of the Genesis Cosmogony" *BZ* 204/4 (1991); "Iron Age Pits and the Lahav (Tell Halif) Grain Storage Project" *BASOR* 273 (1989); "Why Did the Early Israelites Dig All Those Pits?" *BAR* 14/5 (1988); "Beehive Buildings of Ancient Palestine" *BA* (1986). Awd: NEH Summer Fellow. 1989; Zion Res. Grant 1979; Byington Hebrew Fellow. 1977. Mem: ASOR 1977-; ETS 1985-. Rec: Running, baseball. Addr: (o) Reformed Theological Seminary, 5422 Clinton Blvd., Jackson, MS 39209-3099; (h) 603 Winding Hills Dr., Clinton, MS 39056.

CURTIS, Adrian H. W., b. Swindon, UK, January 12, 1945, s. of Kenneth & Gill, m. Hilary Margaret (Dean), chil: Daniel James Adrian; Jonathan Michael. Educ: U. of Manchester, BA 1966, PhD 1975. Emp: U. of Manchester, 1970- Lect., OT. Spec: Archaeology, Hebrew Bible. Pub: "Some Observations on 'Bull' Terminology in the Ugaritic Texts and the Old Testament" *OS* 26 (1990); "The Hebrew World" in *Creating the Old Testament* (Blackwell, 1989); "God as 'Judge' in Ugaritic and Hebrew Thought" in *Law and Religion* (Clarke, 1988); *Ugarit (Ras Shamra)*, Cities of the Bibl. World Ser. (Lutterworth, 1985); "The 'Subjugation of the Waters' Motif in the Psalms: Imagery or Polemic?" *JSS* 23 (1978); and others. Mem: SOTS; Anglo-Israel Arch. Soc. 1985-. Rec: Theatre, crossword puzzles, ornithology, watching rugby. Addr: (o) U. of Manchester, Dept. of Religions & Theology,

Manchester M13 9PL, England 061-275-3606; (h) 5 Hurstville Rd., Chorlton-cum-Hardy, Manchester M21 2DJ, England.

CUSTIS, John R., Jr., b. Chesapeake, VA, July 26, 1914, s. of John & Esther (Keeling), m. Elizabeth (Bond), chil: Mary June; John III; Esther. Educ: Andover Newton Theol. Sch., BD 1940; Temple U., MST 1946, DST 1957; Princeton Theol. Sem., ThM 1949. Emp: Va. Theol. Sem. & Coll., 1940-41 Prof.; New Era Theol. Inst., 1941- Prof.; Villanova U., 1973- Lect., Black Relig. Experience. Spec: New Testament. Mem: SBL 1958-; AAR 1980-. Rec: Hymns, cryptograms, watching sports. Addr: (o) Villanova U., Dept. of Religious Studies, Villanova, PA 19085 215-645-4730; (h) 435 E Washington Ln., Apt. 3, Philadelphia, PA 19144 215-843-4819.

DAHMS, John V., b. Zurich, ON, Canada, April 23, 1919, s. of Nelson & Hilda (Voelzing), m. Dorothy (Burns), chil: Daniel; Esther. Educ: Evang. Theol. Sem., BD 1945; Victoria U., Emmanuel Coll., ThM 1960, ThD 1965. Emp: Evang. United Brethren, United Ch. of Canada, 1940-82 Parish Min.; Canadian Theol. Sem., 1971-89 Prof., 1989- Prof. Emeritus. Spec: New Testament. Pub: "The Johannine Use of Monogenes Reconsidered" NTS 29 (1983); "Isaiah 55:11 and the Gospel of John" EQ; and others. Addr: (o) 4400 Fourth Ave., Regina S4T OH8, Canada 306-545-1515; (h) 863 Connaught St., Regina S4T 6S3, Canada 306-545-2641.

DALLEY, Stephanie M., b. United Kingdom, d. of Katharine (Dohan) & Denys Page, m. Christopher Dalley, chil: Katharine; Rebecca; Ian. Educ: Cambridge U., BA 1965; U. of London, PhD 1970. Excv: Jerusalem, 1964 Site Supr.; Can Hasan, 1965 Site Supr.; Aphrodisias, 1966 Site Supr.; Saliagos, 1965 Cataloguer; Tell Al Rimah, 1967 Epigraphist. Spec: Hebrew Bible, Mesopotamian Studies, Semitic Languages, Texts and Epigraphy, Apocrypha and Post-biblical Studies. Pub: "Gilgamesh in the Arabian Nights" JRAS (1991); "Yahweh in Hamath in the 8th Century B.C." VT 60 (1990); Myths from Mesopotamia (1989); "The God Salmu and the Winged Disk" IRAQ 48 (1986); "Foreign Chariotry and Cavalry in the Armies of Tiglath-pileser III and Sargon II" IRAQ 47 (1985); The Tablets from Fort Shalmaneser: Cuneiform Texts from Nimrud vol. III, co-auth. (1984); Mari and Karana: Two Old Babylonian Cities (1984); The Old Babylonian Tablets from Tell Al Rimah, co-auth. (1976); "A Stela of Adad-Nirari III and Nergal-Eres" IRAQ 30 (1968); and others. Awd: Somerville Coll., Sr. Res. Fellow in Assyriology 1988-. Mem: Soc. of the Antiquaries, Fellow 1989-. Rec: Tennis, piano-playing, sewing, walking. Addr: (o) Oriental Institute, Pusey Ln., Oxford 0X1 2LE, England.

DALTON, William J., b. Benalla, Australia, November 8, 1916, s. of William & Mary (Egan).

Educ: U. of Melbourne, BA 1942, MA 1944; Pont. Bibl. Inst., Rome, Lic. in Sacred Scripture 1953, DSS 1964. Emp: Canisius Coll., Sydney, 1954-68 Prof., Scripture; United Faculty of Theol., Melbourne, 1969-75 Prof., NT; Pont. Bibl. Inst., Rome, 1976-81 Prof., NT; Pont. Bibl. Inst., Jerusalem, 1981-83 Dir.; Cath. Theol. Coll., Melbourne, 1985- Lect., NT. Spec: New Testament. Pub: Galatians Without Tears (St. Paul, 1992); "Pseudepigraphy in the New Testament" Cath. Theol. Rev. 5 (1983); "The Interpretation of 1 Peter 3:19 and 4:6: Light from 2 Peter" Biblica 60 (1979); Salvation and Damnation (1977); Mary in the New Testament (Spectrum, 1974); Christ's Proclamation to the Spirits, Analecta Biblica (1965); and others. Mem: SNTS 1965-; CBA 1965-. Rec: Walking, classical music. Addr: (h) Jesuit Theological College, 175 Royal Parade, Parkville, 3052 Victoria, Australia 03-347-6366.

DANIELI, Giuseppe, b. Montebello Vicentino, December 1, 1923, s. of Giuseppe & Eugenica (Paiusco). Educ: Pont. U. Gregoriana, Lic. Theol. 1950; Pont. Bibl. Inst., Lic. Holy Scripture 1952; Pont. Bibl. Commn., D. Holy Scripture 1967. Emp: Istituto Filosofico-Teologico San Pietro, 1952- Prof., Holy Scripture, 1964-78 Dean of Inst.; Parole di Vita, 1977-87 Ed. Bd.; RivB, 1986- Ed. Bd.; Bibbia della Conferenza Episcopale Italiana, 1988- Sec., Rev. group. Spec: New Testament. Pub: Matteo (Queriniana, 1980); AA.VV., Il messaggio della Salvezza vol. 6, contb. (LDC, 1979); "Maria e i fratelli di Gesu nel Vangelo di Marco" Marianum 40 (1978); "Ipotesi recenti sull'indissolubilita del matrimonio nel NT" Asprenas 22 (1975); Esdra e Neemia (Paoline, 1972); Giuseppe figlio di Davide (Messaggero, 1971); "A proposito delle origini della tradizione sinottica sulla concezione verginale" Divus Thomas 72 (1969); "L'influsso reciproco di tradizioni narrative e commenti profetici nel vangelo di Matteo" Divus Thomas 71 (1968); "Mediator autem unius non est (Gal 3,20)" Verbum Domini 33 (1955); and others. Mem: SNTS 1980-. Addr: (o) Istituto San Pietro, Viale Armando Diaz, 25, 01100 Viterbo, Italy 0761-34-31-34.

DANIELS, Dwight R., b. Los Angeles, CA, May 30, 1956, m. Susan C. Educ: U. of Calif., Irvine, BS 1978; Fuller Theol. Sem., MDiv 1982; U. Hamburg, DTh 1987. Emp: U. Hamburg, 1984-92 Instr. Spec: Hebrew Bible. Pub: "The Composition of the Ezra-Nehemiah Narrative" in Ernten, Was Man Sat, Festschrift K. Koch (1991); "Biblische Theologie in den USA: Ein Forschungs und Tagungsbericht" JBTh 6 (1991); Hosea and Salvation History: The Early Traditions of Israel in the Prophecy of Hosea, BZAW 191 (de Gruyter, 1990); "The Creed of Deuteronomy XXVI Revisited" in VTSup 41 (1990); "Is There a 'Prophetic Lawsuit' Genre?" ZAW 99 (1987); and others. Awd: Deutsche Forschungsgemeinschaft, res. grant 1991-92. Mem: SBL 1982-; Wissenschaftliche Gesellschaft fur Theol. 1984-; ASOR 1989-. Rec: Tennis, golf, soccer, chess, travel. Addr: (h) 1331 Dorothy Dr., Glendale, CA 91202 818-242-7793.

DANIN, Avinoam, b. Haifa, Israel, January 13, 1939, s. of Sara & Hiram, m. Drora, chil: Iris; Morit; Barak; Shira. Educ: Hebrew U., Jerusalem, BS 1962, MSc, Botany 1964, PhD 1970. Emp: Hebrew U., Dept. of Evolution, Systematics & Ecology, 1967-69 Asst., 1969-71 Instr., 1973-79 Lect., 1979-88 Sr. Lect., 1988-Assoc. Prof., OPTIMA, 1979-88 Reg. Adv. on flora of Israel & Sinai. Pub: *Analytical Flora of Eretz-Israel*, co-auth. (Cana, 1991); "Flora and Vegetation of Israel" in *The Zoogeography of Israel* (Dordrecht, 1988); "Revision of the Plant Geographical Territories of Israel and Sinai," co-auth., *Plant Systematics and Evolution* 150 (1987); "Palaeoclimates in Israel: Evidence from Weathering Patterns of Stones in and near Archaeological Sites" *BASOR* 259 (1985); *Desert Vegetation of Israel and Sinai* (Cana, 1983); *Pictorial Flora of Israel* (Massada, 1983); *The Vegetation of the Negev, North of Nahal Paran* (Sifriat Poalim, 1977); "The Vegetation of the Northern Negev and the Judean Desert of Israel" *Israel J. Bot.* 24 (1975); and others. Rec: Flowers, photography. Addr: (o) Hebrew U. of Jerusalem, Dept. of Evolution, Systematics and Ecology, Jerusalem 91904, Israel 02-584319; (h) 11 Bet Hakerem St., Jerusalem 96343, Israel 02-520471.

DANKER, Frederick W., b. Frankenmuth, MI, s. of William & Wilhelomina, m. Lois (Dreyer), chil: Kathleen; James. Educ: Concordia Sem., BD 1950; U. of Chicago, PhD 1963. Emp: Luth. Ch., 1946-54 Pastor; Concordia Sem., 1954-74 Prof.; Christ Sem.-Seminex, 1974-83 Prof.; Luth. Sch. of Theol., 1983-88 Prof., 1988- Prof. Emeritus. Spec: Archaeology, New Testament. Pub: "2 Peter 1: A Solemn Decree" *CBQ* 40 (1978); *A Greek-English Lexicon of the New Testament and Other Early Christian Literature*, co-ed. (U. of Chicago, 1979); *Benefactor: Epigraphic Study of a Graeco-Roman and New Testament Semantic Field* (Clayton, 1982); "Graeco-Roman Cultural Accommodation in the Christology of Luke-Acts" in *SBL Seminar Papers* (1983); "Reciprocity: Acts 15:23-29" in *Political Issues in Luke-Acts* (Orbis, 1983); *A Century of Greco-Roman Philology* (SBL, 1988); *Second Corinthians* (Augsburg, 1989); and others. Mem: SBL 1956-; SNTS 1960-; CBA 1964-. Rec: Travel, chess. Addr: (h) 3438 Russell Blvd. 203, St. Louis, MO 63104 314-772-5757.

DARR, John A., b. Greenville, SC, February 28, 1953, s. of Dick L. & Anne M., m. Katheryn (Pfisterer), chil: Joshua P. Educ: Wheaton Coll., BA 1975; Wheaton Grad. Sch., MA 1977; Vanderbilt U., MA 1981, PhD 1987. Emp: Baldwin-Wallace Coll., 1982-83 Asst. Prof.; Boston U. Sch. of Theol., 1984-87 Lect.; Holy Cross Coll., 1987-88 Asst. Prof.; Boston Coll., 1988- Asst. Prof. Spec: New Testament. Pub: *On Character Building: The Reader and the Rhetoric of Characterization in Luke-Acts* (Westminster/John Knox, 1992); "Chronologies of Paul" in *Paul's Faith and the Power of the Gospel* (Fortress, 1983). Mem: SBL 1982-; AAR 1982-; CBA 1992-. Addr: (o) Boston College, Theology Dept., Chestnut Hill, MA 02167 617-552-3883; (h) 512 Beacon St., #4205, Boston, MA 02215 617-352-7459.

DARR, Katheryn P., b. Davison County, KY, May 30, 1952, d. of Fred R. & Ann Rader Pfisterer, m. John Andrew Darr, chil: Joshua Pfisterer. Educ: Ky. Wesleyan Coll., BA 1974; Vanderbilt U., MA 1981, PhD 1984. Emp: Baldwin Wallace Coll., 1982-83 Asst. Prof.; Boston U. Sch. of Theol., 1984-92 Asst. Prof.; Boston U. Grad. Sch., 1986-92 Asst. Prof.; *The New Interpreters Bible*, 1990- Ed. Bd. Spec: Semitic Languages, Texts and Epigraphy. Pub: *"Far More Precious Than Jewels": Perspectives on Biblical Women*, Gender and the Bibl. Tradition 1 (Westminster/John Knox, 1991); "Write or True?: A Response to Ellen Francis Davis" in *Signs and Wonders: Biblical Texts in Literary Focus* (Scholars, 1989); "Like Warrior, Like Woman: Destruction and Deliverance in Isaiah 42:10-17" *CBQ* 49 (1987); "The Wall Around Paradise: Ezekielian Ideas About the Future" *VT* 37 (1987); and others. Awd: AAR, res. grant 1989; Boston U., Hum. Found., Jr. Fellow 1990-91. Mem: SBL, Pres., New England reg. 1989-90; AAR. Addr: (o) Boston U., School of Theology, #49, Boston, MA 02215 617-353-3074; (h) 610 Beacon St., #2083, Boston, MA 02215 617-352-7459.

DART, John S., b. Peekskill, NY, August 1, 1936, s. of Seward H. & Vella M., m. Gloria, chil: Kim; John; Randall; Christopher. Educ: U. of Colo., BA 1958. Emp: Los Angeles Times, 1967-93 Relig. Writer.; Vanderbilt U., First Amendment Ctr., 1992-93 Vis. Professional Schol. Spec: New Testament, Apocrypha and Post-biblical Studies. Pub: *The Jesus of Heresy and History, The Discovery and Meaning of the Nag Hammadi Gnostic Library* (Harper, 1988); "Fragments from an Earthen Jar" *Christian Century* Mar. (1978); *The Laughing Savior, the Discovery and Significance of the Nag Hammadi Gnostic Library* (Harper & Row, 1976); and others. Awd: Stanford U., NEH Fellow. for Journalists, 1973-74; Relig. Newswriters Assn., Supple Memorial Awd., 1980; Jim Merril Relig. Liberty Memorial Awd., 1980. Mem: SBL 1979-; Relig. Newswriters Assn., Pres. 1990-1992. Rec: Tournament-style table tennis. Addr: (o) LA Times, 2000 Prairie St., Chatsworth, CA 91311 818-772-3342; (h) 12122 Bowmore Ave., Northridge, CA 91326 818-360-3458.

DAUPHIN, Claudine M., b. Alexandria, Egypt, February 28, 1950, d. of Jacques M. & Reine H. (Jauffret). Educ: U. of Edinburgh, MA, Near East. Arch. 1971, PhD, Byzantine Art & Arch. 1974; Ecole Pratique des Hautes Etudes, Eléve Diplomée 1978. Emp: Israel Dept. of Antiq. & Mus., 1977-1979 Byzantine Specialist; Ecole Biblique, 1977-79 Prof., Christian Arch. & Art; U. of Oxford, 1979-84 Lady Carlisle Res.

Fellow, Byzantine Art & Arch.; *Bull. of the Anglo-Israel Arch. Soc.*, 1990- Ed. Bd.; Collège de France, Ctr. d'Hist. & Civ. de Byzance, 1985- Chargé de Recherche, Ctr. Natl. de la Recherche Sci. Excv: Khirbet Jannaba et-Tahta, 1975-76 Dir.; Shelomi, 1976-78 Dir.; Kafr Naffakh, Na'aran, Farj & Er-Ramthaniyye, 1978-88 Dir.; Gevulot & Ohad, 1979 Dir.; Dor Ch., 1979-80, 1983 Dir. Spec: Archaeology. Pub: "Mosaic Pavements as an Index of Prosperity and Fashion" *Levant* 12 (1980); "Settlements of the Roman and Byzantine Periods on the Golan Heights: Preliminary Report on Three Seasons of Survey (1979-1981)" *IEJ* 33 (1983); "A VIIth Century Measuring Rod from the Ecclesiastical Farm at Shelomi in Western Galilee (Israel)" *Jahrbuch der Osterreichischen Byzantinistik* 32/3 (1983); "Temple grec, église byzantine, et cimetière musulman: la basilique de Dor en Israël" *Proche-Orient Chrétien* 36 (1986); "Le catalogue des sites byzantins de la Palestine: buts, méthodes et limites d'une étude démographique" *Eretz-Israel* 19 (1987); *L'Eglise byzantine de Nahariya (Israel): Etude archéologique*, Byzantina Mnemeia 5 (U. de Thessalonique, 1984); and others. Awd: U. of Edinburgh, Tweedie Res. Fellow in Arch. & Anthrop. 1974-75; Hebrew U., Lady Davis Fellow 1975-77; Soc. of Antiquaries of Scotland, Elected Fellow 1974; Albright Inst., Fellow 1988-89. Mem: IES; PEF; BSA; Anglo-Israel Arch. Soc. Rec: Class. music (piano), painting, reading. Addr: (o) Collège de France, Centre d'Histoire et Civilisation de Byzance, 52 rue du Cardinal Lemoine, Paris 75005, France 1-44-27-17-77; (h) 18 Résidence La Gailarderie, 78590 Noisy-le-Roi, France 1-34-62-82-96.

DAVIDS, Peter H., b. Syracuse, NY, November 22, 1947, s. of Hugh H. & Doris M. (Dunning), m. Judith L. (Bouchillon), chil: Elaine Marie; Gwenda Lee; Ian Hugh. Educ: Wheaton Coll., BA, Psychology 1968; Trinity Evang. Div. Sch., MDiv 1971; Victoria U. of Manchester, PhD 1974. Emp: Bibelschule Wiedenest, Germany, 1974-76 Theol. Lehrer; Trinity Episc. Sch. for Ministry, 1976-83 Assoc. Prof.; Regent Coll., Vancouver, 1983-89 Adj. Prof.; Canadian Theol. Sem., 1989-91 Prof.; Langley Vineyard Christian Fellow., 1991- Langley BC Schol. in Residence. Spec: New Testament. Pub: *1 Peter* (Eerdmans, 1990); *James* (Hendrickson, 1989); articles in *Baker Ency. of the Bible* (Baker, 1988); "James and Jesus" in *Gospel Perspectives V* (JSOT, 1985); *James*, Good News Comm. (Harper & Row, 1983); *The Epistle of James* (Eerdmans, 1982); "The Meaning of *Apeirastos* in James 1:13" *NTS* 24 (1978); "The Use of the Pseudepigrapha in the Catholic Epistles" in *The Pseudepigrapha and the New Testament* (Sheffield); and others. Awd: Eta Beta Rho 1968. Mem: Tyndale Fellow. 1974-87; SBL 1974-; IBR 1977-; SNTS 1982-; CSBS 1985-. Rec: Computer science, photography, walking. Addr: (o) Langley Vineyard Christian Fellowship, 5708 Glover Rd., Langley, BC V3A 4H8, Canada 604-530-8463; (h) #9, 21965-49th Ave., Langley, BC V3A 3R9, Canada 604-530-8805.

DAVIDSON, Maxwell J., b. Melbourne, Australia, June 13, 1941, s. of John William & Elsie Marjorie, m. Agnes Mary, chil: Deborah Elizabeth; Timothy John. Educ: U. of Melbourne, BS 1961, Dip. of Educ. 1962; Melbourne Coll. of Div., BD 1968; U. of Queensland, PhD 1988. Emp: SIM Intl. in Ethiopia, 1970-78 Missionary; Bapt. Theol. Coll. of Queensland, Australia, 1982-90 Lect., Systematic Theol.; Murdoch U., West. Australia, 1991- Lect., Hebrew & Systematic Theol.; Bapt. Theol. Coll. of West. Australia., 1991- Lect., Head of Systematic Theol. Dept. Spec: Archaeology, Apocrypha and Post-biblical Studies. Pub: *Angels at Qumran: A Comparative Study of 1 Enoch 1-36, 71-108 and Sectarian Writings from Qumran* (Sheffield, 1992). Mem: SBL 1987-; Australian & New Zealand Soc. for Theol. Stud. 1991-. Rec: Tennis, photography, gardening, walking. Addr: (o) Baptist Theological College of Western Australia, 20 Hayman Rd., Bentley, W.A. 6102, Australia 09-361-9962.

DAVIDSON, Richard M., b. Glendale, CA, June 6, 1946, s. of Howard & Evelyn, m. Jo Ann (Mazat), chil: Rahel; Jonathan. Educ: Andrews U., MDiv 1971, PhD 1981. Emp: Andrews U. Theol. Sem., 1980- Prof., OT Exegesis. Spec: Hebrew Bible. Pub: "Sanctuary Typology" in *Symposium on Revelation—Book 1* (Bibl. Res. Inst., 1992); "Typology in the Book of Hebrews" in *Issues in the Book of Hebrews* (Bibl. Res. Inst., 1989); "Theology of Sexuality in the Song of Songs: Return to Eden" *AUSS* 1 (1989); "The Theology of Sexuality in the Beginning: Genesis 3" *AUSS* 2 (1988); "The Theology of Sexuality in the Beginning: Genesis 1-2" *AUSS* 1 (1988); *A Love Song for the Sabbath* (Review & Herald, 1988); *Typology in Scripture: A Study of Hermeneutical Typos Structures* (Andrews U.P., 1981); and others. Mem: SBL; CSBR. Rec: Tennis, backpacking, music. Addr: (o) Andrews U., Theological Seminary, Old Testament Dept., Berrien Springs, MI 49104 616-471-6575; (h) 5354 Hipps Hollow Rd., Rte. 1, Eau Claire, MI 49111.

DAVIES, Graham I., b. Liskeard, Cornwall, UK, September 26, 1944, s. of Ivor Samuel & Pauline, m. Nicola Rina (Galeski), chil: Peter; Stephen; Michael; Anne. Educ: Merton Coll., Oxford, BA, MA 1970; Peterhouse, Cambridge, PhD 1975. Emp: Nottingham U., 1971-78 Lect., Theol.; Cambridge U., 1979- Lect., Div.; Pembroke Coll. & Peterhouse, 1979-87 Dir., Stud. in Theol.; Fitzwilliam Coll., 1983- Fellow, Dir., Stud. in Theol.; Cities of the Bibl. World Ser., Ed.; *PEQ*, 1990- Ed. Excv: Lachish, 1977, 1980. Spec: Archaeology, Hebrew Bible, Semitic Languages, Texts and Epigraphy. Pub: *Hosea*, New Century Bible (HarperCollins, 1992); *Ancient Hebrew Inscriptions: Corpus and Concordance* (Cambridge U.P., 1991); "British Archaeology in the Holy Land" in *Callaway Festschrift* (1988); *Megiddo* (Lutterworth, 1986); "The Wilderness Itineraries and the Composition of the Pentateuch" *VT* 33 (1983); *The Way of the Wilderness* (Cambridge U.P., 1979); "Apocalyptic and Historiography" *JSOT* 5 (1978); "The Wilderness

Itineraries: A Comparative Study" *TB* 25 (1974); "Hagar, el-hegra and the Location of Mount Sinai" *VT* 22 (1972); and others. Awd: Cambridge U., Jeremie Septuagint Prize 1970; Merton Coll., Oxford, Vis. Res. Fellow 1985. Mem: SOTS; PEF; BSA, Jerusalem; SBL; Soc. of Antiquaries, Fellow. Rec: Rugby, steam trains, gardening. Addr: (o) Divinity School, St. John's St., Cambridge CB2 1TW, England 0-223-332589.

DAVIES, John A., b. Sydney, Australia, February 1, 1950, s. of Arthur & Mary, m. Julie, chil: Kathryn; Timothy; Simon. Educ: Sydney U., MA 1975; Westminster Theol. Sem., MDiv 1978. Emp: Presbyn. Theol. Ctr., Australia, 1980-, 1986- Head of Dept., Hebrew & OT Exegesis, 1987- Prin. Spec: Hebrew Bible. Pub: *Ecclesiastes,* Bible Probe Comm. (ANZEA, 1989); "The Heart of the Old Covenant" in *Evangelism and the Reformed Faith* (1980); "A Note on Job xii 2" *VT* 25/3 (1975); and others. Rec: Music. Addr: (o) Presbyterian Theological Centre, 77 Shaftesbury Rd., Burwood, NSW 2134, Australia; (h) 14 Caloola Cresent, Beverly Hills, NSW 2209, Australia.

DAVIES, Philip R., b. Cardiff, Wales, April 20, 1945, s. of William & Joan, m. Birgit, chil: Gareth. Educ: U. of Oxford, England, BA 1967, MA 1970; U. of St. Andrews, Scotland, PhD 1972. Emp: U. of Cape Coast, Ghana, 1970-73 Lect.; U. of Sheffield, England, 1973- Reader; *JSOT,* 1976- Ed. Spec: Hebrew Bible, Apocrypha and Post-biblical Studies. Pub: *In Search of Ancient Israel* (1992); "Eschatology at Qumran" *JBL* 104 (1985); *Daniel* (JSOT, 1985); *The Damascus Covenant* (JSOT, 1982); *Qumran* (Lutterworth, 1982); "Hasidim in the Maccabean Period" *JJS* 28 (1977); and others. Mem: SOTS 1975-; British Assn. for Jewish Stud. 1977-; CBA 1979-; SBL 1979-. Rec: Cricket, golf, gardening. Addr: (o) U. of Sheffield, Dept. of Biblical Studies, Sheffield S10 2UJ, England 0742-78555; (h) 26 Crescent Rd., Nether Edge, Sheffield S7 1HL, England 0742-555496.

DAVIS, Charles T., b. Marion, AL, July 25, 1939, s. of Charles T., Jr. & Ruby D., m. Mary Holland (King), chil: Eric Randolph. Educ: U. of Alabama, BS 1960; Emory U., Candler Sch. of Theol., BD 1963; Emory U., PhD 1967. Emp: Appalachian State U., 1967- Prof. Spec: Hebrew Bible, New Testament. Pub: "Mark: The Petrine Gospel" in *New Synoptic Studies* (Mercer U.P., 1983); "The Fulfillment of Creation: A Study of Matthew's Genealogy" *JAAR* 41/4 (1973); "Tradition and Redaction in Mt. 1:18-2:23" *JBL* 90/4 (1971); and others. Awd: U. of Heidelberg, Dempster Fellow 1964-65. Mem: SBL 1966-; AAR 1991-. Rec: Bicycle racing, century riding, hiking, juggling, textile crafts. Addr: (o) Appalachian State U., Dept. of Philosophy & Religion, Boone, NC 28608 704-262-3089; (h) PO Box 532, Blowing Rock, NC 28605 704-295-7641.

DAVIS, Ellen F., b. Kentfield, CA, November 20, 1950, d. of Frances E. & John H., m. Dwayne Huebner. Educ: U. of Calif., Berkeley, AB 1971; Oxford U., Cert. Theol. 1982; Ch. Div. Sch. of the Pacific, MDiv 1983; Yale U., PhD 1987. Emp: Union Theol. Sem., 1987-89 Asst. Prof.; Yale Div. Sch., 1989- Assoc. Prof. Spec: Hebrew Bible. Pub: "Jacob and Job: The Integrity of Faith" in *Reading Between the Texts: Intertextuality and the Hebrew Bible* (John Knox, 1992); "Exploding the Limits: Psalm 22" *JSOT* Winter (1992); "Psalm 98" *Interpretation* 46 (1992); "Self-Consciousness and Conversation: Reading Genesis 22" *Bull. for Bibl. Res.* 1 (1991); *Swallowing the Scroll: Textuality and the Dynamics of Discourse in Ezekiel's Prophecy* (Almond, 1989); "Messenger of a Metaphorical God: John Donne's Use of Scripture in Preaching" *ATR* 71 Winter (1989); and others. Mem: SBL. Addr: (o) Yale Divinity School, 409 Prospect St., New Haven, CT 06511 203-432-8162; (h) 625 Maple Ave., Cheshire, CT 06410 203-271-0544.

DAVIS, James A., b. Paducah, KY, March 29, 1953, s. of Clifford & Helen, m. Carolyn, chil: Sarah; Elsa; Hope. Educ: Trinity Evang. Div. Sch., MDiv 1979; Nottingham U., England, PhD 1982. Emp: Trinity Evang. Div. Sch., 1978-79 Teaching Fellow; West. Ky. U., 1982-83 Vis. Asst. Prof., NT; Trinity Episc. Sch. for Ministry, 1983-90 Asst. Prof., Bibl. Stud.; Presbyn. Ch., 1990- Assoc. Pastor. Spec: New Testament. Pub: *Wisdom and Spirit. An Investigaion of 1 Corinthians 1:18-3:20 Against the Background of Jewish Sapiential Tradition in the Greco-Roman Period* (U. Press of Amer., 1985). Awd: Tyndale Fellow. 1981. Mem: SBL; CBA; IBR; and others. Rec: Reading, computers, tennis. Addr: (o) Mercer Island Presbyterian Church, 3605 84th Ave. SE, Mercer Island, WA 98040 206-232-5595; (h) 8011 SE 36th St., Mercer Island, WA 98040 206-232-8563.

DAVIS, John J., b. Philadelphia, PA, October 13, 1936, s. of John & Cathrine, m. Carolyn, chil: Deborah. Educ: Grace Theol. Sem., MDiv 1962, ThM 1963, ThD 1967. Emp: Grace Coll. & Theol. Sem., 1963-65 Instr., 1965- Prof., 1976-82 Exec. V.P., 1986- Pres.; Near East Inst. of Arch., Jerusalem, 1970-71 Exec. Dean; Talbot Theol. Sem., 1976 Lyman Stewart Lect.; Far East. Bible Coll., Singapore, 1982-83, 1985 Vis. Lect., OT; Korea Theol. Sem., 1985 Vis. Lect. Excv: Tekoa, 1968, 1970 Area Supr.; Joint Expdn. to Ai, Raddana Excvn., 1974 Supr.; Heshbon, 1976 Area Supr.; Tell Abila, Tomb Excvn., 1982, 1984 Area Supr. Spec: Archaeology, Hebrew Bible. Pub: *Moses and the Gods of Egypt: Studies in the Book of Exodus* (Baker, 1986); *A History of Israel: From Conquest to Exile,* co-auth. (Baker, 1980); *The Perfect Shepherd: Studies in the Twenty-third Psalm* (Baker, 1979); and others. Awd: Trinity Coll., DD 1968. Mem: NEAS; ETS. Rec: Fishing, hunting. Addr: (o) Grace Theological Seminary, 200 Seminary Dr., Winona Lake, IN 46590 219-372-5101; (h) PO Box 635, Winona Lake, IN 46590 219-267-6033.

DAWSEY, James M., b. Spartanburg, SC, December 4, 1947, s. of Cyrus & Marshlea, m. Dixie, chil: James; Jennifer. Educ: Emory U., MDiv 1973, PhD 1983. Emp: Auburn U., 1980- Prof. Spec: New Testament. Pub: *From Wasteland to Promised Land* (Orbis, 1992); *A Scholar's Guide to Academic Journals in Religion* (Scarecrow, 1988); *The Lukan Voice* (Mercer U.P., 1986); and others. Mem: SBL. Addr: (o) Auburn U., Dept of Religion, 8080 Haley Center, Auburn, AL 36849 205-844-4616; (h) 772 Wild Ginger Ln., Auburn, AL 36849 205-821-7960.

DAY, John, b. London, England, September 13, 1948, s. of Horace & Violet, m. Jane Mary (Osborn). Educ: Cambridge U., Christ's Coll., BA, Theol. 1970, MA 1974, PhD 1977. Emp: U. of Durham, 1977-80 Res. Fellow; U. of Oxford, 1980- Lect., OT, 1984 Dahood Memorial Lect. Spec: Hebrew Bible. Pub: *Psalms* (JSOT, 1990); *Molech: A God of Human Sacrifice in the Old Testament* (Cambridge U.P., 1989); "Asherah in the Hebrew Bible and Northwest Semitic Literature" *JBL* 105 (1986); *God's Conflict with the Dragon and the Sea. Echoes of a Canaanite Myth in the Old Testament* (Cambridge U.P., 1985); *Oxford Bible Atlas*, ed. (Oxford U.P., 1984); "A Case of Inner Scriptural Interpretation" *JTS* 31 (1980); "The Earliest Known Interpretation of the Suffering Servant," "The Daniel of Ugarit and Ezekiel and the Hero of the Book of Daniel" *VT* 30 (1980); "New Light on the Mythological Background of the Allusion to Resheph in Habakkuk III 5" *VT* 29 (1979); and others. Awd: Hebrew U. of Jerusalem, John Goodenday Fellow 1972-73; Cambridge U., Sr. Hebrew Prize 1972; SBL & Doubleday, Mitchell Dahood Memorial Prize 1984. Mem: SOTS; Anglo-Israel Arch. Soc.; PEF. Addr: (o) Oxford U., Lady Margaret Hall, Oxford OX2 6QA, England 274380; (h) 6 Richmond Rd., Oxford OX1 2JJ, England 58337.

DAY, Peggy L., b. Winnipeg, Canada, February 26, 1954, d. of Robert David & Renee Caroline. Educ: U. of Brit. Columbia, BA 1975, MA, OT 1977; Harvard Div. Sch., MTS, Hebrew Bible 1979; Harvard U., PhD 1986. Emp: Harvard U., 1981-86 Teaching Fellow; Harvard Div. Sch. Summer Lang. Prog., 1983-86 Instr., Bibl. Hebrew; U. of Toronto, Trinity Coll., Fac. of Div., 1986-89 Asst. Prof., OT; U. of Winnipeg, 1989- Assoc. Prof., Relig. Stud., Grad. Chair, Joint Masters Prog. in Relig. Stud. Excv: Tel Dor, Israel, 1982 Field Recorder & Square Supr. Spec: Hebrew Bible. Pub: "Anat: Ugarit's 'Mistress of Animals'" *JNES* (1992); "Why is Anat a Warrior and Hunter?" in *The Bible and the Politics of Exegesis*, co-ed. (Pilgrim, 1991); "Women's Studies and Biblical Studies" in *Religious Studies: Issues, Prospects and Proposals* (Scholars, 1991); "From the Child is Born the Woman: The Story of Jephthah's Daughter" in *Gender and Difference in Ancient Israel*, ed. (Fortress, 1989); *An Adversary in Heaven: śātān in the Hebrew Bible*, HSM 43 (Scholars, 1988); "Abishai the śātān in 2 Samuel 19:17-24" *CBQ* 49 (1987). Mem: SBL 1976-; Winnipeg Bibl. Colloquium 1989-. Addr: (o) U. of

Winnipeg, 515 Portage Ave., Winnipeg, Man. R3B 2E9, Canada 204-786-9431; (h) 284 Aubrey St., Winnipeg, Man. R3G 2J2, Canada 204-774-3614.

DE JONGE, Henk J., b. Leiden, Netherlands, September 28, 1943, s. of Marinus I. & Maria P. (Braun), m. Mariann (Doelman), chil: Hans; Casper; Lodewijk. Educ: Leiden U., MA, Class. Philol. 1969, DLitt 1983. Emp: U. of Amsterdam, 1970-84 Lect., NT; Leiden U., 1985-90 Sr. Lect., NT, 1987-91 Prof., Hist. of Bibl. Exegesis, 1991- Prof., NT & Early Christian Lit.; *NT*, 1978- Ed. Spec: New Testament. Pub: "The Historical Jesus' View of Himself and of His Mission" in *From Jesus to John*, Festschrift M. de Jonge (Sheffield, 1993); *Visionaire Ervaring en de historische Oorsprong van het Christendom* (Rijksuniversiteit, 1992); "The Loss of Faith in the Historicity of the Gospels: H. S. Reimarus (ca. 1750) on John and the Synoptics" in *John and the Synoptics* (1992); "Augustine on the Interrelations of the Gospels" in *The Four Gospels*, Festschrift F. Neirynck (1992); "De hogepriesterchristologie en Melchizedek in Hebren" *Nederlands Theol. Tijdschrift* 37 (1983); *De Bestudering van het Nieuwe Testament 1575-1700* (1980); "Sonship, Wisdom Infancy: Luke ii.41-51a" *NTS* 24 (1977-78). Mem: SNTS 1973-. Addr: (o) Rijksuniversteit te Leiden, Theologisch Instituut, Postbus 9515, 2300 RA Leiden, Netherlands 071-272579; (h) Zeemanlaan 47, 2313 SW Leiden, Netherlands 071-141720.

DE KRUIJF, Theo C., b. Frankfurt/Main, Germany, April 6, 1928, s. of Dirk & Elisabeth (Franz). Educ: Archdiocese of Utrecht, Ord. 1954; Athenaeum Pont. Angelicum, Rome, LTh 1955; Pont. Bibl. Inst., Rome, Rerum Biblicarum Lic. 1958, Rerum Biblicarum Dr. 1960. Emp: Major Sem. of the Archdiocese of Utrecht, 1961-67 Prof., Bibl. Exegesis; Cath. Theol. U., Utrecht, 1967- Prof., NT; *Bijdragen*, 1969- Ed. Bd. Spec: New Testament. Pub: "Der Olbaum und seine Frucht" *Bijdragen* 51 (1990); "The Literary Unity of Rom 12:16-13:8a" *Bijdragen* 48 (1987); *De Brief van Paulus aan de Romeinen* (KBS, 1985); "Is Anybody Better Off? (Rom 3:9)" *Bijdragen* 46 (1985); "More than a Hundredweight of Spices (Jo 19:39)" *Bijdragen* 43 (1982); "The Perspective of Romans VII" *Miscellania Neotestamentica* 2 (1978); *Der Sohn des lebendigen Gottes*, Analecta Biblica 16 (1962); and others. Mem: SNTS 1972-. Rec: Music, travelling, chess. Addr: (o) Katholieke Theologische U., Transitorium II, Heidelberglaan 2, 3582 CS Utrecht, Netherlands; (h) Comeniuslaan 13, 3706 XA Zeist, Netherlands 03404-59449.

DE LAMOTTE, Roy C., b. LeCompte, LA, December 10, 1917, s. of Octave & Caroline (Jones), m. Araminta (Harper), chil: Eugenia; Rebecca. Educ: Emory U., BD 1950; Yale U., PhD 1953. Emp: 1951-61 Meth. Min.; Paine Coll., 1961- Prof., Phil. & Relig. Spec: New Testament, Apocrypha and Post-biblical Studies. Pub: *The Alien Christ* (U. Press of Amer., 1980);

and others. Mem: SBL. Rec: Photography, carpentry, theater. Addr: (h) 3325 Tanglewood Dr., Augusta, GA 30909 706-736-5506.

DE VILLIERS, Pieter G. R., b. Venterstad, s. of Pieter & Judith, m. Susan, chil: Elizabeth; Elsje; Judith. Educ: U. of Stellenbosch, BA 1966, BTH 1969, Lic. Theol. 1974, DTh 1976; U. of Kampen, Doc. Sacred Theol. 1973. Emp: U. of Stellenbosch, 1971-84 Sr. Lect.; U. of South Africa, 1984-88 Prof., 1989- Rhodes U. Prof. Spec: New Testament. Pub: "Postmodernism and the New Testament" *Neotestamentica* 25 (1991); "The Medium is the Message: Luke and the Language of the New Testament Against a Graeco-Roman Background" *Neotestamentica* 24 (1990); "New Testament Scholarship in South Africa" *Neotestamentica* 23 (1989); *Reading Revelation*, co-auth. (Van Schaik, 1988); *Leviatan aan 'n lintjie: Woord en Wêreld van die Sieners* (Serva, 1987); "The Interpretation of a Text in the Light of Its Sociocultural Setting" *Neotestamentica* 18 (1984); and others. Awd: Human Sci. Res. Coun., 1980, 1987, 1991 res. awd. Mem: NT Soc. of South Africa; SNTS; AAR; SBL; OT Soc. of South Africa. Rec: Squash. Addr: (o) Rhodes U., Divinity Dept., Grahamstown 6140, South Africa 0461-22023; (h) 14 Kota Inten, Grahamstown 6140, South Africa 0461-311228.

DE VRIES, Simon J., b. Denver, CO, December 20, 1921, s. of Peter & Katherine, m. Betty (Schouten), chil: Judith; Garry. Educ: Calvin Theol. Sem., ThB 1949; Union Theol. Sem., STM 1950, ThD 1958. Emp: 1950-61 Pastoral Min.; Drew U. Theol. Sch., 1957-58 Instr., OT; Western Theol. Sem., 1961-62 Assoc. Prof., Relig.; Hope Coll., 1961-62 Instr., Hebrew; Meth. Theol. Sch. in Ohio, 1962- Prof., OT. Spec: Hebrew Bible. Pub: *1-2 Chronicles*, Forms of the OT Lit. XI (1986); *1 Kings*, Word Bibl. Comm. 12 (1985); and others. Awd:, Fulbright Grant 1956-57. Mem: SBL; ASOR; WUJS. Rec: Photography, camping. Addr: (o) Methodist Theological School in Ohio, Delaware, OH 43015 614-363-1146; (h) 35 Darlington Rd., Delaware, OH 43015 614-363-1433.

DE WAARD, Jan, b. Sommelsdijk, April 24, 1931, s. of Cornelis & Wilhelmina (Boekhoven), m. Tine (Kiel), chil: Janine; Emma; Michiel; Jean-Marc. Educ: U. of Leiden, Holland, ThD 1957, PhD 1965. Emp: Teacher's Training Coll., Dokkum, 1959-64 Prof., Geog. & Arch. of the Near East; United. Bible Soc. for French Speaking Cen. Africa, 1966-72 Trans. Cons., United Bible Soc. for Europe, 1972-75 Trans. Cons., 1975-92 Trans. Coord.; *BT*, 1974-76 Ed.; U. of Strasbourg, France, 1983- Prof., Sci. of Trans.; Free U. of Amsterdam, Netherlands, 1988- Prof., Sci. of Trans. Spec: Hebrew Bible, New Testament. Pub: *A Translator's Handbook on Ruth*, co-auth. (United Bible Soc., 1973, 1992); *From One Language to Another*, co-auth. (Thomas Nelson, 1986); *A Translator's*

Handbook on Amos, co-auth. (United Bible Soc., 1979); *A Comparative Study of the Old Testament Text in the Dead Sea Scroll and in the New Testament* (Brill, 1965, 1966); and others. Mem: United Bible Soc. 1978-; IOSCS; Linguistic Soc. of Amer. Rec: Skiing, chess. Addr: (h) L'Estagnol, 84760 St. Martin de la Brasque, France 33-90776312.

DEARMAN, John A., b. Columbia, SC, December 6, 1951, s. of John & Barbara (Wright), m. Kathleen, chil: John W.; James R.; Giles W. Educ: Princeton Theol. Sem., MDiv 1977; Emory U., PhD 1981. Emp: La. State U., 1981-82 Asst. Prof.; Austin Presbyn. Theol. Sem., 1982- Assoc. Prof. Excv: Cen. Moab Survey, Jordan, 1979, 1982; Khirbet Iskander, Jordan, 1982, 1984. Spec: Archaeology, Hebrew Bible, Semitic Languages, Texts and Epigraphy. Pub: *Religion and Culture in Ancient Israel* (Hendrickson, 1992); *Studies in the Mesha Inscription and Moab* (Scholars, 1989); *Property Rights in the Eighth Century Prophets: The Conflict and Its Background* (Scholars, 1988); "The Location of Jahaz" *ZDPV* 100 (1984); "Prophecy, Property and Politics" *SBL Seminar Papers* (1984); "The Melqart Stele and the Ben Hadads of Damascus" *PEQ* 115 (1983); "Hebrew Prophecy and Social Criticism: Some Observations for Perspective" *Perspectives in Relig. Stud.* 9/2 (1982); and others. Awd: Dorot Found. Grant. Mem: SBL; ASOR. Addr: (o) 100 E 27th St., Austin, TX 78705 512-472-6736; (h) 117 Crestview Dr., Austin, TX 78734 512-261-3782.

DEER, Donald S., b. Terre Haute, IN, October 24, 1929, s. of Roy Burton & Emilie (Spencer), m. Barbara (Sloat), chil: Ruth Emily; Marie Frances. Educ: Colgate Rochester Div. Sch., BD 1955; Hartford Sem. Found., STM 1966; U. de Strasbourg, France, Doc. sci. relig. 1973. Emp: 1962-73 Exegete & Coord. for trans. of NT into Kituba; Zaire Protestant Sem., 1974-81, 1983-87 Prof., NT; Colgate Roch. Div. Sch., 1981-82 Vis. Prof.; Amer. Bapt. Sem. of West, 1989 Vis. Prof.; Va. Union U., Sch. of Theol., 1989- Asst. Prof., Bibl. Stud. Spec: New Testament. Pub: "Getting the 'story' Straight in Acts 20.9" *BT* 39 (1988); "Unity and Diversity in the New Testament" *Bull. de théol. africaine* 7 (1985); "La traduction de la Bible par Luther et l'art de traduire selon Luther" *Bull. de théol. africaine* 6 (1984); "Notes on the Translation of Revelation, Chapter 22, into Kituba" *BT* 24 (1973); *A Translator's Handbook on the Gospel of Luke*, contb. (1971). Awd: Denison U., Alumni Citation 1981. Mem: SBL; SNTS. Rec: Cello, singing. Addr: (h) 5904 Brookfield Rd., Richmond, VA 23227.

DEL AGUA, Agustin, b. Becilla de Valderaduey, September 12, 1947, s. of Leopoldo & Sara. Educ: Pont. Bibl. Inst., Rome, Lic. Holy Scriptures 1974; U. Pont. Comillas of Madrid, Dr. Bibl. Theol. 1979; U. Complutense of Madrid, Dr. Bibl. Philol. 1984. Emp: *EstBib*, 1975-85 Ed. Bd.; Colegio U. San Pablo C.E.U., 1987- Prof., Theol. Spec: New

Testament, Apocrypha and Post-biblical Studies. Pub: "Die 'Erzahlung' des Evangeliums im Lichte der Derasch Methode" *Judaica* 47 (1991); *El metodo midrásico y la exégesis del Nuevo Testamento*, Biblioteca Midrásica 4 (1985); *Evangelizar el Reino de Dios* (1984); "El derás cristológico" *Scripta Theol.* 14 (1982); "DerEas lucano de Mc 13 a la luz de su 'Teologia del Reino': Lc 21,5-36" *EstBib* 39 (1981); "El cumplimiento del Reino de Dios en la misión de Jesus: Programa del Evangelio de Lucas (Lc 4,14-44)" *EstBib* 38 (1979/80); and others. Mem: Spanish Bibl. Soc. 1975-; SNTS 1988-. Addr: (o) Universidad San Pablo C.E.U., c/ Julián Romea 23, 28003 Madrid, Spain 91-5-36-02-85; (h) Avda. Dr Federico Rubio y Gali 57, 28040 Madrid, Spain 91 4-50-78-53

DEL OLMO LETE, Gregorio, b. Aranda de Duero, Spain, April 17, 1935, s. of Manuel & Celedonia, m. Isabel. Educ: Salamanca U., ThD 1969; Madrid U., Doc. Semitic Philol. 1972. Emp: Salamanca U., 1970-75 Assoc. Prof.; Barcelona U., 1975- Prof., Hebrew Lang., 1985-90 Chmn., Dept. of Hebrew & Aramaic Stud.; *Aula Orientalis*, 1988- Ed. Spec: Semitic Languages, Texts and Epigraphy. Pub: *La religión cananea según la liturgia de Ugarit. Estudio textual* (Ausa, 1992); *Interpretación de la mitologia cananea. Estudios de Semántica ugaritica* (Inst. San Jeronimo, 1984); *Mitos y Leyendas de Canaan según la tradición de Ugarit* (Cristiandad, 1981); and others. Mem: Assn. Espanola de Orientalistas; WUJS; European Assn. for Jewish Stud. Addr: (o) U. de Barcelona, Facultad de Filologia, 08007 Barcelona, Spain 317-23-80; (h) Tarragona 114 30 1a, 08015 Barcelona, Spain 2-26-80-73.

DELLER, Walter W. G., b. Hamiota, Man., Canada, June 30, 1954, s. of William & May (Turnbull). Educ: Toronto Sch. of Theol., MDiv 1982, ThD 1989. Emp: Toronto Sch. Theol., Regis Coll., 1985, 1987-88 Sessional Lect.; Henry Budd Coll. for Min., Canada, 1990 Acting Dir.; Logos Inst., Diocese of Toronto, 1991- Coord. Spec: Hebrew Bible. Pub: *Suffering and Vision: The Book of Job* (Logos Inst., 1991); *The Beginning of the Good News: A Study of Mark's Gospel* (Logos Inst., 1988); and others. Mem: CSBS 1988-; SBL 1990-. Rec: Music, food, wine. Addr: (o) The Logos Institute, Anglican Diocese, 135 Adelaide St. E, Toronto, ON, Canada 416-363-6021; (h) 867 Dovercourt Rd., Toronto, ON MGH 2X4, Canada 416-537-9383.

DELORME, Jean, b. Vulbens, France, June 17, 1920, s. of Louis & Celine (Mathieu). Educ: Petit Sem. de Thonon, Baccalaureat 1939; U. of Lyon, Fac. of Theol., ThD 1948; Bibl. Inst., Rome, Lic. in Scriptura 1951; Ecole Biblique, Dip. Arch. 1952. Emp: U. of Lyon, Fac. of Theol., 1960-78 Charge de cours; Ctr. pour l'Analyse du Discourse Relig., 1975-91 Prof., 1978-92 Prof., NT Exegesis; *Semiotique et Bible*, 1975- Dir.; *NTS*, 1978-81 Ed. Bd. Spec: New Testament. Pub: "Semiotique" *Dict. de la Bible, Sup.* 12/67 (1993); *Les Paraboles évangéliques: Perspectives Nouvelles*, ed. (Cerf, 1989); "Salut dans les évangiles synoptiques et les Actes des Apôtres" *Dict. de la Bible, Sup.* 11/62 (1988); *Parole—Figure—Parabole: Recherches autour du discours parabolique*, ed. (Presses universitaires de Lyon, 1987); *Signes et paraboles: Sémiotique et texte évangélique, ed. (Seuil, 1977); Lecture de l'Evangile selon saint Marc* (Cerf, 1972); and others. Awd: U. of Tilburg, Dr. 1987; U. of Lausanne, Dr. 1992. Mem: Assn. Catholique Francaise pour l'Etude de la Bible 1966-; SNTS 1973-. Addr: (o) U. Catholique, CADIR, 25, rue du Plat, 69288 Lyon Cedex 02, France 72-32-50-30; (h) 31, rue JJ Rousseau, 74000 Annecy, France 50-45-39-15.

DEMING, Willoughby H., b. Washington, DC, April 5, 1956, s. of Andrew S. & Maidee Elizabeth (Coffman), m. Lauren Lewis (Wellford). Educ: Coll. of William & Mary, BA 1978; U. of Chicago, MA 1979, PhD 1991. Emp: Rhodes Coll., 1989-90 Instr.; Memphis State U., 1991 Asst. Prof.; U. of Portland, 1992- Asst. Prof. Spec: New Testament. Pub: "Mark 9:42-10:12, Matt 5:27-32, and *b. Nid.* 13b: A First Century Discussion of Male Sexuality" *NTS* 36 (1990). Mem: SBL; AAR. Addr: (o) U. of Portland, 5000 N Willamette Blvd., Portland, OR 97203-5798 503-283-7274.

DEMPSTER, Stephen G., b. Simcoe, ON, Canada, September 20, 1952, s. of Samuel & Mary, m. Judy, chil: Jessica; Joanna; Nathan; Michael. Educ: Westminster Theol. Sem., MAR 1977, MTh 1979; U. of Toronto, MA 1980, PhD 1985. Emp: U. of Toronto, 1979-82 Res. Asst., 1980-82 Hebrew Instr.; Atlantic Bapt. Coll., 1974 Lect., 1985- Asst. Prof. Bibl. Stud., 1991- Assoc. Prof., Relig. Stud.; Cen. Bapt. Sem., Canada, 1983- Hebrew Instr. Spec: Hebrew Bible, Mesopotamian Studies, Semitic Languages, Texts and Epigraphy. Pub: "The Lord is His Name: A Study of the Distribution of the Names and Titles of God in the Book of Amos" *RB* (1991); "The Deuteronomic Formula *Ki yimmāsē'* in the Light of Ancient Near Eastern and Biblical Law" *RB* (1984); "Mythology and History in the Song of Deborah" *Westminster Theol. Jour.* (1978); articles in *ABD, Evangelical Dict. of Biblical Theology*; and others. Mem: CSBS 1983-; SBL 1986-; NAPH 1989-. Rec: Sports. Addr: (o) Atlantic Baptist College, Box 1004, Moncton, NB, Canada 858-8970; (h) 27 Pasadena Dr., Moncton, NB E16 1H7, Canada 384-1533.

DEMSKY, Aaron, b. Brooklyn, NY, December 23, 1938, s. of Solomon & Sadie (Meschkow), m. Rosalind, chil: Elisheva; Yonatan; Noam; Miri; Shlomit; Seraya; Ariel. Educ: Columbia U., BS 1961, MA 1965; Jewish Theol. Sem. of Amer., BRE 1961, MHL 1963; Hebrew U., PhD 1977. Emp: Bar Ilan U., 1968- Assoc. Prof. Excv: Tel Shiloh, 1981-84 Epigraphist, Adv. Spec: Archaeology, Hebrew Bible, Mesopotamian Studies, Semitic Languages, Texts and Epigraphy, Apocrypha and Post-biblical Studies. Pub: "From Kezib to the River Near Amanah (Mish. Shebi'it

6:1)" *Shnaton* 10 (1990); "The Education of Canaanite Scribes in the Mesopotamian Cuneiform Tradition" *Assyriological Stud.* (1990); "Writing in Ancient Israel and Early Judaism" in *Compendia Rerum Iudaicarum ad Novum Testamentum*, sect. II, vol. 1 (1988); "The Clans of Ephrath: Their Territory and History" *Tel Aviv* 13 (1986); "On the Extent of Literacy in Ancient Israel" in *Biblical Archaeology Today* (1985). Awd: NEH, grant 1978; Jewish Theol. Sem. of Amer., Louis Ginzberg Fellow 1985, DHL 1991. Addr: (o) Bar Ilan U., Dept. of Jewish History, Ramat Gan 52900, Israel 03-5318353; (h) 3 Rimmon St., Efrat 90962, Israel 02-931878.

DEN EXTER BLOKLAND, Albert F., b. Hilversum, The Netherlands, July 28, 1949, s. of Adriaan Willem & Dingena (de Cock), m. Vicki L. (Bawsel), chil: Rebecca Ann; Elisabeth Adriana. Educ: Erasmus U., Rotterdam, Propaedeutisch Examen 1971; Trinity Evang. Div. Sch., MDiv 1985, ThM, OT 1988; Free U., Amsterdam, Doc. Examen Theol. 1990. Emp: Campus Crusade for Christ, The Netherlands, 1973-82 Dir., Sch. for Evang. & Discipleship. Spec: Hebrew Bible. Pub: "Clause Analysis in Biblical Hebrew Narrative: An Explanation and a Manual for Compilation" *Trinity Jour.* 11 (1990). Mem: ETS 1988-; SBL 1989-. Rec: Music, antique cars, woodworking, gardening. Addr: (h) 310 Channel Dr., Island Lake, IL 60042 708-526-1223.

DENIS, Albert-Marie, b. London, England, October 16, 1915, s. of Georges-Ernest & Berthe (Duquenne). Educ: U. Liege, Cand., Class Phil.; Commn. Biblique Vatican, Dr. Emp: Studium Phil. & Theol. of the Dominicans, La Sarte, 1947-65 Prof., Bibl. Exegesis; U.C.L., 1965- Lect. Pub: *Concordance grecque des pseudépigraphes d'Ancien Testament* (1987); *Introduction aux pseudépigraphes grecs d'Ancien Testament* (1970); *Les themes de connaissance dans le Document de Damas* (1967). Addr: (o) College Erasme, B-1348 Louvain-la-Neuve, Belgium 016-240181; (h) Klooster der Dominikanen, 112 Ravenstraat, B-3000 Leuven, Belgium 016-240181.

DENNISON, William D., b. Pittsburgh, PA, November 13, 1949, s. of James T. & Elizabeth, m. Patricia Ann, chil: William David II; Atria Ann; Ami Lynd. Educ: Geneva Coll., BA, Bible & Phil. 1973; Westminster Theol. Sem., MDiv 1976, ThM, Apologetics 1980; Mich. State U., ABD 1986, PhD, Theol., Phil. 1992. Emp: Calvin Christian High Sch., 1977-90, 1991-93 Head of Bible Dept.; Calvin Coll., 1988, 1990-92 Asst. Prof.; Covenant Coll., 1993- Assoc. Prof., Interdisciplinary Stud. Spec: New Testament. Pub: *Paul's Two-Age Construction and Apologetics* (U. Press of Amer., 1985); "Indicative and Imperative: The Basic Structure of Pauline Ethics" *Calvin Theol. Jour.* 14 (1979); "Miracles as 'Signs': Their Significance for Apologetics" *BTB* 6 (1976);

and others. Mem: AAR; SBL; ETS; Intl. Christian Stud. Assn.; Amer. Phil. Assn. Rec: Sports, film criticism. Addr: (o) Covenant College, 1500 Scenic Highway, Lookout Mountain, GA 30750 706-820-1560.

DENTAN, Robert C., b. Rossville, IN, November 27, 1907, s. of Claude & Maud (Parry), m. Dealome (Knox), chil: Robert. Educ: Berkeley Div. Sch., BD 1932, STD 1954. Emp: Berkeley Div. Sch., 1943-54 Prof.; *JBL,* 1949-54 Ed; ASOR, 1956-57 Dir.; Gen. Theol. Sem., 1964-73 Prof., OT, 1973- Prof. Emeritus. Excv: El Jib, 1956 Area Supr. Spec: Archaeology, Hebrew Bible, Apocrypha and Post-biblical Studies. Pub: "The Literary Affinities of Exodus XXXIV, 6f" *VT* (1963); *The Knowledge of God in Ancient Israel* (Seabury, 1968); *The Apocrypha, Bridge of the Testaments* (Seabury, 1954); *Preface to Old Testament Theology* (Yale U.P., 1950); articles in *Interpreter's Bible, IDB, Interpreter's 1-Vol. Bible Comm.;* and others. Mem: SBL 1937-; AOS 1943-73; AAR 1943-73. Rec: Travel, music, English lit. Addr: (h) 318 Beard Ave., Buffalo, NY 14214 212-716-8176.

DENYER, David A., b. Colville, WA, October 27, 1933, s. of Charles & Hannah, m. Dorothy, chil: Debra; Donna; Douglas. Educ: Simpson Coll., BA 1955; Wheaton Coll., BA 1958; Golden Gate Bapt. Theol. Sem., MDiv 1968; South. Bapt. Theol. Sem., PhD 1976. Emp: Simpson Coll., 1962-72 Assoc. Prof., OT; Columbia Bible Coll., 1976-77 Prof., OT; Alliance Theol. Sem., 1977- Prof., OT & Arch. Excv: Ai, Israel, 1974 Staff. Spec: Archaeology. Pub: *A Reconstruction of the Religion at Ai and Raddana in the Period of the Hebrew Settlement* (U. Microfilms, 1976). Mem: ASOR; SBL; IES; Rec: Sports. Addr: (o) Alliance Theological Seminary, Nyack, NY 10960 914-634-7429; (h) 25 Short Hill Rd., New City, NY 10956.

DEROCHE, Michael P., b. Medicine Hat, AB, Canada, January 19, 1955, s. of Leonard & Alice, m. Teresa. Educ: U. Laval, MTh 1979; McMaster U., MA 1979, PhD 1986. Emp: McMaster U., 1984-85 Lect.; U. of Calgary, 1985- Asst. Prof., Post-doc. Fellow. Spec: Hebrew Bible. Pub: "Isaiah XLV 7 and the Creation of Chaos?" *VT* 42 (1992); "Structure, Rhetoric and Meaning in Hos IV 4-10" *VT* 33 (1983); "Jeremiah 2:2-3 and Israel's Love for God During the Wilderness Wanderings" *CBQ* 45 (1983); "Yahweh's Rib Against Israel: A Reassessment of the So-Called Prophetic Lawsuit in the Pre-Exilic Prophets" *JBL* 102 (1983); and others. Mem: SBL; CBA; CSBS. Addr: (o) U. of Calgary, Dept. of Religious Studies, Calgary, AB T2N 1N4, Canada 403-220-5886.

DERRETT, John D. M., b. London, England, August 30, 1922, s. of John & Fay (Martin), m. Margaret E., chil: Elizabeth; Paul; Christopher; Robin; Jonathan. Educ: Oxford U., Jesus Coll., BA

1945, MA 1947; London U., Sch. of Oriental & African Stud., PhD 1949. Emp: London U., Sch. of Oriental & African Stud., 1949-82 Prof., Oriental Laws; Oxford U., 1979-81 Wilde Lect. Spec: New Testament. Pub: *The Victim: Johannine Passion Narrative* (Drinkwater, 1993); *Studies in the New Testament*, 5 vol. (Brill, 1977-89); "Recht und Religion im Neuen Testament (bis zum Jahr 135)" in *Max Webers Sicht des antiken Christentums* (Suhrkamp, 1985); *The Anastasis* (Drinkwater, 1985); *The Making of Mark* (Drinkwater, 1985); "Law and Society in Jesus' World" *ANRW* 25 (1982); *Law in the New Testament* (Darton, Longman & Todd, 1970); and others. Awd: London U., DD 1983. Mem: SNTS 1971-. Addr: (h) Half Way House, High St. Blockley, Moreton in Marsh, Gloucester GL56 9EX, England.

DEVER, William G., b. Louisville, KY, November 27, 1933, s. of Lonnie Earl & Claudine (Watts), m. Pamela J. (Gaber), chil: Sean William; Jordana Lee Saletan; Hannah Susan Saletan; Evan Jacob. Educ: Milligan Coll., BA, Relig. 1955; Butler U., MA, Semitics (summa cum laude) 1959; Christian Theol. Sem., BD, Hebrew & Greek 1959; Harvard U., PhD, Syro-Palestinian Arch. 1966. Emp: Nelson Glueck Sch. of Bibl. Arch., Jerusalem, 1964-67 Exec. Officer, 1968-71 Dir.; W.F. Albright Inst. of Arch. Res., Jerusalem, 1971-75 Dir., 1973-75 Prof.; Hebrew U., Jerusalem, 1973-75 Assoc. Prof., Arch., 1981-82 Vis. Prof.; U. of Ariz., 1975- Prof., Near East. Arch. & Anthrop.; *AASOR,* 1984- Ed.; *ABD,* 1991-93 Prin. Ed. Adv. Excv: Kh. el-Kom, Jebel Qaaqir, 1967-71 Dir.; Gezer, 1966-71 Dir., 1972-74 Sr. Adv., 1984, 1990 Dir.; Cen. Negev Highlands Project, 1978-80 Co-dir.; Tell el-Hayyat, 1981-85 Prin. Investigator; Tel Wawiyat Reg. Project, 1986 Prin. Investigator. Spec: Archaeology. Pub: *The 1953 Jordan Valley Survey: Some Unpublished Soundings conducted by James Mellaart,* ed. (1991); "Tell ed-Daba and Levantine Middle Bronze Age Chronology" *BASOR* 281 (1991); "The End of the Middle Bronze Age in Palestine: A Reply to J.K. Hoffmeier" *Levant* 22 (1990); "Of Myths and Methods" *BASOR* 277/278 (1990); *Recent Archaeological Discoveries and Biblical Research* (Washington U.P., 1990); *Recent Excavations in Israel: Studies in Iron Age Archaeology, AASOR* 49, co-ed. (ASOR, 1989); "Yigael Yadin: Prototypical Biblical Archaeologist" *Eretz-Israel* 20 (1989); "Palestine in the Middle Bronze Age: The Zenith of the Urban Canaanite Era" *BA* 50 (1987); and others. Awd: Harvard U., Robert H. Pfeiffer Travelling Fellow 1962, 1964-65; Israel Mus., Percia Schimmel Prize 1982; Guggenheim Memorial Fellow 1981-82. Mem: ASOR, V.P. 1982-88; AIA; AOS; IES; SBL. Rec: Music, sailing, cabinetmaking. Addr: (o) U. of Arizona, Dept. of Near Eastern Studies, Franklin Bldg., Tucson, AZ 85721 602-621-8012; (h) 2302 E Mitchell, Tucson, AZ 85719 602-327-4521.

DEXINGER, Ferdinand, b. Vienna, Austria, April 24, 1937, s. of Ferdinand & Valerie, m.

Siglinde, chil: Johanna. Educ: U. of Vienna, Dr. Theol. Stud. 1964, Dr. Judaic Stud. 1974. Emp: U. of Vienna, 1966- Prof., Hist. of Jewish Relig. Spec: Apocrypha and Post-biblical Studies. Pub: *Die Samaritaner,* co-auth. (Darmstadt, 1992); *Als die Heiden Christen wurden,* co-auth. (1992); "Samaritan Eschatology" in *The Samaritans* (1988); *Der Taheb* (1986); *Jordanien,* co-auth. (1985); "Der Profet wie Mose in Qumran und bei den Samaritanern" in *Festschrift M. Delcor,* AOAT 215 (1985); "Limits of Tolerance in Judaism: The Samaritan Example" in *Jewish Christian Self Definition II* (Sanders, 1981); "A Hebrew Lead Seal from the Period of Sassanian Occupation of Palestine (614-629 A.D.)," co-auth., *Rev. des etudes juives* 40 (1981); and others. Mem: WUJS. Addr: (o) Institut fuer Judaistik der U. Wien, Ferstelgasse 6/12, A-1090 Wien, Austria 40103-2502; (h) Landstr.-Hauptstr., 33A/12, A-1030 Wien, Austria.

DI LELLA, Alexander A., b. Paterson, NJ, August 14, 1929, s. of Alessandro & Adelaide (Grimaldi). Educ: St. Bonaventure U., BA 1953; Cath. U., STL 1959, PhD 1962; Pont. Bibl. Inst., Rome, SSL 1964. Emp: Holy Name Coll., 1964-69 Lect., OT; Cath. U., 1966-76 Assoc. Prof., Semitic Lang., 1976- Prof., Bibl. Stud.; *CBQ,* 1966-92 Assoc. Ed.; *Theol. Bull.,* 1968-72 Ed.; Washington Theol. Union, 1969-72 Adj. Prof., OT; *OT Abstracts,* 1978- Assoc. Ed. Excv: Araq el-Emir, 1962 Field Supr.; Wadi Daliyeh, 1963 Field Supr. Spec: Hebrew Bible, Semitic Languages, Texts and Epigraphy, Apocrypha and Post-biblical Studies. Pub: "The Structure and Composition of the Matthean Beatitudes" in *To Touch the Text: Biblical and Related Studies in Honor of Joseph A. Fitzmyer, S.J.* (Crossroad, 1989); "The Newly Discovered Sixth Manuscript of Ben Sira from the Cairo Geniza" *Biblica* 69 (1988); *The Wisdom of Ben Sira,* AB vol. 39 (Doubleday, 1987); "Sirach 51:1-12: Poetic Structure and Analysis of Ben Sira's Psalm" *CBQ* 48 (1986); "Genesis 1:1-10: A Formal Introduction to P's Creation Account" *Alter Orient und Altes Testament* 215 (1985); "Sirach 10:19-11:6: Textual Criticism, Poetic Analysis, and Exegesis" in *The Word of the Lord Shall Go Forth: Essays in Honor of David Noel Freedman in Celebration of His Sixtieth Birthday* (ASOR/Eisenbrauns, 1983); "Daniel 4:7-14: Poetic Analysis and Biblical Background" *Alter Orient und Altes Testament* 212 (1981); *Proverbs, in The Old Testament in Syriac According to the Peshitta Version,* Part II, fasc. 3 (Brill, 1979); *The Book of Daniel,* AB vol. 23 (Doubleday, 1978); and others. Awd: ASOR, Jerusalem, Fellow 1962-63; Guggengeim Fellow 1972-73; Assn. of Theol. Sch. in the US & Canada, Fellow. 1979-80. Mem: CBA; SBL; RSV Bible Com. Rec: Bird-watching, astronomy, photography. Addr: (o) Catholic U., 420 Caldwell, Washington, DC 20064 202-319-5867; (h) Catholic U., Curley Hall, Washington, DC 20064 202-319-5657.

DI MARCO, Angelico Salvatore, b. Linguaglossa, Italy, January 2, 1929, s. of

Antonino & Rosa-Giuseppa (Vecchio). Educ: Pont. Bibl. Inst., Rome, Lic. Sci. Bibl. 1959; Pont. U. Gregoriana, Rome, ThD 1974. Emp: Theol. Inst. of Messina, Italy, 1955- Prof., Bibl. Hebrew & NT Greek. Pub: "La recezione del Nuovo Testamento nei padri apostolici" *ANRW* 27/1 (1993); "Ipsissima verba Jesu: Mc 1:45-Risvolti Linguistici ed ermeneutici" in *Salvezza Cristiana e Cultura Odierne* (1984); "Ef 5:21-6:9: Teologia della Famiglia" *RB* 31 (1983); "Dikaiosyne-Dikaioma-Dikaiosis in Rm: Linguistica ed esegesi" *Laurentianum* 23 (1983); *Il "perfetto" nei vangeli* (1981); *Il chiasmo nella Bibbia-Contributi di stilistica strutturale* (1980). Mem: Assn. Bibl. Italiana 1960-; SBL1982-; SNTS 1985-; Soc. Linguistica Italiana 1986-. Addr: (h) Viale Regina Margherita 25, I-98121 Messina, Italy 41986.

DICKINSON, Charles C., III, b. Charleston, WV, May 13, 1936, s. of Charles Cameron, Jr., & Frances Ann (Saunders), m. JoAnne (Walton), chil: Richard Essex Perigrene Eaton; John Walton Tristram Eaton; Edward Valentine Hollingsworth Eaton. Educ: Dartmouth College, BA 1958; Pittsburgh Theol. Sem., BD 1965; U. of Pittsburgh, PhD 1973. Emp: Union Theol. Sem., Va., 1974-75 Vis. Prof.; Morris Harvey Coll., 1975-79 Asst. Prof., Dir. of Hon. Prog.; Amer. Coll. of Rome, 1979 Prof.; U. of Charleston, 1980-81 Res. Prof.; Hebei Teachers' U., China, 1983-84 Prof. Spec: New Testament, Apocrypha and Post-biblical Studies. Pub: "What is Myth?" *Encounter* Spring (1982); "A Passus in Christology" *Encounter* Summer (1982); *Pre-existence, Resurrection, and Recapitulation: An Examination of the Pre-existence of Christ in Karl Barth, Wolfhart Pannenberg, and the New Testament* (Xerox U. Microfilms, 1974); and others. Awd: Chicago Theol. Sem., Entrance Fellow. 1962. Mem: Royal Soc. of Arts, Fellow.; Amer. Phil. Assn.; AAR; SBL; ASOR. Rec: Theology, linguistics, humanities, travel. Addr: (o) 1111 City National Bldg., Wichita Falls, TX 76301-3309 817-322-5941; (h) 2100 Sante Fe, Apt. 903, Wichita Falls, TX 76309 817-767-3187.

DILLARD, Raymond B., b. Louisville, KY, January 7, 1944, s. of Raymond E. & Ruth (Wallace), m. Ann A., chil: Joel Bryan; Jonathan Bruce; Joshua Albrecht. Educ: Bob Jones U., BA 1966; Westminster Theol. Sem., BD 1969; Dropsie U., PhD 1975. Emp: Westminster Theol. Sem., 1971-86 Prof., OT; Myerstown Evang. Sch. of Theol., 1980 Vis. Prof.; Gordon-Conwell Sem., 1980 Vis. Prof.; Winnipeg Theol. Sem., 1986 Vis. Prof. Spec: Hebrew Bible, Mesopotamian Studies, Semitic Languages, Texts and Epigraphy. Pub: *2 Chronicles*, Word Bibl. Comm. 15; "Reward and Punishment in Chronicles: The Theology of Immediate Retribution" *Westminster Theol. Jour.* 46 (1984); "The Literary Structure of the Chronicler's Solomon Narrative" *JSOT* 30 (1984); "The Chronicler's Solomon" *Westminster Theol. Jour.* 43 (1980); "The Reign of Asa: An Example of the Chronicler's Theological Method" *JETS* 23 (1980); and others. Mem: SBL; NAPH; IBR.

Rec: Computers, cabinetmaking, bow hunting. Addr: (o) Westminster Theological Seminary, Chestnut Hill, Philadelphia, PA 19118 215-887-5511; (h) 2001 Limekiln Pike, Dresher, PA 19025 215-643-2889.

DILLENBERGER, Jane Daggett, b. Hartford, WI, February 27, 1916, d. of John & Blanche (Morris), chil: Patricia; Christopher. Educ: U. of Chicago, BA 1940; Radcliffe Coll., MA 1944. Emp: San Francisco Theol. Sem., 1963-71 Assoc. Prof., Christianity & the Arts; Grad. Theol. Union, 1967- Prof., Theol. & Visual Arts, 1978- Prof. Emerita; Stud. in Hum. Ser., Ed. Pub: "The Magdalen: Reflections on the Images of the Saint and Sinner in Christian Art" in *Women, Religion and Social Change* (State U. of N.Y., 1985); "Images of God in Western Art" *BR* 1/2 (1985); "George Segal's Abraham and Isaac: Some Iconographic Reflections" in *Art Creativity and the Sacred* (Crossroad, 1984); *Style and Content in Christian Art* (Abingdon, 1965; Crossroad, 1986); and others. Mem: AAR. Addr: (h) 1536 LeRoy Ave., Berkeley, CA 94708 510-848-7487.

DIMANT, Devorah, b. Jerusalem, Israel, June 4, 1939, d. of Itzhak & Batiah. Educ: Hebrew U., Jerusalem, BA 1963, MA 1967, PhD 1974. Emp: U. of Haifa, Israel, 1974- Assoc. Prof.; U. de Lille III, France, 1982-83 Vis. Prof. Spec: Apocrypha and Post-biblical Studies. Pub: "The Merkabah Vision in Second Ezekiel (4Q385 4)" *RQ* 14 (1990); "Use and Interpretation of Mikra in the Apocrypha and Pseudepigrapha" *Mikra* (1988); "4Q Second Ezekiel (4Q385)," co-auth. *RQ* 13 (1988); "Qumran Sectarian Literature" in *Jewish Writings of the Second Temple Period* (1984); "The Biography of Enoch and the Books of Enoch" *VT* 33 (1983). Mem: SBL; IOSCS. Addr: (o) Haifa U., Dept. of Biblical Studies, Haifa 31999, Israel 04-240187; (h) Brener 8, Haifa, Israel 04-223288.

DION, Paul E., b. Québec, Canada, September 28, 1934, s. of J. Omer & Cécile (Rouleau), m. Michéle (Daviau). Educ: Sém. de Québec, BA 1953; U. of Ottawa, Canada, Lic. Th. 1961; Ecole Biblique, Jerusalem, Lic. SS 1963; U. of Toronto, PhD, Near East. Stud. 1973. Emp: Coll. Dominicain, Canada, 1964-80 Prof.; U. of Toronto, 1980-93 Prof. Spec: Hebrew Bible, Semitic Languages, Texts and Epigraphy. Pub: "Les KTYM de Tel Arad: Grecs ou Phoniciens?" *RB* 99 (1992); "YHWH as Storm-God and Sun-God" *ZAW* 103 (1991); "The Suppression of Alien Religious Propaganda" in JSOTSup 124 (1991); "La Lettre araméenne passe-partout et ses sous-espéces" *RB* 89 (1982); "Tu feras disparaitre le mal du milieu de toi" *RB* 88 (1980); *Dieu universel et peuple élu* (Cerf, 1975); *La Langue de Ya'udi* (Wilfred Laurier U.P., 1974); and others. Mem: SBL; ASOR. Rec: Music, entomology, ornithology. Addr: (o) U. of Toronto, Dept. of Near Eastern Studies, 4 Bancroft Ave, Toronto, ON M5S 1A1, Canada

416-978-6599; (h) 44 St. Joseph, #616, Toronto, ON M4Y 2W4, Canada 416-929-4734.

DOERMANN, Ralph W., b. Kodaikanal, India, June 25, 1930, s. of Carl & Cora (Knupke), m. Laurel (Ackerman), chil: Roger; Gail; Richard; William. Educ: Luth. Theol. Sem., BD 1958; Duke U., PhD 1962. Emp: Trinity Luth. Ch., 1961-63 Pastor; Luth. Theol. Sem., 1963-78 Prof., OT; Trinity Luth. Sem., 1978- Prof., OT & Arch.; Capital U., 1982 Staley Lect. Excv: Gezer, 1969-70 Area Supr.; Issawyeh, 1970 Photographer; Tell el-Hesi, 1970-71, 1973, 1975, 1977, 1979, 1981, 1983 Arch. Dir.; Idalion, Cyprus, 1972, 1974 Field Supr. Spec: Archaeology, Hebrew Bible. Pub: "Archaeology and Biblical Interpretation: Tell el-Hesi" in *Archaeology and Biblical Interpretation* (John Knox, 1987); "Tell el-Hesi, 1983," co-auth., *PEQ* (1985); "Salvation in the Hebrew Scriptures: A Christian Perspective" in *Yearbook of the Institute for Ecumenical Research* (Tantur, 1977); "The Hellenistic Buildings on the East Terrace" in *The American Expedition to Idalion, Cyprus,* BASORSup 18; *God's Hand Stretched Out: A Study of the Book of Isaiah* (Augsburg, 1976). Awd: Albright Inst. of Arch. Res., Ann. Prof. 1976-77; ASOR, NEH, Fellow 1985. Mem: ASOR; SBL; AIA. Rec: Photography, visiting arch. sites and museums. Addr: (o) Trinity Lutheran Seminary, Columbus, OH 43209 614-2325-4136; (h) 2474 Seneca Park Pl., Columbus, OH 43209 614-237-2661.

DOMERIS, William R., b. Johannesburg, South Africa, February 17, 1950, s. of William E. & Kima D. (Wilson), m. Shona Ann, chil: Kima L. Educ: U. of the Witwatersrand, BA 1971, BA 1975, MA 1978; U. Durham, PhD 1983. Emp: Johannesburg Coll. of Educ., 1978-81 Lect., 1987-88 Assoc. Head of Dept.; U. of Cape Town, 1981-86 Lect.; U. of the Witwatersrand, 1989- Sr. Lect., Relig. Stud. Excv: City of David, 1983 Square Supr. Spec: Archaeology, Hebrew Bible, New Testament. Pub: "Reading the Bible Against the Grain" *Scriptura 37* (1991); "The Paraclete as an Ideological Construct" *JThSA* 67 (1989); "Two Pre-exilic Passages in Isaiah 40-55" *OTE* 1/3 (1988); *The Portraits of Jesus: John,* (Collins, 1988); *The Portraits of Jesus: Matthew* (Collins, 1987); "The City of David: A Testcase for Biblical Archaeology" *JThSA* 48 (1984); "Christology and Community: The Social Matrix of the Fourth Gospel" *JThSA* 64 (1988); and others. Mem: SBL; Tyndale Fellow.; NT Soc. of South Africa; OT Soc. of South Africa. Rec: Photography, hiking in the mountains. Addr: (o) U. of the Witwatersrand, PO Box 3, 2050 Wits, South Africa 011-716-3416; (h) 6 Fifth St., Linden 2195, Johannesburg, South Africa 011-782-0717.

DONALDSON, Terence L., b. Iroquois Falls, ON, Canada, June 15, 1948, s. of Chester I. & Marion D., m. Lois A., chil: Meredith J.; Graeme B. Educ: U. of Toronto, BS 1970; Wycliffe Coll.,

MRE 1977; Wycliffe Coll. & U. of Toronto, ThM 1979, ThD 1982. Emp: Inst. for Christian Stud., Canada, 1982 Lect.; Coll. of Emmanuel & St. Chad, Canada, 1982- Prof.; U. of SK, Canada, 1982- Assoc. Mem. Spec: New Testament. Pub: "The Mockers and the Son of God (Matt 27:37-44): Two Characters in Matthew's Story of Jesus" *JSNT* 41 (1991); "Rural Bandits, City Mobs and the Zealots" *JSJ* 21 (1990); "Proselytes or 'Righteous Gentiles'? The Status of Gentiles in Eschatological Pilgrimage Patterns of Thought" *JSP* 7 (1990); "Zealot and Convert: The Origin of Paul's Christ-Torah Antithesis" *CBQ* 51 (1989); "The 'Curse of Law' and the Inclusion of the Gentiles, Galatians 3.13-14" *NTS* 32 (1986); *Jesus on the Mountain: A Study in Matthean Theology* (JSOT, 1985); and others. Mem: SBL; CSBS. Addr: (o) College of Emmanuel & St. Chad, Saskatoon, SK S7N OW6, Canada 306-343-0750.

DONFRIED, Karl P., April 6, 1940, m. Katharine (Krayer), chil: Paul; Karen; Mark. Educ: Harvard Div. Sch., BD 1963; Luth. Ch. in Amer., Ord. 1963 Union Theol. Sem., STM 1965; U. of Heidelberg, ThD 1968. Emp: Smith Coll., Dept. of Relig. & Bibl. Lit., 1968- Prof., 1980-83 Chair; *JBL,* 1974-80 Ed. Bd. Spec: New Testament. Pub: *The Romans Debate: New and Expanded Edition* (Hendrickson, 1991); "The Cults of Thessalonica and the Thessalonian Correspondence" *NTS* 31 (1985); *Mary in the New Testament,* co-auth. (Fortress/Paulist, 1978); *The Setting of Second Clement in Early Christianity* (Brill, 1974); and others. Mem: AAR; SBL, Pres., New England Reg. 1975-76; SNTS. Addr: (o) Smith College, Dept. of Religion & Biblical Literature, Northampton, MA 01063 413-585-3662.

DORMEYER, Detlev, b. Leoben-Osterreich, May 12, 1942, s. of Robert & Marga, m. Hildegard, chil: Julia; Sophia. Educ: U. Munster, Lic.Theol. 1968, ThD 1972, Habil., Bibelwis-senschaft & Didaktik 1973. Emp: U. Munster, Kath.-Theol. Fakultat, 1980- Prof. Spec: New Testament. Pub: "Mt 1,1 als Uberschrift zur Gattung und Christologie des Matthaeusevangeliums" in *The Four Gospels,* Festschrift F. Neirynck, BETL 100 (1992); "The Implicit and Explicit Readers and the Genre of Philippians 3:2-4:3,8-9" *Semeia* 48 (1990); "Dialogue with the Text (Mk 3:20f, 31-35)" *Interactional Bible Interpretation* 33 (1990); *Weltuntergang und Gottesherrschaft,* co-auth. (1990); *Evangelium als literarische und theologische Gattung* (1989); "'Evangelium Jesu Christi, des Sohnes Gottes' Mk 1,1 Ihre theologische und literarische Aufgabe in der Jesus-Biographie des Markus" *NTS* 33 (1987); *Der Sinn des Leidens Jesu: Historisch-kritische und textpragmatische Analysen zur Markuspassion,* SBS 96 (1979); *Die Bibel antwortet: Einfuhrung in die interaktionale Bibelauslegun,* Pfeiffer Werkbucher 144 (1978). Mem: SNTS 1986-. Addr: (o) Institut fur Lehrerausbildung, Scharnhorststr. 103-109, 4400 Munster, Germany 02-51-83-92-35; (h) Bahnhofstr. 56 b, 4403 Senden, Germany 0-25-36-15-98.

DORN, Louis O., b. Detroit, MI, July 1, 1928, s. of Theodore & Thekla (Frederking), m. Erna (Koessel), chil: Margaret; Peter; Martin; Judith. Educ: Concordia Theol. Sem., BA 1951, MDiv 1962; Luth. Sch. of Theol. at Chicago, ThD 1980. Emp: Luth. Ch., Philippines, 1953-74 Missionary; United Bible Soc., 1979- Trans. Cons. Spec: Hebrew Bible. Pub: "Chronological Sequence in Two Hebrew Narratives" *BT* 29 (1978); "Philippine Language Trends" *Practical Anthrop.* 114 (1967); and others. Mem: SBL. Rec: Music, photography. Addr: (o) American Bible Society, 1865 Broadway, New York, NY 10023 212-408-1208; (h) 32 Larch Ave., Dumont, NJ 07628 201-385-6165.

DORNISCH, Loretta, b. Washington, DC. Educ: Edgewood Coll., BA; Marquette U., ME, PhD. Emp: Edgewood Coll., 1969- Prof. Spec: New Testament. Pub: "The Book of Job and Ricoeur's Hermeneutics" *Semeia* 19 (1981); "Paul Ricoeur and Biblical Interpretation: A Selected Bibliography," "Symbolic Systems and the Interpretation of Scripture: An Introduction to the Work of Paul Ricoeur" *Semeia* 4 (1975); and others. Mem: AAR; SBL; CSBR. Addr: (o) 855 Woodrow St., Madison, WI 53711 608-257-4861.

DORSEY, David A., b. Charleston, WV, July 17, 1949, s. of Alden & Opal, m. Janet L., chil: Jonathan; Benjamin; Sarah. Educ: Trinity Evang. Div. Sch., MA, OT Stud. 1973; Dropsie U., PhD 1981. Emp: Evang. Sch. of Theol., 1979- Prof, OT. Excv: South. Wall, Jerusalem, 1974. Spec: Archaeology, Hebrew Bible, Semitic Languages, Texts and Epigraphy. Pub: *The Roads and Highways of Ancient Israel* (Johns Hopkins U.P., 1991); "Literary Structuring in the Song of Songs" *JSOT* 46 (1990); "Shechem and the Road Network of Central Samaria" *BASOR* 268 (1987); "Another Peculiar Term in the Book of Chronicles: Mesillâ, 'Highway'?" *JQR* 75 (1985); "The Location of Biblical Makkedah" *Tel Aviv* 7 (1980); and others. Mem: SBL. Addr: (o) Evangelical School of Theology, Myerstown, PA 17067 717-866-5775; (h) 728 Frystown Rd., Myerstown, PA 17067 717-933-5318.

DOTHAN, Moshe, b. Cracow, Poland, September 13, 1919, s. of Salomon & Helena, m. Trude, chil: Daniel; Uriel. Educ: Hebrew U., MA 1950, PhD 1959. Emp: Dept. of Antiq. & Mus., Jerusalem, 1950-73 Dir. of Excvn. & Surveys, Acting Dir. of the Dept.; The Technion, Haifa, 1960-65 Lect.; U. of Haifa, 1972-89 Prof., Chmn., Dept. of Arch., Assoc. Prof., Dept. of Maritime Civ. Excv: Tell Mor, 1959 Dir.; Tell Azor, 1959-60 Dir.; Hammat Tiberias, 1961-63 Dir.; Tell Ashdod, 1962-72 Dir.; Tell Akko, 1973-88 Dir. Spec: Archaeology. Pub: *People of the Sea: The Search for the Philistines,* co-auth. (Macmillan, 1992); *Hammat Tiberias* (IES/U. of Haifa, 1983); *Ashdod IV, 'Atiqot,* Eng. Ser. 15, co-auth. (1982); *Ashdod II-III: The Second and Third Seasons of Excavations, 'Atiqot,* Eng. Ser. 9-10 (1971); and others. Awd: Hebrew U., Fulbright Fellow. 1965-

66. Mem: IES; Arch. Coun.; German Arch. Inst. Addr: (o) Israel Antiquities Authority, Jerusalem, Israel 02-638-421; (h) 24 29th of November St., Jerusalem, Israel 02-632-096.

DOTHAN, Trude, Educ: Hebrew U., Jerusalem, BA, MA, PhD. Emp: Hebrew U., Jerusalem, 1960- E.L. Sukenik Prof. of Arch., Dir. of Berman Ctr. for Bibl. Arch.; N.Y. U., Vis. Prof. Excv: Tel Qasile; Hazor; En-Gedi; Deir el-Balah, Dir.; Tel Miqne/Ekron, Co-dir. Spec: Archaeology. Pub: *People of the Sea: The Search for the Philistines,* co-auth. (Macmillan, 1992); "Ekron of the Philistines," co-auth., *BAR* 16/1 (1990); *Excavations at Athienou, Cyprus, 1971-72,* co-auth. (Hebrew U., 1983); *The Philistines and Their Material Culture* (Yale U.P., 1982); "What We Know About the Philistines" *BAR* 8/4 (1982); and others. Awd: U. of Chicago, Oriental Inst., Ryerson Fellow; Israel Mus., Percia Schimmel Awd. 1991; BAS Pub. Awd., Best Popular Book on Arch. 1993. Addr: (h) 24 29th of November St., Jerusalem, Israel 02-632-096.

DOTY, William G., b. Raton, NM, August 7, 1939, s. of William & Marcia, m. Joan T. Mallonee. Educ: San Francisco Theol. Sem., BD 1963; Drew U. Grad. Sch., PhD 1966. Emp: Rutgers Coll., 1965-66 Instr., Relig.; Garrett Theol. Sem., 1966-67 Instr., NT; Vassar Coll., 1967-68 Instr., Relig.; Rutgers U., 1968-75 Asst. Prof., Relig.; U. of Ala., 1981- Prof., Chmn., Dept. of Relig. Stud.. Spec: New Testament. Pub: "The Epistles" in *The Bible as Literature* (Zondervan, 1993); *The Daemonic Imagination* (Scholars, 1991); *Mythography: The Study of Myths and Rituals* (Alabama U.P., 1986); *Letters in Primitive Christianity* (Fortress, 1977); *Contemporary New Testament Interpretation* (Prentice-Hall, 1972); "Linguistics and Biblical Criticism" *JAAR* 41/1 (1973); "The Classification of Epistolary Literature" *CBQ* 31/2 (1969); "The Literature and Discipline of New Testament Form Criticism" *Anglican Theol. Rev.* 51/4 (1969); and others. Mem: AAR; SBL. Addr: (o) U. of Alabama, Dept. of Religious Studies, 212 Manly, Tuscaloosa, AL 35487-0264 205-348-8511; (h) 4343 Springhill Dr., Tuscaloosa, AL 35405 205-556-3257.

DOUKHAN, Jacques B., b. Constantine, Algeria, November 17, 1940, s. of Albert & Fortunee (Attal), m. Lilianne (Uebersax), chil: Myrte Abigail. Educ: Adventist Sem., France, Lic. Theol. 1967; U. of Strasbourg, France, MA, Hebrew, PhD, Hebrew Letters 1973; Andrews U., ThD 1978. Emp: Adventist Sem., France, 1970-73, 1978-80 Tchr.; France-Belgian Union, 1974-76 Pastor; Adventist Sem., Mauritius, 1980-84 Pres., Tchr.; Andrews U. Theol. Sem., 1984- Prof., OT Interpretation; *L'Olivier,* Chief Ed. Spec: Hebrew Bible. Pub: *Daniel, the Vision of the End* (1986); "The Seventy Weeks of Daniel 9: An Exegetical Study" *AUSS* 17/1 (1979); and others. Rec: Gymnastics. Addr: (o) Andrews U. Theological Seminary, Berrien

Springs, MI 49104 616-471-3349; (h) 4797 Kimber Ln., Berrien Springs, MI 49103 616-473-2410.

DOUMAS, Christos G., b. Patras, Greece, February 17, 1933, s. of George & Dorothy (Avgeros), m. Alexandra (Macfarlane), chil: Electra Ioanna; Ekavi Dorothea; Priamos Iakovos. Educ: U. of Athens, Dip., Hist. & Arch. 1958; U. of London, Inst. of Arch., PhD 1972. Emp: Greek Arch. Service, 1960-84 Cur., Admn.; U. of Athens, 1980- Prof., Arch. Excv: Cyclades, 1960-63 Dir.; Class. sites, Dodecanese, 1973-77 Dir.; Akrotiri, Thera, 1968-73 Asst. Dir., 1975- Dir. Spec: Archaeology. Pub: "Luxury Vessels and Aegean Society" *Archaeognosia* (1993); *The Wall-Paintings of Thera* (Thera Found., 1992); *Thera: Pompeii of Ancient Aegean* (Thames & Hudson, 1983); *Cycladic Art* (Benaki Mus., 1978); *Early Bronze Age Burial Habits in the Cyclades* (1977); "The Minoan Eruption of the Santorini Volcano" *Antiq.* (1974); and others. Mem: Greek Arch. Soc. of Athens; Union Intl. des Sci. Hist. & Protohist.; German Arch. Inst.; Soc. of Antiquaries of London; Acad. Europaea. Rec: Photography, music, gardening, walking. Addr: (o) U. of Athens, Dept. of Archaeology & History of Art, Athens 15784, Greece 01-721-3203; (h) Lambrou Photiadi 27, Athens 11636, Greece 01-922-9264.

DOWD, Sharyn E., b. Atlanta, GA, February 14, 1947, d. of Edward James & Doris (Dellinger). Educ: Wake Forest U., BA 1969; SE Bapt. Theol. Sem., MDiv 1980; Emory U., PhD 1986. Emp: Wake Forest U., 1984-87 Instr.; Lexington Theol. Sem., 1987-91 Assoc. Prof., 1992- Prof. Spec: New Testament. Pub: Articles in *Mercer Dict. of the Bible, The Women's Bible Comm.*; "New Testament Theology and the Spirituality of Early Christianity" *Lexington Theol. Quar.* 14 (1989); "The Theological Function of Petitionary Prayer in the Thought of Philo" *Perspectives in Relig. Stud.* 10 (1983); and others. Awd: Emory U., Grad. Fellow. 1980-83. Mem: SBL; AAR; NABPR; SPS. Rec: Walking, music. Addr: (o) Lexington Theological Seminary, 631 S Limestone St., Lexington, KY 40508 606-252-0361; (h) 157 Montmullin St., Lexington, KY 40508 606-253-1641.

DOYLE, B. Rod, b. Melbourne, Australia, March 9, 1932, s. of Gerald & Veronica (Mahady). Educ: Lateran U., Rome, LRSc 1965; Angelicum U., Rome, STL 1966; Pont. Bibl. Inst., Rome, BSS 1967, LSS 1968; Melbourne U., MA 1970, PhD 1984. Emp: Christian Brothers Tchr. Coll., Melbourne, 1970-75 Lect.; *Australian Bibl. Rev.*, 1975-90 Book Rev. Ed.; Natl. Pastoral Inst., Melbourne, 1976-80 Team Mem.; Melbourne Coll. of Div., 1984- Lect. Spec: New Testament. Pub: *Biblical Studies in Australia: A Catholic Contribution* (Lovell, 1990); "Matthew's Intention as Discerned by His Structure" *RB* 95 (1988); "A Concern of the Evangelist: Pharisees in Matthew 12" *Australian*

Bibl. Rev. 34 (1986); "Matthew 11.12—A Challenge to the Evangelist's Community" *Colloquium* 18/1 (1985); "Disciples as Sages and Scribes in Matthew's Gospel" *Word in Life* 32/4 (1984); "'Crowds' in Matthew: Texts and Theology" *Cath. Theol. Rev.* 6 (1984); and others. Mem: Fellow. of Bibl. Stud. 1969-, Pres. 1978; CBA 1969-, Pres., Australia 1988; SBL 1990-. Rec: Jogging, tennis, squash, music, opera. Addr: (o) Catholic Theological College, PO Box 302, Clayton, Victoria 3168, Australia 03-543-1858; (h) 974 Canterbury Rd., Box Hill, Victoria 3128, Australia 03-890-7005.

DRANE, John W., b. Hartlepool, England, October 17, 1946, s. of John W. & Marjorie (Ireland), m. Olive Mary (Fleming), chil: Andrew J.J.; Mark S.P.; Alethea J.F. Educ: U. of Aberdeen, Scotland, MA 1969; U. of Manchester, England, PhD 1972. Emp: U. of Stirling, Scotland, 1973- Lect., 1992- Dir., Ctr. for the Study of Christianity and Contemporary Soc.; Scottish Ch. Coun., 1984-90 Mission Convener; World Coun. of Ch., 1990- Cons. in Christian Evang. Spec: New Testament. Pub: *The Bible: Fact or Fantasy?* (1989); *Introducing the Old Testament* (1987); *Introducing the New Testament* (1986); "Why did Paul Write Romans?" in *Pauline Studies in Honor of F.F. Bruce* (1980); "Theological Diversity in the Letters of St. Paul" *TB* 27 (1976); "Simon the Samaritan and the Lucan Concept of Salvation History" *EQ* 47 (1975); "Tradition Law and Ethics in Pauline Theology" *NT* 16 (1974); and others. Mem: SNTS. Rec: Gardening, skiing, travel. Addr: (o) U. of Stirling, Center for the Study of Christianity & Contemporary Society, Stirlingshire FK9 4LA, Scotland 44786-467594; (h) 39 Fountain Rd., Bridge of Allan, Stirlingshire FK9 4AU, Scotland 44786-833028.

DRAZIN, Israel, b. Baltimore, MD, December 5, 1935, s. of Nathan & Celia (Hoenig), m. Dina, chil: Daniela; Michele; Sarena; Stephen. Educ: Ner Israel Rabbinical Coll., Ord., BA 1957; Loyola Coll., MA 1966; U. of Baltimore, JD 1974; Baltimore Hebrew Coll., MA 1978; St. Mary's U., PhD 1981. Emp: Soc. for Targumic Stud. Inc., 1983- Pres. Spec: Hebrew Bible, Semitic Languages, Texts and Epigraphy, Apocrypha and Post-biblical Studies. Pub: *Targum Onkelos to Leviticus* (Ktav, 1993); *Targum Onkelos to Exodus* (Ktav, 1990); *Targum Onkelos to Deuteronomy* (Ktav, 1982); *Targumic Studies* (1981). Mem: SBL. Rec: Jogging, swimming. Addr: (h) 10915 Swansfield Rd., Columbia, MD 21044 410-730-6715.

DRESNER, Samuel H., b. Chicago., IL, November 7, 1923, s. of Julius & Maude, m. Ruth, chil: Hannah; Miriam; Nehama; Rachel. Educ: U. of Cincinnati, BA 1945; Jewish Theol. Sem., MHL, Rabbinical Ord. 1951, DHL 1954. Emp: *Conservative Judaism*, 1960-70 Ed.; Hebrew U., 1985 Vis. Prof.; Hebrew Union Coll., 1986 Vis. Prof.; Jewish Theol. Sem., 1987- Vis. Prof. Pub:

"Rachel and Leah—Sibling Tragedy or the Triumph of Piety and Compassion?" *BR* 6/2 (1990); *The Zaddik* (Abelard-Schuman, 1960; Schocken 1972); *The Jewish Dietary Laws* (Burning Bush, 1960); and others. Awd: Spertus Coll. of Judaica, DHL 1984. Mem: AJS. Addr: (h) 3777 Independence Ave., Riverdale, NY 10463 212-543-2528.

DRUMMOND, Richard H., b. San Francisco, CA, December 14, 1916, s. of John Albert & Clara (Jacobson), m. Pearl Estella, chil: Donald Craig; Angela Claire (Pfeifer); Lowell Henry. Educ: U. of Calif., BA 1938, MA 1939; U. of Wis., PhD 1941. Emp: Meiji Gakuin U., Japan, 1957-62 Prof., Christian Stud. & Class Lang.; U. of Dubuque Theol. Sem., 1962-86 Prof., Comparative Relig.; *Japan Christian Quar.*, 1957-62 Ed. Bd; Intl. Christian U., Japan, Vis. Prof.; Luther Theol. Sem., Vis. Prof. Spec: New Testament. Pub: *Toward a New Age in Christian Theology* (1980); and others. Awd: U. of Wis., Res. Fellow. in Class. 1940-41; Gettysburg Theol. Sem., Teaching Fellow. 1941-44; Sealantic Fund, Japan, ATS Fac. Fellow. 1968-69; Outstanding Educators of Amer. 1972-74. Mem: Prof. of Mission, MidW Fellow.; AAR; Amer. Soc. of Missiology; N Amer. Acad. of Ecumenists; Intl. Assn. for Mission Stud. Rec: Hiking, music, travel. Addr: (o) U. of Dubuque, 2000 University Ave., Dubuque, IA 52001 319-589-3114; (h) 135 Croydon Crest, Dubuque, IA 52001 319-588-1927.

DU TOIT, Andries B., b. Boshof, Orange Free State, November 19, 1931, s. of Hermanus Carel & Jacoba Aletta Catharina, m. Lydia, chil: Magdalena; Jacoba; Hermanus; George; Andries. Educ: U. of Pretoria, BA 1951, BD 1954, MA, Greek 1962; U. of Basel, ThD 1959. Emp: Dutch Reformed Ch., 1959-70 Min.; U. of Pretoria, 1970- Prof., Head of NT Dept., 1984-87 Dean, Fac. of Theol.; *Neotestamentica*, 1965-80 Ed. Spec: New Testament. Pub: *Guide to the New Testament*, vol. 1, 4-6, co-auth., ed. (Orion, 1979, 1983, 1985, 1992); "Faith and Obedience in Paul" *Neotestamentica* 25 (1991); "Persuasion in Romans 1, 1-17" *BZ* 13 (1989); "Gesetzesgerechtigkeit und Glaubens-gerechtigkeit in Rm 4:13-25: In Gespräch mit E.P. Sanders" *Hervormde Teologiese Stud.* 44 (1988); "Dikaiosyne in Röm 6" *ZTK* 76 (1979); "The Significance of Discourse Analysis" *Neotestamentica* 8 (1974); and others. Awd: U. of Pretoria, Special Awd. for Acad. Achievement 1989; Ds Pieter van Drimmelen Medal 1992. Mem: NT Soc. of South Africa 1965-; SNTS 1975-. Rec: Tennis, gardening. Addr: (o) U. of Pretoria, Dept. of New Testament, Faculty of Theology (B), 0002 Pretoria, South Africa 012-4202358; (h) PO Box 11191, 0011 Brooklyn, Pretoria, South Africa 012-9912406.

DUGGAN, Michael W., b. Calgary, AB, Canada, July 8, 1948, s. of William J. & Mary Eileen. Educ: U. of SK, BA, (summa cum laude), Phil. 1969; Gregorian U., Rome, STB (magna cum laude) 1972; Pont. Bibl. Inst., Rome, SSL (magna cum laude) 1975. Emp: R.C. Diocese of Calgary, Canada, Lect.; *The Word Among Us*, Contb. Writer. Spec: Hebrew Bible. Pub: *The Consuming Fire* (Ignatius, 1991). Mem: CBA; SBS; CSBS. Rec: Golf, skiing, hiking. Addr: (o) PO Box 2206, Gaithersburg, MD 20886 301-990-2082; (h) 20501 Goshen Rd., Gaithersburg, MD 20879 301-990-8996.

DULING, Dennis C., b. Coshocton, OH, April 7, 1938, s. of Lester & Alice, m. Gretchen (Smith), chil: Teddie; Stephen. Educ: McCormick Theol. Sem., BD 1963; U. of Chicago, MA 1967, PhD 1970. Emp: U. of Detroit, 1969-72 Asst. Prof., Relig. Stud.; Boston U., 1972-76 Asst. Prof., Sch. of Theol.; Ohio North. U., 1976-78 Assoc. Prof.; Canisius Coll., 1978- Prof., Dept. of Relig. Stud. Spec: New Testament, Apocrypha and Post-biblical Studies. Pub: *The New Testament: An Introduction*, co-auth. (Harcourt, Brace, Jovanovich, 1972, 1993); "Kingdom of God/Heaven" in *ABD* (1992); "'[Do Not Swear]...by the City of the Great King' (Matthew 5:35)" *JBL* 110/2 (1991); "The Testament of Solomon: Retrospect and Prospect" *JSP* 2 (1988); "The Eleazar Miracle and Solomon's Magical Wisdom in Flavius Josephus' *Antiquitates Judaicae* 8:42-49" *HTR* (1985); *Jesus Christ Through History* (Harcourt, Brace, Jovanovich, 1978); and others. Awd: U. of Heidelberg, NEH Fellow 1985. Mem: SBL; CBA; SNTS. Addr: (o) Canisius College, Tower 1013, Buffalo, NY 14208 716-883-7000; (h) 146 Mt. Vernon Rd., Snyder, NY 14226 716-839-0682.

DUMAIS, Marcel, b. Drummondville, Que., Canada, s. of Philippe & Jeannette (Corriveau). Educ: St. Thomas U., Rome, LPh 1959, LTh 1963; Pont. Bibl. Inst., Rome, LSS 1966; Cath. Inst. of U. of Paris, DTh 1974. Emp: U. of Ottawa, 1963-64 Lect.; St. Paul U., Ottawa, 1968- Prof., NT. Spec: New Testament. Pub: *Communauté et Mission: Une Lecture des Actes des Apôtres pour Aujourd'hui* (Desclée, 1992); *Homelies sur l'Ecriture a l'époque apostolique* (Desclée, 1989); "Langage sexiste et traductions de la Bible" *Eglise et Theol.* 19 (1988); "The Church of the Acts of the Apostles: A Model of Inculturation?" *Acta* (1985); "L'évangélisation des pauvres dans l'oeuvre de Luc" *Sci. et Esprit* 36 (1984); "Les deux lettres de Paul aux Thessaloniciens" in *Lettres de Paul, de Jacques, Pierre et Jude* (1983); *L'actualisation du Nouveau Testament: De la réflexion a la pratique* (Cerf, 1982); *Le langage de l'évangélisation: L'annonce missionnaire en milieu juif* (Desclée/Bellarmin, 1976); and others. Awd: Pont. Bibl. Commn., 1984-. Mem: CBA 1970-; CSSR 1975-; SNTS 1978-. Rec: Theatre, tennis, skiing, swimming. Addr: (o) 223 Rue Main, Ottawa, ON K1S 1C4, Canada 613-236-1393; (h) 175 Rue Main, Ottawa, ON K1S 1C3, Canada 613-237-0580.

DUMM, Demetrius R., b. Carrolltown, PA, October 1, 1923, s. of Gordon & Esther (Kirsch).

Educ: St. Vincent Coll., BA 1945; Collegio di Sant'Anselmo, Rome, STD 1950; Pont. Bibl. Inst., SSL 1952. Emp: St. Vincent Sem., 1952- Prof., NT. Spec: New Testament. Pub: *Flowers in the Desert: A Biblical Spirituality* (Paulist, 1987); "Witness of Benedictines in Ministry: An Expression of Biblical Prophecy and Apocalyptic" *Amer. Benedictine Rev.* 35/4 (1984); "Work and Leisure: Biblical Perspectives" *Amer. Benedictine Rev.* 28/4 (1977). Mem: CBA 1952-; SBL 1954-. Rec: Gardening. Addr: (h) St. Vincent Archabbey, Latrobe, PA 15650 412-532-6600.

DUNHAM, Sally S., b. New York, NY, September 15, 1944, d. of Robert & Elizabeth (Cooper). Educ: Columbia U., MA, Anc. Near East. Art & Arch. 1971, MPhil 1974, PhD 1980. Emp: Columbia U., 1983-84, 1986-87 Adj. Asst. Prof. Excv: Nahr Ibrahim Cave, Lebanon, 1973 Site Supr.; Selenkahiya, Syria, 1975 Site Supr.; Al-Hiba, Iraq, 1975-76 Site Supr., Faunal Analyst; Tell Raqa'i, Syria, 1986-90 Site Supr., & Registrar; Hammam er-Turkman, Syria, 1986- Site Supr. Spec: Archaeology, Mesopotamian Studies. Pub: "Sumerian Words for Foundation: Part I: Temen" *Revue d'Assyriologie* 80 (1986); "The Monkey in the Middle" *Zeitschrift fur Assyriologie* 75 (1985); "Notes on the Relative Chronology of Early Northern Mesopotamia" *JANES* 15 (1983); "Bricks for the Temples of Shara and Ninurra" *Revue d'Assyriologie* 76 (1982); and others. Mem: AOS; AIA. Rec: Horses. Addr: (h) 5 Longview Ln., Westport, CT 06880 203-227-2493.

DUNKLY, James W., b. Alexandria, LA, August 1, 1942, s. of James & Frances (Jones), m. Nancy Rose, chil: Margaret Rose; Michael Benjamin. Educ: Tex. Christian U., BA 1963; Vanderbilt U., MA 1968, PhD 1982. Emp: Episcopal Theol. Sch., 1969-71 Lect.; Boston U. Sch. of Theol., 1971-72 Lect.; *NT Abstracts*, 1972-75 Managing Ed.; Nashotah House, 1975-83 Assoc. Prof., Lbrn.; *ATR*, 1977- Ed.; Episcopal Div. Sch. & Weston Sch. of Theol., 1983-93 Dir. of Lib. Spec: New Testament. Mem: SBL; CBA. Addr: (o) 99 Brattle St., Cambridge, MA 02138 617-868-3450; (h) 7 Fairway Rd., Acton, MA 07120 508-263-5447.

DUNN, James D. G., b. Birmingham, England, October 21, 1939, s. of Agnes & David, m. Meta, chil: Catrina Clare; David George; Fiona Margaret. Educ: U. of Glasgow, MA 1961, BD 1964; U. of Cambridge, PhD 1968. Emp: U. of Nottingham, 1970-82 Lect., Reader in Theol.; U. of Durham, 1982-89 Prof. of Div., 1989- Lightfoot Prof. of Div.; Oxford U., 1991 Henton Davies Lect.; Gregorian Pont. U., Rome, 1990 McCarthy Vis. Prof.; London U., 1993 Ethel M. Wood Lect. Spec: New Testament. Pub: *Jesus' Call to Discipleship* (Cambridge U.P., 1992); *The Partings of the Ways between Christianity and Judaism and their Significance for the Character of Christianity* (SCM/Trinity, 1991); "Once More, PISTIS CHRISTOU" in *SBL 1991 Seminar Papers* (Scholars, 1991); *Jesus, Paul and the Law: Studies in Mark and Galatians* (SPCK/Westminster, 1990); *Unity and Diversity in the New Testament* (SCM, 1977, 1990); *Christology in the Making* (SCM, 1980, 1989); "Let John be John—A Gospel for its Time" in *Das Evangelium und die Evangelien* (Mohr, 1983); "Prophetic 'I'-Sayings and the Jesus Tradition: The Importance of Testing Prophetic Utterances within Early Christianity" *NTS* 24 (1977-78); "The Messianic Secret in Mark" *TB* 21 (1970); "2 Corinthians 3.17—'The Lord is the Spirit'" *JTS* 21 (1970); and others. Awd: U. of Cambridge, BD 1976, DD 1991. Mem: SNTS; SBL; SST; Tyndale Fellow. Rec: Choral singing, fell walking, touring & sight-seeing. Addr: (o) U. of Durham, Dept. of Theology, Abbey House, Palace Green, Durham DH1 3RS, England 091-374-2062; (h) 4 Fieldhouse Terrace, Durham DH1 4NA, England 091-386-4080.

DUNNETT, Walter M., b. Tayport, Fife, Scotland, July 5, 1924, s. of Daniel M. & Jemima K., m. Delores E., chil: Sharon; Mark. Educ: Wheaton Coll., BA 1949, MA 1950, BD 1953; Case West. Reserve U., PhD 1967; NW Luth. Theol. Sem., STM 1980. Emp: Cornus Hill Bible Coll., 1953-58 Acad. Dean, Prof. of Bible; Moody Bible Inst., 1958-66, 1972-76 Tchr.; Wheaton Coll., 1966-69 Asst. Prof.; Trinity Coll., 1969-72 Assoc. Prof.; NW Coll., 1976-92 Prof., Bible & Greek. Spec: New Testament, Apocrypha and Post-biblical Studies. Pub: *Revelation: God's Final Word to Man* (Meridian, 1991); "Scholarship and Spirituality" *JETS* 31/1 (1988); "The Hermeneutics of Jude and 2 Peter: The Use of Ancient Jewish Traditions" *JETS* 31/3 (1988); *The Interpretation of Holy Scripture* (Thomas Nelson, 1984); *The Book of Acts* (Baker, 1981); *An Outline of New Testament Survey* (Moody, 1960); *New Testament Survey* (E.T.T.A., 1958, 1963). Mem: ETS 1955-, Pres. 1987; IBR 1988-; SBL 1989-. Rec: Golf, swimming, gardening. Addr: (o) 1651 Ford Parkway, St. Paul, MN 55116 612-698-2590; (h) 3651 N Snelling Ave., St. Paul, MN 55112 612-631-3758.

DUTCHER-WALLS, Patricia N., b. Glen Ridge, NJ, March 17, 1952, d. of Ruth Y. & C. Mason Dutcher, m. Timothy, chil: Ruth Marie; Wesley David. Educ: Coll. of Wooster, BA 1974; Harvard Div. Sch., MDiv 1978. Emp: Colgate U., 1978-81 Instr., Phil. & Relig. Dept., Asst. Chaplain; San Francisco Theol. Sem., 1988-89 Vis. Instr. Spec: Hebrew Bible. Pub: "The Social Location of the Deuteronomists: A Sociological Study of Factional Politics in Late Pre-Exilic Judah" *JSOT* 52 (1991); "Cultural Conflict in the Book of Amos" *Creation Mag.* 2/5 (1986); "Incarnation: Interaction as a Means of Grace" in *Of Human Bondage and Divine Grace: A Global Testimony* (Open Court, 1992). Awd: Phi Beta Kappa 1974. Mem: AAR; SBL; CBA. Rec: Gardening, camping, choral music, sci. fiction. Addr: (h) PO Box 603, Fort Recovery, OH 45846 419-375-4049.

EAKINS, J. Kenneth, b. Ozark, MO, February 22, 1930, s. of A. Homer & Pearl A. (Meadows), m. Marian (McInnes) (dec.), chil: Douglas G.; Nancy L.; Sheri L.; Laurie L. Educ: U. of Ill. Coll. of Medicine, MD 1956; South. Bapt. Theol. Sem., BD 1967, PhD 1970. Emp: South. Bapt. Theol. Sem., 1969-70 Instr.; Golden Gate Bapt. Sem., 1970- Prof., Arch. & OT.; *Trowel and Parish*, Ed.; Golden Gate Bapt. Sem., Marian Eakins Arch. Collection, Cur. Excv: Tel el-Hesi, 1973- Osteologist. Spec: Archaeology, Hebrew Bible, Semitic Languages, Texts and Epigraphy. Pub: "Anthropomorphisms in Isaiah 40-55" *Hebrew Stud.* 20-21 (1979-80); "Human Osteology and Archeology" *BA* 43 (1980); "Pathologies among the Population at Tel el-Hesi, Israel" *Amer. Jour. of Physical Anthrop.* 52 (1980); "Biblical Archaeology in Transition" *Perspectives. in Relig. Stud.* 10 (1983); and others. Awd: Albright Inst. of Arch. Res., Jerusalem, Ann. Prof. 1983. Mem: SBL 1970-; ASOR 1970-; Paleopathology Assn. 1977-. Rec: Astronomy, flute. Addr: (o) Golden Gate Baptist Seminary, Mill Valley, CA 94941 415-388-8080; (h) 78 LaBrea Way, San Rafael, CA 94903 415-479-9642.

EASLEY, Kendell H., b. Durant, OK, September 14, 1949, s. of Charles & Pauline (Brock), m. Nancy (Maulden), chil: Jordan. Educ: Trinity Evang. Div. Sch., MDiv 1975; SW Bapt. Theol. Sem., PhD 1978. Emp: SW Bapt. Theol. Sem., 1977-78 Teaching Fellow; East. N. Mex. U., 1980 Vis. Instr.; Toccoa Falls Coll., 1980-88 Assoc. Prof.; Mid-Amer. Bapt. Theol. Sem., 1988- Assoc. Prof. Spec: New Testament. Pub: Articles in *Holman Bible Dict.* (Broadman, 1991); articles in *Nelson's Illustrated Bible Dict.* (Thomas Nelson, 1986); "The Pauline Usage of *Pneumati* as a Reference to the Spirit of God" *JETS* 27 (1984); and others. Mem: SBL; ETS; IBR. Rec: Jogging, photography. Addr: (o) Mid-American Baptist Theological Seminary, Box 3624, Memphis, TN 38173-0624 901-726-9171; (h) 4271 Beechcliff Ln., Memphis, TN 38128 901-372-0019.

ECKLEBARGER, Kermit A., b. Chicago, IL, December 10, 1935, s. of Kermit Arthur & M. Marie (Wilson), m. Shirley Jean (Hawkins), chil: Kae Anne; Kermit Andrew. Educ: Wheaton Coll., MA 1961; U. of Chicago, PhD 1987. Emp: London Coll. of Bible & Missions, Canada, 1960-68 Assoc. Prof.; ON Bible Coll., 1968-72 Prof.; Denver Sem., 1972- Assoc. Prof., NT. Spec: New Testament, Apocrypha and Post-biblical Studies. Pub: *Thomas Nelson's Illustrated Bible Dict.*, co-ed. Mem: ETS 1963-; SBL 1973-; IBR 1990-. Rec: Bicycling, photography, sports. Addr: (o) Box 10,000, Denver, CO 80250 303-761-2482; (h) 8981 S Coyote St., Highlands Ranch, CO 80126 303-791-2986.

ECONOMOU, Elly H., b. Thessalonica, Greece, d. of George & Helen. Educ: Andrews U., MA 1967; U. de Strasbourg, France, PhD 1975. Emp: Andrews U., 1967- Prof., Relig. & Bibl. Lang. Spec: New Testament. Pub: *Greek Papyri (c. 300 B.C.)* (Natl. Lib. of Strasbourg, France, 1975-76); and others. Mem: AAR; SBL; Coun. on Study of Relig. Rec: Translating for publication, photography, traveling. Addr: (o) Andrews U., Griggs Hall, Berrien Springs, MI 49103 616-471-3189; (h) 260 University Blvd., Berrien Springs, MI 49103 616-473-1066.

EDELSTEIN, Gershon, b. Argentina, November 14, 1930, s. of Catalina (Kogan) & Israel, m. Lydia (Aflalo), chil: Daniel; Helena. Educ: Hebrew U. of Jerusalem, BA 1963. Emp: Israel Dept. of Antiq., 1962-89 Field Arch.; U. of Tel Aviv, 1967-72 Vis. Lect.; Israel Antiq. Authority, 1989-92 Sr. Arch. Excv: Nahariya, 1969 Dir.; Tel Ridan, 1972 Dir.; Mevaseret Yerushalaiym, 1977 Co-dir.; Ein Yael, 1973-87 Dir.; Manahat, 1987-89 Dir. Spec: Archaeology. Pub: "The 'Philistine' Tomb at Tell 'Eitun," co-auth., *Atiqot* 21 (1992); "What's a Roman Villa Doing Outside Jerusalem?" *BAR* 16/6 (1990); "Investigating Rural Landscape," co-auth. *Levant* 17 (1985); *L'Eglise Byzantine de Nahariya (Israel)*, Etude Arch. Byzantina, co-auth. (1984); "Ancient Jerusalem's Rural Food Basket," co-auth., *BAR* 8/4 (1982); "Mevasseret Yerushalayim—The Ancient Settlement and its Agricultural Terraces" *BAR* (1981); and others. Mem: Ein Yael Living Mus., Bd. Mem. Rec: Painting, drawing, weaving, pottery. Addr: (o) Israel Antiquites Authority, PO Box 586, Jerusalem 91004, Israel 02-638421.

EDWARDS, Douglas R., b. Superior, NE, January 9, 1950, s. of Russell D. & Marjorie Ann, m. Mary Edith Lynn, chil: Jessica Ann; Samuel Robert; Helen Valmere. Educ: U. of Nebr., BS 1972; Boston U., MDiv 1978, PhD 1987. Emp: U. of Vt., 1984-85 Vis. Instr.; Coll. of the Holy Cross, 1985-87 Instr.; U. of Puget Sound, 1987- Asst. Prof. Excv: Sepphoris, 1986-89, 1991, 1993 Square Supr., Field Dir.; Kefar Hananya, 1989 Square Supr.; Joint Jotapata Expdn., 1992 Co-dir. Spec: Archaeology, New Testament. Pub: "The Socio-economic and Cultural Ethos of the Lower Galilee in the First Century: Implications for the Nascent Jesus Movement" in *The Galilee in Late Antiquity* (Harvard U.P., 1992); "Surviving the Web of Roman Power: Religion and Politics in the Acts of the Apostles, Josephus, and *Chaereas and Callirhoe*" in *Images of Empire* (JSOT, 1991); "Acts of the Apostles and the Graeco-Roman World" in *SBL Seminar Papers* (1989); "First Century Urban/Rural Relations in Lower Galilee" in *SBL Seminar Papers* (1988); "Religion, Power, and Politics: Jewish Defeats by the Romans in Iconography and Josephus" in *Diaspora Jews and Judaism* (U. of S Fla., 1992); and others. Awd: ASOR, travel grant 1986; ACLS, travel grant 1990; AAR Fellow. 1991; NEH Fellow. 1991-92. Mem: AIA; ASOR; AAR; SBL; CBA. Addr: (o) U. of Puget Sound, Dept. of Religion, Tacoma, WA 98416 206-756-3748; (h) 3421 N 30th St., Tacoma, WA 98407 206-756-9422.

EDWARDS, James R., b. Colorado Springs, CO, October 28, 1945, s. of Robert Emery & Mary Eleanor (Callison), m. Mary Jane (Pryor), chil: Corrie Jane; Mark James. Educ: Princeton Theol. Sem., MDiv 1970; Fuller Theol. Sem., PhD 1978. Emp: Jamestown Coll., 1978- Chmn., Dept. Relig. & Phil. Spec: New Testament. Pub: *Romans,* New Intl. Bibl. Comm. vol. 6 (Hendrickson's, 1992); *Nelson's Illustrated Bible Dict.,* contb. (Thomas Nelson, 1986); and others. Mem: SBL. Rec: Mountaineering, hiking, camping. Addr: (o) Jamestown College, Box 6020, Jamestown, ND 58401; (h) 524 5th St. NE, Jamestown, ND 58401 701-252-3096.

EDWARDS, Richard A., b. West Mahony, PA, December 31, 1934, s. of Francis Reed & Helen Irene (Mates), chil: Jennifer Lynne; Emily Katharine; Jonathan Alan. Educ: Princeton U., BA 1956; U. of Chicago, MA 1962, PhD 1968. Emp: Thiel Coll., 1968-72 Assoc. Prof., Relig.; Va. Polytechnic Inst., 1972-78 Assoc. Prof., Relig.; Marquette U., 1978- Assoc. Prof., Asst. Chmn., Theol. Dept. Spec: New Testament. Pub: *Matthew's Story of Jesus* (Fortress, 1985); *The Sentences of Sextus,* co-auth. (Scholars, 1981); *A Theology of Q: Eschatology, Prophecy and Wisdom* (Fortress, 1976); *The Sign of Jonah in the Theology of the Evangelists and Q* (SCM, 1971). Mem: SBL; SNTS; CBA. Addr: (o) Marquette U., Theology Dept., Milwaukee, WI 53233 414-288-7156; (h) 1732 N Prospect Ave., #603 Milwaukee, WI 53202 414-873-7304.

EDWARDS, Sarah A., b. New York, NY, February 17, 1921, d. of James S. Alexander, m. Robert L., chil: Edith H.; James D. Educ: Bryn Mawr Coll., AB 1943; Union Theol. Sem., MDiv 1950; Hartford Sem., STM 1966, PhD 1974. Emp: Hartford Sem., 1977- Adj. Prof., Bibl. Stud. Spec: New Testament. Pub: *Christological Perspectives,* co-ed., contb. (Pilgrim, 1982); "P. 75 Under the Magnifying Glass" *NT* 18 (1976); and others. Mem: AAR 1974-; SBL 1974-. Rec: Swimming, canoeing, vis. arch. sites. Addr: (o) Hartford Seminary, 77 Sherman St., Hartford, CT 06105 203-232-4451; (h) 63 Bayberry Hill Rd., Avon, CT 06001 203-677-4235.

EFIRD, James M., b. Kannapolis, NC, May 30, 1932, s. of James R. & I.Z. (Christy), m. Vivian Lee (Poythress), chil: Anthony; Whitney Michelle. Educ: Louisville Presbyn. Theol. Sem., MDiv 1958; Duke U., PhD 1962. Emp: Duke Div. Sch., 1962- Prof., Bibl. Interpretation. Spec: Hebrew Bible, New Testament. Pub: *Revelation for Today* (Abingdon); *A Grammar for New Testament Greek* (Abingdon); *The Old Testament Writings: History, Literature, and Interpretation* (John Knox); *The New Testament Writings: History, Literature, and Interpretation* (John Knox); and others. Mem: SBL 1957-; ASOR; AAR. Rec: Sports, flowers, meteorology. Addr: (o) Duke Divinity School, Durham, NC 27706 919-660-3410; (h) 2609 Heather Glen Rd., Durham, NC 27712 919-383-1142.

EHRLICH, Carl S., b. New Haven, CT, May 15, 1956, s. of Leonard H. & Edith, m. Michal (Shekel), chil: Joseph Emanuel; Simeon David. Educ: U. of Mass., BA 1976; Harvard U., MA 1984, PhD 1991. Emp: Oberlin Coll., 1982-83 Lect., Hebrew, Dir. Hebrew House; Vassar Coll., 1987 Lect., Relig.; Hochschule fuer Juedische Stud. & Arch., Germany, 1991- Lect., Bible. Excv: Tel Miqne, 1981 Staff; Tel Lachish, 1981 Staff; City of David, 1983 Staff. Spec: Archaeology, Hebrew Bible, Semitic Languages, Texts and Epigraphy. Pub: "Coalition Politics in Eighth Century BCE Palestine: The Philistines and the Syro-Ephraimite War" *ZDPV* 107 (1991); articles in *ABD, Oxford Companion to the Bible*; "The Text of Hosea 1:9" *JBL* 104 (1985). Awd: Harvard, Dorot Found. Arch. Grant 1981. Mem: ASOR; SBL. Addr: (o) Hochschule fuer Juedische Studien, Friedrichstrasse 9, D-6900 Heidelberg, Germany 06221-22576; (h) 22 Madison St., Newton, NJ 07860 201-579-7367.

EICHLER, Barry L., b. New York, NY, February 6, 1940, s. of Samson & Sylvia, m. Linda (Frisch), chil: Elise Miriam; Rachel Grace; Sara Hope; Bezalel. Educ: Yeshiva U., BA (magna cum laude) 1960, BRE (summa cum laude) 1960; U. of Pa., PhD 1967. Emp: Yale U., 1968-69 Res. Fellow in Mesopotamian Law; U. of Pa., 1969- Assoc. Prof., Dept. of Asian & Middle East. Stud., Assoc. Cur., Babylonian Tablet Collections, Chair, Jewish Stud. Prog.; *Pennsylvania Sumerian Dict., Jewish Law Annual,* Ed. Publ., Babylonian Sect.; Hebrew U., Dept. of Assyriology, 1977-78 Vis. Lect.; Yeshiva U., Bernard Revel Grad. Sch., 1981- Vis. Lect., Bible & Mesopotamian Stud. Spec: Hebrew Bible, Mesopotamian Studies. Pub: "On Weaving Etymological and Semantic Threads: The Semitic Root q1^{C}" in *Lingering Over Words: Studies in Ancient Near Eastern Literature in Honor of William Moran,* HSS 37 (1990); "Nuzi and the Bible: A Retrospective" in *DUMU-E2-DUB-BA-A: Studies in Honor of Ake W. Sjöberg,* (1989); "Literary Structure in the Laws of Eshnunna" in *Language, Literature and History: Philological and Historical Studies Presented to Erica Reiner,* AOS Ser. 67 (1987); "Of Slings and Shields, Throw-sticks and Javelins" *JAOS* 103 (1983); "Another Look at the Nuzi Sistership Contract" in *Ancient Near Eastern Studies in Honor of J.J. Finkelstein* (1977); *Cuneiform Studies in Honor of Samuel Noah Kramer,* ed. (Butzon & Bercker Kevelaer, 1976); *Indenture at Nuzi* (Yale U.P., 1973); and others. Mem: SBL; AOS. Addr: (o) U. of Pennsylvania, Asian & Middle Eastern Studies Dept., 847 Williams Hall, Philadelphia, PA 19104 215-898-7466; (h) 246 Lloyd Ln., Wynnewood, PA 19096 215-642-8410.

EILBERG-SCHWARTZ, Howard, b. Baltimore, MD, February 19, 1956, chil: Penina. Educ: Duke U., BA; Jewish Theol. Sem., MA, Rabbinic Ordination; Brown U., PhD. Emp: Indiana U., 1986-89 Asst. Prof.; Temple U., 1989-90 Asst. Prof.; Stanford U., 1990- Asst.

Prof. Spec: Hebrew Bible, Apocrypha and Post-biblical Studies. Pub: *The Savage in Judaism: An Anthropology of Israelite Religion and Ancient Judaism* (Indiana U., 1990). Awd: NEH, Fellow. 1989; John Simon Gugenheim Fellow. 1992-93. Mem: AAR. Addr: (o) Stanford U., Dept. of Religious Studies, Stanford, CA 94305 415-723-3322; (h) 4294-P Wilkie Way, Palo Alto, CA 94306 415-363-8797.

EISENMAN, Robert H., b. NJ, February 15, 1937, m. Heather, chil: Lavi; Hanan; Nadav; Sarah. Educ: Cornell U., BA 1958; N.Y. U., MA, Hebrew & Near East. Stud. 1966; Columbia U., PhD, Middle East Lang. & Cultures 1971. Emp: Hebrew U. & U. of Tel Aviv, 1970-73 Lect.; Calif. State U., Long Beach, 1973- Prof. of Middle East Relig., Chair of Dept. of Relig. Stud., Dir. of Inst. for Judeo-Christian Origins, Second Temple History & Christian Origins. Spec: Archaeology, Hebrew Bible, New Testament, Apocrypha and Post-biblical Studies. Pub: *The Dead Sea Scrolls Uncovered*, co-auth. (Element, 1992); *A Facsimile Edition of the Dead Sea Scrolls*, co-ed. (BAS, 1991); "Interpreting *Abeit-Galuto* in the Habakkuk *Pesher*" in *MOGILANY 1989: Papers on the Dead Sea Scrolls* (1991); "The Desecrecation of the Scrolls" *Midstream* Dec. (1991); "The Testament of Kohath" BAR 17/6 (1991); "A Response to Schiffman on MMT" *The Qumran Chronicle* 2 (1990-91); "Eschatological 'Rain' Imagery in the War Scroll and the Letter of James" *Near East. Stud.* Spring (1990); *James the Just in the Habakkuk Pesher* (Brill, 1986); *Maccabees, Zadokites, Christians and Qumran* (Brill, 1983); and others. Awd: NEH/Albright Inst., Fellow 1985-86; Linacre Coll., Oxford & Oxford Ctr. for Post-grad. Hebrew Stud., Sr. Fellow 1986-87. Mem: SBL; ASOR; AJS Addr: (o) California State U., Chair, Dept. of Religious Studies, Long Beach, CA 90840 310-985-5341; (h) 10771 La Batista Ave., Fountain Valley, CA 92708.

EITAN, Avi, Addr: (o) Israel Antiquities Authority, PO Box 586, Jerusalem, Israel 02-285151; (h) 20 Neve Sha'anan, Jerusalem, Israel 02-527736.

ELAYI, Josette, b. Bordes sur Lez, France, March 29, 1943, d. of Pierre & Marguerite Escaich, m. Alain G. Elayi, chil: Claude; Laurent. Educ: U. of Toulouse, Lic. de Lettres Class. 1965, Dip. de grec 1966; U. of Lyon, Doc., Greek Stud. 1973; U. of Paris, Cert. d'akkadien et d'hebreu 1982; Inst. Cath. de Paris, Dip. d'arameen 1983; U. of Nancy, Doc.-Es-Lettres 1984. Emp: Cours Notre-Dame, Lyon, 1968-72 Prof., Class. Stud.; U. Beyrouth, 1973-75 Prof.; U. Baghdad, 1975-78 Prof.; French Natl. Coun. of Sci. Res. of Paris, 1982- Res.; *Transeuphratene* 1989- Ed. Spec: Archaeology, Semitic Languages, Texts and Epigraphy. Pub: "Etude paléographique des légendes monétaires phéniciennes d'époque perse" *Transeuphraténe* 5 (1992); *Nouveaux regards sur la Transeuphratene*, co-auth. (Brepols, 1991); *Economie des cités phéniciennes sous l'Empire perse* (Istituto U. Orientale, 1990); *Sidon, cité autonome de l'Empire perse* (Idéaphane, 1989); *Pénétration grecque en Phénicie sous l'Empire perse* (Presses Univesitaires, 1988); "Les sarcophages phéniciens d'époque perse" *Iranica Antiqua* 23 (1988); "Name of Deuteronomy's Author Found on Seal Ring" *BAR* 13/5 (1987); "A Treasure of Coins from Arados," co-auth., *JANES* 17 (1986); "Studies in Phoenician Geography during the Persian Period" *JNES* 41 (1982); and others. Mem: Soc. Asiatique 1981-; Fondation Assyriologique Georges Dossin 1981-; Soc. Francaise de Numismatique 1982-; Soc. d'Etudes Numismatiques et Archeologiques 1985-; Soc. de Prof. d'hist. anc. de l'Université 1986-. Rec: Archaeology, painting, theater, swimming. Addr: (o) CNRS, 15 Quai Anatole France, 75700 Paris, France 1-47 53 15 15; (h) 92 rue de Lourmel, 75015 Paris, France 1-45 57 43 09.

ELGVIN, Torleif, b. Steigen, Norway, February 21, 1950, s. of Torbjorn & Hjordis (Overland), m. Kirsti Melkeraen, chil: Olav; Johannes Djonne; Svein. Educ: Luth. Sch. of Theol., Oslo, MTh 1977. Emp: Ch. of Norway, 1980-85 Min.; Caspari Ctr. of Bibl. & Jewish Stud., Jerusalem, 1986-93 Dir.; *Mishkan*, 1986- Assoc. Ed.; Luth. Sch. of Theol., Oslo, 1993- Res. Fellow. Spec: Hebrew Bible, Semitic Languages, Texts and Epigraphy, Apocrypha and Post-biblical Studies. Pub: *Israel and Yeshua*, ed. (Caspari Ctr., 1993); "The Qumran Covenant Festival and the Temple Scroll" *JJS* 36/1 (1985); *Moderne Trosretninger*, co-auth. (Credo, 1974, 1976); and others. Rec: Mountain hiking, cross-country skiing. Addr: (o) Lutheran School of Theology, Gydas vei 4, 0363 Oslo, Norway 47-22467900; (h) Aasterudsletta 45, 1344 Haslum, Norway.

ELLENS, J. Harold, b. McBain, MI, s. of John S. & Grace (Kortman), m. Mary Jo (Lewis), chil: Deborah; Jacqueline; Daniel; Rebecca; Harold; Brenda. Educ: Calvin Coll., BA 1953; Calvin Sem., MDiv 1956; Wayne State U., PhD 1970. Emp: Christian Assn. for Psychological Stud., 1974-89 Exec. Dir.; Drew U., 1980-90 Adj. Prof., Pastoral Psychology; *Jour. of Psychology & Christianity*, 1982-88 Ed.; Claremont Grad. Sch., Alexandria Res. Project of the Inst. for Antiquity & Christianity, Chmn. Spec: Archaeology, Mesopotamian Studies, New Testament, Apocrypha and Post-biblical Studies. Pub: Articles in *Ency. of Pastoral Care* (Abingdon, 1985), *ISBE* (Eerdmans, 1985); and others. Awd: Knights of Malta. Mem: SBL; AAR; AIA. Rec: Sailing, fiction, equestrian arts. Addr: (h) 26705 Farmington Rd., Farmington Hills, MI 48018 313-474-0514.

ELLIOTT, J. Keith, b. Liverpool, England, March 19, 1943, s. of James & Lillian (Blackler), m. Carolyn Frances (Tull), chil: Rosamund Veronica. Educ: U. of Wales, BA

1964, DD 1988; U. of Oxford, DPhil 1967. Emp: U. of Leeds, 1967- Sr. Lect.; *NTS*, 1983- Ed. Bd. Spec: New Testament. Pub: *The Gospel According to St. Luke*, ed. (Oxford, 1984, 1987); "Old Latin Manuscripts in Printed Editions of the Greek New Testament" *NT* 26 (1984); *Questioning Christian Origins* (SCM, 1982); "An Examination of the 26th Edition of Nestle-Aland *Novum Testamentum* Graece" JTS 32 (1981); "Plaidoyer pour un Eclecticisme integrale Appliqué á la Critique Textuelle du Nouveau Testament" *RB* 83 (1977). Mem: SNTS 1971-. Rec: Squash, walking, music. Addr: (o) U. of Leeds, Dept. of Theology, Leeds LS2 9JP, England 431-751.

ELLIOTT, Mary Timothea, b. Detroit, MI, October 16, 1938, d. of Ernest A. & May E. (Mitchell). Educ: Mercy Coll. of Detroit, BA 1960; St. Mary's Grad. Sch. of Sacred Theol., MA 1965; Pont. Bibl. Inst., Rome, SSL 1979, SSD (magna cum laude) 1988. Emp: Loyola U. of Chicago, 1980, 1984-85 Lect.; Pont. Bibl. Inst., Rome, 1984-91 Asst. Prof.; Pont. Gregorian U., Rome, 1987-91 Asst. Prof.; St. Joseph Sem., 1991- Prof. Spec: Hebrew Bible, New Testament. Pub: *The Literary Unity of the Canticle*, European U. Stud. Ser. 23, vol. 371 (Lang, 1989); "Lo sposo e la sposa nel Cantico dei Cantici" in *Parola Spirito e Vita* vol. 13 (1986); and others. Mem: CBA; SBL. Rec: Music, opera. Addr: (o) St. Joseph Seminary, Dunwoodie, Yonkers, NY 10704 914-968-6200; (h) 63 Crane Hollow Rd., Bethlehem, CT 06751 203-266-5411.

ELLIS, E. Earle, b. Ft. Lauderdale, FL, March 18, 1926, s. of Lindsey Thornton & Lois Bell (McBride). Educ: U. of Va., BS 1950; Wheaton Grad. Sch., MA, BD 1953; U. of Edinburgh, PhD 1955. Emp: Aurora Coll., 1955-58 Asst. Prof., Bible & Phil.; South. Bapt. Theol. Sem., 1958-60 Asst. Prof., NT; Bethel Theol. Sem., 1960-61 Vis. Prof.; New Brunswick Theol. Sem., 1962-64 Vis. Prof., 1964-70 Assoc. Prof., 1970-85 Res. Prof., Bibl. Stud.; SW Sem., 1985- Res. Prof.; *NTS*, 1987-89 Ed. Bd. Spec: New Testament. Pub: "The Making of Narratives in the Synoptic Gospels" in *Jesus and the Oral Gospel Tradition* (Sheffield, 1991); "The End of the Earth (Acts 1:8)" *Bull. for Bibl. Res.* 1 (1991); "Gospels Criticism" in *The Gospel and the Gospels* (1991); *The Old Testament in Early Christianity*, WUNT 54 (1991); "Soma in First Corinthians" *Interpretation* 44 (1990); "Eschatology in Luke Revisited" in *L'evangile de Luc* (1989); *Pauline Theology: Ministry & Society* (1989); *The Gospel of Luke* (1987); *Prophecy and Hermeneutic in Early Christianity* (1978); and others. Awd: U. Tubingen, von Humboldt Schol., 1975-76, 1990; Guggenheim Fellow 1975-76; Cambridge U., Robinson Coll. 1982-83 Vis. Fellow; Fulbright Schol. 1990. Mem: IBR, Founder; SBL; SNTS. Rec: Pool, chess, swimming, travel. Addr: (o) PO Box 22238, Fort Worth, TX 76122 817-923-1921.

ELLIS, Robert R., b. Fort Worth, TX, July 8, 1955, s. of Dr. & Mrs. W. Ray, m. Teresa (Cardin). Educ: Hardin Simmons U., BS 1977; SW Bapt. Theol. Sem., MDiv 1981, PhD 1988. Emp: Hardin Simmons U., Logsdon Sch. of Theol., 1984-86 Instr., OT; SW Bapt. Theol. Sem., 1986- Asst. Prof., OT. Spec: Hebrew Bible, Semitic Languages, Texts and Epigraphy. Pub: "The Remarkable Suffering Servant of Isaiah 40-50" *SW Jour. of Theol.* (1991); articles in *Holman Bible Dict.* (Holman, 1991), *Mercer Dict. of the Bible* (Mercer, 1990); "An Annotated Bibliography for the Book of Malachi" *SW Jour. of Theol.* (1987). Mem: SBL; NABPR. Rec: Tennis, racquetball. Addr: (o) PO Box 22508, Fort Worth, TX 76122-0508 817-923-1921.

ENDRES, John C., b. Tacoma, WA, June 16, 1946, s. of John & Patricia (Ansley). Educ: Coll. of the Holy Cross, AB 1968; Weston Sch. of Theol., MDiv 1977; Vanderbilt U., PhD, OT. Emp: Jesuit Sch. of Theol. at Berkeley, 1982-89 Asst. Prof., 1989- Assoc. Prof.; Grad. Theol Union, 1982-89 Asst. Prof., 1989- Assoc. Prof. Spec: Hebrew Bible, Apocrypha and Post-biblical Studies. Pub: *Temple, Monarchy and Word of God* (Glazier, 1988); *Biblical Interpretation in the Book of Jubilees*, CBQ Mon. Ser. 18 (1987). Mem: SBL; CBA. Addr: (o) Jesuit School of Theology at Berkeley, 1735 LeRoy Ave., Berkeley, CA 94709 510-841-8804.

ENGBERG-PEDERSEN, Troels, b. Skive, Denmark, December 22, 1948, s. of Harald & Ingrid, m. Jonna, chil: Anna; Anders; Astrid. Educ: Copenhagen U., MA 1967-74, PhD 1976-82. Emp: Copenhagen U., 1989- Prof., NT. Spec: New Testament. Pub: "Proclaiming the Lord's Death: 1 Corinthians 11:17-34 and the Forms of Paul's Theological Argument" in *SBL 1991 Seminar Papers* (Scholars, 1991); "1 Corinthians 11:16 and the Character of Pauline Exhortation" *JBL* 110/4 (1991); *The Stoic Theory of Oikeiosis: Moral Development and Social Interaction in Early Stoic Philosophy*, Stud. in Hellenistic Civ. 2 (Aarhus U.P., 1990); *Religion and Religious Practice in the Seleucid Kingdom*, Stud. in Hellenistic Civ. 1, co-ed. (Aarhus U.P., 1990); "Ephesians 5,12-13: *elenchein* and Conversion in the New Testament" *ZNW* 80 (1989); and others. Mem: South. Assn. for Anc. Phil., England, 1977-; SBL 1987-. Rec: Music, literature, art. Addr: (o) Institute of Biblical Exegesis, Koebmagergade 44-46, DK-1150 Copenhagen K, Denmark 33-15-28-11; (h) Duevej 3, DK-4000 Roskilde, Denmark 42-35-55-04.

ENGLE, James R., b. Campbelltown, PA, November 12, 1940, s. of John & Anna, m. Anna Margaret (Groff), chil: David; Michael; Jesse; Karis; Jonathan; Charles; Joseph. Educ: Pittsburgh Theol. Sem., PhD 1979. Emp: Brethren in Christ Ch., 1967-70 Pastor; Freeman Jr. Coll., 1979-84 Prof., Bible; East. Mennonite Coll. & Sem., 1984- Assoc. Prof., OT. Excv:

Bab edh-Dhra, Jordan, 1975 Square Supr., 1977, 1981 Field Supr. Spec: Archaeology, Hebrew Bible. Mem: SBL 1967-; ASOR 1967-. Rec: Gardening, sports. Addr: (o) Eastern Mennonite Seminary, Harrisonburg, VA 22801 703-432-4275; (h) 520 Rockingham Dr., Harrisonburg, VA 22801 703-433-9889.

ENGLERT, Donald M., b. Allentown, PA, October 10, 1909, s. of George & Elsie, m. Ethel, chil: David; Thomas. Educ: Muhlenberg Coll., BA 1929; Princeton U., AM 1932; Princeton Theol. Sem., ThB 1932; Dropsie Coll., PhD 1947. Emp: 1934-43, Parish Min.; Lancaster Theol. Sem., 1943-80 Prof., Hebrew, OT. Spec: Hebrew Bible. Pub: *The Peshitto of Second Samuel,* SBL Mon. Ser. 3 (1949). Mem: SBL 1935-; AOS 1935-50. Addr: (h) 571 Kensington Terrace, Apartment 6, Lancaster, PA 17603 717-394-3120.

ENOCH, S. Ifor, b. Ciliau Aeron, Cardiganshire, December 26, 1914, s. of John Aeronydd & Jennie, m. Margaret Mary, chil: Desmond John; Helen Margaret. Educ: U. of Wales, Swansea, BA 1937; U. of Cambridge, BA 1940, MA 1943; Columbia U., MPhil 1949. Emp: Trinity English Presbyn. Ch., 1941-1948, 1950-1953 Min.; United Theol. Coll., Aberystwyth, 1953-1964 Prof., Greek, 1964-1977 Prin.; U. of Wales, Fac. of Theol., 1970-1974 Dean, 1975-1986 Lect., NT Stud. & Early Christian Thought. Spec: New Testament, Apocrypha and Post-biblical Studies. Pub: *The New Welsh Bible,* trans. (1988); *Jesus in the Twentieth Century* (1979); *The Second Epistle to the Corinthians* (1973); and others. Mem: SNTS. Rec: Sports, intl. politics, hist. & biographical lit. Addr: (h) Hendre, Brynymor Rd., Aberystwyth Dyfeb, SY23 2HX, Wales.

EPP, Eldon J., b. Mountain Lake, MN, November 1, 1930, s. of Jacob Jay & Louise (Kintzi), m. Eldoris M. (Balzer), chil: Gregory T.; Jennifer E. Educ: Wheaton Coll., AB (magna cum laude) 1952; Fuller Theol. Sem., BD (magna cum laude) 1955; Harvard U., STM 1956, PhD 1961. Emp: U. of South. Calif., 1962-68 Assoc. Prof., Relig. & Class.; *Hermeneia,* 1966- Ed. Bd.; Case Western Reserve U., 1968-, 1977-85 Dean of Hum. & Soc. Sci., 1982- Harkness Prof. of Bibl. Lit. & Chmn., Dept. of Relig.; *JBL,* 1971-90 Assoc. Ed.; SBL Centennial Pub. Ser., 1975-86 Ed. Bd.; *Critical Rev. of Books in Relig.,* 1991- Ed.; *Stud. & Documents,* 1991- Ed. Spec: New Testament. Pub: *Studies in the Theory and Method of New Testament Textual Criticism,* co-auth. (Eerdmans, 1993); "New Testament Textual Criticism" in *ABD* (Doubleday, 1992); "New Testament Papyrus Manuscripts and Letter-Carrying in Greco-Roman Times" in *The Future of Early Christianity: Essays in Honor of Helmut Koester* (Fortress, 1991); "The Significance of the Papyri for Determining the Nature of the New Testament Text in the Second Century" in *Gospel Traditions in the Second Century* (U. of Notre Dame, 1990); *The New Testament and Its Modern Interpreters,* co-ed. (Fortress/Scholars, 1989);

New Testament Textual Criticism: Its Significance for Exegesis: Essays in Honour of Bruce M. Metzger, co-ed. (Clarendon, 1981); "The Eclectic Method in New Testament Textual Criticism: Solution or Symptom?" *HTR* 69 (1976); "The Twentieth Century Interlude in New Testament Textual Criticism" *JBL* 93 (1974); *The Theological Tendency of Codex Bezae Cantabrigiensis in Acts* (Cambridge U.P., 1966); and others. Awd: Guggenheim Fellow 1974-75; Phi Beta Kappa. Mem: AAR 1961-, Pres., Pacific Coast Sect. 1965-66; SBL 1956-, Chmn., Textual Crit. Sect. 1971-84; SNTS 1966-; CBA 1969-; Amer. Soc. of Papyrologists 1989-. Addr: (o) Case Western Reserve U., Dept. of Religion Cleveland, OH 44106 216-368-2221; (h) 22399 Shelburne Rd., Shaker Heights, OH 44122 216-464-7927.

ERICKSON, Richard J., b. Everett, WA, June 1, 1947, s. of Howard C. & Betty (Morris), m. Randee L. (Trowbridge), chil: Ingrid M. Educ: Luth. Brethren Sem., BD 1972; Princeton Theol. Sem., ThM 1973; Fuller Theol. Sem., PhD 1980. Emp: Triumph Luth. Ch., 1980-84 Pastor; Fuller Theol. Sem., 1984- Assoc. Prof., NT. Spec: New Testament. Pub: *James Barr and the Beginnings of Biblical Semantics* (Foundations/Windham Hall, 1984); "Linguistics and Biblical Language: A Wide Open Field" *JETS* (1983); "Oida and Ginōskō and Verbal Aspect in Pauline Usage" *Westminster Theol. Jour.* (1982). Mem: ETS 1979-; SBL 1982-87; IBR 1985-92. Rec: Organic gardening, English lit., fiction writing, linguistics. Addr: (o) Fuller Theological Seminary Ext., 101 Nickerson St., Suite 330, Seattle, WA 98109 206-284-9000; (h) 11521 Evanston Ave. N, Seattle, WA 98133 206-363-2146.

ERLING, Svante Bernhard, b. Underwood, ND, April 15, 1922, s. of Svante A. & Edla M. (Larson), m. Marilyn M. (Siersbeck), chil: Maria; Birgitta; Paul; Anne. Educ: Gustavus Adolphus Coll., AB 1943; Augustana Theol. Sem., BD 1946; U. of Chicago, AM 1946; Yale U., PhD 1955; U. of Lund, ThL 1956, ThD 1960. Emp: Upsala Coll., 1956-57 Acting Chaplain, Asst. Prof.; Gustavus Adolphus Coll., 1957-88 Prof., Relig. Spec: Hebrew Bible. Pub: "First-Born and Firstlings in the Covenant Code" in *SBL 1986 Seminar Papers* 25 (1986); "Martin Luther and the Jews in Light of His Lectures on Genesis" *Immanuel* 18 (1984); "Creation and the Motifs" in *Creation and Method* (U. Press of Amer., 1981); "Ezekiel 38-39 and the Origins of Jewish Apocalyptic" in *Ex Orbe Religionum,* Festschrift G. Widengren (1972); *Nature and History, A Study in Theological Methodology with Special Attention to Motif Research* (Gleerup, 1960). Mem: AAR; SBL; Amer. Theol. Soc., Pres., MidW div. 1971-72. Rec: Jogging. Addr: (h) 1412 S Washington Ave., St. Peter, MN 56082 507-931-3878.

ERON, Lewis J., b. Englewood, NJ, July 26, 1951, s. of Abbot & Adele, m. Gail B.

(Trachtenberg), chil: Abby Rebecca; Andrew Michael. Educ: Johns Hopkins U., BA, Bible & Anc. Hist. 1973; Yale U., MA, Semitic Lang. 1975; Temple U., MA 1980, PhD, Relig. 1987; Reconstructionist Rabbinical Coll., Rabbinical Ord. 1981. Emp: Reconstructionist Rabbinical Assn., 1986-87 Exec. Dir.; Temple U., 1987-88 Instr., Relig. Dept. Spec: New Testament, Apocrypha and Post-biblical Studies. Pub: "On the Dating of Isaiah 13 and 14" in *Jewish Civilization, Essays and Studies*, vol. 1 (Reconstructionist Rabbinical Coll., 1979); and others. Awd: W.F. Albright Inst., ASOR, Jerusalem, Res. Fellow 1975-76. Mem: SBL 1976-; AJS 1978-; Reconstructionist Rabbinical Assn. 1981-; AAR 1984-. Rec: Gardening, jogging. Addr: (o) Temple B'nai Abraham, 300 E Northfield Rd., Livingston, NJ 07039 201-994-2290; (h) 27 Longview Rd., Livingston, NJ 07039 201-716-9098.

ESHEL, Esther, b. Nir-Etzion, Israel, February 11, 1958, d. of Shlomoh & Shoshanah (Duvdevan), m. Hanan Eshel, chil: Avshalom; Michal. Educ: Hebrew U., Jerusalem, BA 1986, MA 1991. Emp: Res. Asst. to Ed.-in-Chief of the Dead Sea Scrolls, 1990- Editing Dead Sea Scroll Documents; Israel Antiquities Authority, Jerusalem, 1992-. Spec: Hebrew Bible, Semitic Languages, Texts and Epigraphy, Apocrypha and Post-biblical Studies. Pub: "Fragments of Two Aramaic Documents Which Were Brought to Abi'or Cave During the Bar-Kokhba Revolt," co-auth., *Eretz-Israel* 23 (1992); "4QDeut—A Text That Has Undergone Harmonistic Editing" *HUCA* 62 (1991); "A Scroll from Qumran Which Includes Part of Ps 154 and a Prayer for King Jonathan," co-auth., *Tarbiz* 60 (1991); "4Q471 Fragment 1 and Ma'amadot in the War Scroll" in *Proceedings of the Madrid Congress of the Dead Sea Scrolls* (1991); "A Polemic Qumran Fragment" *JJS;* and others. Awd: Hebrew U., Jerusalem, Golda Meir Fellow. Fund 1989. Addr: (o) Israel Antiquities Authority, Jerusalem, Israel 02-892284; (h) 17 Arlosorov St., 92181 Jerusalem, Israel 02-633516.

ESHEL, Hanan, b. Rehovot, Israel, July 25, 1958, s. of Jacob & Shulamit, m. Esther, chil: Avshalom; Michal. Educ: Hebrew U., Arch. Inst., Jerusalem, BA 1984, MA 1989. Emp: Bar-Ilan U., 1990- Instr., Dept. of Land of Israel Stud. Excv: Ketef-Jericho, 1986 Dir.; Mackuk Cave, 1987 Dir.; Cemetery of the Qumran Type, north of Wadi Muraba'at, 1990 Dir.; Nahal Hever, 1991 Dir.; Jotapata, 1992 Area Supr. Spec: Archaeology, Semitic Languages, Texts and Epigraphy. Pub: "Fragments of Two Aramaic Documents Which Were Brought to Abi'or Cave During the Bar-Kokhba Revolt," co-auth., *Eretz-Israel* 23 (1992); "The Historical Background of the Pesher Interpreting Joshua's Curse on the Rebuilder of Jericho" *RQ* 15/59 (1992); "A Scroll from Qumran Which Includes Part of Ps 154 and a Prayer for King Jonathan," co-auth., *IEJ* 42 (1992); "The Prayer of Joseph from Qumran, a Papyrus from Masada and the

Samaritan Temple on APTAPIZIN" *Zion* 56 (1991); "Isaiah 8:23—A Historical-Geographical Analogy" *VT* 60 (1990); and others. Addr: (o) Bar-Ilan U., Dept. of Land of Israel Studies, 52 900 Ramat-Gan, Israel 03-531350; (h) 17 Arlosorov St., 92181 Jerusalem, Israel 02-633516.

ESLINGER, Lyle M., b. Calgary, Canada, June 4, 1953, s. of Harold & Mary, m. Gloria, chil: A. Cole; A. Jane. Educ: McMaster U., MA, PhD. Emp: U. of Calgary, 1984- Assoc. Prof. Spec: Hebrew Bible. Pub: "Inner-biblical Exegesis and Inner-biblical Allusion: The Question of Category" *VT* 42 (1992); "Freedom or Knowledge? Perspective & Purpose in the Exodus Narrative (Exodus 1-15)" *JSOT* 52 (1992); *Into The Hands of the Living God* (Sheffield, 1989); "A Change of Heart: 1 Sam 16" in *Ascribe to the Lord: Biblical and Other Essays in Memory of Peter C. Craigie*, co-ed. (Sheffield, 1988); "The Education of Amos" *Hebrew Ann. Rev.* 11 (1987); *Kingship of God in Crisis: A Close Reading of 1 Samuel 1-12* (Almond, 1985); and others. Mem: SBL 1976-; CSBS 1976-. Addr: (o) U. of Calgary, Dept. of Religious Studies, Calgary, AB T2N 1N4, Canada 403-220-5886; (h) 104 Riverview Circle, Cochrane, AB T0L 0W4, Canada 403-932-3025.

ESTES, Daniel J., b. Honesdale, PA, January 22, 1953, s. of Ernest & Katherine, m. Carol (Towle), chil: Jonathan; Christiana; Joel. Educ: Cedarville Coll., BA 1974; Dallas Theol. Sem., ThM 1978; Cambridge U., PhD 1988. Emp: Bapt. Ch., 1978-84, 1989-; Cedarville Coll., 1984- Assoc. Prof., Bible. Spec: Hebrew Bible. Pub: "Like Arrows in the Hand of a Warrior—Psalm 127:4-5a" *VT* 41/3 (1991); "Metaphorical Sojourning in 1 Chronicles 29:15" *CBQ* 53/1 (1991); "Looking for Abraham's City" *BS* Oct. (1990). Mem: SBL; AAR; ETS. Rec: Running, hiking, gardening, travel. Addr: (o) Cedarville College, Box 601, Cedarville, OH 45314 513-766-7978; (h) 6619 McVey Blvd., West Worthington, OH 43235 614-798-0914.

ESTRADA, Bernardo, b. Frontino, Colombia, February 17, 1950, s. of Asdrubal Estrada & Laura (Barbier). Educ: Universidad Nacional de Colombia, BS 1973; Ordained Priest 1979; U. of Navarre, Spain, STD, Bibl. Theol. 1981; U. of Salamanca, Lic. degree, Trilingual Bibl. Philol. 1988. Emp: Opus Dei Prelature, Colombia, 1981-84 Prof. of Holy Scripture; Roman Athenaeum of the Holy Cross, Faculty of Theol., Lect. Spec: New Testament. Pub: "La autoridad del Espiritu Santo en las homilias de San Juan Crisostomo sobre los Hechos de los Apostoles" in *Excerpta ex dissertationibus Sacrae Theologiae*, vol. IX (1985); "Il Comandamento dell'amore e le sue conseguenze alla luce di Mt 5,17-20" *Annales Theologici* 1 (1987); "Il binomio kalein-akoloythein nei Vangeli Sinottici" *Divus Thomas* 91 (1988); "A Century of Interpreting Parables: The Legacy of Adolf Julicher" *Annales Theologici* 6 (1992); and others. Awd: U. de Navarra, Premio

Extraordinario de Doctorado 1981. Mem: SBL 1988-; Assn. Bibl. Italiana 1988-; CBA 1989-. Rec: Classical Music, tennis, history of art. Addr: (o) Piazza di Sant'Apollinare 49, 00186 Rome, Italy 06-6861592; (h) Via della Camilluccia 603, 00135 Rome, Italy 06-36304905.

EVANS, Craig A., b. Ontario, CA, January 21, 1952, s. of Richard J. & Betty J., m. Viginia Anne, chil: Carrie L.; Jill Anne. Educ: West. Bapt. Sem., MDiv 1977; Claremont Grad. Sch., MA 1980, PhD 1983. Emp: McMaster U., Canada, 1980-81 Vis. Asst. Prof.; Trinity West. U., 1981- Prof., NT. Spec: New Testament, Apocrypha and Post-biblical Studies. Pub: *Luke* (Peabody, 1990); "Jesus' Action in the Temple: Cleansing or Portent of Destruction?" *CBQ* 51 (1989); *To See and Not Perceive: Isaiah 6:9-10 in Early Jewish and Christian Interpretation* (JSOT, 1989); *Life of Jesus Research: An Annotated Bibliography* (Leiden U.P., 1989); *Early Jewish and Christian Exegesis,* ed. (Scholars, 1987); "An Interpretation of Isaiah 8:11-15 Unemended" *ZAW* 97 (1985); "On the Vineyard Parables of Isaiah 5 and Mark 12" *BZ* 28 (1984); "The Function of Isaiah 6:9-10 in Mark and John" *NT* 24 (1982); "On the Prologue of John and the *Trimorphic Protennoia*" *NTS* 27 (1981); and others. Mem: SBL. Rec: Fishing, sports. Addr: (o) Trinity Western U., 7600 Glover Rd., Langley, BC V3A 6H4, Canada 604-888-7511; (h) 3674 Dunsmuir Way, Abbotsford, BC V2S 6G4, Canada 604-852-3265.

EVERSON, A. Joseph, b. McVille, ND, March 22, 1937, m. Susan (Corey), chil: Paul Corey; Philip John; Sarah Kathryn. Educ: St. Olaf Coll., BA 1959; Luther NW Sem., BD 1965; Union Theol. Sem., MTh 1966, PhD 1969. Emp: Luther Coll., 1968-76 Assoc. Prof.; St. John's U., 1970-71 Vis. Prof.; United Sem., 1980-88 Adj. Prof.; U. of St. Thomas, St. Paul Sem., 1987-90 Adj. Prof.; Calif. Luth. U., 1990- Assoc. Prof. Spec: Hebrew Bible, New Testament, Semitic Languages, Texts and Epigraphy. Pub: "Ezekiel and the Glory of the Lord Tradition" in *Sin, Salvation and the Spirit* (Liturgical, 1979); "To Give Them a Garland Instead of Ashes" *Interpretation* 32/1 (1978); "Day of the Lord" *IDB Sup.* (1976); "The Days of Yahweh" *JBL* 93/3 (1974); and others. Awd: U. of Heidelberg, Fellow. 1959-60; Union Theol. Sem., Herbert Worth Jackson Fellow. 1967-68. Mem: SBL; CBA; Natl. Workshop on Christian-Jewish Relations. Rec: Downhill skiing, mountain biking, travel, class. music. Addr: (o) California Lutheran U., 60 W Olsen Rd., Thousand Oaks, CA 91360 805-493-3239; (h) 841 Calle Catalpa, Thousand Oaks, CA 91360 805-492-6233.

EXUM, J. Cheryl, b. Wilson, NC, May 6, 1946. Educ: Columbia U., MA 1970, MPhil 1975, PhD 1976. Emp: Yale U., 1975-76 Asst. Prof. of OT, Div. Sch., 1976-77 Lect.; Boston Coll., 1977- Assoc. Prof., Hebrew Bible; *Semeia,* 1981-87 Assoc. Ed.; *CBQ,* 1983-90 Assoc. Ed.; *JBL,* 1992- Assoc. Ed; *Bibl. Interpretation,* 1992-

Exec. Ed. Spec: Hebrew Bible. Pub: *Tragedy and Biblical Narrative: Arrows of the Almighty* (Cambridge U.P., 1992); "The Centre Cannot Hold: Thematic and Textual Instabilities in Judges" *CBQ* 52 (1990); "Murder They Wrote: Ideology and the Manipulation of Female Presence in Biblical Narrative" in *The Pleasure of Her Text* (Trinity Press Intl., 1990); *Signs and Wonders: Biblical Texts in Literary Focus,* ed. (Scholars, 1989); "The Book of Judges" in *Harper Biblical Comm.* (Harper & Row, 1988); "The Mothers of Israel" *BR* 2/1 (1986); *Tragedy and Comedy in the Bible,* ed. (Scholars, 1985); and others. Awd: ASOR, NEH Fellow. 1980-81; Albright Inst. of Arch. Res., Jerusalem, Hon. Postdoc. Fellow 1983-84. Mem: AAR 1968-; SBL 1973-; CBA 1977-; ASOR 1978-. Addr: (o) Boston College, Dept. of Theology, Chestnut Hill, MA 02167 617-552-3880.

FABRIS, Rinaldo, b. Pavia (UD), Italy, December 12, 1936, s. of Enrico & Rosalia (Spizzamiglio). Educ: Pont. Lateranense U. & Pont. Bibl. Inst., ThD 1963, Dr.S.Script 1973. Emp: Archbishop's Sem. of Udine, 1967-; *RivBiblt,* 1986- Ed. Spec: New Testament. Pub: *La Bibbia nell'epoca contemporanea* (EDB, 1992); "Il Dio di Gesù Cristo nella Teologia di Matteo" *ScCatt* 117 (1989); "Gesù Cristo" in *Nuovo Dizionario di Teologia Biblica* (1988); *Gesú di Nazareth: Storia e interpretazione* (Cittadella, 1988); "La lettera agli Ebrei e l'AT" *RivBiblt* 32 (1984); *Matteo* (Borla, 1982); "Messianismo escatologico e apparizione di Cristo" in *Dizionario Teologico Interdisciplinare* (1977); *La legge della libertà in Giacomo* (Paideia, 1977). Mem: SNTS 1981-. Addr: (o) Viale Ungheria 20, 33100 Udine (I), Italy 0432-26230.

FAIRCHILD, Mark R., b. Corry, PA, July 23, 1954, s. of Donald & Ethel M., m. Darlene A., chil: Peter N.; Hannah E.; Ennea A.. Educ: Pa. State U., BS 1976; Toccoa Falls Coll., BA (summa cum laude) 1980; Asbury Theol. Sem., MDiv 1982; Drew U., MPhil 1985, PhD 1989. Emp: Drew U., 1984-85 Teaching Asst.; Huntington Coll., 1986- Asst. Prof., Bible & Relig. Spec: New Testament. Pub: "History and the Historical Jesus in the Nag Hammadi Literature" *Asbury Seminarian* 37/4 (1982). Mem: SBL; CBA; ETS. Rec: Baseball, tennis. Addr: (o) Huntington College, Huntington, IN 46750 219-356-6000; (h) 1531 Avon Pl., Huntington, IN 46750 219-356-7874.

FALKOWITZ, Robert S., b. New York, NY, April 9, 1952. Educ: Brown U., AB (magna cum laude) 1974; U. of Pa., PhD 1980. Emp: Emory U., 1982-83 Asst. Prof., Relig.; U. of Chicago Div. Sch., Inst. Advanced Stud. of Relig., 1983-84 Res. Fellow; Yale U., 1984-85 Vis. Lect., Near East. Stud.; U. of Pa., 1984- Res. Assoc., U. Mus. Spec: Mesopotamian Studies. Pub: "Discrimination and Condensation of Sacred Categories: The Fable in Early Mesopotamian Literature" in *La Fable* (Vandoeuvres, 1984); "Round Old Babylonian School Tablets from Nippur" *Archiv für*

Orientforschung 29-30 (1983-84); "Notes on 'Lugalbanda and Enmerkar'" *JAOS* 103 (1983); "Paragraph 59 of the 'Laws of Esnunna'" *Rev. d'Assyriologie* 72 (1970); and others. Mem: AAR; SBL; AOS. Addr: (o) 106, Route de Compois, CH1254 Jussy, Switzerland.

FALLA, Terry C., b. Guernsey, Channel Islands, March 31, 1940, s. of Clifford Wilson & Annette (Collenette), m. Berris Joan, chil: Matthew Clifford; Lynette Ruth; Daniel Bruce; Jeremy Paul. Educ: Melbourne U., BA 1966, MA 1967, PhD 1972. Emp: U. of Melbourne, Whitley Coll., 1971-81 Lect., OT Stud., Ridley Coll., 1983-84 Lect., Bibl. Hebrew; La Trobe U., 1984 Lect.; U. of Auckland, New Zealand Bapt. Theol. Coll., 1985-92 Prof., OT. Spec: New Testament. Pub: *A Key to the Peshitta Gospels*, vol. 1 (Brill, 1991); "Poetic Features of the Peshitta Gospels" *Rev. d'Etudes Orientales* (1977); "Demons and Demoniacs in the Peshitta Gospels" *Abr-Nahrain* 9 (1970); and others. Mem: SBL 1979-; Fellow. of Bibl. Stud., Melbourne. Rec: Music, bush-walking. Addr: (o) Whitley College, 271 Royal Parade, Parkville, Victoria 3050, Australia 00613-347-8388; (h) 1 Sumner Ave., Northcote, Victoria 3050, Australia 00613-481-6855.

FARBER, Gertrud, b. Schweina, Germany, May 29, 1945, d. of Siegfried & Charlotte Flügge, m. Walter, chil: Gregor. Educ: U. of Munich, PhD, Assyriology 1971. Emp: U. of Tuebingen, 1971-75; U. of Chicago, Oriental Inst., 1980- Res. Assoc. Spec: Mesopotamian Studies. Pub: "Konkret, Kollektiv, Abstract" *Aula Orientalis* (1992); "me", in *Reallexikon der Assyriologie* 7 (1990); "al-tar im Edubba: Notwendige Arbeitsgänge beim Bau eines Schulhauses" in *Studies Sjoeberg* (1989); "Another Old Babylonian Childbirth Incantation" *JNES* 43 (1984); *Répertoire Géographique des Textes Cunéiformes*, vol. 1 & 2 (Wiesbaden, 1974, 1977); *Der Mythos "Inanna und Enki" unter besonderer Berücksichtigung der Liste der me* (1973); and others. Addr: (o), U. of Chicago, Oriental Institute, 1155 E 58th St., Chicago, IL 60637 312-702-9548; (h) 5435 S Hyde Park Blvd., Chicago, IL 60615 312-752-0937.

FARBER, Walter, b. Stuttgart, Germany, October 3, 1947, s. of Klemens & Hedwig, m. Gertrud (Flügge), chil: Gregor. Educ: U. of Tübingen, PhD, Assyriology 1973. Emp: U. of Munich, 1974-80 Asst. Prof.; U. of Chicago, Oriental Inst., 1980-89 Assoc. Prof., 1990- Prof., Assyriology. Spec: Mesopotamian Studies. Pub: "Magic at the Cradle: Babylonian and Assyrian Lullabies" *Anthropos* 85 (1990); "Vorzeichen aus der Waschschüssel" *Orientalia* 58 (1989); "(W)ardat-lili(m)" *ZA* 79 (1989); "Lamaštu" in *Reallexikon der Assyriologie und vorderasiatischen Archäologie* (1983); "Die Vergottlichung Naram-Sins" *Orientalia* 52 (1983); "Zur älteren akkadischen Beschwörungsliteratur" *ZA* 71 (1981); *Beschwörungsrituale an Istar und Dumuzi* (Steiner, 1977); and others. Addr: (o) U. of Chicago, Oriental Institute, 1155 E 58th St.,

Chicago, IL 60637 312-702-9546; (h) 5435 S Hyde Park Blvd., Chicago, IL 60615 312-752-0937.

FARMER, Kathleen A., b. Sioux Falls, SD, September 3, 1943, d. of John Douglas Robertson & Phyllis (Gleason), m. Edward R. Farmer, chil: Anna Marie. Educ: Perkins Sch. of Theol., MRE 1967, BD 1970; South. Meth. U., PhD 1978. Emp: United Theol. Sem., 1978-93 Prof. Spec: Hebrew Bible. Pub: "Psalms" in *Womens Bible Comm.* (Westminster/John Knox, 1992); *Who Knows What is Good? A Commentary on Proverbs and Ecclesiastes* (Eerdmans, 1991); "Ungodly Habits of Identification" *United Theol. Sem. Jour. of Theol.* 91 (1987); "The Call to Spiritual Adulthood in the Old Testament" *United Theol. Sem. Bull.* 89 (1985); *Isaiah*, Bible Lives of Faith Ser. (United Meth., 1980). Awd: Woodrow Wilson Fellow 1965; Dempster Grad. Study Fellow. 1974-75. Rec: Fishing, canoeing. Addr: (o) 1810 Harvard Blvd., Dayton, OH 45406 513-278-5817.

FARMER, William R., b. Needles, CA, February 1, 1921, s. of William & Elsie (Vaughan), m. Nell (Cochran), chil: Richard; William; Donald; Rebecca. Educ: Occidental Coll., AB 1942; Cambridge U., BA 1949, MA 1956, BD 1964; Union Theol. Sem., BD 1950, ThD 1952. Emp: Drew U., 1955-59 Asst. Prof.; South. Meth. U., 1959-91 Prof., 1991- Prof. Emeritus. Excv: Shechem, East Gate, 1956-58 Supr. Spec: Archaeology, New Testament, Apocrypha and Post-biblical Studies. Pub: *Jesus and the Gospel* (Fortress, 1982); *The Last Twelve Verses of Mark* (Cambridge U.P., 1974); *The Synoptic Problem* (Macmillan, 1964); "Notes on a Literary and Form-Critical Analysis of Some of the Synoptic Material Peculiar to Luke" *NTS* (1962); "Soundings at Khirbet Wadi Ez-Zaraniq" *BASOR* (1957); "The Geography of Ezekiel's River of Life" *BA* (1956); and others. Awd: Guggenheim Fellow 1964. Mem: SBL 1950-, Pres., SW Sect., 1960, 1973; SNTS 1958-; Intl. Inst. for the Renewal of Gospel Stud., co-chmn., 1980-. Rec: Hiking. Addr: (o) U. of Dallas, Research Scholar, PO Box 684, Irving, TX 75062; (h) 4103 Emerson, Dallas, TX 75205.

FARRELL, Hobert K., b. Charleston, WV, February 15, 1939, s. of Kenneth H. & Juanita (Bowling), m. Carol (Dondit), chil: David Kenneth; John Douglas. Educ: Wheaton Coll., BA 1961; Wheaton Grad. Sch., MA 1964; Gordon Div. Sch., BD 1964; Union Theol. Sem., ThM 1966; Boston U., Grad. Sch., PhD 1972. Emp: Boston U., 1967-71 Instr.; John Wesley Coll., 1971-78 Asst. Prof.; LeTourneau U., 1978- Prof. Spec: New Testament. Pub: "The Structure and Theology of Luke's Central Section" *Trinity Jour.* 7/2 (1986); articles in *Baker Ency. of the Bible.* Mem: ETS 1960-; SBL 1964-; IBR 1970-. Rec: Sports, jogging, camping. Addr: (o) LeTourneau U., PO Box 7001, Longview, TX 75607 903-753-0231; (h) 3012 Keystone St., Longview, TX 75605 903-759-0418.

FARRIS, Stephen C., b. Brampton, Canada, June 21, 1951, s. of Allan & Muriel (Neale), m. Patricia (White), chil: Allan; Daniel. Educ: Union Theol. Sem., DMin 1977, ThM 1978; Cambridge U., PhD 1982. Emp: Presbyn. Ch., 1981-86 Min.; Queen's U., 1983-86 Adj. Lect.; Knox Coll., Toronto, 1986-90 Assoc. Prof., 1990- Prof. Spec: New Testament. Pub: *The Hymns of Luke's Infancy Narratives* (JSOT, 1985); "On Discerning Semitic Sources in Luke 1-2" in *Gospel Perspectives* vol. 2 (1981); and others. Mem: CSBS 1985-; AH 1986-; World Alliance of Reformed Ch., Exec. Com. 1989- Rec: Gardening, sports. Addr: (o) Knox College, 59 St. George St., Toronto, ON M55 2E6, Canada 416-978-4500; (h) 70 Livingston Rd., West Hill, ON, Canada.

FASSBERG, Steven E., b. Washington, DC, March 28, 1956, s. of Harold & Vera, m. Celia (Wasserstein), chil: Teddy Jonathan; Sarah Magda; Miriam Regina. Educ: Harvard U., AB 1978, PhD 1984. Emp: Hebrew U., Jerusalem, 1981- Sr. Lect., Dept. of Hebrew Lang. Spec: Hebrew Bible, Semitic Languages, Texts and Epigraphy. Pub: "The Adverbials 'Miyyad' and 'Al-yad 'Al-yad' in Rabbinic Hebrew" *Lang. Stud.* 5-6 (1991); "Negative Pupose Clauses in Biblical Hebrew" in *Chaim Rabin Festschrift* (1990); *A Grammar of the Palestinian Targum Fragments from the Cairo Genizah*, HSS 38 (Scholars, 1990); "The Origin of the Ketib/Qere in the Aramaic Portions of Ezra and Daniel" *VT* 19 (1989); "Miscellanea in Western Aramaic" *Lang. Stud.* 2-3 (1987); "Determined Forms of the Cardinal Number 'One' in Three Pentateuchal Targumim" *Sefarad* 45 (1985); and others. Awd: Lady Davis Fellow. 1981-83; Allon Fellow. 1987- 90. Mem: WUJS; AJS; AOS; SBL. Rec: Amateur radio. Addr: (o) Hebrew U. of Jerusalem, Dept. of Hebrew Language, Mt. Scopus, Jerusalem, Israel 2-883565; (h) Mevo Dakar 5, French Hill, Jerusalem 97855, Israel 2-323-182.

FAY, Gregory L., b. Magnolia, AK, November 25, 1960, s. of Thomas E. & Rachel (Wallis), m. Cheryl L., chil: Paul D.; Bethany A. Educ: Freed Hardeman U., BA (summa cum laude) 1982; Harding Grad. Sch. of Relig., MA 1987. Emp: Ch. of Christ, 1988-90, 1992- Min.; Marquette U., 1991-92 Fellow. Spec: New Testament. Pub: "Introduction to Incomprehension: The Literary Structure of Mark 4:1-13" *CBQ* 51 (1989). Mem: SBL 1987-. Rec: Tae Kwon Do, tennis, fishing, sports. Addr: (o) Kirkwood Ave. Church of Christ, 1320 Kirkwood Ave., Iowa City, IA 52240 319-338-8780; (h) 915 Boston Way, #4, Coralville, IA 52241 319-339-0647.

FEE, Gordon D., b. Ashland, OR, May 23, 1934, s. of Donald H. & Grace I. (Jacobson), m. Maudine (Lofdahl), chil: Mark; Cherith; Craig; Brian. Educ: Seattle Pacific U., BA 1956, MA, Bibl. Lit. 1958; U. of South. Calif., PhD, NT Stud. 1966. Emp: South. Calif. Coll., 1966-69 Assoc. Prof., Relig.; Wheaton Coll., 1969-74

Assoc. Prof., Bibl. Stud.; Gordon-Conwell Theol. Sem., 1974-86 Prof., NT; Regent Coll., 1986- Prof., NT. Spec: New Testament. Pub: "*Eidolothuta* Once Again—An Interpretation of 1 Corinthians 8-10" *Biblica* 61 (1980); *New Testament Textual Criticism: Its Significance for Exegesis: Essays in Honor of Bruce M. Metzger*, co-ed. (Oxford U.P., 1981); "Origen's Text of the New Testament and the Text of Egypt" *NTS* 28 (1982); *How to Read the Bible for All Its Worth: A Guide to Understanding the Bible*, co-auth. (Zondervan, 1982); *1 and 2 Timothy and Titus: A Good News Commentary* (Harper & Row, 1984); *The First Epistle to the Corinthians: New International Comm.* (Eerdmans, 1987); and others. Mem: SBL; SNTS 1970-. Addr: (o) Regent College, 5800 University Blvd., Vancouver, BC V6T 2E4, Canada.

FELD, Helmut, b. Dillingen-Saar, Germany, August 25, 1936, s. of Alois & Charlotte (Schwendler), chil: Karl M.; Peter D. Educ: Gregoriana U., Rome, Lic. Phil. 1959; U. of Tubingen, ThD 1970; Saarland U., PhD 1976. Emp: U. of Wurzburg, 1974-78 Res.; Saarland U., 1975-; European Inst. & Acad. of Baden- Wurttemberg, 1978-81 Dir.; U. of Tubingen, 1978-91; Inst. of European Hist., Mainz, 1991-. Spec: New Testament, Apocrypha and Post-bib- lical Studies. Pub: *I. Calvini Opera omnia, II/16: Commentarii in Pauli epp. ad Gal, Eph, Phil, Col* (Droz, 1992); *Der Ikonoklasmus des Westens* (Brill, 1990); *Der Hebraerbrief* (1985); *Wendelini Steinbach Opera Exegetica quae supersunt omnia*, 3 vol. (Steiner, 1976-1987); *Das Verstandnis des Abendmahls* (Wiss. Buchges. Darmstadt, 1976); and others. Mem: SNTS 1979-. Addr: (h) Marienburgerstrasse 38, D-72116 Mossingen 1, Germany 07473-6611.

FELDER, Cain H., Educ: Howard U., BA 1966; Oxford U., Mansfield Coll., Dip. Theol. 1968; Union Theol. Sem., N.Y., MDiv 1969; Columbia U., PhD 1982. Emp: Princeton Theol. Sem., 1978- 81 Instr.; Howard U., Sch. of Div., 1981- Prof. of NT, 1982- Ed., *Jour. of Relig. Thought*; Bibl. Inst. for Social Change, 1990- Founder & Chmn. Pub: *African Heritage Study Bible*, gen. ed. (Winston Derek, 1993); "Afrocentric Biblical Interpretation" in *Dict. of Biblical Interpretation* (Abingdon, 1992); *Stony the Road We Trod: African-American Biblical Interpretation* (Fortress, 1991); *Troubling Biblical Waters: Race, Class and Family* (Orbis, 1989); and oth- ers. Awd: Staley Disting. Christian Schol. 1991. Mem: SBL; AAR; Soc. for the Study of Black Relig.; Middle East Stud. Assn. Addr: (o) Howard U., School of Divinity, 1400 Shepherd St. NE, Washington, DC 20017 202-806-0642.

FELDMAN, Louis H., b. Hartford, CT, October 29, 1926, s. of Sam & Sarah (Vine), m. Miriam, chil: Moshe; Sara; Leah. Educ: Trinity Coll., BA 1946, MA 1947; Harvard U., PhD 1951. Emp: Trinity Coll., 1951-53 Instr.; Hobart & William Smith Coll., 1953-1955 Instr.; Yeshiva Coll.,

1955- Prof. of Class.; *EJ*, 1967-71 Dept. Ed., Hellenistic Lit. Pub: *Jew and Gentile in the Ancient World* (Princeton U.P., 1993); "Proselytes and 'Sympathizers' in the Light of the New Inscriptions from Aphrodisias" *Revue des Etudes juives* 148 (1989); "Use, Authority, and Exegesis of Mikra in the Writings of Josephus" in *Mikra: Text, Translation, Reading and Interpretation of the Hebrew Bible in Ancient Judaism and Early Christianity*, Compendia Rerum Iudaicaram ad NT, sec. 2, vol. 1 (1988); "Pro-Jewish Intimations in Anti-Jewish Remarks Cited in Josephus' *Against Apion*" *JQR* 78 (1987-88); *Josephus: A Supplementary Bibliography* (1986); "How Much Hellenism in Jewish Palestine?" *HUCA* 57 (1986); *Josephus and Modern Scholarship (1937-80)* (1984); "Josephus' Portrait of Saul" *HUCA* 53 (1982); *Scholarship on Philo and Josephus* (Yeshiva U., 1963); and others. Awd: Judaica Ref. Book Award. 1985; Guggenheim Fellow. Addr: (o) 500 W 185th St., New York, NY 10033 212-960-5314; (h) 69-11 Harrow St., Forest Hills, NY 11375 718-263-2959.

FENTON, John C., b. Liverpool, England, June 5, 1921, s. of Cornelius & Claudine (O'Connor), m. Linda Winifred. Educ: Queen's Coll., Oxford, BA 1943; Oxford, MA 1947, BD 1954. Emp: Lincoln Theol. Coll., England, 1947-54 Chaplain, Sub-warden; Holy Trinity, Wentworth, Yorkshire, 1954-58 Vicar; Lichfield Theol. Coll., 1958-65 Prin.; St. Chad's Coll., Durham, 1965-78 Prin.; Christ Ch., Oxford, 1978-91 Canon. Spec: New Testament. Pub: *The Gospel According to John* (Clarendon, 1970); *The Gospel of St. Matthew* (Penguin, 1963). Mem: SNTS. Addr: (h) 8 Rowland Close, Lower Wolvercote, Oxford OX2 8PW, England 243-887.

FERGUSON, Wm. Everett, b. Montgomery, TX, February 18, 1933, s. of W.E. & Edith, m. Nancy (Lewis), chil: Everett Ray; Edith Ann; Patricia. Educ: Abilene Christian U., BA 1953, MA 1954; Harvard U., STB 1956, PhD 1960. Emp: NE Christian Jr. Coll., 1959-62 Dean; Abilene Christian U., 1962- Prof.; *Restoration Quar.*, 1987-92 Ed.; *SC*, 1981- Ed. Spec: New Testament, Apocrypha and Post-biblical Studies. Pub: *Ency. of Early Christianity*, ed. (Garland, 1990); "Irenaeus' *Proof of the Apostolic Preaching* and Early Catechetical Instructions" *Studia Patristica* 18/3 (1989); "Spiritual Circumcision in Early Christianity" *SJT* 41 (1988); *Backgrounds of Early Christianity* (Eerdmans, 1987); "Athanasius' 'Epistola ad Marcellinum in Interpretationem Psalmorum'" *Studia Patristica* 16/2 (1985); "Inscriptions and the Origin of Infant Baptism" *JTS* 30 (1979); *Gregory of Nyssa: The Life of Moses*, co-auth. (Paulist, 1978); *Early Christians Speak* (Abilene Christian U.P., 1971); "Jewish and Christian Ordination" *HTR* 56 (1963); and others. Mem: SBL; Amer. Soc. of Ch. Hist.; Eccles. Hist. Soc.; NAPS, Pres. 1990-92. Addr: (o) ACU Station, Box 8402, Abilene, TX 79699 915-674-3734; (h) 609 E.N. 16th St., Abilene, TX 79601 915-677-3893.

FERNANDEZ-MARCOS, Natalio, b. Villanueva de las Manzanas, November 1, 1940, s. of Bernardo & Leocadia. Educ: Phil. Hochschule, Munich, Lic. Phil. 1964; Salamanca U., Lic. Class. Philol. 1966; Complutensian U., Madrid, Lic. Bibl. Philol. 1970, Doc. Class. Philol. 1970. Emp: Consejo Superior de Investigaciones Cientificas, 1972- Prof. de Investigacion, Coord. de Hum. y C. Soc.; *Sefarad*, 1975- Ed. Bd.; *Textos y Estudios Cardenal Cisneros de la Biblia Poliglota Matritense*, 1983- Ed. Bd.; *Septuagint & Cognate Stud.*, 1983- Ed. Bd.; U. of Oxford, 1991-92 Grinfield Lect. on the Septuagint. Spec: Hebrew Bible. Pub: *El texto antioqueno de la Biblia Griega.*, vol. 1-2 (CSIC, 1989, 1992); "La uncion de Salomon y la entrada de Jesus en Jerusalem" *Biblica* 68 (1987); *La Septuaginta en la Investigacion Contemporanea* (CSIC, 1985); "El Protolucianico, revision griega de los judios de Antioquia?" *Biblica* 64 (1983); "[Elpizein] or [eggizein] in Prophetarum Vitae Fabulosae and in the Septuagint" *VT* 30 (1980); *Introduccion a las versiones griegas de la Biblia* (CSIC, 1979); *Los Thaumata de Sofronio. Contribucion al estudio de la Incubatio cristiana.* (CSIC, 1975); and others. Mem: Soc. Esp. Estud. Clasicos 1968-; IOSCS 1971-; Fund Bibl. Espanola 1983-. Rec: Swimming. Addr: (o) Duque de Medinaceli 6, 28014 Madrid, Spain 91-5854839; (h) San Leopoldo 8, 28029 Madrid, Spain 91-3150228.

FERRIS, Paul W., Jr., b. IL, March 25, 1944, s. of Paul Wayne & Isabel Sarah (Gibson), m. Lois Anne (Fransen), chil: Paul W.; Heide L.; Jeremy T. Educ: Trinity Evang. Div. Sch., MA 1969, MDiv 1971; Dropsie Coll. of Hebrew & Cognate Learning, PhD 1985. Emp: Moody Bible Inst., 1968-71 Instr.; *Wycliffe Bible Ency.*, 1969-71 Contb. Ed.; Trinity Evang. Div. Sch., 1971 Vis. Prof.; Columbia Grad. Sch. of Bible & Missions, 1975-92 Prof.; Prairie Bible Inst., 1992- Pres. Spec: Archaeology, Hebrew Bible. Pub: "Genre of Communal Lament" in *ABD;* and others. Mem: SBL; AAR; ETS; NAPH. Rec: Woodworking. Addr: (o) Box 3122, Columbia, SC 29230 803-754-4100.

FESPERMAN, Francis I., b. Rockingham County, NC, October 19, 1921, s. of Luther A. & Beulah (Beaver), m. Kathleen (Castor), chil: Martha; Paul. Educ: Lenoir-Rhyne Coll., AB 1941; Luth. Theol. South. Sem., MDiv 1945; Luth. Sch. of Theol., STM 1962; Vanderbilt U., PhD 1969. Emp: Newberry Coll., 1957- Prof. Spec: Hebrew Bible, New Testament. Pub: *From Torah to Apocalypse* (U. Press of Amer., 1983); "Jefferson's Bible" *Ohio Jour. of Relig. Stud.* Oct. (1976). Awd: Martin Luther Fellow 1962-64; Vanderbilt U., Hillel Fellow 1963-64. Mem: SBL 1958-; S.C. Acad. of Relig. 1967-, Pres. 1976-77. Rec: Tennis. Addr: (o) Newberry College, Newberry, SC 29108 803-321-5199; (h) 2113 Springdale Dr., Newberry, SC 29108 803-276-1598.

FIEDLER, Peter, b. Mariaschein, Bohemia, August 29, 1940, s. of Karl & Marianne

(Plundrich), m. Ursula (Hollaender), chil: Max; Lucia; Astrid; Marisa; Beatrice. Spec: New Testament. Pub: "Probleme der Abendmahlsforschung" *ALW* 24 (1982); "Rom. 8, 31-39 als Brennpunkt paulinischer Frohbotschaft" *ZNW* 68 (1977); *Jesus und die Suender*, BET 3 (Lang, 1976); "Die uebergebenen Talente (Mt. 25, 14-30)" *Bibel & Liturgie* 11 (1970); *Die Formel <und siehe> im Neuen Testament*, STANT 20 (Kosel, 1969); and others. Mem: SNTS 1989-. Addr: (o) Paedagogische Hochschule, D79117 Freiburg, Germany 0761-682-224; (h) Langen Wangen 2, D79112 Freiburg, Germany 0766-4587.

FIELDS, Weston W., b. Long Beach, CA, January 16, 1948, s. of De Witt & Wanda, m. Beverly, chil: Tamie Marie; De Witt Charles. Educ: Faith Bapt. Bible Coll., BA 1970; Grace Theol. Sem., MDiv (magna cum laude) 1973, ThM 1975, ThD 1979; Hebrew U. of Jerusalem, PhD 1992. Emp: Grace Coll. & Theol. Sem., 1975-85 Assoc. Prof.; Inst. of Holy Land Stud., Jerusalem, 1985-91 Prof.; *Grace Theol. Jour.*, 1983-85 Ed. Spec: Hebrew Bible, Semitic Languages, Texts and Epigraphy. Pub: "The Motif 'Night as Danger' in Three Biblical Destruction Narratives" in *Sha'arei Talmon*, co-ed. (Eisenbrauns, 1992); "Sodom and Gomorrah in Intertestament and New Testament Literature" in *New Testament Studies in Honor of Homer Kent* (1991); and others. Mem: SBL. Rec: Private pilot, travel, reading. Addr: (o) PO Box 24265, Jerusalem, Israel 972-2-819337; (h) PO Box 25, Kodiak, AK 99615 907-486-3949.

FIENSY, David A., b. McCleansboro, IL, November 7, 1948, s. of Arthur & G. Maxine (Minor), m. Molly Jean (French), chil: Amanda G.; Jeannie D. Educ: Xavier U., MA 1974; Duke U., PhD 1980. Emp: Kentucky Christian Coll., 1980-87 Asst. Prof.; Inst. for the Study of Christian Origins, Germany, 1987-89 Inst. Schol.; Christian Ch., 1989- Pastor. Spec: New Testament, Apocrypha and Post-biblical Studies. Pub: "Lex Talionis in the Apocalypse of Peter" *HTR* (1983); "Redaction History and the Apostolic Constitutions" *JQR* (1982); articles in *Psuedepigrapha of the Old Testament*, vol. 1 & 2 (1983, 1985); *Prayers Alleged to Be Jewish: An Examination of the Constitutiones Apostolorum* (Scholars, 1985); *The Social History of Palestine in the Herodian Period: The Land is Mine* (Mellen, 1991). Mem: SBL 1978-. Rec: Tennis, hiking. Addr: (o) 6626 Grape Grove Rd., Jamestown, OH 45335.

FINEGAN, Jack, b. Des Moines, IA, July 11, 1908, s. of Henry & Clarissa A., m. Mildred (Meader), chil: Jack R. Educ: Drake U., BA 1928, MA 1929, BD 1930, LLD 1953; Colgate Rochester Div. Sch., BD 1931, MTh 1932; Friedrich Wilhelms U., Berlin, Lic. Theol. (magna cum laude) 1934; Chapman Coll., LittD 1964. Emp: Iowa State U., 1939-46 Prof., Chmn., Dept. of Relig. Educ.; Pacific Sch. of Relig., 1946-75 Frederick Billings Prof. of NT

Hist. & Arch., Inst. of Bibl. Arch., Dir.; *Jour. of Bible & Relig.*, Arch. Ed.; *BAR*, Ed. Adv. Bd. Spec: Archaeology, New Testament. Pub: *The Archaeology of the New Testament*, 2 vol. (Princeton U.P., 1969, 1992; Westview, 1981); *Myth and Mystery, An Introduction to the Pagan Religions of the Biblical World* (Baker, 1989); *Discovering Israel* (Eerdmans, 1981); "Crosses in the Dead Sea Scrolls" *BAR* 5/6 (1979); *Encountering New Testament Manuscripts* (Eerdmans, 1974); and others. Awd: India, Fulbright Res. Schol. 1952-53. Mem: SNTS. Rec: Flying, sailing, mountain climbing. Addr: (o) Pacific School of Religion, 1798 Scenic Ave., Berkeley, CA 94709 415-848-0528; (h) 33 Linda Ave. #1701, Oakland, CA 94611 415-654-9129.

FINKELSTEIN, Israel, b. Tel Aviv, Israel, March 29, 1949, s. of Zvi & Miriam, m. Joelle (Cohen), chil: Adar. Educ: Tel Aviv U., Inst. of Arch., BA 1974, MA 1978, PhD 1983. Emp: Bar Ilan U., Dept. for the Land of Israel Stud., 1976-90; U. of Chicago, Oriental Inst., 1986-87; Tel Aviv U., Inst. of Arch., 1990-. Excv: 'Izbet Sartah, 1976-78 Field Dir.; Tel 'Ira, 1979-80 Co-dir.; Land of Ephraim Survey, 1980-87 Dir.; Shiloh, 1981-84 Dir. Spec: Archaeology. Pub: "Early Arad—Urbanism of the Nomads" *ZDPV* 106 (1991); *From Nomadism to Monarchy: Archaeological and Historical Aspects of Early Israel*, co-ed. (1990); "Further Observations on the Socio-Demographic Structure of the Intermediate Bronze Age" *Levant* 21 (1989); "The Land of Ephraim Survey 1980-87: Preliminary Report" *Tel Aviv* 15-16 (1988-89); *The Archaeology of the Israelite Settlement* (1988); "Arabian Trade and Socio-Political Conditions in the Negev in the Twelfth-Eleventh Centuries B.C.E." *JNES* 47 (1988); *Izbet Sartah: An Early Iron Age Site Near Rosh Ha'ayin, Israel*, Brit. Arch. Reports 299 (Oxford U.P., 1986); *Sinai in Antiquity*, co-ed. (1980); and others. Mem: Hebrew U., Inst. for Advanced Stud. 1983-84. Addr: (o) Tel Aviv U., Institute of Archaeology, Ramat Aviv, Tel Aviv, Israel 03-6409417; (h) 11 Ha'oniversita St., Ramat Aviv 69975, Tel Aviv, Israel 03-6421876.

FIORE, Benjamin, b. New York, NY, August 26, 1943, s. of Philip & Jane (Roszkowski). Educ: Fordham U., MA 1969; Pont. Gregorian Inst., STB 1974; Yale U., MA 1975, PhD 1982. Emp: Canisius Coll., 1979- Prof. Spec: New Testament. Pub: "Invective in Romans and Philippians" *Proc. of East. Great Lakes & MidW Bible Soc.* (1990); *Marxism and Christianity*, co-auth. (Georgetown U., 1987); *Personal Example in the Socratic and Pastoral Epistles* (Bibl. Inst., 1986); "'Covert Allusion' in Corinthians 1-4" *CBQ* 47 (1985); and others. Mem: SBL; CBA. Rec: Calligraphy, sketching, choral singing. Addr: (o) Canisius College, 2001 Main St., Buffalo, NY 14208.

FISCHER, Moshe L., b. Brasov, Romania, s. of Benjamin & Frida, m. Greta, chil: Yair; Shay.

Educ: U. of Bucuresti, Romania, MA 1968; Tel Aviv U., Israel, PhD 1979. Emp: Inst. of Arch., Romania, 1968-70 Asst.; Tel Aviv U., Israel, 1972-87 Lect., 1987- Sr. Lect. Excv: Histros, Romania, 1965-68 Area Supr.; Tamar, Israel, 1973-75 Co-dir.; En Boq eq, Israel, 1972, 1977, 1980 Co-dir.; Quedesh, Israel, 1981-83 Dir; Zikrim, Israel, 1982-89 Dir. Spec: Archaeology. Pub: *Das Korinthische Kapitell im Alten* (1990); "The Corinthian Capitals of the Capernaum Synagogue" *Levant* (1986); and others. Rec: Lit., lang. Addr: (o) Tel Aviv U., Dept. of Classical Study, Tel Aviv, Ramat Aviv, Israel 03-6409938; (h) Petach Tikva, 15 Salant, 49530, Israel 03-9302293.

FISHBANE, Michael A., b. Cambridge, MA, February 18, 1943, s. of Philip & Bernice, m. Mona (DeKoven), chil: Eitan; Elisha. Educ: Brandeis U., PhD 1971. Emp: Brandeis U., 1969-90; U. of Chicago, 1990- Nathan Cummings Prof. of Jewish Stud.; Harvard U., Vis. Prof.; Hebrew U., Vis. Prof.; Stanford U., Vis. Prof.; State U. of N. Y. Press, Jewish Hermeneutics, Mysticism & Relig. Ser., Ed. Spec: Hebrew Bible, Apocrypha and Post-biblical Studies. Pub: "The Holy One Sits and Roars: Mythopoesis and the Midrashic Imagination" *Jewish Thought* (1991); *The Garments of Torah: Essays in Biblical Hermeneutics* (Indiana U.P., 1989); *Biblical Interpretation in Ancient Israel* (Clarendon, 1985, 1988); *Judaism: Revelation and Traditions* (Harper & Row, 1987); "Form and Reformulation of the Biblical Priestly Blessing" *JAOS* (1983); *Text and Texture: Studies in Biblical Literature* (Schocken, 1979); "Composition and Structure in the Jacob Cycle" *JJS* 26 (1975); "Numbers 5:11-31: A Study of Law and Scribal Practice in Israel and the Ancient Near East" *HUCA* 45 (1974); and others. Awd: Lady Davis Fellow 1974-75; Guggenheim Fellow 1984-85; Natl. Jewish Book Awd. for Schol. 1986; Seventh Ann. Kenneth B. Smilen Jewish Lit. Awd. 1986; BAS, Publ. Awd. 1986. Mem: SBL, Pres., New England reg. 1984-85; AJS; CBA; Colloquium for Bibl. Res.; AAJR. Addr: (o) U. of Chicago Divinity School, 1025 E 58th St., Chicago, IL 60637 312-702-8234; (h) 294 Central Ave., Highland Park, IL 60035 708-432-1940.

FISHER, Eugene J., b. Grosse Pointe, MI, September 10, 1943, s. of Eugene & Caroline (Damm), m. Catherine (Ambrosiano), chil: Sarah. Educ: U. of Detroit, MA 1968; New York U., MA, Hebrew Stud. 1971, PhD 1976. Emp: Archdiocese of Detroit, 1971-77 Dir., Catechist Formation; U. of Detroit, 1969-77 Adj. Prof.; St. John's Sem., 1973-75 Adj. Prof.; Natl. Conf. of Cath. Bishops, 1977- Exec. Dir.; *JES*, 1983- Ed. Spec: Hebrew Bible, New Testament. Pub: "The Church's Teaching on Supersessionism" *BAR* 17/2 (1991); *Jewish Roots of Christian Liturgy* (Paulist, 1990); "Nag Hammadi" *BT* (1982); "Lex Talionis" *JES* (1983); *Formation of Social Policy in Catholic and Jewish Traditions*, 2 vol., co-auth. (U. of Notre Dame, 1980-1982); and others. Awd:

Edith Stein Guild Awd., 1983. Mem: SBL, Pres., Chesapeake Bay reg. 1980-81; CBA 1971-. Rec: Sailing, swimming, science fiction. Addr: (o) National Conference of Catholic Bishops, 1312 Mass. Ave. NW, Washington, DC 20005 202-659-6857; (h) 11296 Spyglass Cove Ln., Reston, VA 22091 703-476-4579.

FITCH, Alger M., b. Cornelius, OR, October 18, 1919, s. of Alger M., Sr., & Clara Elsie (Aune), m. Betty Jean (Chitwood), chil: Luana Charlene (Hendrickson); David Alger; Marcia Jean (McKee). Educ: NW Christian Coll., BTh 1945; Phillips U., BD 1949; U. of South. Calif., MA 1964; Sch. of Theol. at Claremont, RelD 1967. Emp: NW Christian Coll., 1968-78 Assoc. Prof., NT; Pacific Christian Coll., 1978- Prof., NT. Spec: New Testament. Pub: *Best of All is Jesus: A Study of Hebrews* (College, 1991); *One Father, One Family: A Biblical Study of Unity* (College, 1990); and others. Addr: (o) Pacific Christian College, 2500 E Nutwood Ave., Fullerton, CA 92631 714-879-3901; (h) 2545 SW Terwilliger Blvd. #610, Portland, OR 97201 503-299-4610.

FITZGERALD, John T., Jr., b. Birmingham, AL, October 2, 1948, s. of J.T. & A.M., m. Karol (Bonneaux), chil: Kirstin L.; Kimberly A. Educ: Abilene Christian U., BA 1970, MA 1972; Yale Div. Sch., MDiv 1975; Yale U., MA 1979, MPhil 1981, PhD 1984. Emp: Yale U., 1979 Instr.; Yale Div. Sch., 1980-81 Instr.; U. of Miami, 1981-88 Asst. Prof., 1988- Assoc. Prof.; Brown U., 1992 Vis. Assoc. Prof. Spec: New Testament. Pub: "Paul, the Ancient Epistolary Theorists, and 2 Corinthians 10-13" in *Greeks, Romans, and Christians* (Fortress, 1990); *Cracks in an Earthen Vessel: An Examination of the Catalogues of Hardships in the Corinthian Correspondence* (Scholars, 1988); *The Tabula of Cebes*, co-auth. (Scholars, 1983); and others. Mem: SBL. Addr: (o) U. of Miami, Dept. of Religious Studies, PO Box 248264, Coral Gables, FL 33124 305-284-4733; (h) 1003 Granada Blvd., Coral Gables, FL 33134 305-461-3389.

FITZMYER, Joseph A., b. Philadelphia, PA, November 4, 1920, s. of Joseph & Anna (Alexy). Educ: Loyola U., Chicago, AB 1943, AM 1945; Facultes St. Albert de Louvain, Belgium, STL 1952; Johns Hopkins U., PhD 1956; Pont. Bibl. Inst., SSL 1957. Emp: Woodstock Coll., 1958-69 Prof., NT & Bibl. Lang.; U. of Chicago, 1969-71 Prof., Aramaic & Hebrew; *JBL*, 1970-76 Ed.; Fordham U., 1971-74 Prof., NT; Weston Sch. of Theol., 1974-76 Prof., NT; Cath. U., 1976-86 Prof., NT; *CBQ*, 1980-84 Ed. Spec: New Testament, Semitic Languages, Texts and Epigraphy, Apocrypha and Post-biblical Studies. Pub: *A Christological Catechism: New Testament Answers* (Paulist, 1982, 1991); *An Introductory Bibliography for the Study of Scripture*, Subsidia Biblica 3 (Pont. Bibl. Inst., 1991); *The Gospel According to Luke*, AB 28, 28A (Doubleday, 1981, 1985); and others. Awd: U. of Scranton, LHD 1979;

Coll. of the Holy Cross, DLitt 1979; Lunds U., Sweden, Teol. H. Dr. 1981; Fairfield U., LHD 1981. Mem: CBA 1955-, Pres. 1969-70; SBL 1955-, Pres. 1979; SNTS 1959-, Pres. 1992; Amer. Theol. Soc. 1980-. Addr: (o) Catholic U. of America, Caldwell Hall, Washington, DC 20064 202-319-5665; (h) Georgetown U., Jesuit Community, Washington, DC 20057 202-687-4273.

FLANDERS, Henry J., Jr., b. Malvern, AR, October 2, 1921, s. of Mr. & Mrs. Henry Jackson, m. Tommie Lou (Pardew), chil: Janet; H.J. Educ: Baylor U., BA 1943; South. Bapt. Theol. Sem., BD 1948, PhD 1950. Emp: Furman U., 1950-62 Prof.; First Bapt. Ch., 1962-69 Pastor; Baylor U., 1969- Prof., Chmn., Relig. Dept. Spec: Anatolian Studies, Hebrew Bible, New Testament. Pub: *People of the Covenant: An Introduction to the Old Testament*, co-auth. (Random, 1963, 1988); *Introduction to the Bible*, co-auth. (Random, 1973); and others. Mem: SBL; AAR; Soc. of Relig. & Ethics; NABPR; Inst. for Antiquity & Christianity. Rec: Golf, flying. Addr: (o) Baylor U., Box 295, Waco, TX 76798 817-755-3735; (h) 3820 Chateau, Waco, TX 76710.

FLEMING, James W., b. Portland, OR, November 21, 1943, s. of John & June. Educ: U. of Guam, AA 1963; Westmont Coll., BA 1965; SW Sem., 1973 EDD. Emp: Bibl. Resources Study Ctr., Jerusalem, 1976- Dir.; Government of Israel Guide Sch., Tel Aviv, 1977- Lect.; Hebrew U., Jerusalem, 1978- Lect.; Jerusalem Ctr. for Bibl. Stud., 1980-86 Acad. Dean; Ecumenical Inst., Jerusalem, 1985- Prof. Excv: Aphek/Antipatris, 1977 Instr.; City of David, 1978-80 Instr.; Mount Zion, 1980 Coord.; Ketef Hennom, 1980 Coord.; Julias, 1987-89 Coord. Spec: Archaeology, New Testament, Apocrypha and Post-biblical Studies. Pub: "Putting the Bible on the Map" *BAR* 9/6 (1983); "Undiscovered Gate Beneath Jerusalem's Golden Gate" *BAR* 9/1 (1983); "Reorganization of the Bible" *Educ. Aids for Bibl. Stud.* (1980); and others. Mem: Ecumenical Fraternity 1975-; Meletz Ctr. for Christian Encounter with Israel 1988-. Addr: (o) PO Box 19556, Jerusalem, Israel 972-276-7361; (h) c/o 1320 Main at Clay, Houston, TX 77002 713-652-2999.

FLESHER, Hubert L., b. Elyria, OH, s. of O. Jay & Armide (de Saulles), m. Mary (Mosher), chil: Erika; Jonathan. Educ: Yale Div. Sch., MDiv 1958; Yale U., MA 1961. Emp: Episc. Theol. Sem., 1963-65 Instr.; Millersville State Coll., 1967-71 Chaplain; Lancaster Theol. Sem., 1969-71 Vis. Prof.; Lehigh U., 1971-90 Prof., Relig. Stud., U. Chaplain; Smith Coll., 1990- Dean of the Chapel, Adj. Prof., Relig. Excv: Akko, Israel, 1980 Fac. Asst. Spec: Hebrew Bible, New Testament, Apocrypha and Post-biblical Studies. Mem: AAR; SBL. Rec: Tennis, photography. Addr: (o) Smith College, Chapel, Northampton, MA 01063 413-585-2750; (h) 16 Paradise Rd., Northampton, MA 01060 413-586-1321.

FLESHER, Paul V. M., b. Morgantown, WV, May 30, 1957, s. of Virgil & Ellen, m. Caroline E. (McCracken). Educ: U. of Rochester, BA, Relig. Stud. 1979; Oxford U., MPhil, Jewish Stud. 1982; Brown U., PhD, Hist. of Judaism 1988. Emp: Wittenberg U., 1988 Vis. Instr., Relig. Stud.; NW U., 1988- Asst. Prof., Relig. Spec: Apocrypha and Post-biblical Studies. Pub: "Palestinian Synagogues Before 70 C.E.: A Review of the Evidence" in *Approaches to Ancient Judaism* vol. 6 (Scholars, 1990); *New Perspectives on Ancient Judaism* vol. 5, ed. (U. Press of Amer., 1990); *Religion, Science, and Magic in Concert and in Conflict: Perspectives of Judaism, Christianity, Philosophy, and Social Science*, co-ed. (Oxford U.P., 1989); "Are Women Property in the System of the Mishnah?" in *From Ancient Israel to Modern Judaism: Intellect in Quest of Understanding* (U. Press of Amer., 1989); *Oxen, Women or Citizens? Slaves in the System of the Mishnah* (Scholars, 1988); *New Perspectives on Ancient Judaism*, vol. I & III, contb. (U. Press of Amer., 1987); and others. Mem: AAR 1978-; SBL 1978-; MidW Jewish Stud. Assn. 1989-. Rec: Travel, camping, sailing. Addr: (o) Northwestern U., Dept. of Religion, 1940 Sheridan Rd., Evanston, IL 60208-4050 708-491-2620.

FLINT, Peter W., b. Johannesburg, South Africa, January 21, 1951, s. of Alwyn & Edelweiss (Hoesch), m. Erica (Smuts), chil: Claire; Amy; Abigail; Jason. Educ: Witwatersrand U., Johannesburg, BA 1972; Johannesburg Coll. of Educ., Tchr. Dip. 1973; U. of South Africa, BA 1979, MA 1983; U. of Notre Dame, MA 1990, PhD 1993. Emp: U. of Transkei, 1984-87 Lect.; *OT Essays*, 1988-89 Ed. Bd.; Rockefeller Museum, Jerusalem, 1989-90 Res. Asst., Qumran Scrollery, 1991-93 Bibl. scrolls from Cave 4, Asst. to Dir., Bibl. scrolls from Nahal Hever & Wadi Seiyal, Ed., Psalms scrolls, Pseudo-Daniel scrolls from Qumran Cave 4, Co-ed. Spec: Hebrew Bible, Semitic Languages, Texts and Epigraphy, Apocrypha and Post-biblical Studies. Pub: "The Psalms Scrolls from the Judaean Desert: Relationships and Textual Affiliations" in *Proceedings of the Congress of the International Organization for Qumran Studies, Paris 18-19 July, 1992* (1993); "The Septuagint Version of Isaiah 23:1-14 and the Massoretic Text" *Bull. of the IOSCS* (1988); "Theological Greek in an African Context" *Ekklesiastikos Pharos* (1986-87); "Old Testament Scholarship from an African Perspective" *Jour. of the OT Soc. of South Africa* (1986). Awd: Transvaal Ed. Dept., teaching awd. 1978, 1989; U. of South Africa, Awd. for Acad. Excellence 1987; ASOR, grants 1991. Mem: OT Soc. of South Africa 1983-; IOSCS 1986-; CBA 1988-; SBL 1988-; ASOR 1991-. Rec: Travel, swimming, Mozart, poetry, computers. Addr: (o) Southwestern College, Biblical Studies Dept., 2625 East Cactus Rd., Phoenix, AZ 85032.

FOCANT, Camille L. A. G., b. Lavaux-Sainte Anne, August 3, 1946, s. of Joseph & Cornélis Louise. Educ: U. Cath. de Louvain, Theol.

Degree 1971, Bibl. Philol. Degree 1973, ThD 1975. Emp: U. Cath. de Louvain, 1981 Prof., 1991- Pres. of Inst. Supérieur des Sci. Relig. Spec: New Testament. Pub: *The Synoptic Gospels: Source Criticism and the New Literary Criticism*, BETL 110, ed. (Peeters, 1993); "La fonction narrative des doublets dans la section des pains: Mc 6,6b-8,26" in *The Four Gospels 1992, Festschrift F. Neirynck*, BETL 100 (Peeters, 1992); "7Q5 = Mk 6,52-53: A Questionable and Questioning Identification?" in *Christen und Christliches in Qumran*, Eichstätter Studien 32 (Pustet, 1992); *La famille de Jésus à Saint Paul*, ed. (Connaitre la Bible, 1989); "La chute de Jérusalem et la datation des evangiles" *Rev. Théol. de Louvain* 19 (1988); "Tromper le Mamon d'iniquite (Lc 16,1-13) in *A cause de l'Evangile, Festschrift J. Dupont*, Lectio Divina 123 (Cerf, 1985); "L'incompréhension des disciples dans le deuxiéme evangile: Tradition et rédaction" *RB* 82 (1975); and others. Mem: Assn. Cath. Francaise pour l'etude de la Bible. Addr: (o) Grand-Place, 45, B-1348 Louvain-la-Neuve, Belgium 010/473605; (h) Rue de Fernelmont, 37, B-5020 Champion, Belgium 081-210139.

FOERSTER, Gideon, b. Israel. Educ: Hebrew U., Jerusalem, BA 1959, MA, Arch. 1961, PhD 1973. Emp: Dept. of Antiq. & Mus., 1963-84 Arch., North Dist.; Haifa Technion, 1965-66 Lect., Arch. of Palestine; Hebrew U., Inst. of Arch., 1969-73 Tchr., 1973-82 Lect., 1982- Sr. Lect., Classical Arch.; Haifa U., 1971-73 Tchr., 1973-75 Lect., Roman Arch. & Hist. of the Jewish People; *Journal of Jewish Art*, Ed. Bd. Excv: Tiberias, 1973-74 Dir.; Roman fort, Tell Shalem, 1976, 1978 Dir.; Beth-Shean (Scythopolis), 1980- Co-dir.; Hamat Gader, 1982 Dir.; Horvat Shura, 1983 Dir. Spec: Archaeology. Mem: IES 1973-; Deutsches Archaologisches Institut 1987-. Addr: Hebrew U., Institute of Archaeology, Mt. Scopus, Jerusalem 91905, Israel 972-2-882-423.

FOHR, Samuel D., b. Brooklyn, NY, March 30, 1943, s. of Henry & Jenny, m. Rena, chil: Sherry; Brad. Educ: Brooklyn Coll., BA 1963; U. of Mich., MA 1967, PhD 1968. Emp: Va. Polytechnic Inst. & State U., 1968-71; U. of Pittsburgh at Bradford, 1972- Prof. Spec: Hebrew Bible. Pub: *Adam and Eve: The Spiritual Symbolism of Genesis and Exodus* (U. Press of Amer., 1986); and others. Mem: AAR. Rec: Classical & jazz music, tennis. Addr: (o) U. of Pittsburgh at Bradford, 300 Campus Dr., Bradford, PA 16701 814-362-7586; (h) 810 W Corydon St., Bradford, PA 16701 814-368-7823.

FOHRER, Georg, b. Krefeld-Uerdingen, September 6, 1915, s. of Wilhelm & Adelheid (Kranz), m. Natanja (Naegele), chil: Eberhard; Irene; Judith; Rahel; David; Miriam. Educ: DPhil 1939; DTh 1944. Emp: U. of Marburg, Germany, 1949-54 Lect., Assoc. Prof.; U. of Vienna, 1954-62 Prof.; U. of Erlangen-Nuenburg, 1962-79 Prof.; *ZAW*, 1960-81 Ed.;

BZAW, 1960-81 Ed. Spec: Hebrew Bible. Pub: *Studien zum Alten Testament (1966-88)*, contb. (de Gruyter, 1991); *Geschichte der Israelitischen Religion* (de Gruyter, 1969); "Prophetie und Magic" *ZAW* 78 (1966); "Prophetie und Geschichte" *TLZ* 89 (1964); "Tradition und Interpretation im Alten Testament" *ZAW* 73 (1961); "Die Struktur der alttestamentlichen Eschatologie" *TLZ* 85 (1960); and others. Awd: U. Marburg, DTh 1954; U. Aberdeen, DDiv 1969; Glasgow, DDiv 1970. Mem: IOSOT 1970-; SBL 1972-. Addr: (h) 36, Chabad Rd., Jewish Quarter, Jerusalem, Israel 287-954.

FOKKELMAN, Jan P., b. Jakarta, Indonesia, March 23, 1940, s. of Joannes & Ans Fokkelman-Bochanen, m. Margriet (Geerts), chil: Mariette Heleen; Bastiaan Johannes; Maarten Geert; Michiel. Educ: U. of Leiden, MA, Semitic Stud. 1963, PhD 1973. Emp: U. Leiden, 1963-73 Jr. Lect., 1973- Sr. Lect. Spec: Hebrew Bible. Pub: *Narrative Art in Genesis, Specimens of Stylistic and Structural Analysis* (Sheffield, 1991); "The Structure of Ps. 68" *OS* 26 (1990); "Time and the Structure of the Abraham Cycle" *OS* 25 (1989); *Narrative Art and Poetry in the Books of Samuel*, vol. 1-4 (1981-1993); "Every Day Life as Creation, A Stylistic Analysis of b.Ta^C^anit 23a-b" *Jaarbericht Ex Oriente Lux* 26 (1979); and others. Awd: Hebrew U., Fellow of the Inst. for Adv. Stud. 1982-83; Natl. Hum. Ctr., Fellow 1990-91. Mem: Dutch Soc. for OT Stud. 1973-. Addr: (o) Dept. of Hebrew, Matthias de Vrieshof 4, 2311 BZ Leiden, Netherlands 071-272257; (h) Willinklaan 14, 2341 LW Oegstgeest, Netherlands 071-171408.

FONTINOY, Charles J. M. E. C., b. Stavelot, Belgium, March 12, 1920, s. of Charles & Marie (Gouders). Educ: U. de l'Etat á Liége, Lic. Phil. & Lettres 1941, Degré Supérieur 1941, PhD 1963. Emp: Athénée Royal d'Aywaille, Belgium, 1945-66 Secondary Sch. Tchr.; State U. of Liége, 1966-85 Prof., Chair, Dept. of Oriental Stud. Spec: Hebrew Bible, Semitic Languages, Texts and Epigraphy. Pub: "Les Formes inférieures de la mystique dans l'Ancien Testament" in *Mélanges Armand*, ABEL (1978); "Le dualisme dans la communauté de Qumran" in *Gnosticisme et monde hellénistique* (Louvain-la-Neuve, 1982); "L'anéantissement des damnés" in *Vie et survie dans les civilisations orientales* (1983); *Le duel dans les langues sémitiques* (Les Belles Lettres, 1969); and others. Awd: Commission mixte des Echanges culturels franco-belges 1954-55, 1957, 1959, 1966; Le Patrimonie de l'U. de Liege 1960. Mem: SBL; Soc. Belge d'Etudes Orientales; L'Inst. Iudaicum; Cercle Belge de linguistique. Rec: Lit., psychology, ornithology. Addr: (o) Place du 20 Aout, 32, B-4000 Liege, Belgium 41-66-55-44; (h) La Bovière, 3, B-4920 Aywaille, Belgium 41-84-40-99.

FORBES, A. Dean, b. Pomona, CA, March 2, 1941, s. of Paul E. & Lela R., m. Ellen (Moss). Educ: Harvard Coll., BA 1962; Pacific Sch. of

Relig., MDiv 1969. Spec: Hebrew Bible. Pub: *Studies in Hebrew and Aramaic Orthography*, co-auth. (Eisenbrauns, 1992); *The Vocabulary of the Old Testament*, co-auth. (Pont. Bibl. Inst., 1989); "Statistical Research on the Bible" in *ABD* (Doubleday, 1992); "Syntactic Sequences in the Hebrew Bible" in *Perspectives on Language and Text* (Eisenbrauns, 1987); *Spelling in the Hebrew Bible*, co-auth. (Pont. Bibl. Inst., 1985); *The Word of the Lord Shall Go Forth: Essays in Honor of David Noel Freedman*, contb.; and others. Mem: SBL 1970-. Addr: (o) 1502 Page Mill Rd., Palo Alto, CA 94304 415-857-4488; (h) 820 Loma Verde Ave., Palo Alto, CA 94303 415-494-6152.

FORESTELL, J. Terence, b. Bridgeburg, Canada, November 22, 1925, s. of Tobias F. & Agnes Irene (O'Driscoll). Educ: U. of Toronto, Canada, BA 1948, Ordained, CSB 1951; Angelicum, Rome, STL 1953; Pont. Bibl. Inst., Rome, SSL 1955; Pont. Bibl. Commn., SSD 1974. Emp: U. of St. Michael's Coll., St. Basil's Sem., 1956-86, Prof., NT Stud.; U. of Alta., St. Joseph's Coll., Edmonton, 1986-91 Prof. of Sacred Scripture. Excv: Ophel, 1965. Spec: New Testament, Semitic Languages, Texts and Epigraphy. Pub: *As Ministers of Christ: The Christological Dimension of Ministry in the New Testament* (Paulist, 1991); *The Book of Proverbs* (Paulist, 1980); *Targumic Traditions and the New Testament: An Annotated Bibliography with a New Testament Index* (Scholars, 1979); *The Word of the Cross: Salvation as Revelation in the Fourth Gospel* (Pont. Bibl. Inst., 1974); and others. Mem: CBA; SBL; SNTS. Rec: Swimming, cycling. Addr: (o) U. of Alberta, St. Joseph's College, Edmonton, AB T6G 2J5, Canada (403) 492-7681.

FORNBERG, Tord, b. Halmstad, Sweden, December 5, 1943, s. of Bertil & Eva, m. Gunnel (Gramner), chil: Mattias; Sofia; Erik. Educ: Uppsala U., BD 1968, MA 1971, ThD, NT Exegesis 1977. Emp: Swedish Bible Commn., 1973-76 Asst.; Uppsala U., 1977-86 Asst. Prof., 1986- Assoc. Prof.; Luth. Theol. Sem., Hong Kong, 1984-85 Guest Prof.; United Theol. Coll., India, 1990 Guest Prof. Spec: New Testament. Pub: "The New Missiology and the Bible" *Bangalore Theol. Forum* 22/4-23/1 (1990-91); "Jag ar vagen, sanningen och livet. Ingen kommer till Fadern utom genom mig. Om Bibeln i indisk religionsteologi" *Religion och Bibel* 48-50 (1989-91); *Matteusevangeliet 1:1-13:52* (EFS-forlaget, 1989); *Jewish—Christian Dialogue and Biblical Exegesis* (Teologiska institutionen, 1988); "Peter—The High Priest of the New Covenant?" *East Asia Jour of Theol.* 4 (1986); "Textual Criticism and Canon" *Studia Theologica* 40 (1986); "Recent Trends in New Testament Research" *Theol. & Life* 8 (1985); *Evangelium enligt Matteus* (Teologiska institutionen, 1981, 1986); *An Early Church in a Pluralistic Society. A Study in 2 Peter* (Gleerup, 1977); and others. Mem: SNTS 1988-. Addr: (o) Teologiska institutionen, Box 1604, S-751 46 Uppsala,

Sweden 46-18-182500; (h) Malmkorarvagen 138, S-740 33 Vattholma, Sweden 46-18-350456.

FOSSUM, Jarl E., b. Oslo, Norway, June 12, 1946, s. of Ruth (Soensteng), m. Ellen (Johns), chil: Maria (Johns). Educ: U. of Bergen, MA 1971; U. of Utrecht, ThD 1982. Emp: U. of Mich., 1988- Assoc. Prof.; C.G. Jung Inst., Zurich, 1991- Vis. Prof. Spec: New Testament, Apocrypha and Post-biblical Studies. Pub: "Col. 1.15-18a in the Light of Jewish Mysticism and Gnosticism" *NTS* 35 (1989); "Sects and Movements" in *The Samaritans* (Mohr, 1989); "The Simonian Sophia Myth" *Studie Materiali di Storia delle Relig.* 53 (1987); "The Magharians" *Henoch* 9 (1987); "Kyrios Jesus as the Angel of the Lord in Jude 5-7" *NTS* 33 (1987); *The Name of God and the Angel of the Lord*, WUNT 1/36 (Mohr, 1985); and others. Mem: SNTS 1985-; Société D'Etudes Samaritaines 1986-; SBL 1988-. Addr: (o) U. of Michigan, Dept. of Near Eastern Studies, 3074 Frieze Bldg., Ann Arbor, MI 48109-1285 313-764-0314; (h) 2759 Page Ave., Ann Arbor, MI 48104 313-677-3263.

FOSTER, Julia A., b. Jacksonville, FL, May 21, 1937, d. of George A. & Aultie B. Educ: Duke U., AB 1958; Boston U., PhD 1969; U. of N.C., Chapel Hill, MSLS 1975. Emp: Boston U., 1968-69 Instr.; Pfeiffer Coll., 1969-83 Assoc. Prof., Reference Lbrn.; Meth. Theol. Sch., 1983- Lbrn. Spec: Hebrew Bible, Semitic Languages, Texts and Epigraphy. Pub: *Variant Versions of Targumic Traditions in Codex Neofiti 1*, co-auth. (Scholars, 1977). Awd: Boston U., Roswell R. Robinson Fellow 1964. Mem: SBL 1968-; East. Great Lakes Bibl. Soc. 1983-. Rec: Choral singing, birdwatching. Addr: (o) Methodist Theological School in Ohio, Box 1204, Delaware, OH 43015 614-363-1146; (h) 72 W Winter St., Apt. #7, Delaware, OH 43015 614-363-3562.

FOUTS, David M., b. Ft. Worth, TX, January 1, 1952, s. of W.E. & Patsy (Strong), m. Marlene (Rahn), chil: Jason Karl; Heidi Rochelle. Educ: Austin State U., BA 1974; Dallas Theol. Sem., ThM 1979, ThD 1992. Emp: Yellowstone Bapt. Coll., 1982-86 Instr.; Dallas Theol. Sem., 1988-90 Instr.; William J. Bryan College, 1993- Asst. Prof. Spec: Hebrew Bible, New Testament. Pub: "Added Support for Reading '70 Men' in I Sam. VI,19" *VT* 42 (1992); *The Use of Large Numbers in the Old Testament* (1992); "A Suggestion for Isaiah xxvi 16" *VT* 41 (1991); and others. Mem: SBL 1989-; ETS 1989-. Rec: Metal detecting, Civil War, softball. Addr: (h) Box 7000, Dayton, TN 37321-7000 615-775-2041.

FOWLER, David C., b. Louisville, KY, January 3, 1921, s. of Earle B. & Susan C., m. Mary (Gene), chil: Sandra C. (dec.); Caroline S. Educ: U. of Fla., BA 1942; U. of Chicago, MA 1947, PhD 1949. Emp: U. of Pa., 1949-51 Instr.; U. of Wash., 1952- Prof. Spec: New Testament, Apocrypha and Post-biblical Studies. Pub: *The*

Bible in Middle English Literature (U. of Wash., 1984); The Bible in Early English Literature (U. of Wash., 1976); "The Meaning of 'Touch Me Not' in John 20:17" EQ 47/1 (1975); "John Trevisa and the English Bible" Modern Philol. 58 (1960); "Some Biblical Influences on Geoffrey of Monmouth's Historiography" Traditio 14 (1958); and others. Awd: ACLS, Schol. Awd. 1951-52; Guggenheim Fellow 1962-63, 1975-76. Mem: SBL. Addr: (o) U. of Washington, Dept. of English GN-30, Seattle, WA 98195 206-543-2690; (h) 6264 19th Ave. NE, Seattle, WA 98115 206-524-8372.

FOWLER, Robert M., b. Emporia, KS, November 29, 1950, s. of Wayne & Jo Anne, m. Mary Sue, chil: Geoffrey; Amanda. Educ: U. of Kans., BA 1972, MA 1974; U. of Chicago, Div. Sch., PhD 1978. Emp: Yankton Coll., 1978-80 Asst. Prof.; Baldwin-Wallace Coll., 1980- Assoc Prof. Spec: New Testament. Pub: *Let the Reader Understand: Reader-Response Criticism and the Gospel of Mark* (Fortress, 1991); "The Rhetoric of Direction and Indirection in the Gospel of Mark" *Semeia* 48 (1989); "Postmodern Biblical Criticism" *Foundations and Facets Forum* 5 (1989); "Who is 'The Reader' in Reader-Response Criticism?" *Semeia* 31 (1985); *Loaves and Fishes: The Function of the Feeding Stories in the Gospel of Mark* (Scholars, 1981); and others. Mem: SBL 1973-; AAR 1979-; CBA 1981-; SNTS 1992-. Rec: Reading, computers, running. Addr: (o) Baldwin-Wallace College, Dept. of Religion, Berea, OH 44017 216-826-2173; (h) 271 Pineview Dr., Berea, OH 44017-1423 216-826-1162.

FOX, Everett, b. New York, NY, May 27, 1947, s. of Barnett S. & Lillian (Goldner), m. Cherie (Koller), chil: Akiva; Leora; Ezra. Educ: Brandeis U., BA 1968, MA 1972, PhD 1975. Emp: Boston U., 1973-84 Asst. Prof.; Clark U., 1986- Assoc. Prof., Dir., Jewish Stud. Prog. Spec: Hebrew Bible. Pub: "The Bible and Its World" in *The Schocken Guide to Jewish Books* (Schocken, 1992); *Genesis and Exodus: A New English Rendition with Commentary and Notes* (Schocken, 1991); "Can Genesis Be Read as a Book?" *Semeia* 46 (1989); "The Samson Cycle in an Oral Setting" *Alcheringa: Ethnopoetics* 4/1 (1978); and others. Mem: AAR 1979-; SBL 1979-. Rec: Class. music. Addr: (o) Estabrook Hall 406, Clark U., 950 Main St., Worcester, MA 01610 508-793-7355; (h) 354 Kenrick St., Newton, MA 02158 617-244-4090.

FOX, Michael V., b. Detroit, MI, December 9, 1940, s. of Leonard & Mildred, m. Jane, chil: Joshua; Ariel. Educ: U. of Michigan, BA 1962, MA 1963; Hebrew Union Coll.-Jewish Inst. of Relig., Ordination 1968; Hebrew U. of Jerusalem, PhD 1972. Emp: Haifa U., Ben Gurion U., 1971-74 Lect.; Hebrew U. of Jerusalem, 1975-77 Lect.; U. of Wis., 1977- Weinstein-Bascom Prof. in Jewish Stud., Dept. of Hebrew & Semitic Stud.; *Hebrew Studies*, 1985- Ed. Spec: Hebrew Bible, Egyptology. Pub: *The Redaction of the Books of Esther*, SBL Mon. Ser. 40 (1991); Character and

Ideology in the Book of Esther (U. of S.C., 1991); *Qoheleth and his Contradictions*, JSOTSup 71 (1989); *The Song of Songs and the Ancient Egyptian Love Songs* (U. of Wis., 1985); *Shirey Dodim Mimitzrayim Ha-atiqa* (Magnes, 1985); "Ancient Egyptian Rhetoric" *Rhetorica* 1 (1983); "The Rhetoric of Ezekiel's Vision of the Valley of the Bones" *HUCA* 51 (1980); "The Identification of Quotations in Biblical Literature" *ZAW* 92 (1980). Mem: SBL 1977-. Rec: Scottish country dancing, choral singing. Addr: (o) U. of Wisconsin-Madison, 1220 Linden Dr., Room 1338, Madison, WI 53706 608-262-2089.

FOX, Samuel J., b. Cleveland, OH, February 25, 1919, s. of Joseph & Yetta (Mandel), m. Edith (Muskin), chil: Joseph Rafael. Educ: Yeshiva Coll., BA 1940; Yeshiva U., Rabbi 1941; Butler U., MA 1944; Harvard U., PhD 1959. Emp: Congregation Chevra Tehillim, 1959- Rabbi; SE Mass. U., 1969-79 Prof.; Merrimack Coll., 1968- Assoc. Prof., Chmn., Dept. of Relig. Stud. Spec: Archaeology, Hebrew Bible, Mesopotamian Studies, Semitic Languages, Texts and Epigraphy, Egyptology. Pub: *Hell in Jewish Literature*. Mem: AAR; Coll. Theol. Soc. Addr: (o) Merrimack College, Dept. of Religious Studies, North Andover, MA 01845 617-683-7111; (h) 145 Lynn Shore Dr., Lynn, MA 01902 617-598-2964.

FRAIKIN, Daniel J., b. Brussels, November 21, 1933, s. of Leon & Mary, m. Frances (McArthur), chil: Jean-Luc. Educ: Inst. Cath. de Paris, BPhil 1954; Facultés du Saulchoir, LTh 1961; Ecole Biblique, Jérusalem, LSS 1963; Harvard U., ThD 1974. Emp: Coll. Dominicain de Phil. et de Théol., Canada, 1964-69 Prof., NT; Queen's Theol. Coll., Canada, 1974- Prof., NT, Vice-Prin. Spec: New Testament. Pub: *Religious Studies in Ontario: A State-of-the-Art Review*, co-auth. (Waterloo U.P., 1992); "The Rhetorical Function of the Jews in Paul's Epistle to the Romans" in *Anti-Judaism in Early Christianity: Paul and the Gospels* (Waterloo U.P., 1986); "Ressemblance (Période Hellénistique et Nouveau Testament)" in *Supplément au Dictionnaire de la Bible* X, 12 (1982); "Jésus ressuscité: phénom'rne observé ou mystère révélé" in *Résurrection* (Desclee, 1971); and others. Mem: SBL 1969-; CBA 1969-; CSSR 1972-; SNTS 1976-; Canadian Corp. for Stud. in Relig., Pres. 1990- .Rec: Sailing, woodworking. Addr: (o) Queen's Theological College, Kingston, ON K7L 3N6, Canada 613-545-2110; (h) 284 Frontenac St., Kingston, ON K7L 3S8, Canada 613-544-9423.

FRANCE, Richard T., b. Londonderry, North Ireland, April 2, 1938, s. of Edgar & Doris W., m. Barbara, chil: David M.; Susan J. Educ: Balliol Coll., Oxford, BA 1960, MA 1963; Tyndale Hall, Bristol, BD 1962; U. of Bristol, PhD 1967. Emp: U. of Ife, Nigeria, 1969-73 Lect.; Tyndale House, Cambridge, 1973-76 Lbrn., 1978-81 Warden; Ahmadu Bello U., Nigeria, 1976-77 Sr. Lect.; London Bible Coll., 1981-88 Vice Prin.; Wycliffe Hall, Oxford,

1989- Prin. Spec: New Testament. Pub: *Divine Government: God's Kingship in the Gospel of Mark* (SPCK, 1990); *Matthew: Evangelist and Teacher* (Paternoster/Zondervan, 1989); "Liberation in the New Testament" *EQ* (1986); *Matthew*, Tyndale Comm. (InterVarsity/Eerdmans, 1985); *Jesus and the Old Testament* (Tyndale/InterVarsity 1971; Baker, 1982); "The Formula-Quotations of Matthew 2 and the Problem of Communication" *NTS* (1981); "The Uniqueness of Christ" *Churchman* (1981); "Herod and the Children of Bethlehem" *NT* (1979); and others. Mem: SNTS 1977-; Tyndale Fellow. 1965-. Rec: Travel, mountains, wildlife. Addr: (o) Wycliffe Hall, 54 Banbury Rd., Oxford OX2 6PW, England 0865-274205; (h) 2A Norham Gardens, Oxford OX2 6QB, England 0865-57539.

FRANKEMOELLE, Hubert, b. Stadtlohn, Westfalen, October 1, 1939, s. of Anna & Paul, m. Renate (Stieler), chil: Anja; Peter. Educ: U. Munster, Katholisch-Theol. Fac., ThD 1972. Emp: U. Munster, Katholisch-Theol. Fac., 1968-78 Akademischer Oberrat; U. Paderborn, 1979- Prof., NT. Spec: New Testament. Pub: *Der Brief des Jakobus I-II* (1993); "Die Entstehung des Christentums aus dem Judentum" in *Christen und Juden* (1992); "Judisch-christlicher Dialog: Interreligiose und innerchristliche Aspekte" *Catholica* (1992); "Evangelium und Wirkungsgeschichte: Das Problem der Vermittlung von Methodik und Hermeneutik in neueren Auslegungen zum Matthaeuslium" in *Salz der Erde—Licht der Welt: Exegetische Studien zum Matthaeusevangelium*, Festschrift A. Voegtle (1991); "Jesus als deuterojesajanischer Freudenbote? Zur Rezeption von Jes 52,7 und 61,1 im Neuen Testament, durch Jesus und in den Targumim" in *Vom Urchristentum zu Jesus*, Festschrift J. Gnilka (1989); *Evangelium, Begriff und Gattung: Ein Forschungsbericht* (1988); *1. Petrusbrief, 2. Petrusbrief, Judasbrief* (1987); *Jahwe-Bund und Kirche Christi* (1974, 1984); and others. Mem: SNTS; Deutschsprachige Katholische Neutestamentler; Wissenschaftlicher Beirat des Katholischen Bibelwerkes. Addr: (o) U.—GH Paderborn, N 3.134, Warburger Str. 100, Germany 0-52-51-602358; (h) D-4790 Paderborn, Helmarshauser Weg 2, Germany 0-52-51-63940.

FRANKFURTER, David T. M., b. New York, NY, February 24, 1961, s. of Eleanor (Munro) & Alfred M., m. Anath C. (Golomb), chil: Raphael G. Educ: Wesleyan U., BA 1983; Harvard Div. Sch., MTS 1986; Princeton U., MA 1988, PhD 1990. Emp: Princeton U., 1987-88 Preceptor; U. of Mich., 1989 Adj. Lect., NT; Coll. of Charleston, 1990- Asst. Prof., Relig. Spec: New Testament, Egyptology, Apocrypha and Post-biblical Studies. Pub: "The Origin of the Miracle-List Tradition and Its Medium of Circulation" in *SBL Seminar Papers* (Scholars, 1990); "Tabitha in the Apocalypse of Elijah" *JTS* 41 (1990); "Stylites and *Phallobates:* Pillar Religions in Late Antique Syria" *VC* 44 (1990); and others. Awd: Wesleyan U., Giffin Prize in Relig. 1983; Princeton U.,

Fellow. 1986-90; Coll. of Charleston, Summer Res. Grant 1991; NEH, Summer Stipend 1992. Mem: SBL; AAR. Rec: Hiking/backpacking, community action, music, film. Addr: (o) The College of Charleston, Dept. of Religion, Charleston, SC 29424 803-792-8033; (h) 90-B Ashley Ave., Charleston, SC 29401 803-853-5714.

FRANKOWSKI, Janusz, b. Warsaw, Poland, September 24, 1928, s. of Antoni & Kazimiera. Educ: Ordained Cath. Priest 1952; U. of Warsaw, ThM 1953; Pont. Bibl. Inst., Rome, D. of Bible 1966. Emp: Sem. of Gniezno, 1965-70 Prof., OT; Sem. of Warsaw, 1983-86 Prof., NT; Akademia Teologii Katolickiej, Warsaw, 1966- Docente, NT Exegesis. Spec: New Testament. Pub: "Problem of the Origins of the Corpus Paulinum. Confrontation with Hypothesis of H.M. Schenke" *Studia Theologica* 26 (1988); *Songs of Israel* (1988); *Pentateuch* (ATK, 1987); *Currents and "Entwicklungslinien" of the New Testament Christological Thought in the Light of Heb. 1,3* (ATK, 1984); "Early Christian Hymns Recorded in the New Testament: A Reconsideration of the Question in the Light of Heb. 1,3" *BZ* 27 (1983); *Warsaw Biblical Studies*, co-ed. (1976); and others. Mem: SNTS 1989. Rec: Hiking. Addr: (o) Akademia Teologii Katolickiej, ul. Dewajtis 3, 01-653 Warszawa, Poland; (h) ul. 3 Maja 40/42, 05-081 Laski Warszawskie, Poland.

FRANZ, Gordon W., b. Ridgewood, NJ, February 11, 1954, s. of Kenneth & Edna. Educ: Florida Bible Coll., BA, Bible 1976; Christian Heritage Coll., BA, Hist. & Soc. Sci. 1978; Columbia Bibl. Sem., MA, OT Stud. 1987. Emp: Inst. of Holy Land Stud., 1988- Field Trip Instr. Excv: Ketef Hinnom, Jerusalem, 1979-80, 1988-89 Area Supr., Asst. to Dir.; Lachish, 1980-81, 1983, 1985, 1987 Educ. Coord.; Kiryat Menachem Tumuli, Jerusalem, 1983 Staff; Ramat Rahel, 1984 Asst. to Dir.; Tel Jezreel, 1990 Staff. Spec: Archaeology. Pub: "Ancient Harbors of the Sea of Galilee" *Arch. & Bibl. Res.* 4/4 (1991); "Divine Healer: Jesus vs. Eshmun (John 5)" *Arch. & Bibl. Res.* 2/1 (1989); "The Excavations at St. Andrews, Jerusalem" *NEAS Bull.* 27 (1986). Mem: ASOR; Assn. for Bibl. Res.; ETS; IES; NEAS, Bd. of Dir. 1989-. Rec: Reading, hiking, canoeing. Addr: (h) 41 Garwood Rd., Fair Lawn, NJ 07410 201-797-6359.

FRANZMANN, Majella M., b. Charleville, Australia, October 13, 1952, d. of John Alfred & Mary Patricia. Educ: U. of Queensland, BA 1980, BA, Relig. 1984, PhD, Relig. 1990. Emp: Brisbane Coll. of Theol., Lect.; Australian Cath. U., Brisbane, Lect.; U. of Queensland, 1990- Lect., Relig. Spec: Hebrew Bible, New Testament, Apocrypha and Post-biblical Studies. Pub: "Of Food, Bodies and the Boundless Reign of God in the Synoptic Gospels" *Pacifica* 5 (1992); *The Odes of Solomon: An Analysis of the Poetical Structure and Form* (Vandenhoeck & Ruprecht, 1991); "The Wheel in Prov. XX 26 and Ode of Solomon XXIII 11-16" *VT* 41 (1991);

"Strangers from Above: An Investigation of the Motif of Strangeness in the Odes of Solomon and Some Gnostic Texts" *Museon* 103 (1990); "The Parable of the Vine in Odes of Solomon 38.17-19? A Response to Richard Bauckham" *NTS* 35 (1989); "Living Water: Mediating Element in Mandaean Myth and Ritual" *Numen* 36 (1989); and others. Awd: U. of Tuebingen, DAAD Schol. 1986-87; Charles Strong Trust, Young Australian Schol. 1988; U. of Tuebingen, Alexander von Humboldt Found., Res. Fellow 1992-93. Mem: Australian Assn. for the Study of Relig. 1983-; CBA, Australia 1984-. Rec: Reading, painting, music, Tai Chi, swimming. Addr: (o) U. of Queensland, Dept. of Studies in Religion, Q. 4072, Australia 07-3652154; (h) 23 Randolph St., Graceville, Q. 4075, Australia 07-3792181.

FREDERICKS, Daniel C., b. Minneapolis, MN, October 25, 1950, s. of Carl Glenn & Yvonne Emily, m. Maribeth Ann, chil: Autumn Brook; Ryan Daniel Carl; Justin Volden; Sean Kristian. Educ: U. of Minn., BA 1975; Covenant Theol. Sem., MDiv 1978; U. of Liverpool, PhD 1983. Emp: U. of Liverpool, 1979-81 Instr., Hebrew; Belhaven Coll., 1983- Assoc. Prof., Bibl. Stud., 1989- V.P., Acad. Affairs; Reformed Theol. Sem., 1990- Adj. Prof. Spec: Hebrew Bible, Semitic Languages, Texts and Epigraphy. Pub: "Life's Storms and Structural Unity in Qoheleth 11:1-12:8" *JSOT* 52 (1991); "Chiasm and Parallel Structure in Qoheleth 5:9-6:9" *JBL* 108 (1989); *Qoheleth's Language: Re-evaluating its Nature and Date* (Mellen U.P., 1989); and others. Awd: Alpha Theta Teaching Awd. 1984. Mem: Tyndale Fellow. 1980-; SBL 1984-; IBR 1985-; Chief Acad. Officers of the South. States 1989-. Rec: Travel, water sports. Addr: (o) 1500 Peachtree St., Jackson, MS 39202 601-968-5916; (h) 1242 Pinehurst Pl., Jackson, MS 39202 601-969-3268.

FREDRIKSEN, Paula, b. RI, d. of John & Erselia (Borrelli), m. Richard Landes, chil: Aliza; Noa; Hannah. Educ: Wellesley Coll., BA 1973; Oxford U., Dip. Theol. 1974; Princeton U., PhD 1979. Emp: U. of Calif., 1981-86 Asst. Prof.; U. of Pittsburgh, 1986-89 Assoc. Prof. Spec: New Testament. Pub: "Apocalypse and Redemption in Early Christianity: From John of Patmos to Augustine of Hippo" *VC* (1991); "Judaism, the Circumcision of Gentiles, and Apocalyptic Hope: Gal. 1 & 2" *JTS* (1991); "Jesus and the Temple, Mark and the War" in *SBL 1990 Seminar Papers* (1990); *From Jesus to Christ* (Yale, 1988); "Beyond the Body/Soul Dichotomy: Augustine on Paul" *Recherches Augustiniennes* (1988); "Paul and Augustine: Conversion Narratives, Orthodox Traditions and the Retrospective Self" *JTS* (1986); "Tyconius and the End of the World" *REA* (1982); *Augustine on Romans* (Scholars, 1982). Mem: AAR; SBL. Addr: (o) Boston U., Dept. of Religion, Boston, MA 02215 617-353-2635.

FREED, Edwin D., b. Beavertown, PA, November 29, 1920, s. of Edwin Ritzman & Mary Ellen (Dreese), m. Ann (Wetzel), chil:

Julie Ann (Gitt); Jane Marie (Roberts). Educ: Gettysburg Coll., BA 1943; Luth. Theol. Sem., BD 1945; Harvard U., PhD 1959. Emp: Gettysburg Coll., 1948-51 Instr., 1953-86 Amanda Rupert Strong Prof. of Relig.; Oberlin Coll., 1989 Vis. Prof. Spec: New Testament, Apocrypha and Post-biblical Studies. Pub: *The New Testament: A Critical Introduction* (Wadsworth, 1986, 1991); "The Parable of the Judge and the Widow (Luke 18:1-8)" *NTS* 33 (1987); "Psalm 42/43 in John's Gospel" *NTS* 29 (1983); "The Son of Man in the Fourth Gospel" *JBL* 86 (1967); *Old Testament Quotations in the Gospel of John* (Brill, 1965); "Variations in the Language and Thought of John" *ZNW* (1964); "The Entry into Jerusalem in the Gospel of John" *JBL* 80 (1961); and others. Awd: Mellon Grant 1977; Lindback Found. Awd. for Disting. Teaching 1984. Mem: SBL; SNTS 1975-. Rec: Reading & writing, hiking, lawn & garden work. Addr: (h) 1527 Willoughby Dr., Wooster, OH 44691 216-264-8127.

FREEDMAN, David Noel, b. New York, NY, May 12, 1922, m. Cornelia Anne (Pryor), chil: Meredith Anne; Nadezhda; David Micaiah; Jonathan Pryor. Educ: Princeton Theol. Sem., ThB, OT 1944; Johns Hopkins U., PhD, Semitic Lang. & Lit. 1948. Emp: *JBL,* 1952-59 Ed.; Anchor Bible Ser., 1956- Ed.; *Interpreter's Dict. of the Bible,* 1957-60 Ed. Cons.; Pittsburgh Theol. Sem., 1960-64 James A. Kelso Prof. of Hebrew & OT; San Francisco Theol. Sem., 1964-71 Dean, Gray Prof. of OT Exegesis; Grad Theol. Union, 1964-71 Prof., OT; Albright Inst. of Arch. Res., Jerusalem, 1969-70, 1976-77 Ann. Dir.; U. of Michigan, 1971- Dir., Program on Stud. in Relig., Arthur F. Thurnau Prof. of Bibl. Stud.; U. of California, San Diego 1985-86 Vis. Prof., 1987-92 Endowed Chair in Hebrew Bibl. Stud.; Anchor Bible Reference Lib., 1988- Ed.; *ABD,* 6 vol., Ed.-in-chief. Excv: Ashod Excvn. Project, 1962-64 Dir. Spec: Hebrew Bible. Pub: *The Unity of the Hebrew Bible* (1991); *Amos,* AB, co-auth. (1989); *The Paleo-Hebrew Leviticus Scroll,* co-auth. (1985); *Pottery, Poetry, and Prophecy* (1981); *Hosea,* AB, co-auth. (1980); *An Explorer's Life of Jesus,* co-auth. (1975); and others. Awd: Guggenheim Fellow. 1958-59; Carey-Thomas Awd. 1965; U. of Pacific, DLitt 1973. Mem: SBL 1947-; AOS 1947-; ASOR 1947-, V.P., 1970-82; AAR 1971-; AIA 1973-. Addr: (o) U. of California at San Diego, Dept. of History, La Jolla, CA 92093-0104 619-534-3542.

FREEMAN, Arthur J., b. Green Bay, WI, October 11, 1927, s. of Arthur & Ethel (Bins), m. Carole Jean, chil: Stephen Boucher; David Freeman. Educ: Lawrence Coll., BA 1949; Moravian Theol. Sem., BD 1952; Princeton Theol. Sem., PhD 1962. Emp: Moravian Ch., 1953-61 Founding Pastor, 1990 Consecrated Bishop; Moravian Theol. Sem., 1961-66 Assoc. Prof., 1966- Prof., Bibl. Theol. & NT; Ecumenical Com. for Continuing Educ., 1974-90 Admin. Spec: New Testament, Apocrypha and Post-biblical Studies. Pub: "Brüderische

Glaubensidentität und die Weitergabe des Evangeliums" *Unitas Fratrum* 27/28 (1991); and others. Mem: SBL 1950-; Moravian Hist. Soc. 1950-; Soc. for the Advancement of Continuing Educ. in Min. 1974-90. Rec: Organ & piano, carpentry, photography & multi-media production. Addr: (o) Moravian Theological Seminary, 60 W Locust St., Bahnson Center, Bethlehem, PA 18018 215-861-1520; (h) 1753 North Blvd., Bethlehem, PA 18017 215-866-4749.

FREND, William H. C., b. Surrey, UK, January 11, 1916, s. of Edwin G.C. & Edith (Bacon), m. Mary G. (Crook), chil: Sarah Ann; Simon William. Educ: Oxford U., MA, Modern Hist. 1937, PhD 1940, DD 1966; Cambridge U., BD 1964. Emp: 1940-51 government service; Cambridge U., 1953-69 Lect., 1956-69 Fellow, Gonville & Caius Coll.; Glasgow U., 1969-84 Prof., Ecclesiastical Hist. Excv: Kherbet Bahrarous, Algeria, 1939 Site Supr.; Knossos, Crete, 1957-61 Dir.; Qasr Ibrim (Nubia), 1963-64 Assoc. Dir.; Carthage, 1976-77 Advisor. Spec: Archaeology, Anatolian Studies, Egyptology. Pub: *The Early Church* (SCM, 1965, 1991); *The Donatist Church* (Oxford U.P., 1951, 1985); *The Rise of Christianity* (Fortress/Dartons, 1984); "A Note on Religion and Life in a Nubian Village in the Later Roman Empire" *Bull. arch. du Comite des Travaux bibl.* (1984); "The Early Christian Church in Carthage" in *Excavation at Carthage in 1976, Conducted by the University of Michigan*, vol. 3 (1977); *Martyrdom and Persecution in the Early Church* (Blackwell, 1965); "A Byzantine Church at Knossos" in *Papers of the British School at Athens*, vol. 56 (1962); and others. Awd: Edinburgh U., DD 1974. Mem: Soc. of Antiq. of London 1952-; Royal Soc. of Edinburgh 1979-; Brit. Acad. 1983-. Rec: Roman-Brit. arch. Addr: (h) The Clerb Cottage, Little Wilbralan, Cambridge CB1 5LB, England.

FRERICHS, Ernest S., b. Staten Island, NY, April 30, 1925, s. of Ernest V. & Eva S., m. Sarah C., chil: John A.; David S.; Elizabeth A. Educ: Brown U., AB 1948; Harvard U., AM 1949; Boston U., STB 1952, PhD 1957. Emp: Brown U., 1964-70 Chmn., Relig. Stud. Dept., 1976- Dean, Grad. Sch., Prof. & Dir. of Prog. in Judaic Stud.; Boston U., 1966-67 Adj. Prof.; U. of Newcastle-upon-Tyne, 1970-71 Vis. Prof.; Albright Inst. of Arch. Res., Jerusalem, 1976-82 Pres., 1983 Ann. Prof., 1989- Chmn., Coun. on Grad. Stud. in Relig.; Brown Judaic Stud., 1976- Ed.; *BR*, 1984- Ed. Bd. Excv: Tel Gezer, Israel 1966; Tel Miqne, 1983- Natl. Dir., Volunteer & Consortium Relationships. Spec: Archaeology, Hebrew Bible. Pub: *Good Enough on the History of Religion and on Judaism*, co-ed. (Scholars, 1986); *The Bible and Bibles in America*, ed. (Fortress, 1986); *To See Ourselves as Others See Us*, co-ed. (Scholars, 1985); and others. Awd: Lilly Post-doc. Fellow 1962-63; Hebrew Union Coll., DHL 1992. Mem: SBL 1967-; AAR 1970-, Pres., New England reg. 1970-71. Rec: Swimming, philately. Addr: (o) Brown U.,

Program in Judaic Studies, Box 1826, Providence, RI 02912 401-863-3900; (h) 32 Vassar Ave., Providence, RI 02906 401-274-9849.

FRERICHS, Wendell W., b. Harris, IA, August 14, 1925, s. of Wallace & Alma (Rehborg), m. Jeanne (Opsahl), chil: Wendy; Rachel; Heidi; Grant; Daniel. Educ: Luther Theol. Sem., BTh 1951; Oberlin Grad. Sch. of Theol., STM 1955; U. of Basel, Switzerland, ThD 1966. Emp: Luther Theol. Sem., 1958-82 Prof., OT; *Dialog*, 1966-69 Managing Ed.; *Luther Sem. Rev.*, 1973-78 Ed.; Gbaya Bible Trans. Ctr., West Africa, 1973, 1976 Cons.; Luther NW Theol. Sem., 1982- Prof., OT. Spec: Hebrew Bible, Apocrypha and Post-biblical Studies. Pub: *The People of God* (Augsburg, 1969); and others. Awd: Inst. for Ecumenical & Cultural Res., Fellow 1972-73. Mem: SBL; ASOR; CBA. Rec: Gardening, travel. Addr: (o) 2481 Como Ave. W, St. Paul, MN 55108 612-641-3201; (h) 1776 Chatsworth, St. Paul, MN 55113 612-489-8947.

FRETHEIM, Terence E., b. Decorah, IA, January 27, 1936, s. of Erling & Marie, m. Faith, chil: Tanya; Andrea. Educ: Luther Coll., BA 1956; Luther Theol. Sem, MDiv 1960; Princeton Theol. Sem., PhD (magna cum laude) 1967. Emp: Augsburg Coll., 1961-63, 1967-68 Asst. Prof., Relig.; Princeton Theol. Sem, 1966-67 Instr., OT; Dennison Luth. Parish, 1968-71 Pastor; Luther NW Theol. Sem., 1968- Prof., OT; *JBL*, 1984-92 Assoc. Ed. Spec: Hebrew Bible. Pub: *Exodus* (John Knox, 1991); "The Reclamation of Creation: Redemption and Law in Exodus" *Interpretation* (1991); "The Plagues as Ecological Signs of Historical Disaster" *JBL* (1991); "The Repentance of God: A Study of Jeremiah 18:7-10" *HAR* (1987); "Divine Foreknowledge, Divine Constancy, and the Rejection of Saul's Kingship" *CBQ* (1985); *The Suffering of God: An Old Testament Perspective* (Fortress, 1984); *Deuteronomic History* (Abingdon, 1983); "Old Testament Commentaries, Their Selection and Use" *Interpretation* (1982); *The Message of Jonah: A Theological Commentary* (Augsburg, 1977); and others. Awd: U. of Durham, England, Fulbright Schol. 1960-61. Mem: SBL 1963-; CBA 1984-. Rec: Stamps, Racquetball. Addr: (o) 2481 Como Ave., St. Paul, MN 55108 612-641-3247.

FRETZ, Mark J. H., b. Lansdale, PA, December 4, 1958, s. of Merrill E. & Nancy C., m. Angela (Hochestetler), chil: Elyse A. H. Educ: East. Mennonite Coll., BA, Bible 1979; Mennonite Bibl. Sem., MDiv 1984; U. of Mich., PhD 1993. Emp: Freeman Jr. Coll., 1984-86 Instr., Bible & Relig.; U. of Mich., 1986-89 Grad. Teaching Asst.; *ABD* Project, 1987-90 Ed. Asst. & Writer; Bluffton Coll., 1990-91 Asst. Prof., Relig.; East. Mennonite Coll., 1991-93 Asst. Prof., Bible & Relig. Spec: Hebrew Bible, Semitic Languages, Texts and Epigraphy. Pub: Articles in *ABD* (Doubleday, 1992); "*Herem* in the Old Testament: A Critical Reading" in *Essays on War and Peace: Bible and Early*

Church (Inst. of Mennonite Stud., 1986). Awd: U. of Mich., U. Fellow., Waterman Awd. 1986-89. Mem: SBL 1984-; AAR 1984-; ASOR 1990-; NAPH 1990-. Rec: Walking, swimming, travel to hist. sites, class. music. Addr: (h) 1641 Park Rd., Apt. C., Harrisonburg, VA 22801 703-434-6951.

FRIEDMAN, Richard Elliott, Educ: Harvard U., ThD 1978. Emp: U. of Calif.-San Diego, 1976-; Oxford Ctr. for Postgrad. Hebrew Stud., 1984 Vis. Schol.; U. of Cambridge, Clare Hall, 1988 Vis. Fellow. Spec: Hebrew Bible, Semitic Languages, Texts and Epigraphy. Pub: "Torah and Covenant" in *The Oxford Study Bible* (Oxford U.P., 1992); *The Future of Biblical Studies: The Hebrew Scriptures,* co-ed. (Scholars, 1987); *Who Wrote the Bible?* (Summit, 1987); *The Poet and the Historian,* HSS, ed. (1983); "From Egypt to Egypt: Dtr 1 and Dtr 2" in *Traditions in Transformation: Turning-Points in Biblical Faith,* Frank Moore Cross Festschrift (Eisenbrauns, 1981); *The Exile and Biblical Narrative,* HSM (1981); "The Tabernacle in the Temple" *BA* 43 (1980); "The MRZH Tablet from Ugarit" *MAARAV* 2 (1980); "Composition and Paronomasia in the Book of Jonah" *HAR* 4 (1980); and others. Mem: Bibl. Colloquium 1987-. Addr: (o) U. of California-San Diego, La Jolla, CA 92093-0410 619-534-3210.

FRIESEN, Steven J., b. Pasadena, CA, June 18, 1954, s. of John E. & Anne Miriam (Schultz), m. Janice Marie (Reamey), chil: David John; Daniel Alan. Educ: Fresno Pacific Coll., BA (magna cum laude) 1976; Fuller Theol. Sem., MDiv 1979; Harvard U., AM 1986, PhD, Study of Relig. 1990. Emp: Fuller Theol. Sem., 1991-92 Adjunct Faculty; Inst. of Culture & Communication, 1990-93 Fellow; U. of Mo., Columbia, 1993- Vis. Asst. Prof. Spec: Archaeology, New Testament. Pub: *Twice Neokoros: Ephesus, Asia, and the Cult of the Flavian Imperial Family,* Religions in the Graeco-Roman World 116 (Brill, 1993); "Corinth A: Architectural Monuments of the Roman City," "Olympia" in *Archaeological Resources for New Testament Studies* 1 (Fortress, 1987); and others. Awd: Jens Aubrey Westengard Fund 1985; Pfeiffer Fund 1985, 1989; Makana Disting. Service Awd. 1991-92. Mem: AAR; SBL. Addr: (o) U. of Missouri, Dept. of Religious Studies, 405 GCB, Columbia, MO 62511 314-882-4769; (h) 1105 8th Ave., Honolulu, HI 96816 808-732-7139.

FRITZ, Volkmar O., b. Dueren, Germany, February 12, 1938. Educ: U. of Marburg, Germany, PhD 1968. Emp: U. of Mainz, 1967-87 Assoc. Prof.; U. of Giessen, 1987- Prof. Excv: Arad, 1965, 1967; Lachish, 1966, 1968; Tell es-Seba', 1970-71 Area Supr.; Khirbet el-Meshash, 1972-75 Co-dir.; Kinneret, 1982-85 Dir. Spec: Archaeology, Hebrew Bible. Pub: *Einfuehrung in die Biblische Archaeologie* (1985); "Palaeste waehrend der Bronze un Eisenzeit in Palaestina" *ZDPV* (1983); "The 'List of Rehoboam's

Fortresses' in 2 Chr. 11:5-12—A Document from the Time of Josiah?" *Eretz-Israel* (1981); "Bestimmung und Herkunft des Pfeilerhauses in Israel" *ZDPV* (1977); "Erwaegungen zu dem spaetbronzezeitlichen Quadratbau bei Amman" *ZDPV* (1971); "Die sogenannte Liste der besiegten Konige in Josua 12" *ZDPV* (1969). Mem: Deutsche Orient-Gessellschaft; Deutscher Palastina-Verein; ASOR. Addr: (o) U. of Giessen, FB 07, Karl-Gloeckner Strasse 21H, 6400 Giessen, Germany; (h) Kapuzinerstrasse 18, 6500 Mainz, Germany 06131-220158.

FRIZZELL, Lawrence E., b. Calgary, Canada, May 28, 1938, s. of Walter John & Mary Angela (Long). Educ: U. of Ottawa, St. Paul's Sem., STL 1962; Pont. Bibl. Inst., Rome, SSL 1967; Oxford U., England, DPhil 1974. Emp: St. Joseph's Sem., Canada, 1962-64, 1967-70 Asst. Prof.; Seton Hall U., 1974- Assoc. Prof. ; Ecole Biblique, Vis. Prof. 1983; Pont. Bibl. Inst., Rome, 1990 Vis. Prof. Spec: Hebrew Bible, New Testament, Apocrypha and Post-biblical Studies. Pub: "Elijah the Peacemaker: Jewish and Christian Interpretations of Malachi 3:23-24" *SIDIC* 17 (1984); *Standing Before God: Studies on Prayer in Scriptures and Tradition,* co-ed. (1981); and others. Awd: Canada Coun. Fellow for Doctoral Stud. 1970-74. Mem: CBA 1968-; SBL 1975-. Rec: Hiking. Addr: (o) Seton Hall U., Dept. of Jewish-Christian Studies, South Orange, NJ 07079 201-761-9469.

FRYE, Richard N., b. Birmingham, AL, January 10, 1920, s. of Nels & Lillie (Hagman), m. Eden (Naby), chil: Jeffrey L.; Rebecca; Robert G.; Nels M.N. Educ: Harvard U., MA 1940, PhD 1946. Emp: Harvard U., 1946- Aga Khan Prof. of Iranian; Pahlavi U., Iran, 1969-74 Dir., Asia Inst.; Persepolis, 1971-72 Lect. Spec: Archaeology. Pub: *The History of Ancient Iran* (Beck, 1984); and others. Mem: AOS 1939-; German Arch. Inst., Berlin 1971-. Rec: Fencing. Addr: (o) 6 Divinity Ave., Cambridge, MA 02138 617-495-2684; (h) 8 Tower Hill Rd., Brimfield, MA 01010.

FRYMER-KENSKY, Tikva Simone, Educ: City Coll. of N.Y., AB, Anc. World 1965; Jewish Theol. Sem., BHL, Bible-Talmud 1965; Yale U., MA, West Semitics 1967, PhD, Assyriology 1977. Emp: Yale U., 1968-69 Asst., Elementary Sumarian; Mount Vernon Coll., 1969-71 Lect., Phil. & Relig.; Wayne State U., 1971-82 Asst. Prof., 1982 Assoc. Prof., Near East. Stud.; U. of Mich., 1978-79 Vis. Asst. Prof., Near East. Stud., 1983-85, 1987 Vis. Assoc. Prof.; Reconstructionist Rabbinical Coll., 1988- Dir., Bibl. Stud.; Jewish Theol. Sem., 1988, 1991- Vis. Assoc. Prof.; *BA,* Ed. Bd. Spec: Mesopotamian Studies. Pub: *In the Wake of the Goddesses* (Free, 1992); *The Judicial Ordeal in The Ancient Near East,* 2 vol., Bibliotheca Mesopotamica; "The Trial Before God of an Accused Adulteress" *BR* 2/3 (1986); "Atrahasis: A Translation" in *In the Beginning: Creation Myths from Ancient Mesopotamia, Israel and*

Greece (1982); "The Patriarchal Family and Near Eastern Law" *BA* 44 (1981); "Unusual Legal Procedures in Elam and Nuzi" in *Hurrian and Nuzi Studies in Honor of Ernest Lacheman* (1981); "What the Babylonian Flood Stories Can and Cannot Teach Us About the Genesis Flood" *BAR* 4/4 (1978); and others. Awd: Woodrow Wilson Grad. Fellow. 1965; Danforth Found., Grad. Fellow. 1965; Mary Isabel Sibley Phi Beta Kappa Fellow. 1971; Wayne State U., Fac. Res. Grant 1978; Annenberg Res. Fellow. 1990-91. Mem: SBL, V.P. MidW. reg.; Amer. Anthrop. Assn.; AOS; Bibl. Colloquium. Addr: (h) 28 Henley Rd., Wynnewood, PA 19096 215-642-4890.

FUCHS, Albert, b. Putzleinsdorf, Austria, October 14, 1937, s. of Josef & Theresia. Educ: U. Salzburg, ThD 1966, PhD 1968; Paepstliches Bibelinstitut Rom, Lic. 1970; U. Regensburg, Habil., Wissenschaft des NT 1977. Emp: Katholisch-Theol. Hochschule Linz, 1972- Ordenlicher Prof., NT; Theol. Hochschule St. Poelten, 1975 Vorlesungen; Theol. Fakultat Tubingen, 1989-90 Vorlesungen. Spec: New Testament, Apocrypha and Post-biblical Studies. Pub: "Die 'Seesturmperikope' Mk 4,35-41 parr im Wandel der urkirchlichen Verkundigung," "Offene Probleme der Synoptikerforschung" *SNTU* 15 (1990); *Konkordanz zu Gespraech Jesu mit dem Teufel* (1983); "Die Ueber-schneidungen von Mk und Q nach B.H. Streeter und E.P. Sanders und ihre wahre Bedeutung (Mk 1,1- 8 parr)" in *Wort in der Zeit: Neutestamentliche Studien* (1979); *Die traditionsgeschichtliche und redaktionsgeschichtliche Entwicklung der Beelzebulkontroverse* (1979); "Die Behandlung der mt/lk Uebereinstimmungen gegen Mk durch S. McLoughlin und ihre Bedeutung fuer die Synoptische Frage" *SNTU* 3 (1978); *Das Petrusevangelium* (1978); *Konkordanz zum Protoevangelium des Jakobus* (1978); and others. Mem: SNTS; Paepstlichen Bibelkommission 1990. Addr: (o) Katholisch-Theol. Hochschule Linz, Bethlehemstrasse 20, A-4020 Linz, Austria 0043-7322375482; (h) Bluetenstrasse 17, A-4040 Linz, Austria.

FUCHS, Stephen L., b. East Orange, NJ, March 16, 1946, s. of Leo & Florence (Goldstein), m. Victoria, chil: Leo; Sarah; Benjamin. Educ: Hamilton Coll., BA 1968; Hebrew Union Coll., Los Angeles, BHL 1970; Hebrew Union Coll., Cincinnati, MAHL 1974, Rabbinic Ord., 1974; Vanderbilt U., DMin 1992. Emp: Temple Isaiah, 1974-86 Rabbi; Congregation Ohabai Sholom, 1986- Sr. Rabbi. Spec: Hebrew Bible. Pub: "Solomon—The King Without a Prophet" *BR* 3/2 (1987); "Abraham eine Auslegung" *Gesprechen in Israel* (1984); "De Verbondsidee—De Noodzaak van het Verbond" *Gesprekken in Israel* 5 (1983); and others. Mem: Cen. Conf. of Amer. Rabbis 1974-; Nashville Assn. of Rabbis, Priests & Min. 1986-, Pres. 1992-93. Rec: Tennis. Addr: (o) Congregation Ohabai Sholom, 5015 Harding Rd., Nashville, TN 37205 615-352-7620; (h) 1209 Canterbury Dr., Nashville, TN 37205 615-292-4278.

FULCO, William J., b. Los Angeles, CA, February 24, 1936, s. of Herman J. & Clelia M. (DeFeo). Educ: Gonzaga U., AB 1959, MA, PhL 1960; U. of Santa Clara, STM, STL 1967; Yale U., PhD 1970. Emp: Grad. Theol. Union, Jesuit Sch. of Theol., 1971-84 Assoc. Prof., Bibl. Stud.; U. of Calif., 1971-85 Vis. Assoc. Prof., Semitics & Arch.; Pont. Bibl. Inst., Jerusalem, 1974-1989 Cur., Arch. & Numismatic Mus.; Jordanian Dept. of Antiq., 1979- Numismatic Cons.; Ecole Biblique, Jerusalem, 1974-75 Vis. Prof.; U. of South. Calif., 1989- Prof. of Arch., Cur. Excv: Syria, 1977 ASOR Arch. Survey Team. Spec: Archaeology, Hebrew Bible, Semitic Languages, Texts and Epigraphy. Pub: *Maranatha: Reflections on the Mystical Theology of John the Evangelist* (Paulist, 1973); *The Canaanite God Resep* (AOS, 1976); "The Amman Citadel Inscription: A New Collation" *BASOR* 230 (1978); "The Amman Theater Inscription" *JNES* 39/1 (1979); "A Seal from Umm el Qanafid, Jordan: G'YHW 'BD HMLK" *Orientalia* 48 (1979); Articles in *The Encyclopedia of Religion* (Macmillan, 1987); and others. Mem: SBL 1971-; AOS 1968-; ASOR 1971-; CBA 1970-. Rec: Photography, orchidiculture, travel. Addr: (o) 8170 Redlands St. #310, Playa del Rey, Los Angeles, CA 90293 310-305-7051; (h) Jesuits at Loyola U., PO Box 45041, Los Angeles, CA 90045 310-338-2746.

FULLER, Michael J., b. Springfield, MO, December 30, 1953, s. of Charles & Wilma, m. Neathery (Batsell). Educ: SW Mo. State U., BS 1976; Washington U., St. Louis, MA 1980, PhD, Anthrop. 1987. Emp: SW Mo. State U., 1975-78 Arch. Res. Assoc.; St. Louis Community Coll., 1982- Prof., Anthrop.; U. of Mo., 1985-91 Adj. Assoc. Prof., Anthrop.; Washington U., St. Louis, 1988, 1992 Adj. Assoc. Prof., Anthrop. Excv: Tell er-Retaba, Egypt, 1978-81 Architect, Geoarchaeologist; Ithaka, Greece, 1985-86 Surveyor, Architect; Tell Abila, Jordan, 1980-86 Field Dir., Architect; Tell Tuneinir, Syria, 1986-93 Co-dir. Spec: Archaeology, Mesopotamian Studies, Egyptology. Pub: "Tuneinir," co-auth., in *Archaeology in Syria*, AJA 95 (1991); "Tell Tuneinir on the Khabur: Preliminary Report on Three Seasons," co-auth., *AAS* 37-38 (1987-88); "Abila Pottery Types" *NEAS Bull.* 27 (1986); "Report of the Survey-Architectural Investigations (Abila)" *NEAS Bull.* 25 (1985). Awd: Mo. Hum. Coun. Schol. 1990-93. Mem: ASOR; AIA, Pres., St. Louis Soc. 1988-90; AOS; Soc. for Amer. Arch.; Amer. Anthrop. Assn. Rec: Scuba diving, jogging, collecting stereoview cards & early photographs. Addr: (o) St. Louis Community College, Dept. of Anthropology, 3400 Pershall Rd., St. Louis, MO 63135 314-595-4414; (h) 13530 Clayton Rd., St. Louis, MO 63141 314-434-4471.

FULLER, Neathery B., b. Tulsa, OK, May 4, 1953, d. of Ned & Martha Batsell, m. Michael J. Educ: Washington U., St. Louis, BS 1979, MA, Anthrop. 1985. Emp: St. Louis Community Coll., 1989-90 Adj. Instr., Sociology. Excv: Odyssey Project, Ithaka, Greece, 1985-86

Archaeobotanist; Tell Abila, Jordan, 1980-86 Area Supr., Ethnoarchaeologist; Tell Tuneinir, Syria, 1986-93 Co-dir. Spec: Archaeology, Mesopotamian Studies. Pub: "Tuneinir," co-auth., in *Archaeology of Syria*, AJA 95 (1991); "Tell Tuneinir on the Khabur: Preliminary Report on Three Seasons," co-auth., *AAS* 37-38 (1987-88); "Abila Tomb Excavations: 1986" *NEAS Bull.* 29 (1987); "1984 Excavations at Abila: Glass Analysis" *NEAS Bull.* 26 (1986). Mem: AIA; Mo. Assn. of Professional Arch. Rec: Scuba diving, painting, sculpture, photography, ceramics. Addr: (o) St. Louis Community College, Dept. of Anthropology, 3400 Pershall Rd., St. Louis, MO 63135 314-595-4414; (h) 13530 Clayton Rd., St Louis, MO 63141 314-434-4471.

FULLER, Reginald H., b. Horsham, Sussex, England, March 24, 1915, s. of Horace & Cora, m. Ilse (Barda), chil: Caroline; Rosemary; Sarah. Educ: Peterhouse, Cambridge, BA 1938, MA 1941. Emp: St. David's U. Coll., Wales, 1950-55 Prof. of Theol.; Seabury-West. Theol. Sem., 1955-56 Prof. of NT; Union Theol. Sem., 1966-72 Baldwin Prof. of Sacred Lit.; Episc. Theol. Sem. of Va., 1972-85 Molly Laird Prof. of NT, 1985- Prof. Emeritus; *SNTS,* Ed. Bd. Spec: New Testament. Pub: *He That Cometh* (1990); and others. Awd: Cambridge U., Schofield Prize 1938; STD 1960, 1962, DD 1983; AATS Fellow 1969. Mem: SBL 1958-; SNTS 1955-, Pres. 1983. Rec: Gilbert & Sullivan. Addr: (h) 5001 E Seminary Ave., Richmond, VA 23227 804-266-6010.

FUNK, Robert W., b. Evansville, IN, July 18, 1926, s. of Robert Joseph & Ada (Adams), m. Charlene (Matejovsky), chil: Andrea Elizabeth; Stephanie McFarland. Educ: Butler U., AB, Relig., Class. 1947, MA, Semitics, Class. 1951; Butler U. Sch. of Relig., BD 1950; Vanderbilt U., PhD, NT 1953. Emp: ASOR, Israel, 1957-58 Ann. Prof.; Emory U., 1958-59 Asst. Prof., Bibl. Theol.; Drew U., 1959-66 Assoc. Prof., NT; Vanderbilt Div. Sch., 1966-69 Prof., NT; U. of Mont., 1969-86 Prof., Relig. Stud.; *Semeia,* 1974-80 Ed.; *The Fourth R,* 1986- Ed. Excv: Shechem, Balatah, 1957 Field Supr.; Beth-zur, 1957-58 Field Supr.; Pella, 1958 Co-dir. Spec: New Testament, Apocrypha and Post-biblical Studies. Pub: *The Gospel of Mark: Red Letter Edition* (Polebridge, 1991); "Unraveling the Jesus Tradition: Criteria and Criticism" *Forum* 5/2 (1989); *The Poetics of Biblical Narrative* (Polebridge, 1988); "The Watershed of the American Biblical Tradition: The Chicago School, First Phase, 1892-1920" *JBL* 95/1 (1976); "Beth-zur" in *EAEHL* (IES/Massada, 1975); *Jesus as Precursor* (Fortress/Scholars, 1975); "A History of Beth-zur," "The Bronze and Iron Age Pottery" in *The 1957 Excavations at Beth-zur, AASOR* 38 (1969); *Language, Hermeneutic, and Word of God* (Harper & Row, 1966); and others. Awd: U. of Tubingen, Fulbright Sr. Schol. 1965-66; Guggenheim Fellow 1965-66; Amer. Coun. of Learned Soc., Fellow. 1973-74; SBL, Fellow. 1980-81. Mem: SBL, Pres. 1974-75; AAR; Amer. Coun. of Learned Soc. Rec: Fly fish-

ing, gardening, reading. Addr: (o) Polebridge Press, 19678 Eighth St. E, Sonoma, CA 95476 707-996-9228; (h) 251 W MacArthur, Sonoma, CA 95476 707-938-0237.

FUNK, Wolf-Peter Paul, b. Oederan, Germany, December 30, 1943, s. of Wolfgang & Johanna. Educ: Humboldt U., dip. theol. 1968, dip. English philol. 1970, ThD, NT 1971. Emp: Humboldt U., 1980-85 Asst. Lect.; U. Laval, 1986-88 Vis. Prof., 1990- Res. Assoc.; Annenberg Inst., 1988-89 Fellow; Ecole Pratique des Hautes Etudes, 1990 Vis. Prof. Spec: New Testament, Egyptology, Apocrypha and Post-biblical Studies. Pub: "Formen und Funktionen des interlokutiven Nominalsatzes in den koptischen Dialekten" *Langues Orientales Anciennes* 3 (1991); *The Chester Beatty Codex ac. 1390: Mathematical School Exercises and John 10:7-13:38 in Subachmimic,* co-auth. (Peeters, 1990); "Dialects Wanting Homes: A Numerical Approach to the Early Varieties of Coptic" in *Historical Dialectology: Regional and Social*(de Gruyter, 1988); "Der Anfang des Johannesevangeliums auf faijumisch" *APF* 34 (1988); "How Closely Related are the Subakhmimic Dialects?" *ZAS* 112 (1985); "Toward a Synchronic Morphology of Coptic" in *The Future of Coptic Studies* (Brill, 1978); *Die zweite Apokalypse des Jakobus aus Nag-Hammadi-Codex V* (Akademie-Verlag, 1976); and others. Mem: IACS 1976-; Societas Linguistica Europaea 1980-; Intl. Assn. of Manichaean Stud. 1989-. Rec: Gardening, swimming. Addr: (o) U. Laval, Projet Nag Hammadi, FAS 1036, Quebec City, Que. G1K 7P4, Canada 418-656-5637; (h) 620 ch. St. Louis, app. 6, Quebec City, Que. G1S 1B8, Canada 418-681-2943.

FURNISH, Victor Paul, b. Chicago, IL, November 17, 1931. Educ: Cornell Coll., AB 1952; Garrett Theol. Sem., BD 1955; Yale U., MA 1958, PhD, Relig. 1960. Emp: South. Meth. U., Perkins Sch. of Theol., 1959-71 Assoc. Prof., 1971- Prof., 1988- U. Disting. Prof. of NT. Spec: New Testament. Pub: "Corinth in Paul's Time: What Can Archaeology Tell Us?" *BAR* 14/3 (1988); *The Moral Teaching of Paul: Selected Issues* (Abingdon, 1985); *The Pauline Letters,* co-auth. (Eerdmans, 1985); *II Corinthians* (Doubleday, 1984); *The Interpreter's Dictionary of the Bible,* co-ed. & contb. (Abingdon, 1976); *The Love Command in the New Testament* (1972); *The Interpreter's One-Volume Commentary on the Bible,* contb. (1971); *Theology and Ethics in Paul* (1968); and others. Awd: U. of Bonn, Alexander von Humbolt Found., Res. Fellow. 1965-66; BAS Publ. Awd., Best Comm. on a Book of the NT 1986. Mem: SBL, Pres. 1993; AAR; SNTS. Addr: (o) Southern Methodist U., Perkins School of Theology, Dallas, TX 75275 214-768-2390.

FUSCO, Vittorio, b. Campobasso, Italy, April 24, 1939, s. of Antonio & Rosina (Sassi). Educ: Pont. U. Gregoriana, Rome, STL 1967; Pont. Bibl. Inst., Rome, SSL 1969, SSD 1980. Emp: Pont. Fac.

Teologica dell'Italia Meridionale, 1969- Prof. Ordinario; *Rassegna di Teologia*, 1981-82 Redaction; *Aloisiana*, 1982-84 Dir.; *Rivista Bibl.*, *Supplementi alla Rivista Bibl.*, 1987- Redaction, 1993- Dir. Spec: New Testament. Pub: *Povertà e sequela. La pericope sinottica della chiamata del ricco (Mc 10, 17-31)* (Paideia, 1991); *Dalla missione di Galilea alla missione universale. La tradizione del discorso missionario*, (Atti 30 sett.bibl.) (EDB, 1990); "Tendances recentes dans l'interpretation des paraboles" in *Les paraboles evangeliques* (Cerf, 1988); "Il valore salvifico della croce nell'opera lucana" in *Testimonium Christi. Studi in onore di Jacques Dupont* (Paideia, 1985); "Lc 21:32 alla luce dell'espressione 'questa generazione'" *Asprenas* (1984); "L'idea di successione nel discorso di Mileto (At 20: 18-35)" in *Una Hostia. Studi in Onore del Cardinale Corrado Ursi* (1983); *Oltre la parabola. Introduzione alle parabole di Gesúio* (Borla, 1983); and others. Mem: Assn. bibl. italiana 1970-; SNTS 1981-. Rec: Classical music. Addr: (o) Pont. Fac. Teol. dell'Italia Meridionale, Via Petrarca 115, 80122 Naples, Italy 081-5750015; (h) Corso Mazzini, 129, 86100 Campobasso, Italy 0874-60385.

GAFNI, Isaiah M., b. Brooklyn, NY, July 11, 1944, s. of Reuben & Betty (Feldman), m. Naomi, chil: Tamar; Chanan; Reuven; Chava. Educ: Hebrew U., BA, Talmud, Jewish Hist. 1966, MA, Jewish Hist. 1969, PhD 1978. Emp: Hebrew U., 1967- Assoc. Prof., Jewish Hist.; Bar-Ilan U., 1978-80 Lect., Jewish Hist.; Jewish Theol. Sem., 1980-81, 1985-86 Vis. Prof., Jewish Hist.; Harvard U., 1989, 1991 Vis. Prof., Jewish Stud.; Yale U., 1981, 1992 Vis. Prof., Jewish Hist. Spec: Semitic Languages, Texts and Epigraphy, Apocrypha and Post-biblical Studies. Pub: *Jews and Judaism in the Second Temple, Mishna and Talmud Period—Studies in Honor of S. Safrai*, ed. (Yad Ben-Zvi, 1993); *Sanctity of Life and Martyrdom—Studies in Memory of Amir Yekutiel*, ed. (Mercaz Shazar, 1992); "The World of the Talmud: From the Mishnah to the Arab Conquest" in *Christianity and Rabbinic Judaism—A Parallel History of Their Origins and Early Development* (BAS, 1992); *The Jews of Babylonia in the Talmudic Era—A Social and Cultural History* (Mercaz Shazar, 1990); "Expressions and Types of Local Patriotism among the Jews of Sasanian Babylonia" *Irano-Judaica* 2 (1990); "The Institution of Marriage in Rabbinic Times" in *The Jewish Family— Metaphor and Memory* (Oxford, 1989); "Josephus and I Maccabeus" in *Josephus, the Bible and History* (1989); "Pre-Histories of Jerusalem in Hellenistic, Jewish and Christian Literature" *JSP* 1 (1987); *Babylonian Jewry and Its Institutions in the Period of the Talmud* (Mercaz Shazar, 1975); and others. Awd: Warburg Prize in Jewish Stud. 1971-1974; Israel Com. for Higher Educ., Barecha (Alon) Prize 1980-83; Holon Municipality, Prize for Schol. in Judaica 1992; Hebrew U., Inst. for Advanced Stud., Fellow & Group Coord. 1992-93. Mem: SBL; AJS; Israel Hist. Soc.; IES; WUJS. Addr: (o) Hebrew U., Dept. of Jewish History, Mt.

Scopus, Jerusalem, Israel 972-2-883560; (h) 22 Hatibonim St., Jerusalem 92386, Israel 972-2-636193.

GAILEY, James H., b. Atlanta, GA, October 17, 1916, s. of J. Herbert & Edna (Bryan), m. Virginia (Templin), chil: L. Landen; J. Bryan. Educ: Davidson Coll., BA 1937; Columbia Theol. Sem., BD 1941; Princeton Theol. Sem., ThM 1942, ThD 1945. Emp: Presbyn. Ch., 1945-53 Pastor; Columbia Theol. Sem, 1953-81 Prof., OT; U. of Ibadan, Nigeria, 1978-79 Vis. Prof. Excv: Tel Zeror, 1966 Dir. Spec: Hebrew Bible, Semitic Languages, Texts and Epigraphy. Pub: *The Layman's Bible Comm.* vol. 15 (John Knox, 1962); "Old Testament Literature, 1957-58" *Interpretation* (1959); "The Sword and the Heart, Evil from the North—and Within" *Interpretaton* (1955). Mem: SBL 1941-; AAR; NAPH. Rec: Woodworking, music, travel. Addr: (h) 37 East Dr. NE, Atlanta, GA 30305 404-233-7755.

GALITIS, George A., b. Volos, Greece, November 8, 1926, s. of Anton & Georgia, m. Zafiria (Stavrakaki), chil: Georgia; Kalliope; Lydia. Educ: U. of Athens, MA 1950, ThD 1960. Emp: U. of Athens, 1964-66 Lect., 1966-69 Asst. Prof., 1979- Prof.; U. of Thessaloniki, 1969-79 Prof.; *Anaplasis*, 1987- Ed. Spec: New Testament. Pub: *The Epistle to Titus* (1992); *Christology of the St. Petrus Speeches I-II* (1990); "Revelation and the Word of God: Apophaticism and Demythologising" *Epist. Epet. Theol. Sch. Thessalon* (1988); "Zu einer Theologie der Materie" *Epist. Epet. Theol. Sch. Thessalo* (1985); "Die Hist.-Kritische Bibelwissenschaft und die orth. Theologie" *Etudes Theol.* 4 (1984); "Das Wesen der Freiheit Eine Untersuchung zu 1Ko9 und seinem Kontext" in *Freedom und Love* (1981); "The Christological Hymne of the Epistle to the Philippians and Ps. 109" *Deltion Bibl. Meleton* 1 (1980); *The Use of the Term* Archegos *in the New Testament* (1960); and others. Awd: Ecumenical Patriarchate of Constantinople, Officer Great Master of the Gospel 1970. Mem: SNTS; Colloquium Paulinum; Wissenschaftliche Gesellschaft fuer Theol.; Greek Soc. for Bibl. Stud., Pres. Addr: (o) U. of Athens, Faculty of Theology, U. Campus, 15772 Athens, Greece 01-7794356; (h) J. Sechou 4, 11524, Athens, Greece 01-6923092.

GALLERY, Maureen L., b. FL, August 26, 1945, d. of William O. & Elizabeth S., m. Frank L. Kovacs. Educ: U. of Toronto, BA 1969, MA 1971; Yale U., PhD 1975. Emp: U. of Chicago, Oriental Inst., 1976-80 Asst. Prof., Res. Assoc., 1981-82 Asst. to Prof. I.J. Gelb. Excv: Tell Leilan, Syria, 1979 Epigrapher. Spec: Mesopotamian Studies. Pub: "The Office of the *satammu* in the Old Babylonian Period" *Archiv fur Orientforschung* 27 (1981); "Kutha," co-auth., *Reallexikon der Assyriologie* 5 (1983); *The Epic of Gilgamesh* (Stanford U.P., 1989); and others. Mem: AOS. Addr: (h) 1832 Lexington Ave., San Mateo, CA 94402 415-573-9352.

GANE, Roy E., b. Sydney, Ausralia, August 31, 1955, s. of Erwin & Winsome, m. Connie, chil: Sarah. Educ: Pacific Union Coll., BA 1977, BMus 1977; U. of Calif., Berkeley, MA 1983, PhD 1992. Emp: U. of Calif., Berkeley, 1989-90 Instr.; Pacific Union Coll., 1992- Asst. Prof. Spec: Hebrew Bible. Pub: "'Bread of the Presence' and Creator-in-Residence" *VT* (1992); "qrb", co-auth., in *Theologisches Woerterbuch zum Alten Testament* (1990); "The Laws of the Seventh and Fiftieth Years" *Jour. of the Assn. of Grad. Near East. Students* (1990); "paroket," co-auth., in *Theologisches Worterbuch zum Alten Testament* (1988); and others. Mem: SBL 1985-; AOS 1989-. Rec: Tennis, hiking, backpacking. Addr: (h) PO Box 206, Angwin, CA 94508 707-965-3463.

GARBER, Paul L., b. Johnstown, PA, April 27, 1911, s. of John A. & Iva L., m. Carolyn (White), chil: Paul L.; David W.; Carter. Educ: Louisville Presbyn. Theol. Sem., MDiv 1936, ThM 1937; Duke U., PhD 1939. Emp: Presbyn. Ch., 1939-43 Pastor; Agnes Scott Coll., 1943-76 Prof., Bible & Relig., Emeritus, Chmn. of Dept.; Howland-Garber Scale Model Reconstruction of Solomon's Temple, 1950 Res. Spec: Archaeology, Hebrew Bible, New Testament. Pub: Articles in *Dict. of Bible and Religion* (1985), *ISBE* (1980); "Reconsidering the Reconstruction of Solomon's Temple" *JBL* (1958); "Reconstructing Solomon's Temple" *BA* (1951); and others. Awd: Duke U., Guerny G. Kearns Fellow. 1937-39. Mem: AAR; SBL; AIA; Oriental Inst.; ASOR. Rec: Travel, photography. Addr: (h) Clairmont Pl., 1800 Clairmont Lake #403, Decatur, GA 30033 404-377-3454.

GARBER, Zev, b. Bronx, NY, March 1, 1941, s. of Morris & Pearl (Borko), m. Susan (Ehrlich), chil: Asher; Dorit. Educ: U. of South. Calif., MA 1968. Emp: Los Angeles Valley Coll., 1970- Prof., Jewish Stud.; U. of Calif. at Los Angeles, 1972-76 Asst. Prof., Hebrew; U. of Calif. at Riverside, 1983- Vis. Prof., Relig. Stud.; *Iggeret,* 1981- Ed.; *Methodology in the Academic Teaching of Judaism,* 1986- Ed. Spec: Hebrew Bible. Pub: "Jethro, Father-in-Law of Moses: Summary of Biblical and Rabbinical Material" *Forum* (1984); articles in *EJ* (1971); and others. Awd: Sir Simon Marks Israel Fellow. 1980-81; NEH, Reviewer 1979-. Mem: AOS 1963-; ASOR 1964-; AAR 1965-; SBL 1965-; NAPH 1970-, Pres. 1988-90. Rec: Films, plays, physical fitness. Addr: (o) Los Angeles Valley College, 5800 Fulton Ave., Van Nuys, CA 91401 818-781-1200; (h) 4540 Stern Ave., Sherman Oaks, CA 91423 818-907-0681.

GARCIA-MORENO, Antonio, b. Badajoz, Spain, September 10, 1932, s. of Andres & Maria Dolores. Educ: U. de Sevilla, Lic. en Derecho Civil 1957; Pont. Bibl. Inst., Lic. en Sagradas Escrituras 1964; U. Gregoriana, ThD 1970. Emp: Sem. Diocesano de Badajoz, 1964-92 Prof.; U. de Navarra, 1971-92 Prof., NT Exegesis. Spec: New Testament. Pub: "Autenticidad e Historicidad del IV Evangelio," "Adorar al Padre en Espiritu y verdad" *ScrTheol* 23 (1991); *Sentido del dolor en Job* (1990); "Aspectos teológicos del Prólogo de S.Juan" *ScrTheol* 21 (1989); *La Neovulgata. Precedentes y actualidad* (1986); *Pueblo, Iglesia y Reino de Dios* (1982); "La realeza y senoria de Cristo en Tesalonicenses" *EstBib* 39 (1979); "Vocación de Jeremias" *EstBib* 27 (1969); and others. Mem: Assn. Bibl. Espanola 1980-; SNTS 1988-. Addr: (o) U. de Navarra, Facultad de Teologia, 31080 Pamplona, Spain; (h) Sancho el Fuerte 17, 70, 31007 Pamplona, Spain 948-265257.

GARNET, Paul, b. Lincoln, England, March 20, 1932, s. of Alfred & Florence Emily (Chilvers), m. Eunice Mary (Mason), chil: Marcus Paul; Jeremy McVeigh; Stephanie Mary. Educ: U. of Sheffield, BA 1954, Cert. in Educ. 1954, MA 1963; McGill U., PhD 1971. Emp: Concordia U., Montreal, 1965- Assoc. Prof. Spec: New Testament. Pub: "The Parable of the Sower: How the Multitudes Understood It" in *Spirit within Structure: Essays in Honor of George Johnston,* Pittsburgh Theol. Mon., New Ser. 3 (1983); "Qumran Light on Pauline Soteriology" in *Pauline Studies: Essays Presented to F.F. Bruce* (Eerdmans, 1980); "The Baptism of Jesus and the Son of Man Idea" *JSNT* 9 (1980); *Salvation and Atonement in the Qumran Scrolls,* WUNT II, 3 (Mohr, 1977). Mem: SBL; CSBS. Rec: Gardening, swimming. Addr: (h) 597 Church St., Beaconsfield, Que. H9W 3T7, Canada.

GARR, W. Randall, b. Norwalk, CT, December 21, 1954, s. of Leon J. & Celeste L. Y., m. Laura Kalman. Educ: Vassar Coll., AB, Relig. 1977; Yale U., MA 1979, MPhil 1980, PhD 1982. Emp: U. of Pa., Dept. of Oriental Stud., 1982-85 Lect.; U. of Chicago, 1986-87 Asst. Prof.; U. of Calif., Santa Barbara, 1987-89 Asst. Prof., 1989- Assoc. Prof. Spec: Hebrew Bible, Semitic Languages, Texts and Epigraphy. Pub: "*ay a* in Targum Onqelos" *JAOS* 111 (1991); "Aspect, Affectedness, and Biblical Hebrew '*et*" *ZAH* 4 (1991); "On the Alternation Between Construct and *Di* Phrases in Biblical Aramaic" *JSS* 35 (1990); *Dialect Geography of Syria-Palestine, 100-586 BCE* (U. of Pa., 1985); and others. Awd: Mitchell Dahood Memorial Contest Prize 1987. Mem: AAJR; AOS; ASOR; CBA; SBL. Rec: Art collecting, book collecting, alternative music, motorcycling. Addr: (o) U. of California, Santa Barbara, Dept. of Religious Studies, Santa Barbara, CA 93106 805-893-8428; (h) 901 W Campus Ln., Goleta, CA 93117 805-685-5529.

GARRETT, Duane A., b. New Orleans, LA, August 4, 1953, s. of Robert & Frances, m. Patricia (Brown), chil: Melissa Diane; Kristin Renee; Jesse Robert. Educ: Rice U., BA 1976; Trinity Evang. Div. Sch., MDiv 1978; Baylor U., PhD 1981. Emp: Korean Bapt. Sem., 1982-85 Asst. Prof.; Houston Bapt. U., 1985-86

Missionary in Residence; Mid-Amer. Bapt. Theol. Sem., 1986-88 Asst. Prof., OT; Canadian South. Bapt. Sem., 1988- Prof., OT & Hebrew. Spec: Hebrew Bible, Semitic Languages, Texts and Epigraphy. Pub: *An Analysis of the Hermeneutics of John Chrysostom's Commentary on Isaiah 1-8 With an English Translation* (Mellen, 1992); *Rethinking Genesis* (Baker, 1991); "Votive Prostitution Again: A Comparison of Proverbs 7:13-14 and 21:28-29" *JBL* 109 (1990); "The Structure of Joel" *JETS* (1985); "The Structure of Amos as a Testimony to its Integrity" *JETS* (1984); "Qoheleth on the Use and Abuse of Political Power" *Trinity Jour.* 8; "Ecclesiastes 7:25-29 and the Feminist Hermeneutic" *Criswell Theol. Jour.* 2 (1988); *Authority and Interpretation*, co-ed. (Baker, 1987); and others. Mem: SBL 1986-; IBR 1988-; NAPH 1990-. Rec: Skiing, hiking. Addr: (o) Canadian Southern Baptist Seminary, PO Box 512, Cochrane, AB T0L 0W0, Canada 403-932-6622; (h) 139 Glenhill Dr., Cochrane, AB T0L 0W3, Canada 403-932-4148.

GARSIEL, Moshe, b. Israel, January 6, 1936, s. of Yonah & Leah, m. Bat-Sheva, chil: Adi; Galit; Nili. Educ: Tel-Aviv U., BA, Bible & Hebrew Lit. 1965, MA 1968, PhD, Bible 1974. Emp: Bar Ilan U., Israel, 1969- Assoc. Prof.; Hebrew Theol. Coll., 1977-78; U. of Wis., 1985-86; Jew's Coll., London, 1992-93 Vis. Prof, Bible & Bibl. Arch.; *Beit Mikra, Bikoret U-Parasanut*, Ed. Bd. Excv: Izbet Sartah, 1975-77 Coord. Spec: Archaeology, Hebrew Bible. Pub: *Biblical Names: A Literary Study of Midrashic Derivations and Puns* (Bar-Ilan U.P., 1991); *The First Book of Samuel: A Literary Study of Comparative Structures, Analogies and Parallels* (Rubin Mass, 1983, 1990); *The Kingdom of David: Studies in History and Inquiries in Historiography* (1975); and others. Addr: (o) Bar-Ilan U., Chairman, Dept. of Bible, Ramat Gan, Israel 03-5318258; (h) 110 Rothschild St., Petach-Tiqvah, Israel 03-9223544.

GASQUE, W. Ward, b. Conway, SC, October 7, 1939, s. of Claude Jackson & Catherine (Ward), m. Laurel (Sandfor), chil: Michelle. Educ: Wheaton Coll., BA 1960; Fuller Theol. Sem., BD 1964, MTh 1965; Manchester U., PhD 1969. Emp: Regent Coll., 1969-72 Asst. Prof., NT Stud., Registrar, 1972-79 Assoc. Prof., NT, 1982-86 Vice Prin., Prof., NT, 1986-90 E. Marshall Sheppard Prof. of Bibl. Stud.; New Coll. Berkeley, 1979-82 Founding Pres. & Prof. of NT; Juniata Coll., J. Omar Good Vis. Disting. Prof. of Evang. Christianity 1987-88; Princeton Theol. Sem., Vis. Schol. 1988-89; East. Coll., 1990- Provost & Prof., Bibl. Stud. Spec: New Testament. Pub: *A History of the Interpretation of the Acts of the Apostles* (Hendrickson, 1989); *A Guide to Biblical Prophecy*, co-ed., contb. (Hendrickson, 1989); "A Fruitful Field: Recent Study of the Acts of the Apostles" *Interpretation* 42 (1988); "Philippi" in *Major Cities of the Biblical World* (Thomas Nelson, 1985); *Pauline Studies Presented to F.F. Bruce by his Students on the Occasion of his Seventieth Birthday*, contb. (Paternoster, 1980);

"Images of Paul in the History of Biblical Interpretation" *Crux* 16 (1980); *Scripture, Tradition and Interpretation: Festschrift for Everett F. Harrison*, co-ed. (Eerdmans, 1978); *Apostolic History and the Gospel: Biblical and Historical Studies Presented to F.F. Bruce on the Occasion of His Sixtieth Birthday*, co-ed. (Paternoster, 1970); and others. Awd: Earhart Found., Res. Schol. 1989; Oxford Ctr. for Mission Stud., Fellow 1990-. Mem: SBL 1969-; AAR 1970-; CSBS 1970-; SNTS 1972-; IBR 1973-. Rec: Travel, walking, hospitality. Addr: (o) Eastern College, St. Davids, PA 19087 215-341-1567; (h) 1300 Eagle Rd., St. Davids, PA 19087 215-688-5908.

GATES, Marie-Henriette, b. Portland, ME, December 8, 1949, d. of Jeffrey J. Carre & Marie-Rose (Durret), m. Charles W. Gates, chil: Caroline R.; Irene B. Educ: Bryn Mawr Coll., AB 1970; Yale U., MA, MPhil 1973, PhD 1976. Emp: Amer. Res. Inst. in Turkey, 1977-78 Dir., Ankara Branch; U. of N.C.–Chapel Hill, 1979-90 Asst. Prof.; Bilkent U., Ankara, 1990- Prof. Excv: Gritille, Turkey, 1981-82 Asst. Dir., 1983-84 Field Dir. Spec: Archaeology, Mesopotamian Studies. Pub: "Casting Tiamat into Another Sphere: Sources for the 'Ain Samiya Goblet'" *Levant* 18 (1986); "Dura-Europos: A Fortress of Syro-Mesopotamian Art" *BA* 47 (1984); "The Palace of Zimri-Lim at Mari" *BA* 47 (1984); "Alalakh Levels VI and V: A Chronological Reassessment" *SMS* 4/2 (1981); and others. Mem: AIA 1970-; ASOR 1979-; AOS 1980-. Rec: Guiding tours. Addr: (o) Bilkent U., Faculty of Humanities & Letters, Dept. of Archaeology and History of Art, 06533 Bilkent, Ankara, Turkey 4 266-44-09.

GAVENTA, Beverly R., b. Humboldt, TN, September 14, 1948, d. of Margaret & Harold Roberts, m. William Carter, chil: Matthew Roberts. Educ: Phillips U., BA 1970; Union Theol. Sem., MDiv 1973; Duke U., PhD 1978. Emp: Colgate Rochester Div. Sch., 1976-87 Assoc. Prof.; Columbia Theol. Sem., 1987-92 Prof.; Princeton Theol. Sem., 1992- Assoc. Prof.; *JAAR*, 1984-87 Book Rev. Ed.; *Critical Rev. of Books in Relig.*, 1987-90 Ed. Spec: New Testament. Pub: "The Singularity of the Gospel: A Reading of Galatians" in *Pauline Theology: Vol. I* (Fortress, 1991); "Apostles as Babes and Nurses in 1 Thessalonians 2:7" in *Faith and History in the New Testament: Essays in Honor of Paul W. Meyer* (Scholars, 1991); *The Conversation Continues: Studies in Paul and John in Honor of J. Louis Martyn*, co-ed. (Abingdon, 1990); "Toward a Theology of Acts: Reading and Rereading" *Interpretation* 42 (1988); "The Rhetoric of Death in the Wisdom of Solomon and in Paul" in *The Listening Heart: Essays in Wisdom and the Psamls in Honor of Roland E. Murphy, O.Carm.* (JSOT, 1987); *From Darkness to Light: Aspects of Conversion in the New Testament* (Fortress, 1986); "Galatians 1 and 2: Autobiography as Paradigm" *NT* 28 (1986); and others. Awd: Assoc. of Theol. Sch., Awd. for Theol. Schol. & Res. 1981-82; Kalamazoo Coll.,

DD 1983. Mem: SBL; SNTS; CBA; AAR; Scholars Press, Bd. of Trustees 1989-. Addr: (o) Princeton Theological Seminary, CN 821, Princeton, NJ 08542; (h) 31 Alexander St., Princeton, NJ 08540 609-497-7765.

GELSTON, Anthony, b. Gillingham, Kent, England, April 5, 1935, s. of Arthur Percival & Katie Winifred, m. Anne (Tombling). Educ: Oxford U., BA 1957, MA 1960, BD, DD 1985. Emp: U. of Durham, 1962-, 1989- Reader. Spec: Hebrew Bible, Semitic Languages, Texts and Epigraphy. Pub: *The Eucharistic Prayer of Addai and Mari* (1992); "Isaiah 52:13-53:12: An Eclectic Text and a Supplementary Note on the Hebrew Manuscript Kennicot 96" *JSS* 35 (1990); "Some Readings in the Peshitta of the Dodekapropheton" in *The Peshitta: Its Early Text and History* (1988); *The Peshitta of the Twelve Prophets* (1987); "A Note on Psalm lxxiv 8" *VT* 34 (1984). Mem: SOTS 1961-, Pres. 1991; British AJS 1976-. Rec: Music, walking, family history. Addr: (o) Dept. of Theology, Abbey House, Palace Green, Durham DH1 3RS, England 091-374-2050; (h) Lesbury, Hetton Rd., Houghton-Le-Spring, Tyne & Wear, DH5 8JW, England 091-584-2256.

GENEST, Olivette, b. Quebec City, Canada, September 14, 1931, d. of Arthur & Jeanne (Couillard-Despres). Educ: U. Laval, Canada, BA 1951, BTh 1968, MTh 1970; U. Gregorienne, Rome, ThD 1974; Ecole des Hautes-Etudes en Sci. Sociales, Paris, Eleve titulaire, Semantique Structurale 1983. Emp: U. of Montreal, 1975- Prof.; *Stud. in Relig.*, 1986- Ed. Adv. Bd.; *Laval Theol. & Phil.*, 1988- Ed. Adv. Bd.; *Stud. in Christianity & Judaism*, 1989 Ed. Bd. Spec: New Testament. Pub: "Analyse structurale et exégèse biblique" in *Dict. de Théol. fondamentale* (Cerf/Bellarmin, 1992); *Femmes du Nouveau Testament. Exégèse sémiotique* (1990); "Langage Religieux chretien et differénciation sexuelle" *Recherches feministes* 3 (1990); "L'actorialisation de Jésus dans l'épitre aux Colossiens" *LTP* 48 (1992); "L'interprétation de la mort de Jésus en situation discursive" *NTS* 34 (1988); "Femmes et Ministeres dans le Nouveau Testament. Réflexions d'ordre méthodologique" *SR* 16 (1987); *De Jésus et des femmes. Lectures semiotiques suivies d'une entrevue avec A.J. Greimas* (Cerf/Bellarmin, 1987); *Le Christ de la Passion. Perspective structurale* (Desclée/Bellarmin, 1978); and others. Awd: Ordre souverain des Chevaliers de Malte, Titre de Dame de Grâce 1992. Mem: Assn. Cath. des Etudes Bibl. au Canada 1976-; SNTS 1982; Soc. Canadienne de Theol. 1978-; CBA 1981-. Rec: Theatre, music. Addr: (o) U. de Montréal, Faculté de Théologie, CP 6128, Succursa A, Montréal, Que. H3C 3J7, Canada 514-343-7794; (h) 4911 Cote-des-Neiges, App. 705, Montréal, Que. H3V 1H7, Canada 514-738-0770.

GEORGI, Dieter, Emp: U. of Frankfurt, 1989- Prof. Addr: (o) Fachbereich Evangelische Theologie, Robert Mayerstr. 5, 6000 Frankfurt, Germany 69-798-2515.

GERATY, Lawrence T., b. St. Helena, CA, April 21, 1940, s. of Thomas S. & Hazel M., m. Gillian Anne (Keough), chil: Julie (Piller); Brent G.T. Educ: Pacific Union Coll., BA, Theol. 1962; Andrews U., MA (summa cum laude), OT 1963, BDiv (summa cum laude) 1965; Harvard U., PhD, Hebrew Bible & Syro-Palestinian Arch. 1972. Emp: Andrews U., 1972-85 Prof., Arch. & Hist. of Antiq.; Siegfried H. Horn Arch. Mus., 1976-85 Cur.; Andrews U., Inst. of Arch., 1981-85 Dir.; *BA*, 1984- Assoc. Ed.; Atlantic Union Coll., 1985-93 Prof. of Arch., Pres.; La Sierra U., 1993- Prof. of Arch., Pres. Excv: Tell Hesban, 1974, 1976 Sr. Adv.; Ein-gedi, 1979 Sr. Adv.; Tell Jalul, 1982 Project Dir.; Tell el-Umeiri, 1984, 1987, 1989, 1992 Project Dir. Spec: Archaeology, Hebrew Bible, Semitic Languages, Texts and Epigraphy. Pub: *Historical Foundations: Studies of Literary References to Hesban and Vicinity*, ed. (Inst. of Arch., 1989); "The Joint Madaba Plains Project: A Preliminary Report on the 2nd Season at Tell el-Umeiri and Vicinity, 1987," co-auth., *AUSS* 26 (1988); "Biblical Archaeologist Celebrating Its 50th Year" *BA* (1987); *The Archaeology of Jordan and Other Studies*, co-ed. (Andrews U.P., 1986); "Andrews University Madaba Plains Project: Preliminary Report, 1st Season at Tell el-Umeiri, Jordan" *Amer. Jour. of Arch.* 89/2,4 (1985); "The Archaeological Field Grid," co-auth., in *The Answers Lie Below* (1984); *Heshbon 1974: The 4th Campaign at Tell Hesban, a Preliminary Report* (Andrews U.P., 1976); "Third Century B.C. Ostraca from Khirbet el-Kom" *HTR* (1972); and others. Awd: Baker Book House Awd. 1965; U.S. Chamber of Commerce, Outstanding Young Man of the Year 1973; Andrews U., Tchr. of the Year 1985. Mem: Amer. Assn. of U. Prof. 1975-; ASOR 1976-; AIA 1978-; SBL, Pres., MidW reg. 1988-90. Rec: Reading, hiking. Addr: (o) La Seirra U., 4700 Pierce St., Riverside, CA 92515 909-785-2020.

GERHARD, Dautzenberg H., b. Koln, January 30, 1934, s. of Leonhard & Elisabet. Educ: Julius Maximilians U. Wuerzburg, ThD 1964, Habil. 1972. Emp: Johannes Duns Scotus Akademie Moenchengladbach, 1965-68 Lect.; Justus Liebig U. Giessen, 1972- Prof.; Stuttgarter Biblische Aufsatzbaende, 1988 Herausgeber. Spec: New Testament. Pub: "Mk 4,1-34 als Belehrung uber das Reich Gottes. Beobachtungen zum Gleichniskapitel" *BZ* 34 (1990); "Pheygete ten Porneian (1 Kor 6,18). Eine Fallstudie zur paulinischen Sexualethik in ihren Verhaeltuis zur Sexualethik des Fruhjudentums" in *Neues Testament und Ethik*, Festschrift fur Rudolf Schnack; "Der zweite Korintherbrief als Briefsammlung. Zur Frage der literarischen Einheitlichkeit und des theologischen Gefueges von 2 Kor 1-8" *ANRW* 25/4 (1987); "Da ist nicht maennlich und weiblich" Zur Interpretation von Gal 3,28" *Kairos* 24 (1982); "Der Wandel der Reich-Gottes-Verkuendigung in der urchristlichen Mission" in *Zur Geschichte des Urchristentums* (1979); and others. Mem: Katholische deutschsprachige Neutestamentler 1970- Rhein-Main-Exegetentreffen 1971-; SNTS 1974-; Gesellschaft fur Christlich-Juedische Zusammenarbeit 1978-. Addr: (o) Institut fur Katholische Theologie, Karl-Gloeckner-Str. 21, Haus H, 35394 Giessen, Germany 0641-702-6068; (h) Loeberstrasse 9, 35390 Giessen, Germany 0641-74891.

GERHARDSSON, Birger, b. Vannas, Sweden, September 26, 1926, s. of J. Gerhard Abelsson & Edith (Sandstrom), m. Kerstin (Eidolf), chil: Orjan; Torbjorn; Krister. Educ: Uppsala U., ThD 1961. Emp: *Svenska Jerusalemsforeningens tidskrift*, 1955-60 Ed.; *Svenskt Bibliskt Uppslagsverk*, 1959-63 Ed. Sec.; Uppsala U., 1961-65 Doc., NT Exegesis; Lund U., 1965- Prof., Exegesic Theol.; *NTS*, 1967-72, 1989-92 Ed. Bd.; *JSNT* 1981-90 Ed. Bd. Spec: New Testament. Pub: "Illuminating the Kingdom" in *Jesus and the Oral Gospel Tradition* (JSOT, 1991); "The Narrative Meshalim in the Synoptic Gospels" *NTS* 34 (1988); *The Gospel Tradition* (Liber, 1986); *The Ethos of the Bible* (Fortress, 1981; Darton, Longman & Todd, 1982); "Gottes Sohn als Diener Gottes" *Studia Theol.* 27 (1973); "The Parable of the Sower and Its Interpretation" *NTS* 14 (1967-68); *The Testing of the God's Son* (Gleerup, 1966); *Memory and Manuscript* (Gleerup, 1961); and others. Awd: U. of Edinburgh, Scotland, DD 1978. Mem: SNTS 1962-, Pres. 1990-91; WUJS 1971-; Royal Soc. of Letters at Lund 1966-; New Soc. of Letters 1972-; Royal Physiographical Soc. of Lund 1983-. Rec: Books, sports. Addr: (o) Theologicum, S-223 62 Lund, Sweden 046-10-90-49; (h) Vapplingevagen 2D, S-227 38 Lund, Sweden 046-11-36-80.

GERSTENBERGER, Erhard S., b. Rheinhausen, Germany, June 20, 1932, s. of Fritz & Anna, m. Rita (Buttgereit), chil: Bjoern L.; Dennis M.; Debora A.G. Educ: U. of Bonn, ThD 1962; U. of Heidelberg, Habil. 1971. Emp: Yale Div. Sch., 1961-64 Prof., Asst. Prof.; City of Essen, 1965-75 Pastor; Faculdade de Teologia, Brasil, 1975-81 Prof., OT; U. of Giessen, 1981-85 Prof., OT; U. of Marburg, 1985- Prof., OT. Spec: Hebrew Bible. Pub: *Leviticus*, ATD 6 (1993); *Jahwe-Ein Patriarchaler Gott?* (Kohlhammer, 1988); *The Psalms*, FOTL 14/1 (Eerdmans, 1988); "Der Realitatsbezug alttestamentlichen Exegese" in VTSup 36 (1985); "Psalm 12: Gott hift den Unterdrueckten" in *Anwalt des Menschen* (Giessen, 1983); *Der Bittende Mensch*, WMANT 51 (Neukirchen/Vluyn, 1980); "Os Sofrimentos do homen no Antigo Israel" *Estudos Teologicos* 15/3 (1975); "Jeremiah's Complaints" *JBL* 82 (1963); "The Woe-Oracles of the Prophets" *JBL* 81 (1962); and others. Awd: Fulbright Travel Grant & Ecumenical Coun. Schol. 1959-60. Mem: SBL 1962-; Inst. for Christianity & Antiq. 1967-. Rec: Swimming, hiking, literature. Addr: (o) Alte Universitat Lahntor 3, D- 3550 Marburg, Germany 06421-28 24 55; (h) Fasanenweg 29, D-Giessen, Germany 0641-47196.

GEVA, Hillel, b. Rehovot, Israel, August 21, 1946, s. of Jeremiah & Ester, m. Ruthie, chil: Jettonathan; Ithai. Educ: Hebrew U., BA 1974. Excv: Jewish Quarter, 1969-84; Tel Yarmuth, 1970; David's Citadel, Jerusalem, 1976-80. Spec: Archaeology. Pub: "'The First Wall' of Jerusalem During the Second Temple Period" *Eretz-Israel* 18 (1985); "The Camp of the Tenth Legion in Jerusalem: An Archaeological Reconsideration" *IEJ* 34 (1984); "Excavations in the Citadel of Jerusalem, 1979-80: Preliminary Report" *IEJ* 33 (1983); "'The Tower of David'—Phasael or Hippicus?" *IEJ* 31 (1981); "The Western Boundary of Jerusalem at the End of the Monarchy" *EJ* 29 (1979). Addr: (h) 27 Nisan St., Jerusalem 96821, Israel 02-419912.

GIACUMAKIS, George, Jr., b. New Castle, PA, July 6, 1937, s. of George & Stavroula, m. Joan (Gillies), chil: Stephen; Deborah; Mark; Andrew. Educ: Brandeis U., MA 1961, PhD 1963. Emp: Calif. State U., 1963-78, 1985- Prof., Near East Hist.; Inst. Holy Land Stud., Jerusalem, 1978-84 Pres. & Exec. Dir.; Lockman Found., 1985- Ed. Dir. Spec: Hebrew Bible, Mesopotamian Studies, New Testament, Apocrypha and Post-biblical Studies. Pub: *Young's Bible Dict.*, co-ed. (Tyndale, 1984); *Zondervan Pictorial Biblical Ency.*, contb. (Zondervan, 1975); "The Gate Below the Gate" *NEAS Bull.* (1974); *The Akkadian of Alalah* (Mouton, 1970). Mem: AIA; ASOR; ETS; IBR. Rec: Jogging, tennis. Addr: (o) California State U., Mission Viejo Campus, 28000 Marquerite Pkwy, Mission Viejo, CA 92692 714-582-4995; (h) P.O. Box 1053, Yorba Linda, CA 92686.

GIANTO, Agustinus, b. Solo, September 23, 1951. Educ: Driyarkara Sch. of Phil., Indonesia, BPhil 1975; U. of Indonesia, MA 1978; Pont. Gregorian U., BTh 1981; Ord. 1981; Pont. Bibl. Inst., SSL 1983; Harvard U., PhD 1987. Emp: Pont. Bibl. Inst., 1988-90 Lect., 1991- Assoc. Prof. Spec: Hebrew Bible, Semitic Languages, Texts and Epigraphy. Pub: *Word Order Variation in the Akkadian of Byblos*, Studia Pohl 15 (Pont. Bibl. Inst., 1990); and others. Mem: CBA 1984-; SBL 1984-; Linguistic Soc. of Amer. 1990-. Rec: Cycling, cross-country. Addr: (o) Pontifical Biblical Institute, Via Della Pilotta 25, 00187 Roma, Italy 06-679-64-53.

GIBBS, James M., b. Chicago, IL, April 17, 1928, s. of Frank C. & Edna A., m. Dorothy Anne (Hart), chil: Stephen James; Jenna Marie; Thomas Wayne. Educ: Seabury-West. Theol. Sem., BD 1957; U. of Nottingham, England, PhD 1968. Emp: Lichfield Theol. Coll., England, 1965-71 Vice Prin.; United Theol. Coll., India, 1972-77 Asst. Prof., NT, 1975-76 Dir., Div. of Postgrad. Stud.; *Bangalore Theol. Forum*, 1975-76 Assoc. Ed.; Queen's Coll., England, 1978-84 Sr. Tutor. Spec: New Testament. Pub: "Wisdom, Power and Wellbeing: A Set of Biblical Parameters for Man..." in *Studia Biblica 1978* III, JSNTSUP 3

(Sheffield, 1980); "Matthew's Use of 'Kingdom', 'Kingdom of God' and 'Kingdom of Heaven'" *Bangalore Theol. Forum* 8/1 (1976); "Luke 24:13-33 and Acts 8:26-39: The Emmaus Incident and the Eunuch's Baptism as Parallel Stories" *Bangalore Theol. Forum* 7/1 (1975); "The Son of God as the Torah Incarnate in Matthew" in *Studia Evangelica IV* (Akademie, 1968); "Purpose and Pattern in Matthew's Use of the Title 'Son of David'" *NTS* 10 (1964); and others. Mem: SBL 1967-; CBA 1978-. Rec: Class. music, choral singing, model railroads, crossword puzzles, swimming. Addr: (o) The Vicarage, Albert Rd., Stechford, Birmingham B33 8UA, England 021-783-2463.

GIBBS, John G., b. Asheville, NC, August 25, 1930, s. of Robert S. & Isabella (Gamble), chil: Elizabeth Cecker; Suzanne Robins; Ian; Patrick; Anne. Educ: Davidson Coll., AB 1952; Union Theol. Sem., MDiv 1955, ThM 1958; Princeton Theol. Sem., PhD, NT Stud. 1966. Emp: Presbyn. Ch., 1956-64, 1990- Pastor; Macalaster Coll., 1964-65 Interim Instr.; Moorhead State U., 1967-83 Prof., Hum.; Westminster/John Knox Press, 1983-90 Acquisitions Ed., 1988- Ed. of Acad. & Ref. Books. Spec: New Testament. Pub: "Excuse," "Fiery Ordeal," "Forsake," "Hour," "Human," "Just-Justice" in *ISBE* (1981); "Pauline Theology and Rehumanization" *Stud. in Relig.* (1976); "The Cosmic Scope of Redemption According to Paul" *Biblica* 1975; "Pauline Cosmic Christology and Ecological Crisis" *JBL* (1971); *Creation and Redemption, A Study in Pauline Theology*, NTSup 26 (Brill, 1971); "The Relation Between Creation and Redemption According to Phil. 2:5-11" *NT* (1970); and others. Awd: Union Theol. Sem., Fellow. 1955-56; Inst. for Ecumenical & Cultural Res., Fellow 1973-74; Yeshiva U., NEH Fellow 1980. Mem: SBL 1962-; SNTS 1971-; CBA 1985-. Rec: Hiking, photography, class. music concerts, art museums, politics. Addr: (h) Route 1, Box 104-B, Park Rapids, MN 56470 218-732-9633.

GIBSON, Shimon, b. London, England, September 21, 1958, s. of George & Fiona. Educ: U. Coll., London, Inst. of Arch., BA, Arch. of West. Asia 1986. Emp: Israel Dept. of Antiq. & Mus., 1978-81 Arch.; Arch. Survey of Israel, 1981-82 Arch.; Israel Mus., 1982-83 Post-excvn. Res.; *Bull. of the Anglo-Israel Arch. Soc.*, 1986- Chief Ed.; PEF, 1989- Archive Photographic Officer. Excv: En Shadud, 1979 Co-dir.; Raset-Tawil, 1981 Dir.; Survey east of Tell el-Ful, 1981-82 Dir.; Ras Amar/Tell el-Ful, 1987 Dir.; Sataf Project of Landscape Arch., 1987-89 Dir. Spec: Archaeology. Pub: "The Tell Sandahannah Ship Graffito Reconsidered" *PEQ* 124 (1992); "Three Coins of Alexander Jannaeus from El 'Al in the Golan Heights," co-auth., *Bull. of the Anglo-Israel Arch. Soc.* 10 (1990-91); "The Sataf Project of Landscape Archaeology in the Judaean Hills: A Preliminary Report on Four Seasons of Survey and Excavation (1987-89)," co-auth., *Levant* 23

(1991); "Tell el-Hesi and the Camera: The Photographs of Petrie and Bliss," co-auth., *PEQ* 122 (1990); "Landscape Archaeology at Er-Ramthaniyye," co-auth., in *Archeologie et Espaces* (1990); and others. Mem: BSA, Jerusalem; PEF; Brit. Assn. for Near East. Arch.; IES; ASOR. Addr: (o) Palestine Exploration Fund, 2 Hinde Mews, Marylebone Ln., London W1M 5RR, England 071-935-5379; (h) 11A Aubrey Rd., Hornsey, London N8 9HH, England 081-348-5414.

GIESE, Ronald L., Jr., b. Madison, WI, January 15, 1960, s. of Ronald L. & Maureen F., m. Karla K., chil: Danielle; Benjamin; Jared. Educ: Liberty U., BS 1982; U. of Wis.-Madison, MA 1985, PhD 1990. Emp: Liberty U., 1989- Assoc. Prof., Bibl. Stud. Spec: Hebrew Bible, Semitic Languages, Texts and Epigraphy. Pub: "Qualifying Wealth in the Septuagint of Proverbs" *JBL* 111/3 (1992); "Strength Through Wisdom and the Bee in LXX-Prov 6,8[a-c]" *Biblica* 73/3 (1992); "Further Evidence for the Bisection of 1QIs[a]" *Textus* 14 (1988). Awd: Wis. Soc. for Jewish Learning, Mansoor Awd. for Acad. Excellence 1987; Interuniversity Fellow. in Jewish Stud. 1988. Mem: NAPH; SBL; CBA; IOSCS. Addr: (o) Liberty U., School of Religion, Lynchburg, VA 24506 804-582-2569; (h) 110 Baldwin Cir., Lynchburg, VA 24502 804-525-5241.

GILBERT, Martin J., b. London, October 25, 1936, s. of Peter & Miriam (Green), m. Susan M. (Sacher), chil: Natalie; David; Joshua. Educ: Magdalen Coll., Oxford, MA, Hist. 1960. Emp: St. Antony's Coll., Oxford, 1960-62 Sr. Res. Schol.; Churchill biography, 1962-67 Res. Asst. Spec: Apocrypha and Post-biblical Studies. Pub: *Jewish History Atlas* (Dent/Morrow, 1968, 1993); *Jerusalem: Rebirth of a City* (Chatto & Windus/Viking, 1984); *Children's Illustrated Bible Atlas* (Allen, 1979); *Jerusalem Illustrated History Atlas* (Macmillan, 1978). Awd: Merton Coll., Oxford, Fellow 1962-. Mem: Royal Soc. of Lit., Fellow 1970. Addr: (o) Merton Coll., Oxford, England.

GILBERT, Maurice, b. Gilly, Belgium, March 12, 1934, s. of Auguste & Suzanne (Derclaye). Educ: Cath. U. of Louvain, Lic. Class. Philol. 1958; Eegenhoven-Louvain, Jesuit Fac., Lic. Phil. 1960, Lic. Theol. 1966; Pont. Bibl. Inst., Rome, Doc. Sacred Scripture 1973. Emp: Cath. U. of Louvain, 1971-75 Prof.; Pont. Bibl. Inst., 1975-93 Prof.; *Biblica*, 1975-78 Ed. & Redactor; Ecole Biblique, Jerusalem, 1984-93 Vis. Prof.; U. Notre-Dame de la Paix, Namur, Belgium, 1993- Rector Fac. Spec: Hebrew Bible, Apocrypha and Post-biblical Studies. Pub: *Les louanges du Seigneur* (Desclee, 1991); *La Sagesse de l'Ancien Testament*, ed. (1990); "Sagesse de Salomon" in *Dictionnaire de la Bible, Supplément* (1986); "Wisdom Literature" in *Jewish Writings of the Second Temple Period* (1984); "La description de la vieillesse en

Qohelet XII 1-7 est-elle allégorique?" in VTSup (1981); "'Une seule chair' (Gn 2:24)" *Nouvelle Rev. Théol.* (1978); *Morale et Ancien Testament,* co-auth. (Ctr. Cerfaux-Lefort, 1976); "La critique des dieux dans le Livre de la Sagesse (Sg. 13-15)" in *Analecta Biblica* (Bibl. Inst., 1973); and others. Addr: (o) U. Notre-Dame de la Paix, rue de Bruxelles 61, 5000 Namur, Belgium 724111.

GILLMAN, Florence M., b. Utica, NY, April 27, 1947, d. of Ann (Malone) & Wesley B. Morgan, m. John Gillman. Educ: Cath. U., BA 1974, MA, Relig. 1976; U. of Louvain, Belgium, BA, Relig. Stud. 1977, MA, STB, Theol 1978, STL 1980, PhD, Relig. Stud. 1982, STD 1984. Emp: Gonzaga U., 1982-84 Asst. Prof.; Mundelein Coll., 1985-86 Adj. Asst. Prof.; U. of San Diego, 1986- Assoc. Prof. Spec: New Testament. Pub: *United to a Death Like Christ's: A Study of Rom 6:5a,* Disting. Diss. Ser. (Mellen, 1993); *Women Who Knew Paul* (Liturgical, 1992); "Matthew 27:19: The Wife of Pilate" *Louvain Stud.* 17 (1992); "Early Christian Women at Philippi" *Jour. of Gender in World Relig.* 1 (1990); "Jason of Thessalonica" in *The Thessalonian Correspondence* (Louvain U.P., 1990); "Another Look at Rom 8:3 'In the Likeness of Sinful Flesh'" *CBQ* 49 (1987); "Romans 6:5a: United to a Death Like Christ's" *ETL* 59 (1983); and others. Awd: U. of Louvain, 1979-82 doc. grant. Mem: CBA 1979-; SBL 1982-. Rec: Travel. Addr: (o) U. of San Diego, Dept. of Religious Studies, San Diego, CA 92110 619-260-4525; (h) 7030 Hilton Pl., San Diego, CA 92111.

GILLMAN, John L., b. IN, December 25, 1948, s. of Georgene (Hirt) & Carl, m. Florence (Morgan). Educ: St. Meinrad Coll., BA, Phil. 1971; U. of Louvain, Belgium, BA 1973, MA, STB, Theol. 1974, PhD, Relig. Stud. 1980. Emp: Gonzaga U., 1983 Adj. Asst. Prof.; East. Wash. U., 1983-84 Adj. Asst. Prof.; Purdue U., St. Thomas Ctr., 1985 Theologian-in-residence; Mercy Hospital, 1986- Chaplain; San Diego State U., 1988- Lect. Spec: New Testament. Pub: "Hospitality in Acts 16" *Louvain Stud.* 17 (1992); "A Thematic Comparison: 1 Cor 15:50-57 and 2 Cor 5:1-5" *JBL* 107 (1988); "Signals of Transformation in 1 Thess 4:13-18" *CBQ* 47 (1985); "A Temptation to Violence: The Two Swords in Lk 22:35-38" *Louvain Stud.* 9 (1982); "Transformation in 1 Cor 15, 50-53" *ETL* 58 (1982); and others. Mem: CBA 1980-; SBL 1980-. Rec: Running. Addr: (o) Mercy Hospital, San Diego, CA 92103 619-260-7020; (h) 7030 Hilton Pl., San Diego, CA 92111.

GINGRICH, F. Wilbur, b. Annville, PA, September 27, 1901, s. of Felix & Minnie (Shiffer), m. Lola (Engel) (dec.), chil: John; Barbara; Carol. Educ: U. of Chicago, AM 1927, PhD 1932. Emp: Albright Coll., 1923- Prof., Greek, Prof. Emeritus. Spec: New Testament. Pub: "The Contributions of Walter Bauer to New

Testament Lexicography" *NTS* (1962); "The Greek New Testament as a Landmark in Semantic Change" *JBL* (1954); *Shorter Lexicon of the Greek New Testament* (U. of Chicago, 1965); *A Greek-English Lexicon of the New Testament and Early Christian Literature* (U. of Chicago, 1957). Mem: SBL. Addr: (h) 1502 N 12th St., Reading, PA 19604 215-376-0561.

GITAY, Yehoshua, b. Rehovot, Israel, October 2, 1938, m. Zefira, chil: Zemer. Educ: Hebrew U., Jerusalem, BA, Bible & Jewish Hist. 1967; Haifa U., Tchr. Dip. 1968; Emory U., PhD, Bibl. Stud. 1978. Emp: U. of N.C., Chapel Hill, 1978-79 Lect., 1979-82 Vis. Asst. Prof., Hebrew & Bibl. Stud.; Columbia U., 1980-81, 1983 Vis. Asst. Prof., Bibl. Lit. & Relig. Stud.; Duke U., 1981-82 Vis. Asst. Prof., Bibl. Stud.; Jewish Theol. Sem. of Amer., 1984 Vis. Asst. Prof., Bible; U. of Cape Town, South Africa, 1992- Prof., Isidore & Theresa Cohen Chair of Hebrew Lang. & Lit., Dept. of Hebrew & Jewish Stud. Spec: Hebrew Bible. Pub: *Prophecy and Persuasion,* Forum Theologiae Linguisticae 14 (Linguistica Biblica, 1981); articles in *Harper's Bible Dict.* (1985); "The Effectiveness of Isaiah's Speech" *JQR* 75 (1984); "Reflections on the Study of the Prophetic Discourse: The Question of Isaiah I 2-20" *VT* 33 (1983); "A Study of Amos's Art of Speech: A Rhetorical Analysis of Amos 3:1-15" *CBQ* 42 (1980); "Deutero-Isaiah: Oral or Written?" *JBL* 99 (1980); *Israelite and Judaean History,* co-trans. (Westminster, 1977); *The Book of Job: An Anthology of Critical Studies* (Haifa U., 1973); and others. Awd: Hebrew U., Fellow. 1964-65; Wesleyan U., Fellow. grant 1984-85. Mem: SBL; AJS; WUJS; ASOR. Addr: (o) U. of Cape Town, Dept. of Hebrew & Jewish Studies, Private Bag, Rondebosch 7700, South Africa 021-650-2945.

GITAY, Zefira, b. Israel, m. Yehoshua. Educ: Emory U., PhD. Emp: Prehistoric Mus., Haifa, Cur.; Teachers Coll., Israel, Fac.; U. of N.C., Chapel Hill, Fac.; Wesleyan U., Grad. Liberal Stud. Prog., Vis. Prof.; Rhodes Coll., Dept. of Relig. Stud., Vis. Prof. Pub: "Hagar's Expulsion—A Tale Twice-Told in Genesis" *BR* 2/4 (1986); "Two Master Portraits of Isaiah" *BR* 4/6 (1988); and others. Mem: AAR; Coll. of Art Assn. Addr: (o) c/o U. of Cape Town, Dept. of Hebrew & Jewish Studies, Private Bag, Rondebosch 7700, South Africa.

GITIN, Seymour, b. Buffalo, NY, January 12, 1936, s. of Harry & Ida, m. Cheryl, chil: Michal; Adam; Talya. Educ: U. of Buffalo, BA 1956; HUC-Jewish Inst. of Relig., BHL 1959, MHL/Rabbinic Ord. 1962, PhD 1980. Emp: Nelson Glueck Sch. of Bibl. Arch., Jerusalem, 1976-79 Dir. of Gezer Publ. Project; HUC-Jewish Inst. of Relig., Jerusalem, 1977-78 Sr. Lect. in Arch., 1977-79 Cur., Nelson Glueck Study Collection; Brandeis U., Jerusalem, Dept. of Class. & Oriental Stud., 1979-80 Adj. Asst. Prof., 1981-82 Adj. Assoc. Prof., Hiatt Inst.,

1980-82 Dir. of Brandeis/ASOR Joint Arch. Prog. in Jerusalem; W.F. Albright Inst. of Arch. Res., 1980- Dir., Prof. of Arch.; ASOR Diss. Ser., 1981-89 Ed. Com.; *BA*, 1985- Ed. Bd., 1987-90 Assoc. Ed. Excv: Tel Gezer, 1970-71 Area Supr., 1972-73 Field Arch.; Jebel Qa'aqir, 1971 Field Arch.; Tel Dor, 1980- Co-dir.; Tel Miqne-Ekron Excvn. & Publ. Project, 1981- Co-dir. Spec: Archaeology, Semitic Languages, Texts and Epigraphy. Pub: "Seventh Century BCE Cultic Elements at Ekron" in *Proceedings of the II International Congress on Biblical Archaeology, Jerusalem, 1990* (1993); "The Last Days of Philistia" *Arch.* (1992); "New Incense Altars from Ekron: Typology, Context and Function" *Eretz-Israel* 23 (1992); "Scoops: Corpus, Function and Typology" in *Moshe Dothan Festschrift* (U. of Haifa, 1992); *Gezer III*, Ann. of the Nelson Glueck Sch. of Bibl. Arch. (1990); "Tel Miqne-Ekron: A Type Site of the Inner Coastal Plain in the Iron II Period" in *Recent Excavations in Israel: Studies in Iron Age Archaeology, AASOR* 49, co-ed. (1989); *Gezer IV*, Ann. of the Nelson Glueck Sch. of Bibl. Arch., contb. (1986); "Stratigraphy and its Application to Chronology and Terminology" in *Biblical Archaeology Today, Proceedings of the International Congress of Biblical Archaeology, Jerusalem, 1984* (1985); and others. Awd: Hebrew U., Dept. of Arch., Vis. Schol. 1982; HUC-Jewish Inst. of Relig., DD 1988; Annenberg Res. Inst., Post-Doctoral Fellow 1991-92. Mem: ASOR; IES; PEF. Rec: Tennis, bridge. Addr: (o) W.F. Albright Institute of Archaelogical Research, Box 19096, Jerusalem 91190, Israel 288956; (h) 87 Bar Kochba, Apt. 1, Tzameret HaBira, Jerusalem, Israel 810271.

GITTLEN, Barry M., b. Norfolk, VA, May 21, 1943, s. of J. Leon & Ruth, m. Elaine G., chil: Lisa S. Educ: Wayne State U., Monteith Coll., PhB 1965; U. of Pa., PhD 1977. Emp: Balt. Hebrew U., 1972- Prof. Excv: Tell Gezer, 1969-70 Area Supr.; Jenin-Meggido Survey, 1969 Survey Team Leader.; Tell esh-Shari'a, 1974-75 Field Supr.; Cen. Negev Highlands Project, 1978 Field Arch., 1980 Off-site Dir.; Tel Miqne/Ekron, 1982- Field Arch. & Arch. Coord. Spec: Archaeology, Hebrew Bible. Pub: "The Late Bronze Age 'City' at Tel Miqne/Ekron" *Eretz- Israel* 23 (1992); "The Massacre of the Merchants Near Akko" in *Biblical and Related Studies Presented to Samuel Iwry* (1985); *Tel Miqne/Ekron: Report of the 1984 Excavations, Field III-SE* (Albright Inst., 1985); "Form and Function in the New Late Bronze Age Temple at Lachish" *Eretz-Israel* 16 (1982); "The Cultural and Chronological Implications of the Cypro-Palestinian Trade During the Late Bronze Age" *BASOR* 241 (1981); "Cypriote White Slip Pottery in its Palestinian Stratigraphic Context" in *The Archaeology of Cyprus—Recent Developments* (1975). Awd: NEH Fellow 1989; ASOR, W.F. Albright Fellow 1969-70; Hebrew Union Coll., 1960-70 Arch. Fellow. Mem: ASOR 1966-; IES 1966-; AIA 1971-; AOS 1971-; AJS 1971-. Rec: Music, poetry. Addr: (o) Baltimore Hebrew U., 5800 Park Heights Ave., Baltimore, MD 21215 410-578-6907.

GLADSON, Jerry A., b. Dalton, GA, April 21, 1943, s. of Howard J. & Laura E., chil: Johanna; Paula. Educ: South. Coll., BA 1965; Vanderbilt U., MA, OT 1973, PhD, OT 1978. Emp: Ky.-Tenn. Conf., Seventh-Day Adventists, 1965-72; South. Coll., 1972-87 Prof., Relig.; *These Times*, 1979-84 Contb. Ed.; Psychological Stud. Inst., 1987- Dean. Spec: Hebrew Bible. Pub: *Who Said Life Is Fair? Job and the Problem of Evil* (Rev. & Herald, 1985); and others. Mem: SBL; CBA. Rec: Freelance writing, computers. Addr: (o) Psychological Studies Institute, 2055 Mt. Paran Rd. NW, Atlanta, GA 30327 404-233-3949; (h) 1565 Bakers Glen Dr., Atlanta, GA 30350 404-913-9722.

GLASSWELL, Mark E., b. Darlington, England, May 16, 1938, s. of William & Edith (Charlesworth). Educ: U. Durham, St. Chad's Coll., BA 1960, PhD 1965. Emp: U. Sierra Leone, Fourah Bay Coll., 1965-74 Lect., Theol.; U. of Durham, 1974-75 Lect.; U. of Nigeria, 1975-85 Sr. Lect., NT Stud., 1980-84 Head, Dept. of Relig.; *West African Relig.*, 1980-84 Chmn., Ed. Bd. Spec: New Testament. Pub: Articles in *Exegetical Dict. of the New Testament* 1 (1978, 1990); "The Relation Between John and Mark" *JSNT* (1985); "Some Issues of Church and Society in the Light of Paul's Eschatology" in *Paul and Paulinism* (SPCK, 1982); *New Testament Christianity for Africa and the World*, co-ed. (SPCK, 1974); "The Use of Miracles in the Markan Gospel" *Miracles: Cambridge Studies in their Philosophy and History* (Mowbrays, 1965); and others. Mem: SNTS 1966-. Rec: Music. Addr: (h) The Rectory, Little Sampford, Saffron Walden, Essex CB10 2QT, Great Sampford, England 079-986-437.

GLENNY, W. Edward, b. Rockford, IL, April 28, 1949, s. of William F. & Geraldine J., m. Jacqueline J., chil: Brittany Joy; Courtney Jean. Educ: Pillsbury Coll., BA 1972; Cen. Bapt. Sem., MDiv 1976, ThM 1982; Dallas Theol. Sem., ThD 1987. Emp: Pillsbury Coll., 1975-82 Prof., Bible; Cen. Bapt. Sem., 1984- Prof. of NT, Dir. of Postgrad. Stud. Spec: New Testament. Pub: "The Israelite Imagery of I Peter 2" in *Dispensationalism, Israel and the Church* (Zondervan, 1992); "I Corinthians 7:29-31 and the Teaching of Continence in the Acts of Paul and Thecla" *Grace Theol. Jour.* Fall (1990). Awd: Cen. Sem. Alumni Citation 1989. Mem: ETS 1980-; SBL 1985-. Rec: Jogging, basketball, fishing, reading. Addr: (o) Central Seminary, 1250 W Broadway, Minneapolis, MN 55411 612-522-3628; (h) 3546 Xerxes Ave. N, Minneapolis, MN 55412 612-588-4185.

GNUSE, Robert K., b. Quincy, IL, December 4, 1947, s. of Karl Arthur & Margaret Elizabeth, m. Elizabeth (Hammond), chil: Rebecca Elizabeth; John Robert Jacob; Adam Joseph Neary. Educ: Concordia Sr. Coll., BA 1970; Concordia Sem. in Exile, MDiv 1974, STM 1975; Vanderbilt U., MA 1978, PhD 1980. Emp: U. of Va., 1978-79 Asst. Prof.; N.C. Wesleyan Coll., 1979-80 Asst. Prof.; Loyola U., New Orleans, 1980- Prof.; *BTB*, 1986-

Assoc. Ed.; JSOT reprint series, 1991- Co-ed. Spec: Hebrew Bible. Pub: "Israelite Settlement of Canaan: A Peaceful Internal Process" *BTB* 21 (1991); "The Jewish Dream Interpreter in a Foreign Court" *JSP* 7 (1990); "Contemporary Evolutionary Theory as a New Heuristic Model for the Social Scientific Method in Biblical Studies" *Zygon* 25 (1990); "Dream Genre in the Matthean Infancy Narratives" *NT* 32 (1990); "Dream Reports in the Writings of Flavius Josephus" *RB* 96 (1989); *Heilsgeschichte as a Model for Biblical Theology* (1989); *Jewish Roots of Christian Faith* (Loyola, 1983); and others. Awd: Harold Sterling Vanderbilt Awd. 1975-78. Mem: SBL 1976-; CBA 1976-; ASOR 1978-91; Coll. Theol. Soc. 1980-, Reg. Pres. 1985-87; AOS 1985-91. Addr: (o) Loyola U., Dept. of Religious Studies, 6363 St. Charles Ave, New Orleans, LA 70118 504-865-3057; (h) 7731 Wave Dr., New Orleans, LA 70128 504-243-0739.

GOEDICKE, Hans, b. Vienna, Austria, August 7, 1926, m. Lucy (McLaughlin). Educ: U. of Vienna, PhD 1949. Emp: UNESCO, Egypt, 1957-58 Tech. Asst.; U. of Gottingen, 1958-60 Asst.; Johns Hopkins U., 1960-, 1969-93 Prof., 1979-84 Chmn., Dept. of Near East. Stud.; U. of Vienna, 1978-79, 1985 Guest Prof.; *Jour. of the Amer. Res. Ctr. in Egypt,* Rev. Ed.; *Records of the Anc. Near East,* Ed.; *Near East. Stud.,* Ed. Excv: Giza 1972, 1974 Field Dir.; Wadi Tumilat, 1977-78, 1981 Dir. Spec: Egyptology. Pub: *Studies About Amehotep III* (1992); *The Quarrel of Apophis and Seqenenre* (1988); *Perspectives on the Battle of Kadesh* (1985); "Symbolische Zahlen" *Lexikon der Aegyptologie* 6 (1985); "Sinuhe's Foreign Wife" *Soc. D'Egytologie* 9-10 (1985); "Rudjet's Delivery" *Varia Egyptica* 1 (1985); *Studies in the Hekanakhte Papers* (1984); and others. Awd: Guggenheim Fellow, 1966-67; Amer. Res. Ctr. in Egypt, Governor; Natl. Hum. Ctr., Adv. Addr: (o) Johns Hopkins U., Dept. of Near Eastern Studies, Baltimore, MD 21218 401-516-7497; (h) 3959 Cloverhill Rd., Baltimore, MD 21218 401-467-8186.

GOEHRING, James E., b. CA, January 31, 1950, s. of John G. & Dorothea, chil: Nathan W.; Matthew E. Educ: U. of Calif., BA 1972, MA, Relig. Stud. 1976; Claremont Grad. Sch., PhD, NT 1981. Emp: Akademie der Wissenschaften, Germany, 1978-81 Wissenschaftlicher Mitarbeiter, Kommission zur Erforschung altchristlichen Monchtum, 1989-90 Alexander von Humboldt Stipendiat; Claremont Grad. Sch., Inst. Antiq. & Christianity, 1981-85 Asst. Dir., Asst. Prof.; Mary Washington Coll., 1985- Assoc. Prof. Excv: Nag Hammadi Arch. Expdn., 1978, 1980 Numismatist. Spec: Archaeology, New Testament, Egyptology. Pub: *Gnosticism and the Early Christian World,* co-ed. (Polebridge, 1990); *Gospel Origins and Christian Beginnings,* co-ed.; *The Crosby-Schoyen Codex. Ms 193 in the Schloyen Collection,* CSCO 521 (Peeters, 1990); *The Roots of Egyptian Christianity,* co-ed. (Fortress, 1986); *The Letter of Ammon and Pachomian*

Monasticism, PTS 27 (de Gruyter, 1986); "A New Coptic Fragment of Melito's Homily on the Passion" *Museon* 97 (1984); "Pachomius' Vision of Heresy: A Study of the Development of a Pachomian Tradition" *Museon* 95 (1982); "A Classical Influence on the Gnostic Sophia Myth" *VC* 35 (1981); and others. Mem: SBL; AAR; IACS. Rec: Hiking, canoeing, tennis. Addr: (o) Mary Washington College, 1301 College Ave., Fredericksburg, VA 22401 703-899-4853.

GOLB, Norman, b. Chicago, IL, January 15, 1928. Educ: Roosevelt Coll., BA 1948; Johns Hopkins U., PhD 1954. Emp: U. of Wis., 1957-58 Vis. Lect., Semitic Lang.; Hebrew Union Coll., 1958-63 Asst. Prof., Medieval Jewish Stud.; U. of Chicago, 1963-73 Assoc. Prof., 1973- Prof. of Medieval Jewish Stud. Pub: *Spertus College of Judaica Yemenite Manuscripts* (Spertus Coll., 1972); "Topography of the Jews of Medieval Egypt" *JNES* (1965, 1974). Awd: Hebrew U., Warburg Res. Fellow., Judeo-Arabic Stud. 1955-57; Amer. Phil. Soc., grant 1959, 1963, 1967; Amer. Coun. Learned Soc., grant 1963, 1965; Guggenheim Memorial Found., Fellow. 1964-65, 1966-67; NEH, grant 1970-72. Addr: (o) U. of Chicago, Oriental Institute, 1155 E 58th St., Chicago, IL 60637 312-702-9526.

GOLDMAN, Edward A., b. Toledo, OH, March 25, 1941, s. of Beryl & Ida (Mostov), m. Roanete (Naamani), chil: Ariel; Dalia. Educ: Harvard Coll., AB 1963; Hebrew Union Coll., Rabbinical Ord., MAHL 1969, PhD 1974. Emp: B'nai B'rith Hillel Found., U. of Cincinnati, 1965-67 Dir.; Hebrew Union Coll., 1972- Prof. Spec: Apocrypha and Post-biblical Studies. Pub: *The Talmud of the Land of Israel: A Preliminary Translation and Explanation,* Chicago Stud. in the Hist. of Judaism, vol. 16 Rosh Hashanah, trans. (U. of Chicago, 1987); "Who Raises Up the Fallen" *Hebrew Stud.* 20 (1980); and others. Mem: SBL; AJS. Rec: Piano, organ. Addr: (o) Hebrew Union College, 3101 Clifton Ave., Cincinnati, OH 45220 513-211-1875.

GOLDSTEIN, Jonathan A., b. New York, NY, July 19, 1929, s. of David & Rose (Berman), m. Helen (Tunik), chil: Rise; Rachel. Educ: Harvard, AM 1951; Jewish Theol. Sem. of Amer., Rabbinical Ord., MHL 1955; Columbia U., PhD 1959. Emp: U. of Iowa, 1962- Prof., Anc. History & Class.; U. of Chicago., 1975 Lester Aronberg Judaica Lect.; Augustana Coll., 1986 Stone Lect., Judaism. Spec: Hebrew Bible, Mesopotamian Studies, Semitic Languages, Texts and Epigraphy, Apocrypha and Post-biblical Studies. Pub: *Semites, Iranians, Greeks and Romans* (Scholars, 1990); "I Maccabees," "II Maccabees" in *AB* (Doubleday 1976, 1983); "The Apocryphal Book of Baruch" *Proc. of the Amer. Acad. for Jewish Res.* 46/47 (1980); "The Syriac Bill of Sale from Dura-Europos" *JNES* 25 (1966); and others. Awd: Fulbright Grant 1959-60; Amer. Acad. of Jewish Res., 1977 Fellow;

Jewish Theol. Sem. of Amer., 1987 DHL. Mem: Amer. Assn. of U. Prof.; IES; AIA; AJS. Rec: Singing, Jewish community affairs. Addr: (o) U. of Iowa, Dept. of History, Schaeffer Hall, Iowa City, IA 52242 319-335-2329; (h) 312 Windsor Dr., Iowa City, IA 52245 319-338-1252.

GOLEBIEWSKI, Marian, b. Trzebuchow, Poland, September 22, 1937, d. of Wladyslaw & Cecylia. Educ: Cath. U., Poland, MTh 1968; Pont. Bibl. Inst., Rome, Doc. Bibl. Sc. 1976. Emp: Priest's Sem., Prof., OT Exegesis; Acad. of Cath. Theol., Warsaw, Lect.; *Ateneum Kaplanskie,* 1979- Ed. Bd. Spec: Hebrew Bible. Pub: "Greckie i lacinskie tlumaczenia psalterza" *Coll. Theol.* 60 (1990); "Objawienie Boga w Starym Testamencie" *Stud. Theol. Vars.* 23 (1985); "Jednosc Pisma Swietego jako zada hermeneutyczna" *Coll. Theol.* 53 (1983); "L'alliance éternelle en Is 54-55 en comparaison avec d'autres textes prophétiques" *Coll. Theol.* 50 (1980); "Le sens de la Parole divine chez le Deutére-Isaie" *Coll. Theol.* 49 (1979); and others. Addr: (o) ul. S Karnkowskiego 3, 87-800 Wloclawek, Poland.

GONEN, Rivka, b. Vienna, Austria. Educ: Hebrew U., Jerusalem, BA, Arch. & Geography 1968, PhD 1979. Emp: Brandeis U., Hiatt Inst., Tchr.; Bezalel Acad. of Art & Design, Jerusalem, Sr. Lect., Arch. & Anc. Cultures; Israel Museum, Jerusalem, Dept. of Jewish Ethnography, 1986- Curator; Ben-Gurion U., Dept. of Bible & Near East. Stud., Lect. Excv: Efrat, MB I-II Cemetery, 1979 Dir. Spec: Archaeology. Pub: *Burial Patterns and Cultural Diversity in Late Bronze Canaan,* ASOR Diss. Ser. 7 (Eisenbrauns, 1992); "Visualizing First Temple Jerusalem" *BAR* 15/3 (1989); "Megiddo in the Late Bronze Age— Another Reasment" *Levant* 19 (1987); "Structural Tombs in 2nd Millenium B.C. Canaan" in *Architecture in Ancient Israel* (IES, 1987); "Urban Canaan in the Late Bronze Period" *BASOR* 253 (1984); "Tell el-Ajjul in the Late Bronze Age—City or Cemetery?" *Eretz-Israel* 15 (1981); and others. Mem: IES; Israel Arch. Assn.

GOOCH, Paul W., b. Toronto, Canada, June 24, 1941, s. of George F. & Ruth (Lovering), m. Pauline A. (Thompson). Educ: Bishop's U., Canada, BA 1963; U. of Toronto, Canada, MA 1965, PhD 1970. Emp: U. of Toronto, Canada, Scarborough Coll., 1967- Prof., Phil., 1977-82 Chmn., Div. of Hum., 1986-88 Dir., Ctr. for Relig. Stud., 1988- Assoc./Asst. Dean, Grad. Stud. Spec: New Testament. Pub: "Sovereignty and Freedom: Some Pauline Compatibilisms" *SJT* (1987); *Partial Knowledge: Philosophical Studies in Paul* (U. of Notre Dame, 1987); "'Conscience' in I Corinthians 8 and 10" *NTS* (1987); "On Disembodied Resurrected Persons" *Relig. Stud.* (1981); "The Ethics of Accommodation: A Study in Paul" *TB* (1978); "Divine Love and the Limits of Language," co-auth., *JTS* (1972); and others. Mem: CSSR; IBR; CSBS. Addr: (o) U. of Toronto, Scarborough

College, Division of Humanities, Scarborough, ON M1C 1A4, Canada 416-284-3141; (h) 116 Sutherland Dr., Toronto, ON M4G 1H9, Canada 416-429-0189.

GOOD, Deirdre J., b. Nairobi, Kenya, July 12, 1953, d. of Robert Stanley & Joan (Walker). Educ: St. Andrews U., Scotland, MTh 1975; Union Theol. Sem., STM 1976; Harvard Div. Sch., ThD 1983. Emp: Valparaiso U., 1982-83 Instr., Theol.; Agnes Scott Coll., 1983-86 Asst. Prof., Chmn., Bible & Relig. Dept.; Gen. Theol. Sem., 1986-92 Asst. Prof., 1992- Prof., NT. Spec: New Testament, Apocrypha and Post-biblical Studies. Pub: "Gender and Generation: Observations on Coptic Terminology, with Particular Attention to Valentinian Texts" in *Images of the Feminine in Gnosticism* (Fortress, 1988); *Reconstructing the Tradition of Sophia in Gnostic Literature* (Scholars, 1987); "Divine Noetic Faculties in Eugnostos the Blessed and Related Documents" *Le Museon* (1986); "Sophia and Valentinianism" *SC* 4/4 (1984); and others. Awd: Harvard U., Clarence E. Campbell Awd. 1978-79; Intl. Assn. of U. Women Fellow. 1978-79; Josephine de Karman Fellow. 1981-82. Mem: SBL; IACS. Rec: Swimming, tennis, golf. Addr: (o) General Theological Seminary, 175 Ninth Ave., New York, NY 10011 212-243-5150.

GOODRICK, Edward W., b. Appleton, WI, March 11, 1913, s. of John B. & Mary Althea (Wood), m. Gwendolyn H. (Davidson), chil: Janet M.; John B.; Lynda D.; Cynthia L.; James W. Educ: Bible Inst. of Los Angeles, BTh 1940; Westmont Coll., BA 1943; U. of Mont., MSE 1956. Emp: Mont. Inst. of the Bible, 1953-54; Multnomah Sch. of the Bible, 1956-. Spec: Archaeology, Anatolian Studies, New Testament. Pub: *The NIV Exhaustive Concordance,* co-ed. (Zondervan, 1990); "Let's Put 2 Timothy 3:16 Back in the Bible" *JETS* (1982); *The NIV Complete Concordance,* co-ed. (Zondervan, 1981); and others. Awd: West. Conservative Bapt. Sem., DDiv 1980. Mem: ETS 1979-, Chmn., NW Sect. 1982. Rec: Reading, studying, chess. Addr: (h) 16321 NE Oregon, Portland, OR 97230 503-255-2819.

GOODWIN, Charles, b. Hartford, CT, May 5, 1913, s. of Charles A. & Ruth (Cheney). Educ: Yale Coll., BA 1935; Episc. Theol. Sch., BD 1939; Yale Grad. Sch., PhD 1960. Emp: Berkeley Div. Sch., 1955-58 Instr.; Yonsei U., Seoul, 1961-78 Prof.; St. Michael's Anglican Sem., Seoul, 1961-78 Prof. Spec: Hebrew Bible, New Testament, Apocrypha and Post-biblical Studies. Pub: "What is the Point of the Book of Job?" *Theol. Forum* 12 (1974); "On St. Paul's Idea of Justification" *Theol. Forum* 9 (1961); "How Did John Treat His Sources?" *JBL* 73 (1954); and others. Mem: SBL 1938-; ASOR 1951-; AAR 1979-90. Rec: Sailing, calligraphy, lit. Addr: (h) Haeundae, PO Box 42, Pusan 612-600, Korea.

GORANSON, Stephen C., b. Surrey, England, s. of Harold & Brinkley, chil: Anna. Educ: Brandeis U., BA; Duke U., MA, PhD. Emp: Wake Forest U., Vis. Asst. Prof. Excv: Sepphoris. Spec: Archaeology, Hebrew Bible, New Testament, Apocrypha and Post-biblical Studies. Pub: "Sectarianism, Geography, and the Copper Scroll" *JJS* 43 (1992); "Nazarenes," "Ebionites" in *ABD* (Doubleday, 1992); "Further Qumran Archaeology Publications in Progress" *BA* 54 (1991); "'Essenes': Etymology from 'asah" *RQ* 11 (1984). Addr: (h) 706 Louise Cir. 30J, Durham, NC 27705.

GORDON, Cyrus, b. Philadelphia, PA, June 29, 1908. Educ: U. of Pa., AB 1927, AM 1928, PhD 1930. Emp: Johns Hopkins U., 1936-38 Instr. of Semitic Lang.; Smith Coll., 1938-41 Vis. Lect., Bible & Ancient Hist.; Dropsie Coll., 1946-56 Prof. of Assyriology & Egyptology; Brandies U., 1956-73 Prof. of Mediterranean Stud.; New York U., 1973- Prof. of Hebrew Stud., Gottesman Prof. of Hebraic Stud. Excv: Jerusalem, 1931-35. Pub: "The Double Paternity of Jesus" *BAR* 4/2 (1978); "Where is Abraham's Ur?" *BAR* 3/2 (1977); *Ugaritic Textbook* (1967); *Ugarit and Minoan Crete* (Norton, 1966); *The Ancient Near East* (Norton, 1965); *The Common Background of Greek and Hebrew Civilizations* (Norton, 1965); *Hammurabi's Code* (Holt, 1957); and others. Awd: Royal Asiatic Soc., Hon. Fellow.; Am. Acad. of Arts & Sci., Fellow. Mem: AOS; SBL; AIA. Addr: (o) New York U., East Bldg. Rm. 637, New York, NY 10003 212-598-2824.

GORDON, Victor R., b. Fort Dodge, IA, November 29, 1950, s. of Lyle, m. Susan, chil: Joshua; Nathan; Jonathan; Joy. Educ: Stanford U., AB 1973; Fuller Theol. Sem., MDiv 1975, PhD, NT Theol. 1979. Emp: N Amer. Bapt. Sem., 1979-82 Adj. Prof.; Wheaton Coll., 1983-88 Asst. Prof., Bibl. Stud.; North. Bapt. Sem., 1984-88 Adj. Prof.; Bapt. Ch., Sr. Pastor. Spec: New Testament. Pub: Articles in *ISBE*, vol. 3, 4 (Eerdmans, 1986); *Studies in the Covenantal Theology of the Epistle to the Hebrews in the Light of its Setting* (U. Microfilms, 1979); and others. Mem: SBL; AAR; CBA; SBL. Addr: (o) First Baptist Church, Wichita, KS 67202 316-263-5285; (h) 7116 Greenbriar Cir., Wichita, KS 67226 316-687-4551.

GOTTLIEB, Isaac B., b. New York, NY, May 18, 1945, s. of Emanuel & Peshe, m. Shelley, chil: Ariella; Avinoam; Hoshea; Tzivia. Educ: Yeshiva U., BA 1966, MA 1969; N.Y. U., PHD 1972. Emp: Ben-Gurion U., Israel, 1972-78 Lect., Dept. of Hebrew Lang.; Bar-Ilan U., Inst. for the Hist. of Jewish Bibl. Interpretation, 1979- Sr. Lect., Dept. of Bible. Spec: Hebrew Bible, Semitic Languages, Texts and Epigraphy. Pub: "Biblical Endings" *Prooftexts* 11 (1991); "Pirke Abot and Wisdom" *VT* 40 (1990); "Genesis 18 and 19" in *Aharon Mirsky Jubilee Volume* (1986); "Midrash as Biblical Philology" *JQR* (1984); and others. Awd: Mazer Fellow. 1969-

70; Jewish Mem. Found. Fellow. 1985-86. Addr: (o) Bar-Ilan U., Ramat-Gan, Israel 03-718229; (h) Yad Mordecai 4, Jerusalem, Israel 02-665065.

GOTTSCHALK, Alfred, b. Oberwesel, Germany, March 7, 1930, s. of Max & Erna (Nussbaum), m. Deanna (Zeff), chil: Marc H.; Rachel L. Educ: Brooklyn Coll., AB 1952; Hebrew Union Coll., Jewish Inst. of Relig., BHLit 1954, MA 1956, Rabbinic Ord. 1957; U. of South. Calif., PhD 1965. Emp: Hebrew Union Coll., Jewish Inst. of Relig., 1957- Prof., Dean, Pres. Spec: Hebrew Bible. Pub: *Ahad Ha'Am: v'haruah ha-leumi* (Hasifriyah Hazionit, 1992); *The Image of Man in Genius and in the Ancient Near East* (1976); *Hesed in the Bible*, trans. (Hebrew Union Coll., 1967); and others. Awd: Smithsonian Inst., research grants 1963, 1967; Bertha Guggenheimer Fellow 1967, 1969. Mem: AIA; ASOR. Rec: Travel, reading. Addr: (o) Hebrew Union College, 3101 Clifton Ave., Cincinnati, OH 45220 513-221-1875; (h) 17 Belsaw Pl., Cincinnati, OH 45200 513-281-5880.

GOTTWALD, Norman K., b. Chicago, IL, October 27, 1926, s. of Norman & Carol (Copeland), m. Laura, chil: Sharon; Lise. Educ: Union Theol. Sem., MDiv 1951; Columbia U., PhD 1953. Emp: Columbia U., 1953-55 Asst. Prof., Relig.; Andover Newton Theol. Sch., 1955-66 Samuel Lowry Prof. of OT; Grad. Theol. Union, Berkeley, 1966-82 Prof., OT, Bibl. Theol. & Ethics, 1966-67 Assoc. Dean; N.Y. Theol. Sem., 1980- Wilbert W. White Prof. of Bibl. Stud.; *Semeia*, 1984-89 Ed. Bd.; JSOTSup, 1992- Ed. Bd. Spec: Hebrew Bible. Pub: *The Bible and Liberation: Political and Social Hermeneutics*, co-ed. (Orbis, 1983, 1993); "Social Class as an Analytic and Hermeneutical Category in Biblical Studies" *JBL* 112/1 (1993); "Literary Criticism of the Hebrew Bible: Retrospect and Prospect" *Bucknell Rev.* 37/2 (1990); "Religious Conversion and the Societal Origins of Ancient Israel" *Perspectives in Relig. Stud.* 15 (1988); "The Participation of Free Agrarians in the Introduction of Monarchy to Ancient Israel: An Application of H.A. Landsberger's Framework for the Analysis of Peasant Movements" *Semeia* 37 (1986); *The Hebrew Bible—A Socio-Literary Introduction* (Fortress, 1985); "Social Matrix and Canonical Shape" *Theol. Today* 42 (1985); *The Tribes of Yahweh: A Sociology of the Religion of Liberated Israel, c. 1250-1050 B.C.E.* (Orbis, 1979); *A Light to the Nations: An Introduction to the Old Testament* (Harper & Row, 1959); and others. Awd: Hebrew U., Fulbright Res. Schol. 1960-61; Gottwald festschrift 1991. Mem: SBL 1960-, Pres. 1992; AAR 1960-; CBA 1980-. Addr: (o) New York Theological Seminary, Dept. of Biblical Studies, 5 W 29th St., New York, NY 10001 212-532-4012; (h) 175 Ninth Ave., New York, NY 10011 212-924-3459.

GOURGUES, Michel, b. Saint-Michel, Que., Canada, August 22, 1942, s. of Henri & Thérèse (Laverdière). Educ: U. Laval, Canada, BA 1963;

Coll. U. Dominicain, BPh 1966, MATh 1971; Ecole Biblique, Jerusalem, Dip. d'élève titulaire 1974; Inst. Cath. de Paris, ThD 1976. Emp: Coll. Dominicain, Fac. de Theol., Canada, 1976-80 Prof., 1976-78 Vice-doyen, 1978-87 Doyen, 1980- Prof. Titulaire, 1988- Prés. du Coll. Excv: Tell Qeisan, 1975 Asst. de recherche. Spec: New Testament. Pub: "Le père prodigue (Luc 15, 11-32)" *Nouvelle Rev. Théol.* 114 (1992); *Le Crucifié: Du scandale a l'exaltation* (Desclée/Bellarmin, 1989); "Esprit des commencements et Esprit des prolongements dans les *Actes*" *RB* 93 (1986); "The Thousand-Year Reign (Rev. 20:1-6)" *CBQ* 47 (1985); "*Pour que vous croyiez"—Pistes d'exploration de l'evangile de Jean* (Cerf, 1982); "A propos du symbolisme christologique et baptismal de Marc 16:5" *NTS* 27 (1981); *A la droite de Dieu: Résurrection de Jésus et actualisation du Psaume 110:1 dans le Nouveau Testament* (Gabalda, 1978); "Lecture christologique du Psaume CX et fête de la Pentecote" *RB* 83 (1976); and others. Awd: Rome, Maitrise en Sacrée Théol. 1989. Mem: CBA 1976-; Assn. canadienne des études bibl. au Canada 1977-; Soc. canadienne de théol. 1977-; SNTS 1979-. Addr: (o) Collège dominicain de phil. et de théol., 96 Ave. Empress, Ottawa, ON K1R 7G3, Canada 613-233-5696; (h) Dominican Priory, 96 Empress Ave., Ottawa, ON K1R 7G3, Canada 613-232-7363.

GOWAN, Donald E., b. Cleghorn, IA, January 31, 1929, s. of Elmer G. & Lucile (Woodcock), m. Darlene G., chil: Douglas A.; Pamela S. Educ: U. of S.D., BA 1951; U. of Dubuque Theol. Sem., BD 1957; U. of Chicago, PhD 1964. Emp: North Texas State U., 1962-65 Head of Bible Dept.; Pittsburgh Theol. Sem., 1965- Robert Cleveland Holland Prof. of OT; *Horizons in Bibl. Theol.*, 1990- Co-ed. Excv: Ashod, 1968 Asst. Area Supr. Spec: Hebrew Bible, Apocrypha and Post-biblical Studies. Pub: *Bridge Between the Testaments* (Pickwick, 1976, 1986); *Eschatology in the Old Testament* (Fortress, 1986); *Ezekiel* (John Knox, 1985); *Shalom: A Study of the Biblical Concept of Peace* (Creative Edge, 1984); and others. Mem: SBL. Addr: (o) 616 N Highland Ave., Pittsburgh, PA 15206 412-362-5210; (h) 4184 Timberlane Dr., Allison Park, PA 15101 412-487-2404.

GOWLER, David B., b. Mt. Vernon, IL, September 24, 1958, s. of Cedric M. & Betty L., m. Rita K., chil: Camden D. Educ: U. of Ill., BA 1981; South. Sem., MDiv 1985, PhD 1989. Emp: South. Sem., 1988-89 Instr.; Berry Coll., 1989-90 Asst. Prof.; Chowan Coll., 1990- Asst. Prof.; Emory Stud. in Early Christianity, 1991- Assoc. Ed. Spec: New Testament. Pub: *Host, Guest, Enemy and Friend: Portraits of the Pharisees in Luke and Acts*, Emory Stud. in Early Christianity vol. 1 (Lang, 1991); "Characterization in Luke: A Socio-Narratological Approach" *BTB* 19/2 (1989); and others. Mem: SBL 1985-; Westar Inst. 1987-; CBA 1991-. Rec: Chowan Coll. varsity tennis coach, racquetball. Addr: (o) Chowan College, Murfreesboro, NC 27855 919-398-

4101; (h) 514 Merriman Ave., Murfreesboro, NC 27855 919-398-3641.

GRABBE, Lester L., b. TX, November 5, 1945, s. of Warner B. & Opal D. (Chappell), m. Elizabeth H. (Wood), chil: Heather; Bruce. Educ: Ambassador Coll., England, BA 1968, Calif., MA 1970; Claremont Grad. Sch., PhD, Relig. 1976. Emp: Ambassador Coll., 1971-82 Assoc. Prof.; U. of Hull, Dept. of Theol., England, 1982- Sr. Lect. Spec: Hebrew Bible, Semitic Languages, Texts and Epigraphy, Apocrypha and Post-biblical Studies. Pub: *Judaism from Cyrus to Hadrian* (Fortress, 1992); "Maccabean Chronology" *JBL* 110 (1991); *Etymology in Early Jewish Interpretation: The Hebrew Names in Philo* (Scholars, 1988); "Another Look at the *Gestalt* of Darius *the Mede*" *CBQ* 50 (1988); "Josephus and the Reconstruction of the Judean Restoration" *JBL* 105 (1987); "Aquila's Translation and Rabbinic Exegesis" *JJS* 33 (1982); *Comparative Philology and the Text of Job: A Study in Methodology* (Scholars, 1977); "The Seasonal Pattern and the 'Baal Cycle'" *UF* 8 (1976); and others. Mem: SBL 1971-; CBA 1976-; SOTS 1983-; Assn. for Targumic Stud. Rec: Mystery novels. Addr: (o) U. of Hull, Dept. of Theology, Hull HU6 7RX, England 0482-465997; (h) 68 Newland Park, Hull HU5 2DS, England 0482-445706.

GRAF, David F., b. Detroit, MI, December 3, 1939, s. of Carl O. & Rose Lou, m. Linda (Conner), chil: John D.; Jennifer L. Educ: Harding Coll., BA 1965; McCormick Theol. Sem., BD 1970; U. of Mich., MA 1975, PhD 1979. Emp: *BA*, 1980-82 Assoc. Ed.; U. of Mich., 1982-83 Vis. Lect., 1984-86 Adj. Assoc. Prof.; Montana State U., 1983-84 Adj. Asst. Prof.; U. of Miami, 1986- Prof.; King Saud U., Saudi Arabia, Vis. Lect. Excv: Hisma Survey, Jordan, 1978-81 Dir.; Humayma Survey, Jordan, 1983 Co-dir.; Tel Anafa, 1981 Asst. Supr.; Abila of the Decapolis Project, 1980-85 Epigraphic Cons.; Roman Road Project, Jordan, 1986-92 Dir. Spec: Archaeology, Semitic Languages, Texts and Epigraphy. Pub: *Palestine in Transition: The Emergence of Ancient Israel*, co-ed.; *ABD*, assoc. ed. (Doubleday, 1992); "Hellenization and the Decapolis" *ARAM* 4 (1992); "The Origin of the Nabataeans" *ARAM* 2 (1990); "Les routes romaines d'Arabie Petree" *Le Monde de la Bible* 59 (1989); "Inscriptions from the Southern Hawran Survey, 1985 (Dafyana, Umm al-Quttayn, Dayr al-Qinn)" *Ann. of the Dept. of Antiq. of Jordan* 33 (1989); "Qura Arabiyya and Provincia Arabia" in *Geographie Historique au Proche Orient* (Monographies Techniques, 1988); "The Nabateans and the Hisma: In the Steps of Glueck and Beyond" in *The Word of the Lord Shall Go Forth: Essays in Honor of David Noel Freedman* (Eisenbrauns, 1983); and others. Awd: NEH Fellow. 1979-80. Mem: SBL 1970-; ASOR 1978-. Addr: (o) U. of Miami, Dept. of History, PO Box 248107, Coral Gables, FL 33124 305-284-3660; (h) 11411-Y SW 109th Rd., Miami, FL 33176 305-596-5450.

GRAGG, Douglas L., b. Huntsville, AL, October 26, 1957, s. of Lloyd O., Jr. & Amelia H. (Harris), m. Sandra Michelle (Mays). Educ: David Lipscomb U., BA 1978; Abilene Christian U., MA 1981, MDiv 1983; Emory U., PhD 1990. Emp: Abilene Christian U., 1978-79 Adj. Instr., Hebrew; Emory U., Candler Sch. of Theol., 1985-87 Adj. Instr., NT; Inst. for Christian Stud., 1987-92 Asst. Prof., Bible; East. European Mission & Bible Found., Austria, 1992- Writer & Ed. Spec: Hebrew Bible, New Testament. Pub: "Discourse Analysis of 1 Corinthians 1:10-2:5" *Linguistica Biblica* 65 (1991); "The Community of Believers in 1 Corinthians" *Christian Stud.* 9 (1988). Mem: SBL. Addr: (o) Eastern European Mission, Heizwerkstrasse 12, A-1232 Vienna, Austria; (h) Sechshauserstrasse 21/13, A-1150 Vienna, Austria.

GRASSMICK, John D., b. Rocky Ford, CO, September 7, 1944, s. of Jonathan & Vivian, m. Karen, chil: Lisa; Jonathan; Heather; Andrew. Educ: Dallas Theol. Sem., ThM 1974. Emp: Dallas Theol. Sem., 1974-. Spec: New Testament. Pub: "Mark" in *Bible Knowledge Comm.* (Victor, 1983); *Principles and Practice of Greek Exegesis* (Millet, 1974). Rec: Sports. Addr: (o) Dallas Theological Seminary, 3909 Swiss Ave., Dallas, TX 75204 214-824-3094; (h) 4152 Arbor Court, Mesquite, TX 75150 214-226-2852.

GRAUDIN, Arthur F., b. Philadelphia, PA, s. of Jacob & Mildred (Cepurneek), m. Marlyn Elinor (Bangert), chil: David; Deborah; Elisabeth; Mark. Educ: Concordia Sem., BA 1947, MDiv 1956. Emp: Concordia Coll., 1956-58 Asst. Prof.; Concordia Tchr. Coll., 1961-64 Asst. Prof.; Concordia Sem., 1974- Assoc. Prof. Spec: Hebrew Bible, New Testament. Pub: "A Lutheran Response to Authority of the Scripture—One Lutheran Perspective" *Covenant Jour.* (1983); and others. Mem: SBL 1976-; ETS 1976-. Rec: Tennis, volleyball. Addr: (o) Concordia Seminary, 801 De Mun Ave., Clayton, MO 63105 314-721-5934; (h) 18 N Seminary Terrace, Clayton, MO 63105 314-727-4477.

GRECH, Prospero, b. Malta, December 24, 1925, s. of Vincent & Amelia (Gatt). Educ: Gregorian U., Rome, ThD 1951; Pont. Bibl. Inst., Rome, Lic. 1953. Emp: Augustinian Theol. Sem., Malta, 1959-61 Lect.; Vicarate Vatican City, 1961-65 Sec.; Pont. Patristic Inst. Augustinianum, Rome, 1965- Prof., NT, 1968- Pres.; Pont. Bibl. Inst., 1971- Guest Lect.; Lateran U., Rome, 1968-85 Guest Lect. Spec: New Testament. Pub: *Ermeneutica e teologia biblica* (1986); "Jewish Christianity and the Purpose of Acts" *Studia Evangelica* 7 (1982); *Metodologia per lo studio della teol., NT,* co-auth. (1978); *Il Gesu storico e l'ermeneutica esistenziale* (1977); "The Testimonia and Modern Hermeneutics" *NTS* 19 (1976); *Acts of the Apostles Explained* (1966); and others. Mem: SNTS 1966-; Italian Bibl. Assn. 1968-. Rec:

Photography, music. Addr: (o) College S. Monica, Via Paolo VI, 00193 Rome, Italy 06-680069.

GREEN, H. Benedict, b. Oxford, England, January 9, 1924, s. of Frederick Wastie & Marjorie Susan (Gosling). Educ: Merton Coll., Oxford, BA 1949, MA 1952. Emp: King's Coll., London, 1955-60 Lect.; Coll. of the Resurrection, 1965-75 Vice Prin., 1975-84 Prin.; U. of Leeds, 1967-87 Assoc. Lect. Spec: New Testament. Pub: "Matthew 28.19, Eusebius and the Lex Orandi" in *The Making of Orthodoxy* (1989); "Matthew, Clement, and Luke: Their Sequence and Relationship" *JTS* 40 (1989); "The Credibility of Luke's Transformation of Matthew," "Matthew 12:22-50: An Alternative to Matthaean Conflation" in *Synoptic Studies,* JSNTSup 7 (JSOT, 1984); *The Gospel of Matthew,* New Clarendon Bible (Oxford U.P., 1975, 1980); "The Structure of St. Matthew's Gospel" *Studia Evangelica* IV, TU 102 (1968); and others. Mem: SNTS 1989-. Rec: Music, travel, architecture, walking, swimming. Addr: (h) House of the Resurrection, Mirfield, West Yorkshire WF14 OBN, England 0924-494318.

GREEN, Henry A., b. Ottawa, Canada, November 25, 1949, s. of Murray & Sarah, m. Elizabeth, chil: Jordan; Trevor; Fiona. Educ: Carleton U., Canada, BA 1970, MA 1973; St. Andrew's U., Scotland, St. Mary's Coll., PhD 1982. Emp: Hebrew U. of Jerusalem, 1977-79 Res. Assoc.; U. of Alberta, Canada, 1979-80 Vis. Asst. Prof.; Carleton U., Canada, 1981-83 Vis. Asst. Prof., Relig., Sociology; Dickinson Coll., 1983-84 Asst. Prof., Relig., Class.; U. of Miami, 1984- Assoc. Prof., Relig., Sociology, Dir. of Judaic Stud. Prog. Spec: Apocrypha and Post-biblical Studies. Pub: "Power and Knowledge: A Study of the Social Development of Early Christianity" *Stud. in Relig.* 20/2 (1991); "The Socio-Economic Background of Christianity in Egypt" in *The Roots of Egyptian Christianity* (Fortress, 1986); *The Economic and Social Origins of Gnosticism* (Scholars, 1985); "Ritual in Valentinian Gnosticism: A Sociological Interpretation" *Jour. of Relig. Hist.* 12/2 (1982); "Suggested Sociological Themes in the Study of Gnosticism" *VC* 31 (1977); "Gnosis and Gnosticism: A Study in Methodology" *Numen* 24 (1977); and others. Awd: St. Andrews U., Russel Trust Awd. 1976; Government of Israel, Fellow. 1978. Mem: SBL 1977-; CSSR 1979-; AJS 1984-. Addr: (o) U. of Miami, Judaic Studies Program, PO Box 248645, Coral Gables, FL 33124 305-284-4375; (h) 3601 Justison Rd., Coconut Grove, FL 33133.

GREEN, Ronald M., b. New York, NY, December 16, 1942, s. of Daniel & Beatrice (Friedlander), m. Mary Jean (Matthews), chil: Julie; Matthew. Educ: Brown U., AB (summa cum laude) 1964; Harvard U., PhD 1973. Emp: Dartmouth Coll., 1969- Prof.; *Jour. of Relig. Ethics,* 1973- Ed. Bd.; U. of Chicago, 1980 Hoover Lect.; Stanford U., 1984-85 Vis. Prof.; *JAAR,* 1985- Ed. Bd. Spec: Hebrew Bible. Pub:

"Theodicy," "Religion and Ethics" in *Ency. of Religion* (1986); "Abraham, Isaac and the Jewish Tradition" *Jour. of Relig. Ethics* 10/1 (1982); *Religious Reason* (Oxford U.P., 1978); *Religion and Moral Reason* (Oxford U.P., 1978); and others. Awd: Fulbright Fellow 1964-65. Mem: AAR. Rec: Sailing, travel. Addr: (o) Dartmouth College, Dept. of Religion, Hanover, NH 03755 603-646-3141; (h) PO Box 418, Norwich, VT 05055 802-649-1983.

GREENBERG, Moshe, b. Philadelphia, PA, July 10, 1928, s. of Simon & Betty (Davis), m. Evelyn Doris (Gelber), chil: Joel; Raphael; Ethan. Educ: U. of Pa., BA 1949, PhD 1954; Jewish Theol. Sem. of Amer., Rabbi, MHL 1954. Emp: U. of Pa., 1954-70 Ellis Prof. of Hebrew & Semitic Lang. & Lit.; Hebrew U. of Jerusalem, 1961, 1968, 1970- Vis. Prof. of Bible; *EJ,* 1968-71 Div. Ed.; U. of Calif. at Berkeley, 1981-82 Vis. Prof., Jewish Stud.; Yale U., 1986-87 Vis. Prof., Relig. Stud.; *JBL,* 1959-66 Ed. Bd. Spec: Hebrew Bible. Pub: "The Design and Themes of Ezekiel's Program of Restoration" *Interpretation* 38 (1984); *Ezekiel 1-20, AB* (Doubleday, 1983); *Biblical Prose Prayer* (U. of Calif., 1983); "On the Refinement of the Conception of Prayer in Hebrew Scriptures" *Assn. for Jewish Stud. Rev.* 1 (1976); *Understanding Exodus* (Jewish Theol. Sem., 1969); and others. Awd: Guggenheim Fellow 1961; Danforth Found., Harbison Award 1968; and others. Mem: BC; AAJR; Amer. Acad. of Arts & Sci.; and others. Addr: (o) Hebrew U. of Jerusalem, Dept. of Bible, 91905 Jerusalem, Israel 2-883605; (h) 29 Mitudela St. #8, 92305 Jerusalem, Israel 2-666075.

GREENE, Michael D., b. Boone, NC, July 23, 1957, s. of Earl & Nora, m. Carolyn, chil: Patricia; Meredith. Educ: Campbell U., BA 1979; Wake Forest U., MA 1982; U. of Va., PhD 1987. Emp: Appalachian State U., 1986 Instr.; Chowan Coll., 1986-90 Asst. Prof.; Lees-McRae Coll., 1990- Asst. Prof. Spec: New Testament. Pub: "A Note on Romans 8:3" *BZ* 1 (1991); "Acco," "Bartholomew," "Great Tribulation," "Kidron," "New Birth," "Reconciliation," "Sergius Paulus" in *Mercer Dict. of the Bible* (1990). Awd: U. of Va., DuPont Fellow 1983-86. Mem: SBL; NABPR; N.C. Relig. Stud. Assn. Rec: Piano, horseback riding, hiking. Addr: (o) Lees-McRae College, PO Box 3762, Banner Elk, NC 28604 704-898-8792; (h) Rt. 2, PO Box 613, Boone, NC 28607 704-264-1057.

GREENFIELD, Jonas, Spec: Semitic Languages, Texts and Epigraphy. Addr: (o) Hebrew U., Dept. of Semitic Languages, Jerusalem, Israel; (h) 8 Aharoni, Jerusalem, Israel 039-226.

GREENGUS, Samuel, b. Chicago, IL, March 11, 1936, s. of Eugene & Thelma, m. Lesha (Bellows), chil: Deana; Rachel; Judith. Educ: U. of Chicago, MA 1959, PhD 1963. Emp: Hebrew Union Coll.-Jewish Inst. of Relig., 1963- Prof. of Semitic

Lang., 1979-84 Dean of Rabbinic Sch., 1985-90 Dir., Sch. of Grad. Stud., 1987- Dean of Faculty, 1990- V.P. for Acad. Affairs. Excv: Tell Gezer, 1966-67 Area Supr. Spec: Archaeology, Hebrew Bible, Mesopotamian Studies, Semitic Languages, Texts and Epigraphy. Pub: "Bridewealth in Sumerian Sources" *HUCA* 61 (1990); "The Akkadian Calendar at Sippar" *JAOS* (1987); *Studies in Ishchali Documents,* Bibl. Mesopotamica 19 (Undena, 1986); *Old Babylonian Tablets from Ishchali and Vicinity* (1979); "A Textbook Case of Adultery in Ancient Mesopotamia" *HUCA* (1969-70); "The Old Babylonian Marriage Contract" *JAOS* 89 (1969); "Old Babylonian Marriage Ceremonies and Rites" *JCS* 20 (1966); and others. Awd: Phi Beta Kappa 1959; Amer. Coun. of Learned Soc., Fellow 1970-71; Amer. Assn. of Theol. Sch., Fellow 1976-77. Mem: AOS; AJS; SBL; MidW Jewish Stud. Assn. Addr: (o) 3101 Clifton Ave., Cincinnati, OH 45220 513-221-1875; (h) 3976 Beechwood, Cincinnati, OH 45229 513-281-4567.

GREENHUT, Zvi, b. Jerusalem, December 20, 1958, s. of Zvi & Eva (Blau), chil: Nadav; Hila; Omer. Educ: Hebrew U., BA 1984; Tel Aviv U., MA 1992. Emp: IES, 1985-86 Ed., Pesakh Bar Adon material from the Judean desert; Israel Antiq. Auth., 1989- Arch. Excv: Tel Yoqneam, Israel, 1983 Area Supr.; Jerusalem Manhat, Israel, 1987 Supr.; Hurvat Hermeshit, Israel, 1988-90 Dir.; Caiaphas' Tomb, Israel, 1990 Dir. Spec: Archaeology. Pub: "Caiaphas' Tomb in North Talpiot, Jerusalem" *Atiqot* 21 (1992); "Burial Cave of the Caiaphas Family" *BAR* 18/5 (1992); "Jerusalem, Ezrat Torah" *Hadashot Arch.* 96 (1991); "Discovery of the Caiaphas Family Tomb" *Jerusalem Perspective* 4 (1991); "Hurvat Hermeshit" *Hadashot Arch.* 93, 95, 97 (1989-90). Addr: (o) PO Box 586, Jerusalem 91004, Israel; (h) Kadish Luz St., Jerusalem 96920, Israel.

GREENSPAHN, Frederick E., b. Los Angeles, CA, October 7, 1946, s. of Gerald M. & Bunne B., m. Barbara (Nirenberg), chil: Rachel I.; Daniel S. Educ: U. of Calif., BA 1968; Hebrew Union Coll., Jewish Inst. of Relig., MHL 1973; Brandeis U., PhD 1977. Emp: Assumption Coll., 1977-79 Lect., Relig. Stud.; Brandeis U., 1978 Vis. Lect.; U. of Denver, 1979- Prof., Judaic & Relig. Stud.; Iliff Sch. of Theol., 1980 Vis. Lect.; *JBL,* 1988- Ed. Bd.; *Hebrew Stud.,* 1993- Ed. Spec: Hebrew Bible, Semitic Languages, Texts and Epigraphy. Pub: *When Brothers Dwell Together* (1993); "How Modern Are Modern Biblical Studies?" in *Minhah le-Nahum* (1993); *Essential Papers on Israel and the Ancient Near East,* ed. (N.Y. U.P., 1991); "Why Prophecy Ceased" *JBL* 108 (1989); "Biblical Scholars, Medieval and Modern" in *Judaic Perspectives on Ancient Israel* (1986); "Abraham ibn Ezra and the Origin of Some Medieval Grammatical Terms" *JQR* 76 (1986); "The Theology of the Framework to the Book of Judges" *VT* (1986); *Hapax Legomena in Biblical Hebrew* (Scholars, 1984); "An Egyptian Parallel to Judges 17:6 and 21:25" *JBL* 101 (1982); and others. Mem: SBL

1981-, Rocky Mt./Great Plains reg., V.P. 1981-82, Pres. 1982-83; AJS; NAPH. Rec: Reading. Addr: (o) U. of Denver, Center for Judaic Studies, 2199 S University Blvd., Denver, CO 80208 303-871-3020; (h) 3146 S Newport St., Denver, CO 80224 303-759-8753.

GREENSPOON, Leonard J., b. Richmond, VA, December 5, 1945, s. of Alvin L. & Rose L., m. Eliska M., chil: Gallit Rena; Talya Louisa. Educ: U. of Richmond, BA 1967, MA 1970; U. of Rome., 1967-68 Fulbright Fellow. for Class. Stud.; Harvard U., PhD, Near East. Lang. & Civ. 1977. Emp: Clemson U., 1975- Prof., Relig.; *RSRev*, 1990- Book Rev. Ed.; Septuagint & Cognate Stud. Mon. Ser., 1991- Ed. Spec: Hebrew Bible, Semitic Languages, Texts and Epigraphy, Apocrypha and Post-biblical Studies. Pub: "On the Jewishness of Modern Jewish Biblical Scholarship: The Case of Max L. Margolis" *Judaism* 39 (1990); "Biblical Translators in Antiquity and in the Modern World: A Comparative Study" *HUCA* 60 (1989); *Max Leopold Margolis: A Scholar's Scholar*, Bibl Schol. in N Amer. 15 (Scholars, 1987); "The Warrior God, or God, the Divine Warrior" in *Religion and Politics in the Modern World* (N.Y. U.P., 1983); *Textual Studies in the Book of Joshua*, HSM 28 (Scholars, 1983); "Theodotion, Aquila, Symmachus, and the Old Greek of Joshua" *Eretz-Israel* 16 (1982); "The Origin of the Idea of Resurrection" in *Traditions in Transformation: Turning Points in Biblical Faith* (Eisenbrauns, 1981); *Ezekiel*, vol. 1 & 2, Hermeneia Ser., assoc. ed. (Fortress, 1979, 1983); and others. Awd: ASOR 1986; Annenberg Res. Inst. Fellow. 1988; Oxford Ctr. for Postgrad. Hebrew Stud., Skirball Fellow. 1992-93. Mem: ASOR; AJS; CBA; IOSCS; SBL. Rec: Exercise, swimming, collecting just about everything. Addr: (o) Clemson U., Dept. of Philosophy & Religion, Clemson, SC 29634-1508 803-656-5358; (h) 300 Hunting Hill Cir., Greer, SC 29650 803-268-9312.

GREENSTEIN, Edward, b. Rockville Centre, NY, January 18, 1949, s. of Samuel & Goldie, m. Beverly (Gribetz), chil: Batsheva L.; Avraham Zev. Educ: Jewish Theol. Sem., BHL 1970, MA 1974; Columbia U., MPhil 1975, PhD 1977. Emp: *JANES*, 1974- Ed.; Jewish Theol. Sem., 1976- Prof., Bible; *Prooftexts*, 1981-90 Assoc. Ed.; Yale U., 1987, 1990 Vis. Prof.; Hebrew U., 1992-92 Vis. Prof.; Tel Aviv U., 1992-93 Vis. Prof. Spec: Hebrew Bible, Mesopotamian Studies, Semitic Languages, Texts and Epigraphy. Pub: "Misquotation of Scripture in the Dead Sea Scrolls" *Frank Talmage Memorial Volume* (1993); "Mixing Memory and Design: Reading Psalm 78" *Prooftexts* (1990); "The Formation of the Biblical Narrative Corpus" *AJS Rev.* (1990); *The State of Jewish Studies*, co-ed. (1990); "Deconstruction and Biblical Narrative" *Prooftexts* (1989); *Essays on Biblical Method and Translation* (1989); *The Hebrew Bible in Literary Criticism*, co-ed. (1986); "How Does Parallelism Mean?" *JQR Sup.* (1983); and others. Awd: Jewish Theol. Sem., Res. Fellow 1983-84; Mem.

Found. for Jewish Culture, Fellow 1983-84, 1991-93; NEH, Fellow 1991-92; Guggenheim Fellow 1992-93. Mem: AOS 1972-; SBL 1977-. Rec: Music, reading, swimming. Addr: (o) Jewish Theological Seminary, 3080 Broadway, New York, NY 10027 212-678-8847; (h) 57 W 93 St., #1C, New York, NY 10025 212-663-3843.

GRELOT, Pierre, b. Paris, France, February 6, 1917, s. of Louis & Helene (Paty). Educ: Inst. Cath. de Paris, Doc. theol. 1949. Emp: Grand Sem. d'Orléans, 1943-45 Prof.; Ecole des Lang. Orientales anc., 1951-83 enseignement de l'araméen; Sem. St. Sulpice de Paris, 1955-61; Cath. fac. theol., 1962-83; Pont. Bibl. Commn., 1972-86 Mem. Spec: Hebrew Bible, New Testament, Semitic Languages, Texts and Epigraphy, Apocrypha and Post-biblical Studies. Pub: *Introduction critique au Nouveau Testament*, co-auth. (1977, 1991); *Les Poèmes du Serviteur* (1981); *Documents araméens d'Egypte* (1972); and others. Awd: Prix de l'Acad. des Inscriptions et Belles-Lettres 1972. Mem: Assn. Cath. Francaise pour l'Etude de la Bible; SNTS. Rec: Organ. Addr: (h) 7, rue Dupanloup, 45057 Orleans CEDEX 1, France 548-0516.

GRIGGS, C. Wilfred, b. Pocatello, ID, October 5, 1942, s. of L.W. & Loal (Hendricks), m. Karen Ann (Smith), chil: Brian W.; Deborah K.; Stephen Smith; Kent D.; Kathryn A.; Julie D.; Michael J. Educ: Brigham Young U., BA 1966, MA 1968; U. of Calif., PhD, Anc. Hist. & Mediterranean Arch. 1978. Emp: U. of Utah, 1970-82 Vis. Res. Prof.; Intl. Coptic Ency. Project, 1979-82 Asst. Ed.; Brigham Young U., 1980-85 Assoc. Prof., Relig. Stud. Ctr., 1982-88 Dir. of Anc. Stud., 1985-87 Prof., 1987- U. Prof. of Anc. Stud. Excv: Nag Hammadi, Egypt, 1975-76 Staff; Seila, Fayum, Egypt, 1981 Field Dir., 1982- Project & Field Dir. Spec: Archaeology, New Testament, Egyptology. Pub: Artices in *Coptic Ency.* (Macmillan, 1991); *Early Egyptian Christianity* (Brill, 1990); "Excavating a Christian Cemetery Near Seila, in the Fayum Region of Egypt" *Coptic Stud.* (1990); *Excavations at Seila, Egypt, 1981-84*, ed. (Brigham Young U., 1988); *Ramses II: The Pharaoh and His Time, an Exhibition Catalogue*, ed. (U. Press of Amer., 1985); and others. Awd: Stanford U., NDEA & Ford Found. Fellow. 1968-70. Mem: Mormon Arch. & Res. Found.; IACS; Assn. of Anc. Hist.; SBL. Rec: Piano, choral singing, sports activist. Addr: (o) Brigham Young U., Ancient Studies, 4012 HBLL, Provo, UT 84604 801-378-3498; (h) 427 East 500 South, Orem, UT 84057 801-224-1157.

GROH, Dennis E., b. Chicago, IL, August 9, 1939, s. of Edward & Anne, m. Lucille (Sider), chil: Jeremy D.; Sara E. Educ: Ill. Wesleyan U., BA 1961; Garrett Theol. Sem., BD 1965; NW U., PhD 1970. Emp: Garrett-Evang. Theol. Sem., 1968- Prof., Hist. of Christianity; NW U., 1970- Adv. Mem., Grad. Fac.; Ctr. for the Study of East. Mediterranean Relig. & Culture, 1976-82, 1984-86 Dir.; *SC*, Ed. Bd.; *Anglican Rev.*, 1979- Asst.

Ed. Excv: Caesarea Maritima, 1972, 1974-75; Gush Halav, 1977-78 Field Staff; Sepphoris, 1987 Sr. Field & Publ. Staff, Assoc. Dir.; Tel Nessana, Co-dir. Spec: Archaeology, Apocrypha and Post-biblical Studies. Pub: "The Religion of the Empire: Christianity From Constantine to the Arab Conquest" in *Christianity and Judaism—A Parallel History of Their Origins and Early Development* (BAS, 1992); "The Late Roman Fine Wares of the Gush Halav Synagogue" in *Excavations of the Ancient Synagogue of Gush Halav* (Eisenbrauns, 1990); *Augustine: Religion of the Heart* (Graded, 1988); "Jews and Christians in Late Roman Palestine: Towards a New Chronology" *BA* 51 (1988); *In Between Advents: Biblical and Spiritual Arrivals* (Fortress, 1986); *The Living Text: Essays in Honor of Ernest W. Saunders*, co-ed. (U. Press of Amer., 1985); *Early Arianism—A View of Salvation,* co-auth. (Fortress/SCM, 1981); "The Fine Wares from the Patrician and Lintel Houses" in *Excavations at Ancient Meiron, Upper Galilee, Israel, 1971-72, 1974-75, 1977,* Publ. of the Meiron Excvn. Project III (ASOR, 1981); "The Meiron Excavation Project: Archaeological Survey in Galilee and Golan, 1976," co-auth., *BASOR* 230 (1978); and others. Awd: Rockefeller Doc. Fellow in Relig. 1967-68; ASOR, James Alan Montgomery Fellow 1974-75; Albright Inst. of Arch. Res., Jerusalem, Annual Prof. 1982; Ben Gurion U., Humphrey Inst. for Social Ecology, Humphrey Fellow 1988-89; Assn. of Theol. Sch. of the United States & Canada, Sr. Fac. Fellow. 1992. Mem: ASOR; Amer. Soc. of Ch. Hist.; NAPS, V.P. 1980-81, Pres. 1981-83; AIA, V.P., Chicago Soc. 1985-92. Rec: Boating. Addr: (o) 2121 Sheridan Rd., Evanston, IL 60201 708-866-3900; (h) 2743 Meadowlark Ln., Evanston, IL 60201 708-869-2377.

GROMACKI, Robert G., b. Erie, PA, September 20, 1933, s. of Sylvester & Thelma, m. Gloria (Julyan), chil: Gary; Gail. Educ: Dallas Theol. Sem., ThM 1960; Grace Theol. Sem., ThD 1966. Emp: Cedarville Coll., 1960- Prof., Bible & Greek, Chmn. of Bibl. Educ.; Grace Theol. Sem., Bapt. Bible Coll., Guest Prof., Lect.; Appalachia Bible Coll., 1981 Staley Lect.; Grand Rapids Bapt. Sem., 1972, 1984 Staley Lect. Spec: New Testament. Pub: *The Virgin Birth: Doctrine of Deity* (Baker, 1981); *New Testament Survey* (Baker, 1974); and others. Mem: ETS; Creation Res. Soc.; NEAS. Rec: Golf, tennis, travel. Addr: (o) Cedarville College, Box 601, Cedarville, OH 45314 766-2211; (h) 178 Palmer Dr., Box 601, Cedarville, OH 45314 766-5155.

GROS LOUIS, Kenneth R. R., b. Nashua, NH, December 18, 1936, s. of Albert & Jeannette, m. Dolores (Dee), chil: Amy; Julie. Educ: Columbia Coll., BA (magna cum laude) 1959; Columbia U., MA 1960; U. of Wis., PhD 1964. Emp: Ind. U., 1964- Prof., English & Comparative Lit., 1970-73 Assoc. Dean, Coll. of Arts & Sci., 1973-78 Chair, Dept. of English, 1978-80 Dean, Coll. of Arts & Sci., 1988- V.P. & Chancellor; Ind. Stud. in Bibl. Lit., 1985- Adv. Bd. Spec: Hebrew Bible, New Testament. Pub: "Different Ways of Looking at

the Birth of Jesus" *BR* 1/1 (1985); *Literary Interpretations of Biblical Narrative*, vol. 1-2 (Abingdon, 1974, 1982); "Critical Presuppositions in Approaching the Bible as Literature" *Christianity & Lit.* 24 (1979); "The Difficulty of Ruling Well: King David of Israel" *Semeia* 8 (1977). Awd: Phi Beta Kappa 1959; Ind. U., Ulysses G. Weatherly Awd. for Disting. Teaching 1970; Leopold & Clara Fellner Awd., Co-winner 1985-86. Mem: Modern Lang. Assn. Rec: Tennis, jogging. Addr: (o) Indiana U., Vice President's Office, Bryan Hall 100, Bloomington, IN 47405 812-855-4602; (h) 1119 E 1st St., Bloomington, IN 47401 812-336-6792.

GROSS, Walter, b. Wurzburg, June 30, 1941, s. of Walter & Anneliese (Tumma). Educ: Pont. U. Gregoriana, Rome, Lic. Phil. 1964, Lic. Theol. 1968; Pont. Bibl. Inst., Lic. Bibl. 1969; U. of Munich, ThD 1973, Habil. 1975. Emp: Bibl. Exegesis, Munich, 1974-76 Asst. Prof.; U. of Munich, 1975 Assoc. Prof.; Johannes-Gutenberg U. Mainz, 1976-80 Prof., OT Stud.; U. of Tuebingen, Dept. of Cath. Theol., 1980- Prof., OT Stud. Spec: Hebrew Bible. Pub: "Israel und die Voelker: Die Krise des YHWH-Volk-Konzepts im Jesajabuch" *QD* 146 (1993); "Die Gottebenbildlichkeit des Menschen nach Gen 1,26.27 in der Diskussion des letzten Jahrzehnts" in *Lebendige Ueberlieferung: Prozesse der Annaeherung und Auslegung, Festschrift fuer Hermann-Josef Vogt zum 60 Geburstag (1993)*; "Prophet gegen Institution im alten Israel? Warnung vor vermeintlichen Gegensaetzen" *Theol. Quar. Tubingen* 171 (1991); "Israel's Hope for the Renewal of the State" *JNSL* 14 (1988); *Die Pendenskonstruktion im Biblischen Hebraeisch*, Arbeiten zu Text und Sprache im Alten Testament 27 (1987); "Otto Roessler und die Diskussion um das althebraeische Verbalsystem" *Bibl. Notizen* 18 (1982); *Verbform und Funktion: Wayyiqtol fur die Gegenwart? Ein Beitrag zur Syntax poetischer althebraeischer Texte*, Arbeiten zu Text und Sprache im Alten Testament 1 (1976); *Bileam: Literar- und formkritische Untersuchung der Prosa in Num. 22-24*, SANT 38 (1974); and others. Rec: Kammermusik. Addr: (o) Kathol.-Theolog. Seminar, Abtlg. Altes Test., Liebermeisterstr. 12, D-72076 Tuebingen, Germany 07071-296974; (h) Mallestr. 24, D-72072 Tuebingen, Germany 07071-72010.

GROSSBERG, Daniel, b. New York, NY, December 12, 1942, s. of Max & Sophie, m. Millie F., chil: Penina; Yaffa Shira; Sharona. Educ: Columbia U., BS 1965; Jewish Theol. Sem., BRE 1965; U. of Rochester, MA 1967; N.Y. U., PhD 1977. Emp: State U. of N.Y. at Albany, 1977- Assoc. Prof.; St. Anthony on the Hudson, 1978-79 Vis. Adj. Prof., Bible; Siena Coll., 1986-87, 1989, 1991-92 Vis. Adj. Prof., Relig. Stud.; Union College, 1988 Vis. Adj. Prof., Hebrew. Spec: Hebrew Bible, Semitic Languages, Texts and Epigraphy. Pub: *Centripetal and Centrifugal Structures in Biblical Poetry*, SBL Mon. Ser. 39 (Scholars, 1989); "Pivotal Polysemy in Jer. 25:10-11a" *VT* 36 (1986); "The Dual Glow/Grow Motif" *Biblica* 67 (1986); "The Disparate Elements of the

Inclusio in Psalms" *HAR* 6 (1982); "Noun/Verb Parallism in Hebrew Bible" *JBL* 99 (1980); "Nominalization in Biblical Hebrew" *Hebrew Stud.* 20 (1979-80); and others. Awd: Oxford Ctr. for Postgrad. Hebrew Stud., Vis. Sch. 1992. Mem: AJS 1977-; NAPH 1977-; SBL 1977-. Rec: Swimming. Addr: (o) State U. of N.Y. at Albany, HU 283, 1400 Washington Ave., Albany, NY 12222 518-442-4134; (h) 12 Stonehenge Dr., Albany, NY 12203 518-482-7118.

GRUBER, Mayer I., b. Schenectady, NY, November 23, 1944, s. of David S. & Mathilde (Nover), m. Judith (Friedman), chil: David; Benjamin; Hillel; Tamara; Shlomit. Educ: Duke U., AB 1965; Jewish Theol. Sem. of Amer., MHL 1968; Columbia U., PhD, Anc. Semitic 1977. Emp: Spertus Coll. of Judaica, 1972-80 Assoc. Prof., Bibl. Stud.; Ben-Gurion U. of the Negev, Israel, 1980- Sr. Lect., Bible & Anc. Near East; U. of Chicago, Oriental Inst., 1985-86, 1992 Vis. Schol. Spec: Hebrew Bible. Pub: *The Solomon Goldman Lectures*, vol. 6 (Spertus Coll. of Judaica, 1993); *The Motherhood of God and Other Studies*, U. of S Fla. Stud. in Judaica (Scholars, 1992); "What Happened to Rashi's Pictures?" *Bodleian Library Record* April (1992); *Aspects of Nonverbal Communication in the Ancient Near East*, Studia Pohl 12, vol. 2 (Pont. Bibl. Inst., 1980); and others. Mem: AOS; SBL; NAPH; AJS. Rec: Swimming, bicycling, music. Addr: (o) Ben-Gurion U. of the Negev, Dept. of Bible & Ancient Near East, Beersheva, Israel.

GUINAN, Michael D., b. Cincinnati, OH, February 16, 1939, s. of Henry G. & Ursula (Maggini). Educ: Old Mission Theol. Sem., STB 1965; Catholic U., STL 1967, MA 1970, PhD 1972. Emp: Grad. Theol. Union, Franciscan Sch. of Theol., 1972- Prof., Semitic Lang., OT; St. Patrick's Sem., Our Lady of the Angels Sem., Philippines, 1972-86 Vis. Prof.; *CBQ*, 1983-90 Ed. Bd. Spec: Hebrew Bible. Pub: "Book of Lamentations" in *New Jerome Biblical Comm.* (1990); *The Pentateuch* (Liturgical, 1990); *The Book of Job*, Collegeville Bible Comm. 19 (Liturgical, 1986); "Lachish Letters" in *ISBE* (1985); *Gospel Poverty: Witness to the Risen Christ* (Paulist, 1981); *Covenant in the Old Testament* (Franciscan Herald, 1975); "Jacob of Sarug (Serugh)" in *New Catholic Ency.* vol. 16; and others. Mem: SBL; CBA. Rec: Theater, music. Addr: (o) Franciscan School of Theology, 1712 Euclid Ave., Berkeley, CA 94709 415-848-5232; (h) 1708 Euclid Ave. #8, Berkeley, CA 94709 415-540-7566.

GUNN, David M., b. Te Awamutu, New Zealand, September 7, 1942, s. of L. Farquhar & Jean B., m. Margaret I., chil: Rebecca M.; Jonathan F. Educ: U. of Melbourne, Australia, BA 1964, MA 1965; U. of Otago, New Zealand, BD 1967; U. of Newcastle-upon-Tyne, England, PhD 1975. Emp: U. of Sheffield, England, Dept. of Bibl. Stud., 1970-84 Sr. Lect.; Columbia Theol. Sem., 1984-

Prof., OT; *JSOT,* 1976- Co-ed.; JSOTSup, 1976-84 Co-gen. Ed.; Bible & Lit. Ser., 1981-91 gen. Ed.; Literary Currents in Biblical Interpretation, 1990- Co-gen. Ed. Spec: Hebrew Bible. Pub: *Narrative in the Hebrew Bible*, co-auth. (1993); *Gender, Power, and Promise: The Subject of the Bible's First Story*, co-auth. (Abingdon, 1993); *Compromising Redemption: Relating Characters in the Book of Ruth*, co-auth. (Westminster/John Knox, 1990); *The Fate of King Saul: An Interpretation of a Biblical Story* (JSOT, 1980); *The Story of King David: Genre and Interpretation* (JSOT, 1978); and others. Mem: SOTS 1970-; SBL 1972-. Rec: Music, movies, jogging, canoeing, fishing. Addr: (o) Columbia Theological Seminary, PO Box 520, Decatur, GA 30031-0520 404-378-8821; (h) 1728 Vickers Circle, Decatur, GA 30030.

GUTMANN, Joseph, b. Wuerzburg, Germany, August 17, 1923, s. of Henry & Selma (Eisemann), m. Marilyn B., chil: David H.; Sharon D. Educ: N.Y. U., Inst. of Fine Arts, MA 1952; Hebrew Union Coll.–Jewish Inst. of Relig., Rabbi 1959, PhD 1960. Emp: Hebrew Union Coll.–Jewish Inst. of Relig., 1960-69 Assoc. Prof., Jewish Art; Wayne State U., 1969-89 Prof., Art Hist.; U. of Windsor, Canada, 1990- Vis. Prof., Relig. Stud. Spec: Archaeology, Hebrew Bible. Pub: *The Dura-Europos Synagogue: A Re-evaluation (1932-92)*, ed. (Scholars, 1992); *Sacred Images: Studies in Jewish Art from Antiquity to the Middle Ages* (Varorium, 1989); *The Jewish Sanctuary* (Brill, 1983); *The Temple of Solomon*, ed. (Scholars, 1976); and others. Awd: Wayne St. U., Fac. Recog. Awd. 1980, DD 1984; Gershenson Disting. Fac. Fellow 1986-88. Mem: Cen. Conf. of Amer. Rabbis 1959-; SBL 1970-80. Rec: Tennis, reading, drawing. Addr: (h) 13151 Winchester, Huntington Woods, MI 48070 313-547-1067.

HAACKER, Klaus B., b. Wiesbaden, Germany, August 26, 1942, s. of Bernhard & Erna, m. Dorothea, chil: Markus; Christoph. Educ: U. of Mainz, Germany, DTh 1970. Emp: Mainz U., Inst. for Bibl. Arch., 1969-70 Asst.; *Theologische Beitrage*, 1970- Co-ed.; U. of Tubingen, Germany, Institutum Judaicum, 1970-74 Asst. Prof.; Kirchliche Hochschule Wuppertal, 1974- Prof. Spec: Hebrew Bible, New Testament, Apocrypha and Post-biblical Studies. Pub: *Neutestamentliche Wissenschaft. Eine Einfuehrung in Fragestellungen und Methoden* (1981, 1985); "Glaube II: Altes und Neues Testament" *TRE* (1984); "Leistung und Grenzen der Formkritik" *Theologische Beitrage* (1981); "Art. Samaritan, Samaria" *NIDNTT* (1978); *Die Stiftung des Heils. Untersuchungen zur Struktur der johanneischen Theologie* (1972); and others. Mem: SNTS 1976-. Rec: Poetry. Addr: (o) Missionsstrasse 1b, 5600 Wuppertal 2, Germany 0202-85865.

HAAG, Herbert, b. Singen-Hohentwiel, Germany, February 11, 1915, s. of Reinhold & Stephanie. Educ: Pont. Gregorian U., Italy, Lic. Phil. 1937; Institut Catholique, France, Lic. Theol.

1941; U. of Fribourg, Switzerland, Dr. Theol. 1942; Pont. Bibl. Commn., Lic. Bibl. 1947. Emp: Theol. Fac. Lucerne, Switzerland, 1948-60 Prof., OT; U. of Tuebingen, Germany, 1960-80 Prof., OT. Spec: Hebrew Bible. Addr: (h) Haldenstr. 26, 6006 Lucerne, Switzerland 041-311373.

HAAK, Robert D., b. Springfield, IL, January 16, 1949, s. of Rudolph & Lenora, chil: Michael; Robert. Educ: Concordia Tchr. Coll., BS 1970; Luth. Sch. of Theol. at Chicago, MTS 1974; U. of Chicago, PhD 1986. Emp: Luth. Sch. of Theol. at Chicago, 1978-80 Lect.; Ill. Benedictine Coll., 1982 Lect.; St. Xavier Coll., 1982-83 Lect.; McCormick Theol. Sem., 1983 Lect., Augustana Coll., 1983- Asst. Prof. Excv: Tel Lachish, 1981, 1985, 1987; Tel Miqne-Ekron, 1992-93 Pottery Manager, Artifact Registrar. Spec: Hebrew Bible, Semitic Languages, Texts and Epigraphy. Pub: *Habakkuk,* VTSup 44 (Brill, 1992); "Altar" in *ABD* (Doubleday, 1992); "At the Borders of the Text" *Bibl. Res.* (1990); "Poetry in Habakkuk 1:1-2:4?" *JAOS* (1988); "The Shoulder of the Temple" *VT* (1983); "A Study and New Interpretation of QSR NPS" *JBL* (1982); and others. Awd: NEH, Albright Inst. of Arch. Res., Jerusalem, Fellow 1990-91, Annual Prof. 1992-93; Cyprus American Arch. Res. Inst., Augustana Coll. Res. Found. Grant 1988. Mem: ASOR; SBL; CSBR. Addr: (o) Augustana College, Old Main, Rock Island, IL 61201 309-794-7345.

HABEL, Norman C., b. Hamilton, Victoria, Australia, July 9, 1932. Educ: Concordia Sem., BD, STT, ThD. Emp: Concordia Sem., 1960-73 Assoc. Prof., Bibl. Stud.; Adelaide Coll. of Advanced Educ., 1974-83 Prin. Lect., Relig. Stud.; Kodiakanal Intl. Sch., India, 1984-87 Prin.; South Australia Coll. of Advanced Educ., 1987-90 Prin. Lect., Relig. Stud.; U. of South Australia, 1991- Prof., Relig. Stud. Spec: Hebrew Bible. Pub: "The Suffering Land: Ideology in Jeremiah" *Luth. Theol. Jour.* 26 (1992); "Conquest and Dispossession: Justice, Joshua and Land Rights" *Pacifica* 4 (1991); *Job: The Old Testament Library* (Westminster, 1985); "Appeal to Ancient Tradition as a Literary Form" *ZAW* 88 (1976); "Yahweh, Maker of Heaven and Earth" *JBL* 91 (1972); "The Symbolism of Wisdom in Proverbs 1-9" *Interpretation* 26 (1972); *Literary Criticism of the Old Testament* (Fortress, 1971); *Yahweh Versus Baal* (Bookman, 1964); and others. Mem: SBL; Australian Assn. for the Study of Relig., Founding Pres.; Australian & New Zealand Soc. for Theol. Stud. Rec: Fishing. Addr: (o) U. of South Australia, Holbrooks Rd., Underdale, SA 5032, Australia 08-302-6232; (h) 39 Alexander St., Largs Bay, SA 5016, Australia 08-49-8694.

HACHLILI, Rachel, Emp: Tel Aviv U., Tchr., Anc. Jewish & Greek Art; U. of Haifa. Excv: Jericho Hills; Ashdod; Arad; Masada; Caesarea; Katzrin Synogogue. Spec: Archaeology. Pub: *Ancient Jewish Art & Archaeology in the Land of Israel* (Brill, 1988); "The Saga of the Goliath

Family—As Revealed in Their Newly Discovered 2,000-Year-Old Tomb," co-auth., *BAR* 9/1 (1983); "Ancient Burial Customs Preserved in Jericho Hills" *BAR* 5/4 (1979); and others. Addr: (o) U. of Haifa, Dept. of Archaeology, Haifa, Israel 285151; (h) 32 Elkahi St., East Talpiot, Jerusalem, Israel 714905.

HADLEY, Judith M., b. Toledo, OH, December 21, 1956, d. of John Bothwell & Dorothy Ruth (Reynolds). Educ: Wheaton Coll., BA, Bibl. Stud. & Arch. 1977; Inst. of Holy Land Stud., Jerusalem, MA, Hist. of Anc. Israel 1984; U. of Cambridge, PhD, Div. 1989. Emp: Cambridge U., Fac. of Div., 1986-89 Supr. in OT Stud., Arch., Anc. Near East. Texts, 1987-90 Lect., Hebrew & OT; Westminster & Westcott House Theol. Coll., UK, 1988-90 Lect., OT; Villanova U., 1990- Asst. Prof., Bibl. Stud. & Arch. Excv: Tel Gerisa, 1980 Asst. Staff; Khirbet el-Hammam, 1981 Asst. Staff; Tel Lachish, 1981-85 Arch. Recorder; Ramat Rahel, 1984 Site Recorder; Tel Jezreel, 1991 Acting Area Supr. Spec: Archaeology, Hebrew Bible, Semitic Languages, Texts and Epigraphy. Pub: "Some Drawings and Inscriptions on Two Pithoi from Kuntillet 'Ajrud" *VT* 37 (1987); "The Khirbet el-Qom Inscription" *VT* 37 (1987). Mem: ASOR; IOSOT; IES; SBL; Amer. Assn. of U. Prof. Rec: Music, sports, gardening. Addr: (o) Villanova U., Dept. of Religious Studies, Villanova, PA 19085 215-645-7462; (h) 2815 Belmont Ave., Ardmore, PA 19003 215-645-0789.

HAGELIA, Hallvard, b. Gjerstad, Norway, June 29, 1944, s. of Jakob & Teresie, m. Kirsten, chil: Marianne; Nina. Emp: Mission Covenant Ch. of Norway, 1966- Pastor; Ansgar Theol. Sem., 1980- Lect., OT & NT. Spec: Hebrew Bible. Pub: "Gamla Testamentets tro," rev., *Tro och Liv* (1992); "Kvinner i Bibelen, i Kirken, i Misjonen," rev., *Misjonsbladet* (1992); *Apent Brev Fra Fengslet. Brevkurs over Efeserbrevet* (Ansgar Brevshole, 1987); "Kvinnen i Bibelen" *Sirkel* 1 (1985); "Bibelsk og praktisk basis for menighetsplanting" *Sirkel* 2 (1985); *Veien Videre,* co-auth. (Ansgar, 1984); *Liv Og Vekst* (Gyldendal/Land Og Kirke, 1980; Ansgar, 1982); and others. Mem: Fedn. of European Evang. Theol. 1980-; SBL 1981-; Uppsala Exegetiska Sallskap 1987-; Norsk Gammeltestamentlig Selskap 1988-. Rec: Travelling, skiing, fishing. Addr: (o) Fredrik Fransons Vei 4, N-4635 Kristiansand, Norway 42-43900; (h) Nedre BrattBakken 14, N-4635 Kristiansand, Norway 380-47886.

HAGNER, Donald A., b. Chicago, IL, July 8, 1936, s. of Carl & Marie (Gondek), m. Beverly (Smith). Educ: Fuller Theol. Sem., BD 1966, ThM 1967; U. of Manchester, England, PhD 1969. Emp: Wheaton Coll., 1969-76 Assoc. Prof., Bibl. Stud.; Fuller Theol. Sem., 1976- Prof., NT, 1977- Dean, Summer Inst. Spec: New Testament, Apocrypha and Post-biblical Studies. Pub: "Apocalyptic in the Gospel of Matthew:

Continuity and Discontinuity" *Horizons in Bibl. Theol.* 7 (1986); "The Sitz-im-Leben of the Gospel of Matthew" in *SBL Seminar Papers* (1985); *The Jewish Reclamation of Jesus* (Zondervan, 1984); *Hebrews: A Good News Comm.* (Harper & Row, 1983); "Interpreting the Gospels: The Landscape and the Quest" *JETS* 25 (1982); *The Use of the Old and New Testaments in Clement of Rome* (Brill, 1973). Mem: SNTS 1974-; SBL 1969-; Tyndale Fellow., 1967-; IBR 1972-. Rec: Hiking. Addr: (o) Fuller Theological Seminary, Pasadena, CA 91182 818-584-5247; (h) 3056 N Mount Curve, Altadena, CA 91001 818-794-0873.

HAHN, Roger L., b. McCook, NE, February 8, 1950, s. of Lee, m. Dorothy, chil: Jonathan; Matthew; Timothy. Educ: Bethany Nazarene Coll., MA 1974; Nazarene Theol. Sem., MDiv 1976; Duke U., PhD 1984. Emp: South. Nazarene U., 1979- Assoc. Prof., Relig. Spec: New Testament. Pub: "Imprisonment in First Century Palestine" in *Illustrated Bible Life* (1988); "Pneumatology in Romans 8" *WTJ* 21 (1986); "Joel: History or Prophecy" *Emphasis* (1985); and others. Mem: SBL 1979-; AAR 1979-; WTS 1979-; IBR 1987-. Rec: Woodworking. Addr: (o) Southern Nazarene U., 6729 NW 39th Expwy., Bethany, OK 73008 405-789-6400; (h) 6804 NW 27th St., Bethany, OK 73008 405-495-2742.

HAIK-VANTOURA, Suzanne, b. Paris, France, July 12, 1912, d. of Ezra Vantoura & Alice (Ullmann), m. Maurice. Educ: Conservatoire natl. superieur de Musique de Paris, laureate de composition 1939. Emp: Paris, 1937-61 Hon. Prof., Music Educ.; Synagogue de l'Union liberale Israelite, 1946-53 Organist; Eglise Saint-Helene, 1966-79 Organist. Spec: Hebrew Bible. Pub: *Message biblique integral dans son chant retrouvé* (Fondation Roi David, 1992); *La Musique de la Bible Revelee* (Dumas, 1976, 1990); *Les Cinq Meghilot* (Fondation Roi David, 1987); *Les 150 Psaumes dans leurs melodies antiques* (Fondation Roi David, 1985, 1992); "La Cantilation Synagogle et ses Problems" *Le Monde de la Bible* 39 (1985); "La Cantilation Biblique et ses Problemes" *Revue des Etudes Juives* 40 (1981); "La Musique de la Bible" *Les Cahiers de l'Alliance Israelite Universelle* (1981); and others. Awd: Paris Professeur Recruitment, 1st Prize 1937; Institute of France, Prix Bernier 1978. Addr: (h) 9, rue d'Artois, 75008 Paris, France 33-1-43-598538.

HALL, Robert G., b. Manhattan, KS, January 25, 1953, s. of John Watson & Barbara (Givin), m. Jacqueline (Anderson), chil: John Anderson; Sarah Kristin; Nathan Matherly. Educ: Davidson College, BA 1975; Gordon-Conwell Theol. Sem., MDiv 1978; Duke U., PhD 1986. Emp: Hampden-Sydney Coll., 1985-90 Vis. Asst. Prof., 1990- Asst. Prof., Relig. Spec: New Testament, Apocrypha and Post-biblical Studies. Pub: "Circumcision" in *ABD* (Doubleday, 1992);

Revealed Histories: Techniques for Ancient Jewish and Christian Historiography, JSPSup 6 (Sheffield, 1991); "Historical Inference and Rhetorical Effect: Another Look at Galatians 1 and 2" in *Persuasive Artistry: Studies in New Testament Rhetoric in Honor of George A. Kennedy,* JSNTSup 50 (Sheffield, 1991); "Living Creatures in the Middle of the Throne: Another Look at Revelation 4:6" *NTS* 36/4 (1990); "The Ascension of Isaiah: Community Situation, Date and Place in Early Christianity" *JBL* 109/2 (1990); "Epispasm and the Dating of Ancient Jewish Writings" *JSP* 2 (1988); and others. Mem: SBL 1984-; CBA 1985-. Rec: Music, reading, hiking, woodworking, sailing. Addr: (o) Hampden-Sydney College, H.S. Box 72, Hampden-Sydney, VA 23943 804-223-6249.

HALL, Stuart G., b. London, England, June 7, 1928, s. of George Edward & May Catherine (Whale), m. Brenda Mary (Henderson), chil: Lindsay George; Nicola Mary; Edith May; Walter Stuart. Educ: U. of Oxford, BA 1952, MA 1955, BD 1973; Ord. Priest 1955. Emp: Queen's College, Birmingham, 1958-62 Tutor; U. of Nottingham, 1962-73 Lect., Theol., 1973-78 Sr. Lect., 1978 Reader; U. of London at King's Coll., 1978-90 Prof., Eccles. Hist.; Scottish Episc. Ch., 1990- Priest. Spec: New Testament, Apocrypha and Post-biblical Studies. Pub: *Doctrine and Practice in the Early Church* (SPCK, 1991); *Melito of Sardis On Pascha and Fragments* (Clarendon, 1978); "Paschal Baptism" *Studia Evangelica VI* (1973); "Melito in the light of the Passover Haggadah" *JTS* 22 (1971); "Melito *Peri pascha* 1 and 2, Text and Interpretation" *Kyriakon* (1970); "The Melito Papyri" *JTS* 19 (1968); and others. Mem: SNTS 1970-90; SST 1975-; Eccles. Hist. Soc. 1978-; Assn. Intl. d'Etudes Patristiques 1980-, V.P. 1987-91; Acad. Intl. des Sci. Relig. 1986-. Rec: Gardening, swimming. Addr: (h) 15 High Street, Elie, Leven, Fife KY9 1BY, Scotland 0333-330145.

HALLO, William W., b. Kassel, Germany, March 9, 1928, s. of Rudolf & Gertrude, m. Edith (Pinto), chil: Ralph Ethan; Jacqueline Louise. Educ: Harvard Coll., BA (magna cum laude) 1950; U. of Chicago, MA 1953, PhD, Near East. Lang. & Lit. 1955. Emp: Hebrew Union Coll.–Jewish Inst. of Relig., 1956-58 Instr., 1958-62 Asst. Prof., Bible & Semitic Lang.; Yale U., 1962- William M. Laffan Prof. of Assyriology & Babylonian Lit., 1975-82, 1985-89 Chair, Dept. of Near East. Lang. & Civ., Yale Babylonian Collection, Cur.; Morse Coll., 1982-87 Master. Spec: Mesopotamian Studies. Pub: *The Tablets of Ebla: Concordance and Bibliography* (Eisenbrauns, 1984); *Scripture in Context,* 4 vol., ed. (Eisenbrauns, 1980-1991); *Early Near Eastern Seals* (1981); *The Torah: A Modern Commentary* (Union of Amer. Hebrew Cong., 1981); *Sumerian Archival Texts* (1973); *The Exaltation of Inanna* (1968); and others. Awd: Fulbright Grant 1950-51; Guggenheim Fellow 1965-66; Yale U., MA 1965; Hebrew Union Coll.–Jewish Inst. of Relig., Dr. of Humane Letters 1986. Mem: AOS, Pres.

1988-89; AJS, V.P. 1971-74; SBL; WUJS; AAJR. Addr: (o) Yale U., Babylonian Collection, New Haven, CT 06520 203-432-1840; (h) 245 Blake Rd., Hamden, CT 06517 203-865-1660.

HALPERN, Baruch, b. Philadelphia, PA, April 9, 1953, s. of Sidney & Phyllis, m. Lynne, chil: Jesse; Orly. Educ: Harvard Coll., AB 1973; Harvard U., MA 1976, PhD 1978. Emp: York U., 1976- Prof.; U. of Calif., 1978, 1986, 1991 Vis. Prof.; ASOR Diss. Ser., 1985- Ed.; Pa. State U., 1992- Prof., Chair. Spec: Hebrew Bible, Semitic Languages, Texts and Epigraphy. Pub: "Jerusalem and the Lineages in the 7th Century BCE: Kinship and the Rise of Individual Moral Liability" in *Law and Ideology in Monarchic Israel* (Sheffield, 1991); *The First Historians: The Hebrew Bible & History* (Harper & Row, 1988); "The Resourceful Israelite Historian: The Song of Deborah and Israelite Historiography" *HTR* (1983); "Doctrine By Misadventure: Between the Israelite Source and the Biblical Historian" in *The Poet and the Historian* (Scholars, 1983); *The Emergence of Israel in Canaan* (Scholars, 1983); *Traditions in Transformation: Turning-Points in Biblical Faith* (Eisenbrauns, 1981); *The Constitution of the Monarchy in Israel* (Scholars, 1981); and others. Awd: NEH, Fellow 1983-84; Alexander von Humboldt-Stiftung Fellow 1984-85. Mem: ASOR 1978-; SBL 1976-; IES 1983-. Addr: (o) Pennsylvania State U., Dept. of History, University Park, PA 16802.

HAMLIN, E. John, b. Iron River, MI, November 9, 1915, s. of Earle & Marjorie (Howes), m. Frances (Cade). Educ: Oberlin Coll., BA 1936, MA 1941; Union Theol. Sem., BD 1941, STM 1952, ThD 1961. Emp: Cheeloo U. Sch. of Theol., China, 1949-51 OT Tchr.; Thailand Theol. Sem., 1955-74 OT Tchr.; Trinity Theol. Coll., Singapore, 1974-80 OT Tchr. Spec: Hebrew Bible. Pub: *At Risk in the Promised Land: A Commentary on Judges* (Eerdmans, 1989); *Inheriting the Land: A Commentary on Joshua* (Eerdmans, 1983); *Guide to Isaiah 40-66* (SPCK, 1979); and others. Mem: SBL 1941-. Rec: Writing, gardening, music. Addr: (h) 426 Robin Rd., Waverly, OH 45690 614-947-5567.

HAMM, M. Dennis, b. Cincinnati, OH, January 18, 1936, s. of Victor M. & Agnes (Curren). Educ: Marquette U., AB 1958; St. Louis U., MA 1964, PhL 1964, PhD, Bibl. Lang. & Lit. 1975. Emp: Creighton Preparatory High Sch., 1964-65 Instr.; Creighton U., 1965-67 Instr., Dept. of Theol., 1975- Prof., NT; St. Louis U., 1970 Instr., NT; *Theol. Digest*, 1967-71 Ed. Bd., 1969 Asst. Ed., 1970 Managing Ed. Spec: New Testament. Pub: *The Beatitudes in Context: What Luke and Matthew Meant* (Glazier, 1990); "Faith in the Letter to the Hebrews: The Jesus Factor" *CBQ* 52/2 (1990); "Paul's Blindness and Its Healing: Clues to Symbolic Intent (Acts 9:22 and 26)" *Biblica* 71/1 (1990); "Luke 19:8 Once Again: Does Zacchaeus Defend or Resolve?" *JBL* 107

(1988); "The Healing of the Bent Woman and the Restoration of Israel: Luke 13:10-17 As Narrative Theology" *JSNT* 31 (1987); "Acts 3,1-10: The Healing of the Temple Beggar as Lucan Theology" *Biblica* 67 (1986); and others. Awd: Hebrew Union Travel Fellow. 1970; Yale Sch. of Div., Res. Fellow. 1973-75. Mem: CBA 1970-; SBL 1974-; Coll. Theol. Soc. 1985-. Rec: Theater, music, film, swimming. Addr: (o) Creighton U., Dept. of Theology, 2500 California St., Omaha, NE 68178 402-280-2507; (h) Creighton U., Jesuit Community, 2500 California St., Omaha, NE 68178 402-280-2700.

HANDELMAN, Susan, Pub: *Fragments of Redemption: Jewish Thought and Literary Theory in Benjamin, Scholem and Levinas* (Ind. U., 1991); *The Slayers of Moses: The Emergence of Rabbinic Interpretation in Modern Literary Theory* (State U. of N.Y., 1982); and others. Addr: (o) U. of Maryland, English Dept., College Park, MD 20742 301-405-3809; (h) 2400 Virginia Ave. NW, C 901, Washington DC1 20037.

HANDY, Lowell K., b. Fort Dodge, IA, July 18, 1949, s. of Ora Addison & Doris Mary-Alice Leamon. Educ: U. of Iowa, BA 1971, MA 1974; U. of Chicago, MA 1980, PhD 1987. Emp: Iowa Cen. Community Coll., 1975-79 Instr.; Disciples Div. House of the U. of Chicago, 1980-87 Asst. House Admn.; Loyola U. of Chicago, 1987 Sr. Lect.; Amer. Theol. Lib. Assn., 1988- Ed.; *Proc. East. Great Lakes & MidW Bibl. Soc.*, 1990-92 Ed. Bd. Spec: Hebrew Bible. Pub: "The Reconstruction of Biblical History and Jewish-Christian Relations" *SJT* (1991); "Dissenting Deities or Obedient Angels: Divine Hierarchies in Ugarit and the Bible" *BR* 35 (1990); "Sounds, Words and Meanings in Psalm 82" *JSOT* 47 (1990); "Speaking of Babies in the Temple" *Proc. East. Great Lakes & MidW Bibl. Soc.* 8 (1988); "Hezekiah's Unlikely Reform" *ZAW* 100 (1988); and others. Mem: ASOR 1991-; CSBR 1988-; SBL 1975-. Rec: Reading, artwork in construction paper. Addr: (o) ATLA, 820 Church St., Evanston, IL 60201; (h) 615 Case Place #1 SE, Evanston, IL 60202 708-332-1030.

HANHART, Karel, b. Tilburg, The Netherlands, February 16, 1927, s. of Karel & Sara, m. Johanna (van de Grampel), chil: Anna; Karel; Mark. Educ: U. Amsterdam, The Netherlands, Drs. 1959, PhD 1966; West. Theol. Sem., Michigan, BD 1949. Emp: Dubuque Theol. Sem., 1964-72 Prof.; Verenigde Protestanse Kerk, Brussels, 1972- Pastor. Spec: New Testament. Pub: *Open Tomb—New Approach* (Liturgical, 1993); "'Son, your sins are forgiven': Mark 2:5" in *The Four Gospels,* vol. 2, Festschrift Neirynck (Leuven U.P., 1992); "The Tenth Hour on Nisan 15, John 1:10" in *L'Evangelie de Jean* (Leuven U.P., 1976); "The Structure of John 1:35-4:54" in *Studies in John,* Festschrift J.N. Sevenszer (Brill, 1970); "Paul's Hope in Face of Death" *JBL* (1969); *Intermediate State in the New Testament* (Wever, 1966). Mem: SBL 1966-80; SNTS

1974-. Rec: Piano, tennis. Addr: (o) Euripideslaan 5, 5216 CK 's-Hertogenbosch, The Netherlands 073-128902.

HANSON, Paul D., m. Cynthia Jane (Rosenberger), chil: Amy; Mark; Nathaniel. Educ: Gustavus Adolphus Coll., BA 1961; Yale U., BD 1965; Harvard U., PhD 1970. Emp: Harvard U., Div. Sch. & Dept. of Near East. Lang. & Civ., 1971-75 Asst. Prof., 1975-81 Prof., OT, 1981-87 Bussey Prof. of Div., 1987- Florence Corliss Lamont Prof. of Div.; *Hermeneia,* OT Ed. Bd. Spec: Hebrew Bible, Semitic Languages, Texts and Epigraphy. Pub: "Israelite Religion in the Early Postexilic Period" in *Ancient Israelite Religion: Essays in Honor of Frank Moore Cross* (Fortress, 1987); "War, Peace and Justice in Early Israel" *BR* 3/3 (1987); "In Defiance of Death: Zechariah's Symbolic Universe" in *Love and Death in the Ancient Near East: Essays in Honor of Marvin H. Pope* (Four Quarters, 1987); *Old Testament Apocalyptic* (Abingdon, 1987); *The People Called: The Growth of Community in the Bible* (Harper & Row, 1986); "Conflict in Ancient Israel and its Resolution" in *Understanding the Word: Essays in Honor of Bernhard W. Anderson,* JSOTSup 37 (JSOT, 1985); "Apocalyptic Literature" in *The Hebrew Bible and Its Modern Interpreters* (Fortress, 1985); *Visionaries and their Apocalypses,* Issues in Relig. & Theol. 2 (Fortress, 1983); *The Dawn of Apocalyptic: The Historical and Sociological Roots of Jewish Apocalyptic Eschatology* (Fortress, 1975, 1979); and others. Awd: Fulbright Fellow. 1961; ASOR, John Henry Thayer Fellow. 1969-70; Amer. Council of Learned Soc., Fellow. 1973; NEH, Fellow. 1978-70; Alexander von Humboldt Stiftung Fellow. 1981-82. Mem: ASOR; CBA; SBL; Colloquium for Bibl. Res. Addr: (h) 27 Cushing Ave., Belmont, MA 02178.

HARAN, Menahem, b. Moscow, USSR, December 4, 1924, s. of Moshe & Fani (Dyman), m. Raya (Twersky), chil: Tali; Shai. Educ: Hebrew U., MA 1947, PhD 1956. Emp: Hebrew U., Jerusalem, Y. Kaufmann Prof. of Bible Stud.; Cambridge U., Fac. of Oriental Stud., 1973 Vis. Prof.; U. of Wis.-Madison, 1986 H.F. Johnson Res. Prof. in the Hum.; *Ency. Biblica,* 1960-68 Assoc. Ed.; *EJ,* 1969-71 Cons. Ed.; *Tarbiz,* 1981-86 Ed. Bd.; *VT,* 1983- Adv. Com. Spec: Hebrew Bible. Pub: "On the Diffusion of Literacy and Schools in Ancient Israel" in VTSup (1988); *Temples and Temple Service in Ancient Israel* (Eisenbrauns, 1985); "Book-Size and the Device of Catch Lines in the Biblical Canon" *JJS* (1985); "Bible Scrolls in Jewish Communities from Qumran to the High Middle Ages" *HUCA* (1985); "Seething a Kid in its Mother's Milk" *JJS* (1979); "The Law-Code of Ezekiel 40-48 and its Relation to P" *HUCA* (1979); *Ages and Institutions in the Bible* (Am Oved, 1973); *Between 'Former Prophecies' and 'New Prophecies'* (Magnes, 1963); and others. Awd: SOTS, Hon. Mem.; AAJR, Corr. Fellow. Mem: IOSOT; WUJS; AJS. Addr: (o) Hebrew U., Dept. of Bible, Jerusalem 91905, Israel 02-883-515; (h) 37 Alfasi St., Jerusalem 92302, Israel 02-634-245.

HARNER, Philip B., b. Lancaster, PA, April 2, 1932, s. of Nevin C. & Flora B., m. Willa Jean, chil: Heather; Ariana. Educ: Princeton U., AB 1954; Yale U., BD 1957, MA 1959, PhD 1964. Emp: Yale Div. Sch., 1958-60 Asst. Instr., NT Greek; Heidelberg Coll., 1962- Prof., Relig.; Winebrenner Theol. Sem., 1975-76 Vis. Lect., NT. Spec: Hebrew Bible, New Testament. Pub: *"I Am the Lord"—Grace and Law in Second Isaiah* (Mellen, 1988); "Exposition of Matthew 6:5-15" *Interpretation* 41/2 (1987); "Notes on the Accusative Absolute" *Proc. East. Great Lakes and MidW Bibl. Soc.* 6 (1986); *An Inductive Approach to Biblical Study* (U. Press of Amer., 1982); *Understanding the Lord's Prayer* (Fortress, 1975); "Qualitative Anarthrous Predicate Nouns: Mark 15:39 and John 1:1" *JBL* 92 (1973); *The "I Am" of the Fourth Gospel* (Fortress, 1970); "The Salvation Oracle in Second Isaiah" *JBL* 88 (1969); "Creation Faith in Deutero-Isaiah" *VT* 17 (1967); and others. Mem: SBL. Addr: (o) Heidelberg College, Dept. of Religion, Tiffin, OH 44883 419-448-2040; (h) 30 Elmwood St., Tiffin, OH 44883.

HARRELSON, Walter, b. North Carolina, November 28, 1919, m. Idella (Aydlett), chil: Marianne H. (McIver); David A.; Robert J. Educ: U. of N.C., Chapel Hill, AB 1947; Union Theol. Sem., BD 1949, ThD 1953. Emp: Andover Newton Theol. Sch., 1951-55 Prof. of OT; U. of Chicago Div. Sch., 1955-60 Assoc. Prof. of OT, Dean of Div. Sch.; Vanderbilt U. Div. Sch., 1960-75 Prof., 1967-75 Dean of Div. Sch., 1975- Disting. Prof. of OT; Ecumenical Inst. for Theol. Res., Jerusalem, 1977-79 Rector. Spec: Hebrew Bible. Pub: "What Is a Good Bible Dictionary?" *BAR* 12/6 (1986); *From Fertility Cult to Worship* (Doubleday, 1969; Scholars, 1980); *Interpreting the Old Testament* (Holt, Rinehart & Winston, 1964); *Jeremiah, Prophet to the Nations* (Judson, 1959); and others. Awd: Phi Beta Kappa 1946; Amer. Council of Learned Soc., Fellow. 1950, 1970; Fulbright Res. Grant 1962-63; NEH, travel grant 1970, Sr. Fellow. 1983-84. Mem: SBL, Pres. 1972-73. Addr: (h) 305 Bowling Ave., Nashville, TN 37205 615-383-8218.

HARRINGTON, Daniel J., b. Arlington, MA, July 19, 1940, s. of Florence Daniel & Mary Agnes (Brady). Educ: Boston Coll., BA 1964, MA 1965; Harvard U., PhD 1970; Weston Sch. of Theol., MDiv 1971. Emp: Weston Sch. of Theol., 1971- Prof., NT; *NT Abstracts,* 1971- Gen. Ed. Excv: Samaria, 1968 Area Supr. Spec: Hebrew Bible, New Testament, Semitic Languages, Texts and Epigraphy, Apocrypha and Post-biblical Studies. Pub: "Polemical Parables in Matthew 24-25" *Union Sem. Quar. Rev.* 44 (1991); "Second Temple Exegesis and the Social Sciences" *BTB* 18 (1988); *The Gospel of Matthew* (Liturgical, 1991); *The Maccabean Revolt* (Glazier, 1988); "Sociological Concepts and the Early Church" *Theol. Stud.* (1980); "The Original Language of Pseudo-Philo's *Liber*

Antiquitatum Biblicarum" HTS (1970); *A Manual of Palestinian Aramaic Texts*, co-auth. (Bibl. Inst., 1978); *Pseudo-Philon: Les Antiquités Bibliques* (Cerf., 1976); and others. Mem: ASOR 1966-76; SBL 1966-; CBA 1969-; SNTS 1978-. Addr: (o) Weston School of Theology, 3 Phillips Pl., Cambridge, MA 02138 617-492-1960; (h) 12 Linnaean St., Cambridge, MA 02138 617-547-0931.

HARRIS, J. Gordon, b. Bunkie, LA, November 1, 1940, s. of Dr. & Mrs. James G., m. Joyce (Behm), chil: Donna Joy; Jami Ruth. Educ: Baylor U., BA 1962; SW Bapt. Sem., BD 1965, ThM 1967; South. Bapt. Sem., PhD 1970. Emp: Philippine Bapt. Theol. Sem., 1971-75 Prof.; N Amer. Bapt. Sem., 1975- Prof., Acad. V.P. Excv: Ketef Hinnom, 1988 Supr. Spec: Archaeology, Hebrew Bible. Pub: "Aging, Old Age" in *ABD;* "Biblical Hermeneutics and the Aging Experience" in *Research on Adulthood and Aging* (SUNY, 1989); *Overtures to Biblical Theology* (Fortress, 1987); *Biblical Perspectives on Aging*; and others. Mem: NAPH, V.P. 1985-; SBL, V.P., Upper MidW reg. 1978-79, Pres., 1983-86; ASOR; IBR. Rec: Golf, softball, music. Addr: (o) North American Baptist Seminary, 1321 W 22nd St., Sioux Falls, SD 57105 605-336-6588; (h) 1300 Otonka Trail, Sioux Falls, SD 57103 605-334-9866.

HARRIS, Rivkah, b. Toronto, Canada, March 18, 1928, d. of Joel Brickman & Dora (Grafstein), m. Monford O., chil: Abigail; Michael. Educ: U. of Chi., Oriental Inst., PhD 1954. Emp: U. of Chi., 1959-61 Res. Asst.; NW U., 1973-78 Assoc. Prof.; Sch. of the Art Inst. of Chi., 1985- Assoc. Prof. Spec: Mesopotamian Studies. Pub: "The Conflict of Generations in Ancient Mesopotamian Myths" *Compar. Stud. in Soc. & Hist.* 34/4 (1992); "Inanna-Ishtar as Paradox and a Coincidence of Opposites" *Hist. of Relig.* 30/3 (1991); "Notes on the Slave Names of Old Babylonian Sippar" *JCS* 29/1 (1977); "Kinship and Inheritance in Ancient Sippar" *Iraq* 38/2 (1976); *Ancient Sippar: A Demographic Study of an Old Babylonian City (1894-1595 BC)* (Nederlands Hist.-Arch. Inst., 1975); "Notes on the Babylonian Cloister and Hearth: A Review Article" *Orientalia* 83/4 (1969); and others. Awd: Guggenheim Fellow. 1965-66; Natl. Sci. Found., grant 1962-64; Rosary Coll., Doc. of Letters 1973. Mem: AOS 1965-. Addr: (o) School of the Art Institute of Chicago, Liberal Arts, 37 S Wabash Ave., Chicago, IL 60603 312-899-5187; (h) 6258 N Talman, Chicago, IL 60659 312-274-7092.

HARRIS, Robert Laird, b. Brownsburg, PA, March 10, 1911, s. of Walter & Pearl (Graves). Educ: Westminster Theol. Sem., ThB 1935, ThM 1937; U. of Pa., AM 1941; Dropsie Coll., PhD 1947. Emp: Faith Theol. Sem., 1937-56 Prof.; Covenant Theol. Sem., 1956-81 Prof., 1981- Prof. Emeritus; China Grad. Sch. of Theol., 1981 Vis. Prof.; Freie Theol. Akademie,

Germany, 1982-85 Vis. Prof.; Japan Christian Theol. Sem., 1981 Foxwell Lect. Excv: Dothan, 1962 Area Supr. Spec: Archaeology, Hebrew Bible, Semitic Languages, Texts and Epigraphy. Pub: *Theological Wordbook of the Old Testament* (Moody, 1980); *Inspiration and Canonicity of the Bible* (Zondervan, 1969); "The Bible and Cosmology" *JETS* (1962); *Introductory Hebrew Grammar* (Eerdmans, 1950); and others. Awd: Zondervan, Textbook Awd. 1957. Mem: SBL 1937-; ASOR 1939-; ETS 1949-. Rec: Traveling, swimming. Addr: (h) 9 Homewood Rd., Wilmington, DE 19803 302-478-7703.

HARRISVILLE, Roy A., III, b. Mason City, IA, November 26, 1954, s. of Roy A. & Norma A., m. Mary L., chil: Kendra M.; David A. Educ: Concordia Coll., BA 1977; Luther NW Sem., MDiv 1981; Union Sem. in Va., PhD 1990. Emp: Luther NW Sem., 1981 Instr., Greek; Wartburg Coll., 1984 Instr., NT Lit.; Union Sem., 1986, 1988 Vis. Instr., Greek; First Luth. Ch., 1989- Assoc. Pastor; *Luth. Matters*, 1991- Ed. Bd. Spec: New Testament. Pub: *In the Footsteps of Abraham: The Figure of Abraham in the Epistles of St. Paul*, Disting. Diss. Ser. (Mellen Res. U.P., 1992). Mem: SBL 1988-. Addr: (o) First Lutheran Church, 703 S Sibley Ave., Litchfield, MN 55355 612-693-2487; (h) 101 E Weisel St., Litchfield, MN 55355 612-693-7159.

HARROP, Clayton K., b. Berryton, KS, February 18, 1924, s. of Joseph & Rose (Fetrow), m. Shirley (Jacobs), chil: Judith; Joyce; Janice. Educ: William Jewell Coll., AB 1949; South. Bapt. Theol. Sem., BD 1952, PhD 1956. Emp: Birmingham Bapt. Ch., 1947-49 Pastor; New Hope Bapt. Ch., 1951-55 Pastor; Golden Gate Bapt. Theol. Sem., 1955- Prof., 1991- V.P., Acad. Affairs, Dean of Fac. Spec: New Testament. Pub: *History of the New Testament in Plain Language* (Word, 1984); *The Letter of James* (Convention, 1969). Mem: SBL 1964-; NABPR 1986-. Rec: Golf, bowling, jigsaw puzzles. Addr: (o) Golden Gate Baptist Theological Seminary, Mill Valley, CA 94941-3197 415-388-8080; (h) 16 Platt Ct., Mill Valley, CA 94941 415-383-7769.

HARTIN, Patrick J., b. Johannesburg, South Africa, December 7, 1944, s. of Thomas & Sheila. Educ: BA 1966, BSTh 1969, LSTh 1971, DTh 1981. Emp: U. of the Witwatersrand, South Africa, 1984-89 Lect.; U. of South Africa, 1990- Assoc. Prof. Spec: New Testament, Apocrypha and Post-biblical Studies. Pub: *James and the Q Sayings of Jesus*, co-ed. (Sheffield U.P., 1991); *Text and Interpretation*, co-ed. (Brill); and others. Mem: AAR 1984-; NT Soc. of South Africa 1984-; South African Soc. for Promotion of Bibl. Stud. 1984-; SNTS 1992-. Rec: Popular music. Addr: (o) U. of South Africa, Dept. of New Testament, PO Box 392, Pretoria 0001, South Africa 012-429-4705.

HARTLEY, John E., b. Meadville, PA, May 9, 1940, s. of Walter & Mary Elizabeth, m. Dorothy, chil: Joyce; Johannah. Educ: Asbury Theol. Sem., BD 1965; Brandeis U., MA 1968, PhD 1969. Emp: Asbury Theol. Sem., 1970 Guest Prof.; Fuller Theol. Sem., 1973-83 Vis. Prof., OT; Azusa Pacific U., 1969- Prof. Spec: Hebrew Bible. Pub: *Leviticus*, Word Bibl. Comm. (Word, 1992); *The Book of Job*, NICOT (Eerdmans, 1988); articles in *ISBE* (Eerdmans, 1979); "The Kingdom and the Early Prophets" in *Arnold's Comm.* (1979); "Textual Affinities of Papyrus Bopdmer XIV" *Evang. Theol. Quar.* (1968); *Issues in Theology from a Wesleyan Perspective*, co-auth. (Warner); and others. Mem: SBL; ASOR. Rec: Cycling, stamps. Addr: (o) Azusa Pacific U., 901 E Alosta, Azusa, CA 91702 818-969-3434; (h) 1737 Acorn Ln., Glendora, CA 91740 818-963-2348.

HARTMAN, Lars O., b. Uppsala, Sweden, March 2, 1930, s. of Olov F. & M. Ingrid (Olsson), m. Ulla (Ohlson), chil: Anders; Goran; Erik; Anna. Educ: Uppsala U., Fil kand 1953, Teol kand 1957, Fil mag 1959, Teol lic 1961, Teol dr 1966. Emp: Uppsala U., 1967-71 Docent, 1971-77 Acting Prof., 1978- Prof., NT Exegesis; Harvard U., 1968-69 Vis. Prof.; Ch. of Sweden, 1990- Dir., Res. Dept.; *Svensk Exeg. Arsbok*, 1984-90 Ed., 1972-90 Ed. Bd. Spec: New Testament, Apocrypha and Post-biblical Studies. Pub: *Auf den Namen des Herrn Jesus* (Katholisches Bibelwerk, 1992); *Kolosserbrevet* (EFS-Forlaget, 1985); "An Attempt at a Text-Centered Exegesis of John 21" *Studia Theologica* 38 (1984); "An Early Example of Jewish Exegesis: 1 Enoch 10:16-11:2" *Neotestamentica* 17 (1983); *Asking for a Meaning. A Study of 1 Enoch 1-5* (Gleerup, 1979); "The Functions of Some So-Called Apocalyptic Timetables" *NTS* 22 (1975-76); "Into the Name of Jesus" *NTS* 20 (1973-74); *Prophecy Interpreted* (Gleerup, 1966); and others. Mem: Nathan Soderblomsallskapet 1966-, Pres. 1977; Royal Acad. of Arts & Sci. of Uppsala 1973-; Royal Acad. of Letters, Hist. & Antiquities 1989-; SNTS 1966-. Rec: Music, fishing. Addr: (o) Church of Sweden, Research Dept., Box 65, S-751 03 Uppsala, Sweden 18-169726; (h) Tuvangsvagen 4, S-756 45 Uppsala, Sweden 18-309689.

HARTZFELD, David F., b. Wilkensburg, PA, October 9, 1941, s. of Fred & Ruth, m. Linda, chil: Stephanie; Anita; Julie. Educ: Nyack Coll., BS 1963; Jaffary Sch. of Missions, Dip. 1964; Bethel Theol. Sem., MDiv 1967; Pittsburgh Theol. Sem., ThM 1975; Sheffield U., PhD 1990. Emp: Nhatrang Theol. Inst., Vietnam, 1970-72 Missionary; Canadian Bible Coll., 1973-79 Asst. Prof.; Canadian Theol. Sem., 1979-89 V.P., Dean of Faculty; Alliance Theol. Sem., 1989- Prof. Spec: Hebrew Bible. Pub: *Birth of a Vision: Essays in Honour of A.B. Simpson, Founder of the Christian and Missionary Alliance*, contb. (Buena, 1986); and others. Mem: CSBS; SBL. Rec: Basketball, racketball, golf. Addr: (o) Alliance

Theological Seminary, 122 S Highland Ave., Nyack, NY 10960-4121 914-358-1710.

HARVEY, Van A., b. Hankow, China, April 23, 1926, s. of Earle & Mary, m. Margaret (Lynn), chil: Jonathan; Christopher. Educ: Occidental Coll., BA 1948; Yale U., BD 1951, PhD 1957. Emp: Princeton U., 1954-58 Asst. Prof.; South. Meth. U., 1958-68 Prof.; U. of Pa., 1968-77 Prof.; Stanford U., 1977- Prof.; *JAAR*, 1970-79 Ed. Bd. Spec: New Testament. Pub: "Some Problematical Aspects of Peter Berger's Theory of Religion" *JAAR* (1973); *Il Problema di dio: Nella Theologia Americana Contemporanea* (1970); *The Historian and the Believer* (Macmillan, 1966); *A Handbook of Theological Terms* (Macmillan, 1964); and others. Awd: John Simon Guggenheim Fellow 1966, 1972. Mem: AAR. Rec: Sailing. Addr: (o) Stanford U., Building 70, Palo Alto, CA 94305 415-497-3322; (h) 860 Marshall Dr., Palo Alto, CA 94303 415-493-7951.

HARVIAINEN, Tapani, b. Kuopio, Finland, January 2, 1944, s. of Mauri & Kastehelmi, m. Rea, chil: Tuomas; Hanna. Educ: U. of Helsinki, MA 1970, PhD 1977. Emp: Bible Trans. Com., OT, 1977-91; U. of Helsinki, 1985- Prof., Semitic Lang.; *Scandinavian Jewish Stud.*, 1976- Ed. Bd.; *Abr-Nahrain*, 1989- Adv. Bd. Spec: Semitic Languages, Texts and Epigraphy. Pub: "De Karaitis Lithuaniae: Transcriptions of Recited Biblical Texts, Description of the Pronunciation Tradition and the Peculiarities of Shewa" *Orientalia Suecana* 38-39 (1991); "Pseudo-pausal Forms of Passive Stems in Palestinian Punctuations and the Position of Stress in Hebrew" *Abr-Nahrain* 25 (1987); "Diglossia in Jewish Eastern Aramaic: The Aramaic of Targumim, Incantation Bowls, Tractate Nedarim, and Geonim vs. Standard Babylonian Talmudic Aramaic" *Studia Orientalia* 55/2 (1983); "On the Vocalism of the Closed Unstressed Syllables in Hebrew" *Studia Orientalia* 48 (1977); "On the Loss of the Greek /h/ and the So-called Aspirated Rhō" *Studia Orientalia* 45 (1976); and others. Awd: Helsinki, State Awd. of Trans. 1989. Mem: Finnish Oriental Soc., Sec. Gen. 1977-; WUJS; Finnish Exegetical Soc. 1987-. Addr: (o) U. of Helsinki, Dept. of Asian & African Studies, SF-00100 Helsinki, Finland 1-1912214; (h) Osuuskunnantie 26, SF-00660 Helsinki, Finland 0-748956.

HASEL, Gerhard F., b. Vienna, Austria, July 27, 1935, s. of Franz & Helene (Schroeter), m. Hilde (Schafer), chil: Michael; Marlene; Melissa. Educ: Andrews U., MA 1960, BD 1962; Vanderbilt U., PhD 1970. Emp: South. Coll., 1963-66 Prof., Relig.; Andrews U. Theol. Sem., 1967- Dir., PhD/ThD Prog. Excv: Tell Hesban, Jordan, 1971 Assoc. Area Supr. Spec: Archaeology, Hebrew Bible, Semitic Languages, Texts and Epigraphy. Pub: "Major Recent Issues in Old Testament Theology 1978-1983" *JSOT* (1985); *Biblical Interpretation Today* (Bibl. Res. Inst., 1985); "Biblical Theology Movement" in *Evangelical Dict. of Theology* (1984); and others. Mem: SBL;

AAR; ASOR. Rec: Jogging, boating, swimming. Addr: (o) Andrews U., Theological Seminary, Berrien Springs, MI 49104 616-471-3536; (h) 9984 Red Bud Trail, Berrien Springs, MI 49103.

HATA, Gohei, b. Tokyo, Japan, November 19, 1942, s. of Tsuneo & Kikuko, m. Kazuko, chil: Yumiko; Teppei; Sohei; Keiko; Syuhei. Educ: Intl. Christian U., Tokyo, BA 1968; Kyoto U., Japan, MA 1970; Dropsie U., PhD 1975. Emp: Kyoto Sangyo U., 1976-78 Lect., 1979-80 Asst. Prof., Lect. in Grad. Sch.; Tama Bijyutsu U., 1980-86 Asst. Prof., 1987- Prof. Spec: Apocrypha and Post-biblical Studies. Pub: *Eusebius, Christianity, and Judaism,* co-ed. (Wayne State U.P., 1992); *Josephus, the Bible, and History,* co-ed. (Wayne State U.P., 1989); *Josephus, Judaism, and Christian,* co-ed. (Wayne State U.P., 1987); *Ecclesiastical History,* 3 vol., trans. (Yamamoto Shoten, 1986-1988); "Josephus and his Use of Greek Bibles" *The Study of the Bible* (Japan Bible Soc., 1986); "A Story of Moses Told by Josephus" *Jour. of Christian Stud.* (Kyoto U., 1983); "Is the Greek Version of Josephus's Jewish War a Translation or a Rewriting of the First Version?" *Jewish Quar. Rev.* (1975); and others. Mem: Soc. of Christian Stud. 1970-; SBL 1988-. Rec: Fishing. Addr: (o) Tama Bijyutsu U., Hachioji-City, Tokyo 192-03, Japan 0426-76-8611; (h) 4 chome, 28-21, Funabashi, Setagayaku, Tokyo 156, Japan 3483-2802.

HAUER, Christian E., Jr., b. Huntsville, AL, August 22, 1930, s. of Christian, Sr. & Ann Lee (Cotton), m. Elizabeth (Buchanan), chil: John; Anna. Educ: Birmingham-South. Coll., AB 1952; Vanderbilt Div. Sch., BD 1955, PhD 1959. Emp: Westminster Coll., 1959- Prof. of Relig., Chair of Dept. of Relig. Excv: Westminster Coll., Arch. Project, 1973- Co-dir. Spec: Archaeology, Hebrew Bible, Apocrypha and Post-biblical Studies. Pub: *An Introduction to the Bible: A Journey Through Three Worlds,* co-auth. (Prentice-Hall, 1990); "David and the Levites" *JSOT* (1982); "The Economics of National Security in Solomonic Israel" *JSOT* (1980); "When History Stops: Apocalypticism and Mysticism in Judaism and Christianity" in *The Divine Helmsman: Studies in God's Control of Human Events, Presented to Lou H. Silberman* (Ktav, 1980); *The Priests of Qumran* (U. Microfilms, 1959); and others. Mem: AAR 1955-76; ASOR 1965-; CBA 1968-; AIA 1968-; Society of Antiquaries of London, Fellow 1991. Rec: Tennis, biking, gardening. Addr: (o) Westminster College, Fulton, MO 65251 314-642-3361.

HAUSER, Alan J., b. Chicago, IL, October 15, 1945, s. of Edward & Esther, m. Gail (Greene), chil: Deborah; Mary; Stacie; Jacqueline. Educ: Concordia Sem., MAR 1968; U. of Iowa, PhD 1972. Emp: Appalachian State U., 1972- Chair, Dept. of Phil. & Relig; *Currents in Research: Biblical Studies,* 1991- Ed. Spec: Hebrew Bible. Pub: "Unity and Diversity in Early Israel Before Samuel" *JETS* (1979); "Judges 5: Parataxis in

Hebrew Poetry" *JBL* (1980); *Art and Meaning: Rhetoric in Biblical Literature,* co-ed. (JSOT, 1982); "Jonah: In Pursuit of the Dove" *JBL* (1985); *From Carmel to Horeb: Elijah in Crisis* (Sheffield, 1990); and others. Mem: SBL. Rec: Music, softball. Addr: (o) Appalachian State U., Philosophy/Religion Dept., 116 I.G. Greer, Boone, NC 28608 704-262-3089; (h) Rt. 7, 9 Raven's Ridge, Boone, NC 28607 704-264-6936.

HAWKIN, David J., b. Yorkshire, England, October 4, 1944, s. of John & Jessie, m. Eileen, chil: Karen; John. Educ: London U., BD 1966; Leeds U., PGCE 1967; McMaster U., MA 1970, PhD 1974. Emp: Temple Moor Sch., England, 1967-69 Head, Dept. of Relig. Stud.; McMaster U., 1969-74 Tutor, Relig. Stud.; Memorial U. of Newfoundland, 1974-75, 1979- Prof., 1992- Head, Relig. Stud. Dept.; Sir Wilfred Grenfell Coll., 1975-79 Coord., Relig. Stud. Spec: New Testament. Pub: *Self-Definition and Self-Discovery in Early Christianity,* ed. (Mellen, 1990); "Ideological Commitment and Johannine Theology" *ExpTim* (1990); *The Word of Science,* co-auth. (Epworth, 1989); *Christ and Modernity,* (Wilfred Laurier U.P., 1985); "Johannine Theology and the Johannine Transposition" *Laval Theol. & Phil.* (1980); "The Function of the Beloved Disciple Motif in the Johannine Redaction" *Laval Theol. et Phil.* (1977); and others. Mem: CSSR; CSBS. Rec: Films, rugby, football. Addr: (o) Memorial U. of Newfoundland, Dept. of Religious Studies, St. John's, NF, Canada 709-737-8170; (h) 9 Burke Place, St. John's, NF A1B 3G9, Canada 709-753-2648.

HAYAMI, Paul Toshihiko, b. Taipei, Taiwan, China, January 7, 1927, s. of Hisahiko & Nakako, m. Hanna (Naoko), chil: Agnes Midori (Akamatsu); Margaret Izumi (Kobayashi). Educ: Doshisha U., Japan, BA 1950; Cen. Theol. Coll., Japan, BD 1954; Union Theol. Sem., STM 1957. Emp: St. Paul's U., 1960-70 Chaplain, 1970-89 Prof., 1985-89 Dean, Dept. of Art, 1990- Prof. Emeritus; St. Margaret's Jr. Coll., 1989- Pres. Spec: New Testament. Pub: *The Teaching of Jesus—Matthew's Angle* (1992); *New Testament Comm. II* (1991); "St. Paul and 'The Spiritual Men' in Corinth" *Christian Stud.* (1989); *The World of the Bible* (1984); "Exegetical Comment on the Fourth Gospel" *Christian Stud.* (St. Paul's U.P., 1961); and others. Addr: (o) St. Margaret's Junior College, 4-29-23 Kugayama, Suginami-ku, Tokyo 168, Japan 03-3334-5104; (h) 2226-6 Mimuro, Urawa-shi, Saitama-ken 336, Japan 048-873-7986.

HAYDEN, Roy E., b. Rockville, UT, January 20, 1932, s. of James & Gladys (DeMille), m. Mary E. (Richardson), chil: Helen Olynda. Educ: Fuller Theol. Sem., BD 1956, ThM 1959; Brandeis U., MA 1961, PhD 1962. Emp: Huntington Coll., 1962-67 Assoc. Prof.; Oral Roberts U., 1967- Prof. Spec: Anatolian Studies, Hebrew Bible. Pub: Articles in *Zondervan Pictorial Ency. of the Bible* (1975); "Hurrians" in *The Biblical World: A Dict. of Biblical Archaeology*; and others. Mem: SBL 1956-; ASOR 1958-. Addr: (o) Oral Roberts U., Tulsa, OK 74171 918-495-6099; (h) 7805 S College Ave., Tulsa, OK 74136 918-492-5922.

HAYES, Christine E., b. Frederick, MD, December 6, 1960, d. of Victor C. & Marjorie (Fulton), m. Michael Della Rocca. Educ: Harvard U., BA (summa cum laude), Relig. 1984; U. of Calif., Berkeley, MA 1988, PhD, Near East. Stud. 1993. Emp: *Jour. of the Assn. of Grad. Near East. Stud.*, 1989-90 Founding Co-ed.; U. of Calif., Berkeley, 1989, 1991 Instr.; Princeton U., Near East. Stud. Dept., 1993- Asst. Prof., Hebrew Stud. Spec: Hebrew Bible, Semitic Languages, Texts and Epigraphy. Pub: "Word Order in Biblical Aramaic" *Jour. of the Assn. of Grad. Near East. Stud.* Fall (1990); and others. Awd: Harvard U., Phi Beta Kappa 1984; Benjamin Goor Prize for Essay in Jewish Stud. 1989-91; Taubman Fellow. for Talmudic Stud. 1990-91. Mem: SBL 1989-; AAR 1989-; NAPH 1989-. Rec: Singing. Addr: (o) Princeton U., Near Eastern Studies Dept., Jones Hall, Princeton, NJ 08544.

HAYES, John H., b. Camp Hill, AL, February 6, 1934. Educ: Samford U., BA 1956; Princeton Theol. Sem., BD 1960, PhD, OT 1964. Emp: Trinity U., 1964-68 Asst. Prof., 1968-72 Assoc. Prof. of Relig.; Emory U., Candler Sch. of Theol, 1972-76 Vis. Prof., 1977- Assoc. Prof. of OT. Spec: Hebrew Bible. Pub: *A History of Ancient Israel and Judah*, co-auth. (Westminster, 1986); *An Introduction to Old Testament Study* (Abingdon, 1979); *Jesus the Christ* (United Methodist, 1976); *Israelite and Judean History*, co-auth. (Westminster, 1977); *Understanding the Psalms* (Judson, 1976); *Son of God to Superstar: Twentieth Century Interpretations of Jesus* (Abingdon, 1976); *Old Testament Form Criticism* (Trinity U., 1974); and others. Mem: SBL; AIA; ASOR; AAR. Addr: (o) Emory U., Candler School of Theology, Suite 102, Bishop's Hall, Atlanta, GA 30322 404-727-4181.

HAYS, Richard B., b. Oklahoma City, OK, May 4, 1948, s. of Miller & Barbara, m. Judith (Cheek), chil: Christopher; Sarah. Educ: Yale U., BA 1970, MDiv 1977; Emory U., PhD 1981. Emp: Emory U., Candler Sch. of Theol., 1978-80 Instr.; Yale U. Div. Sch., 1981-91 Assoc. Prof.; Duke U. Div. Sch., 1991- Assoc. Prof. Spec: New Testament. Pub: "Scripture-Shaped Community" *Interpretation* (1990); *Echoes of Scripture in the Letters of Paul* (Yale U.P., 1989); "Christology and Ethics in Galatians" *CBQ* (1987); "Have We Found Abraham to be Our Forefather?" *NT* 27 (1985); *The Faith of Jesus Christ: An Investigation of the Narrative Substructure of Gal. 3:1-4:11* (Scholars, 1983); "Psalm 143 and the Logic of Romans 3" *JBL* (1980); and others. Awd: Yale U., A. Whitney Griswold Awd. 1982; Cokesbury Grad. Awd. 1979. Mem: SBL, Pres., New England Reg. 1988-89; CBA. Rec: Baseball, music. Addr: (o)

Duke Divinity School, Durham, NC 27706 919-660-3411; (h) 3605 Stonegate Dr., Durham, NC 27705 919-490-3056.

HAYWARD, Robert C., b. Shrewsbury, England, February 19, 1948, s. of Charles Frederick & Magaret Hannah. Educ: U. of Durham, England, BA 1971, MA 1973; U. of Oxford, DPhil 1975. Emp: U. of Lancaster, England, 1977-79 Lect., Jewish Stud.; U. of Durham, 1979-89 Lect., 1989- Sr. Lect., Theol. Spec: Apocrypha and Post-biblical Studies. Pub: "Red Heifer and Golden Calf: Dating Targum Pseudo-Jonathan" *Targum Stud.* vol. 1 (Scholars, 1992); "The Fourth Philosophy: *Sicarii* and Zealots" in *The History of the Jewish People in the Age of Jesus Christ* (1979); *Divine Name and Presence: The Memra* (Allenheld Osmun, 1981); "The Jewish Temple at Leontopolis: A Reconsideration" *JJS* (1982); *The Targum of Jeremiah* (Glazier, 1987); "Targum Pseudo-Jonathan and Anti-Islamic Polemic" *JSS* (1989); and others. Mem: SOTS; Brit. Assn. for Jewish Stud. Rec: Music. Addr: (o) Abbey House, Palace Green, Durham, England 091-374-2055.

HEDRICK, Charles W., b. Bogalusa, LA, April 11, 1934, s. of Charlie Schreve & Harriet Eva (Smith), m. Peggy S., chil: Charles W.; Janet L.; Lois K. Educ: Mississippi Coll., BA 1958; Golden Gate Bapt. Theol. Sem., BD 1962; U. of South. Calif., MA 1968; Claremont Grad. Sch., PhD 1977. Emp: Claremont Grad. Sch., 1977-78 Lect. in Relig.; Wagner Coll., 1978-80 Asst. Prof. of Relig. Stud.; SW Mo. State U., 1980- Prof. of Relig. Stud., 1992- Disting. Schol.; *Perspectives in Relig. Stud.*, 1985-91 Ed. Bd. Excv: Banias, 1990, 1992 Area Supr. Spec: Archaeology, New Testament. Pub: *The Historical Jesus and the Rejected Gospels*, ed. (Scholars, 1988); *Nag Hammadi Codices XI, XII, XIII* (Brill, 1988); *Nag Hammadi, Gnosticism, and Early Christianity* (Hendrickson, 1986); "The Role of 'Summary Statements' in the Composition of the Gospel of Mark: A Dialog with Karl Schmidt and Norman Perrin" *NT* 26 (1984); "What is a Gospel? Geography, Time, and Narrative Structure" *Perspectives in Relig. Stud.* 11 (1984); "Kingdom Sayings and Parables of Jesus in the Apocryphon of James: Tradition and Redaction" *NTS* 29 (1983); "Christian Motifs in the Gospel of the Egyptians: Method and Motive" *NT* 23 (1981); "Paul's Conversation/Call: A Comparative Analysis of the Three Reports in Acts" *JBL* 100 (1981); *The Apocalypse of Adam: A Literary and Source Analysis* (Scholars, 1980); and others. Awd: NEH, summer stipend 1979; Wagner Coll., Faculty Res. Grant 1980; NEH, Res. Conference Grant 1982; SW Missouri State U., Excellence in Res. Awd. 1988. Mem: SBL; IACS; NABPR, Pres. 1988-89; SNTS; Egyptian Explor. Soc. Rec: Jogging. Addr: (o) Southwest Missouri State U., Dept. of Religious Studies, Springfield, MO 65804 417-836-4148; (h) 963 S Delaware, Springfield, MO 65802 417-831-4548.

HEFLIN, Boo, b. Little Rock, Ark., January 23, 1942, s. of Jay & Lynn, m. Mary (Bishop), chil: Judy Lynn (Malone); Sherry Marie (Stanley); David Carl. Educ: Ouachita Bapt. U., BA 1963; SW Bapt. Theol. Sem., MDiv 1966, PhD 1971. Emp: SW Bapt. Theol. Sem., 1969-71 Instr., 1972-77 Asst. Prof., 1977-87 Assoc. Prof., 1987- Prof., OT & Hebrew. Spec: Hebrew Bible. Pub: "The Prophet Malachi, His World and His Book" *SW Jour. of Theol.* 30 (1987); *Nahum, Habakkuk, Zephaniah and Haggai,* Bible Study Comm. (Zondervan, 1985); "The World of Hosea" *SW Jour. of Theol.* 18 (1975); and others. Mem: Tex. Bapt. Hist. Soc.; NABPR; South. Bapt. Hist. Soc.; NAPH; SBL. Rec: Travel, running, fishing. Addr: (o) Southwestern Baptist Theological Seminary, PO Box 22187, Fort Worth, TX 76122 817-923-1921; (h) 6717 Morning Dew Dr., Forth Worth, TX 76132 817-294-8866.

HEGG, Timothy J., b. Boise, ID, October 23, 1950, s. of Oscar & Pearl, m. Paulette Susan, chil: Joshua Joel; Caleb McCheyne. Educ: Cedarville Coll., BS 1973; NW Bapt. Sem., MDiv 1976, ThM 1980. Emp: Ctr. for Bibl. Stud., 1986- Dir.; West. Reformed Sem., 1987-90 Adj. Fac.; Faith Sem., 1990- Adj. Fac., Hebrew & Judaic Stud. Spec: Hebrew Bible, New Testament, Apocrypha and Post-biblical Studies. Mem: ETS 1986-, Pres., NW reg. 1990; SBL 1988-. Rec: Bicycling. Addr: (o) 3806 Portland, Tacoma, WA 98404; (h) 4105 N 25th, Tacoma, WA 98404.

HEIDER, George C., b. Washington, DC, June 13, 1953, s. of George C., Jr. & Doris H., m. Carolyn (Wolters), chil: Kristen Naomi; Matthew Aaron. Educ: Concordia Sr. Coll., BA 1975; Concordia Sem., MDiv 1979; Yale U., MA 1980, MPhil 1982, PhD 1984. Emp: Concordia Coll., 1984-89 Asst. Prof., 1987- V.P. for Acad. Affairs, 1990- Assoc. Prof.; *OT Abstracts,* 1991- Abstracter. Spec: Hebrew Bible. Pub: "A Further Turn on Ezekiel's Baroque Twist in Ezek 20:25-26" *JBL* 107 (1988); *The Cult of Molek: A Reassessment,* JSOTSup 43 (JSOT, 1985); and others. Mem: SBL; ASOR; CBA. Addr: (o) Concordia College, 800 N Columbia Ave., Seward, NE 68434 402-643-7377; (h) 1564 Plainview Ave., Seward, NE 68434 402-643-2816.

HEINE, Ronald E., b. Liberty, IL, December 25, 1939, s. of Russell & Emma, m. Gillian, chil: Gail; Pamela; Robert. Educ: Lincoln Christian Sem., MA 1963, BD 1966; U. of Ill., MA 1968, PhD 1974. Emp: Lincoln Christian Sem., 1968-86 Prof.; Dallas Christian Coll., 1986-89 Prof.; U. of Birmingham, England, Inst. for the Study of Relig. & Culture, 1986-89 Dir.; Inst. zur Erforschung des Urchristentums, Germany, 1989- Dir. Spec: New Testament, Apocrypha and Post-biblical Studies. Pub: "A Note on the Text of Origen: *Commentary on John* 19.III.16" *JTS* (1991); *The Montanist Oracles and Testimonia* (Mercer U.P., 1989); *Origen: Commentary on the Gospel According to John, Books 1-10* (Cath. U.P., 1989); "The Role of the Gospel of John in the Montanist Controversy"

SC (1987-88); "Can the Catena Fragments of Origen's Commentary on John be Trusted?" *VC* (1986); "Gregory of Nyssa's Apology for Allegory" *VC* (1984); *Origen: Homilies on Genesis and Exodus* (Cath. U.P., 1982); and others. Mem: SBL 1967-; NAPS. Rec: Running, swimming. Addr: (o) Institut zur Erforschung des Urchristentums, Wilhelmstr. 100, d-7400 Tuebingen, Germany 07071-51475; (h) Ulmenweg 4, D-7400 Tuebingen, Germany 07071-64477.

HEINE, Susanne L., b. Prague, Czechoslovakia, January 17, 1942, chil: Alexander. Educ: U. of Vienna, DD, NT 1973; Ord. 1968. Emp: U. of Vienna, Evang.-Theol. Faculty, 1968-79 Asst., Dept. for NT Stud., 1979-82 Lect., 1982-90 Prof., 1984-90 Dir., Dept. for Relig.; Educ.; U. of Augsburg, 1985-86 Guest Prof.; U. of Zurich, 1990- Prof.; U. of Birmingham, 1992 E. Cadbury Lect. Spec: New Testament, Apocrypha and Post-biblical Studies. Pub: *Frauen der Fruhen Christenheit* (Vandenhoeck & Ruprecht, 1986, 1990); *Matriarchs, Goddesses and Images of God* (Augsburg, 1989); *Women and Early Christianity* (SCM, 1987; Augsburg, 1988); *Christianity and the Goddesses* (SCM, 1988); and others. Rec: Painting, pottery-work. Addr: (o) Kirchgasse 9, CH-8001 Zurich, Switzerland 01-2576732; (h) Hohenbuhlstrasse 4, CH-8032 Zurich, Switzerland 01-2614582.

HELTZER, Michael, b. Tallin, Estonia, May 1, 1928, s. of Leib & Ida, m. Shoshanah, chil: Ida; Aryeh; Rafael. Educ: Oriental Inst. of the Acad. of Sci. of the USSR, 1969 Dr. of Hist. Sci. Emp: Higher Educ. Inst., Lithuania, 1959-71 Lect.; U. of Haifa, 1972- Prof. Spec: Hebrew Bible, Mesopotamian Studies, Semitic Languages, Texts and Epigraphy, Apocrypha and Post-biblical Studies. Pub: *Die Organization des Handwerks* (1992); "An Old Aramean Seal-Impression and Some Problems of the History of the Kingdom of Damascus in Arameans, Aramaic and Aramaic Literary Tradition" *Ramat Gan* (1983); *The Suteans* (1981); *The Internal Organization of Ugarit* (1982); *The Extra-Biblical Tradition of Hebrew Personal Names* (Haifa, 1978); and others. Addr: (o) U. of Haifa, Haifa 31999, Israel 04-240-951; (h) Rechov Haperachim 11/10, Haifa 34733, Israel 04-253-974.

HENDEL, Ronald S., b. New London, CT, January 7, 1958, s. of Murray & Marjorie, m. Ann (Eberhardt), chil: Edward Stephen; Nathan Lawrence. Educ: Harvard U., AB 1981, AM 1984, PhD 1985. Emp: South. Meth. U., 1985- Assoc. Prof.; U. of Calif., 1992-93 Vis. Asst. Prof.; *BR,* 1992- Ed. Bd.; *BA,* 1993- Ed. Bd. Spec: Hebrew Bible. Pub: The Text of Genesis 1-11: Masoretic Text, Samaritan Text, Septuagint, and Qumran, HSS (Scholars, 1993); "Genesis, Book of" in *ABD,* vol. 2 (Doubleday, 1992); "When God Acts Immorally: Is the Bible a Good Book?" *BR* 7/3 (1991); "Sacrifice as a Cultural System: The Ritual Symbolism of Exodus 24:3-8" *ZAW*

101 (1989); "The Social Origins of the Aniconic Tradition in Early Israel" *CBQ* 50 (1988); "Of Demigods and the Deluge: Toward an Interpretation of Genesis 6:1-14" *JBL* 106 (1987); *The Epic of the Patriarch: The Jacob Cycle and the Narrative Traditions of Canaan and Israel*, HSM 42 (Scholars, 1987); and others. Awd: SBL, Mitchell Dahood Memorial Prize 1985; South. Meth. U., Faculty Res. Grants 1986, 1988; NEH, Summer Stipend 1988, Fellow. for U. Tchr. 1991-92. Mem: SBL; ASOR; CBA. Rec: Swimming, hiking, playing with sons. Addr: (o) Southern Methodist U., Dept. of Religious Studies, Dallas, TX 75275 214-692-2130; (h) 6718 Santa Anita Dr., Dallas, TX 75214 214-692-0609.

HENDRICKX, Herman N., b. Tienen, Belgium, May 23, 1933, s. of Armand & Emma (Neyrinck). Educ: Cath. U. of Louvain, Lic. in Theol., NT Exegesis 1963. Emp: San Carlos Sem., Manila, 1967-72 Prof., NT; Assumption Sem., 1971 Guest Lect.; Maryhill Sch. of Theol., 1972- Prof., NT Exegesis; St. Paul's Natl. Sem., Australia, 1974 Guest Lect.; E Asian Pastoral Inst., Ateneo de Manila U., 1980- Prof., NT. Spec: New Testament. Pub: *The Household of God* (Claretian, 1992); *From One Jesus to Four Gospels* (Claretian, 1991); *The Parables of Jesus* (Chapman, 1986); *The Resurrection Narratives* (Chapman, 1984); and others. Mem: SBL. Addr: (o) Maryhill School of Theology, PO Box 1323, 1099 Manila, Philippines 721-26-95.

HENDRIX, Holland L., b. Tyler, TX, June 23, 1948, s. of Ernest & Lucille (Dyer), m. Alison. Educ: Columbia U., BA 1971; Union Theol. Sem., MDiv, STM 1975; Harvard Div. Sch., ThD 1984. Emp: MIT, 1977 Instr.; Harvard Div. Sch., 1979 Instr.; Haverford Coll., 1980-82 Instr.; Barnard Coll., 1982- Asst. Prof.; Union Theol. Sem., 1990 Acad. Dean, 1991 Pres. Excv: Tsoukalorio, Greece, 1980 Field Supr. Spec: Archaeology, New Testament. Pub: "Philippi," "Thessalonica" in *ABD*, vol. 5-6 (Doubleday, 1992); "Archaeology and Eschatology at Thessalonica" in *The Future of Early Christianity: Essays in Honor of Helmut Koester* (Fortress, 1991); "Benefactor/Patron Networks in the Urban Environment: Evidence from Thessalonica" *Semeia* 56 (1991); "On the Form and Ethos of Ephesians" *Union Sem. Quar. Rev.* 42/4 (1988); *Archaeological Resources for New Testament Studies*, co-ed. (Fortress, 1986); "Graeco-Roman Libraries" *BI* (1983); and others. Mem: SBL 1977-; AAR 1984-. Rec: Music. Addr: (o) Union Theological Seminary, 3041 Broadway, New York, NY 10027 212-280-1403; (h) 250 W 88th St. #601, New York, NY 10024 212-721-2197.

HENRICKSON, Robert C., b. Lexington, KY, June 14, 1951, s. of Carl & Esther, m. Elizabeth, chil: Sarah. Educ: Vanderbilt U., BA 1973; U. of Toronto, MA 1976, PhD 1984. Emp: Royal Ontario Mus., 1974-86 Res. Asst., 1986-89 Asst. Cur.; U. of Toronto, 1977-81 Teaching Asst.; Smithsonian Inst., 1992- Vis. Scientist. Excv:

Mahidasht Project, Iran, 1978 Site Supr.; Tell Madhhur, Iraq, Site Supr.; Yimneyeh, Iraq, 1982 Asst. Dir.; Kommos, Crete, 1984 Trenchmaster; Gordion, 1988- Project Ceramic Analyst. Spec: Archaeology, Mesopotamian Studies. Pub: "Scale and Paste: Investigating Production of Godin II Buff Ware," co-auth., in *Chemical Characterization of Ceramic Pastes in Archaeology* (1992); "Pottery, Economics and Ceramic Continuity at Gordion in the Late Second and First Millennia B.C." in *Social and Cultural Contexts of New Ceramic Technologies* (1992); "Wheelmade or Wheel Finished? Interpretation of 'Wheelmarks on Pottery'" in *Materials Issues in Art and Archaeology II* (1991); "The Godin III Revised Chronology for Central Western Iran, ca. 2600-1400 B.C." *Iranica Antiqua* (1987); "Workshops and Pottery Production in Bronze Age Central Western Iran" in *Technology and Style* (1986); and others. Awd: Royal Ontario Mus., Post-Doc. Res. Fellow 1985-86; Smithsonian Inst., Post-Doc. in Materials Analysis 1989-90. Mem: AOS 1975-; BSA, Iraq 1975-; AIA 1984-. Rec: Maritime history, residential stained glass. Addr: (o) Smithsonian Institution, Conservation Analytical Lab, Washington, DC 20560; (h) 6617 Westmoreland Ave., Takoma Park, MD 20912.

HENRY, Carl F. H., b. New York, NY, January 22, 1913, s. of Karl & Johanna (Vaethroeder), m. Helga (Bender), chil: Paul; Carol. Educ: Wheaton Coll., BA 1938, MA 1940; North. Bapt. Theol. Sem., BD 1941, ThD 1942; Boston U., PhD 1949. Emp: North. Bapt. Theol. Sem., 1942-47 Prof.; Fuller Theol. Sem., 1947-56 Prof., Theol. & Christian Phil.; *Christianity Today*, 1956-68 Founding Ed.; East. Bapt. Theol. Sem., 1969-74 Prof.; Trinity Evang. Div. Sch., 1974- Vis. Prof., Theol. Spec: New Testament. Pub: "The Priority of Divine Revelation" *JETS* (1984); "The Interpretation of the Scriptures: Are We Doomed to Hermeneutical Nihilism?" *Rev. & Expositor* (1974); *God, Revelation and Authority*, 6 vol. (Word, 1976-1983); and others. Awd: Seattle-Pacific Coll., LittD 1963; Houghton Coll., LHD 1978; NW Coll., DD 1979; Gordon-Conwell Div. Sch., DD 1984; Hillsdale Coll., LLD 1989. Mem: AAR; Amer. Theol. Soc., V.P. 1974-75, Pres. 1979-80; Amer. Soc. of Christian Ethics. Rec: Reading, antiques, azaleas. Addr: (h) 3824 N 37th St., Arlington, VA 22207 703-528-2401.

HENTSCHEL, Georg, b. Rengersdorf, December 18, 1941, s. of Paul & Gertrude. Educ: Erfurt Sem., ThL 1970, ThD 1978. Emp: Peter & Paul Ch., 1968-71 Chaplain; Erfurt Sem., 1971-78 Asst. Lect., 1978-90 Dozent, 1991- Prof., OT Exegesis. Spec: Hebrew Bible. Pub: *Gott, Koenig und Tempel: Beobachtungen zu 2 Sam 7,1-17*, Erfurter Theol. Schriften 22 (1992); *2 Koenige, Neue Echter Bibel* (Wuerz-burg, 1985); *1 Koenige, Neue Echter Bibel* (Wuerzburg, 1984); *Die Elijaerzaehlungen*, Erfurter Theol. Stud. 33 (1977). Addr: (o) Domstrasse 10, 5020 Erfurt/DDR 26577, Germany; (h) Kartaeuserstrasse 28, 5020 Erfurt/DDR 28487, Germany.

HERIBAN, Jozef M., b. Selpice, Czechoslovakia, May 7, 1925, s. of Ignác & Mária (Bohovičová). Educ: Pont. Ateneo Salesiano, Turin, STL 1955; Pont. Bibl. Inst., SSL 1957; Salesian Pont. U., Rome, ThD 1983. Emp: Salesian Theol. Coll., Tokyo, 1957-65 Prof.; Sophia U., Tokyo, 1965-73 Prof., NT Exegesis; Sapientia U., Osaka, 1973-76 Prof., NT Exegesis; Don Bosco Ctr. of Stud., Manila, 1984 Vis. Prof.; Salesian Pont. U., 1978- Prof., NT Exegesis. Spec: New Testament. Pub: *Priručn'y lexikón biblick'yh vied* (Slovak Inst., 1992); *Uvodné poznámky k spisom Nováho zákona* (USCM, 1989); *Bibliografická prirучka pre štúdium Svätého pisma* (USCM, 1986); *Retto phronein e kenosis* (LAS, 1983); and others. Mem: Slovak Inst. 1988-; SNTS 1989-. Addr: (o) U. Pontificia Salesiana, Piazza dell' Ateneo Salesiano, 1, I-00139 ROMA RM, Italy 06-8729-0242.

HERION, Gary A., b. Chapel Hill, NC, August 20, 1954, s. of John & Mary, m. Carol (Creath), chil: Melissa; Samuel; Daniel. Educ: U. of Mich., MA 1977, PhD 1982. Emp: Albion Coll., 1983 Vis. Assoc. Prof.; U. of N.C., 1984-87 Lect.; U. of Mich., 1987-91 Adj. Asst. Prof.; Hartwick Coll., 1991- Asst. Prof. Spec: Hebrew Bible. Pub: *ABD*, assoc. ed. (1992); "Social Science Assumptions in the Study of Ancient Israel" *JSOT* (1986); "Role of Historical Narrative in Biblical Thought" *JSOT* (1981); and others. Mem: ASOR; SBL. Addr: (o) Hartwick College, Dept. of Philosophy & Religion, Oneonta, NY 13820 607-431-4875; (h) 31 Central Ave., Oneonta, NY 13820 607-431-1047.

HERR, Larry G., b. Decatur, IL, September 3, 1946, s. of Theodore and June (Layman), m. Denise (Dick), chil: Garrick. Educ: Andrews U., BA 1970; Harvard U., PhD 1971. Emp: Seventh-Day Adventist Theol. Sem., Far East, 1978-84 Asst. Prof.; Canadian Union Coll., 1984- Prof., Relig. Stud. Excv: Hesban, 1974, 1976 Area Supr.; Amman Airport Project, 1976 Dir.; Hesban North Ch. Project, 1978 Chief Arch.; Madaba Plains Project, 1984 Chief Arch., Ceramic Typologist; Tell el-Umeiri, Jordan, Dir. Spec: Archaeology, Semitic Languages, Texts and Epigraphy. Pub: "What Ever Happened to the Ammonites?" *BAR* 19/6 (1993); *Madaba Plains Project 2: The 1987 Season at Tell el-Umeiri and Vicinity*, co-auth.; "The Servant of Baalis" *BA* (1985); "Paleography and Identification of Seal Owners" *BASOR* (1980); *The Amman Airport Excavations, 1976* (ASOR, 1983); *The Scripts of Ancient Northwest Semitic Seals* (Scholars, 1978); and others. Awd: ASOR, Fellow. 1974-75; Zapara Awd. for Excellence in Teaching 1989; Albright Inst. of Arch. Res., Jerusalem, Ann. Prof. 1993-94. Mem: ASOR 1969-; SBL 1971-; Assn. of Field Arch. Rec: Sailing, music, backpacking. Addr: (o) Canadian Union College, Box 589, College Heights, AB T0C O2O, Canada 403-782-3381.

HERZOG, William R., II, b. Rutland, VT, March 10, 1944, s. of Charles & Helen, m. Mary, chil: Daniel; Catherine. Educ: Harvard U., AB 1966; Amer. Bapt. Sem. of the West, MDiv 1969; Claremont Grad. Sch., PhD 1976. Emp: Amer. Bapt. Sem. of the West, 1974-88 Horace Austin Johnson & Helen Kennedy Johnson Prof. of NT Interpretation; Cen. Bapt. Theol. Sem., 1988-91 Dean & Prof.; Keuka Coll. Forum Ser., 1983 Lect.; Colgate Rochester. Div. Sch., 1991- V.P. for Acad. Life, Dean of Faculty, Prof., NT Interpretation. Spec: New Testament. Pub: "From the End of the World to the End of World: Apocalyptic as a Social Hermeneutic" *Pacific Theol. Rev.* (1985); "Apocalyptic and the Historical Jesus Reconsidered" *Pacific Theol. Rev.* (1984); "The Origins of Ministry in the New Testament" *Amer. Bapt. Quar.* (1984); "Interpretation as Discovery and Creation: Sociological Dimensions of Biblical Interpretation" *Amer. Bapt. Quar.* (1983). Mem: SBL 1974-; AAR 1974-; CBA 1984-. Addr: (o) 1100 S Goodman St., Rochester, NY 14620 716-271-1320; (h) 21 Hidden Creek Cir., Pittsford, NY 14534.

HERZOG, Ze'ev, b. Buchara, Russia, November 10, 1941, s. of Marek & Matilda, m. Hanna, chil: Ken; Ben; Stav. Educ: Hebrew U., Jerusalem, BA 1970; Tel Aviv U., PhD 1977. Emp: Tel Aviv U., 1983- Sr. Lect., Arch.; U. of Pa., 1978-79 Vis. Prof., Anc. Hist.; Harvard U., 1984-85, 1989-90 Vis. Schol., Near East. Lang. & Civ. Excv: Megiddo, Area Supr.; Arad, Area Supr.; Beer-Sheba, 1976 Dir.; Tel Michal, 1977-80 Dir.; Tel Gerisa, 1981-91 Dir. Spec: Archaeology. Pub: "The Valley of Beer Sheba from Nomadism to Monarchy" in *The Land of Israel from Nomadism to Monarchy* (Yad Ben Zvi, 1990); "The Reconstruction of Solomon's Temple according to Recent Discoveries" in *Jerusalem in the Biblical Period* (Yad Ben Zvi, 1990); *Excavations at Tel Michal, Israel*, co-ed. (U. of Minn., 1989); "Archaeology and History at Tel Michal" *Mediterranean Hist. Rev.* 3 (1988); "City Planning and Fortifications in the Iron Age" in *The Architecture of Ancient Israel* (IES, 1987); "Arad—An Ancient Israelite Fortress with A Temple to Yahweh," co-auth., *BAR* 13/2 (1987); *Beer-sheba II: The Early Iron Age Settlements*, co-auth. (Ramot, 1984); and others. Rec: Hiking. Addr: (o) Tel Aviv U., Dept. of Archaeology & Ancient Near Eastern Cultures, 69978 Tel Aviv, Israel 972-3-6409417; (h) 43 Hamlachim St., 47271 Ramat Hasharon, Israel 972-3-5494941.

HESS, Richard S., December 17, 1954, s. of Samuel & Edna. Educ: Wheaton Coll., BA 1976; Trinity Evang. Div. Sch., MDiv 1979, ThM 1980; Hebrew Union Coll., PhD, W Semitic Lang. & Lit. 1984. Emp: Xavier U., 1983-84 Lect., OT; Loyola U. of Chicago, 1984-85 Lect., OT; Tyndale House, Cambridge, 1986-88 Res. Fellow, Genesis 1-11 Project; U. of Sheffield, 1988-89 Res. Asst., Class. Hebrew Dict. Project; Glasgow Bible Coll., 1989- Lect., OT. Spec: Hebrew Bible, Semitic Languages, Texts and Epigraphy. Pub: "Eden—A Well-Watered Place" *BR* 7/6 (1991); "Yahweh and His Asherab? Epigraphic Evidence for Religious Pluralism in Old Testament Times" in *One God,*

One Lord in a World of Religious Pluralism (Tyndale, 1991); "Hiphil Forms of *qwr* in Jeramiah vi 7" *VT* 41 (1991); "The Operation of Case Vowels in the Personal Names of the Amarna Texts" in *Mesopotamie et Elam: Actes de la xxxvieme rencontre assyriologique internationale Gand, 10-14 juillet 1989* (1991); "Splitting the Adam: The Usage of *ADAM* in Genesis i-v" in *Studies in the Pentateuch*, VTSup 61 (Brill, 1990); and others. Awd: U. of Muenster, NEH Summer Travel Grant 1990; Fulbright Post-doc. Res. Fellow, Jerusalem 1986; NEH/ASOR Fellow, Jerusalem 1985. Mem: ASOR; CBA; IBR; IES; SBL. Addr: (o) Glasgow Bible College, 731 Great Western Rd., Glasgow G12 8QX, Scotland 041-334-9849; (h) Flat 1/1, 76 Hotspur St., Glasgow G20 8LP, Scotland.

HESSE, Brian C., b. Pittsburgh, PA, December 15, 1944, s. of Frank McNeil & Elizabeth (Wylie), m. Paula (Wapnish), chil: Arielle Leah. Educ: Columbia U., BA 1970, MPhil 1973, PhD, Anthrop. 1978. Emp: Smithsonian Inst., Mus. of Natural Hist., 1976-78 Anthrop.; U. of Ala., Birmingham, 1979-83 Asst. Prof., 1983-90 Assoc. Prof., 1990- Prof., Anthrop., 1991- Dir., Intl. Stud. Prog.; Field Sch. of Animal Bone Arch., 1991 Dir. Excv: Ganj Dareh, Iran, 1974 Zooarchaeologist; San Pedro de Atacama, Chile, 1978, 1983 Zooarchaeologist; Tel Miqne/Ekron, Israel, 1982- Zooarchaeologist; Ashkelon, Israel, 1985- Zooarchaeologist. Spec: Archaeology, Mesopotamian Studies. Pub: "Pig Lovers and Pig Haters: Patterns of Palestinian Pork Production" *Jour. of Ethnobiology* 10/2 (1990); "Domestication of Hyrax (*Procavia capensis*) in Yemen," co-auth., *Jour. of Ethnobiology* 10/1 (1990); "Paleolithic Faunal Remains from Ghar-i-Khar, Western Iran" in *Early Animal Domestication and its Cultural Context*, MASCA Res. Papers in Arch. (1989); "The Detection of Chronological Mixing in Samples from Stratified Archaeological Sites," co-auth. in *Recent Developments in Environmental Analysis in Old and New World Archaeology*, Brit. Arch. Reports 416 (1988); "Animal Use at Tel Miqne-Ekron in the Bronze and Iron Age" *BASOR* 264 (1986); *Animal Bone Archaeology: From Objectives to Analysis*, co-auth. (Taraxacum, 1985); and others. Awd: Smithsonian Inst., Predoc. Fellow. 1975, Latin Amer. Fund Grant 1981; NEH, Fellow. 1984; Fulbright Fellow. 1986; Natl. Sci. Found., Grant 1989-91. Mem: AOS; ASOR; Assoc. for Field Arch.; IES; PES. Rec: Gardening, travel, reading, sailing. Addr: (o) U. of Alabama at Birmingham, Dept. of Anthropology, Birmingham, AL 35294 205-934-3508; (h) 3700 Crestbrook Rd., Birmingham, AL 35223 205-969-2801.

HESTRIN, Ruth, b. Ben-Shemen, Israel, June 12, 1918, d. of Yehiel & Batya Gluzman, m. Shlomo, chil: Shaul; Michal. Educ: MA, Arch., Greek & Hebrew Stud. 1951. Emp: Israel Mus., 1965-83 Cur. of Israelite & Persian periods; Israel Dept. of Antiq., Inspector of local and reg. mus.; Bronfman Bibl. & Arch. Mus., Israel

Mus., 1973-74 Chief Cur. Spec: Archaeology, Semitic Languages, Texts and Epigraphy. Pub: "Understanding Asherah" *BAR* 17/5 (1991); "The Lachish Ewer and the Asherah" *IEJ* 37 (1987); "The Cult Stand from Taanach and its Religious Background" *Studia Phoenicia* 5 (1987); "Hebrew Seals of Officials" in *Symposium on Ancient Seals and the Bible* (1983); "Two Assyrian Bowls," co-auth., *IEJ* 23 (1979); *Inscribed Seals, First Temple Period—Hebrew, Ammonite, Moabite, Phoenician and Aramaic*, co-auth. (Israel Mus., 1979); *Museum Guide for Israel* (1975); *Inscriptions Reveal*, Israel Mus. Catalogue 100 (1973); *The Philistines and the Other Sea Peoples*, Israel Mus. Catalog 68 (1970); and others. Mem: IES; Israel Assn. of Arch. Rec: Reading, nature walks. Addr: (o) Mitudela St. 34, Jerusalem, Israel 02-619892.

HEZSER, Catherine, b. Wuppertal, Germany, June 30, 1960, d. of Marianne & Tibor. Educ: U. of Heidelberg, PhD 1986; Jewish Theol. Sem., PhD, Anc. Judaism 1992. Emp: King's College, England, 1992- Res. Fellow, Interdisciplinary Early Christianity Project. Spec: New Testament. Pub: *Lohnmetaphorik und Arbeitswelt in Mt 20:1-16: Das Gleichnis von den Arbeitern im Weinberg im Rahmen rabbinischer Lohngleichnisse*, NTOA 15 (1990); and others. Mem: SBL 1987-; AJS 1987-; WUJS 1993-. Rec: Modern art, lit., dance. Addr: (o) King's College, Cambridge CB2 1ST, England 0223-350411.

HIBBITTS, John B., b. Halifax, NS, Canada, May 12, 1918, s. of John & Ethel (Wambolt), m. June (Hilchey), chil: Bernard; Paul. Educ: Dalhousie U., BA 1945, MA 1946; U. of King's Coll., Halifax, MS, Litt. 1948; Gen. Theol. Sem., MDiv 1949, MTS 1951; Oxford U., PhD 1954. Emp: Gen. Theol. Sem., 1949-51 Fellow & Tutor; U. of King's Coll., 1954-59 Dean, Div. Fac.; Seabury-West. Theol. Sem., 1962 Winslow Memorial Lect.; Atlantic Sch. of Theol., Halifax, 1971-83 Prof., Scripture Stud.; *Dalhousie Rev.*, 1965-92 Ed. Adv. Bd. Spec: Hebrew Bible, New Testament, Apocrypha and Post-biblical Studies. Awd: Pine Hill Div. Hall, Canada, DD 1970; U. of King's Coll., DD 1983. Mem: Canadian SBL 1956-; SBL 1982-; AAR 1982-; CBA 1982-. Rec: Travel, walking. Addr: (o) U. of Kings College Halifax, NS B3H 2AI, Canada 902-422-1271; (h) 1625 Preston St., Halifax, NS B3H 3V2, Canada 902-423-1424.

HIDAL, Sten L., b. Landskrona, Sweden, October 5, 1946, s. of Gunnar Hidal & May Larsson, m. Malin (Loman). Educ: U. of Lund, BA 1968, BD 1969 ThD 1974. Emp: Ch. of Sweden, 1969-75 Priest; U. of Lund, 1975- Lect., OT; Royal Swedish Bible Trans. Commn., 1976-85 Mem. Spec: Hebrew Bible, Apocrypha and Post-biblical Studies. Pub: *Gregorios au Nyssa, Mose liv—översätning med inledning och Kommentar* (1991); *Israel och Hellas: Studier kring Gamla testamentet och dess verkningshistoria* (1988); *Bibeltro och bibelkritik* (1979); "Some

Reflections on Deuteronomy 32" *Ann. of the Swedish Theol. Inst.* 11 (1978); "The Land of Cusb in the Old Testament" *SEA* 41 (1977); and others. Mem: Humanistiska Vetenskapssocieteten 1983-. Addr: (o) Lunds U., Teologiska Institut, Alhelgona Kyrkogata 8, S-223 62 Lund, Sweden 046-10-97-54; (h) Karl XI-g 11 B, S-222 20 Lund, Sweden 046-14-67-12.

HIEBERT, D. Edmond, b. Corn, OK, July 21, 1910, s. of D.K. & Katie, m. Ruth (Kopper), chil: Larry; Dorothy; Alice. Educ: South. Bapt. Theol. Sem., ThM 1939, ThD 1942. Emp: Tabor Coll., 1942-55 Prof., NT; Mennonite Brethren Bibl. Sem., 1955- Prof., NT, 1975- Prof. Emeritus. Spec: New Testament. Pub: *James* (Moody, 1992); *The Thessalonian Epistles* (Moody, 1992); "The Significance of Christian Intercession" *BS* Jan. (1992); *The Epistles of John* (Bob Jones U.P., 1991); "Romans 8:28-29 and the Assurance of the Believer" *BS* April (1991); *An Introduction to the New Testament* (Moody, 1977); and others. Mem: ETS. Rec: Collecting relig. poetry. Addr: (h) 4864 E Townsend, Fresno, CA 93727-5005 415-251-7261.

HIEBERT, Robert J. V., b. Vancouver, BC, Canada, November 1, 1951, s. of Robert & Johanna, m. Karen F, chil: Diana R. E. Educ: U. of Toronto, BA 1978, MA 1979, PhD 1986. Emp: ON Bible Coll., Canada, 1986- Prof., OT; ON Theol. Sem., 1987- Adj. Prof. Spec: Hebrew Bible, Semitic Languages, Texts and Epigraphy. Pub: *The 'Syrohexaplaric' Psalter*, SBLSCS 27 (Scholars, 1989); and others. Awd: Social Sci. & Hum. Res. Coun. of Canada, Fellow. 1982-84. Mem: SBL 1984-; IOSCS 1984-. Rec: Sports, photography, fishing, travel. Addr: (o) Ontario Bible College & Theological Seminary, 25 Ballyconnor Ct., North York, ON M2M 4B3, Canada 416-226-6380; (h) 69-2766 Folkway Dr., Mississauga, ON L5L 3M3, Canada 416-607-2088.

HIEBERT, Theodore, b. Paraguay, July 24, 1946. Educ: Fresno Pacific Coll., BA 1968; Princeton Theol. Sem., MDiv 1976; Harvard U., PhD 1984. Emp: St. John's Sem., 1980 Lect.; Boston Coll., 1980-82 Lect.; Gustavus Adolphus Coll., 1982-85 Vis. Asst. Prof.; La. State U., 1985-86 Asst. Prof.; Harvard Div. Sch., 1986- Asst. Prof. Spec: Hebrew Bible. Pub: *God of My Victory: The Ancient Hymn in Habakkuk 3* (Scholars, 1986); and others. Mem: SBL 1980-. Addr: (o) Harvard U., The Divinity School, 45 Francis Ave., Cambridge, MA 02138.

HIERS, Richard H., b. Chestnut Hill, PA, April 8, 1932, s. of Glen & Mildred (Douthitt), m. Jane (Gale), chil: Peter; Rebecca. Educ: Yale Coll., BA 1954; Yale Div. Sch., BD 1957; Yale U., MA 1959, PhD 1961. Emp: Yale Div. Sch., 1958-61 Asst. Instr.; U. of Florida, 1961- Prof., 1971- Doctoral Res. Faculty. Spec: New Testament. Pub: "Day of Judgment," "Day of the Lord" in *ABD* (1992); *Reading the Bible Book by Book* (Fortress, 1988); "Pivotal Reactions to the Eschatological Interpretations: Rudolf Bultmann and C. H. Dodd" in *The Kingdom of God in 20th Century Interpretation* (Hendrickson, 1987); "'Binding and Losing': The Matthean Authorization" *JBL* (1985); "Kingdom of God" in *Harper's Bible Dict.* (1985); "The Problem of the Delay of the Parousia in Luke-Acts" *NTS* (1974); *The Kingdom of God in the Synoptic Tradition* (U. of Fla., 1970); and others. Mem: AAR, Pres., SE Reg. 1969-70; SBL, Pres., SE Reg. 1981-82. Rec: Swimming, hiking. Addr: (o) U. of Florida, Dept. of Religion, 125 Arts & Sciences Building, Gainesville, FL 32611 904-392-1625; (h) 506 SW 40th Terrace, Gainesville, FL 32607 904-376-1765.

HILBURN, Glenn O., b. Plain Dealing, LA, March 27, 1930, s. of Guy & Estella, m. Martell, chil: Vicki; Jeffrey; Kelly. Educ: SW Bapt. Theol. Sem., BD 1956, ThD 1960. Emp: SW Bapt. Theol. Sem., 1958-60 Instr.; Baylor U., 1961- Prof., Chair, Dept. of Relig.; *Jour. of Ch. & State*, 1965- Ed. Bd.; *The Circle*, 1968-78 Ed.; Markham Press, 1970-75 Ed. Spec: New Testament, Semitic Languages, Texts and Epigraphy, Apocrypha and Post-biblical Studies. Mem: Amer. Soc. of Ch. Hist. 1962-; AAR 1964-; SBL 1970-. Rec: Fishing, hiking, photography. Addr: (o) Baylor U., Dept. of Religion, Waco, TX 76798 817-755-3735; (h) 8402 Woodcreek, Waco, TX 76712.

HILGERT, Earle, b. Portland, OR, May 17, 1923, s. of William & Katie, m. Elvire (Roth). Educ: Adventist Theol. Sem., MA 1946, BD 1955; U. of Basel, Switzerland, ThD 1962; U. of Chicago., MA 1970. Emp: Adventist Theol. Sem. 1952-59 Assoc. Prof.; Andrews U., 1959-69 Vice Pres.; *AUSS*, 1963-70 Assoc. Ed.; McCormick Theol. Sem., 1969-75 Ref. Lbrn., 1972-90 Prof., 1990- Prof. Emeritus; *Studia Philonica*, 1971-80 Co-ed.; Philo Inst., 1976-90 Dir. Spec: New Testament, Apocrypha and Post-biblical Studies. Pub: "Bibliographia Philoniana, 1935-81" *ANRW* (de Gruyter, 1984); "Central Issues in Contemporary Philo Studies" *Bibl. Res.* (1978); *The Ship and Related Symbols in the New Testament* (Van Gorcum, 1962); *Nourished with Peace: Studies in Memory of Samuel Sandmel*, co-ed. (Scholars, 1984); and others. Mem: SBL 1953-; CSBR 1960-, Pres. 1980-81; SNTS 1964-. Addr: (o) McCormick Theological Seminary, 5555 S Woodlawn Ave., Chicago, IL 60637 312-947-6300; (h) Rte. 3, PO Box 364, Whitewater, WI 53190 608-883-6631.

HILL, Charles E., b. Syracuse, NE, May 15, 1956, s. of R. Merlyn & Iris, m. Marcy (McPheeters), chil: Séan Christopher; Charity Rose; James Lloyd Burton. Educ: U. of Nebr., BA 1978; Westminster Theol. Sem., MA 1985, MDiv 1985; U. of Cambridge, PhD 1988. Emp: NW Coll., 1989- Asst. Prof., Relig. Spec: New Testament, Apocrypha and Post-biblical Studies. Pub: *Regnum Caelorum: Patterns of Future Hope in Early Christianity* (Oxford U.P., 1992); "Hippolytus and Hades: The Authorship of the Fragment *De Universo*" *Studia Patristica* 21

(1990); "Hades of Hippolytus or Tartarus of Tertullian: The Authorship of the Fragment *De Universo*" *VC* 43 (1989); "Paul's Understanding of Christ's Kingdom in I Corinthians 15:20-28" *NT* 30 (1988). Awd: U. of UK, Overseas Res. Awd. 1985, 1986, 1987; NW Coll., Summer Res. Grant 1990, 1991. Mem: SBL; NAPS. Addr: (o) Northwestern College, Orange City, IA 51041 712-737-4821; (h) 303 Third St. NW, Orange City, IA 51041 712-737-8846.

HILL, Craig C., b. Moline, IL, July 31, 1957, s. of Walter & Virginia, m. Robin Ann, chil: Arthur Lyle. Educ: Ill. Wesleyan U., BA 1978; Garrett Evang. Theol. Sem., MDiv 1982; U. of Oxford, PhD 1989. Emp: Yale U. Div. Sch., 1990-91 Henry R. Luce Fellow; Presbyn. Coll., 1992-. Spec: New Testament. Pub: *Hellenists and Hebrews: Reappraising Division Within the Earliest Church* (Fortress, 1992); *From Alpha to Omega*, co-auth. (Wesleyan U.P., 1978). Mem: SBL 1982-. Rec: Scuba diving, collecting antiques, computers, ceramics, poetry. Addr: (o) Presbyterian College, Clinton, SC 29325 800-476-7272; (h) 209 Belmont Stakes, Clinton, SC 29325 803-893-1114.

HILL, David, b. Coleraine, N Ireland, June 14, 1935, s. of Robert & Mary. Educ: Queens U., N Ireland, BA 1956; St. Andrew's U., Scotland, BD 1959, PhD 1964; Union Theol. Sem., STM 1960. Emp: U. of Sheffield, England, 1964-89 Sr. Lect., Reader; *JSNT,* 1978- Ed. Bd.; *Irish Bibl. Stud.*, 1981- Adv. Ed.; Union Theol. Coll., N Ireland, 1981 Vis. Lect.; U. of Cardiff, Wales, 1986 Vis. Lect. Spec: New Testament. Pub: "To Offer Spiritual Sacrifices, 1 Peter 2:5" *JSNT* (1982); "Son and Servant: An Essay on Matthean Christology" *JSNT* (1980); *New Testament Prophecy* (Eerdmans, 1979); *Matthew*, New Century Bible Comm. (Eerdmans, 1974); *Greek Words and Hebrew Meanings* (Cambridge U.P., 1967); and others. Mem: SNTS 1966-. Rec: Football, music, travel. Addr: (h) Ashdell Court, 26 Westbourne Rd., Sheffield S1O 2QQ, England 0742-668003.

HILLS, Julian V., b. London, England, November 9, 1953. Educ: U. of Durham, England, BA 1975; McCormick Theol. Sem., STM 1977; Harvard U., ThD 1985. Emp: Harvard Div. Sch., 1984-85 Lect.; Marquette U., 1985- Asst. Prof.; *CBQ,* 1991- Assoc. Ed. Spec: New Testament, Apocrypha and Post-biblical Studies. Pub: "A Genre for I John" in *The Future of Early Christianity: Essays in Honor of Helmut Koester* (Fortress, 1991); "The Three 'Matthean' Aphorisms in the *Dialogue of the Savior* 53" *HTR* 84 (1991); "Parables, Prophecies, and Pretenders: Translation and Interpretation in the *Apocalypse of Peter* 2" *RB* 98 (1991); "Proverbs as Sayings of Jesus in the *Epistula Apostolorum*" *Semeia* 49 (1990); *Tradition and Composition in the Epistula Apostolorum* (Fortress, 1990); "'Little Children, Keep Yourselves from Idols': I John 5:21

Reconsidered" *CBQ* 51 (1989); and others. Mem: SBL 1978-; CBA 1985-; Conf. of Anglican Theol. 1986-. Addr: (o) Marquette U., Dept. of Theology, Milwaukee, WI 53233 414-288-3776.

HINSHAW, Verlin O., b. Wichita, KS, November 15, 1925, s. of Orval & Ethel, m. Annabelle (Bowers), chil: Daryl; Kathleen. Educ: Nazarene Theol. Sem., BD 1951; Vanderbilt U., PhD 1964. Emp: William Penn Coll., 1953-58 Prof.; Friends U., 1958- Prof. Spec: New Testament. Pub: "The Church in the New Testament" in *The Church in Quaker Thought and Practice* (Friends World Com., 1979); "An Evangelical Friend Looks at Christology" in *Quaker Understanding of Christ and of Authority* (Friends World Com., 1974); "A Response to 'What is Theology?'" *Quaker Relig. Thought* (1964). Mem: SBL 1959; NEA 1968. Addr: (o) Friends U., 2100 University, Wichita, KS 67213 261-5800; (h) 9900 Bekemeyer, Wichita, KS 67212 722-8605.

HIRSCHFELD, Yizhar, b. Jerusalem, February 6, 1950, s. of Eli & Zafrira, m. Hannah, chil: Tamar; Daphna; Irit. Educ: Hebrew U., BA, Arch. 1974, MA, Class. Arch. 1981, PhD, Monastic Arch. 1987. Emp: Hamat Gader, 1979-82 Dir.; Survey of Judean Desert, 1981-83 Surveyor; Ramat Hanadiv, 1984-92 Dir.; Tiberias, 1989- Dir. Spec: Archaeology. Pub: *The Judean Desert Monasteries during the Byzantine Period* (Yale U.P., 1992); *The Palestinian Dwelling House* (IES, 1987); and others. Addr: (o) Israel Antiquities Authority, POB 586, Jerusalem 91004, Israel; (h) Harazim 6, Motza 90820, Israel 02-342965.

HIRUNUMA, Toshio, b. Osaka, Japan, February 2, 1914, s. of Chikashi & Tori. Educ: U. of Tokyo, BA 1939; Harvard U., LittD 1960. Emp: Kwansei Gakuin U., 1949-82 Prof., Class. Philol., 1982- Prof. Emeritus. Spec: New Testament. Pub: "Aneu tou Patros" *Filologia Neotestamentaria* 3 (1990); *Luke* I (1989); *The Diction of the Greek New Testament* (1989); "Matthew 16:2b-3" in *New Testament Textual Criticism: Its Significance for Exegesis—Essays in Honour of Bruce M. Metzger* (Oxford U.P., 1981); *Mark* (1976); and others. Mem: SBL 1955-; SNTS 1956-. Rec: Classical music. Addr: (h) 13-7, Shibagaki I-chome, Matsubara-shi, Osaka, 580, Japan 0723-31-8383.

HOBBS, Trevor R., b. Pontypridd, Wales, UK, January 31, 1942, s. of Leonard George & Nancy Amelia (Lloyd), m. Heather Sharon, chil: Catherine Joy; Gregory Paul. Educ: U. of London, Spurgeon's Coll., BD 1966; Bapt. Sem., Switzerland, MTh 1968; U. of London, PhD 1973. Emp: McMaster Div. Coll., 1969-70 Sessional Lect., 1970-74 Asst. Prof., 1974-78 Assoc. Prof., Bibl. Stud., 1978- Prof., OT Interpretation, Hon. Prof., Fac. of Theol. Excv: Tel Dor, 1986-89 Dir., Canadian team. Spec: Hebrew Bible. Pub: "The Enemy in the Psalms," co-auth., *BTB* 21 (1991);

"Reflections on 'The Poor' and the Old Testament" *ExpTim* 100 (1989); *1, 2 Kings*, Word Bibl. Themes (Word, 1989); *A Time of War: A Study of Warfare in the Old Testament*, OT Stud. 3 (Glazier, 1989); "The Search for Prophetic Consciousness: Some Comments on Method" *BTB* 15 (1985); *2 Kings*, Word Bibl. Comm. 13 (Word, 1985); "2 Kings 1-2: Unity and Pupose" Stud. in Relig. 13 (1984); "Some Proverbial Reflections in the Book of Jeremiah" *ZAW* 91 (1971); and others. Mem: CSBS 1970-; SBL 1970-; SOTS 1973-. Rec: Music, reading, writing, military hist. Addr: (o) McMaster U., McMaster Divinity College, Hamilton, ON L8S 4K1, Canada 416-525-9140; (h) 35 Dromore Cresent, Hamilton, ON L8S 4A8, Canada 416-572-1104.

HODGE, Carleton T., b. Springfield, IL, November 27, 1917, s. of Clarence & Nina, m. Patricia, chil: Philip; Nina; Nicholas; Charles. Educ: U. of Pa., PhD 1943. Emp: Indiana U., 1943-44 Instr., 1964-83 Prof., Linguistics & Anthrop.; U. of Pa., 1945-46 Instr.; U.S. Dept. of State, Foreign Service. Inst., 1946-64 Prof., Linguistics; *Anthrop. Linguistics*, 1983- Ed. Bd. Spec: Semitic Languages, Texts and Epigraphy, Egyptology. Pub: "Consonant Ablaut in Egyptian" in *Discussions in Egyptology* (1992); "Miktam" in *Semitic Studies in Honor of Wolf Leslau*, vol. 1 (Harrassowitz, 1991); "Thoth and Oral Tradition" in *General and Amerindian Ethnolinguistics in Remembrance of Stanley Newman* (Mouton/de Gruyter, 1989); "Indo-Europeans in the Near East" *Anthrop. Linguistics* (1981); "Akhenaton: A Reject" *Scripta Mediterranea* (1981); and others. Awd: DePauw U., Rector Scholar 1935-1939; U. of Pa., Harrison Scholar 1939-42; Phi Beta Kappa 1939. Mem: AOS 1941-; ASOR 1943-. Rec: Book collecting, including old Bibles. Addr: (o) Indiana U., Memorial 322, Bloomington, IN 47405 812-335-5457; (h) 3291 S Spring Branch Rd., Bloomington, IN 47401 812-332-2540.

HODGES, Louis I., b. Dayton, TN, December 24, 1946, s. of Louis & Louise (Walker), m. Linda (Leinenweber). Educ: Trinity Evang. Div. Sch., MDiv 1970; Princeton Theol. Sem., ThM 1971; U. of Edinburgh, Scotland, PhD 1975. Emp: Tocca Falls Coll., 1975-78 Prof.; Columbia Bibl. Sem., 1978- Prof., Systematic Theol. Pub: *Dict. of Scottish Church History and Theollogy*, contb. Mem: SBL 1975-; ETS 1975-, Chmn., SE Reg. 1981; Evang. Phil. Soc., Pres. 1992. Rec: Sports, photography, travel. Addr: (o) Columbia Biblical Seminary, P.O. Box 3122, Columbia, SC 29212 803-754-4100; (h) 1521 Murraywood Dr., Columbia, SC 29212 803-732-2117.

HODGSON, Robert, Jr., b. Seattle, WA, July 13, 1943, s. of Robert, Sr. & Eileen (Campbell), m. Mary (Downs), chil: Mary; Robert III; Jennifer. Educ: Marquette U., MA 1970; U. of Heidelberg, Germany, ThD 1976. Emp: SE Asia Grad. Sch. of Theol., 1977-80 Prof.; St. Andrews Theol. Sem., 1977-80 Prof., Bibl. Stud.; SW Mo. State U., 1980-90 Assoc. Prof.; Amer. Bible Soc., 1991-

Staff Trans. Spec: New Testament, Apocrypha and Post-biblical Studies. Pub: *Nag Hammadi, Gnosticism and Early Christianity* (Hendricksons/Brill, 1985); "The Social Setting of Holiness in Late Judaism and Early Christianity" in *Reaching Beyond: Chapters in the History of Perfectionism* (Hendrickson, 1985); "On the *Gattung* of Q.A. Dialogue with James M. Robinson" *Biblica* (1985); "Paul the Apostle and First-Century Tribulation Lists" *ZNW* (1983); "1 Thess. 4:1-12 and the Holiness Tradition" in *SBL Seminar Papers* (1982); and others. Mem: CBA 1980-; SBL 1980-. Rec: Skiing, tennis, writing. Addr: (o) 1943 E Swallow, Springfield, MO 65804 417-887-4324.

HOEHNER, Harold W., b. Sangerfield, NY, January 12, 1935, s. of Walter, m. Virginia, chil: Stephen; Susan; David; Deborah. Educ: Dallas Theol. Sem., ThM 1962, ThD 1965; Cambridge U., England, PhD 1968. Emp: Dallas Theol. Sem., 1968-73 Asst. Prof. of Bible Exposition, 1973-77 Assoc. Prof. of NT Lit., 1975- Dir., ThD Stud., 1977 Chmn., Prof. of NT Stud.; *BS*, 1969-74 Asst. Ed. Spec: New Testament. Pub: *Chronological Aspects of the Life of Christ* (Zondervan, 1977); *Herod Antipas*, SNTS Mon. Ser. 17 (Cambridge U.P., 1972); "Duration of Egyptian Bondage" *BS* (1969). Mem: SNTS; SBL; ETS; Tyndale Fellow.; IBR. Addr: (o) 3909 Swiss Ave., Dallas, TX 75204 214-824-3094; (h) 6538 Ridgemont Dr., Dallas, TX 75214 214-369-3592.

HOERBER, Robert G., b. St. Louis, MO, August 25, 1918, s. of Eugene T. & Adele, m. Ruth (Hanser), chil: Robert G. Educ: Washington U., MA 1942, PhD 1944; Concordia Sem., BA 1942, STM 1944. Emp: Bethany Coll., 1944-47; Westminster Coll., 1947-65, 1967-74 Chmn., Disting. Service Prof. of Classics; St. Olaf Coll., 1965-67 Chmn., Prof. of Classics; Concordia Sem., 1974-89 Prof., NT Exegesis; *Concordia Jour.*, 1976-82 Ed. Spec: New Testament. Pub: *Studies in the New Testament* (Biblion, 1990); *Reading the New Testament for Understanding* (Concordia, 1986); *Concordia Self-Study Bible* (Concordia, 1986); "Implications of the Imperative in the Sermon on the Mount" *Concordia Jour.* (1981); "Immortality and Resurrection" *Concordia Jour.* (1977); "New Wine in Old Bottles" *Concordia Theol. Quar.* (1977); "The Decree of Claudius in Acts 18:2" *Concordia Theol. Monthly* (1960); "Galatians 2:1-10 and the Acts of the Apostles" *Concordia Theol. Monthly* (1960); *Saint Paul's Shorter Letters* (Ovid Bell, 1954). Awd: Washington U., Fellow in Greek 1942-44; Phi Beta Kappa 1944; Churchill Fellow 1970; John W. Behnken Presidential Fellow 1985. Mem: APA 1944-; Amer. Class. League 1947-74; SBL 1974-89; CBA 1976-80; SNTS 1978-. Rec: Tennis, walking, jogging, grandchildren. Addr: (h) 802 Bradley Ln., Fulton, MO 65251 314-642-7363.

HOFFMANN, Paul, b. Brunn, February 14, 1933, s. of Ludwing & Martha (Paulczinski). Educ: U. Munchen, Theol. Promotion 1959; U.

Munster, Habil., NT Exegesis 1968. Emp: U. Munster, 1969 Dozent; U. Bamberg, 1970- Prof., NT. Spec: New Testament. Pub: *Das Erbe Jesu und die Macht-in der Kirche* (1991); "Zukunftserwartung und Schopfungsglaube in der Basileia-Verkundigung Jesu" *RhS* 31 (1988); *Priesterkirche* (1987, 1989); "Zur Verbindlichkeit des Gebots der Feindesliebe" in *Ethik im Neuen Testament* (1984); *Studien zur Theologie der Logienquelle* (1972, 1982); "Jesu Einfache u.konkrete Rede von Gott" *SBS* 100 (1981); *Die Toten in Christus* (1966, 1978); "Der Petrusprimat im Matthausevangelium" in *Festschrift Schnackenburg* (1974); and others. Mem: SNTS. Addr: (o) U. Bamberg, An der Universitat 2, D-8600 Bamberg, Germany 0951-8631710; (h) Babenberger Ring 64 b, D-8600 Bamberg , Germany 0951-8631005.

HOFFNER, Harry A., Jr., b. Jacksonville, FL, November 27, 1934, s. of Harry & Madaline (Wolford), m. Winifred (Way), chil: David; Karen; Lee. Educ: Dallas Theol. Sem., ThM 1960; Brandeis U., MA 1961, PhD 1963. Emp: Wheaton Coll., 1963-64 Instr.; Brandeis U., 1964-69 Asst. Prof.; Yale U., 1969-74 Assoc. Prof.; U. of Chicago., 1974- Prof., Hittitology. Spec: Anatolian Studies, Hebrew Bible, Mesopotamian Studies, Semitic Languages, Texts and Epigraphy. Pub: *Akkadian Grammar*, trans. (Scholars, 1992); *Hittite Myths* (Scholars, 1990); "Hittite Religion" in *Religions of Antiquity* (Macmillan, 1989); *Kanissuwar: A Tribute to H.G. Guterbock*, ed. (U. of Chicago., 1986); *The Hittite Dict. of the Oriental Institute of the University of Chicago* (U. of Chicago., 1980); *Alimenta Hethaeorum* (AOS, 1974); and others. Mem: AOS 1963-76. Rec: Photography, jogging. Addr: (o) U. of Chicago, Oriental Institute, 1155 E 58th St., Chicago, IL 60637 312-702-9527; (h) 8421 Creekside Ln., Darien, IL 60561.

HOFFNUNG, Frayda D., b. Hollywood, CA, d. of Joseph Deitchman & Jennie (Lott), m. Warren Ira, chil: Derek; Gregory. Educ: U. of Calif., Irvine, BA (magna cum laude) 1974, MA 1976, PhD 1980. Emp: Calif. State U., 1981-93 Asst. Prof.; Whittier Coll., 1993 Prof. Spec: New Testament. Pub: *The Family of Jesus* (U. of Mich., 1980); and others. Awd: U. of Calif. Regents' Fellow.; Leon Goodman Regents' Diss. Fellow.; Danforth Fellow. Mem: Assn. of Anc. Hist.; Friends of Anc. Hist.; SBL; AAR; ASOR. Rec: Sailing, skiing, computer programming. Addr: (h) PO Box 3405, Newport Beach, CA 92659 714-968-1571.

HOFIUS, Otto Friedrich, b. Siegen, Germany, July 22, 1937, s. of Karl & Helene (Hauser), m. Elisabeth (Bock), chil: Christoph; Antje. Educ: U. of Gottingen, ThD 1969. Emp: Evang. Kirche von Westfalen, 1962-75 Vikar, 1965-72 Pfarrer Gesamthochschule Paderborn, 1972-80 Prof.; U. of Tubingen, 1980- Prof., NT. Spec: New Testament. Pub: *Philipper 2:6-11* (Mohr, 1991); "Unknown Sayings of Jesus" in *The Gospel and*

the Gospels (1991); *Paulusstudien* (Mohr, 1989); "Struktur und Gedankengang des Logos-Hymnus in Joh 1:1-18" *ZNW* 78 (1987); *Katapausis, Die Vorstellung vom endzeitlichen Ruheort im Hebraeerbrief* (Mohr, 1970); and others. Mem: SNTS 1971-. Rec: Baroque music, the art of icons of the Orthodox Ch. Addr: (o) Evangelical-Theological Sem., Liebermeisterstrasse 12, D-7400 Tubingen 1, Germany 07071-292872; (h) Kleiststrasse 1, DV-7400 Tubingen 1, Germany 07071-26828.

HOFRICHTER, Peter L., b. Vienna, Austria, May 24, 1940, s. of Arthur & Christine (Horny), m. Hilde (Polak), chil: Katharina; Veronika; Joachim; Pia. Educ: U. Wien, PhD, Hist. 1967; U. Salzburg, ThD 1977; U. Graz, Habil. 1985. Emp: Intl. Forschungszentrum, Salzburg, 1964-71; U. Salzburg, 1971-81 Asst., 1984-93 Assoc. Prof., 1993- U. Prof. fuer Patrologie; U. Mainz, Germany, 1981-84 Lehrstuhlvertreter fur NT. Spec: New Testament, Apocrypha and Post-biblical Studies. Pub: "Gottesbild und Logoslehre bei Apologeten, Modalisten und Gnostikern: Johanneische Christologie in ihrer fruhesten Rezeption" in *Monotheismus und Christologie, Zur Gottesfrage im hellenistischen Judentum und im Urchristentum*, Quaestiones disputatae 138 (1992); "Von den zwei Speisungen des Markus zu den zwei Aussendungen des Lukas" in *Theologie im Werden*, Gedenkschrift fur O. Kuss (1992); "Johannesevangelium" in *Neues Bibellexikon*, Lieferung 8 (1992); *Im Anfang war der "Johannesprolog": Das urchristliche Logosbekenntnis—die Basis neutestamentlicher und gnostischer Theologie*, Biblische Untersuchungen 17 (1986); *Nicht aus Blut, sondern monogen aus Gott geboren: Textkritische, dogmengeschichtliche und exegetische Untersuchung zu Joh 1,12-14*, Forschung zur Bibel 31 (1978); and others. Mem: SNTS; Assn. Intl. d'etudes patristiques; Collegium Bibl. Munchen; Osterreichisches Katholisches Bibelwerk. Rec: Traveling. Addr: (o) U. Salzburg, Theologische Fakultat, Universitatplatz 1, A-5020 Salzburg, Austria 0043 662 8044; (h) Wallmannhofstrasse 3, A-5400 Hallein, Austria 0043 6245 5010.

HOGLUND, Kenneth G., b. Providence, RI, April 25, 1954, s. of Stanley F. & Phyllis, m. Karen (Spradling), chil: Chace; Meagan. Educ: Wheaton Coll., BA 1975; Duke U., MA 1989, PhD 1989. Emp: Duke U., 1987-88 Instr.; U. of N.C., 1988-89 Vis. Prof.; Wake Forest U., 1990-91 Vis. Asst. Prof., 1991- Asst. Prof. Excv: Giza, Egypt, 1974 Area Supr.; Sepphoris Project, 1985-86 Area Supr., Computer Programmer. Spec: Archaeology, Hebrew Bible, Egyptology. Pub: *Achaemenid Imperial Administration and the Missions of Ezra and Nehemiah*, SBL Diss. Ser. (Scholars, 1992); "The Achaemenid Context" in *Second Temple Studies, vol. 1: The Persian Period* (Sheffield, 1991); *The Listening Heart: Essays on Wisdom and Psalms in Honor of Roland E. Murphy.*, ed. (Sheffield, 1987). Mem: CBA; SBL. Rec: Hiking, fishing. Addr: (o) Wake

Forest U., Dept. of Religion, Winston-Salem, NC 27109 919-759-5461; (h) 2713 Elgin St., Durham, NC 27704 919-220-3428.

HOHLFELDER, Robert L., Educ: Bowdoin Coll., BA 1960; Ind. U., MA 1962, PhD 1966. Emp: Anatolia Coll., Greece, Inst. of Hellenic Stud., 1978-81 Fac.; U. of Colo., 1978- Prof., Hist.; U. of Haifa, Ctr. for Maritime Stud., 1981- Adj. Prof.; E European Mon., Byzantine Ser., Ed. Excv: Kenchreai, Greece; Halieis, Greece; Humayma, Jordan, 1982; Carthage, Tunisia, 1982; Caesarea Anc. Harbor Excv. Proj., Co-dir. Spec: Archaeology. Awd: Dumbarton Oaks, Ctr. for Byzantine Stud., Vis. Fellow; NEH, grant; ACLS, grant; Amer. Phil. Soc., grant. Addr: (o) U. of Colorado, Dept. of History, Campus Box 234, Boulder, CO 80309 303-492-8431.

HOLDREGE, Barbara A., b. Caldwell, ID, d. of George & Elizabeth Louise. Educ: Vassar Coll., AB 1973; Harvard Div. Sch., MTS, Hist. of Relig. 1982; Harvard U., AM 1985, PhD, Study of Relig. 1987. Emp: Harvard U., 1981-86 Res. Asst., 1982-87 Teaching Fellow, Com. on the Study of Relig.; U. of Calif., Santa Barbara, Dept. of Relig. Stud., 1987-93 Asst. Prof., 1993- Assoc. Prof. Spec: Apocrypha and Post-biblical Studies. Pub: *Veda and Torah: Transcending the Textuality of Scripture* (SUNY, 1993); "The Bride of Israel: The Ontological Status of Scripture in the Rabbinic and Kabbalistic Traditions" in *Rethinking Scripture: Essays from a Comparative Perspective* (SUNY, 1989); and others. Awd: Harvard U., Mentorship Grant 1987; U. of Calif., Santa Barbara, Regents' Jr. Fac. Fellow. 1988-89, 1992-93, Fac. Career Development Awd. 1989-90, 1990-91, Harold J. Plous Memorial Awd. 1989-90; Regents' Hum. Fac. Fellow. 1993-94. Mem: SBL; AAR; AOS; Assn. for Asian Stud.; Intl. Assn. for the Hist. of Relig. Addr: (o) U. of California, Santa Barbara, Dept. of Religious Studies, 4711 South Hall, Santa Barbara, CA 93106 805-893-3578; (h) 964 West Campus Ln., Goleta, CA 93117 805-968-6100.

HOLLADAY, John S., Jr., b. Chiengmai, Thailand, October 15, 1930. Educ: U. of Ill., BS 1952; McCormick Theol. Sem., BD 1959; Harvard U., ThD, OT 1966. Emp: Princeton U., 1963-65 Instr. of Relig.; Melanethon Jacobus, 1965-66 Instr., 1966-68 Asst. Prof., 1968-78 Assoc. Prof.; U. of Toronto, 1978- Prof. of Arch. Spec: Archaeology. Pub: "Of Sherds and Strata: Contributions Toward an Understanding of the United Monarchy" in *Magnalia Dei: The Mighty Acts of God* (Doubleday, 1976); *A Technical Aid to Pottery Drawing: On Cutting the Gordian Pot* (1976); *Gezer II: Report of the 1967-70 Seasons in Fields I and II,* contb. (1974); "Further Excavations at Gezer, 1967-71" *BA* (1971). Mem: SBL; ASOR; Colloquium OT Res., Pres. 1972-73; Canadian SBL. Addr: (o) U. of Toronto, Dept. of Near Eastern Studies, Toronto, ON M5S 1A1, Canada.

HOLLADAY, William L., b. Dallas, TX, June 23, 1926, s. of William & Louise (Cook). Educ: U. of Calif., BA 1948; Pacific Sch. of Relig., BD 1951; State U. of Leiden, Netherlands, ThD 1958. Emp: Elmhurst Coll., 1960-63 Asst. Prof., Relig.; Near East Sch. of Theol., Lebanon, 1963- 70 Prof., OT; Andover Newton Theol. Sch., 1970- Lowry Prof. of OT; *VT,* 1973- Ed. Bd.; *JBL,* 1975-78 Assoc. Ed. Spec: Hebrew Bible, Semitic Languages, Texts and Epigraphy. Pub: *The Psalms Through Three Thousand Years* (Fortress, 1993); *Jeremiah 2* (Fortress, 1989); *Jeremiah 1* (Fortress, 1986); *A Concise Hebrew and Aramaic Lexicon of the Old Testament, Based on the Lexical Work of Ludwig Koehler and Walter Baumgartner* (Brill, 1971); and others. Mem: SBL 1958-. Addr: (o) 210 Herrick Rd., Newton Centre, MA 02159 617-964-1100.

HOLLAND, Glenn S., b. Santa Monica, CA, July 14, 1952, s. of Glen A. & Marjorie S., m. Sandra S., chil: Nathaniel I.; Gregory T. Educ: Stanford U., BA 1974; U. of Oxford, MA, Theol. 1982; U. of Chicago, PhD, Bible, NT 1986. Emp: St. Xavier Coll., 1984 Lect., Relig. Stud.; Allegheny Coll., 1985-92 Asst. Prof., Relig. Stud., 1992- Assoc. Prof., Bishop James Mills Thoburn Chair of Relig. Stud. Spec: New Testament. Pub: "Anti-Judaism in Paul: The Case of Romans" *Proc. East. Great Lakes Bibl. Soc.* 10 (1990); *The Tradition that You Received from Us: 2 Thessalonians in the Pauline Tradition,* Hermaneutische Untersuchungen zur Theol. 24 (Mohr, 1988); "Augustine's Hermeneutics as Polemic and Apologetic: the Case of *De Sermone Domine in Monte*" *Proc. East. Great Lakes Bibl. Soc.* 7 (1987); "Let No One Deceive You in Any Way: 2 Thessalonians as a Reformulation of the Apocalyptic Tradition" in *SBL Seminar Papers* (1985); and others. Mem: SBL; East. Great Lakes Bibl. Soc.; Luth. Theol. Soc. of N Amer. Rec: Comedy. Addr: (o) Allegheny College, Box 90, Meadville, PA 16335 814-332-3316; (h) 347 Ravine St., Meadville, PA 16335 814-724-6861.

HOLLANDER, Harm W., b. Leiderdorp, Netherlands, September 6, 1949, s. of H. & C. (van den Berg), m. M.J. (Azcona), chil: Rafael; Edward. Educ: U. of Leiden, DTh 1981. Emp: Netherlands Bible Soc., 1977-80, 1983-91 Res., Exegesis & Trans.; U. of Leiden, 1991- Lect., Res. Schol. Spec: New Testament, Apocrypha and Post-biblical Studies. Pub: *The Testaments of the Twelve Patriarchs: A Commentary,* co-auth. (Brill, 1985); *Joseph as an Ethical Model in the Testaments of the Twelve Patriarchs* (Brill, 1981); "Hebrews 7.11 and 8.6: A Suggestion for the Translation of *Nenomothetetai Epi*" *BT* 30 (1979); *The Testaments of the Twelve Patriarchs. A Critical Edition of the Greek Text* (Brill, 1977); "The Ethical Character of the Patriarch Joseph" in *Studies on the Testament of Joseph* (1975); "The Relationship between Ms. Athos Laura I 48 and Ms. Athos Laura K 116" in *Studies on the Testaments of the Twelve Patriarchs* (1975); and others. Mem: SNTS

1987-. Rec: Fishing. Addr: (o) Theologisch Instituut, MatthDeVrieshof 1, Postbus 9515, 2300 RA Leiden, Netherlands 071-272578; (h) Kempen 66, 2036 EM Haarlem, Netherlands 023-365108.

HOLLERAN, J. Warren, b. San Francisco, CA, April 23, 1928, s. of John M. & Margaret (Heenan). Educ: St. Patrick's Coll., BA 1949; Gregorian U., STB 1951, STL 1953, STD (summa cum laude) 1972; U. of Calif., Berkeley, MA, Phil. 1960; U. of San Francisco, MA 1977. Emp: St. Patrick's Sem., 1968- Prof., Sacred Scripture; U. of Notre Dame, Ctr. for Continuing Formation in Min., 1976- Vis. Prof., Scripture; Franciscan Sch. of Theol., 1986-87 Vis. Prof., NT Stud.; Grad. Theol. Union, 1988-90 Vis. Prof., Scripture; Seton Hall U., 1989-90 Vis. Prof., Scripture. Spec: New Testament. Pub: "The Bible and the Ongoing Education of Priests" *Bull. de Saint-Sulpice* (1992); "The Saint and the Scoundrel (Luke 18:9-14)" *The Bible Today* 25 (1987); *The Synoptic Gethsemane: A Critical Study* (1973); and others. Awd: Apptd. Prelate of Honor by Pope Paul VI 1972; Gregorian U., Papal Medal of Honor 1972; U. of Notre Dame, Ctr. for Pastoral & Social Min., Fellow. 1982. Mem: CTSA; CBA; SBL. Rec: Music, theater, skiing. Addr: (o) St. Patrick's Seminary, 320 Middlefield Rd., Menlo Park, CA 94025 415-325-5621.

HOLLIS, Susan T., b. Boston, MA, March 17, 1939, d. of James & Dorothy, chil: Deborah; Harrison. Educ: Smith Coll., AB 1962; Harvard U., PhD 1982. Emp: Harvard U., 1980-88 Instr.; Scripps Coll., 1988-91 Asst. Prof., Dir., Hum. Internship Prog.; Union Inst., Coll. of Undergrad. Stud., 1991- Prof. Spec: Egyptology. Pub: *The Ancient Egyptian Tale of Two Brothers, The Oldest Fairy Tale in the World* (U. of Okla., 1990); "On the Nature of Bata, the Hero of the Papyrus d'Orbiney" *Chronique d'Egypt* (1985); and others. Mem: SBL 1981-; AAR 1981-. Rec: Music, sailing, reading. Addr: (o) The Union Institute, 4801 Wilshire Blvd., Ste. 250, Los Angeles, CA 90010 213-936-8328; (h) 1233 Woodbury Ct., Apt D, Upland, CA 91786-4322 909-931-9341.

HOLMAN, Charles L., b. Oxnard, CA, March 30, 1935, s. of Charles & Lois, m. Hyacinth Rose, chil: Dorothy Annette; Emily Yvette (Crawford). Educ: Westmont Coll., BA 1957; Fuller Theol. Sem., BD 1962, ThM 1967; U. of Nottingham, PhD 1982. Emp: Regent U., 1982-93 Assoc. Prof., 1993- Prof. Spec: New Testament. Pub: "A Lesson from Matthew's Gospel for Charismatic Renewal" in *Faces of Renewal* (Hendrickson, 1988); "The Idea of an Imminent Parousia in the Synoptic Gospels" *Studia Biblica et Theologica* 3 (1975). Mem: Soc. for Pentecostal Stud. 1982-; Tyndale Fellow. 1983-; SBL 1984-. Rec: Violin playing, reading. Addr: (o) Regent U., Virginia Beach, VA 23464 804-523-7435; (h) 501 Sarah Cir., Virginia Beach, VA 23464 804-499-2697.

HOLMBERG, Bengt V., b. Uppsala, Sweden, June 10, 1942, s. of Tage & Inger, m. Solweig (Johansson), chil: Charlotta; Andreas; Rebecka; Katarina. Educ: U. of Lund, BDiv 1965, MDiv 1966, DTheol 1978. Emp: Luth. Theol. Coll., Tanzania, 1979-83, 1989-92 Lect., Head of Bibl. Dept.; U. of Lund, 1983- Docent. Spec: New Testament. Pub: *Sociology and the New Testament: An Appraisal* (Augsburg, 1990); "Sociologiska perspektiv pa Gal. 2:11-14 (21)" *SEA* 55 (1990); "Reciprocitetsnyanser i *allelon*" *SEA* 51-52 (1986-87); *Paul and Power: The Structure of Authority in the Primitive Church as Reflected in the Pauline Epistles* (Fortress, 1980); "Sociological Versus Theological Analysis of the Question Concerning a Pauline Church Order" in *Paulinische Literatur und paulinische Theologie* (1980). Mem: SNTS 1990-. Addr: (o) Lunds U., Teologiska Inst., Allhelgona kyrkogata 8, S-223 62 Lund, Sweden; (h) Naktergalen 21, S-245 62 Hjaerup, Sweden 040-461170.

HOLMES, Michael W., b. Delano, CA, December 14, 1950, s. of William & Shirley, m. Mary Patricia. Educ: U. of Calif. at Santa Barbara, BA 1973; Trinity Evang. Div. Sch., MA 1976; Princeton Theol. Sem., PhD 1984. Emp: Trinity Evang. Div. Sch., 1977 Teaching Fellow, NT; Princeton Theol. Sem., 1981 Instr., NT; Bethel Coll., 1982- Prof., Bibl. Stud. Spec: New Testament. Pub: *The Text of the Fourth Gospel in the Writings of Origen,* co-auth. (Scholars, 1992); *The Apostolic Fathers* (Baker, 1992); "The Text of the Matthean Divorce Passages" *JBL* (1990); "The Text of Matthew 5:11" *NTS* (1986); "The 'Majority Text Debate': New Form of an Old Question" *Themelios* (1983); "Origen and the Inerrancy of Scripture" *JETS* (1981); "Paul's Soteriological *Pas:* Universal or Limited? An Examination of Three Pauline Texts" *Trinity Jour.* (1977); and others. Mem: SBL 1978-; IBR 1981-. Rec: Fishing, woodworking. Addr: (o) Bethel College, 3900 Bethel D., St. Paul, MN 55112 612-638-6349.

HOLMGREN, Fredrick C., b. Cadillac, MI, April 1, 1926, s. of Charles & Freda, m. Betty Jean (Carlson), chil: Mark; Margaret. Educ: North Park Theol. Sem., Dip. 1952; Union Theol. Sem., BD (magna cum laude) 1955, STM (summa cum laude) 1957, ThD 1963. Emp: North Park Theol. Sem., 1960- Prof., Bibl. Lit.; *The Covenant Quar.,* 1960-64, 1968-72, 1980-84 Ed. Bd.; *Intl. Theol. Comm.,* 1982- Co-Ed. Spec: Hebrew Bible. Pub: "Faithful Abraham and the 'Amanah Covenant (Neh. 9:6-10:1)" *ZAW* (1992); "Holding Your Own Against God (Gen.32)" *Interpretation* 44 (1990); "The God of History: Biblical Realism and the Lectionary" in *Remembering for the Future* I (Pergamon, 1989); *Israel Alive Again: A Commentary on Ezra and Nehemiah* (Eerdmans, 1987); *With Wings as Eagles: Isaiah 40-55* (1973); and others. Awd: Rockefeller Doc. Fellow Relig. 1960; Ruprecht-Karl U., Germany, 1968-69 Vis. Schol. Mem: SBL. Rec: Boating, swimming, travel.

Addr: (o) North Park Theological Sem., 5125 N Spaulding Ave., Chicago, IL 60625 312-794-5271; (h) 5536 N Sawyer Ave., Chicago, IL 60625 312-463-3941.

HOLTZ, Traugott, b. Germany, July 9, 1931, s. of D. Gottfried & Elisabeth (Seyer), m. Regina (Muecke), chil: Christane; Stephan; Annegret; Barbara. Educ: Martin Luther U., Germany DTh 1960, Habil. 1964. Emp: Humboldt U., Berlin, 1964-65 Docent, NT; Ernst Moritz Arndt U., Germany, 1965-71 Prof.; Martin Luther U., 1970- Prof., NT. Spec: New Testament. Pub: *Geschichte und Theologie des Urchristentums,* Ges. Aufsaetze (1991); *Der erste Brief an die Thessalonicher* (EKK, 1986); *Jesus aus Nazaret* (1981); *Die Christologie der Apokalypse des Johannes* (1971); "Christliche Interpolationen in 'Joseph und Aseneth'" *NTS* (1967-68); and others. Mem: SNTS 1965-. Addr: (h) Bergschenkenweg 5, 0-4050 Halle, Germany 03-45-30449.

HOMAN, Martin J., b. Hammond, IN, October 12, 1953, s. of Marten & Beverly (Smeltzer), m. Lisa C. (Loeffler). Educ: Concordia Sr. Coll., BA 1976; Concordia Sem., MDiv 1980, STM 1982; Lutheran Sch. of Theol., ThM 1986. Emp: Concordia Coll., 1981-84 Instr., 1984-87 Asst. Prof.; Grace Luth. Ch., 1988-1990 Pastor; God's Word to the Nations Bible Soc., 1990- In-house Hebrew Trans. Spec: Hebrew Bible, Apocrypha and Post-biblical Studies. Pub: "A Comparative Study of the Psalter in Light of 11QPSA" *Westminster Theol. Jour.* (1977); and others. Addr: (o) God's Word to the Nations Bible Society, PO Box 26343, Cleveland, OH 44126-0343 216-779-9050; (h) 5568 Decker Rd., North Olmstead, OH 44070.

HOMERSKI, Joseph, b. Roznow, Poland, August 20, 1922, s. of Thomas & Catherine (Rojek). Educ: Cath. U. Lublin, Doc. 1957, Habil. 1971; Pont. Bibl. Inst., Lic. 1960; Ecole Biblique, Jerusalem, Eleve Titulaire 1961. Emp: Theol. Inst., Tarnów, 1961-72 Prof., OT Exegesis; Cath. U., Lublin, 1972- Prof., OT Exegesis, 1984-87 Dean, Theol. Fac. Spec: Hebrew Bible. Pub: *Ewangelia wedlug sw.Mateusza: Wstep-Przeklad-Komentarz* (1979); *Ezechiel i Daniel: Przeklad-Komentarz* (1975); *Ksiega Zachariasza. Wstep-Preklad-Komentarz* (1968); and others. Mem: Cath. U. Lublin, Learned Soc. 1984-. Addr: (h) ul. I. Radziszewskiego 7, 20-039 Lublin, Poland.

HOOKER, Morna D., b. Croydon, Surrey, England, May 19, 1931, d. of Percy & Lily (Riley), m. W. David Stacey. Educ: U. of Bristol, BA 1953, MA 1956; U. of Manchester, PhD 1966. Emp: U. of Durham, 1959-61 Res. Fellow; U. of London, King's Coll., 1961-70 Lect., NT Stud.; U. of Oxford, 1970-76 Lect.; U. of Cambridge, 1976- Lady Margaret's Prof. of Div.; *JTS,* 1985- Jt. Ed. Spec: New Testament.

Pub: *A Commentary on St. Mark* (A & C Black, 1991); *From Adam to Christ* (Cambridge U.P., 1990); "Traditions About the Temple in the Sayings of Jesus" *BJRL* 70 (1988); *Continuity and Discontinuity* (Epworth, 1986); *The Message of Mark* (Epworth, 1983); "Trial and Tribulation in Mark XIII" *BJRL* 65 (1982); and others. Mem: SNTS 1959-, Pres. 1988-89; SOTS 1968-. Rec: Molinology, walking. Addr: (o) The Divinity School, St. John's St., Cambridge CB2 1TW, England 0223-33.

HOOPS, Herlin H., b. Byron, NE, October 2, 1926, s. of Henry & Anna, m. Elizabeth (Obermeyer), chil: Pamela; Amy. Educ: Evang. Luth. Sem., BD 1955; U. of Hamburg, Germany, DTh 1958. Emp: Trinity Luth. Sem., 1960- Prof., NT. Spec: New Testament. Pub: "The Concept of Liberation" *Luth. Quar.* (1976); "Translating the Bible: The Challenge of an Ongoing Process" *Trinity Sem. Rev.* (1982); "First Peter: A Renewed Appreciation" *Trinity Seminary Review* (1983); "Christ and Mission: The Fourth Gospel and Our Witness" in *Bible and Mission* (Augsburg, 1986); "First Peter: A Community at Witness" *Trinity Sem. Rev.* (1985). Mem: SBL 1962-; Luth. Acad. for Scholarship 1972-84; Theol. of Amer. 1977-. Rec: Walking, volleyball. Addr: (o) Trinity Lutheran Seminary, 2199 E Main St., Columbus, OH 43209 614-235-4136; (h) 3051 Scottwood Rd., Columbus, OH 43227 614-235-2494.

HOOVER, Roy W., b. Everett, MA, January 1, 1932, s. of Virgil Merritt & Ruth (Hoover), m. Elizabeth A. (Killgore), chil: Richard Roy. Educ: Pasadena Coll., BA 1953; Harvard U., ThD 1968. Emp: Whitman Coll., 1967- Weyerhaeuser Prof. of Bibl. Lit. Spec: New Testament. Pub: "The Harpagmos Enigma: A Philological Solution" *HTR* (1971); and others. Mem: AAR 1967-; SBL 1967-; AIA 1967-. Addr: (o) Whitman College, 345 Boyer Ave., Walla Walla, WA 99632 509-527-5246; (h) 1406 S Division St., Walla Walla, WA 99362.

HOPKINS, David C., b. Mineola, NY, November 25, 1952, s. of Alvin C. & Jean (Lewis), m. Denise (Dombkowski), chil: Brian David; Ariel Eliza. Educ: Trinity Coll., BS 1974; Vanderbilt U., MA, OT 1979, PhD, OT 1984. Emp: Lancaster Theol. Sem., 1980-86 Asst. Prof., OT; Wesley Theol. Sem., 1986- Prof., Hebrew Scripture; St. Mary's Sem. & U., 1987-Adj. Prof., Bibl. Lit.; *BA,* 1991- Assoc. Ed., 1993- Ed. Excv: Tel-el-Umeiri, 1989 Square Supr.; Madaba Plains Project, 1992 Survey Field Supr. Spec: Archaeology, Hebrew Bible. Pub: "Economics in Old Testament Times" in *Mercer Dict. of the Bible* (Mercer U.P., 1990); *Early Israelite Agriculture,* co-ed. (Andrews U.P., 1988); "Life on the Land: The Subsistence Struggles of Early Israel" *BA* 50 (1987); *The Highlands of Canaan: Agricultural Life in the Early Iron Age,* Social World of Bibl. Antiq. 3

(Almond/ASOR, 1985); "The Dynamics of Agriculture in Monarchical Israel" *SBL 1983 Seminar Papers* (Scholars, 1983); "A Concise History of the Judaica Collection" *Tennessee Lbrn.* 33 (1981); "Between Promise and Fulfillment: Von Rad and the 'Sacrifice of Abraham'" *BZ* 23 (1980); and others. Awd: Amer. Coun. of Learned Soc. Res. Grant 1989; Amer. Phil. Soc. Res. Grant 1984, 1992. Mem: SBL, Pres., Chesapeake reg. 1988-89; ASOR; AIA. Rec: Swimming. Addr: (o) Wesley Theological Seminary, 4500 Massachusetts, Ave. NW, Washington, DC 20016 202-885-8699; (h) 13815 Flint Rock Rd., Rockville, MD 20853 301-871-9101.

HOPPE, Leslie J., b. Chicago, IL, September 22, 1944, s. of Daniel & Florence (Kapuscinski). Educ: Aquinas Inst. of Theol., MA 1971; NW U., PhD 1978. Emp: Aquinas Inst. of Theol., 1976-79 Asst. Prof.; St. Mary of the Lake Sem., 1979-81 Assoc. Prof.; Cath. Theol. Union, 1981- Prof.; *The Bible Today*, 1982-91 Ed. Bd., 1991- Ed. Excv: Meiron Excvn. Project, 1977-81 Area Supr.; Sepphoris, 1989-90. Spec: Archaeology, Hebrew Bible. Pub: *What Are They Saying About Biblical Archaeology?* (Paulist, 1984); "Isaiah 58:1-12" *BTB* (1983); "Elders and Deuteronomy—A Proposal" *Eglise et Theol.* (1983); "The Levitical Origins of Deuteronomy Reconsidered" *Bibl. Res.* (1983); *Joshua and Judges* (Glazier, 1982); and others. Mem: CBA; SBL; ASOR. Rec: Stamp collecting, music. Addr: (o) 5401 Cornell Ave., Chicago, IL 60615 312-753-5345; (h) 5103 S Ellis Ave., Chicago, IL 60615 312-752-7540.

HOPPE, Rudolf, b. Recklinghausen, Germany, August 8, 1946. Educ: Freiburg, Promotion 1977; U. Bamberg, Habil. 1991. Emp: Monheim/Cologne, 1976-81 Curate; Leverkusen, 1981-84 Tchr.; Cath. Bible Inst., Stuttgart, 1984-86 Referent; Bamberg U., 1986-92 Acad. Tchr.; U. of Passau, Cath. Fakultat, 1992 Prof. Spec: New Testament. Pub: "Der unausweichliche Konflikt—Uberlegungen zur urchristlichen Rezeption der Jesusverkundigung im Spannungsfeld zwischen Widerspruch und Anpassung" *BN* 66 (1993); "Vollkommenheit bei Matthaus als theologische Aussage" in *Salz der Erde—Licht der Welt*, Festschrift Anton Vogtle (1991); "Der Vorlaufer und die Nachfolger" in *Faszination Bibel* (1991); "Der Jakobusbrief" in *Glaube in der Bewährung* (1990); *Jakobusbrief*, SKK 15 (1989); "Das Mysterium und die Ekklesia: Aspekte zum Mysterium-Verstandnis im Epheser-und Kolosserbrief" in *Gottes Weisheit im Mysterium*; (1989); *Epheserbrief/Kolosserbrief*, SKK 10 (1987); *Der theologische Hintergrund des Jakobusbriefes* (1985); "Gleichnis und Situation" *BZ* 28 (1984); and others. Mem: Arbeitsgemeinschaft der deutschsprachigen Katholischen NT. Rec: Class. music. Addr: (o) U. Passau, Kath.-Theol. Fakultat, Michaeligasse 13, D-W 94030 Passau, Germany 0851-509615;

(h) Kleberstr. 33, D-W 8600 Bamberg, Germany 0951-25558.

HORN, Siegfried H., b. Wurzen, Germany, March 17, 1908, s. of Alwin & Klara, m. Elizabeth. Educ: Walla Walla Coll., BA 1947; Andrews U., MA 1948; U. of Chicago, PhD 1951. Emp: Andrews U., 1951-76 Prof., Arch. & History of Antiq.; *Andrews U. Sem. Stud.*, Vol. 1-12, 1963-74 Ed. Excv: Shechem, 1960, 1962, 1964 Field Supr.; Heshbon, 1968, 1971, 1973 Dir., 1974, 1976 Sr. Adv.; Tell Umeiri, 1984, 1989 Sr. Adv. Spec: Archaeology. Pub: "Why the Moabite Stone was Blown to Pieces" *BAR* 12/3 (1986); *Biblical Archaeology—A Generation of Discoveries* (BAS, 1978); "The Crown of the King of Ammonites" *AUSS* 11 (1973); "Scarabs from Shechem, I-III" *JNES* (1962, 1966, 1973); *The Chronology of Ezra 7*, co-auth. (Rev. & Herald, 1970); "The Amman Citadel Inscription" *BASOR* 193 (1967); "Who Was Solomon's Father-in-Law?" *Bibl. Res.* 12 (1967); *Records of the Past Illuminate the Bible* (Rev. & Herald, 1963); *SDA Bible Dict.* (Rev. & Herald, 1960); *Light from the Dustheaps* (Rev. & Herald, 1955); and others. Awd: Charles Weniger Awd. for Excellence 1979; Festschrift 1986. Mem: PEF 1938-; ASOR 1938-; AOS 1950-; SBL 1951-. Addr: (o) 601 Pope St., St. Helena, CA 94574 707-963-3688.

HORNING, Estella B., b. Havelock, NE, March 18, 1929, d. of Calvin & Carrie (Showalter), m. John S., chil: Ann Elizabeth; James; Judith; Kathleen; Carolyn. Educ: Bethany Theol. Sem., MDiv 1972; NW U. & Garrett Evang. Theol. Sem., PhD 1983. Emp: Bethany Theol. Sem., 1977-91 Dir. of Special Stud.; N Park Coll., 1983-86 Adj. Fac.; North. Bapt. Theol. Sem., 1980, 1986-92 Affiliate Prof.; Believer's Church Bible. Spec: Archaeology, New Testament. Pub: "Chiasmus, Creedal Structure, and Christology in Hebrews 12:1-2" *Bibl. Res.* (1978); and others. Mem: SBL 1982-; AAR 1982-. Rec: Swimming, photography, painting. Addr: (o) Northern Baptist Theological Seminary, 660 E Butterfield, Lombard, IL 60148 708-620-2174; (h) 631 Rochdale Circle, Lombard, IL 60148 708-629-0304.

HORSLEY, Richard A., Spec: New Testament. Pub: *Jesus and the Spiral of Violence: Popular Resistance in Roman Palestine* (Harper & Row, 1987); *Bandits, Prophets, and Messiahs*, co-auth. (Winston-Seabury, 1985); and others. Awd: BAS Publ. Awd. 1986. Addr: (o) U. of Massachusetts at Boston, Dept. of Classics, 100 Morissey Blvd., Boston, MA 02125-3393.

HORSNELL, Malcolm J. A., b. London, England, January 31, 1939, s. of John & Muriel, m. Janet. Educ: Wilfred Laurier U., Canada, BA 1967; Princeton Theol. Sem., ThM 1968; U. of Toronto, Canada, PhD 1974. Emp: U. of Toronto, 1973-78 Asst. Prof.; McMaster Div.

Coll., Canada, 1978- Prof. Spec: Hebrew Bible, Semitic Languages, Texts and Epigraphy. Pub: "Paul's Apocalyptic Gospel: A Review Article" *Theodolite* (1984); "Ebla" in *Major Cities of Bible Times*; "Myth," "Mythology" in *The International Standard Bible Ency.*, 2nd Ed.; and others. Mem: SBL; AOS; CSBS; Soc. of Mesopotamian Stud. Rec: Skiing, golf, swimming, model railroads. Addr: (o) McMaster Divinity College, Hamilton, ON L8S 4K1, Canada 416-525-9140; (h) 200 Cline Ave. N Hamilton, ON L8S 3Z9, Canada 416-526-9101.

HORTON, Fred L., Jr., b. Alexandria, VA, February 4, 1944, s. of Fred & Loetta (Willis), m. Patricia (Hildebrand), chil: E. Kristina (dec.); Joseph. Educ: Union Theol. Sem., BD 1967; Duke U., PhD 1971. Emp: Wake Forest U., 1970- Prof. Excv: Caesarea, 1978 Area Supr., 1991- Supr. Area TP; Hesi, 1979, 1981, 1983 Area Supr. Spec: Archaeology, New Testament, Semitic Languages, Texts and Epigraphy, Apocrypha and Post-biblical Studies. Pub: "Reflections on the Semitisms of Luke-Acts" in *Perspectives on Luke-Acts* (T & T Clark, 1978); *The Melchizedek Tradition* (Cambridge U.P., 1976); "A Reassessment of the Legal Forms in the Pentateuch and Their Functions" in *SBL Seminar Papers* (Scholars, 1971); "Formulas of Introduction of the Qumran Literature" *RQ* (1971); and others. Mem: AAR; SBL; ASOR; IES. Rec: Flying, amateur radio, meteorology. Addr: (o) Box 7468, Reynolda Station, Winston-Salem, NC 27109 919-761-5460.

HORTON, Stanley M., b. Huntington Park, CA, May 6, 1916, s. of Harry & Myrle, m. Evelyn, chil: Stanley, Jr.; Edward; Faith. Educ: U. of Calif., BS 1937; Gordon-Conwell Theol. Sem., MDiv 1944; Harvard U., STM 1945; Cen. Bapt. Theol. Sem., ThD 1959. Emp: Metropolitan Bible Inst., 1945-48 Instr.; Cen. Bible Coll., 1948-78 Prof.; Assemblies of God Theol. Sem., 1978-91 Prof.; Pentecostal Textbook Project, 1991- Coord. Excv: Dothan, 1962 Guest Prof. Spec: Archaeology, Hebrew Bible, New Testament. Pub: *The Ultimate Victory: An Exposition of the Book of Revelation* (Gospel, 1991); and others. Mem: ETS 1946-; NEAS. Addr: (o) 1445 Boonville Ave., Springfield, MO 65802 417-862-3344; (h) 615 W Williams, Springfield, MO 65803 417-833-3135.

HOSCH, Harold E., b. Cleveland, OH, April 11, 1929, s. of Herbert & Hazel, m. Mary Louise, chil: Stephen; Rebecca. Educ: Wheaton Coll., BA 1967, MA 1969. Emp: St. Paul Bible Coll., 1970-71 Instr.; Assoc. of Free Luth. Sch., 1971-77 Instr., OT; Luth. Brethren Sch., 1977-88 Prof. & Chair, Dept. of Bibl. Lang. & Exposition; Amer. Assn. of Luth. Ch., 1988- Dir. of Ch.-Based Theol. Educ. Spec: Hebrew Bible. Pub: "Exodus 12:41: A Translational Problem" *Hebrew Stud.* (1982); "The Concept of Prophetic Time in the Book of Joel" *JETS* (1972); "Theophany" in *The Wycliffe Bible Encyclopedia*. Mem: SBL 1970-; NAPH

1976-. Rec: Scale models. Addr: (o) 2605 Nimitz St., Eau Claire, WI 54701 715-835-4777.

HOSKISSON, Paul Y., b. Urbana, IL, September 1, 1943, m. Joaquina. Educ: Brigham Young U., BA 1969, MA 1973; Brandeis U., PhD 1986. Emp: U. Zurich, 1978-80 Lect., Akkadian & Ugaritic; Brigham Young U., 1991- Assoc. Prof., Anc. Scripture. Excv: Qarqur, Syria, 1983 Epigrapher. Spec: Semitic Languages, Texts and Epigraphy. Pub: "The Nisum Oath in Mari" in *Mari at Fifty: Studies in Honor of the 50th Anniversary of the Discovery of Tell Hariri-Mari* (Eisenbrauns, 1991); "Emar as an Empirical Model of the Transmission of Canon" in *The Biblical Canon in Comparative Perspective*, Scripture in Context IV (Mellen, 1991); and others. Mem: ASOR; SBL; AOS; Found. Assyriologique Georges Dossin. Rec: Backpacking, fishing. Addr: (o) Brigham Young U., 270 F JSB, Provo, UT 84602 801-378-4329; (h) 741 E 3900 N, Provo, UT 84604 801-224-0956.

HOULDEN, James Leslie, b. Knutsford, Cheshire, March 1, 1929, s. of James & Lily Alice. Educ: The Queen's Coll., Oxford, BA 1952, MA 1956. Emp: Trinity Coll., Oxford, 1960-70 Chaplain Fellow; Cuddesdon Theol. Coll., 1970-77 Prin.; King's Coll., London, 1977-87 Lect., 1987-94 Prof., Theol.; *Theol.*, 1984-91 Ed. Spec: New Testament. Pub: *Ethics and the New Testament* (T & T Clark, 1992); *Dict. of Biblical Interpretation*, co-ed. (SCM, 1990); *Johannine Epistles* (Black, 1973); *Paul's Letters from Prison* (Penguin, 1970); and others. Mem: SNTS. Addr: (o) King's College, Strand, London WC2R 2LS, England 071-873-2393; (h) 33 Raleigh Ct., Lymer Ave., London SE19 1LS, England 081-670-6648.

HOWARD, George E., b. Holdenville, OK, June 3, 1935, s. of F.S. & Ann, m. Teresa, chil: Allison; Lindsey; Mandy; Heath. Educ: Harding Grad. Sch., BA 1958, MTh 1961; Hebrew Union Coll., PhD 1964. Emp: David Lipscomb Coll., 1964-68 Assoc. Prof.; U. of Ga., 1968- Head, Dept. of Relig. Spec: New Testament, Apocrypha and Post-biblical Studies. Pub: *Paul: Crisis in Galatia. A Study in Early Christian Theology* (Cambridge U.P., 1979, 1990); "Was the Gospel of Matthew Originally Written in Hebrew?" *BR* 2/4 (1986); *The Teaching of Addai* (Scholars, 1981); "The Name of God in the New Testament" *BAR* 6/1 (1978); "The Tetragram and the New Testament" *JBL* (1977); "Romans 3:21-31 and the Inclusion of the Gentiles" *HTR* (1970); and others. Mem: SNTS; SBL, Pres., SW reg. 1980-81; Intl. Pseudepigrapha Project. Rec: Weight lifting, gardening, class. music. Addr: (o) U. of Georgia, Dept. of Religion, Peabody Hall, Athens, GA 30602 404-542-5356; (h) 305 Red Fox Run, Athens, GA 30605 404-549-7324.

HOWARD, Tracy L., b. Little Rock, AR, August 25, 1954, d. of Clyde & Peggy, m. Lee, chil: Stephanie; Melanie; Gregory. Educ: Tex. Christian U., MA 1983; Dallas Theol. Sem., ThM 1984; La.

State U., JD 1991. Emp: Arlington Bapt. Coll., 1980-84 Prof.; Grace Theol. Sem., 1984-88 Instr.; Vinson & Elkins, 1991- Attorney. Spec: New Testament. Pub: "The Literary Unity of 1 Thessalonians 4:13-5:11" *Grace Theol. Jour.* (1988); "Suffering in James 1:2-12" *Criswell Theol. Rev.* (1986); "The Use of Hosea 11:1 in Matthew 2:15: An Alternative Solution" *Bibliotheca Sacra* (1986); "The Meaning of 'Sleep' in 1 Thess. 5:10: A Reappraisal" *Grace Theol. Jour.* (1985); and others. Mem: SBL; ETS. Rec: Golf, guitar. Addr: (o) Vinson & Elkins, L.L.P., 1001 Fannin St., Houston, TX 77002 713-758-4512; (h) 7 E Summer Storm, The Woodlands, TX 77381.

HUBBARD, Benjamin J., b. Tacoma, WA, February 11, 1937, s. of Benjamin & Margaret (Wolfe), m. Judy, chil: Susan; David. Educ: Marquette U., MA 1967; U. of Iowa, PhD 1973. Emp: Gonzaga U., 1966-67 Lect.; Mount Mercy Coll., 1971-72 Lect.; U. of Waterloo, St. Jerome's Coll., 1972-81 Assoc. Prof.; Marquette U., 1983-85 Prof.; Calif. State U., Fullerton, 1985- Prof. Spec: Hebrew Bible, New Testament. Pub: "Geza Vermes's Contribution to Historical Jesus Studies: An Assessment" in *SBL Seminar Papers* (Scholars, 1985); "Luke, Josephus and Rome: A Comparative Approach to the Lukan *Sitz im Leben*" in *SBL Seminar Papers* (Scholars, 1979); *The Matthean Redaction of a Primitive Apostolic Commissioning: An Exegesis of Matt. 28:16-20* (Scholars, 1974); and others. Mem: SBL; AAR. Rec: Tennis, cycling, music. Addr: (o) California State U., Dept. of Religious Studies, Fullerton, CA 92634 714-773-3452; (h) 1880 Parkview Circle, Costa Mesa, CA 92627 714-646-3282.

HUBBARD, David A., b. Stockton, CA, April 8, 1928, s. of John King & Helena (White), m. Ruth (Doyal), chil: Mary Ruth. Educ: Conservative Bapt. Assn., Ord. Bapt. Min. 1952; Fuller Theol. Sem., BD 1952, ThM 1954; St. Andrews U., Scotland, PhD 1957. Emp: St. Andrews U., Scotland, 1955-56 Lect., OT Stud.; Westmont Coll., 1957-63 Asst. Prof., Chair, Dept. of Bibl. Stud.; Word Bibl. Comm. Ser., 1977- Gen. Ed.; Fuller Theol. Sem., 1963-93 Pres. & Prof., OT. Spec: Hebrew Bible, Semitic Languages, Texts and Epigraphy. Pub: *The Communicator's Commentary: Ecclesiates, Song of Solomon* (Word, 1991); *Hosea*, Tyndale Comm. (InterVarsity, 1989); *Joel, Amos*, Tyndale Comm. (InterVarsity, 1989); articles in *Evangelical Dict. of Theology* (Baker, 1984); articles in *The Illustrated Bible Dict.* (InterVaristy, 1980); *Book of James: Wisdom that Works* (Word, 1980); articles in *The New International Dict. of the Christian Church* (Zondervan, 1974); and others. Awd: Rockford Coll., LHD 1975; John Brown U., DD 1975; King Sejong U., Korea, DLitt 1985; Hope Coll., DLitt 1990; Friends U., EdD 1990; N Park Coll. & Theol. Sem., DD 1993. Mem: AAR 1959-; SBL 1959-; SOTS 1976-. Addr: (o) 658 Chelham Way, Santa Barbara, CA 93108 805-969-9874.

HUBBARD, Robert L., b. Reedley, CA, July 3, 1943, s. of Robert & Verna, m. Pamela Joan (Iverson), chil: Matthew; Benjamin. Educ: Wheaton Coll., AB 1965; Fuller Theol. Sem., BD 1969; Claremont Grad. Sch., MA 1977, PhD 1980. Emp: Denver Conservative Bapt. Sem., 1976-Prof., OT. Spec: Hebrew Bible. Pub: "The Go'el in Ancient Israel: Theological Reflections on an Israelite Institution" *Bull. for Bibl. Res.* (1991); *1-2 Kings* (Moody, 1991); "Theological Reflections on Naomi's Shrewdness" *TB* (1989); "Ruth iv.17: A New Solution" *VT* (1988); *The Book of Ruth* (Eerdmans, 1988); "The Hebrew Root PG' as a Legal Term" *JETS* (1984); "Is the *Tatshäre* Always a Sphere?" *JETS* (1982); "Dynamistic and Legal Processes in Psalm 7" *ZAW* (1982); *Old Testament Comm. Survey*, co-auth. (Theol. Students Fellow., 1981); and others. Mem: SBL 1974-; IBR 1980-. Rec: Jogging, tennis. Addr: (o) Denver Seminary, Box 10,000 UPS, Denver, CO 80250 303-761-2482; (h) 6837 S Birch Way, Littleton, CO 80122-2128.

HUDDLESTUN, John R., b. Delaware, OH, July 2, 1955, s. of Gladys & Lloyd, Jr., m. Birgit, chil: David L.; Peter A. Educ: Ohio State U., BM 1977; U. of Mich., MA, Bibl. & Near East. Stud. 1988. Emp: East. Mich. U., 1991-92 Lect., Rel. Stud.; *ABD*, 1992 Ed. Asst. Spec: Hebrew Bible, Egyptology. Pub: "Red Sea (OT)," "Nile (OT)" in *ABD* (Doubleday, 1992); *The Unity of the Hebrew Bible*, co-auth. (U. of Mich., 1991); *ISBE* vol. 4, contb. (Eerdmans 1988); *Eerdmans Bible Dict.*, contb. (Eerdmans, 1987); and others. Mem: Amer. Res. Ctr. in Egypt 1992-; ASOR 1991-; SBL 1988-; Soc. for the Study of Egyptian Antiq. 1990-. Rec: Racquetball, chess. Addr: (o) U. of Michigan, Dept. of Near Eastern Studies, 3074 Frieze Bldg., Ann Arbor, MI 48109 313-764-0314; (h) 1648 McIntyre, Ann Arbor, MI 48105 313-764-7092.

HUEY, F. B., Jr., b. Denton, TX, January 12, 1925, s. of F.B. & Gwendolyn, m. Nonna Lee, chil: Mary Anne; Linda; David. Educ: U. of Tex., BA 1945; SW Bapt. Theol. Sem., MDiv 1958, PhD 1961. Emp: South Brazil Bapt. Theol. Sem., Rio de Janeiro, 1962-65 Prof., OT; SW Bapt. Theol. Sem., 1965-90 Prof., OT; Bapt. Theol. Sem., Switzerland, 1971-72 Vis. Prof.; *SW Jour. of Theol.*, 1970-73 Book Rev. Ed., 1975-1978 Managing Ed. Spec: Hebrew Bible. Pub: *Numbers*, Bible Study Comm. (Zondervan, 1981); *Yesterday's Prophets for Today's World* (Broadman, 1980); *Zondervan Pictorial Ency. of the Bible*, contb. (Zondervan, 1975); "A Igreja na Europa de hoje" *O Jornal Batista* (1972); and others. Mem: SBL 1967-; NAPH 1983-. Rec: Reading, travel. Addr: (o) 2001 W Seminary, Fort Worth, TX 76122 817-923-1921; (h) 6128 Whitman Ave., Fort Worth, TX 76133 817-292-4991.

HUGENBERGER, Gordon P., b. Boston, MA, October 6, 1948, s. of Paul & Janet, m. Jane, chil: Nathan; Joel; Noah; Esther. Educ: Harvard U., BA 1973; Gordon-Conwell Theol. Sem., MDiv 1974;

Cheltenham & Oxford, PhD 1991. Emp: Gordon-Conwell Theol. Sem., 1974- Adj. Prof.; Lanesville Congl. Ch., 1974- Pastor. Spec: Hebrew Bible. Pub: "Women in Church Office: A Survey of Approaches to 1 Tim 2:8-15" *JETS* 35 (1992); Articles in *ISBE*, vol. 3, 4 (Eerdmans, 1986, 1988). Awd: Gordon-Conwell Theol. Sem., Pres. James Forrester Awd. 1974. Mem: SBL; ASOR; BAS; ETS. Rec: Running, carpentry. Addr: (h) 25 Leverett St., Gloucester, MA 01930 617-283-6878.

HUGHES, Frank W., b. Texarkana, TX, February 23, 1954, s. of William Morris & Mary (Witt). Educ: Hendrix Coll., BA, Relig. 1975; Seabury-West. Theol. Sem., MDiv 1979; U. of Chicago, MA 1981; NW U., PhD 1984. Emp: U. of North. Ia., 1985 Vis. Prof., Relig.; U. of N.C., Greensboro, 1985-86 Vis. Asst. Prof., Relig. Stud.; Episc. Diocese of Pa., 1988-91 Fac., Sch. of the Diaconte; La Salle U., 1990- Adj. Fac.; St. Mark's Episc. Ch., 1991- Rector. Spec: New Testament. Pub: "The Rhetoric of 1 Thessalonians" in BETL 87 (1990); "Rhetorical Criticism" in *Mercer Dict. of the Bible* (1990); *Early Christian Rhetoric and 2 Thessalonians,* JSNTSup 30 (JSOT, 1989); "Feminism and Early Christian History" *ATR* 69 (1987); "The Rhetoric of Reconciliation: 2 Corinthians 1:1-2:13 and 7:5-8:24" in JSNTSup 50; and others. Awd: U. of Gottingen, Fulbright Res. Grant 1986-87. Mem: SBL; NAPS; Intl. Soc. for the Hist. of Rhetoric. Rec: Photography, music (organist), computers. Addr: (o) 21 S Main St., Lewistown, PA 17044-2116 717-248-8327; (h) 454 S Juniata St., Lewistown, PA 17044-2321 717-242-4451.

HUGHES, John J., b. Memphis, TN, February 10, 1947, s. of John & Nell (Jones), m. Claire (McCaskill), chil: John; Ryan; Allen. Educ: Vanderbilt U., BA 1969; Westminster Theol. Sem., MDiv 1973. Emp: Westmont Coll., 1977-82 Asst. Prof.; 1982-86 Technical Writer; *Bits & Bytes Rev.,* 1986-92 Ed., Publ.; Bits & Bytes Computer Resources, 1986-92 Pres. Spec: New Testament. Pub: "Concordances to the Bible: A History and Prospective," co-auth. in *Analytical Concordance of the Greek New Testament* vol. I (Baker, 1991); *Bible Source Reference Manual* (Zondervan, 1991); *macBible Reference Manual* (Zondervan, 1990); "Computers and the Bible" *BAR* 16/6 (1990); "Beyond Word Processing" in *Critical Review of Books in Religion* (Scholars, 1990); *NIV Reference Manual* (Zondervan, 1989); *Bits, Bytes, and Biblical Studies: A Resource Guide for the Use of Computers in Biblical and Classical Studies* (Zondervan, 1987); "Hebrew IX 15ff. and Galatians III 15. A Study of Covenant Practice and Procedure" *NT* 21 (1979); and others. Awd: *Humanities Computing Yearbook,* 1988-90 Adv. Bd., Sect. Ed.; NEH, Ancient, Medieval & Renaissance Stud., Panelist 1990; Tyndale Fellow., Cambridge. Mem: SBL; Assn. for Computing in Hum.; Assn. for Lit. & Linguistic Computing. Rec: Music, sports, backpacking. Addr: (o) 623 Iowa Ave., Whitefish, MT 59937 406-862-7280.

HUGHES, Paul A., b. Tulsa, OK, September 14, 1957, s. of J. Barrie & Naomi (Kinard). Educ: Tex. A&M U., BS 1980; Assemblies of God Theol. Sem., MDiv 1986. Emp: Accuracy in Rel., 1991- Pres. Spec: New Testament. Pub: "How Did Man Change When Adam Fell?" *Paraclete* 23 (1989); "Worship in the Second Century: The Spiritual Dimension" *Paraclete* 21 (1987); and others. Mem: Soc. for Pentecostal Stud. 1986-; SBL 1987-; AAR 1987-. Rec: Class. & jazz music, anc. hist., civil war hist., photography, hiking. Addr: (o) 1111 Woods Dr., Liberty, TX 77575 409-336-7289; (h) Rt. 4, Box 469, Livingston, TX 77351-9404 409-685-4445.

HULL, William Edward, b. Birmingham, AL, May 28, 1930, s. of William E. & Margaret J. (King), m. Wylodine (Hester), chil: David; Susan. Educ: Samford U., BA 1951; South. Bapt. Theol. Sem., MDiv 1954, PhD 1960. Emp: South. Bapt. Theol. Sem., 1954-75 Prof.; *Rev. & Expositor,* 1964-68 Ed. Bd.; *Bapt. Message,* 1977-78 Contb. Ed.; NW La. Bapt. Assn., 1975-87 Exec. Bd.; Samford U., 1987- Provost. Spec: New Testament. Pub: *The Bible* (Covenant, 1974); "John" in *Broadman Bible Comm.* vol. 9 (Broadman, 1970); *The Gospel of John,* Alpa-Omega Ser. (Broadman, 1964); and others. Awd: Samford U., Denom. Service Awd. 1974. Mem: ASOR 1955-73; SBL 1956-; AAR 1957-. Addr: (h) 435 Vesclub Way, Birmingham, AL 35216 205-822-7958.

HULTGREN, Arland J., b. Muskegon, MI, July 17, 1939, s. of Arnold & Ina (Wold), m. Carole (Benander), chil: Peter; Stephen; Kristina. Educ: Augustana Coll., BA 1961; U. of Mich., MA 1963; Luth. Sch. of Theol. at Chicago, MDiv 1965; Union Theol. Sem., ThD 1971. Emp: Wagner Coll., 1969-77 Assoc. Prof.; Luth. NW Theol. Sem., 1977-86 Assoc. Prof., 1986- Prof., NT; *Woid & World,* 1981-88 Ed. Spec: New Testament. Pub: "The Johannine Footwashing (13:1-11) as Symbol of Eschatological Hospitality" *NTS* (1982); "The *Pistis Christou* Formulation in Paul" *NT* (1980); *Paul's Gospel and Mission* (Fortress, 1975); *I and II Timothy, Titus* (Augsburg, 1974); and others. Mem: SBL; SNTS. Addr: (o) Luther Northwestern Theological Seminary, 2481 Como Ave., St. Paul, MN 55108 612-641-3269; (h) 609 Ryan Ave. W, Roseville, MN 55113 612-488-9626.

HUNDERSMARCK, Lawrence F., b. Passaic, NJ, June 3, 1951, s. of Fred & Katherine, m. Kathleen, chil: Christopher; Maria; Kathleen. Educ: Providence Coll., MA 1974; U. of Dayton, MA 1976; Fordham U., PhD 1982. Emp: Pace U., 1980- Prof., Dir. of Ctr. for Relig. Stud. Spec: New Testament. Pub: *Great Thinkers of the Western World,* contb. (HarperCollins, 1992); "A Study of Luke 2:8-20: The Significance of Seeing (eidon) in the Lucan Portrait of the Shepherds" *ABAC Journ.* (1991); "Preaching the Passion. Late Medieval Lives of Christ as Sermon Vehicles" in *De Ore Domini: Preacher and Word* *in the Middle Ages* (West. Mich. U., 1989); and others. Mem: AAR; SBL. Addr: (o) Pace U., 78 N Broadway, White Plains, NY 10603.

HUNT, Harry B., Jr., b. Marshall, TX, July 16, 1944, s. of Harry, m. Patricia (Blackwell), chil: Patrick; Amy. Educ: SW Bapt. Theol. Sem., MDiv 1968, ThD 1972. Emp: SW Bapt. Coll., 1973-76 Asst. Prof.; SW Bapt. Theol. Sem., 1976- Prof. Spec: Archaeology, Hebrew Bible, Semitic Languages, Texts and Epigraphy. Pub: *Old Testament Background Material* (Scripta, 1990); "From Cyrus to Darius" *BI* (1985); "An Examination of the Current Emphasis on the Canon in the Old Testament Studies" *SW Jour. of Theol.* (1980); and others. Mem: ASOR 1978-; SBL 1976-. Rec: Gardening, golfing. Addr: (o) Southwestern Baptist Theological Seminary, PO Box 22388, Fort Worth, TX 76122 817-923-1921; (h) 1313 Country Manor Rd., Fort Worth, TX 76134 817-293-3288.

HUNT, Patrick N., b. San Diego, CA, February 9, 1951, s. of Donald & Patricia (Rhodes), m. Pamela (Sommerfeldt), chil: Hilary Ann; Allegra Christina; Beatrice Patricia. Educ: Simpson Coll., BA (magna cum laude) 1977; Dallas Theol. Sem., MA 1982; U. of London, Inst. of Arch., PhD 1991. Emp: Simpson Coll., 1984-92 Assoc. Prof.; Stanford U., Class. Dept., 1992- Vis. Schol.; U. of Calif.-Berkeley, 1992- Res. Fellow, Near East. Stud., U. of Calif.-Berkeley Extension., Instr. Excv: Jericho, 1990 Provenance Analysis; Olompali Petroglyph Project, 1986 Dir. Spec: Archaeology, New Testament, Semitic Languages, Texts and Epigraphy, Apocrypha and Post-biblical Studies. Pub: "Subtle Paronomasia in Canticum Canticorum" *BEATAJ* 20 (1992); "Mt. Saphon in Myth and Fact" in *Phoenicia and the Bible*, Studia Phoenicia XI, OLA 44 (1991); "Optical Petrology in the Field" *World Arch.* 21/1 (1989); "The International Summer School in Papyrology" *Bull. of the Inst. of Class. Stud.* 35 (1988). Mem: AIA 1984-; ASOR 1986-; Royal Geog. Soc. 1989-. Rec: Numismatics, philately, bibliophily, tennis, hiking. Addr: (o) Stanford U., Classics Dept., Bldg. 310, Stanford, CA 94305 408-338-7570; (h) 711 Elm Ave., San Bruno, CA 94066 916-222-6102.

HUNTER, A. Vanlier, b. Huntingdon, PA, March 28, 1939, s. of Austin & Twila. Educ: Pittsburgh Theol. Sem., MDiv 1964, ThM 1968; U. of Tubingen, 1969-70; U. of Basil, Switzerland, ThD 1981. Emp: Pittsburgh Theol. Sem., 1964-68 Teaching Fellow; St. Mary's Sem. & U., 1972- Prof. of Bibl. Stud., Assoc. Dean, Ecumenical Inst. Spec: Archaeology, Hebrew Bible. Pub: "A Case for Learning Biblical Languages Inductively" in *Proclaimer of the Word: Essays in Honor of James Arthur Walther* (Pickwick, 1983); *Seek the Lord: A Study of the Meaning and Function of the Exhortations in Amos, Hosea, Isaiah, Micah, and Zephaniah* (St. Mary's Sem., 1982). Mem:

SBL 1965-; CBA 1973-; SOTS 1978-. Rec: Photography, travel. Addr: (o) St. Mary's Seminary and U., 5400 Roland Ave., Baltimore, MD 21210 410-323-3200; (h) 336-B1 Stevenson Ln., Baltimore, MD 21204 410-823-9269.

HURD, John C., b. Boston, MA, March 26, 1928, s. of John & Mary (Hough), m. Helen (Porter), chil: Elisabeth; Louisa; Lyman. Educ: Episc. Theol. Sch., BD 1952; Yale U., MA, NT 1957, PhD, NT 1961. Emp: Princeton U., 1958-60 Instr., Relig.; Episc. Theol. Sem. of the SW, 1960-67 Prof., NT; *Anglican Theol. Rev.*, 1966-69 Ed.-in-Chief; Trinity Coll., 1967-93 Prof., NT, 1992-93 Dean (pro tem). Spec: New Testament. Pub: "Paul Ahead of His Time: 1 Thess. 2:13-16" in *Anti-Judaism in Early Christianity* (1986); *Targum Pseudo-Jonathan of the Pentateuch: Text and Concordance*, co-auth. (Ktav, 1984); *The Origin of 1 Corinthians* (1965, 1984); "'The Jesus Whom Paul Preaches' (Acts 19:13)" in *From Jesus to Paul: Studies in Honour of Francis Wright Beare*, co-ed. (Wilfrid Laurier U.P., 1984); "Isaiah's Curse According to Mark" *Bull. of the CSBS* 33 (1973); "The Sequence of Paul's Letters" *Canadian Jour. of Theol.* 14/3 (1968); "Pauline Chronology and Pauline Theology" in *Christian History and Interpretation: Studies Presented to John Knox* (1967); and others. Awd: Christian Res. Found. Awd. 1964; Coun. of Ontario U., awd. for curr. innovation 1974; Assn. of Theol. Sch., awd. for development of computer-assisted instr. materials for Greek 1977-78. Mem: SBL 1956-; CSBS 1967-; CSSR 1979-. Rec: Scottish country dancing, sailing. Addr: (o) Trinity Coll., 6 Hoskin Ave., Toronto, ON M5S 1H8, Canada; (h) 49 Wanless Ave., Toronto, ON M4N 1V5, Canada 416-485-2429.

HUROWITZ, Victor B., b. Philadelphia, PA, April 19, 1948, s. of Bertram & Sadie (Shapiro), m. Ann, chil: Daniel. Educ: Temple U., BA 1969; Hebrew U., MA 1975, PhD 1983. Emp: Hebrew Union Coll., 1977-79 Instr., Bibl. Hebrew; Hebrew U., 1978-91 Instr., Assyriology; Ben Gurion U., 1978- Sr. Lect., Bible & Anc. Near East. Stud. Spec: Hebrew Bible, Mesopotamian Studies, Semitic Languages, Texts and Epigraphy. Pub: "Urim and Thummim in Light of an Akkadian Psephomancy Text (LKA 137)," co-auth. *JANES* 21 (1993); *I Have Built You an Exalted House: Temple Building in the Bible in Light of Mesopotamian and Northwest Semitic Writings* (Sheffield, 1992); "Some Literary Observations on the Sitti-Marduk Kudurru (BBS6)" *ZA* 88 (1992); "Isaiah's Impure Lips and Their Purification in Light of Akkadian Sources" *HUCA* 60 (1989); "The Priestly Account of Building the Tabernacle" *JAOS* 105 (1985); "Literary Structures in Samsuiluna A" *JCS* 36 (1984); and others. Awd: BAS, Publ. Awd. 1986; Hebrew U., A. Z. Shkop Publ. Awd. 1991. Mem: AOS 1983-; AJS 1983-. Addr: (o) Ben Gurion U., Dept. of Bible & Ancient Near Eastern Stud., Beer Sheba, Israel 057-461-092; (h) Mishol Psamon 47, Beer Sheba, Israel 057-413-124.

HURTADO, Larry W., b. Kansas City, MO, December 29, 1943, s. of Weir & Bonnie, m. Shannon, chil: Tiffany; Elisse; Jesse. Educ: Trinity Evang. Div. Sch., MA 1967; Case West. Reserve U., PhD 1973. Emp: Regent Coll., Canada, 1975-78 Asst. Prof., NT; U. of Manitoba, 1978- Prof., Relig. Spec: New Testament, Apocrypha and Post-biblical Studies. Pub: "The Gospel of Mark: Evolutionary or Revolutionary Document?" *JSNT* 40 (1990); *One God, One Lord: Early Christian Devotion and Ancient Jewish Monotheism* (Fortress, 1988); "New Testament Christology: Retrospect and Prospect" *Semeia* 30 (1985); "Revelation 4-5 in the Light of Jewish Apocalyptic Analogies" *JSNT* 25 (1985); "Jesus as Lordly Example in Philippians 2:5-11" in *From Jesus to Paul: Studies in Honour of Francis Wright Beare* (Wilfrid Laurier U.P., 1984); *Mark: A Good News Commentary* (Harper & Row, 1983); "The Jerusalem Collection and the Book of Galatians" *JSNT* 5 (1979); "New Testament Christology: A Critique of Bousset's Influence" *Theol. Stud.* 40 (1979); and others. Mem: SBL; CSBS; IBR. Rec: Tennis, skiing, archery. Addr: (o) U. of Manitoba, Dept. of Religion, Winnipeg, Man. R3T 2N2, Canada 204-474-9516; (h) 11 Rutgers Bay, Winnipeg, Man. R3T 3C9, Canada 204-269-5223.

HURVITZ, Avi, b. Tel-Aviv, Israel, August 30, 1936, s. of Elhanan & Zipora, m. Gila, chil: Naama; Osnat; Tamar. Educ: Hebrew U., BA 1960, MA 1962, PhD 1967. Emp: Hebrew U., 1967- Lect., 1978- Prof.; U. of Pa., 1978-79 Vis. Prof.; U. of CA, San Diego, 1983 Vis. Prof.; Harvard U., 1988 Vis. Prof.; Brandeis U., 1988 Vis. Prof. Spec: Hebrew Bible, Semitic Languages, Texts and Epigraphy. Pub: *Wisdom Language in Biblical Psalmody* (Magnes, 1991); "Dating the Priestly Source in Light of the Historical Study of Biblical Hebrew a Century After Wellhausen" *ZAW* 100 (1988); "Wisdom Vocabulary in the Hebrew Psalter" *VT* 38 (1988); "The History of a Legal Formula—*Kol'asher hapes 'a'sah* (Psalms cxv 3, cxxxv 6)" *VT* 32 (1982); *A Linguistic Study of the Relationship Between the Priestly Source and the Book of Ezekiel—A New Approach to an Old Problem,* Cahiers de la Rev. Bibl. 20 (Gabalda, 1982); "The Date of the Prose-Tale of Job Linguistically Reconsidered" *HTR* 67 (1974); *The Transition Period in Biblical Hebrew—A Study in Post-Exilic Hebrew and its Implications for the Dating of Psalms* (Bialik Inst., 1972); "The Chronological Significance of 'Aramaisms' in Biblical Hebrew" *IEJ* 18 (1968); and others. Awd: J. Klausner Awd. for Jewish Stud. 1968. Mem: IOSOT. Addr: (o) Hebrew U., Dept. of Bible and Hebrew Language, Jerusalem 91905, Israel 02-883569; (h) 32 Tchernichovsky St., Jerusalem 92585, Israel 02-638991.

HUTTENMEISTER, Frowald G., b. Remscheid-Lennep, Germany, March 2, 1938, s. of Josef & Elisabeth, m. Hilleke, chil: Nathanja; Jochanan; Michael. Educ: U. Saarbrucken, DPhil 1970. Emp: U. of Tubingen, Inst. Judaicum, 1972-84; Tubinger Atlas des Vorderen Orients, 1985- Res. Prog.; Ctr. natl. de la recherche scientifique, Paris, 1984-85. Spec: Archaeology, Semitic Languages, Texts and Epigraphy. Pub: *Megilla Schriftrolle* (1987); "The Tora-Shrine and the Development of Ancient Synagogues" in *Proceedings of the Eighth World Congress of Jewish Studies* (1982); *Die antiken Synagogen in Israel, Teil I: Die judischen Synagogen* (Lehrhäuser & Gerichtshöfe, 1977). Mem: WUJS 1980-; Verband der Judaisten in Deutschland. Addr: (o) Institutum Judaicum, Liebermeisterstr. 12, D-7400 Tubingen, Germany 07071/292874; (h) Tessinstr. 39, D-7400 Tubingen 3, Germany 07071-72317.

HUUHTANEN, Pauli Taisto, b. Jaaski, November 13, 1930. Educ: U. of Helsinki, Theol. Cand. 1956, Theol. Licentiate 1969, Theol. Doctor 1976. Emp: U. of Helsinki, 1975-81 Tchr., Greek, 1984- Docent, NT Stud. Spec: New Testament. Pub: *John the Baptist in the New Testament and in Josephus,* contb. (1992); *The Secret Sayings of Jesus,* co-auth. (1992); *Jerusalem and Rome: The History of New Testament Times* (1989); "The Report of Josephus about the Mass Suicide on Masada" *Teologinen Aika-Kauskirja* 4 (1988); "A Heathen in the Holy of Holies: The Blasphemy of Pompeius 63 B.C." *Teologinen Aika-Kauskirja* 3 (1987); *The Jewish War 66-74 C.E.: The Motives of the War and the Groups Participating in It* (1984); "Die Perikope vom 'Reichen Jungling' unter Beruecksichtigung der Akzentuierungen des Lukas" *Stud. zur Umwelt des NT* (1977); and others. Addr: (h) Metsolantie 14, Helsinki 00610, Finland.

HYLDAHL, Niels, b. Lemvig, Denmark, December 30, 1930, s. of Richardt & Ragnhild, m. Solveig, chil: Peter; Anders; Astrid. Educ: Aarhus U., Denmark, DTh 1966. Spec: New Testament. Pub: "The Corinthian 'Parties' and the Corinthian Crisis" *Studia Theologica* (1991); *Die paulinische Chronologie* (1986); "Die Frage nach der liter-arischen Einheit des Zweiten Korintherbriefes" *ZNW* (1973); *Philosophie und Christentum. Eine Interpretation der Einleitung zum Dialog Justins* (1966); "Hegesipps Hypomnemata" *Studia Theologica* (1960). Mem: SNTS. Addr: (o) Kobenhavns U., Teologiske Fakultet, Kobmagergade 44-46, DK-1150 Kobenhavn, Denmark 33-152811; (h) Nivaavaenge 20-6, DK-2990 Nivaa, Denmark 42-246165.

IBACH, Robert D., Jr., b. Lynch, NE, December 31, 1940, s. of Robert & Mabel, m. Paula. Educ: Detroit Bible Coll., BRE 1963; Grace Theol. Sem., BD 1966, ThM 1969; Indiana U., MLS 1975. Emp: Grace Coll. & Theol. Sem., 1969-86 Lib. Dir., Assoc. Prof.; Dallas Theol. Sem., 1986- Lib. Dir. Excv: Heshbon, 1971 Square Supr., 1973 Survey Supr., 1974, 1976 Survey Dir. Spec: Archaeology, Hebrew Bible. Pub: *Archaeological Survey of the Hesban Region (Hesban 5)* (Andrews U., 1987); "An Intensive Surface Survey at Jalul," "Expanded Archaeological Survey of the Heshbon Region" *AUSS* 16 (1978); "Heshbon 1974: Area G.8

(Umm Es-Sarab)" *AUSS* 14 (1976); and others. Mem: ASOR 1969-; NEAS 1969-; Amer. Theol. Lib. Assn. 1976-; SBL 1976-. Rec: Radio controlled model aircraft. Addr: (o) Dallas Theological Seminary, 3909 Swiss Ave., Dallas, TX 75204 214-841-3753; (h) 3229 Colby Circle, Mesquite, TX 75149.

IDESTROM, Rebecca G. S., b. Sweden, April 9, 1963, d. of Manne & Gunvor. Educ: Cen. Pentecostal Coll., Canada, BTh 1985; U. of Toronto, Trinity Coll., BA, Jewish Stud. 1987; U. of Toronto, Wycliffe Coll., MA, OT 1990. Emp: U. of Toronto, 1989-1990 Teaching Asst.; U. of Sheffield, 1990-1992 Teaching Asst. Spec: Hebrew Bible. Pub: "Addendum to the Bibliography of Peter C. Craigie," co-auth., *JSOT* 51 (1991); "Asherah and Yahweh" *Prolegomena* 1/1 (1989). Awd: Fourth Bishop of Toronto Prize in Hebrew 1988; Social Sci. & Hum. Res. Coun. of Canada, Doc. Fellow. 1990-; Overseas Res. Students Awd. 1990-92. Mem: SBL 1990-; Tyndale Fellow. 1990-. Rec: Art, sports, music, hiking. Addr: (o) U. of Sheffield, Dept. of Biblical Studies, PO Box 595, Arts Tower, Sheffield, England 0742-768-555.

VAN IERSEL, Bastiaan M. F., b. Heerlen, The Netherlands, September 27, 1924, s. of Adrianus Hendricus & Maria Gertrudis (Stalman). Educ: Cath. U. Nijmegen, DTh 1961. Emp: Het Heilige Land, 1954-68 Ed.; Cath. U. Nijmegen, 1960-66 Asst. Prof., 1966-71, Lect., NT Exegesis, 1969-73, 1979-80 Dean, Dept. of Theol, 1971-89 Prof., 1987-90; Vice Chancellor; Schrift, 1969- Ed.; Tijdschrift voor Theol., 1969-1989. Spec: New Testament. Pub: "The Reader of Mark as Operator of a System of Connotations" *Semeia* 48 (1989); *Reading Mark* (T & T Clark, 1989); "Les Recits-Paraboles et la Fonction du Secret pour les Destinataires de Marc" *Semiotique et Bible* 45 (1987); Marcus (Katholieke Bijbelstichting, 1986, 1990); "Locality, Structure and Meaning in Mark" *Linguistica Biblica* 53 (1983) "The Gospel According to St. Mark—Written for A Persecuted Community?" *Nederlands Theologisch Tijdschrift* 34 (1980); *'Der Sohn' in den synoptischen Jesusworten* (Brill, 1961, 1964); and others. Awd: Ridder Nederlandse Leeuw 1989. Mem: SNTS 1964-; SBL 1980-; Natl. Dutch Org. for Sci. Res. in the Field of Theol., Pres., 1986-92. Addr: (h) Mgr. Suyslaan 4, NL-6564 BV, H. Landstichting, Netherlands 080-222723.

ILAN, David, b. Los Angeles, CA, October 7, 1956, s. of Leon & Sybil (Goldenblank), m. Ornit, chil: Yoav; Guy. Educ: Hebrew U., BA, Arch. & Geog. 1980, MA, Bibl. Arch. 1991. Emp: Israel Antiq. Auth., 1978-79 Res. Arch.; Hebrew U., 1981-91 Lect.; Israel Mus., 1983-86 Res. Arch.; Hebrew Union Coll., 1986- G.E. Wright Schol. Excv: Tel Qasis, 1979 Field Supr.; Tel Malhata, 1979 Field Supr.; Damascus Gate, 1985 Co-dir.; Tel Dan, 1988 Field Supr.; Sha'at Cave, 1988 Dir. Spec: Archaeology. Pub: "A Middle Bronze Age Glass Bead from Tel Dan," co-auth. *IEJ* 43

(1993); "A Middle Bronze Age Cultic Cache from Tel Dan" *Eretz-Israel* 23 (1991); "Stepped-rim Juglets from Tel Dan and the MBI-II (MBIIA-B) Transition" *IEJ* 41 (1991); "The Rampant Rape of Israel's Archaeological Sites" *BAR* 15/2 (1989); and others. Awd: Ahvat Yosef Found. Grant 1985-86; Hebrew Union Coll., Ernest G. Wright Fellow 1987-. Mem: IES 1980-92; Assn. of Arch. in Israel, Pres. 1989-90. Addr: (o) Nelson Glueck Sch./Arch., 13 King David St., Jerusalem 94101, Israel 972-2-203333; (h) 40 Haneviim St., Jerusalem 95103, Israel 972-2-240759.

ILLMAN, Karl-Johan, b. Helsinki, June 27, 1936, s. of Karl Uno & Svea Augusta, m. Siv. G., chil: Johan Mika; Hanna Liv; Sara Augusta; Ruth Gunhild. Educ: Abo Acad. U., Cand.Theol. 1961, BA 1965, Lic. Theol. 1969, ThD 1975. Emp: Abo Acad., 1963-65 Lect., NT Greek, 1966-75 Lect., Bibl. Hebrew & OT Exegesis, 1975-80 Acting Prof., OT, 1980- Prof., OT Exegesis & Jewish Stud.; *Svensk Teologisk Kvartalskrift*, 1975-90 Ed. Bd.; *Nordisk Judaistik*, 1975-91 Ed. Bd., 1992 Ed.; *Teologisk tidskrift*, 1984- Ed. Bd. Spec: Hebrew Bible. Pub: *Judendomen i ljuset av dess högtider* (Abo Acad., 1992); "Pa'al, Po'al" in *Theologisches Wörterbuch zum Alten Testament* 6 (1988); "Mut, mawet" in *Theologisches Wörterbuch zum Alten Testament* 4 (1983); *Old Testament Formulas about Death* (1979); *Thema und Tradition in den Asaf-Psalmen* (1976); *Leitwort-Tendenz-Synthese: Programm und Praxis in der Exegese Martin Bubers* (1975); "Anfänge der judischen Bibelwissenschraft" in *Opuscula exegetica in honorem Rafael Gyllenberg octogenarii* (Abo Acad., 1973); and others. Mem: WUJS 1970-; Soc. for Scandinavian Jewish Stud. 1974-, Chmn. 1985-; Finnish Exegetical Soc. 1977-; Uppsala Exegetical Soc. 1978-. Rec: Lit., sports. Addr: (o) Biskopsgatan 16 A, SF-20500 ABO, Finland 358-21-654-283; (h) Sirkkalagatan 6 C 42, SF-20520 ABO, Finland 358-21-328-468.

INCH, Morris A., b. Wytopitlock, ME, October 21, 1925, s. of Clarence & Blanche, m. Joan (Parker), chil: Deborah; Lois; Thomas; Joel; Mark. Educ: Gordon Div. Sch., MDiv 1951; Boston U., PhD 1955. Emp: Gordon Coll., 1955-62 Assoc. Prof.; Wheaton Coll., 1962-86 Prof.; Inst. of Holy Land Studies, Jerusalem, 1986- Exec. Dir. Spec: Apocrypha and Post-biblical Studies. Pub: *Saga of the Spirit: A Biblical, Systematic, and Historical Theology of the Holy Spirit* (Baker, 1985); *My Servant Job* (Baker, 1979); and others. Mem: Coll. Theol. Soc.; ETS. Rec: Tennis, swimming. Addr: (h) 221 E Union, Wheaton, IL 60287.

IRVINE, Stuart A., b. Los Angeles, CA, May 11, 1954, s. of Alexander Ray & Louise (Yoder), m. Elizabeth (Tobie), chil: Maxwell M.; Alexander T.; Samuel M. Educ: Pomona Coll., BA 1976; Yale Div. Sch., MDiv 1980; Emory U., PhD 1989. Emp: La. State U., 1986- Asst. Prof. Spec: Hebrew Bible. Pub: *Isaiah, Ahaz, and the Syro-Ephraimitic Crisis* (Scholars,

1990); *Isaiah, the Eighth Century Prophet*, co-auth. (Abingdon, 1987). Mem: SBL; CBA. Addr: (o) Louisiana State U., 309 Coates Hall, Baton Rouge, LA 70803 504-388-2220; (h) 1645 St. Rose Ave., Baton Rouge, LA 70808 504-336-9023.

ISAAC, Ephraim, b. Ethiopia. Educ: Concordia Coll., BA; Harvard Div. Sch., MDiv; Harvard U., PhD, Near East. Lang. Emp: Hebrew U., Vis. Lect., Anc. Semitic Lang. & African Stud.; Princeton U., Vis. Lect., Near East. Stud. & African Lang.; Harvard U., 1968-71 Asst. Prof., 1972-77 Assoc. Prof.; Inst. of Semitic Stud., 1985- Dir.; Princeton Theol. Sem., 1992- Fellow. Spec: Semitic Languages, Texts and Epigraphy. Pub: *An Ethiopic History of Joseph* (Sheffield, 1990); *The Book of Enoch*, trans. (Doubleday, 1983); and others. Awd: Harvard U., Fellow; Inst. for Advanced Study, Vis. Fellow; City U. of N.Y., John Jay Coll., DHL. Mem: Natl. Literacy Campaign, Ethiopia, Founder & Dir. 1963-71. Addr: (h) 9 Grover Ave., Princeton, NJ 08540 609-921-9062.

ISAACS, Marie E., b. London, England, March 13, 1936, d. of Elizabeth Mary (Allen) & Albert Edward. Educ: London U., King's Coll., BD 1958; Oxford U., BA 1962, MA 1967, DPhil 1973; Bapt. Union of Ch. of Great Britain & Ireland, 1962 Ord. Min.; Emp: Birmingham U., 1963-68 Ecumenical Chaplain; Lady Spencer-Churchill Coll., Oxford, 1969-70 Lect., Relig. Educ.; Rachel McMillan Coll., London, 1970-72 Lect., Relig. Educ.; London U., Heythrop Coll., 1973- Lect., NT Stud., 1978- Head of Bibl. Stud. Dept.; McGill U., Canada, 1978, Vis. Prof., NT. Spec: New Testament. Pub: *Sacred Space: An Approach to the Theology of the Epistle to the Hebrews*, JSNTSup 73 (Sheffield, 1992); "Exegesis and Homiletics" in *Spirituality and Scripture*, The Way Sup. 72 (1991); "The Prophetic Spirit in the Fourth Gospel" *Heythrop Jour.* (1983); *The Concept of Spirit: A Study of Pneuma in Hellenistic Judaism and its Bearing on the New Testament*, Heythrop Mon. 1 (Heythrop Coll., 1976); "Mary in the Lucan Infancy Narrative" in *God and Mary*, The Way Sup. 25 (1975). Awd: St. Hugh's Coll., Yates Sr. Schol. 1960-62, 1970-72. Mem: SNTS 1976-; SBL 1978-. Rec: Sharing good food, wine and conversation with friends, music, theatre, gardening. Addr: (o) London U., Heythrop College, 11-13 Cavendish Square, London, W1M 0AN, England 071-580-6941; (h) 44B Great Percy Street, London, WC1X 9QR, England 071-278-8809.

ISHIDA, Tomoo, b. Tokyo, Japan, December 14, 1931, s. of Tomoji & Mitsuji, m. Kazuko. Educ: Waseda U., BA 1954; Tokyo Union Theol. Sem., MD, Bibl. Theol 1959; Hebrew U., Jerusalem, PhD 1974. Emp: U. of Tsukuba, 1976- Prof., Hist. of Anc. Near East. Spec: Hebrew Bible. Pub: "The Succession Narrative and Esarhaddon's Apology: A Comparison" in *Ah, Assyria*, Tadmor Festschrift (1991); "Royal Succession in the Kingdoms of Israel and Judah

with Special Reference to the People under Arms As a Determining Factor in the Struggles for the Throne" *SVT* 40 (1988); "Solomon Who is Greater Than David: Solomon's Succession in the Light of the Inscription of Kilamuwa, King of Y'DY-Sam'al" *SVT* 36 (1985); *Studies in the Period of David and Solomon and Other Essays*, ed. (Yamakawa-Shuppansha/Eisenbrauns, 1982); *A History of Judaism* (Yamakawa-Shuppansha, 1980); "The Structure and Historical Implications of the Lists of Pre-Israelite Nations" *Biblica* 60 (1979); *The Royal Dynasties in Ancient Israel*, BZAW 142 (de Gruyter, 1977); "The Leaders of the Tribal Leagues 'Israel' in the Pre-Monarchic Period" *RB* 80 (1973); and others. Mem: WUJS; SOTS; SBL; IOSOT. Rec: Ch. Music in the Baroque Period, especially J.S. Bach's Ch. Cantata. Addr: (o) U. of Tsukuba, Institute of History & Anthropology, Tsukuba-shi 305, Japan 0298-53-4069; (h) 2-7-10 Tokodai, Tsukuba-shi 300-26, Japan 0298-47-8696.

IWRY, Samuel, b. Bialystok, Poland, December 25, 1910, s. of Jacob & Dinah, m. Nina (Rochman), chil: J. Mark. Educ: Vilno Teacher Sem., BS 1929; Warsaw Higher Inst. of Judaic Stud., MA 1937; Johns Hopkins U., PhD 1951. Emp: Baltimore Hebrew Coll., 1947-85 Disting. Prof. of Lit.; Johns Hopkins U., 1951-91 Prof., Near East. Stud.; Hebrew U. of Jerusalem, 1964-65 Fulbright Exchange Prof. of Bibl. Stud. Spec: Archaeology, Hebrew Bible, Semitic Languages, Texts and Epigraphy, Apocrypha and Post-biblical Studies. Pub: "Turning New Ground in the Debate on the Language of Qumran Literature" *Eretz Israel* 16 (1982); "Was There a Migration to Damascus?" *Eretz Israel* 9 (1969); "The Masoretes" in *Ency. Britannica* (1966); "A Striking Variant Reading in IQ Isaiah" *Textus* vol. 5 (1966); *Reading in the Phoenician Inscriptions from Byblus* (U. of Haifa, 1965); "New Evidence for Belomancy in Ancient Israel and Phoenicia" *JAOS* 81 (1961); "Massebah and Bamah in IQ Isaiah 6:13" *JBL* 76 (1957); "The Qumran Isaiah and the End of the Dial of Ahaz" *BASOR* 147 (1957); and others. Awd: Johns Hopkins U., Phi Beta Kappa 1951, Samuel Iwry Hebraic Lectureship established 1985; Baltimore Hebrew U., DHL 1987; Festschrift on Bibl. & Related Stud. presented to Samuel Iwry 1985. Mem: ASOR; Hebrew U. Bible Project 1966-; WUJS 1979-. Addr: (o) Johns Hopkins U., Dept. of Near Eastern Studies, Baltimore, MD 21218 410-516-7023; (h) 2401 Brambleton Rd., Baltimore, MD 21209 410-664-1153.

JACKSON, Kent P., b. Salt Lake City, UT, August 9, 1949, s. of Richard W. & Hazel P., m. Nancy Ellen, chil: Sarah; Rebecca; Jennifer; Jonathan E.; Alexander K. Educ: Brigham Young U., BA 1974; U. of Mich., MA 1976, PhD 1980. Emp: Brigham Young U., 1980- Prof., Anc. Scripture. Spec: Hebrew Bible, Semitic Languages, Texts and Epigraphy. Pub: "The Text of the Mesha Inscription," "The Language of the Mesha Inscription" in *Studies in* the *Mesha Inscription and Moab* (Scholars, 1989); *The Ammonite Language of the Iron Age* (Scholars, 1983); "Ammonite Personal Names in the Context of the West Semitic Onomasticon" in *The Word of the Lord Shall Go Forth: Essays in Honor of D.N. Freedman* (Eisenbrauns, 1983); and others. Mem: SBL, Reg. Pres. 1985. Rec: Reading, hiking, camping, visiting historic sites. Addr: (o) Brigham Young U., 270G JSB, Provo, UT 84602 801-378-2761; (h) 1493 S 100 West, Orem, UT 84058 801-226-8082.

JACOBS, Lambert D., b. Bellville, South Africa, February 22, 1962, s. of Daniel Jacobus & Johanna Magdalena (Visser), m. Isabella (Grobler). Educ: Potchefstroom U., BA 1982, BA, Class. Lang. 1983; U. of the Orange Free State, MA, Greek 1985; U. of Pretoria, BD 1987 Emp: U. of South Africa, Inst. for Theol. Res., 1986-87 Res. Asst., 1988 Jr. Lect., Dept. of NT; U. of Zululand, 1989-1991 Lect., Dept. of Class.; Dutch Reformed Ch., 1991- Min. Spec: New Testament. Pub: "The Textual Criticism of the New Testament (1): The Current Methodological Situation" *Skrif en Kerk* 12/2 (1991); "Minister of the Word, Perform Your Duties with Sobriety! 2 Timothy 4:1-8" *Acta Theologica* 11/1 (1991); "The Macro Discourse Strategy in 1 Corinthians 1-4" *Skrif en Kerk* 7/2 (1986); "The Success of Paul's Teaching to the Corinthians," "The Nature of the Discourse in 1 Corinthians 1-4" in *On Style and Rhetoric; in Paul,* Acta Academica D 6 (1986); and others. Awd: U. of Pretoria, Andrew Murray Awd. 1987. Mem: NT Soc. of South Africa 1986-; South African Acad. for Sci. & Arts 1991-; SBL 1991-; AAR 1991-. Rec: Singing, rugby, cricket, athletics. Addr: (o) DR Church, PO Box 161, 3880 Empangeni, South Africa 0351-2-3644; (h) PO Box 1494, 3880 Empangeni, South Africa 0351-2-1654.

JACOBS, Paul F., b. Lockhaven, PA, June 20, 1942, s. of Glenn & Lois, m. Nancy (Naugle), chil: Jonathan; Katherine. Educ: Drew U., BD 1967; Union Theol. Sem., PhD 1972. Emp: U. of St. Thomas, 1974-88 Prof.; John Carroll U., 1986-87 Touhy Chair of Interrelig. Stud.; Miss.State U., 1988-. Excv: Tel Gezer, 1970-72 Asst.Field Supr.; Lahav Res. Project, 1976- Field Supr.; Lahav Res. Project III, Co-dir. Spec: Archaeology, Hebrew Bible. Pub: "'Cows of Bashan'—A Note on the Interpretation of Amos 4:1" *JBL* 104 (1985); "Tel Halif: 1983 Season" *IEJ* 34 (1984); "Tel Halif: 1979-80," co-auth. *RB* (1981). Awd: NEH Fellow 1985. Addr: (o) Mississippi State U., Box JS, MS 39759; (h) 618 Hospital Rd., Starkville, MS 39759 601-324-1904.

JACOBSON, Arland D., b. Mitchell, SD, September 25, 1941, s. of Olaf & Ruth, m. Wilhelmine (Treadwell), chil: Erik Eugene; Karin Inga. Educ: Augustana College, BA 1963; Luther Theol. Sem., BD 1967; Claremont Grad. Sch., PhD 1978. Emp: Scranton, ND, 1967-71 Pastor; Humboldt, SD, 1974-76 Pastor; Loyola

Marymount U., 1978-79 Vis. Prof.; Concordia Coll., 1979-83 Asst. Prof.; Concordia Coll., CHARIS Ecumenical Ctr., 1983- Exec. Dir. Spec: New Testament. Pub: *The First Gospel: An Introduction to the Sayings Gospel Q* (Polebridge, 1992); *The Complete Gospels,* contb. (Polebridge, 1992); "Apocalyptic and the Sayings Source Q" in *The Four Gospels: 1992. Festschrift Frans Neirynck* (Leuven U., 1992); "Proverbs and Social Control: A New Paradigm for Wisdom Studies" in *Gnosticism and the Early Christian World* (Polebridge, 1990); "The Literary Unity of Q" *JBL* 101 (1982); and others. Mem: SBL 1968-; CBA 1981-; Westar Inst. 1988-. Addr: (o) Concordia College, CHARIS Ecumenical Center, Moorhead, MN 56562 218-299-3566; (h) 1915 12th Ave. S, Moorhead, MN 56560 218-236-6275.

JACOBY, Ruth, b. Jerusalem, Israel, February 6, 1942, d. of Richard & Martha. Educ: Hebrew U., Jerusalem, BA 1967, MA 1976. Emp: Ben-Gurion U., U. of Bar-Ilan, 1974-77 Instr.; Hebrew U., Rotheberg Sch. for Overseas Students, Jerusalem, Lect. in Arch., Dir., Index of Anc. Jewish Art. Excv: Coral Island, Field Dir.; Arad, 1965; Megiddo, 1965-66 Registrar in Chief. Spec: Archaeology. Pub: *Ancient Jewish Synagogues: Plans and Illustrations* (1984); *Archives of Ancient Jewish Art,* co-auth. (1984); *The Synagogue of Bar'am—Jerusalem Ossuaries* (1987); *Ancient Jewish Synagogues: Architectural Glossary,* co-auth. (1988); "The Ornamented Stone Near the Fountain of Qayatbay: A Sarcophagus or a Frieze?" *IEJ* 39 (1989); "The Representation and Identification of Cities on Assyrian Reliefs" *IEJ* 41 (1991); and others. Addr: (o) Hebrew U., Center of Jewish Art, Jerusalem 91904, Israel 02-754605; (h) 6 Molcho St., Jerusalem 92185, Israel 02-664-818.

JAMIESON-DRAKE, David W., b. Columbia, MO, December 21, 1954, s. of Dennis C. & Elizabeth A., m. Victoria K., chil: Rebeccah Elizabeth; Abigail Wieting; Samuel David. Educ: Stanford U., BA 1976; Yale U., MDiv 1981; Duke U., PhD 1988, MBA 1991. Emp: Duke U., 1983-86 Asst. to Dean for Residential Life, 1986-92 Asst. Dean for Residential Life, 1992- Dir. of Inst. Res. Excv: Joint Sepphoris Excvn. Project, 1985 Area Coord. Spec: Archaeology, Hebrew Bible. Pub: *Scribes and Schools in Monarchic Judah: A Socio-Archaeological Approach,* JSOTSup. 109 (Sheffield/Almond, 1991); "Literary Structure, Genre, and Interpretation in Job 38" in *The Listening Heart: Festschrift for Roland Murphy* (Almond, 1986). Mem: CBA 1986-; AAR 1990-; SBL 1990-. Rec: Golf, tennis, swimming, bicycling. Addr: (o) Duke U., Office of the Provost, 220 Allen Bldg., Durham, NC 27706 919-684-2631; (h) 1525 Acadia St., Durham, NC 27701 919-682-2497.

JAMME, Albert J., b. Senzeilles, Belgium, June 27, 1916, s. of Alfred & Albine (Roulin). Educ: Catholic U., Louvain, STD 1946, PhD, Oriental Hist. & Philol. 1952; Ecole Biblique, Lic., Bibl.

Stud. 1948. Excv: Marib, N Yemen, 1951-52 Epigrapher; Salalah, Oman, 1952 Epigrapher; Wadi Hadramawt, S Yemen, 1961-62 Epigrapher; Sana, N Yemen, 1974-76 Epigrapher; Wadi al-Jubah, N Yemen, 1981-87 Epigrapher. Spec: Archaeology, Semitic Languages, Texts and Epigraphy. Pub: "The Bethel Inscribed Stamp Again: A Vindication of Mrs. Theodore Bent" *BASOR* 280 (1990); *Miscellanees d'ancient arabe*, vol. 1-17, (1971-1989); "A New Qatabanian Dedicatory Inscription to the God Basamum, Ja 3198" in *On Both Sides of al-Mandab, Istanbul* (1988); "A New Inscribed Sabaean Offering Table" *Record of the Art Mus., Princeton U.* 31 (1972); "Safaitic Vogue 402" *JNES* 31 (1972); "Lihyanite, Sabaean and Thamudic Inscriptions from Western Saudi Arabia" *RSO* 45 (1971); *Sabaean and Hasaean Inscriptions from Saudi Arabia* (U. of Rome, 1966); *Sabaean Inscriptions from Mahram Bilqis (Marib)* (Amer. Found. for the Study of Man, 1962); *Les antiquites sud-arabes du Museo Nazionale Romano* (Acad. Nazionale dei Lincei, 1955); and others. Mem: AOS 1955-; CBA 1955-. Addr: (o) Catholic U. of America, Dept. of Semitic & Egyptian Lang. & Lit., Washington, DC 20064 202-319-5514; (h) 1624 21st St. NW, Washington, DC 20009 202-232-5154.

JANECKO, Benedict F., b. Latrobe, PA, November 22, 1938, s. of Frank & Margaret (Kralik). Educ: St. Vincent Sem., BA 1961; Collegio de Sant'Anselmo, Rome, STL 1966; Pont. Bibl. Inst., Rome, SSL 1969. Emp: St. Vincent Sem., 1969- Assoc. Prof., Theol. & Scriptures; St. Vincent Coll., 1969- Assoc. Prof., Relig. Stud. Spec: Hebrew Bible. Pub: "Ecology, Nature, and the Psalms" in *The Psalms and Other Studies on the Old Testament*, Fs. Joseph I. Hunt (Forward Movement, 1990); *The Psalms: Heartbeat of Life and Worship* (Abbey, 1986); "Israel, Prophecy and Politics" *BTB* 8/4 (1978); "Myth, History, God and Jesus" *Amer. Benedictine Rev.* 23/2 (1972). Mem: SBL; CBA. Addr: (h) St. Vincent Archabbey, Latrobe, PA 15650 412-532-6600.

JANKOWSKI, Augustyn B., b. Zlatoust, Russia, September 1, 1916, s. of Franciszek & Modesta. Educ: U. of Warsaw, MA 1939, MDiv 1946, DDiv 1953; Eccles. Sem. of Warsaw, Ord. 1943; Pont. Bibl. Inst., Rome, Lic. Scripture 1948. Emp: Eccles. Sem. of Warsaw, 1945-55 Instr.; Pont. Acad. of Theol., Cracow, 1963- Prof., NT; *Analecta Cracoviensia*, Ed. Spec: New Testament. Pub: *Duch Dokonawca* (1983); *Zarys pneumatologii NT* (1982); *Listy wiezienne 'sw. Pawla* (1962); *Apokalipsa sw. Jana* (1959); and others. Mem: SNTS 1975-; Pont. Bibl. Commn. 1978-89. Addr: (o) Papieska Akademia Teologiczna, Wydz. Teol. Szujskiego 4, PL 31-123, Krakow, Poland 22-90-92; (h) Opactwo Benedyktynow Benedyktynska 37/39, PL 30-375 Krakow, Poland 66-09-77.

JASTRAM, Nathan R., b. Japan, December 3, 1957. Educ: U. of S.Dak., BA 1980; Concordia

Theol. Sem., MDiv 1984; Harvard U., PhD 1990. Emp: Concordia U., 1990- Asst. Prof. Spec: Hebrew Bible. Pub: "The Text of 4QNum^b" in *Studies in the Text of the Judean Desert* (Brill); "4QNum^b" in *Discoveries in the Judean Desert* (Clarendon); and others. Mem: SBL 1990-. Addr: (o) Concordia U., 7400 Augusta St., River Forest, IL 60305 708-209-3624; (h) 1107 Monroe Ave., River Forest, IL 60305 708-366-4279.

JEFFERY, Peter, b. New York, NY, October 19, 1953, s. of Grant & Mathilde (Matano), m. Margot (Fassler), chil: Joseph; Francis. Educ: CUNY, Brooklyn Coll., BA 1975; Princeton U., MFA 1977, PhD 1980. Emp: Hill Monastic Manuscript Lib., 1980-82 Cataloguer, Publ. Ed.; U. of Delaware, 1984- Assoc. Prof.; Harvard U., 1990-92 Vis. Schol., 1992- Vis. Prof.; Princeton U., 1993- Prof. Spec: Semitic Languages, Texts and Epigraphy, Apocrypha and Post-biblical Studies. Pub: "The Liturgical Year in the Ethiopian *Degg^wa* (Chantbook)" in *Eulogêma: Studies in Honor of Robert Taft, S.J.*, Analecta Liturgica, Studia Anselmiana (Pont. Ateneo Sant'Anselmo, 1993); "Christian Liturgical Music from the Bible to the Renaissance," co-auth., in *Sacred Sound and Social Change: Liturgical Music in Jewish and Christian Experience*, Two Liturgical Traditions 3 (U. of Notre Dame, 1992); "The Lost Chant Tradition of Early Christian Jerusalem: Some Possible Melodic Survivals in the Byzantine and Latin Chant Repertories" *Early Music Hist.* 11 (1992); "The Sunday Office of Seventh-Century Jerusalem in the Georgian Chantbook (Iadgari): A Preliminary Report" *Studia Liturgica* 21; (1991); and others. Awd: Harvard U., Mellon Faculty Fellow 1982-83; NEH, grants 1984, 1986-88; MacArthur Fellow., 1987-92; Amer. Coun. of Learned Soc., Travel Grant 1990. Mem: NAPS 1978-; N Amer. Acad. of Liturgy 1980-; SBL 1987-. Rec: Computers, camping with family. Addr: (h) 33 Jasset St., Newton, MA 02158 617-244-6002.

JEFFORD, Clayton N., b. Greenwood, SC, September 23, 1955, s. of Jack & Beth (Nance), m. Susan (Sanders). Educ: SE Bapt. Theol. Sem., MDiv 1980, ThM 1983; Claremont Grad. Sch., MA 1986, PhD 1988. Emp: Inst. for Antiq. & Christianity, 1985-89 Asst. Dir.; Calif. State U. at Long Beach, 1988-89 Adj. Asst. Prof.; St. Meinrad Sch. of Theol., 1989-91 Asst. Prof., 1991- Assoc. Prof. Spec: Archaeology, New Testament. Pub: "Obedience and the Life of Apa Silvanus in the *Apophthegmata Patrum*" *Bulletin de la Societe d'Archeologie Copte* 28 (1986-89); *The Sayings of Jesus in the Teaching of the Twelve Apostles* (Brill, 1989); "The Dangers of Lying in Bed: Luke 17:34-35 and Parallels" *Forum* 5/1 (1989); "Presbyters in the Community of the *Didache*" *Studia Patristica* 21 (1989); and others. Mem: SBL 1980-; AAR 1985-; IACS 1987-; NABPR 1987-; SNTS 1992-. Rec: Tennis, hiking, water skiing. Addr:

(o) St. Meinrad School of Theology, St. Meinrad, IN 47577 812-357-6631.

JENKINS, Allan K., b. Port Talbot, Wales, September 1, 1940, s. of Kenneth & Muriel. Educ: U. of London, King's Coll., BD, AKC 1963; U. of London, MTh 1970, PhD 1985. Emp: U. of Serampore, India, 1970-76 Lect., Bibl. Stud.; Chichester Theol. Coll., England, 1978-83 Dir. of Stud.; E Anglian Min. Training Course, 1984-87 Sr. Tutor; Cardiff, 1987- Sr. Anglican Chaplain. Spec: Hebrew Bible. Pub: "Hezekiah's Fourteenth Year. A New Interpretation of 2 Kings 18:13-19:37" VT 26 (1976); "A Great Name: Genesis 12:2 and the Editing of the Pentateuch" JSOT 10 (1978); "Isaiah 14:28-32—An Issue of Life and Death" Folia Orientalia 21 (1980); "The Development of the Isaiah Tradition in Isaiah 13-23" in The Book of Isaiah (Leuven U.P., 1989). Mem: SOTS 1970-. Addr: (h) 61 Park Pl., Cardiff CF1 3AT, Wales 0222-232550.

JENKINS, Ferrell, b. Huntsville, AL, January 3, 1936, s. of B.M. & Vera (Mann), m. Elizabeth (Williams), chil: Ferrell, Jr.; Stanley. Educ: Harding Grad. Sch. of Relig., MA 1971. Emp: Ordained Min., 1953-; Florida Coll., 1969-84 Bible Faculty, 1991- Chmn., Dept. of Bibl. Stud.; Study tours to Bible Lands, 1967- Dir. Excv: Lachish Expdn., 1980 Staff. Spec: Archaeology, New Testament. Pub: The Theme of the Bible (Fla. Coll., 1990); New Smith's Bible Dict.; Studies in Revelation; The Old Testament in the Book of Revelation (Baker, 1976); and others. Mem: SBL; ETS; ASOR. Rec: Photography, racquetball, travel. Addr: (h) 9211 Hollyridge Pl., Tampa, FL 33637 813-988-8485.

JENKS, Gregory C., b. Lismore, NSW, Australia, March 11, 1952, s. of Douglas Crawford & Lilian Mae, chil: Danelle Maree; Adam Douglas; Clare Therese. Educ: U. of Queensland, BA 1978, MA 1979, PhD 1989. Emp: St. Barnabas' Coll., Australia, 1986-89 Lect.; St. Francis' Coll., Australia, 1990-92 Lect.; Colloquium, 1990- Assoc. Ed.; Directory of Grad. Stud. & Res. in Australian & New Zealand Inst., 1991- Ed.; 1992- Networking Cons. Spec: Hebrew Bible, New Testament, Apocrypha and Post-biblical Studies. Pub: The Origins and Early Development of the Antichrist Myth, BZNW 59 (1990); "Maundy Thursday and the Passover" Australian Jour. of Liturgy 1 (1988). Mem: SBL 1977-; Australian & New Zealand Soc. for Theol. Study 1981-; Higher Educ. Res. & Development Soc. of Australasia 1987-. Rec: Gardening, reading, interfaith dialogue. Addr: (h) PO Box 63, Everton Park, 4053, Australia 07-354-1761.

JENNINGS, Louis B., b. Lancaster, SC, May 5, 1917, s. of Arthur & Selma (Helms), m. Grace (Allen), chil: Carolyn; Sharon. Educ: Duke U., AB 1938; Crozer Theol. Sem., BD 1945; U. of Chicago, PhD 1964. Emp: Marshall U., 1948-79 Prof.,

Chmn., Dept. Bible & Relig., 1980- Prof. Emeritus; Ohio U., 1961-72 Prof. Spec: New Testament. Pub: The Function of Religion: An Introduction (U. Press of Amer.); and others. Awd: Ford Found. Fellow 1951-52. Mem: SBL; AAR. Rec: Travel, reading, walking. Addr: (h) 2 Kirknewton Dr., Salisbury, MD 21801 410-749-1286.

JENSEN, Joseph N., b. Mannheim, IL, November 22, 1924, s. of Harry & Annette. Educ: Coll. San Anselmo, Rome, STL 1955; Pont. Bibl. Inst., Rome, SSL 1968; Catholic U., STD 1971. Emp: St. Anselm's Abbey Sch. & Sem., 1955-66 Tchr., Prof. of OT; Catholic U., 1961- Assoc. Prof.; New Catholic Ency., Asst. Ed.; OT Abstracts, 1977- Managing Ed. Spec: Hebrew Bible, Semitic Languages, Texts and Epigraphy. Pub: Isaiah 1-39 (Glazier, 1983); God's Word to Israel (Allyn & Bason, 1968; Glazier, 1986); The Use of Tôra by Isaiah: His Debate with the Wisdom Tradition, CBQ Mon. Ser. 3 (CBA, 1973); and others. Mem: CBA 1970-; Coun. on the Study of Relig. 1970-; SBL 1972-. Rec: Reading, sports. Addr: (o) Catholic U. of America, Dept. of Religion & Religious Education, Washington, DC 20064 202-319-5519; (h) St. Anselm's Abbey, 4501 S Dakota Ave. NE, Washington, DC 20017 202-269-2300.

JEPPESEN, Knud O., b. Vodskov, Denmark, September 26, 1938, s. of Marius & Kristine J. (Christensen), m. Ida (Bang), chil: Grete (Wigh-Poulsen); Lars; Anders. Educ: U. of Aarhus, Fac. of Theol., Cand. Theol. 1965, ThD 1987. Emp: U. of Aarhus, Denmark, 1966- Asst. Prof., 1974- Assoc. Prof.; The New Danish Authorized Bible, 1984-91 Co-ed.; Scandinavian Jour. of the OT, 1986- Co-ed.; U. of Kiel, Germany, 1992 Guest Prof. Spec: Hebrew Bible. Pub: "You are a Cherub, but no God" JSOT (1991); "From 'You, my Servant' to 'The Hand of the Lord is with my Servants'" SJOT (1990); Skriv synet tydeligt paa tavler!, Festschrift S. Holm-Nielsen, co-ed. (1989); Jesajas bog fortolket (1988); Grader ikke saa saare: Studier i Mikabogens sigte, I-II (1987); "The Massa' Babel in Isaiah 13-14" Proc. of the Irish Bibl. Assn. 9 (1985); "Micah v13 in the Light of a Recent Archaeologic Discovery" VT 34 (1984); The Productions of Time, Tradition History in Old Testament Scholarship, co-ed. (1984); "How the Book of Micah Lost its Integrity" Studia Theologica 33 (1979); and others. Awd: Aarhus U., Golden Medal 1967; Arthur Christensens legat for Orientalister 1988. Mem: Danish Collegium Biblicum 1972-; British SOTS 1980-; SBL 1988-. Rec: Traveling. Addr: (o) U. of Aarhus, Inst. for Gammel Testamente, Fac. of Theol., DK 8000 Aarhus C, Denmark 45 86136711; (h) Ingasvej 46, DK 8220 Brabrand, Denmark 45 86253231.

JERVELL, Jacob Stephan, b. Fauske, Norway, May 21, 1925, s. of Sverre & Thora, m. Kari, chil: Stephan. Educ: U. of Oslo, BD 1951, DTh 1959. Emp: U. of Oslo, 1960-87 Prof. of NT, 1976-80 Vice Chancellor; Yale U., 1970; Aarhus

U., 1973 Vis. Prof.; *Norsk Teologisk Tidssrift*, 1960- Ed.; *Studia Theologica*, 1966-87 Ed. Spec: Hebrew Bible, New Testament, Apocrypha and Post-biblical Studies. Pub: *The Unknown Paul* (Augsburg, 1984); "Die Mitte der Schrift" in *Festschrift for E. Schweizer* (1983); "Der Schwache Charismatiker" in *Festschrift for E. Kasemann* (1976); *Luke and the People of God* (Augsburg, 1972); "The Law in Luke-Acts" *HTR* (1971); "The Divided People of God" *Studia Theologica* (1965); *Imago Dei* (Ruprecht, 1960); and others. Awd: Aarhus U., DTh 1973. Mem: SNTS 1961; Soc. Royal des Lettres de Lund 1972; Norwegian Acad. of Sci. & Letters 1975. Addr: (o) Seterstoa, 2150 Ames, Norway 06-907187; (h) Industrigata 38A, 0357 Oslo, Norway 02-464014.

JERVIS, L. Ann, b. Edmonton, AB, Canada, October 11, 1953, d. of Beverley & Shirley Johnston, m. Peter Robert Jervis, chil: Dylan Michael; Bronwen Leigh. Educ: York U., Canada, BA 1976; Queen's U., Canada, MDiv 1980; U. of Toronto, Sch. of Theol., ThD 1990. Emp: Wycliffe Coll., 1989- Asst. Prof., NT. Spec: New Testament. Pub: *The Purpose of Romans: A Comparative Letter Structure Investigation* (Sheffield, 1991); and others. Mem: SBL; CSBS. Addr: (o) Wycliffe College, 5 Hoskin Ave., Toronto, ON M5S 1H7, Canada 416-979-2870; (h) 320 Indian Valley Trail, Mississauga, ON L5G 2K8, Canada 416-271-6569.

JEWETT, Robert, b. Lawrence, MA, December 31, 1933, m. Janet (Miller), chil: Ellen Elizabeth. Educ: Nebr. Wesleyan U., BA 1955; U. of Chicago, BD 1958; U. of Tuebingen, DTh 1964. Emp: United Meth. Ch., 1964-66 Min.; Morningside Coll., 1965-80 Prof., Relig. Stud.; Garrett-Evang. Theol. Sem., 1980- Prof., 1987- Harry R. Kendall Prof. of NT Interpretation; *Semeia*, 1980-86 Ed. Bd.; JSOTSup, 1991- Ed. Bd. Spec: New Testament. Pub: "A Matrix of Grace: The Theology of 2 Thessalonians as a Pauline Letter" in *Pauline Theology* (Fortress, 1991); "Numerical Sequences in Paul's Letter to the Romans" in *Persuasive Artistry: Studies in New Testament Rhetoric in Honor of George A. Kennedy* (JSOT, 1991); "Jesus as the Apocalyptic Benefactor in Second Thessalonians," co-auth. in *The Thessalonian Correspondence* (Leuven U.P., 1990); *A Chronology of Paul's Life* (Fortress, 1979); *Paul's Anthropological Terms: A Study of Their Use in Conflict Settings* (Brill, 1971); and others. Awd: Morningside Coll., DD 1985; Kalamazoo Coll., DD 1989. Mem: SBL, Pres., MidW reg. 1986-88. Rec: Sailing, music. Addr: (o) Garrett-Evangelical Theological Seminary, 2121 Sheridan Rd., Evanston, IL 60201 708-866-3979; (h) 729 Emerson, Evanston, IL 60201 708-475-2770.

JOACHIM PILLAI, Christie A., b. Jaffna, Sri Lanka, January 6, 1931, s. of K. Krishnapillai & Regina (Tiruchelvam). Educ: Angelico U., Rome, LPh 1953, STL 1957; Pont. Bibl. Inst., Rome, LSS 1960; Gregorian U., Rome, STD 1961. Emp: Oblate Coll. of the SW, 1972-76 Assoc. Prof.,

Doctrinal Theol.; St. Paul U., Canada, 1976-80 Prof., NT; Oblate Sch. of Theol., 1980-85 Prof.; St. Augustine's Sem. of Toronto, 1985- Fac.; Toronto Sch. of Theol., 1985- Prof., Systematics & Bibl. Theol. Spec: New Testament. Pub: *Apostolic Interpretation of History* (1979); and others. Mem: CBA 1976-; AAR 1976-; SBL 1978-; CTSA 1978-; Amer. Soc. of Missiology 1988-. Rec: Travel, social work, music. Addr: (o) Toronto School of Theology, 47, Queen's Park Crescent, Toronto, ON M5S 2C3, Canada 416-978-4039; (h) St. Augustine's Seminary, 2661 Kingston Rd., Scarborough, ON M1M 1M3, Canada 416-267-4572.

JOBES, Karen H., b. Trenton, NJ, July 2, 1952, d. of Robert F. & Dorothy E. (Hill), m. Dr. Forrest C. Jobes. Educ: Trenton State Coll., BA 1974; Rutgers U. Grad. Sch., MS 1979; Westminster Theol. Sem., MAR, 1989. Emp: Westminster Theol. Sem., 1989- Lect. Spec: Hebrew Bible, New Testament. Pub: "Rhetorical Achievement in the Hebrews 10 'Misquote' of Psalm 40" *Biblica* 72/3 (1991); "Distinguishing the Meaning of Greek Verbs in the Semantic Domain for Worship" *Filologia Neotestamentaria* 4 (1991). Mem: SBL; ETS; IBR. Rec: Swimming, sailing, skiing. Addr: (o) Westminster Theological Seminary, PO Box 27009, Philadelphia, PA 19118 215-887-5511.

JOHNSON, Alfred M., Jr., b. Fuquay-Varina, NC, June 16, 1942, s. of Alfred, m. Tullie (Hoyle), chil: Jeffrey. Educ: Wake Forest U., BBA 1964; SE Bapt. Theol. Sem., MDiv 1968; U. of Pittsburgh, Theol. Sem., PhD, Relig. 1978. Emp: South. Bapt. Ch., 1966- Min.; Pickwick Press, 1973-78 Asst. to Ed. Spec: New Testament, Apocrypha and Post-biblical Studies. Pub: "Structuralism, Biblical Hermeneutics and the Role of Structural Analysis in Historical Research" in *Structuralism and Biblical Hermeneutics*; "Philip the Evangelist and the Gospel of John" *Abr Nahrain* 16 (1976); *The Semiotics of the Passion Narrative*, trans. (Pickwick, 1980); *Structuralism and Biblical Hermeneutics*, ed. (Pickwick, 1979); *The New Testament and Structuralism*, ed. (Pickwick, 1976). Mem: SBL 1971-; CBA 1979-. Rec: Stamp collecting, microcomputers. Addr: (h) 1247 Kimbolton Dr., Cary, NC 27511 919-469-1758.

JOHNSON, Bo E., b. Jorlanda, Sweden, April 8, 1928, s. of Anna & Sune, m. Birgitta (Jannert), chil: Signild (Risenfors); Hedvig (Eriksson); Erland; Inger (Bergstrom). Educ: Doc. 1963. Emp: U. of Lund, Sweden, 1988 Prof., Theol. Spec: Anatolian Studies, Hebrew Bible, Semitic Languages, Texts and Epigraphy. Pub: *Rattfardigheten i Bibeln* (1985); "Form and Message in Lamentations" *ZAW* 97 (1985); *Hebraisches Perfekt und Imperfekt mit vorangehendem W* (1979); *Die hexaplarische Rezension des l. Samuelbuches der Septuaginta* (1963); and others. Addr: (o) Theologicum Allhelgona Kyrkogata 8, S-22362 Lund, Sweden 46 46 1090

38; (h) Skolradsvagen 17, S-22467 Lund, Sweden 46 46 11 4318.

JOHNSON, E. Elizabeth, b. Morgantown, WV, November 29, 1951, d. of C. Bosworth & Dorothy R., chil: Carol Grace; Sarah Ruth. Educ: Ohio U., BGS 1973; Princeton Theol. Sem., MDiv 1977, PhD 1987. Emp: Yale U. & Div. Sch., 1977-79 Teaching Fellow, NT; Queens Coll., 1979-83 Chaplain, Instr., Hum.; Princeton Theol. Sem., 1983-86 Teaching Fellow, NT; New Brunswick Theol. Sem., 1986- Assoc. Prof., NT; *BR,* 1992- NT Book Rev. Ed. Spec: New Testament. Pub: "Ephesians," "Colossians," "2 Thessalonians" in *The Women's Bible Comm.* (Westminster/John Knox, 1992); "The Wisdom of God as Apocalyptic Power" in *Faith and History: Essays in Honor of Paul W. Meyer,* co-ed. (Scholars, 1991); *Good News to the Poor: Peacemaking in the Gospel of Luke* (Presbyn. Peacemaking Prog., 1991); *The Function of Apocalyptic and Wisdom Traditions in Romans 9-11,* SBL Diss. Ser. 109 (Scholars, 1989); "Jews and Christians in the New Testament: John, Matthew, and Paul" *Reformed Rev.* 42 (1988-89); *The Miracle of Pentecost: Peacemaking in the Acts of the Apostles* (Presbyn. Peacemaking Prog., 1988); "Not in Vain: I Corinthians 15:51-58" *Perspectives* 3 (1988); and others. Mem: SBL 1983-; Bibl. Theologians 1991-. Rec: Intl. & single-parent adoptive families, Latin Amer. culture & hist. Addr: (o) 17 Seminary Place, New Brunswick, NJ 08901 908-247-5241; (h) 29 Seminary Place, New Brunswick, NJ 08901 908-846-7403.

JOHNSON, Marshall D., b. Middle River, MN, November 15, 1935, s. of Ingvald & Bertha (Maijala), m. Alice Joy (Peterson), chil: Nathan; Catherine; Jennifer. Educ: Augsburg Theol. Sem., BTh 1961; Union Sem., ThD 1966. Emp: Luth. Sem., 1965-66 Vis. Instr.; Wartburg Coll., 1966-85 Prof., Relig.; U. Bergen, 1976 Fulbright Lect.; Augsburg Publ., 1985-88 Ed.; Fortress Press, 1989 Ed., 1990- Ed. Dir. Spec: New Testament, Apocrypha and Post-biblical Studies. Pub: *The Purpose of the Biblical Genealogies* (Cambridge U.P., 1988); "Power Politics and New Testament Scholarship in the National Socialist Period" *JES* (1986); "The Life of Adam and Eve" in *Old Testament Pseudepigrapha* (Doubleday, 1985); "The Paralysis of Torah in Habakkuk 1:4" *VT* (1984). Awd: Rockefeller Fellow of Relig. 1963-65. Mem: SBL 1961-; AAR 1990-; SNTS 1991-. Rec: Travel, music, swimming. Addr: (o) Fortress Press, Box 1209, Minneapolis, MN 55440 612-330-3436; (h) 5413 Morgan Ave. S, Minneapolis, MN 55419.

JOHNSON, R. Francis, b. Bedford, VA, May 1, 1923, s. of Robert & Florence (Saunders), m. Parthenia (Grier), chil: Thomas; Abigail; Sarah; Hannah; Parthenia; Bosworth; Ashley. Educ: Union Theol. Sem., BD 1946, ThD 1953. Emp: Lexington Theol. Sem., 1953-55 Assoc. Prof., OT; Smith Coll., 1955-56 Asst. Prof., Relig.; Episcopal Theol. Sem. of the SW, 1956-69 Prof.,

OT; Amherst Coll., 1968-69 Vis. Prof., Relig.; Connecticut Coll., 1969-89 Prof., Relig. Stud., 1989- Prof. Emeritus. Spec: Hebrew Bible. Pub: "Bible" in *World Book Ency.* (1978); articles in *IDB* (1962); "More on Heidegger and Bultmann" *Encounter* 18 (1957); and others. Awd: Ecumenical Inst. for Advanced Theol. Stud., Jerusalem, Resident Fellow 1976; Epis. Theol. Sem. of the SW, DD 1986. Mem: SBL; AAR. Rec: Gardening, music, sailing. Addr: (h) 39 Meadowlark Ln., Hilton Head, SC 29926 803-689-2805.

JOHNSSON, William G., b. Adelaide, Australia, June 20, 1934, s. of Joel & Edith, m. Noelene, chil: Terence B.; Julie Margaret. Educ: Adelaide U., BTech 1954; Avondale Coll., BA 1959; Andrews U., MA 1966; London U., BD 1969; Vanderbilt U., MA 1972, PhD, Bibl. Stud. 1973. Emp: Spicer Coll., India, 1963-73 Relig. Tchr., 1973-75 Dean, Sch. of Theol.; Andrews U., 1975-80 Prof., NT; SDA Theol. Sem., 1978-80 Assoc. Dean; *Adventist Rev.,* 1980-82 Assoc. Ed., 1982- Ed. Spec: New Testament. Pub: *Clean: The Meaning of Christian Baptism* (South. Publ. Assn., 1980); *Hebrews* (John Knox, 1980); "The Pilgrimage Motif in the Book of Hebrews" *JBL* 97/2 (1978); "The Cultus of Hebrews in Twentieth Century Scholarship" *ExpTim* 89 (1978); "The Nature of New Testament Ethics" *Pers Relig. Stud.* 5 (1978); "Issues in the Interpretation of Hebrews" *AUSS* 15 (1977); and others. Mem: SBL; AAR. Rec: Long-distance running, gardening. Addr: (o) 12501 Old Columbia Pike, Silver Spring, MD 20904-6600 301-680-6561; (h) 2808 Red Lion Ln., Silver Spring, MD 20904 301-572-2850.

JOHNSTON, George, b. Clydebank, Scotland, June 9, 1913, s. of William George & Jenny Connolly (McKeown), m. Alexandra (Gardner), chil: Christine; Ronald; Janet. Educ: U. of Glasgow, MA 1935, BD 1938,; U. of Cambridge, PhD 1941. Emp: Hartford Theol. Sem., 1947-52 Assoc. Prof.; Emmanuel Coll., Toronto, 1952-59 Prof., NT; McGill U., Montreal, 1959-81 Prof., NT, 1970-75 Dean, Relig. Stud., 1982- Emeritus Prof.; United Theol. Coll., Montreal, 1959-70 Prin.; *Canadian Jour. of Theol.,* 1960-67 Chair. Spec: New Testament. Pub: "Should the Synoptic Evangelists be Considered as Theologians?" *Tokyo Jour. of Theol.* 50 (1988); "Christ as Archegos" NTS 27/3 (1981); *The Spirit-Paraclete in the Gospel of John* (1970); *Ephes., Col., Phil. and Philemon,* New Century Bible (1967); "*Oikoumene* and *Kosmos* in the New Testament" NTS 10/3 (1964); *The Doctrine of the Church in the New Testament* (1943); and others. Awd: Glasgow U., Black Theol. Fellow. 1938, DD 1960; AATS, Fellow. 1967; Mount Allison U., LLD 1974; Canada Coun., Fellow. 1976. Mem: CSBS, Pres. 1963; Canadian Theol. Soc., Pres. 1966; SBL; Hum. Res. Coun. of Canada 1971-75. Rec: Golf, art hist., travel, music. Addr: (o) Faculty of Religious Studies, 3250 University St., Montreal, Que. H3A 2A7, Canada 514-398-4121; (h) 399 Clarke Ave., Apt. 1c, Westmount, Que. H3Z 2E7, Canada 514-935-2186.

JOHNSTON, Robert M., b. Palo Alto, CA, May 8, 1930, s. of Arthur & Mary Elizabeth (Butler), m. Madeline (Steele), chil: Paul; Robert T.; Elizabeth Ann; Margaret. Educ: Pacific Union Coll., BA 1952; Seventh-Day Adventist Theol. Sem., MA 1955; Andrews U., BD 1966; Hartford Sem., PhD 1977. Emp: Korean Union Coll., 1959-69 Prof., Chmn., Dept. of Theol.; Philippine Union Coll., 1969-70; Andrews U., 1973- Prof., NT & Christian Origins; *AUSS*, 1985- Assoc. Ed. Spec: New Testament, Apocrypha and Post-biblical Studies. Pub: "The Rabbinic Sabbath" in *The Sabbath in Scripture and History* (Rev. & Herald, 1982); "Patriarchs, Rabbis, and Sabbath" *AUSS* 12 (1974); "Greek Patristic Parables" *SBL Seminar Papers* 11 (1977); *Drinking at the Sources*, co-trans. (Pacific, 1981); *They Also Taught in Parables: Rabbinic Parables From the First Centuries of the Christian Era*, co-auth. (Zondervan, 1990); and others. Mem: SBL 1970-; AAR 1973-; CSBR 1975-. Rec: Classical music, travel, languages. Addr: (o) Andrews U., Berrien Springs, MI 49104 616-471-3418; (h) 8742-1 N Ridge Ave., Berrien Springs, MI 49103 616-471-1109.

JONES, Brian C., b. Turlock, CA, November 29, 1957, s. of Virgil & Ruth, m. Judith Anne, chil: Marcus N. Educ: Merced Jr. Coll., Assoc. of Sci. 1980; Point Loma Coll., BA 1981; Princeton Theol. Sem., MDiv 1986. Emp: Candler Sch. of Theol., 1989-90, 1992 Instr. Spec: Hebrew Bible. Pub: "In Search of Kir Hareseth: A Case Study in Site Identification" *JSOT* 52 (1991). Awd: Emory U., Non-Service Fellow. 1986-1989; Princeton Theol. Sem., Henry Snyder Gehman Awd. in OT 1986. Mem: SBL 1987-. Rec: Backpacking, ham radio. Addr: (o) 433 S Candler St., Decatur, GA 30030 404-371-8776.

JONES, Bruce W., b. Palo Alto, CA, August 28, 1935, s. of Harry C. & Allene (Kankel), chil: Timothy F.; Samuel S.; Nicholas D. Educ: Amherst Coll., BA 1956; Union Theol. Sem., MDiv 1959; Grad. Theol. Union, OT 1972. Emp: Pacific Sch. of Relig., 1968-69 Lect., OT; Mills Coll., 1969-73 Lect., Relig. Stud.; Calif. State U., 1973-83 Assoc. Prof., 1983- Prof., Relig. Stud. Spec: Hebrew Bible. Pub: *The Bible in the Light of Cuneiform Literature: Scripture in Context III*, Anc. Near East. Texts & Stud. vol. 8, co-ed. (Mellen,; 1990); "Antiochus Epiphanes and the Persecution of the Jews" in *Scripture in Context: Essays on the Comparative Method* (Pickwick, 1980); "The So-Called Appendix to the Book of Esther" *Semitics* 6 (1978); "Two Misconceptions About the Book of Esther" *CBQ* 38 (1977); "The Prayer in Daniel 9" *VT* 18 (1968); and others. Mem: SBL 1965-. Addr: (o) California State U., Dept. of Religious Studies, Bakersfield, CA 93311-1099 805-664-2214; (h) PO Box 9501, Bakersfield, CA 93309-9501 805-833-9821.

JONES, Donald L., b. Xenia, OH, August 7, 1938, s. of Alice & Dana, m. Susan (Haas), chil:

Douglas; Kevin; Darin. Educ: Ohio Wesley U., BA 1960; Meth. Theol. Sch. in Ohio, MDiv, NT 1963; Duke U., PhD 1966. Emp: Earlham Coll. & Sch. Relig., 1966-67 Asst. Prof.; U. of S.C., 1967- Prof., Chmn., Grad. Dir.; Luth. Theol. Sem., Adj. Prof. Spec: New Testament. Pub: "Roman Imperial Cult" in *ABD* vol. 5 (1992); "The Legacy of Henry Joel Cadbury" in *Cadbury, Knox and Talbert: American Contributions to the Study of Acts* (Scholars, 1992); "Luke's Unique Interest in Historical Chronology" in *SBL 1989 Seminar Papers* (Scholars, 1989); "The Title 'Son of God' in the Acts of the Apostles" in *SBL 1985 Seminar Papers* (Scholars, 1985); "The Title 'Servant' in Luke-Acts" in *Luke-Acts: New Perspectives from the SBL Seminar* (Crossroad, 1984); and others. Mem: SBL 1963-; AAR 1965-. Rec: Tennis, basketball, swimming. Addr: (o) U. of South Carolina, Dept. of Relig., Columbia, SC 29208 803-777-2283; (h) 848 Malibu Dr., Columbia, SC 29209 803-776-1542.

JONES, F. Stanley, m. Britt. Educ: Yale U., BA 1975; U. of Oxford, BA 1978, MA 1982; U. Goettingen, DTheol 1987; Vanderbilt U., PhD 1989. Emp: U. Goettingen, 1984-88 Instr. & Res.; Calif. State U. at Long Beach, 1988- Asst. Prof. Spec: New Testament, Apocrypha and Post-biblical Studies. Pub: "Evaluating the Latin and Syriac Translations of the Pseudo-Clementine *Recognitions*" *Apocrypha: Le Champ des Apocryphes* 3 (1992); "The Martyrdom of James in Hegesippus, Clement of Alexandria, and Christian Apocrypha, Including Nag Hammadi: A Study of the Textual Relations" in *SBL 1990 Seminar Papers* (Scholars, 1990); *Pseudo-Clementine Recognitions 1.27-71: Early Jewish Christian Perspectives on the Nature and History of Christianity* (U. Microfilms, 1989); "Freiheit" in *den Briefen des Apostels Paulus: Eine historische, exegetische und religionsgeschitliche Studie*, Goettinger Theologische Arbeiten 34 (Vandenhoeck & Ruprecht, 1987); *Paul, Apostle to the Gentiles: Studies in Chronology* (Fortress, 1984); and others. Awd: Ecole Pratique des Hautes Etudes, Sect. des Sci. Relig., Paris, Guest Prof. 1990. Mem: AAR; Assn. pour L'etude de la lit. apocryphe chretienne; Intl. Assn. of Manichaean Stud.; SBL. Addr: (o) California State U., Dept. of Religious Studies, 1250 Bellflower Blvd., Long Beach, CA 90840 310-985-4587.

JONES, Richard N., b. Oakland, CA, November 12, 1950, s. of Normand & Marcia, m. Kathryn, chil: Nicholas. Educ: Utah State U., BSc 1976; U. of Utah, MA, Arabic 1981, PhD 1993. Emp: U. of Utah Medical Ctr., Associated Regional & U. Pathologists, 1983- Res. & Development Technologist, Dept. of Trace Metals Analysis. Excv: Tell el-Shuqafiya, Egypt, 1982 Epigrapher & Paleopathologist. Spec: Archaeology, Semitic Languages, Texts and Epigraphy, Apocrypha and Post-biblical Studies. Pub: "Balm," "Embalming," "Lame/Lameness," "Leprosy," "Discharge," "Paleopathology," "Tahpanhes" in *ABD* (Doubleday, 1992). Mem: ASOR; SBL; Soc. for

Coptic Arch. Rec: White water rafting, mountaineering, skiing. Addr: (o) Association of Regional & U. Pathologists, 500 Chipeta Way, Salt Lake City, UT 84108 801-583-2787; (h) 9231 Stone Ridge Cir., Sandy, UT 84093 801-942-6983.

JORDAN, Gregory D., b. Jackson, MS, December 19, 1951, s. of Wallace & Nell, m. Sally (Franze), chil: Benjamin; Gregory S.; Jonathan. Educ: Trinity Evang. Div. Sch., MA 1976, MDiv 1977; Hebrew Union Coll., Jewish Inst. of Relig., PhD 1986. Emp: King Coll., 1980- Prof., Bible & Relig.; Inst. of Holy Land Stud., 1985- Bd. of Dir., 1986 Adj. Prof. Spec: Hebrew Bible. Pub: Articles in *Baker Dict. of the Bible, ISBE.* Mem: SBL 1985-. Rec: Hiking. Addr: (o) King College, Bible and Religion Dept., Bristol, TN 37620 615-968-1187; (h) 1353 King College Rd., Bristol, TN 37670 615-968-1359.

JOSSA, Giorgio, b. Napoli, Italy, July 27, 1938, s. of Franco & Olga (Pensa), m. Concetta (Palmesano), chil: Stefano; Emanuela; Roberta; Andrea; Francesca. Educ: U. of Naples, Dr. in Jurisprudence 1959. Emp: U. of Naples, 1981- Prof., Hist. of Early Ch. Spec: New Testament. Pub: *I Cristiani e l'Impero Romano da Tiberio a Marco Aurelio* (D'Auria, 1991); *Dal Messia al Cristo: Le Origini della Cristologia* (Paideia, 1989); *Gesù e i Movimenti di Liberazione della Palestina* (Paideia, 1980). Mem: SNTS; Accademia Pontaniana, Naples. Addr: (h) Via G. Piscicelli 77, 80121 Napoli, Italy 081-682040.

JOUKOWSKY, Martha S., b. Cambridge, MA, September 2, 1936, d. of Waitstill Sharp & Martha (Ingham Dickey), m. Artemis W. Joukowsky, chil: Nina; Artemis III; Michael. Educ: N.Y. U., BA 1959; Amer. U., Beirut, MA 1972; U. de Paris, Sorbonne, PhD 1982. Emp: City U. of New York, Hunter Coll., 1982, 1984-85 Adj. Asst. Prof.; N.Y. U., 1987 Adj. Asst. Prof.; Brown U., 1980-85 Trustee, 1985- Trustee Emerita, 1988- Assoc. Prof., 1990-91 Acting Dir., Ctr. for Old World Arch. & Art; Amer. U., Beirut, 1987-93 Trustee. Excv: Tell el Ghassil, Lebanon 1969-70 Supr., Pottery Dir.; Sarepta, Lebanon, 1969-73 Supr., Pottery Dir.; Aphrodisias, Turkey, 1975-86 Supr., Prehist. Excvn.; Kasfiki, Palaiopolis, Kokotos, Greece, 1987-90 Field Dir.; South. Temple at Petra, Jordan, 1993- Dir. Spec: Archaeology, Anatolian Studies, Mesopotamian Studies. Pub: "A Celebration of Archaeology at Boston University" *Context* 45/6 (1992-93); *The Crisis Years—The 12th Century B.C.,* ed. (Kendall-Hunt, 1992); *The Heritage of Tyre,* ed. (Kendall-Hunt, 1992); "Ethics in Archaeology: An American Perspective" *Berytus* 39 (1991); "Prehistoric Developments in the Acropolis (Theater Hill)" *Jour. of Roman Stud.,* Aphrodisias Papers 3, Sup. 2 (1991); *La Muculufa, the Early Bronze Age Sanctuary,* co-auth. (Brown U.P., 1990); "Exchange at Prehistoric Aphrodisias: Considerations" in *Eski Onasya'da Anadolu— Anatolia in the Ancient Near East* (1989);

Prehistoric Aphrodisias: An Account of the Excavations and Artifact Studies (Louvain, 1986); and others. Awd: R.I. Coun. for the Hum. Awd. 1989-90; Brown U., PhB 1982, LhD 1985, Lect. Com. Awd. 1989-90, Watson Travel Grant 1993; Wayland Collegium Development Grant 1993-94. Mem: Soc. of Professional Arch. 1980-; AIA, Pres., 1989-91; Oriental Inst.; ASOR. Rec: Travel. Addr: (o) Brown U., Dept. of Old World Archaeology & Art, Box 1837, Providence, RI 02912 401-863-2306; (h) 79 Prospect St., Providence, RI 02906 401-274-7006.

JUNACK, Klaus K. M., b. Berlin, Germany, March 10, 1927, s. of Johannes & Katharina (Hunius), m. Susanne (Bahn), chil: Matthias J.; Dorothea S.; Karola K. Emp: Deutsche Akademie der Wissenschaften zu Berlin, 1952-58 Asst.; Westf. Wilhelms-U. Munster, 1958-66 Asst.; Inst. fur NT Textforschung Munster, 1966-83 Kustos, 1984-90 Akademischer Dir. Spec: New Testament. Pub: *Das Neue Testament auf Papyrus II,1, Paulin. Briefe (Rm - 2. Kor),* ANTF 12 (de Gruyter, 1989); *Das Neue Testament auf Papyrus I, die Kath. Briefe,* ANTF 6 (de Gruyter, 1986); "Abschreibpraktiken und Schreibgewohnheiten" in *Essays in Honor of B. M. Metzger* (Clarendon, 1981); "Bibelhandschriften II, Neues Testament" *TR* (de Gruyter, 1980); "The Reliability of the New Testament Text from the Perspective of Textual Criticism" *BT* 29 (1978); "Eine Fragmentsammlung mit Teilen aus 1.Tim. (0241)" in *Essays in Honour of G. D. Kilpatrick* (Brill, 1976); "Zu den griechischen Lektionaren und ihrer Uberlieferung" in *Alte Ubersetzungen des NT, Kirchenvaeterzitate und Lektionare,* ANTF 5 (de Gruyter, 1972); and others. Awd: Wartburg Theol Sem., DD 1973. Mem: SNTS 1968-. Rec: Astronomy, sailing. Addr: (h) Am Schutthook 59, D-48167 Munster, Germany 0251-614-553.

JYOO, Yeong-Heum, b. Seoul, Korea, March 3, 1934, s. of Soo-Kyeom & O-Am (In-Deok). Educ: Seoul Natl. U., Coll. of Educ., BSC 1956; Korea U. Grad. Sch., MSC 1959; Kon-Kuk U. Grad. Sch., DSC 1972. Emp: Presbyn. Coll. & Theol. Sem., Lect.; Chong-Shin U., Grad. Sch. of Theol., Lect.; Kon-Kuk U., Prof., Physics. Spec: Hebrew Bible, New Testament. Pub: *The Genesis Creation of the Heavens and the Earth* (1991); *The Second Coming of Jesus Christ* (Kairos, 1991); *The Proper Course of the Bible Translation* (Jesus Christ Holiness Ch., 1976); and others. Mem: SBL; Japan Soc. for the Study of Bible Trans.; Japan Bible Soc. Addr: (o) Kon-Kuk U., Dept. of Physics, Seoul 133-701, Korea 02-450-3405.

KADDARI, Menahem Z., b. Hungary, May 18, 1925, s. of Yehosua & Shoshana (Schwarcz), m. Leah (Goldstein), chil: Miriam (Shapira); Mikhal (Ferencz); Ruth (Halperin). Educ: Hebrew U., Jerusalem, MA 1950, PhD 1955. Emp: Hebrew U., Jerusalem, 1957-59 Tchr. of Stylistics; Bar-Ilan U., Israel, 1959- Prof., Hebrew; U. of Witwatersrand, 1979-81 Prof.; *Bar-Ilan Ann. in the Hum.,* 1968 Ed., 1970-83 Joint Ed., Vol. 11-

21. Spec: Hebrew Bible. Pub: *Post-Biblical Hebrew Syntax and Semantics (Studies in Diachronic Hebrew)*, vol. 1 (Bar-Ilan U.P., 1991); "On Deontic Modality in Biblical and Post-Biblical Hebrew" in *Occident and Orient* (1988); "The Lexical Entry of BH *HU* in Monolingual Dictionaries" *Intl. Jour. of Lexicography* 1 (1988); "Concessive Connectors in the Language of Isaiah" *OTWSA* 23 (1980); *Studies in BH Syntax* (Bar-Ilan U.P., 1976); *'Otzar Leshon Hamiqra*, Thesaurus of BH vol. 3 (1968); *Semantic Fields in the Language of the Dead Sea Scrolls* (1968); "The Nominal Phrases of 'Lev, Levav' in BH" *Bar-Ilan Ann.* 4-5 (1967); and others. Awd: Hebrew U., Gelber Prize 1955; Tel-Aviv, Bene Herzl Prize in Jewish Stud. 1971. Mem: AOS 1967-; Soc. Linguistica Europaea 1969-; Israel Soc. of Applied Linguistics 1976-, Pres. 1982. Rec: Tourism. Addr: (o) Bar-Ilan U., Dept. of Hebrew & Semitic Languages, Ramat-Gan 52100, Israel 03-5318226; (h) 16 Sanhedrin St., Ramat-Gan 52376, Israel 03-741695.

KAISER, Walter C., Jr., b. Folcroft, PA, April 11, 1933, s. of Walter & Estelle (Jaworsky), m. Margaret (Burk), chil: Walter; Brian; Kathleen; Jonathan. Educ: Wheaton Coll., BA 1955, BD 1958; Brandeis U., MA 1962, PhD 1973. Emp: Wheaton Coll., 1961-65 Asst. Prof., Bible, 1983-Bd. of Trustees; Trinity Evang. Div. Sch., 1966-Prof., OT & Semitic Lang.; Talbot Theol. Sem., 1985 Lyman Stewart Lect.. Spec: Archaeology, Hebrew Bible, Mesopotamian Studies, Semitic Languages, Texts and Epigraphy, Egyptology. Pub: *Communicator's Commentary: Micah to Malachi* (Word, 1992); *More Hard Sayings of the Old Testament* (IVP, 1992); *Hard Sayings of the Old Testament* (IVP, 1988); *Uses of the Old Testament in the New* (Moody, 1985); "The Promised Land: A Biblical-Historical View" *Bibl. Sacra* 138 (1981); "The Old Promise and the New Covenant: Jeremiah 31:31-34" *JETS* 15 (1972); and others. Awd: Gold Medallion Book Awd. of Merit 1985. Mem: ETS, Pres. 1977; NEAS; SBL; IBR. Rec: Gardening, woodcutting, furniture restoration. Addr: (o) Trinity Evangelical Divinity School, 2065 Half Day Rd., Deerfield, IL 60015 708-317-8002; (h) 1150 Linden Ave., Deerfield, IL 60015 708-945-4959.

KALLUVEETIL, Paul, b. Trichur, India, January 21, 1940, s. of Lazar & Anna. Educ: Pont. Atheneum, Poona, India, MA, Phil 1961, MA, Theol. 1965; Pont. Bibl. Inst., Rome, DSS 1980. Emp: Dharmaram Pont. Inst., Bangalore, 1980-Prof., OT & Semitic Relig.; *Journal of Dharma*, Rev. Ed.. Spec: Anatolian Studies, Hebrew Bible, Mesopotamian Studies, Semitic Languages, Texts and Epigraphy. Pub: *Declaration and Covenant* (Bibl. Inst., 1982); and others. Mem: SBL; CBA, India; SBS. Addr: (h) Dharmaram College, Bangalore 560029, India.

KALMIN, Richard, b. Bridgeport, CT, October 28, 1953, s. of Irving & Regina, m. Freda (Kleinburd), chil: Rachel; Michael. Educ: Brown

U., BA 1975; Jewish Theol. Sem., MA 1978, PhD 1985. Emp: Jewish Theol. Sem., 1982- Assoc. Prof., 1991 Acting Dean; Hebrew Union Coll., 1987 Vis. Asst. Prof.; Union Theol. Sem., 1992 Adj. Assoc. Prof. Spec: Semitic Languages, Texts and Epigraphy, Apocrypha and Post-biblical Studies. Pub: "Friends and Colleagues, or Barely Acquainted? Relations Between Fourth-Generation Masters in the Babylonian Talmud" *HUCA* 61; (1990); "Saints or Sinners, Scholars or Ignoramuses?" *AJS Rev.* 15/2 (1990); "The Talmudic Story: Aggada as History" in *Proceedings of the World Congress of Jewish Studies* (1990); *The Redaction of the Babylonian Talmud: Amoraic or Saboraic?* (Hebrew Union Coll., 1989); "Quotation Forms in the Babylonian Talmud" *HUCA* 59 (1988); "The Post-Rav Ashi Amoraim: Transition or Continuity? A Study of the Role of the Final Generations of Amoraim in the Redaction of; the Talmud" *AJS Rev.* 2/2 (1986); and others. Awd: Jewish Theol. Sem., Stroock Fac. Fellow. Mem: AJS 1982-; AAR 1982-; SBL 1982-; WUJS 1987-. Addr: (o) Jewish Theological Seminary, 3080 Broadway, New York, NY 10027 212-678-8018; (h) 4525 Henry Hudson Pkwy., Riverdale, NY 10471 212-548-1337.

KAMPEN, John I., b. Rosetown, Canada, April 10, 1946, s. of Peter & Hertha, m. Margaret Ann. Educ: U. of Saskatchewan, Canada, BA 1968; Mennonite Bibl. Sem., MDiv 1975; Hebrew Union Coll., PhD 1985. Emp: Payne Theol. Sem., 1984-Asst. Prof., 1986- Assoc. Prof., 1989- Academic Dean, Prof., Bible. Spec: New Testament, Apocrypha and Post-biblical Studies. Pub: "A Reexamination of the Relationship between Matthew 5:21-48 and the Dead Sea Scrolls" in *SBL 1990 Seminar Papers* (1990); *The Hasideans and the Origin of Pharisaism: A Study in 1 and 2 Maccabees*, Septuagint & Cognate Ser. 24 (Scholars, 1988); "The Temple Scroll: The Torah of Qumran?" *Proc. of the East. Great Lakes Bibl. Soc.* 1 (1981); and others. Mem: SBL; AAR; AJS; CSBS. Addr: (o) Payne Theological Seminary, PO Box 474 Wilberforce, OH 45384 513-376-2946; (h) 30-E Seminary Ave., Dayton, OH 45403 513-253-4841.

KAPELRUD, Arvid S., b. Lillehammer, Norway, May 14, 1912, s. of Gustav & Ingeborg (Schou), m. Brynhild Havig (Bommen), chil: Rannveig K. (Eriksen); Jon Gunnar. Educ: Oslo U., Cand. theol. 1938, BA, Linguistics 1941; Uppsala U., ThD 1948. Emp: Oslo U., 1935-46 Lib. Asst., 1946-52 Lbrn., 1952-54 Assoc. Prof., OT, 1954-82 Prof., 1969-72 Dean of Fac.; *Norsk teologisk tidsskrift*, 1966-82 Co-ed.; *Studia Theologica*, 1966-88 Ed.; *Temenos*, 1968- Co-ed. Excv: German Warka Expdn., Iraq, 1957. Spec: Archaeology, Hebrew Bible, Mesopotamian Studies, Semitic Languages, Texts and Epigraphy. Pub: "Ba'al, Schöpfung and Chaos" *UF* 11, C.F.A. Schaeffer festschrift (1979); *The Message of the Prophet Zephaniah* (1975); *The Violent Goddess: Anat in the Ras Shamra Texts* (1969); "The Role of the Cult in Old Israel" in *The Bible in Modern Scholarship* (SBL, 1966); "Temple Building, a Task for Gods and Kings"

Orientalia 32 (1963); "The Interrelationship between Religion and Magic in Hittite Religion" *Numen* 6 (1959); *Central Ideas in Amos* (1956, 1961); "The Gates of Hell and the Guardian Angels of Paradise" *JAOS* 70 (1950); and others. Awd: Fridtjof Nansen Awd. 1975; U. of Aberdeen, Scotland, DD 1979. Mem: SBL 1950-; Det Norske Videnskaps-Akademi 1959. Rec: Nature photography, cross-country skiing. Addr: (o) Rektorhaugen 15, N-0876 Oslo 8, Norway.

KAPERA, Zdzislaw, b. Krakow, Poland, March 14, 1942, s. of Konstanty & Maria (Banach), m. Wieslawa, chil: Krzysztof; Anna; Michal. Educ: Jagiellonian U., Krakow, MA, Mediterranean Arch. 1964, PhD 1978. Emp: Polish Acad. of Sci., Cracow Branch, 1972- Sec., *Folia Orientalia*; Wydanictwo Naukowe PWN, 1989- Sec., *Filomata*; Enigma Press, 1990- Ed., *The Qumran Chronicle.* Spec: Archaeology, Apocrypha and Post-biblical Studies. Pub: *The Third Battle of the Scrolls* (Enigma, 1993); "Khirbet Qumran: No More a Monastic Settlement" *The Qumran Chronicle* 2/2 (1993); *Mogilany 1989: Papers on the Dead Sea Scrolls Offered in Memory of Jean Carmignac,* vol. I-II, ed. (Enigma, 1991-93); *Intertestamental Essays in Honor of Józef Toudeusz Milik,* ed. (Enigma, 1992); "AMS Carbon-14 Dating of the Scrolls" *The Qumran Chronicle* 2/1 (1992); "The Unfortunate Story of Qumran Cave Four" *The Qumran Chronicle* 1/2-3 (1990-91); "How Not to Publish 4QMMT in 1955-1991" *The Qumran Chronicle* 1/2-3 (1990-91); *Qumran Cave IV and MMT: Special Report,* co-auth., ed. (Enigma, 1991); "The Present State of Qumranology" *Folia Orientalia* 26 (1990); and others. Mem: Polish Soc. of Orientalists 1975-; Polish Acad. of Sci., Oriental Com. 1979-. Rec: Traveling. Addr: (o) Jagiellonian U., Inst. of Oriental Philology, Al. Mickiewicza 9/11, Krakow, Poland 48-12-336377; (h) Borsucza 3/58, Krakow 31-408, Poland 48-12-674124.

KARAGEORGHIS, Vassos, b. Trinomo, Cyprus, April 29, 1929, s. of George & Panagiota, m. Jacqueline, chil: Clio; Andreas. Educ: U. of London, U. Coll., BA 1952, PhD 1957; U. of London, Inst. of Arch., Cert. Practical Arch. 1952. Emp: Cyprus Mus., 1960-63 Cur.; Republic of Cyprus, 1963-89 Dir. of Antiq.; Ecole des Hautes Etudes, 1983-84 Dir. d'Etudes; Inst. for Advanced Study, 1989-90 Vis. Mellon Prof.; U. of Cyprus, 1992- Prof., Arch. Excv: Salamis, 1952-73; Akhera, Pendayia, Necropolis, 1960; Necropolis of Salamis, 1962-67; Kition, 1962-81; Maa-Palaeokastro, Pyla-Kokkinokremos, 1979-87. Spec: Archaeology. Pub: *The Coroplastic Art of Ancient Cyprus I, Chalcolithic-Late Cypriote I* (1991); "Miscellanea from Late Bronze Age Cyprus" *Levant* 22 (1990); "A new 'Geryon' terracotta statuette from Cyprus" *Eretz-Israel* 20 (1989); *Excavations at Maa-Palaeokastro 1979-86,* co-auth. (1988); *Archaeology in Cyprus 1960-85,* ed. (A.G. Leventis Found., 1985); "Exploring Philistine Origins on the Island of

Cyprus" *BAR* 10/2 (1984); "Cyprus" in *Cambridge Ancient History* Parts 1, 3 (Cambridge U.P., 1982); *Excavations in the Necropolis of Salamis,* vol. I-IV (1967-78); and others. Awd: Chevalier de l'Ordre Natl. de la Legion d'Honneur 1971; Soc. of Antiquaries of London, Hon. Fellow 1983; Oxford U., DLitt 1990; Royal Order of the Polar Star, Commander 1990; Commandeur de l'Ordre des Arts et Lettres 1990. Mem: Greek Arch. Soc. 1973, Hon. Mem. of Coun.; Royal Soc. of Arts, Fellow 1977; Austrian Acad. of Sci. 1977; Acad. des Inscriptions et Belles Lettres 1984; AIA 1990-, Hon. Mem. Rec: Gardening. Addr: (o) Leventis Foundation, Sofoulis Str. 28, Chanteclair Bldg., Office 114, Nicosia, Cyprus 02-461706; (h) Kastorias Str., 16, Nicosia 133, Cyprus 02-465249.

KARRIS, Robert J., b. Chicago, IL, January 25, 1938, s. of Henry & Hannah (Altmann). Educ: Pont. Athenaeum Antonianum, STB 1965; Cath. U., STL 1966; Harvard U., ThD 1971. Emp: Cath. Theol. Union, 1971-87 Prof., NT Stud.; *CBQ,* 1974-76 Assoc. Ed., 1977-81 NT Book Rev. Ed.; CBQ Mon. Ser., 1983-91 Gen. Ed., 1992-93 Pres. Spec: New Testament. Pub: *Jesus and the Marginalized in John's Gospel* (Liturgical, 1990); *Luke: Artist and Theologian* (Paulist, 1985); *The Pastoral Epistles* (Glazier, 1979); "Missionary Communities: A New Paradigm for the Study of Luke-Acts" *CBQ* 41 (1979); and others. Mem: SNTS; SBL. Rec: Cooking, walking. Addr: (o) Curia Generalizia O.F.M., Via S Maria Mediatrice, 25, 00165 Rome, Italy 396-68491-290.

KAUFMAN, Asher S., b. Edinburgh, Scotland, s. of Isaac & Zlate, m. Josephine (Corman), chil: Rachel; Shmuel. Educ: U. of Edinburgh, BS 1948, PhD 1954. Emp: Hebrew U., Jerusalem, 1959-87 Assoc. Prof. Spec: Archaeology, Hebrew Bible, Apocrypha and Post-biblical Studies. Pub: *The Temple of Jerusalem. Tractate Middot* (Har Yera'eh, 1991); "Fixing the Site of the Tabernacle at Shiloh" *BAR* 14/6 (1988); "Determining the Length of the Medium Cubit" *PEQ* 116 (1984); "Where the Ancient Temple of Jerusalem Stood" *BAR* 9/2 (1983); "The Eastern Wall of the Second Temple at Jerusalem Revealed" *BA* 44 (1981); "New Light Upon Zion: the Plan and Precise Location of the Second Temple" *Ariel* 43 (1977); and others. Mem: IES; AJS. Rec: Nature study, *halakhah,* weather in anc. lit. Addr: (o) Hebrew U., Racah Inst. of Physics, Jerusalem 91904, Israel 02-58-4470; (h) 54 Rehov Hehaluz, Jerusalem 96269, Israel 02-43-5082.

KAUFMAN, Stephen A., b. Minneapolis, MN, September 11, 1945, s. of Leo J. & Rosetta, m. Rosalind (Newman), chil: Batya Sharon; Joshua Saul. Educ: U. of Minn., BA 1966; Yale U., PhD 1970. Emp: U. of Chicago, 1971-76 Asst. Prof.; Haifa U., 1974-76 Vis. Sr. Lect.; Hebrew Union Coll., 1976- Prof.; *JAOS,* 1988-92 Anc. Near East Sect. Ed.; *The Comprehensive Aramaic Lexicon,* 1986- Ed. Spec: Hebrew Bible, Mesopotamian

Studies, Semitic Languages, Texts and Epigraphy, Apocrypha and Post-biblical Studies. Pub: *An Aramaic Bibliography: Part I*, co-auth. (1992); *The Comprehensive Aramaic Lexicon: Text Entry and Format Manual* (1987); "The Pitfalls of Typology: On the Early History of the Alphabet" *HUCA* 57 (1986); "Reflections on the Assyrian-Aramaic Bilingual from Tell Fakhariyah" *MAARAV* 3 (1982); "The Temple Scroll and Higher Criticism" *HUCA* 53 (1982); "The Structure of the Deuteronomic Law" *MAARAV* 1 (1978-79); *The Akkadian Influences on Aramaic*, Assyriological Stud. 19 (U. of Chicago, 1974); "The Job Targum from Qumran" *JAOS* 93 (1973); and others. Addr: (o) Hebrew Union Coll., 3101 Clifton Ave., Cincinnati, OH 45220 513-221-1875; (h) 6507 Brackenridge, Cincinnati, OH 45213 513-731-4382.

KAWAMURA, Akinori, b. Tokyo, Japan, October 20, 1928, s. of Koi & Sachiko, m. Etsusko. Educ: U. of Tokyo, BA 1953; Tokyo Union Theol. Sem., MDiv 1956. Emp: Tokyo Woman's Christian U., 1964- Prof.; Tokyo Union Theol. Sem., 1981- Lect., NT. Spec: New Testament. Rec: Piano. Addr: (o) 3-1, Mure 4-chome Mitaka-shi, Tokyo 181, Japan 0422-45-4145; (h) 20-2, Setagaya 1-chome Setagaya-ku, Tokyo 154, Japan 03-3429-9803.

KEARNEY, Peter J., b. New York, NY, September 16, 1935, s. of Peter & Rose (Cassidy), m. Clare (Senecal). Educ: Pont. Gregorian U., STL 1960; Pont. Bibl. Inst., SSL 1962. Emp: St. Joseph's Coll., 1966-67 Asst. Prof.; Cath. U., 1967-81 Assoc. Prof.; Lib. of Congress, 1982-. Spec: Hebrew Bible. Pub: "He Appeared to 500 Brothers (I Cor. XV 6)" *NT* (1980); "Creation and Liturgy: The P Redaction of Exodus 25-40" *ZAW* (1977); and others. Mem: CBA 1963-86; SBL 1974-86; Cath. Theol. Assn. 1977-86. Rec: Jungian psychology, mythology. Addr: (o) Library of Congress, Hebraica Cataloging, Washington, DC 20540 202-707-7499; (h) 317 Riley St., Falls Church, VA 22046 703-534-9247.

KEATHLEY, Naymond H., b. Memphis, TN, September 25, 1940, s. of Maurice & Rubye, m. Carolyn (Griffin), chil: Kevin; Craig; Kristen. Educ: Baylor U., BA 1962; South. Bapt. Theol. Sem., BD 1966, PhD 1971. Emp: Palm Beach Atlantic Coll., 1972-76 Asst. Prof.; Golden Gate Bapt. Theol. Sem., 1976-81 Assoc. Prof.; Baylor U., 1981-89 Assoc. Prof., 1989- Prof. Spec: New Testament. Pub: *Discovering Romans*; *With Steadfast Purpose*, ed.; articles in *Mercer Dict. of the Bible*, *Holman Bible Dict.* Mem: SBL. Rec: Photography. Addr: (o) Baylor U., Dept. of Religion, Waco, TX 76798 817-755-3735; (h) 310 Trailwood Dr., Waco, TX 76712 817-776-7337.

KECK, Leander E., b. Washburn, ND, March 3, 1928. Educ: Linfield Coll., BA 1949; Andover Newton Theol. Sch., BD 1953; Yale U., PhD

1957. Emp: Wellesley Coll., 1957-59 Asst. Prof., Bibl. Hist.; Vanderbilt U., Div. Sch., 1959-72 Prof. of NT; Emory U., Candler Sch. of Theol., 1972- Prof. of NT, 1972- Chmn. of Relig. Dept. & Grad. Sch.; *SBL*, 1973- Ed. Spec: New Testament. Pub: *The Pauline Letters*, co-auth. (Abingdon, 1984); *The Bible in the Pulpit* (Abingdon, 1978); *The New Testament Experience of Faith* (Bethany, 1977); "Exegesis" in *Interpretive Dictionary of the Bible* (1975); *A Future for the Historical Jesus* (Abingdon, 1971; SCM, 1972); and others. Mem: AAR; SBL. Addr: (o) Yale Divinity School, 409 Prospect St., New Haven, CT 06511.

KEDAR-KOPFSTEIN, Benjamin E., b. Seesen, Germany, July 15, 1948, s. of Felix & Gertrud (Eckert), m. Miriam (Heymann), chil: Tamara; Daniela. Educ: U. of London, BA 1954; Hebrew U., MA 1961, PhD 1968. Emp: Hebrew U. Bible Project, 1962-; U. of Haifa, 1966- Prof.; Temple U., 1973-74 Vis. Prof.; Heidelberg U., Hochschule fur Judische Stud. 1983-84 Rector; *Hebrew Ann. Rev.*, Ed. Bd. Spec: Hebrew Bible. Pub: *Mikra, Compendia Rerum Iudaicarum ad Novum Testamentum*, trans. (Fortress, 1988); "Die Stammbildung *qotel* als Ubersetzungsproblem" *ZAW* 93 (1981); *Biblische Semantik* (Kohlhammer, 1981); and others. Mem: WUJS 1968-; IOSOT 1986-. Rec: Mathematics, formal logic, computers. Addr: (o) Haifa U., Dept. of Bible Studies, Haifa 31 999, Israel 04-240-187; (h) Oren St. 23/81, Haifa 34 734, Israel 04-244043.

KEE, Howard Clark, b. Beverly, NJ, July 28, 1920, s. of Walter L. & Regina V., m. Janet (Burrell), chil: H. Clark, III; Christopher A.; Sarah Leslie. Educ: Bryan Coll., BA 1940; Dallas Theol. Sem., ThM 1944; Yale U., PhD 1951. Emp: U. of Pa., 1951-53 Instr., Relig. & Class., 1989- Sr. Res. Fellow; Drew U., 1953-68 Prof., NT; Boston U., 1968-88 William Goodwin Aurelio Prof. of Bibl. Stud., 1988- Prof. Emeritus; SBL Diss. Ser., Ed. Excv: Herod's Palace at Jericho, 1949; Shechem 1958-62; Mt. Gerizim, Co-dir.; Ashdod, 1966-67; Pella, Jordan, 1967. Spec: Archaeology, New Testament, Apocrypha and Post-biblical Studies. Pub: "After the Crucifixion—Christianity Through Paul" in *Christianity and Rabbinic Judaism* (BAS, 1992); *Understanding the New Testament* (Prentice-Hall, 1992); "The Transforming of the Synagogue after 70 C.E." *NTS* (1990); "Magic and Messiah" in *Judaism and Messiahs* (1987); *Medicine, Miracle and Magic in New Testament Times* (Cambridge U.P., 1986); "Synoptic Studies" in *The New Testament and its Modern Interpreters* (Epp, 1984); "The Socio-Cultural Setting of 'Joseph and Asenath'" *NTS* (1983); *Christian Origins in Sociological Perspective*, trans. (Westminster, 1980); *Community of the New Age: Studies in Mark's Gospel* (Mercer U.P., 1983); and others. Awd: Marburg U., Assn. of Theol. Sch. Fellow 1959-60; Israel Antiq. Dept., Guggenheim Fellow. 1966-67, 1968; NEH, Summer Fellow. 1984. Mem: SBL, Pres., NE reg. 1983-84; AAR,

Pres., NE reg. 1985; SNTS; ASOR. Rec: Piano, bicycling, hiking. Addr: (h) 220 W Rittenhouse Square, Philadelphia, PA 19103.

KEEL, Othmar, b. Einsiedeln, Switzerland, December 6, 1937, s. of Joseph & Andree (Sutter), m. Hildi (Leu), chil: David; Sara. Educ: U. of Fribourg, Switzerland, ThD 1967. Emp: U. of Fribourg, 1967- Prof.; Orbis Biblicus et Orientalis ser., 1973- Ed.; Orbis Biblicus et Orientalis Archaeologica ser., 1980- Ed.; U. of Zurich, 1981-82 Vis. Prof.; U. of Bern, 1983-84 Vis. Prof. Spec: Archaeology, Hebrew Bible, Egyptology. Pub: *Götter, Göttinnen und Gottessymbole (1992); Altorientalische Miniaturkunst*, co-auth. (1990); *Studien zu den Stempelsiegeln aus Palästina/Israel*, 1-3 (1985-1990); *Symbolism of the Biblical World* (1978); and others. Mem: Schweizerische Gesellschaft für Orientalische Altertumswissenschaft. Rec: Gardening, poetry, arts. Addr: (o) Biblisches Institut der U., CH-1700 Fribourg, Switzerland 037-219385; (h) Grand Torry 16, CH-1700 Fribourg, Switzerland 037-251215.

KEENER, Craig S., b. Massillon, OH, July 4, 1960, s. of John & Gail. Educ: Cen. Bible Coll., BA 1982; Assemblies of God Theol. Sem., MA, Bibl. Lang. 1987; Duke U., PhD 1991. Emp: Duke U., 1989-91 Grad. Asst.; Hood Theol. Sem., 1992-94 Assoc. Prof., NT. Spec: New Testament. Pub: *...And Marries Another: Divorce and Remarriage in the Teaching of the New Testament* (Hendrickson, 1991); "Matthew 5:22 and the Heavenly Court" *ExpTim* 99 (1987). Mem: SBL 1990-. Rec: Writing, playing guitar. Addr: (h) 808 W Monroe St., Salisbury, NC 28144 704-639-1752.

KELLOGG, Frederic R., b. San Angelo, TX, December 16, 1939, s. of John & Lucille, m. Jeannette, chil: Christopher; Mark. Educ: South. Methodist U., MTh 1965; Yale U., PhD 1972. Emp: Emory & Henry Coll., 1969- Prof., Relig. Spec: New Testament. Mem: AAR 1969-; SBL 1969-. Addr: (o) Emory and Henry Coll., Emory, VA 24327 703-944-4121; (h) Box 24, Emory, VA 24327 703-944-5422.

KELM, George L., b. Hanna, AB, Canada, February 26, 1931, s. of G. Fred & Alma, m. Linda. Educ: Pacific Coll., BA 1955; Denver Sem., BD 1958; NYU, MA 1965, PhD 1968. Emp: Amer. Inst. of Holy Land Stud., Jerusalem, 1962-64 Acad. & Adm. Field Dir.; New Orleans Bapt. Sem., 1968-80 Prof., Bibl. Intro. & Arch.; SW Bapt. Theol. Sem., 1980- Prof., Bibl. Backgrounds & Arch. Excv: Arch. Expdn. to Aphek-Antipatris, Israel, 1972-76 Co-Dir.; Arch. Expdn. to Tel-Batash, Timnah 1977-89 Dir. Spec: Archaeology. Pub: *Escape to Conflict* (1991); "Tel Batash (Timnah) Excavations: Third Preliminary Report, 1984-89" *BASORSup* 27 (1991); "Excavating in Samson Country—The Philistines and Israelites at Tel Batash" *BAR* 15/1 (1989); "Tel Batash (Timnah) Excavations: Second

Preliminary Report (1981-83)" *BASORSup* 23 (1985); "Timnah—A City of Conflict Within the Traditional Buffer Zone of the Shephelah" *Bull. of the Anglo-Israel Arch. Soc.* (1985); "Tell Batashi (Tel Batash) 1979 á 1983" *RB* 3 (1984); and others. Mem: AIA 1968-, Pres., New Orleans Chap. 1972-77; ASOR 1971-; IES 1982-. Addr: (o) PO Box 22417, Fort Worth, TX 76122 817-923-1921; (h) 6505 S Hulen St., Fort Worth, TX 76133 817-294-7223.

KEMPINSKI, Aharon, b. Haifa, Israel. Educ: Hebrew U., BA, Arch. & Hist. of Israel 1962, MA Arch. & Assyriology 1967, PhD 1975. Emp: *Ency. Biblica*, 1966-67 Arch. Ed.; U. of Tubingen, 1975 Vis. Schol.; Tel Aviv U., 1979 Sr. Lect., Prof. of Arch. & Anc. Near East. Hist.; Ben Gurion U., 1979 Sr. Lect., Prof. of Arch.; Harvard U., 1981-82 Vis. Prof., Near East. Lang. & Civ. Excv: Megiddo 1963, 1965; Tel Masos, 1972-75, 1979 Co-dir.; Bet-Haémeq, 1973 dir.; Tell Kabri, 1975, 1986-88 Dir., 1989 Co-dir.; Tell Erani, 1985, 1987-88 Co-dir. Spec: Archaeology. Pub: "Reconstructing the Canaanite Tower-Temple" *Eretz-Israel* 20 (1989); "Urbanisation and Metallurgy in Southern Canaan" in *L'urbanisation de la Palestine a l'age de Bronze ancien*, Brit. Arch. Reports 527 (1989); *Megiddo, A City State and Royal Center in North Israel* (Beck, 1989); "Jacob in History" *BAR* 14/1 (1988); *The Architecture of Ancient Israel*, co-ed., contb. (1987); "Joshua's Altar—An Iron Age I Watchtower" *BAR* 12/1 (1986); *Syrier und Palästina (Kanaan) in der letzen phase der Mittlebronze II B Zeit* (Bamberg, 1983); *The Rise of an Urban Culture—Palestine in the Third Millennium B.C.*, IES Stud. 4 (1978). Mem: IES; AIA; ASOR; Deutsches Palestina Vereins; Israel Assn. of Arch. Rec: Science fiction, desert touring.

KENNEDY, Charles A., June 19, 1929, s. of Watson & Emily (Schweser), m. Virginia, chil: Catherine; Susan; Betsy. Educ: Yale U., BA 1951, BD 1956, PhD 1961. Emp: Austin Coll., 1961-67; Va. Polytechnic Inst. & State U., 1967- Prof. of Relig., Dept. Head; BAR, Ed. Adv. Bd. Spec: Archaeology, Hebrew Bible, New Testament, Apocrypha and Post-biblical Studies. Pub: "Isaiah 57:5-6: Tombs in the Rocks" *BASOR* 275 (1989); "Were Christians Buried in Roman Catacombs to Await the Second Coming?" *BAR* 6/3 (1980); "Early Christians and the Anchor" *BA* 38 (1975); and others. Mem: ASOR; SBL; AAR. Rec: Photography, music. Addr: (o) Virginia Polytechnic Institute, Dept. of Religion, Blacksburg, VA 24061 703-231-5118; (h) 805 Broce Dr. NW, Blacksburg, VA 24060 703-552-0030.

KENT, Dan G., b. Palestine, TX, October 13, 1935, s. of Tom & Hazel, m. Barbara Jo (Wilkerson), chil: Blake W.; Barrett (Border); Leslie (Cappo). Educ: Baylor U., BA 1957; SW Bapt. Theol. Sem., BD 1959, ThD 1965. Emp:

Wayland Bapt. U., 1975-80 Assoc. Prof., Relig.; SW Bapt. Theol. Sem., 1980- Prof., OT; *SW Jour. of Theol.*, 1983-89 Ed. Spec: Hebrew Bible. Pub: *Layman's Bible Book Comm.* vol. 4 (Broadman, 1980); "Jeremiah: The Man and His Times" *SW Jour. of Theol.* 24/1 (1981); *Lamentations,* Bible Study Comm. (Zondervan, 1983); "The Rechabites: What Do We Know?" *SW Jour. of Theol.* 32/3 (1990); and others. Mem: SBL; NABPR, Pres., SW reg. 1978. Addr: (o) PO Box 22,338, Fort Worth, TX 76122-0338 817-923-1921.

KEOWN, Gerald L., b. Anniston, AL, February 10, 1946, s. of Dr. & Mrs. Harlice E., m. Sharon Diane (Alverson), chil: Stephanie Lyn; Allison Lee. Educ: U. of Ala., BS 1968; South. Bapt. Theol. Sem., MDiv 1975, PhD 1979. Emp: South. Bapt. Theol. Sem., 1977-79 Instr., 1982-86 Asst. Prof., 1986- Assoc. Prof., OT Interpretation, 1990- Assoc. Dean, Master of Div. Sch.; U. of Mo., Bapt. Student Ctr., 1979-82 Prof., Bible. Spec: Hebrew Bible. Pub: "Biblical Criticism and the Hermeneutical Task," "Jeremiah 40:1-6" *Rev. & Expositor* 88/1 (1991); "Theological Introduction to 'Ruth'" *Disciple's Study Bible* (Holman, 1988); "Messianism in the Book of Malachi" *Rev. & Expositor* 84/3 (1987); and others. Mem: NAPH; SBL; Amer. Assn. of U. Prof. Rec: Golf, running, fishing. Addr: (o) SBTS, PO Box 8-1960, 2825 Lexington Rd., Louisville, KY 40280 502-897-4224; (h) 12024 Ancient Spring Dr., Louisville, KY 40245 502-241-6832.

KERN-ULMER, Brigitte A. A., b. Braunschweig, West Germany, March 14, 1951, d. of Lisa & Fritz Sonnenbrodt, m. Moshe Ulmer, chil: Michael S.F. Kern. Educ: Goethe U., Frankfurt, MA 1980, PhD, Judaic Stud. 1985. Emp: Goethe U., 1980-86 Seminar fuer Judaistik; Juedische Hochschule, Heidelberg, 1986 Vis. Prof.; Brown U., 1988-91 Vis. Schol.; Hebrew Union Coll., Jewish Inst. of Relig., 1991- Vis. Schol. Pub: "The Midrashim for Hanukkah: A Survey and a Sample Analysis" in *Approaches to Ancient Judaism,* N.S. III (Scholars, 1993); "Eine Anfrage uber Homosexualitaet im juedischen Gesetz," co-auth. *Zeitschrift fuer Relig.-und Geistesgeschichte* 43 (1991); "Shekhinah" in *Ency. Philosophique* II (Presses U., 1991); "The Power of the Evil Eye and the Good Eye in Midrashic Literature" *Judaism* 40 (1991); *Rabbinische Responsen zum Synagogenbau* (Olms, 1990); "Gattungstheorie und rabbinische Literatur" *Linguistica Biblica* 61 (1988); *Troestet, troestet mein Volk! Zwei rabbinische Homilien zu Jesaja 40,1* (Gesellschaft zur Foerderung Judaistischer Studien, 1986); *Diskussionsbeitraege aus dem Juedischen Lehrhaus in Frankfurt am Main* (Lehrhaus, 1986); and others. Awd: NEH Summer Seminar 1992; Hebrew Union Coll., Jewish Inst. of Relig., Frances Grabow Goldman Fellow. in Advanced Judaic Stud. for Women 1987. Mem: WUJS 1984-; Soc. of Jewish Stud. 1982-; European AJS 1982-86; AJS 1985-; SBL 1991-. Rec: Egypt. Addr: (h) 24 Community Rd., Bay Shore, NY 11706 516-666-8645.

KERSHAW, Norma, Educ: Queens Coll., BA; Columbia U., MA, Art Hist. & Arch. Emp: Hofstra U., Art Hist. Dept., 1974-88 Fac.; *BAR,* 1974- Ed. Adv. Bd. Excv: Gezer; Aphek; Salamis, Cyprus. Pub: *Ancient Art from Cyprus* (Ringling Mus. of Art, 1983); "The Bible Comes to Life at the Jewish Museum" *BAR* 3/1 (1977); and others. Awd: Phi Beta Kappa; Hofstra U., Conger-Patterson Awd. for Disting. Teaching; AIA, Disting. Service Awd. Mem: Amer. Res. Center in Egypt, Trustee; Albright Inst. of Arch. Res., Jerusalem, Hon. Trustee; AIA, Pres., Orange County Soc., Trustee; ASOR, Hon. Trustee; Cyprus Amer. Arch. Res. Inst., Hon. Trustee; Addr: (h) 25686 Morales, Mission Viejo, CA 92691 714-951-5586.

KHANJIAN, John, b. Aleppo, Syria, December 3, 1932, s. of Georgis & Sayoud, m. Pauline Lucy, chil: Tanya Joy; Jonathan Alex. Educ: Amer. U. of Beirut, BA 1962, MA 1968; Near East Sch. of Theol., BD 1963; Claremont Grad Sch., PhD 1974. Emp: Claremont Grad. Sch., 1966-71 Res. Asst. to Dean; Near East Sch. of Theol., Beirut, 1971-76 Assoc. Prof., OT, Lbrn.; Pasadena City Coll., 1976-77 Instr.; Kans. Wesleyan, 1977-87 Assoc. Prof., Chmn., Relig. Dept.; U. of La Verne, Amer. Armenian Intl. Coll., 1987- Dean, Assoc. Prof., Relig. Stud. Spec: Hebrew Bible, Mesopotamian Studies, Semitic Languages, Texts and Epigraphy. Mem: SBL; Inst. of Antiq. & Christianity. Rec: Jogging, organ, piano. Addr: (o) U. of La Verne, 1950 3rd St., La Verne, CA 91750 714-593-3511; (h) 1825 Rosemount, Claremont, CA 91711 714-624-3042.

KHOURI, Rami G., b. New York, NY, October 22, 1948, s. of George & Zubaida, m. Ellen (Kettaneh), chil: Haitham; Raja. Educ: Syracuse U., BA 1970. Emp: Al Kutba Publ., 1986- Owner & Gen. Manager; *Jordan Times,* 1976-82 Ed. in Chief. Spec: Archaeology. Pub: Arch. Guides: *Amman, Jerash, Petra, Desert Castles, Pella* (Al Kutba Publ., 1990); *Antiquities of the Jordan Rift Valley* (Al Kutba Publ., 1988). Mem: Friends of Arch. Soc., Pres. 1989-91; Petra Natl. Trust 1989- . Rec: Arch., sports, travel, reading, playing guitar. Addr: (o) PO Box 9446, Amman, Jordan.

KIDD, Reggie M., b. Gainesville, FL, July 18, 1951, s. of Rex C. & Linnie G., m. Sharon S., chil: T. Charles; Robert M.; Randall S. Educ: Coll. of William & Mary, AB 1973; Westminster Theol. Sem., MAR 1975, MDiv 1977; Duke U., PhD 1989. Emp: Duke Div. Sch., 1981-86 Instr.; U. of N.C., Chapel Hill, 1984-90 Vis. Lect., Relig. Stud., Instr., Independent Stud. by Extension; Reformed Theol. Sem., Orlando, 1990- Assoc. Prof., NT. Spec: New Testament. Pub: *Wealth and Beneficence in the Pastoral Epistles: A "Bourgeois" Form of Early Christianity?* SBL Diss. Ser. 122 (Scholars, 1990). Mem: SBL; ETS. Rec: Acoustic guitar, running. Addr: (o) Reformed

Theological Seminary, Orlando, PO Box 945120, Maitland, FL 32794 407-875-8388; (h) 371 White Oak Circle, Maitland, FL 32751 407-539-1670.

KIEFFER, René J. J., b. Aumetz, Moselle, France, September 22, 1930, s. of Eugene & Marie (Fournier), m. Margareta (Lundborg), chil: Mirjam; Anna; Helena. Educ: Luxembourg, Doc. 1955; Rome, Baccalaureus & Lic. in sci. bibl. 1964; Ecole Biblique, Jerusalem, Dip. 1964; Uppsala, ThD 1968. Emp: Lund, Sweden, 1970-89 Asst. Prof.; Uppsala, Sweden, 1990- Prof.; *Lumen*, 1967-71 Ed. Bd.; *Svensk Exegetisk Arsbok*, 1990- Co-ed.; *Acta U. Upsalienis*, 1990- Co-ed.; *Conjectanea Bibl.*, NT ser., 1990- Co-ed. Spec: New Testament. Pub: *Nytestamentlij teologi* (Verbum, 1991); "L'eschatologie en 1 Thessaloniciens dans une perspective rhetorique" in *The Thessalonian Correspondence*, BETL 87 (1990); *Johannes evangelist*, vol. 1-2 (1987, 1988); "L'espace et le temps dans l'evangile de Jean" *NTS* 31 (1985); *Foi et justification á Antioche* (Le Cerf, 1982); "Deux types d'exegese a base linquistique" *Concilium* 158 (1980); "Analyse semiotique et commentaire" *NTS* 25 (1979); *Essais de methodologie neo-testamentaire* (Berlingska, 1971); "Vishet och välsignelse som grundmotiv i salig prisningarna hos Matteus och Lukas" *Svensk Exegetisk Arsbok* 34 (1969); and others. Mem: ACFEB 1968-; SNTS 1969-; Svensk Exegetisk Soc. 1969-; Vetenskapssocieteten Lund 1975-; Nathan Soderblom Soc. 1990-. Rec: Music (piano), lit., phil. Addr: (o) Teologiska Institutionen, Box 1604, 75136 Uppsala, Sweden 0-18-182235; (h) Paprikagatan 3, Sweden 0-18-242033.

KIEHL, Erich H., b. Lone Elm, MO, August 27, 1920, s. of Henry G. H. & Clara L. (Kuecker), m. Dorothy L., chil: David; Kathryn; Sharon; Daniel; Mark; Thomas. Educ: Concordia Sem., BA 1942, MDiv 1945, STM 1951, ThD 1959. Emp: Concordia Coll., 1965-74 Prof., Relig.; Concordia Sem., 1974- Prof., Exegetical Theol.; *Greek-English Theological Dictionary*, 6 vol., Complete Bibl. Lib. Ser., Bd. of Rev. Spec: Hebrew Bible, New Testament. Pub: "The 'Lost' Parables in Luke's Gospel Account" *Concordia Jour.* July (1992); "Why Jesus Spoke in Parables" *Concordia Jour.* July (1990); *The Passion of Our Lord* (Baker, 1990); *Building Your Biblical Studies Library: A Survey of Current Resources* (Concordia, 1988); "Comm. on Galatians" in *New Testament Study Bible*, Complete Bibl. Library Ser. (1986); and others. Mem: SBL; ETS; AIA; NEAS; PES. Rec: Travel, esp. in the Mediterranean area. Addr: (o) Concordia Seminary, 801 De Mun Ave., St. Louis, MO 63105 314-721-5934.

KIILUNEN, Jarmo V., b. Vaasa, Finland, April 12, 1948, s. of Veikko & Aino (Perko), m. Ulla (Pohjolan-Pirhonen), chil: Liisa-Maria; Jaakko. Educ: U. of Helsinki, Cand. Theol. 1971, Lic. Theol. 1974, ThD 1985. Emp: U. of Helsinki, 1977-89 Asst., 1986- Docent, Bibl. Exegetics; Diocese of

Helsinki, 1990- General Sec. Spec: New Testament. Pub: "Der nachfolgewillige Schriftgelehrte. Matthaus 8:19-20 im Verstandnis des Evangelisten" *NTS* 37 (1991); *Das Doppelgebot der Liebe in synoptischer Sicht. Ein redaktionskritischer Versuch*, AASF B 250 (Academia Scientiarum Fennica, 1989); *Die Vollmacht im Widerstreit. Untersuchungen zum Werdegang von Mk 2,1-3,6*, AASF 40 (Academia Scientiarum Fennica, 1985). Mem: Finnish Exegetical Soc. 1979-92; SNTS 1987-. Rec: Music, steam engines. Addr: (o) PO Box 142, SF-00121 Helsinki, Finland 0-601-117; (h) Vapaalantie 72 A, SF-01650 Vantaa, Finland 0-8534 157.

KIKAWADA, Isaac M., b. Sendai, Japan, April 16, 1937, s. of John & Katsuko. Educ: Kenyon Coll., BD 1965; U. of Calif., Berkeley, PhD 1979. Emp: U. of Calif., Berkeley, 1972-92 Vis. Lect., Near East. Stud.; U. of Ariz., 1984-85 Vis. Asst. Prof. Spec: Hebrew Bible, Mesopotamian Studies, Semitic Languages, Texts and Epigraphy. Pub: *Before Abraham Was*, co-auth. (Abingdon, 1985); "Jonah and Genesis," co-auth. *Ann. of the Japanese Bibl. Inst.* 10 (1984); "The Double Creation of Mankind in *Enki and Ninmah*, *Atrahasis* I 1-351 and Genesis 1-2" *Iraq* 45 (1983); and others. Mem: ASOR; AOS; SBL, Pres., W Coast Reg., 1984-85. Rec: Collection of antique Japanese porcelain, skiing. Addr: (o) U. of California, Near Eastern Studies, Berkeley, CA 94720 510-642-3757; (h) 1787 Sonoma Ave., Berkeley, CA 94707 415-525-8767.

KILEY, Mark C., b. Syracuse, NY, October 13, 1953, s. of William & Cecilia. Educ: Harvard U., MTS 1977, PhD 1983. Emp: Emmanuel Coll., 1981-83 Lect.; St. Jerome Coll., Canada, 1983-91 Asst. Prof.; St. John's U., Staten Island 1992 Asst. Prof. Spec: New Testament. Pub: "Catholic Epistles" in *New Catholic Ency.* Sup. vol. 18 (Cath. U.P., 1989); "The Exegesis of God: Jesus' Signs in John 1-11" in *SBL Seminar Papers* (Scholars, 1988); "Like Sara: The Tale of Terror Behind 1 Peter 3:6" *JBL* 106 (1987); "Melchisedek's Promotion to 'archiereus' and the translation of *ta Stoicheia tes Arches* (Heb. 5:12)" in *SBL Seminar Papers* (Scholars, 1986); *Colossians as Pseudepigraphy* (JSOT, 1986); "Why 'Matthew' in Matt 9:9-13?" *Biblica* 3 (1984). Mem: SBL; CBA. Rec: Swimming, ice skating, travel. Addr: (o) St. John's U., Dept. of Philosophy & Theology, 300 Howard Ave., Staten Island, NY 10301.

KILLEBREW, Ann E., b. Los Angeles, CA, November 4, 1954, d. of Alfred & Jeanne (Bennewitz). Educ: U. of Calif., Irvine, BA 1976; Hebrew U., Jerusalem, Inst. of Arch., MA 1989. Emp: U. of Haifa, 1991- Instr.; Hebrew U., Jerusalem, 1987- Instr.; W.F. Albright Inst. of Arch. Res., 1983- Res. Fellow. Excv: Deir el-Balah, Israel, 1978-82 Field Arch.; Tel Miqne/Ekron, Israel, 1981-89 Field Arch.; Qasrin Village, Israel, 1983-90 Dir.; Tel Beth

Shean, Israel, 1983, 1990- Field Arch., Field Sch. Instr.; Katzion, Israel, 1992- Co-dir. Spec: Archaeology. Pub: "Qatzrin—Reconstructing Village Life in Talmudic Times," co-auth., *BAR* 17/3 (1991); "Pottery from Dabiyye" *'Atiqot* 20 (1991); "Archaeological Treasures in the Golan Archaeological Museum," co-auth., *BAR* 14 (1989); *Tel Miqne—Report of the 1984 Excavations in Field INE/ISE* (W.F. Albright Inst., 1986); "Comparison of Neutron Activation and Thin Section Analysis on Late Bronze Age Ceramics from Deir el-Balah," co-auth., in *Proceedings of the 24th International Archaeometry Symposium* (1986); "Jewish Funerary Customs during the Second Temple Period, in Light of the Excavations at the Jericho Necropolis," co-auth., *PEQ* (1983); and others. Awd: Hebrew U., Inst. of Arch., Zinder Prize 1990, Berman Prize 1992. Mem: ASOR 1992-. Rec: Dancing, horseback riding, weightlifting. Addr: (o) Hebrew U., Institute of Archaeology, Jerusalem, Israel; (h) Shimoni 30/B, Jerusalem 92623, Israel.

KIM, Ee Kon, b. Manchuria, December 22, 1940, s. of Yong Duk & Suk Ee (Sung), m. Pok Ja Kwon, chil: George; Michael. Educ: Hankuk Theol. Sem., Korea, ThB 1964; United Grad. Sch. of Theol., Yonsei U., Korea, ThM 1967; Union Theol. Sem., STM 1979, PhD 1984. Emp: Hanshin U., Korea 1969- Prof. of OT, Dean. Spec: Hebrew Bible. Pub: *A Theology of Suffering in the Old Testament* (Korea Theol. Study Inst., 1989); *A Theology of Suffering in the Book of Exodus* (Korea Theol. Study Inst., 1989); "'Outcry': Its Context in Biblical Theology" *Interpretation* 42/3 (1988); *The Rapid Change of Mood in the Lament Psalms: A Matrix for the Establishment of a Psalm Theology* (Korea Theol. Study Inst., 1985); "The Contextual Usage of the Morpheme *'WAW'*" *Theol. Stud.* 21 (1979); "The Israelite Adaptation of the Shemesh-motif in Psalm 19A" *Theol. Thought Quar.* 18 (1977); and others. Mem: Assn. of OT Stud. Addr: (o) Hanshin U., 411 Yangsanri, Osanup, Hwasungkun, Kyunggido, Seoul 170-83, Korea 233-9438; (h) 129 Suyudong, Dobong-ku, Seoul 132, Korea 902-2824.

KIMBROUGH, S T, Jr., b. Athens, AL, December 17, 1936, s. of S T & Dorothy (Butterley), m. Sarah Ann (Robinson), chil: David R.; Timothy E.; Steven F.; Mark S. Educ: Duke U. Div. Sch., BD 1962; Princeton Theol. Sem., PhD 1966. Emp: Princeton Theol. Sem., 1964-70 Asst. Prof., OT; Kaiser Friedrich Wilhelm U., Germany, 1975-78, 1992 Vis. Prof.; M. Flavius Illiricus Theol. Fac., Yugoslavia, 1978 Vis. Prof.; Ctr. of Theol. Inquiry, 1985- Mem. Spec: Archaeology, Hebrew Bible. Pub: *Psalms for Praise and Worship* (Abingdon, 1992); "Bible Translation and the Gender of God" *Theol. Today* 46 (1989); *Israelite Religion in Sociological Perspective* (Harrassowitz, 1978); *The Old Testament as the Book of Christ*, trans. (Westminster, 1976); "A Non-Weberian Approach to Old Testament Religion" *JNES* 31 (1972); "Une conception sociologique de la

Religion d'Israel" *Revue d'Histoire et de philosophie Religieuse* 49 (1969); "The Ethic of the Qumran Community" *RQ* 6 (1968); and others. Rec: Squash, tennis, walking. Addr: (h) 128 Bridge Ave., Bay Head, NJ 08742.

KIMURA, Hiroshi, b. Kawaguchi, Japan, May 14, 1936, s. of Shigeo & Chiyo, m. Gunilla Marta (Svensson), chil: Magnus Yuzo; Wilhelm Shoji. Educ: Doshisha U., Kyoto, BA 1959, MD 1961; Uppsala U., DD 1981, ThD 1981. Emp: United Ch. of Christ in Japan, 1961-64 Pastor; Kyoai Gakuen Jr. Coll., 1988- Dean of Chaplains. Spec: Hebrew Bible. Pub: *Israels Profeter*, co-auth. (Barnum, 1974). Rec: Fishing. Addr: (o) Kyoai Gakuen Women's Junior College, 1154-4, Koyahara, Maebashi, Japan 0272-66-7575; (h) 1525-2 Koyahara, Maebashi, Japan 0272-66-4982.

KINDER, Donald M., b. Charleston, WV, June 23, 1953, s. of Cebert & Rosemary, m. Vicki, chil: Brandon. Educ: Abilene Christian U., BA (summa cum laude) 1975, MA 1976; U. of Iowa, PhD 1987. Emp: Columbia Christian Coll., 1989- Asst. Prof., Bible, 1990- Chair, Div. of Bible & Relig. Spec: New Testament. Pub: "Clement of Alexandria: Conflicting Views on Women" *SC* 7/4 (1989-90). Mem: SBL 1990-. Rec: Hiking, music, computers, racquetball. Addr: (o) Columbia Christian College, 9101 E Burnside, Portland, OR 97216 503-257-1243; (h) 9102 NE Glisan, Portland, OR 97220 503-253-8758.

KING, Philip J., b. Newton, MA, March 26, 1925. Educ: St. John Sem. Coll., AB 1945; Cath. U. of Amer., STL 1954; Pont. Bibl. Inst., Rome, SSL 1957; Pont. Lateran U., Rome, STD 1959. Emp: Boston Coll., Prof. of Bibl. Stud.; *CBQ*, 1974-77 Assoc. Ed.; SBL/ASOR, Arch. & Bibl. Stud. Ser., 1985- Ed.; *BR*, 1985- Ed. Bd. Excv: Tell er-Rumeith, Jordan, 1967; Tell Taanach, West Bank, 1968; Tell Gezer, Israel, 1968-69; Tell el-Hesi, Israel, 1970-71, 1973; Wadi el-Jubah, North Yemen, 1984. Spec: Archaeology, Hebrew Bible. Pub: *Jeremiah: An Archaeological Companion* (Westminster/John Knox, 1993); "The Marzeah Amos Denounces—Using Archaeology to Interpret a Biblical Text" *BAR* 14/4 (1988); *Amos, Hosea, Micah—An Archaeological Companion* (Westminster, 1988); "The Contribution of Archaeology to Biblical Studies" in *A Companion to the Bible* (1985); "Revealing Biblical Jerusalem: An Introduction" in *Biblical Archaeology Today* (1985); "Archaeology at the Albright Institute" *BA* 38 (1975); "The American Archaeological Heritage in the Near East" *BASOR* 217 (1975); *The Book of Numbers*, OT Reading Guide (1966); *The Book of Psalms* (1962); and others. Awd: ASOR, Jerusalem, William F. Albright Fellow 1966-67; NEH, Jerusalem, Post-doc. Fellow 1986. Mem: ASOR, Pres. 1976-82; AIA; CBA, Pres. 1981-82; IES; SBL, Pres., New England reg. 1965-66, 1983-84, Pres. 1988. Addr: (o) Boston College, Dept. of Theology,

Carney Hall, Room 407, Chestnut Hill, MA 02167 617-552-4240.

KIRCHSCHLAGER, Walter, b. Kamegg, Austria, April 27, 1947, s. of Rudolf & Herma, m. Heidi K., chil: Barbara M.; Andreas R.; Thomas J.; Peter G. Educ: Pont. Gregorian U., Rome, BA, Phil. 1968; Pont. Gregorian U., Vienna, ThD 1972, Habil. 1981. Emp: Sec. to Archbishop of Vienna, 1970-73; U. of Vienna, Inst. for NT Stud., 1972-79 Asst.; Archdiocese of Vienna, 1980-82 Dir., Theol. Adult Educ.; Theol. Fac. in Lucerne, 1982- Prof., NT Stud., 1990-93 Rector. Spec: New Testament. Pub: *Gott spricht verbindlich* (Paulusverlag, 1992); *Die Anfaenge der Kirche* (Styria, 1990); *Ehe und Ehescheidung im Neuen Testament* (Herold, 1987); "Zwanzig Jahre Dei Verbum" *BiLi* 59 (1986); *Dogmatische Konstitution uber die Goettliche Offennbarung "Dei Verbum":* *Kommentar* (Katholisches Bibelwerk, 1985); "Die Geburt Jesu von Nazaret (Lk 2,1-20)" *TQ* 131 (1983); "Die Losloesung der gekruemmten Frau Lk 13,10-17" *Arzt und Christ* 24/25 (1978/1979); "Exorzismus in Qumran?" *Kairos* 18 (1976); and others. Awd: Kardinal-Innitzer-Forderungspreis fur Theol. 1981. Mem: SNTS 1986-; Arbeitsgemeinschaft der deutschsprachigen katholischen Neutestamentler 1981-; Europaische Akademie fur Wissenschaft & Kunste 1992-. Rec: Do-it-yourself-carpentry, skiing, model trains. Addr: (o) Seestrasse 93, CH 6047 Kastanienbaum, Switzerland 041-47-38-85.

KIRKEBY, Oliver M., b. Henning, MN, September 14, 1930, s. of Ole & Minnie, m. Judith D. (Hillestad), chil: Paul; Beth; Jayne. Educ: Luther Sem., BTh 1957; U. of Windsor, Canada, MA 1972; Trinity Sem., DMin 1980; Wayne State U., PhD 1982. Emp: Luth. parish, campus min., 1958-80; Highland Park Sch., 1982-85 Instr.; Wayne State U., 1985- Intl. Counselor, Adj. Prof.; *Michigan Social Studies Teacher,* 1986- Assoc. Ed. Spec: New Testament. Mem: AAR; SBL; Assn. Sociology of Relig.; Soc. for the Sci. Stud. of Relig. Rec: Marksmanship. Addr: (o) Wayne State U., International Services Office, 5460 Cass Ave., Detroit, MI 48202 313-577-3422.

KISLEV, Mordechai E., b. Haifa, Israel, May 8, 1937, s. of Arie & Sara, m. Rachel, chil: Ithamar; Shamai; Eliakim. Educ: Hebrew U. of Jerusalem, MSc 1963, PhD 1972. Emp: Hebrew U. of Jerusalem, 1961-71 Instr., Botany; Bar-Ilan U., 1973-90 Sr. Lec., 1990- Assoc. Prof., Life Sci. Spec: Archaeology, Hebrew Bible, Apocrypha and Post-biblical studies. Pub: "Vegetal Food of Bar Kokhba Rebels at Abi'or Cave near Jericho" *Rev. of Palaeobotany & Palynology* 73 (1992); "Origins of the Cultivation of *Lathyrus sativus* and *L. cicera* (Fabaceae)" *Economic Botany* 43 (1989); "*Pinus pinea* in Agriculture, Culture and Cult" *Forschungen und Berichte zur Vor- und Fruhgeschichte in Baden-Wurttemberg* 31; (1988); "Emergence of Wheat Agriculture" *Paleorient* 10 (1984); "Stem Rust of Wheat 3300 Years Old

Found in Israel" *Science* 216 (1982); and others. Addr: (o) Bar-Ilan U., Dept. of Life Sciences, Ramat-Gan 52900, Israel 03-531-8245; (h) Etzion Gaver St. 2, Jerusalem 97803, Israel 02-81-0206.

KITCHEN, Kenneth A., b. Aberdeen, Scotland, s. of Leslie & Hannah (Sheen). Educ: U. of Liverpool, BA, Egyptology & Semitics 1956, PhD 1974. Emp: U. of Liverpool, 1957-87 Reader, Egyptian & Coptic; 1987- Prof., Egyptology. Excv: Ramesside inscriptions, Egypt, 1962-76 Epigrapher. Spec: Archaeology, Anatolian Studies, Hebrew Bible, Semitic Languages, Texts and Epigraphy, Egyptology. Pub: *Pharaoh Triumphant (Ramses II)* (Aris & Phillips, 1982); *The Bible in its World* (Paternoster, 1977); *Ramesside Insciptions I-VIII* (Blackwells, 1969-90); and others. Mem: Egypt Exploration Soc. 1949-; PEF 1952-; BSA 1952-; BIA, Ankara 1956-; Soc. Stud. Egypt. Antiq. 1977-. Addr: (o) U. of Liverpool, Dept. of Egyptology, P.O. 147, Liverpool, L69 3BX, England 051-794-2468.

KIYOSHIGE, Naohiro, b. Tokyo, Japan, May 14, 1939, s. of Kuchi & Kiyoye, m. Keiko, chil: Tadahiro; Tomoko; Kazuhiro. Educ: Tokyo U., BA 1964; St. Paul U., Tokyo, MTh 1966; Union Theol. Sem., Doc. 1972-75. Emp: Japan Evang. Luth. Ch., 1968-72 Pastor; Japan Luth. Theol. Coll./Sem., 1975- Prof., Pres. Excv: Tel Zeror, 1965-66 Area Supr. Spec: Archaeology, Hebrew Bible. Pub: *Methods of Biblical Criticism* (1979). Mem: SOTS 1975-; Soc. for Bible Translators 1970. Addr: (o) Ohsawa 3-10-20, Mitaka-Tokyo, Japan 0422-31-6696.

KLASSEN, William, b. Halbstadt, Canada, May 18, 1930, s. of David & Susan (Heinrichs), m. Dona (Harvey), chil: Jarold; Kirsten L.; Karis L. Educ: Goshen Sem., BD 1954; Princeton Sem., PhD (magna cum laude) 1960. Emp: Mennonite Bibl. Sem., 1959-69 Prof.; U. of Manitoba, 1969-81 Prof., NT, Dept. Head; Simon Fraser U., 1982-84 Instr., Relig.; Ecumenical Inst., Interfaith Acad. of Peace, Jerusalem, 1984- Dean; St. Paul's United Coll., 1989- Prin. Spec: New Testament, Apocrypha and Post-biblical Studies. Pub: "Love," "War," "Peace," "Judas Iscariot," "Kiss" in *ABD* (1992); "Musonius Rufus, Jesus and Paul: Three First Century Feminists" in *From Jesus to Paul: Studies in Honour of Francis Beare* (Wilfrid Laurier U.P., 1984); "Humanitas as Seen by Epictetus and Musonius Rufus" in *Studi Storico Religiosi* (Rome, 1977); "Vengeance in the Apocalypse" *CBQ* (1966); and others. Mem: AAR; SBL; SNTS. Rec: Tennis, golf, cooking. Addr: (o) St. Paul's College, Westmount Rd. N, Waterloo, ON N2L 365, Canada; (h) 550 Glasgow St., Kitchener, ON, Canada 519-744-9924.

KLAUS, Natan, b. Tel-Aviv, Israel, January 12, 1941, s. of Akiva & Nehama, chil: Erez; Oren; Hadas; Dikla. Educ: Tel-Aviv U., BA 1965, MA

1969. Spec: Hebrew Bible. Pub: "A Play on Language in the Bible" Beit Mikra 129 (1992); "Simultaneity in the Bible" Beit Mikra 127 (1991); *Studies in the Biblical Narrative* (Am Oved, 1990); "The Pivotal Structure and its Influence on the Structure of the Story (2 Sam. 20)" *Bisde Hemed* 7-8 (1989); *The Book of Numbers* (Even Yehuda, 1988); *The Book of Jonah* (Even Yehuda, 1987); and others. Addr: (o) Hasharam School, Dubnov St., Ra'anana, Israel 052-440432; (h) Akiva St., 68, Ra'anana, Israel 052-432665.

KLEIN, Michael L., b. Brooklyn, NY, August 5, 1940, s. of Charles & Esther (Beckenstein), m. Shoshana (Silber), chil: Mattan; Elad; Rachel; Ruth. Educ: U. of Pa., MA 1975; Hebrew U., Jerusalem, PhD 1979. Emp: HUC-Jewish Inst. of Relig, 1970- Prof., Bible & Targumic Lit., Dean. Spec: Hebrew Bible, Semitic Languages, Texts and Epigraphy. Pub: *Targumic Manuscripts in the Cambridge Genizah Collections* (1992); *Genizah Manuscripts of Palestinian Targum to the Pentateuch* (HUC, 1986); "Associative and Complementary Translation in the Targumim" *Eretz-Israel* 16 (1982); *The Translation of Anthropomorphisms in the Targumim*, VTSup (Brill, 1981); *The Fragment-Targums of the Pentateuch*, 2 vol., Analecta Bibl. 76 (1980); "Converse Translation: A Targumic Technique" *Biblica* 57 (1976); "The Extant Sources of the Fragmentary Targum to the Pentateuch" *HUCA* 46 (1975); and others. Awd: Memorial Found. for Jewish Culture Fellow 1979-81; Cambridge U. Lib., Vis. Res. Assoc. 1987-88; Soviet Acad. of Sci., Sr. Schol. Exchange 1987, 1989. Mem: SBL; WUJS; Assn. for Targumic & Cognate Stud. Addr: (o) Hebrew Union College, 13 King David St., Jerusalem, Israel 02-203331; (h) 4 Bodenheimer St., Jerusalem, Israel 02-416247.

KLEIN, Ralph W., b. Springfield, IL, December 1, 1936, s. of George & Pauline (Doroh), m. Marilyn, chil: Martha; Rebecca. Educ: Concordia Sem., MDiv 1962; Harvard Div. Sch., ThD 1966. Emp: Concordia Sr. Coll., 1966-68 Asst. Prof.; Concordia Sem., 1968-74 Asst. Prof.; Luth. Sch. of Theol./Christ Sem., 1974- Prof. *Currents in Theology and Mission*, 1974 Ed. Spec: Hebrew Bible, Semitic Languages, Texts and Epigraphy. Pub: *Ezekiel: The Prophet and His Message* (U. of S.C., 1988); "Abijah's Campaign Against the North (II Chr 13)- What Were the Chronicler's Sources?" *ZAW* 95 (1983); *I Samuel* (Word, 1983); "The Message of P" in *Die Botschaft und die Boten, Festshrift fur Hans Wolff* (1981); *Israel in Exile* (Fortress, 1979); *Textual Criticism of the Old Testament* (Fortress, 1974); "Jeroboam's Rise to Power" *JBL* 89 (1970); and others. Awd: Harvard U., Rockefeller Fellow. 1965-66, Humboldt Fellow. 1977-78, 1993. Mem: CBA 1969-; SBL 1962-. Addr: (o) Luth. Sch. of Theol. 1100 E 55 St., Chicago, IL 60615 312-753-0721; (h) 10700 S Seeley, Chicago, IL 60643 312-238-1856.

KLEIN, William W., b. Weehawken, NJ, February 11, 1946, s. of William & Eleanor, m. Phyllis G., chil: Alison; Sarah. Educ: Denver Conservative Bapt. Sem., MDiv 1970; U. of Aberdeen, Scotland, PhD 1978. Emp: Columbia Bible Coll., 1977-78 Instr., NT; Denver Sem., 1978- Prof. Spec: New Testament. Pub: "Noisy Gong or Acoustic Vase? A Note on 1 Corinthians 13.1" *NTS* 32 (1986); "Paul's Use of *kalein*: A Proposal" *JETS* 27 (1984); and others. Mem: SBL; IBR; Tyndale Fellow.; ETS. Rec: Skiing, hiking. Addr: (o) PO Box 10,000 UPS, Denver, CO 80250 303-761-2482; (h) 2590 S Adams St., Denver, CO 80210.

KLONER, Amos, b. Israel, February 26, 1940, s. of Pesah & Dina. Educ: Hebrew U., Jerusalem, MA 1973, PhD 1980. Emp: Dept. of Antiq., 1972- District Arch.; Haifa U., 1975-78, Bar-Ilan U., 1981- Lect., Arch. Spec: Archaeology. Pub: "Lead Weights of Bar Kokhba's Administration" *IEJ* 40/1 (1990); "The Synagogues of Horvat Rimmon, Ancient Synagogues in Israel" *British Arch.* Records 499 (1989); "The Roman Amphitheatre at Beth-Guvrin" *IEJ* 38/1-2 (1988); *The Hiding Complexes in the Judean Shephelah* (1988); "Jerusalem Tombs from the Days of the First Temple," coauth. *BAR* Mar./Apr. (1986); "The 'Third Wall' in Jerusalem and the 'Cave of the Kings'" (Josephus War v. 147) *Levant* 18 (1986); "ABCDerian Inscriptions in Jewish Rock-Cut Tombs" in *Proceedings of the Ninth World Congress of Jewish Studies* (1986); "A Monument of the Second Temple Period West of the Old City of Jerusalem" *Eretz Israel* 18 (1985); and others. Addr: (h) 1 Mevo Dakar, Jerusalem 97855, Israel 02-81-7871.

KNIGHT, Douglas A., b. Cortland, NY, May 1, 1943, s. of Allan R. & Pearl P., m. Catherine W. (Snow), chil: Lisa I.; Jonathan W. Educ: Ottawa U., BA 1965; Calif. Bapt. Theol. Sem., MDiv 1968; Georg-August U., Germany, Dr.theol. (magna cum laude) 1973. Emp: American Bapt. Sem. of the West, 1973 Adj. Prof., OT; Vanderbilt U. Div. Sch. & Grad. Dept. of Relig., 1973- Prof., Hebrew Bible; SBL Diss. Ser. 1974-78 Ed.; *JBL*, 1991- Ed. Bd.; The Bible & Its Modern Interpreters Ser., SBL, 1975-89 Gen. Ed.; Issues in Relig. & Theol. Ser., 1980-87 Co-ed. Excv: Aphek-Antipatris, 1984. Spec: Hebrew Bible, Semitic Languages, Texts and Epigraphy. Pub: "The Ethics of Human Life in the Hebrew Bible" in *Justice and the Holy: Essays in Honor of Walter Harrelson*, co-ed. (Scholars,; 1989); "Cosmogony and Order in the Hebrew Tradition" in *Cosmogony and Ethical Order: New Studies in Comparative Ethics* (U. of Chicago,; 1985); "The Pentateuch" in The Hebrew Bible and Its Modern Interpreters, co-ed. (Scholars/Fortress, 1985); "Jeremiah and the Dimensions of the Moral Life" in *The Divine Helmsman: Studies on God's Control of Human Events, Presented to Lou; H. Silberman* (Ktav, 1980); "Revelation through Tradition" in

Tradition and Theology in the OT (Fortress/SPCK, 1977); *Tradition and Theology in the OT*, ed. (Fortress/SPCK, 1977); *Rediscovering the Traditions of Israel* (SBL, 1973, 1975); and others. Awd: Assn. of Theol. Sch. in the United States & Canada, Basic Theol. Schol. & Res. Awd. 1981-82; Vanderbilt U., U. Fellow. Awd. 1981-82; Fulbright Awd., 1981-82; NEH, Fellow. for U. Teachers 1987-88. Mem: AAR 1972-; ASOR 1978-; CBA 1976-; SBL 1972-; Scholars Press, Mem. Bd. of Trustees 1981-82. Rec: Skiing, tennis, fishing, travel. Addr: (o) Vanderbilt U., Divinity School, Nashville, TN 37240 615-343-5008; (h) 1106 Clifton Ln., Nashville, TN 37204 615-292-6078.

KNIGHT, George A. F., b. Perth, Scotland, May 12, 1909, s. of George & Annie (Baillie), m. Agnes, chil: David B.; E.H. Ann. Educ: U. of Glasgow, Scotland, MA, Class. Lang. 1930, MA, Semitics 1932, BD 1935. Emp: Knox Coll., New Zealand, 1947-58 Prof., OT; Pacific Theol. Coll., Fiji, 1965-72 Prin.; McCormick Theol. Sem., 1960-65 Prof., OT; U. of St. Andrews, Scotland, 1959-60 Lect., OT & Semitic Lang.; Ferrie, Sydney and Melbourne, 1972 Lect. Spec: Hebrew Bible, Semitic Languages, Texts and Epigraphy. Pub: *Theology as Narration: A Commentary on Exodus* (Handsel/Eerdmans, 1976); "The Maccabees" in *Ency. Britannica* (1971); *Deutero-Isaiah: A Theological Commentary* (Abingdon, 1965); *A Christian Theology of the Old Testament* (1959); and others. Awd: U. of Glasgow, Melbourne,; Coe Coll., DD. Mem: SBL 1960-; SOTS 1940-. Rec: Gardening. Addr: (h) 22 Gladstone Rd., Gardens, Dunedin, New Zealand 3-4737-043.

KNOBLOCH, Frederick W., b. Troy, NY, August 28, 1956, s. of Fred & Martha, m. Atsuko Hattori. Educ: U. of Del., BA (magna cum laude) 1980; U. of Pa., MA, Oriental Stud. 1987. Emp: U. of Pa., 1989-92 Lect.; La Salle U., 1990-91 Lect.; Computer-Assisted Tools for Septuagint Stud., 1981-92 Res. Asst. Excv: City of David Excvn., 1984 Square Supr.; Qazrin Excv., 1984 Square Supr., Vol. Coord. Spec: Hebrew Bible. Pub: Articles in *ABD* (Doubleday, 1992); articles in *Illustrated Dict. and Concordance of the Bible* (Macmillan, 1986). Awd: Phi Beta Kappa 1980; Phi Kappa Phi 1980; Hebrew U. of Jerusalem, Rabbi Israel Goldstein Fellow 1983-84; Albright Inst. of Arch. Res., Res. Fellow 1984-85. Mem: SBL 1983-; NAPH 1989-; IOSCS 1989-. Addr: (o) U. of Pennsylvania, 847 Williams Hall, Philadelphia, PA 19104-6305 215-898-7466.

KNOCH, Otto B., b. Sindelfingen, Germany, January 7, 1926, s. of Franz and Hedwig (Speer). Educ: U. Tubingen, Dipl. Theol. 1951, Dr.Theol. 1959. Emp: U. of Tubingen, 1967-71 Docent, Bibl. Intro.; Philos.-Theol. Hochschule Passau, 1971-78 Prof., Bibl. & Kerygmatics; U. of Passau, 1978- Prof.; *Bibel und Kirche,* Ed. Spec: New Testament, Apocrypha and Post-biblical Studies.

Pub: "Im Namen des Petrus und Paulus: Der Brief des Clemens Romanus und die Eigenart des roemischen Christentums" *ANRW* II, 27/1 (1993); *Die Petrusbriefe, Der Judasbrief* (1990); *1. und 2. Timotheusbrief. Titusbrief,* Echter Bibel. NT 14 (1988); *Die Botschaft der Gleichnisse Jesu* (1987); *Die Botschaft der Wundererzaehlungen der Evangelien* (1986); and others. Awd: Papal medal 'bene merenti' 1965; Papal honorary prelate 1979; Bundesrepublik Deutschland, Medal of Honor 1985. Mem: Assn. of Cath. German-speaking Scholars of NT 1968-; SNTS 1970-; Scholars of NT, Bavarian Theol. Faculty & Acad. 1976-. Rec: Collecting early bibl. translations in German dialects. Addr: (h) Stiftsstr. 5, 7056 Weinstadt-Beutelsbach, Germany 07151-66-07-31.

KOBAYASHI, Nobuo, b. Yamaguchi, Japan, October 15, 1922, s. of Setsuzo & Misao (Takebayashi), m. Haruko, chil: Kei. Educ: Kyushu Imperial U., MA 1945; Emmanuel Coll., Toronto, BD 1952. Emp: Kwansei Gakuin U., Sch. of Theol., 1954- Prof., NT. Spec: New Testament. Pub: *Shingaku Kenkyu Kwansei: Baptism in the New Testament,* contb. (1956); and others. Mem: SBL 1980; Soc. of Relig. Stud., Japan 1950-; Soc. of Christian Stud., Japan 1955-. Rec: Golf. Addr: (o) Kwansei Gakuin U., Uegahara, Nishinomiya 662, Japan 0798-53-6111; (h) 2 Kotoen, Nishinomiya 662, Japan 0798-51-0948.

KOCH, Dietrich-Alex G., b. Koenigsberg/Ostpreussen, October 22, 1942, s. of Hans-Werner & Charlotte (Bohm), m. Ruth (Metzger), chil: Cecilie; Marianne. Educ: ThD 1973. Emp: U. Mainz, 1977-85 Wiss. Mitarbeiter, 1984 Prof., NT; U. Muenster, 1985- Prof., NT. Spec: New Testament. Pub: "Source Criticism (NT)" in *ABD* vol. 6 (Doubleday, 1992); *Der Taeufer als Zeuge des Offenbarers,* Festschrift F. Neirynck, BETL 100 (Peeters, 1992); *Jesu Tischgemeinschaft mit Zoellner und Suendern,* Festschrift W. Marxsen (Gerd Mohn, 1989); *Die Schrift als Zeuge des Evangeliums: Untersuchungen zur Verwendung und zum Verstaendnis der Schrift bei Paulus,* BHT 69 (Mohr, 1986); "Geistbesitz, Geistverleihung und Wundermacht: Erwaegungen zur Tradition u.z. luk. Redaktion in Act 8,5-25" *ZNW* 77 (1986); "Der Text von Hab 2,4 in der Septuaginta und im Neuen Testament" *ZNW* 76 (1985); "Inhaltliche Gliederung u. geographischer Aufrisse im Markusevangelium" *NTS* 29 (1983); "Beobachtungen z. christologischen Schriftgebrauch in den vorpl. Gemeinden" *ZNW* 71 (1980); *Die Bedeutung der Wundererzaehlungen fuer die Christologie des Markusevangeliums,* BZNW 42 (de Gruyter, 1975); and others. Mem: Wissenschaftliche Gesellschaft fuer Theol. 1984-; SNTS 1985-. Addr: (o) Ev.-Theol. Fakultaet, Universitaetsstr. 13-17, D-48143 Muenster, Germany 0251-83-2542; (h) Nicolaistr. 4, D-48161 Muenster-Roxel, Germany 02534-8968.

KOCHAVI, Moshe, b. Bucharest, Romania, October 26, 1928, s. of Shmuel & Agatha, m.

Nora, chil: Noam; Uri; Tal. Educ: Hebrew U., Jerusalem, MA 1961, PhD 1968. Emp: Tel-Aviv U., Inst. of Arch., 1969-77 Sr. Lect., 1977- Assoc. Prof.; Inst. of Arch., TAV, 1976-80, 1985-90 Dir.; Bar-Ilan U., 1975-83. Excv: Tel Zeror, 1964-66; Kh. Rabud, 1968-69; Tel Malhata, 1967, 1971; Aphek-Antipatris, 1972-85; Land of Geshur Project, 1987- Dir. Spec: Archaeology. Pub: "Some Connections Between the Aegean and the Levant in the Second Millennium BC" in *Greece Between East and West* (Von Zabern, 1993); *Aphek in Canaan: The Egyptian Governors Residence and its Finds* (Israel Museum, 1990); *Aphek-Antipatris: Five Thousand Years of History* (Hakkibutz Hameuchad, 1989); *History of the Land of Israel*, vol. 2, co-auth. (Keter, 1985); "Aphek-Antipatris, Tel Poleg, Tel Zeror and Tel Burga: Four Fortified Sites of the MBIIA in the Sharon Plain," co-auth. *ZDPV* (1979); "An Ostracon of the Period of the Judges from Izbet Sartah" *Tel-Aviv* (1977); "Kh. Rabud-Debir" *Tel-Aviv* (1974); *Judea, Samaria & Golan, Archaeological Survey in 1967-8*, ed., co-auth. (Carta, 1972); "The Middle Bronze Age I (Intermediate Bronze Age) in Eretz-Israel" *Qadmoniot* (1969); and others. Mem: IES 1978-. Addr: (o) Institute of Archaeology, TAV, Tel-Aviv, Israel 03-6409417; (h) 93, University St., Tel-Aviv, Israel 03-6418731.

KODELL, Jerome, b. Clarksville, AR, January 19, 1940, s. of Frank & Clara (Spanke). Educ: New Subiaco Abbey, BA 1961; Collegio Sant' Anselmo, Rome, STL 1967; Pont. Bibl. Inst., Rome, SSL 1969. Emp: New Subiaco Abbey, Stud. Prog. 1969-; Providence Coll., Relig. Stud., 1971-72, 1974; *BTB*, 1973- Ed. Bd. Spec: New Testament. Pub: *The Eucharist in the New Testament* (Glazier, 1988); "Luke and the Children: The Beginning and End of the Great Interpolation (Lk 9:46-56; 18:9-23)" *CBQ* 49 (1987); *The Catholic Bible Study Handbook* (Servant, 1985); *The Gospel according to Luke* (Liturgical, 1983); "Luke's Theology of the Death of Jesus" in *Sin, Salvation and the Spirit* (Liturgical, 1979); and others. Mem: CBA 1970-; SBL 1973-. Addr: (h) Subiaco Abbey, Subiaco, AR 72865 501-934-4295.

KOESTER, Craig R., b. Northfield, MN, August 25, 1953, s. of Richard & Gloria, m. Nancy, chil: Matthew; Emily. Educ: Luther Theol. Sem., MDiv 1980; Union Theol. Sem., PhD 1986. Emp: Augsberg Publ. House, 1980- Writer; Luth. Ch., 1980-83 Asst. Pastor; Luther NW Theol. Sem., 1986- Assoc. Prof. Spec: New Testament. Pub: *A Beginners Guide to Reading the Bible* (Augsberg, 1991); "John Six and the Lord's Supper" *Luth. Quar.* 4 (1990); "The Savior of the World (John 4:42)" *JBL* 109 (1990); *The Dwelling of God*, CBQ Mon. Ser. 22 (CBA, 1989); "Hearing, Seeing and Believing in the Gospel of John" *Biblica* 70 (1989); "Messianic Exegesis and the Call of Nathaniel" *JSNT* 38 (1989); "A Qumran Bibliography 1974-1984" *BTB* 15 (1985); and others. Mem: SBL. Rec: Hiking. Addr: (h) 527 Riverside Dr., New York, NY 10027 212-866-7952.

KOESTER, Helmut, b. Hamburg, Germany, December 18, 1926, s. of Karl & Marie-Luise (Eitz), m. Gisela (Harrassowitz), chil: Reinhild E. (Haak); Almut J.; Ulrich C.; Heiko J. Educ: U. of Marburg, Germany, Dr. theol. 1954; U. of Heidelberg, Habil. 1956. Emp: U. of Heidelberg, 1956-58 Asst. Prof.; Harvard U., 1958-59 Vis. Prof., 1959-63 Assoc. Prof., 1963- John H. Morison Prof. of NT Stud., 1968- Winn Prof. of Eccles. Hist.; Drew U., 1963 Vis. Prof.; *HTR*, 1975- Ed.; *JBL*, 1977-81 Ed. Bd.; U. of Minn. 1990 Vis. Prof. Spec: Archaeology, New Testament, Apocrypha and Post-biblical Studies. Pub: *Ancient Christian Gospels: Their History and Development* (Trinity/SCM, 1992); *Genese de l'ecriture chretienne*, co-auth. (Memoires premieres, 1991); "The Gospel of Thomas—Does It Contain Authentic Sayings of Jesus?" co-auth. *BR* 6/2 (1990); *Introduction to the New Testament*, 2 vol. (de Gruyter, 1980; Fortress, 1982); "Using Quintilian to Interpret Mark" *BAR* 6/3 (1980); "Apocryphal and Canonical Gospels" *HTR* 73 (1980); "Apostel und Gemeinde in den Briefen an die Thessalonicher" in *Kirch, Festschrift fuer Guenther Bornkamm* (1980); *Trajectories Through Early Christianity*, co-auth. (Fortress, 1971). Awd: Guggengeim Fellow 1963-64; Amer. Coun. of Learned Soc., Fellow 1971-72, 1978-79; U. of Geneva, Dr. theol. 1989. Mem: Amer. Acad. of Arts & Sci.; SNTS 1957-; ASOR; SBL 1958-, Pres. 1991; Inst. for Antiq. & Christianity. Addr: (o) Harvard Divinity School, 45 Francis Ave., Cambridge, MA 02138 617-495-5926; (h) 12 Flintlock Rd., Lexington, MA 02173 617-862-4166.

KOHLENBERGER, John R., III, b. Chicago, IL, April 6, 1951, s. of John & Doris, m. Carolyn (Nelson), chil: Sarah; Joshua. Educ: Multnomah Sch. of the Bible, BTh, Greek & Bible 1973-76; West. Conservative Bapt. Sem., MA, Hebrew & OT 1980. Emp: Multnomah Sch. of the Bible, 1977- Instr., Bibl. Lang. Spec: Hebrew Bible. Pub: *The NIV Complete and Handy Concordances*, co-auth. (Zondervan); *NRSV Concordance Unabridged* (Zondervan, 1991); *NIV Exhaustive Concordances* (Zondervan, 1990); *NIV Cross Reference Bible*, OT, ed. (Zondervan, 1984); and others. Rec: Running, cycling. Addr: (o) 2107 SE 180th, Portland, OR 97233 503-761-6720.

KOKKINOS, Nikos, b. Alexandria, Egypt, September 6, 1955, s. of Theodosios & Pagona, m. Hariclia, chil: Sarah; Theodosios; Rachel. Educ: London U., Inst. of Arch., BA 1987; U. of Oxford, DPhil 1992. Emp: Chrysê Tomê Publ., Athens, 1975-77 Ed.; London, 1977-84 Cons. numismatist. Excv: Tell es-Samarat, Jericho, 1985 Supr.; Tell Nebi Mend, Syria 1986- Supr. Spec: Archaeology, New Testament. Pub: "The Greek Inscriptions from Senaim, Mount Hermon" *PEQ* 124 (1992); *Antonia Augusta* (Routledge, 1992); *Centuries of Darkness*, co-auth. (Cape, 1991); "A Fresh Look at the Gentilicium of Felix, Procurator of Judea" *Latomus* 49 (1990); "Crucifixion in AD 36: The

Keystone for Dating the Birth of Jesus" in *Chronos, Kairos, Christos* (Eisenbrauns, 1989); "Which Salome Did Aristobulus Marry?" *PEQ* 118 (1986); *The Enigma of Jesus the Galilean* (Athens, 1983); and others. Awd: St. Hugh's Coll., Oxford, 1988-90 Dorothea Gray Sr. Scholar. Mem: SBL 1982-; PEF 1982-. Rec: Philately, photography, music. Addr: (h) 11 Okeburn Rd., Tooting, London SW17 8NJ, England 081-767-6274.

KOLARCIK, Michael F., b. New Westminster, Canada, October 10, 1950, s. of Michael & Mary (Chmura). Educ: U. of Guelph, Canada, BA 1973; U. of Toronto, MDiv 1979; Pont. Bibl. Inst., Lic. Sacred Scripture 1983, Doc. Sacred Scripture 1989. Emp: Regis Coll., 1989- Assoc. Prof., Bibl. Dept.; U. of Regina, Campion Coll., 1992 Vis. Lect. Spec: Hebrew Bible, Apocrypha and Post-biblical Studies. Pub: *The Ambiguity of Death in the Book of Wisdom (1-6): A Study of Literary Structure and Interpretation,* Analecta Biblica 127 (Pont. Bibl. Inst., 1991). Mem: CBA 1983-. Addr: (o) Regis College, 15 St. Mary St., Toronto, ON M4Y 2R5, Canada 416-922-5474; (h) 105 Madison Ave., Toronto, ON M5R 2S3, Canada 416-960-9214.

KOLASNY, Judette Marie, b. Tiffin, OH, October 15, 1938. Educ: Mary Manse Coll., BA (magna cum laude) 1960; U. of Detroit, MA 1963; U. of Dayton, MA 1980; Marquette U., PhD, Relig. Stud. 1985. Emp: U. of Notre Dame, 1985-87 Asst. Prof., NT; Marquette U., 1987-90 Asst. Prof., NT. Spec: New Testament. Pub: "An Example of Rhetorical Criticism, Luke 4:16-30" in *New Views on Luke and Acts* (Liturgical, 1990). Mem: CBA 1981-; CTSA 1984-; NAPS 1984-. Rec: Ballet, sports, reading. Addr: (h) 1129 N Jackson St. #212, Milwaukee, WI 53202 414-289-0105.

KOLENKOW, Anitra Bingham, b. Cambridge, MA, September 5, 1934, d. of Robert Bingham & Anita (Cross), m. Robert J. Educ: Harvard Div. Sch., STB 1960; Harvard U., PhD 1972. Emp: Boston U., 1969-72 Lect., OT & NT; U. of Calif., Santa Cruz, 1975-76 Lect., Jewish Stud.; Grad. Theol. Union, 1976- Vis. Schol.; U. of Calif., Berkeley, 1979-81 Vis. Schol.; Dominican Sch. of Phil., 1981- Lect. Spec: New Testament, Apocrypha and Post-biblical Studies. Pub: "The Testament of Abraham as a Testament" in *Studies on the Testament of Abraham* (1976); "The Narratives of the Testament of Joseph and the Organization of the Testaments of the Twelve Patriarchs" in *Studies in the Testament of Joseph* (1975); and others. Mem: SBL 1969-, V.P., West. Reg. 1991, Pres., 1992; CBA 1974-; SNTS 1984-. Rec: Painting, music, study of monasticism. Addr: (o) 2401 Le Conte Way, Berkeley, CA 94709 848-3788; (h) 2435 Virginia St., Berkeley, CA 94709 549-2963.

KOTANSKY, Roy D., b. Montreal, Canada, February 3, 1953, s. of Daniel. Educ: Fuller Theol. Sem., MA, Semitic Stud. 1977; U. of

Chicago, PhD, Early Christian Lit. 1988. Emp: J. Paul Getty Mus., 1984-88 Ed. Adv.; U. of Koeln, Inst. fuer Altertumskunde, 1990-91 Humboldt Fellow. Spec: Archaeology, New Testament, Semitic Languages, Texts and Epigraphy, Apocrypha and Post-biblical Studies. Pub: "A Greek-Aramaic Silver Amulet from Egypt in the Ashmolean Museum" *Le Mus´won* 105 (1992); "Two Inscribed Jewish-Aramaic Amulets from Syria" *IEJ* 41 (1991); "An Inscribed Copper Amulet from 'Evron" *'Atiqot* 20 (1991); "Magic in the Court of the Governor of Arabia" *Zeitschrift fuer Papyrologie und Epigraphik* 88 (1991); "Incantations and Prayers for Salvation on Inscribed Greek Amulets" in *Magika Hiera* (Oxford U.P., 1991); and others. Mem: SBL 1975-; CSBR 1980-. Rec: Karate, chess, music. Addr: (o) U. Koeln, Institut fuer Altertumskunde, D-5000 Koln 41, Germany; (h) 902 Idaho Ave., Santa Monica, CA 90403.

KOUCKY, Frank L., b. Chicago, IL, June 24, 1927, s. of Frank & Ella (Harshman), m. Virginia (Ruhl), chil: Frank; David; Walter; Jonathan. Educ: U. of Chicago, PhB 1949, MS 1953, PhD 1956. Emp: U. of Ill., 1949-60; U. of Cincinnati, 1960-72; Coll. of Wooster, 1972-92 Prof., Geology; MIT 1978, 1983 Res. Assoc. Excv: Jordan, Cyprus, Israel, 1972-87 Geologist; ACOR, Amon, Jordan, 1987 NEH Fellow. Spec: Archaeology. Pub: "The Ancient Slags of Cyprus," co-auth. in *Metallurgy in Cyprus* (1983); "Ancient Mining and Mineral Dressing on Cyprus" in *Early Pyrotechnology* (Smithsonian, 1982); "The Serpent Mound Disturbance," co-auth *Amer. Jour. of Science* 282 (1982); and others. Awd: NEH fellow, ACOR, Jordan 1987. Mem: Geological Soc. of Amer., Fellow; ACOR; ASOR; Amer. Assn. for the Advancement of Sci., Fellow. Rec: Arch. field work, gardening. Addr: (o) College of Wooster, Dept. of Geology, Wooster, OH 44691; (h) 122 W Easton Rd., Burbank, OH 44214 216-435-4049.

KOVACS, Judith L., b. Defiance, OH, November 10, 1945, d. of Keith Tustison & Mary (Carey), m. P. David Kovacs, chil: Mark Daniel; Ellen Ruth. Educ: Coll. of Wooster, BA 1967; Columbia U., Union Theol. Sem., MA 1969, PhD 1978. Emp: Springfield Coll., 1974-75 Instr., Relig.; Georgetown U., 1981-82 Asst. Prof., Theol.; Union Theol. Sem., 1979, 1984 Vis. Asst. Prof., NT & Greek; U. of Va., 1977- Lect., Relig. Stud. & Class. Spec: New Testament. Pub: "A Reader's Guide to the Bible" in *NRSV* (Oxford U.P., 1990); "Women in the New Testament" in *What the Bible Really Says* (Prometheus, 1989); "The Archons, the Spirit, and the Death of Christ: Do We Need the Hypothesis of Gnostic Opponents to Explain 1 Corinthians 2:6-16?" in *Apocalyptic and the New Testament: Essays in Honor of J. Louis Martyn* (JSOT, 1989); and others. Awd: Phi Beta Kappa, 1967; Columbia U., Fac. Fellow. 1967-71. Mem: SBL 1970-; NAPA 1993-. Rec: Swimming, travel, children. Addr: (o) U. of Virginia, Dept. of Religious Studies, Cocke Hall, Charlottesville, VA 22903 804-924-3741;

(h) 1621 Rugby Ave., Charlottesville, VA 22903 804-977-8527.

KRAABEL, Alf T., b. Portland, OR, November 4, 1934, s. of Alf & Marie (Swensen), m. Janice, chil: Allen; Thomas; Sarah. Educ: Luther Coll., BA, Class. 1956; U. of Iowa, MA, Class. 1958; Luther Theol. Sem., BD 1961; Harvard U., ThD 1968. Emp: U. of Minn., 1967-82 Prof., Class. & Relig. Stud.; *HTR*, 1974- Bd. of Cons.; *RSRev*, 1977- Ed., Book Rev. in Class.; Luther Coll., 1983- V.P. & Dean of Coll., 1988- Qualley Prof. of Class. Excv: Sardis, Turkey, 1966 Staff Arch.; Khirbet Shema', Israel, 1969-73 Assoc. Dir. Spec: Archaeology, Anatolian Studies, New Testament. Pub: *The Future of Early Christianity: Essays in Honor of Helmut Koester*, ed., contb. (Fortress, 1991); *Goodenough on the Beginnings of Christianity*, ed. (Scholars, 1990); "Unity and Diversity Among Diaspora Synagogues" in *The Synagogue in Late Antiquity* (1987); "Greeks, Jews, and Lutherans in the Middle Half of Acts" in *Christians Among Jews and Gentiles: Essays in Honor of Krister Stendahl on His Sixty-Fifth Birthday* (1986); "Archaeology, Iconography and Nonliterary Written Remains," co-auth., in *Early Judaism and Its Modern Interpreters* (1986); "*Synagoga caeca*: Systematic Distortion in Gentile Interpretations of Evidence for Judaism in the Early Christian Period" in *To See Ourselves As Others See Us: Christians, Jews, and "Others" in Late Antiquity* (1985); *Ancient Synagogue Excavations at Khirbet Shema', Upper Galilee, Israel, 1970-72*, co-auth. (Duke U.P., 1976); and others. Awd: Oxford U., Wolfson Coll., Vis. Fellow 1981, 1990; Amer. Coun. of Learned Soc., Fellow. 1977-78; Oxford U., Mansfield Coll., Vis. Fellow 1977-78. Mem: SBL 1973-81; SNTS; Class. Assn. of the Middle W and S. Addr: (o) Luther College, Dean's Office, 700 College Dr., Decorah, IA 52101 319-387-1005; (h) 708 Ridge Rd., Decorah, IA 52101 319-382-4443.

KRAEMER, David C., b. Newark, NJ, October 23, 1955, s. of Paul & Phyllis (Ferster), m. Susan (Boxerman), chil: Talia; Liviya. Educ: Brandeis U., BA (summa cum laude) 1977; Jewish Theol. Sem., MA 1978, PhD 1984. Emp: Jewish Theol. Sem., 1979- Assoc. Prof. Spec: Apocrypha and Post-biblical Studies. Pub: "The Formation of Rabbinic Canon: Authority and Boundaries" *JBL* 110 (1991); *The Mind of the Talmud: An Intellectual History of the Bavli* (Oxford U.P., 1990); "On the Reliability of Attributions in the Bavli" *HUCA* 60 (1989); "Scripture Commentary in the Babylonian Talmud: A Primary or Secondary Phenomenon?" *AJS Rev.* 14 (1989); "Composition and Meaning of the Bavli" *Prooftexts* 8 (1988). Awd: Rabbi Judah Nadich Assoc. Prof. in Talmud 1983. Mem: SBL; AJS. Addr: (o) Jewish Theological Seminary, 3080 Broadway, New York, NY 10027 212-678-8844; (h) 312 W 105th St., New York, NY 10025 212-666-9347.

KRAEMER, Ross S., b. New York, NY, October 28, 1948, d. of Herman Shepard and Harriet (Plager), m. Michael, chil: Jordan. Educ: Princeton U., MA 1973, PhD 1976. Emp: Stockton St. Coll., 1979-84 Asst. to the Pres.; Medical Coll. of Pa., 1984-88 Dir. of Alumni Relations; NEH, 1988-89 Sr. Fellow.; Princeton U., 1989-90 Lect., Relig.; Franklin and Marshall Coll., 1990- Vis. Assoc. Prof. of Relig. Stud. Spec: New Testament, Apocrypha and Post-biblical Studies. Pub: *Her Share of the Blessings: Women's Religions Among Pagans, Jews and Christians in the Greco-Roman World* (Oxford U. P., 1992); "Jewish Tuna and Christian Fish: Identifying Religious Affiliation in Epigraphic Sources" *HTR* (1991); "On the Meaning of the Term 'Jew' in Greco-Roman Inscriptions" *HTR* (1989); "Monastic Jewish Women in Greco-Roman Egypt: Philo, Judaeus on the Therapeutrides" *Signs* (1989); Maenads, Martyrs, Matrons, Monastics: A Sourcebook of Women's Religions in the Greco-Roman World (Fortress, 1988); "Non-literary Evidence for Jewish Women in Rome and Egypt" *Helios* (1986); "A New Inscription From Malta and the Question of Women Elders in Diaspora Jewish Communities" *HTR* (1985); and others. Mem: SBL 1970-; AAR 1976-; Women's Caucus in Relig. Stud. Addr: (o) Franklin & Marshall College, Dept. of Religious Studies, Lancaster, PA 17604-3003 717-291-4234; (h) 7703 Lincoln Dr., Philadelphia, PA 19118.

KRAFT, Robert A., b. Waterbury, CT, March 18, 1934, s. of Howard & Marian (Northrop), m. Carol L. (Wallace), chil: Cindy L.; Scott W.; Todd A.; Randall J. Educ: Wheaton Coll., BA (summa cum laude) 1955, MA 1957; Harvard U., PhD 1961. Emp: U. of Manchester, England, 1961-63 Asst. Lect.; U. of Pa., 1963- Prof., Relig. Stud.; SBL, 1967-78 Ser. Ed. Spec: Apocrypha and Post-biblical Studies. Pub: "Biblical Studies," (co-ed.) in *The Humanities Computing Yearbook 1989-90* (Clarendon, 1991); *Early Judaism and its Modern Interpreters*, co-ed. (Scholars/Fortress, 1986); "Christian Transmission of Greek Jewish Scriptures: A Methodological Probe" in *Paganisme, Judaisme, Christianisme: Melanges M. Simon* (De Boccard, 1978); "The Multiform Jewish Heritage of Early Christianity" in *Christianity, Judaism and Other Greco-Roman Cults III* (Brill, 1975); "In Search of 'Jewish Christianity' and its 'Theology': Problems of Definition and Methodology" in *Recherches de Sciences; Religieuse, Festschrift J. Danielou* (1972); and others. Awd: Guggenheim Fellow 1969-70. Mem: SBL 1956-; SNTS 1963-. Rec: Antiques, historical renovation. Addr: (o) U. of Pennsylvania, Box 36, College Hall, Philadelphia, PA 19104-6303 215-898-5827.

KREMER, Jacob, b. Kohlscheid, Germany, December 8, 1924, s. of Wilhelm. Educ: U. Bonn; Pont. U. Gregoriana, Rome. Emp: U. of Vienna, 1972- Prof. Spec: New Testament. Pub: *Das Lukasevangelium*, NEB.NT 3 (1988, 1991); *2. Korintherbrief* SKK.NT 8 (1990); *Das*

Evangelium von Jesu Tod und Auferstehung
(1988); *Lazarus—die Geschichte einer
Auferstehung* (1985); and others. Mem: SNTS;
Deutschsprachige NT. Addr: (o) Institut fur
Neutestamentliche Bibelwissenschaft, Schottenring
21, A-1010 Wien, Austria; (h) Boltzmanngasse 9,
A-1090 Wien, Austria.

KRENTZ, Edgar M., b. Macomb County, MI,
May 27, 1928, s. of Arnold & Magdalena
(Droegemueller), m. Marion (Becker), chil:
Peter; Michael; Elizabeth; Susanna; Matthew;
Christopher. Educ: Concordia Sem., BA 1949,
MDiv 1952; Washingotn U., MA 1953, PhD
1960; U. of Chicago, SS 1955. Emp: Concordia
Sem., 1953-75 Prof., NT; *Concordia Theol.
Monthly*, 1968-74 Ed. Com.; Christ Sem.-
Seminex, St. Louis, 1975-83 Prof.; Luth. Sch. of
Theol., Christ Sem.-Seminex, 1983- Prof. Excv:
Joint Expdn. Caesarea Maritima, 1972 Area
Supr., 1974-87 Field Supr., Exec. Com., 1978-
Assoc. Dir. Spec: Archaeology, New Testament.
Pub: "The Joint Expedition to Caesarea
Maritima: Tenth Season, 1982," co-auth. in
*Preliminary Reports of ASOR-Sponsored
Excavations 1982-1989*, BASORSup 27 (Johns
Hopkins U.P./ASOR, 1991); "Traditions Held
Fast: Theology and Fidelity in 2 Thessalonians"
in *The Thessalonian Correspondence*, BETL 87
(Leuven U.P./Peeters, 1990); "Roman Hellenism
and Paul's Gospel" *The Bible Today* 26 (1988);
Galatians, Augsburg NT Comm. (Augsburg,
1985); "New Testament Commentaries: Their
Selection and Use" *Interpretation* 36 (1982); *The
Historical-Critical Method*, Guides to Bibl.
Schol. (Fortress, 1975); "The Extent of
Matthew's Prologue" *JBL* 83 (1964); and others.
Awd: Lilly Found., Res. Fellow 1963-64. Mem:
AIA 1954-; SBL 1956-; SNTS 1965-. Rec:
Photography, tennis, opera. Addr: (o) Lutheran
School of Theology, 1100 East 55th St., Chicago, IL
60615 312-753-0752; (h) 5433 S. Ridgwood Ct.,
Chicago, IL 60615 312-947-8015.

KRESS, Robert L., b. Jasper, IN, September
22, 1932, s. of Oscar, m. Stella (Schutz). Educ:
U. of Innsbruck, Austria, STB 1956, STL 1958;
U. of Notre Dame, MA 1964; U. of St. Thomas,
Rome, STD (summa cum laude) 1968. Emp: U.
of Evansville, 1967-70, 1973-78; U. of San
Diego, 1986-92 Assoc. Prof., Relig. Stud.; U. of
Ill., 1984-86 Assoc. Prof., Relig. Stud.; *Theol.
Digest*, 1971-75 Cons. Ed. Spec: New
Testament. Pub: "Leise Treten: An Eirenic
Ecumenical Hermenuetic" *Theol. Stud.* (1983);
and others. Mem: AAR; CTSA. Addr: (o) St.
Paul's Church, Theologian in Residence, 214
Nassau St., Princeton, NJ 08542 609-924-1743;
(h) 6371 Caminito TELMO, San Diego, CA
92111 619-278-6612.

KSELMAN, John S., b. New York, NY,
February 16, 1940, s. of Joseph & Rosemary
(Correll). Educ: St. Mary's Sem., BA 1961, STB
1963, STL 1967; Harvard U., PhD 1971. Emp: St.
Mary's Sem., 1971-77 Assoc. Prof.; *CBQ*, 1976-

1983, 1985-1989 Assoc. Ed., 1989-1992 Gen. Ed.;
St. Patrick's Sem., 1977-80; Catholic U., 1981-
87; Weston Sch. of Theol., 1987- Assoc. Prof.
Spec: Hebrew Bible. Pub: "Psalm 146 in Its
Context" *CBQ* (1988); "Royal Confession and
Divine Oracle in Psalm 101" *JSOT* (1985);
"Psalm 77 and the Book of Exodus" *JANES*
(1984); "'Why Have You Abandoned Me?' A
Rhetorical Study of Psalm 22" in *Art and
Meaning: Rhetoric in Biblical Literature* (1982);
"New Exodus, Covenant, and Restoration in
Psalm 23," co-auth. in *The Word of the Lord
Shall Go Forth: Essays in Honor of David Noel
Freedman* (1980); and others. Mem: SBL; CBA;
SOTS. Addr: (o) Weston School of Theology,
Cambridge, MA 02138 (617) 492-1960; (h)
2222 Massachusetts Ave., Cambridge, MA
02140 (617) 868-5032.

KUAN, Jeffrey K., b. Malaysia, December 7,
1957, s. of Choon-Hock & Geok-Luen (Ong), m.
Valentine P. (Toh), chil: Valene M. Educ:
Emory U., PhD 1993; Trinity Theol. Coll.,
Singapore, BTh 1980; South. Meth. U., MTS
1986. Emp: Pacific Sch. of Relig., 1991- Asst.
Prof., OT. Spec: Hebrew Bible. Pub: "The Final
Years of Samaria (730-720 BC)," co-auth.
Biblica 72 (1991); "Hosea 9:13 and Josephus's
Antiquities IX, 277-287" *PEQ* 123 (1991);
"Third Kingdoms 5:1 and Israelite-Tyrian
Relations During the Reign of Solomon" *JSOT*
46 (1990). Awd: ASOR, SE reg., Joseph A.
Callaway Award in Bibl. Arch. 1991. Mem: SBL
1987-; ASOR 1989-. Rec: Racquetball. Addr: (o)
Pacific School of Religion, 1798 Scenic Ave.,
Berkeley, CA 94709 510-848-0528; (h) 2380
Virginia St., Berkeley, CA 94709 510-649-8949.

KUBO, Sakae, b. Honolulu, HI, May 8, 1926, s.
of Kumashichi & Teki, m. Hatsumi, chil:
Wesley; Charlene; Calvin. Educ: Emmanuel
Missionary Coll., BA 1947; Seventh-day
Adventist Theol. Sem., MA 1954, BD 1955; U.
of Chicago, PhD 1964; West. Mich. U., MLS
1968. Emp: Andrews U., 1955-78 Prof., NT;
Walla Walla Coll., Dean, Sch. of Theol., Prof.,
NT; Newbold Coll., Pres. & Prof., NT; Atlantic
Union Coll., V.P., Acad. Affairs, Prof., NT.
Spec: New Testament. Pub: "The New Revised
Standard Version" *AUSS* 29 (1991); "Jude 22-
23: Two Division Form or Three?" in *New
Testament Textual Criticism: Its Significance for
Exegsis: Essays in Honor of Bruce M. Metzger*
(Clarendon, 1981); *A Beginner's New Testament
Greek Grammar* (U. Press of Amer., 1979); "I
Cor 7:14: Optimistic or Pessimistic?" *NTS* 24
(1978); "Textual Relationships in Jude" in
*Studies in New Testament Language and Text:
Essays in Honour of George D. Kilpatrick on the
Occasion of His Sixty-fifth Birthday* (Brill,
1976); *A Reader's Greek-English Lexicon to
the New Testament* (Brill, 1971); "I John 3:8:
Absolute or Habitual?" *AUSS* 7 (1969); *P72
and Codex Vaticanus* (U. of Utah, 1965); and
others. Mem: SBL. Rec: Gardening, sports.
Addr: (o) 207 Autumn Gold Dr., Chico, CA
95926 916-893-5580.

KUECHLER, Max B., b. Sulgen, TG, August 27, 1944, s. of Max & Josephine (Schmuki), m. Bernadette (Schwarzen), chil: Katharina; Micha; Benjamin; Samuel. Educ: ThD 1979, Habil. 1987. Emp: 1988 Assoc. Prof.; Novum Testamentum et Orbis Antiquus, Ed. Spec: Archaeology, New Testament, Apocrypha and Post-biblical Studies. Pub: "Wir haben seinen Stern gesehen... (Mt 2,2)" *Bibel & Kirche* 44 (1989); "Moschee und Kalifenpalaeste Jerusalems nach den Aphrodito-Papyri" *ZDPV* 101 (1992); *Orte und Landschaften der Bibel: Ein Handbuch und Studienreisefuehrer zum Heiligen Land*, vol. 1-2, co-auth. (1982, 1984); *Herders Grosser Bibelatlas*, co-auth. (Herder, 1989); *Schweigen, Schmuck und Schleier: Drei Neutestamentliche Vorschriften zur Verdraengung der Frauen auf dem Hintergrund einer frauenfeindlichen Exegese des Alten Testaments im Antiken Judentum*, Novum Testamentum et Orbis Antiquus 1 (Vavdenhoeck & Ruprecht, 1986); and others. Mem: SNTS 1987-; Societe Suisse des Etudes Juives; Deutscher Palaestina-Verein 1991-. Addr: (o) Biblisches Institut, Buero 4216, Universitaet Misericorde, CH-1700 Fribourg, Switzerland 0041-37-21-9384; (h) Rue Marcello 3, CH-1700 Fribourg, Switzerland 0041-37-22-8867.

KUFELDT, George, b. Chicago, IL, November 4, 1923, s. of Henry & Lydia, m. Lydia (Borgardt), chil: Anita Kay (Shelton); Kristina Sue (Schmidt). Educ: Anderson U., AB 1945, ThB 1946, MDiv 1953; Dropsie U., PhD 1974. Emp: Ch. of God, 1948-61 Pastor; Anderson U., 1961-90 Prof., 1990- Prof. Emeritus. Spec: Hebrew Bible, Mesopotamian Studies, Semitic Languages, Texts and Epigraphy. Pub: "The Book of Ezekiel" *Asbury Bible Comm.* (1992); "The Prophets: Divine Words or Human Words?" *Listening to the Word of God* (1990); "Were There People Before Adam and Eve?" in *The Genesis Debate* (1986); *Vine's Expository Dict. of Biblical Words*, contb. (1985); "Commentary on Book of Proverbs" *Wesleyan Bible Comm.* (1968); and others. Awd: Anderson U., Hodges Awd. 1953; Dropsie U., Fellow 1957, 1961. Mem: SBL; NAPH. Rec: Gardening, photography, travel. Addr: (h) 907 N Nursery Rd., Anderson, IN 46012 317-643-2401.

KUGEL, James L., Educ: Yale U., BA 1968; City U. of N.Y., PhD 1977. Emp: City U. of N.Y., 1977-78 Andrew Mellon Fac. Fellow; Harvard U., Ctr. for Jewish Stud., 1978-79 Fellow; Yale U., 1979-82 Asst. Prof., Relig. Stud. & Comparative Lit.; *Prooftexts*, Assoc. Ed.; Harvard U., Dept. of Near East. Lang. & Civ., 1982- Prof. Spec: Hebrew Bible. Pub: *Poetry and Prophecy: The Beginnings of a Literary Tradition*, ed. (Cornell U.P., 1991); *In Potiphar's House: The Interpretive Life of a Biblical Text* (Harper San Francisco, 1990); *Early Biblical Interpretation*, co-auth. (Westminster, 1986); *The Idea of Biblical Poetry: Parallelism and Its History* (Yale U.P., 1981); and others. Awd: Phi Beta Kappa; Fulbright Fellow.; Danforth Grad. Fellow.; Woodrow Wilson Fellow. Addr: (o) Harvard U.,

Dept. of Near Eastern Languages & Civilizations, 6 Divinity Ave., Cambridge, MA 02138 617-495-1681.

KUMMEL, Werner G., b. Heidelberg, Germany, May 16, 1905, s. of Werner & Marie (Ulmann), m. Auguste (Bender), chil: Werner; Hans; Katharina; Dorothea; Barbara. Educ: Heidelberg U., DTh, Ord. 1929. Emp: Zurich U., 1932-51 Prof.; Mainz U., 1951-52 Prof.; Marburg U., 1952-73 Prof., 1973- Prof. Emeritus; *Theologische Rundschau*, 1957-81, 1982-83 Ed. Spec: New Testament, Apocrypha and Post-biblical Studies. Pub: *Jesus der Menschensohn?* (Steiner, 1983); *Theologie des Neuen Testaments nach seinen Hauptzeugen* (Vandenhoeck & Ruprecht, 1980); "Lukas in der Anklage der heutigen Theologie" *ZNW* 63 (1972); "Futurische und praesentische Eschatologie im aeltesten Christentum" *NTS* 5 (1958); and others. Awd: U. of Glasgow, D.D. 1969; Burkitt Medal for Bibl. Stud. 1973. Mem: SNTS, Pres. 1963-64. Addr: (h) von Harnackstrasse 23, D-3550 Marburg/Lahn, Germany 06421-67965.

KUNG, Hans, b. Surse, Lucerne, Switzerland, March 19, 1928. Educ: Pont. Gregorian U., Rome, Lic. Phil. 1951, Lic. Theol. 1955; Sorbonne & Inst. Catholique, Paris, Dr. Theol. 1957. Emp: Second Vatican Coun., 1962-65 Official Theol. Cons.; U. of Tuebingen, 1960- Prof., Dir., Inst. for Ecumenical Res.; Okumenische Forschungen and Okumenische Theologie, Co-ed.; *Tubinger Theologische Quartalschrift*, *JES*, Assoc. Ed. Spec: New Testament. Pub: *Judaism* (SCM/Crossroad, 1992); *Theology for the Third Millenium: An Ecumenical View* (Doubleday, 1988; HarperCollins, 1991); *The Incarnation of God* (T & T Clark, 1987); and others. Awd: U. of Toronto, DDL 1984; U. of Mich., LHD 1985; U. of Cambridge, DD 1985. Addr: (h) Waldhauserstrasse 23, D-7400 Tuebingen, Germany.

KUNTZ, J. Kenneth, b. St. Louis, MO, January 20, 1934, s. of John & Zula (Reed), m. Ruth M. (Stanley), chil: David; Nancy. Educ: Yale U. Div. Sch., BD 1959; Union Theol. Sem., PhD 1963. Emp: Wellesley Coll., 1963-67 Asst. Prof., Bibl. History; U. of Iowa, Sch. of Relig., 1976- Prof. Spec: Hebrew Bible. Pub: "King Triumphant: A Rhetorical Study of Psalms 20 and 21," *Hebrew Ann. Rev.* 10 (1986); "How Does the Bible Present Women?: A Crucial Dimension in Investigating the Bible as Literature" *Relig. & Public Educ.* 14 (1987); "Psalm 18: A Rhetorical-Critical Analysis" *JSOTSup* 26 (1983); "The Contribution of Rhetorical Criticism to Understanding Isaiah 51:1-16" in *Art and Biblical Meaning: Rhetoric in Biblical Literature* (JSOT, 1982); "The Retribution Motif in Psalmic Wisdom" *ZAW* 89 (1977); *The People of Ancient Israel: An Introduction to Biblical Literature, History, and Thought* (Harper & Row, 1974); *The Self-Revelation of God* (Westminster, 1967); and others. Awd: U. of Iowa, Mellon Found. Fellow

1982; Bonn, Alexander von Humboldt-Stiftung Awd. 1971-73, 1979. Mem: AAR; ASOR; SBL; CBA. Rec: Photography, music, cycling. Addr: (o) U. of Iowa, School of Religion, Iowa City, IA 52242 319-335-2164; (h) 321 Koser Ave., Iowa City, IA 52246 319-338-2762.

KUNTZMANN, Raymond, b. Strasbourg, France, August 1, 1936, s. of Antoine & Josephine (Kirmser). Educ: Gregorian Pont. U., Rome, Lic. Th. 1964; Bibl. Pont. Inst., Rome, Lic. Sc. Bibl., Doctorandus Sc. Bibl. 1968; U. des Sciences Humaines, France, Doc. de Third Cycle en Sci. Relig. 1971, Doc. d'Etat, Theol. Cath. 1979. Emp: U. des Sciences Humaines, Faculte de theol. cath., France, 1983- Prof. Hist. & Bibl. Arch. Spec: Hebrew Bible. Pub: *Nag Hammadi: Evangile de Thomas,* Coll. Cahiers Evangile Sup. 58 (Cerf, 1987); *Le Livre de Thomas,* Nag Hammadi II, 7 (Peeters, 1986); "Pessimisme et paraphrase dans le livre de Thomas" *Archaeologia* 70 (1983); *Le Symbolisme des Jumeaux. Naissance, evolution et fonction d'un symbole* (Beauchesne, 1983). Awd: Officer de l'ordre national du merite. Mem: Assn. des Biblistes de France, Pres. Rec: Hill-walking, skiing. Addr: (o) Palais U., 9, Place de l'Universite, 67086 Strasbourg, France 88-25-97-28; (h) 22, Avenue du General de Gaulle, 67000 Strasbourg, France.

LAATO, Antti J., b. Turku, Finland, August 9, 1961, s. of Heimo & Eeva, m. Anni Maria, chil: Katariina Debora; Samuli Daniel; Martti Sakari Paulus. Educ: Abo Acad., Cand. Theol. 1983, Lic. Theol. 1984, ThD 1988; Turku U., Cand. Phil. 1986. Emp: Finnish Acad., 1989- Younger Schol. Spec: Hebrew Bible. Pub: "The Chronology in the Damascus Document of Qumran" *RQ* 57 (1993); *The Servant of YHWH and Cyrus: A Reinterpretation of the Exilic Messianic Programme in Isaiah 40-55* (Almquist & Wiksell, 1992); "The Eschatological Act of *kipper* in the Damascus Document" in *Milik Festschrift* (1992); "Psalm 132 and the Development of the Jerusalemite/Israelite Royal Ideology" *CBQ* 54 (1992); *Josiah and David Redivivus: The Historical Josiah and the Messianic Expectations of Exilic and Postexilic Times* (Almquist & Wiksell, 1992); "The Seventy Yearweeks in the Book of Daniel" *ZAW* 102 (1990); "The Composition of Isaiah 40-55" *JBL* 109 (1990); *Who is Immanuel? The Rise and the Foundering of Isaiah's Messianic Expectations* (Abo Acad., 1988); and others. Rec: Chess. Addr: (o) Dept. of Exegetics, Piispank 16 Turku 50, SF-20500, Finland 21-65-4292; (h) Jaanintie 36 B 10, 20540 Turku 54, Finland 21-374-286.

LABERGE, Leo, b. Quebec, Canada, January 2, 1932, s. of Cyrille & Lucienne (Fiset). Educ: Angelicum, Rome, BPh, LPh 1954, BTh, LTh 1958; Pont. Bibl. Commn., Rome, BSS 1963, LSS 1966, DSS 1968. Emp: U. of Ottawa, 1958- Prof.; *Eglise & Theol.,* 1970- Ed.; CBQ, 1981-89 Assoc. Ed.; CBQ Mon. Ser., 1990- Assoc. Ed. Spec: Hebrew Bible. Pub: "Le texte de

Deuteronome 31 (Dt 31,1-29; 32,44-47)" in *Pentateuchal and Deuteronomistic Studies* (1990); "Micah" in *New Jerome Biblical Comm.* (1989); "Le lieu que YHWH a choisi pour y mettre son Nom" *EstBib* (1985); *La Septante d'Isaie 28-33* (1978); and others. Mem: CBA; SBL; IOSOT. Rec: Music, literature. Addr: (o) St. Paul U., Faculty of Theology, 223 Main, Ottawa, ON K1S 1C4, Canada 613-236-1393; (h) Residence Deschatelets 175 Main, Ottawa, ON K1S 1C3, Canada 613-237-0580.

LA BIANCA, Oystein S., b. Kristiansand, Norway, September 10, 1949, s. of Olav & Kirsten (Olson), m. Asta Ellen (Sakala), chil: Erik; Aren; Ivan. Educ: Loma Linda U., MA 1976; Brandeis U., PhD, Anthrop. 1987. Emp: Andrews U., 1980- Prof., Anthrop., 1981- Chair, Dept. of Behavioral Sci. Excv: Hesban, 1971-76, 1980-81 Anthrop.; Wadi Tumilat, Egypt, 1979 Chief Anthrop.; Madaba Plains, 1984-92 Dir. of Reg. Survey & Ecology Lab. Spec: Archaeology. Pub: "Food Systems Research: An Overview and a Case Study from Madaba Plains, Jordan" *Food and Foodways* 4 (1991); *Madaba Plains Project,* vol. 1 & 2, ed. (Andrews U.P., 1989, 1991); *Hesban,* vol. 1 & 2 (Andrews U.P., 1986, 1990); "The Madaba Plains Project: Three Seasons of Excavation at Tell el-'Umeiri and Vicinity, Jordan," co-auth. *Echos du Monde Classique* 34/9 (1990); "The Diachronic Study of Animal Exploitation at Hesban: The Evolution of a Research Project" in *The Archaeology of Jordan and Other Studies* (Andrews U.P., 1986); "The Local Environment and Human Food-Procuring Strategies in Jordan: The Case of Tell Hesban and its Surrounding Region," co-auth., in *Studies in the History and Archaeology of Jordan II* (Amman Dept. of Antiq., 1985); "Man, Animals and Habitat at Hesban: An Integrated Overview" *AUSS* 16 (1978); and others. Awd: Albright Fellow 1980-81. Mem: ASOR; AAS; ACOR, Jordan. Rec: Swimming. Addr: (o) Andrews U., Institute of Archaeology, Berrien Springs, MI 49104 616-471-3273; (h) 2470 Lake Chapin Rd., Berrien Springs, MI 49103 616-473-5093.

LACH, Jan, b. Gorzkow, Poland, June 15, 1927, s. of Faliks & Katarzyna (Bajda). Educ: Jagiellonian U., ThM 1952; Cath. U. of Lublin, ThD 1957; Pont. Bibl. Inst., Rome, Lic. re biblica 1968, Cand. ad Lauream 1969; Acad. of Cath. Theol. Habil. 1971. Emp: Higher Sem., Tarnow, 1959-67 Lect.; Acad. of Cath. Theol., Warsaw, 1969- Prof., 1980- Chmn. of Bibl. Theol. Dept.; Dean, Theol. Fac. 1980-83, 1986-90, Rector, Acad. of Cath. Theol. 1990-. Spec: Hebrew Bible, New Testament. Pub: *Comm. to the Book of Psalms* (1990); *Studies on Theology of the Gospel of Jesus' Childhood* (1978); *1-2 Samuel Book Comm.* (1973); *Jesus Son of David* (1973); and others. Addr: (o) Akademia Teologii Katolickiej, ul. Dewajtis 5:01 815 Warszawa, Poland 39-52-21; (h) ul. Reymonta 10/238, 01-842 Warszawa, Poland 34-93-73.

LACOCQUE, André, b. Belgium, October 26, 1927, m. Claire, chil: Michel; Pierre E.; Elisabeth. Educ: U. of Strasbourg, France, DLit 1957, DTh 1961. Emp: Faculte de Théologie Protestante, Belgium, 1958-69 Prof., OT; Spertus Coll. of Judaica, 1969-73 Vis. Prof.; Chicago Theol. Sem., 1966- Prof., OT. Spec: Hebrew Bible, Apocrypha and Post-biblical Studies. Pub: *Jonah, A Psycho-Religious Approach,* co-auth. (U. of S.C., 1990); *Daniel in His Time* (U. of S.C., 1988); "Haman in the Book of Esther" *HAR* (1988); *The Book of Daniel* (John Knox/SPCK, 1979); and others. Awd: Assn. of Theol. Schol., grant 1984. Mem: SBL 1967-, Pres., MidW sect. 1973-75; AAR 1967-; CSBR 1967-; AJS 1982-. Rec: Forest farming in Michigan. Addr: (o) Chicago Theological Seminary, 5757 University Ave., Chicago, IL 60637 312-752-5757; (h) Jackson Towers, 5555 S Everett #8C, Chicago, IL 60637 312-955-0396.

LAFFEY, Alice L., b. Pittsburgh, PA, December 1, 1944, d. of John & Marion (Caveney). Educ: Pont. Bibl. Inst., Italy, SSB, SSL, SSD. Emp: Regina Mundi, Rome, 1978-80 Lect.; Gregorian U., 1978-80 Adj. Prof.; Assumption Coll., 1982, 1989 Lect.; St. Michael's Coll., 1989-90 Lect.; Coll. of Holy Cross, 1981- Assoc. Prof. Spec: Hebrew Bible. Pub: *Lent: Proclamation Series B* (Fortress, 1990); *Introduction to the Old Testament: A Feminist Perspective* (Fortress, 1988); *The Books of Kings and Chronicles* (Liturgical, 1986); *A Study of the Literary Function of 2 Samuel 7 in the Deuteronomistic History* (Gregorian U., 1981); and others. Mem: CBA 1976-; SBL 1982-; AAR 1982. Rec: Music, crocheting, feminism. Addr: (o) College of the Holy Cross, Stein 429, Worcester, MA 01610 508-793-3359.

LAGRAND, James, b. Grand Rapids, MI, April 24, 1941, s. of James, Sr., & Katherine (Tornga), m. Virginia V. M., chil: David Martin; John Patrick; Paul Damien; Peter Lambert. Educ: Calvin Coll. & Sem., AB 1962, ThM 1975; U. of Mich., AM 1968; Yale U., BD 1968; Basel U., ThD (magna cum laude) 1989. Emp: Christian Reformed Ch., 1969-74, 1977-87 Pastor; Chicago Metropolitan Ctr., 1991-92 Instr.; Luth. Sch. of Theol. at Chicago, 1992-93 Lect., NT. Spec: Hebrew Bible, New Testament, Apocrypha and Post-biblical Studies. Pub: "'Hebrews' in the Tanakh" *Proceedings,* MidW SBL (1991); "The Water of Baptism and the Wine of Communion" *Calvin Theol. Jour.* (1989); *The Earliest Christian Mission to 'All Nations' in the Light of Matthew's Gospel* (Basel U., 1989); "How was the Virgin Mary 'Like a Man'? A Note on Mr.i.18b and Related Syriac Christian Texts" *NT* 22 (1980); *TO MYCTHPION: The New Testament Development of the Semitic Usage* (Calvin Theol. Sem., 1975); and others. Awd: Calvin Coll. Alumni, Outstanding Service Awd. 1986. Mem: Amer. Soc. of Ch. Hist. 1968-; SBL 1968-; Tyndale Fellow. 1976-; Soc. of Christian Phil. 1989-. Rec: Swimming, tennis, community organizing. Addr: (o) Lutheran School of Theology at Chicago, 1100 E 55th, Chicago, IL 60615 312-753-0774; (h) 5338 S Kimbark #2, Chicago, IL 60615 312-493-5374.

LAMPE, Peter, b. Detmold, Germany, January 28, 1954, s. of Dr. Karl-Heinrich & Helga, m. Margaret (Birdsong), chil: Daniel; Jessica. Educ: U. of Gottingen, Germany, Cand. Theol. 1977; U. of Bern, Switzerland, PhD 1983, Dr.Habil. 1991. Emp: U. of Bern, Switzerland, 1981-87 Wissenschaftl. Asst.; Union Theol. Sem., Va., 1987-92 Prof., NT, 1989-92 Chair, Bibl. Stud. Dept.; Christian-Albrechts U., 1992- Prof., NT, 1992- Dir., Inst. of Early Christian & Judaic Stud.; *Interpretation,* 1991-92 Ed. Bd. Spec: Archaeology, New Testament, Apocrypha and Post-biblical Studies. Pub: "Acta 19 im Spiegel der ephesischen Inschriften" *BZ* (1992); "Das Korinthische Herrenmahl im Schnittpunkt hellenistisch-roemischer Mahlpraxis" *ZNW* (1991); "Theological Wisdom and the 'Word about the Cross'" *Interpretation* (1990); *Die stadtroemischen Christen in den ersten beiden Jahrhunderten* (Mohr, 1989); "Keine Sklavenflucht des Onesimus" *ZNW* (1985); *Eschatologie und Friedenshandeln,* co-auth. (Kath. Bibelwerk, 1982); "Das Spiel mit dem Petrusnamen" *NTS* (1978/79); and others. Mem: SBL 1987-; SNTS 1991-. Rec: Sailing, painting, playing the piano & cello. Addr: (o) Institut Neutest. Wiss., Universitaet, Olshausenstr, D-24118 Kiel, Germany.

LANDES, George M., b. Kansas City, MO, August 2, 1928, s. of George & Margaret, m. Carol, chil: George, Jr.; Margaret; John. Educ: McCormick Theol. Sem., MDiv 1952; Johns Hopkins U., PhD 1956. Emp: Union Theol. Sem., 1956- Prof.; Columbia U., 1977- Adj. Prof.; BASOR Sup. Ser., 1979-82 Ed.; *JBL,* 1983-88 Ed. Bd. Excv: Araq el-Emir, Jordan, 1962 Field Supr.; ASOR Rescue Operation, Suwwanet eth-Thaniya, Jordan Valley, 1968 Arch. Dir. Spec: Archaeology, Hebrew Bible, Semitic Languages, Texts and Epigraphy. Pub: "Matthew 12:40 as an Interpretation of the 'Sign of Jonah' Against its Biblical Background" in *The Word of the Lord Shall Go Forth* (1983); "Linguistic Criteria and the Date of the Book of Jonah" *Eretz-Israel* 16 (1982); "Jonah: A Masal?" in *Israelite Wisdom: Theological and Literary Essays in Honor of Samuel L. Terrien* (1978); *Report on Archaeological Work at Suwwnet Eth-Thaniya* (1975); *A Student's Vocabulary of Biblical Hebrew* (1961); and others. Mem: AOS; SBL, Reg. Pres. 1981-82; ASOR, V.P. for Amman Sch. 1969-79. Rec: Tennis. Addr: (o) 3041 Broadway, New York, NY 10027 212-280-1391; (h) 606 W 122nd St., Apt. 6-E, New York, NY 10027 212-864-0764.

LANG, Bernhard, b. Stuttgart, Germany, July 12, 1946, s. of Gert & Stefanie (Germautz). Educ: Tubingen, Dr. Th. 1975; Freiburg, Dr. Theol. Habil. 1977. Emp: U. of Tubingen, 1977-82 Prof.; U. of Mainz, 1982-85 Prof.; U. of Paderborn, 1985- Prof.; Sorbonne, Paris, 1992-93 Vis. Prof.; *Internationale Zeitschriftenschau fur Bibelwissenschaft und Grenzgebiete,* 1980- Exec. Ed. Spec: Apocrypha and Post-biblical

Studies. Pub: *Neues Bibel-Lexikon*, co-auth. (Benziger, 1991); *Heaven*, co-ed. (Yale, 1988); "Afterlife—Ancient Israel's Changing Vision of the World Beyond" *BR* 4/1 (1988); *Paradise Found*, co-auth. (Yale U.P., 1988); *Wisdom and the Book of Proverbs: A Hebrew Goddess Redefined* (Pilgrims, 1986); *Anthropological Approaches to the Old Testament* (Fortress, 1985); and others. Mem: SBL 1968-. Rec: Anthropology, sociology. Addr: (o) U. of Paderborn, FB 1, D-33098 Paderborn, Germany.

LAPERROUSAZ, Ernest-Marie, b. Raymond, France, August 2, 1924, m. (Halfon). Educ: Sorbonne, Paris, Faculte des Lettres, diplome 1946, Lic., PhD. Emp: U. of Cairo, Egypt, 1950-56 Prof.; CNRS, Paris, 1957-63 Prof.; Sorbonne, Paris, 1963- Prof. & Dir., Ecole Pratique des Hautes-Etudes, Sect. des Sci. Relig.; U. de Paris-Sud-Orsay, 1975- Prof. & Dir., Ctr. Interdisciplinaire d'Etude de l'Evolution des idées, des sci. et techniques; *Revue* of the "Soc. Ernest-Renan. Soc. Francais d'Hist. des Relig.," Ed. Excv: Saint-Rémy de Provence, Glanum, 1946-50 Asst.; Qumran, 1954, 1970- Asst. & Vis. Prof.; Masada, 1963 Asst. Prof. Spec: Archaeology, Apocrypha and Post-biblical Studies. Pub: *Les Esséniens selon leur témoignage direct* (Desclée, 1982); *L'attente du Messie en Palestine à la veille et au début de l'ère chrétienne, à la lumière des documents récemment découverts* (Picard, 1982); *Qumrân: L'établissement essénien des bords de la mer Morte: Histoire et archéologie du site* (Picard, 1976); *Le Testament de Moise*, Semitica 19 (Adrien-Maisonneuve, 1970); and others. Awd: Ordre des Palmes Acad., Commandeur 1982. Mem: Intl. Assn. for the Hist. of Relig., Soc. Ernest-Renan 1968-; Soc. des Etudes juives, Pres. 1990-92. Rec: Architecture, music, promenades in forests. Addr: (o) Sorbonne, Ecole Pratique Haute Etudes, Sect. des Sci. Relig., 45 rue des Ecoles, Paris, France; (h) 20 rue de Vanves, 92140 Clamart, France 1-46-42-69-72.

LATTKE, Michael S., b. Stettin, Germany, May 12, 1942, s. of Kurt & Maria (Kanski), chil: Frank; Birgit. Educ: U. of Tuebingen, Dipl. Theol. 1968; U. of Freiburg, DTh 1974; U. of Augsburg, DTh Habil. 1979; U. of Queensland, Brisbane, DLitt 1992. Emp: Speyer 1970-/1 Lect.; Muenster, Inst. NT Res., 1972-73 Fellow; Augsburg, 1974-80 Res. Asst.; U. of Queensland, Australia, 1981- Reader. Spec: New Testament, Semitic Languages, Texts and Epigraphy, Apocrypha and Post-biblical Studies. Pub: *Hymnus* (Vandenhoeck & Ruprecht, 1991); "Heiligkeit III. NT" *TRE* (1985); "Rudolf Bultmann on Rudolf Otto" *HTR* (1985); "Joh 20,30f als Buchschluss" *ZNW* (1987); *Die Oden Salomos* (Vandenhoeck & Ruprecht, 1979, 1986); "Haggadah & Halachah" in *Reallexikon fuer Antike und Christentum* (1985) "Salz der Freundschaft in Mark 9,50c" *ZNW* (1984); *Register zu Rudolf Bultmans Glauben und Verstehen I-IV* (Mohr, 1984); and others. Mem: SNTS 1976-; IACS 1977-; SBL 1980-; Australian Assn. for the Study of Relig. 1981-. Rec: Cooking, music, tennis. Addr: (o) U. of Queensland, Studies in Religion, St. Lucia, Brisbane QLD 4072,

Australia 07-365-3331; (h) 3/64 Sisley St., St. Lucia, Brisbane, Australia 07-371-8239.

LAUGHLIN, John C. H., b. Asheboro, NC, September 5, 1942, s. of Charles & Alice, m. Janet, chil: John. Educ: Wake Forest U., BA 1967; South. Bapt. Theol. Sem., MDiv 1971, PhD 1975. Emp: Hardin-Simmons U., 1976-77 Asst. Prof.; Palm Beach Atlantic Coll., 1977-79 Asst. Prof.; Averett Coll., 1979- Prof. of Relig. Excv: Capernaum, 1981-87 Area Supr., Vis. Prof. of Arch; Banias, 1988- Area Supr., Vis. Prof. of Arch. Spec: Archaeology, Hebrew Bible. Pub: "Zedekiah: His Life and Times" *BI* (1985); "Ancient Crowns" *TBI* (1984); "The Remarkable Discoveries at Tel Dan" *BAR* 8/5 (1981); *Excavations at Capernaum, vol. 1 (1978-82)*, co-auth.; "The 'Strange Fire' of Nadab and Abihu" *JBL* (1976). Mem: ASOR; SBL; NABPR. Rec: Photography, gardening, jogging. Addr: (o) Averett College, Danville, VA 24541 804-791-5707; (h) 153 Beverley Rd., Danville, VA 24541 804-797-2093.

LAVERDIERE, Eugene A., b. Waterville, ME, April 7, 1936, s. of Laurier & Gladys. Educ: John Carroll U., MA 1963; U. of Fribourg, STL 1965; Pont. Bibl. Inst., SSL 1967; U. of Chicago, PhD 1977. Emp: John Carroll U., 1969-76; Jesuit Sch. of Theol., 1976-81; Cath. Theol. Union, 1981- Adj. Prof.; *Emmanuel Magazine*, 1983-88 Ed., 1988- Sr. Ed.; U. of St. Mary of the Lake, 1988-89 Adj. Prof., 1990- Margaret & Chester Paluch Chair of Theol. Spec: New Testament. Pub: *Luke* (Glazier, 1980); *The New Testament in the Life of the Church* (Ave Maria, 1980); and others. Mem: CBA 1969-; SBL 1969-. Addr: (h) 184 E 76th St., New York, NY 10021 212-288-5082.

LAWLOR, John I., b. Winona Lake, IN, December 16, 1941, s. of George & Mildred (Rex), m. Mary Ellen, chil: Karis; Nancy; Renee. Educ: Cedarville Coll., BA 1963; Grace Theol. Sem., MDiv 1966, ThM 1969; Drew U., PhD 1990. Emp: Bapt. Bible Coll. of Pa., 1970-80 Asst. Prof.; Bapt. Bible Theol. Sem., 1980- Prof. Excv: Heshbon N Ch. Project, 1978 Field Dir.; Madaba Plains Project, Tell el Umeiri, 1984, 1987, 1989, 1992 Field Supr. Spec: Archaeology. Pub: "Theology and Art in the Narrative of the Ammonite War" *Grace Theol. Jour.* (1982); "The Test of Abraham: Genesis 22:1-19" *Grace Theol. Jour.* (1980); "The Excavation of the North Church at Hesban, Jordan: A Preliminary Report" *AUSS* (1980); "The 1978 Excavation of the Hesban North Church" *Ann. of the Dept. of Antiq. of Jordan* (1980); *The Nabataeans in Historical Perspective* (Baker, 1974); and others. Mem: ASOR 1978-; NEAS 1978-; SBL 1980-. Rec: Class. music, golf, family. Addr: (o) 538 Venard Rd., Clarks Summit, PA 18411 717-587-1172; (h) 116 Maple Ave., Clarks Summit, PA 18411 717-587-5885.

LAWS, Sophie S., b. Brixham, Devon, England, September 1, 1944, d. of Peter & Margaret

Marshall, m. John G. Laws, chil: Margaret. Educ: Oxford U., BA 1963, BLitt 1969, MA 1970. Emp: Leeds U., 1968-69 Asst. Prof.; U. of London, King's Coll., 1969-82 Lect.; *Theology*, 1971-75 Rev. Ed.; John Carroll U., 1984 Walter and Mary Tuohy Prof. of Inter-Relig. Stud.; Regent's Coll., London, 1985- Fellow. Spec: New Testament. Pub: *ABD*, contb. (Doubleday, 1992); *A Dict. of Bibl. Interpretation*, contb. (SCM, 1990); *The Books of the Bible* (Scribner's, 1989); "The Doctrinal Basis of the Ethics of James" *Studia Evang.* (1982); "The Blood-Stained Horseman: Revelation 19:11-13" *JSNT* (1980); *A Commentary on the Epistle of James* (Harper & Row, 1980); "Can Apocalyptic be Relevant?" in *What About the New Testament?* (1975); and others. Mem: SNTS 1971-. Rec: Sewing, Greece, Jane Austen. Addr: (h) 19 Longmoore St., Pimlico, London SW1V 1JQ, England 071-834-4719.

LAYMAN, Fred D., b. Marshfield, MO, September 27, 1931, s. of Lee Roy & Winnie Amanda (Thomas), m. Donna (Roberts), chil: Steven R. Educ: Asbury Theol. Sem., BD 1956; Princeton Theol. Sem., ThM 1957; U. Iowa, PhD 1972. Emp: Friends U., 1957-64 Prof.; Asbury Coll., 1967-68 Assoc. Prof.; Asbury Theol. Sem., 1968- Prof. Spec: New Testament. Pub: Articles in *New 20th Cent. Ency. of Religious Knowledge* (1991); "Contemporary Issues in Theological Education" *Asbury Theol. Jour.* 41 (1986); articles in *Beacon Dict. of Theology* (1983); "Theology and Humor" *Asbury Seminarian* (1984); "Salvation in the Book of Revelation" in *An Inquiry into Soteriology* (Warner, 1981) and others.; "Male Headship in Paul's Thought" *WTJ* (1980); "Man and Sin in the Perspective of Biblical Theology" *Asbury Seminarian* (1975); and others. Mem: SBL. Rec: Music, outdoor sports. Addr: (o) Asbury Theological Seminary, Wilmore, KY 40390 606-858-3581; (h) 210 Linden Ln., Nicholasville, KY 40356 606-885-3701.

LAYTON, Bentley, b. Jackson, MS, August 12, 1941, s. of Reber & Gray. Educ: Harvard U., PhD 1971. Emp: Ecole Biblique, Jerusalem, 1971-76 Vis. Prof.; Yale U., 1976- Prof.; *The Second Century*, 1981- Ed. Cons. Bd.; *HTR*, 1980- Ed. Cons. Bd.; *Jour. of Coptic Stud.*, 1991- Ed. Cons. Bd. Spec: New Testament, Egyptology, Apocrypha and Post-biblical Studies. Pub: *Catalogue of Coptic Literary Manuscripts in the British Library* (British Lib., 1986); *Nag Hammadi Codex II, 2-7* (Brill, 1986); "Vision and Revision: A Gnostic View of Resurrection" *Colloque Intl. sur Les Textes de Nag Hammadi* (1981); "Compound Prepositions in Sahidic Coptic" in *Festschrift for Hans Jakob Polotsky* (Pirtle and Polson, 1981); *The Gnostic Treatise on Resurrection* (Fortress, 1978); "The Text and Orthography of the Coptic Hypostasis of the Archons" *Zeitsehrift fuer Papyrologie und Epigraphik* (1970); and others. Awd: Guggenheim Fellow 1979-80. Mem: SBL 1976-, Chmn. Nag Hammadi Sect.; IACS 1976-80 V.P., Pres. 1980-84; British Sch. of Arch. in Jerusalem 1971-. Addr: (o) Yale U., Dept. of Religious Studies,

Box 2160, Yale Station, New Haven, CT 06520-2160 203-432-0828.

LEACH, Donn A., b. St. Louis, MO, January 26, 1929, s. of Vern & Nora (Leavitt), m. Joan (Baldwin), chil: Dann; John. Educ: Lincoln Christian Coll., AB 1950; Butler U., MDiv 1953, MA 1954; North. Bapt. Theol. Sem., ThD 1960. Emp: Lincoln Christian Coll., 1957-72 Prof., NT; Manhattan Christian Coll., 1972-88 Prof., Bible; Springdale Coll., England, 1988- Lect., Bibl. Stud. & Greek. Spec: New Testament. Pub: *What the Bible Says About Jesus* (College, 1989). Mem: AAR 1958-66; SBL 1958-. Rec: Gardening, photography, travel. Addr: (o) 54 Weoley Park Rd., Birmingham B29 6RB, England 021-472-0726; (h) 1 Middle Park Rd., Birmingham B29 4BE, England 021-475-3196.

LEANEY, Alfred R. C., b. Birmingham, England, June 8, 1909, s. of Alfred & Violet (Dickinson), m. Mary Elizabeth, chil: Christopher Laurence John. Educ: Hertford Coll., England, BA 1932, MA 1939, BD 1952, DD 1966. Emp: Eastwood, Notts, 1946 Rector; Wishaw, Birmingham, 1948-52 Rector; Ripon Hall, 1952-55 Vice-Prin.; Nottingham U., 1956- Lect., 1969- Prof., NT, 1970-74 Prof., Christian Theol., Head, Dept. of Theol. Spec: New Testament, Apocrypha and Post-biblical Studies. Pub: *The Jewish and Christian World 200 BC to AD 200* (Cambridge U.P., 1984); *The New Testament* (Hodder & Stoughton, 1972); *Biblical Criticism*, co-auth. (Penguin, 1970); "The Experience of God in Qumran and in Paul" *BJRL* (1969); *1 and 2 Peter and Jude*, Cambridge Bible Comm. Ser., (1967); and others. Mem: SNTS; SOTS; SBL. Rec: Music, gardening. Addr: (o) 3 King St., Newport, Pembs., Dyfed SA42 OPY, England 0239-820211.

LEASE, Gary L., b. Hollywood, CA, September 27, 1940, s. of Rex & Isabelle (Riehle), chil: Dylan. Educ: Loyola U. of Los Angeles, BA 1962; U. of Munich, Germany, Dr. Theol. 1968. Emp: St. Xavier Coll., 1968-69 Asst. Prof.; Loyola U. of Los Angeles, 1969-73 Asst. Prof.; U. of Munich, 1971-72 Res. Fellow; U. of Calif., 1973- Prof. & Dean of Humanities. Excv: Caesarea Maritima, 1974 Asst. Area Supr., 1975 Area Supr.; Nag Hammadi, Egypt, 1979-80 Supr., 1989 Co-dir., Ed. of Excvn. Reports. Spec: Archaeology, Egyptology. Pub: *Traces of Early Egyptian Monasticism: The Faw Qibli Excavations* (Claremont, 1991); "Religiöses Bewusstsein und Kultur: Ein vergleichende Untersuchung von Ueberlebungs-Strategien" in *Paradoxien, Dissonanzen, Zusammenbruche* (1991); "Mithra in Egypt" in *The Roots of Egyptian Christianity* (Fortress, 1986); "Mithraism and Christianity: Borrowings and Transformations" *ANRW* (de Gruyter, 1980); "The Caesarea Mithraeum" *BA* 38 (1975); and others. Awd: Fulbright Fellow. 1984. Mem: NAASR; ASOR; AAR; Amer. Res. Ctr., Egypt; Gesellschaft fuer Geistesgeschichte. Rec: Hunting. Addr: (o) U. of California, Humanities

Division, Santa Cruz, CA 95064 408-459-2696; (h) 248 Dickens Way, Santa Cruz, CA 95064 408-423-0546.

LEE, Archie Chi Chung, b. Canton, China, September 15, 1950, s. of Tak Choi & Lai Bun (Kwong), m. Alison S. M., chil: Lee Yu Hin. Educ: Chinese U. of Hong Kong, BA 1973, MDiv 1975; Edinburgh U., PhD 1980. Emp: Chinese U. of Hong Kong, 1980-92 Lect., 1992- Sr. Lect., 1984-92 Dir. of Stud. in Relig., 1989-92 Assoc. Dean, Prog. for Theol. & Cultures in Asia. Spec: Hebrew Bible, Mesopotamian Studies. Pub: "The David-Bathsheba Story and the Parable of Nathan" in *Voices from the Margin: Interpreting the Bible in the Third World* (SPCK, 1991); "Creation Narratives and the Movement of the Spirit" *ATESEA Occasional Papers* 11 (1991); *A Commentary on the Book of Koheleth* (Chinese Christian Lit. Coun., 1990); "The Context and Function of the Plague Tradition in Ps. 78" *JSOT* 48 (1990); "Genesis One and the Plagues Tradition in Ps. 105" *VT* 40 (1990); *The Old Testament in Context* (Chung Chi Theol. Div., 1989); "The Dragon, the Deluge and Creation Theology" *ATESEA Occasional Papers* 8 (1989). Mem: SBL. Addr: (o) Chinese U. of Hong Kong, Religion Dept., Shatin, New Territories, Hong Kong 852-6096497; (h) Chinese U. of Hong Kong, A11 Chung Chi College Staff Quarters, Shatin, New Territories, Hong Kong 852-6036791.

LEE, Dorothy A., b. Scotland, UK, March 23, 1953, d. of Edwin & Barbara Lee, m. David Pollard, chil: Miriam E.; Irene M. Educ: Newcastle U., NSW, Australia, BA 1976, Dip. in Educ. 1977; Sydney U., BD 1983, PhD 1991; Uniting Ch. of Australia, 1984 Ord. Min. Emp: United Theol. Coll., Sydney, 1984-89 Lect., NT; United Fac. of Theol., Melbourne, 1990- Lect., NT; *Australian Bibl. Rev.*, 1991 Acting Ed., 1992- NT Book Ed. Spec: New Testament. Pub: *The Last Days of Jesus According to Mark* (Albatross, 1992); "The Blindness of the Disciples (Mark 6:7-8:26)" in *The Year of Mark* (Desbooks, 1984); "The Prologue to John's Gospel (John 1:1-18)" in *The Years of John* (Desbooks, 1985); "Powerlessness as Power: A Key Emphasis in the Gospel of Mark" *SJT* 40 (1987); and others. Awd: Sydney U., U. Medal 1983. Mem: Fellow. for Bibl. Stud. Rec: Reading, music. Addr: (o) MacLean House, Ormond College, Parkville, Victoria 3052, Australia 03-347-7199; (h) 3 Queen's College, Parkville, Victoria 3052, Australia.

LEE, Jong Keun, b. Korea, January 30, 1951, s. of Kyo Won & Jin Pil, m. Kyoung Bae Kim, chil: Hong Lak; Koo Lak. Educ: Sahmyook U., ThB 1973; Seoul Natl. U., MBA 1976; Philippine Union Coll., MPH 1982; Asia Adventist Inst. of Advanced Stud., MA 1982, MDiv 1987; Harvard U., ThM 1989; Boston U., ThD 1992. Emp: Seoul, 1980-82 Pastor; Pusan, 1982-84 Hospital Chaplain; Sahmyook U., 1984-86 Instr., 1986- Asst. Prof.; Harvard U., 1993

Vis. Schol. Spec: Hebrew Bible, Mesopotamian Studies, Semitic Languages, Texts and Epigraphy. Pub: *The Theological Concept of Divine Ownership of the Land in the Hebrew Bible* (Boston U.P., 1992); "A Study on Oral Tradition Based on Biblical Genealogy" *Jour. of Sahmyook Stud.* (1988); *A Study on Sanctuary Truth* (Jungmun, 1987); and others. Mem: SBL; AAR; Soc. for the Anc. Near East. Stud. in Korea. Addr: (o) Sahmyook U., Chung Ryang PO Box 118, Seoul, South Korea 02-972-3606; (h) 29-1, Hwikyung-dong, Dongdaemun-ku, Seoul, South Korea 02-248-9856.

LEESEBERG, Martin W., b. Milwaukee, WI, September 7, 1915, s. of Ralph & Ella (Klein), m. Irma (Christophel), chil: Karen; Lynette; Marilyn. Educ: Wartburg Sem., BD, MDiv 1947; Princeton Sem., ThM 1950; Yale U., MA 1952; Concordia Sem., ThD 1961. Emp: Luth. Sem., Canada, 1952-80. Spec: Hebrew Bible, Semitic Languages, Texts and Epigraphy. Pub: "Ezra and Nehemiah: A Review of the Return and Reform" *Concordia Theol. Monthly* (1962); "On the Road to Gaza" *The Shepherd* (1970); and others. Mem: SBL 1952-. Rec: Reading, poetry, woodcarving. Addr: (h) #605-2311 McEown Ave., Saskatoon, SK S7J 2H3, Canada 306-374-5759.

LEHMAN, Israel Otto, b. Berlin, March 6, 1912, s. of Max & Constance. Educ: Hochschule fur die Wissenschaft des Judentums, ord. Rabbi 1938; U. of Oxford, St. Catharine's Coll., BA 1944, BLitt 1947, MA 1948, PhD 1960. Emp: Hebrew Lang. Inst., 1936- Lect.; Bodleian Lib., Oxford, 1947- Asst. to the Keeper; Baeck Coll., London, 1956-64 Lect.; Coll. of Jewish Stud., 1964-65 Vis. Prof.; Hebrew Union Coll., Cincinnati, 1968- Cur. of Manuscripts & Special Collections; Miami U., Adj. Prof., Dept. of Relig. Spec: Hebrew Bible, Semitic Languages, Texts and Epigraphy. Pub: "Aspects of the Experience of God through Buildings and Manuscripts in Christianity, Judaism and Islam" in *Approaches to Ancient; Judaism* vol. 1 (1990); articles in *EJ*; *Handbook of Hebrew and Aramaic Manuscripts*, ed. (1975); Pentateuch and Haftorahs, trans. (1937); and others. Awd: Royal Asiatic Soc., London, Fellow; John F. Kennedy Lib., Fellow. Mem: AOS; SBL; SOTS, England. Rec: Book collecting, walking, art. Addr: (o) 3101 Clifton Ave., Cincinnati, OH 45220-2404 221-1875; (h) 3655 Middleton Ave., Cincinnati, OH 45220.

LEHMANN, Manfred R., b. Stockholm, Sweden, August 28, 1922, s. of Hans & Fannie, m. Sara Anne (Moskovits), chil: Barbara (Siegel); Karen (Eisner). Educ: Johns Hopkins U., MA 1946; Ner Israel Rabbinical Coll., Rabbinical Ord. 1954, D. of Talmudic Law 1980. Spec: Hebrew Bible, Apocrypha and Postbiblical Studies. Pub: "The Temple Scroll as a Source of Sectarian-Sadducee Halakha" *RQ* 36/9 (1978); "Identification of the Copper Scroll Based on Its Technical Terms" *RQ* 17/5 (1964);

"Studies in the Muarabba'at and Nahal Hever Documents" *RQ* 13/4 (1963); *Ohel Hayim* vol. I & II, MSS Catalogue (1988, 1990); *Torah from Kenya* (1985); *Critical Edition of Rashi Based on Yemenite MS* (1981); "Ben Sira and the Dead Sea Literature" *RQ* 8/3 (1961); "Talmudic Material Relating to the Dead Sea Scrolls" *RQ* 3/1 (1959); and others. Awd: Bar Ilan U., Doc. 1991; Maimon Inst., Jerusalem, Maimon Prize 1990. Mem: JBS; ASRL. Rec: Collecting manuscripts. Addr: (o) 5500 Collins Ave., Miami Beach, FL 33140 305-866-1094.

LEHMANN-HABECK, Martin H. G., b. Karwesee, Germany, June 22, 1936, s. of Martin & Hildegard, m. Erika, chil: Martin; Christiane. Educ: U. Heidelberg, Kirchliche Hochschule Berlin, I. Theol. Exam 1960, II Theol. Exam 1963, ThD, NT 1968; Protestant Episc. Theol. Sem., STM 1961. Emp: Evang. Ch. of Berlin West, 1964-65 Pastor; Kirchliche Hochschule Berlin, 1964-70 Teaching Asst., Lect.; Ch. Head Office Berlin, 1964-76 Sec. for Theol. Educ.; U. of Zimbabwe, 1988- Sr. Lect., 1991- Assoc. Prof., Bibl. Stud. Spec: New Testament. Pub: "Das Gesetz als der gute Gotteswille fuer meinen Naechsten" in *Treue zur Thora*, Festschrift fuer Guenther Harder zum 75 Geburtstag; (1979); *Synoptische Quellenanalyse und die Frage nach dem historischen Jesus, BZNW* 38 (1970); and others. Mem: SNTS 1971-; Gesellschaft fur Evang. Theol. 1971-; Intl. Assn. for Mission Stud. 1985-. Rec: Choir singing, hiking, swimming. Addr: (o) U. of Zimbabwe, Dept. of Religious Studies, Classics & Philosophy, PO Box M P 167 Mt. Pleasant, Harare, Zimbabwe 2634-303211; (h) 50 Norfolk Rd., Mt. Pleasant, Harare, Zimbabwe 2634-38069.

LEITH, MaryJoan W., b. Edinburgh, Scotland, March 11, 1956, d. of William E. & Barbara P. Winn, m. Royal W. Leith, III, chil: William Winn; Thomas Bell. Educ: Harvard U., Radcliffe Coll., AB (magna cum laude) 1977; Harvard U., MA 1983, PhD, Near East. Lang. & Civ. 1990. Emp: Stonehill Coll., 1988-89 Asst. Prof.; Mass. Inst. of Technology, 1990-92 Lect.; Brandeis U., 1991-92 Lect. Excv: Numeira, Jordan, 1983 Field Supr., 1981 Area Supr.; North. Orontes Valley, 1979 Staff Mem.; Wadi Tumeilat Project, Tell Maskhuta, 1978 Area Supr. Spec: Archaeology, Hebrew Bible. Pub: "Verse and Reverse: The Woman, Israel, in Hosea 1-3" in *Gender and Difference in Ancient Israel* (Augsburg/Fortress, 1989); and others. Awd: Phi Beta Kappa 1976; Zion Res. Found. Travel Grant 1979, 1981; Harvard U., Pfeiffer Fellow. for Bibl. Arch. 1979, 1981, 1983; NEH, Travel to Collections Fellow. 1991; Hess & Helyn Kline Found., Pub. Fellow. 1992. Mem: ASOR; SBL; AAR; AIA, V.P. Boston Chap. 1989-91. Addr: (h) 131 Huron Ave., Cambridge, MA 02138 617-491-5396.

LEMAIRE, André, b. Neuville, France, January 2, 1942, s. of Pierre & Louise, m.

Urszula, chil: Viviane; Guillaume. Educ: Cath. Inst. Paris, Lic. Theol. 1967; Ecole Pratique des Hautes Etudes, Sorbonne, Dip. 1970, 1973, Doc., Oriental Stud. 1973. Emp: Cath. Inst., Paris, 1969-73 Charge de cours; Ctr. Natl. de la Recherche Sci., 1973-87 Dir. de Recherche, Semitic Stud.; Ecole Pratique des Hautes Etudes, Hist. & Philol., 1987- Dir. d'etudes; *VT*, 1976- Ed. Bd.; VTSup, 1989- Ed. Bd. Excv: Sebastyeh-Samaria, Gezer; Tel Megaddim; Beersheba; Lachish; Tel Yarmut. Spec: Archaeology, Hebrew Bible, New Testament, Semitic Languages, Texts and Epigraphy. Pub: *Les Inscriptions arameennes de Sfire et l'Assyrie de Shamshi-ilu* (Hautes Etudes Orient., 1984); "Probable Head of Priestly Sceptor from Solomon's Temple Surfaces in Jerusalem" *BAR* 10/1 (1984); and others. Awd: Inst. de France, Prix d'Aumale 1973. Mem: Soc. asiatique; Soc. des Etudes Juives. Addr: (o) College de France, Institute d'Etdues Semitiques, 11, Pl. Marcelin Berthelot, Paris 75231, France 1-4271051.

LEMCHE, Niels P., b. Copenhagen, September 6, 1945, s. of Svend E. & Lise W., m. Elsebeth, chil: Frederik; Nikolaj; Valdemar; Joakim. Educ: U. of Copenhagen, MA, Theol. 1971, ThD 1985. Emp: U. of Copenhagen, 1972-78 Res. Asst., 1978-86 Asst. Prof., 1987- Prof., Theol.; U. of Hamburg, 1986-87 Vis. Prof.; *Scandinavian Jour. of the OT*, 1987- Founder & Ed. Spec: Archaeology, Hebrew Bible, Mesopotamian Studies. Pub: *The Canaanites* (JSOT, 1991); "On the Use of 'System Theory'" *SJT* (1990); "Rachel and Lea I-II" *SJT* (1987-88); *Ancient Israel* (JSOT, 1988); *Early Israel* (Brill, 1985); "Israel in the Period of the Judges" *Studia Theol.* 38 (1984); *"Andurarum* and *Misarum" JNES* 38 (1979); "The Hebrew Slave" *VT* 25 (1975); *Israel i Dommertiden* (Gad, 1972); and others. Awd: U. of Copenhagen, Silver Medal 1969. Mem: Coll. Bibl., Denmark 1973-; Wissenschaftliche Gesellschaft fur Theol. 1987-; Nathan Söderblom Selskapet, Uppsala 1988-; SBL 1989-. Rec: Full Captain, Danish Home Guard, gardening, opera. Addr: (o) U. of Copenhagen, Dept. of Biblical Studies, Kobmagergade 46, DK-1150 Copenhagen, Denmark 45-35323649; (h) "Smedebakken", Smedebakken 12, DK-3490 Kvistgaard, Denmark 45-49138124.

LEMKE, Werner E., b. Berlin, Germany, January 31, 1933, s. of Erich & Minna, m. Sandra J., chil: Kathryn Anne; Michael John; Elizabeth. Educ: NW U., BA 1956; North Park Theol. Sem., BD 1959; Havard U. Div. Sch., ThD 1964. Emp: McCormick Theol. Sem., 1960-94 Dir., Summer Lang. Prog. in Greek & Hebrew; Harvard U., 1965 Vis. Asst. Prof.; North Park Coll. & Theol. Sem., 1963-66 Asst. Prof., Bibl. Lit.; Colgate Rochester Div. Sch., 1966- Prof., OT Interpretation; U. of Rochester, 1970, 1974, 1977,19 83 Vis. Prof., Hebrew Bible. Excv: Hebrew Union Coll. in Jerusalem, Tel Gezer, 1970 Arch. Fellow & Field Supr.; ASOR, William F. Albright Inst., Jerusalem, 1973 Ann. Prof. Spec: Hebrew Bible. Pub: "Theology, Old Testament" in *ABD* vol. 6

(Doubleday 1992); "Is Old Testament Theology an Essentially Christian Theological Discipline?" *Horizons in Bibl. Theo.* 11 (1989); "Revelation Through History in Recent Biblical Theology" *Interpretation* 36 (1982); "The Near and the Distant God: A Study of Jeremiah 23:23-24 in Its Biblical Theological Context" *JBL* 100 (1981); *Magnalia Dei/ The Mighty Acts of God: Essays on the Bible and Archaeology in Memory of G. Ernest Wright*, contb. (Doubleday, 1976); "Nebuchadrezzar, My Servant" *CBQ* 28 (1966); "The Synoptic Problem in the Chronicler's History" *HTR* 58 (1965); and others. Awd: Rockefeller Doctoral Fellow. in Relig, 1961-63; William F. Albright Inst. of Arch. Res. in Jerusalem, Ann. Prof. 1973. Mem: SBL; ASOR; CBA; Colloquium for Bibl. Res.; CSBR. Rec: Hiking, camping, cross country skiing, classical music, farming. Addr: (o) Colgate Rochester Divinity School, 1100 S Goodman St., Rochester, NY 14620 716-271-1320; (h) 167 Crosman Terrace, Rochester, NY 14620 716-244-0825.

LEON-DUFOUR, Xavier, b. Paris, France, July 3, 1912, s. of Bernard & Suzanne Genty de Bussy. Emp: Enghien, Belgium, Fac. de Theol. 1948-1957; Lyon-Fourviere, Fac. de Theol. 1957-1973; Centre. Sevres, Paris, Fac. de Theol. 1974-1992. Spec: New Testament. Pub: "New Testament Studies: Presidential Address" *NTS* 27 (1981); *Resurrection and the Message of Easter* (1975); *The Gospels and the Jesus of History* (1970); *Dict. of Biblical Theology*, contb. Awd: Consuoteur de la Pont. Bibl. Commn. Mem: SNTS, Pres. 1980. Addr: (o) 35 rue de Sevres, Paris 75006, France 1-45-44-58-91.

LESKE, Adrian M., b. Gumeracha, S Australia, April 14, 1936, s. of Wilhelm & Lenora (Zacker), m. Patricia (Kowald), chil: Kylie-Anne; Jane Patricia; Andrew Christopher. Educ: Concordia Coll., S Australia, Class. Dipl. 1955; Concordia Luth. Sem., S Australia, Grad. Dipl. 1958; Concordia Sem. Grad. Sch., St. Louis, MDiv 1960, ThD 1971. Emp: New Zealand & S Australia, 1960-69 Pastor; Concordia Coll., Canada, 1971- Prof., Relig. Stud.; Luth. Coun. in Canada, 1978-81 Chair, Div. of Theol.; St. Stephen's Coll., U. of AB, Canada, 1976- Bd. of Managers. Spec: Hebrew Bible, New Testament. Pub: "The Beatitudes, Salt and Light in Matthew and Luke" 1991 SBL Seminar Papers (Scholars, 1991); "Righteousness as Relationship" in *Festschrift: A Tribute to Dr. William Hordern* (U. of SK, 1985); "Exegetical Case Study: 1 Corinthians 11:2-16" *Consensus* (1980); and others. Mem: Canadian Soc. for the Study of Relig. 1975-; CSBS 1977-; SBL 1979-. Rec: Travel. Addr: (o) Concordia College, 7128 Ada Blvd., Edmonton, AB T5B 4E4, Canada 403-479-8481; (h) 10323 134 St., Edmonton, AB T5N 2A9, Canada 403-452-9949.

LETIS, Theodore P., b. Wilmington, DE, July 15, 1951, s. of George & Grace, m. Laura Susan, chil: Grace Elizabeth; Theodore Peter, II. Educ:

Evang. Coll., BA 1981; Emory U., Candler Sch. of Theol., MTS (magna cum laude) 1987. Emp: *Bull. of the Inst. for Reformation Bibl. Stud.*, 1989- Ed.; U. of Edinburgh, 1990 Lect. Spec: New Testament. Pub: *The Revival of the Ecclesiastical Text and the Claims of the Anabaptists*, ed. (Inst. for Reformation Bibl. Stud., 1992); "The Ecclesiastical Text Redivivus?" *Bull. of the Inst. for Reformation Bibl. Stud.* 1/2 (1990); and others. Awd: U. of Edinburgh Theol. Soc., Pres. Mem: SBL 1978-; AAR 1985-; Eccles. Hist. Soc. 1990-. Rec: Photography, running. Addr: (o) U. of Edinburgh, New College, The Mound, Edinburgh EH12LU, Scotland; (h) 12 Dovecot Park, Edinburgh EH142LN, Scotland.

LEVENSON, David B., b. Oklahoma City, OK, October 12, 1948, s. of Joseph & Claire, m. Cathy W. Educ: Princeton U., AB (summa cum laude) 1970; Harvard U., MA 1975, PhD 1980. Emp: Fla. State U., 1976- Assoc. Prof. Spec: New Testament, Apocrypha and Post-biblical Studies. Pub: "Julian's Attempt to Rebuild the Temple: An Inventory of Ancient and Medieval Sources" in *Of Scribes and Scholars: Studies on the Hebrew Bible, Intertestamental Judaism, and Christian Origins* (U. Press of Amer., 1990); "Different Texts or Different Quests: The Contexts of Biblical Studies" in *Hebrew Bible or Old Testament?* (Notre Dame U.P., 1990); "Julian, the Emperor" in *Ency. of Early Christianity* (Garland, 1990); "Elijah, Apocalypse of (Hebrew)" in *ISBE* (1982); and others. Awd: Phi Beta Kappa 1970. Mem: SBL; AJS; NAPS; Assn. of Anc. Hist.; AAR. Rec: Golf. Addr: (o) Florida State U., Religion Dept., Tallahassee, FL 32306 904-644-0212; (h) 3566 Gardenview Way, Tallahassee, FL 32308 904-893-5088.

LEVENSON, Jon D., Spec: Hebrew Bible. Addr: (o) Harvard Divinity School, 45 Francis Ave., Cambridge, MA 02138 617-495-5955.

LEVIN, Saul, b. Chicago, IL, July 13, 1921, s. of Nathan & Rose (Finkel), m. Ruth (Harris), chil: Nathaniel; Eve; Margaret; Anne; Daniel; Victoria. Educ: U. of Chicago., AB 1942, PhD 1949; Harvard U., Jr. Fellow 1946-49. Emp: U. of Chicago., 1949-51 Instr.; Washington U., 1951-61 Assoc. Prof.; Harpur Coll., 1961- Prof. 1990- Disting. Prof.; *General Linguistics*, 1983- Co-ed. Spec: Hebrew Bible, New Testament, Semitic Languages, Texts and Epigraphy. Pub: *Guide to the Bible* (SUNY, 1990); "An Unattested 'Scribal Correction' in Numbers 26:59" *Biblica* (1990); "In What Sense Was Hebrew a Primeval Language?" *Gen. Linguistics* (1989); "The Hebrew of the Pentateuch" in *Focus: A Semitic/Afrasian Gathering in Remembrance of Albert Ehrman* (1988); "Defects, Alleged or Real, in the Tiberias Pointing" *Hebrew Stud.* (1982); "The Correspondence Between Hebrew and Arabic Pausal Verb-Forms" *Zeitschrift der Deutschen Morgenlaendschen Gesellschaft* (1981); *The Father of Joshua/Jesus* (SUNY, 1978); *The*

Indo-European and Semitic Languages (SUNY, 1971); and others. Mem: SBL; NAPH; IOSCS. Addr: (o) SUNY, Dept. of Classical and Near Eastern Studies, Binghamton, NY 13902-6000 607-777-6776; (h) 517 Harvard St., Vestal, NY 13850 607-797-2294.

LEVINE, Amy-Jill, b. New Bedford, MA, June 29, 1956, d. of Saul & Anne H., m. Jay Geller, chil: Sarah Elizabeth; Alexander David. Educ: Smith Coll., BA 1978; Duke U., MA 1981, PhD 1984. Emp: Duke U., 1982-85 Instr.; U. of N Carol., 1984-85 Vis. Instr.; Swarthmore Coll., 1985-90 Asst. Prof., 1991-92 Assoc. Prof., 1993-James A. Michener Assoc. Prof. Spec: Hebrew Bible, New Testament, Apocrypha and Post-biblical Studies. Pub: "Sacrifice and Salvation: Otherness and Domestication in the Book of Judith" in *No One Spoke Ill of Her: Essays on Judith*, EJL 2 (Scholars, 1992); "Diaspora as Metaphor: Bodies and Boundaries in the Book of Tobit" in *Diaspora Jews and Judaism* (Scholars, 1992); *'Women Like This': New Perspectives on Jewish Women in the Greco-Roman World*, ed. EJL 1 (Scholars, 1991); "Who's Catering the Q Affair? Feminist Observations on Q Paraenesis" *Semeia 50* (1990); *The Social and Ethnic Dimensions of Matthean Salvation History: 'Go Nowhere Among the Gentiles' (Matt.10:5b)* (Mellen, 1988); and others. Awd: Duke U., Gurney Harris Kearns Fellow. 1978-81; Andrew Mellon Diss. Fellow. 1983-84; Brand Blanchard Fac. Fellow 1988-89; NEH Res. Grant for Coll. Tchr. 1992-93; ACLS grant 1992-93. Mem: AAR 1987-; SBL 1989-; CBA; AJS. Rec: Running, swimming, knitting, ballroom dancing. Addr: (o) Swarthmore Coll., Dept. of Religion, 500 College Ave., Swarthmore, PA 19081 215-328-8054; (h) 316 Ogden Ave., Swarthmore, PA 19081 215-543-0724.

LEVINE, Lee I. A., b. Bangor, Maine, February 1, 1939, s. of Harry & Irene, m. Mira, chil: David; Elana; Talya; Dafna. Educ: Columbia U., BA 1961, MA 1966, PhD 1970; Jewish Theol. Sem., BHL 1961, MHL 1963, Rabbinic Ord. 1965. Emp: Jewish Theol. Sem., 1967-71 Instr.; Hebrew U. of Jerusalem, 1971- Prof.; Sem. of Judaic Stud., 1987- Dean & Dir. Excv: Caesarea, 1975, 1976 Co-Dir.; Synagogue at Horvat Ammudim, 1979 Dir. Spec: Archaeology, Apocrypha and Post-biblical Studies. Pub: "Judaism from the Destruction of Jerusalem to the End of the Second Jewish Revolt: 70-135 C.E." in *Christianity and Rabbinic Judaism* (BAS, 1992); "The Sages and the Synagogue in Late Antiquity: The Evidence of the Galilee" in *The Galilee in Late Antiquity*, ed. (1992); "The Interior of the Ancient Synagogue and its Furnishings: From Communal Center to 'Lesser Sanctuary'" *Cathedra* 60 (1990); *The Rabbinic Class of Roman Palestine in Late Antiquity* (Jewish Theol. Sem., 1989); *Ancient Synagogues Revealed* (IES, 1981); "R. Simeon bar Yohai and the Purification of Tiberias" *HUCA* 49 (1978); *Caesarea under Roman Rule* (Brill, 1975);

Roman Caesarea: An Archaeological-Topographical Study (Hebrew U.P., 1975); and others. Awd: Guggenheim Found., Fellow 1976-77; Harvard U., Ctr. for Jewish Res., Fellow 1986-87; Rockefeller Found., Bellagio Ctr., Fellow 1991. Mem: IES 1972-; Israel Hist. Soc. 1975-; SBL 1978-; WUJS 1989-. Addr: (o) Hebrew U., Institute of Archaeology, Jerusalem 91905, Israel 02-882-436; (h) 27 Mevo Hamaavaq, Jerusalem 97877, Israel 02-813164.

LEVINSON, Bernard M., b. S Porcupine, ON, Canada, June 13, 1952, s. of Ulysses & Molly. Educ: York U., BA 1974; McMaster U., MA 1978; Brandeis U., PhD 1985. Emp: Middlebury Coll., 1984 Vis. Lect.; U. of Wash., 1987-88 Stroum Fellow in Advanced Jewish Stud.; Pa. State U., 1988-90 Instr., Relig. Stud. Prog.; Ind. U., 1990- Asst. Prof., Near East. Lang. & Cultures. Spec: Hebrew Bible, Semitic Languages, Texts and Epigraphy. Pub: "The Right Coralé: From the Poetics of Biblical Narrative to the Hermeneutics of the Hebrew Bible" in *'Not in Heaven': Coherence; and Complexity in Biblical Narrative* (Indiana U.P., 1991); "Calum M. Carmichael's Approach to the Laws of Deuteronomy" *HTR* 83 (1990). Mem: AOS; AJS; CSBS; SBL. Addr: (o) Indiana U., Goodbody Hall 216, Near Eastern Languages & Cultures, Bloomington, IN 47405 812-855-4323.

LEVISON, John R., b. Glen Cove, NY, August 8, 1956, s. of John & Norma (Buffington), m. Priscilla (Pope), chil: Chloe. Educ: Wheaton Coll., Ill., BA 1978; Cambridge U., BA 1980, MA 1984; Duke U., PhD 1985. Emp: Ohio North. U., 1984-85 Instr., Relig.; U. of St. Andrews, St. Mary's Coll., 1985-86 Hon. Vis. Lect.; St. Paul Sch. of Theol., 1986-89 Asst. Prof., NT; N Park Coll., 1989- Asst. Prof., 1993- Assoc. Prof., Bibl. Stud. Spec: New Testament, Apocrypha and Post-biblical Studies. Pub: *Jesus in Global Contexts*, co-auth. (Westminster/John Knox, 1992); "The Use of the New Testament in Third World Christologies," co-auth. *Bibl. Res.* 37 (1992); "2 Apoc. Bar. 42:1-52:7 and the Apocalyptic Dimension of Colossans 3:1-6" *JBL* 108 (1989); "The Exoneration of Eve in the Apocalypse of Moses 15-30" *JSJ* 20 (1989); *Portraits of Adam in Early Judaism: From Sirach to 2 Baruch* (JSOT, 1988); "Responsible Initiative in Matthew 5:21-48" *ExpTim* 98 (1987); "Is Eve to Blame? A Contextual Analysis of Sirach 25:24" *CBQ* 47 (1985); and others. Awd: Alexander von Humbolt Res. Fellow. 1992; NEH, Summer Sem. 1992. Mem: SBL 1980-. Rec: Travel, hiking, parenting. Addr: (o) North Park College, Dept. of Religion, 3225 W Foster Ave., Chicago, IL 60625 312-583-2700.

LEVY, Thomas E., b. N Hollywood, CA, September 11, 1953, s. of Howard & Phyllis, m. Alina Maria (Nazareth), chil: Ben Howard; Gil Asher. Educ: U. of Ariz., BA, Anthrop. 1975; U. of Sheffield, UK, PhD, Arch. & Prehist. 1981. Emp: Negev Mus., 1981-85 Ethnographic Cur.; W.F. Albright Inst. of Arch. Res., ASOR,

Jerusalem, 1985-87 Asst. Dir.; Nelson Gleuck Sch. of Bibl. Arch., HUC-Jewish Inst. of Relig., 1987-92 Asst. Dir.; U. of Calif., San Diego, 1992- Asst. Prof., Dept. of Anthrop. & Judaic Stud. Excv: Shiqmim, Negev Desert, 1982-89 Prin. Investigator; Gilat, Negev Desert, 1990-92 Prin. Investigator; Ethnoarch. Res. Proj., North. Cameroon, 1988-91 Co-Dir. Spec: Archaeology. Pub: *Spatial Boundaries and Social Dynamics— Case Studies from Agrarian Societies*, co-ed., Intl. Mon. in Prehist. (1993); *Eretz-Israel*, co-auth. 23 (IES, 1992); "Transhumance, Subsistence, and Social Evolution in the Northern Negev Dersert" in *Pastoralism in the Levant: Archaeological Materials in Anthropological Perspective* (Prehistory, 1992); "Subterranean Settlement and Adaptation in the Northern Negev Desert, ca. 4500-3700 B.C." *Res. & Exploration* 7 (1991); "Prehistoric Metalworking in the Southern Levant: Archaeometallurgical and Social Perspectives," co-auth. *World Arch.* 20 (1989); *Shiqmim I— Studies Concerning Chalcolithic Societies in the Northern Negev Desert, Israel (1982-1984)*, 2 vol., British Arch. Reports 356 (1987); "Archaeological Sources for the History of Palestine—The Chalcolithic Period" *BA* 49 (1986); "The Emergence of Specialized Pastoralism in the Southern Levant" *World Arch.* 15 (1983); and others. Awd: W.F. Albright Inst. of Arch. Res., NEH Post-Doc. Fellow. 1982-83; Natl. Geog. Soc., Res. Grant 1982, 1983, 1984, 1989, 1992; NEH Matching Grant 1987, 1989, 1992. Mem: ASOR; Israel Arch. Coun. Rec: Camping, hiking, scuba diving. Addr: (o) U. of California, San Diego, Dept. of Anthropology, 9500 Gilman Dr., La Jolla, CA 92093.

LEWIS, Arthur H., b. Kalamazoo, MI, August 25, 1923, s. of Arthur & Gertrude (Duddles), m. Helen (Drake), chil: Jonathan Drake; Jewel Ann; Theodore Gordon. Educ: Wheaton Coll., BA 1947; Gordon Div. Sch., BD 1950; Harvard Grad. Sch., MA 1951; Brandeis U., PhD 1966. Emp: Gordon Coll., 1947-51 Asst. Prof.; Seminario Teologico de Leiria, Portugal, 1952-64 Prof.; Bethel Coll., 1966-88 Prof. Spec: Archaeology, Hebrew Bible, New Testament, Semitic Languages, Texts and Epigraphy. Pub: "The New Birth under the Old Covenant" *EQ* (1984); "Israel in New Testament Prophecy" *Standard* (1982); *Judges/Ruth: A Commentary* (Moody, 1979); "Resurgent Semitisms in New Testament Theology" *JETS* (1974); "The Localization of the Garden of Eden" *JETS* (1968); and others. Mem: SBL 1951-; ETS 1952-, Pres. 1974. Addr: (h) 1282 Silverthom Dr., St. Paul, MN 55126.

LEWIS, Jack P., b. Midlothian, TX, March 19, 1919, s. of Pearl & Anna (Holland), m. Annie May (Alston), chil: John; Jerry. Educ: Abilene Christian U., BA 1941; Sam Houston State Teachers' U., MA 1944; Harvard Div. Sch., STB 1947; Harvard U., PhD 1951; Hebrew Union Coll., PhD 1962. Emp: Harding U., Harding Grad. Sch. of Relig., 1954- Prof., Bible; U. Christian Ctr., 1962- Bd. of Dir.; *Restoration Quar.*, 1957- Ed. Bd.; West

Texas State U., 1983 Williston Lect. Excv: Tell Suwwanet Eth-Thaniya, 1968 Field Supr. Spec: Archaeology, Hebrew Bible, New Testament. Pub: "William Francis Lynch, Explorer of the Dead Sea" *NEAS Bull.* 37 (1992); "James Turner Barclay, Explorer of Nineteenth-Century Jerusalem" *BA* 51 (1988); "The Text of the New Testament" *Restoration Quar.* 27 (1984); "Noah and the Flood in Jewish, Christian and Muslim Tradition" *BA* 47 (1984); *Archaeological Backgrounds to Bible People* (Baker, 1981); *Archaeology and the Bible* (Bibl. Res., 1975). Awd: ASOR, Thayer Fellow 1967-68; Albright Inst. of Arch. Res., Hon. Sr. Fellow 1983-84. Mem: AAR; SBL; ETS, Chair, South. sect. 1969-70; NAPH, Exec. Coun. 1975-. Rec: Travel, woodwork, writing. Addr: (o) 1000 Cherry Rd., Memphis, TN 38117 901-761-1350; (h) 1132 S Perkins Rd., Memphis, TN 38117 901-683-1678.

LEWIS, Joe O., b. Waco, TX, October 5, 1935, s. of Ollin & Juanita, m. Shirley (Pigg), chil: Paul; Page. Educ: South. Bapt. Theol. Sem., PhD 1965. Emp: Bapt. Ch., 1959-65 Pastor; South. Bapt. Theol. Sem., 1965-66 Instr., OT & Hebrew; Cumberland Coll., 1966-68 Assoc. Prof.; Georgetown Coll., 1968-, 1974-80 Chmn. of Relig. Dept., 1975-80, 1992- Prof., 1980-1992 Acad. Dean. Spec: Hebrew Bible. Pub: *I & II Samuel, I Chronicles*, Layman's Bible Book Comm. vol. 5 (Broadman, 1980); "Yahwistic Kerygma in the Jacob Narratives" *Perspectives in Relig. Stud.* 5 (1978); "Genesis 32:23-33, Seeing a Hidden God" in *SBL Proceedings* vol. 2 (1972); and others. Mem: SBL; NABPR, Pres 1977-78. Rec: Tennis, art. Addr: (o) Georgetown College, Georgetown, KY 40324 502-863-8011; (h) 1003 Arapaho Trail, Georgetown, KY 40324 502-863-2573.

LEWIS, Theodore J., b. Green Bay, WI, September 21, 1956, s. of Harland R. & Jean M., m. Anita M., chil: Eric T.; Meghan C.; Hannah E. Educ: U. Wis.-Madison, BA, Hebrew & Semitic Stud. 1978, MA 1979; Harvard U., PhD, Near East. Lang. & Civ. 1986. Emp: Harvard U., 1983-85 Teaching Fellow, 1986-87 Vis. Lect.; U. of Ga., 1987-92 Asst. Prof., 1992- Assoc. Prof.; *Hebrew Ann. Rev.*, 1990- Ed.; SBL, 1993- Co-Chair, Hebrew Scriptures & Cognate Lit. Sect. Spec: Hebrew Bible, Semitic Languages, Texts and Epigraphy. Pub: "The Textual History of the Song of Hannah: 1 Samuel 2:1-10" *VT* (1993); "Israelite Religion" in *The Oxford Companion to the Bible* (1993); articles in *ABD* (Doubleday, 1992); "The Ancestral Estate (nahalat elohim) in 2 Samuel 14:16" *JBL* 110 (1991); *Cults of the Dead in Ancient Israel and Ugarit* (Scholars, 1989); "Death Cult Imagery in Isaiah 57" *Hebrew Ann. Rev.* 11 (1987); "Notes on Some Problems in the Aramaic Text of The Hadd-Yith'i Bilingual," co-auth. *BASOR* 259 (1985). Awd: Inst. for Intl. Educ., ITT Intl. Fellow. to Israel 1979-80; U. of Ga., Jr. Fac. Res. Awd. 1989, 1992, Sr. Fac. Res. Awd. 1993; Sarah H. Moss Fellow. 1992-93. Mem: SBL 1978-; ASOR 1991-; AOS; IOSCS; IBR. Addr: (o) U. of Georgia, Dept. of Religion, 217 Peabody Hall, Athens, GA 30602

706-542-5356; (h) 430 Ponderosa Dr., Athens, GA 30605 706-353-8857.

LIAO, Paul S. H., b. Kobe, Japan, November 11, 1937, s. of Joseph & Mary (Hwang), m. Janice, chil: Irene; Isaac. Educ: Faith Theol. Sem., STM 1968; Hartford Sem. Found., PhD 1973. Emp: Taiwan Theol. Coll., 1976-79 Dean of Student Affairs, 1979-82 Dean of Acad. Affairs, 1980-Prof. NT, 1981-87 VP, 1987-, Pres.; *Taiwan Jour. of Theol.*, 1979-82, 1984-87, Founding Ed. Spec: New Testament. Pub: *Rapid Learning of Biblical Greek* (Yeang Wang, 1993); *Comentary on Matthew* (Chinese Christian Lit. Coun., 1986); *New Tesatament Theology* vol. 1 (Yeang Wang, 1984); "The Parables of Jesus: A Contemporary Hermeneutical Problem" *Taiwan Jour. of Theol.* 2 (1980); and others. Rec: Sports. Addr: (o) Taiwan Theological College & Seminary, 20, Lane 2, Sec 2, Yang Teh Ta Rd., Shihlin, Tapei, Taiwan 02-882-2370.

LIBACKYJ, Anfir, b. Mosuriwci, Ukraine, September 8, 1926, s. of Serhij & Kateryna (Slowinskyj). Educ: Liege U., Belgium, MSc 1954; Polytechnic Inst. of Brooklyn, PhD 1965; Union Theol. Sem., MDiv 1977. Emp: Polytechnic Inst. of Brooklyn, 1959-63 Res. Fellow; E.I. du Pont de Nemours Co., 1963-67 Res. Sci.; N.Y. Inst. of Tech., 1968-73 Adj. & Asst. Prof.; St. Sophia Sem., 1977- Prof. Spec: Apocrypha and Post-biblical Studies. Pub: *The Ancient Monasteries of Kiev Rus* (Vantage, 1978). Mem: AAR 1970-; Amer. Assn. of U. Prof. 1973-. Addr: (h) 84, 22, 107 Ave., Jamaica, NY 11417 718-641-3434.

LIEBERMAN, Stephen J., b. Minneapolis, MN, March 21, 1943, s. of Martin & Selma, m. Joelle (Wallach). Educ: U. of Minn., AB 1963; Harvard U., PhD 1972. Emp: N.Y. U., 1971-75 Assoc. Prof.; U. of Pa., U. Mus., 1976-79 Res. Specialist; Jewish Theol. Sem. of Amer., 1983-84 Vis. Assoc. Prof.; Dropsie Coll., 1982-86 Prof. Spec: Hebrew Bible, Mesopotamian Studies, Semitic Languages, Texts and Epigraphy. Pub: "The Years of Damiqilishu, King of Isin" *Revue d'Assyriologie et d'Archeologie Orientale* (1983); "Of Clay Pebbles, Hollow Clay Balls and Writing: A Sumerian View" *Amer. Jour. of Arch.* (1980); "Response On the Historical Periods of the Hebrew Language" in *Jewish Languages: Themes and Variations* (1978); *The Sumerian Loanwords in Old-Babylonian Akkadian* (Scholars, 1977); and others. Awd: Guggenheim Fellow 1979-80. Mem: SBL; Amer. Hist. Assn.; AOS; ASOR. Rec: Piano. Addr: (o) P.O. Box 28824, Philadelphia, PA 19151 215-667-1830.

LIEBOWITZ, Harold A., March 16, 1934, s. of Samuel & Nettie, m. Judith, chil: Esther; Naomi; Deborah; Dina. Educ: Yeshiva U., BA 1955; N.Y. U., Inst. of Fine Arts, MA 1965; U. of Pa., PhD 1972. Emp: Duke U., 1972-73; Bar Ilan U., 1973-74, 1984-85; U. of Texas at Austin, 1974-. Excv: Khirbet Shema, 1972 Field Supr.; Tel Yin'am, 1976-77, 1979-81, 1983-89 Dir.; Beit Gan, 1988-89, 1992. Spec: Archaeology, Hebrew Bible, Egyptology. Pub: "Early Bronze Age IV Tombs at Yavne'el" *'Atiqot* 21 (1992); "Two Assyrianizing Ivories from Megiddo" in *Proceedings of the Tenth World Congress of Jewish Studies* (1990); *Terra Cotta Figurines and Model Vehicles* (Undena, 1988); "Late Bronze Age Ivory Working in Palestine" *BASOR* 265 (1987); "The Dawn of Iron Smelting in Palestine: The Late Bronze Age Smelter at Tel Yin'am, Preliminary Report" co-auth. *JFA* 7 (1984); "Excavations at Tel Yin'am: 1976 and 1977 Seasons of Excavation: Preliminary Report" *BASOR* 241 (1981); *Daily Life in Ancient Israel* (Yeshiva U., 1980); "Military and Feast Scenes in Late Bronze Age Palestinian Ivories" *IEJ* 30 (1980); and others. Mem: IES; ASOR. Rec: Reading, travel, painting, walking, gardening. Addr: (o) U. of Texas at Austin, 2601 University Ave., Austin, TX 78712 512-471-1365; (h) 3102 Carlisle Dr., Austin, TX 78731 512-453-7417.

LIEU, Judith M., m. Samuel, chil: Esther. Educ: Durham U., BA 1972, MA 1973; Birmingham U., PhD 1980. Emp: Queen's Coll., Birmingham, 1981-84 Lect., Bibl. Stud.; King's Coll., London, 1985- Lect., Christian Origins & Early Judaism. Spec: New Testament, Apocrypha and Post-biblical Studies. Pub: *The Jews Among Pagans and Christians*, co-ed. (Routledge, 1992); *The Theology of the Johannine Epistles* (Cambridge U.P., 1991); "Blindness in the Johannine Tradition" *NTS* 34 (1988); "Epiphanius on the Scribes and Pharisees" *JTS* 39 (1988); *The Second and Third Epistles of John* (T & T Clark, 1986); "'Grace to You and Peace': The Apostolic Greeting" *BJRL* 68 (1985); "Authority to Become Children of God" *NT* 23 (1981). Mem: SOTS; SNTS; Brit. Assn. for Jewish Stud. Rec: Cycling. Addr: (o) Kings College London, Dept. of Theology & Religious Studies, Strand, London W62R 2LS, England 071-873-2467.

LILLIE, Betty Jane, b. Cincinnati, OH, April 11, 1926, d. of Harrison & Hilda Rose. Educ: Coll. of Mt. St. Joseph, BS, Ed. 1955, BA 1961; Providence Coll., MA, Theol. 1967, MA, Bibl. Stud. 1975; Hebrew Union Coll., PhD 1982. Emp: Providence Coll., 1979-86 Adj. Faculty; Coll. of Mt. St. Joseph, 1980 Adj. Faculty; Mt. St. Mary Sem., 1982- Faculty; United Theol. Sem., 1983-84 Adj. Faculty; U. of Cincinnati, 1984- Lect. Spec: Hebrew Bible, New Testament, Apocrypha and Post-biblical Studies. Pub: *A History of the Scholarship on the Wisdom of Solomon from the Nineteenth Century to Our Time* Microfilms Intl., 1983); and others. Mem: CBA 1982-; SBL 1984-; East. Great Lakes Bibl. Soc. 1985-. Addr: (o) Athenaeum of Ohio/Mt. St. Mary's Seminary, 6616 Beechmont Ave., Cincinnati, OH 45230 513-231-2223; (h) 2704 Cypress Way, #3, Cincinnati, OH 45212-1773 513-531-1309.

LIM, Timothy H., April 24, 1960, s. of Benjamin & Josephine, m. Laura Adrienne (Perler), chil: Jonathan Christopher. Educ: U. of Brit. Columbia, BA 1982; Regent Coll., MCS 1985; Macquarie U., Dip., Anc. Hist. 1986; U. of Oxford, MPhil, Jewish Stud. 1988, DPhil, Jewish Stud. 1991. Emp: U. of Oxford, Oriental Inst., 1991- Kennicott Hebrew Fellow; Oxford Ctr. for Postgrad. Hebrew Stud., 1991- Jr. Res. Fellow. Spec: Hebrew Bible, New Testament, Apocrypha and Post-biblical Studies. Pub: "A Chronology of the Flood Story from Qumran" *JJS* (1992); "11 QMelch, Luke 4 and the Dying Messiah" *JJS* 43 (1992); "Eschatological Orientation and the Alteration of Scripture in the Habakkuk Pesher" *JNES* 49 (1990); "Nevertheless these were men of piety (Sir xliv 10)" *VT* 38/3 (1988); "Not in Persuasive Words of Wisdom, But in the Demonstration of the Spirit and Power" *NT* 29 (1987); and others. Awd: Regent Coll., Bd. of Governors' Prize 1985; Comm. of Vice Chancellors & Prin. of the U. of the United Kindgom, Overseas Res. Scheme Awd. 1986-89; Social Sci. & Hum. Res. Coun. of Canada, Doc. Fellow. 1988-90; Hebrew U., Jerusalem, Lady Davis Doc. Fellow. 1989-90; U. of Oxford, Wolfson Coll., Jr. Res. Fellow. 1990-92. Mem: Brit. Assn. for Jewish Stud.; SBL; European Assn. for Jewish Stud.; ASOR; IOSCS. Rec: Squash, music. Addr: (o) U. of Oxford, St. Hugh's College, Oxford OX2 6LE, England 0865-274981.

LIMBURG, James W., b. Redwood Falls, MN, March 2, 1935, s. of Stanley & Ella, m. Martha (Ylvisaker), chil: Kristi; David; Mark; Paul. Educ: Luther Theol. Sem., BD 1961; Union Theol. Sem., ThM 1962, ThD 1969. Emp: Augustana Coll., 1962-78 Prof.; Luther NW Theol. Sem., 1978- Prof. Spec: Hebrew Bible. Pub: "The Responsibility of Royalty: Genesis 1-11 and the Core of the Earth" *Word & World* (1991); "Jonah and the Whale, Through the Eyes of Artists" *BR* 6/4 (1990); *Hosea—Micah. Interpretation: A Bible Commentary for Teaching and Preaching* (John Knox, 1988); *Psalms for Sojourners* (Augsburg, 1986); "Psalm 121: A Psalm for Sojourners" *Word & World* (1985); *Old Stories for a New Time* (John Knox, 1983). Awd: Luther Coll., Disting. Service Awd. 1978. Mem: SBL. Rec: Fishing, sailing, trombone. Addr: (o) Luther Northwestern Seminary, 2481 Como Ave., St. Paul, MN 55108 612-641-3460; (h) 152 Windsor Ct., New Brighton, MN 55112.

LINCOLN, Andrew T., b. Wolverhampton, England, May 17, 1944, s. of Arnold & Margaret (Cooper), chil: David G.; Paul M. Educ: Trinity Coll., Cambridge, BA 1966, PhD 1974; Westminster Theol. Sem., BD 1971. Emp: Gordon-Conwell Theol. Sem., 1975-79 Asst. Prof., NT; St. John's Coll., England, 1979-85 Lect., NT; U. of Nottingham, 1982-83 Lect.; U. of Sheffield, 1985- Lect., NT. Spec: New Testament. Pub: *The Theology of the Late Pauline Letters* (Cambridge U.P., 1993); *Ephesians*, Word Bibl. Comm. 42 (Word, 1990); "The Promise and the Failure: Mark 16:7,8" *JBL*

108 (1989); "Theology and History in the Interpretation of Luke's Pentecost" *ExpTim* (1985); "Ephesians 2:8-10: A Summary of Paul's Theology?" *CBQ* (1983); *From Sabbath to Lord's Day*, contb. (Paternoster, 1982); "The Use of the Old Testament in Ephesians" *JSNT* (1982); *Paradise Now and Not Yet* (Cambridge U.P., 1981); and others. Mem: Tyndale Fellow 1973; SBL 1975-; SNTS 1981-. Rec: Cricket, badminton, music. Addr: (o) U. of Sheffield, Dept. of Biblical Studies, Sheffield S10 2TN, England 0742-76855; (h) 31 Elmore Rd., Sheffield S10 1BY, England 0742-678697.

LIND, Millard C., b. Bakersfield, CA, October 10, 1918, s. of Norman & Sarah, m. Miriam (Sieber), chil: Dan; Jonathan; Timothy; Matthew; James; Sarah; Dirk. Educ: Goshen Bibl. Sem., BD 1947; Pittsburgh-Xenia Theol. Sem., ThM 1955; Pittsburgh Theol. Sem., ThD 1965. Emp: Hopewell Mennonite Ch., 1943-47 Pastor; Mennonite Publ. House, 1947-60 Ed.; *Christian Living*, 1955-60 Ed.; Goshen Bibl. Sem., 1959- Prof. Spec: New Testament. Pub: *The Revised Standard Version, An Examination and Evaluation* (Herald, 1953); *Yahweh is A Warrior* (Herald, 1980); "Hosea 5:8-6:6" *Interpretation* (1984); *Monotheism, Power, Justice: Collected Old Testament Essays* (Inst. of Mennonite Stud., 1990); and others. Mem: SBL 1960-; CSBR 1960-; ASOR. Rec: Reading, walking, writing. Addr: (o) AMBS, 3003 Benham Ave., Elkhard, IN 46517 219-295-3726; (h) 1123 S Eighth St., Goshen, IN 46526 219-533-6098.

LINDEMANN, Andreas, b. Leer, Ostfriesland, October 18, 1943, s. of Renate & Rolf, m. Erdmute (Hartel), chil: David. Educ: U. Gottingen, ThD 1975, Habil. NT 1977. Emp: U. Gottingen, 1974-78 Wiss. Asst.; Kirchliche Hochschule Bethel, 1978- Prof., NT; *Handbuch zum NT*, 1983- Ed; *NTS*, 1992- Ed. Bd. Spec: New Testament. Pub: *Die Clemensbriefe* (Mohr, 1992); "Paul in the Writings of the Apostolic Fathers" in *Paul and the Legacies of Paul* (1990); *Interpreting the New Testament*, co-auth. (Hendrickson, 1988); "Erwagungen zum Problem einer 'Theologie der Synoptischen Evangelien'" *ZNW* 77 (1986); *Der Epheserbrief*, TVZ (1985); "Literaturbericht zu den Synoptischen Evangelien 1978-83" *Theol. Rundschau* 49 (1984); *Der Kolosserbrief*, TVZ (1983); "Zur Gleichnisinterpretation im Thomas-Evangelium" *ZNW* 71 (1980); and others. Mem: SNTS 1978-; Wiss. Gesellschaft fur Theol. 1978-. Rec: Stamp collecting. Addr: (o) Kirchliche Hochschule Bethel, PO Box 130440, D-33544 Bielefeld, Germany 0521-144-3948; (h) An der Rehwiese 38, D-33617 Bielefeld, Germany 0521-144-3956.

LINSS, Wilhelm C., b. Erlangen, Germany, March 21, 1926, s. of Hans & Ingeborg, m. Margaret, chil: Camilla; Jeannie; Andrew. Educ: Erlangen U., MDiv 1950; Boston U., ThD 1955. Emp: Gustavus Adolphus Coll., 1954-57 Asst. Prof.; Augsburg Theol. Sem., 1954-57 Instr.; Cen. Luth. Theol. Sem., 1957-67 Prof.; Luth.

Sch. of Theol. at Chicago, 1967- Prof. Spec: New Testament. Pub: "The Lenten Cycle: Series A" *Luth. Quar.* (1974); and others. Mem: SBL 1957-; CSBR 1967-. Rec: Music. Addr: (o) Lutheran School of Theology, 1100 E 55th St., Chicago, IL 60615 312-753-0777; (h) 10534 S Hamilton Ave., Chicago, IL 60643 312-779-7489.

LIPINSKI, Edouard, b. Lodz, Poland, June 18, 1930, s. of Szmul-Hersz & Gabrielle (Beghon). Educ: U. Louvain, MA, Oriental Phil. & Hist. 1960, DD 1962; U. Rome, MA 1963, PhD, Bibl. Sci. 1964. Emp: U. of Louvain, 1967- Ord. Prof. Spec: Hebrew Bible, Semitic Languages, Texts and Epigraphy. Pub: "Les Japhétites selon Gen 10,2-4 et 1 Chr 1,5-7" *ZAH* (1990); "The Syro-Palestinian Iconography of Woman and Goddess" *IEJ* (1986); *Recherches Archéologiques en Israël* (Peeters, 1984); *Studies in Aramaic Inscriptions and Onomastics* (Leuven U.P., 1975); "Healer" *AION* (1973); *La Royauté de Yahwé dans la poésie et le culte de l'Ancien Israel* (Paleis der Acad., 1965, 1968); *Le Poeme royal du Psaume 89* (Gabalda, 1967); and others. Awd: Belgian Royal Acad., Prize 1963. Rec: Collector. Addr: (o) Blijde Inkomststraat 21, B-3000 Leuven, Belgium 016-284936; (h) Adolphe Lacomblelaan 50/11, B-1040 Brussels, Belgium 02-7361347.

LIVINGSTON, George H., b. Russell, IA, July 27, 1916, s. of George & Clara (Baker), m. Maria (Saarloos), chil: Burton; Nellie; David. Educ: Asbury Theol. Sem., BD 1948; Drew U., PhD 1955. Emp: Wessington Springs Coll., 1951-53 Dean; Asbury Theol. Sem., 1953-87 Prof., OT, 1987- Prof. Emeritus; Inst. of Holy Land Stud., Jerusalem, 1959 Dir.; Central Coll., 1982 Staley Lect. Excv: Ai, West Bank, Israel, 1966 & 1968 Area Supr.; Tell Qasile, Israel, 1972 Area Supr. Spec: Archaeology, Hebrew Bible, Semitic Languages, Texts and Epigraphy. Pub: *The Pentateuch in its Cultural Environment* (Baker, 1972); and others. Mem: AAR 1955-87; SBL 1955-87; ETS 1970-89; NAPH 1970-89. Rec: Fishing, woodworking. Addr: (o) Asbury Theological Seminary, Wilmore, KY 40390 606-858-3581; (h) 502 Bellvue Ext., Wilmore, KY 40390 606-858-3070.

LJUNGMAN, Henrik, b. Goteborg, Sweden, July 28, 1917, s. of Gustaf & Lotten (Cullberg), m. Anna-Elisabeth (Nygren), chil: Kristina; Anders; Ragnhild; Maria; Helena; Lars. Educ: Lund U., BD 1941, MA 1943, Lic. 1947, ThD 1950. Emp: Ch. of Sweden, 1943- Min.; Lund U., 1951- Docent, NT Exegesis, 1951-58 Sr. Lect., 1957 Acting Prof.; 1958- Parish clergyman; Karlstad, 1972-82 Domprost, 1982- Domprost Emeritus. Spec: New Testament. Pub: *Sifre Deuteronomium übersetzt und erklärt von Hans Bietenhard*, co-auth., Judaica & Christiana 8 (Lang, 1984); *Pistis. A Study of Its Presuppositions and Its Meaning in Pauline Use* (Gleerup, 1964); *Das Gesetz erfüllen. Matt. 5,17 ff. und 3,15 untersucht* (Gleerup, 1954); *Guds bärmhartighet och dom. Fariseernas lära om de*

två "matten" (Gleerup, 1950). Mem: SNTS 1956-. Rec: Books, sports. Addr: (h) Varvädersvägen 6 A, S 22227 Lund, Sweden 046-151982.

LOADER, William R. G., b. Auckland, New Zealand, January 6, 1944, s. of Nelson & Elizabeth, m. Gisela, chil: Stefanie; Christopher. Educ: U. of Auckland, BA 1966; U. of Otago, BD 1969; Johannes Gutenberg U., Mainz Drtheol 1972. Emp: Auckland, 1968-78 Meth. Min.; St. Johns Coll., New Zealand, 1973-78 Lect.; Uniting Ch. in Australia, 1978- Lect. NT. Spec: New Testament. Pub: *The Christology of the Fourth Gospel: Structure and Issues* (Lang, 1992); *The Johannine Epistles* (Epworth, 1992); "John 1:51 and 'the greater things' of Johannine Christology" in *Anfeange der Christologie*, FS fuer F. Hahn (Vandenhoeck & Ruprecht, 1991); "Jesus and the Rogue in Luke 16:1-8A. The Parable of the Unjust Steward" *RB* (1989); "The Central Structure of Johannine Christology" *NTS* 1984; "Son of David, Blindness, Possession, and Duality in Matthew" *CBQ* (1982); *Sohn und Hoherpriester: Eine traditionsgeschichtliche Untersuchung zur Christologie des Hebraeerbriefes* (Neukirchen, 1981); and others. Mem: SBL; Australian/New Zealand Soc. for Theol. Stud.; SNTS. Rec: Music, gardening. Addr: (o) St. Columba College, Perth Theological Hall, Stirling Hwy., Nedlands WA 6009, Australia 09-386-8878; (h) 37 Eastwood Way, Hamersley WA 6022, Australia 09-447-4994.

LOEHR, Gebhard, b. Eitorf/Sieg, April 3, 1958, s. of Martin & Marianne, m. Heike. Educ: U. Goettingen, MA, Dip.Theol. 1986, PhD 1989. Spec: New Testament. Pub: *Das Problem des Einen und Vielen in Platons "Philebos,"* Hypomnemata 93 (Vandenhoeck & Ruprecht, 1990); "1. Thess. 4,15-17: Das 'Herrenwort,'" *ZNW* 71 (1980); and others. Mem: Gesellschaft fur analytische Phil. 1991-; AAR; SBL. Rec: Class. music, lit. Addr: (o) U. Goettingen, Platz der Goettinger, Sieben 2 D-3400 Goettingen, Germany 0551-397132; (h) Steinweg 5, D-3406 Bovenden, Germany 0551-83005.

LOH, I-Jin, b. Taiwan, Republic of China, January 16, 1935, s. of Sian Loh & Bin Ang, m. Lucy, chil: Theodore; Grace. Educ: Princeton Theol. Sem., PhD, NT 1968. Emp: 1958-60 Min.; Taiwan Theol. Coll., 1968-71 Dean, Assoc. Prof.; SE Asia Grad. Sch. of Theol., 1968-71 Taiwan Area Dean; Amer. Bible Soc., 1971-78 Trans. Res. Assoc.; United Bible Soc., 1974- Trans. Cons., Asia Pacific Reg., 1978- Trans. Coord. Spec: New Testament. Pub: *A Concise Greek-Chinese Dictionary of New Testament*, ed. (United Bible Soc., 1989); "Which Possum to Catch? Further Thoughts on a Hermeneutical Approach to Study Bibles" *Current Trends in Scripture Trans.* (1988); "Today's Chinese Version Luke—a Study Edition" *Current Trends in Scripture Trans.* (1985); *Today's Chinese Version Bible*, co-trans.

(United Bible Soc., 1981); *A Translator's Handbook on Paul's Letter to the Philippians*, co-auth. (United Bible Soc., 1977); *Today's Taiwanese Version, New Testament, co-trans.* (Bible Soc. in Rep. of China, 1972); and others. Mem: SBL 1971-. Addr: (o) 7/F., No. 18, Alley 14, Lane 283, Roosevelt Rd., Sect. 3, Taipei, Taiwan; (h) Apt. 3, 6/F, No. 14, Alley 14, Ln. 283, Roosevelt Rd., Sect. 3, Taipei, Taiwan.

LOHFINK, Norbert F., b. Frankfurt a.M., July 28, 1928, s. of Franz A. & Maria. Educ: Berchmanskolleg, Munchen, PhL 1953; Hochschule St. Georgen, Frankfurt, ThL 1957; Pont. Bibl. Inst., Rome, SSD 1962. Emp: St. Georgen Sch. of Theol., 1962-66, 1970- Prof.; Pont. Bibl. Inst., 1966-70 Prof. Spec: Hebrew Bible. Pub: "Der Begriff *Bund* in der biblischen Theologie" *ThPh* 66 (1991); "Poverty in the Laws of the ANE and of the Bible" *ThSt* 52 (1991); *The Covenant Never Revoked* (Paulist, 1991); *Die Vaeter Israels im Deuteronomium*, OBO 111 (Universitaetsverlag, 1991); *Studien zum Deuteronomium und zurdeuteronomistischen Literatur*, 2 vol. (Kath. Bibelwerk, 1990, 1991); "Welches Orakel gab den Davididen Dauev?" in *Lingering over Words: Studies in Honor of W.L. Moran* (Scholars, 1990); *Lobgesgaenge der Armen*, SBS 143 (Kath. Bibelwerk, 1990); "2 Koen 23,3 und Dtn 6,17" *Biblica* 71 (1990); "Qoheleth 5:17-19— Revelation by Joy" *CBQ* 52 (1990); and others. Mem: CBA 1969-; SOTS 1972-; SBL 1972-. Addr: (o) Offenbacher Ldstr. 224, D-6000 Frankfurt a.M. 70, Germany 49-69-6061-234.

LONG, Burke O., b. Richmond, VA, September 17, 1938, s. of Eugene & Emily, m. Judith (Holstein), chil: Melissa; Timothy. Educ: Yale U., BD 1964, MA 1966, PhD 1967. Emp:Bowdoin Coll., 1968- Prof.; Emory U., 1982 Prof.; Hebrew U., Jerusalem, 1983-84 Prof., Sr. Fulbright Lect.; *Sources for Bibl. Study*, 1977-85 Ed.; *JBL*, 1978-83 Ed. Bd.;*JSOT*, 1982- Ed. Bd.; *Semeia*, 1983-88 Ed. Bd.; *Writings from the Ancient World*, 1988- Ed. Bd. Spec: Hebrew Bible. Pub: *2 Kings* (Eerdmans, 1991); "The 'NEW' Biblical Poetics of Alter and Sternberg" *JSOT* (1991); "Framing Repetitions in Biblical Historiography" *JBL* (1987); *1 Kings with an Introduction to Historical Literature* (Eerdmans, 1984); *Canon and Authority: Essays in Old Testament Religion and Theology*, co-ed. (Fortress, 1977); "Recent Field Studies in Oral Literature and their Bearing on Old Testament Criticism" *VT* (1976); *The Problem of Etiological Narrative in the Old Testament* (de Gruyter, 1968); and others. Mem: SBL 1963-; IOSOT 1974-; WUJS 1974-; Inst. for Antiquity & Christianity 1975-. Rec: Music, antiquing. Addr: (o) Bowdoin College, Dept. of Religion, 38 College St., Brunswick, ME 04011 207-725-3538; (h) 16 McLellan St., Brunswick, ME 04011 207-725-8920.

LONGACRE, Robert E., b. Akron, Ohio, August 13, 1922, s. of William & Sylvia, m.

Gwendolyn M. S., chil: Roberta; William; Stephen; David. Educ: Houghton Coll., BA 1943; U. of Pa., MA 1953, PhD, Linguistics 1955. Emp: Summer Inst. of Linguistics, Mexico, 1947-1972 Field Worker & Cons., 1968- Intl. Linguistic Cons.; U. of Tex. at Arlington, 1972- Prof., Linguistics. Spec: Hebrew Bible. Pub: "Two Hypotheses Regarding Text Generation and Analysis" *Discourse Processes* 12 (1989); *Joseph: A Story of Divine Providence: A Text Theoretical & Text Linguistic Study of Genesis 37 and 39-48* (Eisenbrauns, 1989); "Interpreting Bible Stories" in *Discourse and Literature* (Benjamins, 1985); "The Discourse Structure of the Flood Narrative" *JAAR* 47/1 (1979); and others. Awd: Inst. for Advanced Christian Stud. Awd. 1973; Houghton Coll., DLitt 1979; U. of Tex. at Arlington, Disting. Record of Res. 1990; Recipient of Festschrift vol., *Language in Context: Essays for Robert E. Longacre* 1992. Mem: Linguistic Soc. of Amer.; SBL; Linguistic Assn. of the SW. Rec: Music, poetry, swimming. Addr: (o) U. of Texas at Arlington, Linguistics Program, Arlington, TX 76010 817-273-3133; (h) Summer Institute of Linguistics, 7500 W Camp Wisdom Rd., Dallas, TX 75236 214-709-2457.

LONGENECKER, Richard N., b. Mishawaka, IN, July 21, 1930, s. of Ward & Ruth, m. Frances Lee (Wilson), chil: Elizabeth; David; Bruce. Educ: Wheaton Grad. Sch., MA 1956; U. of Edinburgh, New Coll., Scotland, PhD 1959. Emp: Wheaton Coll., 1960-63 Asst. Prof.; Trinity Evang. Div. Sch., 1963-72 Prof., NT; U. of Toronto, Wycliffe Coll., 1972- Ramsay Armitage Prof. of NT, 1976- Dir. Advanced Degree Stud., St. Michael's Coll., 1976-78; Prof. of Scripture. Excv: Dothan Excvn., 1958 Area Supr. Spec: New Testament. Pub: *Galatians* (Word, 1990); "'Who is the Prophet Talking About?' Some Reflections on the New Testament's Use of the Old" *Themelios* (1987); "The Nature of Paul's Early Eschatology" *NTS* (1985); "The Pedagogical Nature of the Law in Galatians 3:19-4:7" *JETS* (1982); *Acts,* EBC 9 (Zondervan, 1981); *Biblical Exegesis in the Apostolic Period* (Eerdmans, 1975); and others. Mem: SNTS; SBL. Rec: Carpentry, travel, sports. Addr: (o) U. of Toronto, Wycliffe College, Toronto, ON M5S 1H7, Canada 416-979-2870; (h) 34 Johnson St., Niagara-on-the Lake, ON LOS 1JO, Canada 416-468-7298.

LONGSTAFF, Thomas R. W., b. Nashua, NH, October 9, 1935, s. of William & Evelene (Hayes Mulliken), m. Cynthia (Curtis), chil: Thomas; David; Sarah; Anna; William. Educ: U. of Maine, BA 1964; Bangor Theol. Sem., MDiv 1964; Columbia U., PhD 1973. Emp: Meth. Ch., 1960-64 Min.; Bangor Theol. Sem., 1963-64 Lect.; Union Theol. Sem., 1965-69 Tutor; Colby Coll., 1969- Charles A. Dana Prof. of Relig. Stud.; Mass. Inst. of Technology, Ctr. for Materials Res. in Arch. & Ethnology, 1984-85 Vis. Schol.; Harvard U., Semitic Mus., 1991-92 Vis. Schol. Excv: Meiron Excvn. Project, 1977-81 Area Supr.; Sepphoris, 1982- Assoc. Dir.;

Nessana, 1992- Staff Arch. Spec: Archaeology, New Testament. Pub: "Excavations: Sepphoris (Sippori) 1983," co-auth. *IEJ* (1984); "The Women at the Tomb" *NTS* (1981); "Mark and Roger of Hovedon: A Response" *CBQ* (1979); "At the Colloquium's Conclusion" in *Synoptic and Text-Critical Studies 1776-1976*; and others. Awd: Bangor Theol. Sem., Jonathan F. Morris Prize 1961, 1963; Woodrow Wilson Fellow, 1964. Mem: ASOR; CBA; IES. Rec: Skiing, sailing, theater. Addr: (o) Colby College, Waterville, ME 04901 207-872-3150; (h) 39 Pleasant St., Waterville, ME 04901 207-872-6617.

LOPEZ RIVERA, Francisco, b. Guadalajara, November 26, 1938, s. of Francisco Lopez Gonzalez & Luz Maria Rivera De. Educ: Inst. Libre de Filosofia, Lic. Filosofia 1963; Jesuit Inst. of Theol., Theol. Lic. 1972; Pont. Bibl. Inst., Holy Scripture Lic. 1975. Emp: Interdiocesan Sem. of Our Lady of Guadalupe, 1975-77 Prof.; Jesuit Novitiate, Guadalajara, 1977-84 Novice Master; Iberoamericana U., 1985-87 Vis. Prof., OT; Jesuit Inst. of Theol., 1975-77, 1985- Prof., OT, 1986-89 Rector; Mexican Province of the S. J., 1989- Dir. of Formation. Spec: Hebrew Bible. Pub: "Proyecto de Dios y Discernimiento, la perspectiva profética" *Christus* 635-636 (1990); "Los profetas y el conflicto" *Christus* 607-608 (1987); "Narrativa e Historia en la Biblia" *Christus* 591-592 (1985-86); *Biblia y Sociedad* (Centro de Reflexion Teologica, 1977); and others. Mem: SBL 1987-; Assn. de Biblistas de Mexico 1990-. Rec: Music, lit. Addr: (o) Rio Churubusco 434, Col. El Carmen, Coyoacan, 04100 DF, Mexico 5-524-47-42; (h) Seneca 310, Col. Los Morales, 11510, Mexico 5-280-70-75.

LOUBSER, Johannes A., b. Cape Town, South Africa, July 27, 1947, chil: Coenraad; Jacques; Johannes; Sanmari. Educ: MA 1975; DTh 1980. Emp: DR Ch. Min., 1978-89; U. of Zululand, Dept. of Bibliological Stud., 1989- Prof., Dept. Head. Spec: New Testament. Pub: "Winning the Struggle (or How to Treat Heretics) (2 Corinthians 12:1-10)" *Jour. of Theol. for Southern Africa* 75 (1991); "Paulus as Kontekstuele teoloog. 'n Hermeneutiese verkenning van 2 Korintiers 1:3-11" *Ned. Geref. Teologiese Tydskrif* 32 (1991); *A Critical Review of Racial Theology in Southern Africa: The Apartheid Bible* (1991). Awd: Dautsche Akademische Austauschdienst Stipend 1975-76. Mem: NT Soc. of South Africa 1977; SBL 1989-; AAR 1989-. Rec: Hiking, scuba diving. Addr: (o) Private Bag X1001, Kwadlangezwa 3886, South Africa 027-351-93911.

LOVESTAM, O. Evald, b. Lysvik, Sweden, December 7, 1921, s. of Nils & Alma, m. Maj (Ringdahl), chil: Eva M.; K. Monica; N.E. Goeran. Educ: Lund U., Sweden, Cand. Theol. 1944, Lic. Theol. 1946, DD 1950, MA 1953. Emp: Karlstad, 1956-62 Lect., Relig.; Gothenburg, 1966-69 Lect., Relig. & Phil.; Lund

U., 1951, 1958-66 Docent, 1966-69 Res. Docent, 1969-87 Prof., Early Christian Lit. Spec: New Testament. Pub: *Apostlagärningarna* (1988); "Divorce and Remarriage in the New Testament" *The Jewish Law Annual IV* (1981); "The he genea haute Eschatology in Mk 13,30 parr." *ETL* 53 (1980); "Jésus Fils de David chez les Synoptiques" *Studia Theologia* 28 (1974); *Spiritus Blasphemia* (1968); *Spiritual Wakefulness in the New Testament* (1963); "Wunder und Symbolhandlung: Eine Studie über Matth. 14,28-31" *KerDog* 8 (1962); *Son and Saviour* (1961); and others. Mem: SNTS; Jewish Law Assn. Addr: (h) Stora Tomegatan 25, S-223 51 Lund, Sweden 046-121660.

LUC, Alex T., b. South Vietnam, June 6, 1945, s. of Dang & Thuankieu (Phan), m. Trina, chil: Michael; Stephen. Educ: Theol. Coll. of Vietnam, BTh 1972; Trinity Coll., BA; Trinity Evang. Div. Sch., MDiv 1977; U. of Wis., MA 1979, PhD 1982. Emp: Phuoc Au Vien Orphanage Sch., South Vietnam, 1968-70 Prin.; Chinese Christian Alliance Ch., 1969-73 Pastor; Columbia Bib. Sem. & Grad. Sch. of Missions, 1982- Res. Faculty, OT. Spec: Hebrew Bible. Pub: "Isaiah 1 as Structural Introduction" *ZAW* 101 (1989); "The Structure and Message of Job" *China Theol. Jour.* 1 (1985); *Basic Bible Hermeneutics* (AFC, 1984); "A Theology of Ezekiel" *JETS* 26 (1983); and others. Mem: ETS 1981-; SBL 1982-; NAPH 1983-. Rec: Jogging, gardening. Addr: (o) Columbia Bible Seminary, Box 3122, Columbia, SC 29230 803-754-4100; (h) 3550 Bronte Road, Columbia, SC 29210 803-772-3534.

LUDLOW, William L., b. Elyria, OH, February 16, 1905, s. of Linnaeus, m. Cora, chil: David; Martha. Educ: Oberlin Coll., AB 1928, AM 1934, BD 1934; U. of Chicago, PhD 1948. Emp: Oberlin Coll., 1932-34 Prof., Theol.; Muskingum Coll., 1936-73 Prof. Spec: New Testament. Pub: *The Story of Bible Translations* (1990); "Paraphrases on First Corinthians 13" (1958). Awd: AHA, Hon. Life Mem. Mem: Amer. Soc. of Ch. Hist.; SBL. Addr: (h) Box 1346, 527 N 10th St., Cambridge, OH 43725 614-826-4852.

LUEHRMANN, Dieter H., b. Lingen/Ems, Germany, March 13, 1939, s. of Karl & Kaete, m. Renate (Stockhusen), chil: Silke; Susanne; Sonja. Educ: U. Heidelberg, ThD 1964, Ord. Pastor 1965. Emp: U. Heidelberg, 1965-69 Asst. Prof., 1969-74 Docent, Prof.; Bethel Theol. Sem., 1974-82 Prof.; *NTS*, 1978-81 Ed. Bd.; U. Marburg, 1982- Prof., NT; Yale U., 1989 Vis. Prof. Spec: New Testament. Pub: *Galatians* (Fortress, 1992); *Das Markusevangelium* (Mohr/Siebeck, 1987); *Auslegung des Neuen Testaments* (Theologischer Verlag Zurich, 1984); *Kirche, Festschrift fur Guenther Bornkamm zum 75 Geburtstag,* co-ed. (Mohr/Siebeck, 1980). Mem: SNTS 1969-; Wissenschaftliche Gesellschaft fuer Theol. 1975-. Addr: (o) U. Marburg, Fachbereich 05

Evangelische Theologie, Lahntor 3, 35032 Marburg, Germany 06421-284275; (h) Im Hainbach 9, 35043 Marburg-Cyriaxweimar, Germany 06421-31306.

LUKER, Maurice S., Jr., b. Louisville, KY, June 4, 1934, s. of Maurice S. & Bee (Hartley), m. Jean (Knarr), chil: Maurice S., III; Amy (Cloud); Marc Anton. Educ: South. Meth. U., BA 1956; Drew U., BD, Theol., Bible 1959, PhD, Theol., Bible 1968. Emp: Upsala Coll., 1963 Vis. Instr.; Ohio Wesleyan U., 1964-65 Instr.; Emory & Henry Coll., 1965- Prof.; Meth. Ch., 1961-64, 1988-92 Pastor. Excv: Shechem, 1960 Asst. Field Supr.; Gezer, 1968 Staff Mem.; Tell el-Hesi, 1971, 1973, 1975, 1977 Area Supr.; Caesarea Maritima, 1985, 1987 Area Supr., Asst. to Dir. Spec: Archaeology, Hebrew Bible. Pub: *The Figure of Moses in the Plague Traditions* (U. Microfilms, 1968); and others. Mem: ASOR; CBA; SBL. Rec: Reading, travel, tennis, flower gardening. Addr: (o) Emory & Henry College, Emory, VA 24327 703-944-4121; (h) 216 Stonewall Heights, Abingdon, VA 24210 703-628-5063.

LULL, David J., b. Mount Kisko, NY, October 14, 1944, s. of John & Viola, m. Karen. Educ: Perkins Sch. of Theol., BD 1969; Claremont Grad. Sch., PhD 1978. Emp: Ctr. for Process Stud., 1975-81 Project Dir.; Sch. of Theol. at Claremont, 1979 Lect.; Yale U. Div. Sch., 1981- Assoc. Prof., NT & Relig. Stud. Spec: New Testament. Pub: "Salvation History: Theology in 1 Thess, Phlm, Phil, and Gal" in *Pauline Theology* vol. 1 (Fortress, 1991); *Biblical Preaching on the Death of Jesus* (Abingdon, 1989); "'The Law Was Our Pedagogue': A Study in Gal 3:19-25" *JBL* (1986); "The Servant-Benefactor as a Model of Greatness (Luke 22:24-30)" *NT* (1986); "To Set at Liberty: The Challenge of an Inclusive-Language Lectionary" *Reflection* (1985); "What is 'Process Hermeneutics'?" *Process Stud.* (1983); *Old Testament Interpretation from a Process Perspective* (Scholars, 1982); *The Spirit in Galatia: Paul's Interpretation of Pneuma as Divine Power* (Scholars, 1980); and others. Mem: AAR; SBL, Exec. Dir. 1987-. Addr: (o) Society of Biblical Literature 1549 Clairmont Rd., Ste. 204, Decatur, GA 30033 404-636-4744; (h) 2221 Shasta Way NE, Atlanta, GA 30345.

LUND, Jerome A., b. Willmar, MN, September 12, 1948, s. of Clarence & Lyla, m. Anne Margrethe (Underdal, chil: Petter Immanuel; Jon Michael Jerome. Educ: Los Angeles Bapt. Theol. Sem., MDiv (summa cum laude) 1973; Hebrew U. of Jerusalem, MA 1982, PhD 1989. Emp: Caspari Center, 1983-88 Lect.; Inst. of Holy Land Stud., 1984 Lect.; Hebrew U. Bible Project, 1984-85 Res.; Free Fac. of Theol., Denmark, 1989; Hebrew Union Coll., Cincinnati, Comprehensive Aramaic Lexicon, 1990- Assoc. Res. Schol. Spec: Hebrew Bible. Pub: "The Language of Jesus" *Mishkan* 17-18 (1992-93); *Sepher Bereshit* (Caspari Ctr., 1991); "The Syntax of the Numeral 'One' as a

Noun Modifier in Jewish Palestinian Aramaic of the Amoraic Period" *JAOS* 106, 108 (1986,; 1988); "The Problem of Expressing 'Three Hundred' and the Like in the Language of Codex Neofiti I" *Sefarad* 47 (1987); "On the Interpretation of the Palestinian Targumic Reading WQHT in Genesis 32:25" *JBL* (1986); "The Interchange of (d / (l in Targum Neofiti 1" *Bull. of Sch. of Oriental & African Stud.* 42 (1979); and others. Mem: SBL; AOS. Rec: Camping, hiking. Addr: (o) 3101 Clifton Ave., Cincinnati, OH 45220 513-221-1875.

LUNDBOM, Jack R., b. Chicago, IL, July 10, 1939, s. of C. Russell & Dorothy (Ohlson), m. Linda (Larson), chil: Jean. Educ: North Park Theol. Sem., BD 1967; Grad. Theol. Union, PhD 1973. Emp: Andover Newton Theol. Sch., 1974-75 Vis. Prof.; Harvard Div. Sch., 1981-82 Vis. Schol.; Yale Div. Sch., 1983-85 Vis. Prof. & Res. Fellow; Marburg U., 1988-89 Sr. Fulbright Prof.; Uppsala U. & Cambridge U., 1990-92 NEH Fellow. Spec: Hebrew Bible, New Testament. Pub: Articles in *ABD, Theological Dict. of the Old Testament*; "Psalm 23: Song of Passage" *Interpretation* (1986); "Contentious Priests and Contentious People in Hosea IV:1-10" VT 36 (1986); "The Double Curse in Jeremiah 20:14-18" *JBL* (1985); "Abraham and David in the Theology of the Yahwist" in *The Word of the Lord Shall Go Forth* (Eisenbrauns, 1983); *Jeremiah: A Study in Ancient Hebrew Rhetoric* (Scholars, 1975); and others. Mem: SBL 1965-; CBA 1968-; ASOR 1974-84. Rec: Waterskiing, racquetball, boating. Addr: (o) Lutheran School of Theology, 1100 E 55th St., Chicago, IL 60625 312-753-0700; (h) 5254 N Spaulding Ave., Chicago, IL 60625 312-588-6818.

LUNDQUIST, John M., b. Twin Falls, ID, September 22, 1938, s. of Milton & Mildred, chil: Jennifer; Emily; Eric; Margaret; John; Jack. Educ: Portland State U., BA 1970; Brigham Young U., MLS 1972; U. of Mich., MA 1974, PhD 1983. Emp: Lang. & Lang. Behavior Abstracts, 1972-73 Trans.; U. of Mich., 1973-78 Teaching Fellow; Jordan Valley Authority, USAID, 1978 Field Arch.; Brigham Young U., 1979-83 Asst. Prof.; New York Public Lib., 1985- Susan & Douglas Dillon Chief Lbrn., Oriental Div. Excv: Dibsi-Faraj, Syria, 1973 Area Supr.; Tall Hadidi, Syria, 1974-76 Area Supr.; Jordan Valley Authority, 1978 Co-dir.; Orontes Valley, Syria, 1979 Field Arch.; Tell Qarqur, Syria, 1982- Dir. Spec: Archaeology, Mesopotamian Studies. Pub: *The Temple: Meeting Place of Heaven and Earth* (Thames & Hudson, 1993); *By Study and Also By Faith, Essays in Honor of Hugh Nibley*, co-ed. (Deseret, 1990); "Tell Qarqur—The 1983 Season" in *Annales Archeologiques Arabes Syriennes* (1983); "The Legitimizing Role of the Temple in the Origin of the State" in *SBL Seminar Papers* (1982); "What is a Temple? A Preliminary Typology" in *George E. Mendenhall Festschrift* (1983); *Archaeological Reports from the Tabqa Dam Project—Euphrates Valley, Syria* (ASOR, 1979); "An Archaeological Survey of Three Reservoir Areas in Northern Jordan—1978" in *Ann. of the Dept. of Antiq. of Jordan* (1977); and others.

Mem: ASOR 1975-; AOS 1975-; SBL 1976-; CBA 1984-. Rec: Marathon running, children. Addr: (o) New York Public Library, Oriental Division, Fifth Ave. & 42 St., New York, NY 10018 212-930-0721; (h) 881 7th Ave., #1001, New York, NY 10019 212-262-7041.

LUPIERI, Edmondo F., b. Torino, Italy, November 10, 1950, s. of Gallieno & Onodia R. (Moscone), m. Linda L. (Foster), chil: Sigrid M.; Nikol A.; Erika M. Educ: U. degli Studi di Pisa, Laurea in Lettere 1973. Emp: U. of Turin, Italy, 1979-83 Asst. Prof., Storia del Cristianesimo, 1983-90 Assoc. Prof., Storia delle Origini Cristiane; U. of Udine, Italy, 1990- Prof., Storia della Chiesa Med. e Mod. Spec: New Testament, Apocrypha and Post-biblical Studies. Pub: "John the Baptist in New Testament Traditions and History" *ANRW* (1992); *Giovanni e Gesu: Storia di un Antagonismo* (Mondadori, 1991); *Esegesi e simbologie apocalittiche" ASE* 7/2 (1990); *Giovanni Battista fra storia e leggenda* (Paideia, 1988); *Giovanni Battista nelle tradizioni sinottiche* (Paideia, 1988); "Modelli scritturistici di comportamento ereticale" *Mem. Acc. Naz. Lincei* 383 (1986); "La purita impura: Giuseppe Flavio e le purificazioni degli Esseni" *Henoc* 7 (1985); *Il cielo e il mio trono: Isaia 40,12 e 66,1 nella tradizione testimoniaria* (Storia e Letteratura, 1980); "La morte di croce (Phil. 2,6-11)" *RB* 27 (1979); and others. Mem: SNTS 1988. Addr: (o) Dipartim. di Studi Storici e Documentari, Via Antonini 8, 33100 Udine, Italy 0432.501318; (h) Via Liruti 30, 33100 Udine, Italy 0432.512422.

LUST, Johan, b. Bruges, Belgium, October 12, 1937, s. of Jozef & Laura (Wintein). Educ: K. U. Leuven, Lic. Bibl. Philol. 1966, ThD 1967. Emp: K. U. Leuven, 1984- Prof., OT Lit.; *Ephemerides Theol. Lovanienses*, Co-Ed. Spec: Hebrew Bible. Pub: *A Greek-English Lexicon of the Septuagint, Part 1: A-I*, (Deutsche Bibelgesellschaft 1992); "Messianism and the Greek Version of Jeremiah" in *VII Congress of the IOSCS 1989, Leuven* (1991); "J.F. Schleusner and the Lexicon of the Septuagint" *ZAW* 102 (1990); *Ezekiel and his Book*, ed., BETL 74 (1986); *The Story of David and Goliath: Textual and Literary Criticism*, OBO 73 (1986); "Messianism and Septuagint: Ez 21,30-32" in *Congress Volume Salamanca 1983* VTSup. 36 (1985); and others. Awd: Laureate of the Koninklijke Acad. voor Wetenschappen, Letteren en Schone Kunsten van Belgie 1967; Fellow of the Von Humboldt Stiftung 1976. Mem: Colloquium Bibl. Lovaniense; OT Werkgesclap. Addr: (o) Faculty of Theology, K. U. Leuven, St. Michielsstraat 2-6, B.3000 Leuven, Belgium 016.283820; (h) Van 't Sestichstraat 34, B.3000 Leuven, Belgium 016.237468.

LUTTIKHUIZEN, Gerard P., b. Schoorl, April 29, 1940, s. of G.P. & C.M.C. (Schoone), m. M.M. (Mineur), chil: Peter; Daniel; Marike. Educ: U. of Groningen, ThD 1984. Emp: U. of Groningen, 1988- Prof., NT, Early Christian Lit.

& Interpretation. Spec: New Testament, Apocrypha and Post-biblical Studies. Pub: *Op zoek naar de samenhang van Paulus' gedachten* (Kok, 1990); "Intertextual References in Readers' Responses to the Apocryphon of John" in *Intertextuality in Biblical Writings* (Kok, 1989); "The Jewish Factor in the Development of the Gnostic Myth of Origins: Some Observations" in *Text and Testimony* (Kok, 1988); *Gnostische Geschriften I* (Kok, 1988); "The Evaluation of the Teaching of Jesus in Christian Gnostic Revelation Dialogues" *NT* 30 (1988); "The Book of Elchasai: A Jewish Apocalypse" *Aula Orientalis* 5 (1987); *The Revelation of Elchasai* (Mohr, 1985); and others. Mem: SNTS; IACS. Addr: (o) Theologische faculteit, Nieuwe Kijk in't Jatstraat 104, 9712 SL Groningen, Netherlands 050-635568; (h) Marktstraat 6, 9712 PC Groningen, Netherlands 050-185619.

LYONS, George L., b. Richmond, IN, December 9, 1947, s. of Galen & Georgia, m. Terre (Hickok), chil: Kara; Nathanael. Educ: Nazarene Theol. U., MDiv 1973; Emory U., PhD 1982. Emp: Olivet Nazarene U., 1977-91 Prof.; NW Nazarene Coll., 1991- Prof. Spec: New Testament. Pub: *A Dictionary of the Bible and Christian Doctrine in Everyday English*, co-auth. (1985); *Pauline Autobiography: Toward a New Understanding* (Scholars, 1985); "Hermeneutical Bases for Theology: Higher Criticism and the Wesleyan Interpreter" *WTJ* (1983); and others. Mem: SBL 1972-; WTS 1977-, First V.P. 1992-93. Rec: Travel, photography. Addr: (o) Northwest Nazarene College, Nampa, ID 83686 208-467-8450; (h) 4012 Ivy Dr., Nampa, ID 83686 208-467-9242.

LYONS, Melvin K., b. Concord, NH, June 22, 1920, s. of Morris & Anna, m. Celia, chil: Beth; Robert; Joshua. Educ: Boston U. Sch. of Medicine, MD 1943. Excv: Tel Gezer, 1969-70; Tel Hesi, 1970, 1972-73, 1975; Idalion, Cyprus, 1971. Spec: Archaeology. Pub: *The Care and Feeding of Dirt Archaeologists: A Manual of Field Medicine, Sanitation, and Hygiene for Excavations in the Near East* (ASOR, 1978). Mem: ASOR; ACOR, Medical Dir. Addr: (h) 12 Ninth St., Medford, MA 02155 617-395-3240.

MAAHS, Kenneth H., b. Peoria, IL, June 19, 1940, s. of Silas & Lydia (Heinold), m. Vivian (Englert), chil: Kirsten; Kenneth. Educ: Simpson Coll., BA 1962; Fuller Theol. Sem., ThM 1966; South. Bapt. Theol. Sem., PhD 1972. Emp: Pastor; Tour Guide, Israel & Egypt; Nyack Coll., 1966-67 Instr.; Bethel Coll., 1968 Instr.; East. Coll., 1972- Prof., Clemens Chair of Bibl. Stud. Spec: Hebrew Bible, New Testament. Pub: Articles in *ISBE*, vol. 1-3; "Male & Female in Pauline Perspective: A Study in Biblical Ambivalence" *Dialogue & Alliance* 2 (1988). Awd: Lindback Awd., Disting. Teaching 1984. Mem: SBL. Rec: Tennis, golf, swimming. Addr: (o) Eastern College, St. Davids, PA 19087 215-

341-5895; (h) 346 E Valley Forge Rd., King of Prussia, PA 19406 215-265-2992.

MACCOULL, Leslie S. B., b. New London, CT, August 7, 1945. Educ: Vassar, AB 1965; Yale U., MA 1966; Cath. U., PhD 1973. Emp: Cath. U., Inst. of Christian Oriental Res., 1973-77 Cur.; Soc. for Coptic Arch., 1978- Sr. Res. Schol.; *Bull. of the Soc. for Coptic Arch.*, 1982-86 Ed.; Macquarie U., Australia, 1983 Vis. Lect. Spec: Archaeology. Pub: *Coptic Perspectives on Late Antiquity* (1993); "Towards an Appropriate Context for the Study of Late Antique Egypt" *Anc. Hist. Bull.* 6 (1992); "The Era of the Martyrs," co-auth. in *Miscellanea Papyrologica* (1990); *Dioscorus of Aphrodito: His Work and His World* (1988); "Coptic Sources: A Problem in the Sociology of Knowledge" *BS* 26 (1984); *Coptic Documentary Papyri in the Beinecke Library, Yale* (Soc. for Copt. Arch., 1986); and others. Awd: Amer. Numismatic Soc., Summer Fellow 1967; NEH Fellow. 1993-94. Mem: IACS 1976-. Rec: Singing Bach cantatas & early choral music, Star Trek, Monty Python, Dr. Who. Addr: (o) Soc. for Coptic Archaeology 2800 Wisconsin Ave. NW, Washington, DC 20007 202-363-3480.

MACDONALD, Burton, b. Beauchastel, Canada, September 13, 1939, s. of Daniel & Christena. Educ: St. Francis Xavier U., BA 1960; U. of Ottawa, Canada, STB 1962, STL 1964, MA 1965; Ecole Biblique, Jerusalem, Eleve Titulaire 1970; Catholic U., PhD 1974. Emp: Xavier Coll., NS, 1965-66, Lect.; St. Francis Xavier U., 1972-, 1979-89 Assoc. Prof., 1989- Prof., Theol.; ACOR, Jordan, 1979-80, 1986-87 Ann. Prof., 1991-92 Dodge Fellow. Excv: Wadi el-Hasa Survey, 1979-83 Dir.; South. Ghors & NE Arabah Survey 1985-86 Dir. Spec: Archaeology, Hebrew Bible, Egyptology. Pub: *The Southern Ghors and Northeast 'Arabah Archaeological Survey 1985-1986*, Sheffield Arch. Mon. 5, co-auth. (J.R. Collis, 1992); "Settlement Patterns Along the Southern Flank of Wadi al-Hasa: Evidence From the Wadi al-Hasa Archaeology Survey" in *Studies in the History and Archaeology of Jordan IV* (Amman: Dept. of Antiq., 1992; "L'Occupation nabateenne du Wadi el Hasa" *Archeologia*, Dossiers d'histoire et d'archeologie 163 (1991); *The Wadi el-Hasa Archaeological Survey 1979-83: West-Central Jordan*, co-auth. (Wilfrid Laurier U.P., 1988); "Southern Ghors and Northeast 'Araba Archaeological Survey 1985 and 1986, Jordan: A Preliminary Report," co-auth. *BASOR* 272 (1988); "Deir 'Ain 'Abata: A Byzantine Church/Monastery Complex in Ghor es-Safi" *Liber Annus* 38 (1988); "Exploration du Wadi el-Hasa (1981 et 1982)" *RB* 91 (1984); "Wadi el-Hasa" *Amer. Jour. of Arch.* 88 (1984); "The Wadi el-Hasa Archaeological Survey" in *The Answers Lie Below: Essays in Honor of Lawrence Edmund Toombs* (1984); and others. Mem: ASOR 1971-; SBL 1972-; CBA 1976-. Rec: Genealogical studies, travel, sports. Addr: (o) St. Francis Xavier U., Box 137, Antigonish, NS B2G 1C0, Canada 902-867-2155; (h) MacKinnon's Hollow Antigonish County, NS B2G 2L1, Canada 902-863-6772.

MACDONALD, Dennis R., b. Chicago, IL, July 1, 1946, s. of J. Ronald & Mildred (Friend), m. Diane (Prosser), chil: Katya; Julian. Educ: McCormick Theol. Sem., MDiv 1973; Harvard U., PhD 1978. Emp: Goshen Coll., 1977-80; Iliff Sch. of Theol., 1980- Prof.; Harvard Div. Sch., 1985-86 Vis. Prof.; Union Theol. Sem. of New York, Vis. Prof. Spec: New Testament, Apocrypha and Post-biblical Studies. Pub: *The Acts of Andrew and the Acts of Andrew and Matthias in the City of Cannibals* (Scholars, 1991); *There Is No Male and Female: The Fate of a Dominical Saying in Paul and Gnosticism* (Fortress, 1986); "A Conjectural Emmendation of 1 Cor. 15:31-32" *HTR*; *The Legend and the Apostle: The Battle for Paul in Story and Canon* (Westminster, 1983); and others. Awd: Harvard U., Clarence G. Campbell Fellow. 1975-76. Mem: SBL 1974-; SNTS 1985-; IACS 1986-; Assn. pour l'étude de la lit. apocryphe chrétienne 1988-. Rec: Racquetball, ice hockey. Addr: (o) Iliff School of Theology, 2201 S University Blvd., Denver, CO 80210 303-744-1287.

MACDONALD, Margaret Y., b. St. Jean, Quebec, February 16, 1961, d. of Therese Dufour & Hugh J., m. J. Duncan Macpherson, chil: J. Delia. Educ: St. Mary's U., BA 1983; Oxford U., PhD 1986. Emp: St. Francis Xavier U., 1986-90 Asst. Prof.; U. of Ottawa, 1990- Assoc. Prof. Spec: New Testament, Apocrypha and Post-biblical Studies. Pub: "Early Christian Women Married to Unbelievers" *Stud. in Relig.* 19 (1990); "Women Holy in Body and Spirit: The Social Setting of 1 Corinthians 7" *NTS* 36 (1990); *The Pauline Churches: A Socio-historical Study of Institutionalization in the Pauline and Deutero-Pauline Writings* (Cambridge U.P., 1988). Awd: Oxford U., Commonwealth Schol. 1983-86. Mem: CSBS 1986-; SBL 1986-; AAR 1990-; CBA 1990-. Rec: Jogging, music, dance. Addr: (o) U. of Ottawa, Dept. of Religious Studies, 177 Waller St., Ottawa, ON KIN 6N5, Canada 613-564-2300; (h) 1870 Thistleleaf Crescent, Orleans, ON K1C 5W7, Canada.

MACGREGOR, Geddes, b. Glasgow, Scotland, November 13, 1909, s. of Thomas & Blanche (Geddes), m. Elizabeth (McAllister), chil: Marie; Martin. Educ: U. of Edinburgh, BD 1939, LLB 1943; U. of Oxford, D.Phil 1945, BD 1955, DD 1959; U. Paris, Sorbonne, Docteur-ès-lettres (summa cum laude) 1951. Emp: Bryn Mawr Coll., 1949-60 Rufus Jones Chair of Phil. & Relig.; U. of South. Calif., 1960-66 Prof., Dean, Grad. Sch. of Relig., 1966-75 Disting. Prof., Phil., 1975- Emeritus; Yale U., 1967-68 Vis. Fellow; McGill U., 1976 Vis. Prof.; U. Complutense de Madrid, 1992 Vis. Lect. Spec: New Testament, Apocrypha and Post-biblical Studies. Pub: *Dict. of Religion and Philosophy*, contb. (1989, 1991); and others. Awd: Royal Soc. of Lit. Fellow 1948; Hebrew Union, Hon. LHD 1978; Phi Kappa Phi 1982; U. of South. Calif. Disting. Emeriti Awad. 1993. Mem: AAR; Amer. Phil. Assn.; SBL. Rec: Manual labor, reading, writing. Addr: (h) 876 Victoria Ave., Los Angeles, CA 90005-3751 213-938-4826.

MACHINIST, Peter B., b. Philadelphia, PA, September 3, 1944, s. of Milton & Sylvia, m. Alice, chil: Edith; David. Educ: Harvard U., AB 1966; Yale U., MPhil 1971, PhD 1978. Emp: Case West. Reserve U., 1971-77 Instr.; U. of Ariz., 1977-86 Assoc. Prof.; U. of Mich., 1986-1991 Assoc. Prof.; Harvard U., 1991-92 Prof., 1992- Hancock Prof. of Hebrew & Other Oriental Lang.; *BA,* 1982-90 Ed.; *BASOR,* 1983-90 Ed. Excv: Sardis, Turkey, 1964 Photographer; Gezer, Israel, 1966 Head of Photography. Spec: Mesopotamian Studies. Pub: "The Question of Distinctiveness in Ancient Israel: An Essay" *Ah, Assyria: Studies in Honor of Hayim Tadmor* (Magnes, 1991); "On Self-Consciousness in Mesopotamia" in *The Origins and Diversity of Axial Age Civilizations* (New York U.P., 1986); "Assyria and Its Image in the First Isaiah" *JAOS* 103 (1983); "Rest and Violence in the Poem of Ezra" *JAOS* 103 (1983); "Literature as Politics: The Tukulti-Ninurta Epic and the Bible" *CBQ* 38 (1976); and others. Mem: AOS 1966-; ASOR 1969-; SBL 1972-. Rec: Tennis, travel. Addr: (o) Harvard U. Dept. of Near Eastern Languages, 6 Divinity Ave., Cambridge, MA 02138 617-495-0333; (h) 125 Windermere Rd., Newton, MA 02166 617-527-2607.

MACKENZIE, R. Sheldon, b. New Glasgow, NS, July 26, 1930, s. of Harold S. & Gladys, m. Jenipher I.R., chil: Mark S.; Clare I. Educ: Acadia U., BA 1955; Presbyn. Coll., Montreal, BD 1958; St. Andrew's U., Scotland, PhD 1962. Emp: St. Andrew's Presbyn. Ch., NF, 1969-72; Memorial U. of NF, 1972- Prof.; Queen's Theol. Coll., NF, 1982- Adj. Prof.; *Practice of Ministry in Canada,* Contb. Ed.; *The Presbyterian Record,* Contb. Ed. Spec: New Testament, Apocrypha and Post-biblical Studies. Awd: Knox Coll., Toronto, DDiv 1980; Canada Coun. Leave Fellow. 1980-81. Mem: CSSR 1972-; SBL 1974-. Rec: Golf, class. music. Addr: (o) Memorial U. of Newfoundland, Dept. of Religious Studies, St. John's, NF, A1C 5S7, Canada 709-737-8169; (h) 95 Logy Bay Rd., St. John's, NF, A1A 1J5, Canada 709-722-7130.

MACKY, Peter W., b. Auckland, New Zealand, July 22, 1937, s. of Wallace & Mary (Whitfield), m. Nancy (Space), chil: Cameron; Christopher. Educ: Harvard Coll., AB 1957; Oxford U., BA 1962, MA 1966, PhD 1967; Princeton Theol. Sem., BD 1963, ThD 1970. Emp: Princeton Theol. Sem., 1964-65, 1967 Instr.; Westminster Coll., 1970- Prof., Chmn., Dept. Relig. & Phil.; Chautauqua Inst., 1984 Eugene Ross McCarthy Relig. Lect. Spec: New Testament. Pub: *The Centrality of Metaphor to Biblical Thought* (Mellen, 1990); and others. Awd: Rhodes Schol. 1960. Rec: Coach of college soccer, racquetball. Addr: (o) Westminster College, New Wilmington, PA 16172 412-946-7155; (h) R.D. #1, Susan Trace, New Wilmington, PA 16142 412-946-2962.

MACLENNAN, Robert S., b. Los Angeles, CA, May 20, 1941, s. of Edward & Lucy, m. Jane (Lawther), chil: T. Stewart; Katharine H.

Educ: Occidental Coll., BA, Hist. 1963; Princeton Sem., BD, Bibl. Stud. 1966; U. of Minn., PhD, Anc. Stud. 1988. Emp: Presbyn. Ch., 1966-73 Min., 1983- Sr. Min.; Amer. Protestant Ch., Germany, 1973-77 Min.; Colonial Ch. of Edina, 1977-83 Teaching Min. Pub: *Diaspora Jews and Judaism: Essay in Honor of and in Dialogue with A. Thomas Kraabel,* co-auth. (Scholars, 1992); *Early Christian Texts on Jews and Judaism,* co-auth. (Scholars, 1990); "The God-Fearers: A Literary and Theological Invention?" co-auth. *BAR* 12/5 (1986). Mem: SBL; AAR. Rec: Tennis, travel, museums, music, reading. Addr: (o) 6 Edgehill St., Princeton, NJ 08540 609-683-0909.

MAEIR, Aren M., b. Rochester, NY, s. of David & Sheila, m. Adina, chil: Noam; Uri. Educ: Hebrew U., BA, Hist., Arch. 1986. Emp: Hebrew U., Inst. of Arch., 1985-92 Asst.; Bar-Ilan U., 1990-92 Lect., Dept. of Land of Israel Stud.; Israel Antiq. Authority, Jerusalem, 1989-92 Field Arch. Excv: Hazor, 1986 Area Supr.; Qasile, 1988 Area Supr.; Jerusalem, Municipality, 1989 Dir.; Jerusalem, Mamila, 1989-90 Dir.; T. Beth Shean, 1990-91 Area Supr. Spec: Archaeology, Egyptology. Pub: "The Origin of the Pictorial Krater from the Mycenean Tomb at Tel Dan" *Archaeometry* 34/1 (1992); "A Re-evaluation of the Red and Black Bowl from Parker's Excavations in Jerusalem" *OJA* 11/1 (1992); "Bone and Metal Straw-Tip Beer-Strainers from the Ancient Near East" *Levant* 24 (1992); "Remarks on a Supposed Egyptian Residency at Gezer" *Tel Aviv* 15 (1989). Awd: Hebrew U., Zinder Prize 1991. Mem: IES; AAS; PES; BSA. Rec: Sports. Addr: (o) Hebrew U., Institute of Archaeology, Jerusalem 91905, Israel 02-882404; (h) 31 Reuven St., Jerusalem 93510, Israel 02-710404.

MAGEN, Izchak, m. Yudit. Spec: Archaeology. Addr: (o) Rockefeller Museum, Officer in Charge of Archaeology, Jerusalem, Israel 761-563; (h) Rechov Betar 44, Jerusalem, Israel.

MAGEN, Menahem, b. Jerusalem, Israel. Educ: Hebrew U., Jerusalem, degree in Arch. & Hebrew Lang. Emp: Hillel Acad., Mass., 1965-67 Tchr.; Hebrew High Sch., Providence, R.I., 1967-70 Prin.; Ben Gurion U., 1977-78 Dir., arch. lab., Asst. Excvn Dir.; East Jerusalem Development Co., 1978- Arch. advisor. Excv: Temple Mount, 1970-76 Supr., finds & restorations; Caearea, 1976 Field Supr.; Lions Gate, Dir.; Via Dolorosa, Dir.; Damascus Gate Proj., Proj. Dir. Spec: Archaeology. Addr: (o) Ma'alot Daphna 121/19, Jerusalem, Israel 02-818758.

MAGNE, Jean, b. Charenton-le-Pont, France, July 20, 1910, s. of Henri & Yvonne. Educ: U. Angelica, Rome, Lic. Phil. 1934; Sorbonne, Doc. Sci. des Relig. 1975. Emp: Coll. de France, Inst. d'Etudes Semitiques Bibliothecaire. Spec: Hebrew Bible, New Testament. Pub: *From Christianity to*

Gnosis and from Gnosis to Christianity (Scholars, 1992); "Les récits de la cène et la date de la Passion" *Ephemerides Liturgicae* 105 (1991); "La solution nouvelle du probleme synoptique proposée par Philippe Rolland, et deux omissions de Luc et une de Matthieu" *Rev. de la Soc. Ernest-Renan* 38 (1989); *Logique des dogmes* (1989); *Logique des sacrements* (1989); "La réception de la variante 'Que vienne ton Esprit saint sur nous et qu'il nous purifie' (Lc 11,2)" *Ephemerides Liturgicae* 102; (1988); "Le processus de judaisation au témoignage des reecritures du récit de la multiplication des pains" *Augustinianum* 28 (1988); *Sacrifice et sacerdoce* (1975); "Le texte du psaume XXII et sa restitution sur deux colonnes" *Semitica* II (1961); and others. Addr: (h) 23, Rue Lacharriere, F 75011 Paris, France 1-47007322.

MAGNESS, J. Lee, b. Baltimore, MD, August 14, 1947, s. of James H. & Arlene P., m. Patricia P., chil: Erik L.; Ethan L.. Educ: Milligan Coll., BA 1969; Emmanuel Sch. of Relig., MDiv 1977; Emory U., PhD 1985. Emp: Boise Bible Coll., 1975-1980 Assoc. Prof.; Atlanta Christian Coll., 1980-83 Instr.; Milligan Coll., 1983- Assoc. Prof. Spec: New Testament. Pub: *Sense and Absence: Structure and Suspension in the Ending of Mark's Gospel* (Scholars, 1986); and others. Mem: SBL 1983-. Rec: Hiking, backpacking, white-water rafting. Addr: (o) Milligan College, Milligan College, TN 37682 615-461-8754; (h) Rt. 11, Box 2780, Elizabethton, TN 37643 615-543-6427.

MAGNESS, Jodi, b. Philadelphia, PA, September 19, 1956, d. of Herbert & Marlene. Educ: Hebrew U., BA 1977; U. of Pa., PhD 1989. Emp: Hebrew U. Sch. for Overseas Students, 1984- Instr., Arch.; U. of Miami, 1988-1989 Adj. Prof., Anthrop. & Relig. Stud.; Tufts U., 1992- Asst. Prof., Class. & Near East. Arch. Excv: Hurvat Uza', Israel, 1983 Area Supr.; Ancient Corinth, Greece, 1984 Area Supr.; Kfar Hananiya, Israel, 1986 Area Supr.; Nahal Rephaim, Israel, 1987, 1988, 1989 Area Supr., Instr.; Caesarea Maritima, Israel (CCE), 1989- Late Roman & Byzantine Ceramics Spec. Spec: Archaeology. Pub: *Jerusalem Ceramic Chronology circa 200-800 C.E.* (Sheffield, 1993); "The Late Roman and Byzantine Pottery from the City of David" *Qedem* 33 (1992); "A Reexamination of the Archaeological Evidence for the Sasanian Persian Destruction of the Tyroponean Valley" *BASOR* 287 (1992); "Arms and the Man" *BAR* 18 (1992); "Late Roman and Byzantine Pottery, Preliminary Report, 1990" in *Caesarea Papers: Straton's Tower, Herod's Harbour, and Roman and Byzantine Caesarea*, Jour. of Roman Arch. Sup. Ser. 5 (1992); "Some Observations on the Roman Temple at Kedesh" *IEJ* 40 (1990). Awd: ASOR, George A. Barton Fellow 1984-85, James A. Montgomery Fellow 1985-86, Samuel H. Kress Fellow 1986-87; U. of Pa., Mellon Grad. Fellow 1988-89, 1989-90; Brown U., Mellon Post-doc. Fellow in Syro-Palestinian Arch. 1990-92. Mem: IES 1981-; AIA 1983-; ASOR 1984-; WUJS 1989-. Rec: Soccer, figure skating. Addr: (o) Tufts U., Dept.

of Classics, 321 Eaton Hall, Medford, MA 02155 617-628-5000; (h) 63 Waterhouse St., Apt. 3, Somerville, MA 02144 617-625-7408.

MAIER, John R., b. Charleston, WV, June 14, 1943, s. of James & Dorothy, m. Helen, chil: William. Educ: U. of Pa., AM 1966; Duquesne U., PhD 1970. Emp: Duquesne U., 1966-69 Instr.; Clarion State Coll., 1969-71 Asst. Prof.; State U. of N.Y., 1971- Prof.; *Literary Onomastics Stud.*, 1976-79 Ed.; U. of Aleppo, 1979-80; U. of Jordan, Amman, 1980 Fulbright Sr. Lect.; *Rev. of Relig. Res.*, 1983- Ed.; Sidi Moh. Ben Abdellah U., Fez 1989-90. Spec: Hebrew Bible, Mesopotamian Studies, New Testament. Pub: "Une catégorie de la littérature mondiale: La littérature archaïque" in *Littérature générale/Littérature comparée* (Lang, 1992); "Asia under the Sign of Woman: The Feminization of the Orient in *The Aeneid*" *Works and Days* 18 (1991); *Mappings of the Global Terrain: The Bible as Text*, co-auth. (Bucknell U.P., 1990); *Myths of Enki, The Crafty God*, co-auth. (Oxford U.P., 1989); "Three Voices of Enki: Strategies in the Translation of Archaic Literature" in *Comparative Criticism* (Cambridge U.P., 1984); *Gilgamesh, Translated from the Version of Sin-leqi-unninni*, co-auth. (Knopf, 1984); *The Bible in its Literary Milieu: Contemporary Essays*, co-ed. (Eerdmans, 1980); and others. Mem: SBL; AOS; Soc. Mesopotamian Stud.; Relig. Res. Assn. Rec: Contract bridge, basketball. Addr: (o) SUNY College at Brockport, Brockport, NY 14420 716-395-2503; (h) 20 Trefoil Ln., Brockport, NY 14420 716-637-9253.

MAIER, Walter A., III, b. Buffalo, NY, July 23, 1952, s. of Walter & Leah. Educ: Concordia Theol. Sem., MDiv 1978; Harvard U., PhD 1984. Emp: Concordia U., 1984-89 Asst. Prof., 1989-Assoc. Prof., Concordia Theol. Sem.; Concordia Luth. Ch., 1989-92 Asst. Pastor. Spec: Hebrew Bible. Pub: Articles in *ABD* (Doubleday, 1992); *'Ašerah: Extrabiblical Evidence*, Harvard Sem. Mon. (1986). Mem: ASOR 1981-; SBL 1981-. Rec: Sports, reading, music. Addr: (o) Concordia Theological Seminary, 6600 N Clinton St., Ft. Wayne, IN 46825-4996 219-481-2132.

MALAMAT, Abraham, b. Vienna, January 26, 1922, s. of Nathan & Lore, m. Naama, chil: Taliah. Educ: Hebrew U., MA 1946, PhD 1951. Emp: IEJ, 1956- Ed. Adv. Bd.; Hebrew U., 1964-69 Assoc. Prof., 1970- Prof., Chmn., Dept. of Jewish Hist.; ZAW, 1976- Intl. Ed. Bd.; JSOT, 1981- Intl. Ed. Bd. Spec: Hebrew Bible, Mesopotamian Studies. Pub: "The Divine Nature of the Mediterranean Sea" in *Mari in Retrospect* (1992); "Mari and the Early Israelite Experience" *Schweich Lectures* (1984, 1992); *Mari and Israel—Two West Semitic Cultures* (Magnes, 1991); "New Light from Mari on Biblical Prophecy" *J.A. Soggin Festschrift* (1991); *Israel in Biblical Times* (IES, 1983); "Origins—The Formative Period" in *A History of the Jewish People* (Weidenfeld & Nicholson, 1976); and others. Mem: SBL, hon. mem.;

SOTS; South Africa Bible Soc.; WUJS 1981-; AAJR 1987-. Addr: (o) Hebrew U., Dept. of Jewish History, Jerusalem, Israel; (h) 1 Rashba St., Jerusalem, Israel.

MALATESTA, Edward J., b. Paterson, NJ, May 31, 1932, s. of Edward & Concetta (Caratozzolo). Educ: Gonzaga U., MA 1955; Les Fontaines, France, STL 1962; Pont. Bibl. Inst., Rome, SSL 1965, SSD 1974. Emp: Pont. Gregorian U., Rome, 1966-79 Assoc. Prof.; U. of San Francisco, Inst. for Chinese-West. Cultural Hist., 1984- Co-Found. & Dir. Spec: New Testament. Pub: *The True Meaning of the Lord of Heaven*, ed. (1985); *Interiority and Covenant* (Pont. Bibl. Inst., 1978); *The Epistles of St. John* (Pont. Bibl. Inst., 1973); *St. John's Gospel, 1920-65* (Pont. Bibl. Inst., 1967); and others. Mem: CBA; SBL; Assn. for Asian Stud.; Amer. Cath. Hist. Assn. Rec: Travel, hiking, swimming. Addr: (o) U. of San Francisco, Ricci Institute for Chinese-Western Cultural History, 2130 Fulton St., San Francisco, CA 94117 415-666-6401; (h) 2001 37th Ave., San Francisco, CA 94116.

MALCHOW, Bruce V., b. Chicago, IL, January 7, 1940, s. of Virgil & Ruth, m. Roberta, chil: Timothy; Laura. Educ: Concordia Coll., BA 1961; Concordia Sem., MDiv 1965, STM 1966; Marquette U., PhD 1972. Emp: Concordia Coll., 1968-74 Asst. Prof.; Marquette U., 1974-75 Lect.; Sacred Heart Sch. of Theol., 1975- Prof. Spec: Hebrew Bible. Pub: "A Manual for Future Monarchs" *CBQ* (1985); "The Messenger of the Covenant in Mal 3:1" *JBL* (1984); and others. Mem: SBL 1970-. Rec: Reading, recorder playing, swimming. Addr: (o) Sacred Heart School of Theology, PO Box 429, Hales Corners, WI 53130-0429 414-425-8300; (h) 5407 Butterfield Way, Greenfield, WI 53211 414-282-5543.

MALHERBE, Abraham J., b. Pretoria, South Africa, May 13, 1930. Educ: Abilene Christian Coll., BA 1954; Harvard U., STB 1957, ThD, NT 1963. Emp: Abilene Christian Coll., 1963-69 Assoc. Prof.; Dartmouth Coll., 1969-70 Assoc. Prof.; Yale U., Div. Sch., 1970-78 Assoc. Prof., 1978- Prof. of NT. Spec: New Testament. Pub: *Gregory of Nyssa: Life of Moses* (Paulist, 1978); *Social Aspects of Early Christianity* (1977); *The Cynic Epistles: A Study Edition*, co-auth. (Scholars, 1977); "The Inhospitality of Diotrephes" in *In God's Christ and his People* (Dahl Festschrift, 1977); "Ancient Epistolary Theorists" *Ohio Jour. of Relig. Stud.* (1977). Awd: NEH, grant 1973-74. Mem: SBL; SNTS; Inst. of Antiquity & Christianity. Addr: (h) 71 Spring Garden St., Hampden, CT 06517.

MALLAU, Hans-H., b. Koenigsberg, Germany, March 12, 1930, s. of Hans & Margarete (Muller), chil: Michal; Hans-Tibor. Educ: U. Kiel, Dr.theol. 1963. Emp: U. Kiel, 1963-70 Instr.; Bapt. Theol. Sem., Ruschlikon 1969-70 Guest Prof., 1977- Prof., OT; Instituto Superior

Evangelico de Estudios Teologicos, Argentina, 1970-77 Prof.; Baptist Theological Seminary, Ruschliken 1977- Prof., OT. Spec: Hebrew Bible. Pub: "The Redaction of Ezra 4-6: A Plea for a Theology of Scribes" *Perspectives in Religious Studies* 15 (1988); "Las Diversas Reacciones al mensaje profetico en Israel y su ambiente" *Cuadernos de Teologia* 2 (1972); "Das Tor im Alten Testament" in *Im Lande der Bibel* (1968); *Die Theologische Bedeutung der Wuste im Alten Testament* (Eigenverlag, 1963); and others. Mem: SBL 1977-. Rec: Music. Addr: (o) Baptist Theological Seminary, Gheistrasse 31, CH-8803 Ruschlikon, Switzerland 01-724-00-10; (h) Alemannenweg 1, 8803 Ruschlikon, Switzerland 01-724-14-26.

MALONEY, Elliott C., b. Pittsburgh, PA, April 17, 1946, s. of C. Leo & Barbara F. Educ: St. Vincent Coll., BA 1968; Pont. Athenaeum of St. Anselm, Rome, STL 1972; Fordham U., PhD 1979. Emp: St. Vincent Sem., 1978- Prof., NT Stud.; St. Vincent Coll., 1984- Chmn., Dept. of Relig. Stud. Spec: New Testament. Pub: "The Historical Present in the Gospel of Mark" in *To Touch the Text: In Honor of Joseph A. Fitzmyer*; "Pseudonymity in the New Testament: Who Was the Author of the Pastorals?" *The Bible Today* (1986); *Semitic Interference in Marcan Syntax* (Scholars, 1981); and others. Mem: SBL 1972-; CBA 1974-. Rec: Music, landscaping, forestry. Addr: (o) St. Vincent College, Latrobe, PA 15650 412-539-9761.

MALONEY, Linda M., b. Houston, TX, April 10, 1939, d. of David Bruce & Alta C. Mitchell, chil: Sharon Frances McKee; David Bruce McKee; Vincent Kiltanon. Educ: St. Louis U., BA (summa cum laude) 1965, PhD 1968, MA, Relig. Stud. 1983; Eberhard-Karls-U. Tuebingen, Germany, ThD (magna cum laude) 1989. Emp: South. Ill. U., 1968-69 Asst. Prof.; Our Lady of the Lake Coll., 1971-72 Lect.; Tex. Christian U., 1972-73 Asst. Prof.; U. of S.C., 1973-79 Asst. Prof.; Franciscan Sch. of Theol., 1989-92 Asst. Prof., 1992- Assoc. Prof. Spec: New Testament. Pub: *All That God Had Done With Them: The Narration of the Mighty Works of God in the Acts of the Apostles* (Lang, 1991). Awd: Smithsonian Inst., Postdoc. Fellow 1969-70. Mem: Amer. Hist. Assn. 1965-80, 1990-; CTSA 1982-; SBL 1987-; CBA 1987-. Rec: Hiking, camping. Addr: (o) Franciscan School of Theology, 1712 Euclid Ave., Berkeley, CA 94709 510-848-5232; (h) 1515 Hopkins St. #3, Berkeley, CA 94707 510-525-5932.

MALTSBERGER, David C., b. Fayetteville, NC, February 19, 1960, m. Elaine, chil: Connor; Reuben; Martin. Educ: E Tex. Bapt. U., BA 1981; SW Bapt. Theol. Sem., MDiv 1987, PhD 1992. Emp: SW Bapt. Theol. Sem., 1988-90 Teaching Fellow; *Field Notes* 1992- Ed.; Bapt. Theol. Sem., Ukraine, 1992- Assoc. Prof. Excv: Tel Batash/Timnah, 1985, 1987-89 Area Supr. Spec: Archaeology. Pub: Articles in *Mercer*

Dict. of the Bible (Mercer U.P., 1990), *Holman Bible Dict.* (Holman, 1991); and others. Mem: IES; ASOR. Rec: Hunting, fishing. Addr: (o) 13419 Rockhampton, San Antonio, TX 78232.

MANDELL, Sara R. S., b. New York, NY, May 11, 1938, d. of George & Beatrice Sindel, m. Leon. Educ: N.Y. U., BA 1964, MA 1966, PhD 1969. Emp: Emory U., 1969-72 Asst. Prof., Class.; U. of S Florida, 1986-91 Asst. Prof., 1991 Assoc. Prof., Class., 1991- Assoc. Prof., Relig. Stud. Spec: Hebrew Bible, Mesopotamian Studies, Semitic Languages, Texts and Epigraphy, Apocrypha and Post-biblical Studies. Pub: "Roman Dominion: Desire and Reality" *The Anc. World* 22 (1991); "Did the Maccabees Believe They Had a Valid Treaty with Rome?" *CBQ* (1991); "The Language, Eastern Sources, and Literacy Posture of Herodotus" *The Anc. World* 21 (1990); "Was Rome's Early Diplomatic Interaction with the Maccabees Legal?" *Class. Bull.* 64 (1988); "Who Paid the Temple Tax When the Jews Were Under Roman Rule?" *HTR* 77 (1984); and others. Awd: N.Y. U., Founders' Day Awd. 1970. Mem: ASOR, V.P., SE Sect. 1992; AOS; CBA; SBL; AAR. Addr: (o) U. of South Florida, Religious Studies, CPR 304, Tampa, FL 33620-5550 813-974-2221; (h) 4304 Ashby Ln., Tampa, FL 33624 813-969-0723.

MANN, Christopher S., b. United Kingdom, March 7, 1917, s. of William & Elsie. Educ: U. of London, King's Coll., BD 1956, PhD 1960. Emp: Ch. of England, 1960-65 Gen. Ordination Examiner; SPCK Theological Collections, 1965, 1969 Ed.; Johns Hopkins U., 1965-68 Post-Doc. Fellow, Near East. Stud.; St. Mary's Sem. & U., 1967-68 Prof. of NT Seminars, 1968-70 Dean, Ecumenical Inst. of Theol. Spec: New Testament. Pub: *St. Mark*, AB (Doubleday, 1985); *St. Matthew*, AB (Doubleday, 1971); and others. Mem: SOTS 1956-; SBL 1966-, V.P., Chesapeake sect. 1973, Pres. 1974; CBA 1970-; SNTS 1975-. Rec: Exploring Civil War sites, west. ghost towns, steam railways. Addr: (h) 107 E Chase St., Baltimore, MD 21202 410-837-7362.

MANSOOR, Menahem, b. Port Said, Egypt, August 4, 1911, s. of Asher & Yonah (Shalom), m. Claire (Kramer), chil: Yardena; Daniel. Educ: Trinity Coll., Dublin, MA 1941, PhD 1944. Emp: U. of Wis., Dept. of Hebrew & Semitic Stud., 1955-77 Chmn., 1982- Prof. Emeritus. Spec: Hebrew Bible, Semitic Languages, Texts and Epigraphy. Pub: *Guide to the Dead Sea Scrolls* (Brill/Eerdmans, 1964; BBH, 1984); *The Book and the Spade* (Madison, 1975); *The Thanksgiving Hymns* (Brill/Eerdmans, 1961); "Studies in the New Thanksgiving Hymns: Some Theological Doctrines in the Hoyadot, 1-5" *Bibl. Res.* 5 (1960); *Biblical Hebrew Step by Step*, vol. 1 & 2. Awd: Fulbright Grant 1953-54. Mem: AOS 1969-, MidW Branch Pres. 1969-70; SBL 1970-, MidW Branch Pres. 1970-71; NAPH 1975-. Rec: Swimming, deciphering. Addr: (o)

1346 Van Hise Hall, 1220 Linden Dr., Madison, WI 53706 608-262-3204; (h) 1225 Sweetbriar Rd., Madison, WI 53703 608-233-0565.

MAORI, Yeshayahu, b. Tel Aviv, Israel, April 24, 1937, s. of Arye & Risha, m. Haya, chil: Michal; Boaz; Yoav. Educ: Hebrew U., Jerusalem, BA 1963, MA 1967, PhD 1976. Emp: Haifa U., 1964- Sr. Lect., 1983-85 Head, Dept. of Bible; Hebrew U., Jerusalem, 1964-86 Staff, Bible Project, 1985-86 Study Group on Targumic & Cognate Stud.; Yeshiva U., 1977-79, 1986-87 Vis. Prof.; Bar Ilan U., 1981 Vis. Sr. Lect.; Annenberg Res. Inst., 1988-89 Study Group on Bible Trans. Spec: Hebrew Bible. Pub: "The Targumim to Exodus 20: Reconstructing the Palestinian Targum," co-auth. *Textus* 16 (1991); "The Approach of Classical Jewish Exegesis to Peshat and Derash and its Implications for the Teaching of the Bible Today" *Tradition* 21 (1984); "Sectional Divisions in Ancient Hebrew Manscripts" *Textus* 10 (1982); "Midrashic Influence on the Peshitta's Choice of Words" *Tarbiz* 46 (1977); *The Book of Isaiah*, vol. 1-2, contb. (Magnes, 1975); and others. Mem: SBL; WUJS. Addr: (o) Haifa U., Dept. of Bible, Haifa, Israel 04-240187; (h) 22 Leon Blum St., Ramath Hadar, Haifa 33851, Israel 04-386397.

MA'OZ, Zvi 'Uri, b. Haifa, Israel, March 18, 1949, s. of Moshe & Tamar (Mendelowitz), m. Tova, chil: Yael; Anat; Noaa; Semadar. Educ: Hebrew U., BA 1979, MA 1986, PhD 1993. Emp: IES, 1973-87; Israel Antiq. Auth., 1981-87 Arch., 1988-91 Dir., N Reg. 1993- Arch., Proj. Dir. Excv: Jerusalem, Jewish Quarter, 1973-77 Field Supr.; Golan Synagogues, 1977-83 Dir.; Sanctuary of Pan, Caesarea Philippi, 1988- Dir.; Tel-Qasile, 1991-92 Asst. Dir.; Caesarea Maritima-Herod's Palace, 1993- Field Supr. Spec: Archaeology. Pub: "Golan," "Deir Qruch," "Dabbiyye," "Qasrin," "Ein Nashut," "Givat Urcha, Bar" in *The New Ency. of Archaeological Excavations in the Holy Land* (1993); "The Synagogue in the Second Temple Period" *Eretz-Israel* 23 (1992); "The Golan Heights, Geshur" in *ABD* 2 (1992); "The Praetorium at Musmiye, Again" *Dumbarton Oak Papers* 44 (1990); "Synagogues in the Golan—An Introduction" *BA* 51 (1988); *The Golan in Antiquity—An Historic-Geographical Survey* (Golan Res. Inst., 1986); *The Synagogues and Jewish Settlements in the Golan* (Israel Soc. for the Protection of Nature, 1980); and others. Addr: (o) Israel Antiquities Authority, Excavations & Surveys, Gamla, Qazrin 12900, Israel 972-6-961876; (h) Nimron, Qazrin 12900, Israel.

MARCH, W. Eugene, b. Dallas, TX, July 8, 1935, s. of Wallace & Helen, m. Margaret (Spencer), chil: Judith; Katherine. Educ: Austin Presbyn. Theol. Sem., BD 1960; Union Theol. Sem., PhD 1966. Emp: Austin Presbyn. Theol. Sem., 1966-82 Prof.; Louisville Presbyn. Theol. Sem., 1982- Arnold B. Rhodes Prof. of OT; Mrs.

Jacob H. Horn Arch. Mus., Cur. Spec: Hebrew Bible. Pub: "Micah" in *Harper's Bible Comm.* (1988); "Redaction Criticism and the Formation of Prophetic Books" in *SBL 1977 Seminar Papers* (1981); *Text and Testament: Critical Essays on the Bible and Early Church Fathers*, ed. (Trinity U.P., 1980); *Basic Bible Study* (1978); and others. Mem: AAR; SBL, Pres., SW reg. 1976; ASOR. Rec: Sports, music. Addr: (o) Louisville Presbyterian Theological Seminary, 1044 Alta Vista Rd., Louisville, KY 40205 502-895-3411; (h) 3014 Juniper Hill Rd. Louisville, KY 40206 502-896-4386.

MARCUS, David, b. Dublin, Ireland, June 24, 1941, s. of Jacob & Lilly, m. Joyce (Newman), chil: Jacob; Noah; Rebecca. Educ: Trinity Coll., Dublin, BA 1961; Cambridge U., MA 1963; Columbia U., PhD 1963. Emp: Columbia U., 1970-78 Asst. Prof.; Jewish Theol. Sem., 1979-86 Assoc. Prof., Bible; *JANES*, 1968-1992 Ed. Spec: Hebrew Bible, Semitic Languages, Texts and Epigraphy. Pub: "The Legal Dispute Between Jephthah and the Elders" *HAR* 12 (1990); "'Lifting Up the Head': On the Trail of a Word Play in Genesis 40" *Prooftexts* 10 (1990); *Jephthah and His Vow* (Tex. Tech. U., 1986); *A Manual of Babylonian Jewish Aramaic* (U. Press of Amer., 1981); "Some Antiphrastic Euphemisms for a Blind Person in Akkadian and Other Semitic Languages" *JAOS* 100 (1980); *A Manual of Akkadian* (U. Press of Amer., 1978); and others. Mem: AOS 1964-; SBL 1964-. Rec: Squash. Addr: (o) Jewish Theological Seminary, 3080 Broadway, New York, NY 10027 212-678-8856; (h) 37 Lester Pl., New Rochelle, NY 10804 914-576-3487.

MARE, William H., b. Oregon, July 23, 1918, s. of Scott & Sallie (Knight), m. Elizabeth, chil: Myra; Sally; Nancy; William; Judith. Educ: Wheaton Coll., BA 1941, MA 1946; Faith Theol. Sem., BD 1945; U. of Pa., PhD 1961. Emp: Faith Theol. Sem., 1946-53; Presbyn. Ch., 1953-63 Pastor; Covenant Coll., 1963-65 Prof.; Covenant Theol. Sem., 1963- Prof., NT; Grace Theol. Sem., 1973 Guest Lect. Excv: Near East Sch. of Arch., Jerusalem, 1962, 1964, 1970 Dir., Prof.; Raddana, Israel, 1972; Heshbon, Jordan, 1974, 1976; Moab Survey, Jordan, 1979; Abila of the Decapolis, 1980, 1982, 1984, 1986, 1988, 1990, 1992 Dir. Spec: Archaeology, New Testament. Pub: Articles in *ABD* (Doubleday, 1992); "Abila" in *New Ency. of Archaeological Excavations in the Holy Land* (Simon & Schuster, 1992); *The Archaeology of the Jerusalem Area* (Baker, 1986); "The Abila Excavation. The Seventh Campaign of Abila of the Decapolis" *NEAS Bull.* 24 (1992); *Mastering New Testament Greek* (Baker, 1979); "A Study of the New Testament Concept of the Parousia" in Festschrift, Merrill C. Tenney (Eerdmans, 1975); "Acts 7: Jewish or Samaritan in Character?" *WTJ* 34/1 (1971); and others. Mem: SBL; ASOR; AIA; NEAS, Pres. 1971-. Rec: Photography. Addr: (o) Covenant Theological Seminary, 12330 Conway Rd., St. Louis, MO 63141 314-434-4044; (h) 978 Orchard Lakes Dr., St. Louis, MO 63146 314-569-0879.

MARGALIT, Baruch, b. Montreal, Canada, November 28, 1940, s. of William and Ruth, m. Bina (Rauchberger), chil: Doron Mordechai; Michal Netta; Mérav Rachel; Uri Menachem. Educ: McGill U., BA, Phil. & Political Sci. 1961; PhD, 1967. Emp: Hebrew Teachers Coll., Boston, 1965-68 Fac.; Ben-Gurion U., Israel, 1968 Fac.; Haifa U., Dept. of Biblical Stud., 1969- Prof. Pub: *A Matter of Life and Death* (Neukirchen-Vluyn, 1980); and others. Awd: Woodrow Wilson Fellow. 1961. Rec: bridge, swimming, cantorial music, barbering. Addr: (o) Haifa U., Dept. of Biblical Studies, Mt. Carmel, Haifa, Israel; (h) PO Box 227, Zikhron Ia'aqov 30900, Israel.

MARGOT, Jean-Claude, b. Chateau-d'Oex, Switzerland, June 10, 1924, s. of Willy & Marcelle (Baumgartner), m. Annie (Thomas), chil: Catherine; Henriette; Francois; Daniel; Genevieve. Educ: Faculte de Theologie de l'Eglise libre, Lausanne, Lic.Th. 1951; U. de Lausanne, ThD 1978. Emp: Vaud, Switzerland, 1950-66 Pasteur de l'Eglise libre; United Bible Soc., 1966-89 trans. cons.; *Cahiers de Traduction Biblique*, Paris, 1983- Ed. Spec: New Testament. Pub: *Traduire sans trahir: La Theorie de la Traduction et son Application aux Textes Bibliques* (L'Age d'Homme, 1979, 1990); "L'impot du temple: Matthieu 17:24-27" in *Understanding and Translating the Bible* (1974); "L'indissolubilite du mariage selon le Nouveau Testament" *Revue de Theologie et de Philosophie* (1967); "Heritage" in *Vocabulaire Biblique* (Neuchatel, 1964); *Les Epitres de Pierre. Commentaire* (Labor et Fides, 1960); and others. Mem: Soc. vaudoise de theol. 1951-; Soc. suisse de theol. 1966-. Rec: Music, reading best novels. Addr: (h) Ch. des Ecoliers, 10 CH 1163 Etoy, Switzerland 021-808-58-01.

MARGUERAT, Daniel L., b. Lausanne, Switzerland, October 30, 1943, d. of Michel & Renee, m. Claire Diserens, chil: Isabelle; Laurence. Emp: U. of Lausanne, 1984- Prof., NT, Fac. of Theol. Spec: New Testament. Pub: *L'homme qui venait de Nazareth: Ce qu'on peut aujourd'hui savoir de Jesus* (Moulin, 1993); *La memoire et le temps: Melanges offerts a Pierre Bonnard*, co-auth., Le Monde de la Bible 23 (Labor et Fides, 1991); *Le Dieu des premiers chretiens*, Essais bibl. 16 (Labor et Fides, 1990); *Vivre avec la mort: Le defi du Nouveau Testament* (Moulin, 1990); "La 'source des signes' existe-t-elle?" in *La communaute johannique et son histoire*, Le Monde de la Bible 20 (Labor et Fides, 1990); "2 Corinthiens 10-13: Paul et l'experience de Dieu" *ETR* 63 (1988); "A quoi sert l'exegese? Finalite et methodes dans la lecture du Nouveau Testament" *RThPh* 119 (1987); "El porvenir de la ley: Mateo puesto a prueba ante Pablo" *Selecciones de teologia* 23 (1984); "L'avenir de la Loi: Matthieu a l'epreuve de Paul" *ETR* 57 (1982); and others. Mem: SNTS; Assn. Cath. Francaise pour l'Etude de la Bible; SBL. Addr: (o) U. of Lausanne, Faculty of Theology, BFSH 2, 1015 Lausanne,

Switzerland 21-692-44-83; (h) 9 Ave. Davel, 1004 Lausanne, Switzerland 21-37-37-07.

MARIOTTINI, Claude F., b. Rio de Janeiro, Brazil, December 24, 1942, s. of Waldemiro & Palmyra (Bastos), m. Donna, chil: Claude; Christopher; James. Educ: Calif. Bapt. Coll., BA 1968; Golden Gate Bapt. Theol. Sem., MDiv 1971; South. Bapt. Theol. Sem., PhD 1983. Emp: South. Bapt. Theol. Sem., 1982 Instr.; SW Bapt. U., 1983-88 Asst. Prof.; North. Bapt. Sem., 1988-. Spec: Hebrew Bible, Mesopotamian Studies, New Testament, Apocrypha and Post-biblical Studies. Pub: *Paso a Paso a Traves del Antiguo Testamento*; "1 and 2 Chronicles" in *Mercer Bible Comm.* Mem: SBL; ASOR; CBA. Rec: Soccer, bowling, reading. Addr: (o) Northern Baptist Seminary, 660 E Butterfield Rd., Lombard, IL 60148 708-620-2186.

MARJANEN, Antti, b. Helsinki, Finland, March 28, 1952, s. of Helge & Linnea, m. Solveig, chil: Katja; Jani; Patrik; Jenna. Educ: Bapt. Theol. Sem., Switzerland, BD 1977. Emp: U. of Helsinki, 1983- Lect., Bibl. Exegetics. Spec: New Testament, Apocrypha and Post-biblical Studies. Pub: *Jeesuksen salaiset sanat: Tuomaan evankeliumi* (Helsinki U.P., 1992); "Juutalaiset uskonnolliset velvoitteet Tuomaan evankeliumissa" in *Alkukirkko ja Juutalaisuus* (Finnish Exegetical Soc., 1991); "Maailman synnystä gnostilaisuudessa: Luomismyytti Johanneksen apokryfin mukaan" *TAik* 96 (1991); "Nag Hammadin kirjasto ja varhaiskristillisyyden tutkimus" *TAik* 88 (1983); and others. Mem: Finnish Exegetical Soc. 1982-; IACS 1986-; SBL 1990-. Rec: Jogging, Finnish baseball, basketball, literature. Addr: (o) Eksegetiikan laitos, PL 37 (Neitsytpolku 1b), SF-00014 Helsingin yliopisto, Finland 90-1911; (h) Viertolankatu 49 B 7, SF-05800 Hyvinkaa, Finland 914-452367.

MARKS, Herbert J., b. New York, NY, June 22, 1947, s. of Robert & Rosemary, m. Elizabeth (Hodges), chil: Robert; Jesse. Educ: Princeton U., AB 1969; Oxford U., Dip. 1970; Yale U., PhD 1985. Emp: Yale U., Instr.; Indiana U., Asst. Prof., Assoc. Prof., Dir., Inst. Bibl. & Lit. Stud.; *Indiana Studies in Biblical Literature*, Co-ed. Spec: Hebrew Bible. Pub: "The Twelve Prophets" in *Literary Guide to the Bible* (1987); "On Prophetic Stammering" *Yale Jour. of Criticism* (1987); "Pauline Typology and Revisionary Criticism" *JAAR* 52/1 (1984); and others. Awd: NEH Fellow 1988. Mem: SBL. Addr: (o) Indiana U., Comparative Literature, Ballantine Hall 402, Bloomington, IN 47405 812-855-7070.

MARLOWE, Walter C., b. Mooresville, NC, June 14, 1951, s. of Billy G. & N. Louise, m. Sherry L., chil: Marcus Creighton; Jonathan Michael. Educ: U. of N.C., BA 1973; West. Sem., M.Div. 1977, ThM 1979; Mid-Amer. Sem., ThD 1985. Emp: West. Sem., 1988-89 Vis. Prof.,

Hebrew Scriptures; Tyndale Sem., 1989- Asst. Prof., OT Stud., 1991-92 Acting Acad. Dean, 1992 Asst. to the Pres. for Admin. Spec: Hebrew Bible. Pub: "A Summary Evaluation of OT Hebrew Lexica, Translations, and Philology" *Grace Theol. Jour.* (1991); "Biblical Distinctives Between the Content and Character of Preaching and Teaching," co-auth. *Jour. of Christian Educ.* (1981). Awd: West. Sem., Ch. Hist. Awd. 1978. Mem: ETS 1980-; SBL 1991-; Fellow. of European Evang. Theol. 1992-. Rec: Tennis, reading, camping. Addr: (o) Tyndale Theological Seminary, Egelantierstraat 1, 1171 JM Badhoevedorp, Netherlands 020-6596455; (h) Windstraat 36, 1171 KA Badhoevedorp, Netherlands 020-6595738.

MARROW, Stanley B., b. Baghdad, Iraq, February 10, 1931, s. of Behjet & Victoria (Korkis). Educ: Boston Coll., MA 1955; Weston Coll., STL 1962; Pont. Bibl. Inst., Rome, SSL 1964; Gregorian U., Rome, STD 1966. Emp: Weston Sch. of Theol., 1971- Prof.; *Biblica,* 1968-71 Assoc. Ed.; *NT Abstracts,* 1971- Assoc. Ed.; *CBQ,* 1978-86 Assoc. Ed. Spec: New Testament. Pub: "Principles for Interpreting the New Testament Soteriological Terms" *NTS* 36 (1990); *Paul, His Letters and His Theology* (Paulist, 1986); "A Christological Paraenesis: Philippians 2:5-11" *Word & Spirit* 5 (1983); "*Parrhesia* and the New Testament" *CBQ* 44 (1982); *Basic Tools of Biblical Exegesis* (Bibl. Inst., 1978); and others. Mem: CBA 1965-; SBL 1971-; AAR 1971-; SNTS. Addr: (o) Weston School of Theology, 3 Phillips Place, Cambridge, MA 02138 617-492-1960.

MARRS, Rick R., b. Tucson, AZ, May 28, 1952, s. of Roscoe & Vivian, m. Paula, chil: Staci; Jeremy. Educ: Abilene Christian U., BA 1973, MDiv 1976; Johns Hopkins U., PhD 1982. Emp: Villa Julie Coll., 1979-84 Asst. Prof.; Ecumenical Inst. of Theol., 1982-84 Adj. Prof.; Inst. for Christian Stud., 1984-87 Assoc. Prof.; Pepperdine U., 1987- Assoc. Prof. Spec: Hebrew Bible, Semitic Languages, Texts and Epigraphy. Pub: "The Sons of God (Genesis 6:1-4)" *RQ* 23 (1980). Mem: SBL; CBA. Rec: Tennis. Addr: (o) 24255 Pacific Coast Hwy., Malibu, CA 90263 310-456-4179; (h) 1431 Kirk Ave., Thousand Oaks, CA 91360 805-379-3071.

MARSH, John, b. Brighton, England, November 5, 1904, s. of George Maurice & Florence Elizabeth, m. Gladys (Walker), chil: John; George; Mary. Educ: Edinburgh U., Scotland, MA, Phil 1928; Mansfield Coll., Oxford, DPhil 1931. Emp: Edinburgh U., Scotland, 1926-28 Asst. Lect.; Westhill Training Coll., England, 1932-34 Lect.; Congregational Ch., 1934-38 Min.; Mansfield Coll. Oxford, 1938-48 Tutor, Chaplain, 1953-70 Prin.; Nottingham U., 1949-53 Prof., Christian Theol. Spec: Archaeology, Hebrew Bible. Pub: *Theology of the New Testament,* trans. (1955); *Amos and Micah* (SCM, 1959); *Commentary St.*

John (Pelican, 1963); *Jesus in His Lifetime* (Sidgwick & Jackson, 1981); and others. Awd: Edinburgh U., DD 1955; Commander British Empire, 1964; Nottingham U., DD 1991. Mem: SOTS; SNTS. Rec: Water color painting, poetry. Addr: (h) 5 Diamond Court, 135 Banbury Rd. Oxford OX2 7AA, England.

MARSHALL, I. Howard, b. Carlisle, England, January 12, 1934, s. of Ernest & Ethel, m. Joyce. Educ: U. of Aberdeen, MA 1955, BD 1959, PhD 1963; U. of Cambridge, BA 1959. Emp: Meth. Min. 1960-64; U. of Aberdeen, 1964- Prof., NT Exegesis; *EQ,* 1982- Ed.; *JSNT,* 1981- Adv. Ed.; Manson Memorial Lect. 1989. Spec: New Testament. Pub: *Philippians* (Epworth, 1992); *1 Peter* (InterVarsity, 1991); "Luke's View of Paul" *SW Jour. of Theol.* 33 (1990); "Church and Temple in the New Testament" *TB* 40/2 (1989); "The Christology of the Pastoral Epistles" *SNTU* 13 (1988); *1 and 2 Thessalonians* (Eerdmans, 1983); *The Gospel of Luke* (Eerdmans, 1978); and others. Mem: SNTS; Tyndale Fellow.; Fellow. of European Evang. Theol.; SBL. Addr: (o) The University, Dept of New Testament Exegesis, Aberdeen AB9 2UB, Scotland 0224-272388.

MARSHALL, Robert J., b. Burlington, IA, August 26, 1918, s. of Robert M. & Margaret E., m. Alice (Hepner), chil: Robert E.; Margaret (Niederer). Educ: Wittenberg U., BA 1941; Chicago Luth. Theol. Sem., MDiv 1944. Emp: Muhlenberg Coll., 1947-53 Assoc. Prof.; Chicago Luth. Theol. Sem., 1953-62 Prof.; Luth. Ch. in Amer., 1962-78 Synod Pres./Pres.; Luth. Theol. South. Sem., 1981-88 Prof.; Luth. Sch. of Theol. at Chicago, 1988- Adj. Prof. Spec: Hebrew Bible. Pub: *The Mighty Acts of God* (Augsburg/Fortress, 1964, 1990); "The Structure of Isaiah 1-12" *Bibl. Res.* (1962). Mem: SBL 1950-; CSBR 1953-62; ASOR 1959-. Addr: (o) 1100 E 55th St., Chicago, IL 60615 312-753-0673; (h) 1700 E 56th St., Apt. 901, Chicago, IL 60637-1933 312-363-4587.

MARTENS, Elmer A., b. Main Ctr., SK, Canada, August 12, 1930, s. of J.H. & Susie, m. Phyllis, chil: Lauren; Frances; Vernon; Karen. Educ: U. of Saskatchewan, Canada, BA 1954; U. of Manitoba, Canada, BEd 1956; Mennonite Brethren Bibl. Sem., BD 1958; Claremont Grad. Sch., PhD 1972. Emp: *New American Standard Bible,* 1969-70 Trans. Team; Mennonite Brethren Bibl. Sem., 1970- Prof., 1977-86 Pres.; *New King James Version,* 1977 Trans. Team. Spec: Hebrew Bible. Pub: *The Flowering of Old Testament Theology,* co-ed. (Eisenbrauns, 1992); "Biblical Theology and Normativity" in *So Wide a Sea: Essays in Biblical and Systematic Theology* (Inst. of Mennonite Stud., 1991); *Jeremiah,* Believers Church Bible Comm. (Herald, 1986); *Plot and Purpose in the Old Testament* (InterVarsity Press, 1981); *God's Design: A Theology of the Old Testament* (Baker, 1981); "Tackling Old Testament Theology" *JETS* (1977); and others. Mem: IBR; SBL; NEAS. Addr: (o) 4824 E Butler,

Fresno, CA 93727 209-251-8628; (h) 4850 E Rialto, Fresno, CA 93276 209-291-5904.

MARTENS, John W., b. Vancouver, BC, November 10, 1960, s. of John & Gertrude, m. Jo-Ann Amy, chil: Jacob Peter. Educ: U. of St. Michael's Coll., U. of Toronto, BA 1984; McMaster U., MA 1987, PhD 1991. Emp: Canadian Mennonite Bible Coll., 1991-92 Instr.; Concord Coll., 1991-92 Instr.; U. of Winnipeg, 1992-93 Instr. Spec: New Testament, Apocrypha and Post-biblical Studies. Pub: "Unwritten Law in Philo: A Response to Naomi G. Cohen" *JJS* 43 (1992). Awd: Deutscher Akademischer Austauschdienst 1989-90. Mem: CSBS 1989-; SBL 1991-. Rec: Soccer, hockey, woodwork, painting & drawing. Addr: (h) 1-540 Corydon Ave., Winnipeg, Man. R3L-0P1, Canada 204-284-1451.

MARTIN, Clarice J., b. Los Angeles, CA, d. of Strown & Fannie. Educ: U. of Calif., BA 1972; Wheaton Grad. Sch., MA 1974; San Francisco Theol. Sem., MDiv 1981; Duke U. Grad. Sch. of Relig., PhD 1985. Emp: Princeton Theol. Sem., 1985-92 Asst. Prof., NT; Colgate Rochester Div. Sch., 1992- Assoc. Prof., NT. Spec: New Testament. Pub: "Mary's Song" in *Dict. of Jesus and the Gospels* (InterVarsity, 1992); "The Haustafein (Household Codes) in African-American Biblical Interpretation: 'Free Slaves' and 'Subordinate Women'" in *Stony the Road We Trod: African-American Biblical Interpretation* (Fortress, 1991); "The Rhetorical Function of Commercial Language in Paul's Letter to Philemon (v. 18)" in *Persuasive Artistry: Studies in Honor of George A. Kennedy* (Sheffield, 1991); "Womanist Interpretations of the New Testament: The Quest for Holistic and Inclusive Biblical Translation and Interpretation" *Jour. of Feminist Stud. in Relig.* 6/2 (1990); *Tongues of Fire: Power for the Church Today. Studies in the Acts of the Apostles* (Horizons, 1990); "A Chamberlain's Journey and the Challenge of Interpretation for Liberation" *Semeia* 47 (1989); and others. Mem: AAR; SBL; Soc. for the Stud. of Black Relig.; Fund for Theol. Educ. Rec: Tennis, jogging. Addr: (o) Colgate Rochester Divinity School, 1100 South Goodman St., Rochester, NY 14620 716-271-1320; (h) 3 Watchman Ct., Rochester, NY 14624 716-426-8384.

MARTIN, Ernest L., b. Meeker, OK, April 20, 1932, s. of Joel Chester & Lula Mae (Quinn), m. Ramona Mallett (Kinsey), chil: Kathryn; Phyllis; Samuel. Educ: Ambassador Coll., BA 1957, MTh 1960, PhD 1965. Emp: Ambassador Coll., England, 1960-72 Tchr., Calif., 1972-73 Chmn., Dept. of Theol.; Found. for Bibl. Res., 1974-85 Dir., *Commentary,* Ed.; Assn. for Scriptural Knowledge, 1985- Dir., *Communicator,* Ed.; Manuscript Version of the Bible Project, 1989 Originator. Excv: Temple Mount, 1969-74 Supr. of 450 Students. Spec: Archaeology, New Testament. Pub: *The Original Bible Restored*

(Found. for Bibl. Res., 1984; Assn. for Scriptural Knowledge, 1991); *Secrets of Golgatha* (Assn. for Scriptural Knowledge, 1987); *The Birth of Christ Recalculated* (Found. for Bibl. Res., 1978, 1980); and others. Mem: SBL; PES. Rec: Meteorological & astronomical exploratory activities. Addr: (o) Associates for Scriptural Knowledge, PO Box 25000, Portland, OR 97225 503-292-4352; (h) 7222 SW Scholls Ferry Rd., #1, Beaverton, OR 97005 503-644-6520.

MARTIN, Luther H., Jr., b. Richmond, VA, June 1, 1937, s. of L. Howard & Mary (McKay), m. Rux, chil: Brendan; Hilary. Educ: Drew U., MDiv 1962, STM 1963; Claremont Grad. Sch., PhD 1972. Emp: U. of Vt., 1967- Assoc. Prof., 1987- Prof. Pub: *Hellenistic Religions: An Introductory Essay* (Oxford U.P., 1987); *Essays on Jung and the Study of Religion*, co-ed. (U. Press of Amer., 1985); "Why Cecropian Minerva? Hellenistic Religious Syncretism as System" *Numen* (1983); "Josephus' Use of *Heimurmena* in the *Jewish Antiquities* XII, 171-3" *Numen* (1981); and others. Mem: AAR; SBL; NAASR. Addr: (o) U. of Vermont, Dept. of Religion, Burlington, VT 05405 802-656-3080; (h) Underhill Ctr., VT 05490 802-899-3423.

MARTIN, Ralph P., b. Liverpool, England, August 4, 1925, s. of Philip & Ada, m. Lily, chil: Patricia; Elizabeth. Educ: U. of Manchester, BA 1949, MA 1955; U. of London, PhD 1963. Emp: London Bible Coll., 1955-64 Lect.; Bethel Theol. Sem., 1964-65 Vis. Prof.; U. of Manchester, 1965-69 Lect.; Fuller Theol. Sem., 1969-88 Prof.; U. of Sheffield, 1988- Prof., Bibl. Stud. Dept. Spec: New Testament. Pub: *Ephesians, Colossians, and Philemon* (Westminster, 1991); *Worship of God* (Eerdmans, 1984); *Carmen Christi* (Cambridge U.P./Eerdmans, 1963, 1983); *Reconciliation* (John Knox, 1981). Mem: SNTS; SBL; IBR. Addr: (h) 4 College Close, Birkdale, Southport PR8 4DG, England.

MARTINEZ, Ernest R., b. Denver, CO, December 12, 1931, s. of Belarmino & Nievecitas (Lopez). Educ: Gonzaga U., MA 1956; U. of Santa Clara, MST 1963; Alma Coll., LST 1963; Pont. Bibl. Inst., Rome, SSL 1966; Pontifical Gregorian U., Rome, STD 1970. Emp: Loyola U., 1969-70 Asst. Prof.; Jesuit Sch. of Theol. at Berkeley, 1971-79 Asst. Prof.; Diocese of Oakland, Calif., Dept. Catechetical Min. 1976-89 Cons. for Scripture; Pont. Gregorian U., Rome, 1989- Adj. Prof.; Pont. Bibl. Inst., Rome, 1970, 1979-81 Vis. Prof. Spec: Hebrew Bible, New Testament. Pub: *Hebrew-Ugaritic Index with an Eblaite Index*, vol. I & II (Bibl. Inst., 1967, 1981); "The Identity of Jesus in Mark" *Communio* 1 (1974); *The Gospel Accounts of the Death of Jesus* (Gregorian U.P., 1970); "The Interpretation of 'Oi Mathetai in Matthew 18" *CBQ* 23 (1961); and others. Mem: CBA 1970-; SBL 1970-; CTSA 1970-. Rec: Opera, photography. Addr: (o) Pontificia U. Gregoriana, Piazza della Pilotta, 4, 00187 Rome, Italy 39-6-6701-5317.

MARTOLA, Nils O., b. Helsingfors, March 22, 1943, s. of Karl-Erik & Ester Sofia (Bystrom), m. Yngvill (Johansson), chil: Jutta Maria. Educ: Abo Akademi, Fac. of Theol., MDiv 1968, Lic. Div. 1980, DD 1984; Abo Akademi, U. Lib., Degree 1969; Abo Akademi, Fac. of Hum., MA 1974. Emp: Inst. of Exegetics, Abo Akademi, 1975-77 Lect., Hebrew & OT Stud., 1977-92 Asst. in Exegetics; Finnish Acad., 1985-88 Res. Fellow; *Scandinavian Jour. of Jewish Stud.*, 1985-91 Chief Ed. Spec: Hebrew Bible, Apocrypha and Post-biblical Studies. Pub: "Rabbinatet i historiskt perspektiv" *Nordisk judaistik* 10 (1989); *Kommentar till Paskhaggadan*, Religionsvetenskapliga skrifter 16 (Abo Akademi, 1988); "Litterära former i Mishna" *Nordisk judaistik* 8 (1987); *Capture and Liberation: A Study in the Composition of the First Book of Maccabees*, Acta Acad. Aboensis, Humaniori 63/1 (Abo Akademi, 1984); "Kriget som en purification av det oskärade landet—ett fragment" *Teologisk tidskrift* 89 (1984); "Det heliga kriget i Gamla Testamentet" in *Fredsperspektiv i teologin* (1984); and others. Mem: Soc. for Jewish Stud. 1976-; European Assn. for the Study of Judaism 1990-; Finnish Exegetical Soc. 1991-. Rec: Reading science fiction, walking in the mountains. Addr: (o) Biskopsgatan 16 A, SF-20500 Abo, Finland 9-21-654565; (h) Eskogatan 8 C 102, SF-20340 Abo, Finland 9-21-483508.

MARUCCI, Corrado, b. Bologna, Italy, August 19, 1940, s. of Oreste & Annamaria (Bongiovanni). Educ: Aloisianum, Italy, Lic. Phil. 1966; U. of Padua, Italy, Dr. Math. 1970; Phil.-Theol. Hochschule, ThD 1980. Emp: Pont. Theol. Fac. of South Italy, 1981-87 Adj. Prof., 1993- Prof., NT Exegesis; Leopold Franzens U., Austria, 1987-93 Prof., NT Exegesis. Spec: New Testament. Pub: "Die Haltung der neutestamentlichen Schriftsteller gegenuber dem romischen Reich" *ZKT* 114 (1992); "La rilevanza sapienziale della Torah nel quarto libro dei Maccabei e negli scritti di F. Giuseppe" in *Sapienza e Torah* (1987); "Die implizite Christologie in der sogenannten Vollmachtsfrage (Mk 11,27-33)" *ZKT* 108 (1986); "Matrimonio e divorzio nella teologia di M. Lutero" in *Ecclesiae Sacramentum, Studi in onore di A. Marranzini* (1986); *Il nuovo diritto matrimoniale della Chiesa*, co-auth. (Dehoniane, 1985); *Parole di Gesùsul divorzio*, Aloisiana 16 (Morcelliana, 1982); and others. Mem: SNTS 1984-; Europaische Gesellschaft fur Katholische Theol. 1990-; Intl. Soc. for the Class. Tradition 1992-; Assn. Bibl. Italiana 1992-; SBL 1994. Rec: Music, lit. Addr: (o) Pont. Facolta dell'Italia Meridionale, Via Petrarca 115, I-80122 Napoli, Italy 081-5750015.

MARZAL, Angel, b. Saucedilla, Spain, November 23, 1933, s. of Pedro & Luciana. Educ: Gregorian U., Rome, STL 1958; Pont. Bibl. Inst., SSL 1960; U. of Chicago, PhD 1969. Emp: DePaul U., 1965-72 Asst. Prof.; Central YMCA Community Coll., 1972-, Instr. Spec: Hebrew Bible, Mesopotamian Studies, Semitic Languages, Texts and Epigraphy. Pub: "Nuevas cláusulas 'apodicticas' de Mari" *Sefarad* 38

(1978); *Gleanings from the Wisdom of Mari* (Bibl. Inst., 1976); "Two Officials Assisting the Provincial Governor at Mari" *Orientalia* 41 (1972); "The Provincial Governor at Mari: His Title and Appointment" *JNES* 30 (1971); "Mari Clauses in 'Casuistic' and 'Apodictic' Styles" *CBQ* 33 (1971); "Consideraciones sobre la raiz ugaritica *t l t*" *Biblica* 44 (1963); and others. Awd: Fulbright Fellow. 1962-63. Mem: AOS; CBA. Addr: (h) 16445 S Halsted St., Harvey, IL 60426 708-339-3139.

MASON, John P., b. Martinsville, VA, October 19, 1951, s. of John Felix & Inice (Smith), m. Terri (Paxton). Educ: Averett Coll., BA 1974; SE Bapt. Theol. Sem., MDiv 1976, MTh 1981; South. Bapt. Theol. Sem., DPhil 1989. Emp: South. Bapt. Theol. Sem., 1987-90 Instr., 1988-90 Garrett Teaching Fellow, 1990- Adj. Prof., NT; Bapt. Ch., Pastor. Spec: New Testament. Pub: "Fables and Endless Genealogies" *BI* Summer (1992); "The Heavenly Places" *BI* Spring (1991); *Reading the New Testament: Exercises for Beginning Readers of the Greek New Testament*, co-auth. (Mellen, 1988); and others. Mem: SBL 1989-; IBR 1990-. Rec: Softball, swimming, reading, frisbee. Addr: (o) Trinity Baptist Church, 2808 Ballentine Blvd., Norfolk, VA 23509 804-853-5017; (h) 1156 Pascal Pl., Norfolk, VA 23502 804-461-6685.

MASON, Steve N., b. Scarborough, ON, Canada, September 14, 1957, s. of Terry & Grace, m. Glenna, chil: Cara Lynn; Ian Trevor. Educ: McMaster U., BA 1980, MA 1981; U. of St. Michael's Coll., Canada, PhD 1986. Emp: Memorial U. of Newfoundland, 1987-89 Assoc. Prof.; York U., Canada, 1989- Assoc. Prof.; ASOR Diss. Ser., 1990- Ed. Bd. Spec: New Testament, Apocrypha and Post-biblical Studies. Pub: *Josephus and the New Testament* (Hendrickson, 1992); *Flavius Josephus on the Pharisees: A Composition-Critical Study*, Studia Post-Biblica 39 (Brill, 1991); "Pharisaic Dominance Before 70 CE and the Gospels' Hypocrisy Charge (Matt 23:2-3" *HTR* 83/4 (1990); *An Early Christian Reader*, co-auth. (Canadian Schol., 1990); "Paul, Classical Anti-Judaism, and the Letter to the Romans" in *Self-Definition and Self-Discovery in Early Christianity*, Stud. in the Bible & Early Christianity 26 (Mellen, 1990); "Was Josephus a Pharisee? A Re-examination of *Life* 10-12" *JJS* 40/1 (1990); "Josephus on the Pharisees Reconsidered: A Critique of Smith/Neusner" *Stud. in Relig.* 17/4 (1988); "Priesthood in Josephus and the 'Pharisaic Revolution'" *JBL* 107 (1988); and others. Awd: Social Sci. and Hum. Res. Coun. of Canada, res grant 1991-93. Mem: CSBS 1981-; SBL 1987-. Rec: Sports, swimming. Addr: (o) York U., 219 Vanier College, 4700 Keele St., North York, ON M3J 1P3, Canada 416-736-5158; (h) 4 Viewmark Dr., Richmond Hill, ON L4S 1C9, Canada 416-508-7098.

MATHENEY, M. Pierce, Jr., b. El Dorado, AR, September 24, 1930, s. of M.P. & Harriett

(Waters), m. Katherine E. (Clippard), chil: Susan; Matthew; Kendall. Educ: Baylor U., BA 1952; Brown U., MA 1958; South. Bapt. Theol. Sem., BD 1957, ThD 1965. Emp: South. Bapt. Theol. Sem., 1958-60 Instr.; Midw. Sem., 1960- Prof., OT Hebrew, 1972 Pres. Excv: Tell Halif, 1986-88 Area Supr. Spec: Archaeology, Hebrew Bible, Semitic Languages, Texts and Epigraphy. Pub: "The 'Isles'" *BI* (1984); "The Ark of the Covenant" *BI* (1973); "Major Purposes of the Book of Job" *SW Jour. of Theol.* (1971); "Interpretation of Hebrew Prophetic Symbolic Acts" *Encounter* (1968); "Introduction to 1-2 Kings" & "Commentary on 1 Kings" in *Broadman Bible Commentary* vol. 3; "God's Wounded Love" in *Study Guide to Hosea*; "Studies in Psalms" in *Study Guide to Psalms*; and others. Mem: SBL 1960-; ASOR 1960-. Rec: Travel, photography. Addr: (o) Midwestern Baptist Theological Seminary, 5001 N Oak St. Hwy., Kansas City, MO 64118 816-453-4600; (h) 5221 N Garfield, Kansas City, MO 64118 816-452-5253.

MATSUNAGA, Kikup, b. Nagoya, Japan, May 11, 1933, s. of Torkujiro & Yoshie, m. Junko, chil: Tomoo; Nobutsugu; Yuhko. Educ: Intl. Christian U., BA 1957; Tokyo Union Theol. Sem., Grad. Sch. 1960; Union Theol. Sem., STM 1965; McGill U., PhD 1970. Emp: Kyodan, 1960-83 Min.; Tokyo Union Theol. Sem., 1970- Prof., Pres.; *Seisho to Kyokai*, 1979-83 Ed.; *Pedilabium*, 1979-83, 1988- Ed.; Intl. Christian U., 1983- Lect. Spec: New Testament. Pub: *Jesus in History* (NHK, 1989); "Is John Anti-Sacramental?" *NTS* 27 (1981); "The Theos' Chrisiology as the Ultimate Confession of the Fourth Gospel" *Ann. of the Japan Bibl. Inst.* (1981); "The World of John-Jesus' Enemies in the Fourth Gospel" in *Festschrift fur Dr. Teo Kanda* (1975) "Judas Iscariot in the Fourth Gospel" *Japan Bibl. Inst. Collected Paper* 9 (1972) and others. Rec: Readings, classical music. Addr: (o) Tokyo Union Theological Seminary, 3-10-30 Osawa, Mitaka, Tokyo 181, Japan.

MATTHEWS, Victor H., b. Joplin, MO, November 13, 1950, s. of Harold & Lillie, m. Carol (Mason), chil: Peter; Samuel. Educ: Brandeis U., MA 1973, PhD 1977. Emp: Clemson U., 1978-80 Vis. Asst. Prof.; Anderson Coll., 1980-84 Asst. Prof.; Southwest Mo. State U., 1984- Prof. Spec: Hebrew Bible, Mesopotamian Studies. Pub: "Hospitality & Hostility in Gen 19 & Judg 19" *BTB* 22 (1992); "The King's Call to Justice" *BZ* 35 (1991); *Old Testament Parallels* (Paulist, 1991); *Manners and Customs in the Bible* (Hendrickson, 1988); "Entrance Ways & Threshing Floors" *Fides et Historia* 19 (1987); and others. Mem: SBL. Rec: Editor, *ASOR Newsletter*. Addr: (o) Southwest Missouri State U., Religious Studies Dept., Cheek Hall 17M, Springfield, MO 65804 417-836-5491; (h) 1320 E. Delmar, Springfield, MO 65804 417-865-2405.

MATTIES, Gordon H., b. Chilliwack, BC, December 28, 1951, s. of Henry & Mary, m.

Lorraine E., chil: Zoe; Jesse. Educ: U. of Brit. Columbia, BA 1976; Regent Coll., DipCS 1979; Vanderbilt U., MA 1984, PhD 1989. Emp: Mennonite Brethren Bible Coll., 1984-92 Asst. Prof.; Concord Coll., 1992- Asst. Prof.; Believers Ch. Bible Comm., Ed. Coun. Spec: Hebrew Bible. Pub: *Ezekiel 18 and the Rhetoric of Moral Discourse*, SBL Diss. Ser. 126 (Scholars, 1990). Awd: Regent Coll., Bd. of Governors Prize 1979, Bibl. Stud. Prize 1979; Amer. Bible Soc. Awd. 1983. Mem: SBL 1980-; Canadian Soc. of Bibl. Stud. 1984-; IBR 1991-. Addr: (o) Concord College, 169 Riverton Ave., Winnipeg, Man. R2L 2E5, Canada 204-669-6575; (h) 141 Glenwood Cres., Winnipeg, Man. R2L 1J7, Canada 204-668-2527.

MATTILL, Andrew J., Jr., b. St. Joseph, MO, August 2, 1924, s. of Andrew & Ruth (Hanne), m. Mary (Bedford). Educ: U. of Chicago, BA 1949; Evang. Theol. Sem., BD 1952; Vanderbilt U., PhD 1959. Emp: Berry Coll., 1958-62 Assoc. Prof.; Livingstone Coll., 1962-65 Prof.; Winebrenner Theol. Sem., 1965-75 Bucher Prof. of NT Lang. & Lit.; Universalist Ch., 1977-. Spec: New Testament. Pub: *Jesus and the Last Things: The Story of Jesus the Suffering Servant* (Flatwoods Free, 1983); *Luke and the Last Things: A Perspective for the Understanding of Lukan Thought* (West. N.C., 1979); "The Way of Tribulation" *JBL* 98 (1979); "The Jesus-Paul Parallels and the Purpose of Luke-Acts" *NT* 17 (1975); "*Naherwartung, Fernerwartung,* and the Purpose of the Luke-Acts" *CBQ* 34 (1972); and others. Mem: SBL 1956-90. Rec: Bird watching, travel. Addr: (h) Rt 2, Box 49, Gordo, AL 35466-9516 205-364-7883.

MAUSER, Ulrich W., b. Stuttgart, Germany, October 3, 1926, s. of Wilhelm & Helene (Postruschnigg), m. Margaret (Malcolm), chil: Ulrich W.; Martin A.; George M.; Thomas L. Educ: U. of Tubingen, ThD 1957. Emp: Louisville Presbyn. Theol. Sem., 1964-77 Prof., Bibl. Theol.; Pittsburgh Theol. Sem., 1977-90 Prof., NT, 1981-90 Dean; *Horizons in Bibl. Theol.*, 1979-90 Ed., 1990- Co-Ed.; Princeton Theol. Sem., 1990- Prof., NT. Spec: New Testament. Pub: *The Gospel of Peace* (Westminster/John Knox, 1992); "Historical Criticism: Liberator or Foe of Biblical Theology?" in *Promise and Practice of Biblical Theology* (1991); "One God Alone: A Pillar of Biblical Theology" *Princeton Sem. Bull.* 7/3 (1991); "'Heaven' in the World View of the New Testament" *Horizons in Bibl. Theol.* 9/2 (1987); *Gottesbild und Menschwerdung* (Mohr, 1971); *Der junge Luther und die Haresie* (Gutersloher, 1968); *Christ in the Wilderness* (SCM, 1963); and others. Mem: SBL 1963-; AAR; SNTS 1970-. Rec: Music. Addr: (o) Princeton Theological Seminary, CN 821, Princeton, NJ 08542 609-497-7762; (h) 52 Mercer St., Princeton, NJ 08540 609-497-3232.

MAYERSON, Philip, Educ: New York U., AB 1947, PhD 1956. Emp: New York U., Dept. of

Class., 1948-56 Instr., 1956-60 Asst. Prof., 1960-66 Assoc. Prof., 1966-88 Prof., 1973-78 Dean of Washington Square & U. Coll., 1988- Prof. Emeritus; Hebrew U., Jerusalem, 1956-57 Vis. Schol., 1978-79 Vis. Prof.; *BASOR*, Adv. Ed.; *Jour. of the Amer. Res. Ctr. in Egypt*, Adv. Ed. Spec: Archaeology. Pub: "The Use of the Term *Phylarchos* in the Roman-Byzantine East" *Zeitschrift fuer Papyrologie und Epigraphik* 88 (1991); "Toward a Comparative Study of a Frontier" *IEJ* 40 (1990); "Justinian's Novel 103 and the Reorganization of Palestine" *BASOR* 268 (1987); "Choricius of Gaza on the Water-supply System of Caesarea" *IEJ* 36 (1986); "Codex Sinaiticus: An Historical Observation" *BA* (1983); *Classical Mythology in Literature, Art, and Music* (1971); *The Ancient Agricultural Regime of Nessana and the Central Negeb* (BSA, Jerusalem/Colt Arch. Inst., London, 1961); and others. Awd: Rockefeller Found., Grant 1956-57; Amer. Coun. of Learned Soc., Fellow. 1961-62. Mem: APA; ASOR; Amer. Res. Ctr. in Egypt. Addr: New York U., Dept. of Classics, 25 Waverly Pl., New York, NY 10003 212-998-8592.

MAYES, Andrew D., b. Belfast, Northern Ireland, April 10, 1943, s. of T.D.D. & H., m. Elizabeth (Turbitt), chil: Katherine; Richard. Educ: Trinity Coll., Dublin, BA 1964; U. of Edinburgh, PhD 1969. Emp: Trinity Coll., Dublin, 1967-79 Lect., 1979-92 Assoc. Prof., Hebrew & Semitic Lang., 1992- Erasmus Smith's Prof. of Hebrew. Spec: Hebrew Bible. Pub: *The Old Testament in Sociological Perspective* (Pickering, 1989); "Idealism and Materialism in Weber and Gottwald" *Proc. of the Irish Bibl. Assn.* 11 (1987); *Judges*, OT Guides (JSOT, 1985); *The Story of Israel between Settlement and Exile* (SCM, 1983); "Deuteronomy 4 and the Literary Criticism of Deuteronomy" *JBL* 100 (1981); *Deuteronomy*, New Century Bible (Oliphants, 1979); "The Rise of the Israelite Monarchy" *ZAW* 90 (1978); "Israel in the Pre-Monarchy Period" *VT* 23 (1973); "The Historical Context of the Battle Against Sisera" *VT* (1969); and others. Awd: Fellow, Trinity Coll., Dublin 1974; U. of Tuebingen, Alexander von Humboldt Fellow 1983, 1987; Royal Irish Acad. 1992-. Mem: SOTS 1967-, Pres. 1992. Addr: (o) Trinity College, Dept. of Hebrew, Dublin 2, Ireland 01-772941; (h) 39 Evora Park, Howth, Dublin, Ireland 01-323760.

MAYNARD, Arthur H., b. Centerville, MI, August 28, 1915, s. of Floyd & Harriet (Crumb), m. Pauline (Schroeder), chil: Paulette; Kent. Educ: Boston U., MA 1938, STB 1939; U. of South. Calif., PhD 1959. Emp: Meth. Ch., 1939-50 Pastor; Willamette U., 1950-52 Asst. Prof.; U. of Miami, 1952-58 Prof.; U. of the Pacific, 1958-85 Prof. of Bible. Spec: New Testament. Pub: "Kai emoi Kai Soi" *NTS* (1985); "The Role of Peter in the Fourth Gospel" *NTS* (1984); *The Enduring Word: A Study of the Old Testament in Historical Perspective* (1964); *Understanding the Gospel of John* (Mellen, 1992). Mem: AAR 1947-; SBL 1947-, V.P., W Coast Sect. 1972-73,

Pres. 1973-74. Rec: Fishing, photography. Addr: (h) 2009 Meadow Ave., Stockton, CA 95207 209-477-5380.

MAYNARD-REID, Pedrito U., b. Kingston, Jamaica, July 10, 1947, s. of Harry Reid & E. Maynard, m. Violet, chil: Pedrito II; Natasha. Educ: Andrews U., MA 1973, MDiv 1975, ThD 1981. Emp: West Indies Coll., 1970-85 Prof., Relig.; Andrews U., 1980 Adj. Prof., NT; Antillian Coll., 1985-89 Prof., Relig.; Walla Walla Coll., 1990- Prof., Bibl. Stud. Spec: New Testament. Pub: *Poverty and Wealth in James* (Orbis, 1987). Mem: SBL; AAR. Rec: Gardening, stamp & coin collecting. Addr: (o) Walla Walla College, 204 S College Ave., College Place, WA 99324 509-527-2028; (h) 1030 SE Date Ave., College Place, WA 99324 509-529-0135.

MAZAR, Amihai, b. Haifa, Israel, November 19, 1942, s. of Hanoch & Batyah, m. Orah, chil: Sigal; Ran; Yotam. Educ: Hebrew U. Jerusalem, BA 1967, MA 1973, PhD 1977. Emp: Hebrew U., Inst. of Arch., 1968- Assoc. Prof.. Excv: Tell Qasile, 1972-74, 1982-86 Dir.; Tel Batash, Timnah, 1977-89 Field Dir.; Giloh, 1978-83 Dir.; Hartuv, 1985 Co-dir.; Beth-Shean, 1989-92 Dir. Spec: Archaeology. Pub: *Archaeology of the Land of the Bible 10000-586 B.C.E.* (1990); "Tel Batash (Timnah) Excavations: Third Preliminary Report, 1984-89," co-auth., BASORSup 27 (1990); "The Emergence of the Philistine Culture" *IEJ* 35 (1985); "Tell Batash (Timnah) Excavations, Second Preliminary Report (1981-1983)," co-auth., BASORSup 23 (1985); "Tell Batash (Timnah) Excavations: Third Preliminary Report, 1984-89," co-auth., BASORSup 27 (1990); *Excavations at Tell Qasile, Part Two. Various Objects, The Pottery, Conclusions*, Qedem 12 (1985); "The 'Bull Site': An Iron Age I Open Cult Place" *BASOR* 247 (1982); "Giloh—An Early Israelite Site in the Vicinity of Jerusalem" *IEJ* 31 (1981); *Excavations at Tell Qasile, Part One. The Philistine Sanctuary: Architecture and Cult Objects, Qedem* 20 (1981); and others. Mem: IES; Arch. Coun. of Israel. Rec: Gardening. Addr: (o) Hebrew U., Inst. of Arch., Jerusalem, Israel 02-882403; (h) 84 Derech Hachoresh, Jerusalem 97225, Israel 02-865187.

MAZAR, Benjamin, b. Ciechanowiec, Russia. Emp: Hebrew U. of Jerusalem, 1943- Lect., 1951-73 Prof., 1952-61 Rector, Pres. Excv: Ramath Rahel, 1931; Beit She'arim, 1936-40; Tel Qusileh, 1948-50; Ein Gedi, 1961-64; Temple Mount, Jerusalem, 1968-75. Spec: Archaeology. Pub: *Israel: People and State* (Magnes, 1992); *The Early Biblical Period* (IES, 1986); "Excavations Near Temple Mount Reveal Splendors of Herodian Jerusalem" *BAR* 6/4 (1980); and others. Mem: IES, Hon. Pres.; Israel Acad. of Sci. & Hum. Addr: (o) Hebrew U. of Jerusalem, Jerusalem, Israel; (h) 9 Abarbauel, Jerusalem, Israel 02-639859.

MAZAR, Eilat, b. Jerusalem, Israel. Educ: Hebrew U., Jerusalem, MA 1989. Excv: City of

David, 1981-85 Area Supr.; Ophel, 1986-87 Dir.; Achziv, 1988- Dir. Spec: Archaeology. Pub: "Excavations in the South of the Temple Mount," co-auth., *Qedem* 29 (1989); "Royal Gateway to Ancient Jerusalem Uncovered" *BAR* 15/3 (1989); "Edomite Pottery at the End of the Iron Age" *IEJ* 35 (1985); and others. Addr: (o) Hebrew U., Institute of Archaeology, Jerusalem, Israel.

MBITI, John S., b. Kitui, Kenya, November 30, 1931, s. of Samuel Mutuvi & Velesi (Kiimbi), m. Verena (Siegenthaler), chil: Kyeni; Maria; Esther; Kavata. Educ: Makerere U., Uganda, BA 1953; Barrinton Coll., AB 1956, ThB 1957; U. of Cambridge, PhD 1963. Emp: Makerere U., Uganda, 1964-74 Lect., Prof.; Ecumenical Inst., Switzerland, 1974-80 Prof., Dir.; U. of Bern, Switzerland, 1983- Prof.; U. of Hamburg, Germany, 1966-67 Vis. Lect.; U. of Geneva, Switzerland, 1978 Vis. Prof. Spec: New Testament. Pub: *Bible and Theology in African Christianity* (Oxford U.P., 1986); *New Testament Eschatology in an African Background* (Oxford U.P., 1971) and others. Awd: Barrington, LHD 1973; U. of Lausanne, D. Theol. 1990. Mem: SNTS 1963-. Rec: Reading, writing. Addr: (o) Einschlagweg 11, CH 3400 Burgdorf, Switzerland 034-22-64-20.

MCARTHUR, Harvey K., b. Billingsville, MO, May 9, 1912, m. Elizabeth (Dimock), chil: Harvey K., Jr.; John B.; Pamela S. Educ: Wheaton Coll., 1933, PhB; Hartford Theol. Sem., STM 1940, PhD 1941. Emp: Wellesley Coll., 1947-48; Hartford Theol. Sem., 1948-78 Hosmer Prof. of NT. Spec: New Testament. Pub: *They Also Taught in Parables*, co-auth. (Zondervan, 1990); "Son of Mary" *NT* 15/1 (1973); *In Search of the Historical Jesus* (Scribner's, 1969); "'Kai' Frequency in Greek Letters" *NTS* 15/3 (1969); "The Eusebian Sections and Canons" *CBQ* 27/3 (1965); *Understanding the Sermon on the Mount* (Harper, 1960); and others. Addr: (o) 16 S Sycamore Knolls, South Hadley, MA 01075 413-536-5406.

MCCANE, Byron R., b. Cincinnati, OH, March 1, 1955, s. of Ralph C. & Joan S., m. Linda, chil: Julie; Laura. Educ: U. of Ill., BA 1976; Trinity Evang. Div. Sch., MDiv 1979; Duke Div. Sch., ThM 1987; Duke U., PhD 1992. Emp: Duke U., 1992-93 Vis. Asst. Prof., NT. Spec: New Testament. Pub: "Bones of Contention? Ossuaries and Reliquaries in Early Judaism and Christianity" *SC* 8 (1991); "Let the Dead Bury their Own Dead: Secondary Burial and Mt. 8:21-22" *HTR* 83 (1990). Awd: Phi Beta Kappa 1976; SBL, SE reg., Kenneth Willis Clark Prize 1990. Mem: SBL; AAR; NAPS. Rec: Running, golf, weightlifting. Addr: (o) 118 Gray Bldg., Duke U., Durham, NC 27706 919-660-3520; (h) 3206 Lassiter Pl., Durham, NC 27707 919-490-0740.

MCCANN, J. Clinton, Jr., b. Richmond, VA, August 10, 1951, s. of Jerry & Nan (Carter), m. Nancy (Rowland), chil: Jennifer; Sarah. Educ:

Davidson Coll., AB 1973; Union Theol. Sem., DMin 1977, ThM 1978; Duke U., PhD 1985. Emp: Davidson Coll., 1985-86 Vis. Asst. Prof.; Eden Sem., 1987- Assoc. Prof., OT. Spec: Hebrew Bible, New Testament. Pub: *The Shape and Shaping of the Psalter*, JSOTSup 159, ed. (1993); *A Theological Introduction to the Book of Psalms: The Psalms as Torah* (Abingdon, 1993); "The Psalms as Instruction" *Interpretation* 46 (1992); "Exodus 32:1-14" *Interpretation* 44 (1990); "Psalm 73: A Microcosm of Old Testament Theology" in *The Listening Heart*, JSOTSup 58 (1987). Awd: Duke U., G.H. Kearns Fellow. 1979-82. Mem: SBL 1985-; CBA 1985-. Rec: Running, basketball, tennis. Addr: (o) 475 E Lockwood Ave., St. Louis, MO 63119 314-961-3627; (h) 413 Marion Ave., St. Louis, MO 63119 314-968-7296.

MCCARTER, P. Kyle, Jr., Educ: U. of Oklahoma, BA 1967; McCormick Theol. Sem., MDiv 1970; Harvard U., Dept. of Near East. Lang., PhD 1974. Emp: U. of Va., Dept. of Relig. Stud., 1974-79 Asst. Prof., 1979-82 Assoc. Prof., 1982-85 Prof.; Harvard U., 1978-79 Vis. Lect., Bibl. Hebrew; Dartmouth Coll., 1979 Vis. Assoc. Prof., Relig.; Johns Hopkins U., 1985- William Foxwell Albright Prof. of Bibl. & Anc. Near East. Stud., 1987-89 Assoc. Dean of Arts & Sci., 1991- Chmn., Dept. of Near East. Stud., 1991- Acting Chmn., Dept. of Class. Spec: Archaeology, Hebrew Bible, Semitic Languages, Texts and Epigraphy. Pub: "The Mysterious Copper Scroll: Clues to Hidden Treasure?" *BR* 8/4 (1992); "Canaan, Canaanites," "Canaan, Conquest of," "High Place(s)" in *Oxford Companion to the Bible* (Oxford U.P., 1991); "The Sage in the Deuteronomistic History" in *The Sage in Israel and the Ancient Near East* (Eisenbrauns, 1990); "The Patriarchal Age" in *Ancient Israel: A Short History from Abraham to the Roman Destruction of the Temple* (BAS, 1988); articles in *ISBE* (Eerdmans, 1982, 1988); "Aspects of the Religion of the Israelite Monarchy: Biblical and Epigraphic Data" in *Ancient Israelite Religion: Essays in Honor of Frank Moore Cross* (Fortress, 1987); *Recovering the Text of the Hebrew Bible: An Introduction to Textual Criticism*, Guides to Bibl. Schol., OT Ser. (Fortress, 1986); *I Samuel, II Samuel*, AB, vol. 8, 9 (Doubleday, 1980, 1984); *The Antiquity of the Greek Alphabet and the Early Phoenician Scripts*, HSM 9 (Scholars, 1975); and others. Awd: U. of Va., Summer Res. Fellow. 1975, 1976, 1980; Phi Beta Kappa Book Prize, 1980; NEH, Summer Stipend 1981. Mem: SBL, Past Pres., SE reg.; Bibl. Colloquium; Colloquium for Bibl. Res.; ASOR, Pres., 1988-90. Rec: squash, fly-fishing. Addr: (o) John Hopkins U., 124 Gilman Hall, Baltimore, MD 21218.

MCCARTNEY, Dan G., b. Clarksburg, WV, January 27, 1950, s. of James M. & Janet S., m. Helen Kathleen (Capcara), chil: Christopher John; Cara Elisabeth. Educ: Carnegie Mellon U., BFA 1971; Gordon Conwell Theol. Sem., MDiv 1974; Westminster Theol. Sem., ThM 1977, PhD 1989. Emp: Manna Bible Inst., 1977-81 Instr., Bible &

Theol.; Westminster Theol. Sem., 1983- Assoc. Prof., NT; *Westminster Theol. Jour.*, 1992 Book Rev. Ed. Spec: New Testament. Pub: "*Logikos* in 1 Peter 2,2" *ZNW* 82 (1992); "New Testament Citations of the Pentateuch: Implications for Theonomy" in *Theonomy: A Reformed Critique* (Baker, 1990); "The New Testament Use of the Old Testament" in *Inerrancy and Hermeneutics: A Tradition, A Challenge, A Debate* (Baker, 1988); "Biblical and Allegorical Interpretation in Origen's Contra Celsum" *Westminster Theol. Jour.* Fall (1986). Mem: SBL; ETS; IBR. Addr: (o) Westminster Theological Seminary, Box 27009, Chestnut Hill, Philadelphia, PA 19090 215-572-3818; (h) 22 Elliot Ave., Willow Grove, PA 19090 215-659-7854.

MCCOMISKEY, Thomas E., b. Paterson, NJ, August 22, 1928, s. of Samuel & Christine, m. Eleanor, chil: Karen; Douglas; Bruce. Educ: The King's Coll., BA 1953; Faith Theol. Sem., MDiv 1956; Brandeis U., MA 1963, PhD 1965; Westminster Theol. Sem., ThM 1975. Emp: The King's Coll., 1964-69 Assoc. Prof., Chmn., Bibl. Stud.; Trinity Evang. Sch., 1969-90 Prof. of OT & Semitic Lang., Chmn., OT & Arch., 1990-91 Acting Dir. of the Acad. Doc. Prog., Prof. of OT Exegesis & Bibl. Theol.; Amer. Coll. of Bibl. Theol., 1987- Presiding Fellow. Spec: Hebrew Bible. Pub: "Prophetic Irony in Hosea 1:4: A Study of the Collocation *paqad 'al* and its Implications for the Fall of Jehu's Dynasty" *JSOT* March (1993); *The Minor Prophets: An Exegetical and Expository Commentary*, vol. 1 (Baker, 1992); "Hosea 9:13 and the Integrity of the Masoretic Tradition in the Prophecy of Hosea" *JETS* (1990); "The Hymnic Elements of the Prophecy of Amos—A Study of Form Critical Methodology" *JETS* (1987); "The Seventy 'Weeks' of Daniel Against the Background of Ancient Near Eastern Literature" *WTJ* (1985); *The Covenants of Promise: A Theology of the Old Testament Covenants* (Baker, 1985); "Idolatry" in *ISBE* (1982); and others. Mem: ETS 1969-85; SBL 1984-. Rec: Astronomy, oil painting, bicycling. Addr: (h) 2 Hawthorn Dr., Hawthorn Woods, IL 60047 708-438-2687.

MCCONAUGHY, Daniel L., b. Newport, RI, May 16, 1955, s. of Donald & Janet (Palen), m. Lorraine, chil: Jessica. Educ: Coll. of Charleston, BS 1976; U. of Chicago, MA 1981, PhD 1985. Christian Stud. 1985. Emp: Rosary Coll. Spec: New Testament, Semitic Languages, Texts and Epigraphy. Pub: "An Old Syriac Reading of Acts 1:4 and More Light on Jesus' Last Meal Before His Ascension" *Oriens Christianus* 72 (1988); "The Syriac Manuscripts in the Coptic Museum, Cairo," "An Update on the Syriac MSS Collections in South India" *Oriens Christianus* 71 (1987); "A Recently Discovered Folio of the Old Syriac (SY) Text of Luke 16, 13-17,1" *Biblica* 68/1 (1987); "Syriac Manuscripts in South India: The Library of the Saint Thomas Apostolic Seminary" *Orientalia Christiana Periodica* 52/2; (1986); and others. Mem: SBL 1984-; ETS 1985-. Rec: Beekeeping. Addr: (h) 301 S Euclid Ave., Oak Park, IL 60302.

MCCONVILLE, James G., b. Lurgan, N Ireland, April 30, 1951, s. of Walter & Elizabeth, m. Helen, chil: Alistair; Carys; Andrew; Claire. Educ: Cambridge U., BA 1973, MA 1976; New Coll., Edinburgh, BD 1976; Queen's U., Belfast, PhD 1980. Emp: Trinity Coll., Bristol, 1980-89 Lect.; Wycliffe Hall, Oxford, 1989- Lect. Spec: Hebrew Bible. Pub: "1 Kings viii 46-53 and the Deuteronomic Hope" *VT* 42 (1992); "Narrative and Meaning in the Books of Kings" *Biblica* 70 (1989); "I Chronicles 28:9: Yahweh 'Seeks Out' Solomon" *JTS* 37 (1986); "Ezra-Nehemiah and the Fulfillment of Prophecy" *VT* 36 (1986); *Law and Theology in Deuteronomy* (JSOT, 1984); and others. Mem: SOTS 1982-; Tyndale Fellow. 1978-. Rec: Theatre. Addr: (o) Wycliffe Hall, Oxford OX2 6PW, England 0865-274200; (h) 3 Norham Gardens, Oxford OX2 6PS, England 0865-515796.

MCCOY, Glenn W., b. Hatfield, AR, July 4, 1933, s. of Raymond & Irene, m. Dorla (Medford), chil: Annette; John; Stanley. Educ: SW Bapt. Theol. Sem., BD 1958, MTh 1962, DMin 1980. Emp: Bapt. Ch., 1959-63 Pastor; N. Mex. Highlands U., 1963-71 Campus Min., Bible Tchr.; East. N. Mex. U., 1971- Assoc. Prof., Chmn., Dept. of Relig. Spec: Archaeology, New Testament. Pub: *New Testament Survey*; *Archaeology of St. Paul's Travels*; *Summary of Old Testament History*; and others. Mem: SBL; ASOR. Rec: Gardening, fishing. Addr: (o) Box 2005, Portales, NM 88130 505-356-4252; (h) B 141 Yucca Dr., Portales, NM 88130 505-356-4771.

MCCREESH, Thomas P., b. New York, NY, October 6, 1943, s. of James & Annie. Educ: Providence Coll., BA 1965; Dominican House of Stud., STB 1971, Ord. 1972, STL 1977; Cath. U. of Amer., MA 1974, PhD, Semitics 1982. Emp: Yale U. Div. Sch., 1977-79 Res. Fellow; Dominican House of Stud., 1979- Assoc. Prof., Scripture; *Old Testament Abstracts*, 1987-92 Gen. Ed. Spec: Hebrew Bible. Pub: "Proverbs" *New Jerome Biblical Comm.*; *Biblical Sound and Sense* JSOTSup 128 (Sheffield, 1991); "Salvation History" in *New Dict. of Theology* (Glazier, 1987); "Wisdom as Wife: Proverbs 31:10-31" *RB* 92 (1985). Awd: Yale U. Div. Sch., Res. Fellow. 1977-79. Mem: SBL 1971-; CBA 1975-. Rec: Swimming, scuba diving, hiking, painting, drawing. Addr: (o) Dominican House of Studies, 487 Michigan Ave., NE, Washington, DC 20017 202-529-5300.

MCCULLOH, Gerald W., b. St. Paul, MN, May 3, 1941, d. of Gerald & Evelyn, m. Karen (Smith), chil: Gerald; Heather. Educ: Vanderbilt U., BA (magna cum laude) 1962; Harvard U., MDiv 1965; U. of Chicago, MA 1968, PhD 1973. Emp: Loyola U., 1969- Assoc. Prof., Theol., 1990- Assoc. Dir. Res. Services; *AAR*, 1973-83 Ed. Spec: New Testament. Pub: *Christ's Person and Lifework in the Theology of Albrecht Ritschle*; and others. Mem: AAR 1971-. Rec: Canoeing. Addr: (o) Loyola U. of Chicago, Dept. of Theology, 6525 N Sheridan Rd., Chicago, IL 60626 312-508-2361.

MCCULLOUGH, John C., b. United Kingdom, February 13, 1942, s. of John & Mabel, m. Dorothy, chil: Judith; Jonathan. Educ: Queen's U., Belfast, BA 1963, BD 1966, PhD 1971. Emp: Near East Sch. of Theol., Beirut, 1976-84 Assoc. Prof., Bibl. Stud., Acad. Dean; Knox Coll., New Zealand, Theol. Hall, 1984-87 Prof., NT Stud.; Union Theol. Coll., Belfast, 1987- Prof., NT Stud.; Queen's U., Belfast, 1987- Prof., NT Stud. Spec: New Testament. Pub: "Ancient Syriac Commentaries on the New Testament" *Theol. Rev.* 5 (1982); "Recent Scholarship on the Epistle to the Hebrews" *Irish Bibl. Stud.* 2, 3 (1980, 1981); "The Old Testament in Hebrew" *NTS* 26 (1980); and others. Mem: SBL 1985-. Rec: Photography. Addr: (o) Union Theological College, 26 College Green Belfast, BT7 1IN, North. Ireland 0232-325374; (h) 11 Royal Lodge Park, Belfast, BT8 4YP, North. Ireland 0232-790000.

MCDANIEL, Thomas F., b. Baltimore, MD, March 1, 1931, s. of Walter & Hilda, m. Doris, chil: James. Educ: East. Bapt. Sem., BD 1955; U. of Pa., MA 1956; Johns Hopkins U., PhD 1966. Emp: Kanto Gakvin U., Yokohama, 1956-69 Assoc. Prof.; East. Bapt. Sem., 1969- Prof. of OT Stud. & Hebrew. Spec: Hebrew Bible, Semitic Languages, Texts and Epigraphy. Pub: *Deborah Never Sang* (Makor, 1983); "Philological Studies in Lamentations" *Biblica* (1968); "The Alleged Sumerian Influence Upon Lamentations" *VT* (1968); "The Consonantal Force of *He* in the Tetragrammaton" *Bible & Theol.* (1968). Mem: SBL 1966-; ASOR 1969-; NAPH 1975-. Rec: Racquetball, rare books. Addr: (o) Eastern Baptist Seminary, City and Lancaster Ave, Philadelphia, PA 19151 215-896-5000; (h) 4 Narbrook Park, Narberth, PA 19072.

MCDONALD, James I. H., b. Stonehouse, Scotland, February 7, 1933, s. of James & Joanna (Leishman), m. Jenny (Fleming). Educ: U. of Glasgow, MA 1954, BD 1957, MTh 1969; U. of Edinburgh, PhD 1974, FEIS 1986. Emp: Ch. of Scotland, 1958-63 Min.; Moray House Coll., Edinburgh, 1963-80 Lect., Relig. Stud.; U. of Edinburgh, 1980- Lect., 1989- Sr. Lect., 1992- Reader, NT & Ethics. Spec: New Testament. Pub: *Biblical Interpretation and Christian Ethics* (Cambridge U.P., 1993); *The Resurrection: Narrative and Belief* (SPCK, 1989); *Jesus and the Ethics of the Kingdom*, co-auth. (SPCK, 1987); *Kerygma and Didache* (1980); and others. Mem: SNTS 1981-. Addr: (o) New College, Faculty of Divinity, Mound Pl., Edinburgh EH1 2LX, Scotland 031-225-8400; (h) 23 Ravelston House Rd., Edinburgh EH4 3LP, Scotland 031-332-2172.

MCDONALD, Lee M., b. San Jose, CA, January 24, 1942, s. of Walter & Veleda, m. Mary (Stager), chil: Karl; Heidi (Lum); Marshall; Sharon. Educ: Biola U., BA 1964; Talbot Theol. Sem., BD (magna cum laude) 1969; Harvard U., ThM 1985; U. of Edinburgh,

Scotland, PhD 1976. Emp: Trinity Coll., 1974-75 Asst. Prof., Bibl. Stud.; N Amer. Bapt. Sem., 1975-80 Assoc. Prof., NT Stud.; Fuller Theol. Sem., 1985- Adj. Prof., NT Stud.; Santa Clara First Bapt. Ch., 1985-91 Sr. Min.; Alhambra First Bapt. Ch., 1991- Sr. Min. Spec: New Testament, Apocrypha and Post-biblical Studies. Pub: "Anti-Judaism in the Early Church Fathers" in *Faith and Polemic: Studies in Anti-Semitism in Early Christianity* (Fortress, 1993); "Christianity, History of in Greece" in *ABD* (Doubleday, 1992); "Canon (of Scripture)," "Acts of the Apostles" in *Ency. of Early Christianity* (Garland, 1990); *Formation of the Christian Biblical Canon* (Abingdon, 1988); "Historical-Critical Inquiry and the Resurrection of Jesus" *Theol., News, & Notes* (June, 1983); and others. Awd: Talbot Theol. Sem., Homiletics Awd. 1968; Merchison Found. Grant 1970; N Amer. Bapt. Sem., Outstanding Fac. Awd. 1980. Mem: SBL 1975-; ACT 1977-; IBR 1977-; NABPR 1988-. Rec: Chess, camping, wind surfing, skiing. Addr: (o) First Baptist Church, 101 S Atlantic Blvd., Alhambra, CA 91801 818-570-1511.

MCELENEY, Neil J., b. Charlestown, MA, August 8, 1927, s. of Neil & Mary (McDevitt). Educ: St. Paul's Coll., AB 1950, MA 1953; Cath. U. of Amer., STL 1954; Pont. Bibl. Inst., Rome, SSB 1955, SSL 1956. Emp: St. Paul's Coll., 1956-71 Prof., Bibl. Stud. & Hebrew; Marist Coll., 1965-66 Prof., NT; *CBQ,* 1968-75 Assoc. Ed.; Cath. U. of Amer., 1979- Adj. Prof.; Pont. Bibl. Inst., Rome, 1982 CBA Ann. Prof. Excv: Tell Gezer, 1973-74. Spec: Archaeology, Hebrew Bible, New Testament, Apocrypha and Post-biblical Studies. Pub: "Does the Trumpet Sound or Resound? An Interpretation of Matthew 6:2" *ZNW* 76 (1985); "The Beatitudes of the Sermon on the Mount" *CBQ* 43 (1981); *The Growth of the Gospels* (Paulist, 1979); "Orthodoxy in Judaism of the First Christian Century" *JSJ* 9 (1978); "153 Great Fishes (John 21,11)—Gematriacal Atbash" *Biblica* 58 (1977); "Conversion, Circumcision and the Law" *NTS* 20 (1973); and others. Mem: CBA, V.P. 1978-79, Pres. 1979-80; ASOR; SNTS; AAR; Liturgical Conf. Addr: (h) St. Paul's College, Washington, DC 20017 202-832-6262.

MCEVENUE, Sean E., b. Toronto, Canada, June 10, 1931, s. of Clair & Kathleen (Lang), m. Mary, chil: Patrick; Kate; Timothy. Educ: St. Mary's U., Canada, MA 1961; Pont. Bibl. Inst., Rome, SSL 1964, SSD 1971. Emp: Loyola Coll., Canada, 1954-57 Lect.; Regis Coll., Toronto Sch. of Theol., 1965-72 Prof., Dean; Concordia U., 1972- Assoc. Prof., 1986 Assoc. Vice-Rector Acad. Spec: Hebrew Bible. Pub: *Interpretation Theory and the Old Testament* (1993); *Interpreting the Pentateuch* (Collegeville, 1990); *The Narrative Style of the Priestly Writer* (1971). Mem: SBL; CBA. Rec: Riding. Addr: (o) Concordia U., 7141 Sherbrooke St. W, Montreal, Quebec H4B 1R6, Canada 514-848-2475; (h) 377 Main Rd., Hudson, Que. JOP 1HO, Canada 514-848-2475.

MCGAUGHY, Lane C., b. Washburn, ME, July 24, 1940, s. of Clifford & Irene, chil: Lane, Jr.; Charis. Educ: Ohio Wesleyan U., BA 1962; Drew Theol. Sem., BD 1965; Vanderbilt U., MA 1969, PhD 1970. Emp: U. of Montana, 1969-81 Assoc. Prof.; Willamette U., 1981- Atkinson Prof., Relig. & Ethical Stud.; U. of Nebr., 1977 Cotner Vis. Prof. Spec: New Testament. Pub: "New Testament Greek" in *Harper's Bible Dict.* (1985); "Pagan Hellenistic Literature: The Babrian Fables" *SBL 1977 Seminar Papers*; "The Fear of Yahweh and the Mission of Judaism" *JBL* (1975); *Toward a Descriptive Analysis of Einai as a Linking Verb in New Testament Greek* (Scholars, 1972); and others. Addr: (o) Willamette U., Dept. of Religion D180, Salem, OR 97301; (h) 32640 N Fork Rd., Lyons, OR 97358.

MCGOVERN, Patrick E., b. Corpus Christi, TX, December 9, 1944, s. of Edward & Florence (Brisbin), m. Doris (Nordmeier). Educ: Cornell U., AB 1966; Faith Theol. Sem., MDiv 1969; U. of Pa., PhD 1980. Emp: Archaeoceramics, MASCA, U. Museum, 1979- Res. Specialist; Dropsie Coll., 1982-85 Adj. Asst. Prof.; Rutgers U., 1992- Instr. Excv: Jerusalem, 1972 Field Supr.; Sarepta, Lebanon, 1974, Pottery Supr.; Baq'ah Valley, Jordan, 1977- Dir. Spec: Archaeology. Pub: *Organic Contents of Ancient Vessels,* ed. MASCA Res. Papers 7 (1990); *Cross-Craft and Cross-Cultural Interactions in Ceramics,* Ceramics & Civ. IV (Amer. Ceramic Soc., 1989); *The Late Bronze and Early Iron Ages of Central Transjordan,* U. Mus. Mon. 65 (1986); *Late Bronze Palestinian Pendants:Innovation in a Cosmopolitan Age* (ASOR/JSOT, 1985); and others. Awd: W.F. Albright Fellow. 1976-77. Mem: ASOR 1977-. Rec: Music, golf, reading. Addr: (o) U. of Pennsylvania, University Museum, 34th & Spruce St., Philadelphia, PA 19104; (h) 549 Midvale Rd., Upper Darby, PA 19086.

MCGRAW, Gerald E., b. Oil City, PA, May 26, 1932, s. of Earl & Gladys (Snyder), m. Martha (Swauger), chil: Philip; David. Educ: Wheaton Coll., MA 1958; Chicago Grad. Sch. of Theol., MDiv 1968; SE Bapt. Theol. Sem., DMin 1975; N.Y. U., PhD 1986. Emp: Manahath Educ. Ctr., 1961-63 Prof.; Toccoa Falls Coll., 1968- Prof., Dir., Sch. of Bible & Theol. Spec: Hebrew Bible, New Testament. Mem: AAR; ETS, reg., Pres. 1978-79; WTS. Rec: Fishing, gardening. Addr: (o) Box 800725, Toccoa Falls, GA 30598-0725 706-886-6831; (h) 215 Shoreline Ln., Westminster, SC 29693-9429 803-647-9375.

MCHATTEN, Mary T., b. Castle Hill, ME, October 20, 1931, d. of Herman & Verna. Educ: U. of Maine, BS 1955; Boston Coll., MEd 1963; Providence Coll., MA 1971; U. of Ottawa, PhD 1979; Ecole Biblique, Jerusalem, Eleve Titulare 1984. Emp: St. Joseph Coll., 1964-65 Prof.; Kino Inst., 1973-89 Prof.; Mt. Angel Sem., 1989- Prof., Scripture. Spec: Archaeology, Hebrew Bible, New Testament. Pub: "Turn from

Your Wickedness" *Bible Today* 30 (1992); "Prophetic Call to Women" *Emmanuel* 96/7-8 (1990); "Biblical Roots of Women" *Emmanuel* 89 (1983). Mem: SBL; CBA. Rec: Sports, reading, music. Addr: (o) Mt. Angel Seminary, St. Benedict, OR 97373 503-845-3365; (h) 840 S Main St., Mt. Angel, OR 97362 503-845-6141.

MCHUGH, John F., b. Stalybridge, Cheshire, August 3, 1927, s. of Joseph & Margaret (Buck). Educ: Gregorian U., Rome, Licence Phil. 1949, Dr. Theol. 1955; Bibl. Inst., Rome, BSS 1955; Ecole Biblique, Jerusalem, Bibl. Comm. Lic. 1956. Emp: Ordained R.C. Priest, 1952; Ushaw Coll., 1957-76 Sr. Lect.; U. of Durham, 1976-88 Sr. Lect.; *The Liturgical Psalter*, 1972-77 Co-Trans. Spec: New Testament. Pub: "In Him Was Life" in *Jews and Christians* (1993); "A Reconsideration of Ephesians 1:10b in the Light of Irenaeus" in *Paul and Paulinism: Festschrift C.K. Barrett* (1982); *The Mother of Jesus in the New Testament* (1975); *The Gospel and The Jesus of History*, trans. (1968); *Ancient Israel*, trans. (1961); and others. Mem: SOTS 1957-; SNTS 1976-; Pont. Bibl. Commn. 1984-90. Rec: Dante, travel, classics. Addr: (o) Stamford House, Stamford Rd., Alderley Edge, Cheshire, SK9 7NS, England 0625-582386.

MCIVER, Robert K., b. Hastings, New Zealand, January 14, 1953, s. of Don & Dora, m. Susan M., chil: Althea S.; Skye C. Educ: U. of Canterbury, BSc 1973; Christchurch Tchr. Coll., Dip. 1974; Avondale Coll., BA, Theol. 1981; London U., BD 1983; Andrews U., Avondale, MA 1984, Berrien Springs, PhD 1989. Emp: Warburton SDA Ch., 1982-83 Asst. Pastor; Avondale Coll., 1984, 1988- Lect., NT; Andrews U., 1991- Vis. Prof., NT. Spec: Archaeology, Hebrew Bible, New Testament. Pub: "Cosmology as a Key to the Thought World of Philo of Alexandria" *AUSS* 26 (1988); and others. Mem: SBL 1985-; Australia & New Zealand Soc. for Theol. Stud. 1988-. Rec: Computers, reading, building, joinery. Addr: (o) Avondale College, Theology Dept. Cooranbong, NSW 2265, Australia 49-771107; (h) 1 Minmi St., Stanford Merthyr, NSW 2327, Australia 49-374716.

MCKAY, Heather A., b. Morecambe, Great Britain, November 15, 1941, d. of Jemima C. (Bracken) and Robert H. Ayre, m. David J.A. Clines, chil: Kevin W.M.; Robert R. Educ: U. of Glasgow, BSc 1962, MSc 1965, BD, OT Lang. & Lit. 1985, PhD 1992. Emp: Bishopton Erskine Parish Ch., 1985-86 Asst. Min.; John Leggott Coll., Scunthorpe, 1988 Tchr.; Relig. Stud.; Hungerhill Sch., Doncaster, 1989- Head of Relig. Educ. & Relig. Stud. Dept.; U. of Sheffield, 1990- Hon. Lect., Dept. of Bibl. Stud; Edge Hill Coll., 1992- Sr. Lect., Relig. Stud. Spec: Hebrew Bible, New Testament, Apocrypha and Post-biblical Studies. Pub: "From Evidence to Edifice: Four Fallacies About the Sabbath" in *Text as Pretext: Essays in Honour of Robert Davidson*, JSOTSup 138 (Sheffield, 1992); "New Moon or Sabbath?" in *The Sabbath in Jewish and Christian Tradition* (Crossroad, 1991); "Jacob Makes It across the Jabbok: An Attempt to Solve the Success/Failure Ambivalence in Israel's Self-Consciousness" *JSOT* 38 (1987); and others. Awd: Glasgow U., Cleland & Rae Wilson Gold Medal for Hebrew 1984, Henderson Prize Essay 1985, 1987. Mem: SOTS 1988-; SBL 1990-. Rec: Travel, reading, horse-riding. Addr: (o) The University, Dept. of Biblical Studies, Sheffield, S10 2TN, England 0742-768555; (h) 90 Ashland Rd., Sheffield S7 1RJ, England 0742-550562.

MCKENNA, Margaret M., b. Teaneck, NJ, May 26, 1930, d. of Stella (Schnell) & Walter. Educ: Chestnut Hill Coll., AB 1955; Notre Dame U., MA 1960; Ecole Biblique, Jerusalem, Eleve Titulare 1970; U. of Pa., PhD, Christian Origins 1980. Emp: St. Teresa's Inst., Dean of Women; La Salle U., 1970-75 Lect. Excv: Tel Belata Canaanite Sanctuary, 1967 Area Supr. Spec: Archaeology, Hebrew Bible, New Testament, Apocrypha and Post-biblical Studies. Pub: *The Two Ways in Greco-Roman Literature* (U. of Pa., 1980); *Women of the Church: The History, Role and Spirit of the Ecclesial Order of Women* (Macmillan, 1960). Awd: Chestnut Hill Coll., Phil. Awd. 1954; Ecole Biblique, Hon. Mention 1970. Mem: CBS; SBL; AAR; Coll. Theol. Soc. Rec: Retreats, theol. workshops, educ. in non-violence & peace spirituality, drug & alcohol rehabilitation. Addr: (o) 2011 W Norris St., Philadelphia, PA 19121 215-763-8806.

MCKENZIE, Steven L., b. Denver, CO, October 9, 1953, s. of Wilfred & Germaine, m. Vilma, chil: Christina; Bonnie. Educ: Abilene Christian U., MDiv 1978; Harvard Div. Sch., ThD 1983. Emp: Rhodes Coll., 1983- Asst. Prof., Relig. Spec: Hebrew Bible, Semitic Languages, Texts and Epigraphy. Pub: *The Trouble with Kings: The Composition of the Book of Kings in the Deuteronomistic History* (Brill, 1991); "The Jacob Tradition in Hosea XII 4-5" *VT* 36 (1986); "I Kings 8: A Sample Study" *Bull. of the IOSCS* 19 (1986); "The Prophetic History and the Redaction of Kings" *HAR* 9 (1985); *The Chronicler's Use of the Deuteronomistic History* (Scholars, 1985); "Covenant in Malachi," co-auth. *CBQ* 45 (1983); "'You Have Prevailed': The Function of Jacob's Encounter at Peniel in the Jacob Tradition" *Restoration Quar.* 23 (1980); and others. Mem: SBL 1978-. Rec: Basketball, tennis. Addr: (o) Rhodes College, 2000 N Parkway, Memphis, TN 38117 901-726-3908; (h) 4783 Marlin, Memphis, TN 38117 901-761-5760.

MCKINNEY, Larry E., b. Tulsa, OK, July 19, 1949, s. of E.A. & Lillian (Seyle), m. Janet Kay. Educ: Tex. Tech. U., BFA 1972; MidW Bapt. Theol. Sem., MDiv 1981; Cen. Bapt. Theol. Sem., MA 1985. Emp: MidW Bapt. Theol. Sem., 1981-85 Reader Services Lbrn., 1985-90 Instr., Bibl. Stud., 1990- Asst. Prof., Bibl. Backgrounds

& Arch., Cur. of Morton Mus. of Arch. Excv: Lahav Res. Project, Tel Halif, Israel, 1987-91 Area Supr.; Banias/Caesarea Philippi, Israel, 1991- Area Supr. Spec: Archaeology, Hebrew Bible, New Testament. Pub: "Languages of the Bible," "Logia," "Slaughter of the Innocents" in *Holman Bible Dict.* (Holman, 1991); "Bethsaida" *BI* (1990); "A Late Roman Hoard from the Jerusalem Area" *The Celator* (1990); "The Sandon Monument and Tarsian Coinage" *The Celator* (1989); "Notes on Two Numismatic References in Eusebius' 'Life of Constantine'" *Jour. of the Soc. for Anc. Numismatics* 16 (1985); and others. Awd: Numismatic Fine Arts Lit. Prize 1985; Endowment for Bibl. Res. Travel Awd. 1987. Mem: Amer. Numismatic Soc.; ASOR; Amer. for Middle East Understanding; SBL. Rec: Listening to classical music, tennis, running. Addr: (o) Midwestern Baptist Theological Seminary, 5001 N Oak St. Trafficway, Kansas City, MO 64118 816-453-4600; (h) 5539 N Woodland, Kansas City, MO 64118 816-452-7968.

MCKNIGHT, Edgar V., b. Wilson, SC, November 21, 1931, s. of William & Carrie (DeMars), m. Shirley (Robinson), chil: Lynn; Edgar. Educ: Coll. of Charleston, BS 1953; South. Bapt. Theol. Sem., MDiv 1956, PhD 1960. Emp: Chowan Coll., 1960-63 Chaplain; Furman U., 1963- William R. Kenan, Jr. Prof. of Relig.; South. Bapt. Theol. Sem., 1966-67 Vis. Prof. Spec: New Testament. Pub: *The Bible and the Reader* (Fortress, 1985); "Erhardt Guttgemanns' 'Generative Poetics' as New Testament Hermeneutics" *Semeia* 10 (1978); *Meaning in Texts: The Historical Shaping of a Historical Hermeneutics* (Fortress, 1978); "Can the Griesbach Hypothesis be Falsified?" co-auth. *JBL* 91 (1972); *What is Form Criticism?* (Fortress, 1969); *Introduction to the New Testament*, co-auth. (Ronald, 1969); and others. Mem: SNTS; SBL, Pres., SE reg. 1985; AAR. Addr: (o) Furman U., Greenville, SC 29613 803-294-3297; (h) 201 Alpine Way, Greenville, SC 29609 803-244-6003.

MCLEAN, Bradley H., b. Toronto, ON, Canada, s. of Bevis L. & Gayle H. (Halstead), m. Shauna J. (Pugsley), chil: Hudson B.; Merrill D. Educ: U. of Toronto, Trinity Coll., MDiv 1983, MTh 1987; U. of St. Michael's Coll., Canada, PhD 1989. Emp: St. Gile's Church, England, 1983-85 Curate; Parish of Mono, Toronto, 1985-87 Incumbent; Trinity Coll., 1986-91 Tutor, Div., 1991-92 Lect.; U. of Manitoba, St. John's Coll., 1992- Dean of Theol. Spec: New Testament. Pub: *Citations and Allusions to Jewish Scripture in Early Christian and Jewish Writings through 180 C.E.* (Mellen, 1992); "The Interpretation of the Levitical Sin Offering and the Scapegoat" *Stud. in Relig.* 20/3 (1992); "A Christian Epitaph: The Curse of Judas Iscariot" *Orientalia Christiana Periodica* 58 (1992); "The Absence of an Atoning Sacrifice in Paul's Soteriology" *NTS* 38/4 (1992); "Christ as a Pharmakos Victim in Pauline Soteriology" in

SBL 1991 Seminar Papers (Scholars, 1991); "A Christian Sculpture in Old Corinth" *Orientalia Christiana Periodica* 57 (1991); and others. Awd: Trinity Coll., Howard Clark Memorial Fellow. 1990; CSBS, Joachim Jeremias Prize 1990. Mem: SBL; Intl. Q Project, IAC. Rec: Running. Addr: (o) U. of Manitoba, St. John's College, Winnipeg, Man. R3T 2M5, Canada 204-474-8133.

MCLEAN, Mark D., b. Cincinnati, OH, September 26, 1947, s. of Davis & Kathrine, m. Jun-ko, chil: Scott; Christina. Educ: South. Calif. Coll., BA (summa cum laude) 1974; Harvard Div. Sch., MTS 1976; Harvard U., PhD 1982. Emp: Evangel Coll., 1982- Prof. Spec: Hebrew Bible, Semitic Languages, Texts and Epigraphy. Pub: "Hebrew Scripts," "Paleography" in *ABD* (Doubleday, 1992); "The Initial Issue of Hasmonean Coins" *Amer. Numismatic Soc. Mus. Notes* 26 (1981). Mem: AAR; ASOR; SBL. Addr: (o) Evangel College, Biblical Studies & Phil. Dept., 1111 N Glenstone, Springfield, MO 65802 417-865-2811; (h) 809 S Sparks Ave., Springfield, MO 65802 417-864-6986.

MCMANAMAN, Ray, b. Waukegan, IL, July 14, 1929, s. of Raymond & Frances. Educ: St. Mary's Coll., MA 1956; Seattle U., MA 1972; Aquinas Inst. of Theol., DMin 1977; San Francisco Theol. Sem., STD 1981. Emp: Joliet Sem., 1972-75; Lewis U., 1972- Prof., 1974-76, 1978-92 Chmn., Relig. Stud. Dept.; De La Salle U., Holy Rosary Coll., Philippines, 1985 Guest Lect. Spec: New Testament, Apocrypha and Post-biblical Studies. Pub: *Scripture Interpretation* (Green Hills, 1985); *The Passion Narrative* (Green Hills, 1985); and others. Awd: La Sallian Inst., Rome, Cours Moyen 1954. Mem: Natl. Cath. Evang. Assn. Rec: Reading, hiking. Addr: (o) Lewis U., Romeoville, IL 60441 815-838-0500.

MCMILLION, Phillip E., b. Dallas, TX, June 24, 1947, s. of Mavin & Maud, m. Joyce. Educ: Abilene Christian U., STB 1973; Vanderbilt U., MA 1981, PhD 1985. Emp: East. N. Mex. U., 1973-77 Asst. Prof.; Cen. Coll. of Iowa, 1983-84 Instr.; Bibl. Stud. Ctr., 1984-90 Dir.; Harding U. Grad. Sch. of Relig., 1990- Assoc. Prof., OT. Spec: Hebrew Bible. Pub: "Judges, Book of" in *Mercer Dict. of the Bible*; "An Exegesis of Hosea 4:1-5:7" *Restoration Quar.* 17 (1974). Mem: SBL. Rec: Cross-country skiing. Addr: (o) 1000 Cherry Rd., Memphis, TN 38117 901-761-1350; (h) 4950 Essexshire, Memphis, TN 38117 901-683-9128.

MCNAMARA, Martin J., b. Lahinch, Co. Clare, Ireland, June 26, 1930, s. of Michael & Mary (McMahon). Educ: Gregorian U., Rome, STL 1954; Bibl. Inst., Rome, LSS 1956, DSS 1965; Ecole Biblique, Eleve Titulaire 1958; Natl. U. of Ireland, PhD 1976. Emp: Moyne Park, Ireland, 1958-71 Prof., Scripture; Milltown Inst.

of Theol. & Phil., Dublin, 1972-75 Lect., 1975 Prof., Sacred Scripture, 1976-79, 1982-85 Dean, Fac. of Theol.; *Scripture in Ch.,* 1971- Ed.; *Proc. of the Irish Bibl. Assn.,* 1976- Ed.; *Milltown Stud.,* 1978-84 Ed. Spec: Hebrew Bible, New Testament, Semitic Languages, Texts and Epigraphy, Apocrypha and Post-biblical Studies. Pub: *Targum Neofiti 1: Genesis (The Aramaic Bible 1A)* (Glazier/Liturgical, 1992); "The Text of the Latin Bible in the Early Irish Church: Some Data and Desiderata" in *Ireland and Christendom* (1987); *Glossa in Psalmos: The Hiberno-Latin Gloss on the Psalms of Codex Palatinus Latinus 68* (Bibliotheca Apostolica Vaticana, 1986); "'To de (Hagar) Sina oros estin en tê Arabia': Paul and Petra" *Milltown Stud.* 2 (1978); *The Apocrypha in the Irish Church* (Dublin Inst. for Advanced Stud., 1975); "Psalter Text and Psalter Study in the Early Irish Church (AD 600-1200)" *Proc. of the Royal Irish Acad.* 73C (1973); *Targum and Testament* (Irish Acad., 1972); "Some Early Rabbinic Citations and the Palestinian Targum to the Pentateuch" *RivStudOrient* 41 (1966); "Targumic Studies" *CBQ* 28 (1966); and others. Mem: CBA 1962-; Irish Bibl. Assn., Pres. 1972-75; SNTS; Royal Irish Acad. 1982-; SOTS 1992-. Addr: (o) Milltown Inst. of Theology and Philosophy, Milltown Park, Sandford Rd., Dublin 6, Ireland 01-2698802; (h) Woodview, 34 Mt. Merrion Ave., Blackrock, Co. Dublin, Ireland 01-2881343.

MCRAY, John R., b. Holdenville, OK, December 17, 1931, s. of Marvin & Opal (Roberts), m. Naomi, chil: John R.; David E.; Barrett W. Educ: Harding U., MA 1956; U. of Chicago, PhD 1967. Emp: Harding U., 1958-66 Asst. Prof.; David Lipscomb Coll., 1966-71 Assoc. Prof.; W.F. Albright Inst. of Arch. Res., Jerusalem, 1972-73 Res. Assoc.; Middle Tenn. State U., 1973-80 Prof., Relig. Stud.; Wheaton Coll., 1980- Prof. Excv: Caesarea Maritima, 1972, 1974, 1976, 1978, 1980, 1982 Area Supr.; Sepphoris, 1983 Area Supr.; Herodium, 1985 Area Supr. Spec: Archaeology, New Testament. Pub: *Archaeology and the New Testament* (Baker, 1991); Articles in *ABD* (1992), *Holman's Bible Dict.* (1991), *Ency. of Early Christianity* (1990), *Abingdon Dict. of Bible and Religion* (1986); and others. Mem: ASOR 1972-; SBL 1958-, Pres., SE Sect. 1978; IBR 1980-. Rec: Photography, tennis, travel. Addr: (o) Wheaton College Graduate School, Wheaton, IL 60187 708-752-5177; (h) 1269 Reading Ct., Wheaton, IL 60187 708-653-2768.

MCVEY, Kathleen E., b. Evanston, IL, November 29, 1944, d. of David & Eileen (Entress), m. Paul Finney, chil: Siobhan; Nathaniel. Educ: Harvard U., BA 1966, PhD 1977. Emp: U. of Mo., 1974-76 Instr.; Ecole Biblique, Jerusalem, 1978-79 Vis. Prof.; Princeton Theol. Sem., 1979- Assoc. Prof. Excv: Carthage, 1978 Area Supr.; Idalion, 1978 Area Supr. Spec: Apocrypha and Post-biblical Studies. Pub: "Abgar, Correspondence with Jesus," "Bardaisan of Edessa," "Edessa" in *ABD* (Doubleday, 1992); "A

Fresh Look at the Letter of Mara bar Serapion to his Son" *Orientalia Christiana Analecta* 236 (1990); "The Anti-Judaic Polemic of Ephrem Syrus' Hymns on the Nativity" in *Of Scribes and Scrolls: Studies in Hebrew Bible, Intertestamental Judaism and Christian Origins* (U. Press of Amer., 1990); "The Use of Stoic Cosmogony in Theophilus of Antioch's *Hexaemeron*" in *Viva Vox Scripturae: Essays in Honor of Karlfried Froehlich* (Eerdmans, 1991); *Ephrem the Syrians: Hymns on the Nativity, Hymns on Virginity and on the Symbols of the Lord* (Paulist, 1989); and others. Mem: CBA; Symposium Syriacum; NAPS. Addr: (o) Princeton Theological Seminary, CN 821, Princeton, NJ 08542 609-921-8300; (h) 11 Alexander St., Princeton, NJ 08540 609-683-8378.

MCWILLIAMS, Warren L., b. Fort Smith, AR, December 12, 1946, s. of George & Werdna, m. Patricia, chil: Amy; Karen. Educ: South. Bapt. Theol. Sem., MDiv 1971; Vanderbilt U., MA, PhD 1974. Emp: Stetson U., 1974-76 Asst. Prof.; South. Bapt. Theol. Sem., 1976 Vis. Prof.; Okla. Bapt. U., 1976- Auguie Henry Prof. of Bible. Spec: Hebrew Bible, New Testament. Pub: *Free in Christ: The New Testament Understanding of Freedom* (Broadman, 1984); "The Spread of the Gospel by A.D. 100" *BI* (1984); and others. Mem: AAR. Addr: (o) Oklahoma Baptist U., Shawnee, OK 74801 405-275-2850; (h) 4106 N Chapman, Shawnee, OK 74801 405-273-8316.

MEACHAM, Tirzah Yoreh, b. Shell Lake, WI, January 22, 1949, d. of Marion Reiter (Walls) & Walter J., m. Harry Fox, chil: Tzemah Lapidot Yoreh; Tanhum Siah Yoreh; Yoam Tehila Yoreh. Educ: U. of Wis., BA 1973, Phil., Jewish Stud.; Hebrew U., BA eq. 1973, Talmudic & Rabbinic Lit., MA 1979, PhD 1989. Emp: U. of Toronto, 1987-88 Instr., Near East. Stud., 1988-89 Vis. Prof., 1990- Asst. Prof. Spec: Hebrew Bible, Semitic Languages, Texts and Epigraphy, Apocrypha and Post-biblical Studies. Pub: "Klakh and its Substitutes" *Asufot* 6 (1992); "Neusner's *Talmud of the Land of Israel*" *Jewish Quar. Rev.* LXVII (1986), in *The Origins of Judaism* (Garland, 1992). Mem: AJS; SBL; WCJS. Rec: Karate. Addr: (o) U. of Toronto, Dept. of Near Eastern Stud., 4 Bancroft St., Toronto, ON M5S 1A1, Canada 416-978-3080; (h) 407 Palmerston Blvd., Toronto, ON M6G 2N7, Canada.

MEADE, David G., b. Franklin, PA, March 28, 1950, s. of Robert & Avonell, m. Elizabeth, chil: Kara; Andrew; Nathan. Educ: Houghton Coll., BA 1972; Gordon-Conwell Theol. Sem., MDiv 1975; Princeton Theol. Sem., ThM 1980; U. of Nottingham, England, PhD 1984. Emp: United Meth. Ch., 1975-79, 1990- Pastor; St. John's Theol. Coll., England, 1982-83 Vis. Lect.; Houghton Coll., 1984-90 Asst. Prof., NT. Spec: New Testament. Pub: *Pseudonymity and Canon* (Mohr/Siebeck, 1986; Eerdmans, 1987). Mem: SBL. Rec: Hunting, fishing. Addr: (o) 723 7th St., Niagara Falls, NY 14301 716-284-9961; (h) 748 4th St., Niagara Falls, NY 14301 716-282-1075.

MEALAND, David L., b. Bristol, England, s. of Leonard & Barbara, m. Prue, chil: Anne; Jane. Educ: U. of Oxford, MA; U. of Bristol, MLitt; U. of Edinburgh, PhD. Emp: Wells Theol. Coll., 1966-71 Tutor; Salisbury & Wells 1971-72 Head. of NT Stud.; U. of Edinburgh, 1972-86 Lect., NT, 1987- Sr. Lect., NT. Spec: New Testament. Pub: "Hellenistic Historians and the Style of Acts" *ZNTW* 82 (1991); "The Close of Acts and its Hellenistic Vocabulary" *NTS* 36 (1990); "Positional Stylometry Reassessed: Testing a Seven Epistle Theory of Pauline Authorship" *NTS* 35 (1989); "Computers in New Testament Research" *JSNT* 33 (1988); *Poverty and Expectation in the Gospels* (SPCK, 1980); "The Dissimilarity Test" *SJT* 31 (1978); and others. Awd: Oxford, Ellerton Prize, 1966. Mem: SNTS. Rec: Classical music, hill-walking. Addr: (o) U. of Edinburgh, New College, New Testament Dept., Mound Place, Edinburgh EH1 2LX, Scotland 44-31-225-8400.

MEDALA, Stanislaw, b. Szarwark, Poland, April 5, 1935, s. of Wladyslaw & Maria (Wajda). Educ: Pont. Bibl. Inst., Rome, CD in SS 1963; Gregorian U., Rome, ThD 1964. Emp: Diocesan Sem., Gor´zow Wielkopolski, 1964-71 Prof. of Holy Scriptures; Diocesan Sem., Gda´nsk, 1971-75 Prof. of NT; Theol. Inst. of the Congregation of Mission in Krakow, 1975-80 Prof., Arch., 1975- Prof, NT; Acad. of Cath. Theol. in Warszawa, 1982- Prof., Chmn. of Intertestamental Lit. Spec: Archaeology, New Testament, Apocrypha and Post-biblical Studies. Pub: "Apocryphes de l'Ancien Testament" in *Dictionnaire Encyclopédique de la Bible* (Turnhout, 1987); *The Christological and Ecclesiological Function of the Dialogues of Jesus with Jews in the Fourth Gospel* (Akademia Teol. Kat., 1984); "The Tradition About Eternity of the Messiah and Redaction of John 12,34" *Ruch Biblijny i Liturgiczny* 28 (1975); "The Oldest Palestinian Targumim and Their Value for the Study of Ancient Judaism" *Przeglad Orientalistyczny* 91 (1974); *Studia Gdanskie*, vol. 1, ed. (1973); and others. Mem: Polish Oriental Soc. 1973-; Polish Theol. Soc. 1975-; IOSOT 1978-. Rec: Photography, theater. Addr: (o) Akademia Teologii Katolickiej, ul.Dewajtis 5, 01-653 Warszawa, Poland 39-52-21; (h) ul.Krakowskie Przedmiéscie 3, 00-047 Warszawa, Poland 26-89-10.

MEEKS, Wayne A., b. Aliceville, Ala., January 8, 1932. Educ: U. of Ala., BS 1953; Austin Presbyn. Theol. Sem., BD 1956; Yale U., MA 1963, PhD, NT 1965. Emp: Dartmouth Coll., 1964-65 Instr.; Ind. U., Bloomington, 1966-69 Assoc. Prof.; Yale U., 1969-73 Assoc. Prof., 1973- Prof. of Relig. Stud. Spec: New Testament. Pub: *The First Urban Christians: The Social World of the Apostle Paul* (Yale U.P., 1983); "The Image of the Androgyne" *Hist. Relig.* (1973); *The Writings of St. Paul*, ed. (Norton, 1972); "The Man From Heaven in Johannine Sectarianism" *JBL* 91 (1972); "The Prophet-King, 67 & Moses as God and King" in *Religions in Antiquity* (Brill, 1968); *Go From Your Father's*

House (Knox, 1964); and others. Mem: SBL; AAR; SNTS. Addr: (o) Yale U., Dept. of Religious Studies, New Haven, CT 06520 203-432-0747.

MEGIVERN, James J., b. Johnson City, NY, July 2, 1931, s. of John & Katherine (Gibbons), m. Marjorie L. Educ: Mary Immaculate Coll. & Sem., BA, Phil. 1955, MA Theol. 1959; U. of Fribourg, Switzerland, STL 1960, ThD (summa cum laude) 1962; Gregorian U., Pont. Bibl. Inst., Rome, SSL 1966. Emp: Mary Immaculate Coll. & Sem., 1962-64 Instr., Bibl. Lang. & Lit.; St. John's U., Dept. of Theol., 1966-67, Asst. Prof., 1967-70, Assoc. Prof.; N.Y. City Bd. of Educ., South Bronx, 1970-74 Prog. Dir.; U. of N.C. at Wilmington, 1974-77 Assoc. Prof., Dept. of Phil. & Relig., 1975-92 Chmn., 1977- Prof.; Emory U., 1981 Vis. Prof., Dept. of Relig. Spec: New Testament, Apocrypha and Post-biblical Studies. Pub: "Jacques Ellul's *Apocalypse*" *BTB* (1981); *Bible Interpretation*, co-ed.; *Worship & Liturgy*, co-ed. (Consortium, 1978); "Wrestling with Revelation" *BTB* (1978); "Forgive Us Our Debts" *Scripture* (1966); and others. Awd: Moravian Theol. Sem., DD 1966. Mem: SBL; AAR; Amer. Assn. of U. Prof. Rec: Barbershop harmonizing. Addr: (o) U. of North Carolina at Wilmington, Dept. of Philosophy & Religion, Wilmington, NC 28403 919-395-3407; (h) 5618 Greenville Loop Rd., Wilmington, NC 28409 919-799-3069.

MEIER, John P., b. Bronx, NY, August 8, 1942, s. of Paul & Elizabeth (O'Reilly). Educ: St. Joseph's Sem., BA 1964; Gregorian U., Rome, STL 1968; Pont. Bibl. Inst., Rome, SSD 1976. Emp: St. Joseph's Sem., 1972-85 Prof., Chmn. of Scripture Dept.; *CBQ*, 1975- Ed.; Maryknoll Sem., 1975-85 Guest Lect.; Fordham U., 1980-89 Guest Lect.; Catholic U. of Amer., 1985- Prof. Spec: New Testament. Pub: "The Brothers and Sisters of Jesus" *CBQ* 54 (1992); "John the Baptist in Josephus" *JBL* 111 (1992); *A Marginal Jew* (Doubleday, 1991); "Jesus in Josephus" *CBQ* 52 (1990); *The Mission of Christ and His Church* (Glazier, 1990); "The Historical Jesus: Rethinking Some Concepts" *TS* 51 (1990); "Matthew 5:3-12" *Interpretation* 44 (1990); *Antioch and Rome*, co-auth. (Paulist, 1983); *The Vision of Matthew* (Paulist, 1979); and others. Awd: STL & SSD degrees with Papal Gold Medal. Mem: CBA 1971-; SBL 1971-. Rec: Music, cinema. Addr: (o) Catholic U., Box 39, Curley Hall, Washington, DC 20064 202-635-5717.

MEIER, Samuel A., III, b. Tucson, AZ, September 10, 1952, s. of Samuel Arthur, II & Charlotte Lou, m. Patricia (Eileen), chil: Eris Eileen; Samuel Arthur, IV. Educ: UCLA, BA 1974; Dallas Theol. Sem., ThM 1978; Harvard U., PhD 1986. Emp: Asian Theol. Sem., Philippines, 1978-82 Lect.; Ohio State U., 1986- Assoc. Prof.; *HAR*, 1986- Assoc. Ed. Spec: Hebrew Bible, Semitic Languages, Texts and Epigraphy. Pub: *Speaking of Speaking—Marking Direct Discourse in Biblical Hebrew*, VTSup (Brill, 1992); "Women and Communication in the Ancient Near East" *JAOS* 111 (1991); "Linguistic Clues on the Date and Canaanite Origin of Genesis 2:23-24" *CBQ* 53 (1991); "House Fungus—Mesopotamia and Israel (Lev 14:33-53)" *RB* 96 (1989); "Job 1-2: A Reflection of Genesis 1-3" *VT* 39 (1989); *The Messenger in the Ancient Semitic World*, HSM 45 (Scholars, 1988); "Baal's Fight with Yam (KTU 1.2)—A Part of the Baal Myth as Known in KTU 1.1,3-6?" *UF* 18 (1986); and others. Awd: Asian Theol. Sem., Teaching Excellence Awd. 1982; Ohio State U., Alumni Disting. Teaching Awd. 1989. Mem: SBL 1986-. Addr: (o) 226 Cunz Hall, 1841 Millikin Rd., Columbus, OH 43210 614-292-9255; (h) 1825 Weatherstone Ln., Worthington, OH 43235 614-766-2885.

MEITZEN, Manfred O., b. Houston, TX, December 12, 1930, s. of Otto & Laura, m. Fredrica (Kilmer). Educ: Wartburg Theol. Sem., MDiv 1956; Harvard U., PhD 1961. Emp: Rocky Mountain Coll., 1961-65 Assoc. Prof.; W.Va. U., 1965- Prof., Chmn., Dept. of Relig. Stud., 1991- Clinical Prof. of Psychiatry; U. of Charleston, 1981-82 Guest Lect. Spec: New Testament. Pub: Articles in *Religion in the Southern States* (Mercer U.P., 1983); *Religion in Appalachia* (W.Va. U.P., 1978); "Some Reflections on the Resurrection and Eternal Life" Luth. Quart. 24 (1972); and others. Mem: AAR 1955-. Rec: Organist, hunting, motorcycling. Addr: (o) West Virginia U., 324 Stansbury Hall, PO Box 6324, Morgantown, WV 26506 304-293-4995; (h) 119 Forest Dr., Morgantown, WV 26505 304-599-6364.

MELICK, George F., Jr., b. Morristown, NJ, September 7, 1924, s. of George & Esther (Udall), m. Florence (Bevins), chil: Robert; Linda; Judith; Karen. Educ: Princeton U., BSE 1944; Stevens Inst. of Technology, MS 1955; Columbia U., ME 1963; N.Y. U., MA 1970. Emp: Stevens Inst. of Tech., 1955-58 Asst. Prof.; Columbia U., 1958-61 Assoc. in M.E.; Rutgers U., 1961-77 Assoc. Prof., Dean; Drexel U., 1987-91 Prof., Prog. Dir. Spec: New Testament. Pub: *John Mark and the Origin of the Gospels* (Dorrance, 1979). Mem: AAR 1964-; SBL 1965-. Rec: Swimming. Addr: (h) 6 Raven Ct., Mt. Laurel, NJ 08054 609-234-7093.

MELICK, Richard R., Jr., b. Charleston, SC, December 14, 1944, s. of Richard & Sara (Smith), m. Shera (Smith), chil: Richard III; Kristen D.; Karen E. Educ: Columbia Bible Coll., BA 1966; Trinity Evang. Div. Sch., MDiv 1969; SW Bapt. Theol. Sem., PhD 1976. Emp: Miami Christian Coll., 1977-79 Prof. & Chmn., Bible & Theol. Dept.; Palm Beach Atlantic Coll., 1980-83 Prof. & Chmn., Relig. & Phil. Dept.; Mid-Amer. Bapt. Theol. Sem., 1983-92 Prof. & Chmn., NT & Greek Dept.; Evangelische Theol. Faculteit, Belgium, 1985- Vis. Prof.; Criswell Ctr. for Bibl. Stud., 1992- Pres. Spec: New Testament. Pub: *Philippians, Colossians, and Philemon*, New Amer. Commn. 32; *Authority and Interpretation: A Baptist Perspective*, ed.; and others. Mem: SBL; IBR; ETS. Rec: Sports, music. Addr: (o) Criswell Center for Biblical Studies, 4010 Gaston Avenue, Dallas, TX 75246; (h) 8185 Kimbrook, Germantown, TN 38138.

MENARD, Jacques-Edouard, b. Montreal, Canada, February 21, 1923, s. of Leon-Paul & Alice (LaFrance). Educ: Montreal U., BA 1935; Angelicum, Rome, DTh 1947, Lic. Bibl. Sci. 1949; Practical Sch. of Higher Stud., PhD 1960; Strasbourg, State Doc. 1967. Spec: Apocrypha and Post-biblical Studies. Pub: *Gospel of Thomas* (1975, 1982); *Gospel of Philip* (1967, 1982); *Texts of Nag Hammadi* (1975); *Gospel of Truth* (1961, 1972); and others. Awd: Montreal, Doc. 1978; Malta, Doc. 1980; French Coptic Assn., Hon. Pres. Addr: (o) U. of Human Sciences, Faculty of Catholic Theology, 67084 Strasbourg, Germany 8861-00-46.

MENDELSON, Alan, b. Washington, DC, July 30, 1939, s. of Israel & Harriet (Holstein), m. Sara (Heller), chil: David; Daniel. Educ: Brandeis U., MA 1965; U. of Chicago, PhD 1971. Emp: McMaster U., 1976- Assoc. Prof.; *Studia Philonica Ann.*, Assoc. Ed. Spec: Apocrypha and Post-biblical Studies. Pub: *Secular Education in Philo of Alexandria*, Hebrew Union Coll. Mon. Ser. (1982); *Jewish and Christian Self-Definition: Judaism from the Maccabees to the Mid-Third Century*, co-ed. (1981); *Philo's Jewish Identity*, Brown Judaic Stud. (1988). Mem: The Philo Inst., Bd. Dir. Addr: (o) McMaster U., Dept. of Religious Studies, Hamilton, ON L8S 4K1, Canada 416-525-9140; (h) 82 Whitton Rd., Hamilton, ON L8S 4C8, Canada 416-523-8076.

MENDENHALL, George E., b. Muscatine, IA, August 13, 1916, s. of George & Mary, m. Ethel, chil: George; Lauri; Stanley; Gordon; Stephen. Educ: Midland Coll., BA 1936; Luth. Theol. Sem., BD 1938; Johns Hopkins U., PhD 1947. Emp: Hamma Div. Sch., 1947-51 Assoc. Prof.; U. of Mich. 1951-86 Prof.; Yarmouk U., Inst. of Arch., 1987-92 Part-time Vis. Prof.; Amer. Sch. Oriental Res., Jerusalem, 1955-56 Ann. Prof., 1965-66 Dir.; Amer. U. of Beirut, 1971 Vis. Res. Prof. Excv: Jericho, 1956 Field Supr.; Bab Edh-Dhra, Jordan, 1965 Field Supr.; Umm er-Rujam, Jordan, 1966, 1975 Dir.; Tell Hadidi, Syria 1974 Co-dir., Field Supr. Spec: Archaeology, Hebrew Bible, Semitic Languages, Texts and Epigraphy. Pub: *The Syllabic Inscriptions from Byblos* (Amer. U. of Beirut, 1985); "The Inscription from Catal Huyuk in the Plain of Antakya" *Kadmos* (1975); *The Tenth Generation—The Origins of the Biblical Tradition* (Johns Hopkins U. P., 1973); "The Hebrew Conquest of Palestine" *BA* (1962); "The Census Lists of Numbers 1 and 26" *JBL* (1958); "Ancient Oriental and Biblical Law" *BA* (1954); and others. Awd: Midland Coll., LittD 1959; Uppsala Coll., LittD 1981. Mem: AOS, Pres., MidW Branch 1950-51; SBL, Pres., MidW Sect. 1960; ASOR. Rec: Photography, horticulture. Addr:

(o) U. of Michigan, 3074 Frieze Building Ann Arbor, MI 48105 313-763-1595; (h) 1510 Cedar Bend Dr., Ann Arbor, MI 48105 313-665-5364.

MENKEN, Maarten J. J., b. Leiden, March 13, 1948, s. of Stef & Maria E. J. (Blomert), m. Corja J. (Bekius), chil: Ruben D.; Marco A. Educ: Katholieke Theol. U., Amsterdam, BA 1970, MA 1972; U. van Amsterdam, Fac. of Theol., BA 1970, MA 1972, PhD 1985. Emp: U. voor Theol. en Pastoraat, Heerlen, 1977-88 Lect., NT Exegesis, 1989-92 Prof., NT Exegesis; Katholieke U. Nijmegen, Fac. of Theol., 1992- Prof., NT Exegesis; *NT,* 1989- Ed. Staff & Ed. Sec. Spec: New Testament. Pub: "Paradise Regained or Still Lost? Eschatology and Disorderly Behaviour in 2 Thessalonians" *NTS* 38 (1992); "Die Redaktion des Zitates aus Sach 9,9 in Joh 12,15" *ZNW* 80 (1989); "Die Form des Zitates aus Jes 6,10 in Joh 12,40" *BZ* NF 32 (1988); "The Provenance and Meaning of the Old Testament Quotation in John 6:31" *NT* 30 (1988); *Numerical Literary Techniques in John: The Fourth Evangelist's Use of Numbers of Words and Syllables* NTSup 55 (Brill, 1985); "The References to Jeremiah in the Gospel According to Matthew (Mt 2,17; 16,14; 27,9)" *ETL* 60 (1984); and others. Mem: Bijbelwerkgenootschap Sint Hieronymus 1978-; SNTC 1978-; SNTS 1989-; Werkgemeenschap Bijbelwetenschappen en Judaica 1978-. Rec: Music, long-distance walking. Addr: (o) Catholic Theological U., Heidelberglaan 2, 3584 CS, Utrecht, Netherlands 030-533796; (h) Oude Amhemseweg 315, 3705 BG Zeist, Netherlands.

MERCER, Calvin R., Jr., b. Kinston, NC, August 27, 1953, s. of Calvin Richard & Edna Ruth (Kennedy), m. Marilyn. Educ: U. of N.C., BA 1975; Southeast. Bapt. Theol. Sem., ThM 1979, MDiv 1977; Fla. State U., PhD, Relig. Stud. 1983. Emp: Fla. A&M U., 1979-80 Instr.; Mt. Olive Coll., 1981-84 Prof.; East Carolina U., 1985-90 Asst. Prof., 1990- Assoc. Prof. Spec: New Testament. Pub: "Jesus, the Apostle: 'Sending' and the Theology of John" *JETS* 35 (1992); "*Apostello* and Pempo in John" *NTS* 36 (1990); "Contemporary Language and New Translations of the Bible: The Impact of Feminism" *Relig. & Public Educ.* 17 (1990); "Norman Perrin's Interpretation of the New Testament: From 'Exegetical Method' to 'Hermeneutical Process'" in *Studies in Hermeneutics* 2 (Mercer U.P., 1986); and others. Awd: South. Reg. Educ. Bd. Small Grants Prog., Travel & Res. Awd. 1986; Duke-U. of N.C. Ctr. for Res. on Women, Curr. Development Grant 1987; AAR Res. Assistance Grant 1990; East Carolina U., Teaching Effectiveness Grant 1990. Mem: AAR; SBL; SNTS; Coll. Theol. Soc. Rec: Racketball, skiing, backpacking, canoe camping, hanging out at Trappist monasteries. Addr: (o) East Carolina U., Dept. of Philosophy, Greenville, NC 28518-4357 919-757-6121.

MERKLEIN, Helmut M., b. Wuerzburg, September 17, 1940, s. of Martin & Anna. Educ:

U. Wuerzburg, ThD 1976. Emp: U. Wuerzburg, 1977 Privatdozent; U. Wuppertal, 1977-80 Prof., NT; U. of Bonn, Kath.-Theol. Fakultaet, 1980- Prof., Dir. of NT Seminar. Spec: New Testament. Pub: *Der erste Brief an die Korinther. Kap. 1-4* (Mohn-Echter, 1992); *Jesu Botschaft von der Gottesherrschaft* (Kath. Bibelwerk, 1989); *Studien zu Jesus und Paulus* (Mohr, 1987); *Die Gottesherrschaft als Handlungsprinzip* (Echter, 1984); "Die Auferweckung Jesu und die Anfange der Christologie" *ZNW* 72 (1981); "Die Ekklesia Gottes. Der Kirchenbegriff bei Paulus und in Jerusalem" *BZ* 23 (1979); and others. Mem: SNTS; Kath. Bibelwerk. Addr: (o) U. Bonn, Katholische Theologische-Fakultaet, Regina-Pacis-Weg 1a, 53113 Bonn 1, Germany 0228-737643; (h) Toepferstrasse 6a, 53343 Wachtberg, Germany 02225-13185.

MERKUR, Dan, b. Toronto, Canada, May 26, 1951. Educ: York U., Canada, BA 1981, MA 1982; U. of Stockholm, PhD 1985. Emp: York U., 1984-85 Lect.; Syracuse U., 1986-90 Asst. Prof.; U. of Toronto, 1992 Lect. Spec: Hebrew Bible, Apocrypha and Post-biblical Studies. Pub: "The Visionary Practices of Jewish Apocalyptists" in *Psychoanalytic Study of Society* 14 (1989); "Prophetic Initiation in Israel and Judah" *Psychoanalytic Study of Society* 12 (1988); "The Prophecies of Jeremiah" *American Imago* 42 (1985); and others. Mem: CSBS 1980-; CSSR 1980-; SBL 1984-; AAR 1984-. Rec: Stained glass. Addr: (h) 3 Belsize Dr., Toronto, ON M4S 1L3, Canada 416-480-0119.

MERLING, Paul David, b. Pittsburgh, PA, June 14, 1948, s. of Clark Anderson & Mary Iva (Stover), m. Stephanie C. (Osborne), chil: Paul David, Jr.; Jeremy Daniel. Educ: South. Coll., BA, Theol. 1974; Andrews U., MDiv 1983. Emp: Andrews U., Horn Arch. Mus., 1984-86 Asst. Cur., 1986- Cur., 1986- Asst. Prof. of Arch. & Hist. of Antiq., 1991- Assoc. Dir. for Admn., Inst. of Arch. Excv: Tell Hesban, Jordan, 1974 Square Supr.; Tell el-Umeiri, Jordan, 1984, 1987 Square Supr.; Tell Gezer, 1990 Field Supr.; Tell Jalul, Jordan, 1992 Asst. Dir., Field Supr. Spec: Archaeology, Hebrew Bible. Pub: "Heshbon: A Lost City of the Bible" *Arch. in the Bibl. World* Fall (1991); "The Tell el-Umeiri Inscription" *AUSS* 29/3 (1991); "An Analysis of Charles Warren's Explorations between Na'ur and Khuraybat as Suq" in *The Madaba Plains Project: The Report of the 1984 Season* (Andrews U.P., 1989); "A Tribute to Siegfried H. Horn for His Eightieth Birthday and a Note" *AUSS* 26/1 (1988); and others. Awd: Zion Res. Found. Travel Grant 1984; Andrews U. Fac. Res. Grant 1991-92. Mem: ASOR; NEAS; SBL; BIA, Amman; Andrews Soc. for Relig. Stud. Rec: Canoeing, camping, fly fishing. Addr: (o) Andrews U., Horn Archaeological Museum, Berrien Springs, MI 49104-0990 616-471-3273; (h) 2036 U.S. 31 N, Niles, MI 49120 616-684-1623.

MERRILL, Arthur L., b. Tura, Assam, India, September 14, 1930, s. of Alfred & Ida (Walker),

m. Margaret, chil: Margaret J.; Robert L.; Katherine M. Educ: U. of Chicago, PhD 1962. Emp: United Theol. Sem., 1962- Prof., OT Theol.; *Theol. Markings,* 1971-78 Ed. Bd.; *Prism,* 1984- Ed. Bd. Spec: Hebrew Bible. Pub: "Psalm XXIII and the Jerusalem Tradition" *VT* 15 (1965); and others. Awd: AATS-Lilly Found., Post-doc. Fellow 1966-67. Mem: SBL 1957-, Pres., Upper MidW Reg. 1978-79; ASOR 1968-; IES 1977-. Addr: (o) United Theological Seminary, Twin Cities, 3000 5th St. NW, New Brighton, MN 55112 612-633-4311; (h) 214 Windsor Court, New Brighton, MN 55112 612-633-9330.

MERRILL, Eugene H., b. Anson, ME, September 12, 1934, s. of Orrin & Ruby, m. Janet, chil: Sonya. Educ: Bob Jones U., BA 1957, MA 1960, PhD 1963; NYU, MA 1970; Columbia U., MPhil 1977, PhD 1985. Emp: Bob Jones U., 1958-60, 1963-66 Prof.; NE Bible Coll.,1966-68 Asst. Prof.; Berkshire Christian Coll., 1968-75 Prof.; Dallas Theol. Sem. 1975- Prof. Spec: Hebrew Bible, Mesopotamian Studies, Semitic Languages, Texts and Epigraphy. Pub: *An Historical Survey of the Old Testament* (1966, 1991); *1, 2 Chronicles* (Zondervan, 1988); *Kingdom of Priests: A History of Old Testament Israel* (Baker, 1987); *Qumran and Predestination* (Brill, 1975). Mem: AOS; ASOR; SBL; NEAS; ETS. Addr: (o) Dallas Theological Seminary, 3909 Swiss Ave., Dallas, TX 75204 214-841-3650; (h) 9314 Waterview Rd., Dallas, TX 75218 214-328-2148.

MESHEL, Ze'ev, b. Israel, October 12, 1932, s. of David & Ada, m. Ester, chil: Gili; Yoel; Noga. Educ: Hebrew U., Jerusalem, BA 1960, MA 1964; Tel Aviv U., Jerusalem, PhD 1974. Emp: Tel Aviv U., Inst. of Arch., 1967- Sr. Lect. Excv: Negev sites, Judean Desert, Yotvata, Ajrud, Simai Sites, Ein Gedi, 1964- Dir. Spec: Archaeology. Mem: IES; AIA. Addr: (o) Tel Aviv U., Tel Aviv, Israel 03-420703; (h) 75 Hapalmach St., Jerusalem, Israel 02-632261.

MESHORER, Yaakov, b. Jerusalem, Israel, August 14, 1935, s. of Abraham & Zmira, m. Adaya, chil: Hagit; Nitzan; Ishai. Educ: Hebrew U., Jerusalem, BA, MA, PhD. Emp: Israel Mus., Numismatic Dept., 1969- Cur., 1975-82, 1990- Chief Cur. of Arch.; Hebrew U., Jerusalem, 1970- Assoc. Prof. Spec: Archaeology. Pub: *The Coinage of Samaria in the 4th Century BCE* (1991); *The Coinage of Aelia Capitolina* (1989); *City Coins of Eretz-Israel and the Decapolis* (1985); *Ancient Jewish Coinage,* 2 vol. (Amphora, 1982); *Syllogue Nummorum Graecorum of the American Numimatic Society, Part 6, Palestine-Arabia* (1981); *Nabatean Coins, Qedem* 3 (1975); and others. Awd: Kadman Prize for Numismatic Res. 1973; Girshman Prize of Arch.; Amer. Numismatic Soc., Overseas Fellow. Mem: Royal Numismatic Soc.; Amer. Numismatic Soc. Rec: Playing the violin. Addr: (o) The Israel Museum, Jerusalem, Israel 708812; (h) 8 Louria St., Jerusalem, Israel 713326.

METTINGER, Tryggve N. D., b. Helsingborg, Sweden, June 8, 1940, s. of Allan & Anna M., m. Solvi (Axell). Educ: U. of Lund, Sweden, MA 1963, ThD 1971. Emp: U. of Lund, 1971-78 Asst. Prof., 1978- Prof.; Princeton Theol. Sem., 1984 Guest Prof.; *Coniectanea Biblica,* OT Ser. 1978- Co-ed.; *JSOT,* 1982- Ed. Bd. Spec: Hebrew Bible, Semitic Languages, Texts and Epigraphy. Pub: "The Elusive Essence: YHWH, El and Baal and the Distinctiveness of Israelite Faith" in *Die Hebraeische Bibel und ihre Zweifache; Nachgeschichte,* Festschrift Rolf Rendtorff (Neukirchener, 1990); "The Study of the Gottesbild: Problems and Suggestions" *SEA* 54 (1989); *In Search of God: The Meaning and Message of the Everlasting Names* (Fortress, 1988); *A Farewell to the Servant Songs* (Almqvist, 1983); *The Dethronement of Sabaoth: Studies in the Shem and Kabod Theologies,* ConBOT 18 (Almqvist, 1982); "YHWH Sabaoth—The Heavenly King on the Cherubim Throne" in *Studies in the Period of David and Solomon* (1982); "The Veto on Images and the Aniconic God in Ancient Israel" in *Religious Symbols and Their Functions,* Scripta Inst. Donneriani 10; (1979); *King and Messiah,* ConBOT 8 (Almqvist, 1976); "The Hebrew Verb System: A Survey of Recent Research" *ASTI* 9 (1973); and others. Awd: King Oscar II's Awd. for Outstanding Diss. 1971. Mem: Royal Soc. of Letters, Lund 1981; New Soc. of Letters, Lund 1986. Rec: Walking, class. music, lit. Addr: (o) U. of Lund, Theologicum, Allhelgona Kyrkog. 8, S - 223 62 Lund, Sweden 046-10-90-45; (h) Anders Mollares vag 20, S - 237 41 Bjarred, Sweden 046-29-31-02.

METZGER, Bruce M., b. Middletown, PA, February 9, 1914, s. of Maurice R. & Anna M., m. Isobel Mackay, chil: John M.; James B. Educ: Lebanon Valley Coll., AB 1935; Princeton Theol. Sem., ThB 1938, ThM 1939; Princeton U., MA 1940, PhD 1942. Emp: Princeton Theol. Sem., 1938-84 Tchr. of NT, 1984- George L. Collord Prof. Emeritus of NT Lang. & Lit.; *Theol. Today,* 1945-59 Ed. Sec.; Presbyn. Theol. Sem., Korea, 1986, Caribbean Grad. Sch. of Theol., Jamaica, 1990; Sem. Intl. Teologico Bautista, Argentina, 1991 Vis. Prof. Spec: New Testament, Apocrypha and Post-biblical Studies. Pub: *The Text of the New Testament: Its Transmission, Corruption, and Restoration* (Oxford U.P., 1992); *The Canon of the New Testament: Its Origin, Development, and Significance* (Oxford U.P., 1987); *The Early Versions of the New Testament: Their Origin, Transmission, and Limitations* (Oxford U.P., 1977); *An Introduction to the Apocrypha* (Oxford U.P., 1957); "A Greek and Aramaic Inscription Found at Armazi in Georgia" *JNES* 15 (1956); "Considerations of Methodology in the Study of the Mystery Religions and Early Christianity" *HTR* 48 (1955); "Tatian's Diatessaron and a Persian Harmony of the Gospels" *JBL* 69 (1950); "Recent Spanish Contributions to the Textual Criticism of the New Testament" *JBL* 66 (1947); "Trends in the Textual Criticism of the Iliad, the Mahabharata, and the New Testament" *JBL* 65 (1946); and others. Awd: St. Andrews U., Scotland, DD 1964; U. of Muenster, Germany, DTheol 1971; U. of Potchefstroom (South Africa), DLitt 1985; Ernest Trice Thompson Awd. 1991. Mem: APA 1944-; SBL, Pres. 1970-71; SNTS, Pres. 1971-72; NAPS, Pres. 1972; Brit. Acad., Corresponding Fellow. Rec: Woodworking. Addr: (h) 20 Cleveland Ln., Princeton, NJ 08540 609-924-4060.

MEYER, Ben F., b. Chicago, IL, November 5, 1927, s. of Ben F. & Mary (Connor), m. Denise (Oppliger). Educ: Gonzaga U., BA 1950, MA 1951; Mt. St. Michael's, PhL 1951; Santa Clara U., MST 1958; Alma College, STL 1958; Pont. Bibl. Inst., SSL 1961; U. Gregoriana, STD (summa cum laude) 1965. Emp: Alma Coll., 1963-68 Asst. Prof.; Grad. Theol. Union, 1966-68 Asst. Prof.; McMaster U., 1969- Prof. Spec: New Testament. Pub: *Christus Faber: The Master Builder and the House of God*, Princeton Theol. Mon. Ser. 29 (Pickwick, 1992); "The Challenge of Text and Reader to the Historical-Critical Method" *Concilium* (1991); *Critical Realism and the New Testament*, Princeton Theol. Mon. Ser. 17 (Pickwick, 1989); "The Expiation Motif in the Eucharistic Words: A Key to the History of Jesus?" *Gregorianum* 69 (1988); *The Early Christians: Their World Mission and Self-Discovery* (Glazier, 1986); "The Primacy of Consent and the Uses of Suspicion" *Ex Auditu* 2 (1986); "The Pre-Pauline Formula in Romans 3:25-26a" *NTS* 29 (1983); *The Aims of Jesus* (SCM, 1979); and others. Awd: U. of Gottingen, Fulbright Fellow. 1964-65; Canada Coun. Fellow. 1976-77; Social Sci. & Hum. Res. Coun. of Canada, Res. Fellow. 1983-84. Mem: CBA 1964-; SBL 1965-; CSSR 1972-; CSBS 1973-, Pres.1987-88; SNTS 1974-. Addr: (o) McMaster U., Dept. of Religious Studies, Hamilton, ON L8S 4K1, Canada 416-525-9140; (h) 2160 Lakeshore Rd., Apt. 1008, Burlington, ON L7R 1A7, Canada 416-632-1589.

MEYER, Marvin W., b. Grand Rapids, MI, April 16, 1948, s. of Martin & June, m. Bonita K., chil: Stephen; Jonathan; Elisabeth. Educ: Calvin Coll., AB 1970; Calvin Theol. Sem., MDiv 1974; Claremont Grad. Sch., PhD 1979. Emp: Barnard Coll., 1978-79 Asst. Prof., Relig.; U. of Calif., Santa Barbara, 1979-80 Asst. Prof., Relig. Stud.; Claremont Grad. Sch., Inst. for Antiq. & Christianity, 1980-83 Asst. Dir.; Ferrum Coll., 1983-85 Asst. Prof., Relig.; Chapman U., 1985- Assoc. Prof. of Relig, Dir. of Hon. Prog. Excv: Heshbon, Jordan, 1971 Square Supr.; Nag Hammadi/Faw Qibli, 1976-78, 1980 Square Supr. Spec: Archaeology, New Testament, Apocrypha and Post-biblical Studies. Pub: *The Gospel of Thomas: The Hidden Sayings of Jesus* (HarperCollins, 1992); "The Beginning of the Gospel of Thomas," "The Youth in the *Secret Gospel of Mark*" *Semeia* (1990); *The Ancient Mysteries: A Sourcebook* (HarperCollins, 1987); "The Light and Voice on the Damascus Road" *Foundations & Facets Forum* (1986); "Making Mary Male: The Categories 'Male' and 'Female'

in the *Gospel of Thomas*" *NTS* (1985); "Archaeological Survey of the Wadi Sheikh Ali: December 1980" *Göttingen Miszellen* (1983); *The Letter of Peter to Philip: Text, Translation, and Commentary* (Scholars, 1981); and others. Awd: Ferrum Coll. & Chapman U., res. grants 1983-; NEH Summer Stipend 1988; ACLS, Graves Awd. 1990-91. Mem: AAR; SBL; Amer. Res. Ctr. in Egypt; IACS. Rec: Hiking, coaching soccer & Little League baseball. Addr: (o) Chapman U., Dept. of Religion, Orange, CA 92666 714-997-6602; (h) 2544 E Jackson, Orange, CA 92667 714-633-7727.

MEYERS, Carol L., b. Wilkes-Barre, PA, November 26, 1942, d. of Harry & Irene Lyons, m. Eric M., chil: Julie Kaete; Dina Elisa. Educ: Wellesley Coll., AB, Bibl. Hist., Lit. & Interpretation 1964; Brandeis U., MA 1966, PhD, Near East. & Judaic Stud. 1975. Emp: Duke U., 1977-84 Asst. Prof., 1984-90 Assoc. Prof., 1990- Prof., Relig., Women's Stud. Prog., 1986-90 Assoc. Dir., 1992- Dir.; *Ency. of Near Eastern Archeology*, ASOR & Oxford U.P., Co-ed.; ASOR Diss. Ser., 1978-, *BA*, 1982-92, JSOTSup, 1991- Ed. Bd. Excv: Tell Gezer, Israel, 1964-67 Area Supr.; Khirbet Shema', Israel, 1970-71 Area Supr.; Meiron, Israel, 1971 Area Supr., 1972 Field Supr., 1974-78 Core Staff, Field Arch., 1978- Assoc. Dir.; Joint Sepphoris Proj., 1984- Co-dir. Spec: Archaeology, Hebrew Bible. Pub: *Sepphoris*, co-auth. (Eisenbrauns, 1992); "'To Her Mother's House'—Considering a Counterpart to the Israelite *Bet 'ab*" in *The Bible and the Politics of Exegesis* (Pilgrim, 1991); "Of Drums and Damsels: Women's Performance in Ancient Israel" *BA* 54 (1991); *Excavations at the Ancient Synagogue of Gush Halav*, Meiron Excvn. Project vol. 5, co-auth. (Eisenbrauns/ASOR, 1990); "Women and the Domestic Economy of Early Israel" in *Women's Earliest Records: From Ancient Egypt and Western Asia*, Brown Judaic Stud. 166 (Scholars, 1989); "Expanding the Frontiers of Biblical Archaeology," co-auth. *Eretz-Israel* 20 (1989); *Discovering Eve: Ancient Israelite Women in Context* (Oxford U.P., 1988); "Artistry in Stone: The Mosaics of Ancient Sepphoris," co-auth. *BA* 50 (1987); *Excavations at Ancient Meiron, Upper Galilee, Israel, 1971-72, 1974-75, 1977*, Meiron Excvn. Project vol. 3, co-auth. (ASOR, 1981); and others. Awd: Albright Inst. of Arch. Res., Jerusalem, Thayer Fellow 1975-76; NEH, Fellow. 1982-83, 1990-91; Oxford Ctr. for Postgrad. Hebrew Stud., Vis. Schol. 1982-83; Duke U., Res. Coun., res. grants 1983-84, 1985-86, 1987-88, 1990-91; Princeton U., Ctr. of Theol. Inquiry, Resident Mem. 1990-91. Mem: AAR; ASOR; AIA; IES; PES. Rec: Travel, squash, hiking, cooking. Addr: (o) Duke U., Dept. of Religion, PO Box 90964, Durham, NC 27708-0964 919-660-3510; (h) 3202 Waterbury Dr., Durham, NC 27707 919-489-1746.

MEYERS, Eric M., b. Norwich, CT, June 5, 1940, m. Carol (Lyons), chil: Julie; Dina. Educ: Brandeis U., MA 1964; Harvard U., PhD 1969. Emp: Duke U., 1969- Prof., Relig.; U. of N.C.,

1973- Vis. Assoc. Prof.; Albright Inst. Arch. Res., Jerusalem, 1975-76 Dir.; *BASOR,* 1978- Assoc. Ed.; *BA,* Ed.; Annenberg Res. Inst., 1991-92 Dir. Excv: Khirbet Shema, 1969-72 Dir.; Meiron, 1971- Dir.; En-Nabratein, 1980-81 Dir. Spec: Archaeology. Pub: *Excavation at Gush Halav* (ASOR, 1991); *Archaeology, the Rabbis, and the New Testament,* co-auth. (Abingdon, 1981); *The Excavations at Ancient Meiron* (ASOR, 1981); and others. Mem: AAR; AIA; ASOR, Pres. Pub.; IES; SBL. Addr: (o) Duke U., Dept. of Religion, Duke Station, P.O. Box 4735, Durham, NC 27706.

MICHAELS, J. Ramsey, b. Syracuse, NY, May 1, 1931, s. of Peter & Ethel (Ramsey), m. Betty, chil: Carolyn; Linda; David; Kenneth. Educ: Princeton U., BA 1952; Grace Theol. Sem., BD 1955; Westminster Theol. Sem., ThM 1956; Harvard U., ThD. Emp: Gordon-Conwell Theol. Sem., 1958-84 Prof., NT; SW Mo. State U., 1984- Prof., Relig. Stud. Spec: New Testament, Apocrypha and Post-biblical Studies. Pub: "John" in *New International Biblical Comm.* (1989); "1 Peter" in *Word Biblical Comm.* (1988); "The Level Ground in the Shepherd of Hermas" *ZNW* (1969); "Eschatology in 1 Peter iii.17" *NTS* (1967); and others. Mem: CBA; SBL; SNTS. Rec: Skiing, book collecting. Addr: (o) Southwest Missouri State U., Dept. of Religious Studies, Springfield, MO 65804 417-836-5474; (h) 2706 S Edgewater, Springfield, MO 65804 417-883-7622.

MICHALOWSKI, Piotr, January 9, 1948. Educ: U. of Warsaw, MA, Mediterranean Arch. 1968, MA, Near East. Philol. 1968; Yale U., MPhil 1972, PhD 1976. Emp: Yale U., 1974 Instr., Dept. of Near East. Lang. & Cultures; Harvard U., 1974-75 Res. Fellow; U. of Calif., 1975-79 Asst. Prof., Sumerian; U. of Pa., 1979-81 Res. Assoc., Sumerian Dict. Project; U. of Mich., 1981- George G. Cameron Assoc. Prof. of Anc. Near East. Lang. & Civ., 1987- Chmn., Dept. of Near East. Stud.; *JCS,* 1991- Ed. Spec: Mesopotamian Studies. Pub: "Mari: the View from Ebla" in *Mari in Retrospect* (Eisenbrauns, 1991); "The Shekel and the Vizier" *ZA* 80 (1990); "Presence at the Creation" in *Lingering Over Words: Studies in Ancient Near Eastern Literature in Honor of William L. Moran;* (Scholars, 1990); *The Lamentation Over the Destruction of Sumer and Ur,* Mesopotamian Civ. 1 (Eisenbrauns, 1989); "Magan and Meluhha Once Again" *JCS* 40 (1988); "Divine Heroes and Historical Self-Representation: From Gilgamesh to Shulgi" *Bull. of the Soc. of Mesopotamian Stud.* 16 (1988); *The Tablets of Ebla: Concordance and Bibliography,* co-auth. (Eisenbrauns, 1984); and others. Awd: Yale U., Grad. Fellow. 1968-73, Rackham Res. Grant 1981; Amer. Phil. Soc., Travel Grant 1984, Rackham Res. Grant 1984; NEH, Summer Fellow. 1985; NEH, Trans. Grant 1985-86, 1988-91. Mem: AOS; Linguistic Soc. of Amer.; BSA, Ankara; BSA, Iraq; Found. Assyriologique G. Dossin. Addr: (o) U. of Michigan, 3074 Frieze Bldg., Ann Arbor, MI 48109-1285 313-764-0314; (h) 451 S 4th Ave., Ann Arbor, MI 48104 313-761-7647.

MILAZZO, G. Tom E. J., b. New Haven, CT, May 10, 1954, s. of Pasquale & Marie (Ciaburri), m. Norma Jean, chil: Joshua James; Jeannine Anna-Rose. Educ: Fordham U., BA 1973, MA, Phil. 1978; Yale Div. Sch., MDiv 1982; Emory U., PhD, Bibl. Theol. 1988. Emp: Ga. State U., 1991 Adj. Asst. Prof.; St. Leo Coll., 1992- Asst. Prof., Relig. Stud. Spec: Hebrew Bible, Apocrypha and Post-biblical Studies. Pub: "To an Impotent God: Images of Divine Impotence in Hebrew Scripture" *Shofar* 11/2 (1993); *The Protest and the Silence: Suffering, Death and Biblical Theology* (Fortress, 1991); "For My Heart is Lonely: The Problem of Death in Biblical Theology" *Shibboleth* (1980); "The Human Face of Jesus" *Shibboleth* (1979); and others. Awd: Yale Div. Sch., Timothy Dwight Fellow 1982; Wesleyan U., NEH Fellow 1978. Mem: SBL 1982-; AAR 1984-; Coll. Theol. Soc. 1992-. Rec: Distance bicycling, weight lifting, guitar. Addr: (o) St. Leo College, Dept. of the Humanities, PO Box 2127, Saint Leo, FL 33574 904-588-8296; (h) 1501 Jefferson Ave., Dade City, FL 33525.

MILETIC, Stephen F., b. Windsor, ON, Canada, November 23, 1952, s. of Anica & Mate, m. Joyce Elaine (Bachmeier), chil: Isaac Francis; Heather Ann; Rose Sharon; Frances Clare. Educ: U. of Windsor, BA 1976, MA 1977, BEd 1978; Marquette U., PhD 1985. Emp: U. of Windsor, 1980, 1983 Lect.; U. of St. Thomas, 1983-84 Vis. Asst. Prof.; U. of Lethbridge, 1984-85 Lect., Relig. Stud.; Notre Dame Inst., 1988-90 Asst. Prof., Sacred Scripture, 1988- Acad. Dean, 1990- V.P., 1993- Assoc. Prof., Provost & Acad. Dean; Marymount U., 1991- Adj. Lect. Spec: New Testament. Pub: Articles in *The Catholic Encyclopedia* (1991); *"One Flesh": Ephesians 5.22-24, 31: Marriage and the New Creation,* Analecta Biblica 115 (Pont. Bibl. Inst., 1988); *The Message of the New Testament and the Aramaic Bible (Targum),* trans. (Pont. Bibl. Inst., 1982). Mem: SBL; CSBS; CBA; Assn. Catholique des Etudes Bibliques aux Canada. Rec: Sports, travel, popular media, computers. Addr: (o) Notre Dame Institute, 4420 Sano St., Alexandria, VA 22312-1553 703-658-4304; (h) 19027 Canadian Ct., Gaithersburg, MD 20879 301-977-2872.

MILGROM, Jacob, b. Brooklyn, NY, February 1, 1923, s. of Isaac & Clara, m. Jo, chil: Shira; Jeremy; Etan; Asher. Educ: JTS, BHL 1943, MHL, Rabbi 1946, DHL 1953; U. of Judaism, DHL 1989; Jewish Theol. Sem., DD 1973. Emp: Va. Union U., 1955-65 Prof.; U. of Calif. at Berkeley, 1965-93 Prof. Spec: Hebrew Bible. Pub: *Leviticus 1-16,* AB (Doubleday, 1991); *Numbers* (Jewish Publ. Soc., 1990); *Studies in Cultic Theology and Terminology* (Brill, 1983); *Cult and Conscience* (Brill, 1976); *Studies in Levitical Terminology* (U. of Calif., 1970); and others. Awd: Guggenheim Fellow; Amer. Acad. for Jewish Res., Fellow; Fulbright Fellow; Inst. for Advanced Stud., Jerusalem, Fellow; Hebrew Union Coll., DHL 1993. Mem: SBL. Addr: (o) U. of California at Berkeley, Near Eastern Studies,

Berkeley, CA 94720 510-642-3757; (h) 1042 Sierra St., Berkeley, CA 94702 510-524-3144.

MILIK, J. T., Emp: Ctr. Natl. de Recherche Sci., Paris. Spec: Hebrew Bible, Semitic Languages, Texts and Epigraphy. Pub: "Daniel et Susanne à Qumrân?" in *De la Tôrah au Messie: Etudes d'exégèse et d'herméneutique bibliques offertes à Henri Cazelles* (Desclée, 1981); "Ecrits préesséniens de Qumrân: D'Hénoch à Amram" in *Qumran: Sa piété, sa théologie et son milieu,* BETL 46 (Duculot, 1978); *Discoveries in the Judaean Desert,* vol. 1-3, 6, contb. ed. (Clarendon, 1955-1977); *The Books of Enoch: Aramaic Fragments of Qumran Cave 4,* co-auth. (Clarendon, 1976); "Un fragment mal placé dans l'édition du Siracide de Masada" *Biblica* 47 (1966); "The Copper Document from Cave III of Qumran: Translation and Commentary" *Ann. of the Dept. of Antiq. of Jordan* 4-5 (1960); *Ten Years of Discovery in the Wilderness of Judea,* Stud. in Bibl. Theol. 26 (SCM, 1959); "Le travail d'édition des manuscrits du Désert de Juda" in *Volume du Congrès, Strasbourg 1956,* VTSup 4 (Brill, 1957); "Manuale disciplinae" *Verbum Domini* 29 (1951); and others. Addr: (o) Centre National de Recherche Scientifique, 92 Rue de Lourmel, 75015 Paris, France 43206503.

MILLARD, Alan Ralph, b. Harrow, England, December 1, 1937, s. of Ralph & Joyce, m. Margaret (Sibley), chil: Clare; Stephen; Jonathan. Educ: U. of Oxford, BA 1959; U. of London, MPhil 1967. Emp: British Mus., 1961-63 Asst. Keeper; Tyndale Lib. Bibl. Res., 1963-70 Lbrn.; U. of Liverpool, 1970 Rankin Prof. in Hebrew & Anc. Semitic Lang.; Hebrew U., Inst. for Advanced Stud., Jerusalem, 1983-84 Fellow; *TB,* 1966-78 Ed. Excv: Tell Rifa'at, Syria, 1960 Site Supr.; Petra, Jordan, 1960 Site Supr.; Nimrud, Iraq, 1961 Asst. Epigraphist; Tell Nebi Mend, Syria, 1975, 1977, 1979 Epigraphist, Registrar. Spec: Archaeology, Hebrew Bible, Mesopotamian Studies, Semitic Languages, Texts and Epigraphy. Pub: "Variable Spelling in Hebrew and other Ancient Texts" *JTS* 42 (1991); *Discoveries from the Time of Jesus* (Lion, 1990); "The Bevelled-Rim Bowls: Their Purpose and Significance" *Iraq* 50 (1988); "Sennacherib's Attack on Jerusalem" *TB* 36 (1985); *Treasures from Bible Times* (Lion, 1985); *The Bible B.C.: What Can Archaeology Prove?* (Intervarsity, 1977); "Assyrian Royal Names in the Old Testament" *JSS* 21; "The Practice of Writing in Ancient Israel" *BA* 35 (1972); *Atra-Hasis: The Babylonian Story of the Flood,* co-auth. (Clarendon, 1969); and others. Mem: SOTS; BSA, Iraq; BIA, Jerusalem. Rec: Walking. Addr: (o) The University, Dept. of Oriental Studies, Liverpool L69 3BX, England 051-709-6022; (h) 21 Riversdale Rd., West Kirby, Wirral, Merseyside, L48 4EY, England.

MILLER, Charles H., b. Parsons, KS, October 23, 1933, s. of Charles & Mary (O'Connor).

Educ: San Anselmo Coll., Rome; STD 1973. Emp: St. Louis U., 1970-79 Assoc. Prof.; St. Mary's U., 1979- Prof., 1987- Dean; *Theol. Digest,* 1970-76 Assoc. Ed. Spec: Archaeology, Hebrew Bible. Pub: Articles in *HBD* (1985); *As It is Written: The Use of Old Testament References in Vatican Council II* (Marianist, 1973); and others. Awd: Israel, Fulbright-Hayes Sr. Scholar, 1978-79. Mem: SBL 1970-; ASOR; AAR 1982-; ACOR 1989- Trustee; Tex. Com. for Humanities 1990-. Rec: Hiking, fishing, hunting. Addr: (o) St. Mary's U., San Antonio, TX 78228-8548 210-436-3737; (h) 10910 Wild Grape, San Antonio, TX 78230 210-641-6354.

MILLER, Donald G., b. Braddock, PA, October 30, 1909, s. of C. Herbert & Alma (Gilmore), m. Eleanor (Chambers), chil: Lynne; Douglas; Richard. Educ: Bibl. Sem., STB 1933, STM 1934; NYU, MA 1934, PhD 1935. Emp: Gettysburg Theol. Sem., 1938-39 Vis. Instr.; Union Theol. Sem., 1943-62 Walter H. Robinson Prof. of NT; *Interpretation,* 1947-62 Co-ed.; *Layman's Bible Comm.,* 1957-65 Ed.; Pittsburgh Theol. Sem., 1962-70 Pres. Spec: New Testament. Pub: "Romans, Epistle to" in *ISBE* (Eerdmans, 1988); *The Authority of the Bible* (Eerdmans, 1972); *The Gospel According to Luke* (John Knox, 1959); *Conqueror in Chains: A Story of the Apostle Paul* (Westminster, 1951). Awd: Waynesburg Coll., LLD 1963; Washington and Jefferson Coll., LittD 1965. Mem: SBL 1935-. Rec: Woodwork, classical music. Addr: (h) 401 Russell Ave. #405, Gaithersburg, MD 20877 301-926-2233.

MILLER, Eddie L., b. Los Angeles, CA, April 6, 1937, s. of William D. & Georgia L., m. Cynthia L., chil: Terryl E.; Timothy A.; Tad S.; Sean D. Educ: U. of S Calif., BA 1959, MA 1960, PhD 1965; U. of Basel, Switzerland, Dr. theol. 1981. Emp: Calif. Luth. Coll., 1962-64 Instr.; St. Olaf Coll., 1964-66 Asst. Prof.; U. of Colo., 1966- Prof., 1967- Dir., Theol. Forum. Spec: New Testament. Pub: *Salvation History in the Prologue of John* (Brill, 1989); "The Logic of the Logos-Hymn: A New View" *NTS* (1983); "The Logos Was God" *EQ* (1981); "The Logos of Heraclitus: Updating the Report" *HTR* (1981); "The Christology of John 8:25" *TZ* (1980); and others. Mem: SNTS 1973-; AAR 1975-; Soc. of Christian Phil. 1988-. Rec: Skiing, Colo. Indian Wars. Addr: (o) U. of Colorado, CB 232, Boulder, CO 80309 303-492-8414; (h) 4220 Corriente Pl., Boulder, CO 80301 303-447-2349.

MILLER, James E., b. Minot, ND, October 29, 1957, s. of Thomas & Jean. Educ: Dakota State Coll., BS 1978; Andrew U., MA 1984. Excv: Rujm Selim, Jordan, 1987 Square Supr.; El Dreijat, Jordan, 1989 Square Supr., Asst. Field Supr. Spec: Hebrew Bible, Apocrypha and Post-biblical Studies. Pub: "The Thirtieth Year of Ezekiel 1:1" *RB* 99 (1992); "The Redaction of Daniel" *JSOT* 52 (1991); "Structure and Meaning of the Animal Discourse in the

Theophany of Job" *ZAW* 103 (1991); "Dreams and Prophetic Visions" *Biblica* 71 (1990); "The Vision of Eliphaz as Foreshadowing in the Book of Job" *Proc. of the East. Great Lakes & MidW Bibl. Soc.* 9 (1989). Mem: SBL 1983-; AAR 1984-; ASOR 1987-; Andrews Soc. for Relig. Stud. 1983-88. Rec: Music, classics, science. Addr: (h) 6421 Bridge #203, Madison, WI 53713 608-221-8328.

MILLER, John W., b. Akron, PA, December 22, 1926, s. of Orie O. & Elta, m. Louise, chil: Christopher; Jeanette; Karen. Educ: Goshen Coll., BA 1948; N.Y. U., MA 1951; Princeton Theol. Sem., BD 1951; U. of Basel, ThD 1955. Emp: Goshen Coll. Bibl. Sem., 1954-57 Asst. Prof.; Kendell Coll., 1957-62 Lect.; Garrett Theol. Sem., 1957-62 Lect.; Ecumenical Inst., 1960-61 Staff; U. of Waterloo, Conrad Grebel Coll., 1969-92 Prof., Relig. Stud. Spec: Hebrew Bible, New Testament. Pub: *Meet the Prophets* (Paulist, 1987); "Depatriarchalizing God in Biblical Interpretation: A Critique" *CBQ* 48/4 (1986); "God as Father in the Bible and the Father Image in Several Contemporary Ancient Near Eastern Myths: A Comparison" *Stud. in Relig.* 14/3 (1985); *Step by Step Through the Parables* (Paulist, 1981); "Jesus' Personality as Reflected in His Parables" in *The New Way of Jesus* (Faith & Life, 1980); "Prophetic Conflict in Second Isaiah, the Servant Songs in the Light of Their Context" in *Wort-Gebot-Glaube, BTAT* 59 (1970); and others. Mem: CSBR 1973-; CSBS 1973-; SBL 1973-; AAR 1973-; CBA 1988-. Rec: Tennis, Scrabble. Addr: (h) 18 Heins Ave., Kitchener, ON N2G 1Z8, Canada 519-578-4276.

MILLER, J. Maxwell, b. Kosciusko, MS, September 20, 1937, s. of James & Nora (Cagle), m. Alice (Julene), chil: David; Charles. Educ: Emory U., PhD 1964. Emp: Interdenominational Theol. Ctr., 1962-63 Instr.; Birmingham-Southern Coll., 1964-67 Asst. Prof., OT Stud.; Emory U., 1967- Prof., 1983-92 Dir., Grad. Div. of Relig. Excv: Arch. Survey of Al-Kerak dist., Jordan, 1978-83 Dir. Spec: Archaeology, Hebrew Bible. Pub: *Archaeological Survey of the el-Kerak Plateau*, Ed. (ASOR, 1991); *A History of Ancient Israel and Judah*, co-auth. (SCM/Westminster, 1986); *Introducing the Holy Land* (Mercer U.P., 1982); *Israelite and Judean History*, co-ed., OT Lib. Ser. (SCM/Westminster, 1977); and others. Awd: Millsaps Coll., Hon. DD 1984. Addr: (o) Emory U., Bishops Hall, Atlanta, GA 30322.

MILLER, Patrick D., b. Atlanta, Georgia, October 24, 1935, s. of Patrick D. & Lila (Bonner), m. Mary Ann (Sudduth), chil: Jonathan; Patrick. Educ: Davidson Coll., AB 1952; Union Theol. Sem., BD 1959; Harvard U., PhD 1963. Emp: *Interpretation,* 1966-80 Book Ed. & Assoc. Ed.; Union Theol. Sem., 1966-84 John F. & Mary Jane McNair Prof. of Bibl. Stud., 1980-84 Dean of the Fac.; *Theol. Today,* 1984- Book Ed. & Co-Ed.; Princeton Theol.

Sem., 1984- Charles T. Haley Prof. of OT Theol.; Harvard Div. Sch., 1985-86 Vis. Prof. Spec: Hebrew Bible, Semitic Languages, Texts and Epigraphy. Pub: *Deuteronomy,* Interpretation Comm. (John Knox, 1990); "The Place of the Decalogue in the Old Testament and Its Law" *Interpretation* 43 (1989); "Der Kanon in der gegenwartigen amerikanischer Diskussion" *Jahrbuch fur Bibl. Theol.* 3 (1988); "Prayer and Sacrifice in Ugarit and Israel" in *Text and Context: Old Testament and Semitic Studies for F.C. Fensham* (JSOT, 1988); "Cosmology and World Order in the Old Testament: The Divine Council as Cosmic-Political Symbol" *Horizons in Bibl. Theol.* 9 (1987); *Interpreting the Psalms* (Fortress, 1986); "Eridu, Dunnu, and Babel: A Study in Comparative Mythology" *HAR* 9 (1985); *Sin and Judgment in the Prophets,* SBL Mon. Ser. (Scholars, 1982); *The Divine Warrior in Early Israel,* HSM 5 (Harvard U.P., 1973); and others. Awd: Advanced Relig. Stud. Found. grant 1966; Assn. of Theol. Sch. Res. Grant 1977-78, 1991-92; NEH, Summer Res. Grant 1980. Mem: SBL 1961-; Colloquium for Bibl. Res. 1963-; CBA; Rev. Stand. Bible Trans. Com. 1974-. Addr: (o) Princeton Theological Seminary, CN 821, Princeton, NJ 08540 609-497-7985; (h) 89 Mercer St., Princeton, NJ 08540 609-683-4098.

MILLER, Stuart S., b. Newark, NJ, June 16, 1953, s. of Irving & Eva, m. Laura, chil: Aviva; Rena; Tova. Educ: N.Y. U., MA 1975, PhD 1980. Emp: N.Y. U., 1979-81 Adj. Asst. Prof.; U. of Notre Dame, 1981-82 Vis. Asst. Prof.; U. of Conn., 1982- Asst. Prof., Hebrew & Judaic Stud. Excv: Joint Sepphoris Project, Staff. Spec: Semitic Languages, Texts and Epigraphy, Apocrypha and Post-biblical Studies. Pub: "Sepphoris, the Well Remembered City" *BA* June (1992); "Zippora'ei, Tibera'ei, and Deroma'ei: Their Origins, Interests and Relationship" in *Proceedings of the Tenth World Congress of Jewish Studies* (Magnes, 1990); "Intercity Relations in Roman Palestine: The Case of Sepphoris and Tiberias" *AJS Rev.* 12 (1987); articles in *The Ency. of Religion* (Macmillan, 1986); *In the Margins of the Yerushalmi,* contb. (Scholars, 1983); *Studies in the History and Traditions of Sepphoris* (Brill, 1984). Mem: AJS 1976-; SBL 1979-; ASOR. Rec: Class. guitar, swimming. Addr: (o) U. of Connecticut, Dept. of Modern & Classical Languages, U-57, Storrs, CT 06268 203-486-3386; (h) 21 Wiltshire Ln., West Hartford, CT 06117 203-233-2725.

MILLIGAN, Charles S., b. Sterling, CO, January 30, 1918, s. of Martin & Jonnie (McCown), m. Nancy (Whitnell), chil: Kathleen; Stacia; Deborah; Stuart. Educ: Iliff Sch. of Theol., ThM 1942, ThD 1952; Harvard U., STM 1948, PhD 1951. Emp: U. of Denver, 1939-42 Instr.; Tufts U., 1951-57 Assoc. Prof.; Iliff Sch. of Theol., 1957-88 Prof., 1988- Prof. Emeritus; *Iliff Rev.,* 1958-88 Ed. Pub: "The Modes of God's Causal Activity" *Iliff Rev.* (1988); *A Functional Philosophy of Religion* (Criterion, 1968); and others. Mem: AAR 1960-. Addr:

2201 S University Blvd., Denver, CO 80210
303-744-1287; (h) 2266 S Columbine, Denver,
CO 80210 303-733-1454.

MILNE, Pamela J., Emp: U. of Windsor, ON,
Relig. Stud. Dept., Assoc. Prof., Hebrew Bible;
Social World of Bibl. Antiq. Ser.,
Sheffield/Almond Press, 1986- Ed. Adv. Bd.;
Stud. in Relig., 1990- Ed. Bd.; Stud. in Women
& Relig. Ser., 1992- Adv. Bd. Spec: Hebrew
Bible. Pub: "The Narrative Role of Judith:
Warrior Heroine or Seductive Helper?" *Semeia*
62 (1993); "The Patriarchal Stamp of Scripture:
The Implications of Structuralist Analyses for
Feminist Hermeneutics and Afterword" in
Genesis vol. 1, Feminist Companion to the Bible
Ser. (Sheffield, 1993); "Feminist Interpretations
of the Bible: Then and Now" *BR* 8/5 (1992);
"Naming the Unnameable? A Response to
Russell McCutcheon's Discussion of Inclusive
Language" *Method & Theory in the Study of
Relig.* 3/1 (1991); *Vladimir Propp and the Study
of Structure in Hebrew Biblical Narrative,* Bible
& Lit. Ser. 13 (Almond/Sheffield, 1988); "Eve
and Adam—Is a Feminist Reading Possible?"
BR 4/3 (1988); and others. Mem: SBL; Canadian
Women's Stud. Assn. Addr: (o) U. of Windsor,
Religious Studies Dept., 401 Sunset Ave.,
Windsor, ON N9B 3P4, Canada 519-253-4232.

MINEAR, Paul S., b. Mt. Pleasant, IA,
February 17, 1906, s. of George & Nellie
(Sevier), m. Gladys (Hoffman), chil: Larry;
Richard; Anita. Educ: Iowa Wesleyan Coll., BA
1927; Garrett Bibl. Inst., BD 1930; NW U., MA
1930; Yale U., PhD 1932. Emp: Hawaii Sch. of
Relig., 1933-34; Garrett Bibl. Inst., 1934-44
Prof.; Andover Newton Theol. Sch., 1944-56
Norris Prof. of NT; Yale U. Div. Sch., 1956-71
Winkley Prof. of Bibl. Theol. Spec: New
Testament. Pub: "The Functions of John 21"
JBL 102 (1983); "Holy People, Holy Land,
Holy City" *Interpretation* 37 (1983); *New
Testament Apocalyptic* (Abingdon, 1981); "The
Beloved Disciple in the Fourth Gospel" *NT* 19
(1977); "Ontology and Ecclesiology in the
Apocalypse" *NTS* 12 (1966); *Images of the
Church in the New Testament* (Westminster,
1960); "Revelation and Knowledge of the
Church" *Harvard Div. Sch. Bull.* 20 (1954); and
others. Mem: SBL; SNTS; Amer. Theol. Soc.
Rec: Music, tennis, hiking. Addr: (h) 64 Farm
View Dr., Guilford, CT 06437 203-453-5380.

MINETTE DE TILLESSE, Caetano, b.
Neder-Ockerzeel, Belgium, July 6, 1925, s. of
Georges & Augusta (de Heusch de la Zangrye).
Educ: Pont. U. Gregoriana, Lic. Theol.; Pont.
Bibl. Inst., Lic. Bible 1956; Fortaleza, Lic. Phil.
1978. Emp: Revista Biblica Brasileira, 1984-
Dir. Spec: Hebrew Bible, New Testament. Pub:
Le Secret messianique en saint Marc, Lectio
Divina 47 (Cerf, 1968); "Sections-Tu et
Sections-Vous dans le Deut" *VT* (1962).
Addr: (o) Caixa Postal 1577, BR-60.001,
Fortaleza, CE, Brazil.

MINKOFF, Harvey, b. New York, NY, April
9, 1944, s. of Michael & Mildred (Falk), m.
Evelyn Melamed. Educ: City Coll. of New York,
BA, Linguistics, English 1965; City U. of New
York Grad. Ctr., PhD, Linguistics 1970. Emp:
Iona Coll., New Rochelle, N.Y., 1967-70 Asst.
Prof., Linguistics; Hunter Coll., New York, 1971-
Prof., Linguistics. Spec: Hebrew Bible, Semitic
Languages, Texts and Epigraphy. Pub: "The
Aleppo Codex: Ancient Bible from the Ashes" *BR*
7/4 (1991); "Was the First Feminist Bible in
Yiddish?" co-auth. *Moment* 16/3 (1991); "The
Man Who Wasn't There: Textual Mysteries
Created by Hebrew Spelling" *BR* 6/6 (1990);
"Coarse Language in the Bible: It's Culture
Shocking" 5/2 *BR* (1989); "Problems of
Translations: Concern for the Text Versus
Concern for the Reader" *BR* 4/4 (1988); and oth-
ers. Mem: Linguistic Soc. of Amer. 1970-;
Linguistic Assn. of Canada & U.S. 1987-. Rec:
Drawing, swimming, martial arts. Addr: (o)
Hunter College, Dept. of English, 695 Park Ave.,
New York, NY 10021 212-772-5070.

MIRECKI, Paul A., b. Chicago, IL, February 5,
1950. Educ: Gordon-Conwell Sem., MDiv 1980;
Harvard Div. Sch., ThD 1986. Emp: U. of Mich.,
1986-88 Vis. Asst. Prof.; Albion Coll., 1988-89
Vis. Asst. Prof.; U. of Kans., 1989- Assoc. Prof.
Spec: New Testament, Egyptology, Apocrypha
and Post-biblical Studies. Pub: "The Coptic
Wizard's Hoard" in *Coptic Texts of Ritual Power*
(HarperCollins, 1993); "A Hymn to the 'Light-
Nous' in the Coptic Manichaean Psalm-Book,"
"The 'Nous' in the Greek and Coptic Magical
Papyri" in *Proceedings of the International
Conference of the Manichaean Nous,* Manichaean
Stud. 2 (1992); "The Antithetic Saying in Mark
16:16" in *The Future of Early Christianity*
(Fortress, 1991); "Coptic Manichaean Psalm 278
and Gospel of Thomas 37" in *Manichaeica
Selecta* (1991); and others. Awd: Deutscher
Akademischer Austaudienst, grant 1987; Amer.
Coun. of Learned Soc., grant 1989; U. of Kans.
Res. Fund, grant 1990-93; NEH Summer
Stipend, 1993-94. Mem: AAR; SBL; CBA 1984-;
Amer. Soc. of Papyrologists 1988-; IACS 1991-.
Rec: Reading, film, bicycling, intl. travel. Addr:
(o) U. of Kansas, Dept. of Religion, Smith Hall,
Lawrence, KS 66047 913-864-4663.

MITCHELL, Alan C., b. Brooklyn, NY,
November 16, 1948, s. of Albert. Educ: Fordham
U., AB (summa cum laude) 1972; Weston Sch. of
Theol., MDiv 1979; Yale U., MA 1981, MPhil
1983, PhD 1986. Emp: Wheeling Coll., 1973-76
Instr.; Yale U., 1980-82 Teaching Fellow; Fairfield
U., 1983 Adj. Instr.; Georgetown U., 1984- Instr.,
1992 Assoc. Prof., Theol. Spec: New Testament.
Pub: "The Use of *Prepein* and Rhetorical Propriety
in Hebrews 2:10" *CBQ* 54 (1992); "The Social
Function of Friendship in Acts 2:44-47 and 4:32-
37" *JBL* 111 (1992); "The Use of Zacchaeus's
Defense" *Biblica* 72 (1991); "Zacchaeus Revisited:
Luke 19,8 As a Defense" *Biblica* 71 (1990). Mem:
SBL 1972-; CBA 1972-. Rec: Jogging, photogra-
phy. Addr: (o) Georgetown U., Dept. of Theology,

Washington, DC 20057-0998 202-687-5756; (h) Jesuit Community, Georgetown U., Washington, DC 20057 202-687-4007.

MITCHELL, Christopher W., b. Palo Alto, CA, November 4, 1957, s. of John & Carol, m. Carol (Prentice), chil: David; Noah. Educ: U. of Wis.-Madison, BS 1978, MA 1980, PhD 1983; Concordia Sem., MDiv 1987. Spec: Hebrew Bible, Semitic Languages, Texts and Epigraphy. Pub: "Job and the Theology of the Cross" *Concordia Jour.* 15/2 (1989); *The Meaning of BRK 'To Bless' in the Old Testament* (Scholars, 1987); "The Use of Lexicons and Word Studies in Exegesis" *Concordia Jour.* 11/4 (1985). Mem: SBL; NAPH. Rec: Distance running, hiking, fishing. Addr: (o) Concordia Publishing House, 3558 S Jefferson Ave., St. Louis, MO 63118; (h) 8921 Westhaven Ct., St. Louis, MO 63126.

MOBERLY, Walter R. W. L., b. Caterham, Surrey, England, March 26, 1952, s. of Robert & Eliza, m. Meredith. Educ: Cambridge U., Trinity Coll., PhD, OT 1981. Emp: Knowle Parish Ch., 1981-85 Asst. Curate; U. of Durham, 1985- Lect., Theol. Spec: Hebrew Bible. Pub: *From Eden to Golgotha: Essays in Biblical Theology* (Scholars, 1992); *Genesis 12-50* (JSOT, 1992); *The Old Testament of the Old Testament* (Fortress, 1992); "Yahweh is One: The Translation of the Shema," "Abraham's Righteousness (Genesis 15:6)" in VTSup 41 (1990); "The Earliest Commentary on the Akedah" *VT* 38 (1988); "Did the Serpent Get It Right?" *JTS* 39 (1988); *At the Mountain of God* (JSOT, 1983); and others. Mem: Tyndale Fellow. 1977-; SOTS 1985-; Brit. AJS 1987-. Rec: Chess, swimming, reading, walking, travel. Addr: (o) Abbey House, Palace Green, Durham DHI 3RS, England 091-374-2067; (h) 8 Princes St., Durham DHI 4RP, England 091-386-4255.

MODA, Aldo, b. Giaveno, Italy, February 27, 1944, s. of Mario & Barone, m. Loretta (Alberti), chil: Luca; Emanuele. Educ: Inst. Cath., Paris, Dip. Ecumenical Stud. 1972; Neuchatel U., ThD 1977; U. Cattolica, D. Letters 1981. Emp: Turin, 1975- Prof., Relig. Spec: New Testament. Pub: *Paolo Prigioniero* (Sardini, 1992); *Per una cronologia degli ultimi anni di Paolo* (Sardini, 1989); *Il Cristianesimo nel primo secolo* (Ecumenica, 1986); "La date de la Cène" *Nicolaus* 3 (1975); "Il problema dell'autorità politica secondo Rom. 13,1ss" *Nicolaus* 1 (1973); "La Resurezione di Cristo" *Parole di Vita* 14 (1969). Mem: SNTS 1973-. Addr: (h) Via Bonzo #4, 10148 Torino, Italy 2264363.

MOESSNER, David P., b. Lincoln, NE, January 3, 1949, s. of Samuel & Helen, m. Jeanne (Stevenson). Educ: Princeton U., AB (magna cum laude) 1971; Princeton Theol. Sem., MDiv 1975; U. of Oxford, BA 1976, MA 1989; U. of Basel, ThD 1983. Emp: La. State U., 1982-83 Instr.; Yale U. Div. Sch., 1983-84 Asst. Prof.; Columbia Theol. Sem., 1984- Assoc. Prof.; Emory U., 1985-

Adj. Prof.; U. of Geneva, 1990 Vis. Lect., Theol. Spec: Hebrew Bible, New Testament. Pub: *Lord of the Banquet: The Literary and Theological Significance of the Lukan Travel Narrative* (Fortress, 1989); "Paul in Acts: Preacher of Eschatological Repentance to Israel" *NTS* 34 (1988); "The 'Leaven of the Pharisees' and 'This Generation': Israel's Rejection of Jesus According to Luke" *JSNT* 34 (1988); "'The Christ Must Suffer': New Light on the Jesus" *NT* (1986); "Luke 9:1-50: Luke's Preview of the Journey of the Prophet Like Moses of Deuteronomy" *JBL* 102 (1983); and others. Mem: SBL 1978-; AAR 1978-. Rec: Symphony, ballet. Addr: (o) Columbia Theological Seminary, Decatur, GA 30031 404-378-8821; (h) 232 Northern Ave., Decatur, GA 30030 404-377-1582.

MOIR, Ian A., b. Motherwell, Scotland, June 27, 1914, s. of Alexander & Mary (Strachan), m. Kirsteen, chil: Jean; Elspeth; Alastair. Educ: Aberdeen U., MA 1936, BD 1939; Cambridge U., PhD 1943. Emp: Min. 1942-61; U. of Edinburgh, 1961-81 Sr. Lect. Spec: New Testament, Apocrypha and Post-biblical Studies. Pub: *Codex Climaci Rescriptus Graecus* (Cambridge U.P., 1956); "Tischendorf and the Codex Sinaiticus" *JTS* (1957); "Two Septuagint Palimpsest Fragments" *NTS* (1976); and others. Mem: SNTS 1957-. Rec: Railway modeling, golf, computing. Addr: (h) 26/01 Croft-an-Righ, Edinburgh EH8 8ED, Scotland.

MOLONEY, Francis J., b. Melbourne, Australia, March 23, 1940, s. of Dennis & Mary (O'Connor). Educ: Salesian Pont. U., Rome, STL 1970; Pont. Bibl. Inst., Rome, SSL 1972; Oxford U., DPhil 1975. Emp: Salesian Pont. U., 1975-76 Lect., NT Stud.; Cath. Theol. Coll., Australia, 1977-82 Lect., NT Stud., 1983- Head, Bibl. Stud.; Gregorian U., Pont., Yarra Theol. Union, Vis. Lect. Spec: New Testament. Pub: "A Sacramental Reading of John 13:1-38" *CBQ* 53 (1991); *A Body Broken for a Broken People: Eucharist in the New Testament* (Collins, 1990); "Reading John 2:13-22: The Purification of the Temple" *RB* 97 (1990); "Johannine Theology" in *New Jerome Biblical Comm.* (Prentice-Hall, 1989); "The Reinterpretation of Psalm VIII and the Son of Man Debate" *NTS* 27 (1981-82); "Matthew 19,3-12 and Celibacy: A Redactional and Form Critical Study" *JSNT* 2 (1979); *The Johannine Son of Man* (Libreria Ateneo Salesiano, 1978); and others. Mem: SBL 1976-; CBA 1976-, Pres. 1980; Fellow. for Bibl. Stud., Australian. Pres. 1985. Rec: Jogging, tennis, cricket, art. Addr: (o) Catholic Theological College, PO Box 302, Clayton, Victoria 3168, Australia 03-543-1858; (h) Salesian College, Bosco St., Chadstone, Victoria 3148, Australia 03-807-2473.

MONTEFIORE, Hugh W., b. London, May 12, 1920, s. of Charles and Munel, m. Elisabeth (Paton), chil: Teresa; Janet; Catherine. Emp: Westcott House, 1951-54 Chaplain & Vice Prin.; Caius Coll., 1954-63 Fellow, Dean; Cambridge U., 1956-59 Asst. Lect., 1959-63 Lect., NT; U.

Ch. of Great St. Mary's, 1963-70 Vicar; Birmingham, 1978-87 Bishop. Spec: New Testament. Pub: *Comm. on Epistle to the Hebrews* (Black, 1964); "Jesus and the Temple Tax" *NT* 11/1 (1964); "Thou Shalt Love Thy Neighbor as Thyself" *NT* 2/3 (1962); "Revolt in the Desert?" *NT* 8/2 (1962); *Josephus and the NT* (Monbray, 1962); "God as Father in the Synoptic Gospels" *NT* 3/1 (1956). Awd: St. Andrews U., DD 1977; Birmingham U., DD 1985; St. John's Coll., Oxford, Fellow. 1983. Mem: SNTS. Rec: Reading, walking. Addr: (h) White Lodea, 23 Bellevue Rd., Wandsworth Common, London SW17 7EB, England 081-672-6697.

MOO, Douglas J., b. LaPorte, IN, March 15, 1950, s. of John & Alice (Bartz), m. Jenny Lynn (Larson), chil: Jonathan; David; Lukas; Rebecca; Christy. Educ: DePauw U., BA 1972; Trinity Evang. Div. Sch., MDiv (magna cum laude) 1975; U. of St. Andrews, Scotland, PhD 1980. Emp: Trinity Evang. Div. Sch., 1977- Prof.; *Trinity Jour.*, 1980-87 Book Rev. Ed., 1987- Ed. Spec: New Testament. Pub: *Introduction to the New Testament*, co-auth. (Zondervan,1991); *Romans 1-8*, Wycliffe Exegetical Comm. (Moody, 1991); "Paul and the Law in the Last Ten Years" *Scottish Jour. of Theol.* 40 (1987); "Israel and Paul in Romans 7:7-12" *NTS* 32 (1986); "The Problem of *Sensus Plenior*" in *Hermeneutics, Authority, Canon* (Zondervan, 1986); *The Epistle of James*, Tyndale NT Comm. (IVP/Eerdmans, 1985); "Jesus and the Authority of the Mosaic Law" *JSNT* 20 (1984); *The Rapture: Pre-, Mid-, or Post-Tribulational?*, co-auth. (Zondervan, 1984); "'Law,''Works of the Law' and Legalism in Paul" *Westminster Theol. Jour.* 45 (1983); and others. Mem: CSBR 1984-; ETS 1977-; IBR 1982-; SBL 1988-. Rec: Basketball, bicycling, meteorology. Addr: (o) Trinity Evangelical Divinity School, 2065 Half Day Rd., Deerfield, IL 60015 708-945-8800; (h) 597 Pine Grove Ave., Gurnee, IL 60031 708-244-6480.

MOORE, Carey A., b. Baltimore, MD, March 5, 1930, s. of Carey & Grace (Bell), m. Patricia (Emlet), chil: Kathleen; Stephen; David; Bruce. Educ: Gettysburg Coll., BA 1952; Luth. Theol. Sem., BD 1956; Johns Hopkins U., PhD 1965. Emp: Gettysburg Coll., 1959- Prof., Dept. Relig., 1991- Marshal; Luth. Theol. Sem., 1965-67, 1991 Vis. Prof. Excv: Gezer, 1966-68, 1973 Area Supr.; Tel Dan, 1974 Area Supr. Spec: Archaeology, Hebrew Bible, Apocrypha and Post-biblical Studies. Pub: "Susanna: A Case of Sexual Harassment in Ancient Babylon" *BR* (1992); "Scholarly Issues in the Book of Tobit Before Qumran and After: An Assessment" *JSP* 5 (1989); "You Too Can Read Hieroglyphics" *BAR* (1985); "Judith" *AB* (Doubleday, 1985); *Studies in the Book of Esther* (Ktav, 1982); "Daniel, Esther and Jeremiah: The Additions" in *AB* (1977); "Archaeology and the Book of Esther" *BA* 38 (1975); "Toward the Dating of the Book of Baruch" *CBQ* 36 (1974); "Esther" *AB* (Doubleday, 1971); and others. Awd: Hebrew Union Coll., Post-Doctoral Arch. Fellow. Mem:

SBL; ASOR; IOSCS. Rec: Photography. Addr: (o) Gettysburg College, Box 408, Gettysburg, PA 17325 717-337-6778; (h) 106 E Middle St., Gettysburg, PA 17325 717-334-1214.

MOORE, Rick D., b. Sikeston, MO, October 8, 1953, s. of Ernest B. & Doris N., m. Regina H., chil: Emily Jo; Hannah Elizabeth. Educ: Lee Coll., BA 1976; Vanderbilt U., MA 1982, PhD, OT Stud. 1988. Emp: *Lee Coll. Clarion* 1973, 1976 Ed.; Vanderbilt Div. Lib., 1980-82 OT Bibliographer; Church of God Sch. of Theol., 1982- Assoc. Prof., OT Stud.; *Jour. of Pentecostal Theol.*, 1992- Ed. Spec: Hebrew Bible. Pub: *God Saves: Lessons from the Elisha Stories*, JSOTSup 95 (JSOT, 1990); "The Integrity of Job" *CBQ* 45 (1983). Mem: SBL 1979-; Soc. for Pentecostal Stud. 1980-; ETS 1982-; CBA 1982-. Addr: (o) Church of God School of Theology, 900 Walker St. NE, PO Box 3330, Cleveland, TN 37311 615-478-7039; (h) 4876 Meadow Avenue NW, Cleveland, TN 37312 615-478-2275.

MOORE, Robert R., b. Kittanning, PA, April 6, 1937, s. of Howard & Tirza (Rood), m. D. Lucille, chil: Robert R.; Tania L. Educ: Emory & Henry Coll., BA 1969; Asbury Theol. Sem., MDiv 1972; Emory U., PhD 1982. Emp: Asbury Coll., 1975- Prof., Relig. Spec: New Testament. Pub: "The Gospel of Luke" in *The Wesley Bible* (Nelson, 1990). Mem: SBL; ETS; Wesleyan Theol. Soc. Rec: Reading, sports. Addr: (o) Asbury Coll., Wilmore, KY 40390 606-858-3511; (h) 223 Kimberly Dr., Nicholasville, KY 40356 606-885-6505.

MOORE, Stephen D., b. Limerick, Ireland, April 3, 1954, s. of Brian Moore & Frieda (O'Dea), m. Jane (Hurwitz), chil: Frieda Olivia. Educ: U. Coll., Galway, Ireland, BA 1975; U. of Dublin, BA, Bibl. Stud. 1982, PhD, NT 1986. Emp: Trinity Coll., Dublin, 1982-86 Adj. Lect., Bibl. Stud., 1989-91 Lect., NT; Wichita State U., 1991- Asst. Prof., Relig.; *JSNT*, 1991- Ed. Bd. Spec: New Testament. Pub: *Mark and Method: New Approaches in Biblical Studies*, co-ed. (Fortress, 1992); *Mark and Luke in Poststructuralist Perspectives: Jesus Begins to Write* (Yale U.P., 1992); *Poststructuralism as Exegesis*, co-ed. (Scholars, 1991); "The Gospel of the Look" *Semeia* 54 (1991); *Literary Criticism and the Gospels: The Theoretical Challenge* (Yale U.P., 1989); "Rifts in (a Reading of) the Fourth Gospel, or: Does Johannine Irony Still Collapse in a Reading That Draws Attention to Itself?" *Neotestamentica* 23/1 (1989); "The 'Post-' Age Stamp: Does It Stick? Biblical Studies and the Postmodernism Debate" *JAAR* 57/3 (1989); "Stories of Reading: Doing Gospel Criticism as/with a 'Reader'" *BTB* 19/3 (1989); "Negative Hermeneutics, Insubstantial Texts: Stanley Fish and the Biblical Interpreter" *JAAR* 54/4 (1986); and others. Awd: Yale U., Henry R. Luce Postdoc. Fellow 1987-89. Mem: SBL; AAR; CBA; Modern Lang. Assn.

Addr: (o) Wichita State U., Dept. of Religion, Wichita, KS 67208 316-689-3108; (h) 430 N Clifton St., Wichita, KS 67208 316-685-4002.

MOOREY, P. R. S., b. Bush Hill Park, England, May 30, 1937, s. of Stuart & Freda (Harris). Educ: Corpus Christi Coll., Oxford, BA 1961, MA 1963, DPhil 1967. Emp: Ashmolean Mus., Oxford, 1961- Keeper of Antiq.; *Levant,* 1968-86 Ed.; U. of Pa., 1973 Kevorkian Lect.; British Sch. of Arch., Jerusalem, 1990- Pres. Excv: Jerusalem, 1963 Site Supr.; Abu Salabiqh, Iraq, 1975, 1977, 1981 Site Supr., Cataloguer. Spec: Archaeology, Mesopotamian Studies. Pub: *A Century of Biblical Archaeology* (1991); *Excavations in Palestine* (1981); *Kish Excavations, 1923-33* (Oxford, 1978); "What Do We Know About the People Buried in the Royal Cemetery [at Ur]" *Expedition* (1977); "Iranian Troops at Deve Huyuk in Syria in the Fifth Century B.C." *Levant* 7 (1975); *Biblical Lands* (London, 1975); and others. Awd: Percia Schimmel Prize for Disting. Contb. to Arch. in Eretz Israel and the Lands of the Bible 1989. Mem: British Inst. of Persian Stud. Rec: Walking, travel. Addr: (o) Ashmolean Museum, Oxford, OX1 2PH, England 0865-278019-20.

MORAG, Shelomo, b. Petah-Tiqvah, Israel, July 17, 1926, s. of Moshe Arie & Sarah Mirkin, m. Shoshana (Disenhouse), chil: Rinat Weigler; Ariela Mann. Educ: The Hebrew U., MA 1949, PhD 1955; Cambridge U., MA 1975, DLitt 1991. Emp: Hebrew U., 1950- Asst. Prof., 1975- Prof., 1982- Bialik Prof. of Hebrew; Tel-Aviv U., 1959-77 Prof., Hebrew & Semitic Lang.; Ben-Zvi Inst., 1971-74 Chmn.; *Eda Velashon,* vol. 1-16, 1977-93 Ed.; U. of Calif., Berkeley, Taubman Vis. Prof. 1985; U. of Helsinki, 1987 Ann. Guest Prof. Spec: Hebrew Bible, Semitic Languages, Texts and Epigraphy. Pub: "On Semantic and Lexical Features in the Language of Hosea" *Tarbiz* 53 (1984); "On the Historical Validity of the Vocalization of the Hebrew Bible" *JAOS* 94 (1974); *The Book of Daniel: A Babylonian-Yemenite Manuscript.* (Kiryath-Sepher, 1973); "Biblical Aramaic in Geonic Babylonia: The Various Schools" in *Studies in Egyptology and Linguistics in Honour of H.J. Polotsky* (1964); *The Hebrew Language Tradition of the Yemenite Jews* (Hebrew Lang. Acad., 1963); *The Vocalization Systems of Arabic, Hebrew and Aramaic* (Mouton, 1962); "The Vocalization of Codex Reuchlinianus: Is the 'Pre-Masoretic' Bible Pre-Masoretic?" *JJS* 4 (1959); "Mesha: A Study of Certain Features of Old Hebrew Dialects" in *Eretz-Israel* 5 (1958); and others. Awd: Leib Jaffe Prize for Jewish Stud. 1964; Israel Prize for Scholarly Achievements in the Field of Jewish Stud. 1966; St. John's Coll., Cambridge, Overseas Fellow 1975-76; Annenberg Res. Inst., Fellow 1989; Bialik Prize for Excellence in Jewish Stud. 1989. Mem: AOS; SBL; ISBR; IES; AAJR. Rec: Music. Addr: (o) The Hebrew U., Dept. of Hebrew, Mount Scopus, Jerusalem 91905, Israel 02-883551; (h) Nayot 8, Jerusalem 93704, Israel 02-792619.

MORGAN, Donn F., b. Syracuse, NY, September 12, 1943, s. of Robert Earle & Eloise Farley, m. Alda Marsh, chil: Curtis Matthew; Lauren Michelle. Educ: Oberlin Coll., AB 1965; Yale Div. Sch., BD 1968; Claremont Grad. Sch., MA 1972, PhD 1974. Emp: Ch. Div. Sch., 1972- Prof. of OT, 1985- Dean of Acad. Affairs. Spec: Hebrew Bible. Pub: *Between Text and Community—The "Writings" in Canonical Context* (Augsburg/Fortress, 1990); *Wisdom in Old Testament Traditions* (John Knox, 1980); and others. Mem: SBL; SOTS. Rec: Cycling. Addr: (o) Church Divinity of the Pacific, 2451 Ridge Rd., Berkeley, CA 94709 510-204-0727; (h) 2964 Linden Ave., Berkeley, CA 94905 510-848-8977.

MORGAN, Robert C., b. Oswestry, England, October 24, 1940, s. of Oscar & Kathleen (Chowen), m. Prue (Sykes), chil: Teresa; Catharine; Anna. Educ: St. Catharine's Coll., Cambridge, BA 1963; St. Chad's Coll., Durham, DipTh 1965. Emp: U. of Lancaster, 1967-76 Sr. Lect.; Linacre Coll., Oxford, 1976- Lect., Fellow. Spec: New Testament. Pub: *Biblical Interpretation,* co-auth. (Oxford U.P., 1986); "A Straussian Question to New Testament Theology" *NTS* 23 (1977); *The Nature of New Testament Theology* (SCM, 1973); and others. Mem: SNTS 1968-; SBL 1982-. Rec: Running, fishing. Addr: (o) Linacre College, Oxford, England; (h) Lower Farm, Sandford-on-Thames, Oxford, OX4 4YR, England 0865-748848.

MORIMURA, Nobuko, b. Japan, September 14, 1929, d. of Shigeki & Yuko. Educ: U. of the Sacred Heart, Tokyo, BA 1951; Manhattanville Coll., N.Y., MA 1969. Emp: Acad. of the Sacred Heart, 1963-68 Prin.; U. of the Sacred Heart, 1977-85 Assoc. Prof., 1985- Prof.; Inst. for Res. of Christian Culture, 1978-79, 1983-88 Dir.; *Japan Christian Rev.,* 1992- Assoc. Ed. Spec: Hebrew Bible. Pub: "Tamar and Judah (Gen. 38): A Feminist's Interpretation" *Seishin Stud.* 80 (1993); "Pilgrimage in Ancient Israel—the Fate of the Communitas" in *Pilgrimage & Culture* (1987); "Inner Structure of Book of Amos" *Relig. & Civ.* 12 (1987); Biblical Archaeology, trans., vol. 1-2 (1984-1985); "Old Testament Women" *Bible Mus.* (1984); "A Consideration on P Redaction" *Orient* 22 (1980); and others. Mem: Japan Assn. for Relig. Stud. 1970-; Soc. for Near East. Stud. in Japan 1975-; SOTS in Japan 1978-; SBL 1986-; Soc. of Cath. Theol. in Japan 1989-. Rec: Music, hiking. Addr: (o) U. of the Sacred Heart, Hiroo 4-3-1 Shibuyaku, Tokyo 150, Japan 03-3407-5811.

MORRICE, William G., b. Leitholm, Scotland, May 30, 1929, s. of William & Mary (Gorman), m. Katherine (Morrison). Educ: Aberdeen U., MA 1951, BD 1954, PhD 1957; Union Theol. Sem., STM (summa cum laude) 1955. Emp: Min., 1957-70; Brit. & Foreign Bible Soc., London, 1970-72 Adv.; New Coll., London, 1972-75 Lect.; St. John's Coll., Durham, 1975-90 Tutor, Lbrn. Spec: New Testament. Pub: *Joy in the New*

Testament (Paternoster, 1984; Eerdmans, 1985); and others. Mem: SNTS 1971-. Rec: Reading, writing, photography. Addr: (h) 69 Hallgarth St., Durham DH1 3AY, England 091-3869699.

MORRIS, Leon L., b. Lithgow, NSW, Australia, March 15, 1914, s. of George Coleman & Ivy (Lamb), m. Mildred. Educ: U. of Sydney, BSc 1934; Australian Coll. of Theol., ThL 1937; U. of London, BD 1943, MTh 1946; U. of Cambridge, PhD 1952; U. of Melbourne, MSc 1966. Emp: Minnida Mission, Australia, 1940-45 Priest; Ridley Coll., Melbourne, 1946-59 Vice Prin., 1964-79 Prin.; Tyndale House, England, 1961-63 Warden. Spec: New Testament. Pub: *An Introduction to the New Testament*, co-auth. (Zondervan, 1992); *The Epistle to the Romans* (Eerdmans, 1988); *New Testament Theology* (Zondervan, 1986); *The Apostolic Preaching of the Cross* (Tyndale, 1965); "The Biblical Use of the Term 'Blood'" *JTS* (1952); "The Wrath of God" *ExpTim* Feb. (1952); and others. Awd: Australian Coll. of Theol., ThD 1980. Mem: Fellow. for Bibl. Stud. 1951-; SNTS 1952-. Rec: Gardening, L.A. Dodgers. Addr: (h) 17 Queens Ave., Doncaster, Victoria 3108, Australia 03-848-3318.

MOSCA, Paul G., b. Brooklyn, NY, June 26, 1946, s. of William F. & Dorothy B., m. Eileen (O'Reilly), chil: Matthew W.; Peter D.; John P. Educ: Fordham Coll., BA 1966; Harvard U., MA 1972, PhD, Near East. Lang. 1975. Emp: U. of B.C., 1974- Assoc. Prof. & Head, Relig. Stud.; *CBQ*, 1990- Assoc. Ed. Excv: ASOR Carthage Excav., Punic Team, 1974-79 Punic Epigraphist. Spec: Hebrew Bible, Semitic Languages, Texts and Epigraphy. Pub: "A Phoenician Inscription from Cebel Ires Dagi in Rough Cilicia," co-auth. *Epigraphica Anatolica* 9 (1987); "Ugarit and Daniel 7: A Missing Link" *Biblica* 67 (1986); "Once Again the Heavenly Witness of Ps 89:38" *JBL* 105 (1986); "Psalm 26: Poetical Structure and the Form-Critical Task" *CBQ* 47 (1985); "Once Again CIS I 91" *Revisita di Studi Fenici* 10 (1982); and others. Awd: Fulbright Fellow, Rome 1972-73. Mem: CBA; IES; SBL. Rec: Baseball, hiking, camping. Addr: (o) U. of British Columbia, Religious Studies, E270-1866 Main Mall, Vancouver, BC V6T 1Z1, Canada 604-822-6322; (h) 1150 Rose St., Vancouver, BC V5L 4K8, Canada 604-254-2644.

MOST, William G., b. Dubuque, IA, August 13, 1914, s. of George H. & Mary Fay. Educ: Columbia Coll., AB 1936; Catholic U. of Amer., MA, Relig. Educ. 1940, PhD 1946. Emp: Loras Coll., 1940-89 Prof., Classics; Notre Dame Inst., 1989- Prof., Scripture. Spec: New Testament, Apocrypha and Post-biblical Studies. Pub: "New Light on Isaiah 7:14" *Faith & Reason* (1992); *The Consciousness of Christ* (Christendom, 1990); *Free From All Error* (Prow, 1985, 1990); "Did St. Luke Imitate the Septuagint" *JSNT* (1982); "Apocrypha" in *Corpus Encyclopedia Dict. of Religion* (1979); *Covenant and*

Redemption (Alba, 1977); *New Answers to Old Questions* (St. Paul, 1971); "A Biblical Theology of Redemption in a Covenant Framework" *CBQ* (1967); articles in *New Catholic Ency.*; and others. Mem: CBA 1946-; CTSA 1950-; Assn. of Anc. Hist. 1985-; NAPS 1985-93. Rec: Computers, swimming, diving. Addr: (o) Notre Dame Institute, 4319 Sano St., Alexandria, VA 22312-1553 703-658-4304; (h) 6222 Franconia Rd., Alexandria, VA 22310.

MOTT, Stephen Charles, b. Lakewood, OH, April 9, 1940, s. of Royden & Katherine (Hyde), m. Sandra (Goossen), chil: Adam; Rachel; Sarah. Educ: Wheaton Coll., BA 1962, BD 1965; Harvard U., PHD 1972. Emp: Gordon-Conwell Theol. Sem., 1970- Prof.; *Christian Social Action*, 1990- Contb. Ed. Spec: New Testament. Pub: *Biblical Ethics and Social Change* (Oxford U. P., 1982); "Greek Ethics and Christian Conversion" *NT* 20 (1978); and others. Mem: SBL, 1968-. Rec: Sports, hiking, camping. Addr: (o) Gordon-Conwell Theol. Sem., 130 Essex St., Box 219, S Hamilton, MA 01982 508-468-7111; (h) 11 Miller Rd., Beverly, MA 01915-1315 508-927-5683.

MOULE, Charles F. D., b. Hangchow, China, December 3, 1908, s. of Henry William & Laura Clements (Pope). Educ: U. of Cambridge, BA 1931, MA 1934; Ridley Hall, Cambridge, Ord. 1933. Emp: Ridley Hall, 1936-44 Vice Prin.; Clare Coll., Cambridge, 1944-51 Dean, 1944- Fellow; U. of Cambridge, 1944-51 Lect., 1951-76 Lady Margaret's Prof.; Leicester Cathedral, 1955-76 Canon Theologian. Spec: New Testament. Pub: *Essays in New Testament Interpretation* (Cambridge U.P., 1982); *The Origin of Christology* (Cambridge U.P., 1977); *The Birth of the New Testament* (A & C Black, 1962, 1981); *An Idiom Book of New Testament Greek* (Cambridge U.P., 1953, 1959); and others. Awd: St. Andrew's U., Scotland, DD 1958; British Acad., Fellow 1966-, Burkitt Medal 1970; Commander of the Order of the British Empire, 1985; U. of Cambridge, DD 1988. Mem: SNTS 1945-, Pres. 1967-68; SBL hon. mem. Addr: (h) 1, King's Houses, Pevensey, East Sussex, BN24 5JR, England.

MOWERY, Robert L., b. Rochester, PA, March 22, 1934, s. of Herman V. & M. Margaret (Long), m. Janet (Bartholomew), chil: Philip L.; Patricia Anne. Educ: Purdue U., BSME 1956; Garrett-Evang. Theol. Sem., MDiv 1960; NW U., MA, Relig. 1961, PhD, Early Christian Life & Lit. 1967; U. of Ill., MS 1968. Emp: Meth. Ch., 1963-68 Pastor; Ill. Wesleyan U., 1968- Librn. & Prof. Spec: New Testament. Pub: *New Views on Luke and Acts*, contb. (Liturgical, 1990); "Subtle Differences: The Matthean 'Son of God' References" *NT* (1990); "The Articular Prepositional Attributes in the Pauline Corpus" *Biblica* (1990); "Pharisees and Scribes, Galilee and Jerusalem" *ZNW* (1989); "God, Lord and Father: The Theology of the Gospel of Matthew" *Bibl. Res.* (1988); and others. Mem: SBL; CSBR; CBA.

Addr: (o) Illinois Wesleyan U., PO Box 2899, Bloomington, IL 61702 309-556-3109; (h) 1507 N Fell Ave., Bloomington, IL 61701 309-827-6506.

MOXNES, Halvor, b. Stokke, Norway, September 13, 1944, s. of Halvor & Jorunn. Educ: U. of Oslo, Norway, DTh 1978. Emp: U. of Oslo, 1978- Prof., NT. Spec: New Testament. Pub: "Patron-Client Relations and the New Community in Luke-Acts" in *The Social World of Luke-Acts* (Hendrickson, 1991); *The Economy of the Kingdom. Social Conflict and Economic Relations in Luke's Gospel* (Fortress, 1989); *Theology in Conflict*, NTSup 53 (Brill, 1980); and others. Mem: SBL 1974-; CBA 1983-; SNTS 1983-. Rec: Literature. Addr: (o) Oslo U., PO Box 1023, 0315 Oslo, Norway 22-85-68-64; (h) Neuberggt.6c, 0367 Oslo, Norway 22-55-67-50.

MOYER, James C., b. Norristown, PA, November 30, 1941, s. of Raymond & Mary, m. Roberta, chil: Brenda; Marsha; Rebecca. Educ: Gordon Div. Sch., MDiv 1966; Brandeis U., MA 1968, PhD 1969. Emp: SW Mo. State U., 1970- Prof. & Head, Relig. Stud. Dept. Excv: Gezer, 1969-70 Area Supr.; Ai at Raddana, 1972, 1974 Area Supr., Acad. Coord. Spec: Archaeology, Anatolian Studies, Hebrew Bible. Pub: Articles in *ABD* (1992), *Holman Bible Dict.* (1991), *Mercer Dict. of the Bible* (1990), *ISBE* (1979), *Zondervan Pictorial Ency.* (1975); *Scripture in Context II: More Essays on the Comparative Method*, co-ed. (Eisenbrauns, 1983); and others. Awd: Hebrew Union Coll., Jerusalem, Arch. Fellow. 1969-70. Mem: SBL 1967-; CBA 1973-; ASOR 1975-; NABPR 1988-. Rec: Gardening, reading. Addr: (o) Southwest Missouri State U., Dept. of Religious Studies, Springfield, MO 65804 417-836-5514; (h) 634 E Cardinal, Springfield, MO 65810 417-881-6857.

MUELLER, James R., b. Memphis, TN, July 16, 1951, s. of R.J. & H.J., m. Scarlott. Educ: Duke Div. Sch., MDiv 1977; Duke U., MA 1984, PhD 1986. Emp: U. of N.C.-Greensboro, 1981-82 Lect.; N.C. State U., 1982-86 Vis. Instr.; *RSRev*, 1982- Area Sub-ed.; *JSP*, 1986- Assoc. Ed.; U. of N.C.-Chapel Hill, 1987-88 Vis. Asst. Prof.; U. of Fla., 1988- Asst. Prof. Spec: New Testament, Apocrypha and Post-biblical Studies. Pub: *Oxford Study Bible*, co-ed. (Oxford U.P., 1992); *The New Testament Apocrypha and Pseudepigrapha: A Guide to Publications*, co-auth. (Scarecrow, 1987); "The Apocryphon of Ezekiel: A New Translation and Introduction," co-auth., "The Vision of Ezra: A New Translation and Introduction," co-auth. in *The Old Testament Pseudepigrapha* vol. 1 (1983); and others. Mem: SBL; AAR; ASOR; CBA. Addr: (o) U. of Florida, 125 Dauer Hall, Gainesville, FL 32611 904-392-1625; (h) 9211 SW 42nd Ln., Gainesville, FL 32608 904-336-4600.

MUELLER, John J., b. Denver, CO, January 10, 1945, s. of John & Cecelia. Educ: St. Louis U., BA 1969, MA 1970; Grad. Theol. Union,

PhD, Theol., 1979. Emp: Gonzaga U., 1979-84 Assoc. Prof.; St. Louis U., 1984- Assoc. Prof. Spec: New Testament. Pub: *What Are They Saying About Theological Method?* (Paulist, 1984); and others.. Mem: AAR; CTSA. Addr: (o) St. Louis U., Lindell Blvd., St. Louis, MO 63108-3395.

MUELLER, Mogens, b. Hellerup, Denmark, January 25, 1946, s. of Johannes & Agnete, m. Lisbet, chil: Dorte; Johannes; Agnete. Educ: U. of Copenhagen, Cand. Theol. 1972, ThD 1984. Emp: Inst. for Bibelsk Eksegese, 1982- Prof., Theol.; *Dansk Teologisk Tidsskrift*, Chief Ed. Spec: New Testament. Pub: "The Gospel of St. Matthew and the Mosaic Law—A Chapter of a Biblical Theology" *Studia Theologica* 46 (1992); *Gnostikerne og Bibelen: Ptolemaeus' brev til Flora*, Tekst og Tolkning 9 (Cph. Akademisk Forlag, 1991); "Graeca sive Hebraica Veritas? The Defence of the Septuagint" *SJT* 1-2 (1989); *Mattaeusevangeliet fortolket* (Cph. Bibelselskabet, 1988); *Der Ausdruck "Menschensohn" in den Evangelien: Voraussetzungen und Bedeutung*, ATHD 17 (1984); "The Expression 'The Son of Man' as Used by Jesus" *Studia Theologica* 38 (1984); *Jesus-opfattelser i nytestamentlige forskning* (1978); "Uber den Ausdruck 'Menschensohn' in den Evangelien" *Studia Theologica* 31 (1977); "Der Jesus der Historiker, der historische Jesus und die Christusverkundigung der Kirche" *KuD* 22 (1976); and others. Mem: SNTS. Addr: (o) Institut for Bibelsk Eksegese, Kobmagergade 44-46, DK 1150 Kobenhavn K, Denmark 33152811; (h) Heslegardsvej 47, DK 2900 Hellerup, Denmark 31612404

MUELLER, Paul-Gerhard, b. Sulzbach/Saar, June 29, 1940, s. of Franz & Katharina (Simon). Educ: U. Loewen/Belgien, Dipl. Theol., Lic. Bibl., Lic. Phil. Orient. 1965; U. Regensburg, ThD 1972, Habil., NT Exegese 1976. Emp: U. Regensburg, 1969-76 Asst., 1978- Prof., NT Exegese; CBA, Stuttgart, 1979-89 Dir.; Bible Inst. Trier, 1990- Dir. Spec: New Testament. Pub: *Bibel und Christologie* (1987); *Lexikon exegetischer Fachbegriffe* (1986); *Der Traditionsprozess im Neuen Testament* (1982); *Christos Archegos* (1972); and others. Mem: SNTS 1976-; Commn. Juden-Christen 1980-. Rec: Guiding study-travels to Middle East & bibl. countries. Addr: (h) Im Sabel 25, D-54294 Trier, Germany 0651-8-65-63.

MUHLY, James D., May 6, 1936. Educ: U. of Minn., BA 1958; Yale U., PhD 1969. Emp: U. of Minn., 1964-67 Lect., Hist. Dept.; U. of Pa., 1967-69 Lect., 1969-73 Asst. Prof., 1973-79 Assoc. Prof., 1979- Prof., Dept. of Oriental Stud. Excv: Tel Michal, 1977-80 Proj. Dir.; Tel Gerisha, 1981-83 Proj. Dir. Spec: Archaeology. Pub: "Metal Artifacts," co-auth., in *Excavations at Tel Michal, Israel* (U. of Minn., 1989); "Solomon, the Copper King: A Twentieth Century Myth" *Expedition* 29/2 (1987); "End of the Bronze Age" in *Elba to Damascus: Art and Archaeology of Ancient Syria* (Smithsonian Inst., 1985); "A Steel Pick from Mt.

Adir in Palestine" *JNES* 44 (1985); "The Role of the Sea Peoples in Cyprus During the LCIII Period" in *Cyprus at the Close of the Late Bronze Age* (Nicosia, 1984); "How Iron Technology Changed the Ancient World—and Gave the Philistines a Military Edge" *BAR* 8/6 (1982); and others. Awd: NEH Res. Grant 1980-82, 1984-85; NEH/ASOR Res. Fellow.; Albright Arch. Inst., Jerusalem 1981-82; U. of Pa., Fac. Res. Grant 1983-84; Amer. Phil. Soc., Res. Grant 1983. Mem: AIA; Amer. Sch. of Class. Stud.; ASOR; AOS. Addr: (o) U. of Pennsylvania, Ancient History, 711 Williams Hall, Philadelphia, PA 19104 215-898-6042; (h) 444 S 49th St., Philadelphia, PA 19143 215-472-5431.

MULDER, Martin J., b. Ter Aar, Netherlands, December 25, 1923, s. of Albertus & Johanna (Plettenburg), m. Jitske (Andringa), chil: Ab; Hermien; Sian; Rita; Lydia; Regien; Jan; Heleen; Ben. Educ: Free U., Amsterdam, ThD 1962; State U., Leiden, DLitt 1969. Emp: Dutch Reform Ch., 1949-64 Pastor; Free U., Amsterdam, 1964-79 Prof., Semitic Lit.; State U., Leiden, 1979-89 Prof. of Theol., Dir.; Peshitta-Inst., 1989- Prof. Emeritus; Bibl. Mus., Amsterdam, Chmn. Spec: Hebrew Bible, Semitic Languages, Texts and Epigraphy. Pub: "Von Selden bis Schaeffer" *Ugarit-Forshungen* 11 (1979); "Esekiel xx 39 and the Pesitta Version" *VT* 25 (1975); "Die Partikel *Ya'an*" *Oudtestament Stud.* 18 (1973); and others. Mem: Dutch SOTS 1970-, Pres. 1978-81. Rec: Public heraldry, travel, chess. Addr: (h) Amperestraat 48, 1171 BV Badhoevedorp, Netherlands 020-6594337.

MULHOLLAND, M. Robert, Jr., b. Rutland, VT, September 3, 1936, s. of Moston & Georgine (Schou), m. Gweneth (Scholl), chil: Jeremy; Tareena. Educ: US Naval Acad., BS 1958; Wesley Theol. Sem., MDiv (summa cum laude) 1965; Harvard Div. Sch., ThD 1977. Emp: United Meth. Ch., Pastor; McMurry Coll., 1977-79 Asst. Prof.; Asbury Theol. Sem., 1979- Prof., V.P./Provost; Acad. for Spiritual Formation, 1983- Adj. Prof. Spec: New Testament. Pub: "Acts" in *Asbury Bible Comm.* (Zondervan, 1992); "Sociological Criticism" in *New Testament Criticism and Interpretation* (Zondervan, 1991); *Revelation* (Zondervan, 1990); "The Church in the Epistles" in *The Church: An Inquiry into Ecclesiology from a Biblical Theological Perspective* (Warner, 1984); articles in *Beacon Dict. of Theology* (1983); "The Infancy Narratives in Matthew and Luke— Of History, Theology and Literature" *BAR* 7/2 (1981); and others. Mem: SBL 1963-. Rec: Alpine skiing, spelunking, rollerblading. Addr: (o) Asbury Theological Seminary, 204 N Lexington Ave., Wilmore, KY 40390 606-858-3581; (h) 422 Akers Dr., Wilmore, KY 40390 606-858-4219.

MULL, Kenneth V., b. Wendling, OR, September 16, 1930, s. of Wallace & Ella, m. Carolyn (Sandquist), chil: Mark; David. Educ: U. of Minn., MA 1954; Evang. Theol. Sem., MDiv 1957; NW U., PhD 1962. Emp: Meth. Ch., 1953-

67 Pastor; Aurora U., 1967- Prof., Relig., Arch.; Kampsville Excvn. Sch., 1979 Lect. Excv: Tel Miqne, 1981, 1984 Area Supr. Spec: Archaeology. Awd: ASOR, Thayer Fellow. 1973-74; Harvard U., NEH Fellow. 1983. Mem: AAR; ASOR; IES; SBL. Addr: (o) Aurora U., 347 S Gladstone, Aurora, IL 60506 708-844-5417; (h) 207 S Randall, Aurora, IL 60506 708-892-6206.

MULLEN, Everett T., Jr., b. Lincolnton, NC, January 14, 1948, s. of Everett & Evelyn (Self), m. Grace (Friend). Educ: Davidson Coll., AB 1970; Harvard U., PhD 1976. Emp: Harvard Div. Sch., 1976-77 Instr.; Indiana/Purdue U., 1978- Assoc. Prof. Spec: Hebrew Bible, Semitic Languages, Texts and Epigraphy. Pub: *Narrative History and Ethnic Boundaries: The Deuteronomistic Historian and the Creation of Israelite National Identity* (Scholars, 1993); "The Royal Dynastic Grant to Jehu and the Structure of the Books of Kings" *JBL* 107/2 (1988); "The Sins of Jeroboam: A Redactional Reassessment" *CBQ* 49/2 (1987); "Judges 1:1-36: The Deuteronomistic Reintroduction of the Book of Judges" *HTR* 77/1 (1984); "The Divine Witness and the Davidic Royal Grant: Ps 89: 37-38" *JBL* 102 (1983); "The 'Minor Judges'— Some Literary and Historical Considerations" *CBQ* 44 (1982); *The Assembly of the Gods: The Divine Council in Canaanite and Early Hebrew Literature* (Scholars, 1980); and others. Mem: AAR; ASOR; SBL. Addr: (o) Indiana U., Dept. of Religious Studies, 425 University Blvd., Indianapolis, IN 46202 317-274-5941; (h) 8647 Log Run South Dr., Indianapolis, IN 46234 317-329-1382.

MULLER, Earl C., b. Columbia, SC, August 18, 1947, s. of Philip H. & Catherine C. Educ: Spring Hill Coll., BS 1971; Regis Coll., Canada, MDiv 1977; Marquette U., PhD, Theol. 1987. Emp: Spring Hill Coll., 1984-87 Instr.; Marquette U., 1987- Asst. Prof. Spec: New Testament, Apocrypha and Post-biblical Studies. Pub: *Trinity and Marriage in Paul: The Establishment of a Communitarian Analogy of the Trinity Grounded in the Theological Shape of Pauline Thought* (Lang, 1990). Awd: Arthur J. Schmitt Fellow. 1979-81. Mem: CBA 1978-; SBL 1978-; NAPS 1989-; CTSA 1978-. Addr: (o) Marquette U., Theology Department, Milwaukee, WI 53233 414-288-3745; (h) Jesuit Residence, 1404 W Wisconsin Ave., Milwaukee, WI 53233 414-288-5000.

MULLINS, Terence Y., b. Washington, DC, December 18, 1921, s. of Eber & Beulah (Yoos), m. Beverly (Schultz), chil: Joanna. Educ: U. of Va., BA 1943, MA 1954; Luth. Theol. Sem., BD 1945. Emp: Luth. Ch., 1945-59 Pastor; Luth. Theol. Sem., 1959-60 Lect.; Luth. Ch. in Amer., 1960- Ed.; *SALT*, 1964-70 Ed.; *Augsburg Bible Stud.*, 1970-87 Ed. Spec: New Testament, Apocrypha and Post-biblical Studies. Mem: ASOR 1944-; SBL 1945-. Rec: Chess, photography, nature. Addr: (h) 3206 W Penn St., Philadelphia, PA 19129.

MUNDHENK, Norman A., b. Portland, OR, March 5, 1943, s. of Alvin & Dorothy (Hare), m. Alice (Tegenfeldt), chil: Rita; Rhonda; Renee; Raewyn; Ruthie; Rowan. Educ: Hartford Sem. Found., MA 1968. Emp: United Bible Soc., 1965- Trans. Adv. Pub: *Translator's Handbook on Obadiah and Micah,* co-auth. (United Bible Soc., 1982); "Translation and the Form of the Source Language" *Bull. of United Bible Soc.* (1981); "The Subjectivity of Anachronism" in *On Language, Culture and Religion* (Mouton, 1974); and others. Mem: SBL; CBA. Rec: Stamp collecting, genealogy. Addr: (o) Box 723, Mt. Hagen, Papua 52-1507, New Guinea.

MUNOZ LEON, Domingo, b. Chiclana de Segura (Jaen), October 26, 1930, s. of Juan Angel & Ana Dolores. Educ: Pont. U. of Comillas, Lic. Theol. 1954; Ulpan Etzion of Jerusalem, Dip., Modern Hebrew 1963; Pont. Bibl. Inst., Rome, Doc., Bibl. Sci. 1968; Complutensian U. of Madrid, Lic. Bibl. Philol. (praemium) 1978, Doc. Bibl. Philol. 1984. Emp: Theol. Fac. of Granada, 1968-74 Aggregate Prof., Bibl. Sci., 1969-74 Pro-Dir. of Bibl. Dept.; CSIC, Madrid, 1974- Mem.; *EstBib,* 1974-86 Chief of Redaction. Spec: New Testament, Apocrypha and Post-biblical Studies. Pub: "Jesus y la apocaliptica pesimista (A proposito de Lc 18,8b y Mt 24,12)" *EstBib* 46 (1988); *Deras: Los caminos y sentidos de la Palabra Divina en la Escritura* (CSIC, 1987); *Palabra y Gloria: Excursus en la Biblia y en la Literatura Intertestamentaria* (CISC, 1983); *Gloria de la Shekina en los Targumim del Pentateuco* (1977); "El origen de las formulas ritmicas antiteticas en la Primera Carta de San Juan" *EstBib* (1975); "El 4 de Esdras y el Targum Palestinense" *EstBib* 33 (1974); *Dios-Palabra: Memra en los targumim del Pentateuco* (1974); "Soluciones de los targumin del Pentateuco a los antropomorfismos" *EstBib* 28 (1969); and others. Mem: Pont. Bibl. Commn. 1984-92; SNTS 1990-. Rec: Excursions to bibl. places. Addr: (o) Consejo Superior de Investig. Cient., C/Duque de Medinaceli, 6, 28014 Madrid, Spain 91-5854877; (h) Argueso, 21, 1 B., 28019 Madrid, Spain 91-4699641.

MUNRO, Winsome, b. South Africa, October 23, 1925, d. of Henry & Maria (Borcherds). Educ: Witwatersrand U., South Africa, BA 1945; U. of Birmingham, England, MDiv 1962; Union Theol. Sem., STM 1967; Columbia U., EdD 1974. Emp: Siena Coll., 1979-80; U. of Dubuque, Theol. Sem., 1980-82; Presbyn. Ch., 1982-84 Pastor; Luther Coll., 1984-86; St. Olaf Coll., 1986-91 Asst. Prof., 1991- Emerita. Spec: New Testament. Pub: "Interpolation in the Epistles: Weighing Probability" *NTS* (1990); "Romans 13: 1-7: Apartheid's Last Biblical Refuge" *BTB* 20 (1990); "Women, Text, and the Canon: The Strange Case of 1 Corinthians 14:33-35" *BTB* 18 (1988); Authority in Paul and Peter— The Identification of a Pastoral Stratum in the Pauline Corpus and I Peter (Cambridge U.P., 1983); "Women Disciples in Mark?" *CBQ* 44 (1982); and others. Mem: SBL 1973-; CBA 1984-.

Rec: Theater, swimming, walking. Addr: (h) 206 N Plum, Northfield, MN 55057 507-645-4551.

MUNTINGH, Lukas M., b. South Africa, June 28, 1929, s. of Johannes & Maria, m. Aletta, chil: Narina; Lukas; Wynand; Johannes. Educ: U. of Stellenbosch, BA 1950, MA 1954, Lic. Theol. 1954, DLitt 1963, DTh 1973. Emp: U. of the Orange Free State, 1960-63 Lect.; U. of Stellenbosch, 1963- Sr. Lect., Bibl. Stud. Spec: Archaeology, Hebrew Bible, Mesopotamian Studies, Semitic Languages, Texts and Epigraphy, Egyptology. Pub: "The Role of the Scribe According to the Mari Texts: A Study of Terminology" *Jour. for Semitics* 3/1 (1991); "Syro-Palestinian Problems in Light of the Amarna Letters" in *Essays on Ancient Anatolian and Syrian Studies in the 2nd and 1st Millenium B.C.* vol. IV (Harrassowitz, 1991); "Problems in Connection with the Verbal Forms in the Amarna Letters from Jerusalem, with Special Reference to EA 286" *Jour. for Semitics* 1/2; "Second Thoughts on Ebla and the Old Testament" in *Text and Context,* JSOTSup 48 (Sheffield, 1988); "Amorite Marriage and Family Life According to the Mari Texts" *JNSL* 3 (1974); and others. Mem: OT Soc. of South Africa 1957-; SBL 1983-. Rec: Music, photography. Addr: (o) U. of Stellenbosch, Dept. of Religious Studies, 7600 Stellenbosch, South Africa 02231-772028; (h) 58 Van der Stel St., 7600 Stellenbosch, South Africa 02231-4282.

MURPHY, Frederick J., b. Worcester, MA, August 16, 1949, s. of James F. & Hazel L., m. Leslie Sue, chil: Rebecca; Jeremy. Educ: Harvard U., AM 1981, PhD 1984; U. of London, BD 1977. Emp: Holy Cross Coll., 1983- Asst. Prof., 1989- Assoc. Prof., Dept. Chmn. Spec: New Testament, Apocrypha and Post-biblical Studies. Pub: *The Religious World of Jesus: An Introduction to Second Temple Palestinian Judaism* (Abingdon, 1991); "God in Pseudo-Philo" *JSJ* 19 (1988); "The Eternal Covenant in Pseudo-Philo" *JSP* 3 (1988); "Divine Plan, Human Plan: A Structuring Theme in Pseudo-Philo" *JQR* 77 (1986); "Sapiental Elements in the Syriac Apocalypse of Baruch" *JQR* 76 (1986); "2 Baruch and the Romans" *JBL* 104 (1985); *The Structure and Meaning of Second Baruch* (Scholars, 1985). Mem: SBL 1982-; CBA 1983-. Rec: Music, reading, sports. Addr: (o) Holy Cross Coll., Dept. of Relig. Stud., Worcester, MA 01610 617-793-3404; (h) 196 Beaconsfield Rd., Worcester, MA 01602 617-754-7036.

MURPHY, Roland E., b. Chicago, IL, July 19, 1917, s. of John & Marian. Educ: Cath. U., STD 1948, MA 1949; Pont. Bibl. Inst., SSL 1958. Emp: Cath. U., 1949-69; *CBQ,* 1958-66 Ed.; Duke U., 1971-86 George Washington Ivey Emeritus Prof. of Bibl. Stud.; Pittsburgh Theol. Sem., 1965 Vis. Prof.; Yale Div. Sch., 1966 Vis. Prof.; Princeton Theol. Sem., 1970-71 Vis. Prof.; Notre Dame U., 1985 Vis. Prof. Spec: Hebrew Bible. Pub: *Ecclesiastes* (Word, 1992); *The Tree* of Life (Doubleday, 1990); *The Song of Songs* (Fortress, 1990); "Wisdom and Creation" *JBL* 104 (1985); *Wisdom Literature and Psalms* (Abingdon, 1983); *Wisdom Literature* (Eerdmans, 1981); and others. Mem: CBA 1968, Pres.; SBL 1984, Pres. Rec: Swimming, lit. Addr: (o) Whitefriars Hall, 1600 Webster St. NE, Washington, DC 20017 202-526-1221.

MURPHY-O'CONNOR, Jerome J., b. Cork, Ireland, April 10, 1935, s. of Kerry & Mary (McCrohan). Educ: U. of Fribourg, Switzerland, ThL 1961, ThD 1962; Ecole Biblique de Jerusalem, Eleve Titulaire 1964; Pont. Bibl. Commn., Rome, LSS 1965. Emp: Ecole Biblique, Jerusalem, 1967-72 Lect., 1972- Prof.; NT; U. of Notre Dame, 1984 O'Brien Vis. Prof.; *RB* 1967- Ed. Bd.; *NTS,* 1986-88 Ed. Bd.; *Pacifica,* 1987- Ed. Bd. Spec: New Testament. Pub: *The Holy Land. An Archaeological Guide from Earliest Times to 1700* (Oxford U.P., 1992); *The Theology of the Second Letter to the Corinthians* (Cambridge U.P., 1991); "2 Tim Contrasted with 1 Tim and Titus" *RB* 98 (1991); "The Date of 2 Cor 10-13" *AusBR* (1991); *The Ecole Biblique and the New Testament: A Century of Scholarship (1890-1990),* NTOA 13 (Fribourg U.P., 1990); "Another Jesus (2 Cor 11:4)" *RB* 97 (1990); "John the Baptist and Jesus: History and Hypotheses" *NTS* 36 (1990); "Qumran and the New Testament" in *The New Testament and Its Modern Interpreters* (Scholars, 1989); and others. Awd: Irish Bibl. Assn., Boylan Lect. 1973; U. of Sydney, Australia, MacDonald Lect. 1976; Cath. Theol. Coll., Australia, Knox Lect. 1990. Mem: CBA 1967-; Irish Bibl. Assn. 1967-; SBL 1967-; SNTS 1970-. Rec: Hiking. Addr: (o) Ecole Biblique, P.O.B. 19053, Jerusalem, Israel 972-2-894-468.

MURRAY, Donald F., b. Hornsby, NSW Australia, September 23, 1940, s. of Evelyn & Herbert Augustus, m. Suzanne Grace, chil: Alasdair James; Gaenor Lyn; Susannah Rachel. Educ: U. of Sydney, BA 1968; U. of Cambridge, BA 1970, MA 1973. Emp: U. of Southampton, 1971-88 Lect.; U. of Exeter, 1988- Lect. Spec: Hebrew Bible. Pub: "*MQWM* and the Future of Israel in 2 Samuel VII 10" *VT* 40 (1990); "The Rhetoric of Disputation: Re-examination of a Prophetic Genre" *JSOT* 38 (1987); "Once Again '*T 'HD SBTY YSR' L* in II Samuel 7:7" *RB* 94 (1987); "Narrative Structure and Technique in the Deborah-Barak Narrative (Jdg. IV 4-22)" in *Studies in the Historical Books of the Old Testament,* VTSup 30 (1979); and others. Mem: SOTS 1973-; SBL 1988-. Rec: Music, reading novels, watching soccer. Addr: (o) U. of Exeter, Theology Dept., Queen's Bldg., Queen's Dr., Exeter EX4 4QH, England 392-264238; (h) 2 Charingthay Gate, Sylvan Rd., Exeter EX4 6EW, England 392-437109.

MURRAY, Robert, P. R., b. Beijing, China, June 8, 1925, s. of A. H. Jowett & Mary (Robertson).

Educ: Corpus Christi Coll., Oxford, MA 1951; Heythrop Coll., STL 1960; Gregorian U., Rome, STD 1964. Emp: Heythrop Coll., Oxfordshire, 1963-70, U. of London, 1970-1988 Sr. Res. Fellow; *Heythrop Jour.,* 1971-83 Ed.; U. of London, 1988 E.M. Wood Lect.; U. of Oxford, 1991 D'Arcy Lect. Spec: Hebrew Bible, New Testament, Semitic Languages, Texts and Epigraphy, Apocrypha and Post-biblical Studies. Pub: *The Cosmic Covenant: Biblical Themes of Justice, Peace and the Integrity of Creation* (Sheed & Ward, 1992); *Symbols of Church and Kingdom: A Study in Early Syriac Tradition* (Cambridge U.P., 1975); and others. Mem: British SOTS, Pres. 1986-87; SNTS. Rec: Company of friends, lit., fine arts. Addr: (o) U. of London, Heythrop Coll., Kensington Sq., London W8 5HQ, England 071-795-6600.

MYLLYKOSKI, Matti, b. Karhula, Finland, October 9, 1958, s. of Kosti & Maija, m. Maria. Educ: Helsinki U., DD 1991. Emp: *Teologinen Aikakauskirja,* 1986- Co Ed. Spec: New Testament. Pub: "The Material Common to Luke and John: A Sketch" in *Luke-Acts: Scandinavian Perspectives,* PFES 54 (1991); *Die letzten Tage Jesu: Markus und Johannes, ihre Traditionen und die historische Frage* I, AASF B/256 (1991). Mem: SBL 1990-. Rec: Cats, cooking, Italian opera. Addr: (o) Helsinki U., Faculty of Theology, PO Box 37, 00014 Helsinki, Finland; (h) Katajaharjuntie 5A2 00200 Helsinki, Finland 671-501.

MYRE, André, b. Montreal, Canada, August 14, 1939, s. of Pauline (Bissonnette) & Antonio. Educ: Coll. de l'Immaculee-Conception, Montreal, MA Ph 1964, MA Th 1970; Hebrew Union Coll., Jewish Inst. of Relig., PhD 1968. Emp: U. de Montreal, Fac. de Theol., 1970-71, 1973- Titular Prof. Spec: New Testament. Pub: *Un souffle subversif: l'Esprit dans les lettres pauliniennes,* Recherches NS 12 (Bellarmin/ Cerf, 1987); *Eucharisties* (Bellarmin, 1974, 1977); and others. Addr: (o) U. de Montreal, Fac. de Theol., C.P. 6128, Succursale A, Montreal, Que. H3C 3J7, Canada 514-343-7024.

NA'AMAN, Nadav, b. Jerusalem, Israel, April 2, 1939, s. of Shlomo & Leah, m. Ilana. Educ: Hebrew U., Jerusalem, BA 1967, MA 1970; Tel Aviv U., PhD 1975. Emp: Tel Aviv U., 1971- Prof.; Hebrew U. of Jerusalem, 1971-73, 1979; *Tel Aviv,* 1977- Ed. Bd. Spec: Archaeology, Hebrew Bible, Mesopotamian Studies. Pub: "The Kingdom of Judah under Josiah" *Tel Aviv* 18 (1991); *From Nomadism to Monarchy: Archeological and Historical Aspects of Early Israel,* co-ed. (1990); "The Historical Background to the Conquest of Samaria" *Biblica* 71 (1990); "Habiru and Hebrews: The Transfer of a Social Term to the Literary Sphere" *JNES* 45 (1986); *Borders and Districts in Biblical Historiography* (1986); "Economic Aspects of the Egyptian Occupation of Canaan" *IEJ* 31 (1981); "The Chronology of Alalakh Level VII Once Again" *Anatolian Studies* 29 (1979); and others. Addr: (o) Tel Aviv U., Dept. of Jewish

History, Ramat Aviv 69978, Israel 03-6409277; (h) 19/3 Einstein St., Ramat Aviv 69101, Israel 03-6426962.

NAGAKUBO, Senzo, b. Japan, February 5, 1933, m. Hisako, chil: Masaki; Aki. Educ: Andrews U., BD 1961, MTh 1963; Duke U., PhD 1974. Emp: Saniku Gakuin Coll., 1963- Prof. Spec: Apocrypha and Post-biblical Studies. Pub: "Additions to Daniel," "Greek Ezra," "Latin Ezra" in *Comm. to the New Joint Translation of the Old Testament*, vol. 3, Apocrypha (Nihon Kirisutokyoudan Shuppankyoku, 1993); "Dead Sea Scrolls" in *Oriental Studies* vol. 1 (Gakuseisha, 1984); "World of the New Testament" in *World of the Bible* (Jiyukokuminsha, 1984); "An Aspect of Messianism in the Intertestamental Literature" *Bible & Ch.* 212 (1983); and others. Mem: SBL; Japan Soc. Christian Stud.; Japan Bibl. Inst. Addr: (o) Saniku Gakuin College, 1500 Kugahara, Otaki-machi, Isumi-gun, Chiba-ken, Japan 0470-84-0111; (h) 1090 Ishigami Otaki-machi, Isumi-gun, Chiba-ken 298-02, Japan 0470-84-0458.

NAGATA, Takeshi, b. Aichi, Japan, December 30, 1947, s. of Kunio & Hisae, m. Yaeko, chil: Lisa. Educ: Gordon-Conwell Theol. Sem., MDiv 1974; Princeton Theol. Sem., ThM 1975, PhD 1981. Emp: Intl. Christian U., 1980- Assoc. Prof., NT Stud. Spec: New Testament. Pub: "A Neglected Literary Feature of the Christ-Hymn in Phil 2:6-11" *Ann. of the Japanese Bibl. Inst.* 7 (1982). Mem: SBL; Japan Inst. Bibl. Stud.; SNTS. Rec: Swimming. Addr: (o) International Christian U., 3-10-2 Osawa, Mitaka, 181 Tokyo, Japan 0422-33-3323; (h) 2-12-4-502 Bessho, Hachioji, 192-03, Tokyo, Japan 0426-74-7862.

NAVEH, Nira, b. Jerusalem, Israel, March 8, 1937, d. of Nissan & Rachel, m. Menachem, chil: Gili; Yehuda; Roni; Reuven. Educ: Hebrew U. of Jerusalem, BA, MLS. Emp: Inst. of Arch., Hebrew U. of Jerusalem, 1962-; *Qadmoniot,* 1968-92 Indexer. Spec: Archaeology. Pub: *The New Ency. of Archaeological Excavations in the Holy Land,* contb. (1993); "A Bibliography of Tiberias" *Idan* 11 (1988); "Bibliography of Personal Bibliographies of Scholars of the Archaeology of Palestine" *IEJ* 35 (1985); and others. Mem: Israel Assn. of Arch.; Israel Soc. of Special Libraries & Information Ctrs. Addr: (o) Hebrew University of Jerusalem, Institute of Archaeology, Jerusalem, Israel 02-882415; (h) 27 Habanai St., Jerusalem, Israel 02-522910.

NAYLOR, Peter J., b. Cardiff, Wales, September 22, 1954, s. of John & Joan, m. Pamela, chil: Hannah; Rebecca; Sarah. Educ: Oxford U., England, DPhil 1980. Spec: Hebrew Bible, New Testament, Semitic Languages, Texts and Epigraphy. Pub: *An Introduction to Structuralism* (1983); *The Language of Covenant* (Oxford, 1980). Rec: Badminton, chess. Addr: (h) 15 Aldsworth Rd., Canton, Cardiff CF5 1AA, Wales 0222-569405.

NEBE, Gerhard-Wilhelm, b. Korbach/Waldeck, June 25, 1944, s. of Wilhelm & Eugenie (Muschenborn). Educ: Theol. Examen Bielefeld, 1968; U. of Heidelberg, PhD 1991. Emp: U. Heidelberg, Fakultat fur Orientalistik & Altertumswissenschaft,Qumran-Forschungsstelle, 1968-. Spec: Hebrew Bible, New Testament, Semitic Languages, Texts and Epigraphy, Apocrypha and Post-biblical Studies. Pub: *Text und Sprache der hebraeischen Weisheitsschrift aus der Kairoer Geniza,* (Lang, 1993); *Qumran,* co-ed., Wege der Forschung (Darmstadt, 1981); and others. Rec: Music, singing. Addr: (h) Krahnengasse 12, 69117 Heidelberg, Germany 06221-183912.

NEBE, Gottfried, b. Hagen, Westfalen, Germany, December 15, 1942, s. of Wilhem & Eugenie (Muschenborn), m. Ingrid (Altrock). Spec: New Testament, Egyptology. Pub: "Righteousness in Paul" in *Festschrift B. Uffenheimer* (Sheffield, 1992); and others. Mem: SNTS 1989; Wissenschaftliche Gesellschaft fur Theol. 1988. Rec: Music, sport. Addr: (o) Ruhr-U. Bochum, Evang-Theol. Facultat, Universitatstrasse 150, D 44801 Bochum, Germany; (h) Adolf-Reichwein-Str. 26, D 48159 Munster/Westf, Germany 0251/216050.

NEEDLEMAN, Jacob, b. Philadelphia, PA, October 6, 1934, s. of Benjamin & Ida, m. Gail, chil: Raphael; Eve. Educ: Harvard U., BA 1956; Yale U., PhD 1961. Emp: San Francisco State U., 1962- Prof., Phil.; U. of the Pacific, 1978 Colliver Lect. Spec: New Testament, Apocrypha and Post-biblical Studies. Pub: *Lost Christianity* (Doubleday, 1980); and others. Mem: AAR. Addr: (o) San Francisco State U., Dept. of Philosophy, San Francisco, CA 94132 415-338-1596.

NEGEV, Avraham, b. Pinsk, Poland, August 31, 1923, s. of Jacob Barzilai & Heller (Pola-Penina), m. Rachel (Zeldin), chil: Eilat; Anat. Educ: Hebrew U., BA 1956, MA 1958, PhD 1961. Emp: Hebrew U., 1964-68 Lect., 1968-71 Sr. Lect., 1972-81 Assoc. Prof., 1982-92 Prof.; *IEJ* 1965- Ed. Bd. Excv: Oboda-Avdat, 1958-61, 1976-77, 1989 Dir.; Caesarea, 1961-62 Dir.; Mampsis-Kurnub, 1965-67, 1972 Dir.; Elusa-Haluza, 1973, 1979-80 Dir.; Susiya-Carmel, 1984-85 Dir. Spec: Archaeology, New Testament, Semitic Languages, Texts and Epigraphy. Pub: *Personal Names in the Nabatean Realm* (Hebrew U., Inst. of Arch., 1991); "The Temple of Obodas: Excavations at Oboda in July 1989" *IEJ* 41 (1991); "Mampsis—The End of a Nabatean Town" *ARAM Periodical* 2/1-2 (1990); "The Cathedral of Elusa and the New Typology and Chronology of the Byzantine Churches in the Negev" *Liber Annuus* 39 (1989); *The Architecture of Mampsis: Final Report. Volume I: The Middle and Late Nabatean Periods* (Hebrew U., Inst. of Arch., 1988); *The Architecture of Mampsis: Final Report. Volume II: The Late Roman and Byzantine Periods* (Hebrew U., Inst. of Arch., 1988); "Understanding the Nabateans" *BAR* 14/6

(1988); *Nabatean Archaeology Today* (N.Y. U., 1986); "Obodas the God" *IEJ* 36 (1986); and others. Mem: IES 1958-; ARAM Soc. for Syro-Mesopotamian Stud. 1989-. Addr: (o) Hebrew U., Institute of Archaeology, Mount Scopus, Jerusalem 91905, Israel 02-88-24-22; (h) Gelber 16, Jerusalem 96755, Israel 02-41-71-96.

NEL, Philip J., b. Ladysmith, June 6, 1948, s. of Elizabeth Maria, m. Olivia Margaretha, chil: Philo; Melike; Jeanine; Hilani. Educ: BA 1969; BA 1970; BTh 1973; MA, Semitic Lang. 1974; DLitt 1980. Emp: U. of Stellenbosch, 1970-74 Lect., Dept. of Semitic Lang.; U. of Orange Free State, 1975-82 Sr. Lect., 1982-88 Co-Prof., 1988- Prof., Dept. of Semitic Lang. Spec: Hebrew Bible, Semitic Languages, Texts and Epigraphy. Pub: "Cosmos and Chaos: A Reappraisal of the Divine Discourses in Job 38-41" *OTE* 4/2 (1991); "A Critical Perspective on Old Testament Exegetical Methodology" *OTE* 2/3 (1989); "Psalm 132 and Covenant Theology" in *Text and Context*, Festschrift for F.C. Fensham (JSOT, 1988); "The Riddle of Samson (Judg 14:14-18)" *Biblica* 66/4 (1985); *The Structure and Ethos of the Wisdom Admonitions in Proverbs*, *BZAW* 158 (1982); "Authority in the Wisdom Admonitions" *ZAW* 92/3 (1981); and others. Mem: SBL; OT Werkgemeenskap van Suid-Afrika; South. African Soc. for Semitics; South African Soc. for Gen. Lit. Stud.; Suid-Afrikaanse Akademie vir Wetenskap en Kuns. Rec: Carpentry, furniture making. Addr: (o) U. of the Orange Free State, Dept. of Semitic Languages, PO Box 339, Bloemfontein (RSA), South Africa 051-4012470; (h) Paul Rouxstraat 91, Dan Pienaar, Bloemfontein (RSA), South Africa 051-311468.

NELLER, Kenneth V., b. Corona, CA, February 20, 1954, s. of L.L. & Constance, m. Barbara, chil: Colin; Seth. Educ: Harding Grad. Sch. of Relig., MTh 1979, MA 1980; U. of St. Andrews, Scotland, PhD 1983. Emp: Ch. of Christ, 1978-79, 1981-92 Parish Min.; St. Mary's Coll., U. of St. Andrew's, Scotland, 1979-81 Tutor, NT Greek; Harding U., 1992- Assoc. Prof., NT Greek, Preaching. Spec: New Testament, Apocrypha and Post-biblical Studies. Pub: "Diversity in the Gospel of Thomas: Clues for A New Direction?" *SC* 7 (1989-90); and others. Mem: SBL 1983-. Addr: (o) Harding U., 900 E Center, Searcy, AR 72149; (h) 900 Merritt St., Searcy, AR 72143.

NELSON, Peter K., b. Minneapolis, MN, January 21, 1958, s. of Kenneth & Connie, m. Cheryl B., chil: Elliot L.; Jeremy A. Educ: Bethel Coll., BA 1980; Bethel Theol. Sem., MATS 1984, MDiv 1988; Trinity Coll., Bristol, PhD 1991. Emp: Bethlehem Bapt. Ch., Minneapolis, 1986-87 Interim Pastor; Trinity Coll., Bristol, 1989-91 Lect., NT & Greek; First Bapt. Ch., 1991-92 Interim Pastor; Light of the Gospel Bible Coll., Ukraine, 1992 Vis. Instr. Spec: New Testament. Pub: "The Flow of Thought in Luke 22:24-27" *JSNT* 43 (1991).

Awd: Tyndale House Coun., 1990-91 Res. Funding; Amer. Bible Soc. Awd. 1988. Mem: SBL 1990-; IBR 1990-; ETS 1988-. Rec: Tennis, graphic arts. Addr: (o) First Baptist Church, 309 Holden Ave., Henning, MN 56551 218-583-2161; (h) PO Box 356, Henning, MN 56551 218-583-2526.

NELSON, Richard C., b. Beatrice, NE, September 27, 1938, s. of Harry & Elsie (Hinkleman), m. Marilyn, chil: Stephanie; Gregory. Educ: U. of Minn., MA 1966, PhD 1975. Emp: Macalester Coll., 1965-66 Instr.; U. of Minn., 1967-68 Instr.; Augsburg Coll., 1968- Prof., Hist. Spec: Mesopotamian Studies. Pub: "Inventory of UR III Pisan-Dub-Ba Texts" in *Studies in Honor of Tom B. Jones* (1979). Rec: Photography, gardening. Addr: (o) Augsburg Coll., Chairman, Dept. of History, Minneapolis, MN 55430 612-330-1199; (h) 6707 Colfax Ave. N, Minneapolis, MN 55430 612-561-2834.

NELSON, Richard D., b. Fort Still, OK, October 27, 1945, s. of Donald & Ruth, m. Karen, chil: Daniel; Gretchen; Erica; Johanna. Educ: Trinity Luth. Sem., MDiv 1970; Union Theol. Sem., ThM 1971, PhD 1973. Emp: Ferrum Coll., 1977-80 Prof.; Luth. Theol. Sem., 1980- Assoc. Prof. Spec: Hebrew Bible. Pub: "The Role of the Priesthood in the Deuteronomistic History" in VTSup (Brill, 1991); "The Anatomy of the Book of Kings" *JSOT* (1988); *First and Second Kings* (John Knox, 1987); "The Altar of Ahaz: A Revisionist View" *HAR* (1986); "Realpolitik in Judah (687-609 BC)" in *Scripture and Context* II (Eisenbrauns, 1983); "Josiah in the Book of Joshua" *JBL* (1981); *The Double Redaction of the Deuteronomistic History* (JSOT, 1981); and others. Mem: SBL 1973. Rec: Cycling. Addr: (o) Lutheran Theological Seminary, 61 W Confederate Ave., Gettysburg, PA 17325 717-334-6286; (h) 54 N Hay St., Gettysburg, PA 17325 717-337-1453.

NETZER, Ehud, b. Jerusalem, Israel, m. Dvorah (Dove). Educ: Israel Inst. of Technology, Haifa, qualified 1958. Emp: Architect, 1958-63, 1966-71; Hebrew U., Inst. of Arch., 1971-80 Architect, Tchr., Dept. of Arch., 1981-93 Sr. Lect. Excv: Masada, 1963-65 Co-architect, 1989 Dir.; Herodium, 1972-75, 1978, 1980-84 Dir.; Jericho, 1973-83 Dir.; Sepphoris, 1985-93 Co-dir.; Caesarea, 1990 Dir. Spec: Archaeology. Pub: "New Mosaic Art from Sepphoris," co-auth., *BAR* 18/6 (1992); "The Last Days and Hours at Masada" *BAR* 17/6 (1991); *Masada, The Yigael Yadin Excavation 1963-1965, Final Reports*, 3 vol., co-ed. (IES/Hebrew U., 1989-1991); and others. Addr: (o) Hebrew U., Institute of Archaeology, Jerusalem, Israel.

NEUFELD, Edmund K., b. Vancouver, BC, Canada, November 10, 1954, s. of Elvin & Joanne, m. Marilyn. Educ: Winnipeg Theol. Sem., MA, Bibl. Stud. 1980; Marquette U., PhD,

Scriptural Theol., NT 1986. Emp: Winnipeg Theol. Sem., 1984-90 Instr., NT; Kleefeld Christian Community, 1990-. Spec: New Testament. Mem: CBA 1984-; CSBS 1986-; SBL 1987-; ETS 1989-. Rec: Camping/canoeing, 18th-19th Century English novels. Addr: (o) Kleefeld Christian Community, Box 338, Kleefeld, MB, Canada 204-377-4231; (h) Box 152, Kleefeld, MB R0A 0V0, Canada 204-377-4231.

NEUGEBAUER, Fritz, b. Bunzlau, March 16, 1932, s. of Ernst & Johanna (Rex), m. Erika (Zerling), chil: Maria; Andreas; Antje; Johanna; Ursula. Educ: U. Halle, ThD 1957. Emp: Katechetischen Oberseminar, 1960-64 Dozent; U. Halle, 1984- Lehrbeauftragungen. Spec: New Testament. Pub: "Die wunderbare Speisung (Mk 6,30-44 parr.) und Jesu Identitat" *KuD* 32 (1986); *Jesu Versuchung* (1986); "Die dargebotene Wange und Jesu Gebot der Feindesliebe, Erwaegungen zu Lk 6,27-36/Mt 5,38-48" *ThLZ* 110 (1985); "Zur Deutung und Bedeutung des 1.Petrusbriefes" *NTS* 26 (1980); "Die Davidssohnfrage (Mark 12,35-37 parr.) und der Menschensohn" *NTS* 21 (1975); *Jesus der Menschensohn, Ein Beitrag zur Klarung der Wege historischer Wahrheitsfindung im Bereich der Evangelien* (1972); *Die Entstehung des Johannesevangeliums, Altes und Neues zur Frage seines historischen Ursprungs* (1968); "Geistsprueche und Jesuslogien" *ZNW* 53 (1962); *In Christus, Eine Untersuchung zum Paulinischen Glaubensverstandnis* (1961); and others. Mem: SNTS 1982-. Addr: (o) Dorfstr. 28, D-14913 Seehausen, Germany Bloensdorf 459.

NEUMANN, Kenneth J., b. Albany, MN, February 12, 1940, s. of Kermit & Agnes, m. Velma L., chil: Erika Lynn; Kevin Paul; Timothy Andrew. Educ: Concordia Sr. Coll., BA 1963; Concordia Sem., MDiv, STM 1963-68; Toronto Sch. of Theol., ThD 1988. Emp: Luth. Ch., 1968-72, 1976-81, 1988- Pastor; Luth. Theol. Sem., Canada, 1979-80, 1982-83 Lect. Spec: New Testament. Pub: *The Authenticity of the Pauline Epistles in the Light of Stylostatistical Analysis,* SBL Diss. Ser. 120 (Scholars, 1990); *Romans: The Gospel According to Paul* (1986); "Paul's Use of Authority and Persuasion in the Corinthian Letters" *Consensus* 5/3 (1979); and others. Mem: CSBS 1973-; SBL 1976-. Rec: Basketball, family history, music, computer programming, fishing. Addr: (o) Box 10, Fairy Glen, SK S0E 0T0, Canada.

NEUSNER, Jacob, b. Hartford, CT, July 28, 1932, m. Suzanne (Richter), chil: Samuel; Eli; Noam; Margalit. Educ: Jewish Theol. Sem., MHL 1960; Columbia U., PhD, Relig. 1960. Emp: U. of Wis.-Milwaukee, 1961-62 Asst. Prof., Hebrew; Brandeis U., 1962-64 Res. Assoc.; Dartmouth Coll., 1964-68 Assoc. Prof., Relig.; Brown U., 1968-90 U. Prof. & Ungerleider Disting. Schol. of Judaic Stud., Co-dir. of Prog. in Judaic Stud.; U. of S Fla., 1990- Disting. Res. Prof. of Relig. Stud.; *Stud. in*

Judaism in Late Antiq., 1973- Found. & Ed.; *SC,* 1980- Ed.; *JAAR,* 1985-90 Adv. Bd.; *Relig. & Theol. Stud.,* 1985- Ed. Bd. Spec: Hebrew Bible. Pub: *The Mishnah: A New Translation* (Yale U.P., 1986); *Comparative Midrash: The Plan and Program of Genesis Rabbah and Leviticus Rabbah* (Scholars, 1986); *Judaisms and their Messiahs in the Beginning of Christianity* (Cambridge U.P., 1986); *The Oral Torah: The Sacred Books of Judaism* (Harper & Row, 1985); and others. Awd: Hebrew U., Fulbright Schol. 1957-58; Guggenheim Found. Fellow. 1973-74, 1979-80; U. of Chicago, LHD 1978; U. of Cologne, PhD 1979. Mem: AOS 1960-; AAR, V.P. 1967-68, Pres. 1968-69; Royal Asiatic Soc., Fellow 1968-; AAJR 1972-; Max Richter Found., Founder & Pres. 1969-. Addr: (o) U. of South Florida, Dept. of Religious Studies, Tampa, FL 33620 813-974-2221.

NEWING, Edward G., b. Sydney, Australia, July 12, 1930, s. of Edward & Gertrude (Moore), m. Joyce (Chapman), chil: Paul; Timothy; Miriam; Ruth. Educ: U. of New S Wales, Dip Civ. Eng. 1954; Australia Coll. of Theol., ThLic 1958; London U., BD 1959, MTh 1961; Makerere U., BA 1968; St Andrews U., PhD 1978. Emp: St. Paul's Coll., Kenya, 1961-73 Lect., OT; Macquarie U., New South Wales, 1976-80, 1984-86 Tutor in Anc. Near East. Civ.; Trinity Theol. Coll. & Grad. Sch., S.E.A. Singapore, 1980-83 Lect., OT & Hebrew; Pacific Theol. Coll., Fiji, 1989-91 Head of Dept. of Bibl. Stud.; Adelaide Coll. of Div., 1992- Tutor & Res. Spec: Hebrew Bible. Pub: "Up and Down, In and Out—Moses on Mount Sinai" *Australian Bibl. Rev.* 37/2 (1993); *Essays in Honor of Francis I. Anderson's Sixtieth Birthday,* co-ed. (Eisenbrauns, 1986); "The Rhetoric of Hope: The Structure of Genesis—II Kings" *Colloquium* 17/2 (1985); "A Rhetorical and Theological Analysis of the Hexateuch" *SE Asia Jour. of Theol.* 22/2 (1981); and others. Mem: SBL 1965-; Australia & New Zealand Soc. of Theol. Stud. 1974-; Australia Assn. for the Stud. of Relig. 1975-. Rec: Citroen cars, golf, chess. Addr: (h) PO Box 729, Willunga, S.A. 5172, Australia 085-564-004.

NEWMAN, Carey C., b. Savannah, GA, March 5, 1959, s. of Robert A. & Grace H., m. Leanne (Lewis). Educ: U. of S Fla., BA 1980; SW Bapt. Theol. Sem., MDiv 1983; U. of Aberdeen, Scotland, MTh 1985; Baylor U., PhD 1989. Emp: Palm Beach Atlantic Coll., 1989-93 Asst. Prof., Relig.; South. Bapt. Theol. Sem., 1991 Vis. Prof., 1993- Asst. Prof., NT. Spec: New Testament, Apocrypha and Post-biblical Studies. Pub: *Paul's Glory-Christology: Tradition and Rhetoric,* NTSup 69 (Brill, 1992); "Transforming Images of Paul" *EQ* 64 (1992); "Christophany as a Sign of 'The End': A Semiotic Approach to Paul's Epistles" *Mosaic* 25/3 (1992); "Apocalyptic Pattern and Narrative Horizon in Jewish and Jewish Christian Religion of the First Century" *Opus* 1 (1990-91); "A Matter of Glory or Making Glory Matter?" *Milton Quar.* 23 (1989); and others. Awd: Eddie Dwyer Endowed Acad. Fellow. 1988-89. Mem:

SBL; Tyndale Fellow; IBR. Rec: Jogging, skiing, travel. Addr: (o) Southern Baptist Theological Seminary, 2825 Lexington Rd., Louisville, KY 40280 502-897-4607; (h) 4214 Winchester Rd., Louisville, KY 40207 502-899-7902.

NEWMAN, Louis E., b. St. Paul, MN, July 10, 1956, s. of Marion & Annette. Educ: U. of Minn., BA (magna cum laude) 1976, MA 1979; Brown U., PhD 1983. Emp: Carleton Coll., 1980- Prof. of Relig., Dir. Judaic Stud. Pub: *The Sanctity of the Seventh Year: A Study of Mishnah Tractate Shebiit* (Scholars, 1983). Mem: AAR 1980-; SBL 1980-; AJS 1980-. Rec: Community service, music. Addr: (o) Carleton College, Dept. of Religion, Northfield, MN 55057 507-663-4227; (h) 1933 Fairmount Ave., St. Paul, MN 55105.

NEWMAN, Robert G., b. Blountstown, FL, August 18, 1936, s. of Corley & Margaret (Hirschi). Educ: Columbia Theol. Sem., MDiv 1961; Drew U., PhD 1965. Emp: Drew U. Theol. Sch., 1962-63 Inst.; Lees-McRae Coll., 1964-67 Prof., Chaplain; Morris Harvey Coll., U. of Charleston, 1967- A. J. Humphreys Prof. of Relig. Spec: New Testament. Pub: *Tradition and Interpretation in Mark* (1965). Mem: SBL; AAR; APA. Addr: (o) U. of Charleston, 213C Riggleman Hall, 2300 MacCorkle Ave., SE, Charleston,, WV 25304 304-357-4786; (h) 1508 Bridge Rd., Charleston, WV 25314 304-345-0225.

NEWSOM, Carol, Educ: Birmingham-South. Coll., AB (summa cum laude) 1971; Harvard Div. Sch., MTS 1975; Harvard U., PhD 1982. Emp: Emory U., Candler Sch. of Theol., 1980-82 Instr., 1982-88 Asst. Prof., 1988- Assoc. Prof., OT; *JSP*, 1987- Ed. Bd.; *JBL*, 1989-91 Ed. Bd.; OT Lib. Ser., Westminster/John Knox Press, 1990- Ed. Adv. Bd. Spec: Hebrew Bible. Pub: "4Q374: A Discourse on the Exodus/Conquest Traditions" in *The Dead Sea Scrolls: Forty Years of Research* (Brill, 1992); *Women's Bible Comm.,* co-ed. (Westminster/John Knox, 1992); "The Dead Sea Scrolls and Other Jewish Literature" in *The Oxford Study Bible* (Oxford U.P., 1992); articles in *ABD* (Doubleday, 1992); "'Sectually Explicit' Literature from Qumran" in *The Bible and Its Interpreters* (Eisenbrauns, 1990); "Women in the Discourse of Patriarchal Wisdom: A Study of Proverbs 1-9" in *Gender and Difference in Ancient Israel* (Augsburg/Fortress, 1989); *Harper's Bible Comm.,* co-ed., contb. (Harper & Row, 1988); *Songs of the Sabbath Sacrifice: A Critical Edition,* HSS 27 (Scholars, 1985); "The Masada Fragment of the Qumran Sabbath Shirot," co-auth., *IEJ* 34 (1984); and others. Awd: Phi Beta Kappa 1970; Danforth Fellow. 1975-78; Emory U., Res. Com., Fellow. 1983, Awd. 1985; NEH, Fellow. 1983-84; Amer. Coun. of Learned Soc., Grants 1983-84, 1987, Res. Fellow. 1988-89. Mem: SBL, Pres., SE Reg. 1992. Addr: Emory U., Candler School of Theology, Atlanta, GA 30322 404-727-4053.

NEYREY, Jerome H., b. New Orleans, LA, January 5, 1940, s. of Henry G. & Olga (Lux).

Educ: St. Louis U., BA 1963, MA 1964; Regis Coll., Toronto, MDiv 1970, MTh 1972; Yale U., PhD 1977; Weston Sch. of Theol., STL 1987. Emp: Spring Hill Coll., 1971-73 Lect.; Weston Sch. of Theol., 1977-92 Prof.; Pont. Bibl. Inst., 1989 Vis. Prof.; U. of Notre Dame, 1992- Prof. Spec: New Testament. Pub: "'Without Beginning of Days or End of Life' (Hebrews 7:3): Topos for a True Diety" *Biblica* 53 (1991); *The Social World of Luke-Acts* (Hendrickson, 1991); *Paul, In Other Words* (Westminster/John Knox, 1990); *An Ideology of Revolt* (Fortress, 1988); "Bewitched in Galatia: Paul in Social Science Perspective" *CBQ* 50 (1988); "Jesus the Judge: Forensic Process in John 8:21-59" *Biblica* 68 (1987); *The Passion According to Luke* (Paulist, 1983); "The Jacob Allusions in John 1:51" *CBQ* 44 (1982); "Form and Background of Polemic in 2 Peter" *JBL* 99 (1980); and others. Awd: Yale U. Fellow. 1973-77; ATS, Young Schol. Grant 1984, Res. Grant 1989; Santa Clara U., Bannan Fellow. 1984-85. Mem: SBL, Pres, New England reg. 1990; CBA. Rec: Birdwatching, classical music, hiking, fiction. Addr: (o) U. of Notre Dame, Dept. of Theology, Notre Dame, IN 46556 219-631-7469; (h) 228 Columba Hall, Notre Dame, IN 46556 219-631-9429.

NICKELSBURG, George W. E., b. San Jose, CA, March 15, 1934, s. of George & Elsie (Schwab), m. Marilyn (Miertschin), chil: Jeanne; Michael. Educ: Concordia Sem., BD 1960, STM 1962; Harvard Div. Sch., ThD 1968. Emp: Luth. Ch., 1966-69 Pastor; U. of Iowa, 1969- Prof.; *CBQ,* 1979- Assoc. Ed. Excv: Ta'anek, 1963 Area Supr.; Wadi-ed-Daliyeh, 1964 Area Supr.; Tel el Ful, 1964 Area Supr. Spec: New Testament, Apocrypha and Post-biblical Studies. Pub: *Faith and Piety in Early Judaism,* co-auth. (Fortress, 1983); *Jewish Literature Between the Bible and the Mishnah* (Fortress, 1981); "Apocalyptic and Myth in 1 Enoch 6-11" *JBL* 96 (1977); "Discoveries in the Wadi-ed-Daliyeh" *AASOR* 41 (1976); *Resurrection, Immortality and Eternal Life in Intertestamental Judaism,* HTS 26 (Harvard U.P., 1972); and others. Awd: ASOR, Jerusalem, Thayer Fellow 1963-64; Guggenheim Fellow. 1977-78. Mem: SBL 1959-; SNTS 1969-; CBA 1975-. Rec: Woodworking, music. Addr: (o) U. of Iowa, School of Religion, Gilmore Hall, Iowa City, IA 52242; (h) 1713 E Court St., Iowa City, IA 52245 319-351-2072.

NICKLE, Keith F., b. Keokuk, Iowa, June 10, 1933, s. of George H. & Vena M. (Keith), m. Marie (Love), chil: Neely K.; Stephen R.; John M.; Thomas A. Educ: U. of Tex., BA 1955; Austin Presbyn. Theol. Sem., BD 1958; U. of Basel, ThD 1966. Emp: Presbyn. Ch., 1963-67, 1983-90; St. Louis U., 1967-76 Prof., Bibl. Lang./Lit.; Columbia Theol. Sem., 1975-83 Prof., NT Lang./Lit. & Exegesis; Pittsburgh Theol. Sem., 1990- V.P. for Acad. Affairs, Dean of Fac., Prof., NT Stud. Spec: New Testament. Pub: *The Synoptic Gospels: Conflict and Consensus* (John Knox, 1980); "Romans 7:7-25: An Expository Article" *Interpretation* 33 (1979); *The Collection: A Study in the Strategy of Paul,*

Stud. in Bibl. Theol. (SCM, 1966); and others. Mem: SBL 1967-; CBA 1968-. Addr: (o) Pittsburgh Theological Seminary, 616 N Highland Ave., Pittsburgh, PA 15206 412-362-5610; (h) 6346 Aurelia St., Pittsburgh, PA 15206 412-362-4054.

NICOL, George G., b. Glasgow, Scotland, July 15, 1948, s. of George & Mary, m. Elaine, chil: Callum; Lyle. Educ: U. of Glasgow, Scotland, BD 1977; U. of Oxford, Regent's Park Coll., England, DPhil 1987. Emp: Bapt. Ch., 1982-87; Ch. of Scotland, 1988- Min. Spec: Hebrew Bible. Pub: "Story Patterning in Genesis" in *Text as Pretext, Essays in Honour of Robert Davidson*; "What Are You Doing Here, Elijah?" *Heythrop Jour.* 28 (1987); "The Wisdom of Joab and the Wise Woman of Tekoa" *Studia Theologica* 36 (1982); "Genesis 29.32 and 35.22a: Reuban's Reversal " *JTS* 31 (1980); "Isaiah's Vision and the Visions of Daniel" *VT* 29 (1979); and others. Rec: Sports, computers, spy novels. Addr: (o) St Peter's Parish Church, Inverkeithing, Fife, KY11, Scotland; (h) 20 Struan Dr., Inverkeithing, Fife KY11 1AR, Scotland.

NIEDERWIMMER, Kurt, b. Wien, Austria, November 11, 1929, s. of Ludwig & Anna, m. Erna, chil: Eva; Ruth; Paul. Educ: U. Wien, Habil. 1962. Emp: U. Wien, 1973 Prof., NT; *Rahmen des Meyerschen Kommentarwerkes*, Mitherausgeber des Kommentars zu den Apostolischen Vaetern. Spec: New Testament. Pub: *Die Didache*, KAV 1 (Vandenhoeck & Ruprecht, 1989, 1993); *Askese und Mysterium* (Vandenhoeck & Ruprecht, 1975); *Jesus* (Vandenhoeck & Ruprecht, 1968); *Der Begriff der Freiheit im Neuen Testament* (de Gruyter, 1966); and others. Mem: SNTS; Patristische Kommission der Oesterreichischen Akademie der Wissenschaften; Deutsche Wissenschaftliche Gesellschaft. Addr: (o) Universitaet Wien, Rooseveltplatz 10/10, A 1090 Wien, Austria 0222-435981; (h) Karlweisgasse 41/3/2, A 1180 Wien, Austria 0222-4725645.

NIEDNER, Frederick A., b. Lander, WY, May 5, 1945, s. of Frederick A. & Esther M. (Harting), m. Barbara (Crumpacker), chil: Joshua M.; Rebekah J.C.; Micah F.C. Educ: Concordia Sr. Coll., BA 1967; Concordia Sem., MDiv 1971, STM 1973; Christ Sem., ThD 1979. Emp: Valparaiso U., 1973- Prof. of Theol. Spec: Hebrew Bible, New Testament. Pub: "Rereading Matthew on Jerusalem and Judaism" *BTB* (1989); "Markan Baptismal Theology: Renaming the Markan Secret" *Currents* (1982); *Keeping the Faith: A Guide to the Christian Message*, co-auth. (Fortress, 1981). Mem: SBL; CSBR; MidW Jewish Stud. Assn.; NAPH. Addr: (o) Valparaiso U., Dept. of Theology, Valparaiso, IN 46383 219-464-5281; (h) 1402 Cross Creek Rd., Valparaiso, IN 46383 219-462-5161.

NIEHOFF, Maren, b. Germany, April 16, 1963, d. of Gerd & Ulla. Educ: Oxford U., PhD. Emp: Hebrew U., Lect. Spec: Hebrew Bible. Pub: *The Figure of Joseph in Post-biblical Jewish Literature* (Brill, 1992); "Do Biblical Characters Talk to Themselves? Narrative Modes of Representing Inner Speech in Early Biblical Fiction" *JBL* 111/4 (1992); "A Dream Which is Not Interpreted is Like a Letter Which is Not Read" *JJS* 43 (1992); "The Figure of Joseph in the Targums" *JJS* 34 (1988). Rec: Photography. Addr: (o) The Hebrew U. of Jerusalem, Dept. of Jewish Thought, Jerusalem, Israel 972-2-883605; (h) 17 Balfour St., Jerusalem 92102, Israel 972-2-619569.

NIELSEN, Helge K., b. Resen, June 25, 1937, s. of Emil K. & Marie K., m. Inge K., chil: Henrik; Thomas; Michael; Karin; Morten. Educ: Aarhus U., Grad. in Div. 1969, Doc. 1987. Emp: Aarhus U., Dept. of Bibl. Stud., Fac. of Theol., 1969- Asst. Prof. Spec: New Testament. Pub: *Hjertets Efterklang* (Kbh., 1992); *Heilung und Verkuendigung: Das Verstaendnis der Heilung und ihres Verhaeltnisses zur Verkuendigung bei Jesus und in der aeltesten Kirche* (Brill, 1987); *Nytestamentlig Graesk* (Aarhus, 1984); and others. Mem: SNTS. Addr: (o) Aarhus U., Det Teologiske Fakultet, DK-8000 C, Denmark 86136711; (h) Slotsparrken 10 A, DK-8410 Roende, Denmark 86371326.

NIELSEN, Kirsten, b. Svendborg, Denmark, October 12, 1943, d. of Else & Verner (Schroll), m. Leif. Educ: Aarhus U., Dip. Educ. 1970, Lic. Th. 1976, DTh 1985. Emp: Aarhus U., 1971- Lect.; *Religionsvidenskabeligt Tidsskrift*, 1983-84 Ed. Bd. Spec: Hebrew Bible. Pub: *Tematiske laesninger i Det gamle Testamente*, co-auth. (Gyldendal, 1973); *Yahweh as Prosecutor and Judge* (Sheffield, 1978); "Das Bild des Gerichts (rib-pattern) in Jes. I-XII. Eine Analyse der Beziehungen zwischen Bildsprache und dem Anliegen der Verkundigung" *VT* (1979); "Le Choix contre le droit dans le Livre de Ruth" *VT* (1985); *There is Hope for a Tree. The Tree as Metaphor in Isaiah* (Sheffield, 1989); *Satan— den fortabte son?* (Anis, 1991); and others. Rec: Family, literature, classical music. Addr: (o) Aarhus U., Det teologiske fakultet, 8000 Aarhus C., Denmark 86-136711; (h) Vagogade 5, 8200 Aarhus N, Denmark 86-162394.

NIGOSIAN, Solomon A., b. Egypt, April 23, 1932, s. of Abraham & Alice, m. Henaz, chil: Leo; Diana. Educ: McMaster U., Canada, MA 1970, PhD 1975. Emp: York U., Canada, 1971-73 Lect.; Ctr. Christian Stud., Canada, 1971-74 Lect.; U. of Toronto, 1972- Asst. Prof.; Ontario Coll. of Art, 1978-79 Lect. Spec: Hebrew Bible, Semitic Languages, Texts and Epigraphy. Pub: *Judaism* (Thorsons, 1986); *Occultism in the Old Testament* (Dorrance, 1978); "Zoroastrianism in Fifth Century Armenia" *Stud. in Relig.* 7/4 (1978); and others. Mem: AAR; CSSR; CSBS. Addr: (o) U. of Toronto, Victoria College, 73 Queen's Park Cr.,

Toronto, ON M5S 1K7, Canada 416-585-4572; (h) 140 Haddington Ave., Toronto, ON M5M 2P6, Canada 416-488-3609.

NIKAIDO, Scott K., b. Los Angeles, CA, January 14, 1956, s. of George & Haru, m. Heidi (Brown), chil: Apphia L.; David E. Educ: UCLA, BS 1982; U. of Judaism, MA 1989. Spec: Hebrew Bible. Pub: *Illustrated Dictionary and Concordance of the Bible*, contb. (Jerusalem Publishing House, 1986). Awd: U. of Judaism, Lewis E. Pennish Awd. 1985, Isaac Lipson Awd. 1987, Althea O. Silberman Awd. 1989; U. of Calif., Berkeley, Benjamin Goor Essay Prize 1993. Mem: SBL 1986-. Rec: Swimming, tennis. Addr: (o) U. of Calif. at Berkeley 250 Barrows Hall Berkeley, CA 94720; (h) 3040 Smyth Rd. #23-J, Berkeley, CA 94704 510-649-8313.

NITOWSKI, Eugenia L., b. San Diego, CA, July 17, 1949, d. of Carl F. & Carole (Downs). Educ: Loma Linda U., BA 1971; Andrews U., MA, Relig., Hist., Arch. 1973; U. Notre Dame, MA 1978, PhD 1979. Emp: Andrews U., Horn Arch. Mus., 1971-80 Asst. Cur., 1979-80 Dir., Student Projects in Arch. & Mus. Stud.; Mus. Assistance Prog., Jordan, 1977 Cons., Mus. Planning & Orgn.; U. of S Fla., 1988- Courtesy Prof., Relig.; Mount Carmel Project, Israel, 1987-92 Chief Arch., 1987- Ed., Preliminary Reports, Newsletter. Excv: Heshbon, Jordan, 1971, 1973 Asst. Sq. Supr., Photographer; Tell el-Hesi Exped., Israel, 1975 Asst. Photographer; Wymer Excvn., 1976-77, 1979 Asst. Dir., Aerial Photographer; Environmental Study of the Shroud, Jerusalem, 1986 Dir.; Mt. Carmel, Israel, 1987- Chief Arch. Spec: Archaeology, New Testament, Apocrypha and Post-biblical Studies. Pub: "Mount Carmel Project: Ongoing Report" *Carmelite Digest* 3 (1988-); *Luchnaria, Byzantine Greek Inscribed Lamps*, Andrews U. Mon. Ser. (1986); "Nuevas Excavaciones en el Wadi es-Siah, Monte Carmelo (Haifa)" *Monte Carmelo* 97/1; "New Evidence May Explain Image on Shroud of Turin," co-auth. *BAR* 12/4 (1986); "Rolling Stone Tomb F.1 at Tell Hesban" *AUSS* 18/1 (1980); "Inscribed and Radiated-Type Byzantine Lamps" *AUSS* 12/1 (1974); and others. Awd: Pont. Acad. Science, Official Citation 1987. Mem: ASOR. Rec: Astronomy, natural hist. Addr: (o) 1427 W Alder Rd., Salt Lake City, UT 84123 801-265-8873.

NOLAN, Brian M., b. Cork, Ireland, September 10, 1934, s. of Charles & Helen (Nagle). Educ: University Coll., Dublin, BA 1956; Angelicum, Rome, STL 1961; Pont. Bibl. Inst., Rome, SSL 1963; U. of Fribourg, Switzerland, STD 1975. Emp: All Hallows Coll., Dublin, 1970- Lect.; St. Patrick's Coll., Ireland, 1975-76, 1990-91 Vis. Lect.; Holy Cross Coll., Dublin, 1979 Vis. Lect.; Cath. Theol. U./De Andreis, 1984 Vis. Lect.; St. Thomas Sem., 1985-86 Vis. Lect. Spec: Hebrew Bible, New Testament. Pub: "The Figure of David as a Focus for the Christology of Matthew" *Scripture Bull.* 12 (1981); *The Royal Son of God: The Christology of Matthew 1-2 in the Setting of* *the Gospel* (Vandenhoeck & Ruprecht, 1979); "The Parousia and New Testament Eschatology" *Irish Theol. Quar.* 16 (1969). Mem: Irish Theol. Assn. 1968-; CBA 1979-. Rec: Walking, photography. Addr: (o) All Hallows College, Dublin 9, Ireland 01-373745.

NOLLAND, John L., b. Tamworth, Australia, February 17, 1947, s. of Reginald & Jean, m. Lisa, chil: David; Elizabeth. Educ: U. of New England, Australia, BSc 1967; Australian Coll. of Theol., ThL 1970; U. of London, BD 1971; U. of Cambridge, PhD 1977. Emp: Anglican Min., 1972-74; Regent Coll., Canada, 1978-86 Asst. Prof.; Trinity Coll., England, 1986- Lect., 1991- Vice Prin.; *Crux*, 1979-83 Ed. Spec: New Testament. Pub: *Luke 9:21-18:34*, Word Bibl. Comm. 35b (Word, 1993); *Luke 1-9:20*, Word Bibl. Comm. 35a (Word, 1989); "Grace as Power" *NT* 28 (1986); "Words of Grace (Luke 4, 22)" *Biblica* 65 (1984); "Uncircumcised Proselytes?" *JSJ* 12 (1981); "A Fresh Look at Acts 15:10" *NTS* 27 (1980); and others. Mem: SBL; IBR; CSBS. Addr: (o) Trinity College, Stoke Hill, Bristol, BS9 1JP, England 0272-682803; (h) 129 Reedley Rd., Stoke Bishop, Bristol, BS9 1BE, England 0272-684-053.

NORDLING, John G., b. Portland, OR, March 17, 1957, s. of Don G., m. Sara Anne. Educ: Concordia Coll., AA 1977; Valparaiso U., BA 1980; Concordia Sem., MDiv 1985; Washington U., St. Louis, MA, Class. 1985; U. of Wis.-Madison, PhD, Class. 1991. Emp: Grace English Evang. Luth. Ch., 1990- Pastor. Spec: New Testament. Pub: "*Onesimus Fugitivus*: A Defense of the Runaway Slave Hypothesis in Philemon" *JSNT* 41 (1991). Mem: APA 1987-; CSBR 1992-. Rec: Basketball, walks with my wife, gardening, running. Addr: (o) 2725 N Laramie, Chicago, IL 60639 312-637-1177; (h) 5139 W Parker, Chicago, IL 60639 312-622-0679.

NORTH, Robert, b. Iowa City, IA, March 25, 1916, s. of Grenville & Veva (Grady). Educ: St. Louis U., MA 1939; Pont. Bibl. Inst., Rome, SSD 1954. Emp: Marquette U., 1961-84 Prof.; St. Louis U., 1960-68 Prof.; *Theol. Digest*, 1961-82 Assoc Ed.; *Biblica*, 1968-85 Assoc. Ed.; *Elenchus of Biblica*, 1980- Ed. Excv: Jericho, 1952-53, Dhiban, Jordan, 1953, Byblos, Lebanon, 1953 Field Supr.; Teleilat Ghassul, Jordan, 1959-60 Dir. Spec: Archaeology, Hebrew Bible. Pub: *A History of Biblical Map Making* (Reichert, 1979); *Archeo-Biblical Egypt* (Bibl. Inst., 1967); *Ghassul 1960 Excavation Report* (Bibl. Inst., 1961); *Guide to Biblical Iran* (Bibl. Inst., 1956); "The Damascus of Qumran Geography" *PEQ* 87 (1955); and others. Mem: CBA 1960-, Pres. 1984. Addr: (o) Pontificio Instituto Biblico, Via Pilotta 25, Rome 00187, Italy 06-6701-6117.

NORTON, Gerard J., b. Dublin, Ireland, July 9, 1957, s. of James G. & Alice M. (Butler). Educ: U. Coll. Dublin, BA 1981, PhD, Semitic Lang.

1987; Angelicum, Rome, STL, Bibl. Theol. 1985; Pont. Bibl. Commn., BSS 1987, LSS 1988; Ecole Biblique, Jerusalem, Eleve titulaire 1987, Eleve dip. 1988. Emp: U. Coll. Dublin, 1981-83 Tutor, Class. Greek & Bibl. Hebrew, 1991-92 Vis. Lect.; Ecole Biblique, Jerusalem, 1987- Prof., Hebrew; Ecole Pratique des Hautes Etudes, Paris, 1991- Vis. Dir. of Stud.; *RB*, 1987- Ed. Bd.; *Scripture in Ch.*, 1991- Ed. Bd. Spec: Hebrew Bible, Semitic Languages, Texts and Epigraphy, Apocrypha and Post-biblical Studies. Pub: *Habakkuk 1: An Introduction, Sample Text, and Commentary*, co-auth. (Deutsch Bibelstiftung, 1992); "Psalm 2:11-12 and Modern Textual Criticism" *Proc. of the Irish Bibl. Assn.* 15 (1992); "St. Matthew and the Old Testament" *Scripture in Church* 64 (1986); "Cautionary Reflections on a Re-Edition of Fragment of Hexaplaric Material" in *Tradition of the Text*, Festschrift D. Barthelemy, OBO 109, co-ed. (Vandenhoeck & Ruprecht, 1991); and others. Mem: SBL; SOTS; Irish Bibl. Assn.; Natl. Bible Soc. of Ireland; CBA. Rec: Second-hand bookshops, European hist. & biography, hill-walking, theatre. Addr: (h) St Mary's Priory, Tallaght, Dublin 24, Ireland.

OAKMAN, Douglas E., b. Des Moines, IA, February 11, 1953, s. of Virgil Lee & Dorothy Jean (Rastovac), m. Deborah Lynn, chil: Justin Michael; Jonathan Edward. Educ: U. of Iowa, BA 1975; Christ Sem.-Seminex, MDiv 1979; Grad. Theol. Union, PhD 1986. Emp: Santa Clara U., 1986-87 Vis. Asst. Prof.; Pacific Luth. U., 1988- Asst. Prof. Spec: New Testament. Pub: "The Ancient Economy in the Bible: *BTB* Readers Guide" *BTB* 21 (1991); "The Countryside in Luke-Acts" in *The Social World of Luke-Acts* (Hendrickson, 1991); "Rulers' Houses, Thieves, and Usurpers: The Beelzebul Pericope" *Forum* 3 (1989); *Jesus and the Economic Questions of His Day* (Mellen, 1986); and others. Mem: SBL 1981-; CBA 1988-. Rec: Computer programming, music, train photography. Addr: (o) Pacific Lutheran U., Religion Dept., 121st & Park Ave., Tacoma, WA 98447 206-535-7317; (h) 870-120th St. S., Tacoma, WA 98444 206-537-2376.

O'BRIEN, Julia M., b. Raleigh, NC, November 13, 1958, d. of Harold & Aileen Myers, chil: Anna Catherine. Educ: Wake Forest U., BA, Relig. 1981; Duke Div. Sch., MDiv 1984; Duke U., PhD, Hebrew Bible/Semitics 1988. Emp: U. of N.C.-Chapel Hill, 1985-87 Vis. Lect.; Duke Div. Sch., 1988 Vis. Instr.; Meredith Coll., 1989- Asst. Prof. Spec: Hebrew Bible, Semitic Languages, Texts and Epigraphy. Pub: Articles in *ABD* (Doubleday, 1992); *Priest and Levite in Malachi*, SBL Diss. Ser. 121 (1990); "Because God Heard My Voice: The Individual Thanksgiving Psalm and Vow-Fulfillment" in *The Listening Heart: Essays in Wisdom and the Psalms in Honor of Roland Murphy*, JSOTSup 58 (1987). Awd: Duke U., Andrew Mellon Graduate Fellow. 1987-88. Mem: SBL; ASOR; CBA. Addr: (o) Meredith College, Dept. of Relig., 3800 Hillsborough St., Raleigh, NC

27607 919-829-8559; (h) 3136 Morningside Dr., Raleigh, NC 27607 919-787-7575.

O'CALLAGHAN, Martinez José, b. Tortosa, Tarragona, Spain, October 7, 1922, s. of Juan & Concepcion. Educ: U. of Murcia, Lic. in Phil. & Letters 1957; U. of Madrid, PhD 1959; U. degli Studi, Milan, D. of Letters 1960. Emp: Faculty de Teologia de Barcelona, 1961-72 Prof.; Pont. Inst. Bibl., Rome, 1971- Decano; *Studia Papyrologica*, 1962-83 Dir.; *Papyrologica Castroctaviana*, 1967-88 Dir.; *Estudis de Papirologia i Filologia Bibl.*, 1991- Dir. Spec: Semitic Languages, Texts and Epigraphy. Pub: "El Fondo papirologico Palau-Ribes (Sant Cugat del Valles-Barcelona)" *Aula Orientalis* (1984); "Theocrite I 31-35, 73-78 (P. Berl. inv. 17073)" *Chronique d'Egypte* (1975); *Cartas cristianas griegas del siglo V* (1963); *Las tres categorias esteticas de la cultura clasica* (1960); and others. Awd: Premio "Meneadez Pelayo" 1958. Mem: Found; Egyptologique Reine Elisabeth; Assn. Intl. de Papyrologues. Rec: Music. Addr: (o) Seminari de Papirologia, Llaseres 30, 08190 Sant Cugat del Vallès, Spain 674-1150.

OCHS, Peter W., b. Boston, MA, January 26, 1950, s. of Sidney & Ruth, m. Vanessa (Yablin), chil: Juliana; Elizabeth. Educ: Yale Coll., BA, Anthrop. (summa cum laude) 1971; Jewish Theol. Sem., MA, Jewish Thought 1975; Yale U., PhD 1980. Emp: Colgate U., 1979-86 Asst. Prof., Dept. of Phil. & Relig.; Yale U., 1986-88 Post-Doc. Fellow; Hebrew U., Fulbright Sr. Lect. 1988; Drew U., 1988- Wallerstein Assoc. Prof. of Jewish Stud.; *Postmodern Jewish Phil. Bitnetwork*, Ed. Spec: Hebrew Bible, Apocrypha and Post-biblical Studies. Pub: "Rabbini Semiotics" *Amer. Jour. of Semiotics* Fall (1992); "Postcritical Scriptural Interpretation" in *Torah and Revelation* (Mellen, 1992); "Rabbinic Text Process Theology" *Jewish Thought* 1/1 (1991); "A Rabbinic Pragmatism" in *Theology and Dialogue* (U. of Notre Dame, 1990); *Under-standing the Rabbinic Mind: Essays on the Hermeneutic of Max Kadushin*, ed., contb. (Scholars, 1990); "Scriptural Pragmatism: Jewish Philosophy's Conception of Truth" *Intl. Phil. Quar.* 26/2 (1986); and others. Awd: Kent Fellow. 1974-77; Spencer Found. Grant 1987-88; AAR, Collaborative Res. Grant 1990-91; Ctr. of Theol. Inquiry, Invited Mem. 1992. Mem: Amer. Phil. Assn. 1978-; AAR 1979-; Assn. for Relig. in Intellectual Life 1981-; AJS 1982-; Acad. for Jewish Phil. 1984-. Rec: Sports coaching, wildflowers. Addr: (o) Drew U., Dept. of Religion, Madison, NJ 07940 201-408-3222; (h) 57 Fairmount Ave., Morristown, NJ 07960 201-984-3913.

O'CONNELL, Kevin G., b. Boston, MA, May 22, 1938, s. of George & Mary (Cohan). Educ: Boston Coll., MA 1963; Weston Coll., PhL 1963; Harvard U., PhD 1968; Weston Sch. of Theol., MDiv 1969; Ordained Priest 1969. Emp: *CBQ*, 1969-75 Assoc. Ed.; Weston Sch. of Theol., 1971-80 Assoc. Prof.; Harvard Div. Sch., 1972-80 Vis. Lect.; Albright Inst. Arch. Res.,

Jerusalem, 1980-81 Ann. Prof., Res. Assoc.; John Carroll U., 1981-87 Assoc. Prof., Chmn., Relig. Stud.; *BR*, 1987- Ed. Adv. Bd.; Le Moyne Coll., 1988- Pres., Prof. Excv: Joint Arch. Expdn. to Tell ed-Hesi, Israel, 1971- Bd. Chmn., Gen. Ed., Pub. Ser. Spec: Archaeology, Hebrew Bible, Semitic Languages, Texts and Epigraphy. Pub: "Continuity and Change in Israel's Covenant with God" *BR* 1/4 (1985); "The List of Seven Peoples in Canaan: A Fresh Analysis" in *The Answers Lie Below: Essays in Honor of Lawrence Edmund Toombs* (U. Press of Amer., 1984); "Tell el-Hesi, 1979," co-auth., *PEQ* 112 (1980); "Tell el-Hesi, 1977," co-auth., *PEQ* 110 (1978); *Theodotionic Revision of the Book of Exodus* (Harvard U.P., 1972); and others. Awd: Harvard U. Fellow. 1964-65. Mem: ASOR 1964-; CBA 1964-; SBL 1964-; IOSCS 1968-; AIAR 1982-. Rec: Handball, science fiction. Addr: (o) Le Moyne College, Office of the President, Syracuse, NY 13214-1399 315-445-4120; (h) Le Moyne College, Syracuse, NY 13214-1399 315-445-4638.

O'CONNELL, Robert H., b. Kitchener, ON, Canada, December 4, 1955, s. of Joan Houston (Molloy) & Ronald John, m. Mina Maria (Fain), chil: Nathan Houston. Educ: Dallas Theol. Sem., ThM 1982, ThD 1989; U. of Cambridge, PhD 1993. Emp: Dallas Bible Coll., 1983-85 Instr.; Romsey House Theol. Train. Coll., Cambridge, 1989-90 Instr.; U. of Cambridge, Faculty of Div., 1990-91 Instr.; Colo. Christian U., 1991-93 Asst. Prof., Bibl. Stud. Spec: Hebrew Bible. Pub: "Deuteronomy ix 7-x 7, 10-11: Panelled Structure, Double Rehearsal and the Rhetoric of Covenant Rebuke" *VT* 42/4 (1992); "Deuteronomy vii 1-26: Assymetrical Concentricity and the Rhetoric of Conquest" *VT* 42/2 (1992); "Proverbs vii 16-17: A Case of Fatal Deception in a 'Woman and the Window' Type-Scene" *VT* 41/2 (1991); "Deuteronomy viii 1-20: Asymmetrical Concentricity and the Rhetoric of Providence" *VT* 40/4 (1990); "Isaiah xiv 4b-23: Ironic Reversal through Concentric Structure and Mythic Allusion" *VT* 38/4 (1988); and others. Mem: SBL 1984-93. Rec: Hiking in the Colorado Rockies. Addr: (o) Colorado Christian U., 180 S Garrison St., Lakewood, CO 80226 303-238-5386; (h) 2352 S Garrison St., Denver, CO 80210-5025 303-778-8358.

O'CONNOR, Michael Patrick, b. Lackawanna, NY, April 7, 1950, s. of John & Anna (Crosta). Educ: British Columbia U., Canada, MA 1972; Michigan U., AM 1974, PhD 1977. Spec: Hebrew Bible, Semitic Languages, Texts and Epigraphy. Pub: *Hebrew Verse Structure* (Eisenbrauns, 1980); *Introduction to Biblical Hebrew Syntax*, co-auth. (Eisenbrauns, 1990); and others. Addr: (o) U. of St. Thomas, Saint Paul Seminary School of Divinity, St. Paul, MN 55105-1096 612-647-5715.

ODELL, Margaret S., b. Norfolk, VA, January 18, 1955, d. of Earl H. & Margaret W. Educ: Meredith Coll., BA 1977; Yale Div. Sch., MAR

1979; U. of Pittsburgh, PhD 1988. Emp: Hollins Coll., 1988-89 Asst. Prof., Relig.; Converse Coll., 1989- Asst. Prof., Relig. Spec: Hebrew Bible, New Testament. Pub: "An Exploratory Study of Shame and Dependence in the Bible and Selected Near Eastern Parallels" in *The Biblical Canon in Comparative Perspective*, Scripture in Context IV (Mellen, 1991). Mem: SBL 1984-. Addr: (o) Converse College, Dept. of Religion & Philosophy, Spartanburg, SC 29302 803-596-9106; (h) 126 Ponce de Leon Ave., Spartanburg, SC 29302 803-583-4604.

ODEN, Robert A., Jr., b. Vermillion, SD, September 11, 1946, s. of Robert A. & Ardelle, m. Teresa (Johnston), chil: Robert A., III; Katharine A. Educ: Harvard Coll., AB 1969; Cambridge U., Pembroke Coll., BA 1971, MA 1975; Harvard Div. Sch., ThM 1972; Harvard U., PhD 1975. Emp: Harvard U., 1971-74 Teaching Fellow, Near East. Lang. & OT; Dartmouth Coll., 1975-81 Asst. Prof., 1981-85 Assoc. Prof., 1983-89 Prof., Relig., 1988-89 Dir. of Hum. Inst.; U. of Va., 1984- Vis. Assoc. Prof., Relig. Stud.; Hotchkiss Sch., 1989- Headmaster; *Semeia*, 1984-90 Assoc. Ed. Spec: Hebrew Bible. Pub: *The Bible Without Theology* (Harper & Row, 1987); "The Place of Covenant in the Religion of Israel" in *Ancient Israelite Religion: Essays in Honor of Frank Moore Cross* (Fortress, 1987); "Intellectual History and the Study of the Bible" in *The Future of Biblical Studies* (Scholars, 1987); *The Syrian Goddess (De Dea Syria)*, SBL Texts & Trans., Greco-Roman Relig. Ser. vol. 1, co-ed., trans. (Scholars, 1976, 1986); "Jacob as Father, Husband and Nephew: Kinship Studies and the Patriarchal Narratives" *JBL* 102/2 (1983); "Divine Aspirations in Atrahasis and in Genesis 1-11" *ZAW* 93/2 (1981); *Philo of Byblos: The Phoenician History*, CBQ Mon. Ser. 9, co-auth. (1981); "Theoretical Assumptions in the Study of Ugaritic Myths" *MAARAV* 2/1 (1979); *Studies in Lucian's De Dea Syria*, HSM 14 (Scholars, 1977); and others. Awd: NEH Stipend 1979; Dartmouth Coll., MA 1987. Mem: SBL; AAR, V.P., New England reg. 1989-90. Rec: Fly fishing. Addr: (o) The Hotchkiss School, Route 112, Lakeville, CT 06039 203-435-2591.

OEGEMA, Gerbern S., b. Dokkum, The Netherlands, June 4, 1958, s. of J. &. A. Oegema. Educ: Vrije U., Amsterdam, Kand. 1983, ThD 1985; Freie U., Berlin, MA 1988, PhD 1989. Emp: Vrije U., 1984-85 Asst. Lbrn. Hum., 1986 Lect., Bibl. Stud.; Freie U., 1987-90 Lect., Jewish Stud.; W.W. U. Munster, 1992- Lect., Jewish Stud. Spec: New Testament, Apocrypha and Post-biblical Studies. Pub: *Der Gesalbte und sein Volk: Untersuchungen zum Konzeptualisierungsprozess der messianischen Erwartungen von den Makkabaern bis Bar Kosiba* (Vandenhoeck & Ruprecht, 1993); *De messias in talmoed en midrasj* (Ten Have, 1993); *De Davidster: De geschiedenis van een symbool* (Ten Have, 1992); *De messiaanse verwachtingen ten tijde van Jezus* (Ten Have, 1991); *De bijbel van toen: een boek* *voor nu?* (Ten Have, 1990). Awd: Vrije U., Fellow. 1983, 1989; Freie U., 1986-88. Mem: AAR 1985-; SBL 1985-; Franz Dilitzsch Gesellschaft 1991-; Verband der Judaisten in der B.R.D. 1991-. Addr: (o) W.W. U. Munster, Institutum Judaicum, Wilmergasse 1-4, 4400 Munster, Germany 0251-832561; (h) Lippestrasse 42, 4270 Dorsten 1, Germany 02362-27063.

OGDEN, Graham S., b. Sydney, Australia, July 17, 1938, s. of Sydney W. & Madge, m. Lois Emily (Wilson), chil: Melissa Anne; Timothy Chad. Educ: U. of Sydney, BA 1957; Moore Theol. Coll., ThL 1961; U. of London, BD 1962; U. of Durham, MLitt 1964; Princeton Theol. Sem., PhD 1975. Emp: Trinity Theol. Coll., Singapore, 1968-72 Lect.; United Theol. Coll., Australia, 1976-78 Lect.; Taiwan Theol. Coll., 1978-85 Prof., OT, 1982-85 Acad. Dean; *Taiwan Jour. of Theol.*, Ed.; United Bible Soc., 1985- Trans. Cons. Spec: Hebrew Bible. Pub: "The Use of Figurative Language in Malachi 2:10-16" *Bible Trans.* 39 (1988); *Qoheleth* (JSOT, 1987); *Joel* (Eerdmans, 1987); *Jonah*, co-auth. (Yung Wang, 1985); "Joel 4 and Prophetic Responses to National Laments" *JSOT* 26 (1983); "Qoheleth's Use of the 'Nothing-is-Better' Form" *JBL* 98 (1979); "Moses and Cyrus" *VT* 28 (1978); "Time and the Verb *hayah* in Old Testament Prose" *VT* 21 (1971); and others. Mem: SBL. Rec: Reading, gardening, travel. Addr: (h) RMB 18 Bingley Way, Wamboin, NSW 2620, Australia 06-238-3266.

OLBRICHT, Thomas H., b. Thayer, MO, November 3, 1929, s. of Benjamin & Agnes (Taylor), m. Dorothy (Kiel), chil: Suzanne; Eloise; Joel; Adele; Erica. Educ: U. of Iowa, MA 1953, PhD 1959; Harvard U., STB 1962. Emp: Harding Coll., 1954-55 Asst. Prof., Dir. of Forensics; U. of Dubuque, 1955-59 Asst. Prof., Dept. Chmn.; Pa. State U., 1962-67 Assoc. Prof.; Abilene Christian U., 1967 Prof., Dean of Coll. of Liberal & Fine Arts; Pepperdine U., 1986- Chair, Relig. Div. Spec: New Testament. Pub: "An Aristotelian Rhetorical Analysis of I Thessalonians" in *Greeks, Romans and Christians* (Fortress, 1991); and others. Mem: AAR, Pres., SW Reg. 1976-77; SBL. Addr: (o) Pepperdine U., Malibu, CA 90263 310-456-4352.

OLLEY, John W., b. Sydney, Australia, July 26, 1938, s. of John & Dorothy (Allison), m. Elaine (Waugh), chil: David; Linda; Catherine. Educ: U. of Sydney, Australia, BSc 1959, PhD 1963; Baptist Theol. Coll. of New S Wales, Australia, BD 1965; Melbourne Coll. of Div., ThM 1975. Spec: Hebrew Bible. Pub: "'Righteous' and Wealthy? The Description of the *saddiq* in Wisdom Literature" *Colloquium: Australia-New Zealand Theol. Rev.* 22/2 (1990); "'Righteousness'—Some Issues in Old Testament Translation into English" *Bible Trans.* 38 (1987); "Notes on Isaiah xxxii 1, xlv 19, 23 and lxiii 1" *VT* 33:4 (1983); *'Righteousness' in the Septuagint of Isaiah* (Scholars, 1979);

"Leadership: Some Biblical Perspectives" *SE Asia Jour. of Theol.* 18/1 (1977); and others. Mem: SBL 1973-; IOSCS 1974-; ASOR 1984-. Rec: Crossword puzzles, music. Addr: (o) Baptist Theological College of Western Australia, 20 Hayman Rd., Bentley 6102 Australia 09-361-9962.

OLSON, Dennis T., b. Luverne, MN, January 6, 1954, s. of Toby & Esther, m. Carol, chil: Eric; Kristen. Educ: Augustana Coll., BA (summa cum laude) 1976; Luther Theol. Sem., MDiv 1980; Yale U., MA 1981, PhD 1984. Emp: Yale Div. Sch., 1981-82 Teaching Fellow, 1983 Instr., Hebrew; United Luth. Ch., 1984-87 Pastor; Luther NW Theol. Sem., 1985-87 Instr.; Princeton Theol. Sem., Asst. Prof., OT. Spec: Hebrew Bible. Pub: *Saints and Sojourners: An Old Testament Journey* (Augsburg/Fortress, 1990); "The Book of Numbers" in *HBC* (Harper & Row, 1988); "Biblical Perspectives on the Land" *Word & World* (1986); *The Death of the Old and the Birth of the New, The Framework of the Book of Numbers and the Pentateuch* (Scholars, 1985); and others. Mem: SBL. Rec: Woodcarving. Addr: (o) Princeton Theological Seminary, CN 821, Princeton, NJ 08542 609-497-7769; (h) 56 N Main St., Pennington, NJ 08534 609-737-8066.

OLSON, Howard S., b. St. Paul, MN, July 18, 1922, s. of Oscar L. & Clara J., m. A. Louise, chil: Howard Joseph; Sharon; Timothy; Linda. Educ: Gustavus Adolphus Coll., BA 1943; Augustana Theol. Sem., MDiv 1946; Hartford Sem. Found., PhD 1965. Emp: Luth. Theol. Coll., Tanzania, 1964-88 Prof. Emeritus; Pacific Luth. Theol. Sem., Berkeley, 1977-78 Vis. NT Prof.; *Africa Theol. Jour.*, 1982-88 Ed.; Luth. Sch. of Theol., Chicago, 1986 Vis. Prof.; Wartburg Theol. Sem., 1988-91 Prof., NT, Missiology. Spec: New Testament. Pub: *Teach Yourself NT Greek* (Central Tanganyika, 1972, 1985); "Theology as a Linguistic Discipline" *Africa Theol. Jour.* 13 (1984); and others. Awd: Gustavus Adolphus Coll., Dr. of Letters 1970; Luth. Sch. of Theol., Outstanding Alumnus 1978; Luth. Theol. Coll., Makumira, festschrift, *Essential Essays on Theology in Africa* 1988. Mem: SBL 1988-. Rec: Mountain climbing, swimming, hiking. Addr: (o) 1925 Grand Cypress Ln., Sun City Center, FL 33573 813-634-8022.

OLSSON, Birger O., b. Harnosand, May 11, 1938, s. of Petrus & Birgitta, m. Lena (Malmgren), chil: Stefan; Kristina; Martin. Educ: Fil.Mag. 1963; Theol.Lic. 1967; ThD 1974. Emp: Dept. of Educ., 1963-78 Trans.; Johannelunds Teologiska Inst., 1963-71 Tchr., NT & Greek, 1987-88 Acting Prin.; U. of Uppsala, 1978-87 Docent, NT; Swedish Evang. Mission, 1988-92 Dir.; U. of Lund, 1992- Prof., NT. Spec: New Testament. Pub: "A Decade of Text-Linguistic Analysis of Biblical Texts at Uppsala" *Studia Theologica* 39 (1985); *Structure and Meaning in the Fourth Gospel* (Gleerup, 1974); and others. Mem: SNTS

1976-. Rec: Music. Addr: (o) Lunds U., Teologiska institionen, Allhelgona Kyrkogata 8, 223 62 Lund, Sweden 046-104339; (h) Warholms väg 6A, S-22465 Lund, Sweden 046-152586.

OMANSON, Roger L., b. Kewanee, IL, August 6, 1946, s. of Roland G. & Mary E., m. Marsha Elaine (Kiesow), chil: Cara Nicole; Aaron Jay. Educ: Ill. State U., BA 1968; South. Bapt. Theol. Sem., MDiv 1971, PhD 1975. Emp: United Bible Soc., 1975-79 Trans. Cons., West Africa, 1987- Inter-reg. Trans. Cons.; South. Bapt. Theol. Sem., 1979-87 Assoc. Prof., NT. Spec: New Testament. Pub: "Dynamic Equivalence Translations Reconsidered" *Theol. Stud.* 51 (1990); "The Role of Women in the New Testament Church" *Rev. & Expositor* 83 (1986); "Translations: Text and Interpretation" *EQ* 57 (1985); "The Church" in *Evangelical Dict. of Theology* (Baker, 1984); "A Perspective on the Study of the New Testament Text" *BT* 34 (1983). Mem: SBL; Linguistic Soc. of Amer. Rec: Running, magic. Addr: (h) 1519 Lynndale Dr., Jeffersonville, IN 47130 812-288-8893.

O'NEILL, John C., b. Melbourne, Australia, December 8, 1930, s. of J.A. & B.A. (Cochrane), m. Judith, chil: Rachel; Catherine; Philippa. Educ: U. of Melbourne, BA 1951; Melbourne Coll. of Div., Australia, BD 1954; U. of Cambridge, PhD 1959. Emp: U. of Melbourne 1952-55 Sr. Tutor; Ormond Coll., Australia, 1959-64 Lect.; Westminster Coll., England, 1964-85 Dunn Prof. of NT Lang., Lit. & Theol.; U. of Edinburgh, New Coll., 1975-77 Cunningham Lect., 1985- Prof. of NT Lang., Lit. & Theol. Spec: New Testament, Apocrypha and Post-biblical Studies. Pub: *The Bible's Authority: A Portrait Gallery of Thinkers from Lessing to Bultmann* (T & T Clark, 1991); "The Unforgivable Sin" *JSNT* 19 (1983); *Paul's Letter to the Romans* (Penguin, 1975); *The Recovery of Paul's Letter to the Galatians* (SPCK, 1972); and others. Mem: SNTS. Addr: (o) U. of Edinburgh, New College, The Mound, Edinburgh EH1 2LX, Scotland 031-225-8400.

ONUKI, Takashi, b. Hamamatsu-shi, Japan, April 26, 1945, s. of Sakutaro & Toyo (Oguri), m. Yuko (Abe), chil: Yoshiya; Aogu. Educ: U. of Tokyo Grad. Sch., MA 1972; U. Munchen, ThD 1979. Emp: Tokyo Women's Christian U., 1980-82 Lect., 1982-91 Assoc. Prof.; U. of Tokyo, 1991- Assoc. Prof.; *Ann. of the Japanese Bibl. Inst.*, 1990- Co-ed. Spec: New Testament, Egyptology, Apocrypha and Post-biblical Studies. Pub: *Gnosis und Stoa: Eine Untersuchung zum Apokryphon des Johannes*, NTOA 9 (1991); *Studies in the Gospels and Sociology of Literature* (Iwanami-shoten, 1991); "Traditionsgeschichte von Thomas 17 und ihre christologische relevanz" in *Anfaenge der Christologie*, F. Hahn Festschrift (1991); "Wiederkehr des weiblichen Erloesers Barbelo-Pronoia: Zur Verhaeltnisbestimmung der Kurz und Langversionen des Apokryphon des Johannes"

Ann. of the Japanese Bibl. Inst. 13 (1988); *Gemeinde und Welt im Johannesevangelium*, WMANT 56 (1984); "Zur literatursoziologischen Analyse des Johannesevangeliums: Auf dem Wege yur Methodenintegration" *Ann. of the Japanese Bibl. Inst.* 8 (1982); "Die Johanneischen Abschiedsreden und die synoptische Tradition" *Ann. of the Japanese Bibl. Inst.* 3 (1977); and others. Awd: Soc. for Stud. in Relig. of Japan, Year Awd. 1985. Mem: Intl. Assn. of Manichaean Stud. 1983-; SNTS 1991-; Japanese Bibl. Inst. 1972-. Addr: (o) U. of Tokyo, Faculty of General Arts & Sciences, 3-8-1 Komaba, Meguro-ku, Tokyo 153, Japan 03-3467-1171; (h) Seibu Green Hill 9-104, Kamifujisawa 406, Iruma-shi 358, Japan 0429-65-2391.

OOSTHUIZEN, Martin J., b. Durban, South Africa, October 22, 1953, s. of Marthinus & Juliet, m. Gardi, chil: Louzanne; Marthinus Jacobus. Educ: U. of Stellenbosch, BA 1975, BTh 1979, BA 1980, MTh 1984; U. of South Africa, DTh 1989. Emp: U. of Fort Hare, 1982-86 Lect.; U. of South Africa, 1987-89 Sr. Lect.; U. of Port Elizabeth, 1990- Assoc. Prof. Spec: Hebrew Bible. Pub: "Divine Insecurity and Joban Heroism: A Reading of the Narrative Framework of Job" *OT Essays* 4/3 (1991); "Exodus 4:21-23: A Fusion of Two Narrative Voices" *OT Essays* 1/3 (1989); "Scripture and Context: The Use of the Exodus Theme in the Hermeneutics of Liberation Theology" *Scriptura* 25 (1988); "Some Thoughts on the Interpretation of Exodus 4:24-26" *OTWSA* 29 (1986). Mem: OT Soc. of South. Africa 1983-; South. African Bibl. Stud. Soc. 1982-; SBL 1991-. Rec: Running, swimming, stamp-collecting. Addr: (o) U. of Port Elizabeth, Dept. of Biblical Studies, PO Box 1600, Port Elizabeth 6000, South Africa 041-504-2152; (h) 7 Erasmus Dr., Summerstrand, Port Elizabeth 6001, South Africa 041-532706.

ORCHARD, Dom J. Bernard, b. Bromley, England, May 3, 1910, s. of Henslow & Madge. Emp: U. of Dallas, 1976-78 Vis. Prof. Spec: New Testament. Pub: *The Order of the Synoptics* (Mercer U.P., 1987); *Synopsis of the Four Gospels in Greek* (Edinburgh, 1983); *Synopsis of the Four Gospels in English* (Mercer U.P., 1982); "Why Three Synoptic Gospels?" *Irish Theol. Quar.* 46/4 (1979). Mem: SNTS 1961-. Addr: (h) Ealing Abbey, Ealing W5 2DY, London, England 081-998-2158.

OREN, Eliezer D., b. Petah-Tiqva, Palestine, January 22, 1938, s. of Menasheh & Bella (Hornstein), m. Shulamith, chil: Yarden; Kineret. Educ: Hebrew U., Jerusalem, BA 1963; U. of Pa., MA 1966; U. of London, PhD 1969. Emp: Dept. of Antiquities, Israel, 1969-71 Field Arch.; U. of Haifa, 1971-72 Lect.; Ben Gurion U., 1970- Assoc. Prof., Chmn., Arch. Div., 1986-87 Chmn., Dept. of Bible & Anc. Near East. Stud.; Harvard U., 1980-81 Res. Schol.; U. of Pa., 1988, 1991-92 Vis. Prof. Excv:

Jerusalem, Tiberias, Acre, 1969-71 Dir.; Tel Sera, 1972-78 Dir.; North Sinai Survey, 1972-82 Dir.; Land of Gerar, 1981- Dir. Spec: Archaeology, Egyptology. Pub: "The Necropolis of Maresha-Beit Govrin" *IEJ* 34 (1984); "Migdol—A New Fortress on the Edge of the Eastern Nile Delta" *BASOR* 256 (1984); "Ziklag—A Biblical City on the Edge of the Negev" *BA* (1982); "Chalcolithic Sites in Northeast Sinai" *Tel Aviv* 8 (1981); *The Northern Cemetary of Beth Shan* (Brill, 1973); and others. Mem: IES; ASOR; Amer. Res. Ctr. Egypt; PEF. Rec: Photography, music. Addr: (o) Ben Gurion U., Archaeology Division, Box G53, Beer-Sheva 84105, Israel 057-461091; (h) 9 Sigalon St., Omer 84965, Israel 057-469701.

ORNAN, Tallay, b. Jerusalem, Israel, January 14, 1951, s. of Uzzi & Shoshana, m. Nama. Educ: Hebrew U., BA, MA, Arch. Emp: Rockefeller Mus., Cur.; Israel Mus., West. Asiatic Antiq., Cur. Spec: Archaeology. Pub: "The Dayan Collection" *Israel Mus. Jour.* 2 (1982). Addr: (o) Israel Museum, Jerusalem, Israel 02-708885; (h) 17 Bethlehem Rd., Jerusalem, Israel 02-722758.

OSBORN, Noel D., b. Columbus, OH, December 25, 1927, s. of Rev. C. D. & Marjorie (Sain), m. Emma (Anderson), chil: Philip; Cynthia. Educ: Evang. Theol. Sem., BD 1953; Vanderbilt U., PhD 1978. Emp: Union Christian Coll., 1956-66 Prof.; Interconfessional Trans. of Bible into Ilokano, 1967-73 Coord.; United Bible Soc., 1975- Trans. Cons.; United Theol. Sem., 1986-87, 1992- Adj. Prof. Spec: Hebrew Bible. Pub: "Tent or Tabernacle: Translating Two Traditions" *BT* (1990); "This is My Name Forever: 'I AM' or 'Yahweh'?" *BT* (1988); "Circumspection About Circumcision in Exodus 4:24-26" in *Issues in Bible Translation*, UBS Mon. Ser. (1988); "Principles of Dynamic Equivalence" *The Ilocos Rev.* 14 (1982); "The Wider Context" *BT* (1978); and others. Mem: SBL. Rec: Reading, painting, sculpture. Addr: (o) Philippine Bible Society, 890 United Nations Ave., PO Box 755, Manila 575751, Philippines; (h) 602 E Cooke Rd., Columbus, OH 43214 614-261-9056.

OSBORNE, Grant R., b. New York, NY, July 7, 1942, s. of Thomas & Clara, m. Nancy (Hardy), chil: Amber; Susanne. Educ: Trinity Evang. Div. Sch., MA 1971; U. of Aberdeen, Scotland, PhD 1974. Emp: Winnipeg Theol. Sem., Canada, 1974-77; Trinity Evang. Div. Sch., 1977- Assoc. Prof.; *TSF Bull.*, 1979- Ed.; InterVarsity Press NT Comm. Ser., Gen. Ed. Spec: New Testament. Pub: *The Hermeneutical Spiral: A Comprehensive Introduction to Biblical Interpretation* (InterVarsity, 1991); "Christology and New Testament Hermeneutics" *Semeia* 30 (1985); *The Resurrection Narratives: A Redactional Study* (Baker, 1984); *Handbook for Bible Study*, co-auth. (Baker, 1979); and others. Mem: SBL 1977-; IBR 1979-. Rec: Reading, travel. Addr: (o) Trinity Evangelical Divinity School, 2065 Half Day Rd., Deerfield,

IL 60015 312-945-8800; (h) 743 Garfield Rd., Libertyville, IL 60048 312-680-8813.

OSBURN, Carroll D., b. Arkansas City, KS, September 2, 1941, s. of Jessie & Mattie, m. Linda, chil: Heather; Valerie. Educ: Harding Grad. Sch. of Relig., MTh 1968; Vanderbilt U., DDiv 1970; U. of St. Andrews, Scotland, PhD 1974. Emp: Harding Grad. Sch. of Relig., 1973-83 Prof.; Pepperdine U., 1983-87 Prof., Relig.; U. of St. Andrews, Scotland, 1980 Vis. Prof.; Abilene Christian U., 1987- Disting. Prof. Spec: New Testament. Pub: *The Peaceable Kingdom* (1992); "Discourse Analysis and Jewish Apocalyptic in the Epistle of Jude" in *Linguistics and New Testament Interpretation* (1992); "The Search for the Original Text of Acts" *JSNT* 44 (1991); and others. Mem: SBL; Assn. Intl. d'Etudes Patristiques. Rec: Seaplane & acrobatic pilot. Addr: (o) ACU Station, PO Box 8425, Abilene, TX 79699.

OSIEK, Carolyn A., b. St. Charles, MO, June 11, 1940. Educ: Manhattanville Coll., MAT 1966; Harvard U., ThD 1978. Emp: Maryville Coll., 1974-76 Lect.; Harvard Div. Sch., 1976-77 Res. Assoc.; Cath. Theol. Union, 1977- Prof., NT; *The Bible Today*, 1978- Assoc. Ed.; *CBQ*, 1985-88 Assoc. Ed., 1988- NT Book Rev. Ed. Spec: New Testament, Apocrypha and Post-biblical Studies. Pub: *What Are They Saying About the Social Setting of the New Testament?* (Paulist, 1992); "The Feminist and the Bible: Hermeneutical Alternatives" in *Feminist Perspectives on Biblical Scholarship* (Scholars, 1985); *Rich and Poor in the Shepherd of Hermas: An Exegetical-Social Investigation*, CBQ Mon. Ser. (CBA, 1983); *Galatians*, NT Message Ser. (Glazier, 1980); and others. Mem: SBL; CBA; CSBR; SNTS. Addr: (o) Catholic Theological Union, 5401 Cornell Ave., Chicago, IL 60615 312-324-8000.

OSWALT, John N., b. Mansfield, OH, June 21, 1940, s. of Glenn & Mildred, m. Karen, chil: Elizabeth; Andrew; Peter. Educ: Asbury Theol. Sem., BD 1960, ThM 1965; Brandeis U., MA 1965, PhD 1968. Emp: Barrington Coll., 1968-70 Assoc. Prof.; Asbury Theol. Sem., 1970-82 Prof., 1989- Prof.; Asbury Coll., 1983-85 Pres.; Trinity Evang. Div. Sch., 1986-89 Prof.; United Wesleyan Coll., 1979 Dieter Lec.; Point Loma Nazarene Coll., 1988 Wiley Lect. Spec: Hebrew Bible, Mesopotamian Studies, Egyptology, Apocrypha and Post-biblical Studies. Pub: "God's Determination to Save His People" *Rev. & Expositor* (1991); *The Wesley Bible*, OT ed. (Nelson, 1990); "Golden Calves and the 'Bull of Jacob'" *Israel's Apostasy and Restoration* (1988); *Isaiah* (Eerdmans, 1986); "Recent Studies in Old Testament Eschatology and Apocalyptic" *JETS* (1981); "A Case for Biblical Authority" *Asbury Seminarian* (1977); and others. Mem: SBL; IBR; WTS. Rec: Reading, model railroading. Addr: (o) Asbury Theological Seminary, Wilmore, KY 40390 606-858-3581; (h) 135 Lowry Ln. Wilmore, KY 40390.

O'TOOLE, Robert F., b. St. Louis, MO, June 20, 1936, s. of Mr. & Mrs. William F. Educ: St. Louis U., MA, PhL 1961, STL 1968; Pont. Bibl. Inst., Rome, SSL 1970, SSD 1975. Emp: Regina Mundi, Rome, 1972-74 Instr.; St. Louis U., 1974-91 Prof., Chmn., Dept. of Theol. Stud.; Pont. Bibl. Inst., 1991- Prof.; *Biblica,* 1991- Assoc. Ed. Spec: New Testament. Pub: *Who Is A Christian: A Study in Pauline Ethics* (Liturgical, 1990); "Luke's Message in Luke 9:1-50" *CBQ* 49 (1987); "Parallels Between Jesus and His Disciples in Luke-Acts: A Further Study" *BZ* 27 (1983); "Activity of the Risen Jesus in Luke-Acts" *Biblica* 62 (1981); *The Unity of Luke's Theology: An Analysis of Luke-Acts* (Glazier, 1984); "Acts 2:30 and the Davidic Covenant of Pentecost" *JBL* 102 (1983); "Paul at Athens and Luke's Notion of Worship" *RB* 89 (1982); and others. Mem: SBL; CBA; SNTS. Rec: Hiking, swimming. Addr: (o) Pontifical Biblical Institute, Via della Pilotta 25, 00187 Rome, Italy 06-679-64-53.

OTTOSSON, Magnus Y., b. Kristdala, Sweden, June 17, 1929, s. of Karl-Oskar & Eugenia (Pihl), m. Ann-Marie (Billing), chil: Astrid; Nils. Educ: BTh 1956; Ord. 1956; BPh 1962; ThLic 1962; ThD 1969. Emp: Oslo U., Norway, 1983-85 Prof.; Uppsala U., Sweden, 1983-94 Prof. Excv: Tell el-Fukhar, Jordan, 1990- Dir. Spec: Hebrew Bible. Pub: *Josuaboken-en programskrift for davidisk restauration* (1991); "The Prophet Elijah's Visit to Zarephath" in JSOTSup (1984); "Tradition and History, with Emphasis on the Composition of the Book of Joshua" in *The Productions of Time: Tradition History in Old Testament Scholarship* (1984); *Temples and Cult Places in Palestine* (Boreas, 1980); *Gilead, Tradition and History* (1969); and others. Awd: Nathan Soderblom-Sallskapet 1970; Det Norske Videnskaps-Akademi 1984. Rec: Vacationing on the island of Rosso. Addr: (o) Uppsala U., Theological Institution, Box 1604, 751 46 Uppsala, Sweden 018-182500.

OTZEN, Benedikt, b. Copenhagen, Denmark, December 16, 1929, s. of Povl & Astrid (Lange), m. Sif K. (Korsbaek), chil: Gertrud; Bodil Elisabeth; Thomas. Educ: U. of Copenhagen, MA, Theol. 1955; U. of Aarhus, ThD 1964. Emp: Copenhagen & Aarhus, Theol. Fac., 1957-60 Lbrn.; U. of Aarhus, 1964 Prof., OT Exegesis; *Dansk Teologisk Tidsskrift,* 1965-88 Ed. Bd.; *VT,* 1989- Ed. Bd. Spec: Hebrew Bible, Semitic Languages, Texts and Epigraphy, Apocrypha and Post-biblical Studies. Pub: "The Aramaic Inscriptions" in *Hama: Fouilles et Recherches* 2/2 (1990); *Judaism in Antiquity* (Sheffield, 1990); *Myths in the Old Testament,* co-auth. (SCM, 1980); *Israeliterne i Palaestina* (Gad, 1977); "De tolv Patriarkers Testamenter" in *De gammeltestamentlige Pseudepigrafer* (1974); *Studien über Deuterosacharja* (Munksgaard, 1964); and others. Awd: U. of Copenhagen, Golden Medal 1953; Knighthood of Danneborg II 1973, I 1986. Mem: Uppsala,

Nathan Soderblom Sallskapet 1981-; Wissenschaftliche Gesellschaft fur Theol. 1988-; Royal Danish Acad. of Sci. & Letters 1989-. Addr: (o) U. of Aarhus, Institute for Old Testament, Theology Faculty, (DK) 8000 Aarhus, Denmark 45/86 13 67 11; (h) Haslevangsvej 36, (DK) 8210 Aarhus V, Denmark 45/86 15 62 13.

OVADIAH, Asher, b. Greece, July 2, 1937, s. of Esther & Haim, m. Ruth, chil: Esti. Educ: Hebrew U., Jerusalem, BA, MA, PhD 1971. Emp: Dept. of Antiq. & Mus., Jerusalem, 1969-71 Cur.; Upper Montclair Coll., 1971-72 Vis. Prof.; Tel Aviv U., Israel, 1972-86 Sr. Lect. & Assoc. Prof., 1986- Prof.; Israeli Acad. Ctr. in Cairo, 1987-89 Dir. Excv: Elijah's Cave, Israel, 1966 Dir.; Gaza, 1967, 1976 Dir.; Kedesh, Upper Galilee, 1981, 1983-84 Dir. Spec: Archaeology. Pub: *Mosaic Pavements in Israel,* co-auth. (1987); "Observations on the Origin of the Architectural Plan of Ancient Synagogues" *JJS* 38 (1987); "Art of the Ancient Synagogues in Israel" *Gerion* 4 (1986); "The Roman Temple at Kedesh, Upper Galilee: A Preliminary Study" *Tel Aviv* 11 (1984); *Supplementum to the Corpus of the Byzantine Churches in the Holy Land,* co-auth. (1984); "Some Notes on the Roman Theatre of Beth-Shean (Seythopolis)" in *Scripta Classica Israelica* VI (1981-82); *Geometric and Floral Patterns in Ancient Mosaics* (1980); *Corpus of the Byzantine Churches in the Holy Land* (1970); and others. Mem: Greek Arch. Soc.; Intl. Assn. of Greek & Latin Inscriptions. Rec: Photography, operatic music, traveling. Addr: (o) Tel Aviv U., Dept. of Art History and Classical Studies, Ramat-Aviv, Israel 6409481; (h) 10, Ben-Tabbai St., San-Simon, Jerusalem, Israel 784578.

OWEN, David I., b. Boston, MA, October 28, 1940, s. of Myer & Anna, m. Susan (Kadiff), chil: Joshua; Ethan. Educ: Brandeis U., MA 1963, PhD 1969. Emp: U. Mus., 1969-71 Cur.; Dropsie U., 1971-74 Asst. Prof.; Cornell U., 1974- Prof.; Inst. of Nautical Arch., 1975- Adj. Prof.; *JAOS,* 1984-88 Assoc. Ed.; Stud. on the Civilization & Culture of Nuzi & the Hurrians, 1981- Ed.-in-Chief. Excv: Kyrenia, Cyprus, 1968-69 Asst. Dir.; Porticello, Italy, 1970-71 Dir.; Tel Aphek-Antipatris, Israel, 1978-85 Dir., Epigraphist. Spec: Archaeology, Mesopotamian Studies, Semitic Languages, Texts and Epigraphy. Pub: *Neo-Sumerian Archival Texts Primarily from Nippur in the University Museum, the Oriental Institute and the Iraq Museum* (Winona Lake, 1982); "An Akkadian Letter from Ugarit at Tel Aphek" *Tel Aviv* 8 (1981); "Widows Rights in Ur III Sumer" *Zeitschrift fuer Assyriologie* 70 (1980); *The John Frederick Lewis Collection* (Rome, 1974); and others. Mem: AOS 1962-; ASOR 1978-; IES 1977-. Addr: (o) Cornell U., Dept. of Near Eastern Studies, 360 Rockefeller Hall, Ithaca, NY 14853 607-255-6275; (h) 1326 East State St., Ithaca, NY 14850 607-273-4717.

OWENS, Robert J., Jr., b. Springfield, IL, October 20, 1947, s. of Robert & Betty, m. Mary, chil: Monica; Taylor. Educ: Lincoln Christian Sem., MA, MDiv 1973; Johns Hopkins U., PhD 1981. Emp: Manhattan Christian Coll., 1974-76 Asst. Prof.; St. Mary's Sem., 1978-82 Adj. Faculty; Emmanuel Sch. of Relig., 1980- Prof., Hebrew Bible & OT. Spec: Hebrew Bible, Semitic Languages, Texts and Epigraphy. Pub: "The Early Syriac Text of Ben Sira" *JSS* 34 (1989); "Aphrahat as a Witness to the P Text of Lev 1" in *Monographs of the Peshitta Institute* vol. 4 (Brill, 1986); "The Genesis and Exodus Citations of Aphrahat the Persian Sage" in *Monographs of the Peshitta Institute* vol. 3 (Brill, 1983). Mem: SBL; CBA. Rec: Sailing, canoeing. Addr: (o) Emmanuel School of Religion, One Walker Dr., Johnson City, TN 37601 615-926-1186; (h) 1805 Colonial Ridge Dr., Johnson City, TN 37601.

PACWA, Mitchell C., b. Chicago, IL, July 27, 1949, s. of Mitchell & Lorraine (Szczerba). Educ: U. of Detroit, BA (summa cum laude) 1972; Loyola U., Jesuit Sch. of Theol., MDiv 1979; Vanderbilt U., MA 1962, PhD 1984. Emp: Loyola U., 1985- Asst. Prof., Theol. Spec: Hebrew Bible. Mem: SBL 1980-. Rec: Playing bluegrass mandolin, photography. Addr: (o) 6525 N Sheridan Rd., Chicago, IL 60626 312-274-3000.

PAGAN, Samuel, b. San Juan, PR, July 29, 1950, s. of Luis & Ida, m. Noheme, chil: Samuel; Luis. Educ: U. of PR, BSChE 1973; Evang. Sem., PR, MDiv 1975; Princeton Theol. Sem., ThM 1977; Jewish Theol. Sem., Dr. Heb. Lit. 1988. Emp: Evang. Sem., Puerto Rico, 1982-85 Acad. Dean; United Bible Soc., 1987-. Spec: Hebrew Bible, New Testament, Apocrypha and Post-biblical Studies. Pub: *Comentario a Esdras, Nehemias y Ester* (1992); *Vision y mision* (1992); and others. Rec: Playing guitar. Addr: (o) 7200 NW 19th St. #206, Miami, FL 33126 305-539-0009; (h) 15121 Norfolk Ln., Davie, FL 33331 305-680-3080.

PAGE, Sydney H. T., b. London, Canada, November 27, 1944, s. of Sydney & Audrey (Hull), m. Faith, chil: Jonathan; Kathryn. Educ: Westminster Theol. Sem., MDiv 1970; Princeton Theo. Sem., ThM 1971; U. of Manchester, England, PhD 1974. Emp: N Amer. Bapt. Coll., Canada, 1977-81 Assoc. Prof.; Edmonton Bapt. Sem., Canada, 1981- Acad. V.P., Prof. of NT. Spec: New Testament. Pub: "Ransom Saying" in *Dict. of Jesus and the Gospels* (InterVarsity, 1992); "The Authenticity of the Ransom Logion (Mark 10:45b)" *Gospel Perspectives* (1980); "Revelation 20 and Pauline Eschatology" *JETS* 23/1 (1980). Mem: SBL; ETS; IBR. Rec: Racquetball. Addr: (o) Edmonton Baptist Seminary, 11525 23 Ave., Edmonton, AB T6J 4T3, Canada 437-1960; (h) 14807 108 Ave., Edmonton, AB T5N 1H3, Canada 453-8992.

PAGELS, Elaine, b. Palo Alto, CA, February 13, 1943. Educ: Stanford U., BA 1964, MA 1965;

Harvard U., PhD 1970. Emp: Barnard Coll., 1970-74 Asst. Prof., 1974- Assoc. Prof., Hist. of Relig.; Princeton U. Spec: Apocrypha and Post-biblical Studies. Pub: *Adam, Eve, and the Serpent* (Random, 1988); *The Gnostic Gospels* (Random House, 1979); *Paul the Gnostic: Gnostic Exegesis of the Pauline Letters* (Fortress, 1975); "Mystery of the Resurrection" *JBL* (1974); "Conflicting Reviews of Valentinian Eschatology" *HTR* (1974); *The Johanine Gospel in Gnostic Exegesis* (Abingdon, 1973); and others. Awd: Guggenheim Found., grant 1978. Mem: SBL; AAR; Soc. Bibl. Theol.; Soc. Arts, Relig. & Culture. Addr: (o) Princeton U., 17 Ivy Ln., Room 23, Princeton, NJ 08544.

PAINCHAUD, Louis, b. Quebec City, Canada, March 10, 1950, s. of Robert & Lucille (Parent), m. France (Dion), chil: Genevieve; Anne-Marie; Alexis; Josee. Educ: Petit Sem. de Quebec, DEC, Hum. 1969; U. Laval, Bac., Theol. 1972, MA, Theol. 1975, PhD, Theol. 1979; Ecole Biblique, Jerusalem, Cert. 1988. Emp: Coll. de Sainte-Foy, 1979 Prof.; Hebrew U., Jerusalem, 1988 Vis. Lect.; U. Laval, 1988 Assoc. Prof.; *Bibliotheque Copte de Nag Hammadi*, 1982 Ed. Bd. Spec: Apocrypha and Post-biblical Studies. Pub: "The Redactions of the Writing Without Title (CG II⁵)" *SC* 8 (1991); "Le Sommaire anthropognique de l'*Ecrit sans Titre* (NH II, 117:27-118:2) à la lumière de 1 Co 15:45-47" *VC* 44 (1990); *Le Traité Tripartite*, Bibliotheque Copte de Nag Hammadi 19, co-auth. (1989); "L'ecrit sans titre du Codex II de Nag Hammadi (II.5) et la *Symphonia* d'Epiphane (*Pan.* 40)" *Studia Patristica* 18/1 (1986); "Deux citations vétéro-testamentaires dans l'Ecrit sans Titre" *Le Muséon* 98 (1985); *Le Fragment de la République de Platon*, Bibliotheque Copte de Nag Hammadi (1983); *Le Deuxième Traite du Grand Seth*, Bibliotheque Copte de Nag Hammadi 6 (1982); and others. Mem: Intl. Assn. for Patristic Stud. 1983-; Canadian Assn. for Patristic Stud. 1989-; SBL 1989-; Soc. quebecoise pour l'etude de la relig. 1991-; IACS 1992-. Rec: Skiing, tennis, squash, swimming, camping. Addr: (o) U. Laval, Fac. de theologie, Pavillon Felix-Antoine-Savard, Sainte-Foy, Que. G1K 7P4, Canada 418-656-5637; (h) 1216 avenue Joseph Vezina, Sillery, Que. G1T 2K9, Canada 418-527-8292.

PAINTER, John, b. Bellingen, Australia, September 22, 1935, s. of Edward & Gladys, m. Gillian, chil: Katharine Jane; Janet. Educ: Australian College of Theol., ThL 1961, Th.School. 1963; Melbourne Coll. of Div., Dip. R.E. 1962; London U., BD 1963; U. of Durham, England, PhD 1968. Emp: St. John's Coll., England, 1965-68 Tutor; U. of Cape Town, 1971-76 Assoc. Prof.; La Trobe U., Australia, 1977- Head, Div. of Relig. Stud. Spec: New Testament, Apocrypha and Post-biblical Studies. Pub: *The Quest for the Messiah: The History, Literature and Theology of the Johannine Community* (T & T Clark, 1991); *John: Witness and Theologian* (Beacon Hill, 1986); "The Opponents in 1 John" NTS 32 (1986); *Theology as*

Hermeneutics: Rudolf Bultmann's Interpretation of the History of Jesus (Almond, 1986); *Reading John's Gospel Today* (Knox, 1980); and others. Mem: SNTS 1972-; Fellow of Bibl. Stud. 1977-, Pres. 1979; SBL 1980-; Australian Acad. of the Hum. 1991, Fellow. Rec: Cricket, fishing. Addr: (o) La Trobe U., Division of Religion, 3083, Victoria, Australia 478-3122; (h) 51 Castleton Rd., Viewbank, 3084 Victoria, Australia.

PALS, Daniel L., b. South Holland, IL, October 28, 1946, s. of Herbert & Margaret, m. Phyllis. Educ: Calvin Theol. Sem., BD 1971; U. of Chicago, MA 1973, PhD 1975. Emp: *Ch. Hist.,* 1973-76 Ed. Asst.; Trinity Coll., 1976-77 Asst. Prof.; Centre Coll., 1977-80 Asst. Prof.; U. of Miami, 1980- Assoc. Prof. Spec: New Testament. Pub: "Explanation, Social Science, and the Study of Religion" *Zygon* (1992); "Axioms Without Dogmas" *JAAR* (1991); "Several Christologies of the Great Awakening" *ATR* (1990); "Reductionism and Belief" *JR* (1986); *The Victorian 'Lives' of Jesus* (Trinity U.P., 1982); and others. Mem: AAR. Rec: Golf, running. Addr: (o) PO Box 248264, Coral Gables, FL 33124 305-284-4733; (h) 11116 SW 70th Terrace, Miami, FL 33173 305-279-8803.

PANIMOLLE, Salvatore, b. Agosta, Italy, August 21, 1935, s. of Amerigo & Amalia. Educ: U. Gregoriana, Rome, Laurea, Theol. 1971; Pont. Bibl. Inst., Rome, Laurea, Sacra Scrittura 1977. Emp: U. di Sassari, Prof.; *Dizionario di Spiritualita Biblico-Patristica,* Ed., Dir. Spec: New Testament. Pub: *Apostolo-Discepolo-Missione* (Borla, 1993); *Abba'-pa Dre* (Borla, 1992); *Alleanza-Patto-Testamento* (Borla, 1992); *Amore-Carita'-Misericordia* (Borla, 1992); "La Struttura del discorso della montagna (Mt. 5-7)" *Testimonium Christi* (1985); "Il valore salvifico della morte di Gesu negli scritti di Luca" *Sangue et Antropologia Biblica* (1981); and others. Mem: Assn. Bibl. Italiana; SNTS. Addr: (o) Via Carso 35/B, 07100 Sassari, Italy 079-299909.

PANNELL, Randall J., b. Dallas, TX, April 2, 1950, s. of Dan & Betty, m. Estella (Kelley), chil: John; Shawnee; Karen; Nathan. Educ: Southwest. Bapt. Theol. Sem., MDiv 1975, PhD 1979. Emp: Southwest. Bapt. Sem., 1976-79 Instr.; Seminario Intl. Teologico Bautista, Argentina, 1980-83 Assoc. Prof.; Houston Bapt. Sem., 1983-84 Prof.; Ch. of the Savior, Evang. Presbyn. Ch., 1987- Pastor. Spec: Hebrew Bible, Semitic Languages, Texts and Epigraphy. Pub: "El Deuteronomio y Su Hermeneutica de la Tradicion" *Dialogo Teologico* 21 (1982-83); "La violencia y la politica del Mesias a la luz de Miqueas 4:14-5:5" *Apuntes Pastorales* 1 (1981); and others. Mem: SBL 1976-; CBA 1979-. Rec: Running. Addr: (o) PO Box 11255, Spring, TX 77391-1255 713-355-7044; (h) 3603 Laurel Hollow Dr., Spring, TX 77388 713-350-2207.

PAPADEMETRIOU, George C., b. Thasos, Greece, April 11, 1932, s. of Constantine &

Ourania, m. Athanasia, chil: Constantine; Jane (Kourtis); Anastasios. Educ: Holy Cross Greek Orthodox Sem., BTh 1959; Tex. Christian U., MTh 1966; Temple U., PhD 1977; Simmons Coll., MLS 1983. Emp: 1960- Greek Orthodox Priest; 1981- Lbrn.; 1978- Prof. Spec: New Testament. Pub: *Essays on Orthodox Christian-Jewish Relations* (1990); and others. Mem: Orthodox Theol. Soc., V.P. 1976-78, Pres. 1978-80. Rec: Reading, traveling. Addr: (o) 50 Goddard Ave., Brookline, MA 02146 617-731-3500; (h) 20 Lantern Ln., Needham, MA 02192 617-444-8941.

PARKE-TAYLOR, Geoffrey H., b. Denham, Buckinghamshire, UK, January 22, 1920, m. Mary (Bagshaw), chil: Janet; Michael. Educ: U. of Toronto, BA 1942, MA 1944; Wycliffe Coll., LTh 1944, BD 1961, DD 1967. Emp: Wycliffe Coll., 1946-47 Prof., OT; Parish ministry, 1951-59; Anglican Theol. Coll., 1959-64 Prof., NT; Huron Coll., 1964-76 Prof., OT & Hebrew, 1966-76 Dean of Theol.; Bishop Suffragan, 1976-85. Spec: Hebrew Bible. Pub: *YAHWEH: The Divine Name in the Bible* (Wilfred Laurier U.P., 1975). Awd: Huron Coll., DD 1976; Trinity Coll., DD 1982. Mem: CSBS 1947-, Pres. 1966; SBL 1947-; SOTS 1950-. Rec: Collecting pressed glass goblets. Addr: (h) Cedar Beach, R.R. 1, Beaverton, ON LOK 1A0, Canada 705-426-9330.

PARKER, David C., b. Boston, UK, July 4, 1953, s. of T. H. L. & M., m. Karen, chil: Louise; James; John; Alison. Educ: St. Mary's Coll., U. of St. Andrews, MTh 1975; Emmanuel Coll., Cambridge, Dip. in Theol. 1976; U. of Leiden, Doc. 1990. Emp: St. Paul's, London, 1977-80 Curate; Bladon with Woodstock, 1980-85 Curate; The Queen's Coll., Birmingham, 1985-93 Tutor in Bibl. Stud.; U. of Birmingham, 1986-93 Lect., NT; Intl. Greek NT Proj., 1987- Co-Ed. Spec: New Testament. Pub: *Codex Bezae: An Early Christian Manuscript and its Text* (Cambridge U.P., 1992); "Unequally Yoked: The Present State of the Codex Bobbiensis" *JTS* 42 (1991); "Scripture is Tradition" *Theol.* 94 (1991); "The International Greek New Testament Project: The Gospel of John" *NTS* 36 (1990); *Melanchthon's Scholia on Colossians,* trans., ed. (Almond, 1989); *The New Testament in Greek,* Intl. Greek NT Project, St. Luke, Part 2 (Oxford U.P., 1987); "The Translation of OYN in the Old Latin Gospels" *NTS* 31 (1985); "The Development of Textual Criticism since B.H. Streeter" *NTS* 24 (1977); and others. Rec: Reading, bell ringing, watching cricket and rugby, gardening, music. Addr: (o) U. of Birmingham, Dept. of Theology, Edgbaston, Birmingham B15 2TT, England 021-414-3613.

PARKER, Pierson, b. Shangai, China, May 27, 1905, s. of Alvin & Susie (Williams), m. Mildred Ruth (Sorg), chil: Peter. Educ: U. of Calif., AB 1927; Pacific Sch. of Relig., MA 1933, ThD 1934.

Emp: Pacific Sch. of Relig., 1934-36 Instr.; N Cong. Ch., 1936-44 Pastor; Ch. Div. Sch. of the Pacific, 1940-49 Assoc. Prof.; Gen. Theol. Sem., 1949-74 Glorvina Rossell Hoffman Prof. of NT; Pacific Sch. of Relig., Vis. Prof. Spec: New Testament. Pub: "The Priority of Mark" in *New Synoptic Studies* (Mercer U.P., 1983); *Good News in Matthew* (Collins, 1976); *The Gospel Before Mark* (U. of Chicago, 1953); *Deuteronomy*, co-auth. Interpreter's Bible; and others. Awd: Ch. Div. Sch. of Pacific, STD 1964. Mem: SBL 1934-, Hon. Pres. 1978; Pacific Theol. Group 1940-49; SNTS 1955-. Rec: Bridge, chess, swimming. Addr: (h) 650 W Harrison Ave., Claremont, CA 91711 714-624-9120.

PARKER, Simon B., b. Manchester, England, February 23, 1940, s. of Harold & Irene, m. Sonia, chil: Jonathan; Jeremy. Educ: Asbury Theol. Sem., BD 1963; Johns Hopkins U., PhD 1967. Emp: Reed Coll., 1967-75 Asst. Prof.; U. of Oreg., 1976-77 Vis. Asst. Prof.; Boston U. Sch. of Theol., 1981- Assoc. Prof., 1981-88 Assoc. Dean, 1991- Harrell F. Beck Schol. in Hebrew Scriptures; *Maarav*, 1977-85 Ed. Pub: "Syrian and Palestinian Religions" in *Ency. Britannica* (1992); "Toward Literary Translations of Ugaritic Poetry" *UF* 22 (1990); *The Pre-Biblical Narrative Tradition* (Scholars, 1989); "KTU 1.16 III, The Myth of the Absent God and 1 Kings 18" *UF* 21 (1989); "Possession Trance and Prophecy in Pre-exilic Israel" *VT* 28 (1978); *Enuma Elish. The Babylonian Epic of Creation: The Cuneiform Text*, co-auth. (Clarendon, 1966); and others. Awd: Graves Awd. 1972. Mem: SBL 1966-; AOS 1969-; SOTS 1973-; ASOR 1990-. Rec: Playing piano. Addr: (o) Boston U., School of Theology, 745 Commonwealth Ave., Boston, MA 02215 617-353-3063; (h) 47 Woodland Rd., Newton, MA 02166 617-527-1259.

PARRY, Donald W., b. Nampa, ID, January 15, 1953, s. of Atwell & Elaine, m. Camille, chil: Matthew; Julie; Justin; Kirkham; Stephen. Educ: Brigham Young U., BA, Near East. Stud. 1985, MA 1986; U. of Utah, PhD, Middle E Stud., Hebrew 1992. Emp: Brigham Young U., 1985- Instr., Bibl. Hebrew & Relig. Stud. Spec: Hebrew Bible, Semitic Languages, Texts and Epigraphy. Pub: *A Bibliography on Temples of the Ancient Near East and Mediterranean World*, co-auth. (Mellen, 1991); *A Guide to Scriptural Symbols*, co-auth. (Bookcraft, 1990); "Sinai as Sanctuary and Mountain of God" in *By Study and Also By Faith, Essays in Honor of Hugh W. Nibley*, vol. 1 (Deseret, 1990); "The Garden of Eden: Sacred Space, Sanctuary, Temple of God" *Explorations* 5 (1987); "The Judges of Israel" in *Studies in Scripture: The Old Testament* (Randall, 1985); and others. Mem: SBL. Rec: Camping, racquetball, water activities. Addr: (o) Brigham Young U., PO Box 7113, U. Station, Provo, UT 84602 801-378-3295; (h) 810 N 1220 W, Provo, UT 84601 801-375-3887.

PARUNAK, H. Van Dyke, b. Newport, RI, May 3, 1947, s. of Aram & Orianna, m. Anita, chil: Gene. Educ: Princeton U., A.B. 1969; Dallas Theol. Sem., ThM 1973; Inst. of Holy Land Stud., MA 1978; Harvard U., AM, PhD 1978; U. of Mich., MS 1982. Emp: Harvard U., 1978-79 Res. Asst.; U. of Mich., 1979-82 Asst. Prof.; Comshare, 1982-84 Computer Scientist; Industrial Technology Inst., 1984- Sci. Fellow. Spec: Archaeology, Hebrew Bible, New Testament, Semitic Languages, Texts and Epigraphy. Pub: "The Dimensions of Discourse Structure," in *Linguistics and the New Testament Interpretation* (Broadmans, 1993); "Transitional Techniques in the Bible" *JBL* 102 (1983); "Oral Typesetting: Some Uses of Biblical Structure" *Biblica* 62 (1981); *Linguistic Density Plots in Zechariah* (Bibl. Res. Assn., 1979); *Structural Studies in Ezekiel* (U. Microfilms, 1978); "The Orthography of the Arad Ostraca" *BASOR* 230 (1978); "Was Solomon's Temple Aligned to the Sun?" *PEQ* 110 (1978); and others. Addr: (o) ITI, P.O. 1485, Ann Arbor, MI 48106 313-769-4049; (h) 1027 Ferdon Rd., Ann Arbor, MI 48104 313-996-1384.

PASTOR-RAMOS, Federico, b. Zamora, Spain, January 2, 1939, s. of Felipe & Julia, m. Maria Fernanda (Lopez-Larrea), chil: Emmanuel; Fernanda; Ramon; Federico. Educ: Berchmanskolleg, Munchen, Phil. Lic. 1963; U. P. Comillas, Theol. Lic. 1967; Pont. Bibl. Inst., Rome, SSD 1975. Emp: U. P. Comillas, Madrid, 1970-88 Prof., 1979-85 Dean; St. Louis U. at Madrid, 1988- Prof.; *Estudios Bibl.*, 1987-89 Ed. Spec: New Testament. Pub: *La Salvacion del hombre en la muerte y resurreccion de Cristo* (Verbo Divino, 1992); *Pablo. Un seducido por Cristo* (Verbo Divino, 1991); *Hechos de los Apostoles. Comentario.* (Sigueme, 1989); "Cristo imagen del Padre" *EstTrin* 22 (1988); "Cristo solidario. Aportaciones desde San Pablo a la teologia de la liberacion" *Rev.LatTeol* 5 (1988); "La Cristologia de Galatas. Sinteses y observaciones" *EstBib* 46 (1988); "Ciencias biblicas e increncia en Espana hoy" *RazFe* 74 (1988); "La muerte por otros en el mundo grecoromano" *MisCom* 45 (1987); *La libertad en la Carta a los Galatas* (U. Comillas, 1977). Mem: SNTS; Assn. Bibl. Espanola, Chmn. 1987-89. Addr: (o) St. Louis U., c. Vina 3, 28003 Madrid, Spain; (h) c/ Fernando el Catolico 63 60 D, 28015 Madrid, Spain 549-60-35.

PATHRAPANKAL, Joseph, b. Elamgulam, India, September 29, 1931, s. of Chacko Avirah & Mariamma Abraham. Educ: Papal Athaeneum, India, MTh 1959; Pont. Bibl. Inst., Rome, LSS 1962; Gregorian U., Rome, ThD 1964. Emp: Dharmaram Pont. Inst. of Theol. & Phil., 1968- Dean, Faculty of Theol.; Princeton Theol. Sem., 1972 Vis. Fellow; Dharmaram Vidya Kshetram, India, 1979-85 Pres., 1985-91 Dean, Faculty of Theol. Spec: New Testament. Pub: *Text and Context in Biblical Interpretation* (1992); "Jesus of Nazareth: Paradigm Par Excellence" *Jour. of Dharma* (1992); "Mediation universelle du Christ et pluralisme de religions" *Spiritus* (1991); "L'home de la Pentacote: du particulier à l'universel" *Spiritus* (1988); *Critical and Creative* (1986); *New Testament Perspectives* (1982); and others. Awd: Congregation for Cath. Educ., Rome, Hon. Prof. 1988; Pont. Bibl. Commn., 1984-90. Mem: SNTS 1975-; Katholisches Bibelwerk; CBA 1980-; Conf. of Cath. Theol. Inst., V.P. 1980-. Addr: (o) Dharmaram Vidya Kshetram, Bangalore 560029, India 0812-649095; (h) Dharmaram College, Bangalore 560029, India 0812-643266.

PATRICH, Joseph, b. Romania, May 11, 1947, s. of Michael & Feiga, m. Shoshana, chil: Aviya; Yishai; Michael. Educ: Hebrew U. of Jerusalem, MA 1981, PhD 1989. Emp: Israel Dept. of Antiq., 1981-82 Head, Arch. Survey Team, Mar Saba map; U. of Haifa, 1985- Sr. Lect. Excv: Caves in Judean Desert, 1983-87 Dir., Arch. Survey, 1986-91 Dir., Excvn.; Kh. Beth Loya, 1984-86 Dir. Spec: Archaeology. Pub: *The Formation of Nabatean Art: Prohibition of a Graven Image Among the Nabateans* (Magnes/Brill, 1990); "A Juglet Containing Balsam Oil(?) From a Cave Near Qumran" *IEJ* 39 (1989); "The *mesibbah* of the Second Temple in Jerusalem according to the Tractate *Middot*" *IEJ* 36 (1986); "Les grottes de el-Aleiliyat et la laure de Saint Firmin" *RB* 91-92 (1984-85); "Al 'Uzza Earrings" *IEJ* 34 (1984); "A Sadducean Halakha and the Jerusalem Aqueduct" *Jerusalem Cathedra* 2 (1982); and others. Awd: Hebrew U. of Jerusalem, Inst. of Arch., Teich Awd. 1981, Girschman Awd. 1987; Yad Yizhak Ben Zvi, Jerusaelm, Rachel Yanait Ben Zvi Awd. 1987. Mem: Israel Arch. Soc.; Israel Assn. for Byzantine Stud. Addr: (o) U. of Haifa, Dept. of Archaeology, Mt. Carmel, Haifa 31905, Israel 04-240234.

PATRICK, Dale A., b. Eugene, OR, October 2, 1938, s. of Paul & Grace, m. Mary (Webber), chil: Jeremy. Educ: Drew U., BD 1963; Grad. Theol. Union, ThD 1971. Emp: Mo. Sch. of Relig., 1968-81 Assoc. Prof.; U. of Mo., 1981-82 Vis. Assoc. Prof.; Drake U., 1982- Assoc. Prof. Spec: Hebrew Bible. Pub: *Rhetoric and Biblical Interpretation*, co-auth. (Almond, 1990); "Studying Biblical Law as a Humanities" *Semeia* 45 (1989); *Old Testament Law: An Introduction* (John Knox, 1984); *The Rendering of God in the Old Testament*, Overtures to Bibl. Theol. Ser. (Fortress, 1981); "Job's Address of God" *ZAW* 91/2 (1979); "The Covenant Code Source" *VT* 27/2 (1977); *Arguing with God: The Angry Prayers of Job* (Bethany, 1977); "Short Note: The Translation of Job XLII 6" *VT* 26/3 (1976); "Casuistic Law Governing Primary Rights and Duties" *JBL* 92/2 (1973); and others. Mem: AAR 1968-; SBL 1968-. Addr: (o) Drake U., 208 Medbury Hall, Des Moines, IA 50311 515-271-2885; (h) 4125 Beaver Crest, Des Moines, IA 50310 515-255-5838.

PATTEN, Bebe Rebecca, b. Berkeley, CA, January 30, 1950, d. of Dr. Bebe & C. Thomas. Educ: Patten Coll., BS, Bible 1969; Coll. of Holy Names, BA, Phil. 1971; Wheaton Coll., MA, NT 1972; Drew U., PhD, NT 1976; Dominican Coll.,

MA, Phil. 1990. Emp: Christian Cathedral of C.E.C.A. Inc., 1964- Co-Pastor; Christian Evang. Ch. of Amer., 1964- Bd. of Dir.; Patten Bible Coll., 1975-82 Assoc. Prof., 1977- Acad. Dean, 1982- Prof., NT. Spec: New Testament. Pub: *The World of the Early Church* (Mellen, 1990); *Before the Times* (Strawberry Hill, 1980); and others. Mem: IBR 1981-; Amer. Assn. of U. Prof. 1975-; SBL 1975-; AAR 1975-. Rec: Skiing. Addr: (o) 2433 Coolidge Ave., Oakland, CA 94601 510-533-8300.

PATTERSON, Richard D., b. Aurora, IL, December 14, 1929, m. Anna L., chil: Lois Ann (Grill); Nancy Diana (Lewis); John B. Educ: Wheaton Coll., AB 1956; NW Bapt. Sem., MDiv 1960; Talbot Theol. Sem., ThM 1961; U. of Calif., Los Angeles, MA 1965, PhD 1970. Emp: Los Angeles Bapt. Coll. & Sem., 1962-76 Prof.; Grand Rapids Bapt. Theol. Sem., 1976-77 Prof.; NW Bapt. Sem., 1977-82 Prof.; Liberty U., 1982- Prof., Chmn., Bibl. Stud.; *Wycliffe Exegetical Comm.*, 1984- Co-ed. Spec: Hebrew Bible, Mesopotamian Studies, Semitic Languages, Texts and Epigraphy, Egyptology. Pub: *Nahum, Habakkuk, Zephaniah* (Moody, 1991); "Nahum: Poet Laureate of the Minor Prophets" *JETS* 33 (1990); "Of Bookends, Hinges, and Hooks: Literary Clues to the Arrangement of Jeremiah's Prophecies" *WTJ* 51 (1989); *1, 2 Kings*, Expositor's Bible Comm., vol. 4 (Zondervan, 1988); "The Psalm of Habakkuk" *GTJ* 8 (1987); *Joel*, Expositor's Bible Comm., vol. 7 (Zondervan, 1985); "The Song of Deborah" in *Tradition and Testament* (Moody, 1981); "The Widow, the Orphan and the Poor in the Old Testament and the Extra Biblical Literature" *BS* 130 (1973); and others. Awd: Hebrew Union Coll., Middle East. Stud. Fellow 1968; NW Bapt. Theol. Sem., Alumnus of the Year 1991-92. Mem: ETS 1962-, Chmn., SW reg. 1975-76; Egypt Exploration Soc. 1963-; Oriental Inst. 1966-; ASOR 1970-; NEAS 1971-. Rec: Reading, sports. Addr: (o) Liberty Baptist Theological Seminary, Box 20,000, Lynchburg, VA 24506 804-582-2587; (h) 121 Lafayette Pl., Forest, VA 24551 804-525-4768.

PATTERSON, Stephen J., b. Ft. Worth, TX, November 29, 1957, s. of John W. & Alice Joan (Fitts), m. Deborah L. Educ: Yankton Coll., BA 1981; Harvard U., MTS 1983; Claremont Grad. Sch., MA 1988, PhD 1988. Emp: Eden Theol. Sem., 1988- Asst. Prof., NT; *BR*, 1992- Contb. Ed. Spec: New Testament, Apocrypha and Post-biblical Studies. Pub: *The Gospel of Thomas and Jesus* (Polebridge, 1993); "Paul and the Jesus Tradition: It Is Time for Another Look" *HTR* 84 (1991); "Sources, Redaction, and *Tendenz* in the Acts of Peter and the Twelve Apostles" *VC* 45 (1991); *The Q-Thomas Reader*, co-auth. (Polebridge, 1990); "The Gospel of Thomas: Does It Contain Authentic Sayings of Jesus?," co-auth. *BR* 6/2 (1990); "A Note on Didache 12.2a (Coptic)," co-auth. *SC* 7 (1989-90); "Fire and Dissension: Ipissima Vox Jesu in Q12:49,51-53?" *Forum* 5 (1989); and others.

Awd: Fulbright Fellow. 1986-87. Mem: SBL 1983-; Inst. for Antiq. & Christianity 1983-Pres.; The Jesus Sem. 1986-. Addr: (o) Eden Theological Seminary, 475 E Lockwood Ave., St. Louis, MO 63119 314-961-3627; (h) PO Box 215, Smithton, IL 62285.

PAUL, Maarten J., b. Sliedrecht, March 13, 1955, s. of Hendrik Paul & Aaltje (Bos), m. Neeltje A. (van Dijke), chil: Hendrik J.; Catharina; Abraham J.; Marinus A. Educ: U. of Leiden, Kerkelijk Examen 1982, Doc. 1988. Emp: Oranje Nassau Coll., Zoetermeer, 1977-79 Relig. Instr.; Evang. Hogeschool, Amersfoort, 1979-91 Tchr., OT, Head, Relig. Dept. of Tchr. Training Coll.; Theol. Hogeschool, 1991- Tchr., OT. Spec: Hebrew Bible. Pub: "King Josiah's Renewal of the Covenant (2 Kings 22-23)" in *Pentateuchal and Deuteronomistic Studies* (1990); "Hoedemaker en de uitleg van de Bijbel" in *Hoedemaker herdacht* (Ten Have, 1989); *Het Archimedisch Punt van de Pentateuchkritiek* (Boekencentrum, 1988); "The Order of Melchizedek (Ps 110:4 and Heb 7:3)" *WTJ* 49 (1987); "Hilkiah and the Law (2 Kings 22) in the 17th and 18th Centuries: Some Influences on W.M.L. de Wette" in *Das Deuteronomium* (1985); and others. Mem: Tyndale Fellow. 1980-. Rec: Bicycle, chess, stamps of Israel. Addr: (o) Theologische Hogeschool, Julianalaan 34B, 3721 EG Bennekom, Netherlands; (h) Schoolstraat 1A, 4261 BN Wijk en Aalburg, Netherlands 0-4164-1697.

PAUL, Shalom M., b. Philadelphia, PA, May 2, 1936, s. of Samuel & Celia, m. Yona, chil: Michal; Yael; Benzion. Educ: Temple U., BA (summa cum laude), Gratz Coll., BHL; Jewish Theol. Sem., MHL, Rabbinic Ord. 1962; U. of Pa., PhD 1964. Emp: Jewish Theol. Sem., 1960-70 Assoc. Prof.; Tel Aviv U., Israel, 1971-74 Sr. Lect.; Hebrew U., Jerusalem, 1986- Head of Bible Dept.; 1986-90 Assoc. Prof., 1991- Prof.; Ohio State U., Vis. Disting. U. Schol.; *BAR, BR, Hebrew Ann. Rev.,* Ed. Spec: Hebrew Bible, Mesopotamian Studies, Semitic Languages, Texts and Epigraphy. Pub: *Amos* (Hermeneia, 1991); *Almanac of the Bible,* co-auth. (1991); *Illustrated Dict. & Concordance of the Bible,* co-ed. (1986); "Jerusalem of Gold — A Song and an Ancient Crown" *BAR* 3/4 (1977); *Biblical Archaeology,* ed. (1973); *Studies in the Book of the Covenant in the Light of Cuneiform and Biblical Law* (1970); and others. Awd: Cyrus Adler Schol., 1960; Jewish Theol. Sem., Hon. Doc. 1986; Saul Lieberman Inst. for Talmudic Research, First Hon. Fellow 1987. Mem: SBL; ASOR. Addr: (o) Hebrew U., Bible Dept., Jerusalem 91905, Israel 02-88-35-30; (h) 4 Ben Tabbai St., Jerusalem 93591, Israel 02-63-01-61.

PAULIEN, Jon, b. New York, NY, June 5, 1949, s. of Kurt & Gertrude, m. Pamella, chil: Tammy Kaye; Joel Jonathan; Kimberly Kaye. Educ: Atlantic Union Coll., BA 1972; Andrews U., MDiv 1976, PhD 1987. Emp: Andrews U., 1984-

88 Asst. Prof., 1988-92 Assoc. Prof., 1992- Prof., NT; *AUSS* 1991- Assoc. Ed. Spec: New Testament. Pub: "The Seven Seals," "Interpreting Revelation's Symbolism" in *Symposium on Revelation—Book I* (Bibl. Res. Inst., 1992); *The Book of Revelation: Too Good to be False* (Review & Herald, 1990); "Elusive Allusions: The Problematic Use of the Old Testament in Revelation" *Bibl. Res.* 33 (1988); *Decoding Revelation's Trumpets,* Andrews U. Sem. Doc. Diss. Ser., vol. 11 (Andrews U.P., 1988); "Recent Developments in the Study of the Book of Revelation" *AUSS* 26 (1988); and others. Mem: SBL 1984-; Andrews Soc. for Relig. Stud. 1984-; CSBR 1988-. Rec: Basketball, photography, travel. Addr: (o) Andrews U. Theological Seminary, Berrien Springs, MI 49104-1500 616-471-6574; (h) 8756-1 N Ridge, Berrien Springs, MI 49103 616-471-1058.

PAYNE, Philip B., b. Long Island, NY, July 2, 1948, m. Nancy, chil: David; Kimiko; Brendan. Educ: Trinity Evang. Div. Sch., MA (summa cum laude) 1972, MDiv (summa cum laude) 1973; Cambridge U., PhD 1976. Emp: Cambridge U., 1974-75 Supr., NT Stud.; Trinity Evang. Div. Sch., 1976 Vis. Prof.; Gordon-Conwell Theol. Sem. 1985-87 Vis. Prof.; Fuller Theol. Sem., 1988- Adj. Prof. Spec: New Testament. Pub: *Super Greek, Hebrew and Phonetics* (Linguist's Software, 1985); "Midrash and History in the Gospels with Special Reference to R.H. Gundry's *Matthew*" in *Gospel Perspectives* III (JSOT, 1983); and others. Awd: Cambridge, Higgins Schol. 1974. Mem: Tyndale Fellow. 1974-; ETS 1977-; IBR 1985-; SBL 1984-. Rec: Computers, hiking. Addr: (o) Fuller Theological Seminary, 101 Nickerson St., Suite 200, Seattle, WA 98109-1621 206-284-9000; (h) P.O. Box 580, Edmonds, WA 98020-0580 206-775-1130.

PEARSON, Birger A., b. Turlock, CA, September 17, 1934, s. of Yngve & Mildred, m. Karen, chil: Ingrid; David; Kristin; Daniel; Sven; Anders. Educ: Upsala Coll., BA 1957; U. of Calif., Berkeley, MA 1959; Pacific Luth. Theol. Sem., MDiv 1962; Harvard U., PhD 1968. Emp: Duke U., 1966-69 Asst. Prof.; U. of Calif., Santa Barbara, 1969- Prof.; *BR,* Ed. Bd.; *ABD,* Ed. Bd.; *JBL,* 1983-89 Ed. Bd. Spec: Archaeology, New Testament, Egyptology, Apocrypha and Post-biblical Studies. Pub: *The Future of Early Christianity: Essays in Honor of Helmut Koester,* ed. (Fortress, 1991); *Gnosticism, Judaism and Egyptian Christianity* (Fortress, 1990); *The Roots of Egyptian Christianity,* ed. (Fortress, 1986); *Nag Hammadi Codices IX and X* (Brill, 1981); and others. Mem: SBL; SNTS; ASSR; IACS; Soc. d'Arch. copte. Rec: Music, farming. Addr: (o) U. of California, Dept. of Religious Studies, Santa Barbara, CA 93106.

PECKHAM, J. Brian, b. Montreal, Canada, January 28, 1934, s. of Sidney Brittain & Elizabeth Ann (Caroline). Educ: St. Mary's U., Toronto, BA 1957; U. of Toronto, MA 1958;

Harvard U., PhD 1965; Fourviere, Lyon, France, ThL 1968. Emp: Regis Coll., Toronto, 1969 Asst. Prof., 1975- Assoc. Prof. Spec: Hebrew Bible, Semitic Languages, Texts and Epigraphy. Pub: *History and Prophecy. The Development of Late Judean Literary Traditions* (Doubleday, 1993); "Phoenicia, History of" in *ABD* vol. II (Doubleday, 1992); "The Phoenician Foundation of Cities and Towns in Sardinia" in *Sardinia in the Mediterranean: A Footprint in the Sea, Studies in Sardinian Archaeology Presented to Miriam S. Balmuth* (Sheffield, 1992); "Literacy and the Creation of the Biblical World" *Scripta Mediterranea* 12-13 (1991-92); "The Composition of Hosea" *HAR* 11 (1987); "The Deuteronomistic History of Saul and David" *ZAW* 7 (1985); *The Composition of the Deuteronomistic History*, HSM 35 (Scholars, 1985); *The Development of the Late Phoenician Scripts* (Harvard U.P., 1968); and others. Mem: CBA 1966-; SBL 1969-. Rec: Athletics, gardening, travel. Addr: (o) 339 Bloor St. W, Suite 217, Toronto, ON M5S 1E7, Canada 416-593-9346; (h) 56 Alcorn Ave., Toronto, ON M4V 1E4, Canada 416-925-7889.

PEIFER, Claude J., b. Lincoln, IL, September 20, 1927, s. of John & Armella (Meyer). Educ: Coll. di Sant'Anselmo, Rome, STL 1954; Pont. Bibl. Inst., Rome, SSL 1956. Emp: St. Bede Abbey Sch. of Theol., 1957-69 Instr.; Marquette U., 1961 Vis. Prof.; St. John's U., 1967, 1968, 1974 Vis. Prof.; *The Bible Today*, 1972-85 Assoc. Ed.; St. Paul Sem., 1978, 1980 Vis. Prof. Spec: Hebrew Bible, New Testament. Mem: CBA 1958-; SBL 1962-. Addr: (h) St. Bede Abbey, Peru, IL 61354 815-223-3140.

PELEG, Yehuda, b. Frydek, October 9, 1924, s. of Joseph (Fischer) & Ella (Kornfeld), m. Martha, chil: Naomi; Asaf; Amit. Excv: Caesarea Aqueduct, 1971-73 Surveyor; Susita-Hippos, 1993 Staff. Spec: Archaeology. Pub: "Ancient Pipelines in Israel," ed., in *Future Currents in Aqueduct Studies* (1991); "Die Wasserversorgung der Wuestenfestungen am Jordangraben," co-auth. *Antike Welt* 20 (1989); "Das Stauwerk fuer die untere Wasserleitung nach Caesarea" *Mitteilungen des Leichtweiss Institutes* 89 (1986); "Two Aqueducts to Dor" *Mitteilungen des Leichtweiss Institutes* 82 (1984); "The Water Supply at Caesarea Maritima" *IEJ* 27 (1977); and others. Mem: Frontinus Gesellschaft a.v. 1989-. Addr: (h) Maayan Zvi 30 805, Israel 06-395123.

PENCHANSKY, David, b. Brooklyn, NY, December 3, 1951, s. of Charles & Mimi (Black), m. Joyce (Grigsby), chil: Simon Graham; Maia Lucy. Educ: CUNY, Queens Coll., BA 1974; Assemblies of God Grad. Sch., MA 1980; Vanderbilt U., PhD 1987. Emp: Evang. Coll., 1979-84 Instr.; Vanderbilt U., 1986 Grad. Instr.; West. Ky. U., 1985-89 Instr.; U. of St. Thomas, 1989- Asst. Prof. Spec: Hebrew Bible. Pub: "Up for Grabs: A Tentative Proposal for Ideological Criticism" *Semeia* 59 (1992); "Staying the Night:

Intertextuality in Genesis and Judges" in *Reading Between the Texts* (Westminster/John Knox); *Judges-1 Kings*, Storyteller's Companion vol. 3, co-auth. (Abingdon, 1991); *The Betrayal of God* (John Knox, 1990); and others. Mem: SBL, Pres., Upper MidW Sect., 1992; CBA. Rec: T'ai Chi, science fiction, films. Addr: (o) U. of St. Thomas, Mail #4328, 2115 Summit Ave., St. Paul, MN 55105 612-962-5371; (h) 1480 Blair Ave., St. Paul, MN 55104 612-649-0922.

PERELMUTER, Hayim G., b. Montreal, Canada, June 2, 1914, s. of Benjamin & Tillie, m. Nancy (Goodman), chil: Mayer; Michael. Educ: Harvard U., MA 1940; Hebrew Union Coll., Jewish Inst. of Relig., Rabbi 1939, MHL 1939, DD 1964, DHL 1979. Emp: Cath. Theol. Union at Chicago, 1968- Prof., Jewish Stud.; Pacific Luth. Theol. Sem., 1979-89 Vis. Prof.; Grad. Theol. Union, 1979-89 Vis. Prof.; Luzerne U., 1986-87 Vis. Prof. Spec: Hebrew Bible. Pub: *Siblings: Rabbinic Judaism and Early Christianity at the Beginnings* (Paulist, 1989); *This Immortal People*, co-auth. (Paulist, 1985); and others. Mem: AAJR 1980-; SBL 1983-; AAR 1983-; N Amer. Acad. of Liturgy 1984-. Rec: Jogging, walking. Addr: (o) 5401 S Cornell Ave., Chicago, IL 60615 312-324-8000; (h) 5000 East End Ave., Chicago, IL 60615 312-643-4070.

PERKIN, James R. C., b. Northamptonshire, England, August 19, 1928, s. of William & Lily (Drage), m. Dorothy (Bentley), chil: James; John; Anne. Educ: Oxford U., MA 1955, PhD 1955. Emp: Bapt. Ch., 1956-62 Minister; New Coll., Edinburgh, 1963-65 Lect.; McMaster Div. Coll., Canada, 1965-69 Assoc. Prof.; Acadia U., Canada, 1969- Prof. & Pres., 1982- Vice-Chancellor. Spec: New Testament. Pub: *Handbook for Biblical Studies* (Lancelot, 1974, 1976); *Scripture Then and Now* (Atlantic Bapt. Fellow., 1975); and others. Mem: SNTS; CSSR. Rec: Music, literature. Addr: (o) Acadia U., Office of the President, Wolfville, NS B0P 1X0, Canada 902-542-2201; (h) Box 355, Wolfville, NS B0P 1X0, Canada 902-542-5501.

PERKINS, Pheme, Spec: New Testament. Addr: (o) Boston College, Dept. of Theology, 140 Commonwealth Ave., Boston, MA 02167 617-552-3889.

PERRY, Theodore A., b. Waterville, ME, December 24, 1938, m. Sydney Helene (Alderman). Educ: Bowdoin Coll., BA (summa cum laude) 1960; Yale U., PhD 1966. Emp: U. of Conn., 1967-74 Asst. Prof., 1974-80 Assoc. Prof., 1980- Prof., Modern & Class. Lang.; Hebrew U., Jerusalem, 1986-87 Vis. Fulbright Prof. Pub: "Dialogues with Kohelet: Towards a New Translation of Ecclesiastes" *LIT* 1 (1990); "Quadripartite Wisdom Sayings and the Structure of Proverbs" *Proverbium* 4 (1987); "Metaphors of Sacrifice in the Zohar" *Stud. in Comparative Relig.* 16 (1986); "Bathsheba's Bath: Medieval

Spanish Versions of 2 Samuel 11:1-5" *Hebrew U. Stud. in Lit. & the Arts* 11 (1983); and others. Awd: NEH Grant for Younger Schol. 1969-70; Fulbright Sr. grant 1985-86. Mem: AJS; SBL; Modern Lang. Assn. Addr: (o) U. of Connecticut, Dept. of Modern & Classical Languages U-57, Storrs, CT 06268; (h) 161 McKinley Ave., New Haven, CT 06515 203-387-7619.

PESCE, Mauro, b. Genova, Italy, March 21, 1941, s. of Giancarlo & Maria (Piacentino), m. Adriana (Destro), chil: Stefano; Sara; Simona. Educ: U. di Roma, Laurea in Filosofia 1964; Katholische Theol. Fakultaet, Bonn, BRD 1970. Emp: U. di Bologna, 1968- Prof. Ordinario de Storia del Cristianesimo; *Annali di Storia dell'Esegesi,* 1984- Ed.; *Origini,* Testi e Studi del CISEC, 1991- Ed. Spec: New Testament, Apocrypha and Post-biblical Studies. Pub: "Ricostruzione del kerygma ai tessalonicesi sulla base di 1Ts 1:9-10" *Annali di Storia dell'esegesi* 2 (1985); "La profezia cristiana come anticipazione del giudizio escatologico (1 Cor. 14: 24-25)" in *Testimonium Christi: Scritti in onore di J. Dupont* (1985); *Il 'Regno' di Isaia' non esiste: L'Ascensione di Isaia e le tradizioni giudaiche sull'uccisione del profeta* (1984); *Isaia, Il Diletto e la Chiesa: Visione ed esegesi profetica cristiano-primitiva* (1983); *Dio senza mediatori: Una tradizione teologica dal giudaismo al cristianesimo* (1979); and others. Mem: Assn. italiana per lo studio del giudaismo. Addr: (o) U. di Bologna, CISEC, Strada Maggiore 45, I-40125 Bologna, Italy 051-232892; (h) Via Scornetta 14, I-40068 S. Lazzaro (BO), Italy 051-451113.

PESCH, Rudolf, b. Bonn, Germany, September 2, 1936, s. of Matthias & Elisabeth, m. Ingeborg, chil: Berthold; Friederike. Educ: PhD 1964, ThD, NT 1967, Habil., NT 1969. Emp: U. of Frankfurt, 1970-80 Prof.; U. of Freiburg, 1980-84; U. of Bonn, 1980-84; Akademie fur Glaube und Form, Integrierte Gemeinde, 1984-. Spec: New Testament. Mem: SNTS. Addr: (o) Herzog Heinrich Str. 18, D-8000 Munchen 2, Germany 089-531000.

PETER-CONTESSE, René, b. Bevaix, Switzerland, December 6, 1934, s. of James & Emma, m. Christiane, chil: Claude; Florence; Philippe. Educ: U. de Neuchatel, Lic. Theol. 1958, DTh 1990. Emp: Pasteur, 1960-72; Alliance Bibl. U., 1972- Traducteur Bibl. Spec: Hebrew Bible. Pub: *Manuel du traducteur pour le livre de Ruth* (Alliance Bibl. U., 1990); *Manuel du traducteur pour les livres d'Abdias et de Michee* (Alliance Bibl. U., 1988); *Manuel du traducteur pour le livre de Daniel* (Alliance Bibl. U., 1986); *Manuel du traducteur pour le livre du Levitique* (Alliance Bibl. U., 1985); "L'imposition des mains dans l'Ancien Testament" *VT* 27/1 (1977); "Par et sor: note de lexicographie hebraique" *VT* 25/3 (1975); and others. Addr: (h) CH-2013 Colombier, Switzerland.

PETERSEN, David L., b. Elgin, IL, March 21, 1943, s. of Kermit & Charlotte, m. Sara, chil:

Naomi; Joshua. Educ: Yale U., BD 1968, MPhil 1970, PhD 1972. Emp: U. of Ill., 1972-83 Assoc. Prof.; Iliff Sch. of Theol., 1983- Prof.; *JBL,* Ed. Bd.; *HBC,* Assoc. Ed.; SBL Diss. Ser., Ed.; Aarhus U., Denmark, 1977-78 Fulbright Sr. Lect. Spec: Hebrew Bible. Pub: "Israelite Prophecy: Change Versus Continuity" in VTSup 43 (1991); *Prophecy in Israel* (Fortress, 1987); "Portrait of David" *Interpretation* 40 (1986); "Zechariah's Visions: A Theological Perspective" *VT* 34 (1984); "Biblical Texts and Statistical Analysis: Zechariah and Beyond" *JBL* 103 (1984); *Haggai and Zechariah 1-8* (Westminster, 1984); *The Roles of Israel's Prophets* (JSOT, 1981); "Genesis 6:1-4, Yahweh and the Organization of the Cosmos" *JSOT* 13 (1979); *Late Israelite Prophecy,* SBL Mon. Ser. (1977); and others. Mem: SBL; AAR; ASOR. Rec: Skiing, fishing. Addr: (o) Iliff School of Theology, 2201 S University Blvd., Denver, CO 80210 303-744-1287; (h) 2439 S Lima St., Aurora, CO 80014 303-751-1982.

PETERSEN, Norman R., b. Chicago, IL, August 25, 1933, s. of Norman & Mildred, m. Antoinette, chil: Kristen; Mark; Joanna. Educ: Harvard Div. Sch., STB 1961; Harvard U., PhD 1967. Emp: Wellesley Coll., 1963-69 Asst. Prof.; Williams Coll., 1969- Washington Gladden Prof. of Relig.; *Semeia,* 1974-82 Assoc. Ed. Spec: New Testament. Pub: *Rediscovering Paul* (Fortress, 1985); "The Composition of Mark 4:1-8:26" *HTR* 73 (1980); "Mark's Narrative" *Interpretation* 34 (1980); *Literary Criticism for the New Testament Critics* (Fortress, 1978); and others. Mem: SNTS 1976-; SBL. Addr: (h) 51 Bulkley St., Williamstown, MA 01267.

PETERSEN, William L., b. Laredo, TX, January 19, 1950. Educ: U. of Iowa, BA 1971; Luth. Theol. Sem., Saskatoon, MDiv 1975; Rijksuniversiteit te Utrecht, Netherlands, ThD 1984. Emp: Memorial U., Newfoundland, 1977 Lect.; U. of Notre Dame, 1985-90 Asst. Prof.; Pa. State U., 1990-93 Asst. Prof., 1993- Assoc. Prof. Spec: New Testament, Apocrypha and Post-biblical Studies. Pub: "The Christology of Aphrahat, the Persian Sage: An Excursus on the 17th Dem." *VC* (1992); "Textual Evidence of Tatian's Dependence upon Justin's ATTOMNHMONEYMATA" *NTS* (1990); *Gospel Traditions in the Second Century: Origins, Traditions, Texts and Recensions* (Notre Dame U.P., 1989); *Origen of Alexandria: His World and His Legacy* (Notre Dame U.P., 1988); *The Diatessaron and Ephrem Syrus as Sources of Romanos the Melodist,* CSCO 475 (Peeters, 1985); "The Dependence of Romanos the Melodist upon the Syriac Ephrem: It's Importance for the Origin of the Kontakion" *VC* 39 (1985); "Romanos and the Diatessaron: Readings and Method" *NTS* 29 (1983); "The Parable of the Lost Sheep in the Gospel of Thomas and the Synoptics" *NT* 23 (1981); and others. Mem: SNTS ; SBL; NAPS; Intl. Assn. of Manichaean Stud. Rec: Alpine skiing, alpinism, music, reading. Addr: (o) Pennsylvania State U.,

Relig. Studies Prog., 319 Weaver Bldg., University Park, PA 16802 814-865-7773; (h) 610 Toftrees Ave. #355, State College, PA 16803 814-867-8796.

PETROTTA, Anthony J., b. San Francisco, CA, October 12, 1950, s. of Anthony & Mildred, m. Janet M. (Bell), chil: Brian A.; Jenna A. Educ: Westmont Coll., BA 1975; Fuller Theol. Sem., MA 1977; U. of St. Andrews, MPhil 1984; U. of Sheffield, PhD 1990. Emp: New Coll., 1981-84 Adj. Prof.; Sterling Coll., 1984-91 Asst. Prof.; King Coll., 1991- Assoc. Prof. Spec: Hebrew Bible. Pub: *Lexis Ludens: Wordplay and the Book of Micah* (Lang, 1991); "An Even Closer Look at Matt 2:6 and its Old Testament Sources" *JETS* 33 (1990); "Building an Old Testament Library: Ruth to Job" *Catalyst* 14 (1988); "A Closer Look at Matthew 2:6" *JETS* 28 (1985); "Old Testament Textual Criticism" *TSF Bull.* (1981). Awd: Sterling Coll., Natl. Conf. of Christians & Jews Study Fellow. 1987. Mem: SBL. Rec: Running, softball, basketball, reading. Addr: (o) King College, 1350 King College Rd., Bristol, TN 37620 615-652-4803; (h) 108 Brookwood Dr., Bristol, TN 37620 615-968-3364.

PETZER, Jacobus H., b. Butterworth, South Africa, October 30, 1956, s. of Jacobus H. & Jeanetta, m. Marina. Educ: Potchefstroom U., South Africa, BA 1977, Honns.-BA, Greek 1978, MA, Greek 1980, ThB 1983, DLitt 1987. Emp: Potchefstroom U., 1982-87 Lect., 1988-90 Sr. Lect., Greek, 1991- Sr. Lect., NT; Intl. Project on the Text of Acts, Ed., Latin version. Spec: New Testament. Pub: "St. Augustine and the Latin Version of Acts" *Neotestamentica* 25 (1991); "Tertullian's Text of Acts" *SC* 8 (1991); "Style and Text in the Lucan Narrative of the Institution of the Lord's Supper" *NTS* 37 (1991); *Text and Interpretation: New Approaches in the Criticism of the New Testament*, NT Tools & Stud. 15, co-ed. (Brill, 1991); "A Survey of the Developments in New Testament Textual Criticism Since 1975" *Neotestamentica* 24 (1990); *Die Teks van die Nuwe Testament* (1990); "Contextual Evidence in Favour of KAYXHSOMAI in 1 Cor. 13:3" *NTS* 35 (1989); *A South African Perspective on the New Testament*, co-ed. (Brill, 1986); and others. Mem: SBL 1987-; NTS of South Africa 1984-; Class. Assn. of South Africa 1986-; South African Assn. for Patristic & Byzantine Stud. 1987-. Rec: Model trains. Addr: (o) U. of South Africa, Department of the New Testament, PO Box 392, 0001 Pretoria, South Africa 27-12-4294734; (h) 11 Maroelana St., Maroelana, Pretoria, 0018, South Africa 27-12-464599.

PFAMMATTER, Joseph N., b. Sarnen, Switzerland, October 25, 1926, s. of Theophil & Katharina (Bachmann). Educ: Angelicum, Rome, Lic. Theol. 1956; Pont. Bibl. Inst., Rome, B.Rer.Bibl. 1957; Ecole Biblique, Lic.Rer.Bibl. 1958; Pont. U. Gregoriana, Rome, STD 1959. Emp: Theol. Hochschule Chur, 1959- Prof., NT, 1968-70 Rector; *Theol. Berichte*, 1972-

Mitherausgeber. Spec: New Testament. Pub: *Epheserbrief. Kolosserbrief*, NEB NT 10/12 (1990); "Katholische Jesusforschung im Deutschen Sprachraum" *Theol. Berichte* 7 (1978); *Die Auferstehung Jesu Christi*, trans. (1968); "Eigenschaften und Verhaltensweisen Gottes im Neuen Testament" *MySal* 2 (1967); "Glaube nach der heiligen Schrift" *MySal* 1 (1965); *Die Kirche als Bau: Eine exegetisch-theologische Studie zur Ekklesiologie der Paulusbriefe* (1960); and others. Mem: SNTS; Schweiz. Theol. Gesellschaft; Kreis Kath. Fachexegeten der Schweiz. Addr: (o) Theologische Hochschule Chur, alte Schanfiggerstr. 7, CH-7000 Chur, Switzerland 081-222012; (h) alte Schanfiggerstr. 9, CH-7000 Chur, Switzerland 081-222817.

PFANN, Stephen J., b. Redwood City, CA, August 29, 1952, m. Claire Ruth, chil: Stephen, Jr.; Shoshana; Michael. Educ: De Anza Coll., AA 1972; Bethany Bible Coll., BS 1974; Grad. Theol. Union, MA 1982. Emp: North. Calif. Bible Coll., 1972-82 Instr., Greek & Hebrew; Ctr. for the Study of Early Christianity, 1984- Dir.; Amer. Inst. of Holy Land Stud., 1985-91 Instr., Aramaic & Comparative Semitics; Rothberg Sch. for Overseas Students, 1989 Instr., Bibl. Hebrew; Dead Sea Scrolls Publ. Project, 1991-93 Res., Qumran texts, Ed. Team, Cryptic Texts. Excv: City of David, 1983 Staff; Beth Shean, 1983 Staff. Spec: Semitic Languages, Texts and Epigraphy. Pub: *The Dead Sea Scrolls on Microfiche* (1993); "The Aramaic Text and Language of Daniel and Ezra in the Light of Some Unpublished Manuscripts from Qumran" *Textus* 16 (1991); "A Concordance to Ugaritica VII" *Newsletter for Ugaritic Stud.* 22 (1980); *The Illustrated Dictionary and Concordance to the Bible*, contb. (Jerusalem/Macmillan, 1986). Awd: Albright Inst., Endowment for Bibl. Res. 1984. Mem: SBL 1974-83; ASOR 1977-. Addr: (o) Hebrew U., Dept. of the Bible, Qumran Project, Mt. Scopus Jerusalem, Israel 2-883514; (h) 6 Naomi St., Abu Tor, Jerusalem, Israel 2-723785.

PFATTEICHER, Philip H., b. Philadelphia, PA, October 29, 1935, s. of Ernst & Esther, m. Lois (Sharpless), chil: Carl; Carolyn; Sarah; Linda. Educ: Luth. Theol. Sem., MDiv 1960; U. of Pa., MA 1960, PhD 1966; Union Theol. Sem., STM 1968. Emp: Luth. Ch., 1960-68 Pastor; Luther Coll., 1966-68 Lect.; E Stroudsburg U., 1968- Prof. Spec: Hebrew Bible, New Testament. Pub: *Dict. of Liturgical Terms* (Trinity, 1991); *Festivals and Commemorations* (Augsburg, 1980); *Manual on the Liturgy*, co-auth. (Augsburg, 1979); *The Lesser Festivals*, 2 vol. (Fortress, 1975); and others. Mem: AAR; SBL; N Amer. Acad. of Liturgy. Addr: (o) East Stroudsburg U., East Stroudsburg, PA 18301 717-424-3426; (h) 127 Village Dr., Stroudsburg, PA 18360 717-421-5048.

PFITZNER, Victor C., b. Pinnaroo, S Australia, October 14, 1937, s. of Carl Julius & Elvera Lottie (Keil), m. Valmai B. (Schuster), chil: Suzanne Julie; Matthew Carl; Sarah Louise.

Educ: Adelaide U., BA 1957; Immanuel Sem., BTh 1960; Munster U., DTh 1964. Emp: Luth. Ch. of Australia, 1964-66 Pastor; Concordia Sem., Australia, 1966-67 Lect.; Luther Sem., Australia, 1968-88 Lect., 1989- Prin. Spec: New Testament. Pub: "Proclaiming the Name: Cultic Narrative and Eucharistic Proclamation in 1 Corinthians" *Luth. Theol. Jour.* 25/1 (1991); *John,* Chi Rho Comm. (Luth., 1988); *First Corinthians,* Chi Rho Comm. (Luth., 1982); "Purified Community—Purified Sinner: Expulsion from the Community According to Matt. 18:15-18 and 1 Cor. 5:1-5" *Australian Bibl. Rev.* 30 (1982); "Pneumatic Apostleship? Apostle and Spirit in the Acts of the Apostles" in *Wort in der Zeit* (Brill, 1980); "The School of Jesus: Jesus Traditions in Pauline Paraenesis" *Luth. Theol. Jour.* 13/2-3 (1979); "The Coronation of the King: The Passion in the Gospel of John" *Concordia Theol. Monthly* 4/1 (1977); *Paul and the Agon Motif* (Brill, 1967); and others. Mem: SNTS 1973-; Australian & New Zealand Soc. for Theol. Stud. 1970-. Rec: Ancient numismatics, music. Addr: (o) Luther Seminary, 104 Jeffcott St., N Adelaide, S.A. 5006, Australia 08-267-3233; (h) 89 Winchester St., Malvern, S.A. 5061, Australia 08-271-3202.

PHERIGO, Lindsey P., b. Miami, FL, December 29, 1920, s. of Ezekiel & Dorothy (Price), m. Viola (Schmitt), chil: Linda; Stephen; Ruth; Robert. Educ: U. of Fla., BAE 1942; Boston U., STB 1945, PhD 1951. Emp: Syracuse U., 1949-51 Instr.; Scarritt Coll., 1951-59 Prof.; Vanderbilt U., 1953-59 Lect.; St. Paul Sch. of Theol., 1959- Prof. Spec: New Testament, Apocrypha and Post-biblical Studies. Pub: *The Great Physician* (1983, 1991); "Paul's Life After the Close of Acts" *JBL* (1951); "Paul and the Corinthian Church" *JBL* (1949); and others. Mem: SBL 1945-; Amer. Soc. Ch. Hist. 1945-. Rec: Collecting classical music, coins, & stamps. Addr: (o) 5123 Truman Rd., Kansas City, MO 64127 816-483-9600; (h) 4960 Westwood Rd., Kansas City, MO 64112 816-531-3220.

PHILLIPS, Anthony C. J., b. Falmouth, United Kingdom, June 2, 1936, s. of Arthur & Esmee, m. Victoria, chil: Christopher; James; Lucy. Educ: King's Coll., London, BD, AKC 1963; Cambridge U., PhD 1967. Emp: Trinity Hall, Cambridge, 1969-74 Dean, Chaplain & Fellow; St. John's Coll., Oxford, 1975-86 Chaplain & Fellow; Jesus Coll., Oxford, 1975-86 Lect., Theol.; Hertford Coll., Oxford, 1984-86 Lect., Theol.; The King's Sch., Canterbury, 1986- Headmaster. Spec: Hebrew Bible. Pub: "A Fresh Look at the Sinai Pericope—Part 1 and 2" *VT* 34 (1984); "The Laws of Slavery: Exodus 21:2-11" *JSOT* 30 (1984); "The Decalogue—Ancient Israel's Criminal Law" *JJS* 34 (1983); *Lower than the Angels: Questions Raised by Genesis 1-11* (1983); *Israel's Prophetic Tradition,* co-ed. (Cambridge U.P., 1982); *Deuteronomy,* Cambridge Bible Comm. (Cambridge U.P., 1973); *Ancient Israel's Criminal Law* (Blackwell, 1970); and others. Mem: PES;

SOTS. Rec: Gardening, beachcombing. Addr: (o) The King's School, Canterbury CT1 2ES, England 475-501.

PHIPPS, William E., b. Waynesboro, VA, January 28, 1930, s. of Charles & Ruth, m. Martha (Swezey), chil: Charles; Anna; Ruth. Educ: Union Theol. Sem., MDiv 1952; U. of St. Andrews, Scotland, PhD 1954; U. of Hawaii, MA 1963. Emp: Peace Coll., 1954-56 Prof.; Davis & Elkins Coll., 1956- Prof., Relig. & Phil. Spec: New Testament. Pub: *Assertive Biblical Women* (Greenwood, 1992); "A Woman Was the First to Declare Scripture Holy" 6/2 *BR* (1990); *Genesis and Gender* (Prager, 1989); "Jesus, the Prophetic Pharisee" *JES* (1977); *Was Jesus Married?* (Harper & Row, 1970); and others. Mem: AAR. Addr: (o) Davis & Elkins College, Elkins, WV 26241 304-636-1900.

PIETERSMA, Albert, b. Netherlands, September 28, 1935, s. of Liekele & Martje, m. Margaret (Stadig), chil: Bryan; Kevin; Larisa. Educ: Calvin Theol. Sem., BD 1965; U. of Toronto, Canada, PhD 1970. Emp: U. of Toronto, Canada, 1969- Prof., Dept. of Near East. Stud. Pub: "Septuagint Research: A Plea for a Return to Basic Issues" *VT* (1985); *The Acts of Phileas, Bishop of Thmuis,* Cahiers d'Orientalisme 7 (1984); *De Septuaginta: Studies in Honour of John William Wevers,* co-ed. (1984); *Two Manuscripts of the Greek Psalter,* Analecta Biblica 77 (Bibl. Inst., 1978); and others. Mem: IOSCS 1972-, Pres. 1980-. Addr: (o) U. of Toronto, Dept. of Near Eastern Studies, 4 Bancroft Ave., Toronto, ON M5S 1A1, Canada 416-978-3858; (h) 21 Cross St., Weston, ON M9N 2B8, Canada 416-244-6677.

PIKE, Dana M., b. Boston, MA, June 28, 1953, s. of Ronald & Marilyn, m. Jane, chil: Benjamin; Daniel; Allison. Educ: Brigham Young U., BS; U. of Pa., PhD 1990. Spec: Hebrew Bible, Semitic Languages, Texts and Epigraphy. Pub: Articles in *HBD* (1985) & *ABD* (1992). Mem: SBL; ASOR; BAS. Rec: Gardening, swimming. Addr: (o) Brigham Young U., Dept. of Ancient Scripture, 316-G JSB, Provo, UT 84602.

PILCH, John J., b. Brooklyn NY, August 7, 1936, s. of John & Anna (Wypych), m. Jean (Peters). Educ: St. Francis Coll., BA (summa cum laude) 1959; Marquette U., MA 1968, PhD 1972. Emp: St. Scholastica Coll., 1969-70 Vis. Prof.; Marquette U., 1971 Vis. Prof.; St. Mary of the Lake U., 1971-74 Asst. Prof. Spec: New Testament. Pub: "Understanding Healing in the Social World of Early Christianity" *BTB* 22 (1992); *Dict. of Bible Values,* ed. (Hendrickson, 1992); "Separating Sheep from Goats" *PACE* 22 (1992); *Introducing the Cultural Context of the New Testament and Introducing the Cultural Context of the Old Testament* (Paulist, 1991); "Marian Devotion and Wellness Spirituality" *BTB*

20 (1990); "Understanding Biblical Healing: Selecting the Appropriate Model" *BTB* 18 (1988); "Healing in Mark" *BTB* 15 (1985); *Wellness Spirituality* (Crossroads, 1985); *Galatians and Romans* (Liturgical, 1983); and others. Mem: SBL 1967-; CBA 1967-. Rec: Singing with Baltimore Symphony & Milwaukee Opera Choruses, cooking. Addr: (h) 1318 Black Friars Rd., Catonsville, MD 21228-2710 410-778-5106.

PINERO, Antonio, b. Chipiona, Spain, August 14, 1941, s. of Gregorio & M. Dolores, m. Arminda (Lozano), chil: Zahra; Antonio. Educ: U. Comillas, Lic. en Filologia 1966; U. Complutense, Madrid, Lic. Filologia Clasica 1970; U. Pont. Salamanca, Lic. Filologia Biblica, Dr. Class. Philol., 1974. Emp: U. Complutense, Madrid, 1970-74 Assoc. Prof., 1974-83 Adj. Prof., 1983- Prof.; *Filologia Neotestamentiaria* Ed. Bd. Spec: New Testament, Apocrypha and Post-biblical Studies. Pub: *Los Origenes del Cristianismo* (El Almendro, 1991); "Les conceptions de l'inspiration dans les Pseudepigraphes de L'Ancien Testament" in *Literaterature Intertestamentaire* (PUF, 1985); "Jose Asenet y el Nuevo Testamento" *Actas del I Symposion Biblico Espanol de Salamanca 1982* (1984); *Apocrifos del Antiguo Testamento*, contb. (1986); "El Job apocrifo y la reinterpretacion de la figura del Jesus historico" in *Unidad y pluralidad en el Mundo Antiguo* (1982); and others. Awd: Premio Extraordinario de Licenciatura en Filologia Clasica 1971; Premio "Luis Vives" del Consejo Superior de Investigaciones Cientificas 1976. Mem: SNTS 1984-. Rec: Music, sailing. Addr: (o) U. Complutense, Facultad de Filologia, Seminario A 35, 28040 Madrid, Spain 91-394-5297; (h) c/ Pena Pintada 28, 28034 Madrid, Spain 91-734-6040.

PIPER, Ronald A., b. Washington, March 27, 1948, s. of Harold & Cleo, m. Faith, chil: Lisette. Educ: Pomona Coll., BA (summa cum laude) 1970; U. of London, BD 1975; U. of London, King's Coll., PhD 1986. Emp: U. of Aberdeen, Scotland, 1979-80 Lect., NT Exegesis; U. of St. Andrews, Scotland, 1980-92 Lect., 1992- Reader, NT Lang. & Lit., Head of Sch. of Div., 1992-93 Prin., St. Mary's Coll. Spec: New Testament, Apocrypha and Post-biblical Studies. Pub: "Social Background and Thematic Structure in Luke 16" in *The Four Gospels: Festschrift F. Neirynck* (1992); *Wisdom in Q. Aphorisms in the Sayings of Jesus* (Cambridge U.P., 1989); "Matthew 7:7-11 par. Luke 11:9-13: Evidence of Design and Argument in the Collection of Jesus' Sayings" in *Logia. Les Paroles de Jesus*, BETL 59 (1982). Addr: (o) U. of St. Andrews, St. Mary's College, St. Andrews, Fife KY16 9JU, Scotland 0334-76161; (h) 20 Horseleys Park, St. Andrews, Fife KY16 8RZ, Scotland.

PISANO, Stephen F., b. New York, NY, April 16, 1946, s. of Daniel & Elisabeth. Educ: Centre-Sevres, France, STL 1976; Pont. Bibl. Inst., Rome, SSL 1978; U. de Fribourg, Switzerland,

STD 1984. Emp: Pont. Bibl. Inst., 1982- Prof., Textual Criticism & OT Exegesis; *Biblica*, 1984- Assoc. Ed. Spec: Hebrew Bible. Pub: *Additions or Omissions in the Books of Samuel* (Vandenhoeck & Ruprecht, 1984). Addr: (o) Pontifical Biblical Institute, via della a Pilotta, 25, 00187 Roma, Italy 06-679-6453.

PITARD, Wayne T., b. Knoxville, TN, May 9, 1951, s. of Cecil & Ruby (Snell), m. Angela (McCall), chil: Sarah; Samantha. Educ: Harvard U., MA 1979, PhD 1982. Emp: U. of Ill., 1983-92 Asst. Prof., 1992- Assoc. Prof. Excv: ASOR Syrian Survey of the Ghab & Rouj, 1979 Field Arch. Spec: Hebrew Bible, Semitic Languages, Texts and Epigraphy. Pub: "A New Edition of the 'Rapiuma' Texts: *KTU* 1:20-22" *BASOR* 285 (1992); "The Identity of the Bir-Hadad of the Melgart Stela" *BASOR* 272 (1988); *Ancient Damascus* (Eisenbrauns, 1987); "RS 34.126: Notes on the Text" *Maarav* 3 (1984); "Amarna *ekemu* and Hebrew *naqam*" *Maarav* 3 (1982); and others. Mem: ASOR 1979-. Rec: Cinema. Addr: (o) 3019 Foreign Languages Bldg., 707 S Matthews, Urbana, IL 61801 217-333-2207; (h) 203 Arbours Dr., Savoy, IL 61874 217-398-6544.

PITIGLIANI, Letizia, b. Rome, Italy, November 23, 1935, d. of Fausto & Nelly (Van Straten), m. Marcius K. Benenson, chil: Alexander; Daniela. Educ: Accademia di Belle Arti, Rome, Dipl. 1955. Emp: Savola Roma, 1956-57 Art Instr.; Mus. of Modern Art, N.Y., 1959 Writer; Newark Sch. of Fine & Industrial Art, N.J., 1960-61 Instr., Hist. of Art. Spec: Archaeology. Pub: "A Rare Look at the Jewish Catacombs of Rome" *BAR* 6/3 (1980); and others. Addr: (o) Artist's Loft Studio, 448 W 37th St., Apt. 6C, New York, NY 10024 212-244-1536; (h) 585 W End Ave., Apt. 16F, New York, NY 10024 212-799-7862.

PIXLEY, George V., b. Chicago, IL, March 29, 1937, s. of John & Phebe, m. Janyce (Babcock), chil: Rebecca; Devin; Mark. Educ: U. of Chicago, MA 1962, PhD 1968. Emp: Sem. Evang. de Puerto Rico, 1963-75 Prof.; Sem. Bautista de Mexico, 1975-85 Prof.; Sem. Teol. Bautista, 1986- Prof.; Iliff Sch. of Theol., 1985 Vis. Prof.; Colgate Rochester Div. Sch., 1986 Vis. Prof. Spec: Hebrew Bible. Pub: *Historia de Israel desde los pobres* (DEI, 1989; Fortress, 1992); *Exodo, Lectura Evangélica y Popular* (CUPSA, 1983; Orbis, 1987); "Antecedentes Biblicos a la Lucha Contra el Fetichismo" *Cristianismo y Sociedad* 23 (1985); *El Libro de Job* (Sem. Bibl. Latinoamericano, 1982); *Reino de Dios* (La Aurora, 1977; Orbis, 1981). Mem: SBL 1968-; Soc. Argentina de Prof. de Sagrada Escritura 1969-. Rec: Music, travel. Addr: (o) Seminario Teologico Bautista, Apartado 2555, Managua, Nicaragua 25409.

PIXNER, Virgil B., b. Meran, Italy, March 23, 1921, s. of Luis & Luzia. Emp: Dormition

Abbey, Jerusalem, Theol. Fac., 1973- Bibl. Arch. Excv: Gate of the Essenes, SW Tower, Jerusalem, 1977-. Spec: Archaeology, New Testament, Apocrypha and Post-biblical Studies. Pub: *Wege des Messias und Stätten der Urkirche* (Brunnen, 1991); *With Jesus Through Galilee According the Fifth Gospel* (Corazin, 1991); "Tabgha, Capernaum, Bethsaida" *BA* (1985); "Unravelling the Copper Scroll Code: A Study on the Topography of 3Q15" *RQ* 43 (1983); "Where was the Original *Via Dolorosa?*" *CNI* 27 (1973); *The Glory of Bethlehem* (Jerusalem, 1981); and others. Rec: Hiking, swimming. Addr: (o) Dormition Abbey, PO Box 22, Jerusalem, Israel 02-719927; (h) Benedictine Monastery, PO Box 52, Tiberias, Israel 06-721061.

PLAUT, W. Gunther, b. Munster, Germany, November 1, 1912, s. of Jonas & Selma (Gumprich), m. Elizabeth (Strauss), chil: Jonathan; Judith. Educ: U. of Berlin, LLB 1933, JSD 1934; Hebrew Union Coll., MHL, Rabbi 1939, DD 1964; U. of Toronto, LLD 1978; Cleveland Coll. of Jewish Stud., DLitt 1979; York U., LLD 1987. Emp: Haifa U., Lect.; Ben-Gurion U., Lect.; York U., Adj. Prof. Spec: Hebrew Bible. Pub: *The Torah* (1981); *The Magen David* (1980); *Proverbs—A Commentary* (1961); and others. Mem: Canadian Jewish Congress, Pres. 1977-80; Cen. Conf. of Amer. Rabbis, Pres. 1983-85. Rec: Tennis, golf, chess. Addr: (o) Holy Blossom Temple, 1950 Bathurst St., Toronto, ON M5P 3K9, Canada.

PLUEMACHER, Eckhard, b. Remscheid, Germany, October 23, 1938, s. of Walther & Liselotte (Schiller), m. Doris (Fouquet), chil: Johanna. Educ: U. Goettingen, ThD 1967. Emp: Bibliothek der Kirchlichen Hochschule, Berlin, 1970-73, Bibliotheksrat, 1974- Bibliotheks-direktor. Spec: New Testament, Apocrypha and Post-biblical Studies. Pub: *Identitaetverlust und Identitaetsgewinn: Studien zum Verhaeltnis von Kaiserzeitlicher Stadt und fruehem Christentum* (Neukirchener, 1987); "Apokryphe Apostelakten" *Pauly-Wissowa* Sup. 15 (1978); *Lukas als hel-lenistischer Schriftsteller: Studien zur Apostelgesschichte* (Vandenhoek & Ruprecht, 1972); and others. Mem: SNTS 1980-; Wissenschafliche Gesellschaft fur Theol., 1990-. Addr: (o) Bibliothek der Kirchlichen Hochschule Berlin, Teltower Damm 118, D-100 Berlin 37, Germany 030-816005-31; (h) Fuggerstr. 19, D-1000 Berlin 30, Germany 030-2135154.

POIRIER, Paul-Hubert, b. St. Simeon, Canada, May 2, 1948, s. of Michel & Bernadette (Bourque). Educ: Strasbourg U., PhD. Emp: Laval U., Fac. of Theol., 1979- Prof.; Ecole Pratique des Hautes Etudes, Paris, 1990-91 Vis. Prof. Spec: Semitic Languages, Texts and Epigraphy, Egyptology, Apocrypha and Post-biblical Studies. Pub: *La Version Copte de la Predication et du Martyre de Thomas* (1984); *L'Hymne de la Perle des Actes de Thomas* (1981); and others. Awd: Royal Soc. of Canada,

Fellow 1990-. Mem: SBL 1983-; CSSR 1979-; Intl. Assn. Patristic Stud. 1979-. Rec: Skiing, jogging. Addr: (o) U. Laval, Faculte de Theologie, Quebec, G1K 7P4, PQ, Canada 418-656-5324; (h) 175, 54 E Rue Est, Charlesbourg, Quebec G1H 6S2, Que., Canada 418-626-1180.

POKORNY, Petr, b. Brno, Czechia, April 21, 1933, s. of Blahoslav & Zdenka, m. Věra, chil: Mary; Ann; Cathren; Peter. Educ: Comenius' Fac. of Theol., ThB 1955, ThD 1963, Habil. 1967; Czechoslovak Acad. Sci., CSc 1968. Emp: Comenius' Fac., 1966-67 Lect.; U. of Greifswald, 1967-68 Assoc. Prof.; Charles U., Prague, 1968- Prof. Spec: New Testament. Pub: *Epheserbrief* (EVA, 1992); *Die Zukunft des Glaubens* (1992); *Colossians, A Commentary* (1991); *The Genesis of Christology* (1987); and others. Mem: SNTS 1967-; UBS Bible transl. com. 1986-. Rec: Skiing, jogging. Addr: (h) Horoušanská 7, CZ-190 04 Praha 9, Czech Republic 02-8640021.

POLLEY, Max E., b. South Bend, IN, June 3, 1928, s. of Maynard & Helen, m. Jacquelyn, chil: Vance; Lynn. Educ: Duke Div. Sch., BD 1953, PhD 1957. Emp: Davidson Coll., 1956- Prof. of Relig. Spec: Hebrew Bible. Pub: *Amos and the Davidic Empire* (Oxford U.P., 1989); articles in *Scripture in Context, Essays on the Comparative Method* (Pickwick, 1980), *Science, Faith and Revelation: An Approach to Christian Philosophy* (Broadman, 1979), *The Use of the Old Testament in the New Testament and Other Essays* (Duke U.P., 1972); and others. Mem: AAR 1956-80; SBL 1956-. Rec: Trout fishing, golf. Addr: (o) Davidson College, Davidson, NC 28036 704-892-2000; (h) Box 452, Davidson, NC 28036 704-892-4971.

POLOME, Edgar C., b. Brussels, Belgium, July 31, 1920, s. of Marcel Félicien & Berthe Henry, m. Sharon (Looper), chil: Monique Laure (Ellsworth); André Robert. Educ: Free U. of Brussels, BA 1940, PhD, Germanic Philol. 1949; Catholic U. of Louvain, MA 1943. Emp: Université Officielle du Congo Belge et du Ruanda-Urundi, 1956-61; U. of Tex. at Austin, 1961- Prof.; *Jour. of Indo-European Stud.*, 1972- Co-Ed., 1986- Managing Ed. Spec: Anatolian Studies. Pub: "A Note on Thraco-Phrygian Numerals" *Jour. of Indo-European Stud.* 14 (1986); "The Indo-European Numeral for 'five' and Hittite *panku*—'all'" in *Prātidānam: Indian, Iranian and Indo-European Studies Presented to F.B.J. Kuiper* (Mouton, 1968); "On the Origin of Hittite *h*" *Language* 28 (1952); and others. Awd: U. of Kiel, Germany, Fulbright Vis. Prof. 1968. Mem: Amer. Anthrop. Assn.; AIA; Indogermanische Gesellschaft; Linguistic Soc. of Amer. Addr: (o) U. of Texas at Austin, Dept. of Germanic Languages, E.P. Schoch Bldg., 3.302 Campus 63300 Austin, TX 78712 512-471-4123; (h) 2701 Rock Terrace Dr., Austin, TX 78704-3843 512-326-4146.

POPE, Marvin H., b. Durham, NC, June 23, 1916, s. of Charles & Bessie (Sorrell), m. Ingrid (Bloomquist). Educ: Yale U., PhD 1949. Emp: Duke U., 1947-49 Instr.; Yale U., 1949-55 Asst. Prof., Hebrew Lang. & Lit., 1955-86 Prof., NW Semitic Lang.; U. of Aleppo, 1980 Fulbright Lect.; U. of Muenster, Inst. fuer Ugarit forschung, 1986, 1990, 1991 Fulbright Res. Fellow. Excv: El-Jib (Gibeon), 1959, 1960 Sect. Supr. Spec: Hebrew Bible, Semitic Languages, Texts and Epigraphy. Pub: *Song of Songs*, AB vol. 7C (1977); *The Book of Job*, AB vol. 15 (1965, 1973); *El in the Ugaritic Texts* (Brill, 1955); and others. Awd: Natl. Relig. Book Awd. for AB *Song of Songs* 1978. Mem: Natl. Coun. on Relig. in Higher Educ. 1941-; AOS 1945-; AOS 1945-; ASOR; ASOR; SBL; SBL; RSV Bible Com. 1960-; RSV Bible Com. 1960-. Rec: Fishing, gardening. Addr: (h) 538 Round Hill Rd., Greenwich, CT 06831 203-869-7198.

POPKES, Wiard U., b. Ihren, June 30, 1936, s. of Enno & Elsbeth, m. Irma, chil: Dorothea; Alexander. Educ: Bapt. Sem. Rueschlikon, BD 1962; U. of Zuerich, ThD 1965. Emp: Muenster, 1966-69 Pastor; Hamburg Bapt. Sem., 1969-Tutor/Prof., NT; Hamburg U., 1977- Prof., NT. Spec: New Testament. Pub: *Adressaten, Situation und Form des Jakobusbriefes* (1986); *Gemeinde Raum des Vertrauens* (1984); *Abendmahl und Gemeinde* (1981); *Christus Traditus* (1967); and others. Mem: SNTS; Wissenschaftliche Gesellschaft fuer Theol. Addr: (o) Rennbahnstr. 115, D-22111 Hamburg 74, Germany 040-65585-0; (h) Oberfoersterkoppel 10, D-2055 Aumuehle, Germany 04104-2294.

PORTEN, Bezalel, b. February 14, 1931. Educ: Jewish Theol. Sem., MHL, Rabbi 1957; Columbia U., MA 1954, PhD Jewish Hist. 1964. Emp: U of Calif., Davis, 1965-70 Assoc. Prof., Hebrew & Bible; Haifa U., Israel, 1968-72 Teaching Fellow, Sr. Lect.; Tel-Aviv U., 1970 Teaching Fellow; Hebrew U., 1969-72 Teaching Fellow, 1972-80 Sr. Lect., 1980- Assoc. Prof., Jewish Hist.; U. of Pa., 1979-81 Sr. Fellow. Pub: *Irano-Judaiea II*, ed. (1990); *Textbook of Aramaic Documents from Ancient Egypt*, vol. 1-3, co-auth. (1986-93); "The Bisitun Inscription of Darius The Great: Aramaic Version" *Corpus Inscriptionum Iranicarum* (1982); "The Identity of King Adon" *BA* 44 (1981); "The Scroll of Ruth: A Rhetorical Study" *Gratz Coll. Ann. of Jewish Stud.* (1978); and others. Mem: Amer. Res. Ctr., Egypt; IES; Rabbinical Assembly; SBL. Addr: (o) Hebrew U., Dept. of Jewish History, Jerusalem 91905, Israel.

PORTER, Joshua R., b. Godley, England, May 7, 1921, s. of Joshua & Bessie. Educ: U. of Oxford, MA. Emp: Oriel Coll., Oxford, 1949-62 Chaplain, Lect.; U. of Exeter, 1962-86 Prof., Theol., Dept. Head; SE Sem., 1967 Vis. Prof.; *Folklore*, 1982- Ed. Bd.; Holyrood Sem., 1987-Lect. in OT Stud. Spec: Hebrew Bible, Semitic Languages, Texts and Epigraphy. Pub: "The Seer in Ancient Israel" in *The Seer in Celtic and Other*

Traditions (1989); "The Supposed Deuteronomic Redaction of the Prophets" *Schopfung und Befreiung* (1989); *Presence and Proclamation*, co-auth. (SCM/John Knox, 1970; Mercer U.P., 1984); "Old Testament Historiography" in *Tradition & Interpretation* (1979); *Leviticus* (Cambridge U.P., 1976); *Moses and Monarchy* (Blackwell, 1963); "Pre-Islamic Arabic Historical Traditions and the Early Historical Narratives of the Old Testament" *JBL* (1968); and others. Mem: SOTS, Pres. 1983-84; SBL; WCJS. Rec: Opera, theater. Addr: (h) 36 Theberton St., Barnsbury, London N1 0QX, England 071-354-5861.

PORTER, Stanley E., b. Long Beach, CA, November 23, 1956, s. of Stanley E. & Lorraine D. Educ: Point Loma Coll., BA 1977; Claremont Grad. Sch., MA 1980; Trinity Evang. Div. Sch., MA 1982; U. of Sheffield, England, PhD 1988. Emp: Biola U., 1982-83, 1987-91 Assoc. Prof.; *Filologia Neotestamentaria*, 1990- Ed. Adv. Bd.; Sheffield Acad. Press, 1991-92 Sr. Acad. Ed.; Trinity Western U., 1992- Assoc. Prof. Spec: New Testament. Pub: *"Katallassō" in Ancient Greek Literature, with Reference to the Pauline Writings* (Ediciones El Almendro, 1993); *Idioms of the Greek New Testament* (JSOT, 1992); *The Language of the New Testament: Classic Essays*, Ed. (JSOT, 1991); "The Argument of Romans 5: Can a Rhetorical Question Make a Difference?" *JBL* 110 (1991); "Is *dipsuchos* (James 1:8, 4:8) a 'Christian' Word?" *Biblica* 71 (1990); "*iste ginoskontes* in Ephesians 5:5: Does Chiasm Solve a Problem?" *ZNW* 81 (1990); "Thucydides 1.22.1 and Speeches in Acts: Is There a Thucydidean View?" *NT* 32 (1990); *Verbal Aspect in the Greek of the New Testament, with Reference to Tense and Mood* (Lang, 1989); "The Language of the Apocalypse in Recent Discussion" *NTS* 35 (1989); and others. Awd: U. of Sheffield, Vis. Res. Fellow, Bibl. Stud. 1988, Hon. Lect. in Bibl. Stud. 1991-92. Mem: Tyndale Fellow. 1984-; SBL 1987-; AAR 1987-; Assoc. Intl. de Papyrologues 1988-; APA 1989-. Rec: Used book buying, travel, tennis. Addr: (o) Trinity Western U., 7600 Glover Rd., Langley, B.C. V3A 6H4, Canada 604-888-7511; (h) 4557 204 St., Langley, B.C. V3A 6L3, Canada 604-533-0657.

POSWICK, R. Ferdinand, b. Brussels, Belgium, January 4, 1937, s. of Baron Prosper & Genevieve (de Dieudonne). Educ: Benedictine Monk, Professed 1957; Pont. Inst. for Theol., Rome, Lic. Theol. 1965. Emp: Collection *Bible et Vie Chretienne*, 1967-68 Dir.; "Centre: Informatique et Bible" & Bulletin *Interface* (Maredsous), 1979-80 Found. & Dir.; "Assn. Intl. Bible et Informatique," 1982 Found. & Gen. Sec. Spec: Hebrew Bible, New Testament, Semitic Languages, Texts and Epigraphy, Apocrypha and Post-biblical Studies. Pub: *Concordance de la Traduction ecuménique de la Bible* (Cerf, 1993); "Message chrétien et culture informatique" *Esprit et Vie* (1990); *Dictionnaire Encyclopédique de la Bible* (Brepols, 1987); *Concordance de la Bible de Jérusalem* (Cerf, 1981); *Table Pastorale de la Bible* (Lethielleux, 1974); and others. Mem: SBL 1980-; IOSCS 1980-; Assn. for Literary &

Linguistic Computing 1986-; Cath. Bibl. Fedn., Bd. of Dir. 1986. Rec: Newman & Kierkegaard stud., monastic stud., travel. Addr: (o) Centre Informatique et Bible, Maredsous, B-5537 Denee, Belgium 32-0-82699647.

POTTS, Daniel T., b. New York, NY, February 10, 1953, s. of Morgan & Virginia, m. Hildreth (Burnett), chil: Rowena; Daniel. Educ: Harvard Coll., AB 1975; Harvard U., PhD 1980. Emp: U. of Copenhagen, 1980-81 Vis. Lect., 1986-91 Lect.; Freie U., Berlin, 1981-86 Asst. Prof.; U. of Sydney, 1991- E.C. Hall Prof. of Middle East. Arch. Excv: Tepe Yahya, Iran, 1973, 1975 Site Supr.; Kurban Hoyuk, Turkey, 1981 Site Supr.; Thaj, Saudi Arabia, 1983 Dir.; ed-Dur, 1987-89; Tell Abraq, 1989-. Spec: Archaeology. Pub: *The Pre-Islamic Coinage of Eastern Arabia* (1991); *A Prehistoric Mound in the Emirate of Umm Al-Qaiwain: Excavations at Tell Abraq in 1989* (1990); *The Arabian Gulf in Antiquity* (1990); *Miscellanea Hasaitica* (1989); *Chronologies in Old World Archaeology*, contb. (U. of Chicago, 1987); "Reflections on the History and Archaeology of Bahrain" *JAOS* 105 (1985); "The Road to Meluhha" *JNES* 41 (1982); and others. Mem: AOS 1984-. Rec: Fishing, tennis, piano. Addr: (o) U. of Sydney, Dept. of Archaeology, Sydney, NSW 2006, Australia 61-2-692-3118; (h) 29 Henry St., Waverley, NSW 2024, Australia 61-2-369-1617.

POTTS, Donald R., b. St. Louis, MO, June 10, 1930, m. Jeanne (Daugherty), chil: Cynthia; Donald. Educ: SW Bapt. Sem., BD 1955, ThD 1959, MDiv 1973. Emp: SW Bapt. Sem., 1959-60 Instr.; Bapt. Ch., 1960-76 Pastor; Cameron Coll., 1960-64 Prof.; East Tex. Bapt. U., 1976- Prof., Chmn., Dept. of Relig. Spec: New Testament. Pub: Articles in *Holman Bible Dict.* (1991); and others. Mem: AAR. Rec: Reading, hunting, travel. Addr: (o) East Texas Baptist U., 1209 N Grove, Marshall, TX 75670 214-935-7963; (h) 702 Ambassador, Marshall, TX 75670 214-938-4046.

PRATICO, Gary Davis, b. Rutland, VT, January 6, 1946, m. Mary (Potter), chil: Martha Leigh; Aaron Pasquale. Educ: Berkshire Christian Coll., BA (magna cum laude), Bibl. Greek & NT 1969; Gordon-Conwell Theol. Sem., MDiv (summa cum laude), Bibl. Hebrew & OT 1973; Harvard Div. Sch., ThD, OT & Syro-Palestinian Arch. 1983. Emp: Gordon-Conwell Theol. Sem., 1972- Assoc. Prof., OT 1981- Dir., Hebrew Lang. Prog.; Harvard Semitic Mus., 1976-81 Cur. of Arch. Collections, Artifacts Cataloguer for Nuzi Res. Project, 1979 Dir. of Tell el-Kheleifeh Res. Project, ASOR. Excv: Carthage, 1975, 1977 Square Supr.; Idalion, 1977 Square Supr.; Tell el-Kheleifeh Survey, 1980. Spec: Archaeology, Hebrew Bible. Pub: *Egypt-Sinai-Negev*, Slide Set (BAS, 1987); "Where is Ezion-Geber? A Reappraisal of the Site Archaeologist Nelson Glueck Identified as King Solomon's Red Sea Port" *BAR* 7/5 (1986); "Tell el-Kheleifeh 1937-1940: A Forthcoming Reappraisal" *BA* 45 (1982);

"A Reappraisal of Nelson Glueck's Excavations at Tell el-Kheleifeh" *ASOR Newsletter* 6 (1982); "The Nuzi Collections in the Harvard Semitic Museum," contb., in *Studies on the Civilization and Culture of Nuzi and the Hurrians* (Eisenbrauns, 1981); articles in *ISBE, ABD;* and others. Mem: NEAS, Bd. of Dir. 1980-. Addr: (o) Harvard Semitic Museum, 6 Divinity Ave., Cambridge, MA 02138 617-495-4631; (h) 237 Hale St., Beverly, MA 01915 508-927-2337.

PRATO, Gian-Luigi, b. Bistagno, Italy, April 22, 1940, s. of Renato & Elva (Pesce). Educ: Pont. U. Gregoriana, Rome, STL 1965; Pont. Bibl. Inst., Rome, SSD 1975. Emp: Pont. U. Gregoriana, 1975- Prof., OT. Spec: Hebrew Bible, Semitic Languages, Texts and Epigraphy, Apocrypha and Post-biblical Studies. Pub: "Idolatry Compelled to Search for Its Gods: A Peculiar Agreement Between Textual Tradition and Exegesis (Amos 5:25-27 and Acts; 7:42-43)" in *Luke and Acts* (Mahwah, 1993); "Cosmopolitismo culturale e autoidentificazione etnica nella prima storiografia giudica" *RivB* 34 (1986); "Babilonia fondata dai giganti: il significato cosmico di Gen 11,1-9 nella storiografia dello Pseudo-Eupolemo" in *El misterio de la palabra: Homenaje...Luis Alonso Schokel* (1983); *Il Problema della teodica in Ben Sira: Composizione dei contrari e richiamo alle origini*, Analecta Biblica 65 (1975); and others. Mem: Convegni di Antico Testamento, Dir.; Comm. Storico Esegetico dell'Antico e del NT. Addr: (o) Piazza della Pilotta 4, 00187, Roma, Italy 06-67015336; (h) P. S. Maria Maggiore 5, 00185, Roma, Italy 06-4465563.

PRATSCHER, Wilhelm, b. Redlschlag, August 15, 1947, s. of Wilhelm & Theresia, m. Susanne, chil: Marianne; Georg. Educ: Magister 1972, Doc. 1973, Dozent 1986. Emp: U. of Vienna, 1973-88 Asst. Prof., 1988-92 Assoc. Prof., 1992- U. Prof. Spec: New Testament, Apocrypha and Post-biblical Studies. Pub: "Der Herrenbruder Jakobus und sein Kreis" *ET* 47 (1987); "Der Verzicht des Paulus auf finanziellen Unterhalt durch seine Gemeinden" *NTS* 25 (1979); "Gott ist groesser als unser Herz" *TZ* 32 (1976); and others. Awd: Kardinal Innitzer Foerderungspreis fuer Theol. 1986. Mem: Wissenschaftliche Gesellschaft fuer Theol. 1986-; SNTS 1989-. Rec: Theatre, gardening. Addr: (o) Rooseveltplatz 10, A-1090 Wien, Austria 0222-43-59-81; (h) Schubertgasse 5/13, A-1090 Wien, Austria 0222-319-53-41.

PREGEANT, W. Russell, b. Baton Rouge, LA, October 21, 1937, s. of Victor & Eloise (White). Educ: South. Meth. U., BD 1962; Yale U., STM 1963; Vanderbilt U., PhD 1970. Emp: Meth. Ch., 1968-72 Assoc. Pastor; Curry Coll., 1972- Prof. of Relig. & Phil., Chaplain. Spec: New Testament. Pub: "Christological Groundings for Liberation Praxis" *Modern Theol.* (1989); *Biblical Preaching on the Death of Jesus*, co-auth. (Abingdon, 1988); "Where is the Meaning?

Metaphysical Criticism and the Problem of Indeterminacy" *Jour. of Relig.* (1983); "Grace and Recompense: Reflections on a Pauline Paradox" *JAAR* (1979); *Christology Beyond Dogma: Matthew's Christ in Process Hermeneutic* (Fortress/Scholars, 1978); and others. Mem: SBL; AAR. Rec: Cajun/Creole cooking. Addr: (o) Curry College, Milton, MA 02186 617-333-0500; (h) 735 Adams St., #36, Dorchester, MA 02122.

PREMNATH, Devadasan N., b. India, October 21, 1950, s. of Easter & Saraswathy, m. Dr. Roslyn Karaban, chil: Deepa Lynn; Micah Rayan. Educ: Government Arts & Sci. Coll., Chittoor, India, BA 1970; S.V.U., India, MA 1972; United Theol. Coll., India, BD 1977; Grad. Theol. Union, ThD 1984. Emp: United Theol. Coll., India, 1984-87 Lect., OT; St. Bernard's Inst., 1988-92 Adj. Asst. Prof., OT, 1989- Registrar, 1992- Asst. Prof., OT. Spec: Hebrew Bible. Pub: "Latifundialization and Isaiah 5:8-10" *JSOT* 40 (1988); and others. Mem: SBL 1989-. Rec: Music, gardening, aerobics. Addr: (o) St. Bernard's Institute, 1100 S Goodman St., Rochester, NY 14620 716-271-1320; (h) 30 Gregory Hill Rd., Rochester, NY 14620 716-461-0126.

PRENDERGAST, Terrence, b. Montreal, Quebec, February 19, 1944, s. of John & Marion (Skerry). Educ: Saint Mary's U., Canada, MDiv 1972, ThD 1978; Regis Coll., Canada, STL 1982. Emp: Atlantic Sch. of Theol., 1975-81 Assoc. Prof.; Regis Coll., Canada, 1981- Assoc. Prof., 1991- Acad. Dean. Spec: New Testament. Pub: *Life and Death in the New Testament*, trans. (Harper & Row, 1986); *Dict. of the New Testament*, trans. (Harper & Row, 1981); and others. Mem: SBL 1973-; CBA 1978-. Addr: (o) Regis College, 15 St. Mary St., Toronto, ON, M4Y 2R5, Canada 416-922-5474; (h) 105 Madison Ave., Toronto, ON, M5R 2S3, Canada 416-963-4975.

PRETORIUS, Emil A. C., b. Bloemfontein, South Africa, October 17, 1934, s. of W. J. & G. G. (Kok), m. Isabel (Lindeque), chil: Celia; Ingrid; Anita. Educ: U. of Stellenbosch, BD 1958, ThD 1969; Inst. Judaicum Delitzschianum, Munster, BRD 1968. Emp: Min., 1961-76; U. of Fort Hare, 1976-78; U. of South Africa, 1979- Prof.; *Theol. Evangelica*, 1981-86 Co-Ed. Spec: New Testament. Pub: "Filippense: die evangelie van kerk wees in die skadu van die 'establishment'" in *Geloof en opdrag* (1992); "The Opposition *pneuma* and *sarx* as Persuasive Summons, Galatians 5:13-6:10" *Neotestamentica* (1992); "A Key to the Literature on Philippians" *Neotestamentica* 23/1 (1989); *Die Brief van Jakobus* (1988); "Images of Christ and Models of the Church in Hebrews" *Theologica Evangelica* 15/3 (1982); *From Eden to Rome*, co-auth. (Van Schaik, 1982); *Some Issues in Current New Testament Scholarship* (Fort Hare U.P., 1977); *Die resente Joodse beoordeling van*

die leer van Paulus (Pro Rege, 1972); and others. Mem: NT Soc. South Africa 1966-; SNTS 1984-. Rec: Swimming, gardening. Addr: (o) UNISA, Dept. of New Testament, PO Box 392, Pretoria, South Africa 012-429-4322; (h) 13 Nuwe Hoop St., Alphenpark 0181, Pretoria, South Africa 012-468993.

PRICE, James L., Jr., b. Chase City, VA, September 11, 1915, s. of James & Marguerite, m. Ruth (Watts), chil: James; Linda; Elisabeth. Educ: Princeton Theol. Sem., ThM 1943; U. of Cambridge, PhD 1951. Emp: Wash. & Lee U., 1946-48 Asst. Prof.; SW at Memphis, 1950-52 Assoc. Prof.; Duke U., 1952- Prof. Emeritus; *Interpretation*, 1963-75 Ed. Bd. Spec: New Testament. Pub: *The New Testament: Its History and Theology* (Macmillan, 1987); Articles in *HBD* (1985); "Expository Article: Luke 15:11-32" *Interpretation* (1977); *Interpreting the New Testament* (Holt, Rinehart & Winston, 1961, 1971); *Proclamation* Ser., co-auth. (Fortress); and others. Mem: AAR, Pres. 1965; SBL, Pres., SE Sect. 1961-62; SNTS. Rec: Backpacking, photography. Addr: (h) 500 Avinger Ln., Suite 202, Davidson, NC 28036.

PRICE, Jonathan J., b. St. Louis, MO, November 3, 1956, s. of Elmer & Madelon. Educ: Haverford Coll., BA 1978; Princeton U., MA 1982, PhD, Class. 1987. Emp: Princeton U., 1987-88 Lect.; Middlebury Coll., 1987-90 Asst. Prof.; Hebrew U., 1990-91 Vis. Fulbright Lect.; Tel Aviv U., 1991- Sr. Lect.; *Scripta Classica Israelica*, 1991- Sr. Co-ed. Pub: *Jerusalem Under Siege: The Collapse of the Jewish State* (Brill, 1992); "The Enigma of Philip b. Jakimos" *Historia* 40 (1991); "Who Conquered Masada in 66 C.E., and Who Lived There Until the Fortress Fell?" co-auth. *Zion* 55 (1990). Awd: Phi Beta Kappa 1978; Hebrew U., Jerusalem, Lady Davis Grad. Fellow. 1983-85; Lucius N. Littauer Found. Res. Grant 1990; Fulbright Res. Grant 1990-91; Memorial Found. for Jewish Culture Grant 1990-91. Mem: APA; Assn. of Anc. Hist.; AJS; Class. Assn. of New England; SBL. Addr: (o) Tel Aviv U., Classics Dept., Ramat Aviv, Tel Aviv 69978, Israel 03-640-9779.

PRINSLOO, Willem S., b. Vrede, South Africa, August 19, 1944, s. of Jacobus & Magrieta, m. Avrille, chil: Kobus; Karen; Marieta. Educ: U. of Pretoria, BA 1965, BD 1969, DD 1976. Emp: Dutch Reformed Ch., 1971-74 Min.; U. of Pretoria, 1975- Prof., OT, 1989- Dean, Fac. of Theol.; *Skrif en Kerk,* 1980- Ed. Spec: Hebrew Bible. Pub: *Die Psalms leef* (1991); *Die boek Joel* (1990); *Dialogue with God* (1987); *The Theology of the Book of Joel*, BZAW 163 (de Gruyter, 1985); "The Theology of Jer. 27:1-11" *OTWSA* 24 (1981); "Isaiah 14:12-15: Humiliation, Hubris, Humiliation" *ZAW* 93/3 (1981); "Isaiah 5:1-7: A Synchronic Approach" *OTWSA* 23 (1980); and others. Awd: U. of Tuebingen, Alexander von Humboldt Schol. 1982-83. Mem: South African Soc. for the Study of the OT. Rec: Tennis. Addr: (o) U. of Pretoria, Dept. of the Old Testament, Faculty of Theology, Pretoria 0002, South Africa

012-4202358; (h) 297 The Rand, Menlopark, Pretoria 0081, South Africa 012-476441.

PROPP, William H., Educ: Harvard Coll., AB (magna cum laude) 1979; Harvard U., AM 1983, PhD, Near East. Lang. & Civ. 1985. Emp: U. of Calif., San Diego, 1983-87 Lect., 1986- Coord., Judaic Stud. Prog., 1987- Asst. Prof., Hebrew Lang. & Bibl. Stud. Spec: Hebrew Bible. Pub: articles in *ABD* (Doubleday, 1992); "Did Moses Have Horns?" *BR* 4/1 (1988); *Water in the Wilderness: A Biblical Motif and its Mythological Background,* HSM; and others. Awd: Dorot Found., Travelling Fellow. 1980-81; Israel government, grant 1981-82. Mem: SBL. Addr: (o) U. of California, San Diego, Dept. of History, 0104, 9500 Gilman Dr., La Jolla, CA 92093 619-534-6187.

PROVAN, Iain W., b. Johnstone, Scotland, May 6, 1957, s. of William and Rena (Jamieson), m. Lynette Elizabeth, chil: Andrew Iain; Kirsty Margaret; Duncan William. Educ: U. of Glasgow, MA 1977; London Bible Coll., BA 1980; U. of Cambridge, PhD 1986. Emp: King's Coll., London, 1986-88 Lect., Bibl. Stud.; U. of Wales, 1988-89 U. Fellow; U. of Edinburgh, 1989- Lect., Hebrew & OT Stud. Spec: Hebrew Bible. Pub: "Past, Present and Future in Lamentations 3:52-66: The Case for a 'Precative Perfect' Re-examined" *VT* 41 (1991); *Lamentations,* New Century Bible Comm. (Marshall Pickering, 1991); "Lamentations," "Kings" in *A Dictionary of Biblical Interpretation* (SCM, 1990); "Feasts, Booths and Gardens (Thr 2,6a)" *ZAW* 102 (1990); "Reading Texts Against an Historical Background: The Case of Lamentations 1" *Scandinavian Jour. of the OT* 1 (1990); *Hezekiah and the Books of Kings* (de Gruyter, 1988); and others. Mem: SOTS 1986-; SBL 1988-. Rec: Soccer, golf, chess, hill-walking, reading. Addr: (o) New College, Faculty of Divinity, The Mound, Edinburgh EH1 2LX, Scotland 031-225-8400; (h) 9 Pleasance Court, Dunfermline, Fife KY12 0TT, Scotland 0383-734120.

PRYOR, John W., b. Sydney, Australia, December 18, 1943, m. Lynn, chil: Timothy; Julia; Andrew. Educ: Sydney U., BA 1964; London U., BD 1968; Cambridge U., MA 1974; Australian Coll. of Theol., ThD 1991. Emp: Union Bibl. Sem., India, 1973-76 Lect.; Pacific Theol. Coll., Fiji, 1979-81 Lect.; Bible Coll. of Victoria, Australia, 1981-85 Lect.; Ridley Coll., Australia, 1986-91 Lect.; Australian Coll. of Theol., 1992- Registrar. Spec: New Testament. Pub: *John—Evangelist of the Covenant People* (DLT/InterVarsity, 1992); *In the Fullness of Time: Biblical Studies in Honour of D.W.B. Robinson,* co-ed. (ANZEA, 1992); "The Great Thanksgiving and the Fourth Gospel" *BZ* 199 (1991); "The Johannine Son of Man and the Descent-Ascent Motif" *JETS* 34 (1991); "John 3:3,5—A Study in the Relation of John's Gospel to the Synoptic Tradition" *JSNT* 41 (1991); "Jesus and Israel in the Fourth Gospel—John 1:11" *NT* 37/3 (1990); "Papyrus Egerton 2 and

the Fourth Gospel" *Australian Bibl. Rev.* 37 (1989); and others. Mem: SBL; Fellow. for Bibl. Stud., Melbourne, Pres. 1988. Rec: Biographies, opera. Addr: (o) Australian College of Theology, 6/388 Anzac Parade, Kingsford, NSW 2032, Australia 02-663-2495.

PRZYBYLSKI, Benno, b. Samter, Germany, May 21, 1941, s. of Adolf & Frieda, m. Brigitte, chil: Tiana; Matthew. Educ: U. of BC, Canada, BSc 1965, MA 1971; N Amer. Bapt. Sem., MDiv 1969; McMaster U., PhD 1975. Emp: McMaster U., 1976-81 Res. Asst. Prof.; Edmonton Bapt. Sem., 1981- Prof. Spec: New Testament. Pub: "The Role of Mt. 3:13-4:11 in the Structure and Theology of the Gospel of Matthew" *BTB* 4 (1974); "The Role of Calendrical Data in Gnostic Literature" *VC* 34 (1980); "The Spirit: Paul's Journey to Jesus and Beyond" in *From Jesus to Paul: Studies in Honour of F.W. Beare* (Wilfrid Laurier U.P., 1984); *Righteousness in Matthew and His World of Thought,* SNTS Mon. Ser. 41 (Cambridge U.P., 1980); and others. Mem: SNTS; CSBS; SBL. Rec: Skiing, golf. Addr: (o) Edmonton Baptist Seminary, 11525-23 Ave., Edmonton, AL T6J 4T3, Canada 403-437-1960; (h) 2724-118 St., Edmonton, AB T6J 3P9, Canada 403-430-0377.

PUMMER, Reinhard, b. Znaim, Czechoslovakia, November 30, 1938, s. of Eduard & Maria, m. Lucille. Educ: U. of Vienna, Austria, PhD 1965. Emp: U. of Ottawa, Dept. of Relig. Stud., 1967- Prof.; *Eglise et Theologie,* Ed. Cons. for the OT. Spec: Hebrew Bible, Apocrypha and Post-biblical Studies. Pub: *A Companion to Samaritan Studies,* co-auth. (Mohr, 1993); *Samaritan Marriage Contracts and Deeds of Divorce* vol. I (Harrassowitz, 1993); *Die Samaritaner,* co-auth., Wege der Forschung 604 (Wissenschaftliche Buchgesellschaft, 1992); "Were There Samaritan-Christian Churches?" in *Proc. of the First Intl. Congress of the Soc. d'Etudes Samaritaines* (Tel Aviv U.P., 1991); "ARGARIZIN—A Criterion for Samaritan Provenance?" *JSJ* (1987-88); "Samaritan Amulets from the Roman-Byzantine Period and their Wearers" *RB* (1987); *The Samaritans,* Iconography of Relig. 23, 5 (Brill, 1986); "The Present State of Samaritan Studies" *JSS* (1978); "Genesis 34 in Jewish Writings of the Hellenistic and Roman Periods" *HTR* (1982); and others. Awd: Social Sci. & Humanities Res. Coun. of Can. 1983-84, 1987-88, 1991-92. Mem: CSBS; SBL; ASOR; IOSCS; Soc. d'Etudes Samaritaines. Addr: (o) U. of Ottawa, Dept. of Religious Studies, Ottawa, ON K1N 6N5, Canada 613-564-4213.

PURVIS, James D., b. Chicago, IL, September 18, 1932, s. of Fay & Verda (Appelgate), m. Adele (Germain), chil: James D., Jr.; Jeffrey D.; Gregory R. Educ: Drake U., BA 1954, MA 1954, BD 1956; Harvard U., ThD 1963. Emp: Conn. Coll., 1961-66 Asst. Prof., Relig.; Boston U., 1966- Prof., Relig. Excv: Idalion, Cyprus, 1972 Area Supr.; Dor, Israel, 1980-81 Field Supr., Dir., Vol. Prog. Spec: Archaeology, Hebrew Bible,

Apocrypha and Post-biblical Studies. Pub: *Jerusalem, the Holy City: A Bibliography,* 2 vol. (Scarecrow, 1988-91); "The Barton Collection, the Boston University Library" *BASOR* 248 (1982); "An Early Samaritan Decalogue Inscription," co-auth. *Israel Mus. News* 11 (1976); "The Paleography of the Samaritan Inscription from Thessalonica" *BASOR* 221 (1976); "The Fourth Gospel and the Samaritans" *VT* 17 (1975); *The Samaritan Pentateuch and the Origin of the Samaritan Sect* (Harvard U.P., 1968); "Ben Sira and the Foolish People of Shechem" *JNES* 24 (1965); and others. Awd: Boston U., Metcalf Awd. for Excellence in Teaching 1986. Rec: Philately, landscape gardening, skiing, classical music, baseball. Addr: (o) Boston U., Dept. of Religion, 745 Commonwealth Ave., Boston, MA 02215 617-353-4427; (h) 11 Page Rd., Lexington, MA 02173 617-861-9542.

PUSKAS, Charles B., b. Youngstown, OH, November 3, 1951, s. of Charles B., Sr. & Eva Laura, m. Susan Elaine, chil: Rita Marie; Charles B., III. Educ: Cen. Coll., BA 1974; Wheaton Coll. Grad. Sch., MA 1975; St. Louis U., PhD 1980. Emp: *Theology Digest,* 1975-77 ed. work; Evangel Coll., 1977-80 Asst. Prof.; SW Mo. State U., 1981-86 Adj. Prof.; Drury Coll., 1989-90 Adj. Prof.; Fortress Press, 1990- Acad. Ed. Spec: New Testament. Pub: *The Letters of Paul: An Introduction* (Liturgical, 1993); *An Introduction to the New Testament* (Hendrickson, 1989); and others. Mem: SBL 1975-; CBA 1976-; AAR. Rec: 10K runs, swimming, golf, basketball, boating. Addr: (o) Fortress Press, 426 South Fifth St., Box 1209, Minneapolis, MN 55440 612-330-3255; (h) 6994 W. Shadow Lake Dr., Lino Lakes, MN 55014 612-486-8659.

QIMRON, Elisha, Emp: Ben Gurion U. of the Negev, Prof. Spec: Semitic Languages, Texts and Epigraphy. Pub: "Column 14 of the Temple Scroll" *IEJ* 38 (1988); "Further New Readings in the Temple Scroll" *IEJ* 37 (1987); *The Hebrew of the Dead Sea Scrolls,* HSS 29 (Scholars, 1986); "An Unpublished Halakhic Letter from Qumran," co-auth., in *Biblical Archaeology Today: Proceedings of the International Congress on Biblical Archaeology, Jerusalem, April 1984* (IES, 1985); and others. Addr: (o) Ben Gurion U. of the Negev, Beer-Sheva, Israel.

QUAST, Kevin B., b. Edmonton, AB, Canada, December 5, 1957, s. of John & Olive, m. Sandra A. (Falkenberg), chil: Kira Janelle; Graham Duncan. Educ: N Amer. Bapt. Coll., BA 1979; Acadia U., MDiv 1982; U. of Toronto, DTh 1987. Emp: Ontario Theol. Sem., 1984- Prof., NT. Spec: New Testament. Pub: *Reading the Gospel of John* (Paulist, 1991); "Reexamining Johannine Community" *Toronto Jour. of Theol.* 5/2 (1989); and others. Mem: SBL; CSBS; Canadian Evang. Theol. Assn. Addr: (o) Ontario Theological Seminary, 25 Ballyconnor Court,

Willowdale, ON M2M 4B3, Canada 416-226-6380; (h) 44 Overlord Cres., Scarborough, ON M1B 4P4, Canada 416-282-3576.

QUEEN-SUTHERLAND, Kandy M., b. Gastonia, NC, November 18, 1951, d. of W.J. Queen & Lois J., m. D. Dixon Sutherland, chil: Christa Marie; Caleb Daniel. Educ: Winthrop Coll., BS 1973; South. Bapt. Theol. Sem., MDiv 1976, PhD 1982. Emp: South. Bapt. Theol. Sem., 1981 Instr., Bibl. Hebrew; Stetson U., 1982-83 Vis. Asst. Prof., Relig., 1991- Assoc. Prof., Relig.; Bapt. Theol. Sem., 1984-91 Assoc. Prof., OT. Spec: Hebrew Bible. Pub: "An Exegetical Study of Cultic Calendars in the Old Testament" *Faith & Mission* (1991); articles in *Holman Bible Dict.* (1991); articles in *Mercer Dict. of the Bible* (1990); "Uma Visao da Gloria de Deus" *O Semeador Baptista* June (1989); and others. Mem: SBL; AAR; NABPR. Rec: Golf, swimming, gardening. Addr: (o) Stetson U., Dept. of Religion, Campus Box 8352, DeLand, FL 32720 904-822-8933; (h) 1515 War Admiral Dr., DeLand, FL 32724 904-738-3898.

QUESNEL, Michel, b. Paris, France, June 11, 1942, s. of Maxime & Simonne (Fayet). Educ: Strasbourg U., Maitrise, Theol. 1969; Pont. Bibl. Inst., Rome, Lic., Sacred Scriptures 1971; Ecole Biblique, Elève Titulaire 1978; Cath. Inst., Paris, ThD 1984. Emp: Cath. Inst., Paris, 1988 Vice-Rector, 1991 Prof. Spec: New Testament. Pub: *Jesus-Christ selon saint Matthieu* (Desclé, 1991); "Les Citations de Jérémie dans l'Evangile selon saint Matthieu" *EstBib* 47 (1989); "Le Sacramentel dans le N.T." *RSR* 75 (1987); "Le Baptême" *L'Année Canonique* 29 (1985-86); "Paul en conflit avec les chrétiens de son Temps" *Foi et Vie* 24 (1985); *Baptisés dans l'Esprit, Baptéme et Esprit saint dans les Actes des Apôtres* (Cerf, 1985); *Comment lire un Evangile, saint Marc* (Seuil, 1984); "Le Baptême chrétien et les baptêmes juifs" *Catéchèse* 88-89 (1982); *Aux sources des sacrements* (Cerf, 1977); and others. Awd: Prix Jean et Maurice de Pange, 1985. Mem: SNTS 1988-; Assn. Cath. Francaise pour l'Etude de la Bible 1971-; Anciens et Amis Ecole Biblique, V.P. 1991. Rec: Music, composition of songs, swimming. Addr: (o) Institute Catholique, 21, Rue d'Assas, F. 75270, Paris, Cedex 06, France 33-1-66-39-5211; (h) 2 Bis, Quai des Celestins, F. 75004, Paris, France 33-1-42-74-1778.

RAABE, Paul R., b. KS, April 9, 1953, s. of Bernard & Evelyn. Educ: Concordia Sem., MDiv 1979; Wash. U., MA 1979; U. of Mich., PhD 1989. Emp: Concordia Coll., 1979-83 Instr.; Concordia Sem., 1983- Asst. Prof., 1991- Assoc. Prof.; *Concordia Jour.,* 1985- Ed. Com. Spec: Hebrew Bible, Semitic Languages, Texts and Epigraphy. Pub: "Deliberate Ambiguity in the Psalter" *JBL* (1991); *Psalm Structures: A Study of Psalms with Refrains* (Sheffield, 1990); "The Effect of Repetition in the Suffering Servant Song" *JBL* (1984); "Daniel 7: Its Structure and Role in the

Book" *Hebrew Ann. Rev.* 9. Mem: ASOR 1980-; SBL 1983-; CBA 1990-. Rec: Travel, sports. Addr: (o) Concordia Seminary, 801 DeMun Ave., St. Louis, MO 63105 314-721-5934; (h) 7442 Grant Village Dr., Apt. A, St. Louis, MO 63123 314-849-2490.

RABAN, Avner, b. Ramat David, Israel, May 10, 1937, s. of Ze'ev & Sara, m. Dina, chil: Roee; Semadar; Hagai; Idoe. Educ: Hebrew U., Jerusalem, MA 1974, PhD 1982. Emp: Haifa U., Ctr. for Maritime Stud., 1973-82 Sr. Marine Sci., 1982-87 Chmn., 1991- Head of Ctr., Head of Dept. for Hist. of Maritime Civilizations; Ohel Sara Coll., 1976-84 Tchr.; Haifa U., 1982-88 Lect., 1988- Sr. Lect.; Harvard U., 1987-88 Vis. Schol.; U. of Maryland, 1988 Vis. Schol. Excv: Dor, 1982, 1984 Dir.; Tel Akko, 1983-85 Field Dir., 1989 Co-dir.; Ashkelon, 1985-87, 1990 Dir.; Turkish boat, Sea of Galilee, 1989 Dir.; Caesarea, 1990-91 Dir., Underwater & Coastal Excvn., Co-dir., Land Excvn. Spec: Archaeology. Pub: "The Sea Peoples and Their Contributions to Civilization," co-auth., *BAR* 17/6 (1991); "The Port City of Akko in the MBII Period" *Michmanim* 4/5 (1991); "The Philistines in Western Jezreel Valley" *BASOR* 284 (1991); "The Medinet Habu Ships: Another Interpretation" *Intl. Jour. of Nautical Arch.* 18/2 (1989); *King Herod's Dream—Caesarea on the Sea*, co-auth. (Norton, 1988); *Archaeology of Coastal Changes*, Brit. Arch. Reports 404, ed. (1988); "The Harbor of the Sea Peoples at Dor" *BA* 50/2 (1987); *Harbour Archaeology*, Brit. Arch. Reports 257, ed. (1985); and others. Mem: Israel Soc. of Quaternarian Stud. 1980-; Israel Arch. Exploration Soc. 1981-90; IES 1990-. Addr: (o) U. of Haifa, Ctr. for Maritime Studies, Mt. Carmel, Haifa 31999, Israel 04-240600; (h) Kibbutz Ramat David 30093, Israel 065-49085.

RADDAY, Yehuda T., b. Czechoslovakia, July 21, 1913, s. of Felix & Francisca, m. Ilse, chil: Elinor. Educ: Jewish Theol. Sem., MA 1959; Hebrew U., Jerusalem, PhD 1969. Emp: Technion Israel Inst. of Technology, 1979-82 Dean, Dept. of Gen. Stud., 1982- Prof.; Hochsch. Jud. Studien, Heidelberg, 1982-83 Rektor, 1987-92 Vis. Prof.; U. of Heidelberg, 1992-93 Vis. Prof. Spec: Hebrew Bible. Pub: *On Humour in the Hebrew Bible* (Sheffield, 1990); *Genesis–An Authorship Study in Computer-Assisted Statistical Linguistics* (1985); "The Spoils of Egypt" *Ann. of the Swedish Theol. Inst.* 12 (1983); "The Unity of Zechariah in the Light of Statistical Linguistics" *ZAW* (1975); *The Unity of Isaiah in the Light of Statistical Linguistics* (Hildesheim, 1973); and others. Mem: WUJS 1970-. Rec: Reading, travel. Addr: (o) Technion Israel Institute of Technology, Dept. of General Studies, Haifa 32000, Israel 04-221532; (h) 25a Crusader Ln., Haifa 34373, Israel 04-339801.

RADER, Rosemary, b. St. Leo, MN, d. of Anton & Cecelia (Skrypek). Educ: U. of Minn., MA 1966; Stanford U., PhD 1977. Emp: Ariz. State U., 1977-84 Assoc. Prof.; Stanford U.,

1981 Vis. Prof.; U. of San Diego, U. of St. John, 1985 Vis. Prof. Spec: New Testament, Apocrypha and Post-biblical Studies. Pub: *Breaking Boundaries: Male-Female Friendships in Early Christian Communities* (Paulist, 1983); "Christian Asceticism" in *Dict. of Christian Spirituality* (Westminster, 1983); and others. Mem: AAR 1977-; Amer. Soc. of Ch. Hist. 1977-. Rec: Ballet, classical music. Addr: (o) 2675 E Larpenteur Ave., St. Paul, MN 55109 612-777-5650.

RADL, Walter, b. Aussig, May 10, 1940, s. of Georg & Elisabeth, m. Gertrud, chil: Eckart; Albert; Hildegard. Educ: U. of Innsbruck, Bonn & Bochum, ThD 1968, Habil., NT 1980. Emp: U. of Augsburg, 1984- Prof., NT Exegesis. Spec: New Testament. Pub: *Das Lukas-Evangelium* (Wiss. Buchgesellschaft, 1988); "Kult und Evangelium bei Paulus" *BZ* 31 (1987); *Galaterbrief: Stuttgarter Kleiner Komment* (Kath. Bibelwerk, 1986); "Befreiung aus dem Gefaengnis. Die Darstellung eines biblischen Grundthemas" *BZ* 27 (1983); "'Firmung' im Neuen Testament?" *Communio* 11 (1982); "Das 'Apostelkonzil' und seine Nachgeschichte, dargestellt am Weg des Barnabas" *ThQ* 162 (1982); "Der Tod Jesu in der Darstellung der Evangelien" *Theol. & Glaube* 72 (1982); *Paulus und Jesus im lukanischen Doppelwerk* (Lang, 1975); and others. Mem: SNTS 1984-. Addr: (o) Universitaetsstrasse 10, D-86135 Augsburg, Germany 0821-598-2722; (h) Watzmannstrasse 5, D-8906 Gersthofen, Germany 0821-499294.

RAINEY, Anson F., b. Dallas, TX, January 11, 1930, s. of Anson & Bertie Mae, m. Zipora (Cochavy), chil: Johanan. Educ: Cali. Bapt. Theol. Sem., MA 1953; BD 1954, MTh 1955; Brandeis U., MA 1959, PhD 1962. Emp: Amer. Inst. for Holy Land Stud., 1962- Vis. Prof.; Tel Aviv U., Israel, 1963- Prof.; Bar Ilan U., Israel, 1982- Vis. Prof. Excv: Lachish, 1966, 1968, Arad, 1967, Beer-sheba, 1969-76, Tel Michal, 1977-80 Supr.; Tel Gerisa, 1981-88 Field Supervisor. Spec: Archaeology, Hebrew Bible, Mesopotamian Studies, Semitic Languages, Texts and Epigraphy, Egyptology Pub: *El Amarna Letters 359-379* (AOATS, 1978); *The Society of Ugarit* (Biaik Inst., 1967); and others. Mem: IES; SBL; ASOR. Addr: (o) Tel Aviv U., Inst. of Archaeology, Ramat Aviv, Box 39040, Tel Aviv 69978, Israel 472-3-420703; (h) Yad Hahazaka 4, Ramat Gan 52337, Israel 972-3-74066.

RAISANEN, Heikki M., b. Helsinki, Finland, December 10, 1941, s. of Martti & Saara (Itkonen), m. Leena (Wright), chil: Ilkka; Markku; Päivi; Tuomo. Educ: U. of Helsinki, Finland, STL 1967, MA 1968, STD 1969. Emp: U. of Helsinki, 1975 Prof., NT Exegesis; Finnish Acad., 1984- Res. Prof. Spec: New Testament, Apocrypha and Post-biblical Studies. Pub: *Jesus, Paul and Torah* (Sheffield, 1992); *Beyond New Testament Theology* (SCM, 1990); The 'Messianic Secret' in Mark (T & T Clark, 1990);

Paul and the Law (Fortress, 1986); and others. Awd: Edinburgh, DD 1990. Mem: SNTS 1975-; Finnish Exegetical Soc. Addr: (o) U. of Helsinki, Dept. of Bibl. Exegetics, Neitsytpolku 1 b, SF-00140 Helsinki 14, Finland; (h) Vantaanjänne 1 B 11, SF-01730 Vantaa 73, Finland 0-898422.

RALSTON, Timothy J., b. Toronto, Canada, April 2, 1956, s. of Henry William & Iva Eileen, m. Carol Anne, chil: Briana Leigh. Educ: U. of Waterloo, ON, BS 1978; Dallas Theol. Sem., ThM 1983. Emp: Mount Carmel Bible Sch., AB, 1984 Lect.; Cen. Bapt. Sem., ON, 1985 Instr.; Dallas Theol. Sem., 1988-92 Instr., 1992- Asst. Prof. Spec: New Testament. Pub: "The *Majority Text* and Byzantine Origins" *NTS* 38 (1992); "The Theological Significance of Paul's Conversion" *BS* (1990). Awd: Dallas Theol. Sem., Henry C. Theissen Awd. in NT Stud. 1983. Mem: ETS 1988-; SBL 1988-. Rec: Scuba-diving, sailing, skiing, car repair. Addr: (o) Dallas Theological Seminary, 3909 Swiss Ave., Dallas, TX 75204 214-841-3668; (h) 1525 Bosque Dr., Garland, TX 75040 214-276-5414.

RAMSEY, George W., b. Prescott, AR, December 19, 1937, s. of Harmon & Sarah, m. Ellen, chil: H. Scott. Educ: Union Theol. Sem., BD; Princeton U., MA 1965, PhD 1968. Emp: Carleton U., Canada, 1965-68 Asst. Prof.; Presbyn. Coll., 1968- Herrington Prof. of Relig.; *Presbyn. Outlook*, 1979-81 Ed. Spec: Hebrew Bible. Pub: Articles in *ABD* (1992); "Plots, Gaps, Repetition, and Ambiguity in Luke 15" *PIRS* (1991); "Is Name-Giving an Act of Domination in Genesis 2:23 and Elsewhere?" *CBQ* (1988); *The Quest for the Historical Israel* (John Knox, 1981; SCM, 1982); "Speech Forms in Hebrew Law and Prophetic Oracles" *JBL* (1977); "Amos 4:12–A New Perspective" *JBL* (1970); and others. Mem: SBL 1965-; CBA 1984-. Rec: Tennis, volleyball. Addr: (o) Presbyterian College, Dept. of Religion, Clinton, SC 29325; (h) 911 Calvert Ave., Clinton, SC 29325.

RASCO, Emilio, b. La Habana, Cuba, December 14, 1921, s. of Emilio & Ofelia (Bermudez). Educ: Pont. U., Spain, PhL 1948; Pont. Bibl. Inst., Rome, SSL 1958; Gregorian Pont. U., Rome, STD 1975. Emp: Gregorian Pont. U., Prof. Emeritus. Spec: New Testament. Pub: *La Teologia de Lucas: Origen, Desarrollo, Orientaciones* (U. Gregoriana, 1976); and others. Mem: Assn. Bibl. Italiana 1975-; SNTS 1980-. Addr: (o) Pontifical U. Gregoriana, Piazza della Pilotta 4-00187, Roma, Italy 06-6701-5378.

RASHKOW, Ilona N., b. New York, NY, April 26, 1947, d. of John & Helen Nemesnyik, m. Bruce C. Educ: U. of Maryland, MA 1984, PhD 1988. Emp: U. of Maryland, 1987-88 Instr.; Georgetown U., 1988-89 Lect.; State U. of N.Y. at Stony Brook, Asst. Prof. Spec: Hebrew Bible. Pub: *The Phallacy of Genesis: A Feminist-*

Psychoanalytic Approach (Westminster/John Knox, 1993); "Ruth: The Power of Discourse and the Discourse of Power" in *Feminist Readings of the Book of Ruth* (Sheffield, 1993); "Daughters and Fathers in Genesis...Or, What is Wrong with this Picture?" in *The New Literary Criticism and the Hebrew Bible* (Sheffield, 1993); "Intertextuality, Transference, and the Reader in/of the Biblical Text" in *Reading Between Texts* (Westminster/John Knox, 1992); "Hebrew Bible Translation and the Fear of Judaization" *Sixteenth Century Jour.* 21 (1990); *Upon the Dark Places: Sexism and Anti-Semitism in English Renaissance Biblical Translation* (Sheffield, 1990); "The Rape of Dinah: Crime and Punishment?" *Mid-Hudson Lang. Stud.* 12 (1989); and others. Awd: Meyerhoff Ctr. for Jewish Stud., Vis. Res. Schol. 1992-93. Mem: SBL; AAR; AJS. Addr: (o) State U. of New York at Stony Brook, Dept. of Comparative Studies, Stony Brook, NY 11794 516-632-7460; (h) 1922 Calvert St., Washington, DC 20009 202-234-5189.

RASMUSSEN, Carl G., b. Chicago, IL, September 30, 1942, s. of Walter & Dorothy, m. Mary, chil: John; Peter; Andrew. Educ: Trinity Evang. Div. Sch., BD 1969, ThM 1971; Dropsie U., PhD 1981. Emp: Inst. of Holy Land Stud., Jerusalem, 1973-80 Dean; Bethel Coll., 1980- Prof., OT. Spec: Archaeology, Hebrew Bible. Pub: Articles in *ISBE, Zondervan NIV Atlas of the Bible*; and others. Mem: SBL; IES; ASOR; NEAS. Rec: Camping, fishing, men's soccer coach. Addr: (o) Bethel College, 3900 Bethel Dr., St. Paul, MN 55112 612-638-6351; (h) 2364 17th St. NW, New Brighton, MN 55112 612-636-1235.

RAST, Walter E., b. San Antonio, TX, April 3, 1930, s. of Alfred Otto & Edith Gertrude (Jordan), m. Susanna Marie (Droege), chil: Joel; Timothy; Rebekah; Peter. Educ: Concordia Theol. Sem., MDiv, MSTh 1950-56; U. of Chicago, MA, PhD 1961-66. Emp: Valparaiso U., 1961-92 Prof.; *BASOR*, 1984-90 Ed. Excv: Tell Ta'annek, 1963-68 Core Staff; Tell er-Rumeith, 1967 Staff; Bab edh-Dhra', 1967 Staff; Expdn. to Dead Sea Plain, 1971- Co-Dir. Spec: Archaeology, Hebrew Bible. Pub: "The Problem of Stratigraphy Relating to David" *Eretz-Israel* 20 (1989); *Bab edh-Dhra: Excavations in the Cemetery Directed by Paul W. Lapp (1965-67)*, co-auth. (Eisenbrauns/ASOR, 1989); "Bab edh-Dhra and the Origin of the Sodom Saga" in *Archaeology and Biblical Interpretation: Essays in Memory of D. Glenn Rose*; "Bronze Age Cities Along the Dead Sea" *Arch.* 40 (1987); *Taanach I: Studies in the Iron Age Pottery* (ASOR, 1978); *Tradition History and the Old Testament* (Fortress, 1972); and others. Awd: U. of Chicago, Rockefeller Fellow 1963-65; Amer. Coun. of Learned Soc., Fellow 1971-72; NEH Fellow 1983. Mem: ASOR 1961-; Amman Ctr., Pres. 1979-82; SBL; CSBR. Rec: Woodwork, bicycling. Addr: (o) Valparaiso U., Dept. of Theology, Valparaiso, IN 46383 219-464-5270; (h) 303 Valparaiso St., Valparaiso, IN 46383 219-462-1303.

RATTIGAN, Mary T., b. New York, NY, May 14, 1933, d. of John & Mary. Educ: Fordham U., PhD 1973. Emp: St. John's U., 1979-86 Asst. Prof.; Caldwell Coll., 1987- Assoc. Prof. Spec: New Testament. Pub: "Hazor: Its Significance" *The Bible Today* 23 (1985); "The Concept of God in Process Thought" *Irish Theol. Quar.* 30 (1981) and others. Mem: AAR; CTSA. Rec: Travel, theater. Addr: (h) 102 Magnolia Ave., Jersey City, NJ 07306 201-963-2366.

RATTRAY, Susan, b. Hollywood, CA, June 13, 1956, d. of Rule & Yvonne A. (Vail). Educ: U. of Calif., Berkeley, AB 1978, MA 1982, PhD, Near East. Stud. 1992. Emp: U. of Calif., Berkeley, 1985-89 Instr. Spec: Hebrew Bible, Semitic Languages, Texts and Epigraphy. Pub: "Marriage Rules, Kinship Terms and Family Structure in the Bible" in *SBL 1987 Seminar Papers* (Scholars, 1987); "Worship" in *Harper's Bible Dict.* (Harper & Row, 1985); and others. Awd: Phi Beta Kappa 1976. Mem: SBL 1980-85, 1987-92. Rec: Sci. fiction, linguistics, architecture, gardening, folk dancing. Addr: (h) 3624 Richmond Blvd., Oakland, CA 94611 510-652-1789.

RAY, Paul J., b. Chicago, IL, April 29, 1955, s. of Paul & Anna, m. Barbara Jean, chil: Zechariah David. Educ: U. of Ill., BA, Anthrop. 1977; Andrews U., MA, OT 1981, MA, Arch. 1984. Emp: Bugema Coll., 1990- Instr., Theol. & Bibl. Lang. Excv: Madaba Plains Project, Al Dreijat, 1989 Square Supr.; Gezer, 1990 Square Supr. Spec: Archaeology, Hebrew Bible. Pub: "The Duration of the Israelite Sojourn in Egypt" *AUSS* 24 (1986); "An Evaluation of the Numerical Variants of the Chrono-genealogies of Genesis 5 and 11" *Origins* 12 (1985). Mem: ASOR 1984-; SBL 1985-; IES 1986-. Rec: Reading, bird watching. Addr: (o) Bugema College, PO Box 6529, Kampala, Uganda.

REA, John, b. Pittsburgh, PA, February 18, 1925, s. of James C. & Julia Dodge, m. Elaine (Johnson), chil: Elizabeth (Tebbe); Linda (Tari); Ruth (Donan); Mary (Auch). Educ: Princeton U., BSE 1948; Grace Theol. Sem., MDiv 1951, ThM 1954, ThD 1958; Wheaton Coll. Grad. Sch., MA, Bibl. Lit. 1952. Emp: Grace Coll. & Grace Theol. Sem., 1953-60 Prof.; Moody Bible Inst., 1960-63 Instr.; Melodyland Sch. of Theol., 1977-82 Assoc. Prof., Dean of Acad. Affairs; Regent U., 1982-90 Prof., OT, Coll. of Theol. & Min., 1990- Prof. Emeritus; *Wycliffe Bible Ency.*, 1975 Manuscript Ed. Excv: Dothan, 1953 Surveyor. Spec: Archaeology, Hebrew Bible. Pub: Articles in *Wycliffe Bible Ency.*, *Zondervan Pictorial Ency. of the Bible*; *The Holy Spirit in the Bible* (Creation House, 1990); "Joel, Book of" in *Dict. of Pentecostal and Charismatic Movements* (Zondervan, 1988); "The Personal Relationship of Old Testament Believers to the Holy Spirit" in *Essays on Apostolic Themes: Studies in Honor of Howard M. Ervin* (Hendrickson, 1985); *The Layman's Comm. on the Holy Spirit* (Logos Intl., 1972, 1974);

"Joshua" in *Wycliffe Bible Comm.* (Moody, 1962); "The Time of the Oppression and the Exodus" *Bull. of the ETS* 3 (1960); and others. Awd: Princeton U., Phi Beta Kappa 1948. Mem: ASOR 1953-; SBL 1956-; ETS 1958-. Rec: Travel, hiking, photography. Addr: (h) PO Box 1475, Running Springs, CA 92382 909-867-3830.

REDDISH, Mitchell G., b. Jesup, GA, August 13, 1953, s. of Warren G. & C. Juanita, m. Barbara (Waters), chil: Timothy Glenn; Elizabeth Ann; Michael Jerrell. Educ: U. of Ga., BA, English 1975; South. Bapt. Theol. Sem., MDiv 1978, PhD, NT Stud. 1982. Emp: South. Bapt. Theol. Sem., 1980-82 Instr., NT Greek, 1982-83 Adj. Prof., NT; Stetson U., 1983-86 Asst. Prof., 1986- Assoc. Prof., Relig., 1992- Chair, Dept. of Relig.; *Pulpit Digest*, 1986-1990 NT Book Rev. Ed. Spec: New Testament, Apocrypha and Post-biblical Studies. Pub: Articles in *ABD* (Doubleday, 1992); "Inspiration" in *New Handbook of Christian Theology* (1992); *An Introduction to the Bible*, co-auth. (Abingdon, 1991); articles in *Mercer Dict. of the Bible* (Mercer U.P., 1990); *Apocalyptic Literature: A Reader*, ed. (Abingdon, 1990); "Martyr Christology in the Apocalypse" *JSNT* 33 (1988); and others. Awd: Phi Beta Kappa 1975. Mem: SBL; AAR; NABPR. Rec: Fishing, woodworking, photography. Addr: (o) Stetson U., Campus Box 8354, DeLand, FL 32720-3757 904-822-8930; (h) 537 E Compton Ct., DeLand, FL 32724 904-738-4669.

REDDITT, Paul L., b. Little Rock, AR, August 8, 1942, s. of Paul & Helen, m. Bonnie (Louellen), chil: Pamela; Alan. Educ: South. Bapt. Theol. Sem., MDiv 1967; Vanderbilt U., MA 1971, PhD 1972. Emp: Otterbein Coll., 1972-86 Assoc. Prof.; Georgetown Coll., 1986- Prof., Chmn., Dept. of Relig. Spec: Hebrew Bible, Apocrypha and Post-biblical Studies. Pub: "Zerubbabel, Joshua, and the Night Visions of Zechariah" *CBQ* 54 (1992); "Israel's Shepherds: Hope and Pessimism in Zechariah 9-14" *CBQ* 51 (1989); "The Book of Joel and Peripheral Prophecy" *CBQ* 48 (1986); "The Concept of *Nomos* in Fourth Maccabees" *CBQ* 45 (1983); and others. Mem: SBL. Addr: (o) Georgetown College, Georgetown, KY 40324 502-863-8011; (h) 518 Estill Ct., Georgetown, KY 40324.

REDFORD, Donald B., b. Toronto, Canada, September 2, 1934, s. of Cyril Fitzjames & Kathleen Beryl (Coe), m. Susan (Pirritano), chil: Philip; Christopher; Alexander; Aksel. Educ: U. Coll., BA 1957; U. of Toronto, MA 1958, PhD 1965. Emp: Brown U., 1959-61 Lect.; U. of Toronto, Dept. of Near East. Stud., 1962- Prof.; *Jour. of the Soc. for the Study of Egyptian Antiq.*, 1990- Ed. Excv: Jerusalem, 1964-65, 1967 Site Supr.; Buto, 1968 Epigrapher; Temple of Osiris, Karnak, 1970-72 Dir.; East Karnak, 1975- Dir.; Mendes, 1990- Co-dir. Spec: Archaeology, Egyptology. Pub: *Egypt, Canaan and Israel in Ancient Times* (Princeton U.P., 1992); "The Tod Inscription of Senwosret I..." *Jour. of the Soc.*

for the Study of Egyptian Antiq. 17 (1988); *Akhenaten, the Heretic King* (Princeton U.P., 1984); "A Bronze Age Itinerary in Transjordan" *Jour. of the Soc. for the Study of Egyptian Antiq.* 12 (1982); "The Sun-disc in Akhenaten's Program: Its Worship and Antecedents" *JARCE* 17 (1980); *A Study of the Biblical Joseph Story* (Brill, 1970); "The Hyksos Invasion in History and Tradition" *Orientalia* 39 (1970); *History and Chronology of the Egyptian 18th Dynasty: Seven Studies* (U. of Toronto, 1967); "The Coregency of Tuthmosis III and Amenophis II" *Jour. of Egyptian Arch.* 51 (1965); and others. Awd: Canada Coun. Grants in Aid of Res. 1962-70; Killam Awd., 1975-79. Mem: ASOR; Soc. for Mediterranean Stud.; Canadian Mediterranean Inst., V.P., Egypt 1990-; Soc. for the Study of Egyptian Antiq., Pres. 1990-91. Rec: Baseball, tennis, football. Addr: (o) U. of Toronto, Dept. of Near Eastern Studies, Bancroft Hall, Rm. 418, 4 Bancroft Ave., Toronto, ON M5S 1A1, Canada 416-978-3183; (h) 22 Nesbitt Dr., Toronto, ON M4W 2G3, Canada.

REED, Jeffrey T., b. Billings, Montana, November 14, 1967, s. of Robert & Carol, m. Jamie. Educ: Biola U., BA 1990; Talbot Sch. of Theol., MA 1991. Emp: Talbot Sch. of Theol., 1992- Prof.; Sheffield Acad. Press, 1991-92 Desk Ed. Spec: New Testament. Pub: "Cohesive Ties in 1 Timothy" *Neotestamentica* July (1992); "The Infinitive with Two Substantival Accusatives" *NT* 33 (1991); "Greek Grammar Since BDF" *Filologia Neotestamentaria* 4 (1991). Mem: SBL 1991-. Rec: Fly fishing, hiking, computer programming, weightlifting. Addr: (o) 13800 Biola Ave., La Miranda, CA 90639 310-903-4722.

REEVES, John C., b. Fayetteville, NC, December 1, 1954, s. of William D. & Martha, m. Lu, chil: Daniel. Educ: U. of N.C., BA 1976; SE Sem., MDiv 1982; HUC-Inst. of Relig., MPhil 1986, PhD 1989. Emp: Winthrop U., 1989- Asst. Prof., Relig. Spec: Hebrew Bible, Apocrypha and Post-biblical Studies. Pub: *Jewish Lore in Manichaean Cosmogony: Studies in the Book of Giants Traditions* (Hebrew Union Coll., 1991); "The Elchasaite Sanhedrin of the Cologne Mani Codex in Light of Second Temple Jewish Sectarian Sources" *JJS* 42 (1991); "An Illustration from the Apocrypha in an Eighteenth Century Passover Haggadah" *HUCA* 59 (1988); "What Does Noah Offer in 1QapGen X,15?" *RQ* 12 (1986); and others. Mem: AAR; AOS; Assn. of Manichaean Stud.; SBL. Addr: (o) Winthrop U., Dept. of Philosophy, Religion & Anthropology, Rock Hill, SC 29733 803-323-4652; (h) 520 Union Ave., Rock Hill, SC 29730 803-327-9114.

REICH, Ronny, Educ: Hebrew U., Dept. of Arch., BA, MA, PhD. Emp: Israel Antiq. Authority, 1978-. Excv: Jewish Quarter, Jerusalem, 1969-78 Area Supr.; Iron Age Cemetery, Jerusalem, 1989- Dir., Rescue Excvn. Spec: Archaeology. Pub: "Bozrah," "Tell Abu Salima" in

The New Encyclopedia of Archaeological Excavations in the Holy Land (IES/Carta, 1993); "Caiaphas Name Inscribed on Bone Boxes" *BAR* 18/5 (1992); and others. Addr: (o) Israel Antiquities Authority, PO Box 568, Jerusalem 91911, Israel 972-2-292-627; (h) Shimoni 54, Jerusalem 92630, Israel 972-2-790-198.

REID, Daniel G., b. Los Angeles, CA, May 13, 1949, s. of John & Mary, m. Cynthia M., chil: Lindsey B.; Colin G. Educ: Portland State U., BA 1973; Fuller Theol. Sem., MDiv 1978, PhD 1982. Emp: Asian Theol. Sem., Manila, 1983-85 Asst. Prof.; InterVarsity Press, 1986- Ref. Book Ed.; Fuller Theol. Sem., 1983, 1990- Adj. Prof., Bibl. Stud. Spec: Hebrew Bible, New Testament. Pub: *Dict. of Christianity in America*, co-ed. (InterVarsity, 1990); and others. Awd: *Christianity Today*, Book of the Year Awd. 1990. Mem: SBL; IBR. Rec: Skiing, hiking, mountain climbing. Addr: (o) 28308 SE 451st St., Enumclaw, WA 98022 206-825-0798.

REID, John K. S., b. Leith, March 31, 1910, s. of David & Georgina, m. Margaret W. (Brookes). Emp: Calcutta, Leeds, Aberdeen, Prof. of Theol.; SJT, Co-Ed. Spec: New Testament. Pub: *Christian Apologetics* (H & S, 1969); *The Authority of Scripture* (Greenwood, 1957, 1981); *Baptism in NT*, trans. (SCM, 1950); and others. Awd: Edinburgh, DD 1957. Mem: Scottish Ch. Theol. Soc.; CBE 1970-. Addr: (h) 8 Abbotsford Court, 18 Colinton Rd., Edinburgh, EH10 5EH, Scotland 447-6855.

REIF, Stefan C., b. Edinburgh, January 21, 1944, s. of Peter & Annie, m. Shulamit, chil: Tanya; Aryeh. Educ: U. of London, BA 1964, PhD 1969; U. of Cambridge, MA 1976. Emp: U. of Glasgow, 1968-72 Lect., Dept. of Hebrew & Semitic Lang.; Glasgow Hebrew Coll., 1970-72 Prin.; Dropsie Coll., 1972-73 Asst. Prof. of Hebrew; Cambridge U. Lib., 1973- Dir. of Taylor-Schechter Genizah Res. Unit, Head of Div. of Oriental & Other Lang., Genizah Ser., Ed.; Hebrew U., Jerusalem, 1989 Vis. Prof. Spec: Hebrew Bible, Semitic Languages, Texts and Epigraphy, Apocrypha and Post-biblical Studies. Pub: *Judaism and Hebrew Prayer* (Cambridge U.P., 1993); *Genizah Research After Ninety Years*, co-auth. (Cambridge U.P., 1992); "The Early History of Jewish Worship" in *The Making of Jewish and Christian Worship* (Notre Dame, 1991); "Ibn Ezra on Canticles" in *Abraham Ibn Ezra and His Age: Proceedings of the International Symposium* (1990); *Published Material in the Cambridge Genizah Collections* (Cambridge U.P., 1988); "A Root to Look Up? A Study of the Hebrew ns' 'yn" in *Congress Volume IOSOT* (1985); "Ibn Ezra on Ps. I 1-2" *VT* 34 (1984); *Interpreting the Hebrew Bible*, co-auth. (Cambridge U.P., 1982); "What Enraged Phinehas?—A Study of Num. 25.8" *JBL* 90 (1971); and others. Mem: Royal Asiatic Soc.; Hebraica Libraries Group; SOTS; Jewish Hist. Soc. of England, Pres. 1991-92; Brit. AJS, Pres.

1992. Rec: Squash, cricket, football. Addr: (o) Cambridge U. Library, West Rd., Cambridge CB3 9DR, England 0223-333000; (h) 23 Parsonage St., Cambridge CB5 8DN, England.

REINER, Erica, b. Budapest, Hungary. Educ: Pazmany Peter U., Budapest, Lic. 1948; Ecole Pratique des Hautes Etudes, Paris, Diplome 1951; U. of Chicago, PhD 1955. Emp: U. of Chicago, John A. Wilson Disting. Service Prof.; *The Assyrian Dictionary*, Ed.; The Assyrian Dictionary Project, Dir. Spec: Mesopotamian Studies. Pub: *A Linguistic Analysis of Akkadian* (Mouton, 1966); "Akkadian" in *Current Trends in Linguistics* vol. 6 (Mouton, 1970); "First Millennium Babylonian Literature" in *Cambridge Ancient History* vol. III, part 2 (Cambridge, 1991); and others. Mem: AOS, Pres. 1983-84. Addr: (o) The Oriental Institute, 1155 East 58th St., Chicago, IL 60637 312-702-9550; (h) 5447 Ridgewood Court, Chicago, IL 60615 312-288-1274.

REMUS, Harold E., b. Great Falls, MT, September 20, 1928, s. of Gustav & Wilhelmina (Roesler), m. Alice Croft, chil: Elise; Justin. Educ: Concordia Sem., MDiv 1956; U. of Pa., PhD 1981. Emp: U. of Pa., 1971-73 Lect.; Wilfrid Laurier U., Canada, 1974- Prof., Wilfrid Laurier U. Press, 1978-83 Dir.; *RSRev*, 1975-85, Managing Ed.; *Studies in Religion/Sciences Religieuses*, 1976-79 Managing Ed.; Coun. on Study of Relig., 1977-85 Exec. Officer. Spec: New Testament. Pub: "Miracle (NT)" in *ABD* (Doubleday, 1992); *Religious Studies in Ontario: A State-of-the-Art Review* (1992); "Miracle" in *Ency. of Early Christianity* (1990); "Justin Martyr's Argument with Judaism" in *Anti-Judaism in Early Christianity* vol. 2 (Wilfred Laurier U.P., 1986); *Pagan Christian Conflict Over Miracle in the Second Century* (Philadelphia Patristic Found., 1983); "'Magic or Miracle?' Some Second-century Instances" in *SC* (1982); "Does Terminology Distinguish Early Christian from Pagan Miracles?" *JBL* 101 (1982); and others. Mem: CSBS 1975-; CSSR 1985-; NAPS 1986-; Canadian Soc. Patristic Stud. 1987-; SNTS 1991-. Addr: (o) Wilfrid Laurier U., Waterloo, ON N2L 3C5, Canada 519-884-1970; (h) 85 Longwood Dr., Waterloo, ON N2L 4B6, Canada 519-884-1008.

RENDSBURG, Gary A., b. Baltimore, MD, February 13, 1954, s. of Julius & Irene, m. Susan, chil: David; Rachel; Dina. Educ: NYU, MA 1977, PhD 1980. Emp: Canisius Coll., 1980-86 Asst. Prof.; Cornell U., 1986-89 Asst. Prof., 1989- Assoc. Prof. Spec: Hebrew Bible, Semitic Languages, Texts and Epigraphy. Pub: "The Northern Origin of Nehemiah 9" *Biblica* 72 (1991); *Linguistic Evidence for the Northern Origin of Selected Psalms* (Scholars, 1990); *Diglossia in Ancient Hebrew* (AOS, 1990); "The Internal Consistency and Historical Reliability of the Biblical Genealogies" *VT* 40 (1990); "The Northern Origin of 'The Last Words of David' (2 Sam 23,1-7)" *Biblica* 69 (1988); "The

Ammonite Phoneme /T/" *BASOR* 269 (1988); *The Redaction of Genesis* (Eisenbrauns, 1986); "Late Biblical Hebrew and the Date of 'P'" *JANES* 12 (1980); *The Bible World: Essays in Honor of Cyrus H. Gordon*, ed. (Ktav, 1980); and others. Mem: AOS 1978-; SBL 1978-; AJS 1978-. Addr: (o) Cornell U., Dept. of Near Eastern Studies, 360 Rockefeller Hall, Ithaca, NY 14853 607-255-6275; (h) 11 Davis Street, Binghamton, NY 13905 607-723-4941.

RENDTORFF, Rolf, b. Preetz/Holstein, Germany, May 10, 1925, s. of Heinrich & Hedwig (Besser), m. Helge (Hoefke), chil: Annemarie; Barbara; Klaus; Christian. Educ: U. of Heidelberg, ThD 1950; U. of Gottingen, Habil. 1953. Emp: U. of Gottingen, 1953-58 Dozent; Kirchliche Hochschule, Berlin, 1958-63 Prof.; U. of Heidelberg, 1963-90 Prof.; *Kirche und Israel*, 1986-90 Ed., 1991- Co-ed. Spec: Hebrew Bible. Pub: *Kanon und Theologie: Vorarbeiten zu einer Theologie des Alten Testaments* (Neukirchener, 1991); *The Problem of the Process of Transmission in the Pentateuch*, JSOTSup 89 (Sheffield, 1990); "Toward a Common Jewish-Christian Reading of the Hebrew Bible" in *Hebrew Bible or Old Testament? Studying the Bible in Judaism and Christianity* (U. of Notre Dame, 1990); "'Covenant' as a Structuring Concept in Genesis and Exodus" *JBL* 108 (1989); *The Old Testament: An Introduction* (Fortress, 1986); "Zur Komposition des Buches Jesaja" *VT* 34 (1984); "Der 'Jahwist' als Theologe? Zum Dilemma der Pentateuchkritik" in VTSup 28 (1975); *Studien zur Geschichte des Opfers im Alten Israel* (Neukirchener, 1967); "El, Ba'al und Jahwe: Erwagungen zum Verhaltnis von kanaanaischer und israelitischer Religion" *ZAW* 78 (1966); and others. Mem: Deutscher Verein zur Erforschung Palastinas 1959-; WUJS 1965-; SBL 1987-; AAR 1988-. Rec: Tennis, skiing. Addr: (h) Buchenweg 21, D-61184 Karben 1, Germany 06039-2530.

RENN, Stephen D., b. Sydney, Australia, October 28, 1950, s. of Ernest Norman & Marjorie May, m. Helen, chil: Joshua; Chantelle. Educ: Sydney U., BA 1972, DipEd 1973, MA 1990; Westminster Theol. Sem., MDiv 1979. Emp: Sydney Missionary & Bible Coll., 1986- Lect., OT. Spec: Hebrew Bible. Pub: *The Song of Songs* (Anzea, 1989). Rec: Reading, golf, history, music. Addr: (o) Sydney Missionary & Bible College, PO Box 83, Croydon, NSW 2132, Australia 02-747-4780; (h) 47 Badminton Rd., Croydon, NSW 2132, Australia 02-747-3695.

RESSEGUIE, James L., b. Buffalo, NY, January 1, 1945, s. of Leon & Mabel, m. Dianne (Paulson), chil: Timothy; Carin; Jay. Educ: Princeton Theol. Sem., MDiv 1972; Fuller Theol. Sem., PhD 1978. Emp: Winebrenner Theol. Sem., 1976- J. Russell Bucher Prof. of NT, 1990 Dean of Acad. & Student Affairs. Spec: New Testament. Pub: "Making the Familiar Seem Strange" *Interpretation* 46 (1992); "Automatization and Defamiliarization in Luke 7:36-50" *Lit. & Theol.* 5 (1991); "Defamiliarization and the Gospels" *BTB* 20 (1990); "Reader-Response Criticism and the Synoptic Gospels" *JAAR* 52 (1984); "John 9: A Literary-Critical Analysis" in *Literary Interpretations of Biblical Narratives*, vol. 2 (1982); and others. Mem: SBL; IBR. Addr: (o) Winebrenner Theological Seminary, 701 E. Melrose Ave., Findlay, OH 45840 419-422-4824.

REUMANN, John P., b. Easton, PA, April 21, 1927, s. of W. Paul & Ethel M. (Rauth), m. Martha W. (Brobst), chil: Rebecca Jane (Moore); Amy Elizabeth; Miriam Grace. Educ: Muhlenberg Coll., AB 1947; Luth. Theol. Sem., BD 1950, STM 1951; U. of Pa., MA 1950, PhD, Class. 1957. Emp: Luth. Theol. Sem., 1950-51 Teaching Fellow, 1951-54 Instr., 1954-59 Asst. Prof., 1959- Prof., NT Stud.; Ministerium of Pa., 1962- Prof.; Facet Books, Bibl. Ser., 1963-72. Spec: New Testament. Pub: "Righteousness," "Judaism," "Greco-Roman," "New Testament" in *ABD* (1992); *Stewardship and the Economy of God* (Eerdmans, 1992); "Christology in Philippians, Especially Chap. 3" in *Anfaenge der Christologie*, Festschrift F. Hahn (1991); *Variety and Unity in New Testament Thought* (Oxford U.P., 1991); "Philippians 3.20-21—a Hymnic Fragment?" *NTS* 30 (1984); *"Righteousness" in the New Testament*, co-auth. (Paulist/Fortress, 1982); *Jesus in the Church's Gospels* (Fortress, 1968; SPCK, 1970); "Oikonomia: 'Covenant'" *NT* 3 (1959); "Stewards of God" *JBL* 77 (1958); and others. Awd: Cambridge, AATS Fac. Fellow. 1959-60; Gottingen U., Guggenheim Fellow. 1965-66; Phi Beta Kappa 1976; Wittenberg U., DD 1983; Trinity Sem., Sittler Awd. for Theol. Leadership 1992. Mem: SBL; SNTS 1958-; Philadelphia Sem. on Christian Origins 1963-, co-founder. Rec: Walking, swimming, reading, travel. Addr: (o) 7301 Germantown Ave., Philadelphia, PA 19119 215-248-4616; (h) 7206 Boyer St., Philadelphia, PA 19119 215-242-1418.

REVELL, E. John, b. Bangalore, April 15, 1934, s. of Alfred & Edith (Sheppard), m. Ann, chil: A. John; Bridget. Educ: St. John's Coll., MA 1962; U. of Toronto, PhD 1962. Emp: U. of Toronto, Dept. of Near East. Stud., 1960- Prof. Spec: Hebrew Bible, Semitic Languages, Texts and Epigraphy. Pub: "The System of the Verb in Standard Biblical Prose" *HUCA* 60 (1989); "The Conditioning of Word Order in Verbless Clauses in Biblical Hebrew" *JSS* 34 (1989); *Introduction to the Tiberian Masorah*, trans., Masoretic Stud. 5 (Missoula, 1980); *Biblical Texts with Palestinian Pointing and Their Accents*, Masoretic Stud. 4 (Missoula, 1977); and others. Mem: AOS; SOTS; BSA, Jerusalem. Rec: Growing & water color portraiture of plants. Addr: (o) U. of Toronto, Dept. of Near Eastern Studies, Toronto, ON M5S 1A1, Canada 416-978-6599; (h) 151 Blythwood Rd., Toronto, ON M4S 1A5, Canada 416-482-5036.

REYNOLDS, R. Blair, b. Pittsburgh, PA, March 3, 1947, s. of Robert B. & Marjorie T.,

m. Deborah (Allman). Educ: Muskingum Coll., BA 1969; Purdue U., MS 1972; U. of Pittsburgh, PhD, Theol. 1983. Spec: Hebrew Bible. Pub: "God's Power in Calvin's Sermons on Jeremiah and Micah: Classical Theism Versus Prophetic Exegesis" *Proc. of East. Great Lakes & MidW Bibl. Soc. 10* (1990); *Sermons on Jeremiah*, trans. (Mellen, 1990); *Sermons on Micah*, trans. (Mellen, 1990); *Toward a Process Pneumatology* (Assoc. U. P., 1990). Awd: AAR, Res. Assistance Grant 1988; Harvard U., Ctr. for Cultural & Lit. Stud., Vis. Fellow 1991-92. Mem: AAR 1985-; SBL 1989-; Amer. Phil. Assn. 1991-. Rec: Playing the trumpet, steam locomotives. Addr: (h) 173 Sherman St., Cambridge, MA 02140 617-864-2596.

RHEE, Song N., b. Namwon, Korea, September 10, 1935, s. of Byung-Hong & Choon-Kil (Shin), m. Sue, chil: Pamela Sue; Martha K.; Ruby K. Educ: NW Christian Coll., BTh 1958; Butler U., BA 1960, MA, Semitics 1960; Dropsie Coll., PhD, Anc. Near East. & Hebraic Stud. 1963; U. Oreg., MA 1969, MA 1979, MS 1979, PhD, Anthrop. 1984. Emp: NW Christian Coll., 1963-65 Asst. Prof., 1965-67 Assoc. Prof., 1967- Prof., 1984- Acad. V.P. & Acad. Dean; U. Oreg., 1985 Vis. Prof. Excv: Tel Lachish, 1976-88 U.S. Project Coord. Spec: Archaeology, Hebrew Bible, Mesopotamian Studies. Pub: "Fortifications in the Ancient Levant: Their Origins and Evolution" *Cultura Antiqua* 43/3 (1991); "Sumerian City State" in *City-States in Five Cultures* (ABC Clio, 1981); and others. Awd: NW Christian Coll., Pres. Awd. 1958; 7th Ann. Interfaith Bible Conf. Awd. 1991. Mem: SBL 1988-; Amer. Anthrop. Assn. 1985-; Assn. for Asian Stud. 1985-. Rec: Fishing. Addr: (o) Northwest Christian College, 828 East 11th Ave., Eugene, OR 97401 503-343-1641; (h) 345 East 41st Ave., Eugene, OR 97405 503-344-5528.

RHOADS, David M., b. Altoona, PA, November 17, 1941, s. of Luke & Virginia, m. Sandra (Roberts), chil: Tania; Jessica. Educ: Oxford U., MA 1965; Gettysburg Luth. Sem., BD 1966; Duke U., PhD 1973. Emp: Carthage Coll., 1973-88; Luth. Sch. of Theol. at Chicago, 1988- Prof., Relig. Spec: New Testament. Pub: "Social Criticism: Crossing Boundaries" in *Mark and Method: New Approaches in Biblical Studies* (Fortress, 1992); "The Gospel of Matthew. The Two Ways: Hypocrisy or Righteousness" *Currents in Theol. & Mission* 19 (1992); "Narrative Criticism and the Gospel of Mark" *JAAR* 50 (1982); *Mark as Story: An Introduction to the Narrative of a Gospel*, co-auth. (Fortress, 1982); *Israel in Revolution* (Fortress, 1976). Mem: SBL 1973-; SNTS 1984-; CBA 1985-. Addr: (o) Lutheran School of Theology, 1100 E 55th St., Chicago, IL 60615 312-753-0700; (h) 1436 Park Ave., Racine, WI 53403 414-633-5438.

RHODES, Erroll F., b. Hitachi Omiya Machi, Japan, March 29, 1924, s. of Erroll Allen &

Bessie W., m. Martha (Stowell), chil: Harriet Elizabeth; Erroll Allen; Mary Louise. Educ: George Pepperdine Coll., BA 1943; U. of Chicago Div. Sch., PhD 1948. Emp: Emory U., 1948-50 Instr.; Rikkyo U., Tokyo, 1954-67 Prof.; Amer. Bible Soc., 1968- Scripture Resources Ed. Spec: New Testament. Pub: *The Text of the New Testament*, trans. (Eerdmans, 1986); *Hebrew in the Church*, trans. (Eerdmans, 1984); *The Text of the Old Testament*, trans. (Eerdmans, 1979); "Limitations of Armenian Representing Greek" in *Early Versions of the New Testament* (1977); "Text of New Testament in Jerusalem and New English Bibles" *CBQ* (1970); "The Corrections of Papyrus Bodmer II" *NTS* (1968); "Japanese Bible Translations" *BT* (1967); *An Annotated List of Armenian New Testament Manuscripts* (St. Paul's U.P., 1959); and others. Mem: SBL 1948-; SNTS 1950-. Addr: (o) American Bible Society, Translations, 1865 Broadway, New York, NY 10023 212-408-1247; (h) 19 Comly Ave., Greenwich, CT 06831 203-531-7048.

RIBERA-FLORIT, Josep, b. Barcelona, Spain, October 13, 1935, s. of Ramón & Pilar (Florit), m. Esther (Bartolomé), chil: Ezequiel. Educ: Saint Thomas U., Rome, BA, Theol. 1962; U. of Barcelona, PhD Semitic Lang. 1973. Emp: U. of Barcelona, 1967- Lect., 1988- Prof., Hebrew & Aramaic Lang. Spec: Hebrew Bible, Semitic Languages, Texts and Epigraphy. Pub: *El targum de Jeremias: la versión aramea del Profeta Jeremias* (Verbo Divino, 1992); "El arameo del Targum de los Profetas (Isaias, Jeremias): Morfologia de los Pronombres" *Anuari de Filologia* 14 (1991); "The Babylonian Masoretic Tradition Reflected in the Mss. of the Targum to the Latter Prophets" in *VIII International Congress of the International Organization for Masoretic Studies* (1990); *Targum Jonatán de los Profetas posteriores en tradición babilónica, Isaias* (CSIC, 1988); *El Targum de Isaias: la versión aramea del Profeta Isaias* (Inst. San Jerónimo, 1988); "Breve estudio sobre la Gramática del Arameo del Targum Palestinense" *Aula Orientalis* 6 (1988); "La exégesis judeo-targúmica sobre la resurrección" *EstBib* 46 (1988); "The Image of the Prophet in the Light of the Targum Jonathan and Jewish Literature in the Post-biblical Period" in *Ninth World Congress of Jewish Studies* (1986); *Biblia Babilónica: Profetas Posteriores* (Varona, 1977); and others. Mem: Assn. of Cultural Relations Between Catalonia & Israel, 1987-, V.P. 1987-. Addr: (o) Dept. de Filologia Semitica, Sección de Hebreo, Gran Via 585, Barcelona, 08007, Spain 93-3184266-2740; (h) C/ Oriente 68, at. 4a, Sant Cugat del Vallès, Barcelona, 08190, Spain 93-675-5448.

RICE, Gene, b. Middlesborough, KY, September 12, 1925, s. of Howard & Etta (Wright), m. Betty (Smith), chil: Jane; Jonathan. Educ: Columbia U., PhD 1969. Emp: Howard U. Div. Sch., 1958- Prof.; *The Jour. of Relig. Thought*, 1961- Ed. Spec: Hebrew Bible, Semitic

Languages, Texts and Epigraphy. Pub: *1 Kings. Nations Under God*, Intl. Theol. Comm. (Eerdmans, 1990); "The Integrity of the Text of Psalms 139:20b" *CBQ* 46 (1984); "The African Roots of the Prophet Zephaniah" *Jour. of Relig. Thought* 36 (1979-80); "A Neglected Interpretation of the Immanuel Prophecy" *ZAW* 90 (1978); "The Interpretation of Isaiah 7:15-17" *JBL* 96 (1977); "The Curse that Never Was (Gen. 9:18-27)" *Jour. of Relig. Thought* 29 (1972-73); and others. Mem: SBL 1964-. Rec: Landscape gardening, theater. Addr: (o) Howard U. School of Divinity, 1400 Shepherd St. NE, Washington, DC 20017 202-806-0500; (h) 1634 Argonne Pl., NW, Washington, DC 20009 202-483-9470.

RICHARD, Earl J., b. Arnaudville, LA, December 19, 1940, s. of Lawrence & Wilma, m. Mary Ann (Richter), chil: Elizabeth M.; Marie-Anne N.; Joseph E. Educ: Cath. U. of Amer., BA 1963, PhD 1976; U. of Ottawa, MTh & MA 1967; Johns Hopkins U., MA 1972. Emp: Marycrest Coll., 1968-70 Instr.; Berea Coll., 1974-78 Asst. Prof.; Boston U., 1979-81 Vis. Schol.; Loyola U., 1981- Prof. Spec: New Testament. Pub: "Early Pauline Thought: An Analysis of 1 Thessalonians" in *Pauline Theology* vol. 1 (Fortress, 1991); *New Views on Luke and Acts* (Liturgical, 1990); "Contemporary Research on 1 (& 2) Thessalonians" *BTB* 20 (1990); "Jesus' Passion and Death in Acts" in *Reimaging the Death of the Lukan Jesus* (Hain, 1990); *Jesus: One and Many: Christological Concept of New Testament Authors* (Glazier, 1988); "The Functional Christology of First Peter" in *Perspectives on First Peter* (Mercer, 1986); "Expressions of Double Meaning and Their Function in the Gospel of John" *NTS* 31 (1985); *Acts 6:1-8:4: The Author's Method of Composition* (Scholars, 1978); and others. Mem: SBL 1974-, Pres., SE reg. 1990-91; CBA 1974-; Coll. Theol. Soc. 1981-. Addr: (o) Loyola U., Religious Studies Dept., 6363 St. Charles Ave., New Orleans, LA 70118 504-865-3943; (h) 508 Walnut St., New Orleans, LA 70118 504-861-1605.

RICHARDS, Kent H., b. Midland, TX, July 6, 1939, s. of Eva, m. Kristen (Becker), chil: Lisken; Lisanne. Educ: Sch. of Theol., MTh 1964; Claremont Grad. Sch., PhD 1969. Emp: Inst. for Antiquity/Christianity, 1967-68 Res. Assoc.; U. of Dayton, 1968-72 Asst. Prof.; Iliff Sch. of Theol., 1972- Prof., OT; *Bibl. Schol. in N Amer.*, 1981-92 Ed.; *SBL Seminar Papers*, 1981-85 Ed. Spec: Hebrew Bible. Pub: *Interpreting Hebrew Poetry*, co-auth. (Augsburg/Fortress, 1992); "The Old Testament and Its Inheritors" *Iliff Rev.* 40 (1983); "Cobb's Living Historical Routes: A Response" *Semeia;* and others. Mem: SBL; CBA. Rec: Tennis, skiing. Addr: (o) 2201 S University Blvd., Denver, CO 80210 303-744-1287.

RICHARDSON, Peter, b. Toronto, Canada, January 6, 1935, s. of George & Margaret (Everett), m. Nancy (Cameron), chil: Mary;

Susan; Jonathan; Ruth. Educ: U. of Toronto, Canada, B.Arch 1957; Cambridge U., PhD 1965. Emp: Concordia U., 1969-74 Assoc. Prof.; U. of Toronto, 1977-89 Prin., U. Coll., 1977 Prof.; *Crux*, 1966-78 Ed. Bd.; *ARC*, 1973-74 Ed. Bd.; *Stud. in Relig.*, 1985- Managing Ed. Spec: New Testament, Apocrypha and Post-biblical Studies. Pub: "Why Turn the Tables? Jesus' Protest in the Temple Precincts" *SBL 1992 Seminar Papers* (1992); *Law in Religious Communities in the Roman Period* (Wilfrid Laurier U. P., 1991); "Religion, Architecture and Ethics" *Horizons in Bibl. Theol.* 10 (1988); "Law and Piety in Herod's Architecture" *Stud. in Relig.* 15 (1986); "Judgment in Sexual Matters in 1 Cor. 6:1-11" *NT* 25 (1983); "Pauline Inconsistency in 1 Cor. 9:19-23 and Gal. 2:11-14" *NTS* 26 (1979-80); *Paul's Ethic of Freedom* (Westminster, 1979); *Israel in the Apostolic Church* (Cambridge U.P., 1969); and others. Mem: CSBS, Pres. 1984-85; SNTS; SBL; ASOR. Rec: Carpentry, canoeing. Addr: (o) U. of Toronto, University College, Toronto, ON M5S 1A1, Canada 416-978-7149; (h) 42 St. Andrews Gardens, Toronto, ON M4W 2E1, Canada 416-961-3746.

RICHES, John K., b. London, England, April 30, 1939, s. of Leonard & Freda (Booth), m. Renate (Thermann), chil: Oliver; Susanna; Philip. Emp: Sidney Sussex Coll., Cambridge, 1968-72 Chaplain, Fellow & Dir. of Stud. in Theol.; U. of Glasgow, 1972-86 Lect., Bible Stud., 1986-92 Sr. Lect., 1992- Prof. of Divinity & Bibl. Criticism. Spec: New Testament. Pub: *A Century of New Testament Studies* (Lutterworth, 1993); *The World of Jesus* (Cambridge U.P., 1990); "Interpretation: A Theoretical Perspective and Some Applications," co-auth., *Numen* (1981); "The Sociology of Matthew: Some Basic Questions Concerning Its Relation to the Theology of the New Testament" in *SBL Seminar Papers* (1983); *Jesus and the Transformation of Judaism* (Seabury, 1982); "Ernst Kasemann: An die Roemer" *SJT* 29 (1976); and others. Rec: Hill-walking, Third World self-help groups, travel. Addr: (o) The University, Dept. of Biblical Studies, Glasgow, G12 8QQ, Scotland 01-339-8855; (h) Viewfield, Balmore Torrance, Glasgow, G64 4AE, Scotland 0360-20254.

RICHTER, Hans F., b. Leipzig, Germany, November 5, 1931, s. of Hans & Maria, m. Renate, chil: Andreas; Soren. Educ: Kirchliche Hochschule, Berlin, ThD 1969. Spec: Hebrew Bible, New Testament. Pub: "Zum Problem des Mythos" *ZRGG* 40 (1988); "Zur Urgeschichte des Jahwisten" *BN* 34 (1986); "Die Pferde in den Nachtgesichten Sacharjas" *ZAW* 98 (1986); "Zum Levirat im buch Ruth" *ZAW* 95 (1983); "Auf den Knien Eines Andern Gebaeren?" *ZAW* 91 (1979); *Geschlechtuchyeit ehe und Familie im Alten Testament und Jeiner Umwelt*, 2 vol., BET 10, 1 & 2 (1978); *Auferstehung und Wirylichyeit: Eine Exegetische Hermeneutische und Ontologische Untersuchung zu 1 Kor. 15,1-11* (Augsburg, 1967); and others. Mem: SNTS

1982. Addr: (o) Fregest 12, D-1000 Berlin 41, Germany 030-852-2564.

RICKS, Stephen D., b. Berkeley, CA, January 21, 1952, s. of Marc & Jane, m. Shirley (Smith), chil: Rebecca; Robert; Marc; Lora; Jannifer; Jonathan. Educ: Brigham Young U., BA, Greek 1974, MA, Class. 1976; U. of Calif., Berkeley, PhD, Near East. Relig. 1982. Emp: Brigham Young U., 1981- Assoc. Prof., Hebrew & Semitic Lang. Spec: Hebrew Bible, Semitic Languages, Texts and Epigraphy. Pub: *Western Language Literature on Pre-Islamic Central Arabia: An Annotated Bibliography* (Amer. Inst. of Islamic Stud., 1991); *A Bibliography on Temples of the Ancient Near East and Mediterranean World*, co-auth. (Mellen, 1991); *Lexicon of Inscriptional Qatabanian* (Pont. Bibl. Inst., 1989); and others. Awd: Brigham Young U., Jerusalem Ctr. Fellow 1988. Mem: SBL 1981-; AOS 1981-; NAPH 1984-. Addr: (o) Brigham Young U., Dept. of Asian & Near Eastern Lang., 4067 JKHB, Provo, UT 84602 801-378-5428; (h) 3074 Cherokee Ln., Provo, UT 84604 801-377-8443.

RIDENHOUR, Thomas E., b. Concord, NC, November 11, 1937, s. of Clarence & Elizabeth (Webb), m. Mary (Glass), chil: Thomas; Mary; William. Educ: Luth. Theol. South. Sem., BD 1965; Duke U., PhD 1972. Emp: Newberry Coll., 1968-69 Instr.; Luth. Ch., 1969-74 Pastor; Luth. Theol. Sem., 1974-91 Prof.; Luth. Theol. South. Sem., 1991- Prof. Spec: Hebrew Bible. Pub: *Proclamation 2*, co-auth. (Fortress, 1979); "Immortality and Resurrection in the Old Testament" *Dialog* 15 (1976); and others. Mem: SBL 1965-; ASOR 1965-. Rec: Tennis, basketball. Addr: (o) Lutheran Theological Southern Seminary, 4201 N Main St., Columbia, SC 29203 803-786-5150; (h) 208 Rainsborough Way, Columbia, SC 29223 803-736-5660.

RIEKKINEN, Wille H. J., b. Varpaisjarvi, Finland, July 21, 1946, s. of Heimo A. & Martta (Fohr), m. Seija (Vahakangas), chil: Ulpu Elina; Outi Helena. Educ: Helsinki U., Fac. of Theol., Theol. Cand. 1967-72, Lic. Theol. 1988. Emp: Helsinki U., 1980, 1988 Vis. Asst. Prof., Bibl. Theol.; Finnish Luth. Ch., Ctr. for Advanced Stud., 1985-88, 1992- Tchr., Bibl. Hermeneutics; Joensuu U., 1984- Docent; Helsinki U., 1986-Docent; World Coun. of Ch. 1988-92, Sec. for Bibl. Stud. Spec: New Testament. Pub: *Johdatus eksegetiikkaan: Metodioppi* (1986); *Römer 13: Aufzeichnung und Weiterführung der exegetischen Diskussion* (Helsinki U.P., 1980); and others. Mem: Finnish Exegetical Soc.; SNTS. Addr: (o) Kirkon Koulosuskeskus, 04400 Jarvenpaa, Finland 00358-0-2719915; (h) Vilniementie 12 A 8, Espoo 02940, Finland 00358-0-2719915.

RISSI, Mathias, b. Wienacht, Switzerland, September 29, 1920, s. of Mathias & Fanny, m. Veronica, chil: Mark; Daniel; Hannes; Peter.

Educ: U. of Basel, Switzerland, ThD 1951. Emp:
U. of Basel, Switzerland, 1956-63 Privatdozent;
Union Theol. Sem., 1963-87 Prof., NT;
Interpretation, 1966-76 Ed. Bd. Spec: New
Testament. Pub: "Der Christushymnus in Phil
2,6-11" *ANRW* (1987); *Die Theologie des
Hebraerbriefs* (Mohr, 1987); "Der Aufbau des 4.
Evangeliums" *NTS* 29 (1983); "Die Logoslieder
im Prolog des 4. Evangeliums" *TZ* 31 (1975);
"The Kerygma of the Revelation to John"
Interpretation 22 (1968); "Die Hochzeit in
Kana" in *Oikonomia,* Festschrift O. Cullman
(1967); *Die Zukunft der Welt* (Reinhard, 1966);
Time and History, A Study of the Revelation
(John Knox, 1966); and others. Mem: SNTS;
SBL. Addr: (h) RFD 1 Box 1833, Stonington,
ME 04681 207-348-6235.

RITMEYER, Kathleen M., b. Sligo, Ireland,
June 28, 1952, d. of Edward & Margaret
O'Mahony, m. Leen, chil: Daniel; Nathaniel;
Benjamin; Anna; Joel. Educ: U. Coll., Dublin,
BA 1972; St. Patrick's Training Coll., Dublin,
PGCE 1973. Emp: St. Peter's Sch., Dublin,
1973-75 Tchr.; Ritmeyer Arch. Design Firm,
1983- Partner. Excv: Temple Mount Excvn.,
Jerusalem, 1975-78 Area Supr.; Haifa U., Akko
Excvn. Project, 1978-79 Res. Asst. Spec:
Archaeology. Pub: "Reconstructing Herod's
Temple Mount in Jerusalem," "Reconstructing
the Triple Gate," co-auth., "A Pilgrim's Journey"
BAR 15/6 (1989); and others. Awd: Fellner Awd.
1989. Rec: Bible study, hiking, homemaking.
Addr: (h) 49 Burtree Ave., Skelton, York YO3
6YT, England 0-904-470434.

RITMEYER, Leendert P., b. Rotterdam, The
Netherlands, March 9, 1945, s. of P.A. & E.B., m.
Kathleen, chil: Daniel; Nathaniel; Benjamin;
Anna; Joel. Educ: U. of York, Inst. of Advanced
Architectural Stud., MA 1990; U. of Manchester,
PhD 1992. Emp: Temple Mount Excvn., IES,
1973-77 Field Architect; Jewish Quarter Excvn.,
IES, 1978-83 Field Architect; Arch. Sites in the
Old City of Jerusalem, 1983-87 Chief
Conservation Asst.; York, U.K, 1989-91
Architectural Conservator; Temple Mount, 1991-
Res. Spec: Archaeology. Pub: "Reconstructing
Herod's Temple Mount in Jerusalem,"
"Reconstructing the Triple Gate," co-auth.,
"Quarrying and Transporting Stones for Herod's
Temple Mount" *BAR* 15/6 (1989); "Locating the
Original Temple Mount" *BAR* 18 (1992); and oth-
ers. Awd: Fellner Awd., Second Prize 1989. Mem:
Assn. of Arch. Illus. & Surveyors 1990-. Rec:
Hiking, photography. Addr: (o) 49 Burtree Ave.,
Skelton, York YO3 6YT, England 0-904-470434.

ROBBINS, Vernon K., b. Wahoo, NE, March
13, 1939, s. of Earl & Mildred (Hanson), m.
Deanna (Moritz), chil: Rick; Chimene. Educ:
United Theol. Sem., BD 1963; U. of Chicago
Div. Sch., MA 1966, PhD 1969. Emp: U. of Ill.
at Urbana-Champaign, 1968-84 Assoc. Prof.,
Dir. of Relig. Stud.; Pronouncement Stories Res.
Group, 1981-87 Dir.; *JBL,* 1982-87 Ed. Bd.; U.

of Trondheim, Norway, 1983-84 Fulbright-
Hayes Res. Lect. Fellow; Emory U., 1984- Prof.,
NT. Spec: New Testament, Apocrypha and Post-
biblical Studies. Pub: *Jesus the Teacher*
(Fortress, 1984, 1992); "The Social Location of
the Implied Author of Luke-Acts" in *The Social
World of Luke-Acts* (Hendrickson, 1991);
"Writing as a Rhetorical Act in Plutarch and the
Gospels" in *Persuasive Artistry* (Sheffield,
1991); *Patterns of Persuasion in the Gospels*
(Polebridge, 1989); *Ancient Quotes and
Anecdotes* (Polebridge, 1989); "Pronouncement
Stories and Jesus' Blessing of the Children: A
Rhetorical Approach" *Semeia* 29 (1984); "Mark
I.14-20: An Interpretation at the Intersection of
Jewish and Graeco-Roman Traditions" *NTS* 28
(1982); "The We-Passages in Acts and Ancient
Sea Voyages" *Bibl. Res.* 20 (1975); *Emory
Studies in Early Christianity,* gen. ed. (Lang);
and others. Mem: AAR 1968-77; SBL 1968-;
SNTS 1979-. Rec: Fishing, mountain hiking.
Addr: (o) Emory U., Dept. of Religion, 310
Physics Building, Atlanta, GA 30322 404-727-
6466; (h) 1634 Stonecliff Dr., Decatur, GA
30033 404-982-0174.

ROBERTS, Louis W., b. Denver, CO, April 13,
1930, s. of Wilbur L. & Dorothy Maxine, m.
Pamela (Brown). Educ: St. Louis U., BA 1956,
MA 1958; Innsbruck U., STL 1963; SUNY at
Buffalo, PhD 1970. Emp: St. Bonaventure U.,
1968-69 Asst. Prof., Theol.; Syracuse U., 1970-
74 Asst. Prof., 1974-78 Assoc. Prof., 1979 Prof.;
Merrimack Coll., 1987-88 Prof., Dean; U.
Albany, 1989- Prof. Spec: Semitic Languages,
Texts and Epigraphy, Apocrypha and Post-bibli-
cal Studies. Pub: "Das Sunderproblem des
Passivs bei Reflexiven Verben: Einfluss des
Dynamischen Medio-Passivs auf das Somali"
CILT (1987); "The Literary Form of the
Stromateis" *SC* 3 (1983); "Origen and the
Phoenix Too Frequent" *CF* 20 (1978); *A
Concordance of Lucretius* (Garland, 1976); "The
Unutterable Symbols of Ge-Themis" *HTR* 68
(1975); and others. Awd: NEH Cons. 1985-88.
Mem: APA 1968-; SBL 1990-. Rec: Skiing, hik-
ing, swimming. Addr: (o) State U. of New York,
U. at Albany, HUM 352, Albany, NY 12222
518-442-3978; (h) 55 Eileen St., Albany, NY
12203 518-459-6029.

ROBINSON, James M., b. Gettysburg, PA,
June 30, 1924, chil: Francoise Mary Anne;
James Claude; Joy Odile; Rosemary Kathleen.
Educ: Davidson Coll., AB (summa cum laude)
1945; Columbia Theol. Sem., BD (magna cum
laude) 1946; U. of Basel, Switzerland, ThD
(summa cum laude) 1952; Princeton Theol.
Sem., ThD, NT 1955. Emp: Emory U., Candler
Sch. of Theol., 1952-53 Instr., 1953-56 Asst.
Prof., 1956-58 Assoc. Prof., Bibl. Theol.;
Columbia Theol. Sem., 1955-58 Guest Prof.;
Sch. of Theol. at Claremont, 1958-61 Assoc.
Prof., 1961-64 Prof., Theol. & NT, 1964- Affil.
Prof.; Claremont Grad. Sch., 1959-64 Affil.
Mem. of Fac., 1964- Arthur Letts, Jr., Prof. of
Relig.; ASOR, Jerusalem, 1965-66 Ann. Prof.;

Amer. Res. Ctr. in Egypt, 1974-75 Dir., Nag Hammadi Codices Ed. Project, 1975-89 Prin. Amer. Investigator, Nag Hammadi Excvn. Spec: New Testament. Pub: *A Facsimile Edition of the Dead Sea Scrolls*, 2 vol., co-ed. (BAS, 1991); *The Facsimile Edition of the Nag Hammadi Codices*, 12 vol., co-ed., contb. (1972-1984); *A New Quest of the Historical Jesus*, Stud. in Bibl. Theol. 25 (SCM, 1959; Scholars, 1979); "The Future of Papyrus Codicology" in *The Future of Coptic Studies*, Coptic Stud. 1 (Brill, 1979); "Codicological Analysis of Nag Hammadi Codices V and VI and Papyrus Berolinensis 8502" in *Nag Hammadi Codices V,2-5 and VI*, Nag Hammadi Stud. 11 (Brill, 1979); *The Coptic Gnostic Library*, vol. 1-4, ed. (1974-1979); *Trajectories through Early Christianity*, co-auth. (1971-1979); "The Jung Codex: The Rise and Fall of a Monopoly" *RSRev* 3 (1977); *The Nag Hammadi Library in English*, ed., contb. (1977); and others. Awd: Phi Beta Kappa 1946; U. of Mainz, Germany, D. Theol. 1971; Davidson Coll., D. Lett. 1987. Mem: SBL 1953-, Pres., 1980-81; AAR 1953-; SNTS 1958-; ASSR 1959-; IACS 1976-. Addr: (o) Claremont Graduate School, Harper Hall, Rm. 22, 150 E Tenth St., Claremont, CA 91711 909-621-8000.

ROBINSON, Stephen E., b. Los Angeles, CA, May 23, 1947, s. of Edward & Myrtle (Egan), m. Janet (Bowen), chil: Sarah; Rebekah; Emily; Michael; Mary; Leah. Educ: Duke U., PhD 1978. Emp: Brigham Young U., 1972-74 Instr.; Duke U., 1974 Instr.; Hampden-Sydney Coll., 1978-79 Asst. Prof.; Lycoming Coll., 1979-86 Assoc. Prof.; Brigham Young U., 1986- Dept. Chmn., Prof. of Anc. Scripture. Spec: New Testament, Apocrypha and Post-biblical Studies. Pub: "The Apocryphal Story of Melchizedek" *JSJ* 18 (1987); "The Testament of Adam and the Angelic Liturgy" *RQ* 45 (1985); articles in *The Coptic Encyclopedia*; articles in *The Old Testament Pseudepigrapha*, vol. 1 & 2 (1983, 1985); *The Testament of Adam* (Scholars, 1982); and others. Mem: SBL. Rec: Fishing. Addr: (o) 375A Joseph Smith Bldg., Brigham Young U., Provo, UT 84602; (h) 1605 W, 1170 N, Provo, UT 84604.

ROCHAIS, Gérard G. R., b. La Tessoualle, France, October 24, 1939, s. of M. Augustin. Educ: U. Gregoriana, Lic.Th. 1966; Pont. Bibl. Inst., Lic. Sacred Scripture 1968; Ecole Biblique, Dip. 1969; U. de Montréal, PhD, Etudes Biblique 1973. Emp: U. de Montréal, 1971-74 Fac. de Théol.; Ecole Biblique, 1974-76; U. du Québec, 1978, 1983-84 Dept. de Théol., 1989- Prof. Spec: New Testament, Apocrypha and Post-biblical Studies. Pub: "'Et le Verbe s'est fait chair' (Jn 1,14)" in *Jésus: Christ Universel?* (Montréal Fides, 1990); "Jésus savait-il qu'il était Dieu? Réflexions critiques à propos d'un livre récent" *Sci. Religieuses* 14/1 (1985); "La formation du Prologue (Jn 1,1-18)" *Sci. et Esprit* 37/1 (1985); "Qu'est-ce que l'Apocalyptique?" *Sci. et Esprit* 36/3 (1984); *L'Evangile de Jean*, co-auth. (Cerf, 1977); *Les recits de resurrection des morts dans le*

Nouveau Testament, SNTS Mon. Ser. 40 (Cambridge U.P., 1981); "Les origines de l'Apocalyptique" *Sci. et Esprit* 25/1 (1973); and others. Awd: U. McGill, Montreal, Prix decerne par la CSBS/SCEB 1972; Prix du meilleur etudiant du Canada inscrit en redaction de these biblique. Mem: Assn. Cath. Francaise pour l'etude de la Bible 1969-; Assn. Cath. des Etudes Biblique au Canada 1971-; Soc. Canadienne de Theol. 1982-; Canadian SBS 1986-; SNTS 1986-. Addr: (o) U. du Quebec a Montreal, Dept. des scienes religieuses, CP 8888 Succursale "A", Montreal (Quebec) H3C 3P8, Canada 514-987-8480; (h) 7165 Clark, Appt. 7, Montreal, Que. H2S 3G5, Canada 514-271-4457.

ROCHBERG, Francesca R., b. Philadelphia, PA, May 8, 1952, d. of George & Gene, chil: Jacob; Gemma. Educ: U. of Chicago., PhD 1980. Emp: U. of Chicago, Oriental Inst., 1976- Lect., Res. Assoc., Assyrian Dict.; U. of Notre Dame, 1982- Assoc. Prof., Hist., Hist. & Phil. of Sci. Spec: Mesopotamian Studies, Semitic Languages, Texts and Epigraphy. Pub: "The Cultures of Ancient Science: Some Historical Reflections, Introduction" *ISIS* 83 (1992); "Between Observation and Theory in Babylonian Astronomical Texts" *JNES* 50 (1991); "Babylonian Horoscopes and Their Sources" *Orientalia* NS 58 (1989); *Language, Literature and History: Philological and Historical Studies Presented to Erica Reiner* (AOS/Eisenbraums, 1986); *Aspects of Babylonian Celestial Divination: The Lunar Eclipse Tablets of Enuma Anu Enlil* (Berger, 1986); "Canonicity in Cuneiform Texts" *JCS* 38 (1984); and others. Mem: AOS; ASOR; Amer. Hist. Soc.; Hist. of Sci. Soc. Rec: Music. Addr: (o) U. Notre Dame, Dept. of History, Notre Dame, IN 46556 219-631-7677.

ROFE, Alexander, b. Pisa, Italy, June 29, 1932, s. of Tsvi Gersh Roifer & Matilde (Gallichi), m. Esther (Kessler). Educ: Jerusalem, BA 1956, MA 1961, PhD 1970. Emp: Hebrew U., Jerusalem, 1961-, 1986- Prof. Spec: Hebrew Bible. Pub: "The Name YHWH Seba'ot and the Shorter Recension of Jeremiah" in *Fs. S. Herrmann* (1991); "Ephraimite versus Deuteronomistic History" *Scritti in Onore di J.A. Soggin* (1991); "An Enquiry into the Betrothal of Rebekah" in *Fs. R. Rendtorff* (1990); "The Nomistic Correction in Biblical Manuscripts and Its Occurence in *4QSam[a]*" *RQ* 54 (1989); "How is the World Fulfilled? Isaiah 55:6-11 Within the Theological Debate of Its Time" in *Essays in Honor of B.S. Childs* (1988); *The Belief in Angels in... Early Israel* (Makor, 1979); *The Prophetical Stories* (Magnes, 1988); *Introduction to Deuteronomy* (Academon, 1988); *Introduction to the Prophetic Literature* (Academon, 1992); and others. Addr: (o) The Hebrew U., Dept. of Bible, 91905 Jerusalem, Israel 972-2-88-35-28; (h) 6 Magnes Cr., 92304 Jerusalem, Israel 972-2-63-25-39.

ROFFEY, John W., b. Sydney, Australia, August 10, 1948, s. of Edmond & Gweneth (Medhurst),

m. Bet (Hayward), chil: Melissa; Jennifer; Natalie; Brooke. Educ: U. of Ky., MS 1978, PhD 1980; Lexington Theol. Sem., MDiv 1980; Yale U., STM 1981. Emp: Coll. of the Bible of Ch. in Christ, Australia, 1981-85 Lect.; Melbourne Coll. Div., Dean; Evang. Theol. Assoc., 1986-90 Parish Priest; St. Barnabas' Theol. Coll., 1991- Warden; Adelaide Coll. of Div., 1992- Pres. Spec: Hebrew Bible. Pub: "God's Truth, Jonah's Fish: Structure and Existence in the Book of Jonah" *Australian Bible Rev.* 36 (1988); "On Doing Reflection Theology: Poverty and Revelation 13" *Colloquim* 14/2 (1982); and others. Mem: Fellow of Bible Stud., Melbourne, 1981-, Pres. 1986. Addr: (o) St. Barnabas' College, PO Box 217, Belair, South Australia, Australia 08-2783177.

ROGERS, Cleon L., Jr., b. Ohatchee, AL, February 16, 1932, s. of Cleon L., Sr., & Carrie (Melton), m. Virginia Gail (Martin), chil: Cleon L., III; Charles David; Sharon Gail (Breimhorst); Suzanne Virginia (Rowe). Educ: Bob Jones U., BA 1954; SE Bible Coll., ThB 1955; Dallas Theol. Sem., ThM 1959, ThD 1962. Emp: SE Bible Coll., 1961-65 Instr.; Trinity Evang. Div. Sch., 1969 Guest Prof.; Freie Theologische Akadamie, Founder & Rector, 1974-90; Dallas Theol. Sem., 1978-79 Guest Prof.; World Reach Europe, 1991-. Spec: Hebrew Bible, New Testament, Apocrypha and Post-biblical Studies. Pub: *The Topical Josephus* (Zondervan, 1992); "Moses: Meek or Miserable?" *JETS* 29 (1986); "Erwagungen zur Verfasserschaft des Jesaja" *Fundierte Theologische Abhandlungen* 1 (1983); *A Linguistic Key to the Greek New Testament*, co-auth. (Zondervan, 1982); *Theological Wordbook of the Old Testament*. (Moody, 1980); "The Great Commission" *BS* 130 (1973); "The Covenant with Moses and its Historical Setting" *JETS* 14 (1971); "The Covenant with Abraham and its Historical Setting" *BS* 127 (1970); and others. Mem: ETS; SBL. Rec: Chess, music, sports. Addr: (o) Weingartenstr. 17, 6338 Huttenberg/Weidenhausen, Germany 06441-73900.

ROGERS, Max G., b. Richmond, VA, February 19, 1932, s. of John & Hattie (Gray), m. Hannelore, chil: Deborah; Stephanie; Stefan. Educ: Duke U., BA (summa cum laude) 1955; Union Theol. Sem., BD 1958; Columbia U., PhD 1964. Emp: Columbia U., 1959-60 Lect.; SE Bapt. Theol. Sem., 1960- Prof., OT. Spec: Hebrew Bible. Pub: Articles in *Abingdon Dictionary of Living Religions* (1981), *IDB* (1976); *Yahweh War and Tribal Confederation*, trans. (Abingdon, 1970). Awd: Woodrow Wilson Fellow 1955-56; Danforth Fellow 1955-64; Union Theol. Sem., Travelling Fellow. 1958; Columbia U. Fellow. 1958-59; Wilhelms U., Germany, Alexander von Humboldt Fellow 1966-67. Mem: SBL 1959-; Soc. for Values in Higher Educ. Rec: Tennis, swimming. Addr: (o) Southeastern Baptist Theological Seminary, Wake Forest, NC 27587 919-556-3101; (h) 1022 W Trinity Ave., Durham, NC 27701 919-688-4733.

ROGERS, Robert G., b. Columbus, OH, April 13, 1938, s. of William & Ruby (Baird), m. Gretchen (Lalendorf), chil: Jennifer; Margot. Educ: Boston U., STB 1963, PhD 1969. Emp: Wellesley Coll., 1967-68 Instr.; Newton Coll. of the Sacred Heart, 1969-75 Assoc. Prof.; Hampden-Sydney Coll., 1975- Prof., Relig.; Scarritt Coll., 1975, 1979 Vis. Lect.; Memorial U. of Newfoundland, 1974, 1978 Vis. Prof. Spec: Hebrew Bible, New Testament. Mem: AAR; SBL. Rec: Gardening, drama. Addr: (o) Hampden-Sydney College, Dept. of Religion, Box 685, Hampden-Sydney, VA 23943 804-223-4381; (h) Route #3, Box 400, Farmville, VA 23901 804-223-8443.

ROHDE, Joachim W. A., b. Ruetzow, May 25, 1930, s. of Albert & Berta (Rusch), m. Inge (Gellert), chil: Hartmut; Uta; Andreas. Educ: Dip. Theol. 1957; Humboldt U., Habil. 1970. Emp: *NEUE Zeit*, 1957-58 Journalist; Humboldt U., 1958-66 Wissenschaftlicher Asst., 1966- Wiss. Oberassistent; *THK*, Co-ed. Spec: New Testament. Pub: *Der Brief des Paulus an die Galater* (1989); "Die Diskussion um den Fruehkatholizismus im Neuen Testament, dargestellt am Beispiel des Amtes in den spaet-neutestamentlichen; Schriften" in *Fruehkatholische im oekumen: Gespraech* (1983); *Urchristliche und frukatholische Amter* (1976); *Rediscovering the Teaching of the Evangelists* (1969); "Haeresie und Schisma im 1 Clemensbrief und in den Ignatianen" *NT* 10 (1968); "Pastoralbriefe und Acta Pauli" *Studia Evangelica* 5 (1968); and others. Mem: SNTS; Gesellschaft fuer wissenschaftliche Theol. Addr: (o) Theologische Fakultaet, Burgstr. 25, 0-1020 Berlin, Germany 2468 377; (h) Parkstr. 69, 0-1120 Berlin- Weissensee, Germany 96503 74.

ROHRBAUGH, Richard L., b. Addis Ababa, Ethiopia, s. of James & Marion, m. Miriam, chil: Douglas; Janet. Educ: Pittsburgh Theol. Sem., MDiv 1961; San Francisco Theol. Sem., STD 1977. Emp: Lewis & Clark Coll., 1977- Prof. Excv: Tel Dan, 1986 Area Supr.; Tel Aroer, 1980 Area Supr. Spec: New Testament. Pub: *Social Science Commentary on the Synoptic Gospels*, co-auth. (Fortress, 1992); "A Peasant Reading of the Parable of the Talents: A Text of Terror?" *BTB* (1992); "The Pre-Industrial City: A Reader's Guide" *BTB* (1991); "The Pre-Industrial City in Luke-Acts: Urban Social Relations" in *The World of Luke-Acts* (Hendrickson, 1991); "'Social Location of Thought' as a Heuristic Device in New Testament Interpretation" *JSNT* (1987); *Interpretation* (Creative Edge, 1985); "Methodological Considerations in the Debate Over the Social Class Status of Early Christians" *JAAR* (1984); *The Biblical Interpreter* (Fortress, 1978); and others. Mem: AAR 1977-; SBL 1977-; ASOR 1978-. Rec: Flyfishing, rock climbing. Addr: (o) Lewis and Clark College, Box 41, 0615 SW Palatine Hill Rd., Portland, OR 97219 503-246-6845; (h) 7010 SW 4th, Portland, OR 97219 503-246-6845.

ROLLAND, Philippe, b. Gisors, France, February 25, 1940, s. of Léon & Madeleine (Bellin). Educ: Institut Catholique de Paris, Lic. théologie 1965; Institut Biblique de Rome, Lic. biblique 1967. Emp: Brazzaville, Congo, 1973-78 Prof., Exég.; Reims, France, 1978-81 Prof. Exég.; Jérusalem, 1981-83 Chargé de cours; Séminaire de Saint-Sulpice, 1983-89 Prof., Exég.; Reims, France & N'Djamena, Tchad, 1989- Prof., Exeg. Spec: New Testament. Pub: *A l'écoute de l'Epitre aux Romains* (Cerf, 1991); *Les ambassadeurs du Christ. Ministère pastoral et Nouveau Testament* (Cerf, 1991); *Les premiers évangiles. Un nouveau regard sur le problème synoptique* (Cerf, 1984); *Epitre aux Romains, Texte grec structuré* (Bibl. Pont. Inst., 1980). Mem: Assoc. Cath. Fran. Etude Bibl. Addr: (o) Séminaire Régional, 6, rue du Lieutenant-Herduin, Reims, F-51100, France 26-85-27-17; (h) Séminaire Saint-Luc, N'Djaména, BP 1168, Chad.

ROLLINS, Wayne G., b. Detroit, MI, August 24, 1929, s. of Arthur & Ethel, m. Donnalou (Myerholtz), chil: Michael; Thomas; David. Educ: Yale Div. Sch., BD 1954; Yale U., MA 1956, PhD 1960. Emp: Princeton U., 1958-59 Instr.; Wellesley Coll., 1959-66 Asst. Prof.; Hartford Sem. Found., 1966-74 Prof.; Assumption Coll., 1974- Prof.; Coll. of the Holy Cross, 1976-77 Vis. Prof. Spec: Hebrew Bible, New Testament. Pub: *Jung and the Bible* (Knox, 1983); Articles in *IDB*, Supplement, (1976); "The New Testament and Apocalyptic" *NTS* (1971); *The Gospels: Portraits of Christ* (Westminster, 1964); and others. Mem: SBL; SNTS; AAR, Pres., New England Sect. 1984-5. Rec: Walking, swimming. Addr: (o) Assumption College, 500 Salisbury St., Worcester, MA 01615-0005 508-752-5615; (h) 75 Craigmoor Rd., West Hartford, CT 06107 203-523-8784.

ROMERO, C. Gilbert, b. Dixon, NM, February 15, 1936, s. of J. Tobias & Claudia (Garcia). Educ: St. John's Coll., BA 1957, St. John's Theol. Sem., Dipl.Ord. 1961; Princeton Theol. Sem., PhD 1982. Emp: Wright State U., United Theol. Sem., La Salle Coll., St. Mary's Coll., Adj. Prof.; Seminario Mayor San Carlos, Peru, Vis. Prof. Excv: Gezer, 1968; Ai, 1969 Staff; Lachish, 1983; Tell-el-Hammah, 1988 Staff. Spec: Archaeology, Hebrew Bible, Mesopotamian Studies. Pub: Articles in *ABD* (Doubleday, 1992); *Hispanic Devotional Piety: Tracing the Biblical Roots* (Orbis, 1991); and others. Mem: CBA; SBL; AAR; ASOR; Acad. of Cath. Hispanic Theologians in the U.S. Rec: Hiking, travel, music, Carpe Diem. Addr: (o) CSULA, Catholic Campus Min. Health Center-Rm 221, 5151 State U. Dr., Los Angeles, CA 90032 213-343-2571; (h) 2510 S Fremont Ave., Alhambra, CA 91803.

ROOK, John T., b. Brantford, ON, Canada, May 13, 1948, s. of Thomas & Clair, chil: J. Tyler; Aaron. Educ: McMaster Div. Coll., MDiv 1976; Oxford U., DPhil 1984. Emp: McMaster Div.

Coll., 1979- Assoc. Prof. Spec: New Testament, Apocrypha and Post-biblical Studies. Pub: "A Twenty-eight Day Month Tradition in the Book of Jubilees" *VT* 31 (1981); "Boanerges, Sons of Thunder (Mark 3:17)" *JBL* 100 (1981); "The Names of the Wives from Adam to Abraham in the Book of Jubilees" *JSP* 7 (1990); "Women in Acts: Are They Equal Partners with Men in the Earliest Church?" *McMaster Jour. of Theol.* 2/2 (1991); *A New Testament Greek Workbook* (McMaster, 1985). Mem: SBL 1977-; CSBS 1980-. Addr: (o) McMaster U., Divinity College, Hamilton, ON L8S 4K1, Canada 416-525-9140.

ROOKER, Mark F., b. Dallas, TX, November 23, 1951, s. of George & Dorothy, m. Carole, chil: Nathaniel; Jonathan; Joshua. Educ: Rice U., BA 1974; Dallas Sem., ThM 1978; Brandeis U., MA 1985, PhD 1988. Emp: Dallas Theol. Sem., 1988-92, Asst. Prof.; Criswell Coll., Dallas, 1992- Chmn. & Prof., OT & Hebrew. Spec: Hebrew Bible. Pub: "Genesis 1:1-3: Creation and ReCreation" *BS* 149 (1992); *Biblical Hebrew in Transition: The Language of the Book of Ezekiel* (JSOT, 1990); "Ezekiel and the Typology of Biblical Hebrew" *Hebrew Ann. Rev.* 12 (1990); "The Diachronic Study of Biblical Hebrew" *JNSL* 14 (1988). Awd: Brandeis U., Tuch Fellow. 1987-88. Mem: SBL; NAPH; IBR. Rec: Skiing, camping, sports. Addr: (o) Criswell College, 4010 Gaston Ave. Dallas, TX 75246 214-818-1332; (h) 9571 Spring Branch Dr., Dallas, TX 75238 214-343-2981.

ROOP, Eugene F., b. South Bend, IN, May 11, 1942, s. of Frederic & Lois, m. Delora (Mishler), chil: Tanya; Frederic. Educ: Bethany Theol. Sem., MDiv 1967; Claremont Grad. Sch., PhD 1972. Emp: Claremont Grad. Sch., 1967-70 Resident Asst.; Earlham Coll., Sch. of Relig., 1970-77 Assoc. Prof.; Bethany Theol. Sem., 1977- Prof., Bibl. Stud., 1987-92 Wieand Prof. of Bibl. Stud., 1992- Pres. Spec: Hebrew Bible. Pub: *Commentary on Genesis* (Herald, 1986); "Justice in the Biblical Tradition" *Quaker Relig. Thought* (1977); and others. Mem: SBL; CSBR; AAR. Rec: Tennis, travel. Addr: (o) Bethany Theological Seminary, Oak Brook, IL 60521 312-620-2200; (h) 18W625 22nd St., Lombard, IL 60148 312-620-2254.

ROSEN, Arlene M., b. Los Angeles, CA, February 14, 1950, d. of Leonard Miller & Lilyan (Harris), m. Steven A. Rosen, chil: Yaniv Yacov; Boaz Seth. Educ: U. of N. Mex., BA, Anthrop. 1973; Wash. State U., MA, Anthrop. 1975; U. of Chicago, PhD, Anthrop. 1985. Emp: Albright Inst. of Arch. Res., 1987 NEH Post-Doc. Fellow; Arch. Survey of Israel, 1988-89 Geoarch.; Weizmann Inst. of Sci., 1989-91 Post-Doc. Fellow; Ben Gurion U., 1991- Adj. Lect. in Arch. Excv: Lachish, 1981, 1983 Geoarchaeologist; Ashkelon, 1986 Geoarchaeologist; Miqne-Eqron, 1984-87 Geoarchaeologist; Tel Erani 1987 Geoarchaeologist; Tel Halif, 1992 Geoarchaeologist. Spec: Archaeology. Pub: "Early Bronze Age Tel Erani: An Environmental

Perspective" *Tel Aviv* 18 (1991); "Microartifacts and the Study of Ancient Societies" *BA* 54 (1991); "Environmental Change at the End of the Early Bronze Age in Palestine" in *L'urbanisation de la Palestine a l'age du Bronze ancien*, Brit. Arch. Reports 527 (1989); "Ancient Town and City Sites: A View Through the Microscope" *Amer. Antiq.* 54/3 (1989); "Environmental Change and Settlement at Tel Lachish, Israel" *BASOR* 263 (1986); *Cities of Clay: The Geoarchaeology of Tells* (U. of Chicago, 1986). Mem: Amer. Anthrop. Assn.; AAS; Israel Anthrop. Assn.; Israel Prehist. Soc.; Assn. of Arch. in Israel. Rec: Photography, computers, horseback riding, swimming. Addr: (o) Ben Gurion U., Archaeological Division, PO Box 653, Beer Sheva 84 105, Israel 057-461-093; (h) Negba 73, Beer Sheva 84 232, Israel 057-233562.

ROSEN, Steven A., b. Brooklyn, NY, November 19, 1954, s. of Bernard & Janice, m. Arlene (Miller), chil: Yaniv; Boaz. Educ: U. of Calif. at Berkeley, AB 1975; U. of Chicago, AM 1978, PhD, Anthrop. 1983. Emp: Arch. Survey of Israel, 1980-88 Res. Arch.; *Mitekufat Haeven*, Jour. of the Israel Prehistoric Soc., 1985-90 Co-ed.; Ben Gurion U., 1988-91 Lect., 1991- Sr. Lect. Excv: Nahal Mitnan II, Negev Highlands, 1983 Co-dir.; Givat Hayil, Western Negev, 1987 Dir.; N Oded, Har Oded, Central Negev, 1988 Co-dir.; G'vaot Reved, Cen. Negev, 1989 Dir.; Abu Matar, 1990-91 Co-dir. Spec: Archaeology. Pub: "The Analysis of Early Bronze Age Chipped Stone Industries: A Summary Statement" in *L'Urbanisation de la Palestine a l'Age du Bronze Ancien*, Brit. Arch. Reports (Oxford U.P., 1989); "Notes on the Origins of Pastoral Nomadism: A Case Study from the Negev and Sinai" *Current Anthrop.* 29 (1988); "Finding Evidence of Ancient Nomads" *BAR* 14/5 (1988); "Byzantine Nomadism in the Negev: Results from the Emergency Survey" *Jour. of Field Arch.* 14 (1987); "Demographic Trends in the Negev Highlands: Preliminary Results from the Emergency Survey" *BASOR* 266 (1987); and others. Awd: Hebrew U., Jerusalem, Alexander Babbin Prize in Arch. 1985; Albright Inst., Jerusalem, Hon. Res. Fellow. 1985-86; Amer. Anthrop. Assn., Fellow 1991. Mem: AAS 1978-; Israel Prehistoric Soc. 1980-; ASOR 1983-; Assn. of Arch. in Israel 1988-; Amer. Anthrop. Assn. 1990-. Rec: Lit., camping, raising two children. Addr: (o) Ben Gurion U. of the Negev, Archaeology Division, Beersheva, Israel 057-461092; (h) 73 Negba St., Beersheva, Israel 057-33562.

ROSEN-AYALON, Myriam, b. Paris, France, d. of Ephraim & Clara, m. David. Educ: Sorbonne, Paris, MA 1962, PhD 1970. Emp: Hebrew U. of Jerusalem, 1964- Prof., Head of Inst. of Asian & African Stud. Excv: Kh. al-Minya, 1959; Susa, Iran, 1964-71; Ramla, 1965; Ashkelon, 1985. Spec: Archaeology. Pub: *The Early Islamic Monuments of al-Haram al-Sharif*, *Qedem* 28 (1989); "The Islamic Jewellery from Ashkelon" in *Jewellery and Goldsmithing in the*

Islamic World (1987); "The First Mosaic Discovered in Ramla" *IEJ* (1976); "Une Mosaique Médiéval au Saint-Sépulcre" *RB* (1976); and others. Awd: Schimmel Prize for Arch. 1992. Mem: Assn. Intl. pour l'Hist. du Verre; Soc. Asiatique; Soc. pour l'Avancement des Etudes Iraniennes; Arch. Supreme Coun. Addr: (o) Hebrew U. of Jerusalem, Institute of Archaeology, Mount Scopus, Jerusalem, Israel 02-882420; (h) 7 Kikar Magnes, Jerusalem, Israel 02-633306.

ROSENBAUM, Jonathan, b. Pontiac, MI, March 28, 1947, s. of Milton & Thelma, m. Susan (Gordon), chil: Joseph; Joshua; Jeremy. Educ: U. of Mich., BA; Hebrew Union Coll., BHL 1971, MA, Rabbinic Ord. 1972; Harvard U., PhD 1978. Emp: U. of Nebr., 1976-86 Assoc. Prof., Judaic Stud.; Bur. of Jewish Educ., 1978-86 Exec. Dir.; U. of Hartford, 1986- Maurice Greenberg Prof. & Dir., Maurice Greenberg Ctr. for Judaic Stud. Spec: Hebrew Bible, Semitic Languages, Texts and Epigraphy. Pub: "Hezekiah" in *ABD* (Doubleday, 1992); "Three Unpublished Ostraca from Gezer," co-auth. *BASOR* 262 (1986); "Hezekiah's Reform and the Deuteronomistic Tradition" *HTR* 72 (1979); *Climbing the Steps of Time*, co-auth. (NEH, 1978); and others. Mem: AAR; ASOR; SBL; CBA. Rec: Computers, bicycling. Addr: (o) U. of Hartford, Greenberg Ctr. for Judaic Stud., Auerbach 110 200 Bloomfield, Hartford, CT 06117 203-768-4964; (h) 3 Brownleigh Rd., West Hartford, CT 06117 203-233-0561.

ROSENBERG, Joel W., b. Los Angeles, CA, April 13, 1943, s. of Arthur & Cecile (Lieberman). Educ: U. of Calif., BA 1965, PhD 1978; Hebrew Union Coll., BHL 1968. Emp: U. of Calif., 1973-74 Vis. Lect.; Wesleyan U., 1976-78 Vis. Asst. Prof.; Tufts U., 1980- Assoc. Prof., Hebrew Lit., Judaic Stud. Spec: Hebrew Bible. Pub: "1 and 2 Samuel," "Jeremiah and Ezekiel" in *The Literary Guide to the Bible* (Harvard U.P., 1987); "Biblical Tradition: Literature and Spirit in Ancient Israel" in *Jewish Spirituality from the Bible Through the Middle Ages* (Crossroad, 1986); *King and Kin: Political Allegory in the Hebrew Bible* (Indiana U.P., 1986); "Biblical Narrative" in *Back to the Sources—Reading the Classic Jewish Texts* (Simon & Schuster, 1985); and others. Mem: AJS 1974-; SBL 1981-. Rec: Film, jogging. Addr: (o) Tufts U., Program in Judaic Studies, 325 Olin Hall, Medford, MA 02155 617-628-5000; (h) 35 Oliver St., Watertown, MA 02172 617-924-6547.

ROSENBERG, Roy A., b. Baltimore, MD, December 22, 1930, s. of Harry & Sylvia (Caplan), m. Ruth (Herzberger), chil: Raoul; Risa; Rani; Rianne; Remi. Educ: Hebrew Union Coll., DHL 1964. Emp: Loyola U., 1970-72 Lect. Spec: Hebrew Bible, New Testament. Pub: *The Concise Guide to Judaism: History, Practice, Faith* (Mentor/Penguin, 1991); "The

Slain Messiah in the Old Testament" *ZAW* 99 (1987); *Who Was Jesus?* (U. Press of Amer., 1986); *The Anatomy of God* (Ktav, 1973); "Who is the Moreh Sedeq?" *JAAR* 36 (1968); "Yahweh Becomes King" *JBL* 85 (1966); "Jesus, Isaac and the Suffering Servant" *JBL* 84 (1965); and others. Mem: SBL. Addr: (o) 1010 Park Ave., New York, NY 10028 212-535-0187; (h) 956 E 23 St., Brooklyn, NY 11210 718-253-8386.

ROSENBLATT, Marie-Eloise, b. Boise, ID, February 26, 1944, d. of Ned Klein & Mary Louise (Crum). Educ: U. of Santa Clara, BA 1966; U. of South. Calif., MA 1968; Ecole Biblique, Jerusalem, Eleve Titulaire 1982; Jesuit Sch. of Theol. at Berkeley, STL 1984; Grad. Theol. Union, PhD 1987. Emp: St. Mary's Coll., 1984-87 Chair, Critical Perspectives Prog.; San Francisco Archdiocese, 1985-87 Acad. Dir., Instr. in Scripture; Cath. Theol. Union, 1987-90 Asst. Prof.; Santa Clara U., 1990- Asst. Prof. Spec: New Testament. Pub: "Mission and Money in the New Testament" *Chicago Stud.* 30 (1991); "Recurring Narration as a Lukan Literary Convention in Acts: Paul's Jerusalem Speech in Acts 22:1-22" in *New Views on Luke and Acts* (Glazier/Liturgical, 1990); "The Voice of the One Who Prays in John 17" in *Scripture and Prayer: A Celebration for Carroll Stuhlmueller* (Glazier, 1988); and others. Mem: CBA; CTSA; AAR; SBL. Addr: (o) Santa Clara U., Dept. of Religious Studies, Santa Clara, CA 95053 408-554-4547.

ROSS, James, b. Omaha, NE, December 15, 1927. Educ: Duane Coll., AB 1949; Union Theol. Sem., BD 1952, ThD, OT 1955. Emp: Dartmouth Coll., 1955-59 Asst. Prof.; Drew U., 1959-68 Assoc. Prof. of OT; Princeton U., 1962-63 Vis. Lect.; Hebrew U. Coll., Bibl. & Arch. Sch., 1965-66 Arch. Dir.; Protestant Episcopal Theol. Sem., 1968- Prof. of OT; Albright Inst., Jerusalem, 1970-71 Prof. of Arch. Spec: Hebrew Bible. Pub: *Basic Sources of the Judeo-Christian Tradition* (Prentice-Hall); "Prophesy in Hamath, Mari, and Israel" *HTR* (1970); "Six Campaigns at Biblical Shechem," co-auth., in *Archaeological Discoveries* (Crowell, 1967); "Gezer in the Tell El-Amarna Tablets" *BA* (1967). Mem: SBL; Soc. Relig. Higher Educ. Addr: (o) Virginia Theological Seminary, 3737 Seminary Rd., Alexandria, VA 22304 370-6600.

ROSS, John M., b. Bothwell, Scotland, March 31, 1908, s. of Sir James Stirling & Christina, m. Helen (Wallace), chil: Christina; Helen; Gavin; George; Catherine. Educ: Wadham Coll., England, MA 1930. Spec: New Testament, Apocrypha and Post-biblical Studies. Pub: "The UBS Greek New Testament" *JBL* 95 (1976); "The Status of the Apocrypha" *Theology* 82 (1979); "Some Unnoticed Points in the Text of the New Testament" *NT* 25 (1983); "Amen" *ExpTim* 102 (1991); and others. Awd: CBE

1967. Mem: SST 1954-; SNTS 1984-87. Rec: 18th-century keyboard music, bookbinding. Addr: (h) 64 Wildwood Rd., London NW11 6UU, England 081-455-7872.

ROTHENBERG, Beno, Educ: Hebrew U., Jerusalem, MA 1939; J.W. Goethe U., Frankfurt, PhD 1962. Emp: Tel Aviv U., Inst. of Arch., 1969-75 Sr. Lect.; Arabah Expdn., Inst. of Mining & Metallurgy in the Bibl. World, Tel Aviv, 1973- Dir.; U. Coll., London, Inst. for Archaeo-Metallurgical Stud., 1975- Prof., Dir. Excv: Arabah Expdn., 1959-90 Founder; Arabah Mines and Shelters Excvn., 1964-90; Sinai Expdn., 1967-73 Dir.; Huelva Archaeo-Metallurgical Project, 1973-84 Dir.; Amraru Valley Mines, 1988-90. Spec: Archaeology. Pub: *The Ancient Metallurgy of Copper*, Res. in the Arabah, vol. 2 (1990); *The Egyptian Mining Temple at Timna*, Res. in the Arabah, vol. 1 (1988); *Ancient Mining and Metallurgy in Southwest Spain* (1981); *Sinai, Pharaohs, Miners, Pilgrims and Soldiers* (1979); *Antikes Kupfer im Timna-Tal*, co-auth. (1980); *Timna* (1972); *Negev, Archaeology in the Negev and the Arabah* (1967); "Ancient Copper Industries in the Western Arabah: An Archaeological Survey of the Arabah" *PEQ* 94 (1962); and others. Awd: Soc. of Antiquarians, FSA 1989; Inst. of Mining & Metallurgy, Hon. Fellow. 1992. Mem: IES; PEF; BSA, Jerusalem; ASOR; Hebrew Writers Assn. Addr: (h) PO Box 39113, 61390 Tel Aviv, Israel.

ROWOLD, Henry L., b. St. Louis, MO, July 10, 1939, s. of Henry & Irene, m. Phyllis Ann, chil: Gayle Renee; Jonathan Mark; Sheryl Lynn. Educ: Concordia Sr. Coll., BA 1960; Concordia Sem., MDiv 1964, STM 1965; Christ Sem., ThD 1977. Emp: Concordia Sem., Taiwan, 1972-84; Tainan Sem., 1972-1980; China Evang. Sem., 1978-83; Concordia Sem., Hong Kong, 1984-; Luth. Theol. Sem., Hong Kong, 1984-. Spec: Hebrew Bible. Pub: "Yahweh's Challenge to Rival: The Form and Function of the Yahweh-Speech in 38-39" *CBQ* (1985); "Leviathan and Job in Job 41:2-3" *JBL* (1986). Mem: CBA; SBL; Asia Theol. Assn.; Amer. Soc. of Missiology; Intl. Assn. for Mission Stud. Rec: Racquet sports, walking, jogging, wine-making, Chinese art & calligraphy. Addr: (o) 32 Oxford Rd. G/F, Kowloon, Hong Kong 0118523390587.

RUDOLPH, Kurt H., b. Dresden, Germany, April 3, 1929, s. of Georg & Gertrud, m. Christel, chil: Ulrike; Ekkehard. Educ: U. Leipzig, 1953, Dr Theol. 1956, PhD 1958, DPhilHabil 1961. Emp: U. Leipzig, 1961-63 Dozent, 1963-84 Prof.; U. of Calif. at Santa Barbara, 1984-86 Disting. Prof.; Marburg, 1986- Prof. Spec: Semitic Languages, Texts and Epigraphy, Apocrypha and Post-biblical Studies. Pub: "Geschichte und Probleme der Religionswissenschaft" in *NumenSup* 53 (Brill, 1992); *Die Gnosis* (U. Leipzig, 1977, 1991; Harper & Row, 1987); *Fundamentals and the Study of Religions* (Macmillan, 1985);

Theogonie, Kosmogonie und Anthropogonie in den mandaeischen Schriften (1965); Die Mandaeer, vol. 1 & 2 (Vandenhoeck & Ruprecht, 1961); and others. Awd: St. Andrew's U., Scotland, DD 1983. Mem: Inst. of Antiquity & Christianity, 1975-; SBL 1983-; AOS 1985-; Intl. Assn. for Manichaean Stud., Pres. 1989-. Rec: Travelling, hiking. Addr: (o) Philipps-U., Fachbereich Religionsgeschichte, Am Plan 3, D(W) 3550, Marburg, Germany 06421-28 4286; (h) Holderstrauch 7, D(W) 3550 Marburg, Germany 06421-32523.

RUIZ, Jean-Pierre M., b. Queens, NY, June 12, 1958, s. of Pedro & Reine-Marie. Educ: Cathedral Coll., BA 1978; Pont. Gregorian U., Rome, STB 1981, STL 1983, STD 1989. Emp: Pope John XXIII Natl. Sem., 1989-1991 Prof., Bibl. Stud.; St. Charles Borromeo Sem., 1990-93 Vis. Fac.; St. John's U., 1991- Asst. Prof., Dept. of Theol. & Relig. Stud. Spec: Hebrew Bible, New Testament. Pub: *Ezekiel in the Apocalypse: The Transformation of Prophetic Language in Revelation 16,17-19,10* (Lang, 1989). Mem: CBA 1984-; SBL 1989-; Acad. of Cath. Hispanic Theol. of the U.S. 1992-; AAR 1992-. Rec: Sports, music. Addr: (o) St. John's U., 81-50 Utopia Pkwy., Jamaica, NY 11439 718-990-6424; (h) 139-25 35th Ave., Flushing, NY 11354 718-762-7920.

RUNIA, David T., b. N.O. Polder, Netherlands, December 14, 1951, s. of Klaas & Hendrika, m. Maria Runia-Deenick, chil: Emma; Nicholas; Anthony. Educ: Melbourne U., MA 1975; Free U., Amsterdam, LittD 1983. Emp: Netherlands Orgn. Advancement of Pure Res., 1980-82, 1985 Huggens Res. Fellow; Free U., Amsterdam, 1983-84 Lect., Anc. & Patristic Phil.; Inst. of Advanced Study, 1986-87 Vis. Fellow; U. of Utrect, 1991 C.J. de Vogel Prof. Extraordairius in Anc. Phil.; U. of Leiden, 1992 Prof., Anc. & Medieval Phil. Spec: Apocrypha and Post-biblical Studies. Pub: *Exegesis and Scripture: Studies on Philo of Alexandria* (1990); *Philo of Alexandria: An Annotated Bibliography 1937-86,* co-auth. (1988); *Philo of Alexandria and the Timaeus of Plato* (1986); *The Studia Philonica Annual* (Scholars). Rec: Mozart, travelling, motorcycling. Addr: (o) Leiden U., Faculty of Philosophy, P.O. Box 9515, 2300 RA Leiden,, Netherlands 31-71-272010; (h) Rijnsburgerweg 116, 2333 AD Leiden, Netherlands 31-71-272031.

RUNNING, Leona G., b. Mt. Morris, MI, August 24, 1916, d. of Charles & Leona Glidden, m. Leif. Educ: Andrews U., Emmanuel Missionary Coll., BA 1937; Andrews U., Seventh-Day Adventist Theol. Sem., MA 1955; Johns Hopkins U., PhD 1964. Emp: Andrews U., 1955-81 Prof., Bibl. Lang., 1981- Prof. Emerita. Spec: Hebrew Bible, New Testament, Semitic Languages, Texts and Epigraphy. Pub: "The Dean of Biblical Archaeologists" *Ministry* (1975); "The Problem of the Mixed Syriac Manuscripts of Susanna in the Seventeenth Century" *VT* 19 (1969); "An Investigation of the Syriac Version of Isaiah," Parts 1-3 *AUSS* (1965-66); *William Foxwell Albright: A Twentieth Century Genius* (Morgan, 1975; Andrews U.P., 1991); *From Thames to Tigris* (Wash. Coll., 1958); and others. Mem: SBL 1956-; NAPH 1957-; ASOR 1960-; CSBR 1961-. Rec: Foreign travel, reading, swimming, knitting, crocheting. Addr: (o) Andrews U., Berrien Springs, MI 49104 616-471-7771; (h) 9025 Sunset Dr., Berrien Springs, MI 49103 616-471-1582.

RYBOLT, John E., b. Los Angeles, CA, August 13, 1939, s. of John & Eunice (McLarney). Educ: De Paul U., MA 1967; Harvard U., MA 1968; Cath. U. of Amer., STL 1969; Pont. Bibl. Inst., Rome, SSL 1972; St. Louis U., PhD 1978. Emp: St. Thomas Sem., 1968-69 Instr., 1984-93 Prof., OT, Pres.; Kenrick Sem., 1969-81 Prof.; *OT Abstracts*, 1976-93 Assoc. Ed.; DeAndreis Sem., 1981-84 Prof., Pres. Spec: Hebrew Bible. Mem: SBL 1969-93; CBA 1969-; CSBR 1982-84. Addr: (h) 2904 Arsenal St., St. Louis, MO 63118.

SABOURIN, Leopold, b. St-Jean-Baptiste, Man., Canada, September 7, 1919, s. of Omer & Mathilda (Clement). Educ: U. of Man., BA 1940, Lic. Theol. 1945; Sem. de Phil., Montreal, MA 1941; Pont. Bibl. Inst., Rome, Lic. S.S. 1957; Jesuit Scholasticate, Montreal, ThD 1959. Emp: Grand Sem., Port-au-Prince, 1959-64 Prof., Scripture; Pont. Bibl. Inst., Rome, 1967-78 Prof., Scripture; Grand Sem., Nairobi, Kenya, 1979-80 Prof., Scripture; U. of Calgary, 1980-81 Lect., Relig.; Sem. of Sydney, Australia, 1982-83 Lect., Scripture; Ecumenical Inst. of Theol. Res., Tantur, 1988 Instr., Early Cath. Spec: Hebrew Bible. Pub: "Traits apocalyptiques dans l'Evangile de Matthieu" *Sci. et Esprit* 33 (1981); "La rémission des peches: Ecriture Sainte et pratique ecclésiale" *Sci. et Esprit* 32 (1980); *Il vangelo di Matteo* (1977); *The Psalms, Their Origin and Meaning* (1969); "Un classement littéraire des Psaumes" *Sci. Ecclesiastiques* 16 (1964); *Les noms et les titres de Jésus* (Desclee, 1963); *Redemption Sacrificielle* (Desclee, 1961); and others. Mem: CBA 1964-. Addr: (o) 3200 Ch. Cote Ste. Catherine, Montreal H3T 1C1 PQ, Canada 514-342-1320.

SACK, Ronald H., b. Chicago, IL, November 23, 1943, s. of Herbert & Eleanor. Educ: U. of Minn., MA 1967, PhD 1970. Emp: U. of Wis., 1968-69 Instr.; Coll. of Idaho, 1970-71 Asst. Prof.; N.C. State U., 1971- Prof. Spec: Mesopotamian Studies, Semitic Languages, Texts and Epigraphy. Pub: "The Nabonidus Legend" *Revue d'Assyrologie* (1983); "Nebuchadnezzar and Nabonidus in Folklore and History" *Mesopotamia* 17 (1982); "Amel-Marduk-562-560 B.C." in *Alter Orient und Altes Testament* 4 (1972); and others. Mem: AOS. Rec: Swimming, golf. Addr: (o) North Carolina State U., Dept. of History, PO Box 8018, Raleigh, NC 27695 919-737-2484; (h) 2411 Lake Dr., Raleigh, NC 27609 919-781-6027.

SAFREN, Jonathan D., b. Brooklyn, NY, October 12, 1941, s. of Nathan & Ethel, m. Sarah, chil: Tsippy; Omri; Amnon. Educ: HUC-Jewish Inst. of Relig., MA 1975, PhD 1979. Emp: Hebrew U., Jerusalem, *Textus,* Technical Ed.; Hebrew Union Coll. 1975-78, Instr.; Ben-Gurion U., Israel, 1978-85 Lect., Bible; Bet Berl Coll., Israel, 1985- Lect., Bible. Spec: Hebrew Bible, Mesopotamian Studies. Pub: "'He Restoreth My Soul,' A Biblical Expression and its Mari Counterpart" in *Mari in Retrospect* (1992); "Ahuzzath and the Pact of Beer-Sheba" *ZAW* 101 (1989); "Balaam and Abraham" *VT* 38 (1988); "Dur-Yahdun-Lim—The Raison D'Etre of an Ancient Mesopotamian Fortress-City" *Jour. of the Economic & Soc. Hist. of the Orient* 32; (1988); "Removing the 'Gags' of the Euphrates, *hippam nasahum*" *JANES* 18 (1986); "The Location of Dur-Yahdun-Lim" *Revue Arch.* 78 (1984); *"Merhum* and *Merhutum* in Mari" *Orientalia* 51 (1982); "New Evidence for the Title of the Provincial Governor at Mari" *HUCA* 50 (1979); and others. Mem: SBL; AOS; IES; ISBR. Rec: Computers, jogging. Addr: (o) Bet-Berl College, Bible Dept., Kefar-Sava, Israel 052-906333; (h) 5/3 Nachshon St., Kefar-Sava, Israel 052-970223.

SAGARIN, James L., b. New York, December 31, 1951, s. of Ethel & Lawrence, m. Lori, chil: Eliana Miriam. Educ: State U. of N.Y. at Albany, BA 1974; HUC-Jewish Inst. of Relig., MA 1978, Rabbinic Ord., 1979. Emp: Wash. U., 1985-88 Instr.; Cen. Agency for Jewish Educ., 1982-88 Dir., Continuing Educ.; Temple Beth-El, Chicago, 1988-91 Assoc. Rabbi; Temple Menorah Hebrew & Relig. Sch., Chicago, 1991- Rabbi & Prin. Spec: Hebrew Bible, Semitic Languages, Texts and Epigraphy. Pub: *Hebrew Annual Review: Biblical and Other Studies in Memory of S.D. Goitein,* Hebrew Stud. vol. 9 (NAPH, 1989); *Hebrew Noun Patterns (Mishqalim): Morphology, Semantics, and Lexicon* (Scholars, 1987); and others. Mem: Cen. Conf. of Amer. Rabbis, 1979-; NAPH 1988-. Rec: Swimming, travel, reading, music. Addr: (o) 2800 W Sherwin, Chicago, IL 60645 312-761-5700; (h) 6434 N Kimball, Lincolnwood, IL 60645 708-674-2113.

SAKENFELD, Katharine Doob, Educ: Coll. of Wooster, BA; U. of R.I., MS, Sociology; Harvard Div. Sch., BD; Harvard U., PhD. Emp: Harvard Div. Sch., Teaching Fellow, OT; Harvard U., Teaching Fellow, Early & Oral Lit.; Princeton Theol. Sem., 1970- Assoc. Prof., OT, Dir. of PhD Stud. Spec: Hebrew Bible. Pub: *The Meaning of Hesed in the Hebrew Bible* (Scholars, 1978); and others. Mem: SBL; ASOR; Bibl. Colloquium, Pres. 1985-87; Bibl. Theologians. Addr: (o) Princeton Theological Seminary Princeton, NJ 08540.

SALDARINI, Anthony J., b. Boston, MA, September 18, 1941, s. of Roger & Harriet (Byrne), m. Maureen (Cusack), chil: Daniel; Bryan. Educ: Boston Coll., MA 1966; Weston Coll., PhL 1966; Yale U., MPhil 1970, PhD 1971. Emp: Loyola U., 1972-75 Asst. Prof.; Boston Coll., 1975- Prof.; *CBQ,* 1972-76, 1980-82, 1990- Assoc. Ed. Spec: New Testament, Apocrypha and Post-biblical Studies. Pub: "Delegitimation of Leaders in Matthew 23" *CBQ* 54 (1992); "Jews and Christian in the First Two Centuries: The Changing Paradigm" *Shofar* 10 (1992); "The Gospel of Matthew and Jewish-Christian Conflict" in *Social History of the Matthean Community: Cross-Disciplinary Approaches;* (Augsburg/Fortress, 1991); "Judaism and the New Testament" in *The New Testament and Its Modern Interpreters* (Scholars, 1989); *Pharisees, Scribes and Sadducees* (Glazier, 1988); *Jesus and Passover* (Paulist, 1984); "Adoption of a Dissident: Akabya ben Mahalalel in Rabbinic Tradition" *JSS* 33 (1982). Mem: SBL; CBA; AJS; AAR. Addr: (o) Boston College, Dept. of Theology, Chestnut Hill, MA 02167 617-552-3549; (h) 46 Walker St., Newtonville, MA 02160 617-964-4830.

SALMON, Marilyn J., b. Watertown, SD, May 10, 1948, d. of Guy & Marllys (Campbell), m. Lee S. Wiskochil, chil: Jesse; Isaac. Educ: Concordia Coll., BA 1970; Luther NW Theol. Sem., MDiv 1977; Hebrew Union Coll., Jewish Inst. of Relig., PhD 1986. Emp: Coll. of St. Catherine, 1983-89 Asst. Prof.; United Theol. Sem., 1989- Assoc. Prof., NT. Excv: Bethsaida, 1992 Asst. Area Supr. Spec: New Testament, Apocrypha and Post-biblical Studies. Pub: "Insider or Outsider? Luke's Relationship with Judaism" in *Luke-Acts and the Jewish People* (Fortress, 1988); and others. Mem: SBL 1978-; AJS 1987-. Addr: (o) United Theol. Sem. of the Twin Cities, 3000 5th St. NW, New Brighton, MN 55112 612-633-4311; (h) 1838 Ashland Ave., St. Paul, MN 55104 612-645-8504.

SALOM, Alwyn P., b. Adelaide, Australia, March 23, 1928, s. of Bertram & Gwendolyn, m. Audrey, chil: Melissa; Amanda. Educ: Andrews U., MA 1952; U. of Chicago, PhD 1956. Emp: Avondale Coll., Australia, 1956-64 Lect., 1967-73, 1981- Sr. Lect., Chmn., Dept. of Theol., Dean, Sch. of Relig. Stud.; Walla Walla Coll., 1964-67 Assoc. Prof.; Andrews U., 1981- Vis. Prof., OT. Spec: New Testament. Pub: "The Imperative Use of the Participle in the New Testament" *Australian Bibl. Rev.* 11 (1963); "Some Aspects of the Grammatical Style of 1 John" *JBL* 74 (1955); and others. Mem: ASOR 1951-; SBL 1955-; SNTS 1970-. Rec: Jogging. Addr: (o) 148 Fox Valley Rd., Wahroonga, NSW 2076, Australia 02-489-7122; (h) 9 Lindfield Ave., Cooranbong, NSW 2265, Australia 049-77-1709.

SANDELIN, Karl-Gustav, b. Narpes, April 1, 1940, s. of Adolf & Brita (Rasmussen), m. Ringa (Borg), chil: Benedict; Johanna. Educ: Abo Akademi, Teologie Lic. 1973, ThD 1977. Emp: Helsingfors, 1968-1971 Pastor; Abo Akademi, 1975- Lect. Spec: New Testament, Apocrypha and Post-biblical Studies. Pub: "The Danger of Idolatry according to Philo of Alexandria" *Temenos* 27 (1991); "Mithras=Auriga?" *Arctos* 22 (1988); *Wisdom as Nourisher: A Study of an Old Testament Theme, Its Development within Early Judaism and Its Impact on Early Christianity*,; Acta Acad. Aboensis, Ser. A (1986); "Zwei kurze Studien zum alexandrinischen Judentum" *Studia Theologia* 31 (1977); *Die Auseinandersetzung mit der Weisheit in 1. Korinther 15* (Abo Akademi Foun. Res. Inst., 1976); "Spiritus Vivificans: Traditions of Interpreting Gen 2:7" in *Opuscula Exegetica in Honorem Rafael Gyllenberg Octogenarii* (1973). Awd: Fulbright Schol. 1967-68; Alexander von Humboldt Schol. 1974-75. Mem: SNTS 1984. Rec: Fiction. Addr: (o) Abo Akademi, Domkyrkotorget 3, 20500 Abo, Finland 921-654146; (h) Tallkottsvagen 2 D, 20810 Abo, Finland 921-354181.

SANDERS, E. P., Emp: U. of Oxford, 1984-90 Dean Ireland's Prof. of Exegesis; Duke U., 1990- Prof., Relig. Spec: New Testament, Apocrypha and Post-biblical Studies. Pub: "The Life of Jesus" in *Christianity and Rabbinic Judaism* (BAS, 1992); *Judaism: Practice and Belief, 63 B.C.E.—66 C.E.* (Trinity, 1991); *Jewish Law from Jesus to the Mishnah*; *Paul and Palestinian Judaism* (1977); *Jesus and Judaism* (1985); and others. Awd: Oxford U., DLitt; U. of Helsinki DTh; Relig. Media Today, National Relig. Book Awd., 1977; Grawmeyer Awd. in Relig.; Killam Sr. Res. Fellow.; Guggenheim Fellow. Mem: Amer. Coun. of Learned Soc. Fellow.; Social Sci. & Hum. Res. Coun. of Canada Fellow. Addr: (o) Duke U., Dept. of Religion, Durham, NC 27706 919-660-3510.

SANDERS, Jack T., b. Grand Prairie, TX, February 28, 1935, s. of Eula & Mildred, m. Susan (Plass), chil: Collin. Educ: Emory U., MDiv 1960; Claremont Grad. Sch., PhD 1963. Emp: Claremont Theol. Sch., 1962 Lect.; Emory U., 1964-67 Asst. Prof.; Garrett Theol. Sem., 1967-68 Vis. Asst. Prof.; McCormick Theol. Sem., 1968-69 Vis. Asst. Prof.; U. of Oregon, 1969- Prof.; *JBL,* 1977-82 Ed. Bd. Spec: New Testament. Pub: "Who Is a Jew and Who Is a Gentile in the Book of Acts?" *NTS* (1991); *The Jews in Luke-Acts* (SCM/Fortress, 1987); *Ethics in the New Testament* (SCM, 1986); "The Pharisees in Luke-Acts" in *The Living Text: Essays in Honor of Ernest W. Saunders* (1985); *Ben Sira and Demotic Wisdom* (Scholars, 1983); "Tradition and Redaction in Luke XV. 11-32" *NTS* (1969). Awd: NEH Sr. Res. Fellow 1983-84. Mem: SBL 1960-; SNTS 1971-. Rec: Fly fishing, photography. Addr: (o) U. of Oregon, Dept. of Religious Studies, Eugene, OR 97403 503-686-4971; (h) 2555 Birch Ln., Eugene, OR 97403 503-683-0884.

SANDERS, James A., b. Memphis, TN, November 28, 1927, s. of Robert & Sue (Black), m. Dora (Cargille), chil: Robin. Educ: Vanderbilt U., BA (magna cum laude) 1948; Vanderbilt Div. Sch., BD 1951; Hebrew Union Coll., PhD 1955. Emp: Colgate Rochester Div. Sch., 1954-65 Prof., OT Interpretation; Union Theol. Sem., 1965-77 Auburn Prof. of Bibl. Stud.; Columbia U., 1966-77 Adj. Prof., Relig.; *JBL,* 1970-76 Ed. Bd.; Yale U., 1972 Shaffer Lect.; Claremont Grad. Sch., 1977- Prof. of Relig., Prof. of Intertestamental & Bibl. Stud., Sch. of Theol., 1980- Pres., Anc. Bibl.; Manuscript Ctr.; NRSV, 1981- Bible Com.; Glasgow U., 1990-1991 Alexander Robertson Lect. Spec: Hebrew Bible, New Testament, Semitic Languages, Texts and Epigraphy, Apocrypha and Post-biblical Studies. Pub: *From Sacred Story to Sacred Text* (Fortress, 1987); *Near Eastern Archaeology in the Twentieth Century: Essays in Honor of Nelson Glueck* (Doubleday, 1970); "Text and Canon: Concepts and Method" *JBL* 98 (1979); "The Dead Sea Scrolls—A Quarter Century of Study" *BA* 36 (1973); *Canon and Community: A Guide to Canonical Criticism* (Fortress, 1984); *Torah and Canon* (Fortress, 1972); *The Dead Sea Psalms Scrolls* (Cornell, 1967); *DJD IV: The Psalms Scroll of Qumran Cave ll* (Clarendon, 1965). Awd: Rockefeller Grant 1953-54, 1985-86; Guggenheim Fellow 1961, 1972; Acadia U., LittD 1973; U. of Glasgow, STD 1975; Coe Coll., DHL 1988; Hebrew Union Coll., DHL 1988. Mem: SBL 1954-, 1977-78 Pres.; Albright Inst. Arch. Res., 1970-75 Founding Trustee; SNTS 1971-. Rec: Mysteries. Addr: (o) Ancient Biblical Manuscript Center for Preservation & Res. PO Box 670, Claremont, CA 91711 714-621-6451; (h) PO Box 593, Claremont, CA 91711.

SANDERSON, Judith E., b. Camden, NJ, January 10, 1944, d. of John & Pearl. Educ: Covenant Theol. Sem., MDiv 1972; Inst. of Holy Land Stud., MA, Hebrew 1979; U. of Notre Dame, MA, PhD, Hebrew Bible & Judaica 1985. Emp: Wheaton Coll., 1968-69 Instr.; New Coll. for Advanced Christian Stud., 1984 Vis. Instr., OT Theol.; Princeton Theol. Sem., 1985-91 Asst. Prof., OT; *The Revised Psalms of the New American Bible,* 1991 Steering Com. of Bd. of Ed.; Seattle U., 1991- Asst. Prof., Hebrew Bible. Spec: Hebrew Bible. Pub: *Discoveries in the Judaean Desert* vol. 9, co-ed. (Clarendon, 1992); "Amos," "Micah," "Nahum," "Habakkuk," "Zephaniah" in *The Women's Bible Comm.* (Westminster/John Knox, 1992); "War, Peace, and Justice in the Hebrew Bible: A Representative Bibliography" in *Holy War in Ancient Israel* (Eerdmans, 1991); "The Contributions of 4QpaleoExod^m to Textual Criticism" in *Etudes Qumraniennes: Memorial Jean Carmignac, RQ* 49-52 (1988); *An Exodus Scroll from Qumran: 4QpaleoExod^m and the Samaritan Tradition*, HSS 30 (Scholars, 1986). Addr: (o) 220 24th Ave. East, Seattle, WA 98112.

SANDY, D. Brent, b. Lebanon, PA, March 19, 1947, s. of A. Rollin & Omega (Hartman), m. Cheryl (Ackerly), chil: Jason; Jaron. Educ: Grace Theol. Sem., MDiv 1973; Duke U., PhD

1977. Emp: Grace Coll. & Theol. Sem., 1978-88 Prof.; Bibl. & Anc. Manuscript Ctr., 1985-88 Dir.; Liberty U., 1988- Prof.; *Grace Theol. Jour.*, 1986-88 Managing Ed. Spec: New Testament, Egyptology, Apocrypha and Post-biblical Studies. Pub: "John the Baptist's 'Lamb of God' Affirmation in Its Canonical and Apocalytic Milieu" *JETS* 34/4 (1991); *The Production and Use of Vegetable Oils in Ptolemaic Egypt* (Scholars, 1989); "Egyptian Terms for Castor" *Chronique d'Egypte* 62 (1987); "Oil Specification in the Papyri: What is *Elaion?*" in *Atti del Congresso Internazionale di Papyrologia* (Naples, 1984); and others. Mem: SBL 1978-; ETS 1982-. Rec: Swimming, bicycling. Addr: (o) Liberty U., Lynchburg, VA 24506 804-582-2576; (h) 103 Sparrow Dr., Lynchburg, VA 24502 804-525-3531.

SARASON, Richard S., b. Detroit, MI, February 12, 1948, s. of C. Kenneth & Cornelia, m. Anne (Arenstein), chil: Jonathan; Michael. Educ: Brandeis U., AB 1969; Hebrew Union Coll., MAHL 1974; Brown U., PhD 1977. Emp: Brown U., 1976-79 Asst. Prof.; Hebrew Union Coll. 1979- Prof.; *RSRev*, 1979-88 Ed. Bd.; *HUCA*, 1984- Ed. Bd. Spec: Apocrypha and Post-biblical Studies. Pub: "The Interpretation of Jeremiah 31:31-34 in Judaism" in *When Jews and Christians Meet* (SUNY, 1988); "The Significance of the Land of Israel in the Mishnah" in *The Land of Israel: Jewish Perspectives* (Notre Dame, 1986); "The *Petihot* in Leviticus Rabba: 'Oral Homilies' or Redactional Constructions?" *JJS* (1982); "Developments in the Study of Jewish Liturgy" in *The Study of Ancient Judaism* (Ktav, 1982); and others. Mem: AAR; SBL; AJS; ASOR. Rec: Music, film. Addr: (o) Hebrew Union College, 3101 Clifton Ave., Cincinnati, OH 45220 513-221-1875; (h) 7405 Laurel Oak Ln., Cincinnati, OH 45237 513-731-0554.

SARNA, Nahum M., b. London, England, March 27, 1923, s. of Jacob & Milly, m. Helen, chil: David; Jonathan. Educ: U. of London, MA 1946; Dropsie Coll., PhD 1955. Emp: U. Coll., London, 1946-49 Asst. Lect.; Gratz Coll., 1951-57 Lect.; Jewish Theol. Sem., 1957-65 Assoc. Prof.; Brandeis U., 1965-85 Dora Golding Prof. of Bibl. Stud., 1985- Prof. Emeritus; *EJ,* 1968-72 Dept. Ed. Spec: Hebrew Bible. Pub: *Commentary to Exodus* (Jewish Publ. Soc., 1991); *Commentary to Genesis* (Jewish Publ. Soc., 1989); *Exploring Exodus* (Schocken, 1986); *The Writings (Kethubim)*, co-auth. (Jewish Publ. Soc., 1982); "The Last Legacy of Roland de Vaux" *BAR* 6/4 (1980); "The Biblical Sources for the History of the Monarchy" in *World History of the Jewish People* (Massada, 1979); "Abraham in History" *BAR* 3/4 (1977); and others. Mem: AOS; ASOR; AJS, Pres. 1983-85; IES; PES. Addr: (h) 39 Green Park, Newton, MA 02158 617-332-7968.

SASSON, Jack M., b. Aleppo, Syria, October 1, 1941, m. Diane, chil: David; Noah; Daniel.

Educ: Brandeis U., MA, Mediterranean Stud. 1963, PhD, Mediterranean Stud., OT, Islamic Stud. 1966. Emp: U. of N.C., Chapel Hill, 1966- Prof., Dept. of Relig. Stud., 1991 William R. Kenan Prof.; *JBL*, 1977-82 Ed. Bd.; *BASOR*, 1983- Ed. Bd.; *BA*, 1984- Ed. Bd.; *Mesopotamian Stud.*, 1984- Ed. Bd.; *JAOS*, 1976-84 Ed. Bd. Spec: Anatolian Studies, Hebrew Bible, Mesopotamian Studies, Semitic Languages, Texts and Epigraphy. Pub: *Jonah*, AB (1990); *Ruth* (JSOT, 1990); "Remarks on Ikribum Vows at Mari" *Rev. d'Assyriologie* 79 (1985); "Zimri-Lim Takes the Grand Tour" *BA* 47 (1984); "Mari Dreams," "Musical Settings for Cuneiform Literature: A Discography" *JAOS* 103 (1983); *The Treatment of Criminals in the Ancient Near East*, ed. (Brill, 1977); and others. Awd: Fulbright-Hays 1966-67; Inst. Advanced Stud., Jerusalem, Fellow 1982-83. Addr: (o) U. of North Carolina, Religious Studies Department, 105 Saunders, Chapel Hill, NC 27599-3225 919-962-3925; (h) 1505 Halifax Rd., Chapel Hill, NC 27514 919-929-1202.

SAUNDERS, Ernest W., b. Boston, MA, March 23, 1915, s. of Ernest & Maude (MacDowell), m. Verina, chil: Leslie; Duncan; Charles. Educ: Boston U., BS 1938, STB 1940; Duke U., PhD 1943. Emp: Morningside Coll., 1946-50 Prof.; Garrett-Evang. Theol. Sem., 1950-78 Prof., NT Interpretation; Anc. Bibl. Manuscripts Ctr., 1978- Adv. Bd.; *JBL*, 1983-88 Ed. Bd.; Jerusalem Ctr. for Bibl. Stud., 1985- Bd. Spec: Archaeology, New Testament, Apocrypha and Post-biblical Studies. Pub: *Searching the Scriptures* (Scholars, 1982); *John Celebrates the Gospel* (Abingdon, 1970); *Jesus in the Gospels* (Prentice-Hall, 1967); "Studies in Doctrinal Influences of the Byzantine Text of the Gospels" *JBL* 71 (1952); and others. Awd: Fulbright Res. Fellow. Mem: SBL, Pres., MidW sect. 1949-51, Hon. Pres. 1981; SNTS. Rec: Photography, gardening. Addr: (h) RFD 1, Box 300, Mount Vernon, ME 04352 207-293-2603.

SAVE-SODERBERGH, Torgny, b. Lund, Sweden, June 29, 1914, s. of Gotthard & Inga, m. Brita, chil: Karin Svantesson. Educ: Uppsala U., PhD, Egyptology 1942. Emp: Uppsala U., 1942-50 Asst. Prof., 1950-80 Prof., Egyptology. Excv: Abu Ghalib, Egypt, 1936-37 Asst.; Theban Tombs Project, Egypt, 1956 Documentation, Leader; Scandinavian Joint Expdn., Nubia, Sudan, 1961-64 Leader. Spec: Archaeology, Egyptology, Apocrypha and Post-biblical Studies. Pub: "The Pagan Elements in Early Christianity and Gnosticism" in *Bibl. Copte de Nag Hammadi* (Barc, 1981); "Holy Scriptures or Apologetic Documentations?" in *Les Textes de Nag Hammadi* (Menard, 1975); "Gnostic and Canonical Gospel Traditions" *NumenSup* (1967); "In Gnosticism (Nag Hammmadi): On Evangelium Veritatis" *Symbolae Biblical Uppsalienses* 16 (1959); *Four Eighteenth Dynasty Tombs* (1957); *Studies in the Coptic Manichean Psalmbook* (1949); *Aegypten und Nubien* (1942); and others. Mem: Intl. Assn.

Egyptology, Pres. 1978-82; IACS, Hon. Pres. 1976; Intl. Soc. of Nubian Stud., Hon. Pres. 1990; SBL, Hon. Mem.; Swedish Acad. Letters, Pres. 1978-84. Addr: (o) Uppsala U., Dept. of Egyptology, Gustavianum, 75310 Uppsala, Sweden 018-182080; (h) Kyrkogaridsg 27, 75312 Uppsala, Sweden 018-540140.

SAZAVA, Zdenek, b. Brno, Czechoslovakia, June 28, 1931, s. of Vaclav & Anna, m. Sylvia, chil: Renata. Educ: Hus Faculty of Theol., DD 1969. Emp: Hus Faculty of Theol., 1975-89 Prof., NT; Charles' U., Hussite Faculty of Theol., Prague, 1990- Prof., NT. Spec: New Testament. Pub: *The Teacher and the Lord* (1987); *Stand Up and Walk (Acts, Chpt. 1-12)* (1974); and others. Mem: SNTS 1981-. Rec: Volleyball, music. Addr: (o) 160 00 Prague 6-Dejvice, Wuchterlova 5, Czech Republic 320041-4.

SCAER, David, b. Brooklyn, NY, March 13, 1936, s. of Paul & Victoria (Zimmerman), m. Dorothy (Hronetz), chil: David; Stephen; Peter. Educ: Concordia Sem., MDiv 1960, ThD 1963. Emp: Concordia Theol. Sem., 1966- Prof.; U. of Ill., 1966-76 Adj. Instr.; Concordia Sem., 1974 Vis. Prof.; *Concordia Theol. Quar.*, 1969- Ed.; *Christianity Today*, 1980 Ed. Spec: New Testament. Pub: "He Descended into Hell" *JETS* 34 (1992); "The Relation of Matthew 28:16-20 to the Rest of the Gospel" *Concordia Theol. Quar.* 55 (1991); *Christology* (Intl. Found. for Luth. Confessional Res., 1989); "A Response to Genre Criticism-Sensus Literalis" in *Hermeneutics and Inerrancy* (Zondervan, 1984); *James the Apostle of Faith* (Concordia, 1984). Mem: SBL. Rec: Jogging. Addr: (o) Concordia Theological Seminary 6600 N Clinton St., Ft. Wayne, IN 46825-4996 219-482-9611; (h) 1912 Brandywine Trail, Ft. Wayne, IN 46845-1578 219-637-6201.

SCHABERG, Jane D., b. St. Louis, MO, February 20, 1938, d. of Kenneth Dewar & Helen (Walsh). Educ: Manhattanville Coll., BA 1960; Columbia U., MA 1970; Union Theol. Sem., PhD 1980. Emp: U. of Detroit Mercy, 1977- Prof., Relig. Stud., Chair; *Continuum*, 1990- Assoc. Ed. Spec: New Testament. Pub: "The Gospel of Luke" in *The Women's Bible Comm.* (Westminster/John Knox, 1992); "Thinking Back Through the Magdalene" *Continuum* 1 (1991); *The Illegitimacy of Jesus: A Feminist Theological Interpretation of the New Testament Infancy Narratives* (Harper & Row, 1987;; Crossroad, 1990); "Mark 14:62: Early Merkabah Imagery?" in *Apocalyptic and the New Testament* (JSOT, 1988); "Major Midrashic Traditions in Wisdom 1:1-6:15" *JSJ* 13 (1986); "Daniel 7, 12 and the New Testament Passion-Resurrection Predictions" *NTS* 31 (1985); *The Father, the Son, and the Holy Spirit: The Triadic Phrase in Matthew 18:19* (Scholars, 1982); and others. Mem: SBL; AAR; CBA; Windsor-Detroit Women's Res. Colloquium; Natl. Women's Stud. Assn. Rec: Creative writing, videotaping, travel,

horseback riding, swimming. Addr: (o) U. of Detroit Mercy, Religious Studies Dept., Detroit, MI 39900 313-993-1589; (h) 18202 Fairfield, Detroit, MI 48221 313-864-7957.

SCHALLER, J. Berndt, b. Heidelberg, August 28, 1930, s. of Johann Max & Ilse (Froeschel), m. Kaete (Gossel), chil: Joachim; Jakobe; Rahel. Educ: Theol. Examen 1960; ThD 1960, Habil. 1980. Emp: U. Goettingen, Dept. Antikes Judentum, 1960- Prof.; Heidelberg, 1979-80 Vis. Prof., NT; Hamburg, 1981-82 Vis. Prof., NT; Hebrew U., 1991-92 Vis. Prof. Spec: New Testament, Apocrypha and Post-biblical Studies. Pub: "Philon v. Alexandreia und das Heilige Land" *GThA* 25 (1983); "Das Testament Hiobs und die Septuaginta-Ubersetzung des Buches Hiob" *Biblica* 61 (1980); "Das Testament Hiobs" in *Juedische Schriften aus hellenistischer und roemischer Zeit* 3/3 (1979); "Zur Ueberliefetungsgeschichte des ps-philonischen Liber Antiquitatum im Mittelalter" *JSJ* 10 (1979); "Die Sprueche ueber Ehescheidung und Wiederheirat in der Synoptischen Uberlieferung" in *Der Ruf Jesu und die Antwort der Gemeinde* (1970); "Hekataios von Abdera Uberdie Juden" *ZNW* 54 (1963); and others. Mem: SNTS; Verband der Judaisten in Deutschland. Addr: (o) Institut fuer Spezialforschung, Platz der Goettinger Sieben 2, D 37073 Goettingen, Germany 0551-397145; (h) Ludwig-Beck-Str. 11, D 37075 Gottingen, Germany 0551-22623.

SCHAUB, Marilyn B., b. Chicago, IL, March 24, 1928, d. of Bernard & Helen (Skehan) McNamara, m. R. Thomas, chil: Helen. Educ: U. of Fribourg, Switzerland, PhD 1957; Ecole Biblique, Jerusalem, Diploma 1967. Emp: Duquesne U., 1973- Prof. Excv: Tell er-Rumeith, Jordan, 1967 Area Supr.; Tell Ta'nach, Jordan, 1968 Area Supr.; Idalion, Cyprus, 1972, 1974 Registrar; Bab edh-Dhra, Jordan, 1977, 1979, 1981 Registrar; SE Dead Sea Plain, Feifeh & Khanazir, Jordan, 1989-90 Admin. Dir. Spec: Archaeology, Hebrew Bible. Pub: *Agape in the New Testament* 3 vols., co-trans. (Herder, 1965); *Friends and Friendship for Augustine* (Alba, 1964); and others. Mem: CBA 1963-; SBL 1968-; AAR 1968-; IES 1978-. Rec: Piano, gardening. Addr: (o) Duquesne U., Theology Dept., Pittsburgh, PA 15282 412-434-6530; (h) 25 McKelvey Ave., Pittsburgh, PA 15218 412-242-1219.

SCHAUB, R. Thomas, b. South Bend, IN, March 26, 1933, s. of Raymond & Catherine, m. Marilyn (McNamara), chil: Helen. Educ: Aquinas Inst. Phil., MA (summa cum laude) 1958; Aquinas Inst. Theol., MA 1961; Pont. Bibl. Commn., SSB 1965, SSL 1967; U. of Pittsburgh, PhD 1973. Emp: Aquinas Inst. Theol., 1968-69 Asst. Prof.; Pittsburgh Theol. Sem., 1970-71 Vis. Lect.; Indiana U. of Pa., 1969- Prof., Relig. Stud. Excv: Bab edh-Dhra', Jordan, 1967 Architect, Field Supr.; Tell er-Rumeith, Jordan, 1967- Architect, Area Supr.; Idalion, Cyprus, 1972-74 Architect; SE Plain, Dead Sea, Jordan, 1973 Co-Organizer, 1975 Co-

dir. Spec: Archaeology. Pub: *Bab edh-Dhra':
Excavations in the Cemetery Directed by Paul
W. Lapp (1965-67)* (1989); "Preliminary Report
of the 1981 Expedition to the Dead Sea Plain,
Jordan" *BASOR* 254 (1984); "The Origins of the
Early Bronze Age Walled Town Culture of
Jordan" in *Studies in the History and
Archaeology of Jordan* (Pitman,; 1982);
"Preliminary Report of the 1979 Expedition to
the Dead Sea Plain, Jordan" *BASOR* 240 (1980);
"The Southeastern Dead Sea Plain Expedition:
An Interim Report of the 1977 Season" *AASOR*
46 (1979); "A Preliminary Report of
Excavations at Bab edh-Dhra', 1975" *AASOR* 43
(1976); and others. Mem: SBL; ASOR; AAR;
AIA; CBA. Addr: (o) Indiana U. of
Pennsylvania, 442 Sutton Hall, Indiana, PA
15705 412-357-2310; (h) 25 McKelvey Ave.,
Pittsburgh, PA 15218 412-242-1219.

SCHIFFMAN, Lawrence H., b. New York,
NY, May 4, 1948, s. of Robert & Hilda, m.
Marlene, chil: Daniel; Alyssa; Leah; Esther.
Educ: Brandeis U., MA 1970, PhD 1974. Emp:
N.Y. U., 1972- Prof., Hebrew & Judaic Stud.,
1980-83 Prog. Dir., Tel Dor Excvn.; Ben
Gurion U., 1980-81 Vis. Assoc. Prof.; Hebrew
U., 1989-90 Fellow, Inst. for Advanced Stud.;
Duke U., 1992 Vis. Prof.; Ed. team of Dead Sea
Scrolls. Pub: *Hebrew and Aramaic Magical
Texts from the Cairo Genizah*, co-auth. (1992);
From Text to Tradition (1991); *Archaeology
and History in the Dead Sea Scrolls*, ed.
(1990); *Sectarian Law in the Dead Sea Scrolls*
(1983); *The Eschatological Community of the
Dead Sea Scrolls*, SBL Mon. Ser. 37 (1989);
and others. Mem: AJS; IES; SBL; WUJS; AAJR.
Rec: Travel. Addr: (o) Skirball Dept. of
Hebrew and Judaic Studies, 51 Washington
Square South, New York, NY 10012 212-998-
8980; (h) 20 Edgewood Pl., Great Neck, NY
11024 516-829-5288.

SCHILLE, Gottfried, b. Dresden, Germany,
August 6, 1929, s. of Eva Maria (Klaholz), chil:
Matthias; Maria-Barbara (Franke); Anna-Greta
(Viezens). Educ: U. Gottingen, ThD 1953; U.
Rostock, Habil. 1966. Spec: New Testament.
Pub: "Der Apokalyptiker Johannes und die
Edelsteine" *SNTU* 17 (1992); *Apostelgeschichte*
(1983, 1989); *Frei zu neuen Aufgaben* (1986);
Anfaenge der Kirche (1966); "Das Recht der
Propheten und Apostel (Did 11-13)" *Theol.
Versuche* (1966); "Die Topographie des
Markusevangeliums" *ZDPal* 73 (1957);
"Bemerkungen zur Formgeschichte des
Evangeliums" *NTSt* 58-59 (1958-59); "Das
Leiden des Herrn" *ZTK* 52 (1955); and others.
Mem: SNTS 1983-. Rec: Mineralogy, ornitholo-
gy. Addr: (o) Schulstrasse 12, Borsdorf bei
Leipzig, D-O-7122, Germany Borsdorf 462.

SCHLEY, Donald G., b. Frederick, MD,
February 13, 1953, s. of Donald Gilmer & Helen
(Walker), m. Jan (Sporborg), chil: Elisabeth Jan;

Joshua Sporborg. Educ: Eckerd Coll., BA 1978;
Emory U., MTS (summa cum laude) 1980, PhD
1987. Emp: Emory U., 1984-87 Adj. Instr., Bibl.
Hebrew; Dekalb Coll., 1986-89 Adj. Prof., Hist.;
Scholars Press, 1988-89 Operations Manager;
Coll. of Charleston, 1989-91 Vis. Asst. Prof.; U.
of Colo., 1992- Instr., Relig. Stud. Excv: Survey
of Cen. Moab, 1982 Chief Sherder. Spec:
Hebrew Bible, Mesopotamian Studies, Semitic
Languages, Texts and Epigraphy. Pub:
Introduction to the Ancient World, trans. (1993);
"The *Salisim*: Officers or Special Three-Man
Squads?" *VT* 40/3 (1990); *Shiloh: A Biblical
City in Tradition and History* (1989); "I Kings
10:26-29: A Reconsideration" *JBL* 106/4 (1987);
"'Yahweh will cause you to return to Egypt in
ships' (Dtn. xxviii 68)" *VT* 35 (1985); and oth-
ers. Awd: Boone M. Bowen Awd. for Excellence
in Bibl. Hebrew 1980; U. of Goettingen, Luth.
World Fedn. Grant & Stipend 1981-82. Mem:
SBL 1984-. Rec: Horseback riding, hunting,
travel to crusader fortresses in the Middle East,
motorcycle riding. Addr: (o) U. of Colorado,
Dept. of Philosophy, PO Box 7150, Colorado
Springs, CO 80933-7150 719-593-3615; (h)
2981 El Capitan Dr., Colorado Springs, CO
80918 719-548-0164.

SCHLOSSER, Jacques, b. Lembach, France,
April 23, 1939, s. of Georges & Rose (Isel).
Educ: Fac. de Theol. Cath. de Strasbourg, Lic.
1965, Doc. D'Etat 1978; Pont. Bibl. Inst., Rome,
Lic. Bibl. Sci. 1970; Ecole Biblique, Jerusalem,
Dip. d'Eleve Titulaire 1971. Emp: Fac. de Theol.
Cath. de Strasbourg, 1971 Asst., 1978 Maitre-
Asst., 1980 Prof. Titulaire, 1986-91 Dean. Spec:
New Testament. Pub: "La parole de Jésus sur la
fin du Temple" *NTS* 36 (1990); *Le Dieu de
Jesus*, Lectio Divina (Cerf, 1987); "Lk 17,2 und
die Logienquelle" *SNTU* 8 (1983); "La genèse de
Luc, XXII,25-27" *RB* 89 (1982); *Le Règne de
Dieu dans les dits de ésus*, Etudes Bibliques
(Gabalda, 1980); "Ancien Testament et chris-
tologie dans la Prima Petri" in *Etudes sur la
Première Lettre de Pierre*, Lectio Divina (1980);
"Les jours de Noé et de Lot: A propos de Lc.
XVII,26-30" *RB* 80 (1973); and others. Awd:
Chevalier dans l'ordre des Palmes Acad. 1990.
Mem: Assn. Cath. Francaise pour l'etude de la
Bible 1971-; SNTS 1981-; Arbeitsgemeinschaft
der deutschsprachigen katholischen NT 1983-.
Rec: Music, walking. Addr: (o) Faculte de
Theol. Catholique, 9 Place de l'Universite, F-
67084 Strasbourg, France 88259787; (h) 28 rue
Gounod, F-67000 Strasbourg, France 88615708.

SCHMAHL, Guenther, b. Remagen, March 31,
1939, s. of Wilhelm & Gertrud. Educ: Lic. Phil.
1961, Lic. Theol. 1965, ThD 1972. Emp:
Hochschule Aachen, 1972-80; Studienhaus St.
Lambert, 1976. Spec: New Testament. Pub:
*Trierer Theologische Zeitschrift Bibel und Leben
Pastoralblatt*, contb.; *Die Zwölf im
Markusevangelium* (Trier Theol. Stud., 1974).
Addr: (o) Krayerstr. 15, 5470 Andernach 13,
Germany 02632/8-20-82.

SCHMANDT-BESSERAT, Denise, b. Ay, France, August 10, 1933, d. of Victor Besserat & Jeanne (Crabit), m. Jurgen Schmandt, chil: Alex; Christopher; Phillip. Emp: U. of Tex., 1988- Prof., Middle East. Stud.; *Technology & Culture,* 1978-92 Adv. Ed.; *Visible Lang.,* 1985- Adv. Ed. Spec: Archaeology. Pub: *Before Writing,* 2 vol. (U. of Tex., 1992); "Tokens and Counting" *BA* 46 (1983); *Ancient Persia,* ed. (Undena, 1980); *The Legacy of Sumer,* ed. (Undena, 1976); and others. Mem: AIA 1973-; AOS 1976-; Amer. Anthrop. Assn. 1979-; ASOR 1989-. Rec: Swimming, jogging. Addr: (o) U. of Texas, Art Dept., Austin, TX 78712 512-471-3365; (h) 11 Hull Circle, Austin, TX 78746 512-327-2317.

SCHMELLER, Thomas K., b. Munich, March 2, 1956. Educ: U. of Munich, Dip. Theol. 1981, ThD 1985. Emp: Munich U., 1982-89 Lect.; Emory U., 1989-91 Asst. Prof., NT. Spec: New Testament. Pub: "Der Weg der Jesusbotschaft in die Stadte" *Bibel & Kirche* 47 (1992); "Gottesreich und Menschenwerk: Ein Blick in Gleichnisse Jesu" *Wissenschaft & Weisheit* 54 (1992); "Soziologisch orientierte Exegese des Neuen Testaments" *Bibel & Kirche* 44 (1989); *Brechungen: Urchristliche wander charismatiker im Prisma soziologisch orientierter Exegese,* SBS 136 (Kath. Bibelwerk, 1989); "Zugaenge zum Neuen Testament in lateinamerikanischen Basisgemeinden" *Muenchener Theol. Zeitschrift* 38 (1987); *Paulus und die "Diatribe": Eine vergleichende Stilinterpretation,* NTA NF 19 (Aschendorff, 1987); and others. Mem: SBL 1989-. Addr: (h) Hundsburg Str. 8, 3587 Borken-Kleinenglis, Germany.

SCHMIDT, Andreas, b. Hannover, Germany, April 19, 1960, s. of Gerhard & Margarete (Flader). Educ: U. Gottingen, Dip. Theol. 1987. Emp: U. Gottingen, 1987-88 Wiss. Hilfskraft; Ev-luth. Landeskirche Hannovers, 1988-91 Vikar, 1991- Pastor. Spec: New Testament. Pub: "Das Missionsdekret in Galater 2.7-8 als Vereinbarung vom ersten Besuch Pauli in Jerusalem" *NTS* 38 (1992); "Der mögliche Text von P. Oxy. III 405, Z. 39-45" *NTS* 37 (1991); "Das historische Datum des Apostelkonzils" *ZNW* 81 (1990); "Zwei Anmerkungen zu P. Ryl. III 457" *APF* 35 (1989); "P. Oxy. X 1224, Fragment 2 recto, Col. I: Ein neuer Vorschlag" *ZNW* 80 (1989); and others. Mem: SBL; AAR; ASOR; Deutscher Verein zur Erforschung Palastinas; Assn. Intl. de Papyrologues. Rec: Football, music, traveling. Addr: (o) Ev.-luth. Pfarramt, St. Mauritus Schutzenstr. 11, 4503 Dissen a. TW, Germany 05421-4741; (h) Schutzenstrasse 11, 49201 Dissen a. TW, Germany 05421-4741.

SCHMIDT, Daryl D., b. Sioux Falls, SD, August 12, 1944, s. of Arnold & Jennie. Educ: Associated Mennonite Bibl. Sem., MDiv 1970; Grad. Theol. Union, Berkeley, PhD 1979. Emp: Pacific Sch. Relig., 1977-78 Instr., 1991-93 Vis. Prof.; Tex. Christian U., 1979- Assoc. Prof. Spec: New Testament. Pub: *The Gospel of Mark,* Scholars

Bible 1 (Polebridge, 1991); "Semitisms and Septuagintalisms in the Book of Revelation" *NTS* 37 (1991); "The Syntactical Style of 2 Thessalonians: How Pauline is it?" in *The Thessalonian Correspondence,* BETL 87 (1990); "1 Thess. 2:13-16: Linguistic Evidence for an Interpolation" *JBL* 103 (1983); *Hellenistic Greek Grammar and Noam Chomsky,* SBL Diss. Ser. 62 (Scholars, 1981); "The LXX Gattung 'Prophetic Correlative'" *JBL* 96 (1977); and others. Mem: SBL 1970-; SNTS 1988. Addr: (o) Dept. of Religious Studies Texas Christian U., Fort Worth, TX 76129 817-921-7440.

SCHMIDT, Frederick W., Jr., b. Louisville, KY, June 20, 1953, s. of Frederick W., Sr. & Pauline R., m. Elaine (Melotti), chil: Lindsay Rebekah. Educ: Asbury Coll., BA 1975; Asbury Theol. Sem., MDiv 1978; Oxford U., England, PhD 1986. Emp: Asbury Theol. Sem., 1978-80 Teaching Fellow, NT Greek; U. of Oxford, England, 1984-86 Instr., NT, 1986 Tutor, NT Stud.; Messiah College, 1987- Assoc. Prof., NT Stud. Spec: New Testament. Pub: "Behind Orthodoxy and Beyond It: Recent Developments in Evangelical Christology" *SJT* 45 (1993); "An Unexamined Orthodoxy: Millenialist Interpretations of Apocalyptic Literature" Jour. of the C.S. Lewis Soc. 14 (1992); Articles in *ABD* (Doubleday, 1992); and others. Awd: U. of the U.K., Overseas Res. Stud. Awd. 1980-81, 1981-82, 1982-83; Messiah Coll., Excellence in Teaching Awd. 1990; CBA, Young Schol. Fellow. 1993. Mem: SBL; AAR; WTS; CBA; Soc. for the Sci. Study of Relig. Rec: Reading, chess, tennis, racquetball. Addr: (o) Messiah College, Dept. of Biblical & Religious Studies, Grantham, PA 17027 717-766-2511; (h) 559 Saw Mill Rd., Mechanicsburg, PA 17055.

SCHMITT, John J., b. Milwaukee, WI, May 6, 1938, s. of Silvester & Frances (Knar), m. Roberta (O'Hara), chil: Maria-Kristina; Tara. Educ: U. of Chicago, AM 1970, PhD 1977. Emp: St. Bonaventure U., 1972-80 Asst. Prof.; Marquette U., 1980-86 Asst. Prof., 1987- Assoc. Prof.; U. of Sheffield, England, 1991 Vis. Lect. Spec: Hebrew Bible. Pub: "God's Wife: Some Gender Reflections on the Bible and Biblical Interpretation" in *Constructing and Reconstructing Gender* (SUNY,; 1992); articles in *ABD* (Doubleday, 1992); "Israel and Zion—Two Gendered Images: Biblical Speech Traditions and Their Current Neglect" *Horizons* 18 (1991); "Like Eve, Like Adam: *mshl* in Gen 3:16" *Biblica* 72 (1991); "The Virgin of Israel: Referent and Use of the Phrase in Amos and Jeremiah" *CBQ* 53 (1991); Isaiah and His Interpreters (Paulist, 1986); and others. Mem: CBA 1970-; SBL 1973-; AAR 1973-; CSBR 1980-. Rec: Music, reading. Addr: (o) Marquette U., Theology Dept., Milwaukee, WI 53233 414-288-3739; (h) 1843 N 84th St., Wauwatosa, WI 53226 414-257-3101.

SCHNECK, Richard J., b. San Francisco, CA, September 27, 1941, s. of Thomas & Ruth

(Inda). Educ: Gonzaga U., BA 1965, MA 1969; Jesuit Sch. of Theol. at Berkeley, STM 1973, STL 1985; U. Javeriana, ThD 1990. Emp: St. Ignatius Coll., 1967-69 Instr.; Sem. Regional de Veracruz, 1976-80 Instr., NT; Pot. U. Catolica del Ecuador, 1980-83, 1991- Prof., Sacred Scripture. Spec: New Testament. Pub: "Fundamentalismo: un problema socio-pastoral" *Rev. de la U. Catolica* 11 (1983); "Recensiones Bibliograficas" *Teologica Xaveriana* 39 (1989). Mem: CBA 1981-; SBL 1989-. Rec: Youth soccer matches. Addr: (o) California Jesuit Missionaries, 284 Stanyan St., San Francisco, CA 94118 415-221-1588; (h) Calle Benalcazar 500, Apt. 194, Quito, Ecuador 530-300.

SCHNEIDER, Bernardin V., b. Louisville, KY, October 26, 1917, s. of Otto & Anna (Sanford). Educ: Pont. Bibl. Inst., Rome, SSL 1950; Pontificum Athenaeum Antonianum, Rome, STD 1951; Studium Biblicum Franciscanum, Jerusalem, OFMLG 1951. Emp: St. Anthony Sem., Tokyo, 1954- Tchr.; Studium Biblicum Franciscanum, 1956- Dir. Spec: New Testament. Pub: *The Teacher and the Lord* (1987); *The Teacher and the Lord* (1987); "Esther Revised According to the Maccabees" *Studii Biblici Franciscani Liber Annuus XIII* (1962-63); "The Meaning of St. Paul's Anthesis 'The Letter and the Spirit'" *CBQ* 15 (1953); "*Ho de Kyrios to Pneuma estin*" (*2 Cor. 3, 17a*)—*Studium Exegeticum* (Officium Libri Catholici, 1951); and others. Awd: Japan Bible Soc., Tsuru-Smith Awd., 1977; St. Bonaventure U., DHL 1992. Mem: SNTS; CBA; SBL; ASOR. Rec: Swimming, canoeing. Addr: (o) St. Anthony Seminary, Studium Biblicum Franciscanum, 4-16-1 Seta, Setagaya-ku, Tokyo 158, Japan 03-3707-7764.

SCHNEIDER, Delwin B., b. Oshkosh, WI, m. Katherine, chil: Kathi; Mark; Michael; Lisa. Educ: Concordia Coll., BA; Pepperdine U., MA 1950; Rikkyo U., Tokyo, PhD 1961; Bethlehem Luth. Ch., Ord. 1951. Emp: Harvard U., 1962-65 Chaplain, Lect.; Gustavus Adolphus Coll., 1965-70 Assoc. Prof.; Inst. for E Asian Stud., 1967-70 Dir.; U. of Minn., 1968-69 Prof.; Pacific Luth. Theol. Sem., 1983 Lect. Spec: New Testament. Pub: *Historical Perspectives in Christianity's Relation to Other Religions* (U. San Diego, 1983); and others. Mem: Assn. Asian Stud; AAR. Addr: (o) U. of San Diego, Alcala Park, San Diego, CA 92110 619-260-4600.

SCHNEIDER, Gerhard J., b. Trier, June 15, 1926, s. of Ernst & Josephine (Monzel). Educ: U. of Trier, ThD 1959; U. of Wuerzburg, Habil. 1967. Emp: Koblenz, 1962-65 Dozent, 1966-68 Prof.; Bochum, 1968- Prof. Spec: New Testament. Pub: *Jesusueberlieferung und Christologie*, NTSup 67 (1992); *Lukas, Theologe der Heilsgeschichte*, BBB 59 (1985); "Das Vaterunser des Matthaeus" in *A cause de l'Evangile*, Festschrift J. Dupont (1985); *Das Evangelium nach Lukas*, OTK 3 (1977, 1984); "Jesu uberraschende Antworten. Beobachtungen zu

den Apophthegmen des dritten Evangeliums" *NTS* 29 (1983); *Die Apostelgeschichte*, 2 vol. (1982); "Die Davidssohnfrage (Mk 12,35-37)" *Biblica* 53 (1972); "Urchristliche Gottesverkuendigung in hellenistischer Umwelt" *BZ* 13 (1969); and others. Mem: SNTS; Okumenischer Arbeitskreis evang. und katholischer Theol. Addr: (o) Hustadtring 65, D-4360 Bochum 1, Germany 0234-70-17-95.

SCHNEIDER, Harvey, b. Montreal, Canada, February 8, 1943, s. of Boris & Freda (Clayman), m. Audrey (Schwarzfeld), chil: Naomi Golda; Ron Baruch; Avraham Abba (Avi); Michael Yohanan. Educ: McGill U., BA 1965, MA 1969; U. of West. ON, MLS 1971. Emp: Hebrew U., Inst. of Arch., 1978-81 Assyriology Lbrn., 1983-86 Prehist. Lbrn., 1987- Slide Archivist; Hebrew U., Bloomfield Lib. for the Hum. & Social Sci., 1981- Lbrn. Excv: Mevorakh, 1975; Hazorea, 1976-77 Area Supr.; City of David, 1978 Area Supr.; Yoqneam, 1981 Volunteer Supr. Spec: Archaeology, Hebrew Bible, Semitic Languages, Texts and Epigraphy. Pub: "Six Biblical Signatures: Seals and Seal Impressions of Six Biblical Personages Recovered" *BAR* 17/4 (1991); "'Azariahu son of Hilkiahu' (High Priest?) on a City of David Bulla" *IEJ* 38 (1988); "'Azariahu ben Hilqiahu' (the Priests?) on a Bulla from the City of David" *Qadmoniot* 81-82 (1988); "More on Looking for the Source of Tin in the Ancient Near East" *Qadmoniot* 65 (1984); "Looking for the Source of Tin in the Ancient Near East" *Qadmoniot* 60 (1982). Rec: Music, playing guitar & banjo, English football, reading. Addr: (o) Hebrew U., Institute of Archaeology, Slide Archives, Jerusalem, Israel 02-882415; (h) Mevo Duvdevan 1, PO Box 1673, Mevasseret Zion, 90805, Israel 02-340289.

SCHNEIDER, Paul G., b. Pittsburgh, PA, April 8, 1951, s. of Hope G. & William F. Educ: U. of S Fla., BA 1974; Harvard Div. Sch., MTS 1976; Fla. State U., MA 1978; Columbia U., PhD 1990. Emp: New York Theol. Sem.–Sing Sing Prison, 1987-88 Instr. Spec: New Testament. Pub: *The Mystery of the Acts of John* (Mellen Research U.P., 1991). Mem: AAR 1989-; SBL 1989-. Rec: Computers, video, bowling, music. Addr: (h) 2199 Academy Dr., Clearwater, FL 34624 813-442-4274.

SCHNEIDERS, Sandra M., b. Chicago, IL, November 12, 1936, d. of Alexander & Glen (Ogle). Educ: U. of Detroit, MA 1967; Institut Catholique, Paris, STL 1971; Pont. Gregorian U., Rome, STD (summa cum laude) 1975. Emp: Marygrove Coll., 1965-67, 1971-72 Asst. Prof.; Jesuit Sch. of Theol., 1976- Prof.; U. of Notre Dame, 1985 Vis. Prof.; *CBQ*, 1979-87, *BTB*, 1981-, *Horizons*, 1983- Assoc. Ed. Spec: New Testament. Pub: *The Revelatory Text* (Harper, 1991); "John 21:1-14" *Interpretation* 43 (1989); *Women and the Word* (Paulist, 1986); "The Face Veil: A Johannine Sign (John 20:1-10)" *BTB* (1983); "The Paschal Imagination: Objectivity and Subjectivity in New Testament Interpretation" *Theol. Stud.* 43 (1982); and others. Mem: CTSA 1972-; CBA 1974-; SBL 1976-; AAR 1982-; SNTS 1985-. Rec: Classical music, films. Addr: (o) Jesuit School of Theology, 1735 LeRoy Ave., Berkeley, CA 94709 510-841-8804; (h) 1401 Liberty #12, El Cerrito, CA 94530.

SCHNELLE, Udo, b. Nauen, September 8, 1952, s. of Erwin & Lieschen (Vieth), m. Adelheid (Scola), chil: Carolin; Ricarda. Educ: 1. Theol. Examen 1979, Promotion 1981; 2. Theol. Examen 1984, Habil. 1985. Emp: Ev. Luth., Landeskirche, 1984-86 Pastor; Theol. Fakultaet Erlangen, 1986-92 Prof., NT; Martin-Luther-U. Halle-Wittenberg, Theol. Fakultaet, 1992- Prof., NT. Spec: New Testament. Pub: *Antidocetic Christology in the Gospel of John* (1992); *Neutestamentliche Anthropologie: Jesus—Paulus—Johannes*, BThSt 18 (1991); "Johanneische Ekklesiologie" *NTS* 37 (1991); "Die Abschiedsreden im Johannesevangelium" *ZNW* 80 (1989); "Schriftauslegung Sachgemae " *NT* 30 (1988); "Paulus und Johannes" *ET* 47 (1987); *Antidoketische Christologie im Johannesevangelium*, FRLANT 144 (1987); "Der Erste Thessalonicherbrief und die Entstehung der paulinischen Anthropologie" *NTS* 32 (1986); and others. Mem: SNTS 1986-. Addr: (o) Universitaetsplatz 8/9, O-4020 Halle, Germany 0345-832466; (h) Grossenbuch 125, W-8524 Neunkirchen a.Br., Germany 09134-7469.

SCHOLER, David M., b. Rochester, MN, July 24, 1938, s. of Milton & Bernice (Anderson), m. Jeannette (Mudgett), chil: Emily; Abigail. Educ: Wheaton Coll., MA 1964; Gordon Div. Sch., BD 1964; Harvard Div. Sch., ThD 1980. Emp: Gordon-Conwell Theol. Sem., 1969-81 Assoc. Prof.; North Bapt. Theol. Sem., 1981-88 Julius R. Mantey Prof. of NT; North Park Coll. & Theol. Sem., 1988- Disting. Prof.of NT & Early Ch. Hist.; *Perspectives in Relig. Stud.*, 1982-85 Ed. Bd.; *JBL*, 1991- Assoc. Ed., NT Book Rev. Spec: New Testament, Apocrypha and Post-biblical Studies. Pub: "Bibliographia Gnostica: Supplementum XX" *NT* 34 (1992); "The Function of Apocalyptic Eschatology in Paul" *Ex Auditu* 6 (1990); *Ency. of Early Christianity*, cons. ed. (Garland, 1990); "Issues in Biblical Interpretation" *EQ* 60 (1988); "I Timothy 2:9-15 & the Place of Women in the Church's Ministry" in *Women, Authority and the Bible* (InterVarsity, 1986); "Tertullian on Jewish Persecution of Christians" in *Studia Patristica* 17, 3 vol. (Pergamon, 1982); *Nag Hammadi Bibliography 1948-69* (Brill, 1971); and others. Mem: CBA; IBR; SBL, Pres. New England Reg. 1973-74; SNTS; CSBR, Pres. 1991-92. Rec: Antiquing, theatre. Addr: (o) North Park College & Theological Seminary, 3225 W Foster Ave., Chicago, IL 60625 312-478-2696; (h) 266 S Myrtle, Villa Park, IL 60181 708-530-0899.

SCHORK, R. Joseph, b. Baltimore, MD, April 17, 1933, s. of Rudolph J. & Helen M., chil: Heidi

A. Educ: Coll. of the Holy Cross, AB 1955; Oxford U., DPhil 1957. Emp: Georgetown U., 1960-66 Assoc. Prof., Chair; U. of Minn., 1966-73 Prof.; U. of Mass., Boston, 1975- Prof., 1976-82 Chmn. Pub: "Sung Sermons: Melodies, Morals, and Biblical Interpretations in Byzantium" *BR* 7/2 (1991); "Romanos' Elija: An Apocalyptic Prophet" *Patristic & Byzantine Rev.* 9 (1990); "Romanos, On Joseph I, Stanza: Text and Type" *Byzantion* 45 (1975); "Typology in the Kontakia of Romanos" *Studia Patristica* VI (1962); and others. Awd: Woodrow Wilson Fellow. 1955; Fulbright Schol. 1955-57. Mem: APA 1958-. Addr: (o) U. of Massachusetts-Boston, Classics Dept., Boston, MA 02125-3393 617-287-6120; (h) 961 High St., Dedham, MA 02026 617-329-3849.

SCHOTTROFF, Luise, b. Berlin, April 11, 1934, d. of Rudolf & Elisabeth (Klein), m. Willy, chil: Daniel. Educ: U. Gottingen, DTh 1960; U. Mainz, Habil., NT 1969. Emp: U. Mainz, 1960-1986 Prof., NT; U. Kassel, 1986- Prof., NT. Spec: New Testament. Pub: *Befreiungs erfahrungen, Studien zur Sozialgeschichte des Neuen Testaments* (1990); *Jesus the Hope of the Poor* (Maryknoll, 1986); "Women as Followers of Jesus in NT Times: An Exercise in Social-Historical Exegesis of the Bible" in *The Bible and Liberation.; Political and Social Hermeneutics* (Maryknoll, 1983); *Der Glaubende und die feindliche Welt Beobachtungen zum gnostischen Dualismus und seiner Bedeutung fur Paulus und das Johannesevangelium* (Neukirchen, 1970). Addr: (h) Im Rosental 6, D34132 Kassel, Germany 0561-408844.

SCHOVILLE, Keith N., b. Soldiers Grove, WI, March 3, 1928, s. of Harley & Viva (Banta), m. Merrlyn (Mitchell), chil: Kenneth; Mary; Harley; John; Robert. Educ: U. of Wis., MA 1966, PhD 1969. Emp: U. of Wis., 1968- Prof.; Wis. Inst. in Bibl. Arch., 1983-86 Dir. of Sign, Symbol, Script Trav. Exhib.; Hebrew Stud., 1979-85 Ed.; Emmanuel Sch. of Relig., 1980 Kershner Lect. Excv: Tel Dan, 1976, 79, 81 Area Supr.; Tel Aroer, 1981 Area Supr.; Tel Lachish, 1983, 85 Dir. Spec: Archaeology, Hebrew Bible, Semitic Languages, Texts and Epigraphy. Pub: Biblical Archaeology in Focus (Baker, 1978); "The Problem of Relevancy" ASOR Newsletter 1; "A Note on the Oracles of Amos Against Gaza, Tyre and Edom" VTSup 26; and others. Mem: AOS, Pres., MidW Reg. 1983-85; ASOR; AIA; SBL, Dir., MidW Reg. 1970-; NEAS 1981-, Pres. 1992-. Rec: Horticulture. Addr: (o) 1344 Van Hise Hall, 1220 Linden Dr., Madison, WI 53706 608-262-9785; (h) 5689 Sun Valley Pkwy., Oregon, WI 53575 608-835-7793.

SCHRAGE, Wolfgang, b. Hagen-Haspe, Germany, July 30, 1928, s. of Heinrich & Johanna, m. Elisabeth, chil: Ulrike; Heinrich; Christoph. Emp: U. Bonn, 1964- Prof. Spec: New Testament, Apocrypha and Post-biblical Studies. Pub: Der erste Brief an die Korinther I (Neukirchen, 1991); Ethik des Neuen Testaments (1982); Die Elia-

Apokalypse (1980); and others. Mem: SNTS. Addr: (o) Evang. Theol. Sem. der U., Abtlg. f. Neues Testament, Am Hof 1, 5300 Bonn 1, Germany 0228-737332; (h) Messbeuel 8, 5340 Bad Honnef, Germany 02224-5457.

SCHRAMM, Tim F., b. Zeven, Germany, January 26, 1940, s. of Wilhelm & Aenne (Hueffmeier), m. Annette (Mischkowsky), chil: Caroline; Charlotte. Educ: Abitur, ThD, NT Stud. 1959. Emp: U. of Hamburg, 1971- Prof., NT; Temple U., 1989, 1992 Vis. Prof. Spec: New Testament. Pub: "Das Gleichnis vom guetigen Vater" in *Kieler Entwuerfe fuer Schule und Kirche* (1990); "Bibliodrama und Exegese" in *Bibliodrama* (1987); *Unmoralische Helden: Anstoessige Gleichnisse Jesu*, co-auth. (Vandenhoeck & Ruprecht, 1986); *Selbsterfahrung mit der Biblê: Ein Schluessel zum Lesen und Verstehen*, co-auth. (Pfeiffer/Vandenhoeck & Ruprecht, 1977, 1983); "Distanz und Naehe: Erfahrungen im Umgang mit biblischen Texten" *WPKG* 64 (1975); "Biblische Festlichkeit" *WPKG* 60 (1971); *Der Markus-Stoff bei Lukas: Eine literarkritische und redaktionsgeschichtliche Untersuchung*, SNTS Mon. Ser. 14 (Cambridge U.P., 1971); "Joseph-Christus-Typologie in Thomas Mann's Josephsroman" in *Antike und Abendland XIV* (1968); and others. Mem: SNTS; Wissenschaftliche Gessellschaft fuer Theol. Rec: Reading, music, sports. Addr: (o) Sedanstrasse 19, D-2000 Hamburg 13, Germany 040-4123-3795; (h) Hochkamp 35, D-2110 Buchholz, Germany 04181-31639.

SCHRECK, Christopher J., b. Savannah, GA, May 27, 1952, s. of Joseph C. & Patricia Ann (Barragan). Educ: Coll. of William & Mary, AB 1973; Pont. Gregorian U., Rome, STB 1976; Pont. Bibl. Inst., Rome, SSL 1978; Cath. U. of Leuven, PhD 1990, STD 1990. Emp: St. Vincent de Paul Reg. Sem., 1980-81 Vis. Prof., 1983-90 Assoc. Prof., 1983-86, 1992- Acad. Dean, 1990- Prof., NT. Spec: New Testament. Pub: "The Nazareth Pericope. Luke 4,16-30 in Recent Study" in *L'Evangile de Luc: The Gospel of Luke*, BETL 32 (U. Press of; Amer./Peeters, 1989); "Synthesis of Responses Regarding the Eucharist" *Amer. Bapt. Quar.* 7 (1988); "The Eucharist in International Bilateral Dialogues: Points of Convergence" in *JES* 23 (1986); and others. Mem: CBA 1978-; SBL 1978-. Addr: (o) St. Vincent de Paul Regional Seminary, 10701 S Military Trail, Boynton Beach, FL 33436-4899 407-732-4424.

SCHRIEBER, Paul L., b. Red Bud, IL, April 29, 1949, s. of Oliver & Florence, m. Betty (Koehler), chil: Katherine; Jonathan; Sarah; Deborah; Rachel; Rebekah; Matthew. Educ: Concordia Theol. Sem., MDiv 1975, ThD 1983. Emp: Concordia Coll., 1976-81 Asst. Prof.; Concordia Sem., 1981- Asst. Prof. Spec: Hebrew Bible. Pub: "Priests Among Priests: The Office of the Ministry in Light of the Old Testament Priesthood" *Concordia Jour.* (1988); "Liberation

Theology and the Old Testament: An Exegetical Critique" *Concordia Jour.* (1987); "*Mishken-Mitswah*: Toward a More Unified View of Exodus" *Concordia Jour.* (1977). Mem: SBL 1977-; ETS 1982-; ASOR 1982-. Rec: Running, bicycling, music, swimming. Addr: (o) Concordia Seminary, 801 DeMun, Clayton, MO 63105 314-721-5934; (h) 4307 Roland, Pasadena Hills, MO 63121 314-389-2389.

SCHROEDER, Hans-Hartmut A., b. Kolberg in Pommern, June 22, 1931, s. of Johannes & Eva (Cyrus), m. Rita (Seitz), chil: Elisabeth; Christoph; Eva; Johanna; Cyrus; Onno. Educ: U. of Bochum, Germany, 1. Theol. Exam. 1956, PhD 1960; U. of Kiel, 2. Theol. Exam. 1959. Emp: Evang. Luth. Ch., 1959-60, 1962-67, 1971-76 Pastor; U. of Bochum, Germany, 1967-71 Asst. Prof.; ISEDET, Facultad de Teologia, Argentina, 1976-81 Prof., NT. Spec: New Testament. Pub: "Zum Verhaltnis von Eschatologie und historischer Wirklichkeit" in *Das Wesen des Menschen, Festschrift Karel Vrana* (Minerva, 1985); "La evangelizacien y la justicia" *Revista Biblica* 177 (1980); "'Oikos' y justicia en los evangelios sinopticos" *RivB* 174/4 (1979); "Tienen los dichos de Jesus referentes a la pobreza consecuencias eticas en la realidad social?" in *Los Pobres, Encuentro y compromiso* (La Aurora, 1978); *Eltern und Kinder in der Verkündigung Jesu, eine hermeneutische und exegetische Untersuchung*, Theol. Forschung 53 (Reich, 1972); "Haben Jesu Worte über Armut und Reichtum Folgen für das soziale Verhalten?" in *Studien zum Text und zur Ethik des Neuen; Testaments, Festschrift zum 80 Geburtstag von Heinrich Greeven*. Mem: SNTS 1979-. Rec: Gardening, restoration of old houses. Addr: (o) Aegidienstr. 75, D-2400 Lubeck, Germany 0451-75464; (h) Albertsdorf 18, D-2448 Landkirchen, Germany 04371-1267.

SCHUERMANN, Heinz, b. Bochum, January 18, 1913, s. of Carl & Gertrud (Wilmesmeier). Educ: U. Muenster, Kath. Theol. Fakultat, ThD 1949, Habil. 1952. Emp: U. Muenster, Kath. Theol. Fakultat, 1952-53 Privatdozent; Phil. Theol. Studium Erfurt, 1953-78 Prof., NT Exegesis, 1978- Prof. Emeritus. Spec: New Testament. Pub: *Worte des Herrn* (1955, 1993); *Das Lukasevangelium* vol. I (1969, 1990), vol. II (1993); *Quellenkritische Untersuchung des lukanischen Abendmahlsberichtes Lk 22,7-38*, vol. I-III (1953-1986); *Orientierungen am Neuen Testament* (1978); and others. Awd: U. Louvain la Neuve, U. Uppsala, U. Aberdeen, U. Paderborn, U. Wien, Dr. Mem: Paepstl. Bibelkommission Rom 1965-70; Commissio Theol. Intl. 1969-85. Addr: (o) Phil.-Theol. Studium Erfurt, Domstr. 10, D/ 99084 Erfurt, Germany 0361-26577; (h) Kartaeuserstr. 83, D/99084 Erfurt, Germany 0361-51241.

SCHULLER, Eileen M., b. Edmonton, Canada, November 26, 1946, d. of Norbert & Elizabeth (Deutsch). Educ: U. of Toronto, Canada, MA

1973; Harvard U., PhD 1984. Emp: Newman Theol. Coll., Canada, 1973-77 Asst. Prof.; St. Joseph's Coll., Canada, 1973-77 Lect.; Atlantic Sch. Theol., 1982-90 Assoc. Prof.; McMaster U., 1990-, Assoc. Prof., Relig. Spec: Hebrew Bible, Apocrypha and Post-biblical Studies. Pub: "Psalm of Joseph Within the Context of Second Temple Prayer" *CBQ* 1992; "The Apocrypha" in *Women's Bible Comm.* (Westminster/John Knox, 1992); *Post-Exilic Prophecy*, Message of Bibl. Spirituality Ser. (Glazier, 1987); *Non-Canonical Psalms from Qumran* (Scholars, 1986); and others. Awd: SSHRC Grant 1992-95; Annenberg Res. Inst. Fellow. 1993. Mem: SBL; CBA; CSBS. Addr: (o) McMaster U., Dept. of Religious Studies, Hamilton, ON L8S 4K1, Canada 416-525-9140; (h) 457 Dundurn St. S, Hamilton, ON L8P 4M1, Canada 902-423-6701.

SCHULMAN, Alan R., January 14, 1930, s. of Jacob T. & Hilda, m. Dalia (Sara), chil: Anath Leah; Magen Yakov. Educ: CCNY, BA 1952; U. of Chicago, Oriental Inst., MA 1958, PhD 1962. Emp: CUNY, 1964- Prof.; *Jour. of Amer. Res. Ctr. in Egypt*, 1966-70 Ed., 1970-85 Ed. Bd.; *EJ*, Dept. Ed.; *Bull. of the Egyptological Seminar of N.Y.*, 1979-85 Bd. of Ed.; Natl. Res. Coun. of Argentina, Acad. Com. Overseas Cons. on Egyptological Res. Excv: Egyptian Nubia, 1962 Arch. Spec: Egyptology. Pub: "The Royal Myths of Ancient Egypt" in *Ancient Economy in Mythology East and West* (1992); *Ceremonial Executions and Public Rewards: Some Historical Scenes on New Kingdom Private Stelae*, Orbis Biblicus et Orientalis 75 (1988); "Hittites, Helmets and Amarna: Akhenaton's First Hittite War" in *The Akhenaton Temple Project* II (1988); "The Nubian War of Akhenaton" in *L'Egyptologie en 1979: Axes Prioritaires des Recherches* II (1982); *Military Rank, Title, and Organization in the Egyptian New Kingdom*, Münchner Agyptologische Stud. 6 (1964); and others. Awd: Amer. Phil. Soc., res. grant 1963; Columbia U., publ. subsidy grant 1964. Mem: AIA 1951-58; AOS 1959-72; Amer. Res. Ctr., Egypt 1960-; IES 1969-; Soc. for the Stud. of Egyptian Antiq. 1976-. Rec: Military miniatures & hist., camping, travel, reading. Addr: (o) Queens College, Dept. of History, Flushing, NY 11375; (h) Rehov Wolfsen 51, 46809 Herzliya, Israel 052-541-858.

SCHULTZ, Carl, b. New Castle, PA, September 15, 1930, s. of Carl & Elizabeth, m. Annalee (Price), chil: Barbara; Esther; Carl. Educ: Wheaton Coll., MA 1955; Brandeis U., PhD 1973. Emp: Houghton Coll., 1965- Prof., Chmn., Div. of Relig. & Phil. Spec: Hebrew Bible, Mesopotamian Studies, Semitic Languages, Texts and Epigraphy, Apocrypha and Post-biblical Studies. Pub: "Job," "Ecclesiastes" in *The Evangelical Comm. on the Bible* (Baker, 1986); *An Exegetical Study on Scripture Passages that Relate to Marriage, Divorce, and Remarriage* (Wesley, 1983); "The Political Tensions Reflected in Ezra and Nehemiah" in *Scripture in Context: Essays on*

the Comparative Method (Penguin, 1980); and others. Mem: SBL; AAR. Rec: Travel, fishing. Addr: (o) Houghton College, Houghton, NY 14744 716-567-9452; (h) 17 Park Dr., Houghton, NY 14744 716-567-8192.

SCHULTZ, Donald R., b. Tacoma, WA, June 23, 1927, s. of John & Janna, m. Juanita, chil: Erik; Marta. Educ: Gonzaga U., MA 1955; Santa Clara U., MA 1964; McMaster U., Canada, MA 1969, PhD 1972. Emp: Coll. of Notre Dame, 1964-66 Asst. Prof.; Villanova U., 1969- Asst. Prof.; LaSalle U., 1971 Asst Prof.; St. Joseph U., 1973 Asst. Prof.; Neuman Coll., 1975-77 Asst. Prof. Spec: New Testament, Apocrypha and Post-biblical Studies. Pub: "The Origin of Sin in Irenaeus and Jewish Pseudepigraphical Literature" *VC* (1978); and others. Mem: AAR 1970-. Rec: Curling. Addr: (o) Villanova U., Dept. of Religious Studies, Villanova, PA 19085; (h) 1331 Hermit Cir., Cottonwood, AZ 86326 602-639-0746.

SCHULTZ, Samuel J., b. Mountain Lake, MN, June 9, 1914, s. of David & Anna (Eitzen), m. Eyla (Tolliver), chil: Linda; David. Educ: Faith Theol. Sem., BD 1944; Harvard Div. Sch., MST 1945, ThD 1949. Emp: *JETS*, 1961-74 Ed. Spec: Archaeology. Pub: *The Old Testament Speaks* (Harper & Row, 1960, 1990); *Message of the Old Testament* (Harper & Row, 1986); *The Prophets Speak* (Harper & Row, 1968); and others. Mem: SBL; ETS; ASOR; NEAS. Rec: Swimming, tennis. Addr: (h) 9 Forbes Pl., #802, Dunedin, FL 34698.

SCHUSSLER FIORENZA, Elisabeth, b. Germany, April 17, 1938, m. Francis, chil: Chris. Educ: U. of Wuerzburg, MDiv 1962, Lic. in Pastoral Theol. (summa cum laude) 1963; U. of Muenster, PhD, NT 1970. Emp: U. of Notre Dame, 1970-75 Asst. Prof., Theol., 1975-80 Assoc. Prof., Theol., 1980-84 Prof., Theol.; Episc. Div. Sch., 1984-88 Talbot Prof. of NT; Concilium for Feminist Theol., Co-dir.; Harvard U., 1985- *Jour. of Feminist Stud. in Relig.*, Co-found. & Ed.; Harvard Div. Sch., 1988- Stendahl Prof. of Div. Spec: New Testament. Pub: *Discipleship of Equals: A Critical Feminist Ekklesialogy of Liberation* (Crossroads, 1993); *But She Said: Feminist Practices of Biblical Interpretation* (Beacon, 1992); *Revelation: Vision of a Just World* (Fortress, 1992); "The Twelve and the Discipleship of Equals" in *Changing Women, Changing Church* (Millenium, 1992); "Revelation" in *The Books of the Bible*, vol. 2 (Scribners, 1989); "Text and Reality—Reality as Text: The Problem of a Feminist Historical and Social Reconstruction Based on Texts" *Stud. Theol.* 43; (1989); "I Corinthians" in *Harper's Bible Commentary* (Harper & Row, 1988); "The Ethics of Interpretation: Decentering Biblical Scholarship. SBL Presidential Address" *JBL* 107 (1988); *Bread Not Stone: The Challenge of Feminist Biblical Interpretation* (Beacon, 1985); *The*

Book of Revelation: Justice and Judgment (Fortress, 1985); and others. Awd: St. Bernard's Inst., Hon. Doc. 1990; Guggenheim Fellow. 1983-84. Mem: SBL; AAR; Amer. Theol. Soc. Addr: (o) Harvard Divinity School, Dept. of New Testament, 45 Francis Ave., Cambridge, MA 02138 617-495-5751.

SCHWANK, Benedikt H., b. Karlsruhe, April 16, 1923, s. of Robert & Toni (Daeuwel). Educ: Athenaeum S. Anselmo, Lic. Theol. 1953, ThD 1961; Pont. Bibl. Inst., Lic. Rer. Bibl. 1955. Emp: Theol. Hochschule Beuron, 1955-68 Prof., NT; Hochschule fur Phil., Muenchen, 1968-93 Prof.; Theol. Fac., Jerusalem, 1975-1991 Prof.; *Erbe und Auftrag: Benediktinische Monatsschrift*, 1970- Ed. Spec: Archaeology, New Testament. Pub: "Ein griechisches Jesuslogion? Uberlegungen zur Antwort Jesu auf die Steuerfrage (Mk 12,16-17 parr)" in *XAPICTEION* (1987); "Neue Funde in Nabataerstaedten und ihre Bedeutung fuer die neutestamentliche Exegese" *NTS* 29 (1983); "Das Theater von Sepphoris und die Jugendjahre Jesu" *Lebendiges Zeugnis* 32 (1977); *Florilegia Biblica Africana Saec. V.*, Corpus Christianorum Ser. Lat. XC (1961); and others. Mem: SNTS 1965-. Addr: (o) Abteistr. 2, D-88631 Beuron, Germany 07466-17-190.

SCHWARTZ, Baruch J., b. Philadelphia, PA, July 14, 1954, s. of Fred & Phyllis (Strauss), m. Sema (Tannenbaum), chil: Rachel Naomi; Mordechai Tzvi; Shlomo Ze'ev. Educ: Columbia U., BA 1976; Jewish Theol. Sem. of Amer., BHL, Bible 1976; Hebrew U., Jerusalem, MA 1980, PhD 1988. Emp: Jewish Theol. Sem. of Amer., Jerusalem, 1976-90 Asst. Prof., Bible.; Hebrew U., Jerusalem, 1977-90 Lect., Bible; Gratz Coll., 1987-88 Vis. Asst. Prof., Bible; Leo Baeck Coll., London, 1990 Vis. Lect., Bible; Tel Aviv U., 1991- Lect., Bible. Spec: Hebrew Bible. Pub: "The Prohibitions Concerning the 'Eating' of Blood in Leviticus 17" in *Studies in Cult and Priesthood*, JSOTSup 125 (1991); "The Concentric Structure of Ezekiel 3:1-3:15" in *Proceedings of the Tenth World Congress of Jewish Studies* (1990); "A Literary Study of the Slave-Girl Pericope— Leviticus 19:20-22" in *Studies in Bible*, Scripta Hierosolymitana 31 (1986); "Psalm 50: Its Subject, Form and Place" in *SHNATON* 3 (1979); and others. Awd: Hebrew U., Lady Davis Doc. Fellow 1981-83; U. of Pa., Lady Davis Post-doc. Fellow, Memorial Found., Post-doc. Fellow 1987-88; Hebrew U., Dworsky Res. Fellow 1990-91; and others. Mem: SBL; IOSOT; AJS; NAPH; WUJS. Addr: (o) Tel Aviv U., Dept. of Bible, Ramat Aviv 69978, Israel 03-640 9422; (h) Maaleh Brosh 5, PO Box 1224, Efrat 90962, Israel 02-931 682.

SCHWARTZ, Glenn M., b. Baltimore, MD, May 24, 1954, s. of Sidney & Evelyn. Educ: Yale U., BA 1976, PhD 1982. Emp: Johns Hopkins U., 1986- Asst. Prof., Dept. of Near East. Stud. Excv: Tell Leilan, Syria, 1978-80 Excvn. Supr., 1982 Asst. Dir., 1985 Assoc. Dir.; Tell Brak, Syria,

1983 Excvn. Supr.; Gritille, Turkey, 1984 Ceramics Analyst, Excvn. Supr.; Tell al-Raqai, Syria, 1987-90, 1992- Co-dir. Spec: Archaeology, Mesopotamian Studies. Pub: "Tell al-Raqai 1989 and 1990," co-auth. *AJA* (1992); "Excavations at Tell al-Raqai: A Small Rural Site of Early Urban Mesopotamia," co-auth. *AJA* (1990); "The Origins of the Aramaeans in Syria and Northern Mesopotamia: Research Problems and Potential Strategies" in *To the Euphrates and Beyond* (1989); "Excavations at Karatut Mevkii and Perspectives on the Uruk/Jemdet Nasr Expansion" *Akkadica* (1988); *A Ceramic Chronology from Tell Leilan: Operation 1* (Yale U.P., 1988); "The Ninevite V Period and the Development of Complex Society in Northern Mesopotamia" *Paleorient* (1987); and others. Awd: ASOR, Mesopotamian Fellow. 1983; Amer. Coun. of Learned Soc., Post-doc. Fellow. 1984-85; Mellon Post-doc. Fellow. 1986; Natl. Geog. Soc. grants 1988, 1990; NEH grants 1989-90. Mem: AAS; AOS; Amer. Anthrop. Assn.; AIA; ASOR. Rec: Piano, guitar, songwriting, swimming, squash. Addr: (o) Johns Hopkins U., Dept. of Near Eastern Studies, Baltimore, MD 21218 410-516-8492; (h) 3633 Kimble Rd., Baltimore, MD 21218 410-243-3870.

SCHWEIZER, Eduard R., b. Basel, Switzerland, April 18, 1913, s. of Eduard & Hedwig, m. Elisabeth (Hanhart), chil: Elisabet; Ruth; Eva-Marie; Andreas. Educ: U. of Basel, BD 1936, Dr.theol 1938; U. of Zurich, PhD 1940. Emp: U. of Mainz, Germany, 1946 Prof.; U. of Bonn, 1949 Prof.; U. of Zurich, Switzerland, 1949-79 Prof., NT; Colgate Rochester Div. Sch., San Francisco Theol. Sem., Vis. Prof. Spec: New Testament. Awd: U. of Mainz, Dr. 1950; U. of Wein, Dr. 1972; St. Andrews U., Scotland, DD 1962; U. of Melbourne, Australia, DD 1975. Mem: SNTS, Pres. 1969-70; SBL. Rec: Mountaineering, hiking. Addr: (h) Restelbergstrasse 71, CH 8044 Zurich, Switzerland 01-361-57-20.

SCOGGIN, B. Elmo, b. Harris, NC, October 17, 1915, s. of Johnnie & Pearl (McEntrye), m. Hannah (Pearlman), chil: Scarlett. Educ: S. Bapt. Theol. Sem., ThM 1945, ThD 1955. Emp: Bapt. Ch., 1948-49 Pastor; Bapt. Rep. in Israel 1949-55; SE Bapt. Theol. Sem., 1955-84 Prof., Hebrew & OT, 1984- Prof. Emeritus. Excv: Tel Gezer, 1967-71 Supr., 1984 Co-Dir.; Tel Arad, 1967-68 Field Dir.; Lachish, 1969-70 Field Dir.; Tel Dan, 1981-82 Field Dir., Lect. Spec: Archaeology, Hebrew Bible, Mesopotamian Studies, Semitic Languages, Texts and Epigraphy. Pub: "Commentary on Micah" *Broadman Bible Comm.* 7 (1972); *Geography of the Holy Land*; and others. Mem: ASOR. Rec: Fishing, flying. Addr: (o) Box 1889, Wake Forest, NC 27587 919-556-3101; (h) 2230 Lash Ave., Raleigh, NC 27607 919-787-9232.

SCOPELLO, Madeleine M., b. Turin, Italy, November 4, 1953, d. of Ruggero & Nella (Massucco), m. Carlo Gambacurta. Educ: U. of

Turin, Italy, BA, Lic. Class. 1971, Doc., (magna cum laude) 1977. Emp: U. of Strasbourg, 1980-84 Res. Asst.; Ecole Pratique des Hautes Etudes, Sorbonne, Paris, 1984-86 Res. Asst. Spec: Apocrypha and Post-biblical Studies. Pub: *L'Exégèse de l'âme: Introduction, Traduction, Commentaire* (Brill, 1985); "Ils leur enseignèrent les charmes el les incantations..." in *Historie et Archeologie* (1983); "Le Temple et son Grand Prêtre dans les Enseignements de Silvanos" in *Ecritures et Traditions dans la Littérature Copte* (1983); and others. Mem: Coptic Assn., France, Found. Mem.; IACS; SBL; Soc. d'Hist. des Relig. Addr: (o) Centre de recherche, Lenain de Tillemont, Paris, Sorbonne 75005, France 40462508; (h) 15, rue du Jour, 75001 Paris, France 2362306.

SCOTT, Bernard B., b. Louisville, KY, September 9, 1941, s. of Bernard & Jenny, m. Marilyn K., chil: Mariah Jon; Jonathan Brandon. Educ: St. Meinrad Coll., BA, Class. 1963; Miami U., Ohio, MA, Hellenistic & Roman Relig. 1968; Vanderbilt U., PhD, NT 1971. Emp: St. Meinrad Sch. of Theol., 1971-82 Assoc. Prof., 1975-78 Acad. Dean, 1982- Prof., NT; Yale Div. Sch., 1986 Vis. Prof.; U. of Tulsa, Phillips Grad. Sem., 1988-Darbeth Disting. Prof. of NT; BTB, 1987- Assoc. Ed.; CBQ, 1989- Assoc. Ed.; JBL, 1990- Assoc. Ed. Spec: New Testament. Pub: "The Birth of the Reader" *Semeia* 52 (1991); *Hear Then the Parables* (Fortress, 1989); *The Red Letter Parables*, co-auth. (Polebridge, 1988); "The Empty Jar" *Forum* 3/2 (1987); "Essaying the Rock: The Authenticity of the Parables of Jesus" *Forum* 2/2 (1987); *Jesus: Symbol-Maker for the Kingdom* (Fortress, 1981); "The Kings Accounting: Matthew 18:23-34" *JBL* 40; and others. Awd: Woodrow Wilson Doc. Diss. Fellow. 1970-71. Mem: SBL; AAR; CBA; SNTS. Rec: Cycling, gardening, Native Amer. art. Addr: (o) Phillips Graduate Seminary, 600 S College, Tulsa, OK 74104 918-582-3344; (h) 6306 E 78th, Tulsa, OK 74136 918-488-0515.

SCOTT, J. Julius, Jr., b. Decatur, GA, February 9, 1934, s. of J. Julius & Laverne, m. Florence (Richardson), chil: Mary; Julia; James. Educ: Columbia Theol. Sem., BD 1959; U. of Manchester, U.K., PhD 1969. Emp: Presbyn. Ch., 1955-61 Pastor; Belhaven Coll., 1963-70 Prof.; West. Ky. U., 1970-77 Prof.; Wheaton Coll. Grad. Sch., 1977- Prof., Bibl. Hist. Stud. Spec: Archaeology, New Testament, Apocrypha and Post-biblical Studies. Pub: "The Jewish Backgrounds of the New Testament: Second Commonwealth Judaism in Recent Study" *ABW* 2 (1992); "The Cornelius Incident in the Light of its Jewish Setting" *JETS* 34/4 (1991); and others. Mem: SBL; IBR; ETS. Rec: Hiking and biking, music. Addr: (o) Wheaton Coll. Graduate School, Dept. of Theological Studies, Wheaton, IL 60187 708-752-5280; (h) 924 Eddy Ct., Wheaton, IL 60187 708-682-4126.

SEGAL, Alan F., b. Worcester, MA, August 2, 1945, s. of Bennett & Rose (Sadowsky), m. Meryl (Goldey), chil: Ethan; Jordan. Educ:

Amherst Coll., BA 1967; Brandeis U., MA 1969; Hebrew Union Coll., BHL 1970; Yale U., MA, MPhil 1972, PhD 1975. Emp: Princeton U., 1974-78 Asst. Prof.; U. of Toronto, Canada, 1978-80 Assoc. Prof.; Barnard Coll., Columbia U., 1980- Prof., 1981-84 Chmn., Dept. of Relig.; *SC* 1982- Ed. Bd. Spec: Hebrew Bible, New Testament, Apocrypha and Post-biblical Studies. Pub: *Paul the Convert* (1990); *The Other Judaisms of Late Antiquity* (Scholars, 1988); *Rebecca's Children: Judaism and Christianity in the Roman World* (Harvard U.P., 1986); "Philo and the Rabbis on the Names of God," co-auth. *JSJ* 10 (1979); *Two Powers in Heaven: Early Rabbinic Reports of Christianity and Gnosticism* (Brill, 1977); and others. Awd: Guggenheim Fellow 1977-78; NEH grant 1984-85; Annenberg Res. Inst., Fellow 1992. Mem: SBL; AAR; AJS. Rec: Skiing, tennis. Addr: (o) Barnard College, 219c Milbank Hall, 3009 Broadway, New York, NY 10027-6598 212-854-5419; (h) 5 Beechwood Rd., Ho-Ho-Kus, NJ 07423-1606 201-445-3060.

SEGALLA, Giuseppe, b. Chiuppano, Italy, October 21, 1932, s. of Natalino & Pia (De Muri). Educ: Gregoriana Pont. U., Rome, LT 1959; Pont. U. of Lateran, DT 1965; Pont. Bibl. Inst., D. Bibl. Sci. 1968. Emp: Fac. Teologica dell'Italia Settentrionale, 1968- Prof., NT, 1974-Prof. *Studia Patavina*, 1968- Redactor, 1989- Dir.; *NTS*, Redactor; *Teologia*, 1976- Redactor. Spec: New Testament. Pub: *Giovanni: traduzione e commento del IV vangelo* (Cinisello Balsamo, 1990); *La cristologia del Nuovo Testamento* (1985); *La preghiera de Gesú al Padre*, Giov. 17 (1983); *La volontà di Dio e dell'uomo in Giovanni* (1974). Mem: SNTS 1974-. Addr: (o) Via Seminario, 29, 35122 Padova, Italy 049-658200.

SEGER, Joe D., b. Eau Claire, WI, October 15, 1935, s. of Einar & Esther (Anderson), m. Patricia (O'Connor), chil: Daniel; James; Robert; Kariman. Educ: Elmhurst Coll., BA 1957; Eden Theol. Sem., BD 1960; Harvard Div. Sch., ThD 1965. Emp: Hartford Sem. Found., 1964-69 Assoc. Prof.; Nelson Glueck Sch. Bibl. Arch., Jerusalem, 1969-74 Assoc. Prof.; Hebrew Union Coll., Los Angeles 1974-75,; Calif. State U.-Fullerton 1975 Instr.; U. of Nebraska, 1976-82 Assoc. Prof.; Miss. State U., 1962- Prof. Excv: Tell Balatah (Shechem), 1962, 1964, 1968 Sup. Staff, 1969 Field Dir.; Tell Gezer, 1966-71 Sr. Staff, 1971-74 Dir.; Tell Halif., 1973, 1975- Dir. Spec: Archaeology, Hebrew Bible, Semitic Languages, Texts and Epigraphy. Pub: "The Location of Biblical Ziklag" *BA* 47/1 (1984); "The Lahav Research Project: Investigations at Tell Halif, 1976-1980" *BASOR* 252 (1983); "The Gezer Jar Signs: New Evidence of the Earliest Alphabet" in *The Word of the Lord Shall Go Forth* (ASOR, 1983); "Reflections on the Gold Hoard from Gezer" *BASOR* 221 (1976); "The MB II Fortifications at Shechem and Gezer, A Hyksos Retrospective" *Eretz-Israel* 12 (1975); and others. Mem: ASOR 1957-; AIA 1962-; AAR 1958-85; IES 1960-. Rec: Golf, woodworking. Addr: (o)

Mississippi State U., Drawer AR, Mississippi State, MS 39762 601-325-3286; (h) 810 Howard Rd., Starkville, MS 39759 601-323-8456.

SEGERT, Stanislav, b. Prague, Czechoslovakia, May 4, 1921, s. of Antonin & Marie, m. Jarmila, chil: Eva; Jan. Educ: Charles U., Prague, PhD 1947; Czechoslovak Acad. of Sci., Oriental Inst., Prague, CSc 1958. Emp: John Hus Evang. Theol. Fac., Prague, 1945-52 Lect.; Czechoslovak Acad. of Sci., Oriental Inst., Prague, 1952-70 Res. Assoc.; U. of Chicago, 1966 Vis. Assoc. Prof.; U. of Calif., 1969-91 Prof., 1991- Prof. Emeritus; Ben-Gurion U. of the Negev, Israel, 1985 Vis. Prof. Excv: Ras Shamra/Ugarit, Syria 1963; Carthage, Tunisia 1976; Politiko/Tamassos, Cyprus 1976. Spec: Hebrew Bible, New Testament, Semitic Languages, Texts and Epigraphy, Apocrypha and Post-biblical Studies. Pub: "Unitas Fratrum and the Old Testament" *Communio viatorum* (1990); *Altaramiäsche Grammatik*, Enzyklopädie (1975, 1990); *A Basic Grammar of the Ugaritic Language* (U. of Calif., 1984); *A Grammar of Phoenician and Punic* (Beck, 1976); and others. Awd: Guggenheim Fellow. 1976; Fulbright Awd. 1982-83, 1990; Czechoslovak Acad. of Sci., Josef Dobrovsky's Silver Medal 1991. Mem: AOS 1968-; SBL 1968-; ASOR 1970-; AIA 1972-. Addr: (o) UCLA, Dept. of Near Eastern Languages & Cultures 151105, Los Angeles, CA 90024-1511 310-454-7995.

SEGOVIA, Fernando F., b. Havana, Cuba, April 25, 1948, s. of Fernando & Maria (Guerra), m. Elena (Olazagasti). Educ: U. of Notre Dame, MA 1976, PhD 1978. Emp: Marquette U., 1977-84 Asst. Prof.; Vanderbilt U., 1984-92, Assoc. Prof., 1992- Prof., NT & Early Christianity. Spec: New Testament. Pub: *The Farewell of the Word: Johannine Call to Abide* (Fortress, 1991); "The Journey(s) of the Word: A Reading of the Plot of the Fourth Gospel," "The Final Farewell of Jesus: A Reading of John; 20:30-21:25" *Semeia* 53 (1991); *The Fourth Gospel from a Literary Perspective*, ed. (Scholars, 1991); *Discipleship in the New Testament* (Fortress, 1985); "The Structure *Tendenz*, and *Sitz im Leben* of John 13:31-14:31" *JBL* 104 (1985); "The Theology and Provenance of John 15:1-17" *JBL* 101 (1982); *Love Relationships in the Johannine Traditions* (Scholars, 1982); and others. Mem: SNTS; SBL; CBA. Rec: Opera, classical music, Caribbean art and culture. Addr: (o) Vanderbilt U., The Divinity School, Nashville, TN 37240 615-322-2776; (h) 131 Villa View Ct., Brentwood,, TN 37027 615-371-8812.

SEIDEL, Hans E., b. Breslau, Germany, November 22, 1929, s. of Ewald & Martha-Elisabeth (Quoos), m. Birgit (Geissler), chil: Katrin. Emp: Luth. Ch. of Germany, 1956-72 Min.; Luth. Sem. Leipzig, 1972-92 Prof., OT; U. of Leipzig, 1992 Prof., OT; *Mitteilungen und Beitrage der Forschungsstaelle Judentum*, 1988- Ed. Spec: Hebrew Bible, Apocrypha and Post-

biblical Studies. Pub: "Gen. 4 und der Ursprung der Musik?" *Orbis musicae* 10 (1991); *Musik in Altisrael* (1989); *Auf den Spuren der Beter*; and others. Mem: IES; Intl. Arbeitsgemeinschaft fuer Hymnologie; Hymn Soc. of Amer. Addr: (o) U. of Leipzig, Faculty of Theology, Emil-Fuchs-Str. 1, 04105 Leipzig, Germany; (h) Raschwitzer Str. 56, 04416 Markkleeberg, Germany 0341-327248.

SELAND, Torrey, b. Flekkefjord, Norway, May 30, 1948, m. Anne Margrete, chil: Torgny; Laila Mary; Vidar. Educ: Free Faculty, Oslo, Cand. Theol. 1977; U. of Trondheim, Dr.Artium 1991. Emp: Ch. of Norway, 1977-84 Pastor; Norwegian Res. Coun. for Sci. & the Hum., 1985-87 Res. Fellow; Reg. Coll. of More & Romsdal, Volda, 1988- Assoc. Prof. Spec: New Testament. Pub: "Jesus as a Faction Leader: On the Exit of the Category 'Sect'" in *Context: Essays in Honour of Peder Borgen* (1987); and others. Mem: SBL 1990-. Addr: (o) MRDH-Volda, Pb 188 - 6101 Volda, Norway 47-70075067; (h) Gamletunveien 5, 6100 Volda, Norway 47-70078231.

SELBY, Donald J., b. Kansas City, MO, February 7, 1915, s. of Benjamin W. & Evelyn M. (Wharton), m. Clarice Allene (Beggs), chil: Robert Wallace; Donald Lee. Educ: William Jewell Coll., AB 1946; Andover Newton Theol. Sch., BD 1949; Boston U., PhD 1954. Emp: Pilgrim Cong. Ch., 1948-56 Pastor; Catawba Coll., 1956-80 Prof., Relig., 1970-80 Chmn., Dept. of Relig. & Phil., 1980- Prof. Emeritus; Hood Theol. Sem., 1957-74 Vis. Prof., NT. Spec: New Testament. Pub: *Introduction to the New Testament* (Macmillan, 1971); *Introduction to the Bible*, co-auth. (Selby & West, 1971); *Toward the Understanding of St. Paul* (Prentice-Hall, 1962); "Changing Ideas in New Testament Eschatology" *HTR* (1957). Awd: Outstanding Educ. of Amer. 1972; Algernon Sydney Sullivan Awd. 1980. Mem: SBL 1949-; NABI 1949-88; AAR 1949-88; ASOR 1957-85. Rec: Swimming, sailboating, hiking. Addr: (h) 9 Sargent Pl., Lake Breeze 49, Gilford, NH 03246 603-524-9076.

SELLEW, Philip H., b. Milwaukee, WI, August 16, 1953, s. of Donald & Elgine (Harl), m. Kathleen (Troxell). Educ: Macalester Coll., BA (summa cum laude) 1975; Harvard Div. Sch., MDiv 1978, ThD 1986. Emp: Harvard Div. Sch., 1981-84 Dir., Lang. Stud., Lect.; *HTR*, 1978-81 Managing Ed.; U. of Minn., 1984-90 Asst. Prof., 1990- Assoc. Prof.; *Forum*, 1991- Ed.; *Currents in Research: Biblical Studies*, 1991- NT Ed.. Excv: Tel Dor, Israel, 1988 Staff. Spec: New Testament, Apocrypha and Post-biblical Studies. Pub: "Eusebius and the Gospels" in *Eusebius, Christianity, and Judaism* (Wayne State U.P., 1992); "Interior Monologue as Narrative Device in the Parables of Luke" *JBL* 111 (1992); "Secret Mark and the History of Canonical Mark" in *The Future of Early Christianity: Essays in Honor of Helmut Koester* (Fortress, 1991); "Five Days of Creation? The Origin of an Unusual Exegesis"

ZNW 81 (1990); "Oral and Written Sources in Mark 4" *NTS* 36 (1990). Mem: SBL 1975-; CBA 1984-; ASOR 1992-. Addr: (o) U. of Minnesota, Classical and Near East Studies Dept., 331 Folwell Hall, Minneapolis, MN 55455-0125 612-625-2026; (h) 1756 Lincoln Ave., St. Paul, MN 55105 612-699-7928.

SELLIN, Gerhard, b. Ratzeburg, October 5, 1943, s. of Johanna & Gustav, m. Monika, chil: Julia; Daniel; Jonathan; Benjamin. Educ: U. Munster, Fachbereich Evang. Theol., ThD 1974. Emp: U. Munster, Evang. Theol. Fachbereich 1975-84, Wissenschaftlicher Asst.; U. Oldenburg, 1984- U. Prof., Evangelische Theol. mit dem Schwerpunut NT. Spec: New Testament. Pub: "I Korinther 5-6 und der 'Vorbrief' nach Korinth" *NTS* 37 (1991); "'Gattung' und 'Sitz im Leben' auf dem Hintergrund der Problematik von Mundlichkeit und Schriftlickeit Synoptischer Erzahlungen"; *ET* 50 (1990); *Der Streit um die Auferstehung der Toten*, Eine religionsgeschichtliche und exegetische Untersuchung von 1 Korinther 15; (Vandenhoeck & Ruprecht, 1986); "Das 'Geheimnis' der Weisheit und das Ratsel der 'Christuspartei'" *ZNW* 73 (1982); "Allegorie und 'Gleichnis'" *ZTK* 75 (1978); "Lukas als Gleichniserzahler" *ZNW* 65, 66 (1974-75); and others. Mem: SNTS 1983-; Wissenschaftliche Gesellschaft fur Theol. 1983-. Rec: Lyrics. Addr: (o) U. Oldenburg, Inst. Theologie, Ammerlander Heerstrasse 114-118, D-2900 Oldenburg, Germany 0441-798-2920; (h) Suderdiek 24, D-2900 Oldenburg, Germany 0441-60961.

SENIOR, Donald P., b. Philadelphia, PA, January 1, 1940, s. of Vincent & Margaret (Tiernan). Educ: U. of Louvain, Belgium, STD 1972. Emp: Cath. Theol. Union, 1972- Pres., Prof. of NT; *The Bible Today*, 1973- Assoc. Ed.; *CBQ*, 1975-78 Assoc. Ed., 1980- Book Rev. Ed. Spec: New Testament. Pub: *Jesus: A Gospel Portrait* (Paulist, 1992); *The Passion of Jesus in the Gospel of John* (Liturgical, 1991); *The Catholic Study Bible* (Oxford U.P., 1990); *The Passion of Jesus in the Gospel of Luke* (Liturgical, 1989); and others. Mem: CBA 1970-; CTSA 1970-; SBL 1972-; CSBR 1972-; PCI 1980-. Rec: Walking. Addr: (o) Catholic Theological Union, 5401 S Cornell Ave., Chicago, IL 60615 312-324-8000; (h) 5401 S Cornell Ave., Chicago, IL 60615 312-324-2704.

SEUBERT, August H., b. Marathon, WI, December 25, 1931, s. of Joseph A. & Frances. Educ: Pont. U. Gregoriana, Rome, STL, Bibl. Theol. 1984. Emp: Bluefields, Nicaragua, 1959-81, 1984-92 Vicariato Apostolico; Inst. Teologico de Amer. Cen., Costa Rica, 1987-90 Prof., NT. Spec: Hebrew Bible, New Testament. Pub: *Como Entender el Mensaje del Nuevo Testamento* (Ediciones Paulinas, 1990); "Israel bajo la Dominacion Griega" *Nuevo Mundo* 147 (1990); *Como Entender el Mensaje de Los Profetas* (Ediciones Paulinas, 1988); *Entiendes*

el Mensaje? (Ediciones Paulinas, 1987). Mem: SBL 1985-. Rec: Reading. Addr: (o) Catedral, Apartado 8, Bluefields, Nicaragua 082-575.

SEVRIN, Jean-Marie, b. Marche-en-Famenne, Belgium, July 24, 1942, s. of Aimé Sevrin & Maria Giaux. Educ: U. Cath. de Louvain, BA 1967, Lic. 1969, Lic., Philol. & Hist. Orientales 1970, ThD 1974, Doc. et Maitre en Theol. 1985. Emp: Fonds Natl. de la Recherche Sci., Belgium, 1975-79 Chargé de Recherche; U. Cath. de Louvain, 1979-86 Asst., 1987-89 Charge de cours, 1989- Prof., 1990- Doyen. Spec: New Testament, Apocrypha and Post-biblical Studies. Pub: "L'exégèse critique comme discipline théologique" *Rev. théol. de Louvain* 21 (1990); "Le quatrième Evangile et le gnosticisme: questions de methode" in *La communauté johannique et son histoire* (Labor et Fides, 1990); "L'écriture du ive Evangile comme phénomène de reception" in *The New Testament in Early Christianity*, BETL 86, ed. (Peeters, 1989); *Le dossier baptismal séthien: Etudes sur la sacramentaire gnostique* (U. Laval, 1986); *L'Exégèse de l'âme (N.H. II,6) Introduction, texte, traduction, commentaire* (U. Laval, 1983); "L'Evangile selon Thomas: Paroles de Jésus et révélation gnostique" *Rev. théol. de Louvain* 8 (1977); "Les noces spirituelles dans l'Evangile selon Philippe" *Le Muséon* 87 (1974); and others. Mem: SNTS; IACS. Addr: (o) Collège A. Descamps, Faculté de Theologie, Grand-Place 45, 1348 Louvain la Neuve, Belgium 010-473606.

SEYBOLD, Klaus D., b. Heidenheim/Br., April 28, 1936, s. of Jakob & Margarete (Hofmann), m. Gisela (Vetterlein), chil: Bernhard; Dietrich. Educ: U. Tuebingen, 1.Theol. Examen 1961; U. Kiel, ThD 1968, Habil. 1972. Emp: Evang. Landeskirche, Wuerttemberg, 1961-64 Vikar; U. Kiel, 1964- Wiss. Asst.; U. Basel, 1979- Prof., OT. Excv: Lehrkurs, Israel 1977. Spec: Hebrew Bible. Pub: "Psalm 141: Ein neuer Anlauf" in *Festschrift M. Metzger* (1992); "Habakuk 2,4b und sein Kontext" in *Zur Aktualitat des Ats.*, Festschrift G. Sauer (1992); *Introducing the Psalms* (1990); *Nahum-Habakuk-Zephanja*, ZBK 24,2 (1991); "Der Schutzpanzer des Propheten: Restaurationsarbeiten an Jer 15,11ff." *BZ* 32 (1988); "Der Turmbau zu Babel: Zur Entstehung von Gen XI,1-9" *VT* 26 (1976); "Die Bildmotive in den Visionen des Propheten Sacharja" VTSup 26 (1974); *Bilder zum Tempelbau*, SBS 70 (1974); *Das Gebet des Kranken im Alten Testament*, BWANT 99 (1973); and others. Mem: IOSOT; SBL. Rec: Violin. Addr: (o) Nadelberg 10, CH-4051 Basel, Switzerland 061-267-29-03; (h) Bruderholzrain 62, CH-4102 Binningen BL, Switzerland 061-421-03-67.

SHAFER, Byron E., b. Cincinnati, OH, December 7, 1938, s. of Kenneth & Lucile (Esely), m. Margaret (Loehlin), chil: Stephen; James; Christina. Educ: McCormick Theol. Sem., MDiv 1963; Harvard U., PhD 1968. Emp: Fordham U., 1968- Assoc. Prof. & Co-Dir., Middle East Study

Prog. Spec: Hebrew Bible, Egyptology. Pub: "Relationship to God: Public and Private Worship" in *Oxford Study Bible* (Oxford U.P., 1992); *Religion in Ancient Egypt*, ed. (Cornell U.P., 1991); "The Root *bhr* and Pre-Exilic Concepts of Chosenness in the Hebrew Bible" *ZAW* 89 (1977); articles in *Supplement to the IDB* (Abingdon, 1976); *"Mibhar/Mibhor* 'Fortress'" *CBQ* 33 (1971); and others. Mem: ASOR 1968-; SBL 1968-; AAR 1968-; CBA 1968-. Rec: Yoga, opera music. Addr: (o) Fordham U. at Lincoln Center, 113 W 60th St., New York, NY 10023 212-636-6388; (h) 16 Madeline Pkwy., Yonkers, NY 10705 914-423-8949.

SHANKS, Hershel, b. Sharon, PA, March 8, 1930, s. of A. Martin & Mildred (Freedman), m. Judith A., chil: Elizabeth J.; Julia E. Educ: Haverford Coll., BA 1952; Columbia U., MA 1953; Harvard Law Sch., LLB 1956. Emp: U.S. Dept. of Justice, 1956-59; Glassie, Pewett, Beebe & Shanks 1959-1987; *BAR, BR, Moment,* ed. Spec: Archaeology. Pub: *Understanding the Dead Sea Scrolls* (Random/BAS, 1992); *Christianity and Rabbinic Judaism,* ed. (BAS, 1992); *Ancient Israel,* ed. (BAS, 1986); *Recent Archeology in the Land of Israel,* co-ed. (IES, 1981; BAS, 1984); *Judaism in Stone* (Harper & Row, 1979); *The City of David* (Bazak, 1973); and others. Addr: (o) Biblical Archaeology Society, 3000 Connecticut Ave. NW, Ste. 300, Washington, DC 20008 202-387-8888.

SHARP, Donald B., b. Spokane, WA, July 21, 1940, s. of Malcolm & Elizabeth. Educ: Gonzaga U., AB 1964; Pont. Faculty of Phil. of Mt. St. Michael's, PhL 1965; Coll. de l'Immaculee Conception, Canada, STB 1971; St. Mary's U., Canada, MDiv 1971; Die Leopold-Franzens-U. Innsbruck, Austria, DrTheol 1975. Emp: Gonzaga U., 1966 Instr., 1975- Assoc. Prof., Relig. Stud.; U. of Notre Dame, Austria, 1971-73 Instr. Spec: Hebrew Bible, New Testament, Semitic Languages, Texts and Epigraphy, Apocrypha and Post-biblical Studies. Pub: "In Defense of Rebecca" *BTB* 10 (1980), and others. Mem: CBA 1976-; SBL 1976-. Rec: Hunting, fishing. Addr: (o) Gonzaga U., Spokane, WA 99258 509-328-4220; (h) E 502 Boone Ave., Spokane, WA 99258 509-328-4220.

SHAVER, Judson R., b. Riverside, CA, July 29, 1949, s. of John Robert & Carol Jean, m. D. Page, chil: Nathan R.; Sarah M. Educ: South. Calif. Coll., BA 1975; U. of Notre Dame, MA 1979, PhD 1984. Emp: Wheeling Coll., 1980-85 Asst. Prof.; Seattle U., 1985-90 Assoc. Prof.; Regis U., 1990- Dean of the College & Assoc. Prof. Spec: Hebrew Bible, New Testament. Pub: "Ezra and Nehemiah: On the Theological Significance of Making them Contemporaries" in *Prophets, Priests, and Kings,* Blenkinsopp; Festschrift (JSOT, 1992); "Passover Legislation and the Identity of the Chronicler's Law Book" in *New Perspectives on Ancient Judaism,* (U. Press of Amer., 1990); *Torah and the Chronicler's History Work* (Scholars, 1989); and others. Awd: Layne Fellow. 1974-78; Danforth Fellow. 1979-83; Still Fellow. 1983; NEH Fellow. 1985; Fulbright Fellow. 1988. Mem: AAR; SBL. Addr: (o) Regis U., Dean of the College, Denver, CO 80221 303-458-4040; (h) 325 Albion, Denver, CO 80220 303-320-5405.

SHAVER, Thomas A., b. Healdton, OK, July 9, 1928, s. of Austin & Tessie (Hodges), m. Waunette (Fitzgerald), chil: Sharla; Guy. Educ: South. Meth. U., MA 1953; SW Bapt. Theol. Sem., MRE 1965, DRE 1967. Emp: Abilene Christian U., 1955- Prof., Bible. Spec: Archaeology, New Testament. Pub: *Genesis-Esther, A Study Guide* (Abtex, 1976); and others. Mem: SBL 1967-. Rec: Travel, hunting. Addr: (o) Abilene Christian U., Box 8404, Abilene, TX 79699 915-674-3790; (h) 801 Harrison, Abilene, TX 79601 915-672-5513.

SHAW, Fitzhugh Lewis, b. Oklahoma City, OK, December 16, 1950, s. of Thomas Edward & Sarah Ann, m. Paige Lindsay, chil: Fitzhugh Rivers. Educ: U. of Oklahoma, BA 1973; Yale U., MA 1977; Cambridge U., PhD 1992. Emp: South. Bapt. Theol. Sem., 1985-87, Lect. Spec: Apocrypha and Post-biblical Studies. Pub: *The Fathers of the Church: Biblical Interpretations,* contb. (Glazier, 1988); and others. Awd: Columbia U., Fellow of Grad. Sch. of Arts & Sci., 1978; Albright Inst. of Arch. Res., Jerusalem, Barton Fellow 1982. Mem: AAR 1990-. Rec: Baseball, chess, film, reading. Addr: (o) 1310 Chamberlain Ave., Mobile, AL 36604 205-432-7691.

SHEA, William H., b. Upland, CA, December 31, 1932, s. of Henry & Nette (Lende), m. Karen (Olsen), chil: Josephine; Theodore; Rebecca. Educ: U. of Mich., PhD 1976. Emp: Andrews U., 1972- Prof., 1982-84 Chmn., Dept. of OT, 1985- Dir., Inst. of Arch.; AUSS, 1978- Ed.; Gen. Conf. of SDA, Bibl. Res. Inst., 1986- Res. Assoc. Excv: Gezer, 1966-67; Hesban, 1971. Spec: Archaeology, Hebrew Bible, Semitic Languages, Texts and Epigraphy. Pub: "Sennacherib's Second Palestinian Campaign" *JBL;* "The Eblaite Letter to Hamazi" *Oriens Antiquus* 23 (1984); "Exodus, Date of" in *ISBE,* vol. 2 (1982); "Menahem and Tiglath-Pileser III" *JNES* (1978); "The Date and Significance of the Samaria Ostraca" *IEJ* 27 (1977); and others. Mem: SBL 1976-. Addr: (o) General Conference of SDA, 12501 Old Columbia Pike, Silver Spring, MD 20904 301-680-6794; (h) 808 Bayside Dr., Stevensville, MD 21666 410-643-5673.

SHEARER, Rodney H., b. Reading, PA, September 21, 1944, s. of J. Warren & Helen Rettew (Hain), m. Mary Ellen (Olmsted), chil: Laurabeth; Angela Gail; Sara Helene; Janell Ross (dec.). Educ: Lebanon Valley Coll., BA 1966; United Theol. Sem., MDiv 1969; Drew U., PhD 1985. Emp: St. Paul's United Meth. Ch., 1969-72 Assoc. Pastor; Green Village UMC, 1972-76

Pastor; Lebanon Valley Coll., 1976-80 Chaplain & Adj. Asst. Prof., Relig.; Fritz Memorial United Meth. Ch., 1980-87 Pastor; Ono United Meth. Ch., 1987- Pastor. Spec: Hebrew Bible. Pub: Articles in ABD (Doubleday, 1992); *A Contextual Analysis of the Phrase* 'al-tirā' *as it Occurs in the Hebrew Bible and in Selected Related Literature* (U. Microfilms Intl., 1986). Mem: SBL 1970-. Rec: Piano, reading. Addr: (o) Ono United Methodist Church, PO Box 126, Ono, PA 17077-0126 717-865-7469; (h) PO Box 61, Jonestown & McGillstown Roads, Ono, PA 17077-0061 717-865-2305.

SHEELEY, Steven M., b. Springfield, MO, December 2, 1956, s. of Charles Beecher & Virginia Ruth, m. Elizabeth Ann, chil: Kristen Rebecca; Mary Elizabeth. Educ: SW Mo. State U., BSEd 1979; SW Bapt. Theol. Sem., MDiv 1983; South. Bapt. Theol. Sem., PhD 1987. Emp: South. Bapt. Theol. Sem., 1987-88 Adj. Prof., NT; Shorter Coll., 1988- Assoc. Prof., Relig.. Spec: New Testament. Pub: *Narrative Asides in Luke-Acts* (JSOT/Sheffield, 1992); "The Narrator in the Gospels: Developing a Model" *Perspectives in Relig. Stud.* 16 (1989); "Narrative Asides and Narrative Authority in Luke-Acts" *BTB* 18 (1988). Mem: SBL 1985-; NABPR 1986-. Rec: Basketball, softball, golf, reading. Addr: (o) Shorter College, Box 345, 315 Shorter Ave., Rome, GA 30165 706-291-2121; (h) 3807 Garden Lakes Pkwy., Rome, GA 30165 706-235-5847.

SHELTON, Malcolm W., b. Eckmansville, OH, August 26, 1919, s. of Charles & Mary, m. Muriel (Payne). Educ: Olivet Nazarene Coll., ThB 1951; Pasadena Coll., MA 1952; Nazarene Theol. Sem., MDiv 1971; Phillips U., DMin 1977. Emp: Bethany Nazarene Coll., 1967-85 Prof., OT; SW Coll. of Christian Min., 1985- Prof.; Mid-Amer. Bible Coll., 1985- Prof. Spec: Archaeology. Mem: ASOR; SBL; NEAS; BSA; IES. Addr: (o) Mid-America Bible College, 3500 SW 119th St., Oklahoma City, OK 73170 405-789-7661; (h) 6404 NW 35 St., Bethany, OK 73008 405-787-0503.

SHENHAV, Eli, b. Tel Aviv, Israel, April 15, 1947, s. of Zvi & Bella (Grossman), chil: Shimrat; Dotan; Nadav. Educ: Tel Aviv U., BA, Class. Arch. & Israel Hist. 1969; Bar Ilan U., MA. Emp: Tel Aviv U., Dept. of Class. Arch., 1975-80 Sci. Sec. for Israel Milestone Com.; Jewish National Fund, 1980- Chief Arch. Excv: Tamara, Israel, 1975-76 Supr.; Ein Bokek, Israel, 1976 Supr.; Emmaus, Israel, 1977-79 Supr.; Hanot, Israel, 1984-85 Dir.; Shuni, Israel, 1986- Dir. Spec: Archaeology. Pub: "Le Theatre Romain du Shuni" *Le Monde de la Bible 1991;* "Shuni/Miamas" *Qadmoniot* 89 1991; "Excavation and Survey in Mishkana" *NOFIM* 2 (1982). Addr: (o) Jewish National Fund, Dept. of Archaeology, 11 Zvi Shapira St., Tel Aviv, Israel 03-5261129; (h) 15 Hertzog, Hertzelia, Israel 052-508475.

SHEPHERD, Tom R., b. Van Nuys, CA, February 28, 1951, s. of Allen E. & Irma L., m. Sherry Marie, chil: Amy Marie; Jonathan Jeffrey. Educ: Pacific Union Coll., BA 1973; Andrews U., MA 1986, PhD 1991. Emp: Seventh Day Adventist Ch., 1977-79 Pastor; Malawi, Africa, Missionary-Health Admin. 1979-85; Inst. Adventista de Ensino, Brazil, 1992- Prof., NT. Spec: New Testament. Pub: "Intercalation in Mark and the Synoptic Problem" in *SBL 1991 Seminar Papers* (1991). Mem: SBL 1990-. Rec: Long distance running, reading, amateur radio. Addr: (o) Instituto Adventista de Ensino, Caixa Postal 85, Cep 13160-000 Artur Nog., SP, Brazil 0055-192-67912.

SHERWIN, Byron L., b. New York, NY, February 18, 1946, s. of Sidney & Jean, m. Judith (Schwartz), chil: Jason. Educ: Columbia U., BS 1966; Jewish Theol. Sem., BHL 1966, MHL 1968; Rabbinic Ord., 1970; N.Y. U., MA 1969; U. of Chicago, PhD 1978. Emp: Spertus Coll. of Judaica, 1970- David C. Verson Prof. of Jewish Phil. & Mysticism, 1984- V.P., Acad. Affairs. Spec: Hebrew Bible, Apocrypha and Post-biblical Studies. Pub: *Toward a Jewish Theology* (Mellen, 1992); *No Religion is an Island,* ed. (Orbis, 1991); *The Golem Legend* (U. Press of Amer., 1985); "Portrait of God as a Young Artist" *Judaism* (1984); *Mystical Theology and Social Dissent* (Oxford U.P., 1982). Rec: Cooking. Addr: (o) 618 S Michigan, Chicago, IL 60605 312-922-9012; (h) 6702 N Sheridan Road, Chicago, IL 60626.

SHIELDS, Bruce E., b. Natrona Heights, PA, August 9, 1937, s. of Donald E. & Beatrice S., m. Rosemarie (Klein), chil: Karen E.; James S.; Robert B. Educ: Milligan Coll., BA 1959; Princeton Theol. Sem., BD 1965; U. of Tuebingen, Dr. theol. 1981. Emp: Lincoln Christian Sem., 1977-83 Assoc. Prof.; Emmanuel Sch. of Relig., 1983- Prof. Spec: New Testament. Pub: "The Areopogus Sermon and Romans 1:18ff" *Restoration Quar.* 20/1; *Commentary on Romans* (Standard, 1988); and others. Mem: SBL 1977-; AH 1980-. Rec: Music, gardening. Addr: (o) Emmanuel School of Religion, One Walker Dr., Johnson City, TN 37601 615-461-1505; (h) 224 Pine Ct., Johnson City, TN 37601 615-929-2496.

SHIMADA, Kazuhito, b. Kakogawa, Japan, May 29, 1933, s. of Suekuma, m. Noriye, chil: Nobuhito; Louis. Educ: McCormick Theol. Sem., BD 1960; Union Theol. Sem., STM 1961, ThD 1966. Emp: Meth. Ch., 1966, 1968 Min.; Osaka Christian Coll., 1967-70 Lect. Spec: New Testament. Pub: "Is I Peter Dependent on Ephesians?" *Ann. of the Japanese Bibl. Inst.* 17 (1991); "Is I Peter a Composite Writing?" *Ann. of the Japanese Bibl. Inst.* 11 (1985); "A Critical Note on I Peter 1,12" *Ann. of the Japanese Bibl. Inst.* 7 (1981); "The Christological Credal Formula in I Peter 3,18-22 Reconsidered" *Ann. of the Japanese Bibl. Inst.* 5 (1979); and others. Mem:

Japanese Bibl. Inst.; SBL; Japan Soc. for Christian Stud. Addr: (o) Koh 496-18, Fukura, Nantan-cho, Mihara-gun, Hyogo-ken, Japan 0799-52-3220.

SHIMOFF, Sandra R., b. New York, NY, June 10, 1942, d. of Charlotte & Joseph Steinhardt, m. Eliot, chil: Daniel; Wendy; Randi; Michael. Educ: Yeshiva U., BA, BRE, 1964; City U. of N.Y., MA 1966; St. Mary's Sem. & U., PhD 1981. Emp: U. of Md., Baltimore County, 1981- Asst. Prof. Spec: Hebrew Bible, Apocrypha and Post-biblical Studies. Pub: "Shepherds: Hellenism, Sectarianism and Judaism" in *The Literature of Early Rabbinic Judaism: Issues in Talmudic Redaction and Interpretation*, New Perspectives on Ancient Judaism vol. 4 (U. Press, 1989); "Hellenization among the Rabbis: Evidence from Early Aggadot Concerning David and Solomon" *JSJ* 18 (1988); and others. Mem: SBL 1981-. Addr: (o) U. of Maryland, Baltimore County, Judaic Studies Dept., Baltimore, MD 21228 410-455-2369; (h) 5800 Stuart Ave., Baltimore, MD 21215 410-644-2462.

SHOEMAKER, Melvin H., b. Bryant, IN, February 11, 1940, s. of H. Vaughn & Thelora Avey (Mason), m. Glenna (Cockrell), chil: David Wesley; Diana Marie; Daniel Luther. Educ: Ind. Wesleyan U., BA 1962; Asbury Theol. Sem., MDiv 1967; Drew U., MPhil 1988. Emp: Ind. Wesleyan U., 1966-67 Instr.; Houghton Coll. Wesleyan Ch., 1970-73 Sr. Min.; Free Meth. Ch., 1973-79 Sr. Min.; Bartlesville Wesleyan Coll., 1979-84 Prof.; Azusa Pacific U., 1986- Assoc. Prof. Spec: New Testament. Pub: "Good News to the Poor in Luke's Gospel" *WTJ* 27 (1992); "Jewish Savings & Loan" *Illustrated Bible Life* (1992); *Eerdmans Bible Dict.*, contb. (Eerdmans, 1987); and others. Awd: Spring Arbor Coll., Fellow. 1977. Mem: Marion Area Min. Assn., Pres. 1969-70; Dearborn Area Min. Assn., Pres. 1975-76; WTS 1980-; SBL 1987-. Rec: Travel, hiking, gardening. Addr: (o) Azusa Pacific U., 901 E Alosta Ave., PO Box 7000, Azusa, CA 91702 818-969-3434; (h) 1981 Murfield Ave., Upland, CA 91784 909-931-0604.

SHOTWELL, Willis A., b. Bloomington, IN, August 22, 1920, s. of William & Alta (White), m. Betty (Koch), chil: W. Allen; Kevin. Educ: South. Bapt. Theol. Sem., ThD 1949, ThM 1944; U. of Chicago, PhD 1954. Emp: Cumberland U., 1949-50 Asst. Prof.; Berkeley Bapt. Div. Sch., 1955-66 Prof.; Grad. Theol. Union, 1963-66 Prof.; U. of Calif., 1966-76 Lect. Excv: Wadi ed Dalia, Israel, 1963 Area Supr.. Spec: New Testament. Pub: *The Biblical Exegesis of Justin Martyr* (SPCK, 1965); "The Problem of the Syrian Adra" *BASOR* (1964); and others. Awd: ASOR, Jerusalem, W.F. Albright Fellow 1963. Mem: SBL 1955-. Rec: Cooking, reading. Addr: (h) 505 Thistle Circle, Martinez, CA 94533 510-229-3878.

SIEVERS, Joseph, b. Recklinghausen, Germany, January 18, 1948, s. of Eberhard & Irma

(Pschorn). Educ: U. Wien, Austria, Diss. in Jewish Stud. 1971; Columbia U., MA 1973, MPhil 1975, PhD 1981. Emp: CUNY, Queens Coll., 1974-75 Adj. Lect.; Seton Hall U., 1975-83 Adj. Assoc. Prof.; Pont. Ateneo San Anselmo, Rome, 1989- Vis. Prof.; Pont. Bibl. Inst., 1991- Vis. Prof. Spec: Apocrypha and Post-biblical Studies. Pub: "Chi erano i farisei? Un nuovo approccio a un problema antico" *Nuova Umanita* 75, 76 (1991); *The Hasmoneans and Their Supporters: From Mattathias to the Death of John Hyrcanus I* (Scholars, 1990); "The Role of Women in Hasmonean Dynasty" in *Josephus, the Bible and History* (Wayne State U.P., 1989); "Antiochus IV-XII" in *Ency. Iranica*, vol. 2 (Routledge & Kegan Paul, 1986); "Heidentum" in *Theologische Realenzyklopadie* vol. 14 (de Gruyter, 1986); "'Where Two or Three...': The Rabbinic Concept of *Shekhinah* and Matthew 18:20" in *Standing Before God* (Ktav, 1981); and others. Awd: Studienstiftung des deutschen Volkes, Fellow. 1967-76; Columbia U., President's Fellow. 1973-74; B.Z. Goldberg Fellow. 1974-75. Mem: SBL 1975-; AJS 1981-; CBA 1981-; Assn. Italiana per lo studio del Giudaismo. Addr: (h) Via XXV Luglio 11/A/2, 00046 Grottaferrata, Roma, Italy 39-6-941-1046.

SILBERMAN, Lou H., b. San Francisco, CA, June 23, 1914, s. of Lou Harry & Myrtle (Mueller), m. Helen S. Epstein (dec.), chil: Syrl A.; Deborah S. (Cohn). Educ: U. of Calif., Berkeley, BA 1934; Hebrew Union Coll., BHebL 1939, MHebL 1941, DHebL 1943. Emp: Vanderbilt U., 1952-80 Prof., 1980- Hillel Prof. Emeritus, Jewish Lit. & Thought; U. of Ariz., 1980- Vis. & Adj. Prof., Judaic Stud. Spec: Hebrew Bible, New Testament, Apocrypha and Post-biblical Studies. Pub: "A Theological Treatise of Forgiveness: Chapter Twenty-Three of Pesiqta derab Kahana" in *Studies in Aggadah, Targum and Jewish Liturgy in Memory of Joseph Heinemann* (1981); "Chosen People" in *EJ* 5 (1973); "Unriddling the Riddle: A Study in the Language and Structure of the Habakkuk Pesher (IQpHab)" *RQ* 2 (1961); "Language and Structure in the Hodayot (IQH3)" *JBL* 75 (1956); and others. Mem: SBL, Pres. 1982; AAR; ASSR; Amer. Theol. Soc.; SNTS. Addr: (o) U. of Arizona, Judaic Studies, Franklin Bldg., Tucson, AZ 85721 602-621-9114; (h) 3203 E Third St., Tucson, AZ 85716 602-327-0839.

SILBERMAN, Neil Asher, b. Boston, MA, June 19, 1950, s. of Saul J. & Barbara (Kimball), m. Ellen (Glassburn), chil: Maya. Educ: Wesleyan U., BA 1972. Emp: Israel Dept. of Antiq. & Mus., 1972-74 Field Excavator; Haifa U., Israel, Akko Excvn. Project, 1973-76 Staff Arch.; Hebrew U. of Jerusalem, Inst. of Arch. 1985-87 Vis. Schol.; *BA*, 1987-92 Ed. Bd.; *Arch.*, 1990- Contb. Ed. Excv: Temple Mount Excvn., Jerusalem, 1970, 1972 Staff; Tel Akko Excvn. Project, 1972-76 Area Supr. & Staff Arch.; Akko Lower City Excvn., 1975 Chief Arch. Spec: Archaeology. Pub: "Who Were the

Israelites?" *Arch.* Mar./Apr. (1992); "Desolation and Restoration: The Impact of a Biblical Concept on Near Eastern Archaeology" *BA* June (1991); "The Lure of the Holy Land: Celebrating a Century of Biblical Archaeology" *Arch.* Nov./Dec. (1990); "The Politics of the Past: Archaeology and Nationalism in the Eastern Mediterranean" *Mediterranean Quar.* Jan. (1990); *Between Past and Present* (Holt, 1989); "Measuring Time Archaeologically" *BAR* 15/6 (1989); *Digging for God and Country* (Knopf, 1982); and others. Awd: John Simon Guggenheim Memorial Found., Fellow 1991-92. Mem: ASOR; Soc. for Hist. Arch.; World Arch. Congress; The Author's Guild. Addr: (h) 216 Spruce Hill Rd., Branford, CT 06405 203-481-4141.

SILVA, Moisés, b. Havana, Cuba, September 4, 1945, s. of Rafael & Cristina, m. Patty (Innis), chil: Arla Joy; David Edward; Erika; John Michael. Educ: Westminster Theol. Sem., BD 1969, ThM 1971; U. of Manchester, England, PhD 1972. Emp: Westmont Coll., 1972-81 Assoc. Prof.; Westminster Theol. Sem., 1981-Prof., NT; Fuller Theol. Sem., 1977, 1980 Vis. Adj. Prof.; Trinity Evang. Div. Sch., 1979 Vis. Adj. Prof.; *Westminster Theol. Jour.*, 1982- Ed. Spec: Hebrew Bible, New Testament, Apocrypha and Post-biblical Studies. Pub: *God, Language, and Scripture* (Zondervan, 1991); *Philippians* (Moody, 1990); *Biblical Words and Their Meaning* (Zondervan, 1983); and others. Mem: SBL 1972-; IOSCS 1972-; SNTS 1991-. Rec: Classical music, microcomputers, swimming. Addr: (o) Westminster Theological Seminary, Philadelphia, PA 19118 215-887-5511; (h) 2155 Edge Hill Rd., Huntingdon Valley, PA 19006 215-657-0131.

SILVER, Morris, b. New York, NY, July 9, 1931, s. of Julius & Lilly, m. Sondra, chil: Gerald; Ronald. Educ: Columbia U., PhD 1964. Emp: City Coll. of N.Y., 1963- Prof., Economics. Spec: Hebrew Bible, Mesopotamian Studies, Egyptology. Pub: *Taking Ancient Mythology Economically* (Brill, 1992); *Economic Structures of the Ancient Near East* (Helm, 1985); *Prophets and Markets: The Political Economy of Ancient Israel* (Kluwer-Nishoff, 1983); and others. Mem: AOS 1963-. Rec: Class. music. Addr: (o) City College of New York, Economics Dept., New York, NY 10031 212-650-5404; (h) 25 Joyce Ln., Woodberry, NY 11797 516-921-0072.

SIMIAN-YOFRE, Horacio, b. Santa Fe, Argentina, September 22, 1946, s. of Oscar & Genoveva (Yofre). Educ: U. del Salvador, Buenos Aires, PhL 1970; Iulius Maximillian U., Würzburg, ThD 1974; Pont. Bibl. Comm., Rome, SSL 1976. Emp: Pont. Bibl. Inst., Rome 1974- Prof., OT Exegesis; *Biblica,* 1984- Gen. Ed. Spec: Hebrew Bible. Pub: *El desierto de los dioses: Teologia e historia en el libro de Oseas* (1993); "La métaphore d'Ezéchiel 15" in *BETL* 84 (1986); "Ez 17,1-10 como enigma y parabo-

la" *Biblica* 65 (1984); "La Teodicea del Deuteroisaias" *Biblica* 62 (1981); "Exodo en Deuteroisaias" *Biblica* 61 (1980); *Die Theologische Nachgeschichte der Prophetie Ezechiels* (1974); and others. Rec: Lit., music. Addr: (o) Via della Pilotta, 25, Rome, 00187, Italy 06-679-6453.

SINCLAIR, Lawrence A., b. Chicago, IL, September 19, 1930, s. of James & Helen (Thompson), m. Donna (Behnke). Educ: McCormick Sem., BD 1955; Johns Hopkins U., PhD 1958. Emp: Carroll Coll., 1958- Prof., Chmn., Dept. of Relig. Spec: Archaeology, Hebrew Bible. Pub: "Hebrew Text of the Qumran Micah Pesher and Textual Traditions of the Minor Prophets" *RQ* 42/11 (1983); "A Qumran Biblical Fragment: Hosea 4QXII (Hosea 1:7-2:5)" *BASOR* 239 (1980); "Redaction of Zechariah 1-8" *Bibl. Res.* 26 (1975); and others. Mem: SBL, Pres., MidW sect. 1960-64, 1966; ASOR; CSBR; Cath. Bibl. Soc. Rec: Camping, canoeing. Addr: (o) Carroll College, 100 N East Ave., Waukesha, WI 53186 414-547-1211; (h) W243 S6920 Maple Hill Ave., Waukesha, WI 53186 414-662-4457.

SINCLAIR, Scott G., b. Baltimore, MD, March 29, 1950, s. of James Edward & Pauline (Shoemaker). Educ: Johns Hopkins U., BA 1971, MA 1972; Ch. Div. Sch. of the Pacific, MDiv 1976; Grad. Theol. Union, PhD 1986. Emp: Codrington Coll., Barbados, 1987-91 Tutor. Spec: New Testament. Pub: *Revelation—A Book for the Rest of Us* (BIBAL, 1992); "The Healing of Bartimaeus and the Gaps in Mark's Messianic Secret" *St. Luke's Jour. of Theol.* 33 (1990); *Jesus Christ According to Paul* (BIBAL, 1988). Mem: SBL. Rec: Backpacking, bridge. Addr: (h) c/o Mrs. James Sinclair, PO Box 337, Sewanee, TN 37375 615-598-0332.

SINGER, Itamar, b. Dej, Rumania, November 26, 1946, s. of Zoltan & Gertrud, chil: Jael. Educ: Tel Aviv U., MA 1973; Marburg U., Germany, PhD 1978. Emp: Tel Aviv U., 1975- Assoc. Prof., Dept. of Arch. & Anc. Near East. Stud. Excv: Tel Masos, 1973-74 Field Dir. Spec: Anatolian Studies. Pub: "The Title 'Great Princess' in the Hittite Empire" *UF* 23 (1991); "A Concise History of Amurru" in *Amurru Akkadian,* HSS 41 (1991); *The General's Letter from Ugarit,* co-auth. (1990); "The Origin of the Sea Peoples and Their Settlement on the Coast of Canaan" in *Society and Economy in the Eastern Mediterranean* (1988); "The Political Status of Megiddo VIIA" *Tel Aviv* 15-16 (1988-89); "Merneptah's Campaign to Cannan and the Egyptian Occupation of the Southern Coastal Plain of Palestine in the Ramesside Period" *BASOR* 269 (1988); *The Hittite Ki.Lam Festival,* vol. 1 & 2 (1983, 1984); and others. Mem: IES. Rec: Photography. Addr: (o) Tel Aviv U., Institute of Archaeology, Ramat-Aviv, Tel Aviv, Israel 03-420-417; (h) 30 Sprinzak St., Holon 58330, Israel 03-885307.

SINGER, Suzanne F., b. New York, NY, July 9, 1935, d. of Maurice Fried & Augusta (Ginsberg), m. Max Singer, chil: Saul; Alexander; Daniel; Benjamin. Educ: Swarthmore Coll., BA 1956; Columbia U., MA 1958. Emp: *BAR*, 1977- Managing Ed.; *BR*, 1985- Managing Ed. Spec: Archaeology. Pub: "Against All Odds" *BAR* (1992); "The Power of the Psalms in Our Time" *BR* (1986); "Paper-cuts—An Ancient Art Form Glorifies Biblical Texts" *BR* (1986); "Is the Cultic Installation at Dan Really an Olive Press?" *BAR* (1984); and others. Addr: (o) 3000 Connecticut Ave. NW, Suite 300, Washington, DC 20008 202-387-8888.

SIOTIS, Marcos A., b. Tripotamos, Island Tenos, May 3, 1912, s. of Antonios & Penelope, m. Katherine. Educ: U. of Athens, Theol. Sch., Dip. 1935; U. of Marbourg/Lahn, PhD 1947; U. of Thessaloniki, ThD 1951. Emp: U. of Thessaloniki, 1951-59 Prof.; U. of Athens, Theol. Faculty, 1959-79 Prof., 1979- Prof. Emeritus; Min. of Educ., Dept. of Relig. Affairs, 1964-68 Gen. Dir.; Acad. of Athens, 1993 Mem. Spec: New Testament. Pub: *Gethsemane, Property of the Evangelist St. John* (1989); *Holy Scripture in the Greek Orthodox Church* (1989); *The History of Interpretation of the Sermon on the Mount: A Historical and Critical Search* (1986); "La 'Chrestotes' de Dieu" in *Memoire de Pape Paul VI* (1979); "Luke the Evangelist as St. Paul's Collaborator" in *Neues Testament und Geschichte: Historishes Geschehen und Deutung im NT, Oscar Cullmann zum 70 Geburtstag* (1972); *The Manuscripts of the Dead Sea* (1961); and others. Awd: Cross of Taxiarches of Order Phoenix 1961; Silver Cross of Ecumenical Patriarchate at the Thousand Years of Mount Athos 1963; Highest Taxiarches, Order of the Crusaders of the Holy Sepulchre 1966; Cross of Taxiarches of Order King George I 1967. Mem: SSNT 1962-. Rec: Philately, gardening. Addr: (h) Ravine St. 5, 115 21 Athens, Greece 7217938.

SIRARD, Léas, b. Bromont, Canada, October 11, 1923, s. of Ernest & Léona (Lamothe). Educ: Angelicum, Rome, Lic. Theol. 1951; Pont. Bibl. Inst., Lic. 1953. Emp: Scholasticat Saint-Sacrement, Montreal, 1954-62 Tchr., 1963- Bibl. & Theol. Res. Spec: New Testament. Pub: "La Parousie de l'Antéchrist, 2 Thess. 2, 3-9" in *Studiorum Paulinorum Congressus Internationalis Catholicus* vol. 2 (1961); "Sacrifices et rites sanglants dans l'Ancien Testament" *Sciences ecclésiastiques* 15/2. Addr: (h) 1330 Ch. Ste-Foy, Quebec, Que. G1S 2N5, Canada 418-527-2555.

SLATER, Thomas B., b. Magnolia, AR, July 28, 1952, s. of Thomas Jefferson & Thelma (Bowie), m. Renea D. Educ: South. Meth. U., Perkins Sch. of Theol., MTh 1978, DMin 1981; U. of Va., MA, Relig. Stud. 1992. Emp: Jackson Theol. Sem., 1980-83 Asst. Prof., Acad. Dean; U. of Ga., 1988- Instr. Spec: New Testament, Apocrypha and Post-biblical Studies. Pub: "The Paraclete as Advocate in the Community of the Beloved Disciple" *Africa*

Theol. Jour. 20 (1991); "Notes on Matthew's Structure" *JBL* 99 (1980); and others. Awd: U. of Va., DuPont Fellow 1984-87. Mem: SBL 1984-92; AAR 1988-89. Rec: Softball, science fiction, Hispanic culture. Addr: (o) U. of Georgia, Dept. of Religion, Peabody Hall, Athens, GA 30602 607-542-5356; (h) 330 Jefferson River Rd., Athens, GA 30607 607-353-3124.

SLAYTON, Joel C., b. Gurdon, AR, July 25, 1948, s. of Joe & Doris (Kissinger), m. Dianne, chil: Joey; Amy. Educ: Bapt. Missionary Assoc. Theol. Sem., MDiv 1973; Mid-Amer. Bapt. Theol. Sem., ThD 1982. Spec: Hebrew Bible, Semitic Languages, Texts and Epigraphy, Egyptology. Pub: *The Significance of the Papyrus Discoveries to Old Testament Text* (U. Microfilms, 1983); *ABD*, contb. (1992). Mem: Amer Soc. Papyrologists. Rec: Egyptology. Addr: (o) Vice President for Academic Affairs, 1501 College Ave., Conway, AR 72032 501-329-6872; (h) 3 Rockwood, Conway, AR 72072 501-327-5158.

SLOYAN, Gerard S., b. New York, NY, December 13, 1919, s. of Jerome & Marie (Kelley). Educ: Cath. U. of Amer., STL 1944, PhD 1948. Emp: Cath. U. of Amer., 1950-67 Prof., Head, Dept. of Relig.; Temple U., 1967- Prof.; *JES* 1968- Ed. Bd.; *Horizons*, 1974- Ed. Bd. Spec: New Testament, Apocrypha and Post-biblical Studies. Pub: *What Are They Saying About John?* (Paulist, 1991); *Jesus, Redeemer and Divine Word* (Glazier, 1989); *John* (John Knox, 1988); "Jewish Ritual of the First Century BC and Christian Sacramental Behavior" *BTB* 15/3 (1985); *A[n Exegetical] Comm. on the New Lectionary* (Paulist, 1975); and others. Mem: CBA 1951-; CTSA 1951-; SBL 1967-. Addr: (o) Temple U., Dept. of Religion, Philadelphia, PA 19122 215-204-7210; (h) 2313 Sansom St., Philadelphia, PA 19103 215-561-3126.

SLY, Dorothy I., b. ON, Canada, February 2, 1933, d. of Douglas Cameron & Margaret Winter (Mitchell), m. Douglas M, chil: Gordon; Gregory; Monty; Kenneth; Marnie. Educ: U. of Manitoba, BA 1954, BPaed 1955, MA, Relig. Stud. 1981; McMaster U., PhD, Relig. Stud. 1987. Emp: U. of Windsor, 1989- Assoc. Prof., Relig. Stud. Spec: New Testament. Pub: "I Peter Seen in the Light of Philo and Josephus" *JBL* 110/2 (1991); "Philo's Practical Application of Dikaiosyne" in *SBL 1991 Seminar Papers*; "Changes in the Perception of the Offence in Num 25:1" *Proc. of the East. Great Lakes & MidW Bibl. Soc.* (1991); *Philo's Perception of Women*, Brown Judaic Ser. 209 (Scholars, 1990); and others. Mem: CSBS; AAR; SBL. Addr: (o) U. of Windsor, Dept. of Religious Studies, Windsor, ON N9B 3P4, Canada 519-253-4232; (h) 5800 Ninth St., Windsor, ON N9H 1P2, Canada 519-250-0369.

SMALLEY, Stephen S., b. London, England, May 11, 1931, s. of Arthur Thomas & May Elizabeth, m. Susan Jane, chil: Jovian James

Thomas; Evelyn Mary Michelle. Educ: Jesus Coll., England, BA 1955, MA 1958, PhD 1979; Eden Theol. Sem., BD 1957; Ridley Hall, England, Priest 1959. Emp: U. of Ibadan, Nigeria, 1963-69 Lect.; U. of Manchester, 1970-77 Lect.; Coventry Cathedral, 1977-86 Canon Precentor, 1986 Vice-Provost; Chester Cathedral, 1987- Dean. Spec: New Testament. Pub: "Keeping Up With Recent Studies XII. St. John's Gospel" *ExpTim* 97 (1985-86); *John: Evangelist and Interpreter* (Paternoster, 1978); "Redaction Criticism" in *New Testament Interpretation* (Paternoster, 1977); *1,2,3 John* (Word, 1984); *Christ and Spirit in the New Testament* Festschrift C.F.D. Moule, ed., contb. (Cambridge U.P., 1973); "Spirit, Kingdom and Prayer in Luke-Acts" *NT* 15 (1973); "Diversity and Development in John" *NTS* 17 (1970-71); "The Theatre of Parousia" *SJT* 17 (1964); and others. Awd: U. of Manchester, Manson Memorial Lect. 1986. Mem: SNTS 1965-. Rec: Family, lit., music, drama. Addr: (o) 1 Abbey Sq., Chester, CH1 2HU, England 0244-324756; (h) 7 Abbey St., Chester, CH1 2JF, England 0244-351380.

SMEND, Rudolf, b. Berlin, Germany, October 17, 1932, s. of Rudolf & Gisela (Hubner), m. Dagmar (Erlbruch). Educ: Basel U., ThD 1958. Emp: Berlin Kirchliche Hochschule, 1963-65 Prof.; Munster U., 1965-71 Prof.; Gottingen U., 1971- Prof.; *VT*, 1975- Co-Ed.; FRLANT, 1983- Co-Ed. Spec: Hebrew Bible. Pub: *Gesammelte Studien*, vol. 1-3 (1986-1991); *Deutsche Alttestamentler in drei Jahrhunderten* (Vandenhoek & Ruprecht, 1989); *Die Entstehung des Alten Testaments* (Kohlhammer, 1978, 1989); and others. Awd: St. Andrews U., DD 1979. Mem: Wissenschaftliche Gesellschaft fuer Theol. 1974-; Akademie der Wissenschaffen zu Gottingen 1974-; SBL 1979-; SOTS 1979-. Addr: (o) Theologicum, Platz der Gottingen, Sieben 2, D-3400 Gottingen, Germany 0551-397118; (h) Thomas-Dehler-Wig 6, D-3400 Gottingen, Germany 0551-23332.

SMICK, Elmer B., b. Baltimore, MD, July 10, 1921, s. of Marie & Frank, m. Jane, chil: Peter; Karen; Theodore; Rebecca. Educ: Faith Theol. Sem., ThB 1947, STM 1948; Dropsie Coll., PhD 1951. Emp: Shelton Coll., 1949-56 Prof.; Covenant Coll. & Theol. Sem., 1956-71 Prof.; Near East Sch. of Arch., Jerusalem, 1963 Vis. Lect.; Gordon-Conwell Theol. Sem., 1971-91 Prof., 1991- Prof. Emeritus, OT; Reformed Theol. Sem., 1991- Vis. Prof. Spec: Archaeology, Hebrew Bible, Mesopotamian Studies, Semitic Languages, Texts and Epigraphy, Egyptology. Pub: "Old Testament Theology, The Historio-Genetic Method" *JETS* (1983); *Archaeology of the Jordan Valley* (Baker, 1973); "The Jordan of Jericho" in *Orient and Occident* (1973); "Cuneiform Selections" in *Ugaritic Textbook* (1965); and others. Mem: SBL 1951-; AOS 1951-; IBR 1972-. Rec: Fishing. Addr: (o) Gordon-Conwell Theological Seminary, S Hamilton, MA 01982 617-468-7111; (h) 84 Old Cart Rd., S Hamilton, MA 01982 617-468-3603.

SMITH, Clyde Curry, b. Hamilton, OH, December 16, 1929, s. of Clyde & Ethel, m. Ellen, chil: Harald; Karen. Educ: Miami U., AB, MS 1951; U. of Chicago, DB 1954, MA 1961, PhD 1968. Emp: U. of Manitoba, St. John's Coll., 1958-63 Asst. Prof.; Brandeis U., 1963-65 Instr.; U. of Wis., 1965-1990 Prof., 1990-Emeritus; Culver Stockton Coll., 1990 Vis. Prof.; U. Newcastle-upon-Tyre, England, 1992-93 Vis. Prof. Spec: Hebrew Bible, Mesopotamian Studies, New Testament, Semitic Languages, Texts and Epigraphy, Apocrypha and Post-biblical Studies. Pub: *New Twentieth Century Ency. of Religious Knowledge*, contb. (Baker, 1991), *Ency. of Early Christianity*, contb. (Garland, 1990); *Great Lives from History: Ancient and Medieval Series*, contb. (Salem, 1988); *Who Was Who in Assyriology: A Provisional Biobibliographical Index* (U. of Wis., 1978); "Jehu and the Black Obelisk of Shalmaneser III" in *Scripture in History and Theology: Essays in Honor of John Loert Rybarsdam* (Pickwick, 1977); and others. Mem: BSA, Iraq; Oriental Inst.; NAPS; Hellenic Soc. Rec: Outer space, dinosaurs, theater. Addr: (h) 939 W Maple St., River Falls, WI 54022 715-425-6383.

SMITH, D. Moody, b. Murfreesboro, TN, November 20, 1931, s. of Dwight Moody, Sr. & Nellie (Beckwith), m. Jane (Allen), chil: Cynthia Beckwith; Catherine (Meynardie); David Burton; John Allen. Educ: Davidson Coll., BA 1954; Duke U., BD 1957; Yale U., MA 1958, PhD 1961. Emp: Meth. Theol. Sch., 1960-65 Prof.; Duke U. Div. Sch., 1965- George Washington Ivey Prof. of NT. Spec: New Testament. Pub: *John Among the Gospels: The Relationship in 20th-Century Research* (Fortress, 1992); "Johannine Studies" in *The New Testament and Its Modern Interpreters* (Scholars, 1989); *Anatomy of the New Testament: A Guide to Its Structure and Meaning*, co-auth. (Macmillan, 1988); "The Pauline Literature" in *It is Written: Scripture Citing Scripture: Essays in Honour of Barnabas Lindars* (Cambridge U.P., 1988); *Johannine Christianity: Essays on its Setting, Sources, and Theology* (U. of S.C., 1984); "The Presentation of Jesus in the Fourth Gospel" *Interpretation* 31 (1977); "Johannine Christianity: Some Reflections on its Character and Delineation" *NTS* 21 (1975); "The Historical Jesus in Paul Tillich's Christology" *JR* 46 (1966); *The Composition and Order of the Fourth Gospel: Bultmann's Literary Theory* (Yale U.P., 1965); and others. Awd: Phi Beta Kappa 1953; Lilly Postdoc. Fellow. 1963-64; J.S. Guggenheim Fellow. 1970-71; Davidson Coll., Dr. of Letters, Honoris Causa 1990; Ctr. of Theol. Inquiry 1990-91. Mem: SBL 1957-; SNTS 1966-; Amer. Theol. Soc. 1982-. Addr: (o) Duke U., Box 33 Divinity, Durham, NC 27706 919-660-3466; (h) 2728 Spencer St., Durham, NC 27705 919-489-9574.

SMITH, David W., b. White Plains, NY, s. of A.V. & Katherine. Educ: U. of Thomas Aquinas in the City, Rome, STL 1968, STD 1970; Pont. Bibl. Commn., Rome, SSB 1974, SSL 1975. Emp: U. of St. Thomas, 1970- Assoc. Prof. Spec: New Testament. Pub: Article in *Guidebook for Bible Study* (1981); *Wisdom Christology in the Synoptic Gospels* (1970); and others. Mem: SBL 1970-; CBA 1970-. Rec: Violin, canoeing. Addr: (o) U. of St. Thomas, Mail # 4137, St. Paul, MN 55105-1096.

SMITH, Dennis E., b. Conroe, Texas, December 1, 1944, m. Barbara McBride-Smith, chil: Adam. Educ: Abilene Christian U., BA 1967, MA 1969; Princeton Theol. Sem., MDiv 1972; Harvard U. Div. Sch., ThD 1980. Emp: Princeton Theol. Sem., 1979-81 Asst. Prof.; Okl. State U., 1981-86 Asst. Prof.; Phillips Grad. Sem., 1986- Assoc. Prof. Excv: Caesarea Maritima, 1974, 1976 Area Supr. Spec: Archaeology, New Testament. Pub: "The Messianic Banquet Reconsidered" *The Future of Early Christianity: Essays in Honor of Helmut Koester* (Fortress, 1991); *Many Tables: The Eucharist in the New Testament and Liturgy Today*, co-auth. (SCM & TPI, 1990); *Semeia 52: How Gospels Begin*, ed. (Scholars, 1990); "Table Fellowship as a Literary Motif in the Gospel of Luke" *JBL* (1987); "Field H, 1973 and 1974" in *The Joint Expedition to Caesarea Maritima: Preliminary Reports in Microfiche* (Drew U., 1987); "Meals and Morality in Paul and His World" *SBL 1981 Seminar Papers* (Scholars, 1981); "The Egyptian Cults at Corinth" *HTR* (1977); and others. Mem: AAR; SBL; ASOR, Assoc. Trustee 1988-90. Rec: Camping, backpacking. Addr: (o) Phillips Graduate Seminary, Enid Campus, Box 2335, U. Station, Enid, OK 73702 405-237-4433; (h) Route 2, Box 132, Stillwater, OK 74075 405-624-1155.

SMITH, Mark S., b. Paris, France, Dec. 6, 1955, s. of Donald and Mary Elizabeth (Reichert), m. Elizabeth (Bloch), chil: Benjamin. Educ: Cath. U. of Amer., MA 1978; Harvard Div. Sch., MTS 1980; Yale U., MA 1982, MPhil 1983, PhD 1985. Emp: St. Paul Sem., 1984-86 Asst. Prof., OT; Yale U., 1986- Prof., NW Semitic Lang. & Lit. Spec: Hebrew Bible, Semitic Languages, Texts and Epigraphy. Pub: "Interpreting the Baal Cycle" *UF* 18 (1986); "The Magic of Kothar Wa-Hasis, the Ugaritic Craftsman God, in KTU 1.6 VI 49-50" *RB* 91 (1984); "The 'Son of Man' in Ugaritic" *CBQ* 45 (1983); and others. Mem: CBA; SBL; AOS. Addr: (o) Yale U., Dept. of Near Eastern Language and Literature, PO Box 1504A, Yale Station, New Haven, CT 06520 203-432-2944.

SMITH, Philip E. L., b. Fortune, Canada, August 12, 1927, s. of Frederick & Alice (Lake), m. Fumiko (Ikawa), chil: Douglas. Educ: Harvard U., AM 1957, PhD 1962. Emp: U. of Toronto, 1961-66 Assoc. Prof.; U. of Montreal, 1966- Prof. Excv: Iraq, 1957; Egypt, 1962-63; Iran, 1965, 1967, 1969, 1971, 1974, 1977. Spec: Archaeology, Mesopotamian Studies. Pub:

"Architectural Innovation and Experimentation at Ganj Dareh, Iran" *World Arch.* (1990); *Palaeolithic Archaeology in Iran* (Amer. Inst. Iranian Stud., 1986); "The Late Palaeolithic and Epipalaeolithic of Northern Africa" in *The Cambridge History of Africa* vol. 1 (1982); "The Evolution of Early Agriculture and Culture in Greater Mesopotamia" in *Population Growth: Anthropological Implications* (1972); "Changes in Population Pressure in Archaeological Explanation" *World Arch.* (1972); and others. Awd: Memorial U. of Newfoundland, DLitt. Mem: Canadian Soc. for Arch. Abroad, Pres. 1971-73; Amer. Anthrop. Assn. 1958-; Intl. Union Anthrop. & Ethnological Sci. Rec: Reading. Addr: (o) U. de Montreal, Dep. d'Anthropologie, C.P. 6128, Succ. A, Montreal, Quebec, Canada 514-343-6574; (h) 3955 Ramezay Ave., Montreal, Que. H3Y 3K3, Canada 514-935-6045.

SMITH, Robert H., b. McAlester, OK, February 13, 1931, s. of V. Hubert & Bobbie, m. Geraldine, chil: Vanessa. Educ: Yale Div. Sch., BD 1955; Yale Grad. Sch., PhD 1960. Emp: Coll. of Wooster, 1960- Fox Prof. of Relig. Stud., Chair, Dept. of Relig. Stud., Arch. Program, Pella, Jordan, Dir.; Natl. Geog. Soc., 1985 Grosvenor Lect. Excv: Khirbet Kufin, Jordan, 1960 Dir.; Pella, Jordan, 1967 Dir., 1979- Co-dir. Spec: Archaeology, New Testament. Pub: "The Floruit of Hellenism in the Southern Levant" *Levant* 22 (1990); *Pella of the Decapolis*, vol. 1-2 (Coll. of Wooster, 1973, 1989); "Lake Beisan and the Prehistoric Settlement of the Jordan Valley" *Paléorient* 12 (1986); "Ethics in Field Archaeology" *Jour. of Field Arch.* 1 (1974-75); "An Early Roman Sarcophagus of Palestine and Its School" *PEQ* 105 (1973); "The Household Lamps of Palestine" *BA* 27, 29 (1964, 1966); *Excavations in the Cemetery at Khirbet Kufin, Palestine*, Colt Arch. Inst. Mon. Ser. 1 (1962); and others. Mem: Soc. of Prof. Arch.; SBL; ASOR; ACOR, Jordan. Rec: American local history. Addr: (o) The College of Wooster, Wooster, OH 44691 216-263-2347; (h) 1117 Quinby Ave., Wooster, OH 44691 216-264-7063.

SNELL, Daniel C., b. Jackson, MI, October 1, 1947, s. of Iva & Clair. Educ: Yale U., PhD 1975. Emp: Conn. Coll., 1977-78 Asst. Prof.; Barnard Coll., 1978-80 Asst. Prof.; Gustavus Adolphus Coll., 1981-82 Asst. Prof.; Natl. Mus., Syria, 1982-83 Fulbright Res.; U. of Okla., 1983- Prof. Excv: Tell Leilan, Syria, 1980 Epigrapher, Site Supr.; Tell el-Qitar, Syria, 1983-87 Epigrapher, Site Supr. Spec: Hebrew Bible, Mesopotamian Studies. Pub: *Economic Texts From Sumer*, co-auth., Yale Oriental Ser., Babylonian Texts 18 (Yale U.P., 1991); "Taking Souls in Proverbs XI 30" *VT* 33 (1983); *Ledgers and Prices* (1982); *A Workbook of Cuneiform Signs* (Undena, 1979, 1982); "Why Is There Aramaic in the Bible?" *JSOT* 18 (1980); and others. Mem: SBL 1975-; AOS 1973-. Addr: (o) U. of Oklahoma, Dept. of History, 455 W Lindsey, Norman, OK 73019 405-325-6002.

SNODGRASS, Klyne R., b. Kingsport, TN, December 28, 1944, s. of C. Sidney & Wanda (Lauderback), m. Phyllis (Parks), chil: Nathan; Valerie. Educ: Trinity Evang. Div. Sch., MDiv (magna cum laude) 1969; U. of St. Andrews, Scotland, PhD 1973. Emp: Georgetown Coll., 1973-74 Instr.; N Park Theol. Sem., 1974- Prof., Bibl. Lit. Spec: New Testament. Pub: "The Use of the Old Testament in the New Testament" in *New Testament Criticism and Interpretation* (Zondervan, 1991); *Between Two Truths: Living with Biblical Tensions* (Zondervan, 1990); "Matthew and the Law" in *SBL 1988 Seminar Papers* (Scholars, 1988); "Spheres of Influence: A Possible Solution to the Problem of Paul and the Law" *JSNT* 32 (1988); "Justification by Grace to the Doers: An Analysis of the Place of Romans 2 in the Theology of Paul" *NTS* (1986); *The Parable of Wicked Tenants* (J.C.B. Mohr, 1983); "Western Non-Interpolations" *JBL* 91 (1972); and others. Mem: SBL 1973-; IBR 1974-; SNTS 1984-. Rec: Nature, horseback riding. Addr: (o) North Park Theological Sem., 3225 W Foster Ave., Chicago, IL 60625-4987 312-478-2696; (h) 6147 N Avers, Chicago, IL 60659 312-463-3365.

SNYDER, Barbara W., b. Berkeley, CA, February 6, 1953, d. of Frank B. Wootten, Jr., & Virginia B., m. Steven J. Snyder. Educ: U. of Calif., Riverside, BA 1976; Gordon-Conwell Theol. Sem., MDiv 1982; U. of Calif., Berkeley, with the Grad. Theol. Union, PhD 1991. Emp: Gordon-Conwell Theol. Sem., 1985-89 Adj. Prof., Bibl. Stud.; Ctr. for Urban Min. Educ., 1985-89 Adj. Prof., Bibl. Stud.; Evang. Sch. of Theol., 1989- Assoc. Prof., NT. Spec: Hebrew Bible, New Testament. Pub: "Triple-Form and Space/Time Transitions: Literary Structuring Devices in the Apocalypse" in *SBL 1991 Seminar Papers* 30 (1991); "How Millennial is the Millennium? A Study in the Background of the 1000 Years in Revelation 20" *Evang. Jour.* 9 (1991); *Combat Myth in the Apocalypse: The Liturgy of the Day of the Lord and the Dedication of the Heavenly Temple* (1991). Awd: Grad. Theol. Union grant 1985. Mem: SBL 1985-. Rec: Licensed pilot, swimming, hiking. Addr: (o) Evangelical School of Theology, 121 South College St., Myerstown, PA 17067 717-866-5775; (h) 108 South Locust St., Myerstown, PA 17067 717-866-7876.

SNYDER, Graydon F., b. Peru, IN, April 30, 1930, s. of Clayton & Irene (Fisher), m. Lois (Horning), chil: Jonathan; Anna; Stephen. Educ: Bethany Theol. Sem., MDiv 1954; Princeton Theol. Sem., ThD 1961. Emp: Bethany Theol. Sem., 1959-85 Wieand Prof. of NT Stud.; Chicago Theol. Sem., 1986- Prof., NT; Garrett Theol. Sem., Lutheran Sch. of Theol. at Chicago, Evangelical Theol. Sem., U. of Zimbabwe, Vis. Prof. Spec: Archaeology, New Testament. Pub: *1 Corinthians* (Mercer, 1992); *Ante Pacem* (Mercer, 1985); "John 13:16 and the Anti-Petrinism of the Johannine Tradition" *Bibl. Res.* (1971); "Survey and New Thesis' on the Bones of St. Peter" *BA* (1969); "The *Tobspruch* in the New Testament" *NTS* 23; and

others. Mem: SBL; CSBR, Pres. 1969-70; SNTS. Rec: Photography, racquetball. Addr: (o) Chicago Theological Seminary, 5757 S University Ave., Chicago, IL 60637 312-752-5757.

SOARES-PRABHU, George M., b. Igatpuri, Maharashtra, India, November 17, 1929, s. of Alexander & Georgina (Da Rocha Pinto). Educ: Pont. Athanaeum, India, MTh 1962; Pont. Bibl. Inst., Rome, SSL (summa cum laude) 1966; Lyon-Fourviere, Jesuit Fac., STD (summa cum laude) 1969. Emp: Pont. Athanaeum, India, 1969- Prof., NT; *Jeevadhara,* 1973- Ed. Bd.; *Biblebhashyam,* 1975- Ed. Bd.; Pont. Bibl. Inst., Rome, 1983-84 Vis. Prof. Spec: New Testament. Pub: *Wir werden bei ihm wohnen: Das Johannesevangelium in indischer Detung,* ed. (1984); *The Formula Quotations in the Infancy Narrative of Matthew,* Analecta Biblica 63, (1976); and others. Mem: Indian Theol. Assn. 1974-; SNTS 1977-; Ecumenical Assn. of Third World Theol. 1989-. Addr: (o) DeNobili College, Pune 411014, India.

SOESILO, Daud H., b. Surabaya, Indonesia, August 27, 1952, s. of Rev. H. Hadi, m. Vivian (Andriani), chil: Davi Rafael; Daniel Andi. Educ: Inst. of Tchr. Training Malang, Indonesia, BA 1973, Drs 1976; Asbury Theol. Sem., MDiv 1980; Vanderbilt U., DMin 1981; Union Theol. Sem., PhD 1988. Emp: SE Asia Bible Sem., 1975-77 Vis. Lect.; Indonesian Bible Soc., 1981-83 Trans. Adv., Sec.; Union Theol. Sem., 1985-87 Teaching Asst.; United Bible Soc. Asia-Pacific Reg., 1988- Trans. Cons.; Sabah Theol. Sem., Malaysia, 1991- Vis. Lect. Spec: Hebrew Bible. Pub: "Translating the Poetic Sections of Daniel 1-6" *BT* 41/4 (1990); *Mengenal Alkitab Anda* (Indonesian Bible Soc., 1984, 1990); "Memahami Buku Daniel" *Forum Biblika* 1/1 (1991); "Belshazzar's Scales: Towards Achieving a Balanced Translation of Daniel 5" *BT* 40/4 (1989); "The Story Line in Translating Philemon" *BT* 34/4 (1983). Mem: SBL 1984-. Rec: Photography. Addr: (o) U.B.S. Translations Center, Jalan Anggrek Merpati 12, Malang, E. Java 65141, Indonesia 62-341-44129; (h) Jalan Sartono SH. 2, Malang 65148, Indonesia 62-341-66105.

SOHN, Seock-Tae, b. Korea, August 26, 1945, s. of Jeon-kee Sohn, m. Hee-Sook (Koh), chil: Sooyun; Sunyong. Educ: Korea U., BS 1969; Westminster Theol. Sem., MAR 1981, MDiv 1982; N.Y. U., PhD 1986. Emp: Alliance Theol. Sem., 1983-85 Adj. Prof.; Asia United Theol. Coll., Korea, 1986-90 Asst. Prof., OT; Reformed Theol. Sem., Korea, 1991- Assoc. Prof., OT. Excv: Bethsaida, 1990 staff. Spec: Hebrew Bible. Pub: *The Divine Election of Israel* (Eerdmans, 1991); "Israel, the Son of Yahweh" *ACTS Theol. Jour.* 3 (1988). Mem: SBL; Evang. Theol. Assn., Korea. Addr: (o) Reformed Theological Seminary, 120-3 Chungdam Dong, Gangnam Gu, Seoul 135-100, Korea 02-544-6697; (h) A-103 Hanseong Apt., Yoido dong, Seoul 150-010, Korea 02-783-4605.

SONSINO, Rifat, b. Turkey, September 4, 1938, s. of Albert, m. Ines, chil: Daniel; Deborah. Educ: Istanbul U., LLB 1959; HUC-Jewish Inst. of Relig., MA 1966; U. of Pa., PhD 1975. Emp: Main Line Reform Temple, Wynnewood, Pa. 1969-75; N Shore Cong. Israel, Glencoe, Ill. 1975-80; Temple Beth Shalom, Needham, Mass. 1980-. Spec: Hebrew Bible. Pub: "Characteristics of Biblical Law" *Judaism* 33/1 (1989); "The Bible and Politics" *Judaism* 32/1 (1983); *Motive Clauses in Hebrew Law,* SBL Diss. Ser. 45 (Scholars, 1980); "Towards a Definition of Law in the Pentateuch" *Jour. of Reform Judaism* (1979); and others. Mem: SBL; Cen. Conf. of Amer. Rabbis; AJS. Addr: (o) Temple Beth Shalom, Needham, MA 02194 617-444-0077.

SORDI, Marta, b. Livorno, November 18, 1925, d. of Mario & Anna Maria (Bernardini). Educ: U. of Milano, Laurea in Lettere 1948; Libera docenza, Greek Hist. 1957. Emp: Messina U., 1962-67; Bologna U., 1967-70; Cath. U. of Milan, 1970- Prof., Greek & Roman Hist. Spec: New Testament. Pub: "Tolleranza e intolleranza nel mondo antico" in *La tolleranza religiosa* (1991); "Cristianesimo e paganesimo dopo Costantino" in *L'impero romano-cristiano* (1991); "La tradizione dell'inventio crucis in Ambrogio e in Rufino" *RSCI* 44 (1990); *I Cristiani nell'impero romano* (1983, 1990); "I rapporti fra Ambrogio e il panegirista Pacato" *RIL* 122 (1989); "La lettera di Ambrogio a Studio" in *Polyanthema* (1989); *Paolo a Filemone, o della schiavitù* (1987); *Il cristianesimo e Roma* (1965); and others. Mem: Inst. di Studi Etruschi 1969-; Accademia Ist. Lombardo di Sci. e Lettere 1970-; Pont. Acad. Romana di Arch. 1985-. Rec: Detective stories. Addr: (o) U. Cattolica, Largo Gemelli, 1 Milano, Italy 72342364; (h) Viale E. Caldara 22, 20122 Milano, Italy 55195578.

SPALINGER, Anthony J., b. New York, NY, November 23, 1947, s. of Harold & Elizabeth, m. Gretchen (Altman Lutz). Educ: CUNY, Queens College, BA 1968; Yale U., MPh 1972, PhD 1973. Emp: U. of Calif., 1975-76 Lect.; Yale U., 1976-81, Lect.; U. of Auckland, Auckland, New Zealand, 1981-84 Sr. Lect. Excv: Giza Mastabas, Egypt, 1972 Site Supr.; Malqata, Karnak, 1974-75 Site Supr. Spec: Egyptology. Pub: *Three Studies on Egyptian Feasts* (Halgo, 1992); "A Redistributive Pattern from Assiut" *JAOS* 105 (1985); "The Historical Implications of the Year 9 Campaign of Amenophis II" *Jour. of the Soc. for the Study of Egyptian Antiquities* 11 (1983); *Aspects of the Military Documents of the Ancient Egyptians* (Yale U.P., 1982); "Remarks on the Family of Queen H'.s-nbw..." *Revue d'Egyptolgie* 22 (1980); "The Northern Wars of Seti I" *Jour. of the Amer. Res. Ctr. in Egypt* 16 (1979); and others. Mem: Soc. Study of Egyptian Antiq.; Egypt Exploration Soc.; Amer. Res. Ctr. Egypt. Addr: (o) U. of Aukland, Dept. of Classics & Ancient History, Auckland, New Zealand 3737-599; (h)

6 Rautangi Rd., Mt. Eden, Auckland, New Zealand 6387-480.

SPENCER, Aida Besancon, b. Dominican Republic, January 2, 1947, d. of Frederick & Aida (Besancon), m. William D., chil: Stephen. Educ: Princeton Theol. Sem., MDiv 1973, ThM 1975; South. Bapt. Theol. Sem., PhD 1982. Emp: N.Y. Theol. Sem., 1974-76 Adj. Prof.; King's Coll., 1976-78; Gordon-Conwell Theol. Sem., 1982- Prof. Spec: New Testament. Pub: *Prayer Life of Jesus* (1990); *2 Corinthians* (1989); "The Truly Spiritual in Paul: Biblical Background on 1 Cor. 2:6-16" in *Conflict and Context: Hermeneutics in the Americas* (1986); "Caesarea-by-the-Sea" in *Major Cities of the Biblical World* (1985); *Paul's Literary Style* (1984); "The Wise Fool [And the Foolish Wise]: A Study of Irony in Paul" *NT* 23 (1981); and others. Mem: SBL 1978-; ETS 1973-. Rec: Music, bicycling, fiction. Addr: (o) Gordon-Conwell Theological Seminary, S Hamilton, MA 01982 508-468-7111; (h) 10 Maple St., S Hamilton, MA 01982 508-468-4318.

SPENCER, F. Scott, b. San Antonio, TX, October 22, 1956, s. of Loyd Count & Olga Marie, m. Janet Marie, chil: Lauren Michael; Meredith Leigh. Educ: U. of Tex. at San Antonio, BA (summa cum laude) 1976; SW Bapt. Theol. Sem., MDiv 1979; Westminster Theol. Sem., ThM 1985; U. of Durham, England, PhD 1989. Emp: Wingate Coll., 1989-92 Asst. Prof., Relig. Spec: New Testament. Pub: *The Portrait of Philip in Acts: A Study of Roles and Relations,* JSNTSup 67 (Sheffield, 1992); "Beyond Trench's Study of Synonyms" *ExpTim* 99 (1988); "2 Chronicles 28:5-15 and the Parable of the Good Samaritan" *WTJ* 46 (1984). Awd: Tyndale Fellow. 1987-88. Mem: SBL 1987-; NABPR 1988-; CBA 1991-. Rec: Modern fiction, guitar, tennis. Addr: (o) Wingate College, PO Box 2476, Wingate, NC 28174 704-233-8069; (h) 3215 Karen Ln., Monroe, NC 28110 704-282-0071.

SPENCER, John R., b. Long Beach, CA, January 19, 1945, s. of Frank & Betty, m. Claudia (Avitabile), chil: Beth; Sandra. Educ: Pacific Sch. of Relig., BD, MA 1970; U. of Chicago, MA 1973, PhD 1980. Emp: St. Xavier Coll., 1973 Lect.; Okla. City U., 1975-77 Asst. Prof.; John Carroll U., 1977- Assoc. Prof., 1990- Hon. Prog. Dir. Excv: Tell el-Hesi, Israel, 1983 Area Supr.; Ashkelon, Israel, 1985, 1987, 1989 Area Supr. Spec: Archaeology, Hebrew Bible. Pub: *ABD,* contb. (Doubleday, 1992); "Whither the Bible and Archaeology?" in *Proc. of East. Great Lakes & MidW Bibl. Soc.* 9 (1989); *Illustrated Dict. and Concordance of the Bible,* contb. (Macmillan, 1986); "The Tasks of the Levites: *smr* and *sb*" *ZAW* 96 (1984); *In the Shelter of Elyon,* ed., contb. (JSOT, 1984). Awd: Albright Inst. of Arch. Res., Jerusalem, Ann. Prof. 1985; NEH Summer Res. Grant 1986; John Carrol U., Disting. Fac. Awd. 1991. Mem: SBL 1971-; ASOR 1973-; IES 1983-; AIA 1984-;

Albright Inst. of Arch. Res. Rec: Music, camping. Addr: (o) John Carroll U., Dept. of Religious Studies, University Heights, OH 44118 216-397-4705.

SPENDER, Robert D., b. Waterbury, CT, November 17, 1945, s. of Donald Louise & Grace Towle, m. Aurie A., chil: David D.; Deborah J.; Joshua J. Educ: Barrington Coll., BA 1967; Trinity Evang. Div. Sch., MA 1970; Dropsie U., PhD 1976. Emp: West Woods Christian Acad., 1975-78 Founder, Headmaster; Barrington Coll., 1982-85 Asst. Prof., Bibl. Stud.; The King's Coll., 1985- Prof. & Chair, Dept. of Relig. & Phil. Pub: Articles in *Baker Ency. of the Bible* (Baker, 1988); and others. Mem: ETS 1975-; NEAS 1975-; SBL 1979-. Rec: Computers, gardening, wildflowers. Addr: (o) The King's College, Briarcliff Manor, NY 10537 914-944-5535; (h) 35 Oriole St., Lk. Peekskill, NY 10537 914-528-0152.

SPINA, Frank A., b. Long Beach, CA, September 30, 1943, s. of Frank & Mary (Levato), m. Betty M. (Ehmann), chil: Frank Anthony, II; Stephanie Marie. Educ: Greenville Coll., BA, Phil. & Relig. 1965; Asbury Theol. Sem., MDiv 1968; U. of Mich., MA 1970, PhD, Near East. Stud. 1977. Emp: Seattle Pacific U., 1973- Prof., OT. Spec: Hebrew Bible. Pub: "I-II Samuel" in *Asbury Bible Comm.* (Zondervan, 1992); "A Prophet's 'Pregnant Pause': Samuel's Silence in the Ark Narrative (1 Sam 4:1-7:2)" *Horizons In Bibl. Theol.* 13/1 (1991); "Qoheleth and the Reformation of Wisdom" in *The Quest for the Kingdom of God: Essays in Honor of George E. Mendenhall*, co-ed. (Eisenbrauns, 1983); "Israelites as Gerim, 'Sojourners,' in Historical and Sociological Perspective" in *The Word of the Lord Shall Go Forth: Essays in Honor of David Noel Freedman in Celebration of His Sixtieth Birthday* (Eisenbrauns, 1983); and others. Mem: AAR; SBL, Pres., Pacific NW reg., 1985-86; WTS; ASOR. Rec: Biking, weight lifting, softball umpiring, baseball. Addr: (o) Seattle Pacific U., School of Religion, Seattle, WA 98119 206-281-2161; (h) 414 W Newell, Seattle, WA 98119 206-284-8289.

SPIVEY, Robert A., b. Suffolk, VA, May 25, 1931, s. of Joseph Atwood & Wortley (Roberts), m. Martha (Crocker), chil: Hope Crocker (Stephenson); Matthew Lee; Paul Atwood. Educ: Duke U., BA 1953; Union Theol. Sem., BD 1956; Yale U., MA 1958, PhD 1962. Emp: Williams Coll., 1960-64 Asst. Prof.; Fla. State U., 1964-78 Prof., Relig.; *JAAR,* 1969-72 Ed. Bd.; Randolph-Macon Woman's Coll., 1978-88 Pres., Prof. of Relig.; Va. Found. for Independent Coll., 1988-Pres. Spec: New Testament, Apocrypha and Post-biblical Studies. Pub: *Anatomy of the New Testament*, co-auth. (Macmillan, 1988); "Structuralism and Biblical Studies: The Uninvited Guest" *Interpretation* (1974); *The Good Servant: Guide to First Timothy* (1971); *A Guide to the Bible Reader*, co-auth. (Bruce, 1970); and

others. Awd: Woodrow Wilson Grad. Fellow. 1953; Danforth Grad. Fellow. 1953-60; Fulbright Schol. 1956. Mem: SBL 1960-; AAR 1960-, Exec. Dir. 1972-75; SNTS 1976-. Rec: Tennis. Addr: (o) Virginia Foundation for Independent Colleges, 8010 Ridge Rd., Richmond, VA 23229 804-288-6609; (h) 720 Lakewater Dr., Richmond, VA 23229 804-740-0305.

SPRINKLE, Joe M., b. Oklahoma City, OK, August 18, 1953, s. of Joseph M. & Verna, m. Christilee (Keller), chil: Rebecca; Tamara. Educ: U. of Okla., BS 1976; Trinity Evang. Div. Sch., MDiv (summa cum laude), Bibl. & Pastoral Stud. 1982; HUC—Jewish Inst. of Relig., MPhil 1987, PhD, Hebraic & Cognate Stud. 1991. Emp: Temple Bible Coll., 1985-86 Instr.; HUC—Jewish Inst. of Relig., 1985-86 Teaching Asst., Tutor; Wright State U., 1986-87, Adj. Instr., Relig.; Toccoa Falls Coll., 1988-91 Instr., 1991- Asst. Prof., OT. Spec: Hebrew Bible, Mesopotamian Studies, Semitic Languages, Texts and Epigraphy. Pub: "Literary Approaches to the Old Testament: A Survey of Recent Scholarship" *JETS* 32/3 (1989). Awd: Dr. David Lefkowitz Interfaith Fellow. 1985-87; Workum Found., Fellow. 1983-85. Mem: SBL; ETS. Rec: Hiking, biking, camping, class. music, enjoying children. Addr: (o) Toccoa Falls College, PO Box 800236, Toccoa Falls, GA 30598 706-886-6831; (h) 116 Poplar St., Toccoa, GA 30577 706-886-5039.

SQUIRES, John T., b. Sydney, Australia, April 15, 1954, s. of John & Joan, chil: Erin; Mitchell; Meg. Educ: Sydney U., BA 1976, BD 1980; Yale U., MA 1984, PhD 1987. Emp: Uniting Ch. in Australia, 1981-83, 1988-90 Min.; Sydney U., 1982-83, 1988- Lect.; United Theol. Coll., 1990-Lect. Spec: New Testament. Pub: *The Plan of God in Luke-Acts*, SNTS Mon. Ser. 74 (Cambridge U.P., 1993). Mem: SBL 1986-; Australian & New Zealand Assn. for Theol. Stud. 1988-; Australian Assn. for the Study of Relig. 1988-; Coun. of Christians & Jews 1989-. Rec: Music. Addr: (o) United Theological College, 16 Masons Dr., North Parramatta, NSW 2151, Australia 61-2-683-3655.

STAGER, Lawrence E., b. Kenton, OH, January 5, 1943, m. Susan J. (Simmons), chil: Jennifer; David. Educ: Harvard U., Dept. of Near East. Lang. & Civ., BA (magna cum laude) 1965, MA 1972, PhD 1975. Emp: Harvard U., Dept. of Near East. Lang. & Civ., 1970-72 Teaching Fellow, 1986- Dorot Prof. of the Arch. of Israel; U. of Chicago, Oriental Inst. & Dept. of Near East. Lang. & Civ., 1973-74 Instr., 1974-75 Asst. Prof., 1976-85 Assoc. Prof., 1985-86; Prof., Syro-Palestinian Arch.; Carthage Res. Inst., Tunisia, 1976-80 Dir. Excv: Tell el-Hesi, Tell Gezer, 1966-71 Staff; Beqa'ah Valley Survey and Surroundings, Prin. Investigator; Idalion, Cyprus, 1971-74 Field Dir., 1974-80 Co-Prin. Investigator; Punic Project, Carthage, Tunisia, 1975-80 Field Dir.; Ashkelon, 1985- Project Dir. Spec: Archaeology. Pub: "In the Footsteps of the Philistines and Ashkelon Excavations: The Leon

Levy Expedition" in *History of Ashkelon* (1989); "The Song of Deborah: Why Some Tribes Answered the Call and Others Did Not" *BAR* 15/1 (1989); "The Archaeology of the Family in Ancient Israel" *BASOR* 260 (1985); "Merenptah, Israel & Sea Peoples: New Light on An Old Relief" *Eretz-Israel* 18 (1985); "Archaeology, History and the Bible—The Israelite Settlement in Canaan" *Bibl. Arch. Today* (IES, 1985); and others. Awd: Harvard U., Grad. Prize Fellow. 1968-73; ASOR, Thayer Fellow. 1972-73; NEH, grant 1972-80; Smithsonian Inst., grant 1975-80; Hebrew U., Jerusalem, Inst. for Advanced. Stud., Fellow 1983-84. Mem: ASOR 1988-; AIA, V.P. 1986-88; AOS; SBL; Assn. of Field Arch. Addr: (o) Harvard U., The Semitic Museum, 6 Divinity Ave. Cambridge, MA 02138 617-495-5756; (h) 12 Garden Rd. Concord, MA 01742 508-371-1946.

STALEY, Jeffrey L., b. Kansas City, MO, December 22, 1951, s. of Robert & Mary, m. Barbara, chil: Benjamin; Allison. Educ: Fuller Theol. Sem., MA 1979; Grad. Theol. Union, PhD 1985. Emp: U. of Portland, 1985-1992 Asst. Prof.; U. of Notre Dame, 1992-93 Vis. Asst. Prof. Spec: New Testament. Pub: "Stumbling in the Dark, Reaching for the Light: Reading Character in John 5 and 9" *Semeia* 53 (1991); *The Print's First Kiss: A Rhetorical Investigation of the Implied Reader in the Fourth Gospel*, SBL Diss. Ser. (1988); "The Structure of John's Prologue: Its Implications for the Gospel's Narrative Structure" *CBQ* 48 (1986). Mem: SBL 1980-; CBA 1990-. Rec: Skiing, hiking. Addr: (h) 9255 SW Whitford Ln., Portland, OR 97223 503-245-8411.

STAMPS, Dennis L., b. Hazlecrest, IL, September 3, 1955, s. of Donald & Mary Anna, m. Helen R.C., chil: Jeffrey Donald Lee; Jennifer Elizabeth May. Educ: Biola U., BA (magna cum laude), Bibl. Stud. 1978; Trinity Evang. Div. Sch., MDiv (magna cum laude) 1983, MA (magna cum laude), NT 1987; Durham U., Great Britain, PhD, Theol., NT Stud. 1992. Emp: Trinity Evang. Div. Sch., 1983-84 Teaching Fellow; U. of Durham, 1984-87 Greek Instr., Dept. of Theol.; St. John's Coll., 1987-90 Resident Tutor; Westcott House Theol. Coll., Great Britain, 1990-92 Instr.; West-Midlands Min. Training Course, Great Britain, 1992- NT Examiner. Spec: New Testament, Apocrypha and Post-biblical Studies. Pub: "Rethinking the Rhetorical Situation" in *Rhetoric and the New Testament* (Sheffield, 1993); "Rhetorical Criticism in New Testament Interpretation" in *Literary Criticism and Biblical Hermeneutics* (Attila Jozsep U.P., 1992); "Rhetorical Criticism and the Rhetoric of New Testament Studies" *Lit. & Theol.* 6/3 (1992); "Interpreting the Language of St. Paul" in *Translating Religious Texts* (Macmillan, 1992); and others. Awd: Amer. Bible Soc. Awd. 1987; Trinity Evang. Div. Sch., Prof. L.J. Pedersen Awd. 1987; Tyndale House Res. Grant 1985-86, 1986-87; U. of Durham, Post-grad. Schol. in Theol. for Overseas Students 1984-87. Mem: Brit. NT Soc. 1984-; SBL 1988-; AAR 1988-; Soc. for Study of

Theol.; European Soc. for Lit. & Relig. Rec: Squash, tennis, lit., cinema, harpsicord music. Addr: (o) St. Mary's Church St. Mary's Row, Moseley Birmingham B13 8HW, England 21-449-2243; (h) 4 Woodrough Drive Moseley Birmingham B13 9EP, England 21-449-1336.

STANLEY, Christopher D., b. Birmingham, AL, March 2, 1955, s. of Donald & Mary Evelyn, m. Laurel Virginia, chil: Jeremy Adam; David Joseph. Educ: U. of Va., BS 1976; Regent Coll., MA, Christian Stud. 1983; Duke U., PhD 1990. Emp: U. of N.C., Greensboro, 1990-91 Instr.; N.C. State U., 1991-92 Vis. Asst. Prof.; Hastings Coll., 1992-93 Asst. Prof.; McKendree Coll., 1993- Asst. Prof. Spec: New Testament. Pub: "The Significance of Rom 11:3-4 for the Text-History of the LXX Book of Kingdoms" *JBL* 112 (1993); "The Importance of *4Q Tanhumim*" *RQ* 60 (1992); *Paul and the Language of Scripture* (Cambridge U.P., 1992); "Paul and Homer: Greco-Roman Citation Practice in the First Century C.E." *NT* 32 (1990); "'Under a Curse': A Fresh Reading of Gal 3.10-14" *NTS* 36 (1990); and others. Awd: Phi Beta Kappa 1992. Mem: SBL; IOSCS. Rec: Hiking, basketball, cross-country skiing. Addr: (o) McKendree College, Lebanon, IL 62254 618-537-4481; (h) 2408 Richland Prairie Blvd., Belleville, IL 62221 618-234-3467.

STANTON, Graham N., b. Christchurch, New Zealand, July 9, 1940, s. of Norman & Gladys, m. Esther, chil: Roger; Michael; Nicola. Educ: U. of Otago, New Zealand, MA 1961, BD 1964; U. of Cambridge, PhD 1969. Emp: U. of London, King's Coll., 1970-77 Lect., 1977- Prof.; *NTS*, 1983-90 Ed.; SNTS Mon. Ser., 1983-91 Ed.; U. of Manchester, 1983 Manson Memorial Lect. Spec: New Testament. Pub: *A Gospel for a New People: Studies in Matthew* (T & T Clark, 1992); *The Gospels and Jesus* (Oxford U.P., 1989); *Jesus of Nazareth in New Testament Preaching* (Cambridge U.P., 1974); and others. Mem: SNTS; Brit. Assn. for NT Stud. 1989-92. Rec: Music, cricket. Addr: (o) King's College London, Strand, London WC2R 2LS, England 071-836-5454; (h) 13 Oakwood Rd., Orpington, Kent BR6 8JH, England 0689-856495.

STAUDINGER, Hugo, b. Dresden, July 5, 1921, s. of Gerhard & Margarete (Werner), m. Hilde (Kroeger), chil: Heribert; Maria; Margarete; Mechthild; Gisela; Hiltrud. Educ: U. Munster, Dip. 1950. Emp: Mariengymnasium Werl, 1952-62; U. Paderborn, 1963- Prof. Spec: New Testament, Apocrypha and Post-biblical Studies. Pub: *Gotteswort und Menschenwort* (1993); "Mythos und Geschichte—Uberlegungen zur historisch-kritischen Exegese" *Forum kath. Theol.* 3 (1991); *Die historische Glaubwuerdigkeit der Evangelien* (1988); *Die Glaubwuerdigkeit der Offenbarung und die Krise der modernen Welt*, co-auth. (1987); *An Wunder glauben? Gottes Allmacht und moderne Welterfahrung*, co-auth. (1986); and others. Awd: Komturkreuz des paepstlichen Silvesterordens 1984. Mem: Deutschen

Inst. fuer Bildung und Wissen. Addr: (o) Busdorfwall 16, D-479 Paderborn, Germany 0049-5251-24905; (h) Fuerstenweg 50, D-479 Paderborn, Germany.

STEEGER, William P., b. Brooklyn, NY, June 26, 1945, s. of William E. & Elizabeth T. (Damm), m. Martha Susan (Bowman), chil: W. David; Heidi E.; Liesl R.; Gretchen A. Educ: U. of Fla., BA 1967; S Bapt. Theol. Sem., MDiv 1970, PhD 1983; U. of Louisville, MA 1972. Emp: U. of Louisville, 1969-73 Instr.; Oakland City Coll., Grad. Sch. 1983-84 Prof.; Die Teleogiese Sem. van die Baptiste, S Africa, 1978-86 Lect.; Bapt. Theol. Coll. of S Africa, 1978-86 Lect.; Oachita Bapt. U., 1986- Prof. Excv: Ai Excvn., 1969-73 Garrett Fellow. Spec: Hebrew Bible. Pub: *Old Testament Theology* (Bapt. Theol. Coll. of S Africa, 1984); *Old Testament Introduction, Revised* (Bapt. Theol. Coll. of S Africa, 1980); *Old Testament Exegesis: Psalms* (Bapt. Theol. Coll. of S Africa, 1979); *Old Testament Exegesis: Joshua* (Bapt. Theol. Coll. of S Africa, 1978). Mem: SBL 1967-; ASOR 1967-73; ETS 1986-; NABPR 1986-; IBR 1989-. Rec: Hiking, travel, pipe organ rebuilding. Addr: (o) Ouachita Baptist U., OBU Box 3720, Arkadelphia, AR 71998-0001 501-246-4531; (h) 803 Cupp Dr., Arkadelphia, AR 71923 501-246-7824.

STEGEMANN, Hartmut, b. Gummersbach, Germany, December 18, 1933. Educ: U. of Heidelberg, PhD 1963; 1965 ThD, OT; 1969 Habil., NT. Emp: U. of Bonn, 1963-69 Asst. Lect., 1970-71 Dozent, NT Stud.; U. of Marburg, 1971-80 Prof., NT; Qumran Res. Ctr., Goettingen, 1973- Dir.; U. of Goettingen, 1980- Prof., NT. Spec: Hebrew Bible, New Testament. Addr: Platz der Goettinger, Sieben 2, D-3400 Goettingen, Germany 49-551-397-123.

STEIN, Robert H., b. Jersey City, NJ, March 13, 1935, s. of William & Ella, m. Joan (Thatcher), chil: Julie; Keith; Stephen. Educ: Fuller Theol. Sem., BD 1959; Andover-Newton Theol. Sch., STM 1966; Princeton Theol. Sem., PhD 1968. Emp: Bapt. Ch., 1960-69 Pastor; Bethel Coll., 1969-80 Prof.; Bethel Theol. Sem., 1980- Prof., NT. Spec: New Testament. Pub: *Luke* (Broadman, 1992); "The Argument of Romans 13:1-7" *NT* 31 (1989); *The Synoptic Problem* (Baker, 1987); *Difficult Passages in the Gospels* (Baker, 1984); *An Introduction to the Parables of Jesus* (Westminster, 1981); "Is the Transfiguration (Mark 9:2-8) a Misplaced Resurrection-Account?" *JBL* 95 (1976); "A Short Note on Mark xiv.28 and xvi.7" *NTS* 20 (1973); "What is Redaktionsgeschichte?" *JBL* 88 (1969); and others. Mem: SBL; IBR; ETS. Rec: Fishing, hunting. Addr: (o) Bethel Theological Seminary, 3949 Bethel Dr., St. Paul, MN 55112 612-638-6178; (h) 417 Bear Ave. S, Vadnais Heights, MN 55127 612-429-3507.

STEINHAUSER, Michael G., b. Brooklyn, NY, June 13, 1941, s. of Michael & Agnes (Gallegan).

Educ: U. of Innsbruck, Austria, STL 1967; U. of Wurzburg, Germany, ThD 1978. Emp: Cath. U. of Amer., 1977-79 Asst. Prof.; Toronto Sch. Theol., Canada, 1979- Assoc. Prof., Asst. Dir.; *Toronto Jour. of Theol.*, 1985-91 Ed. Spec: New Testament. Pub: *Q-Thomas Reader* (Polebridge, 1991); "Putting One's Hand to the Plow" *Forum* 5 (1989); "Gal. 4,25a: Evidence of Targumic Tradition in Gal 4:21-31" *Biblica* (1989); "Noah on His Generation: An Allusion to Lb 16: 8b" *ZNW* (1988); *Doppelbidworte in den synoptischen Evangelien* (Verlag, 1981); *Man Before God: Toward a Theology of Man*, co-ed. (1966); *Present and Future: Modern Aspects of New Testament Theology*, trans. (Notre Dame U.P., 1966); and others. Addr: (o) Toronto School of Theology 47 Queens Park, Cres. East, Toronto, ON M5S 2C3, Canada 416-978-4039.

STEINMANN, Andrew E., b. Cincinnati, OH, May 29, 1954, s. of Melvin & Grace, m. Rebecca, chil: Christopher; Jennifer. Educ: U. of Cincinnati, BS 1977; Concordia Theol. Sem., MDiv 1981; U. of Mich., PhD, Near East. Stud. 1990. Emp: St. John Luth. Ch., 1981-86 Assoc. Pastor; Concordia Coll., 1986-90 Instr.; New Evangelical Translation, 1991- Ed. Spec: Hebrew Bible. Pub: "The Order of Amos's Oracles Against the Nations" *JBL* 111 (1992); "The Chronology of 2 Kings 15-18" *JETS* 30 (1987). Mem: SBL; ETS. Rec: Tennis, philately. Addr: (o) God's Word to the Nations Bible Society, 22050 Mastick Rd., Fairview Park, OH 44126 216-779-9050; (h) 30514 Manhassett Dr., Bay Village, OH 44140 216-899-7161.

STENDAHL, Krister, b. Stockholm, Sweden, April 21, 1921, s. of Olof & Sigrid (Ljungquist), m. Brita K. (Johnsson), chil: John Kristofer; Anna Birgitta (Langenfeld); Daniel Kristian. Educ: Uppsala U., Sweden, Teol. kand. 1944, Teol. lic. 1949, Teol. dr. 1954. Emp: Uppsala U., 1948-50 Chaplain, 1951-54 Instr., OT & NT Exegesis, 1954 Docent, Asst. Prof., NT; Harvard Div. Sch., 1954-58 Assoc. Prof., 1958-63 John H. Morison Prof. of NT Stud., 1968-79 Dean, John Lord O'Brian Prof., 1981-84 Andrew W. Mellon Prof., Div., 1989-91 Chaplain; Bishop of Stockholm, Sweden, 1984-88; Brandeis U., 1991-93 Myra & Robert Kraft & Jacob Hiatt Disting. Prof. of Christian Stud. Spec: New Testament. Pub: *Meanings* (Fortress, 1984); *Paul Among Jews and Gentiles* (Fortress, 1976); *The Bible and the Role of Women* (Fortress, 1966); *The School of St. Matthew* (Fortress, 1954); and others. Awd: Brandeis U., LHD 1981; Harvard U., DD 1985; St. Andrews U., DD 1987; Assn. of Theol. Sch., Disting. Service Medal 1988; Loyola U., New Orleans, LHD 1992. Mem: SNTS; Nathan Soederblom Soc.; Amer. Acad. of Arts & Sci. Addr: (h) 85 Trowbridge St., Cambridge, MA 02138 617-868-5572.

STEPHENS, William H., b. Portales, NM, October 11, 1935, s. of W.C. & Oneta, m. Shirley, chil: Laura; Paula; Gregory; Carol. Educ: SW Bapt. Theol. Sem., BD 1964, MDiv 1974; South.

Bapt. Theol. Sem., DMin 1979. Emp: *Upward*, 1968-69 Ed.; *People*, 1969-72 Ed.; Broadman Press, 1972-73 Ed.; *BI*, 1974-84 Ed.; Ch. Training Dept., 1984- Sr. Curr. Coord. Spec: New Testament. Pub: *The Doctrine of Lordship*, co-auth. (Convention, 1991); *The New Testament World in Pictures* (Broadman, 1987); *Where Jesus Walked*, co-auth. (Broadman, 1981); *Elijah* (Tyndale, 1976); and others. Mem: ASOR; SBL; ETS. Rec: Woodsman, cabinbuilding. Addr: (o) 127 Ninth Ave. N, MS #149, Nashville, TN 37234 615-251-2863; (h) 416 Manor View Ln., Nashville, TN 37027 615-370-4936.

STERLING, Gregory E., b. San Jose, CA, November 21, 1954, s. of Kenneth A. & Barbara M., m. Deidra G., chil: Audra M.; Amber F. Educ: Fla. Coll., AA 1974; Houston Bapt. U., BA 1978; Pepperdine U., MA 1980; U. of Calif. at Davis, MA 1982; Grad. Theol. Union, PhD 1990. Emp: *The Exegete*, 1983-85 Co-Ed.; U. of Notre Dame, 1989- Asst. Prof.; *Studia Philonica Ann.*, 1990- Book Rev. Ed.; SBL, Philo of Alexandria Seminar, 1991-96 Chair. Spec: New Testament. Pub: "*Creatio Temporalis, Aeterna, vel Continua*? An Analysis of the Thought of Philo of Alexandria" *Studia Philonica Annual* 4 (1992); *Historiography and Self-Definition: Josephos, Luke-Acts and Apologetic Historiography*, NTSup 64 (Brill, 1992); "Philo's *Quaestiones*: Prolegomena or Afterthought?" in *Both Literal and Allegorical: Studies in Philo of Alexandria's Questions and Answers on Genesis and Exodus*, BJS 232 (Scholars, 1990); "Luke-Acts and Apologetic Historiography" in *SBL Seminar Papers* (Scholars, 1989); "Philo and the Logic of Apologetics: An Analysis of the *Hypothetica*" in *SBL Seminar Papers* (Scholars, 1990). Awd: Lilly Endowment Teaching Fellow 1991-92. Mem: CBA; SBL; NAPS; SNTS. Rec: Athletics, reading, especially about 19th Century Amer. Addr: (o) U. of Notre Dame, Dept. of Theology, Notre Dame, IN 46556 219-631-6607; (h) 14455 Lotus Court, Mishawaka, IN 46545 219-255-3387.

STERN, David M., b. Chicago, IL, July 6, 1949, s. of Kurt & Florence, m. Kathryn (Hellerstein), chil: Rebecca; Jonah. Educ: Columbia Coll., BA 1972; Harvard U., PhD 1980. Emp: U. of Judaism, 1980-83 Asst. Prof.; U. of Pa., 1984-90 Asst. Prof., Oriental Stud., 1990- Assoc. Prof., Rabbinic Lit.; Hebrew U., Jerusalem, 1983-84 Vis. Lect.; Princeton U., 1990 Vis. Asst. Prof.; *Prooftexts*, 1981- Founder & Assoc. Ed. Spec: Hebrew Bible. Pub: "Imitatio Hominis: Anthropomorphism and the Character of God in Rabbinic Literature" *Prooftexts* 12 (1992); *Parables in Midrash: Narrative and Exegesis in Rabbinic Literature* (Harvard U.P., 1991); *Rabbinic Fantasies: Imaginative Narratives from Classical Hebrew Literature* (Jewish Publ. Soc., 1990); "The Parables of Jesus from the Perspective of Rabbinic Literature: The Example of the Wicked Husbandmen" in *Parable and Story in Judaism and Christianity* (Paulist, 1989); "Midrash and Indeterminacy" *Critical Inquiry* 15 (1988); "Midrash and the Language of Exegesis: An

Analysis of Vayikra Rabbah, Chap. 1" in *Midrash and Literature* (Yale U.P., 1986); and others. Awd: Harvard U. Fellow. 1973-76; Memorial Found. for Jewish Culture, Res. Grant 1983-84, 1987-88; U. of Pa., Res. Found. Grant 1986, 1991; Amer. Coun. of Learned Soc. Fellow. 1987-88. Mem: AJS; Oriental Club of Philadelphia; SBL; Modern Lang. Assn. Addr: (o) U. of Pennsylvania, Dept. of Asian & Middle Eastern Studies, 847 Williams Hall, Philadelphia, PA 19104 215-898-6038; (h) 448 S 48th St., Philadelphia, PA 19143 215-471-0873.

STERN, Ephraim, b. Haifa, Israel, January 15, 1934. Educ: Hebrew U., Jerusalem, BA 1958, MA 1962, Inst. of Arch., PhD 1969. Emp: *Ency. Biblica*, 1960- Ed. Bd.; *Qadmoniot*, 1965-77 Assoc. Ed., 1978- Ed.; Tel Aviv U., Inst. of Arch., 1965-71 Lect.; Hebrew U., Inst. of Arch., 1972-84 Prof., 1980-83 Chmn., 1985- Bernard M. Lauterman Prof. of Bibl. Arch.; *EAEHL*, 1973-78, 1988-92 Ed.; *Qedem*, 1981-90 Co-ed. Excv: Masada, 1955 Field Dir.; Hazor, 1956-58 Field Dir.; Ein-Gedi, 1960-65 Field Dir.; Beersheba, 1969-70 Field Dir.; Tel Dor, 1980-92 Dir. of Excvn. Spec: Archaeology. Pub: "New Evidence from Dor for the First Appearance of the Phoenicians Along the Northern Coast of Israel" *BASOR* 279 (1990); "What Happened to the Cult Figurines? Israelite Religion Purified After the Exile" *BAR* 15/4 (1989); *Illustrated Dict. and Concordance to the Bible* (Macmillan, 1987); "Two Phoenician Glass Seals" *JANES* 16-17 (1984-85); *Excavations at Tel Mevorakh (1973-1976)*, vol. 1 & 2, *Qedem* 9, 18 (Hebrew U., 1978, 1984); "A Pottery Group of the Persian Period from Qadum in Samaria" *BASOR* 253 (1984); "The Persian Empire and the Political and Social History of Palestine in the Persian Period," "The Archaeology of Persian Palestine" in *The Cambridge History of Judaism*, vol. 1 (Cambridge U.P., 1984); *The Material Culture of the Land of the Bible in the Persian Period* (Aris & Phillips/IES, 1982); and others. Awd: Hebrew U., Jerusalem, Inst. of Arch., Lucian Teich Prize 1973; Ben-Zvi Inst., Jerusalem, Ben-Zvi Prize 1974; BAS Publ. Awd., Best Schol. Book on Arch. 1984. Addr: (o) Hebrew U., Institute of Archaeology, Jerusalem, Israel 2-639-954; (h) 14 Poltiot St., Arnona, Jerusalem, Israel.

STEYN, Gert J., b. Wolmaransstad, South Africa, March 5, 1962, s. of Gert Jacobus & Gertruida Petronella (Rossouw), m. Ester (Joubert), chil: Jean-Mari; Gert Jacobus. Educ: U. of Pretoria, BA 1983, BA, Greek 1986, BD 1986, MA, Greek 1988. Emp: U. of Pretoria, 1986 Sr. Res. Asst.; U. of South Africa, 1987-90 Jr. Lect.; Federal Theol. Sem., 1992- Lect., Dept. of NT & Greek. Spec: New Testament. Pub: "Intertextual Similarities Between Septuagint Pretexts and Luke's Gospel" *Neotestamentica* 24/2 (1990); "The State of LXX-Research in South Africa (1978-1989) and Its Importance for New Testament Scholarship" *Theologica Evangelica*; 23/2 (1990); "The Occurrence of 'Kainam' in

Luke's Genealogy: Evidence of Septuagint Influence?" *ETL* 65/4 (1989); "The Manifestation of LXX-Influence in the Sondergut-Lukas" *Hervormde Teologiese Studies* 45/4 (1989); "The Exegesis of Old Testament Material in the New Testament: Some Problems and a Possible Model" *Theologica Evangelica* 20 (1987); and others. Awd: Inst. for Res. Development of the Human Sci., Res. Awd. 1989; Deutscher Akademischer Austauschdienst 1990-. Mem: NT Soc. of South Africa 1987-; Pietermaritzburg Com. of Cluster Publ. 1992-. Rec: Community work, hiking, camping, tropical aquaria. Addr: (o) Federal Theological Seminary of Southern Africa, Box 2283, 3200 Pietermaritzburg, South Africa 0331 8-1291.

STIEBING, William H., Jr., b. New Orleans, LA, December 21, 1940, s. of William & Eunice (Perez), m. Ann (Thompson), chil: Kimberly. Educ: U. of Pa., PhD 1970. Emp: U. of New Orleans, 1967- Prof. Excv: Tell es-Sa'idiyeh, Jordan, 1965 Staff mem.; Sarafand, Lebanon, 1974 Pottery Supr. Spec: Archaeology, Hebrew Bible. Pub: *Uncovering the Past: A History of Archaeology* (Prometheus, 1993); *Out of the Desert?: Archaeology and the Exodus/Conquest Narratives* (Prometheus, 1989); "Should the Exodus and the Israelite Settlement be Redated" *BAR* 11/4 (1985); "The Amarna Period" in *Palestine Transition: The Emergence of Ancient Israel* (Almond, 1983); "The End of the Mycenaean Age" *BA* 43/1 (1980); "Hyksos Burials in Palestine: A Review of the Evidence" *JNES* 30 (1971); and others. Mem: Amer. Hist. Assn. 1967-; SBL 1968-; AIA 1974-. Rec: Amateur theatricals, choral singing. Addr: (o) U. of New Orleans, Dept. of History, New Orleans, LA 70148 504-286-6892; (h) 700 Colony Pl., Metairie, LA 70003 504-733-8441.

STIEGLITZ, Robert R., b. Bershad, Ukraine, April 14, 1943, s. of Egon & Paula, m. Dita (Dascal), chil: Daniel; Jonathan. Educ: Brandeis U., MA 1969, PhD 1971. Emp: Natl. Maritime Mus., Haifa, 1971-74 Cur.; Rutgers U., 1978- Assoc. Prof., Hebraic Stud. Excv: Coral Island, Israel, 1971 Asst. Dir.; Crete Coastal Survey, 1981 Dir.; Tel Michmoret, Israel, 1982-84 Co-Dir.; Caesarea, Israel, 1986-90 Co-Dir. Spec: Archaeology, Hebrew Bible, Semitic Languages, Texts and Epigraphy. Pub: *Luke* (Broadman, 1992); *The National Maritime Museum Haifa*, co-auth. (1972); and others. Mem: IES 1971-; AIA 1977-; AOS 1985-. Addr: (o) Rutgers U., Dept. of Class. & Modern Lang. & Lit., Newark, NJ 07102 201-648-5233; (h) 40 Deepdene Rd., Forest Hills, NY 11375 718-268-2497.

STONE, Michael E., b. Leeds, United Kingdom, October 22, 1938, s. of Julius & Reca, m. Nira, chil: Aurit; Dan. Educ: Harvard U., PhD 1965; U. of Melbourne, DLitt 1985. Emp: U. of Calif., 1965-66 Asst. Prof.; Hebrew U., Jerusalem, 1966-76 Prof.; U. of Pa., 1978- Adj. Prof. Spec: Apocrypha and Post-biblical Studies. Pub: *Jewish*

Literature of the Second Temple Period, ed. (Fortress/van Gorcum, 1984); *Faith and Piety in Early Judaism*, co-auth. (Fortress, 1982); *Armenian Apocrypha Relating to Patriarchs and Prophets* (Israel Acad. Sci., 1982); *Scriptures, Sects and Visions* (Blackwell, 1982); and others. Mem: SBL 1962-; Israel Soc. Byzantine Stud.; Soc. Armenian Stud. Rec: Swimming, computers. Addr: (o) Hebrew U., Dept. of Armenian, Jerusalem, Israel 02-883655; (h) PO Box 16174, Jerusalem 91161, Israel 02-412906.

STORFJELL, J. Björnar, b. Ballangen, Norway, s. of Arthur & Margit, m. Judith, chil: Troy; Thor. Educ: Andrews U., BD 1969, PhD 1983. Emp: Middle East Coll., Beirut, 1970-73 Asst. Prof.; Andrews U., 1980- Prof., Arch., Hist. of Antiq. Excv: Tell Hesban, Jordan, 1976; Tell el-Hesi, Israel, 1981 Area Supr.; Tell el-Umeiri, Jordan, 1987 Admn. Dir.; Wadi es-Siah, Israel, 1988-89 Ceramicist. Spec: Archaeology, Hebrew Bible. Mem: ASOR; IES; SBL. Rec: Sailing, skiing. Addr: (o) Andrews U., Berrien Springs, MI 49104-1500 616-471-3205; (h) 4720 E Hillcrest Dr., Berrien Springs, MI 49103.

STORY, Cullen I. K., b. Osceola, IA, July 26, 1916, s. of William & Lenore (Van Scoy), m. Wilma (Pentecost), chil: Edward; John; Donald. Educ: Johns Hopkins U., MA 1943; Dallas Theol. Sem., ThM 1944; Princeton Theol. Sem., PhD 1964. Emp: Dallas Sem., 1943-45 Instr.; Near East Sch. Theol., Beirut, 1954-57 Prin., Prof., NT; Lafayette Coll., 1959-60 Instr.; Princeton Sem., 1961-85 Assoc. Prof., Dir., Bibl. Lang. Prog.; Coll. of the Ozarks, 1965-67 Assoc. Prof., Chmn., Dept. Relig. Spec: Hebrew Bible, New Testament. Pub: "The Mental Attitude of Jesus at Bethany" *NTS* (1991) "The Book of "Amos-Prophet of Praise" *VT* 30/1 (1980); *Greek to Me*, co-auth. (Harper & Row, 1979); *The Nature of Truth in 'The Gospel of Truth' and in the Writings of Justin Martyr* (Brill, 1970); "Proverbs and Northwest Semitic Literature" *JBL* 64 (1945); and others. Mem: SBL. Rec: Basketball. Addr: (h) 78 Edgemore Ave., Plainsboro, NJ 08536 (609) 799-1479.

STOUTENBURG, Dennis C., b. London, ON, Canada, December 16, 1949, s. of Clare Frederick & Elizabeth (Popik), m. Laura Ann (Johnson). Educ: U. de Strasbourg, Doc. 1986. Emp: Regent Coll., 1989 Vis. Prof., NT Greek; Trinity West. Sem., 1988-1990 Adj. Prof., NT; Trinity West. U., 1987-1990 Asst. Prof., Relig. Stud.; Providence Theol. Sem., 1990- Adj. Prof., Bibl. Stud.; Providence Coll., 1990- Assoc. Prof., NT. Spec: Hebrew Bible, New Testament, Apocrypha and Post-biblical Studies. Awd: Brock U., Canada, 1972 Alumni Awd.; U. de Strasbourg, Bourse du gouvernement francais 1983-1986. Mem: SBL 1988-; ETS 1988-; CSBS 1988-1990; IBR 1990-. Addr: (o) Providence College, Dept. of Biblical Studies, Otterburne, Man. R0A 1G0, Canada 204-433-7488.

STOWERS, Stanley K., b. Muncie, IN, February 24, 1948, s. of William & Edith, chil: Lara; Erik. Educ: Abilene Christian U., AB 1970; Princeton Theol. Sem., MA 1974; Yale U., PhD 1979. Emp: Phillips U., 1979-80 Asst. Prof.; Brown U., 1981- Asst. Prof., 1987- Assoc. Prof., 1992- Prof.; *SBL*, 1990-92 Ed. Bd. Spec: New Testament, Apocrypha and Post-biblical Studies. Pub: "Friends and Enemies in the Politics of Heaven: Reading Theology in Phillipians" in *Pauline Theology* (Fortress, 1991); "Paul on the Use and Abuse of Reason" in *Greeks, Romans and Christians* (Fortress, 1990); "*Ek pisteos* and *dia tes pisteos* in Romans 3:30" *JBL* 108 (1989); *Letter Writing in Greco-Roman Antiquity* (Westminster, 1986); "Paul's Dialogue with a Fellow Jew in Romans 3:1-9" *CBQ* 46 (1984); "Social Status, Public Speaking, and Private Teaching: The Circumstances of Paul's Preaching Activity" *NT* 26 (1984); *The Diatribe and Paul's Letter to the Romans* (Scholars, 1981); and others. Awd: NEH Summer Seminar for Coll. Teachers 1980; FIAT Fellow. 1990; Wayland Collegium Grant 1991; NEH Fellow. for U. Tchr., 1991; Woodrow Wilson Ctr. Fellow. 1992. Mem: SBL 1969-; Intl. Numismatics Soc. 1980-85; Soc. for the Sci. Stud. of Relig. 1988-90; SNTS 1988-; APA 1989-. Rec: Opera, bicycling, theater, coastal Maine. Addr: (o) Brown U., Dept. of Religious Studies, Box 1927, Providence, RI 02912 401-863-3569; (h) 106 Blackstone Blvd. #6, Providence, RI 02906 401-272-6046.

STRAND, Kenneth A., b. Tacoma, WA, September 18, 1927, s. of Jens & Bertha (Odegard). Educ: U. of Mich., MA 1955, PhD 1958. Emp: Emmanuel Missionary Coll., 1959-62; Andrews U. Theol. Sem., 1962- Prof., Ch. Hist.; *Andrews U. Sem. Stud.*, 1967- Ed. Spec: New Testament, Apocrypha and Post-biblical Studies. Pub: *The Sabbath in Scripture and History*, contb. ed. (Rev. & Herald, 1982); *Interpreting the Book of Revelation* (Ann Arbor, 1976); *Perspectives in the Book of Revelation* (1975); *Brief Introduction to the Ancient Near East: A Panorama of the Old Testament World* (Braun-Brumfield, 1969). Mem: SBL; Intl. Soc. Comparative Study of Civ. Rec: Photography. Addr: (o) Andrews U., 115 Seminary Hall, Berrien Springs, MI 49104 616-471-3542; (h) 8856 George Ave., Berrien Springs, MI 49103 616-471-3885.

STRANGE, James F., b. Pampa, TX, February 2, 1938, s. of Jerry & Buena (Frost), m. Carolyn (Midkiff), chil: Mary; James; Katherine; Joanna. Educ: Yale Div. Sch., MDiv 1964; Drew U., PhD 1970. Emp: Uppsala Coll., 1965-66 Lect.; Union Coll., 1970 Lect.; U. of S Fla., 1972- Prof., Relig. Stud.; U. of the Orange Free State, S Africa, 1979 Vis. Prof.; *BAR*, 1981- Ed. Bd. Excv: Khirbet Shema', Israel, 1970 Area Supr., 1971-73 Assoc. Dir.; Caesarea, Israel, 1971 Area Supr.; Meiron Excvn. Project, 1974-81 Assoc. Dir.; En Gedi, Israel, 1979 Co-Dir.; Sepphoris, Israel, 1983- Dir. Spec: Archaeology, New Testament. Pub: *The*

Excavations at the Ancient Synagogue of Gush Halav, Israel, co-auth., Meiron Excvn. Project 4 (Eisenbrauns, 1990); *Archaeology, the Rabbis, and Early Christianity* co-auth. (Cerf, 1984); *Excavations at Ancient Meiron, Upper Galilee, Israel, 1971-72, 1974-75 AASOR* 45 (1981); "The Capernaum and Herodium Publications (Part 1)" *BASOR* 226 (1977); *Ancient Synagogue Excavations at Khirbet Shema', Upper Galilee Israel, 1970-72, AASOR* 42 (1976); and others. Awd: W.F. Albright Inst. Arch. Res., Jerusalem, Montgomery Fellow 1970-71. Mem: ASOR; IES; SBL; NABPR; WCJS. Rec: Reading microcomputers, choral music. Addr: (o) U. of South Florida, Dept. of Religious Studies, CPR 304, Tampa, FL 33620 813-974-2221; (h) 9712 Woodland Ridge Drive, Tampa, FL 33617 813-985-3389.

STRECKER, Georg, b. Oldendorf Krs. Melle,, March 15, 1929, s. of Otto & Berta (Romberg), m. Gisela (Schaare), chil: Gabriele; Marianne. Educ: DTh 1955; U. Bonn, Habil., NT 1959. Emp: U. Goettingen, Fac. of Theol., 1953, 1957-59 Faculty Asst., 1959 Lect., 1961 Dozent, 1968- Prof., NT; U. Bonn, 1964 Prof.; *Goettinger Theol. Arbeiten*, 1975- Ed.; *Grundkurs Theol.*, 1989- Ed. Spec: New Testament. Pub: "Literaturgeschichte des Neuen Testaments" *TRE* 21 (1991); "La Conception de L'Histoire chez Mattieu" in *La Mémoire et le temps, Festschrift fur Pierre Bonnard* (Genf, 1991); "Walter Bauers Woerterbuch zum Neuen Testament in neuer Auflage" *TLZ* 116 (1991); "The Historical and Theological Problem of the Jesus Question" *Toronto Jour. of Theol.* (1990); "Chiliasm and Docetism in the Johannine School" *ABR* 38 (1990); *Die Johannesbriefe* (1989); *Einfuehrung in die neutestamentliche Exegese*, co-auth. (1989); *Konkordanz zu den Pseudoklementinen I-II* (1986, 1989); and others. Mem: SNTS. Rec: Hiking, organ music. Addr: (o) Georg-August-U. Goettingen, Platz der Goettinger Sieben 2, D 37073 Goettingen, Germany 0551-39-71-31; (h) Wilhelm-Raabe-Str. 6, D 37120 Bovenden, Germany 0551-88-38.

STRICKLER, Gerald B., b. Wrightsville, PA, June 30, 1921, s. of Francis & Edna (Brenner), m. Margaret (Gotwalt), chil: Susan; Michael. Educ: Luth. Theol. Sem., BD 1946, MDiv 1972; N.Y.U., MA 1949; Temple U., STD 1955; Calif. West. U., PhD 1978. Emp: Luth. Ministry, 1945-55; Midland Coll., 1949-58 Assoc. Prof., Chmn., Dept. of Phil. & Relig., Chaplain; Calif. State U., 1958- Prof., Chmn., Dept. of Phil., Dir., Dept. of Relig. Stud., 1992- Prof. Emeritus. Spec: New Testament. Pub: "A Meaningful Symbol for God" *Exploration Jour.* (1989); and others. Mem: AAR; APA; NABI; Soc. for the Sci. Stud. of Relig.; ASOR. Rec: Fishing, cycling. Addr: (o) California State U., Long Beach, CA 90840 213-498-4331; (h) 11311 Caroleen Ln., Garden Grove, CA 92641 714-539-5403.

STROKER, William D., b. Paris, KY, May 23, 1938, s. of Francis & Josephine (Dettwiller), m.

Mary Ann, chil: Mary. Educ: Transylvania U., BA 1960; Yale U. Div. Sch., BD 1963; Yale Grad. Sch., MA 1966, PhD 1970. Emp: Drew U., 1969- Prof. Spec: New Testament, Apocrypha and Post-biblical Studies. Pub: "Aprapha" in *ABD* (1992); *Extra-Canonical Sayings of Jesus* (Scholars, 1989); "Extracanonical Parables and the Historical Jesus" *Semeia* 44 (1988); "Examples of Pronouncement Stories in Early Christian Apocryphal Literature" *Semeia* 20 (1981); "The Source of an Agraphon in the Manichaean Psalm-Book" *JTS* 28 (1977). Mem: SBL. Rec: Tennis, gardening. Addr: (o) Drew U., 8 Faulkner House, Madison, NJ 07940 201-408-3282; (h) 20 Hoyt St., Madison, NJ 07940 201-377-8217.

STROUD, William J., b. Atkins, AR, March 26, 1937, s. of Joe B. & Carrie L., m. Judith Ann (Beck), chil: Annette; Bruce. Educ: Calif. West. U., BA 1959; Iliff Sch. of Theol., MDiv 1964, ThD 1970. Emp: U. of Denver, Instr.; Wesleyan Coll., Asst. Prof., Phil.; Salem Coll., Assoc. Prof., Phil. & Relig. Spec: New Testament, Apocrypha and Post-biblical Studies. Pub: "New Testament Quotations in the Chenoboskion Gospel of Philip" in *SBL 1990 Seminar Papers* (Scholars, 1990); "Ritual in the Chenoboskion Gospel of Philip" *Iliff Rev.* 28/2 (1971). Mem: SBL 1988-; ASOR 1989-. Rec: Travel, computers. Addr: (o) 9921 Sylvan Hills Highway, Sherwood, AZ 72120 501-835-3410; (h) 225 Reeves Rd., Sherwood, AR 72120 501-835-1796.

STROUSE, Thomas M., b. Indianapolis, IN, March 31, 1945, s. of Thomas & Wilma (Hollowell), m. Janis (Wood), chil: Brent; Aaron; Kristen; Kayla; Mark; Kerith; Joshua; Karis; Luke; Keren; Katy; Kiera; Ryan; Tyler. Educ: Maranatha Bapt. Grad. Sch. Theol., MDiv 1974, ThM 1987; Bob Jones U., 1978 PhD. Emp: Maranatha Bapt. Grad Sch. Theol., 1978- Assoc. Prof., Chmn.; Inst. Bibl. Stud., 1985-88 Guest Lect. Spec: New Testament. Pub: *The Lord God Hath Spoken: A Guide to Bibliography; Biblical, Theological and Religious Glossary;* and others. Rec: Sports, reading. Addr: (o) Maranatha Baptist Graduate School of Theology, 745 W Main St., Watertown, WI 53094 414-261-9300; (h) 1122 Ruth St., Watertown, WI 53094 414-262-0566.

STRUGNELL, John, b. Barnet, Herts, England, May 25, 1930, s. of James & Margaret (MacConochie), m. Cecile (Pierlot), chil: David; Andrew; Anne; Mary; Monique. Educ: Jesus Coll., Oxford, MA 1956. Emp: Jerusalem Palestine Arch. Mus., 1954-60 Epigraphist; Duke U. Div. Sch., 1960-65 Asst. Prof.; Harvard U. Div. Sch., 1966- Prof., Christian Origins; *Discoveries in the Judean Desert,* 1986-90 Chief Ed. Excv: Petra, 1956 Epigraphist; Beidha Survey, 1958 Epigraphist; Hisma Survey, 1959-60 Epigraphist. Spec: Hebrew Bible, New Testament, Semitic Languages, Texts and Epigraphy, Apocrypha and Post-biblical Studies. Pub: *The Books of Elijah, Parts I and II,* Texts & Translations 18, co-auth. (Scholars, 1979); "A

Plea for Conjectural Emendation in the New Testament" *CBQ* 36 (1974); *Concordance to the Corpus Hermeticum: Tractate One,* co-auth. (Boston Theol. Inst., 1971); and others. Awd: Albright Inst, Jerusalem, NEH Fellow 1981-82. Mem: SBL; CBA; BSA, Jerusalem; Albright Inst. Addr: (o) Harvard U. Divinity School, 45 Francis Ave., Cambridge, MA 02138 617-876-7340.

STRUS, Andrzej, b. Siedlce, Poland, April 19, 1938, s. of Mikolaj & Marianna (Sawicka). Educ: Pont. Bibl. Inst., Rome, Dr. Holy Scriptures 1976. Emp: Pont. Salesian U., Rome, 1973- Prof., Holy Scriptures; High Sch. of Theol., Poland, 1976-86 Prof.; St. Paul Theol. Coll., Israel, 1986-90 Pres. Excv: Tell Keisan, Israel, 1972 Asst.; Kh. Samra & Amman, Jordan, 1987-88 Asst. to Dir.; Kh. Fattir (Beit-Jimal), Israel, 1989-. Spec: Hebrew Bible. Pub: "Historia Jozefa-podrecznikiem wychowania mlodego Izraelity" *Seminare* 7 (1985); "Interprétation des noms propres dans les oracles contre les nations" in *Salamanca 1983,* SVT 36 (1985); *Nomen-Omen: Stylistique des noms propres dans le Pentateuque,* Analecta Biblica 82 (1982); "Beit-Gamal può essere il luogo della sepolutra di S. Stefano?" *Salesianum* 54 (1992); and others. Mem: Assn. Bibl. Italiana 1978-; Stowarzyszenie Bibl. Polskich 1979-. Addr: (o) Pontificia U. Salesiana, Piazza Atenio Salesiano 1, 00139 Roma, Italy 06-881-20-41.

STUCKENBRUCK, Earl R., b. Lake City, IA, October 30, 1916, s. of C.O. & May, m. Ottie Mearl (Lawrence), chil: Earl Lee; Vivian Jane; Dale L.; Loren Theo. Educ: Kansas U., BA 1939; Butler Sch. of Relig., MDiv 1946. Emp: Butler Sch. of Relig., 1944-46 Fellow, Missions Dept.; Montpelier Ch. of Christ, 1944-46 Min.; Inst. Zur Erforschung der Ur Christentums, 1950-68 Founder & Dir.; Milligan Coll., 1968-1982 Assoc. Prof. Spec: New Testament. Pub: "The Spirit at Pentecost" in *Essays on New Testament Christianity;* and others. Awd: Phi Beta Kappa 1939. Mem: SBL 1949-. Addr: (h) 1603 Woodridge Dr., Johnson City, TN 37604 615-928-0052.

STUEHRENBERG, Paul F., b. Breckemridge, MN, March 14, 1947, s. of Henry F.E. & Marian (Sandberg), m. Carole L. DeVore. Educ: Concordia Sr. Coll., BA 1968; Concordia Sem., MDiv 1972; Christ Sem, STM 1974; U. of Minn., MA 1976, PhD 1988. Emp: U. of Minn., 1980-82 Asst. Lbrn.; Yale U. Div. Lib., 1982-85 Sr. Catalog Librn., 1985-91 Mon. Librn., 1991- Div. Librn. Spec: New Testament. Pub: "A Guide to the Biographical and Bibliographical Sources for the Study of the Bible before the Reformation" *Jour. of Relig. & Theol. Info.* 1 (1993); "Devout," "Proselyte" in *ABD* (Doubleday, 1992); "The 'God-Fearers' in Martin Luther's Translation of Acts" *Sixteenth Century Jour.* 20 (1989); "The Study of Acts Before the Reformation: A Bibliographical Introduction" *NT* 29 (1987); and others. Mem:

Amer. Theol. Lib. Assn.; SBL; AAR. Addr: (o) Yale Divinity Library, 409 Prospecy St., New Haven, CT 06511 203-432-5292; (h) 280 Bayard Ave., North Haven, CT 06473 203-281-3725.

STUHLMUELLER, Carroll, b. Hamilton, OH, April 2, 1923, s. of William & Alma. Educ: Cath. U., STL 1952; Pont. Bibl. Inst., Rome, SSD 1968. Emp: Passionist Theologate, 1954-65 Asst. Prof.; St. Meinrad Sch. of Theol., 1965-68 Assoc. Prof.; Cath. Theol. Union, 1968- Prof.; Ecole Biblique, 1973 Vis. Prof.; *The Bible Today*, 1965- Assoc. Ed., 1980-85 Ed.; *CBQ*, 1973-77 Assoc. Ed. Spec: Hebrew Bible. Pub: *Haggai, Zechariah* (Eerdmans, 1988); *Psalms*, 2 vol. (Glazier, 1983); *Biblical Meditations*, 6 vol. (Paulist, 1978-85); "Yahweh-King and Deutero-Isaiah" *Bibl. Res.* 15 (1970); *Creative Redemption in Deutero-Isaiah* (Bible Inst., 1970); "The Theology of Creation in Second Isaiah" *CBQ* 21 (1959); and others. Awd: St. Benedict Coll., DHL 1969. Mem: CBA, Pres. 1978-79; CSBR, Pres. 1982-83; SBL. Addr: (o) Cath. Theol. Union, 5401 S Cornell Ave, Chicago, IL 60615 312-324-8000.

STULMAN, Louis, b. Baltimore, MD, August 3, 1953, s. of Seymour & Helene, m. Katherine (Starr), chil: Nathaniel; Timothy; Amy; Michael. Educ: Drew U., MPhil 1981, PhD 1982. Emp: Drew U., 1981-82 Instr.; Winebrenner Theol. Sem., 1982-89 Assoc. Prof., 1989- Prof., OT; U. Findlay, Adj. Prof. Spec: Hebrew Bible. Pub: "Sex and Family Crimes in the D Code" *JSOT* 53 (1992); "Encroachment in Deuteronomy: An Analysis of the Social World of the D Code" *JBL* 109 (1990); *The Prose Sermons of Jeremiah* (Scholars, 1986); *The Other Text of Jeremiah* (U. Press of Amer., 1985); "Some Theological and Lexical Differences Between the Old Greek and the MT of the Jeremiah Prose Discourses" *Hebrew Stud.* 25; (1984). Mem: SBL. Rec: Golf, music. Addr: (o) Winebrenner Theological Seminary, 701 E Melrose Ave., Findlay, OH 45839 419-422-4824; (h) 824 Edgehill Rd., Findlay, OH 45840.

STYLER, Geoffrey M., b. Bradford, Yorkshire, U.K., July 10, 1915, s. of Thomas A. & Gertrude E. (Moreton), m. Audrey H. (Tooth) (dec.). Educ: Corpus Christi Coll., Oxford, BA 1937, MA 1940; Union Theol. Sem., STM 1939. Emp: Corpus Christi Coll., Cambridge, 1948- Fellow; Cambridge U., Faculty of Div., 1950-53 Asst. Lect., 1953-82 Lect. Spec: New Testament. Pub: "The Priority of Mark" in *The Birth of the New Testament* (1981); "Stages in Christology in the Synoptic Gospels" *NTS* 10; and others. Addr: (h) Middleton Cottage, Sidgwick Ave., Cambridge, CB3 9DA, England 0223-358420.

SUGGS, M. Jack, b. Electra, TX, June 5, 1924, s. of Claude & Lottie, m. Ruth, chil: Adena; James; David. Educ: U. of Tex., BA 1946; Tex. Christian U., BD 1949; Duke U., PhD 1954. Emp: Tex. Christian U., Brite Div. Sch., Emeritus Dean & Prof.; Lexington Theol. Sem., 1966 Guest

Lect.; SW Mo. State U., 1978 Carrington Lect. Spec: New Testament. Pub: "Matthew 16:13-20" *Interpretation* 34 (1985); *Wisdom, Christology and Law in Matthew's Gospel* (Harvard U.P., 1970); *The Gospel Story* (Bethany, 1960); "The Eusebian Text of Matthew" *NT* 1 (1956); and others. Mem: SNTS; AAR, Pres., SW Sect. 1960; SBL, Pres., SW Sect. 1969. Addr: (h) 5405 Winifred, Fort Worth, TX 76133 817-292-1473.

SUHL, Alfred Wilhelm, b. Baekken/Ringenenaes-Denmark, January 27, 1934, s. of Otto Bernhard & Helene (Brix), m. Ursala Therese (Gebler), chil: Ulrike Christiane; Michael Peter; Ute Dorothea. Emp: U. Muenster, 1962-70 Sci. Asst., 1970-72 Asst. Prof., 1970- Prof. Spec: New Testament. Pub: "Paulinische Chronologie im Streit der Meinungen" *ANRW* II 26/1; "Der Galaterbrief: Situation und Argumentation" *ANRW* II 25/4; "Zur Auslegung von Mk 1,21-28: Hermeneutische und didaktische Ueberlegungen" *Kairos* (1984); *Der Brief an Philemon* (1981); *Der Wunderbegriff im Neuen Testament*, ed. (1980); *Paulus und seine Briefe: Ein Beitrag zur paulinischen Chronologie* (1975); "Der Philemonbrief als Beispiel paulinischer Paraenese" *Kairos* (1973); "Der konkrete Anlass des Roemerbriefes" *Kairos* (1971); *Die Funktion der alttestamentlichen Zitate und Anspielungen im Markusevangelium* (1965); and others. Mem: SNTS 1975-; Wiss. Gesellschaft fuer Theologie 1987-. Rec: Yachting, flute, singing. Addr: (o) U. Muenster, Evangelisch- Theologische Fakultaet, Universitaetsstr. 13-17, D-4400 Muenster, Germany 0251-832522; (h) Im Muehlenfeld 20, D-4400 Muenster 51, Germany 02501-5200.

SURBURG, Raymond F., b. Chicago, IL, July 3, 1909, s. of Frederick & Hulda, m. Lillian (Werbeck), chil: Paul. Educ: Columbia U., AM 1933; Bibl. Sem. of New York City, MRE 1940; Amer. Theol. Sem., ThD 1942; Fordham U., PhD 1950; Concordia Theol. Sem., DD 1989. Emp: Concordia Teachers Coll., 1954-60 Assoc. Prof.; Concordia Theol. Sem., 1960-85 Prof.; *Concordia Theol. Quar.*, Bk. Ed.; Bethany Luth. Sem., Reformation Lect. 1982. Spec: Hebrew Bible, Apocrypha and Post-biblical Studies. Pub: "The Influence of the Two Delitzches on Biblical and Near Eastern Studies" *Concordia Theol. Quar.* 47/1 (1983); *The Principles of Biblical Interpretation* (Concordia Sem. 1981); *Darwin, Evolution, and Creation* (Concordia Sem., 1959). Mem: ETS; SBL; ASOR. Rec: Sports, travel. Addr: (o) Concordia Theological Seminary, 6600 N Clinton, Ft. Wayne, IN 46825 219-482-9611; (h) 3720 Bobolink Crossover, Ft. Wayne, IN 46815 219-482-3180.

SUSSMAN, Varda, b. Israel. Educ: Hebrew U., BA, MA, Arch. Emp: Israel Dept. of Antiq., Jerusalem, Cur. Pub: "Lighting the Way Through History" *BAR* 11/2 (1987); *Ornamented Jewish Oil-Lamps: From the Destruction of the Second Temple Through the Bar-Kokba Revolt* (Aris & Phillips/IES, 1982); and others. Addr: (o) Israel

Antiquities Authority, PO Box 568, Jerusalem 91004, Israel 02-278-613; (h) 12 Haverey Zion St., Jerusalem 92226, Israel 632-588.

SUTER, David W., b. Staunton, VA, March 1, 1942, s. of Beverly & Sarah (Anderson), m. Kristine (Pearson), chil: Jessica; Aron; Nathan. Educ: U. of Chicago, BD 1967, MA 1970, PhD 1977. Emp: Wichita State U., 1974-81 Asst. Prof.; Pacific Luth. U., 1981-83 Asst. Prof.; St. Martin's Coll., 1983-89 Assoc. Prof., 1989- Prof., Relig. Stud., 1991- Dean of Humanities. Spec: New Testament, Apocrypha and Post-biblical Studies. Pub: "The Measure of Redemption" in *SBL 1983 Seminar Papers* (Scholars, 1983); "Mašal in the Similitudes of Enoch" *JBL* 100 (1981); *Tradition and Composition in the Parables of Enoch*, SBL Diss. Ser. (Scholars, 1979); and others. Mem: SBL 1974-. Rec: Photography. Addr: (o) St. Martin's College, Dept. of Religious Studies, Lacey, WA 98503 206-438-4360; (h) 420 123rd St. E, Tacoma, WA 98445 206-535-9399.

SUTTON, Walter C., b. East McKeesport, PA, April 23, 1927, s. of Harold & Zora (Harvison), m. Edith (McMillan), chil: Harold; Stephanie. Educ: Louisville Presbyn. Theol. Sem., BD 1957, ThM 1963. Emp: First Presbyn. Ch., 1957-76 Pastor; LPTS Admin., 1976-79; *Presbyn. Survey*, 1980-85 Ed.; John Knox Press, 1982-88 Assoc. Ed., Dir.; Westminster/John Knox Press, 1989-92 Assoc. Ed., Dir. Spec: New Testament. Mem: AAR 1982-; SBL 1982-. Rec: Folk dancing, wood carving. Addr: (o) John Knox Press, 341 Ponce de Leon Ave., Atlanta, GA 30365 404-873-1549; (h) 724 Dukehart Ct., Stone Mountain, GA 30083 404-294-7972.

SUZUKI, Yoshihide, b. Kumamoto, Japan, February 26, 1944, s. of Motonobu & Keiko, m. Setsuko, chil: Takako; Hitoshi. Educ: Intl. Christian U., MA 1972; Claremont Grad. Sch., PhD 1982. Emp: Niigata U., Japan, 1982- Asst. Prof., 1990- Prof. Spec: Archaeology, Hebrew Bible. Pub: "Deuteronomic Reformation in View of the Centralization of the Administration of Justice" *Ann. of the Japanese Bibl. Inst.* 13 (1987); *Shinmeiki no bunkengakutekikenkyu* (1987); "A Hebrew Ostracon from Mesad Hashavyahu—A Form-Critical Reinvestigation" *Ann. of the Japanese Bibl. Inst.* 8 (1982); "Deut. 6:4-5. Perspectives as a Statement of Nationalism and of Identity of Confession" *Ann. of the Japanese Bibl. Inst.* 9 (1983); and others. Awd: The Japan Acad. Prize 1990. Mem: SOTS 1972-; Japan Bibl. Inst. 1972-; SBL 1978-; Japan Soc. Christian Stud. 1982-. Rec: Baseball, football. Addr: (o) Niigata U., College of Gen. Ed., 8050 Igarashi-Ninomachi Niigata, Niigata 950-21, Japan 0252-62-7196; (h) 7492-62 Igarashi-Ninomachi Niigata, Niigata 950-21, Japan 0252-62-5864.

SVEINBJORNSSON, Jón, b. Reykjavik, Iceland, July 27, 1928, s. of Sveinbjörn Jonsson & Thórunn

(Bergthorsdóttir), m. Gudrún (Magnúsdóttir). chil: Sveinbjörn; Thorunn; Magnus; Halldor; Ingibjorg. Educ: U. of Uppsala, Sweden, Fil. kand. 1955; U. of Iceland, cand. theol. 1959. Emp: Icelandic Bible Soc., 1962- Trans., NT Trans. Com.; U. of Iceland, 1974- Prof., NT Stud., 1988- Chmn., Inst. of Theol.. Spec: New Testament. Pub: "New Trends in Bible Translation" *Stud. theol. isl.* (1990); "Reading and Exegesis" *Stud. theol. isl.* (1988); "New Trends in Biblical Research" *Timar. Hask.* (1986); "The Bible and New Trends in Literary Criticism" *Otdrid* (1985). Mem: IOSCS 1973-; AAR 1978-; SBL 1978-. Rec: Gardening. Addr: (o) U. of Iceland, Sudurgata, 101 Reykjavik, Iceland 354-1-25088; (h) Artúnsbrekka v/ Ellidaár, 110 Reykjavik, Iceland 354-1-33493.

SWANSON, Reuben J., b. Rockford, IL, April 15, 1917, s. of Joseph & Lorenza, m. Marian, chil: Robert; Timothy; Susan. Educ: Augustana Theol. Sem., BD 1945; Yale U., STM 1951, PhD 1956. Emp: Grand View Sem., 1958-60 Prof.; Lenoir Rhyne Coll., 1960-68 Prof., Relig., Chmn., Dept. of Phil. & Relig.; West. Carolina U., 1968-82 Prof., Phil. & Relig.; Calif. Luth. Coll., 1982-84 Adj. Prof.; St. John's Sem., 1984- Faculty. Spec: New Testament. Pub: *The Horizontal Line Synopsis of the Gospels* (West. N.C., 1975, 1984); and others. Mem: SBL. Rec: Rock collecting. Addr: (h) 16 Tahquitz Ct., Camarillo, CA 93010 805-987-5760.

SWAUGER, James L., b. W Newton, PA, November 1, 1913, s. of John & Katherine (Weaver), m. Helen (Poole), chil: John; Deborah (Handsman); Amy. Educ: U. of Pittsburgh, BS 1941, MLitt 1949; Waynesburg Coll., DSc 1957. Emp: Carnegie Mus. of Natural Hist., 1935-80, 1980- Vol.; U. of Pittsburgh, 1948-50 Lect., 1960 Fac. Mentor, Anthrop., 1971- Adj. Res. Prof., Anthrop. Excv: Timna, Wadi Beihan, West. Aden Protectorate, 1950 Supr.; Ashdod, Israel, 1959 Assoc. Dir.; Jordan, 1959 Investigator; Yemen, 1974 Dir. Spec: Archaeology. Pub: "First International Conference on the History and Archaeology of Jordan" *MERA Forum* 2/3 (1980); "A Visit to the Land of the Queen of Sheba" *Carnegie Mag.* 51/8 (1977); "Ashdoda" *Carnegie Mag.* 50/7 (1976); "Three Dolmen Sites in Jordan" *Almogaren II*, Inst. Canarium (1971); "Dolmen Studies in Palestine" *BA Reader* 3 (Doubleday, 1970); and others. Mem: Soc. for Amer. Arch. 1950-; Soc. for Pa. Arch. 1939-. Rec: Tennis, reading, walking. Addr: (o) Carnegie Museum of Natural History, 5800 Baum Blvd., Pittsburgh, PA 15206-3706 412-665-2606; (h) 179 W Hutchinson Ave., Pittsburgh, PA 15218 412-731-3807.

SWEENEY, Marvin A., b. Springfield, IL, July 4, 1953, s. of Jack & Leonore. Educ: Claremont Grad. Sch., MA, Relig. 1981, PhD 1983. Emp: Anc. Bibl. Manuscript Ctr. for Preservation & Res., 1979-83 Head Cataloguer; U. of Miami,

1983- Assoc. Prof., Relig. Stud.; W. F. Albright Inst., Jerusalem, 1993-94 Dorot Res. Prof. Spec: Hebrew Bible, Apocrypha and Post-biblical Studies. Pub: "Concerning the Structure and Generic Character of the Book of Nahum" *ZAW* 104 (1992); "Habakkuk, Book of" in *ABD* (1992); "A Form-Critical Reassessment of the Book of Zephaniah" *CBQ* 53 (1991); "Puns, Politics, *Perushim* in the Jacob Cycle" *Shofar* 9 (1991); "Structure, Genre, and Intent in the Book of Habakkuk" *VT* 41 (1991); "Isaiah 1-4 and the Post-Exilic Understanding of the Isaianic Tradition" BZAW 171 (1988). Mem: ASOR; AJS; NAPH; WUJS. Addr: (o) U. of Miami, Dept. of Religious Studies, PO Box 248264, Coral Gables, FL 33124 305-284-4733; (h) 6241 SW 78 St., #101 South, Miami, FL 33143 305-661-5215.

SWEET, John P. M., b. Ooticamund, India, June 10, 1927, s. of Jack & Phyllis, m. Mary (Trotman-Dickenson), chil: Richard; Alison; Rosemary. Educ: Oxford U., BA 1949, MA 1952. Emp: Cambridge U., 1958- Lect., Div. Spec: New Testament. Pub: "A Sign for Unbelievers: Paul's Attitude to Glossalalia" *NTS* (1967); "Revelation" in *Pelican Comm.* (SCM, 1979). Mem: SNTS 1961-. Rec: Walking, gardening. Addr: (o) Selwyn College, Cambridge CB3 9DQ, England 0223-335846; (h) 97 Barton Rd., Cambridge CB3 9LL, England 0223-353186.

SWETNAM, James H., b. St. Louis, MO, March 18, 1928, s. of Henry & Helen (Luth). Educ: St. Louis U., MA, PhL 1952; St. Mary's Coll., STL 1960; Pont. Bibl. Inst., Rome, SSL 1962; U. of Oxford, DPhil 1981. Emp: Pont. Bibl. Inst., Rome, 1962- Prof., Vice-Rector, Dean, Sec.; *Analecta Biblica*, 1962-75, 1978- Ed.; *Analecta Orientalia*, 1962-69 Ed.; *Subsidia Biblica*, 1972-75, 1978- Ed.; St. Louis U., 1964-78 Vis. Lect. Spec: New Testament. Pub: *An Introduction to the Study of New Testament Greek*, Subsidia Biblica 16 (1992); *Jesus and Isaac* Analecta Biblica 94 (1981); and others. Mem: CBA 1964-; SNTS 1987-. Addr: (o) Pontifical Biblical Institute, Via della Pilotta 25, 01187 Rome, Italy 06-679-6453.

SYLVA, Dennis D., b. Honolulu, HI, November 30, 1953, s. of Daniel & Winifred, m. Mary Ann, chil: David. Educ: Marquette U., PhD 1985. Emp: St. Francis Sem., 1984-89 Asst. Prof., 1990- Assoc. Prof., Bibl. Stud. Spec: Hebrew Bible, New Testament. Pub: "The Temple Curtain and Jesus' Death in the Gospel of Luke" *JBL* 105 (1986); "The Meaning and Function of Acts 7:46-50" *JBL* 106 (1987); "The Cryptic Clause *en tois tou patros mov* in Luke 2:49b" *ZNW* 78 (1987); "Nicodemus and His Spices (John 19:39)" *NTS* 34 (1988); "The Changing of Images in Psalm 23:5,6" *ZAW* 102 (1990); *Reimaging the Death of the Lukan Jesus*, BBB 73 (Hain, 1990); and others. Mem: SBL 1978-. Rec: Walking. Addr: (o) St. Francis Seminary, 3257 S Lake Dr., Milwaukee, WI 53207 414-481-8468; (h) 11108 Riverland Ct., Mequon, WI 53092 (414) 242-3455.

SYON, Danny, b. Romania, October 2, 1953, s. of Ladislau & Adina, m. Michal. Educ: Technion-Israel Inst. of Tech., Fac. of Aeronautical Engineering, BSc 1981. Emp: Haifa U., Zinman Inst. of Arch., 1989- Res. Fellow; Israel Antiq. Authority, 1991- Arch., Numismatist. Excv: Gamla, 1977-89 Photographer, Area Supr., Admn., Arch.; Caesarea Maritima, 1980-92 Underwater Excavator, Photographer, Area Supr.; Ginnosar Boat, 1986 Photographer, Excavator; Maagan Michael Shipwreck, 1989-90 Photographer, Excavator; Akko, 1991 Asst. Dir., Numismatist. Spec: Archaeology. Pub: "Gamla: Portrait of a Rebellion" *BAR* 18/1 (1992); "Confessions of a 'Nationalist' Archaeologist" in *The Limitations of Archaeological Knowledge*, Etudes et Recherches Arch. de l'Universite de Liege 49 (1992); "Photomosaics of the Boat's Interior," co-auth., in *The Excavation of an Ancient Boat in the Sea of Galilee*, ATIQOT 19; and others. Mem: Amer. Numismatic Soc. 1992-; Israel Numismatic Soc. 1992-. Rec: Photography, natural hist., hiking, diving. Addr: (o) Golan Museum, PO Box 30, Katzrin 12900, Israel 06-961-350; (h) 10 Wingate Ave., Haifa 33724, Israel 04-385-217.

SYREENI, Kari A., b. Helsinki, Finland, July 11, 1952, s. of Esko & Eine M., m. Hilkka-Liisa, chil: Sampo; Ahti. Educ: U. of Helsinki, Cand. Theol. 1976, ThD 1987. Emp: U. of Helsinki, 1976-82 Lect., Bibl. Greek, 1987- Docent, NT Exegesis, 1993-94 Acting Prof.; Acad. of Finland, 1983-91 Res. Asst., Jr. Res. Spec: New Testament. Pub: "The Gospel in Paradigms: A Study in the Hermeneutical Space of Luke-Acts" in *Luke-Acts: Scandinavian Perspectives*, PFES 54 (1991); "Matthew, Luke, and the Law: A Study in Hermeneutical Exegesis" in *The Law in the Bible and in its Environment*, PFES 51 (1990); "Between Heaven and Earth: On the Structure of Matthew's Symbolic Universe" *JSNT* 40 (1990); *The Making of the Sermon on the Mount*, AASF Diss. 44 (1987). Mem: SNTS 1988-; Finnish Exegetical Soc. 1989-. Rec: House building. Addr: (o) U. of Helsinki, Dept. of Bibl. Exegetics, Neitsytpolku 1b, SF-00140 Helsinki, Finland 01-1913961; (h) Haarikkakatu 12, SF-15300 Lahti, Finland 18-7562660.

SYREN, Roger J. B., b. Overmark, April 7, 1948, s. of Runar & Fanny, m. Marianne (Uppgard), chil: Johanna; Joakim; Jon-Anders. Educ: Abo Acad. U., Teol. Kand. 1974, ThD 1986; Helsinki U., BA 1979. Emp: Abo Acad. U., 1982-86 Asst. Tchr., 1986-92 Lect., Bibl. Lang. & Exegetics. Spec: Hebrew Bible, Apocrypha and Post-biblical Studies. Pub: "Targum Isaiah 52:13-53:12 and Christian Interpretation" *JJS* 1989); "The Isaiah Targum and Christian Interpretation" *SJT* (1986); "Vad ar 'targum'?" *Teologinen Aikakavskirja* (1986); *The Blessings in the Targums, A Study on the Targumic Interpretations of Genesis 49 and Deuteronomy 33* (Abo Acad., 1986); "Targumim och Versionerna" *Scandinavian Jewish Stud.* (1985); "Targumisterna som bibeltolkare"

Scandinavian Jewish Stud. (1984); and others. Mem: Scandinavian Soc. of Jewish Stud. 1975-; Scandinavian Assn. of Hum. 1978-. Rec: Music. Addr: (o) Institute of Exegetics, Biskopsg 1b A, SF-20500 Abo, Finland 921-654292; (h) Granboda 6, SF-22610 Lemland, Finland 928-34240.

SZLAGA, Jan, b. Gdynia, Poland, May 24, 1940, s. of Jan & Helena (Sciesinska). Educ: Cath. U. of Lublin, DD 1969. Emp: Catholic Ency., 1969 Redactor; Cath. U. of Lublin, 1970 Asst. Lect., 1983 Prof., 1981-83, Dean of Theol. Faculty., 1984-88 Vice-Rector; Dioces Chelmno 1988-92 Auxiliary Bishop; U. of Gdansk, 1991- Prof.; Dioces Pelplin, 1992- Diocesan Bishop. Spec: New Testament. Pub: Articles in *Catholic Ency.*; *The Newness of the Christ Covenant According the Letter to the Hebrews* (1979); *Studio Lectionem Facere,* co-ed. (1978). Rec: Oratorium & opera music, puzzles. Addr: (o) Ogrod Biskupi 2, PL-83-130 Pelplin, Poland 0-69-36-17-77.

TABET-BALADY, Miguel Angel, b. Caracas, December 24, 1941, s. of Fouad Tábet & Victoria Balady. Educ: Lic., Math 1964; Pont. U. of Laterano, ThD, Dogmatic Theol. 1967; Pont. U. of Salamanca, PhD, Trilingue Bibl. Philol. 1990. Emp: Studium Generale of the Opus Dei Prelature, 1968-69 Prof., Bibl. Exegesis in Spain, 1969-70 in Venezuela, 1970- in Rome; U. of Navarra, Fac. of Theol., 1970- Lect., OT; Fac. of Theol. of Ateneo Romano della Santa Croce, 1985- Prof., Bibl. Exegesis & OT; *Annales Theologici,* 1987- Redactor. Spec: Hebrew Bible. Pub: *Los comentarios de Abraham Ibn Ezra, Moseh ben Nahman y Yishaq Abrabanel a las bendiciones de Jacob (49,1-28)* (1991); "L'eccellenza del dono della vita nell'Antico Testamento" in *Persona, Verita e Morale* (Citta Nuova, 1988); "La distinzione dei peccati secondo la loro gravita nell'insegnamento di Gesu" *Annales Theol.* 2 (1988); "Cristologia e historicidad de los Evangelios en la Const. 'Dei Verbum'" in *Cristo, Hijo de Dios y Redentor del hombre* (Eunsa,; 1982); *Una Introducción a la Sagrada Escritura* (Rialp, 1981); and others. Mem: Assn. Bibl. Italiana 1972-; Assn. Bibl. Espanola 1982-. Rec: Alpinism. Addr: (o) Ateneo Romano della Santa Croce, Pzza. San Apollinare 49, Roma 00186, Italy 06-6861592; (h) Viale Bruno buozzi 73, Italy 06-8079042.

TABOR, James D., b. San Antonio, TX, March 2, 1946, s. of E.L. & Hazel M., m. Lori L. (Woodall), chil: David; Dan; Nathan; Eve; Seth. Educ: Abilene Christian U., BA 1966; Pepperdine U., MA 1971; U. of Chicago, MA 1974, PhD 1981. Emp: U. of Notre Dame, 1981-85 Asst. Prof.; Coll. of William & Mary, 1985-89 Vis. Asst. Prof.; U. of N.C.-Charlotte, 1989-91 Asst. Prof., 1991- Assoc. Prof. Spec: New Testament. Pub: *A Noble Death: Suicide and Martyrdom Among Ancient Jews and Christians,* co-auth. (HarperCollins, 1992); "Reflections on the Hebrew Bible and The New Testament"

Jour. of Reform Judaism (1990); "Returning to the Divinity" *JBL* 108 (1989); "What the Bible Says About the Future" in *What The Bible Really Says* (Prometheus, 1989); *Things Unutterable: Paul's Ascent to Paradise* (U. Press of Amer.); "Paul's Notion of Many 'Sons of God' and Its Hellenistic Contexts" *Helios* 13 (1986); "Resurrection and Immortality: Paul and Poimandies" in *Christian Teachings: Studies in Honor of LeMoine G. Lewis* (Abilene Christian U.P., 1981). Mem: SBL; AAR. Addr: (o) U. of North Carolina, Dept. of Religious Studies, Charlotte, NC 28223 704-547-2783.

TAEGER, Jens W., b. Sondershausen/Thuringia, February 16, 1945, s. of Wilhelm & Ursula. Educ: U. of Munster, Doc. dip. 1979. Emp: Protestant Ch. of Westphalia, 1971-73 Vicar, 1978 Pastor; U. of Munster, 1973-78 Res. Asst., 1978-86 Postdoc. Res. Asst. & Lect.; RWTH, Aachen, 1986-88 Prof., Bibl. Stud., 1989- Prof., NT; U. of Giessen, 1988-89 Prof., Bibl. Stud. Spec: New Testament. Pub: "Der grundsaetzliche oder ungrundsaetzliche Unterschied: Anmerkungen zur gegenwaertigen Debatte um das Gesetzesverstaendnis Jesu" in *Jesus und das juedische Gesetz* (Kohlhammer, 1992); *Johannesapokalypse und johanneischer Kreis, BZNW* 51 (de Gruyter, 1989); "Der konservative Rebell: Zum Widerstand des Diotrephes gegen den Presbyter" *ZNW* 78 (1987); "Einige neuere Veroeffentlichungen zur Apokalypse des Johannes" *Verkundigung und Forschung* 29/1 (1984); *Der Mensch und sein Heil: Studien zum Bild des Menschen und zur Sicht der Bekehrung bei Lukas,* STNT 14 (Mohr, 1982); "Paulus und Lukas uber den Menschen" *ZNW* 71 (1980); and others. Mem: SNTS 1987-; Wissenschaftliche Gesellschaft fur Theol. 1990-. Addr: (o) Institut fur Theologie, Eilfschornsteinstr. 7, D-52056 Aachen, Germany 0241-80-6135; (h) Hoyastr. 21, D-48147 Munster, Germany 0251-271337.

TALBERT, Charles H., b. Jackson, MS, March 19, 1934, s. of Carl & Audrey (Hale), m. Betty (Weaver), chil: Caroline; Richard. Educ: Southern Bapt. Theol. Sem., BD 1959; Vanderbilt U., PhD 1963. Emp: Wake Forest U., 1963- Prof.; *JBL,* 1981-83 Ed. Bd.; SBL, Diss. Ser., NT, 1984-89; *CBQ,* 1991- Assoc. Ed. Spec: New Testament. Pub: *Reading John* (Crossroad, 1992); "Ancient Biography" in *ABD* (1992); *Reading Corinthians* (Crossroads, 1987); "Reimarus" in Ency. of Religion (Macmillan, 1986); "Paul's Understanding of the Holy Spirit: The Evidence of 1 Corinthians 12-14" *Perspectives in Religious Studies* (1984-85); *Acts* (John Knox, 1984); *Reading Luke* (Crossroads, 1982); and others. Mem: SBL 1965-; CBA 1978-; SNTS 1972-. Rec: Travel, sports, fiction. Addr: (o) Wake Forest U., Box 7212, Winston-Salem, NC 27109 919-759-5464; (h) 3091 Prytania Rd., Winston-Salem, NC 27106 919-765-6851.

TALMON, Shemaryahu, b. Skierniwice, Poland, May 26, 1920, s. of Yomtov & Hanna, m. Penina, chil: Efrat; Tamar; Noga; Tammy. Educ:

Hebrew U., Jerusalem, MA 1945, PhD 1955. Emp: Hebrew U., 1961-84 J.L. Magnes Prof. Emeritus of Bibl. Stud.; *Textus,* 1964-82 Ed.; Haifa U., 1968-70, Dean; Hochschule fuer Judische Studien, Heidelberg, 1982-84 Rector; Hebrew U. Bible Project, 1958- Ed.; *VT,* 1972- Adv. Com. Spec: Hebrew Bible, Apocrypha and Post-biblical Studies. Pub: *Juden und Christen im Gespraech* (Neukirchener, 1991); *Jewish Civilization in the Hellenistic Roman Period,* ed. (Sheffield, 1991); *The World of Qumran from Within* (Magnes, 1989); *Gesellschaft und Literatur in der Hebraeischen Bibel* (Neukirchener, 1988); and others. Awd: Munich, Romano Guardini Medal & Prize 1975. Mem: SOTS 1950-; Israel Arch. Soc. 1960-; SBL 1961-. Rec: Swimming, hiking, gardening. Addr: (o) Hebrew U., Dept. of Bible Studies, Mt. Scopus, 5106 Jerusalem, Israel 02-883 510; (h) 5, Jan Smuts St., 93108 Jerusalem, Israel 02-618-893.

TAMBASCO, Anthony J., b. Brooklyn, NY, May 23, 1939, s. of Montana & Filomena, m. Joan (McNeil). Educ: Cath. Inst. of Paris, STL 1968; Pont. Bibl. Inst., SSB 1969, SSL 1970; Union Theol. Sem., N.Y., PhD 1981. Emp: St. Louis U., 1970-73 Asst. Prof.; Maryknoll Sch. of Theol., 1975-79 Asst. Prof.; Georgetown U., 1979- Prof. Spec: New Testament. Pub: *A Theology of Atonement and Paul's Vision of Christianity* (Liturgical, 1991); *In the Days of Paul: The Social World and Teaching of the Apostle* (Paulist, 1991); *What Are They Saying About Mary?* (Paulist, 1984); *In the Days of Jesus: The Jewish Background and Unique Teaching of Jesus* (Paulist, 1983); "Pauline Ethics: An Application of Liberation Hermeneutics" *BTB* (1982); "Jeremiah and the Law of the Heart" *The Bible Today* (1981); and others. Mem: CBA 1970-; SBL 1979-; Coll. Theol. Soc. 1981-. Rec: Travel. Addr: (o) Georgetown U., Theology Dept., Washington, DC 20057 202-687-6234; (h) 3000 Spout Run Pkwy., Apt. B211, Arlington, VA 22201 703-522-0968.

TANNEHILL, Robert C., b. Clay Center, KS, May 6, 1934, s. of Francis & Cecelia, m. Alice, chil: Grace; Celia; Paul. Educ: Yale Div. Sch., BD 1959, Yale U. MA 1960, PhD 1963. Emp: Oberlin Grad. Sch. of Theol., 1963-66 Instr., NT; Meth. Theol. Sch. in Ohio, 1966- Prof., NT; SBL Mon. Ser., 1979-85 Assoc. Ed.; *JBL,* 1988- Ed. Bd. Spec: New Testament. Pub: "The Functions of Peter's Mission Speeches in the Narrative of Acts" *NTS* 37 (1991); *The Narrative Unity of Luke-Acts: A Literary Interpretation,* vol. 1 & 2 (Fortress, 1986, 1990); "Rejection by Jews and Turning to Gentiles: The Pattern of Paul's Mission in Acts" in *Luke-Acts and the Jewish People* (Augsburg, 1988); "Israel in Luke-Acts: A Tragic Story" *JBL* 104 (1985); "Varieties of Synoptic Pronouncement Stories" *Semeia* 20 (1981); "The Disciples in Mark: The Function of a Narrative Role" *JR* 57 (1977); *The Sword of His Mouth: Forceful and Imaginative Language in Synoptic Sayings* (Fortress/ Scholars, 1975); *Dying and Rising with Christ: A*

Study in Pauline Theology (Toepelmann, 1967) and others. Awd: Danforth Fellow. 1956; Assoc. Theol. Sch., Faculty Fellow. 1969; SBL Fellow. 1982. Mem: SBL 1963-; SNTS 1971-; East Great Lakes Bibl. Soc., Pres. 1978-79. Rec: Bird photography. Addr: (o) Methodist Theological School in Ohio, Delaware, OH 43015 614-362-3363; (h) 960 Braumiller Rd., Delaware, OH 43015 614-363-4131.

TATE, Marvin E., b. Hope, AR, May 2, 1925, s. of Marvin Embry & Mary Lou (Merrick), m. Julia (Moorman), chil: Sarah; Martha; Betsey; Andrew; Virginia. Educ: Ouachita Bapt. U., BA 1947; South. Bapt. Theol. Sem., MDiv 1950, PhD 1958. Emp: Wayland Coll., 1959-60 Asst. Prof.; South. Bapt. Theol. Sem., 1960- Prof. Spec: Hebrew Bible, Semitic Languages, Texts and Epigraphy. Pub: "Satan in the Old Testament" *Rev. & Expositor* Fall (1992); *Psalms 51-100,* Word Bibl. Comm. 20 (1991); "War and Peacemaking in the Old Testament" *Rev. & Expositor* (1982); "Promising Paths Toward Biblical Theology" *Rev. & Expositor* (1981); "Proverbs," "Job" in *Broadman Bible Comm.* (1971); and others. Mem: SBL 1958-; NABPH 1959-; NAPH 1975-. Rec: Walking, music, reading. Addr: (o) Southern Baptist Seminary, Box 1916, Louisville, KY 40240 502-897-4309; (h) 3212 Five Oaks Pl., Louisville, KY 40207 502-896-0226.

TATUM, Lynn W., b. Brownfield, TX, January 19, 1954, s. of Delton F. & Freddie J. (Riley), m. Marilyn (Gordon), chil: Talj. Educ: Baylor U., BA 1975; Duke U., PhD 1988. Emp: N.C. Mus. of Life & Sci., 1982 Exhibit Designer; Baylor U., 1986-92 Lect. Excv: Tel 'Ira, 1980 Area Supr.; Horvat 'Uza, 1982-88 Area Supr.; Sepphoris, 1985 Field Supr.; Radum, 1989 Area Supr.; Tel Malhata, 1990 Area Supr. Spec: Archaeology, Hebrew Bible. Pub: "King Manasseh and the Royal Fortress at Horvat 'Uza" *BA* 54 (1991); "Nehemiah's Wall" *BI* 17 (1991). Awd: ASOR, Res. Fellow. 1984-85; Natl. Coun. on U.S.-Arab Relations, Malone Fellow. 1989. Mem: ASOR, Pres., SW reg. 1992-93; SBL; NABPR; IES; Tex. Assn. of Middle East Schol. Rec: Travel, skiing, theatre. Addr: (o) Baylor U., Baylor Box 97294, Waco, TX 76798-7294 817-755-3735; (h) 1317 Dove, Waco, TX 76706 817-662-3574.

TAYLOR, Arch B., Jr., b. Charlotte, NC, December 23, 1920, s. of Archibald Boggs & Margaret (Webb), m. Wanda Rowe (Myers), chil: William; John; Samuel. Educ: Davidson Coll., BA (summa cum laude) 1942; Louisville Presbyn. Theol. Sem., BD 1945, MTh 1954. Emp: Shikoku Gakuin U., Japan, 1950-86 Prof., Bible, 1978-1982 Pres., 1986- Prof. Emeritus; *Japan Christian Quar.,* 1956-57 Ed.; Louisville Presbyn. Sem., 1983-84 Adj. Prof., Missions; Presbyn. Coll., 1990-91 Adj. Prof., Bible, Missionary in Residence. Spec: Hebrew Bible, New Testament. Pub: "Clash of Cultures—Japanese Polytheism vs.

Biblical Monotheism" *Japan Christian Quar.* (1982); "Liberation for Women: A Biblical View" *Japan Christian Quar.* (1974); "Ancient Scripture and Modern Life—A Conciliatory Suggestion Concerning Biblical Authority and Interpretation" *Treatises,* Shikoku Gakuin (1974); "Male-Female-Nature-Scripture" *Treatises,* Shikoku Gakuin (1973); "Decision in the Desert" *Interpretation* (1960); and others. Awd: Davidson Coll., LLD 1964. Mem: SBL; Christian Schol. Assn., Japan. Rec: Travel, peace & justice issues related to Central America & Israel/Palestine. Addr: (h) 2021 Strathmoor Blvd., Louisville, KY 40205 502-454-4105.

TAYLOR, J. Glen, b. Calgary, AB, December 6, 1956, s. of Charles & Margaret Taylor, m. Marion Ann, chil: Peter; Catherine; David. Educ: U. of Calgary, BA 1977; Dallas Theol. Sem., ThM 1981; Yale U., MPhil, PhD, Near East. Lang. & Lit. 1989. Emp: Wycliffe Coll., U. of Toronto, 1987-88 Lect.; 1989- Assoc. Prof., OT. Spec: Archaeology, Hebrew Bible, Semitic Languages, Texts and Epigraphy. Pub: "A First and Last Thing to Do in Mourning: KTU 1.161 and Parallels," "The Two Earliest Known Representations of Yahweh" in *Ascribe to the Lord: Biblical and Other Essays in Memory of Peter C. Craigie,* JSOTSup, co-ed. (Sheffield, 1988); "A Long-Awaited Vocative Singular Noun with Final *Aleph* in Ugaritic" *UF* 17 (1985); "The Song of Deborah and Two Canaanite Goddesses" *JSOT* 23 (1982); and others. Awd: U. of Aberdeen, Henry Foote Prize in OT 1978; ASOR, G.A. Barton Fellow 1986; U. of Toronto, Knox Coll., Blair Teaching Fellow. 1986. Mem: SBL 1982-; ASOR 1986-; CSBS 1987-. Rec: Skiing, camping. Addr: (o) Wycliffe Coll., 5 Hoskin Ave., Toronto, ON M5S 1H7, Canada 416-979-2870.

TAYLOR, J. Justin, b. Wellington, New Zealand, August 26, 1943, s. of John James & Margaret Lilias (Beard). Educ: U. of Cambridge, Downing Coll., England, MA 1970, PhD 1972; Ecole Biblique, Jerusalem, Elève titulaire 1984, Elève dip. 1986. Emp: Cambridge U., Downing Coll., 1970-73 Res. Fellow; Mt. St. Mary's Sem., 1974-78 Lect., Lbrn.; Massey U., New Zealand, 1974-78 Assoc. Lect., Hist.; Ecole Biblique, Jerusalem, 1988-91 Asst. Prof., 1991- Assoc. Prof.; *RB,* Ed. Bd. Spec: New Testament, Apocrypha and Post-biblical Studies. Pub: "The Love of Many Will Grow Cold: Matt 24:9-13 and the Neronian Persecution" *RB* 96 (1989); "The Making of Acts: A New Account" *RB* 97 (1990); "The Coming of Elijah, Mt 17,10-13 and Mk 9,11-13: The Development of the Texts," "Khirbert es-Samra dans l'Histoire" *RB* 98 (1991); *As It Was Written: An Introduction to the Bible* (Paulist, 1987); and others. Mem: SBL 1990-. Rec: Music, walking. Addr: (o) Ecole Biblique et Archeologique Francaise, PO Box 19053, 91190 Jerusalem, Israel 894468.

TAYLOR, Marion A., b. Toronto, ON, d. of Archie & Mary (Finlayson), m. J. Glen Taylor,

chil: Peter; Catherine; David. Educ: U. of Toronto, BA 1975, MA, Near East. Stud. 1977, MDiv 1980; Yale Div. Sch., MSTh 1982; Yale U., MPhil, PhD, Rel. Stud. 1982-88. Emp: Wycliffe Coll., U. of Toronto, 1986-88 Lect., 1988- Assoc. Prof., OT. Spec: Hebrew Bible. Pub: "Working with Wisdom Literature: Joseph Hall and William Henry Green" in *Solomon's Divine Arts: Joseph Hall* (Pilgrim, 1991); "Books of Interest (Old Testament)" *Toronto Jour. of Theol.* 4 (1988); "Jeremiah 45: The Problem of Placement" *JSOT* 37 (1987). Awd: Yale U. Fellow. 1982-86; Social Sci. & Hum. Res. Coun. of Canada, Doc. Fellow. 1985-86. Mem: SBL; CSBS. Rec: Baking, camping. Addr: (o) Wycliffe Coll., 5 Hoskin Ave., Toronto, ON M5S 1H7, Canada 416-979-2870.

TAYLOR, Myron Jackson, b. Goodwill, WV, March 26, 1924, s. of Everett & Lily Mae (Mabry), m. Sarah Jean (Riner), chil: Toni; Tim; Terri. Educ: Christian Theol. Sem., BD 1956; Johnson Bible Coll., DD 1980. Emp: Min., 1942-; Westwood Hills Christian Ch., 1969- Sr. Min.; Westwood Christian Found., 1975- Adj. Prof.; Emmanuel Sch. of Relig., 1980- Adj. Prof. Spec: New Testament. Pub: *Mark—Gospel of Action;* and others. Mem: SBL; AH; Disciples of Christ Hist. Soc. Rec: Gardening, jogging, travel. Addr: (o) Westwood Hills Christian Church, 10808 LeConte Ave., Los Angeles, CA 90024 310-208-8576; (h) 5167 Woodley Ave., Encino, CA 91436.

TAYLOR, Walter F., Jr., b. Omaha, NE, December 15, 1946, s. of Walter & Natalie, m. Dyann Adele (Gottula), chil: Frederick; Jennifer. Educ: Luth. Theol. Sem. at Philadelphia, MDiv 1973; Claremont Grad. Sch., PhD 1981. Emp: Sch. of Theol. at Claremont, 1973-76 Instr.; Luth. Ch., 1978-81 Pastor; Trinity Luth. Sem., 1981- Prof.; *Trinity Sem. Rev.,* 1982-1991 Ed. Spec: New Testament. Pub: "The Pastoral Epistles" in *Later New Testament Writings* (Fortress, 1993); "Humanity, NT View of," "Unity/Unity of Humanity" in *ABD* (1993); *Ephesians* (Augsburg, 1985); and others. Awd: Luth. Theol. Sem., Women's Aux. Schol., 1970-73; ATS Theol. Scholar. and Res. Awd. 1988-89; U. of Heidelberg, Fulbright Prof. 1988-89. Mem: SBL; Soc. for Antiquity & Christianity. Rec: Walking, baseball, gardening. Addr: (o) Trinity Lutheran Seminary, 2199 E Main St., Columbus, OH 43209 614-235-4136; (h) 1461 Kenwick Rd., Columbus, OH 43209 614-231-9822.

TEEPLE, Howard Merle, b. Salem, OR, December 29, 1911, s. of Charles & Etruda (Branchflower), m. Gladys (Windedehl). Educ: Willamette U., BA 1938; U. of Chicago., PhD 1955, MA 1963. Emp: Emory U., 1955-57 Res. Asst.; WV Wesleyan Coll., 1957-61 Assoc. Prof., Chmn. Relig. Dept.; NW U., 1963-69 Sr. Asst. Reference Lbrn.; Chicago State U., 1969-77 Head Reference Dept., Lib. Spec: Archaeology, New Testament. Pub: *How Did Christianity Really Begin?: A Historical-Archaeological Approach* (1992); *The Historical*

Approach to the Bible (Relig. & Ethics Inst., 1982); *The Noah's Ark Nonsense* (Relig. & Ethics Inst., 1978); *The Literary Origin of the Gospel of John* (Relig. & Ethics Inst., 1974); "Methodology in Source Analysis of the Fourth Gospel" *JBL* (1962); and others. Mem: SBL 1954-; AAR 1957-77; Amer. Lib. Assn. 1964-74. Addr: (o) 400 Main St., Evanston, IL 60202 312-328-4049.

TELFORD, William R., b. Glasgow, Scotland, October 15, 1946, s. of William & Marion, m. Andrena (Sandford). Educ: Glasgow U., MA 1968, BD 1971; Union Theol. Sem., STM 1972; Cambridge U., Christ's Coll., PhD 1976. Emp: Mansfield Coll., Oxford, 1977-79 Res. Fellow, Tutor in Bibl. Stud.; U. of Newcastle Upon Tyne, England, 1979- Lect. Spec: New Testament. Pub: "The Pre-Markan Tradition in Recent Research (1980-1990)" in *The Four Gospels: 1992*, Festschrift F. Neirynck (Peeters/Leuven U.P., 1992); "More Fruit from the Withered Tree: Temple and Fig-tree in Mark from a Graeco-Roman Perspective" in *Templum Amicitiae: Essays on the Second Temple*, Festschrift E. Bammel (Sheffield, 1991); "Mark, Gospel of" in *A Dict. of Biblical Interpretation* (SCM, 1990); *The Interpretation of Mark*, ed. (Fortress, 1985); *The Barren Temple and the Withered Tree* (JSOT, 1980); and others. Awd: Union Theol. Sem., Scots Fellow. 1971-72. Mem: SNTS 1981-; Brit. NT Conf. 1981-. Rec: Travel, squash, cinema. Addr: (o) U. of Newcastle Upon Tyne, Religious Studies, Armstrong Bldg, Newcastle Upon Tyne, England 091-222-6729; (h) Ladywell Cottage, 24 West Road, Ponteland, Northumberland NE20 9SX, England 0661-825437.

TEMPLETON, Douglas A., b. Glasgow, Scotland, May 27, 1935, s. of Kenneth & Isabella (Younger), m. Elizabeth (Maclaren), chil: Kirsten; Alan; Calum. Educ: Gonville & Cauis Coll., Cambridge U., BA 1957, MA 1991; U. of Glasgow, BD, PhD 1965. Emp: U. of Edinburgh, 1968- Sr. Lect., NT Lang., Lit., Theol. Spec: New Testament. Pub: "A 'Farced Epistol' to a Sinking Sun of David, *Ecclesiastes* and *Finnegans Wake*: The Synoptic Version" in *Text and Pretext* (Sheffield, 1992); *Re-exploring Paul's Imagination: A Cynical Laywoman's Guide to Paul of Tarsus* (Eisenbrauns, 1988); "Az interpretacio kelta es pannon aspektusai: Pal es Korinthus" *Theologiai Dikevkonyv* (1986-87); "Pauline Investigations" *Heythrop Jour.* 27 (1986); "Kerygma: A Definition" in *God, Secularism and History* (Columbia, 1974); and others. Mem: SNTS 1968-; SST 1968-. Rec: Hill-walking, satire, survival. Addr: (o) New College, The Mound, Edinburgh, EH1 2LX, Scotland 031-225-8400; (h) 22 Royal Circus, Edinburgh EH3 6SS, Scotland 031-225-3084.

TERRIEN, Samuel, b. Saumur, France, March 27, 1911, m. Sara Margaret (Frantz), chil: Georges; Cecile; Alys; Beatrice. Educ: Acad. de Rennes, Baccalaureat es-Lettres 1927, 1928; U. de Paris, Cert. de Lic. es-Lettres en Lang. semitiques 1933; Union Theol. Sem., STM 1936, DTh 1941. Emp: Union Theol. Sem., 1943-47 Asst. Prof., 1947-53 Assoc. Prof., 1953-64; Auburn Prof. of OT, 1964-76 Davenport Prof. of Hebrew & the Cognate Lang.; Columbia U., 1964-76 Adj. Prof. of Relig. Pub: *Proclamation 3: Holy Week* (1986); *Till the Heart Sings: A Bibl. Theol. of Manhood and Womanhood* (1985); *The Elusive Presence: Toward a New Biblical Theol.* (1978); *Oxford Annoted Bible*, contb. (1973); *Interpreter's Dict. of the Bible*, I-IV, assoc. ed. (1962); *Interpreter's Bible*, vol. I-VI, assoc. ed., contb. (1952-56); and others. Mem: SBL, Hon. Pres. 1980. Addr: (h) 12 Stoneleigh Rd., West Newton, MA 02165.

TEUBAL, Savina J., b. Manchester, England, July 25, 1926, d. of Nissim & Violet (Mansour). Educ: Intl. Coll., PhD 1977. Emp: Writer; Lect. Spec: Hebrew Bible, Mesopotamian Studies. Pub: "Simhat Hohmah" in *Four Centuries of Jewish Women's Spirituality: A Sourcebook* (Beacon, 1992); *Hagar the Egyptian: The Lost Tradition of the Matriarchs* (HarperCollins, 1990); "La Mujer, La Ley y El Antiguo Cercano Oriente" in *Maj' Shavot* (1985); *Sarah the Priestess: The First Matriarch of Genesis* (Swallow, 1984). Mem: AAR; SBL. Rec: Archaeology. Addr: (h) 541 Stassi Ln., Santa Monica, CA 90402 213-459-5503.

THEE, Francis C. R., b. Lexington, MO, March 8, 1936. s. of Paul & Yetta (Willer), m. Mary Ellen (Bartlett), chil: Paul. Educ: Cen. Bible Coll., BA 1957, MA 1959; Wheaton Coll., MA 1963; U. of Chicago., PhD 1980. Emp: NW Coll. of the Assemblies of God, 1963- Prof. Spec: New Testament, Apocrypha and Post-biblical Studies. Pub: *The Complete Biblical Library*, contb. (Gospel, 1985); *Julius Africanus and the Early Christian View of Magic* (Mohr, 1984); "'Wherefore Tongues...': An Interpretation of 1 Corinthians 14:20-25" *Paraclete* (1969). Mem: AAR 1970-; Soc. for Pentecostal Stud. 1970-. Rec: Reading, hiking, travel. Addr: (o) Northwest College, PO Box 579, Kirkland, WA 98083-0579 206-822-8266; (h) 5829-112th Pl. NE, Kirkland, WA 98033 206-822-1319.

THEISSEN, Gerd, b. Moenchengladbach, Germany, April 24, 1943, s. of Albert & Else, m. Christa, chil: Oliver; Gunnar. Educ: U. of Bonn, DTh 1968, Habil. 1972. Emp: U. of Bonn, 1973-78 Dozent; U. of Copenhagen, 1978-80 Prof.; U. of Heidelberg, 1980- Prof. Spec: New Testament. Pub: *Lokalkolorit und Zeitgeschichte in den Evangelien* (1989); "Das 'schwankenck Rohr' in Matthew 11,7 und die Grundungmonzen von Tiberias" *ZDPW* (1985); *Biblischer Glaube in evolutionarer Sicht* (1984); *Psychologische Aspekte paulinischer Theologie* (1983); *Studien zur Soziologie des Urchristentums* (1979); and others. Addr: (o) Wissenschaftlich-Theologisches Seminary, Kisselgasse 1, 6900 Heidelberg, Germany 06221-543-311; (h) Max Josef Str. 54/1, 6900 Heidelberg, Germany.

THEOPHILUS, Paul, b. Bandung, Indonesia, January 21, 1943, s. of Tjie Gie & King Leng, m. Jane, chil: Sofia. Educ: Alliance Bible Sem., Hong Kong, ThB 1966; Golden Gate Bapt. Theol. Sem., MDiv 1971; Princeton Theol. Sem., ThM 1972; South. Bapt. Theol. Sem., PhD 1979. Emp: Alliance Bible Sem., Hong Kong, 1980-84 Acad. Dean; China Grad. Sch. of Theol., Hong Kong, 1982 Vis. Prof.; N Amer. Congress of Chinese Evang., 1984-87 Exec. Dir.; Alliance Theol. Sem., 1987- Asst. Prof., OT & Chinese Pastoral Stud. Spec: Hebrew Bible. Pub: "Biblical Creationism Versus Scholars' Creationism" *Chinese Ch. Today* (1982); and others. Mem: SBL. Rec: Swimming, basketball, badminton. Addr: (o) Alliance Theological Seminary, Nyack, NY 10960 914-358-2995.

THIEDE, Carsten P., b. Berlin, Germany, August 8, 1952, m. Franziska (Campbell), chil: Miriam; Emily; Frederick. Educ: Technische U. Berlin, MA 1975; Oxford U., MA 1993. Emp: Oxford U., 1976-77 Res. Fellow; U. de Geneve, 1977-82 Asst. Licencié; London U., Inst. Germanic Stud., 1982-Dir.; Inst. fuer Wissenschaftstheoretische Grundlagenforschung, Germany, 1992-. Spec: New Testament. Pub: *The Earliest Gospel Manuscript? The Qumran Fragment 7Q5 and its Significance for New Testament Studies* (Paternoster, 1992); *Funde, Fakten, Faehrtensuche: Spuren des fruehen Christentums in Europa* (Brockhaus, 1992); *From Christ to Constantine—The Trial and Testimony of the Early Church* (Christian Hist. Inst., 1991); "Papyrus Bodmer L (=p73)" *Museum Helveticum* 47/1 (1990); and others. Rec: Producing TV documentaries, good wine. Addr: (o) Institut fuer Wissenschaftstheoretische Grundlagenforschung, Busdorfwall 16, 33098 Paderborn, Germany 05251-24905; (h) Friedrich-Ebert Str. 52, 33102 Paderborn, Germany 05251-31230.

THIELMAN, Frank S., b. Waynesville, NC, November 18, 1957, s. of Calvin C. & Dorothy B., m. Abigail Rhines, chil: Jonathan. Educ: Wheaton Coll., BA 1980; Cambridge U., BA 1982, MA 1986; Duke U., PhD 1987. Emp: Duke U., 1986-87 James L. Price Instr. in Relig.; King Coll., 1987-89 Asst. Prof.; Beeson Div. Sch., 1989- Assoc. Prof. Spec: New Testament. Pub: "The Coherence of Paul's View of the Law: The Evidence of First Corinthians" *NTS* 38 (1992); "The Style of the Fourth Gospel and Ancient Literary Critical Concepts of Religious Discourse" in *Persuasive Artistry* (Sheffield, 1991); *From Plight to Solution: A Jewish Framework for Understanding Paul's View of the Law in Galatians and Romans* (Brill, 1989); "Another Look at the Eschatology of Eusebius of Caesarea" *VC* 41 (1987). Awd: SBL, SE Kenneth L. Clark Awd. 1986. Mem: IBR; SBL. Addr: (o) Samford U., Beeson Divinity School, Birmingham, AL 35229 205-870-2991; (h) 415 Woodland Dr., Birmingham, AL 35209 205-871-0133.

THIMMES, Pamela L., b. Columbus, OH, July 1, 1948, d. of Leo F. & Margaret (Rohrer). Educ: Ohio U., BS 1970; Canisius Coll., MA 1979;

Vanderbilt U., MA 1986, PhD, Relig. 1990. Emp: U. Dayton, 1985- Asst. Prof. Spec: New Testament. Pub: *Studies in the Biblical Sea-Storm Type-Scene: Convention and Invention* (Mellen, 1992); "The Language of Community: Metaphors, Systems of Convictions, Ethnic and Gender Issues in Luke 10:25-37 and 10:38-42" in *SBL Seminar Papers* (1991); "Fear as a Reaction to Jesus in the Markan Gospel" in *Proc. of the East. Great Lakes & MidW Bible Soc. IX* (1989); and others. Mem: AAR; SBL; CTS. Rec: Golf, camping, needlework, reading. Addr: (o) U. of Dayton, Dept. of Religious Studies, 300 College Park, Dayton, OH 45469-1480 513-229-4321; (h) 2149-F Sidneywood Rd., West Carrolton, OH 45449-2676.

THISELTON, Anthony C., b. Woking, Surrey, England, July 13, 1937, s. of Eric & Hilda (Kevan), m. Rosemary, chil: Stephen; Linda; Martin. Educ: U. of London, BD 1959, MTh 1964; U. of Sheffield, PhD 1977. Emp: U. of Bristol, 1965-70 Tchr., Theol.; U. of Sheffield, 1970-86 Sr. Lect., Bibl. Stud.; St. John's Theol. Coll., Notingham 1986-88 Prin.; *JSNT*, 1981-91 Adv. Ed.; U. of Durham, St. John's Coll., 1988-92 Prin., Hon. Prof., Theol.; U. of Nottingham, 1992- Prof., Christian Theol., & Head, Dept. of Theol. Spec: New Testament. Pub: "Realized Eschatology at Corinth" *NTS* (1978); "Truth" in *New International Dict. of New Testament Theology* (1978); "The 'Interpretation' of Tongues: A New Suggestion in the Light of Greek Usage in Philo and Josephus" *JTS* (1979); *The Two Horizons: New Testament Hermeneutics* (Eerdmans, 1980); *The Responsibility of Hermeneutics,* co-auth. (Eerdmans, 1985); *New Horizons in Biblical Hermeneutics* (HarperCollins, 1992); and others. Mem: SNTS 1976-; SBL 1982-; AAR 1984-. Rec: Choral and organ music. Addr: (o) U. of Nottingham, Dept. of Theology, University Park, Nottingham, NG7 2RD, England 602-515852.

THOMAS, John Christopher, b. Maryville, TN, September 2, 1954, s. of Wayne & Betty (Fritts), m. Barbara Diane (Reckner), chil: Paige Diane; Lori Danielle. Educ: Lee Coll., BA 1976; Ch. of God Sch. of Theol., MA 1977; Ashland Theol. Sem., MDiv 1978; Princeton Theol. Sem., ThM 1979; U. of Sheffield, PhD 1990. Emp: Lee Coll., 1981-82 Vis. Lect.; Ch. of God Sch. of Theol., 1982- Assoc. Prof., NT; *Jour. of Pentecostal Theol.,* & Sup. Ser., 1992- Ed. Spec: New Testament. Pub: "The Kingdom of God in the Gospel According to Matthew" *NTS* 39 (1993); "The Devil, Disease, and Deliverance" *Jour. of Pentecostal Theol.* 2 (1993); "The Fourth Gospel and Rabbinic Judaism" *ZNW* 82 (1991); *Footwashing in John 13 and the Johannine Community* (JSOT, 1991); "Discipleship in Mark's Gospel" in *Faces of Renewal* (Hendrickson, 1988); "A Note on the Text of John 13:10" *NT* 29 (1987); and others. Awd: Ashland Theol. Sem., Alumnus of the Year 1992. Mem: Soc. for Pentecostal Stud. 1981-; ETS 1981-; CBA 1983-; IBR 1985-; SBL 1987-. Rec: Tennis, reading, softball, biking. Addr: (o) Church of God School of Theology, PO Box 3330, Cleveland, TN 37320 615-478-7038; (h) Rt. 2 Box 116 E, Riceville, TN 37370 615-745-2834.

THOMPSON, Henry O., b. Northwood, IA, October 23, 1932, s. of Orrin S. & Martha Mary (Maertens), m. Joyce Elaine (Beebe), chil: Warren Gerald; Howard Orrin. Educ: Iowa State U., BSc 1953; Drew U., MDiv 1958, PhD 1964; Syracuse U., MSc 1971; Jersey City State Coll., MA 1975. Emp: Colgate-Rochester Div. Sch., 1962-63 Instr.; Syracuse U., 1963-67 Lect., OT; N.Y. Theol. Sem., 1967-74 Prof., OT; U. of Jordan, 1971-72 Adj. Prof., Arch.; ACOR, Jordan, 1971-72 Dir., 1972-73 Vis. Prof. Excv: Shechem, 1960, 1962, 1964, 1966 Staff, 1968 Admn. Dir.; Heshbon, 1968, 1971, 1973 Core Staff; Khirbet al Hajjar, 1972. Spec: Archaeology, Hebrew Bible. Pub: *Archaeology in Jordan* (Lang, 1989); *Biblical Archaeology: The World, the Mediterranean, the Bible* (Paragon, 1987); *Put Your Future in Ruins: Essays in Honor of Robert Jehu Bull*, ed. (Wyndham Hall, 1985); *The Answer Lies Below: Essays in Honor of Lawrence Edmund Toombs*, ed. (U. Press of Amer., 1984); "The Excavations of Rujim el-Mekheizin" *ADAJ* 28 (1984); "The Ammonite Remains at Khirbet al Hajjar" *BASOR* 227 (1977); "Thoughts on Archaeological Method" *BAR* 3/2 (1977); "Heshbon 1968: Area C" *AUSS* 7/2 (1969); "Tell el-Husn: Biblical Beth-shan" *BA* 30/4 (1967); "Science and Archaeology" *BA* 29/4 (1966); and others. Awd: Drew U., Dorr F. Dieffendorfer Prize for Excellence in Homiletics 1958; U.S. State Dept., Jordan, grant 1972-73. Mem: ASOR; AIA; Conf. on Faith & Hist.; Global Congress of the World's Relig. Rec: Reading, swimming. Addr: (o) U. of Pennsylvania, Nursing Education Building, #449, Philadelphia, PA 19104 215-898-4335.

THOMPSON, John A., b. Assiut, Egypt, February 24, 1913, s. of F. Scott & May, m. Evelyn Birkel (Aye), chil: Henry; Daniel; Ann; Carol. Educ: Princeton U., AB 1936; Pittsburgh-Xenia Theol. Sem., MDiv 1939, ThM 1941; Johns Hopkins U., PhD 1943. Emp: Bibl. Sem., New York, 1942-48 Prof.; United Presbyn. Missionary, Egypt, 1948-68, 1977-78; Evang. Theol. Sem., Cairo, 1948-67, 1977-78 Prof.; Amer. Bible Soc., Trans. Dept., 1967-81 Cons. Spec: Archaeology, Hebrew Bible, Mesopotamian Studies, New Testament, Semitic Languages, Texts and Epigraphy, Egyptology, Apocrypha and Post-biblical Studies. Pub: "Joel," "Obadiah" in *Interpreter's Bible, Encyclopedia Britannica*; "Egypt" in *The Biblical World*; *Arabic Dict. of the Bible*, co-ed. Awd: Phi Beta Kappa 1935; Pittsburgh-Xenia Theol. Sem., Jamison Fellow. 1939. Mem: SBL; AOS. Rec: Travel, reading, walking. Addr: (h) 1030 Bradbourne Ave., Space 43, Duarte, CA 91010 818-359-2131.

THOMPSON, Leonard L., b. LaFontaine, IN, September 24, 1934, s. of Russell Charles &

Ruth Alice (Dyson), m. Melissa (Ray), chil: Timothy; Daniel; Jennifer. Educ: DePauw U., BA 1956; Drew U., BD 1960; U. of Chicago, MA 1963, PhD 1968. Emp: Lawrence U., 1965-66 Instr., 1968-79 Assoc. Prof., 1980- Prof. of Relig. Stud., 1988-91 Dean of Fac.; Wright State U., 1966-68 Instr. Spec: New Testament. Pub: *The Book of Revelation: Apocalypse and Empire* (Oxford U.P., 1990); "From Tanakh to Old Testament" *Approaches to Teaching the Hebrew Bible as Literature in Translation* (Modern Lang. Assn. of Amer., 1989); "A Sociological Analysis of Tribulation in the Apocalypse" *Semeia* 36 (1986); "Domitianus Dominus: A Gloss on Statius, Silvae 1.6.84" *Amer. Jour. of Philol.* 105 (1984); "The Jordan Crossing: *Sidqot Yahweh* and World Building" *JBL* 100 (1981); *Introducing Biblical Literature: A More Fantastic Country* (Prentice-Hall, 1978); and others. Awd: NEH, Fellow. 1981-82, 1988. Mem: AAR; SBL; CSBR. Addr: (o) Lawrence U., Dept. of Religious Studies, Appleton, WI 54912 414-832-6647; (h) 346 Winnebago Ave., Menasha, WI 54952 414-722-5865.

THOMPSON, Michael B., b. Goldsboro, NC, October 1, 1953, s. of Charles A. & Frances J. (Floyd), m. Susanne K. (Darby), chil: Darby L.; Brittany B.. Educ: U. of N.C., Chapel Hill, BA 1975; Dallas Theol. Sem., ThM, NT 1979; Cambridge U., PhD, NT 1988. Emp: Cambridge U., 1987-88 Instr., NT & Greek; St. John's Coll., Nottingham, 1988- Lect., NT & Greek, 1990- Dir. of Stud. Spec: New Testament. Pub: *Clothed with Christ. The Example and Teaching of Jesus in Romans 12:1-15:13*, JSNTSup 59 (JSOT, 1991); and others. Awd: N.C. Fellow 1971-75; Va. Theol. Sem., Bell Fellow. 1984-86. Mem: SBL 1983-; Tyndale Fellow. 1985-; IBR 1990-. Rec: Music, sports, travel, computing. Addr: (o) St. John's College, Chilwell Ln., Bramcote, Nottingham NG9 3DS, England 0602-251114; (h) 1 Peache Way, Bramcote, Nottingham NG9 3DX, England 0602-229499.

THOMPSON, Yaakov, b. St. Marys, Ohio, December 2, 1954, s. of Herbert & Carolyn, m. Sarah, chil: Adina Michal; Benyamin Asher. Educ: Ohio State U., BA 1977; Jewish Theol. Sem., MA 1983, Rabbi 1983, DHL 1988; N.Y. U., PhD Cand. 1990-. Emp: Cong. B'nai Israel, 1988- Rabbi; Jewish Theol. Sem., 1988-91 Asst. Prof., Dept. of Bible. Spec: Hebrew Bible. Pub: "Rashi, Joseph Qara, et Eliezer de Beaugency: qui etait le Serviteur du Seigneur (Is. 53)?" *Archives Juives* 23/2 (1988); "Samson in Timnah: Judges 14 and 15, Form and Function" *Dor LeDor* 15/4 (1987); "A Missing Hexateuchal Narrative Concerning Child Sacrifice" *Dor LeDor* 15/1 (1986). Mem: Rabbinical Assembly 1983-; AJS 1984-; SBL 1984-; AAR 1984-. Rec: Music, reading. Addr: (o) Congregation B'nai Israel, 30th St. & Pine Ave., Fair Lawn, NJ 07410 201-791-1157; (h) 28-02 Berkshire Rd., Fair Lawn, NJ 07410 201-797-2732.

THORDARSON, Thorir Kr., b. Reykjavik, June 9, 1924, s. of Thordur Nikulasson & Thorbjorg Baldursdottir, m. Jakobina Finnbogadottir, chil: Nanna; Olor; Sveinbjorn; Helga; Gudrun. Educ: Reykjavik Jr. Coll., Grad. 1944; U. of Iceland, Cand. Theol. 1951; U. of Chicago, PhD 1959. Emp: U. of Iceland, 1954-56 Assoc. Prof., 1957- Prof.; McCormick Theol. Sem., 1957-59 Vis. Prof.; U. of Edinburgh, 1972 Tchr. Spec: Hebrew Bible. Pub: "Notes on the Semiotic Context of the Verb *Niham* in the Book of Jonah" *Svensk Exeg. Arsb.* 54 (1989); "The Mythic Dimension: Hermeneutical Remarks on the Language of the Psalter" *VT* 24 (1974); "Abraham," "Covenant in Religion," "Moses" in *Ency. Britannica* (1963); "Biblical Interpretation as Participation: An Essay" *Kirke og Theologi* 6 (1957); and others. Mem: Wissenschaftliche Gesellschaft fur Theol.; SBL. Rec: Theater, lit., Icelandic culture & politics. Addr: (o) Haskoli Islands, Sudurgata, 101 Reykjavik, Iceland 1-694-349; (h) Aragata 4, 101 Reykjavik, Iceland 1-16605.

THROCKMORTON, Burton H., Jr., b. Elizabeth, NJ, February 21, 1921, s. of Harriet Battin (Barrows) & Burton Hamilton, m. Ansley (Coe), chil: Hamilton Coe; Timothy Barrows. Educ: U. of Va., BA 1943; Union Theol. Sem., N.Y., BD 1945; Columbia U., PhD 1955. Emp: Union Theol. Sem., N.Y., 1946-51 Instr.; Princeton U., 1951-53 Instr.; Wellesley Coll., 1953-54 Instr.; Kirchliche Hochschule, Berlin, 1963 Lect.; Bangor Theol. Sem., 1954-88 Prof. Spec: New Testament. Pub: *Gospel Parallels* (Thomas Nelson, 1949, 1992); "The New Revised Standard Version, New Testament, and the Revised English Bible, New Testament" *Theol. Today* 47 (1990); "Language and the Bible" *Relig. Educ.* 80 (1985); "Sozein, Soteria in Luke-Acts" *Studia Evangelica* (1973); *Romans for the Layman* (Westminster, 1961; Oncken, 1968); "The New English Bible" in *The New English Bible* (Epworth, 1965); *The New Testament and Mythology* (Westminster, 1959); "The Longer Reading of Luke 22:19b-20" *ATR* 30/1 (1948); and others. Awd: Lilly Post-doc. Fellow.; Soc. for Values in Higher Educ., Kent Fellow. 1954. Mem: SBL 1945-; AAR. Rec: Music. Addr: (o) Bangor Theological Seminary, 300 Union St., Bangor, ME 04401 207-942-6781; (h) 41 Glencove Ave., Bangor, ME 04401 207-942-8482.

THRONTVEIT, Mark A., b. Chicago, IL, June 20, 1949, s. of Thelford & Louise (Bilstad), m. Carol (Van Regenmorter), chil: Trygve; Trevor. Educ: Luther Theol. Sem., MDiv 1975; Union Theol. Sem. of Va., PhD 1982. Emp: Luther NW Theol. Sem., 1981- Assoc. Prof. Spec: Hebrew Bible. Pub: *Ezra-Nehemiah. Interpretation Commentaries* (John Knox, 1992); "'Minor' Prophets in the Midst of Pentecost" *Word & World* (1989); "Kyrie Eleison: The Penitential Psalms and Lenten Discipline" *Luth. Quar.* (1987); *When Kings Speak: Royal Speech and Royal Prayer in Chronicles* (Scholars, 1987); "Linguistic Analysis and the Question of

Authorship in Chronicles, Ezra and Nehemiah" *VT* (1982). Mem: SBL 1984-. Rec: Guitar, computer programming, athletics. Addr: (o) Luther Northwestern Seminary, 2481 Como Ave., St. Paul, MN 55108 612-641-3272; (h) 520 Branston, St. Paul, MN 55108 612-644-9956.

THUREN, Lauri Tuomas, b. Turku, Finland, November 4, 1961, s. of Jukka Taneli & Liisa Anneli, m. Johanna Katariina, chil: Lotta Maria; Julia Katariina; Sofia Anneli; Otto Tuomas. Educ: Abo Akad., MTh 1984, Lic. Theol. 1988, ThD 1990. Emp: Luth. Evang. Assn., 1985- Pastor; Abo Akad., 1985, 1991 Asst., NT Exegetics; U. of Turku, 1987, 1991 Tchr. Spec: New Testament. Pub: "Vad ar retorisk kritik?" *Teologinen Aikakauskirja* (1991); "Ikkunasta peili?" *Teologinen Aikakauskirja* (1991); *The Rhetorical Strategy of First Peter with Special Regard to Ambiguous Expressions* (Abo Acad., 1990). Addr: (o) Inst. for Exegetik, Abo Akademi, Biskopsgatan 16 A, SF-20500 ABO, Finland; (h) Myllykylantie 21, 20900 Turku, Finland 21-587-334.

THURSTON, Bonnie Bowman, b. Bluefield, WV, October 5, 1952, d. of E.V. & Eleanor (King), m. Burton B. Thurston, Sr. (dec.). Educ: U. of Va., MA 1975, PhD 1979. Emp: Wheeling Coll., 1980-81, 1985 Adj. Prof.; Bethany Coll., 1981-82 Asst. Prof.; Harvard Div. Schol., 1983 Vis. Sch.; Inst. zur Erforschung des urchristentums, 1983-85 Tutor; Wheeling Jesuit Coll., 1986-Assoc. Prof. Spec: New Testament. Pub: *The Widows* (Fortress, 1989); "Christian Socialism and Acts 2.44-45 and 4.32-37" *Mission Jour.* (1984); and others. Mem: CBA; SBL; ASOR. Rec: Gardening, music, travel. Addr: (o) Wheeling College, Dept. of Theology, Wheeling, WV 26003; (h) 260 G.C.P Rd., Wheeling, WV 26003.

TIGAY, Jeffrey H., b. Detroit, MI, December 25, 1941, m. Helene (Zubkoff). Educ: Columbia U., BA 1963; Sem. Coll. of Jewish Stud., Jewish Theol. Sem. of Amer., MHL 1966; Rabbinical Ord. 1968; Yale U., PhD 1971. Emp: Jewish Theol. Sem. of Amer., 1963-66 Curr. Writer, Melton Res. Ctr., 1965-68 Lect., 1980, 1985 Vis. Assoc. Prof.; Yale U., 1968-69 Teaching Asst.; Wesleyan U., 1969-71 Teaching Assoc.; U. of Pa., 1971- Abraham M. Ellis Prof. of Hebrew & Semitic Lang. & Lit.; JBL, 1977-81 Ed. Bd. Spec: Hebrew Bible. Pub: *You Shall Have No Other Gods: Israelite Religion in the Light of Hebrew Inscriptions* (Scholars, 1986); *Empirical Models for Biblical Criticism*, ed. (U. of Pa., 1985); "The Image of God and the Flood: Some New Developments" in *Studies in Jewish Education and Judaica in Honor of Louis Newman* (KTAV, 1984); "An Early Technique of Aggadic Exegesis" in *History, Historiography, and Interpretation* (Magnes, 1983); *The Evolution of the Gilgamesh Epic* (U. of Pa., 1982); "On the Word, 'Phylacteries' (Matthew 23:5)" *HTR* (1979); and others. Awd: ACLS Fellow. 1975-76; Hebrew U., Inst. of Advanced Stud., Fellow 1978-79; Annenberg Res. Inst., Fellow 1991-92. Mem:

ASOR; SBL, Pres., Hudson-Delaware reg. 1975-76; AOS. Addr: (o) U. of Pennsylvania, Dept. of Asian & Middle Eastern Studies, 847 Williams Hall CU, Philadelphia, PA 19104-6305.

TILLEY, Maureen A., b. San Pedro, CA, July 24, 1948, d. of Joseph J. & Elizabeth R. (Kucharik) Molloy, m. Terrence W. Tilley, chil: Elena; Christine. Educ: U. of San Francisco, AB 1970; St. Michael's Coll., MA 1985; Duke U., PhD 1989. Emp: Fla. State U., 1989-. Spec: Apocrypha and Post-biblical Studies. Pub: "Typological Numbers: Taking a Count of the Bible" *BR* 8/3 (1992); "The Ascetic Body and the (Un)making of the Martyr" *JAAR* 59/3 (1991); "Dilatory Donatists or Procrastinating Catholics: The Trial at the Conference of Carthage" *CH* 60/1 (1990); "Scripture as an Element of Social Control: Two Martyr Stories of North Africa" *HTR* 83/4 (1990); and others. Awd: Andrew W. Mellon Diss. Fellow. 1988-89. Mem: NAPS 1986-; SBL 1986-; Coll. Theol. Soc. 1987-; Amer. Soc. of Ch. Hist. 1992-. Rec: Embroidery. Addr: (o) Florida State U., Dept. of Religion R-15, Tallahassee, FL 32306-1029 904-644-1020; (h) 3592 Vicksburg Ct., Tallahassee, FL 32308 904-386-8965.

TILSON, Everett, b. Marion, VA, February 17, 1923, s. of Arthur & Margaret, m. Mary, chil: Stephen; Lee; Hazel; Joe. Educ: King Coll., BA 1944; Vanderbilt U., MDiv 1946, PhD 1952. Emp: Vanderbilt U. Div. Sch., 1951-60 Assoc. Prof.; Meth. Theol. Sch., 1960-88 Prof., 1988 Acting Dean. Spec: Hebrew Bible, New Testament. Pub: "The Eclipse of Faith" *Interpretation* (1963); and others. Awd: Hebrew Union Coll., Horowitz Found. Fellow 1949-50; Yale Div. Sch., Res. Fellow 1954-55. Mem: SBL; ASOR; AAR; NABI, V.P., South. sect. 1959-60, Pres. 1960-61. Rec: Horseshoes, bowling, ping pong, tennis, baseball. Addr: (o) Methodist Theological School, PO Box 1204, 3081 Columbus Pike, Delaware, OH 43015 614-363-1146; (h) 126 Pennsylvania Ave., Delaware, OH 43015 614-369-3957.

TIMBIE, Janet A., b. San Francisco, CA, October 17, 1948, d. of Martin & Margaret (Erjavec), m. James P., chil: Anna; Clare. Educ: Stanford U., BA 1970; U. of Pa., PhD 1979. Emp: Amer. U., 1971 Reader, 1980-81 Lect.; U. of Pa., 1974-76 Teaching Fellow; Wesley Theol. Sem., 1985-86, 1990-91 Lect.; Holy Trinity Ch., 1992 Lect. Spec: Egyptology, Apocrypha and Post-biblical Studies. Pub: "The State of Research in the Career of Shenoute of Stripe" in *The Roots of Egyptian Christianity* (Fortress, 1986); "The Nag Hammadi Library" *Relig. Stud. Rev.* (1982); "The Dating of a Coptic/Sahidic Psalter Codex from the U. Museum in Philadelphia" *Museon* (1975); *The Testament of Job*, co-auth. (Scholars, 1975). Awd: Cath. U., Mellon Fellow. 1979-80. Mem: SBL 1973-; CBA 1979-; AAR 1979-. Rec: Reading, gardening. Addr: (h) 4608 Merivale Rd., Chevy Chase, MD 20815 301-657-8326.

TIMM, Stefan, b. Rostock, Germany, June 26, 1944, s. of Dietrich & Marie-Luise (Neumann), m. Hella (Pohle). Educ: Tuebingen, ThD 1979; Kiel, Habil. 1987, Prof. 1991. Emp: Tuebinger Atlas des Vorderen Orients, 1976-83. Spec: Archaeology, Hebrew Bible, Mesopotamian Studies, Semitic Languages, Texts and Epigraphy, Egyptology. Pub: *Moab zwischen den Maechten, Studien zu historischen Denkmaelern und Texten* (1989); *Die Dynastie Omri, Quellen und Untersuchungen zur Geschichte Israels im 9. Jahrhundert vor Christus* (1982); *Das christlich-koptische Aegypten in arabischer Zeit* vol. 1-6 (1984-92). Addr: (h) Wilhelmplatz 6, D2300, Kiel, Germany 04321-15140.

TINDALL, Philip N., b. Pudsey, Yorkshire, England, December 31, 1910, s. of Thomas & Rose (Noble), m. Maud (Binks). Educ: U. of Manchester, England, BA 1934, BD 1937, MA 1939, PhD 1950; U. of Newcastle-upon-Tyne, MLitt 1979. Emp: Unitarian, Presbyn. Free Christian, Ch., England, Min.; Non-Subscribing Ch. of Ireland, Min.; Manchester Coll., 1948-51 Lect.; Oxford U., 1948-51 Lect.; U. of Newcastle-upon-Tyne, 1977-79 Lect. Spec: Hebrew Bible, New Testament, Semitic Languages, Texts and Epigraphy. Pub: *Gethsemane: Studies in the Passion of Jesus* (Hodder & Stoughton, 1941); and others. Awd: Unitarian Coll., Durning-Smith Schol. 1932-33; U. of Manchester, David S. Bles Hebrew Prizeman 1933. Mem: SOTS 1947-; SBL 1948-. Rec: Stringed musical instruments. Addr: (h) 14, Commercial Villas Pudsey, West Yorkshire, LS28 8BN, England 0532-550-847.

TOBIN, Thomas Herbert, b. Chicago, IL, November 8, 1945, s. of Thomas & Irene (Sheehan). Educ: Xavier U., Litt. B 1967; Loyola U. of Chicago, MA 1973; Harvard U., PhD 1980. Emp: Loyola U., 1980- Assoc. Prof. Spec: New Testament, Apocrypha and Post-biblical Studies. Pub: *Of Scribes and Scrolls*, ed. (U. Press of America, 1990); *The Spirituality of Paul* (Glazier, 1987); *Timaeus of Locri, On the Nature of the World and the Soul* (Scholars, 1985); *The Creation of Man: Philo and the History of Interpretation* (CBA, 1983). Awd: Harvard U., Arthur Darby Nock Fellow 1979. Mem: SBL 1973-; CBA 1978; Philo Inst. 1982-. Addr: (o) Loyola U. of Chicago, 6525 N Sheridan Rd., Chicago, IL 60626 312-508-2343; (h) Ignatius House, 1331 W Albion Ave., Chicago, IL 60626 312-937-1158.

TORJESEN, Karen Jo, b. San Francisco, CA, October 10, 1945, d. of Charles & Mildred (Hall), m. Leif. Educ: Wheaton Coll., BS 1967; Claremont Sch. of Theol., M.Relig 1972; Claremont Grad. Sch., PhD 1982. Emp: George August U., Germany, 1978-82 Asst. Prof.; Mary Washington Coll., 1982-85 Asst. Prof.; Inst. for Antiq. & Christianity, 1985-87 Vis. Schol.; Claremont Grad. Sch., 1987- Assoc. Prof. Pub: "The Teaching Function of the Logos:

Athanasius De Incarnatione xx-xxxii" in *Arianism: Historical and Theological Assessments*, Patristic Mon. Ser. (1985); *Hermeneutical Procedure and Theological Structure in Origen's Exegesis* (de Gruyter, 1985); "'Body,' 'Soul' and 'Spirit' in Origen's Exegesis" *Anglican Theol. Rev.* (1985); "Origen's Interpretation of Gospel" *Vetera Christiana* (1985); "Origen's Interpretation of the Psalms" *Studia Patristica* (1982); "In Praise of Noble Women: Gender and Honor in Ascetic Texts" *Semeia* (1982); and others. Mem: AAR 1982-; Amer. Sch. of Ch. Hist. 1982-; CTSA 1984-. Rec: Travel, hiking. Addr: (o) Institute for Antiquity & Christianity, Claremont, CA 91711 714-621-8066; (h) 2062 Drury Court, Claremont, CA 91711 714-624-3082.

TORRANCE, Iain R., b. Aberdeen, Scotland, January 13, 1949, s. of Thomas F. & Margaret E., m. Moreg Ann, chil: Hew David Thomas; Robyn Alison Meta. Educ: Edinburgh U., MA, Phil. 1971; St. Andrews U., BD, NT 1974; Oxford U., DPhil 1980. Emp: Ch. of Scotland, 1982-85 Min.; SJT, 1982- Co-Ed.; Queen's Coll., UK, 1985-89 Lect., NT; U. of Birmingham, UK, 1989-93 Lect., NT & Patristic Theol.; U. of Aberdeen, 1993- Lect., Patristic Theol. Spec: New Testament, Semitic Languages, Texts and Epigraphy, Apocrypha and Post-biblical Studies. Pub: *Christology after Chalcedon* (Canterbury, 1988). Mem: SST 1972-; Soc. for the Study of Christian Ethics 1988-. Rec: Patristic christology, Scottish hist. Addr: (o) U. of Aberdeen, Dept. of Divinity, Aberdeen AB9 2UB, Scotland 0224-272274.

TOV, Emanuel, b. Amsterdam, September 15, 1941. Educ: Hebrew U., Jerusalem, BA, Bible & Greek Lit. 1964, MA, Bible 1967, PhD (summa cum laude) 1973. Emp: Hebrew U., Jerusalem, 1964-67 Teaching Fellow, 1969-74 Instr., 1974-80 Sr. Lect., 1980- Assoc. Prof.; Harvard U., 1967-69 Teaching Fellow; Dropsie U., 1980-81 Vis. Assoc. Prof.; U. of Pa., 1980-81, 1985-86 Vis. Assoc. Prof.; Oxford U., 1982-88 Grinfield Lect. on the Septuagint. Spec: Hebrew Bible. Pub: *Textual Criticism of the Bible* (Fortress/Van Gorcum, 1992); *Textus*, Stud. of the Hebrew U. Bible Project, vol. 11-15, ed. (Magnes, 1984-1991); "The Textual Base of the Corrections in the Biblical Texts Found in Qumran" in *Forty Years of Research in the Dead Sea Scrolls* (1991); *The Greek Minor Prophets Scroll from Nahal Hever (8HevXIIgr)*, Discoveries in the Judaean Desert 8 (Clarendon, 1990); "The Saga of David and Goliath" *BR* 2/4 (1986); "Hebrew Biblical Manuscripts from the Judaean Desert: Their Contribution to Textual Criticism" *JJS* 39 (1988); "Some Sequence Differences between the MT and LXX and Their Ramifications for the Literary Criticism of the Bible" *JNSL* 13 (1987); "Jewish Greek Scriptures" in *Early Judaism and Its Modern Interpreters* (1986); *The Septuagint Translation of Jeremiah and Baruch—A Discussion of An Early Revision of Jeremiah 29-52 and Baruch*

1:1-3:8, HSM 8 (Scholars, 1976); and others. Awd: Hebrew U., Warburg Awd. 1969-71; Oxford U., Lady Davis Fellow 1974-75; Penn-Israel, Wexler Fellow 1980-81. Mem: SBL 1970-; IOSCS. Addr: (o) Hebrew U., Dept. of Bible, Jerusalem, Israel 2-584-947.

TRAFTON, Joseph L., b. Norfolk, VA, July 1, 1949, s. of W. Elton & Barbara, m. Paula, chil: Jennifer; Joseph; Stephen. Educ: Gordon-Conwell Theol. Sem., MTS 1972, ThM 1974; Duke U., PhD 1981. Emp: Gordon-Conwell Theol. Sem., 1973-74 Teaching Fellow; Duke U., 1976-77 Grad Instr.; West. Ky. U., 1977- Prof.; Fla. State U., 1985-86 Vis. Assoc. Prof.; Princeton Theol. Sem., Subeditor, Dead Sea Scrolls Project. Spec: New Testament, Apocrypha and Post-biblical Studies. Pub: Articles in *ABD* (Doubleday, 1992); articles in *Mercer Dict. of the Bible* (Mercer U.P., 1990); "The Psalms of Solomon: New Light From the Syriac Version?" *JBL* (1986); *The Syriac Version of the Psalms of Solomon: A Critical Evaluation* (Scholars, 1985). Mem: SBL; CBA; IBR; NABPR. Addr: (o) Western Kentucky U., Dept. of Philosophy and Religion, Bowling Green, KY 42101 502-745-3136; (h) 842 Edgefield Way, Bowling Green, KY 42104 502-842-8491.

TRAKATELLIS, Demetrius C., b. Thessalonike, Greece, February 1, 1928, s. of Chrestos & Georgia. Educ: U. of Athens, BD 1950, ThD 1977; Harvard U., PhD 1972. Emp: Theol. Sch. for Priestly Stud., Ch. of Greece, 1972-74 Prof. of Bibl. Stud.; Bishop of Vresthena, 1967-91; Holy Cross Sch. of Theol., 1980-83 Vis. Prof.; Harvard Div. Sch., 1984-85, 1988-89 Vis. Prof.; Hellenic Coll., 1984- Holy Cross Disting. Prof. of Bibl. Stud. & Christian Origins. Spec: New Testament, Apocrypha and Post-biblical Studies. Pub: *The Transcendent God of Eugnostos* (Holy Cross, 1991); "Holy Spirit and Mission in the New Testament" in *Credo in Spiritum Sanctum* (Vaticana, 1983); *The Pre-Existence of Christ in the Writings of Justin Martyr*, Harvard Diss. in Relig. 6 (Scholars, 1976); and others. Awd: Hellenic Coll./Holy Cross Sch. of Theol., Archbishop Iakovos Fac. Awd. 1985. Mem: SBL 1972-; SNTS 1973-; Colloquia Ecumenica Paulina 1978-. Addr: (o) Holy Cross School of Theology, 50 Goddard Ave., Brookline, MA 02146 617-731-3500.

TREACY-COLE, Diane I., b. Pontiac, MI, d. of Kenneth & Irene, m. John F. W. Educ: Principia Coll., BA 1969; NW U., PhD 1984. Emp: Tufts U., 1985-86 Lect.; U. of Wis., Oshkosh, 1986-91 Asst. Prof.; U. of Bristol, England, 1992- Lect. Excv: Gezer, Israel, 1972; Carthage, Tunisia, 1975 Area Supr.; Sepphoris, Israel, 1987- Area Supr., Numismatist. Spec: Archaeology, New Testament. Pub: "Perea" in *ABD* (1992); "Galilee and Regionalism" *Explor.* 3 (1977). Awd: U. of Wis., Oshkosh, Teaching Grant 1989, Res. Grant 1987-88. Mem: ASOR; IES; SBL; CSBR. Rec: Piano, skiing, tennis. Addr: (o) U. Bristol, Dept. of

Theology & Religious Stud, 36 Tyndall's Park Rd., Bristol BS8 1PL, England 0272-303414; (h) 13 Frayne Rd., Ashton Gate, Bristol BS3 1RU, England 0272-666469.

TREAT, Jay C., b. Ithaca, NY, July 31, 1948, s. of Jay E. & Mary Jo, m. Pat, chil: Emily; Jay. Educ: Abilene Christian U., BA 1970; Princeton Theol. Sem., MDiv 1974. Spec: New Testament, Apocrypha and Post-biblical Studies. Pub: "Epistle of Barnabas" in *ABD*; "The Two Manuscript Witnesses to the Gospel of Peter" in *SBL 1990 Seminar Papers*. Awd: Mellon Fellow. 1992-93. Mem: SBL; AAR; IOSCS. Rec: Computers, folk music, hiking. Addr: (o) U. of Pennsylvania, Box 36, College Hall, Philadelphia, PA 19104-6303 215-898-1597; (h) 233 S Bayberry Ln., Upper Darby, PA 19082 215-449-8171.

TREBILCO, Paul R., b. Warkworth, New Zealand, November 3, 1958, s. of George Raymond & Elsme Ruth, m. Gillian Margaret, chil: Fiona Kaye; Stephen George. Educ: U. of Canterbury, New Zealand, BSc 1979; U. of Otago, New Zealand, BD 1982; U. of Durham, England, PhD 1987. Emp: Ch. of Christ, New Zealand, 1983 Min.; Knox Theol. Hall, New Zealand, 1988-90 Lect., Bibl. Stud., 1991- Prof., NT Stud. Spec: Anatolian Studies, New Testament, Semitic Languages, Texts and Epigraphy, Apocrypha and Post-biblical Studies. Pub: "The Church's Lord: Insights from an Early Christian Hymn" *Latimer* 110 (1992); *Jewish Communities in Asia Minor*, SNTS Mon. Ser. 69 (Cambridge U.P., 1991); "Women as Co-workers and Leaders in Paul's Letters" *Jour. of the Christian Brethren Res. Fellow.* 122 (1990); "Paul and Silas, Servants of the Most High God—Acts 16:16-18" *JSNT* 36 (1989). Mem: New Zealand Assn. of Theol. Sch. 1989-; New Zealand Joint Bd. of Theol. Stud. 1991-. Rec: Gardening, stamp collecting, tramping. Addr: (o) Knox College, Arden St., Dunedin, New Zealand 03-4730-109; (h) 168 Evans St., Dunedin, New Zealand 03-4739-629.

TREBOLLE, Julio C., b. Orense, Spain, April 24, 1943, s. of Jose & Marina. Educ: U. Complutense, Madrid, Doc., Semitic Philol. 1980; Pont. U., Salamanca, ThD 1983. Emp: U. Complutense, Madrid, 1984- Prof. Titular, Dir. del Inst. U. de Ciencias de las Relig. Spec: Hebrew Bible. Pub: *La Biblia judia y la Biblia cristiana* (1993); "Textual Variants in 4QJudga and the Textual and Editorial History of the Book of Judges" *RQ* 14 (1989); *Centena in libros Samuelis et Regum* (1989); *Jehu y Joas. Texto y composicion literaria en 2 Reyes 9-11*, Inst. San Jeronimo 17 (1984); "From the Old Latin Through the Old Greek to the Old Hebrew (2 Kgs 10:23-25)" *Textus* 11 (1984); *Salomon y Jeroboan. Historia de la recension y redaccion de 1 Reyes 2-12.14*, Inst. San Jeronimo 10 (1980); and others. Awd: Cross of Isabella I. Mem: Inst. San Jeronimo for Bibl. Res. 1973-, Pres. 1984-; SBL 1985-; Soc. Espanola de Ciencias de Las Relig., V.P. 1993-. Rec: Piano,

organ playing. Addr: (o) U. Complutense, Dept. de Hebreo y Arameo, Facultad de Filologia, 28040 Madrid, Spain 1-3945377; (h) Antonio Lopez Aguado 10, 1 C, 28029 Madrid, Spain 1-3146658.

TRENCHARD, Warren C., b. St. John's, Newfoundland, July 16, 1944, s. of Charles & Violet (Noseworthy), m. Marilyn, chil: Mark; David; Kevin. Educ: Andrews U., MA 1968, BD 1968; U. of Chicago, PhD 1981. Emp: Atlantic Union Coll., 1968-70 Pastor & Instr.; Canadian Union Coll., 1975- V.P. Academic & Prof. of Relig. Stud.; Andrews U., 1981 Vis. Prof. Spec: New Testament, Apocrypha and Post-biblical Studies. Pub: *The Student's Complete Vocabulary Guide to the Greek New Testament* (Zondervan, 1992); *Ben Sira's View of Women: A Literary Analysis* (Scholars, 1982); and others. Mem: SBL 1968-; CBA 1982-. Rec: Photography, computer programming. Addr: (o) Canadian Union College, Box 430, College Heights, Alberta, T0C 0Z0, Canada 403-782-3381; (h) PO Box 458, College Heights, Alberta, T0C 0Z0, Canada 403-783-6675.

TREPP, Leo, b. Mainz, Germany, March 4, 1913, s. of Maier & Selma (Hirschberger), m. Miriam (de Haas), chil: Susan. Educ: Yeshiva, Frankfurt Rabbinic Sem., Berlin, Ord. 1936; Hebrew Union Coll., DD 1985; U. of Wurzburg, PhD (magna cum laude) 1985; U. of Oldenburg, DPhil 1989. Emp: Olenburg Germany, 1936-38 Rabbi; U.S. Communities, 1940- Rabbi; Napa Coll., 1951-89 Prof.; Mainz, 1983, 1985-86, 1988- Prof. Jewish Stud. Spec: Apocrypha and Post-biblical Studies. Pub: *Der Judische Gottesdienst* (Kohlhammer, 1992); *Die Amerikanichen Juden* (Kohlhammer, 1991); *Judaism, Development and Life* (Wadsworth, 1982); *The Complete Book of Jewish Observance* (Summit, 1980); and others. Mem: AAR 1972-; Rabbinical Assembly 1944-; CCAR 1948. Rec: Music, swimming, hiking. Addr: (h) 295 Montecito Blvd., Napa, CA 94559 707-226-2791.

TREVER, John C., b. Milwaukee, WI, November 26, 1915, s. of John H. & Hilda (Carpenter), m. Elizabeth (Burman), chil: John P.; James E. Educ: U. of South. Calif., AB (magna cum laude) 1937; Yale Div. Sch., BD 1940; Yale U., PhD 1943. Emp: Drake U., 1944-47 Assoc. Prof.; Morris Harvey Coll., 1953-59 A.J. Humphreys Prof. of Relig.; Baldwin-Wallace Coll., 1959-75 Prof. of Relig.; Sch. of Theol. at Claremont, 1975- Dir., Dead Sea Scrolls Project; Juniata Coll., 1986-87 J. Omar Good Vis. Disting. Prof. of Evang. Christianity. Excv: Serabit el-Khadem, 1948 Asst. Photographer; Um Rugm, Jordan, 1966 Asst.; Et-Tell, Israel, 1969 Photographer. Spec: Archaeology, Hebrew Bible, New Testament, Semitic Languages, Texts and Epigraphy, Apocrypha and Post-biblical Studies. Pub: "The Qumran Teacher—Another Candidate?" in *Early Jewish and Christian Exegesis: Studies in Memory of William Hugh*

Brownlee (Scholars, 1986); "The Book of Daniel and the Origin of the Qumran Community" *BA* (1985); *The Dead Sea Scrolls: A Personal Account* (Eerdmans, 1978); "1QDanᵃ, The Latest of the Qumran Manuscripts" *RQ* (1970); *The Dead Sea Scrolls of St. Mark's Monastery*, co-auth. (Fleming-Revell, 1965); and others. Awd: Amer. Phil. Soc., John F. Lewis Prize 1955. Mem: ASOR 1937-; SBL 1940-; AAR 1940-. Rec: Photography, gardening. Addr: (h) 176-C Avenida Majorca, Laguna Hills, CA 92653

TREVIJANO, Ramon, b. San Sebastian, Spain, August 13, 1932, s. of Fernando & Manuela. Educ: Gregorian U., Rome, Lic.Phil. 1954, ThD 1959; Pont. Bibl. Inst., Rome, Lic. Holy Scriptures 1961; U. of Zaragoza, Spain, Lic. Hist. 1964. Emp: Theol. Inst. of Cordoba, Argentine, 1964-66 Dir.; Theol. Fac. of the Nord of Spain, 1967-77 Prof.; Theol. Fac. of Buenos Aires, Argentine, 1968-74 Prof.; Theol. Fac. of Salamanca, Spain, 1978- Prof., 1981-84 Dean; *Salmanticensis*, 1978-Dir. Spec: New Testament, Apocrypha and Post-biblical Studies. Pub: *Comienzo del Evangelio: Estudio sobre el prologo de San Marcos* (1971); *En lucha contra las potestades: Exegesis primitiva de Ef 6,11-17 hasta Origenes*, Victoriensia 28 (1968); and others. Mem: SBL. Addr: (o) U. Pontificia, Facultad de Teologia, Compania 5, 37008 Salamanca, Spain; (h) Francisco de Vitoria 19, 37008 Salamanca, Spain 923-215034.

TRIBLE, Phyllis, b. Richmond, VA, October 25, 1932, d. of Samuel & Elsie. Educ: Meredith Coll., BA 1954; Columbia U., Union Theol. Sem., PhD 1963. Emp: Wake Forest U., 1963-71 Assoc. Prof.; Andover Newton Theol. Sch., 1971-79 Hitchcock Prof. of Hebrew Lang. & Lit.; Union Theol. Sem., 1979- Baldwin Prof. of Sacred Lit.; *JBL*, 1977-82 Ed. Bd.; *JAAR*, 1977-85 Ed. Bd.; *Jour. of Feminist Stud. in Relig.*, 1985-90 Ed. Bd. Spec: Hebrew Bible. Pub: *Texts of Terror: Literary-Feminist Readings of Biblical Narratives* (Fortress, 1984); "A Daughter's Death: Feminism, Literary Criticism, and the Bible" *Michigan Quar. Rev.* (1983); *God and the Rhetoric of Sexuality* (Fortress, 1978); "The Gift of the Poem: A Rhetorical Study of Jeremiah 31:15-22" *Andover Newton Quar.* (1977); "Women in the Old Testament" *IDB Sup.* (1976); and others. Awd: Meredith Coll., Alumna Awd. 1977; Franklin Coll., DD 1985. Mem: SBL 1963-; AAR 1963-. Rec: Travel, movies, Japan. Addr: (o) Union Theological Seminary, Broadway at 120th St., New York, NY 10027 212-662-7100; (h) 99 Claremont Ave., #701, New York, NY 10027 212-663-8165.

TRIPOLITIS, Antonia, b. Philadelphia, PA, d. of Constantine & Frances. Educ: U. of Pa., PhD 1971. Emp: U. of Pa., Coll. of Liberal Arts for Women, 1961-69 Asst. Dean; Rutgers U., Douglas Coll., 1975-79 Assoc. Dean of Acad. Affairs, 1980-87 Chair, Grad. Dir., Dept. of Class. & Arch., 1987- Assoc.; Prof., Relig.; Garland Lib.

of World Lit., Adv. Bd. Excv: Patmos Monastery Lib. Project, Greece, 1971-74 Co-coord., Intl. Project Team; Andros Monasteries Project, Greece, 1968-69 Prin. Investigator. Spec: Apocrypha and Post-biblical Studies. Pub: "Porphyry," "Proclus" in *Great Lives from History: Ancient and Medieval* (1988); *Origen: A Critical Reading* (Lang, 1985); "Return to the Divine—Salvation in the Thought of Plotinus and Origen" *Disciplina Nostra*, Patristic Mon. Ser. 6 (1979); *The Doctrine of the Soul in the Thought of Plotinus and Origen* (Libra, 1978); "Discoveries in the Monasteries of Andros, Greece" *Natl. Geographic Soc. Res. Reports* (1976); *Some Uncatalogued Greek Papyri of Theological and Other Interests in the Rylands Collection* (John Rylands Lib., 1968); and others. Mem: Amer. Soc. of Ch. Hist. 1979-; Amer. Soc. of Papyrologists 1967-; Intl. Soc. for Neoplatonic Stud. 1975-; NAPS 1970-; SBL 1968-. Addr: (o) Rutgers U., Dept. of Religion, 116 Loree, Douglas Campus, New Brunswick, NJ 08903 908-932-9637.

TRITES, Allison Albert, b. Fredericton, NB, Canada, September 23, 1936, s. of Borden & Marjorie (Leslie), m. Eugenie, chil: Jonathan; Ian. Educ: U. of New Brunswick, BA 1958; East. Bapt. Theol. Sem., BD 1961; Princeton Theol. Sem., ThM 1962; Oxford U., England, DPhil 1968. Emp: Acadia Div. Coll., Canada, 1965- Prof., 1991- John Payzant Disting. Prof of Bibl. Stud.; U. of King's Coll., Nova Scotia, 1970 Vis. Prof.; South. Bapt. Theol. Sem., 1981, 1990-91 Vis. Prof. Spec: New Testament. Pub: "The Blessings and Warnings of the Kingdom (Matthew 5:3-12; 7: 13-27)" *Rev. & Expositor* (1992); "The Transfiguration in the Theology of Luke: Some Redactional Links" in *The Glory of God in the New Testament* (Clarendon, 1987); "The Transfiguration of Jesus: The Gospel in Microcosm" *EQ* (1979); *The New Testament Concept of Witness* (Cambridge U.P., 1977); "The Prayer Motif in Luke-Acts" in *Perspectives on Luke-Acts* (Mercer U.P., 1977); "The Importance of Legal Scenes and Language in the Book of Acts" *NT* (1975); and others. Awd: Cambridge U., Canada Coun. Leave Fellow. 1972-73. Mem: SBL; NABPR; IBR; CSBS. Rec: Swimming, travel, hunting. Addr: (o) Acadia U., Acadia Divinity College, Wolfville, NS B0P IX0, Canada 902-542-2286; (h) Box 904, Wolfville, NS B0P IX0, Canada 902-542-9172.

TROCME, Etienne P., b. Paris, France, November 8, 1924, s. of Pierre & Aline, m. Ann (Bowden), chil: Suzanne; Claire; Jean-Pierre; Marie. Educ: U. of Paris, Lic. Lettres 1950; Fac. Libre de Theol. Protestante, Paris, BTh 1950; U. of Strasbourg, Lic. Theol. 1955; ThD 1960. Emp: Centre Natl. de la Recherche Scientifique, 1953-56 Attache de Recherche; U. of Strasbourg, 1956- Prof., Pres.; *Revue d'Histoire et de Philosophie Religieuses*, 1967- Dir.; Maison des Sciences de l'Homme, Strasbourg, 1981- Chmn.; *Etudes d'Histoire et de Philosophie Religieuses*, 1981- Ed.; U. of Oxford, 1965-68, Speaker's Lect. in

Bibl. Stud. Spec: New Testament. Pub: "L'Apotre Paul et Rome" *Revue d'Histoire et de Philosophie Religieuses* (1992); "The Beginnings of Christian Historiography and the History of Early Christianity" *Australian Bibl. Rev.* (1983); *The Passion as Liturgy* (SCM, 1983); "Paul-la-Colere, Eloge d'un Schismatique" *Revue d'Histoire et de Philosophie Religieuses* (1981); *Jesus de Nazareth Vu Par les Temoins de se vie* (Delachaux-Niestle, 1971); *Le Formation de l'Evangile Selon Marc* (Presses Universitaires de France, 1963); *Le Livre des Actes et l'Histoire* (Presses Universitaires de France, 1957); and others. Awd: Commandeur, Ordre des Palmes Academiques 1978; Officier de la Legion d'Honneur 1989; and others. Mem: SNTS 1957-, Pres. 1991-92; Soc. de l'Ecole des Chartes 1960-; Soc. Ernest-Renan pour l'Histoire des Religions 1970. Addr: (o) U. Des Sciences Humaines, 22 rue Descartes, 67084 Strasbourg Cedex, France 88-25-97-44; (h) 9, rue Berlioz, 67000 Strasbourg, France 88-61-57-13.

TROOST, Arie C., b. Den Haag, December 31, 1959, s. of Jacob & Maria Theresia, m. Anja Helena Kosterman, chil: Laurens Jacob; Heleen Agnes. Educ: Rijksuniversiteit Utrecht, Fac. of Theol., cand. theol.; Cath. Theol. U. Utrecht, 1988 Doc. Exam. Emp: Cath. U.-Nijmegen, Fac. of Theol., 1988- Res.; Rijksuniversiteit Utrecht, Fac. of Theol., 1991- Instr. Spec: Hebrew Bible, New Testament, Apocrypha and Post-biblical Studies. Pub: "Reading for the Author's Signature: Genesis 21.1-21 and Luke 15.11-32 as Intertexts" in *A Feminist Companion to Genesis* vol. 2 (Sheffield, 1993); "Als Elisabet en Maria elkaar spreken: over het nemen van het woord" *Schrift* 140 (1992); and others. Mem: Netherlands Soc. for Semiotics 1988-; AAR 1989-; SBL 1989-; Found. for Theol. & Relig. Stud. in the Netherlands 1990-. Addr: (o) Katholieke U. Nijmegen, Faculteit der Godgeleerdheid, Erasmusplein 1, 6525 HT Nijmegen, Netherlands 31-80-612479; (h) Ossewagendreef 68, 3564 BS Utrecht, Netherlands 31-30-661768.

TRUDINGER, L. Paul, b. Melut, Sudan, May 5, 1930, s. of Ronald & Lina (Hoopmann), m. Kathleen, chil: Philip; Ashleigh Paul; Bronwen; Caitlin. Educ: U. of Adelaide, BA 1956; Melbourne Coll. of Div., Dip. REd 1957; Andover Newton, STM 1959; Boston U., ThD 1963; Johns Hopkins U., MEd 1971; Intl. U., PhD, MMusA; London U., FPhS, FCollP. Emp: Parkin Theol. Coll., 1963-68 Dean; Marymount U., 1969-71 Prof.; North. Va. Community Coll., 1971-79 Prof.; Coll. of Emmanuel & St. Chad, St. Andrews Coll., Canada 1979-81 Prof., NT; U. of Winnipeg, 1981- Bibl. Stud. Spec: Hebrew Bible, New Testament, Apocrypha and Post-biblical Studies. Pub: "The Historical Jesus: Two Recent Issues for Consideration" *Faith & Freedom* 45 (1992); "Of Women, Weddings, Wells, Waterpots and Wine: Reflections on Johannine Themes" *St. Mark's Rev.* Spring (1992); *Not In the Main-Stream: Biblical Essays*

"in the Eddies" (Frye, 1988); *The Cool Gospel* (Frye, 1988); "Stephen and the Life of the Primitive Church" *BTB* 14 (1984); "The Text of the Old Testament in the Book of Revelation" *JTS* 17 (1966); and others. Awd: McMaster U., Herman Enns Mem. Lect. 1986; Manchester Coll., Oxford, Governor 1988-. Mem: SBL; AAR; Coll. of Preceptors, London 1983-; Phil. Soc. of England 1985. Rec: Reading mysteries, cricket, choral directing, painting, composing hymns. Addr: (o) U. of Winnipeg, Faculty of Theology, 515 Portage Ave., Winnipeg, Man. R3B 2E9, Canada 204-786-9450; (h) 429 Greenwood Pl., Winnipeg, Man. R3G 2P2, Canada 204-775-2375.

TRUMBOWER, Jeffrey A., b. Orlando, FL, June 19, 1960, s. of Jerrold S. & Anita T. Educ: Vanderbilt U., BA (summa cum laude) 1982; U. of Chicago Div. Sch., MA 1984, PhD 1989-. Emp: St. Michael's Coll., 1989- Asst. Prof. Spec: New Testament. Pub: "The Historical Jesus and the Speech of Gamaliel, Acts 5:35-39" *NTS* 39 (1993); *Born From Above: The Anthropology of the Gospel of John* (Mohr, 1992); "Origen's Exegesis of John 8:19-53: The Struggle with Heracleon Over the Idea of Fixed Natures" *VC* 43 (1989). Mem: SBL 1985-; NAPS 1989-. Addr: (o) St. Michael's College, Dept. of Religious Studies, Colchester, VT 05439 802-654-2373; (h) 101 Northshore Dr., Burlington, VT 05401.

TSAFRIR, Yoram, b. Kfar Azar, Israel, January 30, 1938. Educ: Hebrew U., BA (summa cum laude) 1964, MA (summa cum laude), Arch. & Jewish Hist. 1968, PhD 1976 (summa cum laude). Emp: *Qadmoniot,* 1967- Ed. Bd.; Hebrew U., Inst. of Arch., 1969-76 Instr., 1976-78 Lect., 1978-81 Sr. Lect., 1981-87 Assoc. Prof., 1987- Prof. of Arch. 1989- Head of Inst.; Yad Ben Zvi, 1976-83 Head, Res. Dept.; Arch. Survey of Israel, 1976-86 Executive Com.; Harvard U., Dumbarton Oaks Ctr. for Byzantine Stud., 1977-78 Vis. Fellow, 1984-85 Vis. Prof.; *Cathedra,* 1977-78 Ed. Bd., 1978-86 Co-ed. Excv: Bet Shean, 1980-81, 1986-90 Dir.; Sartaba-Alexandrion, 1981-83 Dir.; Bet Loya, 1983-84 Dir.; Horvat Berachot, 1976 Dir.; Rehovot in the Negev 1975-76, 1979, 1986 Dir. Spec: Archaeology. Mem: Israel Arch. Coun. 1989-, Mem. Addr: (o) Hebrew U., Institute of Archaeology, Jerusalem, Israel 2-882-403.

TSAI, Meishi, b. Taiwan, China, January 18, 1942, s. of Shuan & Pan, m. Imei (Chung), chil: Paulus D.; Julius N.; Jeremy H. Educ: Tunghai U., Taiwan, BA 1964; UCLA, MA 1966; U. of Calif.-Berkeley, PhD 1973; U. of Oxford, Dip. Theol. 1984; U. of London, King's Coll., PhD, Theol. 1993. Emp: True Jesus Ch., 1968- Pastor, 1991- Faculty, School of Theol.; Pomona Coll., 1973-78 Chmn., Dept. of Chinese & Asian Stud., 1973-80 Fac.; *Living Water,* 1978-83 Ed.; *Manna,* 1985-87 Ed. Spec: Hebrew Bible, New Testament. Pub: *A Commentary on the Chinese Text of Galatians* (1990); "An Exegesis of Genesis 26: Isaac in Beersheba" *Manna* Sept. (1987); *A Commentary* on the *Chinese Text of Luke* (1983); and others. Awd: Pomona Coll. Res. Grant, Peking, 1974; Claremont Coll., Harriet Bernard Res. Awd. 1978. Mem: AAR; SBL. Rec: Classical music, travel, hiking. Addr: (o) 11236 Dale St., Garden Grove, CA 92641 714-539-1329; (h) 408 Golf View Rd., Wallingford, PA 19086 215-565-2095.

TSEVAT, Matitiahu, b. Kattowitz, Germany, July 15, 1913, s. of Adolf & Lotte, m. Miriam, chil: Joel; David. Educ: Hebrew U., Jerusalem, MA 1948; Hebrew Union Coll., PhD 1953. Emp: Judisch-Theol. Sem., 1937 Instr.; Hebrew Union Coll., 1954-61 Spec. Lbrn., 1961-66 Assoc. Prof., 1966-84 Prof., 1984- Prof. Emeritus; Hochschule fur Judische Studien, Heidelberg, 1983 Guest Prof.; U. of Heidelberg, 1983 Guest Prof., Dir. of Jewish Stud. Spec: Anatolian Studies, Hebrew Bible, Mesopotamian Studies, Semitic Languages, Texts and Epigraphy. Pub: *The Meaning of the Book of Job* (Ktav, 1980); *A Study of the Language of the Biblical Tralius* (SBL, 1955); and others. Mem: WUJS. Addr: (o) Hebrew Union College, 3101 Clifton Ave., Cincinnati, OH 45220 513-221-1875; (h) 764 Red Bud Ave., Cincinnati, OH 45229.

TSUMURA, David Toshio, b. Kobe, Japan, February 4, 1944, s. of Tetsuo & Hatsuyo, m. Susan (Martin), chil: Michio; Makoto. Educ: Hitotsubashi U., BS 1966; Asbury Theol. Sem., MDiv 1969; Brandeis U., MA 1971, PhD 1973. Emp: Japan Bible Sem., 1974 Lect., 1990- Prof, OT; U. of Tsukuba, 1975-90 Assoc. Prof.; Tyndale House, Cambridge, 1986-88 Res. Fellow. Spec: Hebrew Bible, Semitic Languages, Texts and Epigraphy. Pub: *Ugarit and the Old Testament*, trans. (Kyobunkan, 1990); *The Earth and the Waters in Genesis 1 and 2: A Linguistic Investigation*, JSOTSup 83 (Sheffield, 1989); "Niphal with an Internal Object in Hab 3:9a" *JSS* (1986); "Janus Parallelism in Nah 1:8" *JBL* (1983); "Literary Insertion (AXB Pattern) in Biblical Hebrew" *VT* (1983); "Hab 2:2 in the Light of Akkadian Legal Practice" *ZAW* (1982); *Ancient Orient and Old Testament*, trans. (Word of Life, 1979); and others. Mem: SBL 1969-; Soc. for Near East. Stud. in Japan 1974-; SOTS 1983-; Japan ETS 1974-, Bd. Mem. Rec: Hiking, pingpong, tennis. Addr: (o) Japan Bible Seminary, 2-9-3 Hanenishi, Hamura, Tokyo 205, Japan 0425-54-1710; (h) 2-9-3 Hanenishi, Hamura, Tokyo 205, Japan 0425-55-0336.

TUBB, Jonathan, m. Kathryn. Emp: Brit. Mus., West. Asiatic Dept., Cur., Syria-Palestine. Addr: (o) British Museum, Western Asiatic Dept., London WC1B 3DG, England 71-323-8160.

TUBB, Kathryn W., m. Jonathan. Emp: U. of London, Inst. of Arch., Conservator. Spec: Archaeology. Addr: (o) U. of London, Institute of Archaeology, 31-34 Gordon Square, London WC1H 0PY, England 71-387-7050.

TUCK, William P., b. Lynchburg, VA, s. of H.W., m. Emily (Campbell), chil: Catherine; Bill Powell III. Educ: U. of Richmond, BA 1957; SE Bapt. Theol. Sem., BD 1960, ThM 1961; New Orleans Bapt. Theol. Sem., ThD 1965. Emp: Va. Intermont Coll., 1972-75 Adj. Prof.; South. Bapt. Theol. Sem., 1978- Prof.; *Review and Expositor*, 1980-83 Ed. Bd. Spec: New Testament. Pub: "Toward a Theology of the Proclaimed Word" *Rev. & Expositor* (1984); and others. Awd: U. Richmond, DD 1977. Mem: AAR; AH. Rec: Gardening, hiking, writing. Addr: (o) 3515 Grandview Ave., Louisville, KY 40207 502-896-8882; (h) 2322 Thornhill Rd., Louisville, KY 40222 502-425-9385.

TUCKETT, Christopher M., b. Cambridge, England, April 2, 1948, s. of R.F. & E.M., m. Jane, chil: Katherine; Mark; John. Educ: Lancaster U., PhD 1979. Emp: Queen's Coll., 1977-79 Chaplain & Bye-Fellow; Manchester U., 1979-89, Lect., NT Stud., 1989- Sr. Lect., 1991- Prof.; *JSNT*, 1985-91 Ed. Spec: New Testament. Pub: *Reading the New Testament?* (SPCK, 1986); *Nag Hammadi and the Gospel Tradition* (T & T Clark, 1986); *The Revival of the Griesbach Hypothesis* (CUP, 1983); and others. Mem: SBL 1983-; SNTS 1984-. Rec: Walking, music. Addr: (o) U. of Manchester, Dept. of Religions & Theology, Manchester M13 9PL, England 061-275-3607; (h) Kidd Road Farm, Moorfield, Glossop SK13 9PN, England 0457-860150.

TUELL, Steven S., b. East Liverpool, OH, October 3, 1956, s. of Bernard Earl & Mary Louise (Holland), m. Wendy Louise (Rodan), chil: Sean Michael; Anthony Ryan; Mark Anderson. Educ: W. Va. Wesleyan Coll., AB (magna cum laude), Relig. & Psychology 1978; Princeton Theol. Sem., MDiv 1981; Union Theol. Sem., PhD, Hebrew Bible 1989. Emp: United Meth. Ch., 1981-85 Pastor; Coll. of William & Mary, 1988 Instr.; Erskine Coll., 1989-1992 Asst. Prof., 1991- Chair, Dept. of Relig. & Phil.; Randolph-Macon Coll., 1992- Asst. Prof., Relig. Stud. Spec: Hebrew Bible, Mesopotamian Studies, Semitic Languages, Texts and Epigraphy. Pub: *The Law of the Temple in Ezekiel 40-48* (Harvard U.P., 1992); "The Southern and Eastern Borders of Abar Nahara" *BASOR* 284 (1991); "The Temple Vision of Ezekiel 40-48: A Program for Restoration?" *Proc. of the East. Great Lakes Bibl. Soc.* 2 (1982); and others. Mem: SBL 1981-; East. Great Lakes Bibl. Soc. 1981-85; SE Commn. for the Study of Relig. 1990-92. Rec: Folk music of Appalachia and the British Isles, reading mysteries, astronomy. Addr: (o) Erskine College, Due West, SC 29639 803-379-8896; (h) Box 672, Due West, SC 29639 803-379-2877.

TULLOCK, John H., b. Delano, TN, April 24, 1928, s. of William & Ollie, m. Helen (Curtis), chil: Sharon; John Laurens. Educ: SE Bapt. Theol. Sem., BD 1958; Vanderbilt U., PhD 1966. Emp: Pastor 1947-61; Belmont U., 1960-92 Prof.,

1972-85 Dept. Chair. Spec: Hebrew Bible, Semitic Languages, Texts and Epigraphy. Pub: *The Old Testament Story* (Prentice-Hall, 1981, 1992); and others. Mem: ASOR; SBL. Rec: Gardening, folk music, writing. Addr: (h) Box 258, Delano, TN 37325 615-263-2192.

TURNER, George A., b. Willsboro, NY, August 28, 1908, s. of Charles & Bertha, m. Lucile (McIntosh), chil: Allen; Carol. Educ: Greenville Coll., BD 1934; Bibl. Sem. in N.Y., STB 1935, STM 1936; Harvard U., PhD 1946. Emp: Wessington Springs Coll., 1936-38 Prof.; Free Meth. Ch., 1939-42 Prof.; Asbury Theol. Sem., 1945-79 Prof. Bibl. Lit.; *Asbury Seminarian*, 1948-78 Assoc. Ed.; Evangelical Bible Comm., 1956-64 Ed. Excv: Ai, 1968 Field Supr. Spec: Archaeology, New Testament. Pub: "Early Christians?" *Asbury Seminarian* (1983); *Paul, Apostle for Today* (Tyndale, 1981); "Baptism of the Holy Spirit in Wesleyan Tradition" *WTJ* (1979); and others. Mem: SBL 1950-; ETS 1950-; IBR 1965-. Rec: Golf, travel. Addr: (h) 608 Kinlaw Dr., Wilmore, KY 40390 606-858-3216.

TURNER, John D., b. Glen Ridge, NJ, July 15, 1938, s. of Warren & Dorothy, chil: Margaret Angela. Educ: Dartmouth Coll., AB 1960; Union Theol. Sem. at Va., BD 1965, ThM 1966; Duke U., PhD, Relig. 1970. Emp: Claremont Grad. Sch., 1970-71 Vis. Asst. Prof., Asst. Dean; U. of Mont., 1971-76 Assoc. Prof.; U of Nebr., 1976-84 Prof., 1984- Prof., Relig., Class. & Hist. Spec: New Testament, Apocrypha and Post-biblical Studies. Pub: "Gnosticism and Platonism" in *Neoplatonism and Gnosticism*, Stud. in Neoplatonism 6 (SUNY, 1992); "Sethian Gnosticism: A Literary History of Gnosticism" in *Gnosticism and Early Christianity* (Hendrickson, 1986); "The Gnostic Threefold Path to Enlightenment: The Ascent of Mind and the Descent of Wisdom" *NT* 22 (1980); "Thomas The Contender," "Interpretation of Knowledge," "Valentinian Exposition," "Allogenes," "Hypsiphrone," "Trimorphic Protennoia," trans. in *The Nag Hammadi Library in English* (Harper & Row, 1977); *The Book of Thomas the Contender from Codex II of the Cairo Gnostic Library from Nag Hammadi (CG II,7)*, SBL Diss. Ser. 23 (Scholars, 1975); *The Facsimile Edition of the Nag Hammadi Codices: Codices XI, XII and XIII*, contb. (Brill, 1973); "A New Link in the Syrian Judas Thomas Tradition" in *Essays on Nag Hammadi in Honour of Alexander Bölig*, Nag Hammadi Stud. 3 (Brill, 1972); and others. Awd: Rockefeller Doc. Fellow. in Relig. 1968; Amer. Coun. of Learned Soc. Fellow 1976. Mem: SBL; Intl. Soc. for Neoplatonist Stud.; Inst. for Antiq. & Christianity; Soc. for Coptic Arch. Rec: Sailing, swimming, computer programming. Addr: (o) U. of Nebraska–Lincoln, Dept. of Classics, Lincoln, NE 68588-0337 402-472-7008; (h) 3832 Orchard St., Lincoln, NE 68503 402-464-9467.

TURRO, James C., b. Jersey City, NJ, January 26, 1922, s. of Anthony & Sue. Educ: Cath. U., STL 1948; Pont. Bibl. Inst., Rome, SSL 1956;

N.Y. U., MA 1970, PhD 1975. Emp: Immaculate Conception Sem., Prof., NT; Fordham U., LaSalle U., St. Charles Sem., Immaculata Coll., Vis. Prof. Spec: New Testament. Pub: *Reflections* (Paulist, 1970); *Ezekiel* (Liturgical, 1965). Mem: CBA. Addr: (h) Seton Hall U., Seminary, South Orange, NJ 07079 201-761-9575.

TWELFTREE, Graham Hedley, b. Lameroo, South Australia, July 8, 1950, s. of Eric & Iris, m. Barbara Fay, chil: Catherine; Paul. Educ: Adelaide, S Australia, BA 1975; Oxford U., BA 1977; Nottingham, England, PhD 1981, MA 1982. Emp: All Souls Coll. of Applied Theol., London, 1980-83 Lect., Dir. of Stud.; Uniting Ch. in Australia, Min. Spec: New Testament, Apocrypha and Post-biblical Studies. Pub: *Jesus the Exorcist* (Mohr, 1992); "Blasphemy," "Demon...," "Scribes," "Sanhedrin," "Temptation of Jesus" in *Dict. of Jesus and the Gospels* (IVP, 1992); "Ei De...Ego Ekballo Ta Daimonia" in *Gospel Perspectives* (JSOT, 1986); *Christ Triumphant: Exorcism Then and Now* (Hodder & Stoughton, 1985); "Jesus in Jewish Traditions" in *Gospel Perspectives: Studies of History and Tradition in the Four Gospels* (JSOT, 1985); "Demon-Possession and Exorcism in the New Testament" *Churchman* (1980); and others. Mem: SBL. Rec: Music, farming, family. Addr: (h) 26 Scullin Crescent, Hope Valley 5090 Adelaide, S.A., Australia 396-0778.

TYSON, Joseph B., b. Charlotte, NC, August 30, 1928, s. of Joseph B. & Lucy (Lewis), m. Margaret (Helms), chil: Linda Sheridan. Educ: Duke U., BA 1950, BD 1953; Union Theol. Sem., STM 1955, PhD 1959. Emp: South. Meth. U., 1958- Prof.& Chair, Dept. of Relig. Stud. Spec: New Testament. Pub: *Images of Judaism in Luke-Acts* (U. of S.C., 1992); "The Birth Narratives and the Beginning of Luke's Gospel" *Semeia* 52 (1990); *Luke-Acts and the Jewish People: Eight Critical Perspectives*, ed. (Augsburg/Fortress, 1988); "The Emerging Church and the Problem of Authority in Acts" *Interpretation* 42 (1988); "The Problem of Jewish Rejection in Acts" in *Luke-Acts and the Jewish People: Eight Critical Perspectives* (Augsburg/Fortress, 1988); *The Death of Jesus in Luke-Acts* (U. of S.C., 1986); and others. Mem: SBL; AAR; SNTS; CBA. Rec: Gardening, travel. Addr: (o) Southern Methodist U., Dept. of Religious Studies, Dallas, TX 75275-0202 214-768-2105; (h) 8636 Capri Dr., Dallas, TX 75238 214-348-2534.

TZAFERIS, Vassilios E., b. Samos, Greece, April 1, 1936, s. of Emmanuel & Photini, m. Eytychia, chil: Mary; Emmanuel. Educ: Hebrew U., BA, Arch. & Hist. of Anc. Israel, MA, Graeco-Roman Arch., PhD, Byzantine Arch. Emp: Dept of Antiq., 1966-71 Field Arch., 1971-91 Duty Dir. of Excvn.; Israel Antiq. Authority, 1991- Dir. of Excvn./Surveys. Excv: Second Temple Period Tombs, Jerusalem, 1968 Dir.; Kursi-Gergessa, 1970-74 Dir.; Capernaum,

1978-86 Dir.; Caesarea-Philippi, 1987- Dir. Spec: Archaeology. Pub: *Excavations at Capernaum* vol. 1 (1989); *The Monastery of the Holy Cross in Jerusalem* (1987); *The Museum of the Greek Orthodox Patriarchate* (1985); "Jewish Tombs at Giva'at Hamivtar, Jerusalem" *IEJ* 20 (1970); "An Early Christian Church at Magen" *BASOR* 258; "The Greek Inscriptions from the Early Christian Church at Evron" *Israel* 19; "A Pilgrimage to the Site of the Swine Miracle" *BAR* 15/2 (1989); "The Ancient Synagogue at Maoz-Haim" *IEJ* 32; *Excavations at Kursi-Gergessa*, Atiqot 16; and others. Mem: Assn. of Arch. in Israel; Assn. of Arch. of Cyprus. Rec: Swimming, nature walks. Addr: (o) Israel Antiquities Authority, Box 586, Jerusalem, Israel 02-892286-7; (h) Reh. Eliahu beit-zuri 3, Jerusalem, Israel 02-711013.

UCHIDA, Kazuhiko, b. Japan, February 18, 1947, s. of Haruya & Isoko, m. Mizue, chil: Shinobu; Yoshihiko; Shizuka. Educ: Tokyo U., BLitt; Japan Bible Sem., MDiv; Trinity Evang. Div. Sch., ThM; Aberdeen U., PhD. Spec: New Testament. Pub: *Blessed Christian Life according to the Sermon on the Mount* (Word of Life, 1992); *An Exposition of Paul's Epistle to the Colossians* (Word of Life, 1982); "The Authenticity of Matthew 20:16 and the Original Setting of the Parables of the Good Employer" *Evang. Theol.* (1981). Mem: ETS; SBL. Addr: (o) Japan Bible Seminary, 2-9-3 Hanenishi, Hamura, Tokyo 205, Japan 0425-54-1710; (h) 2-9-3 Hanenishi, Hamura, Tokyo 205, Japan 0425-79-3082.

ULRICH, Eugene C., b. Louisville, KY, November 5, 1938. Educ: Xavier U., Litt.B 1961; Loyola U., PhL 1964; Harvard U., MA 1967, PhD 1975; Woodstock Coll., MDiv 1970. Emp: U. of Notre Dame, 1973- Prof.; *Bull. of the IOSCS,* 1980-86 Ed.; *CBQ Mon. Ser.,* 1979- Ed. Bd.; *CBQ,* 1980-87 Assoc. Ed.; *Discoveries in the Judaean Desert,* 1985- Chief. Ed., Bibl. Scrolls; *New Revised Standard Version,* 1982- Ed. Com. Spec: Hebrew Bible, Semitic Languages, Texts and Epigraphy, Apocrypha and Post-biblical Studies. Pub: *Qumran Cave 4.IV: Palaeo-Hebrew and Greek Biblical Manuscripts,* co-auth. (Clarendon, 1992); "The Canonical Process, Textual Criticism, and Latter Stages in the Composition of the Bible" in *Sha'arei Talmon: Studies in the Bible, Qumran, and the Ancient Near East presented to Shemaryahu Talmon* (Eisenbrauns, 1992); "The Greek Manuscripts of the Pentateuch from Qumran, Including Newly-Identified Fragments of Deuteronomy" in *De Septuaginta: Studies in Honour of John William Wevers on his Sixty-Fifth Birthday* (Pietersma & Cox, 1984); "Horizons of Old Testament Textual Research at the Thirtieth Anniversary of Qumran" *CBQ* (1984); "Palimpsestus Vindobonensis: A Revised Edition of 115 for Samuel-Kings," co-auth., *Bull. of the IOSCS* (1983); "4QSam^c: A Fragmentary Manuscript of 2 Samuel 14-15 from the Scribe of the *Serek Hay-yahad* (1QS)" *BASOR* (1979); *The Qumran Text of Samuel and*

Josephus (Scholars, 1978); and others. Awd: Pfeiffer Fellow. for Arch. Res. in Israel 1973; Guggenheim Fellow. 1981-82. Mem: CBA 1967-; SBL 1968-; ASOR 1978-. Addr: (o) U. of Notre Dame, Dept. of Theology, Notre Dame, IN 46556 219-631-6541.

UNTERGASSMAIR, Franz Georg, b. Olang/Sudtirol, Italy, August 11, 1941. Educ: Promotion 1972; Habil. 1978; Prof. 1983. Emp: Prof. of Bibl. Theol., Exegese of NT. Spec: New Testament. Pub: "Gnosis und Neues Testament" in *Erloesung durch Offenbarung oder Erkenntnis? Zum Wiedererwachen der Gnosis,* Vechtaer Beitraege zur; Theol. 1 (1992); "Gemeindemodelle im Neuen Testament" in *Kirche im Jahr 2000: Eine Ringvorlesung des Fachbereichs Katholische Theologie der Universitaet Osnabrueck* (1992); "Volk Gottes zwischen Sammlung und Zerstreuung" in *Volk und Bevoelkerung,* Vechtaer Universitaetsschriften (1992); "Der Spruch vom 'gruenen' und 'duerren' Holz (Lk 23,31)" in *SNTU,* Ser. A 16 (1991); *Im Namen Jesu beten: Biblische Impluse zu christlichem Gebet* (1990); *Kreuzweg und Kreuzigung Jesu,* Paderborner Theol. Stud. 10 (1980); *Im Namen Jesu: Der Namensbegriff im Johannesevangelium (fzb 13)* (1977). Addr: (o) 49364 Vechta, Driverstrasse 26 04441-15-408; (h) 49090 Osnabruck, Ankumer Weg 5 0541-682260.

URBROCK, William J., b. Chicago, IL, September 14, 1938, s. of Ernest & Emma (Kollaritsch), m. Barbara (Wrege), chil: Stephen; Rebecca. Educ: Concordia Sr. Coll., BA 1960; Concordia Theol. Sem., MDiv 1964; Harvard U., PhD 1975. Emp: Lycoming Coll., 1969-71 Asst. Prof.; Susquehanna U., 1971-72 Lect.; U. of Wis., Oshkosh, 1972- Prof., Assoc. Dean of Hum.; *Transactions,* 1992- Ed. Spec: Hebrew Bible. Pub: "Blessings and Curses" in ABD (1992); "Guarding the Walls in Psalm 48 and Haim Gouri's *Nidmeh li...*" *HAR* (1991); "Sisera's Mother in Judges 5 and Haim Gouri's *'Immô'* " *HAR* 11 (1987); "Samson: A Play for Voices" in *JSOTSup* (1986); "Oral Antecedents to Job: A Survey of Formulas and Formulaic Systems" *Semeia* 5 (1976); and others. Awd: Rockefeller Doc. Fellow. 1968; Danforth Assoc. 1980. Mem: SBL 1969-; CSBR 1980-, V.P. 1991-92. Rec: Swimming, music, canoeing, cross-country skiing. Addr: (o) U. of Wisconsin-Oshkosh, Dept. of Religious Studies, Oshkosh, WI 54901 414-424-1186; (h) 608 Elmwood Ave., Oshkosh, WI 54901.

URO, Risto I., b. Imatra, September 22, 1953, s. of Ilmari & Toini, m. Marjatta, chil: Jarkko; Jukka; Ilkka. Educ: U. of Helsinki, ThM 1977, LTh 1984, ThD 1988. Emp: Finnish Luth. Ch., 1977-80 Min.; U. of Helsinki, 1980-83 Tchr., NT Exegetics, 1988-90 Acting Sr. Lect., Bibl. Exegetics, 1991 Docent, NT Exegetics; Finnish Acad., 1984-88 Res. Asst. Spec: New Testament. Pub: *Jeesuksen salaiset sanat: Tuomaan evankeliumi* (Ylipistopaino, 1992); *Sheep Among the Wolves: A*

Study on the Mission Instructions of Q (Suomalainen tiedeakatemia, 1987); and others. Mem: SNTS 1990-. Rec: Jazz, movies. Addr: (o) U. of Helsinki, Dept. of Biblical Exegetics, PO Box 37, SF-00014 U. of Helsinki, Finland 358-0-1911; (h) Marsuntie 10 C 12, SF-04320 Tuusula, Finland 358-0-257438.

USSISHKIN, David, b. Jerusalem, Israel, s. of Samuel & Elsa, m. Ann Naomi (Herzfeld), chil: Iddo; Yoav; Daniel. Educ: Hebrew U., BA 1958, MA 1961, PhD 1964. Emp: Tel Aviv U., 1966- Prof.; Qadmoniot, 1968- Ed. Bd.; BAR, 1975- Ed. Bd.; Tel Aviv, 1977- Ed. Excv: Silwan Necropolis, Jerusalem, 1968-70 Dir.; Tel Lachish, 1973- Dir.; Betar, 1984 Dir.; Tel Jezreel, 1990- Co-dir. Spec: Archaeology. Pub: "Was the 'Solomonic' Gate at Megiddo Built by King Solomon?" *BASOR* (1980); "Hollows, 'Cup-Marks' and Hittite Stone Monuments" *Anatolian Stud.* (1975); *The Conquest of Lachish by Sennacherib* (Tel Aviv U.P., 1982); *The Necropolis from the Period of the Kingdom of Judah in Solwan* (IES, 1986); and others. Mem: IES. Addr: (o) Tel Aviv U., Institute of Archaeology, Tel Aviv, Israel 03-640-9417; (h) 41 Hagefen St., Ramat Hasharon, Israel 03-549-4336.

VAN AARDE, Andries Gideon, b. Pretoria, April 25, 1951, s. of Tienie & Chris, m. Esther, chil: Gideon; Salomie. Educ: U. of Pretoria, BA 1971, BD 1974, BA 1977, MA, Greek & Semitic Lang. 1978, DD 1982. Emp: U. of Pretoria, 1979-80 Lect., NT, Greek, 1980-83 Lect., Bibl. Stud., 1984-89 Assoc. Prof., Dept. of NT Stud., 1989- Prof. & Chair,; Dept. of NT Stud.; Hervormde Teologiese Stud., 1980-92 Ed. Spec: New Testament. Pub: "The Relativity of the Metaphor 'temple' in Luke-Acts" *Neotestamentica* 25 (1991); "Narrative Criticism Applied to Jn 4:43-54" in *Text and Interpretation* (Brill, 1991); "The Struggle against Heresy in the Thessalonian Correspondence" in *The Thessalonian Correspondence* (Leuven U.P., 1990); "Mt 28:7—A Textual Evidence on the Separation of Judaism and Christianity" *Neotestamentica* 23 (1989); "Resonance and Reception: Interpreting Mt 17:24-27 in Context" *Scriptura* 29 (1988); and others. Awd: Human Sci. Res. Coun., South Africa, res. grant 1990; Ctr. for Sci. Development, South Africa, res. grant 1991; Inst. for Ecumenical & Cultural Res., Resident Schol. 1992-93. Mem: NT Soc. of South Africa 1978-92; SBL 1987-92; Westar Inst., Fellow 1990-92. Rec: Reading. Addr: (o) U. of Pretoria, Dept. of New Testament Studies, Faculty of Theology, 0002 Pretoria, South Africa 012-420-2399; (h) 529 Delphi St., Waterkloof Glen, 0010 Glenstania Pretoria, South Africa 012-47-4067.

VAN DAM, Cornelis, b. Zwijndrecht, Netherlands, April 7, 1946, s. of Schalk & Jenny (Van Rijswijk), m. Johanna (Buist), chil: S. Carl. Educ: Wilfrid Laurier U., BA 1968; Westminster Theol. Sem., Theol. Coll. of the Reformed Ch., BD 1971; U. of Toronto, Knox

Coll., ThM 1980; Theol. U., Kampen, The Netherlands, ThD 1986. Emp: Canadian Reformed Ch., 1971-81 Min.; Theol. Coll. of the Canadian Reformed Ch., 1981- Prof. OT. Spec: Hebrew Bible. Pub: "The Meaning of biš'gāgâ" in *Unity in Diversity* (1989); "The Elder as Preserver of Life in the Covenant" in *Proceedings of the International Conference of Reformed Churches* (1989); "Urim and Thummim" in *ISBE* (1988); *The Urim and Thummim: A Study of an Old Testament Means of Revelation* (Van den Berg, 1986); "The Theology of Liberation" *Lux Mundi* 2-3 (1984-85); and others. Mem: SBL 1972-; CSBS 1979-; ETS 1982-; Ex Oriente Lux, Leiden 1984-; Canadian Evang. Theol. Assn. 1991-. Rec: Hiking, music, gardening. Addr: (o) Theol. Coll. Canadian Reformed Churches, 110 West 27th St., Hamilton, ON L9C 5A1, Canada 416-575-3688; (h) 642 Ramsgate Rd., Burlington, ON L7N 2Y1, Canada 416-634-0593.

VAN DER HORST, Pieter W., b. Driebergen, Netherlands, July 4, 1946, s. of Pieter & Jeltje, chil: Bernardine; Mirjam. Educ: State U. of Utrecht, PhD 1978. Emp: Utrecht U., 1969- Sr. Lect., 1991-Prof., NT, Early Judaism; SC, 1980 Ed. Nederlands Theologisch Tydschrift, 1985 Ed. Na de Schriften, 1985 Ed. Spec: New Testament, Apocrypha and Post-biblical Studies. Pub: Ancient Jewish Epitaphs (Kok Pharos, 1991); Essays on the Jewish World of Early Christianity (Vandenhoeck, 1990); Chaeremon (Brill, 1984); "Moses' Throne Vision in Ezekiel the Dramatist" *JJS* 34 (1983); "Hellenistic Parallels to the Acts of the Apostles" *ZNW* 74 (1983); *Aelius Aristides and the New Testament* (Brill, 1980); and others. Mem: SNTC 1971-; SNTS 1975-; European Assn. for Jewish Stud. 1982-. Addr: (o) Theologisch Instituut, P.O.B. 80105, 3508 TC Utrecht, Netherlands 030-531991; (h) Jasmijnstraat 2, 3732 EC De Bilt, Netherlands 030-200455.

VAN DER KOOIJ, Gerrit, b. Schipluiden, Holland, October 22, 1944, s. of Cornelis & Teuntje (Zonneveld), m. Mariette (Schroot), chil: Jeroen; Bram; Hanneke. Educ: U. of Leiden, MA, OT & Arch. 1972, PhD 1986. Emp: U. of Leiden, Fac. of Div., 1974-77 Asst. for Anc. Relig., Fac. of Arts & Hist., Arch. of Palestine, 1977- Wetenschappelijk; Medewerker, U. Docent. Excv: Tell Deir Alla, Jordan, 1967 Pottery Asst., 1976, 1978 Square & Field Supr.; 1979, 1982, 1984, 1987 Co-dir., Field Dir.; Tell Ta'as & Tell el Hadidi, Jebel Aruda, Syria, 1972, 1974 Square Supr., uthography. Spec: Archaeology, Semitic Languages, Texts and Epigraphy. Pub: *The Balaam Text from Deir Alla Re-Evaluated,* co-ed. (Brill, 1991); *Picking up the Threads,* co-auth. (1989); "Artifactual Aspects of Papyrus RMO F 1978/11.4" *OMRO* 68 (1988); "The Identity of Trans Jordanian Alphabetic Writing in the Iron Age" in *SHAJ* 3 (1987); *Early Northwest Semitic Script Traditions: An Archaeological Study of the Linear Alphabetic Scripts Up to c.500 BC,* contb.

(Arch. Ctr., Leiden, 1986); "Some Ethnographical Observations of Archaeological Impact at the Village Hadidi in Syria" *Orientale* 5 (1982); *Aramaic Texts from Deir Alla*, co-auth. (Brill, 1976); and others. Mem: Nederlands Genootschap van Godsdiensthistorici; Ex Oriente Lux; Werkgezelschap voor de arch. van Palestina; ASOR; Oudtestamentisch Werkgezelschap. Rec: Nature, ice skating, music. Addr: (o) Archaeological Centre, Postbus 9515, 2300 RA Leiden, Netherlands 071-272443; (h) Marienpoelstraat 57, 2334 CX Leiden, Netherlands 071-171587.

VAN DER TOORN, Karel, b. The Hague, March 8, 1956, m. Annet De Jong, chil: Judith; Peter. Educ: Free U., Amsterdam, MA 1980, PhD 1985. Emp: Leiden U., Prof., Anc. Relig. Spec: Hebrew Bible, Mesopotamian Studies, Semitic Languages, Texts and Epigraphy. Pub: "Funerary Rituals and Beatific Afterlife in Ugaritic Texts and in the Bible" *Biblica et Orientalia* 48 (1991); "The Babylonian New Year Festival: New Insights from the Cunieform Texts and Their Bearing on OT Study" in VTSup 43 (1991); "The Nature of the Biblical Teraphim in the Light of the Cuneiform Evidence" *CBQ* 52 (1990); "La pureté rituelle au Proche-Orient ancien" *Rev. de l'hist. des relig.* 206 (1989); "Female Prostitution in Payment of Vows in Ancient Israel" *JBL* 108 (1989); *From Her Womb to Her Tomb: Religion in the Lives of Israelite and Babylonian Women* (Ten Have, 1987); *Sin and Sanction in Israel and Mesopotamia: A Comparative Study* (Van Gorcum, 1985); and others. Addr: (o) Leiden U., Faculty of Theology, PO Box 9515, 2300 RA Leiden, Netherlands 011-31-71272569; (h) Spaargarenstraat 36, 2341 JX Oegstgeest, Netherlands 011-31-71157257.

VAN-GEMEREN, Willem A., b. Boskoop, Netherlands, April 7, 1943, s. of Jacobus & Sarah, m. Evona (Adkins), chil: Nurit; Tamara; Shoshanna. Educ: U. of Ill., BA 1968; Westminster Theol. Sem., BD 1971; U. of Wis., MA 1972, PhD 1974. Emp: U. of Wis., 1972-73 Fellow; Geneva Coll., 1974-78 Asst. Prof.; Reformed Theol. Sem., 1978-92 Prof. Pub: *Psalms* in Expositor's Comm. on the Bible (1991); *Interpreting the Prophetic World* (1990); *The Progress of Redemption* (1988); "Israel as the Hermeneutical Crux in the Interpretation of Prophecy" *WTJ* (1983, 1984); "Psalm CXXXI: Kegamul. The Problem of Meaning and Metaphor" *Hebrew Stud.* (1982); "The Sons of God in Genesis 6:1-4" *WTJ* (1981); *The New International Dict. of Old Testament Theology*, Ed.; and others. Awd: Westminster Theol. Sem., Thomas E. Welmers Prize, 1971; U. of Wis., Ford Fellow, 1972-74. Mem: SBL; ETS; IBR. Rec: Gardening, photography. Addr: (o) Trinity Evangelical Divinity School, 2077 Half Day Road, Deerfield, IL 60015 (708) 317-8144; (h) 333 Appley Ave., Libertyville, IL 60048.

VAN HENTEN, Jan Willem, b. Oude Wetering, June 7, 1955, s. of Willem F. & Kitty (Van Den Berg), m. Gieneke (Holland), chil: Coen; Saskia. Educ: Rijksuniversiteit, Leiden, MA, Hist. 1976, MA, Theol. 1981, PhD, Theol. 1986. Emp: Rijksuniversiteit, Leiden, 1981-85 Res. Asst., 1986-91 Lect., Anc. Judaism, 1991- Lect., NT; U. van Amsterdam, 1985-91 Lect., NT. Spec: New Testament, Apocrypha and Post-biblical Studies. Pub: "The Story of Susanna as a Pre-rabbinic Midrash to Dan. 1:1-2" in *Variety of Forms: Dutch Studies in Midrash* (Amsterdam U.P., 1990); "Das jüdische Selbstverstandnis in den ältesten Martyrien" in *Die Entstehung der jüdischen Martyrologie*, SPB 38 (Brill, 1989); "Datierung und Herkunft des Vierten Makkabäerbuches" in *Tradition and Reinterpretation in Jewish and Early Christian Literature: Essays in Honor of Jürgen C.H. Lebram* (Brill, 1986); *De joodse martelaren als grondleggers van een nieuwe orde: Een studie uitgaande van 2 en 4 Makkabeeën* (Van Henten, 1986); "Einige Prolegomena zum Studium der jüdischen Martyrologie" *Bijdragen* 46 (1985); "Der Berg Asdod: Uberlegungen zu 1 Makk. 9,15" *JSJ* 14 (1983). Mem: SNTC 1992-; SBL; European Orgn. of Jewish Schol. Rec: Volleyball, cycling, lit. Addr: (o) Rijksuniversiteit Utrecht Theologisch Instituut, PO Box 80.105, 3508 TC Utrecht, Netherlands 030-531847; (h) Troubadoursborch 19, 3992BE Houten, Netherlands 03403-52412.

VAN HOUTEN, Christiana, b. The Hague, The Netherlands, May 3, 1952, d. of Arie Willem & Maria (Huijssoon), m. Richard Lee, chil: Rose Marie; Nicholas Hiram; Adrianna Mathilda; Katrine Elizabeth. Educ: Loyola U. of Chicago, BA 1973; U. of Chicago Div. Sch., MA 1974; U. of Notre Dame, PhD 1990. Emp: Calvin U., 1980 Instr., 1988- Assoc. Prof., Relig. & Theol.; Hope Coll., 1981-82 Instr. Spec: Hebrew Bible. Pub: *The Alien in Israelite Law* (Sheffield, 1991). Mem: SBL 1982-; CBA 1983-. Addr: (o) Calvin College, Dept. of Religion & Theology, Grand Rapids, MI 49546 616-597-7042; (h) 2031 Godwin SE, Grand Rapids, MI 49507 616-245-0095.

VAN LEEUWEN, Raymond C., b. Artesia, CA, October 2, 1948, s. of Cornelis & Greta (Kruithof), m. Mary (Stewart), chil: K. Dirk; D.S. Neil. Educ: St. Michael's Coll., Toronto, MA 1975, PhD 1984; Calvin Theol. Sem., BD 1976. Emp: Calvin Theol. Sem., 1981-82, 1985- Asst. Prof. Spec: Hebrew Bible, Semitic Languages, Texts and Epigraphy. Pub: "Wealth and Poverty: System and Contradiction in Proverbs" *Hebrew Stud.* 33 (1992); "Liminality and World View in Proverbs 1-9" *Semeia* 50 (1990); *Meaning and Context in Proverbs 25-27* (Scholars, 1988); "What Comes Out of God's Mouth: Theological Wordplay in Deuteronomy 8" *CBQ* (1985); "Isa. 14:12 *Holes 'al Gwym* and Gilgamesh XI,6" *JBL* (1980); and others. Mem: SBL 1976-, Pres., MidW reg. 1992-94; CSBR 1981-. Rec: Music, swimming, cross-country skiing. Addr: (o) Calvin College, 3233 Burton St. SE, Grand Rapids, MI 49506 616-957-6317; (h) 1924 Lenawee SE, Grand Rapids, MI 49506 616-245-4110.

VAN ROOY, Harry F., b. Cape Town, South Africa, August 7, 1949, s. of Bertus & Sientjie, m. Jacoba, chil: Albertus J.; Barend J.; Anna C.; Harry F.; Sinette G.. Educ: Potchefstroom U., BA 1970, BA 1972, MA 1974, ThB 1974, DLitt 1977. Emp: Potchefstroom U. 1980-81 Sr. Lect., 1982-83 Assoc. Prof., Semitics, 1983-, Prof., 1988-91, Dean, Theol.; Koers, 1985- Asst. Ed.; *Old Testament Essays*, 1988- Rev. Ed.; *JNSL*, 1991- Ed. Bd.. Spec: Hebrew Bible, Semitic Languages, Texts and Epigraphy, Apocrypha and Post-biblical Studies. Pub: "Eschatology and Audience: The Eschatology of Haggai" *OT Essays* (1988); "Deuteronomy 28:69—Superscript or Subscript?" *JNSL* (1989); "The Structure of the Aramaic Treaties of Sefices" *Jour. for Semitics* (1989); "The *vox populi* and Structural Aspects of Ezekiel," "Prophetic Utterances in Narrative Texts, with Reference to 1 Samuel 2:27-36" in *Old Testament Essays* (1990). Mem: OT Soc. of South. Africa 1977-; WUJS 1985-; South African Soc. for Semitics 1988-; SBL 1991-. Rec: Chess. Addr: (o) Potchefstroom U. for Christian Higher Ed., Dept. of Semitics 2520 Potchefstroom, South Africa 0148-991605; (h) 5 Goedehoop St., 2520 Potchefstrom, South Africa 0148-5945.

VAN SETERS, John, b. Hamilton, ON, May 2, 1935, s. of Hugo & Anne (Hubert), m. Elizabeth (Malmberg), chil: Peter; Deborah. Educ: Yale U., MA 1959, PhD 1965; Princeton Theol. Sem., BD 1962. Emp: Waterloo Luth. U., 1965-67 Asst. Prof., Near East. Stud.; Andover Newton Theol. Sch., 1967-70 Assoc. Prof., OT; U. of Toronto, 1970-77 Prof.; U. of N.C., 1977- James A. Gray Prof. of Bibl. Lit., 1980-88, 1993- Chmn., Dept. of Relig. Stud. Excv: Tell es' Saideyeh, Jordan, 1965 Field Supr.; Tell el Maskhuta, Ismilia, Egypt, 1978, 1981 Assoc. Dir. Spec: Archaeology, Hebrew Bible, Semitic Languages, Texts and Epigraphy. Pub: *Prologue to History: The Yahwist as Historian in Genesis* (Westminster/John Knox, 1992); *In Search of History: Historiography in the Ancient World and the Origins of Biblical History* (Yale U.P., 1983); *Abraham in History and Tradition* (Yale U.P., 1975); *The Hyksos: A New Investigation* (Yale U.P., 1966); and others. Awd: Yale, Agusta-Hazard Fellow. 1964; Guggenheim Awd. 1979-80. Mem: SBL, Pres., SE reg. 1983-84; AOS; ASOR; Soc. Stud. Egyptian Antiq.; Amer. Assn. of U. Prof. Rec: Gardening. Addr: (o) U. of North Carolina, Dept. of Religious Stud., 101 Saunders, CB 3225, Chapel Hill, NC 27599 919-962-3929; (h) 104 Mullin Ct., Chapel Hill, NC 27514 919-929-1623.

VAN TILBORG, Sjef, b. Tilburg, Netherlands, April 10, 1939, s. of Harrie & Anna (Botermans). Educ: Pont. Bibl. Inst., Rome, Lic. 1967; U. of Nymegen, Doc. 1968, ThD 1972. Emp: Cath. U. of Nymegen, Netherlands, 1968- Fac., Theol. Spec: New Testament. Pub: *Imaginative Love in John* (1993); "Ideology and Text" in *Text and Interpretation* (1991); "Matthew 27:3-10: An Intertextual Reading" in *Intertextuality in Biblical Writings, Essays in Honor of Bas van Jersel* (Kampen, 1989); "The Gospel of John:

Communicative Processes in a Narrative Text" *Neotestamentica* 23 (1989); *The Sermon on the Mount as an Ideological Intervention: A Reconstruction of Meaning* (1986); and others. Mem: Intl. Soc. of NT 1975-. Addr: (o) Erasmusplein 7, Postbus 9103, 6500 HD Nymegen, Netherlands 080-616053; (h) Burghardt van den Berghstraat 109-111, 6512 DH Nymegen, Netherlands 080-241115.

VAN WOLDE, Ellen J., b. Groningen, December 8, 1954, d. of John & Susanna (Lergner). Educ: Kath. U. Nymegen, BA 1976, ThM 1981, ThD 1989. Emp: *Schrift*, 1982- Ed.; Kath. U. Nymegen, 1983-88 Res., 1988-91 Lect, 1991-92, Head Lect., OT; Theol. Faculteit Tilburg, 1992- Prof., OT & Hebrew. Spec: Hebrew Bible, Semitic Languages, Texts and Epigraphy. Pub: *Words Become Worlds, Semantic Studies of Genesis*, Bibl. Interpretation Ser. 6 (Brill, 1993); *Aan de hand van Ruth* (Kok, 1993); *Ruth en Noömi, twee vreemdgangers* (Ten Have, 1993); "The Story of Cain and Abel: A Narrative Study" *JSOT* 52 (1991); *A Semiotic Analysis of Genesis 2-3*, Studia Semitica Neerlandica 25 (Van Gorcum, 1989); "A Reader-Oriented Exegesis, Illustrated by a Study of the Serpent in Gen. 2-3" in *Pentateuchal and Deuteronomistic Studies* (1989); "Trendy Intertextuality?" in *Intertextuality in Biblical Writings*, Festschrift B. Van Iersel (1989); "A Semiotic Analytical Model for Narrative Texts" *Kodikas* 10 (1987); and others. Awd: Marga Klompe-Stichting Awd. 1990. Mem: SBL 1990-; OT Werkgezelschap 1990-; IOSOT 1989-; Nederlandse Vereniging voor Semiotiek 1983-; St. Hieronymus-Bybelwerkgenootschap 1982-. Rec: Sports, music, travel. Addr: (o) Theologische Faculteit Tilburg, Academielaan 9, NL-5037 ET Tilburg, Netherlands 013-662584; (h) Houtlaan 121, NL-6525 ZC Nymegen, Netherlands.

VAN ZYL, Hermias C., b. Rustenburg, Transvaal, June 6, 1947, s. of Petrus L. & Hester Sophia (van der Walt), chil: Annamarie Deborah; Petrus Lodewikus; Barend Nicolas. Educ: U. of Pretoria, BA 1969, BD 1973, DD 1987. Emp: Dutch Reformed Ch., 1975-78 Min.; U. of South Africa, 1979-84 Sr. Lect.; U. of the Orange Free State, 1985- Prof., Dept. of NT; *Neotestamentica*, 1989- Ed. Spec: New Testament. Pub: "The Future of New Testament Studies within the Theological Curriculum" *Acta Academica* (1992); "Die vervreemdings-en toe-eieningstaak van die eksegese" *Nederduitse Gereformeerde Teologiese Tydskrif* (1992); "God se volk in transito-'n Perspektief uit Hebreërs" in *Teologie in konteks* (1991); "Die Nuwe-Testamentiese wetenskap-'n Perspektief" *Tydskrif vir Christelike Wetenskap* (1991); "God se genade verliesbaar? Nogeens Hebreërs 6:4-6" *Nederduitse Gereformeerde Teologiese Tydskrif* (1990); and others. Mem: NT Soc. of South Africa; SBL 1990-; AAR 1990-. Rec: Jogging, reading. Addr: (o) U. of the Orange Free State, Dept. of New Testament, PO Box 339, Bloemfontein, 9300, South Africa

051-401-2789; (h) 21 William Trollip St., Heuwelsig, Bloemfontein, 9301 RSA, South Africa 051-31-4567.

VANDE KAPPELLE, Robert P., b. San Jose, Costa Rica, April 2, 1944, s. of Jacob & Bertha, m. Susan E., chil: R. Peter; Sara E. Educ: The King's College, BA 1965; Ind. U., MA 1967; Princeton Theol. Sem., MDiv 1970, PhD 1977. Emp: Princeton Theol. Sem., 1971-73 Teaching Fellow; First Presby. Ch., 1973-75 Pastor; Grove City Coll., 1975-80 Asst. Prof., Relig.; Washington & Jefferson Coll., 1980- Prof., Chair of Relig. Dept. & Coll. Pastor. Spec: Hebrew Bible, New Testament. Pub: "The Old Testament: The Covenant Between God and Man" in *Building a Christian World View*, vol. 1 (1986); "Prophets and Mantics" in *Pagan and Christian Anxiety: A Response to E.R. Dodds* (U. Press of Amer., 1984); and others. Awd: NEH Summer Grant 1979; ASOR, NEH Summer Inst. in Near East. Arch. 1985. Mem: SBL 1970-; ETS 1975-; AAR 1985-. Rec: Cycling, swimming, reading, tennis, travel. Addr: (o) Washington & Jefferson College, Washington, PA 15301 412-223-6186; (h) 573 Franklin Farms Rd., Washington, PA 15301-5800 412-228-5558.

VANDER HOEK, Gerald W., b. Des Moines, IA, October 26, 1955, s. of William & Mildred, m. Mary L. (Huyser), chil: Natalia Anne; Carrie Christine; Jonathan Arie. Educ: Dordt Coll., BA, Phil. 1977; Calvin Theol. Sem., MDiv 1981, ThM 1982; Claremont Grad. Sch., MA, Relig. 1986, PhD, Bibl. Stud. 1988. Emp: Amer. Bibl. Manuscript Ctr., 1984-85 Res. Assoc.; Calvin Theol. Sem., 1987-88 Lect.; Dordt Coll., 1988-91 Asst. Prof., Theol.; Covenant Christian Reformed Ch., 1989-93 Assoc.; Pine Grove Christian Reformed Ch., 1993- Assoc. Pastor. Spec: New Testament, Apocrypha and Post-biblical Studies. Pub: *The Function of Ps 82 in the Fourth Gospel: A Comparative Midrash Study* (Claremont Grad. Sch., 1988); and others. Mem: SBL 1984-; IBR 1984-. Rec: Jogging, fishing, gardening, basketball, softball. Addr: (o) 8750 Beech, Howard City, MI 49329 616-937-5588.

VANDERKAM, James C., b. Cadillac, MI, February 15, 1946, s. of Henry & Elaine, m. Mary, chil: Jeffrey Mark; Laura Ruth; Daniel Henry. Educ: Calvin Coll., AB 1968; Calvin Theol. Sem., BD 1971; Harvard U., PhD 1976. Emp: N.C. State U., 1976-91 Prof.; *JBL*, 1981-86 Ed. Bd.; *CBQ*, 1985- Ed. Bd.; *JSP*, 1987- Ed. Bd.; *VT*, 1991- Ed. Bd.; U. of Notre Dame, 1991- Prof. Spec: Hebrew Bible, Semitic Languages, Texts and Epigraphy, Apocrypha and Post-biblical Studies. Pub: "Joshua the High Priest and the Interpretation of Zechariah 3" *CBQ* 53 (1991); "The First *Jubilees* Manuscript from Qumran Cave 4: A Preliminary Publication," co-auth., *JBL* 110 (1991); *"No One, Spoke Ill of Her": Essays on Judith*, Early Judaism & Its Lit. 2, ed. (Scholars, 1991); *The*

Book of Jubilees, 2 vol. (Peeters, 1989); *Enoch and the Growth of an Apocalyptic Tradition*, CBQ Mon. Ser. 16 (CBA, 1984); "2 Macc 6,7a and Calendrical Change in Jerusalem" *JSJ* 12 (1981); "Davidic Complicity in the Deaths of Abner and Eshbaal: A Historical and Redactional Study" *JBL* 99 (1980); "The Origin, Character, and Early History of the 364-Day Calendar: A Reassessment of Jaubert's Hypotheses" *CBQ* 41 (1979); *Textual and Historical Studies in the Book of Jubilees*, HSM 14 (Scholars, 1977); and others. Awd: Fulbright Fellow 1971-72; NEH Fellow. 1989-90; NEH Trans. Prog. Grant 1982-83; N.C. State U., Coll. of Hum. & Social Sci., Disting. Res. Awd. 1991. Mem: SBL 1974-; CBA 1974-; ASOR 1990-. Rec: Running, basketball. Addr: (o) U. of Notre Dame, Dept. of Theology, Notre Dame, IN 46556 219-631-5162; (h) 17319 Deerfield Loop, Granger, IN 46530 219-271-1539.

VANHOYE, Albert F., b. Hazebrouck, France, July 24, 1923, s. of Maurice & Collewet Helene. Educ: Sorbonne, Paris, Lic.-es-Lettres 1946; Scolasticat Jesuite, Lic. Phil. 1950, Lic. Theol. 1955; Pont. Bibl. Inst., Rome, Doc. Sci. Bibl. 1961. Emp: Fac. of Theol., Chantilly, 1959-62 Tchr., NT Exegesis; Pont. Bibl. Inst., Rome, 1963- Prof., NT Exegesis, 1969-75 Dean, Bibl. Fac., 1984-90 Rector; *Biblica*, 1978-84 Ed. Spec: New Testament. Pub: *Old Testament Priests and the New Priest According to the New Testament* (St. Bede's, 1986); "L'épitre aux Ephesiens et l'épitre aux Hébreux" *Biblica* 59 (1978); "Situation et signification de Hébreux V.1-10" *NTS* 23 (1976-77); *Situation du Christ: Hébreux 1-2* (Cerf, 1969); *Structure and Theology of the Accounts of the Passion in the Synoptic Gospels* (Liturgical, 1967); *La structure littéraire de l'épitre aux Héreux* (Desclée, 1963); "L'oeuvre du Christ, don du Père (Jn 5,36 et 17,4)" *RSR* 48 (1960); and others. Awd: Chevalier de l'Ordre Natl. du Merite 1989. Mem: SNTS 1965-; Assn. Cath. Francaise pour l'Etude de la Bible 1967-; Pont. Bibl. Commn. 1984-. Rec: Walking, reading poetry & other lit. Addr: (o) Pontificio Istituto Biblico, Piazza della Pilotta, 35, 00187 Rome, Italy 6-67012; (h) Via della Pilotta, 25, 00187 Rome, Italy 6-679-64-53.

VANN, Robert Lindley, b. Greenville, TX, August 8, 1945, s. of Bill & Mary, m. Loetta Marlene. Educ: U. Tex.-Austin, BS 1967; Cornell U., PhD 1976. Emp: U. of Maryland, 1974-92 Assoc. Prof., 1993- Prof.; Haifa U., Ctr. for Maritime Stud., 1982- Adj. Prof.; E Carolina U., 1991- Adj. Prof., Maritime Hist. & Underwater Res.; Cath. U. of Amer., 1991 Vis. Prof. Excv: Sardis, 1970-75 Architect; Carthage, 1976-79 Architect; Joint Expdn., Caesarea Maritima, 1977-81 Architect; Caesarea Anc. Harbor Excvn. Project, 1982-90 Co-dir.; Survey of Anc. Harbors, Turkey, 1991- Dir. Spec: Archaeology, Anatolian Studies. Pub: *Caesarea Papers*, Jour. of Roman Arch. Mon. Ser. (Michigan U.P., 1992); "The Harbor that Herod Built, the Harbor that Josephus Saw" in *Text-Aided Archaeology*

(CRC, 1992); "The Drusion: A Lighthouse in Herod's Harbor at Caesarea Maritima" *Intl. Jour. of Nautical Arch.* 20/2 (1991); "Excavations in the Harbor at Caesarea Maritima" *Arch. News* 16 (1991); "Herod's Ancient Harbor" in *Archaeology in the World of Herod, Jesus and Paul,* Arch. & the Bible vol. 2 (BAS, 1990); "The Application of a Gypsum-based Mortar as an Artificial Building Material in Roman North Africa" in *Studia Pompeiana and Classica, in Honor of Wilhelmina Jashemski* vol. 2 (Karatzas Brothers, 1989); *The Unexcavated Buildings of Sardis,* Brit. Arch. Reports 538 (Oxford U.P., 1989); and others. Awd: Ford Found., grant 1971; Amer. Res. Inst., Turkey 1973; State of Md., Hum. grant 1988; Fulbright Res. Awd. 1991. Mem: ASOR; AIA; Nautical Arch. Soc.; Soc. of Architectural Hist.; Amer. Acad. in Rome. Rec: Skiing, diving. Addr: (o) U. of Maryland, School of Architecture, College Park, MD 20742 301-405-6290; (h) 9205 Harvey Rd., Silver Spring, MD 20910 301-495-8818.

VANNI, Ugo A. V., b. Jesus Maria, Argentina, September 26, 1929, s. of Alfredo & Maria (Ganetti). Educ: Pont. U. Gregoriana, Lic. Phil. 1954, Lic. Theol. 1961; Pont. Bibl. Inst., Rome, Dr. Class. Lit. 1958, Dr. Holy Scripture 1969. Emp: Pont. Bibl. Inst., 1970- Prof. Invitato, NT; Pont. U. Gregoriana, Rome, 1974- Prof. Ordinario, NT. Spec: New Testament. Pub: *L'Apocalisse: ermeneutica, esegesi, teologia* (1991); "Liturgical Dialogue as a Literary Form in the Book of Revelation" *NTS* (1991); "La figura della donna nell'Apocalisse" *Studia Missionalia* (1991); *L'Apocalisse: Un'assemblea interpreta la storia* (1990); "Dalla Venuta Dell'ora Alla Venuta di Christo" *Studia Missionalia* (1983); *La Struttura Letteraria Dell'Apocalisse* (1980); and others. Addr: (o) Piazza Della Pilotta, 4, 00187 Roma, Italy 06-67011.

VANNOY, J. Robert, b. Wilmington, DE, March 3, 1937, s. of Wesley & Margaret, m. Kathe, chil: Margaret Anna; Robert Bruce; Mark Alexander; Jonathan Peter. Educ: Faith Theol. Sem., MDiv 1960, STM 1962; Free U., Netherlands, ThD 1977. Emp: Shelton Coll., 1961-62 Instr.; Faith Theol. Sem., 1965-71 Asst. Prof.; Bibl. Theol. Sem., 1971- Prof.; Westminster Theol. Sem., 1976-77 Lect., OT. Spec: Hebrew Bible. Pub: *Baker Ency. of the Bible,* contb. (1988); *Interpretation and History,* ed., contb. (Christian Life, 1986); *New International Version Study Bible,* contb. (Zondervan, 1985); "The Use of the Word *Haelohim* in Exodus 21:6 and 22:7,8" in *The Law and the Prophets* (1984); *Covenant Renewal at Gilgal* (Mack, 1978). Awd: Faith Theol. Sem., William Allen Chamberlain Awd. 1959; Woodrow Wilson Hon. Fellow 1961-62. Mem: ETS; SBL; Interdisciplinary Bibl. Res. Inst. Rec: Photography, gardening, hiking. Addr: (o) Biblical Theological Seminary, 200 N Main St., Hatfield, PA 19440 215-368-5000; (h) 218 W Walnut St., Souderton, PA 18964 215-723-6258.

VARDAMAN, E. Jerry, b. Dallas, TX, June 18, 1927, s. of Ephraim & Daisy (McCullough, m. Alfalene (Jolly), chil: Carol; Celeste. Educ: SW Bapt. Sem., BD 1952, ThD 1958; Baylor U., PhD 1974. Emp: Tarleton State U., 1952-55 Prof. of Relig.; SW Bapt. Sem., 1955-58 Instr. of Bibl. Intr.; South Bapt. Sem., 1958-72 Asst. Prof. of Bibl. Arch.; Miss. State U., Cobb Inst. of Arch, 1973-84 Dir., 1984-93 Prof., Near East. Arch. & Relig., Dir. of Special Prog. Excv: Machaerus, 1968 Dir.; Elusa, 1980 Dept. Dir. Spec: Archaeology, Anatolian Studies, New Testament. Pub: "Jesus' Life: A New Chronology" in *Chronos, Kairos, Christos; Nativity and Chronological Studies Presented to Jack Finegan.* (Eisenbraun's, 1989); *Archaeology and Living Word* (Sherwood P., 1964, 1980); *Teacher's Yoke: Studies in Memory of H. Trantham,* Joint Ed., (Baylor U.P., 1964); "Index of Scriptural Refrences" *BA* 1-25; and others. Mem: IES; Amer. Numismatic Soc.; ASOR; SBL; PES. Rec: Coin collecting, curation of rare books. Addr: (o) Mississippi State U., Cobb Institute of Archaeology, Box 1,, MS 39762 601-325-7526; (h) 505 Colonial Circle, Starkville, MS 39759 601-323-9198.

VARGAS-MACHUCA, Antonio, b. Mancha Real, Spain, January 20, 1933, s. of Arturo & Catalina. Educ: U. of Murcia & Madrid, Lic. Phil. & Litt. "Sobresaliente" 1958; U. of Innsbruck, Austria, Lic.Theol. (summa cum laude) 1965; ThD; Pont. Bibl. Inst., Rome, Lic. (summa cum laude) 1968; U. of Granada, Spain, PhD 1983. Emp: Comillas U., Spain, 1968-75 Asst. Prof., 1975- Prof.; Theol. Faculty of Granada, 1971-78 Vis. Prof.; *Publicaciones de la U. Pont. Comillas,* 1975- Ed.; *Estudios Eclesiasticos,* 1981- Ed.. Spec: New Testament. Pub: "Why Was Jesus Condemned to Death?" *Theol. Digest* (1981); *Introduccion a los Evangelios Sinopticos* (U.P. Comillas, 1975); "Los Casos de 'divorcio' admitidos por San Mateo" *Estudios Eclesiasticos* (1975); *Escritura, Tradicion e Iglesia como Reglas de fe* (Facultad de Teologia, 1967); and others. Mem: Spanish Bibl. Assn. 1970-; Ctr. for Jewish-Christian Stud. 1975-; SNTS 1978-. Addr: (o) U. Comillas, Facultad de teologia, E-28049 Madrid, Spain 91-734-39-50; (h) U. Comillas 7, E-28049 Madrid, Spain 91-73416-50.

VARGON, Shmuel, b. Israel, February 10, 1940, s. of Shalom & Ita, m. Hadassah, chil: Noam; Nir; Navit; Nethanel. Educ: Bar-Ilan U., BA 1960, MA 1969, PhD 1979. Emp: Bar-Ilan U., 1979- Head, Bible Dept. Spec: Hebrew Bible, Semitic Languages, Texts and Epigraphy. Pub: *The Book of Micah—Studies and Commentaries* (1993); "The City of Ashkelon in the Biblical Period" in *Ashkelon* I (1990); "An Admonition Prophecy to Leaders of Judah (IS. 10:28-32)" *Shnaton* (1987); "The Social Background of Reproach Prophecies from the Latter Half of the 8th Century" in *Proceedings of the Ninth World Congress of Jewish Studies* (1986); "The Oracle for the Philistines (Isaiah

14:28-32)" in *Milet, Everyman's University Studies* (1985); "David's Wanderings: A Geographic-Historical Analysis" in *Reflection on the Bible* (1983); and others. Mem: WUJS; ISBR. Addr: (o) Bar-Ilan U., Bible Dept., Ramat-Gan 52900, Israel 03-5318-229; (h) 8, Rehov Ahiya Hashiloni, Bnei-Braq 51267, Israel.

VEENKER, Ronald A., b. Los Angeles, CA, May 13, 1937, s. of Lillian, m. Beverly, chil: Jonathan. Educ: Bethel Coll., BA 1959; Bethel Theol. Sem., BD 1963; Hebrew Union Coll., PhD 1968. Emp: U. of Miami, 1967-68 Asst. Prof.; West. Ky. U., 1968- Prof. Spec: Hebrew Bible, Mesopotamian Studies. Pub: "Gilgamesh and the Magic Plant" *BA* (1981); "An Old Babylonian Legal Procedure for Appeal" *HUCA* (1974). Awd: Hebrew Union Coll., Lefkowitz Post-Doc. Fellow 1977-78. Mem: AOS; SBL; CBA. Rec: Early music. Addr: (o) Western Kentucky U., Dept. of Philosophy & Religion, Bowling Green, KY 42101 502-745-5755; (h) 562 E Main B3, Bowling Green, KY 42101 502-781-3696.

VELLANICKAL, Matthew, b. Arpookara, India, September 25, 1934, s. of Varkey & Mariam. Educ: Urbanian U., Rome, Lic. in Theol. 1964; Pont. Bibl. Inst., Rome, Doc. in Sacred Scripture 1970. Emp: St. Thomas Apostolic Sem., India, 1970-82 Prof., Sacred Scripture; *Bible Bhashyam,* 1975- Chief Ed.; Pont. Oriental Inst. of Relig. Stud., India, 1982- Pres.; Cong. for Oriental Ch., Rome, 1983-88 Cons. Spec: New Testament. Pub: *Studies in the Fourth Gospel* (1982); "Biblical Theology of Individual Churches" *Christian Orient* 1 (1980); *The Divine Sonship of Christians in the Johannine Writings,* Analecta Biblica (1977); "Jesus of the Fourth Gospel" *Bible Bhashyam* 1 (1975); "Biblical Theology of Evangelization" *Documenta Missionalia* 5 (1972); "Jesus the Word in the New Testament" *Jeevadhara* 2 (1971); and others. Mem: CBA, India 1973-; SBL 1973-, Pres. 1975-77; SNTS 1989-; Intl. Bibl. Commn., Rome 1978-84; Fedn. of Asian Bishops' Conf. 1985-. Addr: (o) Paurastya Vidyapitham, PB No. 10, Vadavathoor, Kottayam, 686 010, Kerala, India 578525-578319; (h) Vellanickal House, Arpookara PO, Kottayam, 686 008, Kerala, India.

VERMES, Geza, b. Mako, Hungary, June 22, 1924, s. of Erno & Terezia (Riesz), m. Pamela (Hobson) (dec.). Educ: Inst. Orientaliste, Louvain, Lic., Oriental Hist. & Philol. 1952; Coll. St. Albert, Louvain, ThD 1953. Emp: Ctr. Natl. de la Recherche Sci., Paris, 1955-57 Res.; U. of Newcastle, 1957-65 Sr. Lect. in Bibl. Stud.; U. of Oxford, 1965-91 Prof., Jewish Stud.; *JJS,* 1971- Ed.; Oxford Ctr. for Postgrad. Hebrew Stud., 1991- Dir., Forum for Qumran Res. Spec: Hebrew Bible, New Testament, Apocrypha and Post-biblical Studies. Pub: *The Religion of Jesus the Jew* (SCM/Fortress, 1993); "Qumran Forum Miscellanea I" *JJS* 43/2 (1992); "The Oxford Forum for Qumran Research:

Seminar on the Rule of War from Cave 4 (4Q285)" *JJS* 43/1 (1992); "Genesis 1-3 in Postbiblical Hebrew and Aramaic Literature" *JJS* 43/1 (1992); "Preliminary Remarks on the Unpublished Fragments of the Community Rule from Qumran Cave 4" *JJS* 42/2 (1991); "Josephus' Treatment of the Book of Daniel" *JJS* 42/2 (1991); *The Essenes According to the Classical Sources* (Sheffield, 1989); *The Dead Sea Scrolls in English* (Penguin, 1987); *Jesus and the World of Judaism* (SCM, 1983); and others. Awd: Brit. Acad., Fellow 1985; Oxford U., DLitt 1988; U. of Edinburgh, Hon. DD 1989; U. of Durham, Hon. DD 1990. Mem: SOTS 1959-; Brit. AJS 1975-, Pres. 1975, 1987; European AJS 1981-, Pres. 1981-84. Addr: (o) Oxford U., Oriental Institute, Pusey Ln., Oxford OX1 2LE, England 865-278200; (h) West Wood Cottage, Foxcombe Ln., Boars Hill, Oxford OX1 5DH, England 865-735384.

VERSEPUT, Donald J., b. Grand Rapids, MI, November 28, 1952, s. of John & Naomi, m. Laura Joan (Altorfer), chil: Elisabeth May; Timothy James. Educ: Wheaton Coll., BA 1974; Dallas Theol. Sem., ThM 1979; U. of Basel, Switzerland, DTh 1986. Emp: Freie Theol. Akadamie, 1985- Dozent fur NT. Spec: New Testament. Pub: "The Faith of the Reader and the Narrative of Matthew 13.53-16.20" *JSNT* 46 (1992); "The Role and Meaning of the Son of God Title in Matthew's Gospel" *NTS* 22 (1987); *The Rejection of the Humble Messianic King: A Study of the Composition of Matthew 11-12* (Lang, 1986). Mem: SBL; ETS; IBR. Addr: (o) Freie Theologische Akademie, Schiffenberger Weg 111, W-6300 Giessen, Germany 641-760-01; (h) Drosselpfad 7, W-6306 Langgoens, Germany 6403-744-23.

VIA, Dan O., b. Charlottesville, VA, December 24, 1928, s. of Dan & Josephine, m. Margaret (Bateman), chil: Dan F.; C. Carter. Educ: South. Bapt. Theol. Sem., BD 1952; Duke U., PhD 1956. Emp: Duke U., 1955-56 Instr.; Wake Forest U., 1956-68 Assoc. Prof.; U. of Va., 1968-84 Prof.; Duke U., 1984- Prof.; Fortress Press Bibl. Schol. Guides, 1968- Ed.; *Semeia Stud.,* 1980-84 Ed. Spec: New Testament. Pub: "Narrative World and Ethical Response: The Marvelous and Righteousness in Matthew 1-2" *Semeia* (1978); *Kerygma and Comedy in the New Testament: A Structuralist Approach to Hermeneutic* (Fortress, 1975); *The Ethics of Mark's Gospel: In the Middle of Time* (Fortress, 1985); *Self-Deception and Wholeness in Paul and Matthew* (Fortress, 1990); and others. Mem: AAR 1956-; SBL 1956-; SNTS 1972-. Rec: Travel, skiing. Addr: (o) Duke U., Divinity School, Durham, NC 27706 919-660-3415; (h) 2824 McDowell St., Durham, NC 27705 919-489-2770.

VINCENT, John J., b. Sunderland, December 29, 1929, s. of David & Ethel, m. Grace (Stafford), chil: Christopher; Helen; James. Educ: London U., BD 1954; Drew U., STM

1955; Basel U., DTh 1960. Emp: Boston U., 1969 Vis. Prof. Theol; N.Y. Theol. Sem., 1970 Vis. Prof. Theol.; Urban Theol. Unit, 1970- Dir.; British Liberation Theol. Project, 1984- Dir.; Sheffield U., Dept. of Bibl. Stud., 1990- Hon. Lect. Spec: New Testament. Pub: *The Bible and the Politics of Exegesis: Essays in Honor of Norman Gottwald*, contb. (Pilgrim, 1992); "Mission in Mark" in *New Testament and Missiology* (Intl. Assn. Mission Stud., 1986); *Mark at Work*, co-auth. (1986); "Pluralism and Mission in the NT" *Studia Biblica* 3 (1978); and others. Mem: SNTS 1961-. Rec: Jogging, writing. Addr: (o) Urban Theology Unit, 210 Abbeyfield Rd. Sheffield, 54 7AZ, England 0742-423438; (h) 178 Abbeyfield Rd. Sheffield, 54 7AY, England 0742-386688.

VINE, Kenneth L., b. England, September 24, 1923, s. of Alfred & Louisa, m. Betty (Jacques), chil: Judy Ann; Terence David. Educ: Newbold Coll., England, Dip. Th. 1945; Andrews U., BA 1950, MA 1951; Columbia U., MA 1954; U. of Michigan, PhD 1965. Emp: Middle East Coll., Lebanon, 1954-71 Pres.; Loma Linda U., 1971-90 Dean, Sch. of Relig.; Columbia Union Coll., G.A. Keough Lect. Ser. on Arch., 1985. Excv: Dolmens of Jordan, 1968 Co-explorer; Caesarea Maritima, 1972- Area Supr.; Et-Tell (Ai), 1966 Co-explorer. Spec: Archaeology, Hebrew Bible. Pub: "Byzantine Written Lamps from Caesarea Maritima" in *Robert Bull Festschrift* (1986); "Ceramic Lamps from the Hippodrome of Caesarea Maritima-1974" in *Horn Festschrift* (1986); *Terracotta Lamps of Caesarea Maritima, 1971-86* (1986); "Terracotta Lamps from Caesarea Maritima (1971-1976) Preliminary Report" in *The Joint Expedition to Caesarea Maritima, Preliminary Reports* (Drew U. Inst. for Arch. Res., 1982). Mem: ASOR; Amer. Soc. for Relig. Study. Rec: Traveling, ham radio, swimming. Addr: (h) 6796 Rolling Hills Dr., Riverside, CA 92505 909-687-7878.

VINSON, Richard B., b. Knoxville, TN, February 1, 1957, s. of Richard G. & Betty B., m. Joan E. (Blackburn), chil: Richard Blackburn; David Bolling; John Lawrence. Educ: Samford U., BA 1976, MA 1977; South. Bapt. Theol. Sem., MDiv 1979; Duke U., PhD 1984. Emp: Averett Coll., 1984- Assoc. Prof.; *Averett Jour.*, Ed. Spec: New Testament. Pub: "A First Century Steward" *BI* Winter (1992); "The Synoptic Enthymemes: A Comparative Study in Style" in *Persuasive Artistry: Studies in New Testament Rhetoric in Honor of George Kennedy* (JSOT, 1991); articles in *Mercer Dict. of the Bible* (Mercer U.P., 1990); "Life Everlasting" *BI* (1989); "An Examination of the Matthean Sayings Doublets with Marcan Parallels" *Studia Biblica et Theologica* (1982). Mem: SBL; NABPR. Rec: Guitar, tennis, softball, basketball, woodworking. Addr: (o) Averett College, Danville, VA 24541 804-791-5752; (h) 204 College Ave., Danville, VA 24541 804-793-1796.

VISOTZKY, Burton L., b. Chicago, IL, October 19, 1951. Educ: U. of Ill., Chicago, BA 1972; Jewish Theol. Sem., MA 1976, Rabbi 1977, PhD 1982; Harvard U., EdM 1976. Emp: Jewish Theol. Sem., 1977- Assoc. Prof., Nathan & Janet Appleman Chair of Midrash & Interrelig. Stud., 1991- Assoc. Dean, Grad. Sch. Spec: Apocrypha and Post-biblical Studies. Pub: *The Midrash on Proverbs* (Yale U.P., 1992); *Reading the Book: Making the Bible a Timeless Text* (Doubleday/Anchor, 1991); *Midrash Mishle* (JTSA, 1990); "Anti-Christian Polemic in Leviticus Rabbah" *Proc. AAJR* 56 (1990); "Prolegomenon to the Study of Jewish-Christianities in Rabbinic Literature" *AJS Rev.* 14 (1989); "Jots and Tittles: On Scriptural Interpretation in Rabbinic and Patristic Literatures" *Prooftexts* 8 (1988); "Overturning the Lamp" *JJS* 38 (1987); "Most Tender and Fairest of Women: A Study in the Transmission of Aggada" *HTR* 76 (1983). Awd: Oxford Ctr. for Post-Grad. Hebrew Stud., Vis. Schol. 1985-86; U. of Cambridge, Clare Hall, Vis. Fellow, Life Member 1985-86; Louis Ginzberg Fellow 1983; Saul Lieberman Fellow 1984-85; Abbell Res. Fellow 1985-86, 1988, 1990. Mem: SBL; AAJR; AJS; Rabbinical Assembly. Addr: (o) Jewish Theological Seminary, 3080 Broadway, New York, NY 10027 212-678-8989.

VIVIANO, Benedict T., b. St. Louis, MO, January 22, 1940, s. of Frank & Carmeline (Chiappetta). Educ: Aquinas Inst., MA, Phil. 1963, MA, Theol. 1967; Duke U., PhD 1976. Emp: Aquinas Inst., 1972-84 Prof., NT; *Newsletter for Targum and Cognate Studies*, 1978-81 Ed.; *CBQ*, 1981-84 Assoc. Ed.; Ecole Biblique, 1984 Prof.; *RB*, 1984- Assoc. Ed. Spec: New Testament, Apocrypha and Post-biblical Studies. Pub: "Matthew" in *New Jerome Biblical Comm.* (Prentice-Hall, 1990); "Matthew 23" *JSNT* 39 (1990); "Rabbouni and Mark 9:5" *RB* 97 (1990); "The Genres of Matthew 1-2" *RB* 97 (1990); "Mark 14:47: The High Priest's Servant's Ear" *RB* 96 (1989); *The Kingdom of God in History* (Liturgical, 1988); "Matthew, Master of Ecumenical Infighting" *Currents* 10 (1983); *Study as Worship: Aboth and the New Testament* (Brill, 1978); and others. Awd: ASOR-Albright Inst., Jerusalem, Thayer Fellow 1971-72. Mem: SBL 1971-; CBA 1976-; SNTS 1991. Rec: Hiking, swimming. Addr: (o) Ecole Biblique, PO Box 19053, 91019 Jerusalem, Israel 927-2-8944689.

VIVIANO, Pauline A., b. Detroit, MI, July 13, 1946, d. of Frank & Elizabeth (Palazzolo). Educ: St. Louis U., MA 1971, PhD, Bibl. Lang. & Lit. 1981. Emp: Loyola U. of Chicago, 1980- Assoc. Prof., Theol. Spec: Hebrew Bible. Pub: *The Book of Genesis*, Collegeville Bible Comm. (Liturgical, 1985); "The Book of Daniel: Prediction or Encouragement" *The Bible Today* (1983); and others. Awd: Natl. Honor Soc. in Phil. 1967; Natl. Jesuit Honor Soc. 1973; Natl. Honor Soc. in Theol. 1976. Mem: CSBR 1982-. Rec: Calligraphy, racquetball. Addr: (o) Loyola

U. of Chicago, Dept. of Theology, 6525 N Sheridan, Chicago, IL 60626 312-508-2346; (h) 3825 Main St., Skokie, IL 60076 312-673-5714.

VOGELS, Walter A., b. Berchem, Belgium, October 14, 1932, s. of Jozef & Maria (Bats). Educ: Gregorian U., Rome, STL 1958; Pont. Bibl. Inst., SSL 1960; U. of Ottawa, PhD 1968; St. Paul U., STD 1970, EPHE, Paris, Elève titulaire 1976. Emp: Intl. Sch. of White Fathers, Ottawa, Canada, 1960-68 Prof.; St. Paul U., 1966- Prof., 1976-82 Vice-Dean, Faculty Théol.; *Eglise & Theol.*, 1980- Ed. Spec: Hebrew Bible. Pub: "The God Who Creates Is the God Who Saves: The Book of Wisdom's Reversal of the Biblical Pattern" *Eglise & Théol.* 22 (1991); "Performance vaine et performance saine chez Qohélet" *Nouvelle Revue Théol.* 113 (1991); *Les Prophetes* (Novalis, 1990); *Job* (Katholieke Bijbelstichting, 1989); "De mens, schepsel en beheerder (Gen. 1,26-28)" *Collationes* 19 (1989); "Hosea's Gift to Gomer (Hos. 3,2): *Biblica*" 69 (1988); *Reading and Preaching the Bible: A New Semiotic Approach* (Glazier, 1986); "Diachronic and Synchronic Studies of Hosea 1-3" *BZ* 28 (1984); and others. Mem: Assn. Cath. des Etudes Bibl. au Canada, V.P. 1980-83; Soc. Cath. de la Bible; CBA; SBL. Rec: Sports, travel. Addr: (o) St. Paul U., 223 Main St., Ottawa, ON K1S 1C4, Canada 613-236-1393; (h) 252 Argyle Ave., Ottawa, ON K2P 1B9, Canada 613-233-8259.

VOGLER, Werner, b. Glashutte, Sa., March 27, 1934, s. of Hans & Margarethe. Educ: U. of Greifswald, ThD 1978, Habil. 1992. Emp: Theol. Sem. Leipzig, 1969- Dozent, 1980-82 Rector, 1990-92 Prof., NT; U. of Leipzig, 1992- Prof. Spec: New Testament. Pub: *Die Briefe des Johannes*, THK 17 (1992); *Juedische Jesusinterpretationen in christlicher Sicht* (1988); "Jesu Tod—Gottes Tat?" *Theol. Literaturzeitung* (1988); "Die 'Naherwartung' Jesu" *Theol. Versuche* 16 (1986); "Daemonen und Exorzismen im Neuen Testament" *Theol. Versuche* 15 (1985); *Judas Iskarioth* (1983, 1985); "Die Bedeutung der urchristlichen Hausgemeinden fuer die Ausbreitung des Evangeliums" *TLZ* (1982). Mem: SNTS 1986-; Wissenschaftliche Gesellschaft fuer Theol. 1991-. Rec: Walking, theatre. Addr: (o) U. of Leipzig, Emil-Fuchs-Str. 1, D 04105 Leipzig, Germany 0341-70946; (h) Stoermthaler Str. 7, D 04299 Leipzig, Germany 0341-80410.

VOLLENWEIDER, Samuel, b. Zurich, September 15, 1953, s. of Max & Helen, m. Elisabeth (Varga). Emp: Bern, Prof. Spec: New Testament, Apocrypha and Post-biblical Studies. Pub: "Grosser Tod und Grosses Leben: Ein Beitrag zum buddhistisch-christlichen Gespraech im Blick auf die Mystik des Paulus" *ET* 51 (1991); *Freiheit als neue Schoepfung: Eine Untersuchung zur Eleutheria bei Paulus und in seiner Umwelt* (1989); "Ich sah den Satan wie einen Blitz vom Himmel fallen (Lk 10,18)" *ZNW*

79 (1988); "Zeit und Gesetz: Erwaegungen zur Bedeutung apokalyptischer Denkformen bei Paulus" *TZ* 44 (1988); "Synesios von Kyrene ueber das Bischofsamt" *Studia Patristica* 18/1 (1986); *Neuplatonische und christliche Theologie bei Synesios von Kyrene* (1985); and others. Mem: SNTS; Intl. Assn. of Patristic Stud. Addr: (o) Evangelical Theological Seminary, Gesellschaftsstr. 25, CH-3012 Bern, Switzerland; (h) Humboldtstr 21, CH-3013 Bern, Switzerland 031-3330278.

VON WAHLDE, Urban C., b. Covington, KY, October 28, 1941, s. of Urban & Louise, m. Carol Anne, chil: Michael; Lisa. Educ: Loyola U., MA 1966; Marquette U., PhD 1975. Emp: Xavier U., 1966-67 Instr.; Brebeuf Prep. Sch., 1967-69 Instr.; St. Mary of the Plains Coll., 1974-76 Asst. Prof.; U. of Scranton, 1976-81 Chair, Dept. of Theol. & Relig. Stud.; Loyola U., 1981-86 Assoc. Prof., 1990- Prof., 1987-93 Chair, Dept. of Theol.. Spec: New Testament. Pub: *The Johannine Commandments* (Paulist, 1990); *The Earliest Version of John's Gospel* (Glazier, 1989); "The Theological Foundation of the Presbyter's Argument in 2Jn (vv4-6)" *ZNW* (1985); "Mark 9:33-50: Discipleship: The Authority That Serves" *BZ* (1985); "The Witnesses to Jesus in 5:31-40 and Belief in the Fourth Gospel" *CBQ* (1981); "The Terms for Religious Authorities in the Fourth Gospel: A Key to Literary Strata?" *JBL* (1979); and others. Mem: CBA 1969-; SBL 1970-. Addr: (o) Loyola U. of Chicago, Dept. of Theol., 6525 N Sheridan Rd., Chicago, IL 60626 312-508-2351; (h) 128 Joyce Pl., Park Ridge, IL 60008-3450.

VOS, Johannes S., b. Gouda, The Netherlands, January 21, 1942, s. of Martinus Cornelis & Cornelia (Vermeulen), m. Jacomina Maria (Oomes). Educ: Rijksuniversiteit Utrecht, ThD 1973. Emp: Evang. Theol. Sem., Tuebingen, 1965-67 Asst.; Leiden U., Fac. of Theol., 1974-75 Lect.; Vrije U., Amsterdam, 1981- Lect. Spec: New Testament. Pub: "Die Hermeneutische Antinomie bei Paulus" *NTS* 38 (1992); "Paulus en de Schrift, Hermeneutiek en retoriek in Gal 3,6-14" in *Jodendom en vroegchristendom* (1991); "Legem statuimus: Rhetorische Aspekte der Gesetzesdebatte zwischen Juden und Christen" in *Juden und Christen in der Antike* (1990); "Antijudaismus/Antisemitismus im Theologischen Woerterbuch zum NT" *NThT* 38 (1984); *Paulus en de andere joden*, co-auth. (Meinema, 1984); *Politiek en Exegese: Gerhard Kittels beeld van het jodendom* (Kok, 1983); *Traditionsgeschichtliche Untersuchungen zur paulinischen Pneumatologie* (Van Gorcum, 1973); and others. Mem: SNTS; SNTC, Holland. Rec: Organ playing. Addr: (o) Vrije U., Faculteit der Godgeleerdheid, De Boelelaan 1105, 1081 HV Amsterdam, Netherlands 020-5485453; (h) Rembrandt van Rijnweg 12, 1191 GG Ouderkerk a/d Amstel, Netherlands 02963-1373.

VOUGA, Francois, October 25, 1948, s. of Paul & Jacqueline (Rochat), m. Anne Fontaine

(Downs), chil: Etienne Paul; Maren Elisabeth; Alexandre Gérard. Educ: U. de Lausanne, Lic. Theol. 1973; U. de Geneve, Doc. Theol. 1985. Emp: L'Eglise Natl. Protestante de Genève, 1975-82 Pasteur; U. de Lausanne, 1973-75 Asst., NT; Faculté libre de Théol. Protestante de Montpellier, 1982-85 Maitre Asst., 1985-88 Prof., NT; U. de Neuchâtel, 1984-85 Vis. Prof.; Kirchliche Hochschule Bethel, 1986- Prof., NT. Spec: New Testament, Apocrypha and Post-biblical Studies. Pub: "Formgeschichtliche Ueberlegungen zu den Gleichnissen und zu den Fabeln der Jesus-Tradition auf dem Hintergrund der hellenistische Literaturgeschichte" in *The Four Gospels* (1992); *Die Johannesbriefe*, HNT 15/3 (Mohr, 1990); "Zur rhetorischen Gattung des Galaterbriefes" *ZNW* 79 (1988); "The Johannine School: A Gnostic Tradition in Primitive Christianity?" *Biblica* 69 (1988); *L'épitre de Jacques*, NT 13a (Labor et Fides, 1984); "La construction de l'histoire en Galates 3-4" *ZNW* 75 (1984); *Le cadre historique et l'intention theologique de Jean* (Beauchesne, 1977, 1981). Mem: SNTS 1986-; Wissenschaftliche Gesellschaft fur Theol. 1986-. Rec: Music. Addr: (o) Kirchliche Hochschule Bethel, Remterweg 45, D-33617, Bielefeld 13, Germany 0521-144-3948; (h) An der Rehwiese 42, D-33617 Bielefeld 13, Germany 0521-144-3176.

VOULGARIS, Christos Sp., b. Kastrakion-Doridos, Greece, October 24, 1937, s. of Spyridon & Georgia, m. Athena (Damianidis), chil: Georgia; Spyridon. Educ: Athens U. Sch. of Theol., MA 1961, ThD 1971; Andover Newton Theol. Sch., STM 1964; Boston U. Sch. of Theol., ThM 1968. Emp: Rizarios Sem., Greece, 1971-73, 1980- Prof.; St. John of Damascus Theol. Sch., Lebanon, 1971-72, 1986-; U. of Athens Sch. of Theol., 1974- Prof. Spec: New Testament. Pub: *The Biblical Doctrine on the Sacrament of Priesthood* (1992); *Chronology of the Life of Paul* (1982); *The Unity of the Apostolic Church* (1974); *Luke's Doctrine on Salvation* (1971); and others. Awd: Pauleios Soc. of Hist. Stud., Greece, Dip. 1980. Mem: AAR 1967-; SBL 1968-; SNTS 1976-. Rec: Mountain climbing. Addr: (o) Panepistimioupolis, Athens 157 72, Greece 7795-177; (h) 16 Eptanisou St., 152 31 Halandrion, Athens, Greece 6473-519.

VYHMEISTER, Nancy Jean, b. Portland, Oregon, August 31, 1937, d. of Charles & Hazel Weber, m. Werner Vyhmeister, chil: Heidi Annette (Grumling); Ronald Elmar. Educ: Pacific Union Coll., BA 1958; Andrews U., MA, Bibl. Lang. 1967, EdD, Relig. Educ. 1978. Emp: River Plate Coll., Argentina, 1961-71 Prof., Bibl. Lang.; Andrews U., 1975-84 Assoc. Prof.; *Comentario Biblico Adventista*, 1978-90 Assoc. Trans. & Ed.; Adventist Intl. Inst. of Advanced Stud., Philippines, 1984-91 Prof., Bibl. Stud.; *AUSS*, 1991- Co-ed. Spec: Hebrew Bible, New Testament. Pub: *Gramatica Elemental de Griego del Nuevo Testamento* (Ceape, 1981). Mem: SBL. Rec: Mission Stud. Addr: (o) Andrews U. Theological Seminary, Berrien Springs, MI

49104 616-471-6281; (h) 4525 Timberland Dr., Berrien Springs, MI 49103 616-473-3439.

WACHOLDER, Ben Zion, b. Poland, m. Touby, chil: Nina; Sholom; David; Hannah. Educ: Yeshiva U., BA 1951; UCLA, PhD 1960. Emp: Hebrew Union Coll., 1956- Prof. Spec: Apocrypha and Post-biblical Studies. Pub: *A Preliminary Edition of the Dead Sea Scrolls: The Hebrew and Aramaic Texts from Cave Four*, Fascicles 1 & 2 (BAS, 1991, 1992); *The Dawn of Qumran* (Hebrew Union Coll., 1983); *Messianism and Mishna* (Hebrew Union Coll., 1979); *Essays in Chronology & Chronography* (Ktav, 1975); and others. Addr: (o) 3101 Clifton, Cincinnati, OH 45220 513-221-1875; (h) 7648 Greenland Pl., Cincinnati, OH 45237 513-761-5836.

WACHSMANN, Shelley, b. Regina, SK, Canada, November 9, 1950, s. of Haskel A. & Friedel, chil: Yonatan; Yishai. Educ: Hebrew U., Inst. of Arch., Jerusalem, BA 1974, MA 1984, PhD, Bibl. Arch. 1990. Emp: Israel Antiq. Authority, 1976-89 Inspector of Underwater Antiq.; Tex. A&M U., 1990- Meadows Asst. Prof. of Bibl. Arch. Excv: Late Bronze Age cargo near Kibbutz Hahotrim, underwater, 1980 Dir.; Byzantine wreck at Dor, 1985 Dir.; Caesarea, Crusader City, 1985 Dir.; Kinneret Boat, 1986 Dir. Spec: Archaeology. Pub: *The Excavations of an Ancient Boat from the Sea of Galilee (Lake Kinneret)*, *'Atiqot* 19 (1990); "The Galilee Boat: 2,000-Year-Old Hull Recovered Intact" *BAR* 14/5 (1988); *Aegeans in the Theban Tombs*, Orientalia Lovaniensia Analecta XX (1987); "Is Cyprus Ancient Alashiya? New Evidence from an Egyptian Tablet" *BA* 49 (1986); "Shfifons—Early Bronze Age Anchor Shaped Cult Stones from the Sea of Galilee Region" *Thracia Pontica* 3 (1986); "The Ships of the Sea Peoples" *Intl. Jour. of Nautical Arch.* 10 (1981); "The Thera Waterborne Procession Reconsidered" *Intl. Jour. of Nautical Arch.* 9 (1980). Mem: ASOR; AIA; Hellenic Inst. of Marine Arch.; Inst. of Nautical Arch.; Nautical Arch. Soc.. Rec: Scuba diving, traveling, reading. Addr: (o) Texas A&M U., Nautical Archeology Program, College Station, TX 77843-4352 409-847-9257; (h) 502 Southwest Pkwy., Apt. 2208 College Station, TX 77840 409-696-8473.

WAETJEN, Herman C., b. Bremen, Germany, June 16, 1929, s. of Henry & Anna, m. Mary (Struyk), chil: Thembisa; Lois; David. Educ: Concordia Coll. Sem., BD 1953; U. of Tubingen, Germany, Dr.Theol. 1958. Emp: U. of South. Calif., 1959-62 Asst. Prof.; San Francisco Theol. Sem., 1962- Robert S. Dollar Prof. of NT; U. of Nairobi, Kenya, 1973-74 Vis. Prof.; U. of Zimbabwe, 1986-87 Vis. Prof.; U. of Namibia, 1993-94 Vis. Prof. Spec: New Testament. Pub: *A Reordering of Power: A Socio-Political Interpretation of Mark's Gospel* (Fortress, 1989); "Jesus, the First Final Human Being" *Pacific Theol. Rev.* (1984); *The Origin and*

Destiny of Humanness: An Interpretation of the Gospel According to Matthew (Omega, 1976); "The Ending of Mark and the Gospel's Shift in Eschatology" *Ann. of the Swedish Theol. Inst.* (1965); and others. Mem: SBL; Pacific Coast Theol. Soc.; Ctr. for Hermeneutical Stud. Rec: Backpacking, photography, travel. Addr: (o) 2 Kensington Rd., San Anselmo, CA 94960 415-258-6581; (h) 83 Jordan Ave., San Anselmo, CA 94960 415-456-0331.

WAGNER, Günter E. A., b. Juterbog, Germany, July 5, 1928, s. of Otto & Martha, m. Doris (Glenn), chil: Undine. Educ: Bapt. Theol. Sem., Switzerland, BLD 1953; U. of Zurich, ThD 1960. Emp: Ecumenical Ctr., Germany, 1956-58 Res. Asst.; Bapt. Theol. Sem., 1958- Prof.; *Una Sancta,* 1971- Co-ed.; *NTS,* 1982-85 Co-ed.; *Die Kirchen der Welt,* 1958- Co-ed.; Cardiff, Wales, 1979- Edward Stephen Griffiths Lect. Spec: New Testament. Pub: *An Exegetical Bibliography of the New Testament* (1983); *Pauline Baptism and the Pagan Mysteries* (1967); *Att dö Och Sedan...* (1966); and others. Mem: SNTS 1963-; SBL 1967-; IACS 1977-. Rec: Travel, music, sports. Addr: (o) Baptist Theological Seminary, CH8803 Ruschlikon, Zurich, Switzerland 01-724-00-10; (h) Vorderi Siten 9, CH-8816 Hirzel, Switzerland 01-729-95-50.

WAINWRIGHT, Elaine Mary, b. Toowoomba, Queensland, August 25, 1948, d. of Norman Thomas & Kathlenn Veronica. Educ: Kelvin Grove Tchr. Coll., Cert. of Teaching 1966; U. of Queensland, BA 1980; Cath. Theol. Union, MA, Theol. 1985; Ecole Biblique, Jerusalem, Eleve Diplome 1986; Pont. Bibl. Commn., Rome, BSS 1986; U. of Queensland, PhD 1990. Emp: Brisbane Archdiocesan & Sisters of Mercy Formation Prog., 1975-78 Lect., Bibl. Stud.; Pius XII Sem., Brisbane, 1981-1983 Lect., Bibl. Stud.; Ecce Homo Ctr. for Bibl. Formation, Jerusalem, 1985-1986 Lect., Bibl. Stud.; Brisbane Coll. of Theol., 1987- Lect., Bibl. Stud. Spec: New Testament. Pub: *Towards a Feminist Critical Reading of the Gospel of Matthew* (de Gruyter, 1991); "A Metaphorical Walk through Scripture in an Ecological Age" *Pacifica* 4 (1991); "The Word is Alive and Active: Gender, Language and Symbol in Our Use of Scripture" *Cath. Sch. Stud.* 64/1 (1991); "In Search of the Lost Coin: Toward a Feminist Biblical Hermeneutic" *Pacifica* 2 (1989); and others. Mem: Australian CBA 1981-, V.P. 1988-89, Pres. 1989-90; CBA 1984-; SBL 1988-; Australian Assn. for Stud. in Relig. 1987-. Rec: Reading, travel, photography. Addr: (o) Catholic Theological College, Approach Rd., Banyo, Queensland 4014, Australia 07-267-5357; (h) 35 Hooker St., Windsor, Queensland 4300, Australia 07-857-6700.

WALKER, William O., Jr., b. Sweetwater, TX, December 6, 1930, s. of William & Frances, chil: Scott; Mary; Neal. Educ: Austin Coll., BA 1953; Austin Presbyn. Theol. Sem., MDiv 1957; U. of Tex. at Austin, MA 1958; Duke U., PhD 1962.

Emp: Austin Coll., 1954-55 Instr.; Duke U., 1960-62 Instr.; Trinity U., 1962 Asst. Prof., Prof, 1988- Dean, Div. of Humanities & Arts. Spec: New Testament. Pub: *Harper's Bible & Pronunciation Guide,* ed. (Harper & Row, 1989); "Text-Critical Evidence for Interpolations in the Letters of Paul" *CBQ* (1988); *Harper's Bible Dict.,* assoc. ed. (Harper & Row, 1985); "Acts and the Pauline Corpus Reconsidered" *JSNT* (1985); *The Relationships Among the Gospels: An Interdisciplinary Dialogue,* ed. (Trinity U.P., 1978); "The Son of Man Question and the Synoptic Problem" *NTS* (1982); "1 Corinthians 11:2-16 and Paul's Views Regarding Women" *JBL* (1975); "The Quest for the Historical Jesus: A Discussion of Methodology" *Anglican Theol. Rev.* (1969); and others. Mem: AAR; SNTS; CBA; SBL. Rec: Tennis, travel, photography. Addr: (o) Trinity U., Division of Humanities & Arts, 715 Stadium Dr., San Antonio, TX 78212 210-736-7650; (h) 315 Cloverleaf Ave., San Antonio, TX 78209 210-842-4911.

WALL, Robert W., b. Seattle, WA, October 21, 1947, s. of Robert & Elizabeth, m. Carla, chil: Zachary; Bartholomew; Cara; Andrew; Benjamin. Educ: Valparaiso U., BA 1969; Dallas Sem., ThM 1973, ThD 1979. Emp: Meth. Ch., 1973-78 Pastor; Seattle Pacific U., 1978- Prof. Spec: New Testament. Pub: *The New Testament as Canon,* JSNTSup (1992); *Commentary on Revelation,* New Intl. Bibl. Comm. (Hendrickson, 1991); "Successors to 'The Twelve' According to Acts 12:1-17" *CBQ* 53 (1991); "The Acts of the Apostles in Canonical Context" *BTB* 18 (1988); "Eschatologies of the Peace Movement" *BTB* (1985); "Introduction: New Testament Ethics" in *Horizons in Biblical Theology* (1983); and others. Mem: SNTS; CBA; SBL. Rec: Jogging, music, gardening. Addr: (o) Seattle Pacific U., Seattle, WA 98119 206-281-2158; (h) 809 N 60th St., Seattle, WA 98103 206-784-8903.

WALLACE, Daniel B., b. Pasadena, CA, June 5, 1952, s. of Beecher & Nayda, m. Pati K., chil: Noah Daniel; Benjamin Baird; Andrew Jon; Zachary Paul. Educ: Biola U., BA 1975; Dallas Theol. Sem., ThM 1979. Emp: Dallas Sem., 1979-81 Instr.; Grace Sem., 1981-83 Instr.; Probe Min., 1984-88 Res. Assoc.; Dallas Theol. Sem., 1988- Asst. Prof. Spec: New Testament. Pub: "John 5,2 and the Date of the Fourth Gospel" *Biblica* 71 (1990); "The *Majority Text:* A New Collating Base?" *NTS* 35 (1989); "Some Second Thoughts on the *Majority Text*" *BS* 146 (1989); *A Scripture Index to Moulton and Milligan's Vocabulary of the Greek Testament* (Dallas Sem., 1988); "The Relation of Adjective to Noun in Anarthrous Constructions in the New Testament" *NT* 26 (1984); and others. Awd: Dallas Sem., Henry C. Thiessen Awd. 1978-79. Mem: ETS 1978-, Second V.P., SW sect. 1992-93; SBL 1978-; IOSCS 1978. Rec: Karate, swimming, football, travel, reading. Addr: (o) Dallas Theological Seminary, 3909 Swiss Ave., Dallas, TX 75204 214-841-3712; (h) 2100 Buckskin Circle, Carrollton, TX 75006.

WALLACE, Howard N., b. Sydney, Australia, July 28, 1948, m. Bronwyn M.. Educ: U. of NSW, Australia, BE 1971; Sydney U., BD 1977; Harvard U., MTh 1978, DTh 1983. Emp: United Theol. Coll, 1983- Lect., OT; Sydney U., 1983-, Lect., OT. Spec: Hebrew Bible. Pub: "Adam," "Eve," "Eden, Garden of," "Garden of God," "Tree of Knowledge/Tree of Life" in *ABD* (Doubleday, 1992); "The Toledot of Adam: Gen. 5:1-6:8" in *Studies in the Pentateuch*, VTSup 41 (Brill, 1990); "Genesis 2:1-3: Creation and Sabbath" *Pacifica* 1/3 (1988); "The Oracles Against the Israelite Dynasties in 1 and 2 Kings" *Biblica* 67 (1986); *The Eden Narrative*, HSM 32 (Scholars, 1985); "Covenant Themes in Malachi," co-auth., *CBQ* 45/4 (1983). Mem: ASOR; CBA; IES; NAPH; SBL. Rec: Calligraphy, golf. Addr: (o) United Theological College, 16 Mason's Dr., Nth Parramatta, NSW 2151, Australia 02-683-3655; (h) 35 Pomeroy St., Homebush, NSW 2140, Australia 02-764-3046.

WALLWORK, Ernest, October 6, 1937, s. of Ernest & Irene, m. Anne (Shere), chil: Adam; Rachel. Educ: Bucknell U., BS 1959; Harvard U., MBA 1961; Yale U., BD 1964, PhD 1971. Emp: Wellesley Coll., 1968-72 Asst. Prof; Union Theol. Sem, 1973-74 Asst. Prof.; Yale U., 1974-79 Assoc. Prof. Spec: Apocrypha and Post-biblical Studies. Pub: *Psychoanalysis and Ethics* (Yale U.P., 1991); "Durkheim's Early Sociology of Religion" *Sociological Analysis* (1985); "Religion and Social Structure" in *The Division of Labor" Amer. Anthrop.* (1984); "Thou Shalt Love thy Neighbor as Thyself—The Freudian Critique" *Jour. of Relig. Ethics* (1982); *Critical Issues in Modern Religion*, co-auth.; *Durkheim: Morality and Milieu* (Harvard U.P. 1972); and others. Awd: Rockefeller Doctoral Fellow 1968. Rec: Swimming, tennis. Addr: (o) Syracuse U., 501 Hall of Languages, Syracuse, NY 13244-1170 315-423-3861; (h) 3021 Davenport St., NW, Washington, DC 20008 202-244-9241.

WALSH, Jerome T., b. Detroit, MI, June 14, 1942, s. of Thomas & Madeleine (Couture). Educ: Catholic U. of Amer., BA 1964, MA 1965; U. of Louvain, BA 1967, MA 1969; Pont. Bibl. Inst., SSL 1975; U. of Mich., PhD 1982. Emp: St John's Provincial Sem., 1975-88 Assoc. Prof.; Mary Immaculate Sem., 1988-89 Assoc. Prof.; St. John's U., 1989- Assoc. Prof. Spec: Hebrew Bible, New Testament. Pub: "I Kings" in *New Jerome Biblical Comm.* (1990); "The Contexts of 1 Kings xiii" *VT* 39 (1989); "The Case for the Prosecution: Isa 41.21-42.17" in *Directions in Biblical Hebrew Poetry* (1987); "From Egypt to Moab: A Source-Critical Analysis of the Wilderness Itinerary" *CBQ* 39 (1977); "Genesis 2:4b-3:24: A Synchronic Approach" *JBL* 96 (1977). Awd: Assn. of Theol. Sch., res. grant 1987; Annenberg Res. Inst. Colloquium 1989; St. John's U., Summer res. grant 1990, Fac. Merit Awd. 1990. Mem: CBA

1975-; SBL 1975-; SOTS 1978-. Rec: Travel, contemporary fantasy lit., computers. Addr: (o) St. John's U., Dept. of Theol. & Relig. Stud., Grand Central & Utopia Pkwy., Jamaica, NY 11439 718-990-6161; (h) 32-23 88th St., Apt. 404, Jackson Heights, NY 11369.

WALTER, Nikolaus, b. Wolfen, Bitterfeld, March 11, 1932, s. of Robert & Caritas, m. Katharina (Wossidlo), chil: Hanna; Bettina. Educ: Martin-Luther-U. Halle, ThD 1961, Habil. 1967. Emp: Kirchliche Hochschule, Naumburg, 1964-86 Docent, NT; Friedrich-Schiller-U. Jena, Theol. Fakultaet 1986- Prof., NT; *NTS,* 1977-80 Ed. Bd. Spec: New Testament, Apocrypha and Post-biblical Studies. Pub: "Jewish-Greek Literature of the Greek Period" in *The Cambridge History of Judaism* (Cambridge U.P., 1989); "Paul and the Early Christian Jesus-Tradition" in *Paul and Jesus* (JSOT, 1989); "Hellenistische Eschatologie" *TLZ* 110 (1985); "Zur Interpretation von Roemer 9-11" *ZTK* 81 (1984); *Fragmente juedisch-hellenistischer Epik* (Mohr, 1983); "Apostelgeschichte 6,1 und die Anfaenge der Urgemeinde in Jerusalem" *NTS* 29 (1983); *Fragmente juedisch-hellenistischer Historiker* (Mohr, 1976, 1980); *Fragmente juedisch-hellenistischer Exegeten* (Mohr, 1975, 1980); *Der Thoraausleger Aristobulos* (Akademie, 1964); and others. Mem: SNTS 1966-; Wissenschaftliche Gesellschaft fuer Theol. 1990-. Addr: (o) Friedrich-Schiller U., Theologische Fakultaet, Ibrahimstr. 24, Jena, Germany 03641-23947; (h) Wilhelm-Wagner-Str. 7, D-06611 Naumburg (Saale), Germany 03445-3068.

WALTKE, Bruce K., b. West New York, NJ, August 30, 1930, s. of Henry & Louise, m. Elaine, chil: Susan; Stephen; Jonathan. Educ: Houghton Coll., BA 1952; Dallas Theol. Sem., ThM 1956, ThD 1958; Harvard U., PhD 1965. Emp: Dallas Theol. Sem., 1958-76 Prof.; Regent Coll., 1976-85, 1991- Prof.; Westminster Theol. Sem., 1985-91 Prof. Excv: Gezer, 1970 Area Supr. Spec: Archaeology, Hebrew Bible, Semitic Languages, Texts and Epigraphy. Pub: "Samaritan Pentateuch" in *ABD* (Doubleday, 1992); "Superscripts, Postscripts, or Both" in *JBL* (1991); *Introduction to Biblical Hebrew Syntax* (1990); "The Date of the Conquest" *Westminster Theol. Jour.* (1989); *Micah* (1988); "Cain and His Offering" *Westminster Theol. Jour.* (1986); "Problems in the Grammatico-Historical Method of Interpretation" *Hermeneutics* (1984); *Biblical Criticism: Historical, Literary and Textual* (1974); and others. Awd: William Anderson Awd. in Grad. Res. 1958; Houghton Coll., Outstanding Alumnus Awd. 1988. Addr: (o) Regents College, 5800 University, Vancouver BC V6T 2E4, Canada.

WALTON, John H., b. Philadelphia, PA, March 11, 1952, s. of Harvey & Eleanore, m. Kim, chil: Jonathan Harvey; Joshua Theodore; Jill Marie. Educ: Wheaton Grad. School, MA 1975; Hebrew Union Coll., PhD 1981. Emp: Moody Bible Inst., 1981- Prof., OT. Spec: Hebrew Bible,

Mesopotamian Studies. Pub: "The Object Lesson of Jonah 4:5-7 and the Purpose of the Book of Jonah" *Bull. for Bibl. Res.* 2 (1992); *A Survey of the Old Testament*, co-auth. (Zondervan, 1991); "Psalms: A Cantata About the Davidic Covenant" *JETS* 24 (1991); *Ancient Israelite Literature in Its Cultural Context* (Zondervan, 1989); "Isaiah 7:14—What is in a Name?" *JETS* 30 (1987); "Deuteronomy: An Exposition of the Spirit of the Law" *Grace Theol. Jour.* 8 (1987); "Daniel's Four Kingdoms" *JETS* 29/1 (1986); *Obadiah—Jonah: A Bible Study Comm.*, co-auth. (Zondervan, 1982, 1988); *Chronological and Background Charts of the Old Testament* (Zondervan, 1978); and others. Mem: SBL; IBR; ETS, MidW Chmn. 1986. Addr: (o) Moody Bible Institute, 820 N LaSalle, Chicago, IL 60610 312-329-4025; (h) 219 Columbia, Park Ridge, IL 60068 708-823-3247.

WANG, Joseph S., b. Taiwan, China, December 17, 1933, s. of John & Ping, m. Esther, chil: David. Educ: Asbury Theol. Sem., BD 1963; Priceton Theol. Sem., MTh 1964; Emory U., PhD 1970. Emp: Asbury Theol. Sem., 1970- Prof. Spec: New Testament. Pub: "Romans" in *Asbury Bible Comm.* (Zondervan, 1992); "Romans" in *The Wesley Bible* (Thomas Nelson, 1990); "Soteriology in the Synoptic Gospels" in *An Inquiry Into Soteriology from a Biblical Theological Perspective* (Warner, 1981); *Peter* (Graded, 1980); and others. Mem: SBL; ETS. Rec: Ping-pong, swimming, photography. Addr: (o) Asbury Theological Seminary, Wilmore, KY 40390 606-858-3581; (h) 216 S Lexington Ave., Wilmore, KY 40390 606-858-4191.

WANSBROUGH, Henry J., b. London, England, September 10, 1934, s. of George & Elizabeth. Educ: Oxford U., St. Benet's Hall, MA 1961; Fribourg U., STL 1964; Ecole Biblique, LSS 1965. Emp: Ampleforth Coll., 1965-90, 1969-90 Housemaster; Ampleforth Abbey, 1966-90 Tutor in Scripture; Oxford U., St. Benet's Hall, 1990- Master. Spec: New Testament. Pub: *New Jerusalem Bible*, gen. ed. (Darton, Longman & Todd, 1985); *Risen from the Dead* (St. Paul's, 1978); "Mark iii.21: Was Jesus Out of His Mind?" *NTS* 18 (1972); and others. Rec: Music, sports. Addr: (o) Oxford U., St. Benet's Hall, Oxford, OX1 3LN, England 0865-513917.

WAPNISH, Paula C., b. Brooklyn, NY, August 27, 1948, d. of Rosalyn & Murray, m. Brian Hesse, chil: Arielle Leah. Educ: City Coll. N.Y., BA (magna cum laude) 1970; Columbia U., MA 1975, MPhil 1978, PhD, Middle East. Lang. & Cultures 1984. Emp: Smithsonian Inst., 1978-90 Res. Collaborator & Res. Assoc., Dept. of Anthrop.; U. of Alabama, Birmingham, 1983-84, 1990-91 Lect., Dept. of Hist., 1990- Res. Assoc., Dept. of Anthrop.; Harvard Semitic Mus., 1988- Res. Assoc.; Philistine Pastoral Production Project, Natl. Sci. Found., 1989-92 Co-investigator. Excv: Tepe Ganj Dareh, Iran, 1974 Square Supr.; Tel Jemmeh, Israel, 1982 zooarchaeologist; Qazrin/Kanaf, Israel, 1985 zooarchaeologist; Tel

Batash, Israel, 1985, 1987 zooarchaeologist; Ashkelon, Israel, 1987, 1989-91 zooarchaeologist. Spec: Archaeology, Semitic Languages, Texts and Epigraphy. Pub: "Pampered Pooches or Plain Pariahs? The Ashkelon Dog Burials" *BA* 56/2 (1993); "Beauty and Utility in Bone: New Light on Bone Crafting" *BAR* 17/4 (1991); "Animal Remains from Tel Dan: Pastoral Production at a Rural, Urban and Ritual Center," co-auth. *Archeozoologia* 4/2 (1991); "Urbanization and the Organization of Animal Production at Tell Jemmeh in the Middle Bronze Age Levant," co-auth., *JNES* 47/2 (1988); *Animal Bone Archaeology: From Objectives to Analysis*, co-auth. (Taraxacum, 1985); "The Dromedary and Bactrian Camel in Levantine Historical Settings: The Evidence from Tell Jemmeh" in *Early Herders and Their Flocks*, Animals & Arch. 3, Brit. Arch. Reports 202 (1984); and others. Awd: Zion Res. Found., res. grant 1975; Memorial Found. for Jewish Culture, res. grant 1977; Natl. Sci. Found., grants 1981, 1989-92; NEH Fellow. 1984. Mem: IES; AOS; ASOR; PES; Intl. Coun. for Archaeozoology. Rec: Reading mysteries, gardening, cooking, traveling. Addr: (o) U. of Alabama at Birmingham, Dept. of Anthropology, Birmingham, AL 35294-3350 205-934-3508; (h) 3700 Crestbrook Rd., Birmingham, AL 35223.

WARD, Richard F., b. Conway, SC, September 19, 1951, s. of Dalton L. & Marjory G., m. Jane Anne (Ferguson), chil: Dylan; Colin. Educ: Okla. Bapt. U., BA (magna cum laude) 1973; Trinity U., MA (magna cum laude) 1976; Christian Theol. Sem., MA, Relig. (summa cum laude) 1987; NW U., PhD 1987. Emp: Okla. Bapt. U., 1976-78 Instr.; NW U., 1982-85 Grad. Asst.; SE Bapt. Theol. Sem., 1983 Adj. Prof.; Emory U., Candler Sch. of Theol., 1985-87 Instr., Speech Communication, 1987-93 Asst. Prof.; Yale Div. Sch., 1993- Assoc. Prof., Communication Arts. Spec: New Testament. Pub: "Pauline Voice and Presence as Strategic Communication" in *SBL Seminar Papers* (1990); "2 Corinthians 10:7-12" *Rev. & Expositor* 87/4 (1990); and others. Awd: NW U., Diss. Year Fellow. 1985-86. Mem: Intl. Network of Bibl. Storytellers 1985-; SBL 1989-; AAR 1989-; Relig. Speech Communication Assn. 1987-; AH 1988-. Rec: Playing guitar, storytelling. Addr: (o) Yale U., The Divinity School, 409 Prospect, New Haven, CT 06511.

WARD, Roy Bowen, Educ: Abilene Christian Coll., BA (summa cum laude), Bible & Greek 1956; Harvard Div. Sch., STB 1959, ThD, NT, Hellenistic-Roman Relig. 1967. Emp: Conn. Coll., 1963-64 Instr., Relig.; Earlham Coll., Sch. of Relig., 1970 Lect., NT; Rice U., 1970-71 Vis. Assoc. Prof., Relig. Stud.; Miami U., Ohio, 1964- Prof., Relig., 1971-78 Chair, Dept. of Relig. Spec: Archaeology, New Testament. Pub: "Women in Roman Baths" *HTR* 85 (1992); "*Porneia* and Paul" *Proc. East. Great Lakes & MidW Bibl. Soc.* 6 (1986); "James, Letter of" in *IDB Sup.* (1976); "Abraham Traditions in Early Christianity" in *Studies on the Testament of Abraham*, Septuagint & Cognate Stud. vol. 6

(Scholars, 1976); "Partially in the Assembly: James 2:2-4" *HTR* 62 (1969); "The Restoration Principle: A Critical Analysis" *RQ* 8 (1965-66); and others. Awd: Rockefeller Doc. Fellow. 1961-63; Harvard U., Teaching Fellow. 1962-63; Danforth Assoc. Fellow. 1969-. Mem: SNTS 1975-; AAR; CSBR; East. Great Lakes Bibl. Soc.; SBL. Addr: (o) Miami U., Dept. of Religion, 12 Old Manse, Oxford, OH 45056 513-529-4303; (h) 103 Oakhill Dr., Oxford, OH 45056 513-523-3991.

WARREN, Virgil, b. Cincinnati, OH, September 25, 1942, s. of Ervin & Elanora, m. Ruth Ann, chil: David; Steve; Tara; Michelle. Educ: Cincinnati Bible Sem., AB, ThB; Wheaton Coll., MDiv. 1971, MA 1973; South. Bapt. Theol. Sem., PhD 1977. Emp: Cincinnati Bible Coll., 1971-74 Assoc. Prof.; Manhattan Christian Coll., 1977- Prof. Spec: New Testament. Pub: *What the Bible Says About Salvation* (College, 1982). Mem: SBL 1978-; AAR 1978-; Evang. Phil. Soc. 1978-. Rec: Basketball, music. Addr: (o) Manhattan Christian College, 1415 Anderson, Manhattan, KS 66502 913-539-3571; (h) 1600 Stewart Ct., Manhattan, KS 66502 913 539-5031.

WASHBURN, David L., b. Stockton, CA, July 20, 1953, s. of LeRoy & Helen, m. Kathryn, chil: Naomi; Becca; Malinda. Educ: Fort Wayne Bible Coll., BA 1981; Denver Conservative Bapt. Sem., MA, OT 1983. Emp: Rockmont Coll., 1985-86 Instr., NT. Spec: Hebrew Bible, Semitic Languages, Texts and Epigraphy. Pub: *A Catalog of Biblical Passages in the Dead Sea Scrolls* (ETS/Eisenbrauns, 1991); "Third Class Conditions in First John" *Grace Theol. Jour.* 11 (1991); "Perspective and Purpose: Understanding the Josiah Story" *Trinity Jour.* 12 (1991); "The Chronology of Judges: Another Look" *BS* 147 (1990). Mem: ETS 1982-; SBL 1990-. Rec: Reading, computer programming, freelance popular writing, walking, bicycling. Addr: (o) 216 N Douglas, Powell, WY 82435 307-754-9851.

WASILEWSKA, Ewa C., b. Gdansk, Poland, February 12, 1958, d. of Czeslaw & Izabela. Educ: Warsaw U., Inst. of Arch., MA 1982; U. of Utah, MA, Turkish Stud. 1989, Ph.D., Anthrop. 1991. Emp: U. of Utah, Dept. of Anthropology, 1986- Assoc. Instr., 1990- Adj. Asst. Prof. Excv: Alexandria, Egypt, 1981 Field Arch.; Palmyra, Syria, 1981 Field Arch.; Petra, Jordan, 1985 Area Supr. Spec: Archaeology, Anatolian Studies. Pub: "Organization and Meaning of the Sacred Space in Prehistoric Anatolia" in *Orientalic Lovanienzia Analecta* (1992); "To Be or Not to Be a Temple? Possible Identification of a Banesh Period Temple at Tall-i Malyan, Iran" in *Mesopotamie et Elam: Actes de la xxxvieme rencontre assyriologique internaionale 1989* (1991); "Archaeology of Religion: Colors as the Symbolic Markers Dividing the Sacred from Profane" in *Jour. of Prehistoric Relig.* (1991); and others. Mem: Amer. Anthrop. Assn.; AOS; ASOR; Soc. for Amer. Arch.; BIA 1984-. Rec: Reading, travel.

Addr: (o) U. of Utah, Dept. of Anthropology, Salt Lake City, UT 84112 801-581-6251; (h) 640 East Brittany Dr. #201, Murray, UT 84107 801-262-7182.

WATSON, Duane F., b. Watertown, NY, May 15, 1956, s. of Frederick & Beverely, m. JoAnn (Ford), chil: Christina Lucille. Educ: Houghton Coll., BA 1978; Princeton Theol Sem., MDiv 1981; Duke U., PhD 1986. Emp: Ashland Theol. Sem., 1984-86 Asst. Prof., Bibl. Stud.; Malone Coll., 1989- Assoc. Prof. Spec: New Testament. Pub: *Persuasive Artistry: Studies in New Testament Rhetoric in Honor of George A. Kennedy*, JSNTSup 50, ed. (JSOT, 1991); "1 Corinthians 10:23-11:1 in the Light of Greco-Roman Rhetoric: The Role of Rhetorical Questions" *JBL* 108 (1989); "A Rhetorical Analysis of 2 John According to Greco-Roman Convention" *NTS* 35 (1989); "A Rhetorical Analysis of 3 John: A Study in Epistolary Rhetoric" *CBQ* 51 (1989); "A Rhetorical Analysis of Philippians and its Implications for the Unity Question" *NT* 30 (1988); *Invention, Arrangement, and Style: Rhetorical Criticism of Jude and 2 Peter*, SBL Diss. Ser. 104 (Scholars, 1988); and others. Awd: Malone Coll. Res. Grant 1991-92; John Wesley Fellow. 1982-85. Mem: SBL; CBA; AAR; East. Great Lakes Bibl. Soc. Rec: Weightlifting, restoration of Victorian antiques. Addr: (o) Malone College, Dept. of Religion & Philosophy, 515 25th St. NW, Canton, OH 44709 216-489-0800; (h) 1527 Old Post Road, Ashland, OH 44805 419-281-5976.

WATSON, JoAnn F., b. Ashland, OH, April 11, 1956, d. of L. W. & Lucille G. (Ford), m. Duane F. Watson, chil: Christina Lucille. Educ: DePauw U., BA (magna cum laude) 1978; Princeton Theol. Sem., MDiv 1981; NW U., PhD 1984. Emp: Ashland Theol. Sem., 1984-86, 1989- Assoc. Prof., Christian Theol. Spec: New Testament. Pub: Articles in *ABD* (Doubleday, 1992); *Mutuality in Christ* (Vantage, 1991); and others. Awd: Phi Beta Kappa 1978. Mem: AAR 1984-; SBL 1984-; Intl. Assn. of Women Min. 1984-. Rec: Music, travel. Addr: (o) Ashland Theological Seminary, 910 Center St., Ashland, OH 44805 419-289-5182; (h) 1527 Old Post Rd., Ashland, OH 44805 419-281-5976.

WATSON, Nigel M., b. Wellington, New Zealand, September 28, 1928, s. of Ronald Sinclair and Clarice Evangeline (Hames), m. Stella (Milnes), chil: Philip Ronald; Janet Linda; Rachel Christine. Educ: U. of Otago, New Zealand, BA 1949, MA 1950; U. of Cambridge, BA 1953, BA, Theol. 1955, MA 1957; U. of Princeton, PhD 1959. Emp: New Zealand, 1959-64 Parish Min.; Ormond Coll., Melbourne, 1965-1992 Prof. of NT & Christian Origins; *Australian Bibl. Rev.*, 1973-92 Ed. Spec: New Testament. Pub: *The First Epistle to the Corinthians* (Epworth, 1992); *Striking Home: Interpreting and Proclaiming the New Testament* (Epworth, 1987); "Justified by Faith; Judged by Works—An Antinomy?" *NTS* 29

(1983); "Simplifying the Righteousness of God" *SJT* 30 (1977); "The Meaning of Righteousness in Paul" *NTS* 20 (1973-74); "Was Zacchaeus Really Reforming?" *ExpTim* 77 (1966); "Some Observations on the Use of AIKAIO in the Septuagint" *JBL* 79 (1960); and others. Awd: Trinity Coll., Cambridge, Sr. Schol. 1953; Princeton U., Charlotte Elizabeth Proctor Fellow. Mem: SNTS 1974-. Rec: Religious drama, tramping. Addr: (o) Ormond College, The Theological Hall, Parkville 3052, Australia.

WATTS, James W., b. Zurich, Switzerland, August 24, 1960, s. of John D.W. & W. Lee, m. Maurine (McTyre). Educ: Pomona Coll., BA 1982; South. Bapt. Theol. Sem., MDiv 1985, ThM 1986; Yale U., PhD 1990. Emp: Yale Div. Sch., 1987-90 Acting Instr.; Stetson U., 1990-91 Vis. Asst. Prof.; Hastings Coll., 1993- Asst. Prof. Spec: Hebrew Bible. Pub: *Psalm and Story: Inset Hymns in Hebrew Narrative*, JSOTSup 139 (JSOT, 1992); "Text and Redaction in Jeremiah's Oracles Against the Nations" *CBQ* 54 (1992); "Psalm 2 in the Context of Biblical Theology" *HBT* 12/1 (1990); "*HNT:* An Ugaritic Formula of Intercession" *UF* 21 (1989); "The Remnant Theme: A Survey of New Testament Research, 1921-1987" *PRS* 15/2 (1988). Mem: SBL 1985-; NABPR. Addr: (o) Hastings Coll. Hastings, NE 68902-0269 402-463-2402.

WATTS, John D. W., b. Laurens, SC, August 9, 1921, s. of James Washington & Mattie Leila, m. Winifred Lee (Williams), chil: Cheryl Lee (Reynolds); Reid McRae; Linda Carol (Cozzolino); James W. Educ: Miss. Coll., BA 1941; New Orleans Bapt. Theol. Sem., ThM 1944; South. Bapt. Theol. Sem., PhD 1948. Emp: Bapt. Theol. Sem., Switzerland, 1948-70 Prof., OT, 1964-70 Pres.; Serampore Dept. of Theol., India, 1972-75 Prof., OT; Fuller Theol. Sem., 1976-81 Prof., OT; South. Bapt. Theol. Sem., 1982-92 Prof., OT. Spec: Hebrew Bible. Pub: *Isaiah 1-33*, *Isaiah 34-66*, Word Bibl. Comm. 24-25 (Word, 1985, 1988); *Obadiah* (Eerdmans, 1969); *Vision and Prophecy in Amos* (Brill/Eerdmans, 1958); and others. Mem: SBL; SOTS; IBR; NABPR. Addr: (o) 2825 Lexington Rd., Louisville, KY 40280 502-897-4393; (h) 401 Godfrey Ave., Louisville, KY 40206 502-897-3191.

WEAD, David W., b. Austin, MN, October 1, 1936, s. of Fred & Alice, m. Marilyn (Osmonson), chil: Michael; Cynthia; Richard. Educ: Basel U., ThD 1968. Emp: Minn. Bible Coll., 1969-71 Prof., Relig.; Emmanuel Sch. of Relig., 1971-73 Asst. Prof., NT; Johnson Bible Coll., 1976-82 Adj. Prof.; Milligan Coll., 1983-84 Adj. Prof.; First Christian Ch., 1984- Sr. Min. Spec: New Testament. Pub: *The Literary Devices of the Gospel of John* (Reinhardt, 1970). Mem: SNTS 1971-; IBR. Rec: Golf, water-skiing. Addr: (o) 4800 Franklin Rd., Nashville, TN 37220 615-832-9259.

WEBBER, Randall C., b. Oak Ridge, TN, November 28, 1961, s. of Brooke B. & Dorothy G.. Educ: Furman U., AB, Hist. 1982; South. Bapt. Theol. Sem., MDiv 1985, PhD 1989. Emp: Salvation Army Family Shelter, 1986-89 Pastoral Counselor, 1992- Emergency Shelter Coord.; *Paradigms*, 1986-89 Manuscript Ed.; U. Microfilms, 1989-92 Asst. Ed.. Spec: New Testament. Pub: "'Why Were the Heathen so Arrogant?' The Socio-Rhetorical Strategy of Acts 3-4" *BTB* 22/1 (1992); "Women and Power in the Jerusalem Church of Acts" *Explorations* 7/3 (1989); "Group Solidarity in the Revelation of John" *SBL Seminar Papers* 27 (1988); and others. Mem: AAR 1988-; SBL 1988-. Rec: Baroque keyboard music, foot races, photography. Addr: (o) 831 S Brook St., Louisville, KY 40203 502-625-1170; (h) 2134 Vernon Ct., Louisville, KY 40206 502-895-3868.

WEBER, Beat, b. Uster, ZH, March 8, 1955, m. Sonya M. (Lehnherr), chil: Rahel S.; Nathanael B.; Noemi R. Educ: Freien Evang.-Theol. Akademie, Riehen-Basel, Lic. Theol. 1981; Kirche Basel-Stadt, Vikariat und Ord. 1991. Emp: Wissenschaftlicher Forschungsassistent SNF, Psalmenprojekt, 1991-. Spec: Hebrew Bible, New Testament. Pub: Schulden erstatten-Schulden erlassen: Zum matthäischen Gebrauch einiger juristischer und monetärer Begriffe" *ZNW* 83 (1992); "...jede Tochter aber sollt ihr am Leben lassen!—Beobachtungen zu Ex 1,15-2,10 und seinem Kontext aus literaturwissenschaftlicher Perspecktive" *BN* 55 (1990); and others. Mem: SBL 1991-. Addr: (o) U. Basel, Theologische Fakultät, Nadelberg 10, CH-4051 Basel, Switzerland 061-267-6900; (h) Ensisheimerstr. 7, CH-4055 Basel, Switzerland 061-321-1938.

WEDDERBURN, Alexander J. M., b. Edinburgh, Scotland, April 30, 1942, s. of Thomas & Margaret, m. Brigitte (Felber), chil: Fiona; Martin. Educ: St. John's Coll., Oxford, BA 1964, MA 1967; New Coll., Edinburgh, BD 1967; King's Coll., Cambridge, PhD 1971. Emp: St. Mary's Coll., 1972-89 Lect.; *SJT*, 1974-85 Dir.; *St. Mary's Coll. Bull.*, 1979-81 Ed.; U. of Durham, 1990- Sr. Lect.; *NTS*, 1991- Ed. Spec: New Testament. Pub: *Paul and Jesus* (1989); *The Reasons for Romans* (1988); *Baptism and Resurrection* (1987); "Paul and Jesus: The Problem of Continuity" *SJT* (1985); "Hellenistic Christian Traditions in Romans 6?" *NTS* (1983); *The New Testament and Gnosis: Essays in Honour of Robert McLachlan Wilson*, ed. (T & T Clark, 1983); "Paul and the Hellenistic Mystery-Cults: On Posing the Right Questions" in *La soteriologia dei culti orientali nell' Impero Romano* (EPRO, 1982); and others. Mem: SNTS 1973-; SBL 1983. Rec: Walking, ornithology, music. Addr: (o) Dept. of Theology, Abbey House, Palace Green, Durham DH1 3RS, England 091-374-2058; (h) 30 Baliol Square, Merryoaks, Durham DH1 3QH, England 091-384-2588.

WEDER, Hans, b. Diepoldsau, Switzerland, December 27, 1946, s. of Johann & Katharina, m.

Veronika (Altherr), chil: Christine; Katharine. Educ: U. Zurich, BD 1971, PhD 1977, Habil. 1979; U. St. Andrews, BPh 1974. Emp: U. Zurich, 1980- Prof., NT; Hermeneutisches Inst., 1990- Dir.; *Zurcher Bibelkommentare*, Ed.; *NT Deutsch*, Ed. Spec: New Testament. Pub: *Einblicke ins Evangelium* (1992); "But I say to you..." in *Text and Logos* (1990); *Die Gleichnisse Jesu als Metaphern*, FRLANT 120 (1978, 1990); *Neutestamentliche Hermeneutik* (1986, 1989); "Exegese und Dogmatik" *ZTK* 84 (1987); "Gesetz und Sünde" *NTS* 31 (1985); "Die Menschwerdung Gottes" *ZTK* 82 (1985); *Das Kreuz Jesu bei Paulus*, FRLANT 125 (1981); "Zum Problem einer 'Christlichen Exegese'" *NTS* 27 (1980); and others. Mem: SNTS; Theol. Kammer der EKD 1989-. Rec: Electronics, computer programming. Addr: (o) Institut fur Hermeneutik, Kirchgasse 9, CH-8001 Zurich, Switzerland 01-257-67-26; (h) Zürichbergstrasse 102, CH-8044 Zurich, Switzerland 01-252-50-78.

WEIGANDT, Peter A. M., b. Dresden, Germany, September 22, 1935, s. of Hanskurt & Alice, m. Ursula, chil: Jochen; Udo; Almut; Gudrun. Educ: U. of Heidelberg, ThD 1962. Emp: U. of Muenster, Inst. of Neutestamentliche Textforschung, 1962-68, 1971-80 Asst. Prof.; Evang. Kirche von Kurhessen-Waldeck, 1972-; Clergyman; U. of Kassel, 1978 Vis. Lect., NT. Spec: New Testament, Apocrypha and Post-biblical Studies. Pub: "Oikos" in *Exegetisches Worterbuch zum Neuen Testament* (1981); "Zur Geschichte der koptischen Bibelubersetzung" *Biblica* 50 (1969); "Zwei griechisch-sahidische Acta-Handschriften" in *Materialien zur neutes-tamentlichen Handschriftenkunde* (1969); "Zur sogenannten Oikos-Formel" *NT* 6 (1963); and others. Mem: SNTS 1966-. Rec: European orchids, ornithology. Addr: (h) Am Hilgenberg 4, D-3500 Kassel, Germany 0561-69592.

WEIMA, Jeffrey A. D., b. Brockville, ON, Canada, July 16, 1960, s. of David & Hinke, m. Bernice, chil: Rebekah Joanne; David Jeffrey (dec.); Allison Carol; Naomi Joy; Samuel David. Educ: Brock U., Canada, BA 1983; Calvin Theol. Sem., MDiv 1986, ThM 1988; U. of Toronto, St. Michael's Coll., PhD 1992. Emp: Redeemer Coll., Canada, 1988-92 Instr., Rel. and Theol.; Calvin Theol. Sem., 1992- Asst. Prof., NT. Spec: New Testament. Pub: "Gal 6:11-18: A Hermeneutical Key to the Galatian Letter" *Calvin Theol. Jour.* 28 (1993); "The Function of the Law in Relation to Sin: An Evaluation of the View of H. Räisänen" *NT* 32 (1990); "The Second Tense in the Gospel of Thomas: The 'Sleeping Beauty' of the Coptic Verbal System" *Orientalia* 59 (1990). Mem: CSBR 1989-92; SBL 1989-; ETS 1989-; IBR 1989-; CSBS 1989-. Addr: (o) Calvin Theological Seminary, 3233 Burton St., SE, Grand Rapids, MI 49546 616-957-6019.

WEINFELD, Moshe, b. Poland, August 27, 1925, s. of Mordechai & Malka, m. Rose, chil: Milka; Adi; Malachi. Educ: Hebrew U., Israel, BA 1955, MA 1959, PhD 1965. Emp: Hebrew U., 1961-69 Lect., 1969-73 Sr. Lect., 1973- Prof.; Brandeis U., 1967- Vis. Prof.; U. Calif., 1981- Vis. Prof.; Ann. for Bibl. & Anc. Near East. Stud., 1976- Ed.; *VT*, 1980- Ed. Bd. Spec: Hebrew Bible. Pub: *From Joshua to Josiah* (Magness, 1992); *Deuteronomy 1-11*, AB (1991); *The Qumran Sect: Its Organization in the Light of Hellenistic Guilds and Associations* (NT/Orbis Antiquus, 1986); *Justice and Righteousness in Israel and the Nations* (Magness, 1985); and others. Mem: SBL. Addr: (o) Hebrew U., Jerusalem 91905, Israel 02-883-512; (h) Aharoni 8, Jerusalem 92549, Israel 02-631-384.

WEIS, Earl A., b. Toldeo, OH, May 5, 1923, s. of Sylvester I. & Louise M. Educ: Loyola U., Chicago, AB 1946, AM 1948; W. Baden Coll., PhL 1948; Weston Coll., STL 1955; Pont. Gregorian U., Rome, STD 1958. Emp: W Baden Coll., 1958-63; U. of Detroit, 1970-71; Loyola U., 1971- Prof. of Theol., 1971-80 Chmn. of Dept.; *New Catholic Ency.*, 1963-66 Staff Ed., Dogmatic Theol.; *Corpus Instrumentorum*, 1966-70 Staff Ed.; *Encyclopedic Dict. of Religion*, 1966-70 Contb. Ed. Spec: Hebrew Bible, New Testament. Mem: CBA; SBL; CTSA; Coll. Theol. Soc.; Fellow. of Cath. Schol. 1976-, V.P. 1983-84, Pres. 1984-85. Addr: (o) Loyola U., Dept. of Theology, 6525 N Sheridan Rd., Chicago, IL 60626 312-508-2347; (h) Loyola U., Jesuit Faculty Residence, 6525 N Sheridan Rd., Chicago, IL 60626 312-508-8800.

WEISER, Alfons, b. Woelfesgrund, Schlesien, February 18, 1934, s. of Franz & Gertrud. Educ: U. of Wurzburg, ThD. Emp: Theol. Coll. Vallendar, Germany, 1970- Prof., NT Exegesis. Spec: New Testament. Pub: *Studien zu Christsein und Kirche* (1990); "Evangelisierung im 'Haus'" *BZ* 34 (1990); *Die Apostelgeschichte*, 2 vol., OTK (1981, 1985); "Die Rolle der Frau in der Urchristlichen Mission" *Die Frau im Urchristentum: Qaestiones Disputatae* 95 (1983); "Neutestamentliche Grundlagen einer kooperativen Pastoral" *Trierer Theol. Zeitschrift* 89 (1980); *Die Knechtsgleichnisse der synoptischen Evangelien* (1971); *Was die Bibel Wunder nennt* (1985); and others. Mem: SNTS 1982-. Rec: Organ playing. Addr: (o) Theologische Hochschule, Pallottistr.3, D-56179 Vallendar, BRD, Germany.

WEISS, Herold D., b. Montevideo, Uruguay, September 5, 1934, s. of Daniel & Maria, m. Aida (Acosta), chil: Herold E.; Carlos. Educ: Andrews U., MA 1957, BD 1960; Duke U., PhD 1964. Emp: Andrews U., 1961-69 Asst. Prof.; St. Mary's Coll., 1969- Prof.; Northern Bapt. Theol. Sem., 1982- Affil. Prof. Excv: Capernaum, 1980, 1982 Asst. Dir. of Vol. Prog. Spec: New Testament. Pub: "The Sabbath in the Fourth Gospel" *JBL* (1991); "Philo on the Sabbath" *Studia Philonica Ann.* (1991); *Paul of Tarsus: His Gospel and Life* (Andrews U.P., 1986, 1989); "Gold Hoard Found at Capernaum" *BAR*

(1983); "The Law in the Epistle to the Colossians" *CBQ* (1972); "The Pagani Among the Contemporaries of the First Christians" *JBL* (1967). Mem: SBL; Philo Inst. Addr: (o) St. Mary's Coll., Madeleva Hall, PO Box 78, Notre Dame, IN 46556 219-284-4505; (h) 9198 Garr Rd., Berrien Springs, MI 49103 616-471-7888.

WEISS, Wolfgang R., b. Berlin-Tempelhof, January 3, 1955, s. of Theodor G.W. & Jutta Irene A. (Szumann), m. Suse A. (Pyroth). Educ: U. Mainz, DTh 1986, Habil. 1991. Emp: Theresianum, Mainz, 1976-84 Tchr., Relig.; U. Mainz, 1979-88 Res. Asst., 1988-92 Lect., 1992- Prof. Spec: New Testament. Pub: *Zeichen und Wunder*, WMANT (1993); "Glaube, Leibe, Hoffnung: Zu der Trias bei Paulus" *ZNW* 84 (1993); "Kenyon, Frederic George" *BBKL* 3 (1992); "Eine neue Lehre in Vollmacht" in *Die Streit- und Schulgespraeche des Markus-Evangeliums*, BZNW 52 (1989); "Friedrich Lang, Die Briefe an die Korinther" *EvErz* 40 (1988); and others. Mem: SBL 1990-. Rec: Reading, enjoying the countryside, dogs, gardening. Addr: (o) Carl v. Ossietzky-U., Inst. Evangelische Theologie, Amerlaender Heerstrasse 114-118, D-26111 Oldenburg, Germany 0441-798-2920; (h) Max Planck-Str. 62, Gonsenheim, D-55124 Mainz 1, Germany 06131-471954.

WELCH, John W., b. Boston, MA, October 15, 1946, s. of John & Unita (Woodland), m. Norma Jean (Sutton), chil: John; Christina; Allison; Gregory. Educ: Brigham Young U., BA 1970, MA 1970; Duke U., JD 1975. Emp: Brigham Young U., Prof. of Law; *Brigham Young U. Stud.*, Ed. Spec: Hebrew Bible, Mesopotamian Studies, New Testament, Apocrypha and Post-biblical Studies. Pub: "Chiasmus in Biblical Law" in *Jewish Law Assn Stud.* (1990); *Religion and Law*, ed. (Eisenbrauns, 1990); *The Sermon on the Mount and the Sermon at the Temple* (Deseret, 1990); *Biblical Law Bibliography* (Mellen, 1990); *Chiasmus in Antiquity*, co-auth. (Gerstenberg, 1981); "Theft and Robbery in Ancient Near Eastern Law and in the Book of Mormon" *FARMS* (1984); "Chiasmus in Ruth," co-auth., *Beth Mikra* (1978); and others. Rec: Skiing, mountains, golf. Addr: (o) Brigham Young U., 522 JRCB, Provo, UT 84602 801-378-3168.

WENHAM, David, b. Oxford, England, December 19, 1945, s. of John & Grace, m. Clare, chil: Alan; Simon. Educ: U. of Cambridge, MA, Theol. 1970; U. of Manchester, PhD 1970. Emp: Union Bibl. Sem., India, 1974-79 Prof.; Tyndale House Gospels Res. Project, 1979-86 Dir.; *Gospel Perspectives* vol. 1-6, 1980-86 Co-ed.; Wycliffe Hall, 1983- Tutor; *Themelios*, 1979-89 Ed. Spec: New Testament. Pub: *The Parables of Jesus* (IVP, 1989); *The Rediscovery of Jesus' Eschatological Discourse*

(JSOT, 1984); "Paul's Use of the Jesus Tradition: Three Samples" in *Gospel Perspectives* (JSOT, 1984); "The Interpretation of the Parable of the Sower" *NTS* 20 (1974); and others. Mem: SNTS 1985-; Tyndale Fellow. Addr: (o) Wycliffe Hall, Banbury Rd., Oxford 0X2 6PW, England 0865-274208; (h) 55 Bainton Rd., Oxford 0X2 7AG, England 0865-58820.

WENHAM, Gordon J., b. Cambridge, UK, May 21, 1943, s. of John & Grace, m. Lynne, chil: John; Mary; Elizabeth; Christopher. Educ: Cambridge U., UK, MA 1969; U. of London, King's Coll., PhD 1970. Emp: Queen's U. of Belfast, 1970-81 Lect. in Semitic Stud.; *Themelios*, 1979-85 OT Ed.; Cheltenham & Gloucester Coll. of Higher Educ., England 1981- Sr. Lect., Relig. Stud.; *Churchman*, 1984- Asst. Ed. Spec: Hebrew Bible. Pub: *The Book of Leviticus*, New Intl. Comm. on OT (Eerdmans, 1979); *Numbers: An Introduction and Commentary*, Tyndale OT Comm. (IVP, 1981); *Jesus and Divorce* (Thomas Nelson, 1985); *Genesis 1-15*, Word Bibl. Comm. (Word, 1987); and others. Mem: Tyndale Fellow. 1968-; SOTS 1973-. Rec: Gardening, walking. Addr: (o) Cheltenham & Gloucester College PO Box 220, The Park, Cheltenham GL50 2QF, England (0242) 532742; (h) 4 Church Walk, Charlton Kings, Cheltenham GL53 8BJ, England (0242) 523961.

WENHAM, John W., b. Surrey, England, December 9, 1913, s. of William Knight & Florence Evelyn, m. Grace, chil: Gordon; David; Peter; Michael. Educ: Cambridge, BA 1935, MA 1939; U. of London, BD 1943. Emp: London Coll. of Div., 1938-41 Tutor; Royal Air Force, 1943-47 Chaplain; St. Nicholas, 1948-53 Vicar; Tyndale Hall, 1953-67 Vice Prin. Spec: New Testament. Pub: *Redating Matthew, Mark and Luke: A Fresh Assault on the Synoptic Problem* (Hodder & Stoughton, 1991; IVP, 1992); "Why Do You Ask Me About the Good? A Study of the Relation Between Text and Source Criticism" *NTS* (1982); "Synoptic Independence and the Origin of Luke's Travel Narrative" *NTS* (1981); *Elements of New Testament Greek* (Cambridge U.P., 1965); and others. Mem: SNTS 1954-. Addr: (h) 55 Bainton Rd., Oxford, OX2 7AG, England 0865-58820.

WENTZ, Herbert S., b. Salisbury, NC, October 22, 1934, s. of Charles & Carolyn May, m. Sofia (Liljencrants). Educ: U. of N.C., AB 1956; Gen. Theol. Sem., STB 1960; U. of Oxford, MA 1963; U. of Exeter, England, PhD 1971. Emp: U. of the South, Dept. of Relig., 1965-. Spec: Hebrew Bible. Mem: AAR 1964-84; SOTS 1971-; SBL 1984-86. Addr: (o) University of the South, Dept. of Religion, Sewanee, TN 37375 615-598-1232.

WESTBROOK, Raymond, b. England, October 1, 1946, s. of Michael & Esther, m. Henie Klara (Leinwand), chil: Baruch; Hasdai. Educ: Magdalen Coll., Oxford, BA 1968; Hebrew U., Jerusalem, LM 1970; Yale U., PhD

1982. Emp: Hebrew U., 1983-86 Lect.; Johns Hopkins U., Dept. of Near East. Stud., 1987-89 Vis. Prof., 1989- Assoc. Prof. Spec: Hebrew Bible, Mesopotamian Studies. Pub: *Property and the Family in Biblical Law* (Sheffield, 1991); "Adultery in Ancient Near Eastern Law" *RB* 97 (1990); "I Samuel 1:8" *JBL* 109 (1990); "Cuneiform Law Codes and the Origins of Legislation" *ZA* 79 (1990); *Old Babylonian Marriage Law*, AFO Beiheft 23 (Berger, 1988); *Studies in Biblical and Cuneiform Law*, Cahiers de la *RB* 26 (Gabalda, 1988); "The Prohibition on Restoration of Marriage in DT 24:1-4" *Scripta Hierosolymitana* 31 (1986); "Lex Talionis and Exodus 21,22-25" *RB* 93 (1986); and others. Mem: SBL; AOS. Addr: (o) Johns Hopkins U., Dept. of Near Eastern Studies, Baltimore, MD 21218 410-516-5220; (h) 19 Belsize Park Gardens, London NW3 4JG, England 44-71-722-3633.

WESTENHOLZ, Joan M. Goodnick, b. Philadelphia, PA, July 1, 1943, d. of Benjamin & Regina (Pollack), chil: Aliza; Dina. Educ: U. of Pa., BA 1964; U. of Chicago, PhD 1971. Emp: U. of Copenhagen, 1980-82 Lect.; U. of Chicago, 1982-84 Assoc.; Hebrew U., 1984-86 Vis. Lect.; Harvard U., 1987-88 Res. Assoc.; Bible Lands Mus. Jerusalem, 1988- Chief Cur. Spec: Mesopotamian Studies. Pub: "The Clergy of Nippur: The Priestesses of Enlil" in *Nippur at the Centennial*, CRRAI 35 (1992); "Oral Traditions and Written Texts in the Cycle of Akkade" in *Mesopotamian Epic Literature: Oral or Aural?* (1992); "Metaphorical Language in the Poetry of Love in the Ancient Near East" in *La circulation des biens, des personnes et des idées dans la Proche-Orient ancien*, CRRAI 38 (1991); "LKA 63: A Heroic Poem in Celebration of Tiglath-Pileser I's Musru-Qumanu Campaign," co-auth., *JCS* 42 (1990); "Towards a New Conceptualization of the Female Role in Mesopotamian Society" *JAOS* 110 (1990); and others. Mem: AOS. Addr: (o) Bible Lands Museum Jerusalem, PO Box 4670, Jerusalem 91046, Israel 972-2-611066; (h) Arlosoroff 16, Jerusalem 92181, Israel 972-2-634684.

WESTERMANN, Claus, b. Berlin, Germany, October 7, 1909, s. of Diedrich & Katharina, m. Anna (Kellner). Emp: Kirchliche Hoch-Schule, Berlin, Prof.; U. of Heidelberg, 1958-76 Prof. Spec: Hebrew Bible. Pub: *Forschung am Alten Testament*, Gesamelte Stud. 1-3 (1964-1984); *Theologie des Alten Testaments in Grundzugen* (1978); *Genesis 1-4* (1974-1986); *Der Segen in der Bibel und im Handeln der Kirche* (1968); *Der Aufbau des Buches Hiob* (1956); and others. Awd: U. of Goettingen, PhD. Mem: SNTS; SBL. Addr: (h) Augustinum, 6900 Heidelberg 1, Jasperstrasse 2, Germany 62-21-388758.

WHEELER, John H., b. Toledo, OH, s. of Floyd James & Mary Madeline. Educ: Ambassador Coll., BA, Theol. 1981. Emp: King David's Harp, Inc., 1988- Dir. Spec: Hebrew Bible. Pub: "Who

Wrote Psalm 23: David or a Canaanite?" *Arch. & Bibl. Res.* 5 (1992); *The Music of the Bible Revealed*, ed. (King David's Harp, 1991); "The Origin of the Music of the Temple," "Music of the Temple" *Arch. & Bibl. Res.* 2 (1989). Mem: SBL 1989-; AOS 1991. Rec: Songwriting, creative writing, hiking, piano, Celtic harp. Addr: (o) King David's Harp, Inc., 750 La Playa, Box 542, San Francisco, CA 94121-3200 415-334-5755.

WHITE, J. Benton, b. Birmingham, AL, September 3, 1931, s. of Job & Edith (Benton), m. Mary Lou (Bloomberg), chil: Thomas; Matthew. Educ: U. of Ala., BS 1953; Candler Sch. of Theol., BD 1956; Pacific Lutheran Theol. Sem., MTh 1969. Emp: 1959-69 Campus Min.; San Jose State U., 1969- Coord., Relig. Stud. Prog. Spec: Hebrew Bible, New Testament, Apocrypha and Post-biblical Studies. Pub: *From Adam to Armageddon: A Survey of the Bible* (Wadsworth, 1986); and others. Mem: AAR 1970-, Pres., West. Reg. 1979-80. Rec: Travel, golf. Addr: (o) San Jose State U., Religious Studies Dept., San Jose, CA 95192 408-924-1367; (h) 2503 Briarwood Dr., San Jose, CA 95125.

WHITE, John Bradley, b. Pulaski, VA, June 25, 1947, s. of Emily & James, m. Dianne (Hardin), chil: Andrew; Sarah. Educ: Emory & Henry Coll., BA 1969; Duke U., MDiv 1972, PhD 1975. Emp: DePauw U., 1977- Prof., Dean of Acad. Affairs. Spec: Hebrew Bible, New Testament, Apocrypha and Post-biblical Studies. Pub: "The Sages' Strategy to Preserve Shalom" in *The Listening Heart: Essays in Wisdom and Biblical Theology*, JSOTSup 58 (1987); *Scripture in Context* vol. 1, co-auth. (Pickwick, 1980); *The Language of Love in the Song of Songs and Ancient Egyptian Poetry* (Scholars, 1978); "Conversing with the Text" *Duke Div. Sch. Rev.* (1974). Awd: Woodrow Wilson Fellow. 1969; Dempster Fellow 1974. Mem: CBA; SBL. Rec: Running, gardening, class. music. Addr: (o) DePauw U., Academic Affairs Office, 500 E Seminary St., Greencastle, IN 46135 317-658-4359; (h) 604 Anderson St., Greencastle, IN 46135 317-653-8960.

WHITE, John L., b. Owensville, MO, May 31, 1940, s. of Frank & Clarice (Mistler), m. Myrna (Wacker), chil: John; Karis; Kristen. Educ: Vanderbilt U., MA 1968, PhD 1970. Emp: Mo. Sch. of Relig., 1969-75 Asst. Prof., 1976-81 Assoc. Prof.; Westminster Coll., 1975-76 Vis. Lect.; U. of Mo.-Columbia, 1970, 1977, 1979 Asst. Prof., Class.; Loyola U. of Chicago, 1981-86 Assoc. Prof. Spec: New Testament, Egyptology. Pub: *Light From Ancient Letters* (Fortress, 1986); "St. Paul and the Apostolic Letter Tradition" *CBQ* 45 (1983); *Form and Structure of the Official Petition*, SBL Diss. Ser. 5 (1972); and others. Mem: Amer. Soc. of Papyrology; Assn. Intl. de Papyrologues; CBA; CSBR; SBL. Rec: Watercolors, acrylics. Addr: (o) Loyola U. of Chicago, Dept. of Theology, 6525 N Sheridan Rd., Chicago, IL 60626 312-508-2342; (h) 6650 N Glenwood, Chicago, IL 60626 312-465-4679.

WHITE, Leland J., b. Charleston, SC, July 25, 1940, s. of Leland S. & Winifred (Budds). Educ: St. Mary's Sem. & U., BA 1962; Pont. Gregorian U., STB 1964, STL 1966; U. of Michigan, MA 1972; Duke U., PhD 1974; Seton Hall U. Law School, J.D. 1992. Emp: Nazareth Coll., 1974-76 Asst. Prof.; Siena Coll., 1976-82 Asst. Prof.; St. John's U., New York, 1982-89 Assoc. Prof., 1989- Prof.; *BTB*, 1984- Ed. Spec: Hebrew Bible, New Testament. Pub: "Grid and Group in Matthew's Community: The Righteousness/Honor Code in the Sermon on the Mount" *Semeia* (1986); *Christ and the Christian Movement: Jesus in the New Testament, the Creeds and Modern Theology* (Alba, 1985); and others. Mem: AAR; SBL; CTSA. Addr: (o) St. John's U., Dept. of Theology & Religious Studies, Grand Central & Utopia, Jamaica, NY 11439 718-990-6161; (h) 149 Walker Rd., West Orange, NJ 07052-3812.

WHITE, Marsha C., b. Boston, MA, April 2, 1950, d. of John Fraser & Grace (Hepler). Educ: Carleton Coll., BA 1973; Andover Newton Theol. Sch., MDiv 1980; Harvard Div Sch., ThM 1983. Emp: Phillips Exeter Acad., 1984-1985 Tchr.; Harvard U., 1986-1991 Teaching Fellow, 1991 Instr.; Coll. of the Holy Cross, 1993-94 Lect. Spec: Hebrew Bible. Pub: "Jonah" in *The Women's Bible Comm.* (Westminster/John Knox, 1992); "The Elohistic Depiction of Aaron: A Study in the Levite-Zadokite Controversy" in *Studies in the Pentateuch,* VTSup 41 (Brill, 1990). Mem: SBL. Rec: Skiing, hiking, bicycling, sea-kayaking. Addr: (o) 6 Divinity Ave., Cambridge, MA 02138; (h) 39 Morrison Ave., Somerville, MA 02144 617-623-3715.

WHITE, Sidnie A., b. Greenwich, CT, January 8, 1960, d. of Earle W. & M. Ottilie. Educ: Trinity Coll., BA 1981; Harvard Div. Sch., MTS 1984; Harvard U., PhD 1988. Emp: Harvard Div. Sch., 1987-88 Instr.; St. Olaf Coll., 1988-89 Asst. Prof.; Albright Coll., 1989- Asst. Prof., Relig.; St. George's Coll., Jerusalem, 1989 Vis. Lect. Pub: "In the Steps of Jael and Deborah: Judith as Heroine" in *No One Spoke Ill of Her: Essays on Judith* (Scholars, 1992); "Important Features of Four Deuteronomy Manuscripts from Cave IV, Qumran" *RQ* (1991); "4QDtn: Biblical Manuscript or Excerpted Text?" in *Of Scribes and Scrolls* (Cath. Theol. Soc. of Amer., 1990); "The All Souls Deuteronomy and the Decalogue" *JBL* 109 (1990); "Esther: A Feminine Model for Jewish Diaspora" in *Gender and Difference in Ancient Israel* (Fortress, 1989); and others. Awd: NEH/ASOR Postdoc. Fellow. 1989-90; W.F. Albright Inst. for Arch. Res., Dorot Fellow 1990; Annenberg Inst. for Near East. Stud., Fellow 1992-93. Mem: AAR; ASOR; SBL; Intl. Org. for the Study of Qumran. Addr: (o) Albright College, Dept. of Religion, Box 15234, Reading, PA 19612 215-921-2381.

WHITEHEAD, Brady B., b. Memphis, TN, February 5, 1930, s. of Brady & Gertrude, m. Emmy Lou (Sessions), chil: Kathy; Diana. Educ:

Rhodes Coll., BS 1952; Emory U., MDiv 1955, MA 1957; Boston U., ThD 1972. Emp: U. of Tenn. at Martin, 1957-62 Dir., Wesley Found.; Lambuth U., 1967- Prof. of Relig. Spec: Hebrew Bible, New Testament. Pub: *Ezra, Nehemiah, and Esther* (Graded); *The Letters of Paul* (Graded); and others. Mem: SBL. Rec: Reading, music, sports. Addr: (o) Lambuth U., Jackson, TN 38301 901-425-3253; (h) 4600 Bells Highway, Jackson, TN 38305 901-668-6552.

WHITELY, Ronald E., Jr., b. Loring A.F.B., Maine, August 5, 1954, s. of Ronald and Yvonne, m. Sally, chil: Ronald E., III; Jonathan E.; Chad E.. Educ: Abilene Christian U., BA, Bibl. Greek 1981. Emp: Port Neches Ch. of Christ, 1983-88 Minister; South Twin Cities Ch. of Christ, 1988- Minister; *Foundations & Facets,* 1992- Asst., Ed. Forum. Spec: New Testament. Pub: "Immersings in the Holy Spirit" *Preceptor* 40,11 (1991); "Lessons from Early Church History" *Christian Bible Teacher* 33 (1989); and others. Mem: SBL 1989-; APA 1989-. Rec: Computers, softball, volleyball, football. Addr: (o) South Twin Cities Church of Christ, 16120 Cedar Ave., South Rosemount, MN 55068-1022 (612) 431-7004; (h) 15343 Dunbar Ave., South Apple Valley, MN 55124-6838 (612) 423-6753.

WHITT, William D., b. Bryn Mawr, PA, December 6, 1963, s. of David & Charlotte, m. Kelli (Kobor). Educ: Duke U., BA 1985; Harvard U., MTS 1987. Emp: N.C. State U., 1991-93 Vis. Lect. Spec: Hebrew Bible. Pub: "The Divorce of Yahweh and Asherah in Hos. 2,4-7.12ff" *SJT* 6 (1992); "The Jacob Traditions in Hosea and their Relation to Genesis" *ZAW* 103 (1991). Mem: AOS 1988-; ASOR 1990-; SBL 1990-; BSA, Jerusalem 1991-. Rec: Bicycling, coffee, *The Economist.* Addr: (o) North Carolina State U., Dept. of Philosophy & Religion, PO Box 8103, Raleigh, NC 27695; (h) 902 Dacian Ave., Durham, NC 27701 919-687-0297.

WHYBRAY, R. Norman, b. Surrey, England, July 26, 1923, s. of Walter & Carrie, m. Mary Elizabeth. Educ: Oxford U., BA 1944, MA 1968, DPhil 1962, DD 1981. Emp: Gen. Theol. Sem., 1948-50 Fellow, Tutor; Central Theol. Coll., Japan, 1952-65 Prof.; U. of Hull, England, 1965-82 Prof., 1982- Prof. Emeritus; Book List, SOTS, 1974-80 Ed.; OT Guides, JSOT Press, 1983- Ed. Spec: Hebrew Bible. Pub: *Wealth and Poverty in the Book of Proverbs* (1991); *Ecclesiastes,* New Century Bible (1989); *Ecclesiastes,* OT Guides (JSOT, 1989); *The Making of the Pentateuch* (1987); "Yahweh-Sayings and their Contexts in Proverbs, 10:1-22, 16" in *La Sagesse de l'Ancien Testament* (1979); "The Joseph Story and Pentateuchal Criticism" *VT* (1968); and others. Awd: Oxford U., Kennicott Hebrew Fellow. 1960-62. Mem: SBL 1949-; SOTS, Pres. 1982. Rec: Music, travel. Addr: (h) 45 Hills Ln. Ely, Cambridgeshire, England 0353-663897.

WIDBIN, R. Bryan, b. St. Louis, MO, September 8, 1948, s. of Robert & Lois, m. Karen (Hanson), chil: Lydia; Zachary. Educ: Trinity Evang. Div. Sch., MDiv 1976, ThM 1977; Brandeis U., MA 1981, PhD 1985. Emp: Brandeis U., 1979-85 Instr.; Alliance Theol. Sem., 1985- Prof. Spec: Archaeology, Hebrew Bible, Semitic Languages, Texts and Epigraphy. Pub: "Salvation for People Outside Israel's Covenant?" in *Through No Fault of Their Own* (Baker, 1991); and others. Mem: SBL 1984-. Rec: Softball, football, running. Addr: (o) Alliance Theological Seminary, Nyack, NY 10960 914-358-1710.

WIDENGREN, Geo, b. Stockholm, Sweden, April 24, 1907, s. of Anna Widengren & Hugo Jakobsson, m. Aina (Bjorkman), chil: Hans. Educ: U. of Stockholm, BA 1930, Lic. Letters 1933; U. of Uppsala, BD 1932, Lic. Theol. 1934, ThD 1936. Emp: U. of Uppsala, 1936 Asst. Prof., 1937-40 Deputy Prof., 1940-73 Prof., 1944-45, 1950-51, 1964-71 Dean, Faculty of Theol. Spec: Hebrew Bible, Mesopotamian Studies, Semitic Languages, Texts and Epigraphy, Apocrypha and Post-biblical Studies. Pub: "Yahweh's Gathering of the Dispersed" in *In the Shelter of Elyon: Essays on Ancient Palestinian Life and Literature* (Sheffield, 1984); "What Do We Know About Moses?" in *Proclamation and Presence* (1970); "Israelite-Jewish Religion: Trends in its History Down to the Maccabean Revolt" in *Historia Religionum* vol. 1 (1969); "Early Hebrew Myths and Their Interpretation" in *Myth, Ritual and Kingship* (1958); "King and Covenant" *JSS* 2; *Sakrales Konigtum im A.T. und im Judentum* (Franz Delitsch Vorlesungen, 1952); "The King and the Tree of Life" in *Ancient Near Eastern Religion*, King & Saviour IV (1951); *Literary and Psychological Aspects of the Hebrew Prophets* (1948); *The Accadian and Hebrew Psalms of Lamentation as Religious Documents: A Comparative Study* (1937); and others. Awd: Amsterdam, DD 1962; Strasbourg, Dr. 1962; Cardiff, DD 1965; Rostock, DD 1969; Uppsala, PhD 1973. Mem: Intl. Assn. for the Hist. of Relig., V.P. 1950-60, Pres. 1960-70; SBL 1972-; Soc. of Exegesis 1974-; Acad. des Inscriptions et Belles Lettres 1976-; WUJS 1983-. Rec: Horsemanship, skiing, swimming. Addr: (h) Karlavagen 95, 115 22 Stockholm, Sweden.

WIEAND, David J., b. Chicago, IL, September 4, 1914, s. of Albert & Katherine (Broadwater), m. Mary Elizabeth (Wertz), chil: Mary; Martha; Jonathan. Educ: Juniata Coll., BA 1936; N.Y.U., MA 1938; Bethany Theol. Sem., BD 1940; U. of Chicago, PhD 1946. Emp: Bethany Theol. Sem., 1939- Prof. Spec: Archaeology, New Testament, Semitic Languages, Texts and Epigraphy. Pub: *Visions of Glory—Studies in Revelation* (Brethren, 1979); and others. Mem: SBL; SNTS; Soc. for the Advancement & Continuing Educ. of Min. Rec: Photography, bridge, reading. Addr: (h) 18 West 711 13th St., Lombard, IL 60148 708-627-3939.

WIFALL, Walter R., Jr., b. St. Paul, MN, September 18, 1935, s. of Elva (Strunk) & Walter, m. Arleen (Mohr), chil: Rachel; Joshua. Educ: Concordia Sem., MDiv 1960, MST 1961; Johns Hopkins U., PhD 1965. Emp: Concordia Coll., 1965-70 Asst. Prof.; St. John's U., 1970- Prof. Spec: Hebrew Bible, Semitic Languages, Texts and Epigraphy. Pub: "The Tribes of Yahweh—A Synchronic Study with a Diachrohnic Title" *ZAW* (1983); "God's Accession Year According to P" *Biblica* (1981); *The Formation of the Old Testament: The Court History of Israel* (Clayton, 1975); and others. Mem: Amer. Assn. of U. Prof. 1965-; SBL 1968-, Pres., Hudson-Delaware Reg. 1978; CBA 1970-. Rec: Tennis, swimming. Addr: (o) St. John's U., Dept. of Theology, New York, NY 11739 718-990-6161; (h) One Claralon Court, Greenlawn, NY 11740 516-757-0862.

WIGTIL, David N., b. Thief River Falls, MN, October 10, 1951, s. of Norval & Marilyn (Fishel), chil: Jessica; Clifton. Educ: U. of Minn., MA 1975, PhD 1980. Emp: Concordia Coll., 1977-81 Instr.; Okla. State U., 1981-84 Asst. Prof.; George Washington U., 1984-86 Vis. Prof. Spec: New Testament, Apocrypha and Post-biblical Studies. Pub: "Incorrect Apocalyptic: The Hermetic 'Asclepius' as an Improvement on the Greek Original" *ANRW* (1984); "The Sequence of the Translations of Apocryphal Psalm 151" *RQ* (1983); "The Ideology of the Greek *Res Gestae*" *ANRW* (1982); "The Translator of the Greek *Res Gestae* of Augustus" *Amer. Jour. of Philol.* (1982); and others. Mem: SBL; APA. Rec: Aviation, computer science. Addr: (h) 11479 Applegrath Way, Germantown, MD 20876 301-540-1121.

WILD, Robert A., b. Chicago, IL, March 30, 1940, s. of John & Mary (Colnon). Educ: Loyola U., BA 1962, MA 1967; Jesuit Sch. of Theol. in Chicago, STL 1970; Harvard U., PhD 1977. Emp: Loyola U., 1968-70, 1984-92 Assoc. Prof.; Marquette U., 1974-84 Assoc. Prof.; Pont. Bibl. Inst., Rome, 1983-84 Vis. Prof.; SJ, Chicago Province, 1985-91 Pres.; Weston Sch. of Theol., 1992- Pres. Pub: *The Sentences of Sextus*, co-auth. (Scholars, 1981); *Water in the Cultic Worship of Isis and Serapis* (Brill, 1981); "The Warrior and the Prisoner: Some Reflections on Ephesians 6:10-20" *CBQ* (1984); "The Pastoral Letters" in *New Jerome Biblical Comm.* (Prentice-Hall, 1990); and others. Mem: SBL 1971-; CBA 1971-. Rec: Swimming, bird watching, hiking. Addr: (o) Weston School of Theology, 3 Phillips Place, Cambridge, MA 02138 617-492-1960.

WILDAVSKY, Aaron, b. Brooklyn, NY, May 31, 1930, s. of Sender & Eva, m. Mary, chil: Adam; Sara; Ben; Dan. Educ: Yale U., MA 1957, PhD 1959. Emp: U. of Calif.-Berkeley, 1963- Prof.; Hebrew U., Jerusalem, 1967 Vis. Prof.; CUNY, 1977 Vis. Prof.; Yale U., 1978 Adj. Prof.; Russell Sage Found., 1977-78 Pres. Spec: Hebrew Bible. Pub: *Assimilation Versus Separation:*

Joseph the Administrator and the Politics of Religion in Biblical Israel (Transaction, 1993); *The Nursing Father: Moses as a Political Leader* (U. of Ala., 1985); and others. Awd: Fulbright 1954-55; Guggenheim 1971; Brooklyn Coll., LLD 1977. Rec: Gardening, hiking. Addr: (o) U. of California, Survey Research Center, 2538 Channing Way, Berkeley, CA 94720 510-642-9974; (h) 4400 Sequoyah Rd., Oakland, CA 94605 510-562-7752.

WILES, John Keating, b. Louisville, KY, September 1, 1950, s. of John C. & Ruth K., m. Carolyn Joy, chil: Sarah Winsett; John Carl. Educ: Okla. Bapt. U., BM 1972; MidW Bapt. Theol. Sem., MDiv 1977; South. Bapt. Theol. Sem., PhD 1982. Emp: South. Bapt. Sch. of Theol., Manila, 1983 Guest Prof.; Sem. Theol. Bapt., Indonesia, 1983-86 Dosen; South. Bapt. Theol. Sem., Louisville, 1987 Vis. Prof.; SE Bapt. Theol. Sem., Wake Forest, 1987-1991 Assoc. Prof.; Shaw Div. Sch., 1991-92 Adj. Prof. Spec: Hebrew Bible. Pub: Articles in *Mercer Dict. of the Bible* (1990); "The Prophetic Critique of the Social and Economic Order" *Faith & Mission* 6/2 (1989); "Wisdom and Kingship in Israel" *Asia Jour. of Theol.* 1 (1987); *Keluarga: Pada Mulanya Hingga Dalam Tuhan* (Sem. Theologia Baptis Indonesia, 1986); and others. Mem: Amer. Assn. of U. Prof.; AAR; NABPR; SBL. Rec: Reading, music, choral singing, needlework. Addr: (o) Shaw Divinity School, PO Box 2090, Raleigh, NC 27602 919-832-1701; (h) 130 N Wingate, Wake Forest, NC 27587 919-556-0582.

WILKEN, Robert L., b. New Orleans, LA, October 20, 1936, m. Carol Faith (Weinhold), chil: Gregory; Jonathan. Educ: Concordia Sem., BA 1957, BD 1960; Washington U., MA, Phil. 1961; U. of Chicago, PhD, Hist. of Christianity 1963. Emp: Luth. Theol. Sem., 1964-67 Asst. Prof.; Fordham U., Dept. of Theol., 1967-71 Asst. Prof.; U. of Notre Dame, Dept. of Theol., 1972-79 Assoc. Prof., 1979-85 Prof., Hist. of Christianity; Hebrew U. of Jerusalem, 1982 Lady Davis Vis. Prof.; U. of Va., 1985- William R. Kenan, Jr., Prof. of Hist. of Christianity, 1985-87 Mem., Ctr. for Advanced Stud.; *RSRev*, Assoc. Ed. Spec: New Testament. Pub: *The Land Called Holy: Palestine in Christian History and Thought* (Yale U.P., 1993); "The Holy Land in Christian Imagination" *BR* 9/2 (1993); *The Christians as the Romans Saw Them* (Yale U.P., 1984); *The Myth of Christian Beginnings* (Doubleday, 1971; U. of Notre Dame, 1980); *Jews and Christians in Antioch,* co-auth. (Scholars, 1978); and others. Awd: U. of Chicago, Fellow. 1960-62; Rockefeller Doc. Fellow 1963; Deutscher Akademische Austauschdienst, Post-doc. Res. Grant 1963-64; Assn. of Theol. Sch., Res. Grant 1975-76; NEH, Fellow. 1981-82. Mem: AAR; NAPS; Amer. Hist. Assn.; Amer. Soc. of Ch. Hist. Addr: (o) U. of Virginia, Dept. of Religious Studies, Cocke Hall, Charlottesville, VA 22903 804-924-3741; (h) 1630 Brandywine Dr., Charlottesville, VA 22901 804-293-8774.

WILKENS, Wilhelm H. F., b. Bethel/Bielefeld, December 1, 1927, s. of Johannes & Hildegard (Stormer), m. Gisela (Lewerenz), chil: Matthias; Johannes; Katharina; Monika; Andreas. Educ: U. of Basel, ThD 1957. Emp: Lienen, Westfalia, 1959-83 Reverend; Kirchenkreis Tecklenburg, 1983-91 Superintendent. Spec: New Testament. Pub: *Die Entstehungsgeschichte des Vierten Evangeliums* (Zollikon, 1958); *Zeichen und Werke. Ein Beitrag zur Theologie des Vierten Evangeliums in Erzahlungs-und Redestoff* (Zwingli, 1969); "Die Komposition des Matthaus-Evangeliums" *NTS* 31 (1985); and others. Mem: SNTS 1980-. Rec: History of the Kirchenkampf 1933-45 in the Kirchenkreis Tecklenburg. Addr: (h) Starenweg 7, D-4543 Lienen 1, Germany 05483-1017.

WILKINS, Michael J., b. Glendale, CA, August 7, 1949, m. Lynne, chil: Michelle; Wendy. Educ: Talbot Theol. Sem., MDiv 1977; Fuller Theol. Sem., PhD 1986. Emp: Evang. Free Ch. of Amer., 1977-83 Pastor; Biola U., Talbot Sch. of Theol., 1983- Prof. & Chair, Dept. of NT Lang. & Lit. Spec: New Testament, Apocrypha and Post-biblical Studies. Pub: *Worship, Theology and Ministry in the Early Church: Essays in Honor of Ralph P. Martin,* JSNTSup 87 (JSOT, 1992); *Following the Master: A Biblical Theology of Discipleship* (Zondervan, 1992); "Disciples," Discipleship," "Sinners" in *Dict. of Jesus and the Gospels* (InterVarsity, 1992); "Named and Unnamed Disciples in Matthew: A Literary/Theological Study" in *SBL Seminar Papers* 30 (Scholars, 1991); "The Concept of Disciple in Matthew's Gospel" in NTSup 59 (Brill, 1988); "The Terminology and Concept of Disciple' in the Post-Biblical Jewish Literature" *JETS* (1986); and others. Mem: SBL 1984-; AAR 1984-; CBA 1984-. Rec: Surfing, snow skiing, family. Addr: (o) Biola U., Talbot School of Theology, 13800 Biola Ave., La Mirada, CA 90639 213-944-0351; (h) 2619 Via Cascadita, San Clemente, CA 92672 714-492-4734.

WILKINSON, John, Pub: *Egeria's Travels to the Holy Land,* ed. (Ariel, 1981); *Jerusalem Pilgrims Before the Crusades* (1978); and others. Addr: (h) 7 Tenniel Close, Queensboro Terrace, London W2 3LE, England 44-71-229-9205.

WILLETT, Michael E., b. Liberty, MO, October 12, 1955, s. of Edward & Eleanor. Educ: South. Bapt. Theol. Sem., MDiv 1981, PhD 1985. Emp: William Jewell Coll., 1985-87 Adj. Instr.; St. Paul Sch. of Theol., 1989-90 Asst. Vis. Prof.; Cen. Bapt. Theol. Sem., 1990-91 Adj. Prof.; Nazarene Theol. Sem., 1990-91 Adj. Prof.; Howard U. Sch. of Div., 1991- Asst. Prof. Pub: "Jung and John" *Explorations* 7/1 (1988); and others. Mem: SBL 1984-; AAR 1985-. Rec: Swimming, walking, reading. Addr: (o) Howard U. School of Divinity, 1400 Shepherd St., NE Washington, DC 20017 202-806-0608; (h) 3220 12th St. NE, #17, Washington, DC 20017 202-529-3983.

WILLIAMS, David Salter, b. Marietta, GA, April 18, 1957, s. of Claude & Jean, m. Jennifer. Educ: U. of Georgia, BA 1979, MA 1982; Hebrew Union Coll., MPhil 1985, PhD 1988. Emp: U. of Georgia, 1981-82 Instr., Relig., 1989- Asst. Prof., Judaica; Chatfield Coll., 1985 Instr., Judaism; Wilmington Coll., Lebanon Correctional Facility, 1986-87 Instr., Phil. & Relig.; Denison U., 1988-89 Instr., Judaism. Spec: New Testament, Apocrypha and Post-biblical Studies. Pub: *Stylometric Authorship Studies in Flavius Josephus and Related Literature* (Mellen, 1992); "On Tertullian's Text of Luke" *SC* 8 (1991); "Reconsidering Marcion's Gospel" *JBL* 108 (1989); and others. Mem: AAR; AJS; MidW Jewish Stud. Assn.; NAPH; SBL. Rec: Reading, listening to music, gardening. Addr: (o) U. of Georgia, Dept. of Religion, Peabody Hall, Athens, GA 30602 706-542-5356; (h) 105 Edgewood Dr., Athens, GA 30606 706-543-0617.

WILLIAMS, Jay G., b. Rome, NY, December 18, 1932, s. of Jay & Mary (Craig), m. Hermine (Weigel), chil: Jay, III; Lynn; Daryl; Ruth. Educ: Union Theol. Sem., MDiv 1957; Columbia U., PhD 1964. Emp: Natl. Coun. of Ch., 1958-60; Hamilton Coll., 1960- Walcott Bartlett Prof. of Relig. Excv: Arad, Israel, Asst. Field Supr.; Dan, Israel, Asst. Field. Supr. Spec: Archaeology, Hebrew Bible. Pub: "The Structure of Judges 2:6-16:31" *JSOT* (1991); "Symphony #1: The Genesis" *Jour. of Relig. Stud.* (1982); "Yahweh, Women and the Doctrine of the Trinity" *Theol. Today* (1975); "Exegesis, Eisegesis: Is There a Difference?" *Theol. Today* (1973); *Understanding the Old Testament* (Barrons, 1972); and others. Mem: AAR; IBSA; ASOR. Rec: Weightlifting, jogging. Addr: (o) Hamilton College, Dept. of Religion, Clinton, NY 13323 315-859-4208; (h) 300 College Hill Rd., Clinton, NY 13323 315-853-8796.

WILLIAMS, Michael A., b. Paducah, KY, August 30, 1946, s. of G. Leon & Mary Sue, m. Mary (Rodriguez), chil: Melissa; Mary Elizabeth. Educ: Abilene Christian Coll., BA 1968; Miami U., MA 1970; Harvard U., PhD 1977. Emp: U. of Wash., 1976- Assoc. Prof., 1985-91 Chair, Comparative Relig. Prog.; *JBL*, 1990- Ed. Bd. Spec: New Testament, Apocrypha and Post-biblical Studies. Pub: *Innovation in Religious Traditions*, co-ed. (de Gruyter, 1992); "Variety in Gnostic Perspectives on Gender" in *Images of the Feminine in Gnosticism* (Fortess, 1988); *The Immovable Race A Gnostic Designation and the Theme of Stability in Late Antiquity* (Brill, 1985); "The Life of Antony and the Domestication of Charismatic Wisdom" in *Charisma and Sacred Biography* (Scholars, 1982); "Stability as a Soteriological Theme in Gnosticism" in *The Rediscovery of Gnosticism* (Brill, 1981); others. Mem: SBL 1972-; IACS 1978-; AAR 1981-. Addr: (o) U. of Washington, Thompson Hall, DR-05, Seattle, WA 98195 206-543-4835; (h) 1504 NE 166th, Seattle, WA 98155.

WILLIAMS, William C., b. Wilkes-Barre, PA, July 12, 1937, s. of Edward & Elizabeth (Schooley), m. Alma Mary (Simmenroth), chil: Linda. Educ: Cen. Bible Coll., BA 1963, MA 1964; NYU, MA 1966, PhD 1975. Emp: New International Version, 1975-76 Trans. Cons.; New Century Version & International Children's Version, 1983- Trans. Cons. & Trans. Ed. of OT; New American Standard Bible, 1969- Trans. Cons.; South. Calif. Coll., 1969- Prof. of OT; Lib. of Congress, Hebraic Sect., 1967-69 Ref. Lbrn. Spec: Hebrew Bible. Pub: *The Complete Biblical Library, New Testament Greek-English Dictionary*, contb. (1990); "Jonah," and "Jonah, Book of" in *ISBE* (Eerdmans, 1982); *Hebrew I and II: A Study Guide*, 2 vol. (Intl. Correspondence Inst., 1980); "How It Looks from Here..." *Agora* 2 (1978); "Writing the Vision: Some Personal Reflections on a Philosophy of Translations for Isaiah 1-14" *Hebrew Stud.* XVII (1976); and others. Awd: Cornell U., NEH Summer Seminar for Coll. Tchr, 1992. Mem: AAR; SBL; ETS; IBR; NAPH. Rec: Photography, hiking, computers. Addr: (o) Southern California College, 55 Fair Dr., Costa Mesa, CA 92626 714-556-3610; (h) 1817 Peninsula Place, Costa Mesa, CA 92627 714-650-8005.

WILLIAMSON, Ronald, December 16, 1927. Educ: U. of Hull, BA, Phil. & Theol. 1949; U. of Cambridge, BA, Theol. Tripos, MA 1952; Leeds U., PhD 1970. Emp: Wesley Coll., 1952-54 Asst. Tutor; Immanuel Coll., Nigeria, 1957-62 NT Lect., Vice Prin.; U. of Leeds., 1970-92 Sr. Lect., NT Stud., Dept. of Theol. & Relig. Stud. Spec: New Testament. Pub: *Philo* (Cambridge U.P., 1989); "The Incarnation of the Logos in Hebrews" *ExpTim* 95/1 (1983); "Philo and New Testament Christology" *ExpTim* 90/12 (1979); *Philo and the Epistle to the Hebrews* (Brill, 1980); *The Epistle to the Hebrews* (Epworth, 1964); and others. Mem: SNTS. Rec: Medieval popular relig. & art. Addr: (h) 38 Gledholt Rd., Huddersfield W Yorkshire HD1 4HR, England.

WILLOUGHBY, Bruce E., b. Newark, OH, November 8, 1948, s. of Harry & Sue Marie, m. Tracy (Blotner), chil: David Bruce; Jamin Andrew. Educ: David Lipscomb Coll., BA 1970; Abilene Christian U., MA 1977. Emp: Abilene Christian U., 1975-77 Lect.; ASOR, 1978-82 Production Manager & Assoc. Ed., *BA, BASOR, ASOR Newsletter*; U. of Michigan, ASOR Books, 1982- Managing Ed. Spec: Hebrew Bible, Semitic Languages, Texts and Epigraphy. Pub: "Amos, Book of" in *ABD*; "I and II Chronicles, Ezra, Nehemiah" in *The Books of the Bible* (Scribners, 1989); "Na'ap," "Mal'ak," "canan," "cammud," "cibri," "Nasa" in *Theologisches Worterbuch zum Alten Testament* (Kohlhammer, 1985); and others. Mem: ASOR 1977-82; AOS 1979-84; SBL 1982-. Addr: (o) U. of Michigan, 108 Lane Hall, Ann Arbor, MI 48109 313-998-7265; (h) 11 N Wallace, Ypsilanti, MI 48197 313-482-2533.

WILSON, J. Christian, b. Winston-Salem, NC, January 17, 1945, s. of T. Woodrow & Kitty L., m. Marianne H., chil: John C.; April W. Educ: Duke U., AB 1967, MDiv (summa cum laude) 1970, ThM (summa cum laude) 1972, PhD 1977. Emp: Tennessee Wesleyan Coll., 1979-83 Asst. Prof.; Greensboro Coll., 1983-86 Asst. Prof.; Elon Coll., 1986- Assoc. Prof. Spec: New Testament, Apocrypha and Post-biblical Studies. Pub: "Tithe," "Polycarp of Smyrna" in *ABD* (1992); "The Dead Sea Scrolls" *The Fourth R.* Jan. (1991); *The Righteousness of God: A Study of Paul's Letter to the Romans* (Graded, 1987); "The Language of the New Testament" in *Profiles: Men and Women of the Bible* (Graded, 1986); "The Promise and Problem of Biblical Commentaries" *Circuit Rider* (1983); and others. Awd: Cokesbury Grad. Awd. in Coll. Teaching 1971-72; Dempster Grad. Fellow. 1973-74. Mem: SBL 1967-; N.C. Relig. Stud. Assn. 1983-; CBA 1992-. Rec: Class. music, travel, gourmet cooking. Addr: (o) Elon College, Box 2209, Elon College, NC 27244 919-584-2242; (h) 5007e Lawndale Dr., Greensboro, NC 27405 919-282-3516.

WILSON, John F., b. Springfield, MO, November 4, 1937, s. of Fred & Jesse, m. L. Claudette (Faulk), chil: Laura; Amy; Emily. Educ: Harding Grad. Sch. of Relig., MA 1961; U.of Iowa, PhD 1967. Emp: SW Mo. State U., 1961-82 Prof.; Pepperdine U., Seaver Coll., 1983- Dean, Prof. of Relig.; Campus Journal, 1964-74 Ed. Excv: Greek Orthodox site, Capernaum, 1982-86 Educ. Dir., Coord.; Banias, 1987- Consortium Dir. Spec: Archaeology, New Testament. Pub: "The Gold Hoard of Capernaum" in *Excavations at Capernaum: Volume I 1978-1982* (Eisenbrauns, 1989); *Religion: A Preface* (Prentice-Hall, 1982, 1988); *Discovering the Bible: Archaeologists Look at Scripture* (Marshall, Morgan & Scott, 1986); "The Contributions of Archaeology to New Testament Interpretation" in *Biblical Interpretation Principles and Practices* (Baker, 1986); and others. Mem: SBL 1968-; AAR 1972-; ASOR 1979-, V.P., Cen. Reg. 1983-84. Addr: (o) Pepperdine University, Seaver Dean's Office, Malibu, CA 90265 213-456-4281; (h) 24410 Tiner Court, Malibu, CA 90265 310-456-4975.

WILSON, John W., b. Manly, NSW, July 12, 1937, s. of Walter & Norma, m. Jill, chil: Susan Jane; Jenny Anne. Educ: Bathurst Tchr. Coll., Tchr. Cert. 1959; Ridley Coll., ThL 1964; U. of London, BD 1966; Yale U., STM 1969; Duke U., PhD 1976. Emp: Ridley Coll., 1973-85 Sr. Lect., OT; Anglican Diocese of Melbourne, 1985- Bishop of the South. Reg.; *Christian Book Newsletter*, 1983-1989 Ed. Spec: Hebrew Bible, New Testament, Apocrypha and Post-biblical Studies. Pub: *Ezekiel: God's Communicator* (Acorn, 1990); and others. Mem: SBL; Fellow. for Bibl. Stud., Melbourne; CBA. Rec: Reading, music, cinema. Addr: (o) St. Paul's Cathedral Buildings, 209 Flinders Ln., Melbourne 3000, Australia 03-653-4220.

WILSON, Marvin R., b. Stoneham, MA, July 17, 1935, s. of Malcom C. & Marion K., m.

Pauline B., chil: Tassa Rose. Educ: Wheaton Coll., BA 1957; Gordon Div. Sch., MDiv 1960; Brandeis U., MA 1961, PhD 1963. Emp: Barrington Coll., 1963-71 Prof., Bibl. Stud., Dept. Chair; Gordon Coll., 1971- Harold J. Ockenga Prof. of Bibl. Stud. Spec: Hebrew Bible. Pub: *Our Father Abraham* (Eerdmans, 1989); "Shema" in *ISBE* (1988); "Passover" in *ISBE* (1986); "Zionism as Theology" *JETS* (1979); "The Jewish Concept of Learning" *CSR* (1976); *Coptic Future Tenses* (Mouton, 1970); and others. Mem: SBL; ETS; IBR. Rec: Travel, reading, sports. Addr: (o) Gordon College, Wenham, MA 01984 508-927-2300; (h) 16 Martel Rd., S Hamilton, MA 01982 508-468-3884.

WILSON, Robert McL., b. Gourock, Scotland, February 13, 1916, s. of Hugh & Janet (Struthers), m. Enid (Bomford), chil: Andrew; Peter. Educ: U. of Edinburgh, MA 1939, BD 1942; U. of Cambridge, PhD 1945. Emp: U. of St. Andrews, St. Mary's Coll., 1954-83 Prof., 1954-64 Lect., 1964-69 Sr. Lect., 1969-83 Prof.; *NTS*, 1967-77 Assoc. Ed. 1977-83 Ed. Spec: New Testament, Apocrypha and Post-biblical Studies. Pub: *Commentary on Hebrews* (Eerdmans, 1987); *Gnosis and the New Testament* (Blackwell, 1968); *The Gospel of Philip* (Mowbray, 1962); *Studies in the Gospel of Thomas* (Mowbray, 1960); and others. Awd: FBA 1977; Aberdeen U., Scotland, DD 1982. Mem: SNTS; SBL. Rec: Golf. Addr: (h) 10 Murrayfield Rd., St. Andrews, Fife KY16 9NB, Scotland 0334-74331.

WILSON, Robert R., b. March 29, 1942. Educ: Transylvania U., AB 1964; Yale Div. Sch., BD 1967; Yale U., MA 1969, PhD 1972. Emp: Yale U., 1970-71 Lect., 1972- Prof., OT; Union Theol. Sem., New York, 1971-72 Instr., OT; Columbia U., Sem. for the Study of the Hebrew Bible, 1978-81 Chair; SBL Diss. Ser., 1978-83 OT Ed. Spec: Hebrew Bible. Pub: *Sociological Approaches to the Old Testament* (Fortress, 1984); "Enforcing the Covenant: The Mechanisms of Judicial Authority in Early Israel" in *The Quest for the Kingdom of God: Essays in Honor of George E. Mendenhall* (Eisenbrauns, 1983); "Israel's Judicial System in the Preexilic Period" *JQR* 74 (1983); "From Prophecy to Apocalyptic: Reflections on the Shape of Israelite Religion," "The Problems of Describing and Defining Apocalyptic Discourse" *Semeia* 21 (1981); *Prophecy and Society in Ancient Israel* (Fortress, 1980); "Between 'Azel' and 'Azel': Interpreting the Biblical Genealogies" *BA* 43 (1979); "Prophecy and Ecstasy: A Reexamination" *JBL* 98 (1979); *Genealogy and History in the Biblical World* (Yale U.P., 1977); and others. Awd: Amer. Coun. of Learned Soc., Post-doc. Fellow. 1975; Yale U., Morse Fellow. 1975; Conn. Acad. of Arts & Sci., Fellow 1978; NEH Summer Seminar for Coll. Tchr., Dir. 1981. Addr: (o) Yale U., Dept. of Religious Studies, PO Box 2160, Yale Station, New Haven, CT 06520 203-432-0828.

WIMBUSH, Vincent L., b. Atlanta, GA, October 26, 1954, s. of Robert & Willie Mae (Rowland), m. Linda (Perkins), chil: Lauren Elizabeth. Educ: Morehouse Coll., BA 1975; Yale Div. Sch., MDiv 1978; Harvard U., AM 1981, PhD 1983. Emp: Sch. of Theol., Claremont, 1983-91 Asst. Prof.; Claremont Grad. Sch., 1983-91 Asst. Prof.; U. of Puget Sound, 1985 Everett W. Palmer Lect.; Union Theol. Sem., 1991-; Princeton Theol. Sem., 1992 Alexander Thompson Lect. Spec: New Testament. Pub: *Asatic Behaviour in Greco-Roman Antiquity: A Sourcebook*, ed. (Fortress, 1990); *Paul the Worldly Ascetic* (Mercer U.P., 1987); and others. Mem: AAR; SBL. Rec: Music, gardening. Addr: (o) Union Theological Seminary, 3041 Broadway, New York, NY 10027 212-280-1390. Addr: (o) Yale U., Dept. of Religious Studies, PO Box 2160, Yale Station, New Haven, CT 06520 203-432-0828.

WIMMER, Donald H., b. WI, September 27, 1932, chil: Richard; Stephanie; Paul. Educ: Marquette U., MA 1966; Notre Dame U., PhD 1973. Emp: Marymount Coll., 1964-65 Asst. Prof.; Seton Hall U., 1965- Prof.; Natl. Coun. on Relig. & Public Educ. Bull., 1974-80 Ed. Excv: Tel Heshbon, 1973 Square/Area Supr., 1976 Area/Field Supr.; Khirbet Iskander, 1981 Area/Field Supr.; Tel Safut, 1982-83, 1985, 1987, 1989, 1992 Dir. Spec: Archaeology, Hebrew Bible, New Testament. Pub: "1984 City of Baal" *Endeavors* 2/2 (1986); and others. Mem: AAR 1966-; SBL 1969-; ASOR 1973-. Rec: Swimming, tennis, camping. Addr: (o) Seton Hall U., Dept. of Religious Studies, Biblical Archaeology, S Orange, NJ 07079 201-761-9608; (h) 101 Ward Place, S Orange, NJ 07079 201-762-3054.

WINBERY, Carlton L., b. Urania, LA, February 15, 1937, s. of Tillman & Elma (Foshee), m. Sarah Ann (Hatten), chil: Stephen; Jerry; Cuong Diet; Shannon. Educ: New Orleans Bapt. Theol. Sem., ThM 1968, ThD 1973. Emp: New Orleans Bapt. Theol. Sem., 1969-73, Instr., NT, 1976-89 Assoc. Prof./Prof.; Baptist Coll. at Charleston, 1973-76 Assoc. Prof.; Bapt. Coll. at Charleston, 1977 Staley Christian Schol. Lecture.; La. Coll., 1989- Chmn., Fogleman Prof. of Relig. Spec: New Testament. Pub: "Introduction to I Peter" *SW Jour. of Theol.* (1981); *Syntax of New Testament Greek*, co-auth. (U. Press of Amer., 1978); and others. Mem: SBL. Rec: Jogging, tennis, golf. Addr: (h) 114 Beall St., Pineville, LA 71360 318-448-6103.

WINDHAM, R. Neal, b. Galveston County, TX, August 10, 1955, s. of John & Iris, m. Miriam (Beaver), chil: Lukas Neal; Melissa Charis. Educ: Lincoln Christian Coll., BA 1978; Lincoln Christian Sem., MA 1980. Emp: Roanoke Bible Coll., 1980-86 Assoc. Prof., NT; Lincoln Christian Coll., 1986- Assoc. Prof., NT. Spec: New Testament. Pub: *New Testament Greek for Preachers and Teachers: Five Areas of Application* (U. Press of Amer., 1991); and others. Mem: SBL 1986-; ETS 1992-. Rec: Running. Addr: (o) Lincoln Christian College, 100 Campus View, Lincoln, IL 62656 217-732-3168; (h) 205 McDivitt, Lincoln, IL 62656 217-732-3140.

WINELAND, John D., b. Hebron, IN, November 9, 1958, s. of Gerald & Marjorie. Educ: Valparaiso U., BS, Biology 1980; Cincinnati Christian Sem., MA, Near East. Antiq. 1987, MDiv, Theol. 1988; Miami U., MA, Anc. Hist. 1988, ABD 1991. Emp: Miami U., 1990- Adj. Instr.; *NEAS Bull.*, 1991- Book Rev. Ed. Excv: Abila of the Decapolis, North. Jordan, 1984 Asst. to Staff Geologist & Field Arch., 1986 Asst. Area Supr., 1988, 1990 Area Supr., Sr. Staff. Spec: Archaeology, New Testament. Pub: "Preliminary Report, Area A, Tell Abil: The 1992 Excavation Season" *NEAS Bull.* (1993); "Archaeological and Numismatic Evidence of Greco-Roman Religions of the Decapolis with Particular Emphasis on Gerasa and Abila" *ARAM* 4 (1993); articles in *ABD* (Doubleday, 1992); "The 1990 Excavation Season, Area A, Tell Abil: Preliminary Report" *NEAS Bull.* 35-36 (1990); "Area A, Tell Abil: Preliminary Report of the 1988 Excavation Season" *NEAS Bull.* 32-33 (1989). Awd: Endowment for Bibl. Res., Travel Grant 1988, 1990. Mem: ASOR; AIA; IBR; SBL; NEAS. Rec: Music, computers, photography. Addr: (o) Miami U., Dept. of History, 281 Upham Hall, Oxford, OH 45056 513-529-5121; (h) PO Box 544, College Corner, OH 45003.

WINK, Walter P., b. Dallas, TX, May 21, 1935, (Gidinghagen), m. June (Keener), chil: Stephen P.; Christopher W.; Rebecca M. Educ: South. Meth. U., BA 1956; Union Theol. Sem., MDiv 1959, PhD 1963. Emp: Meth. Ch., 1962-67 Pastor; Union Theol. Sem., 1967-71 Asst. Prof., 1971-76 Assoc. Prof.; Auburn Theol. Sem., 1976- Prof., Bibl. Interpretation. Spec: New Testament. Pub: *Transforming Bible Study*, 2 vol. (Abingdon, 1990); *Engaging the Powers* (Fortress, 1992); *John the Baptist in the Gospel Tradition* (Cambridge U.P., 1968); and others. Awd: U.S. Inst. of Peace, Peace Fellow 1989-90. Mem: SBL; AAR; SNTS. Rec: Gardening. Addr: (o) Auburn Theological Seminary, 3041 Broadway, New York, NY 10027 212-662-4315; (h) 161 Sandisfield Rd., Sandisfield, MA 02155 413-258-3352.

WINSTON, David S., b. New York, NY, September 3, 1927, s. of Abraham & Sophie, m. Irene, chil: Dani. Educ: Yeshiva U., AB 1948; Columbia U., AM 1949, PhD 1956; Jewish Theol. Sem., Rabbinical Ord., MHL 1955. Emp: U. of Judaism, 1960-66 Assoc. Prof., Rabbinic & Hellenistic Stud.; Grad. Theol. Union, 1966- Prof., Hellenistic & Judaic Stud.; Pacific Sch. of Relig., 1979- Adj. Prof., Hellenistic & Judaic Stud.; Hebrew Union Coll., 1984 Vis. Prof.; Efroymson Lect.; Jewish Theol. Sem., 1984 Henry Rapaport Lect. Spec: Apocrypha and Post-biblical Studies. Pub: *Logos and Mystical*

Theology in Philo of Alexandria (Hebrew Union Coll., 1985); *Two Treatises of Philo of Alexandria*, co-auth. (Scholars, 1983); "Freedom and Determinism in Greek Philosophy and Jewish Hellenistic Wisdom" *Studia Philonica* 2 (1974); "The Book of Wisdom's Theory of Cosmogony" *History of Religions* 11/2 (1971); *The Wisdom of Solomon*, AB (Doubleday, 1971); and others. Awd: Hebrew Union Coll. Bibl. & Arch. Sch., Jerusalem, Fellow; NEH, Sr. Fellow 1978, 1986-87. Mem: SBL, Pres., Pacific Coast reg. 1980-81; AJS; AAJR. Addr: (o) Graduate Theological Union, 2400 Ridge Rd., Berkeley, CA 94709 415-841-9811; (h) 1220 Grizzly, Berkeley, CA 94708 415-548-6734.

WINTER, Willard W., b. Detroit, IL, February 14, 1922, s. of H.L. & Alice Marie (Wilkins), m. Mardell (Reynolds), chil: Willard; Cheryl Ann. Educ: Cincinnati Bible Sem., MA 1946, BD 1948; Xavier U., BS 1956; U. of Cincinnati, MA 1959; HUC-Jewish Inst. of Relig., PhD 1980. Emp: Cincinnati Bible Coll., 1946-71 Prof.; Cincinnati Bible Sem., 1972- Prof.; *Sem. Rev.*, 1975-80 Ed. Excv: Ai, 1968-69; Abila, 1980, 1982, 1984 Registrar & Field Arch. Spec: Archaeology, Hebrew Bible. Pub: "Biblical and Archaeological Data on Ai Reappraised" *Sem. Rev.* (1970); *Studies in Joshua, Judges and Ruth* (College, 1969); *Studies in Samuel* (College, 1968); and others. Mem: NEAS 1969-; SBL 1971-; ASOR 1971-. Rec: Golf, baseball, photography. Addr: (o) 2700 Glenway Ave., Cincinnati, OH 45204 513-244-8198; (h) 8842 Fontainebleau Terr., Cincinnati, OH 45231 513-521-2288.

WISEMAN, Donald J., b. Emsworth, United Kingdom, October 25, 1918, s. of Percy & May (Savage), m. Mary (Ruoff), chil: Gillian; Mary; Catherine. Educ: Wadham Coll., Oxford, MA 1949; Sch. of Oriental & African Stud., D.Lit 1962. Emp: The Brit. Mus., 1948-61 Asst. Keeper; *Iraq*, 1953-78 Ed.; *Reallexikon der Assyriologie*, 1958-78 Joint. Ed.; U. of London, 1961-82 Prof. of Assyriology, 1982- Emeritus Prof.; Brit. Sch. of Arch. in Iraq, 1962- Bonham-Carter Lect. Excv: Nimrud, Iraq, 1949-63 Epigrapher; Tel Rimah, Iraq, 1966 Epigrapher. Spec: Archaeology, Hebrew Bible, Mesopotamian Studies. Pub: *Nebuchadnezzar and Babylon* (Brit. Acad., 1985); *Cylinder Seals from Western Asia* (Batchworth, 1959); *The Babylonian Chronicles* (Brit. Museum, 1956); and others. Mem: SOTS 1956-, Pres. 1981; BSA, Iraq; BIA, Ankara, Amman, Jerusalem. Rec: Gardening, philately. Addr: (h) Low Barn, 26 Downs Way, Tadworth Surrey, KT20 5DZ, England 073-781-3536.

WITHERINGTON, Ben, III, b. High Point, NC, December 30, 1951, s. of Ben & Joyce, m. Ann (Sears), chil: Christy; David. Educ: U. of N.C., BA 1974; Gordon-Conwell Theol. Sem., MDiv 1977; U. of Durham, PhD 1981. Emp: United Meth. Ch., 1980-84 Pastor; Ashland Theol. Sem. 1984- Prof. Spec: New Testament. Pub: *Jesus, Paul, and the End of the World* (InterVarsity,

1992); *Christology of Jesus* (Fortress, 1990); *Women and the Genesis of Christianity* (Cambridge U.P., 1990); *Women in the Earliest Churches* (Cambridge U.P., 1988); "Anti-Feminist Tendencies in the Western Text of Acts" *JBL* (1984); "Galatians 3:28: Rite and Rights for Women" *NTS* (1981); "On the Road with Mary Magdalene, Joanna, Susanna, and Other Disciples: Luke 8:1-3" *ZNW* (1979); and others. Awd: John Wesley Fellow for Life 1977. Mem: SBL; SNTS; IBR. Rec: Jogging, creative writing, music. Addr: (o) Ashland Theolgical Seminary, Center St., Ashland, OH 44805 419-289-5172; (h) 510 Broad St., Ashland, OH 44805 419-289-6686.

WOLFE, Charles E., b. Elk River, MN, November 7, 1931, s. of Raymond & Blanche (Strawser), m. Helen (Bickel), chil: Christian; Hawley; Lewis; David. Educ: North. Iowa U., BA 1952; Austin Presbyn. Theol. Sem., BD 1958; Wesley Theol. Sem., DMin 1977. Emp: 1958- Pastor, Army Chaplain; West. Md. Coll., 1979- Lect.; Wesley Theol. Sem., 1979- Instr.; *Exegetical Resource*, Ed. Spec: New Testament. Pub: *History and Criticism of the Marcan Hypothesis*, contb. (Mercer U.P., 1980); "The 'Second-First Sabbath' (Luke 6:1)" *JBL* (1978); and others. Mem: SBL. Addr: (h) 549 Crossbridge Dr., Westminster, MD 21158 410-857-1011.

WOLFE, Rolland Emerson, b. Hartville, OH, February 25, 1902, s. of Edson & Elta (Henney), m. Esther (Hoff), chil: Frank; Homer. Educ: Manchester Coll., BA 1924; Oberlin Grad. Sch. of Theol., BD 1928, STM 1929; Harvard U., PhD 1933. Emp: Tufts U., 1935-46 Asst. Prof.; Case West. Reserve U., 1946-73 Harkness Prof., Bibl. Lit.; Cleveland State U., 1973-75 Adj. Prof., Bibl. Lit.; *Fifty-Year Golden Jubilee Volume and Index*, 1960 Ed. Spec: Archaeology, Hebrew Bible, New Testament, Semitic Languages, Texts and Epigraphy. Pub: *The Twelve Religions of the Bible* (Mellen, 1982); "Higher Perspectives in Religion" *The Bible & Relig.* (1948); "The Terminology of Biblical Theology" *The Bible & Relig.* (1947); *Meet Amos and Hosea* (Harper, 1945); and others. Mem: AAR 1930-83, Pres. 1947; AOS; AIA; ASOR. Rec: Ornithology, flower gardening, mountain climbing. Addr: (h) The Hermitage, 5000 Fairbanks Ave. #239, Alexandria, VA 22311-1232 703-931-8442.

WOLFE, Samuel R., b. Chicago, IL, June 1, 1950, m. Susan E. (Baskin), chil: Rachel Ann; Jonathan Daniel. Educ: U. of Wisc., Madison, BA 1972; U. of Chicago, MA 1976, PhD, Syro-Palestinian Arch. 1986. Emp: Carthage Res. Inst./ASOR, Tunisia, 1977-79 Dir.; U. of Chicago, Oriental Inst. Mus., 1980-83, 1987 Asst. to Cur.; Ashkelon Publ. Laboratory, 1988-89 Dir.; Ben Gurion U. of the Negev, 1989 Instr.; Israel Antiq. Authority, 1990- Field Arch. Excv: Tell Gezer, 1973 Asst. Area Supr.; Punic Project, Carthage, Tunisia, 1975-79 Area Supr., Pottery Specialist; Tell Ashkelon, 1985, 1987 Field Supr.; Wadi Tut,

Dir. Spec: Archaeology, Semitic Languages, Texts and Epigraphy. Pub: "Carthage and the Mediterranean: Imported Amphoras from the Punic Commercial Harbor" in *Actes du Congrès International sur Carthage, 10-13 October 1984, Trois-Rivières, Canada*, Cahiers des Etudes Anciennes 19 (1986); "Classical and Hellenistic Black Glaze Ware in the Mediterranean: A Study by Epithermal Neutron Activation Analysis," co-auth., *Jour. of Arch. Sci.* 13 (1986); "Child Sacrifice at Carthage: Religious Rite or Population Control?" co-auth., *BAR* 10/1 (1984); "Production and Commerce in Temple Courtyards: An Olive Press in the Sacred Precinct at Tel Dan," co-auth., *BASOR* 243 (1981); "Personal Names from Arad" *UF* 10 (1978); and others. Awd: Ryerson Traveling Fellow. 1977; ASOR, Carthage Fellow. 1977-78, 1978-79; Zion Res. Found., Fellow. 1980; Albright Inst. of Arch. Res., Jerusalem, NEH Fellow. 1987. Mem: ASOR; SBL. Addr: (o) Israel Antiquities Authority, PO Box 586, Jerusalem 91911, Israel 972-2-292-627.

WOLFF, Christian, b. Berlin, June 26, 1943, s. of Friedrich & Charlotte (Jauert). Educ: Ernst Moritz Arndt U. Greifswald, Promotion 1971; Martin Luther U. Halle-Wittenberg, Habil. 1983. Emp: Kirchliche Hochschule Berlin-Brandenburg, Dozent, NT 1972-91; Humboldt U. Berlin, Fac. of Theol., 1991- Prof., NT; *Theologischer Handkommentar zum Neuen Testament*, Co-ed. Spec: New Testament. Pub: "Der Zweite Brief des Paulus an die Korinther" *THK* 8 (1989); "Niedrigkeit und Verzicht in Wort und Werk Jesu und in der apostolischen Existenz des Paulus" *NTS* 34 (1988); "Der Erste Brief des Paulus an die Korinther" *THK* 7 (1982); "Die Gemeinde des Christus in der Apokalypse des Johannes" *NTS* 27 (1981); "Zur Bedeutung Johannes des Taeufers im Markusevangelium" *TLZ* 102 (1977); *Jeremia im Fruehjudentum und Urchristentum* (1976); "Christ und Welt im 1. Petrusbrief" *TLZ* 100 (1975); and others. Mem: SNTS; Gesellschaft fur Wissenschaftliche Theol. Addr: (o) Humboldt U. zu Berlin, Theologische Fakultaet, Burgstr. 25, Berlin, Germany 2468293; (h) Damerowstrasse 20, 0-1100 Berlin-Pankow, Germany 4834809.

WOLTER, Michael, b. Hannover, Germany, July 12, 1950. Emp: U. Bonn, 1988 Prof., Bibl. Theol.; *Texte und Arbeiten zum NT Zeitalter*, Ed. Spec: New Testament. Pub: *Der Brief an die Kolosser, Der Brief an Philemon*, OTK 12 (1993); "Der Apostel und seine Gemeinden als Teilhaber am Leidensgeschick Jesu Christi" *NTS* 36 (1990); "Paulus, der bekehrte Gottesfeind" *NT* 31 (1989); "Die anonymen schriften des Neuen Testaments" *ZNW* 79 (1988); *Die Pastoralbriefe als Paulustradition*, FRLANT 146 (1988); "Verborgene Weisheit und Heil fur die Heiden" *ZTK* 84 (1987); "Apollos und die ephesinischen Johannesjuenger (Act 18,24-19,7)" *ZNW* 78 (1987); *Rechtfertigung und zukuenftiges Heil: Untersuchungen zu Roem 5,1-*

11, BZNW 43 (1978); and others. Mem: SNTS 1982-. Rec: Gardening. Addr: (o) U. Bonn, Am Hof 1, 5300 Bonn, Germany 0228-737366; (h) Kronhuettenweg 64, D-8650 Kulmbach, Germany 09221-64952.

WOLTERS, Albert M., b. Enschede, The Netherlands, September 9, 1942, s. of Siert & Luchiena (Seinen), m. Alice (Van Andel), chil: Victor; Benita. Educ: Calvin Coll., BA 1964; Free U., Amsterdam, PhD 1972; McMaster U., MA 1987. Emp: Inst. for Christian Stud., Canada, 1974-84 Assoc. Prof.; Redeemer Coll., Canada, 1984- Prof. Spec: Hebrew Bible. Pub: "The Riddle of the Scales in Daniel 5" *HUCA* 62 (1991); "Untying the King's Knots" *JBL* 110 (1991); "Not Rescue but Destruction: Rereading Exod 15:8" *CBQ* 52 (1990); "Apocalyptic and the Copper Scroll" *JNES* 49 (1990); "Nature and Grace in the Interpretation of Prov. 31:10-31" *Calvin Theol. Jour.* (1984); and others. Mem: SBL 1984-; CSBS; ETS; IBR. Rec: Movies, novels. Addr: (o) Redeemer College, 777 Hwy. 53, Ancaster, ON L9G 3N6, Canada 416-648-2131; (h) 131 Britten Close, Hamilton, ON L9C 4K1, Canada 416-389-3032.

WONG, Eric K. C., b. Hong Kong, February 5, 1959, s. of Mee-Woon & Han-Yung, m. Mee-Kuen, chil: Thelo Hei-Man; Thea Hoi-Man. Educ: Chinese U. of Hong Kong, BA 1984, MDiv 1986; U. of Heidelberg, ThD 1991. Emp: Amsterdam Chinese Ch. 1991-92 Pastor; Chinese U. of Hong Kong, 1992- Lect., NT. Spec: New Testament. Pub: *Die interkulturelle Theologie des Mattaeusevangeliums und seine bikulturelle Gemeinde* (Vandenhoeck & Ruprecht, 1992); "The Matthaean Understanding of the Sabbath: A Response to G.N. Stanton" *JSNT* 44 (1991). Addr: (o) Chinese U. of Hong Kong, Chung Chi College, Theology Division, Shatin, N.T., Hong Kong 852-609-6705.

WOOD, Bryant G., b. Endicott, NY, October 7, 1936, s. of Harry John Stanley & Nina May (Sheldon), m. Faith Anne (Moore), chil: Dianna May (Haskell); James Bradley; Daniel Gene; Stephen Edward. Educ: Syracuse U., BS 1958; Rensselaer Polytechnic Inst., MS 1964; U. of Mich., MA, Near East. Stud. 1974; U. of Toronto, PhD, Near East. Stud. 1985. Emp: Toronto Bapt. Sem. & Bible Coll., 1977-82, 1989-90 Adj. Prof.; Faith Theol. Sem., 1990-91 Adj. Prof.; Bibl. Theol. Sem., 1991-93 Adj. Prof.; Messiah Coll., 1992-93 Lect., Bible; Assn. for Bibl. Res., 1990- Res. Analyst. Excv: North. Jordan Dam Survey Project, 1978 Co-dir.; Wadi Tumilat Project Survey, Egypt, 1983 Survey Arch.; Khirbet Nisya, Israel, 1985, 1987, 1990-91 Field Supr. Spec: Archaeology. Pub: "Kiln," "Potter's Wheel" in *ABD* (Doubleday, 1992); "The Philistines Enter Canaan" *BAR* 17/6 (1991); "Battle Over Jericho Heats Up—Dating Jericho's Destruction" *BAR* 16/5 (1990); "Did the Israelites Conquer Jericho? A New Look at the Archaeological Evidence" *BAR* 16/2 (1990); *The Sociology of Pottery in Ancient Palestine: The*

Ceramic Industry and the Diffusion of Ceramic Style in the Bronze and Iron Ages, JSOTSup 103 (Sheffield, 1990); "Egyptian Amphorae of the New Kingdom and Ramesside Periods" *BA* 50 (1987); "To Dip or Sprinkle? The Qumran Cisterns in Perspective" *BASOR* 256 (1984); and others. Awd: Endowment for Bibl. Res. Grant 1981; NEH, Travel to Collections Grant 1989; NEH, Summer Stipend 1992. Mem: ASOR 1967-; NEAS 1972-; IBR 1989-; SBL 1991-. Addr: (o) Associates for Biblical Research, Box 125, Ephrata, PA 17522-0125 717-733-3585; (h) 4328 Crestview Rd., Harrisburg, PA 17112-2005 717-652-4516.

WOOD, Richard A., b. Evansville, IN, May 5, 1954, s. of R. Wickliffe & Neree (Hatcher), m. Robbie (Verner). Educ: Ga. Inst. of Tech., BS 1976; New Orleans Bapt. Theol. Sem., MDiv 1979; South. Bapt. Theol. Sem., ThM 1984, PhD, OT Stud. 1989. Emp: Jefferson Community Coll., 1982-87, 1992- Instr. Excv: Tel Dor, 1991 Asst. Area Dir. Spec: Archaeology, Hebrew Bible. Pub: "The Use and Significance" for Models for Historical Reconstruction" in *SBL 1991 Seminar Papers* (Scholars, 1991). Mem: ASOR 1985-; SBL 1988-. Rec: Backpacking, antique restoration, stamp collecting. Addr: (o) Jefferson Community College, Downtown Campus, 101 W Broadway, Louisville, KY 40202 502-584-0181; (h) 315 Ridgedale Rd. #2, Louisville, KY 40206 502-896-4220.

WORGUL, John E., b. Lansing, MI, April 2, 1955, s. of Ernest & Ethel. Educ: Bethel Coll., BA 1977; Westminster Theol. Sem., MA 1979; Dropsie Coll., PhD 1987. Emp: Sem. of the East, 1988- Prof., OT. Spec: Hebrew Bible. Pub: "The Quatrain in Isaianic Poetry" *Grace Theol. Jour.* Fall (1990). Rec: Hiking, racquetball. Addr: (o) Seminary of the East, Philadelphia Center, 1601 Limekiln Pike, Dresher, PA 19025; (h) 208 Hiawatha Ln., Drexel Hill, PA 19026.

WORRELL, John E., b. Indianapolis, IN, November 23, 1933, s. of Fred and Marian, chil: Brad; Bret; Babette; Brenda. Educ: Christian Theol. Sem., BD 1961; Butler U., MA 1963; Claremont Grad. Sch., PhD 1968. Emp: Phillips U., 1966-69 Asst. Prof.; Hartford Sem. Found., 1969-73 Assoc. Prof.; Holy Cross Coll., 1973-77 Assoc. Prof.; Old Sturbridge Village, 1977-, Dir. of Res.. Excv: Tell Balatah, Tell er-Ras, 1966 Area Supr.; Tell Gezer, 1966-69 Area Supr.; Tell el-Hesi, 1969-73 Dir. Spec: Archaeology. Pub: "The Evolution of Holistic Investigation: Phase One of the Joint Expedition to Tell el-Hesi" in *Tell el Hesi, the Site and the Expedition* (1989); "Tell el-Hesi: the Mound of Many Surprises" *ASOR Newsletter* (1971); "Der 'Fruhkatholizismus' im Neuen Testament" *Encounter* (1967); and others. Awd: Layne Arch. Fellow 1966. Rec: Farming. Addr: (o) Dept. of Research, Old Sturbridge Village, Sturbridge, MA 01566 617-347-3362; (h) Wales Rd., Brimfield, MA 01010 413-245-7412.

WRIGHT, Addison G., b. Bridgeport, CT, June 28, 1932, s. of Addison & Anna (Dowd). Educ: Cath. U. of Amer., MA 1962, STD 1965, STL 1975; Pont. Bibl. Inst., Rome, SSL 1963. Emp: St. Mary's Sem. & U., 1963-68, 1971-81 Prof.; St. John's Provincial Sem., 1968-71 Assoc. Prof.; *CBQ*, 1973-76 Assoc. Ed.; Marywood Coll., 1980- Adj. Prof.; Fordham U., 1983- Adj. Prof. Spec: Hebrew Bible, New Testament. Pub: "The Widow's Mites: Praise or Lament? A Matter of Context" *CBQ* (1982); "The Riddle of the Sphinx Revisited" *CBQ* (1980, 1983); "Ecclesiastes," "Wisdom" in *New Jerome Biblical Commentary* (1990); *The Literary Genre Midrash* (Alba, 1967); and others. Mem: CBA 1959-; SBL 1972-. Addr: (h) 24 Killian Ave., Trumbull, CT 06611 203-268-3610.

WRIGHT, Benjamin G., b. Bethesda, MD, January 19, 1953, s. of Terry & Doris (Weber), m. Ann (Phillips), chil: Rachel Leigh; Nathan Christian. Educ: Ursinus Coll., BA, Phil. & Relig. 1975; East. Bapt. Theol. Sem., MDiv (summa cum laude) 1978; U. of Pa., PhD, Christian Origins 1988. Emp: East. Coll., 1981-82 Lect., Relig.; St. Joseph's U., 1982 Lect., Relig.; East. Bapt. Theol. Sem., 1985-86 Lect., Greek; Lehigh U., 1986-87 Vis. Instr., 1990- Asst. Prof., Dept. of Relig. Stud.; Franklin & Marshall Coll., 1989-90 Vis. Asst. Prof., Dept. of Relig. Stud. Spec: Hebrew Bible, New Testament, Apocrypha and Post-biblical Studies. Pub: *No Small Difference: Sirach's Relationship to Its Hebrew Parent Text,* SBLSCS 26 (Scholars, 1989); "The Quantitative Representation of Elements: Evaluating 'Literalism' in the LXX" in *VI Congress of the International Organization for Septuagint and Cognate Studies—Jerusalem 1986,* SCS 23 (Scholars) "Ben Sira 43:11b—To What Does the Greek Correspond?'" *Textus* 13 (1986); "A Previously Unnoticed Greek Variant to Matt 16:14—'Some Say John the Baptist...'" *JBL* 105 (1986); "Computer Assisted Study of the Criteria for Assessing the Literalness of Translation Units in the LXX," co-auth., *Textus* 12 (1985); "A Note on the Statistical Analysis of Septuagintal Syntax" *JBL* 104 (1985); and others. Awd: Penn-Israel Travel Fellow. for Study in Israel 1983-84; Penn-Mellon Diss. Fellow. 1987-88; Lehigh U., Franz Fellow. 1991; Yad Hannadiv/Barecha Found. Fellow. for Jewish Stud. 1992-93. Mem: SBL; IOSCS; Amer. Soc. of Papyrologists. Addr: (o) 9 Lehigh U., Dept. of Religion Studies, 249 Maginnes, Bethlehem, PA 18015 215-758-3344; (h) 1622 W North St., Bethlehem, PA 18018 215-867-8528.

WRIGHT, David P., b. St. Louis, MO, May 20, 1953, s. of Orson & Patricia, m. Dianne (Teerlink), chil: Rebekah; Sarah; Benjamin; Aharon. Educ: U. of Calif., Berkeley, MA 1980, PhD 1984. Emp: Brigham Young U., 1984-89 Asst. Prof.; Middlebury Coll., 1990-91 Asst. Prof.; Brandeis U. 1991- Asst. Prof. Spec: Hebrew Bible. Pub: "The Spectrum of Priestly Impurity" JSOTSup 125 (1991); *The Disposal of Impurity,* SBL Diss. Ser. 101 (Scholars, 1987); "Deuteronomy 21:1-9 as a Rite of Elimination" *CBQ* (1987); "The Gesture of Hand Placement in the Hebrew Bible and in Hittite Literature" *JAOS* (1986); "Purification from Corpse Contamination in Num XXI 19-24" *VT* (1985); and others. Mem: SBL 1978-; CBA 1985-; AOS 1987-; ASOR 1988-; AJS 1990-. Rec: Camping, hiking, woodworking. Addr: (o) Brandeis U., Dept. of NEJS, Waltham, MA 02254 617-736-2950.

WRIGHT, N. Thomas, b. Morpeth, England, December 1, 1948, s. of Nicholas & Rosemary, m. Margaret, chil: Julian; Rosamund; Harriet; Oliver. Educ: Oxford U., BA 1971, 1973, MA 1975, DPhil 1981. Emp: Merton Coll., Oxford, 1975-78 Res. Fellow; Downing Coll., Cambridge, 1978-81 Fellow & Chaplain; McGill U., 1981-86 Asst. Prof.; Oxford U., Worcester Coll., 1986- Fellow, Chaplain, Tutor in Theol., Lect. in NT. Spec: New Testament. Pub: *The New Testament and the People of God* (Fortress, 1992); *The Climax of the Covenant: Christ and the Law in Pauline Theology* (Fortress, 1991); *The Epistles of Paul to the Colossians and Philemon* (Eerdmans, 1986); and others. Mem: SBL; SNTS. Rec: Music, hill walking. Addr: (o) Worcester College, Oxford OX1 2HB, England 0865-278359; (h) 114 Southmoor Rd., Oxford OX2 6RB, England 0865-53923.

WRIGHT, Robert B., b. Jersey City, NJ, April 6, 1934, s. of Leonard & Marion (Macdonald), m. Mary (Halterman), chil: Kevin; Karen. Educ: Drake U., BD 1960; Hartford Sem. Found., STM 1964, PhD 1966. Emp: Boston U., 1966-67 Vis. Lect.; Gettysburg Coll., 1967-69 Asst. Prof.; AAR, 1969-72 Exec. Assoc.; Wilson Coll., 1969-72 Asst. Prof.; Temple U., 1972-, 1984-86 Assoc. Dean for Grad. Affairs. Excv: Tel Gezer 1966-72 Core Staff. Spec: Hebrew Bible, Apocrypha and Post-biblical Studies. Pub: "A New Fragment of Sirac" *JBL* (1976); "The Psalms of Solomon, the Pharisees and the Essenes" *Bull. of the IOSCS* (1972); "The Psalms of Solomon" in *The Pseudepigrapha of the Old Testament* (Doubleday, 1985); *Gezer*, vol. II, IV, V, contb. Mem: SBL; CBA; AAR. Rec: Sailing, period furniture making. Addr: (o) Temple U., 619 Anderson Hall, Philadelphia, PA 19122 215-787-1747; (h) 164 E Main St., Moorestown, NJ 08057 609-235-1170.

WRIGHT, T. John, b. Hawera, New Zealand, June 4, 1940, s. of Trevor & Molly, m. Michaela (Major), chil: Michael; Nicola; Katrina; Stephen. Educ: Victoria U. of Wellington, BS 1963; U. of Otago, BDiv 1966; U. of Manchester, PhD 1973. Emp: Macquarie U., Sydney, 1973-76 Tutor, Anc. Near East; St. John's Coll., Newcastle, Australia, 1977-86 Lect. in OT, Vice Prin.; St. George's Coll., Jerusalem, 1983-84 Vis. Prof.; United Fac. of Theol., Melbourne, 1987- Lect., OT. Spec: Archaeology, Hebrew Bible, Mesopotamian Studies. Pub: "*Rûah*—A Survey" in *The Concept of Spirit* (Prudentia, 1985); "The Concept of Mystery in the Hebrew Bible: An Example of the *Via Negativa*" in *The Via*

Negativa (Prudentia, 1981); "Amos and the Sycamore Fig" *VT* 26 (1976); and others. Mem: Newcastle Theol. Soc. 1973-86; ASOR 1973-; Australian & New Zealand Soc. for Theol. Stud. 1973-; Australian Assn. for the Study of Relig. 1976-; SBL 1990-. Rec: Tennis. Addr: (o) Trinity College, Royal Parade Parkville, Victoria 3052, Australia 3-349-0123.

WUELLNER, Wilhelm H., b. Bochum, Germany, February 21, 1927, s. of Wilhelm & Emma, m. Flora May (Slosson), chil: Christine; Virginia; Lucy. Educ: Marburg U., BD 1951; U. of Chicago, PhD 1958. Emp: Grinnel Coll., 1958-60 Asst. Prof.; Hartford Sem. Found., 1960-65 Asst. Prof.; Pacific Sch. of Relig. & Grad. Theol. Union, 1965-93 Prof.; *Protocols of the Colloquies of the Ctr. for Hermeneutical Stud. in Hellenistic and Modern Culture*, 1969-77 Ed.; Pont. Bibl. Inst., Rome, 1985 Vis. Prof.; NT Soc. of South Africa, 1989 Guest Lect. Spec: New Testament. Pub: *Studies in Paul the Jew*, co-auth. (Berkeley, 1991); *Hermeneutic and Rhetoric* (RSA, 1990); *The Surprising Gospel*, co-auth. (Abingdon, 1984); "Tradition and Interpretation of the 'Wise-Powerful-Noble' Triad in I Cor. 1:26" *Studia Evangelica* (1982); "Toposforschung und Torahinterpretation bei Paulus und Jesus" *NTS* (1978); "Paul's Rhetoric of Argumentation in Romans" *CBQ* (1976); *The Meaning of Fishers of Men* (Westminster, 1967); and others. Mem: SBL 1955-, Pres., Pacific Coast reg. 1968-69; CBA 1959-; SNTS 1968-; Intl. Soc. for the Hist. of Rhetoric 1978-. Rec: Gardening, traveling, poetry. Addr: (o) Pacific School of Religion, 1798 Scenic Ave., Berkeley, CA 97409 510-848-0528.

WYRICK, Stephen V., b. Dallas, TX, March 1, 1952, s. of Floyd A. & Maxine (Clark), m. Janet Lynn (Matthews), chil: Bradley Von; Paul Stephen. Educ: Dallas Bapt. U., BA, Hist. & Relig. 1973; SW Bapt. Theol. Sem., MDiv 1976, PhD, OT & Arch. 1981. Emp: Bapt. Ch., 1982-86 Pastor; Calif. Bapt. Coll., 1986- Assoc. Prof., OT & Hebrew, Chair of Relig. Div.; Golden Gate Bapt. Theol. Sem., 1987- Adj. Prof., Bibl. Stud. Spec: Archaeology, Hebrew Bible. Pub: "Haggai's Appeal to Tradition: Imagination used as Authority" in *Religious Writings and Religious Systems* (Scholar's, 1989); "Leviathan," "Semites" in *Layman's Bible Dict.*; and others. Awd: NEH grant 1988, 1989; W.F. Albright Inst. of Arch. Res., Res. Fellow 1993. Mem: ASOR; SBL; IES; NAPH; NABPR. Rec: Tennis, gold, hunting, skiing. Addr: (o) California Baptist College, 8432 Magnolia Ave., Riverside, CA 92504 714-689-5771; (h) 24089 Canyon Woods Circle, Moreno Valley, CA 92557 714-242-9637.

YAKAR, Jak, b. Istanbul, s. of Moiz & Regina, m. Suzette, chil: Ilan. Educ: Istanbul U., Lic. Arch. 1965; Brandeis U., MA 1966, PhD, Mediterranean Stud. 1968. Emp: Tel Aviv U., 1970-78 Lect., 1978-85 Sr. Lect., 1985- Assoc.

Prof. Anatolian & Near East. Arch., 1988-Chmn., Dept. of Arch., 1990-; Dir., Inst. of Arch. Excv: Catal Hoyuk-Konya, Turkey, 1963 Field Asst.; Beersheba, Israel, 1971 Area Supr.; Ikiztepe-Bafra, Turkey, 1972-75 Co-Field Dir. Spec: Anatolian Studies. Pub: *Prehistoric Anatolia: The Neolithic Transformation and the Early Chalcolithic Period*, Mon. Ser. of the Inst. of Arch., Tel Aviv U. 9 (1991); *The Later Prehistory of Anatolia: The Late Chalcolithic and the Early Bronze Age*, Brit. Arch. Reports 268 (1985); "Regional and Local Schools of Metalwork in Early Bronze Age Anatolia" *Anatolian Stud.* 24-25 (1984-85); "The Indo-Europeans and Their Impact on Anatolian Cultural Development" *Jour. of Indo-European Stud.* 9 (1981); "Recent Contributions to the Historical Geography of the Hittite Empire" *Mitteilungen der Deutschen Orientgesellschaft* 122 (1980); "The Province of Malatya and Sivas: An Archaeological Survey of Pre-Classical Sites," co-auth., *Expedition* 30 (1978); "Hittite Involvement in Western Anatolia" *Anatolian Stud.* 26 (1976); and others. Mem: AOS 1988-; IES 1990-; ASOR 1991-; World Arch. Congress 1991. Rec: Sculpture. Addr: (o) Tel Aviv U., Institute of Archaeology, Ramat Aviv, Tel Aviv 69978, Israel 03-6409417; (h) Rabina St., 15/23, Ramat Aviv, Tel Aviv 69978, Israel 03-6413517.

YAMASHITA, Tadanori, b. Tokyo, Japan, December 23, 1929, s. of Shigeru & Shinae, m. Nobue (Shirakawa), chil: Miki; Takeshi. Educ: U. of Tokyo, Hogakushi Degree 1953; Yale U., BD 1959, PhD 1964. Emp: Yale U., 1959-61 Instr.; Mt. Holyoke Coll., 1963- Prof. Spec: Hebrew Bible, Semitic Languages, Texts and Epigraphy. Pub: *Goddess Asherah* (U. Microfilm, 1964). Mem: SBL; AOS; Assn. of Asian Stud. Addr: (o) Mount Holyoke College, 204 Skinner Hall, South Hadley, MA 01075 413-538-2292; (h) 2 Amherst Rd., South Hadley, MA 01075 413-536-4364.

YAMAUCHI, Edwin, b. Hilo, HI, February 1, 1937, s. of Shokyo & Haruko, m. Kimie, chil: Brian; Gail. Educ: Shelton Coll, BA 1960; Brandeis U., MA 1962, PhD 1964. Emp: Rutgers U., 1964-69 Asst. Prof.; Miami U., 1969- Prof.; *Christianity Today*, Sr. Ed.; *JETS*, 1983- Ed. Com.; West. Conservative Bapt. Sem., Bueerman-Champion Lect. 1980. Spec: Archaeology, Hebrew Bible, New Testament, Semitic Languages, Texts and Epigraphy. Pub: *The Archaeology of New Testament Cities in Western Asia Minor* (Baker, 1980); *The World of the First Christians* (Lion, 1981); *Foes From the Northern Frontier* (Baker, 1982); "The Scythians" *BA* (1983); "Magic in the Biblical World" *TB* (1983); *Persia and the Bible* (Baker, 1990); and others. Mem: AOS; SBL; IBR. Rec: Opera, athletic events. Addr: (o) Miami U., History Dept., Oxford, OH 45056 (513) 529-5141; (h) 807 Erin Dr., Oxford, OH 45056 (513) 523-2819.

YAMAUCHI, Makoto, b. Osaka, Japan, December 8, 1940, s. of Toshio & Chie, m. Anna

Buick (Dickson). Educ: Tokyo Union Theol. Sem., BA 1965, BD 1967; U. of Edinburgh, Scotland, PhD 1972. Emp: Japanese Ch., 1967-Preacher; Tokyo Union Theol. Sem., 1973- Prof. Spec: New Testament, Apocrypha and Post-biblical Studies. Pub: *The Sermon on the Mount* (Tokyo Union Theol. Sem., 1976); *The Easter Texts of the New Testament: Their Tradition, Redaction and Theology* (United Ch. of Christ in Japan, 1979); "On the Method of New Testament Theology" *Jour. of Theol.* (1981, 1982); "The Old Testament in the Gospel According to Mark" *Jour. of Theol.* (1984); *A Commentary on the Epistle to the Philippians* (United Ch. of Christ in Japan, 1987); and others. Mem: SNTS 1973-; Japan Bibl. Inst. 1975-. Addr: (o) Tokyo Union Theological Seminary, 3-10-30, Osawa Mitaka, Tokyo 181, Japan 0422-32-4185.

YANCE, Norman A., b. Ashford, AL, November 28, 1927, s. of C.L. & Annie, m. Gwendolyn (White), chil: Mike; Etoila. Educ: Troy State, BS 1954; South. Bapt. Theol. Sem., BD 1956, ThM 1959; George Washington U., M.Phil. 1969, PhD 1973. Emp: Kentucky Bapt., 1955-57 Missionary; Bapt. Ch., 1959-66 Pastor; George Mason U., 1966- Prof. Emeritus. Spec: New Testament. Pub: *Bible Study for Young Adults* (1968); and others. Mem: NABPR; AAR. Rec: Fishing, bridge, gardening. Addr: (o) George Mason U., 4400 University Dr., Fairfax, VA 22030 703-323-2423; (h) 1805 Courtland Rd., Alexandria, VA 22306 703-768-2772.

YARBROUGH, O. Larry, b. Tuscaloosa, AL, December 19, 1949. Educ: Birmingham South. Coll., BA 1972; Cambridge U., MA 1974; Emory U, Candler Sch. of Theol., MDiv 1975; Yale U., PhD 1984. Emp: Coll. of William & Mary, 1981 Vis. Asst. Prof.; Middlebury Coll., 1983- Assoc. Prof. Spec: New Testament. Pub: *Not Like the Gentiles: Marriage Rules in the Letters of Paul* (Scholars, 1985). Mem: SBL; AAR. Addr: (o) Middlebury College, Dept. of Religion, Middlebury, VT 05753 802-388-3711; (h) RFD 3, Box 899A, Middlebury, VT 05753 802-388-4169.

YARBROUGH, Robert W., b. St. Louis, MO, October 12, 1953, s. of Lewis E. & Dolores B. (Gregory), m. Bernadine, chil: Luke B.; Micah L. Educ: SW Bapt. Coll., BA 1979; Wheaton Coll. Grad. Sch., MA 1982; U. of Aberdeen, Scotland, PhD 1985. Emp: Liberty U., 1985-87 Assoc. Prof.; Wheaton Coll., 1987-91 Assoc. Prof.; Covenant Theol. Sem., 1991- Assoc. Prof. Spec: New Testament, Apocrypha and Post-biblical Studies. Pub: *Is There A Synoptic Problem?*, trans. (Baker, 1992); *John* (Moody, 1991); "Resurrection of Christ" in *Twentieth-Century Ency. of Religious Knowledge* (Baker, 1991); *Historical Criticism of the Bible: Methodology or Ideology?*, trans. (Baker, 1990); "The Date of Papias: A Reassessment" *JETS* 26 (1983); and others. Mem: ETS 1982; Tyndale Fellow. 1984; AAR 1987; SBL 1987; IBR 1988. Rec: Running, timber falling. Addr: (o) Covenant Theological

Seminary, 12330 Conway Rd., St. Louis, MO 63141 314-434-4044; (h) 8267 John McKeever Rd., House Springs, MO 63051 314-285-7306.

YEE, Gale A., b. Cincinnati, OH, April 9, 1949, d. of John & Mary. Educ: Loyola U. of Chicago, BA 1973, MA 1975; U. of St. Michael's Coll., Toronto Sch. of Theol., PhD 1985. Emp: Univ. of St. Thomas, 1984- Assoc. Prof. Spec: Hebrew Bible. Pub: *Jewish Feasts and the Gospel of John* (Glazier, 1989); "I Have Perfumed my Bed with Myrrh: The Foreign Woman in Proverbs 1-9" *JSOT* 43 (1989); "Fraught with Background: Literary Ambiguity in II Sam 11" *Interpretation* 42 (1988); *Composition and Tradition in the Book of Hosea* (Scholars, 1987); "An Analysis of Prov. 8:22-31 According to Style and Structure" *ZAW* (1982); "A Form-critical Study of Isaiah 5:1-7 as a Song and a Juridical Parable" *CBQ* (1981). Mem: CBA; SBL. Rec: Martial arts. Addr: (o) U. of St. Thomas, 2115 Summit Ave., Mail 4362, St. Paul, MN 55105 612-962-5331; (h) 1317 Seminary Ave., St. Paul, MN 55104 612-962-5331.

YEIVIN, Ze'ev, July 11, 1926. Educ: Hebrew U., Israel, BA, Hist. Geog. & Arch. of the Land of Israel 1956, MA, Arch. & Hist. of the People of Israel 1962, PhD, Arch. 1972. Emp: Israel Antiq. Authority, Deputy Dir.; Israel Dept. of Survey & Excvn., Dir.; Arch. Survey of Israel, 1965 Sec., 1972-80 Chmn.; Judea & Samaria, 1967-75 Arch. Field Officer. Excv: Tirat Yehuda; Chorazin; Eshtamoa; Horvat Susiya; Carmel. Spec: Archaeology. Awd: Israel Acad. of Sci. grant. Addr: (h) Rehov Yisrael Aharoni 4, Jerusalem, Israel 2-636-827.

YELLIN, Joseph, b. Tel Aviv, Israel, April 21, 1938, s. of Yitzhak, m. Etta, chil: Irit; Efrat; Tamar. Educ: U. of Del., BD 1960; U. of Calif., Berkeley, PhD 1965. Emp: U. of Calif., Berkeley, 1960-65 Res. Asst.; Lawrence Berkeley Laboratory, 1965-73 Res. Physicist; Hebrew. U., Jerusalem, 1973- Assoc. Prof., Archaeometry & Physics. Spec: Archaeology. Pub: "A Re-Evaluation of the Red and Black Bowl from Parker's Excavations in Jerusalem," co-auth. *Oxford Jour. of Arch.* (1992); "The Origin of Obsidian from Mujahiya," co-auth. *Tel Aviv* (1992); "Preliminary Study of Flint Sources in Israel by Neutron Activation Analysis," co-auth. *Aota Arch. Lovaniensia* (1992); "The Origin of Late Bronze White Burnished Slip Wares from Deir el-Balah," co-auth. *IEJ* (1991); "Correlation Between Petrography, NAA, and ICP....," co-auth. *Geoarch.* (1991); *The Provenience, Typology and Chronology of Eastern Terra Signilata, Qedem,* co-auth. (1984); and others. Mem: Amer. Assn. for the Advancement of Sci.; Israel Physical Soc.; Amer. Physical Soc.; N.Y. Acad. of Sci. Addr: (o) Hebrew U., Institute of Archaeology, Jerusalem, Israel 02-882405; (h) Ha'Chayil 21/9, Jerusalem, Israel 02-810364.

YIEH, John Y. H., b. Taichung, Taiwan, April 20, 1955, s. of Ing-chu & Liu Liu-chih, m. Su M.C..

Educ: Tunghai U., Taiwan, BA 1977; Fu-Jen U., Taiwan, MA 1980; Taiwan Theol. Sem., MDiv (summa cum laude) 1983; Yale U., MA, Relig. 1986, MPhil 1990, NT Stud. Emp: Taiwan Theol Sem. & Coll., 1983-85 Instr., Bibl. Stud.; Yale U., 1986-88 Teaching Fellow in NT Stud.; Bangor Theol. Sem., 1989- Instr., NT Stud. Spec: Archaeology, New Testament. Pub: *New Testament Greek-Chinese Dict.* (United Bible Soc., 1989); "The Use of the Word of God in Second Isaiah: An Investigation of Its Social Function" *Taiwan Jour. of Theol.* 10 (1988); *Romans: A Study Edition of Chinese Bible* (United Bible Soc., 1987); "The Study of Q: A Survey of Its History and Current State" *Taiwan Jour. of Theol.* 8 (1986); "Justice as a Current Theme of Mission: An Old Testament Perspective" *Taiwan Jour. of Theol.* 6 (1984); *Interpreting the New Testament Today,* trans. (Jung Wang, 1982); *The Central Message of the New Testament,* trans. (Jung Wang, 1982); and others. Awd: Tunghai U. Fellow. 1973; Yale U. Fellow. 1985-88; W.F. Albright Inst. of Arch. Res. in Jerusalem, George A. Barton Fellow 1989-90. Mem: SBL; AAR. Rec: Traveling. Addr: (o) Bangor Theological Seminary, 40 College St., Hanover, NH 03755 603-643-5124; (h) 46 Elm St., Lebanon, NH 03766 603-448-0244.

YOUNG, Dwight Wayne, b. Lambert, OK, December 15, 1925, s. of Maurice & Freda (Polson), m. Barbara, chil: Terry; Cecilia. Educ: Hardin-Simmons U., BA 1949; Dropsie Coll. for Hebrew & Cognate Learning, PhD 1955; Dallas Theol. Sem., ThM 1956. Emp: Dallas Theol. Sem., 1954-58 Asst. Prof.; Brandeis U., 1958-87 Prof. Emeritus 1987-; Hebrew U., Jerusalem, 1965 Vis. Prof.; Cornell U., 1967-69 Vis. Prof. Spec: Hebrew Bible, Mesopotamian Studies, Semitic Languages, Texts and Epigraphy, Egyptology, Apocrypha and Post-biblical Studies. Pub: *Coptic Manuscripts from the White Monastery: Works of Shenute,* MPER 25 (1993); *Studies Presented to Hans Jakob Polotsky,* contb. (Pirtle & Polson, 1981); "The Incredible Regnal Spans of Kish I in the Sumerian King List" *JNES* (1991); "The Influence of Babylonian Algebra on Longevity Among the Antediluvians" *ZAW* (1988); *Studies Presented to Hans Jakob Polotsky,* ed., contb. (Pirtl & Polson, 1981); "The Ugaritic Myth of the God Horan and the Mare" *UF* (1979); "The Milieu of Nag Hammadi: Some Historical Considerations" *VC* (1970); "Unfulfilled Conditions in Shenoute's Dialect" *JAOS* (1969); "On Shenoute's Use of Present I" *JNES* (1961); and others. Awd: Dallas Theol. Sem., Solomon Awd. in OT 1951; Brandeis U., Mazur Faculty Res. Awd. 1984. Mem: IACS. Rec: Travel. Addr: (o) Edgewater Beach #617, 5555 N Sheridan Rd., Chicago, IL 60640 312-728-1941.

YOUNG, Fred E., b. Watsontown, PA, s. of Walter & Jessie, m. Sue Kathryn, chil: Patricia; John Paul. Educ: William Jewell Coll., AB 1947; Crozer Thoel. Sem., BD 1950; Dropsie U., PhD 1954. Emp: Bapt. Inst., 1953-54 Prof.; Crozer Theol. Sem., 1954 Vis. Prof.; Cen. Bapt. Theol. Sem., 1955- Prof., Dean. Spec: Hebrew Bible,

Semitic Languages, Texts and Epigraphy, Egyptology. Pub: "I,II Samuel" in *Wycliff Bible Comm.*; "Judges" in *Expositors Bible Comm.* Awd: William Jewell Coll., Disting. Alumnus 1978. Mem: SBL 1955-; NAPH 1960-; ASOR 1966-. Rec: Travel, bibliographies. Addr: (h) 9025 Salem #4, Lenexa, KS 66215 913-599-3702.

YOUNG, Gordon D., b. Philadelphia, PA, May 20, 1936, s. of G. Douglas & Georgina O., m. Barbara J., chil: Susan Elizabeth; Kristin Elizabeth. Educ: U. of Minn., ALA 1955, BA 1960; Brandeis U., MA 1963, PhD 1970. Emp: Purdue U., 1966- Assoc. Prof., Anc. Mediterranean & Near East. Hist.; *Shofar,* Ed. Bd. Spec: Mesopotamian Studies. Pub: *Mari in Retrospect: Fifty Years of Mari and Mari Studies,* ed. (Eisenbrauns, 1992); *Directory of Jewish Studies Scholars in the Midwest,* co-auth. (Purdue U.P., 1990); *The John Frederick Lewis Collection: Texts from the Third Millennium in the Free Library of Philadelphia,* Materiali per il vocabolario Neosumerica, vol. 2, 13, co-auth. (1984); *Ugarit in Retrospect: Fifty Years of Ugarit and Ugaritic,* ed. (Eisenbrauns, 1981); "A Merchant's Balanced Account and Neosumerian Gold" in *Studies in Honor of Tom B. Jones* (1979); "Nuzu Texts in the Free Library of Philadelphia" in *Orient and Occident: Essays Presented to Cyrus Gordon* (1973); "Utu and Justice: A New Sumerian Proverb" *JCS* 24 (1972); "Ur III Texts in the Zion Research Library, Boston," "Cuneiform Texts in the Museum of Fine Arts, Boston," co-auth. *JCS* 23 (1970); and others. Mem: AOS, MidW reg., V.P. 1983-85, Pres. 1985-87; Assn. of Anc. Hist.; ASOR; AIA; SBL. Addr: (o) Purdue U., Dept. of History, West Lafayette, IN 47907 317-494-4151; (h) 815 Windsor Dr., West Lafayette, IN 47906 317-463-2868.

YOUNG, Norman H., b. Perth, Western Australia, April 12, 1938, s. of Hugh & Jessica, m. Eva Elizabeth, chil: Paul; Michelle. Educ: Pacific Union Coll., BA 1965; Manchester U., BD 1970, PhD 1973; U. of New England, MLitt 1981. Emp: Avondale Coll., 1973- Sr. Lect.. Spec: New Testament. Pub: "The Figure of the *Paidagogos* in Art and Literature" *BA* (1990); "*Paidagogos*: The Social Setting of a Pauline Metaphor" *NT* (1987); "Jesus and the Sinners: Some Queries" *JSNT* (1985); *Rebuke and Challenge: The Point of Jesus' Parables* (Rev. & Herald, 1985); "The Commandment to Love Your Neighbor as Yourself and the Parable of the Good Samaritan (Luke 10:25-37)" *Andrews U. Sem. Stud.* (1983); "The Gospel According to Hebrews 9" *NTS* (1981); and others. Mem: SNTS. Rec: Hiking. Addr: (o) Avondale College, Dept. of Theology, Cooranbong, NSW 2265, Australia 049-771-170; (h) 6 Jacaranda Close, Cooranbong, NSW 2265, Australia 049-771-170.

YOUNG, William A., b. Duluth, MN, September 11, 1945, s. of Arthur & Rhoda (Magers), m. Susan (Ammon), chil: Rachel; Matthew. Educ: U. of Tulsa, BA 1967;

McCormick Theol. Sem., MDiv 1970; U. of Iowa, PhD 1974. Emp: Willamette U., 1974-75 Asst. Prof.; Westminster Coll., 1975- Prof. & Chaplain. Spec: Hebrew Bible. Pub: *An Introduction to the Bible: A Journey into Three Worlds* (Prentice-Hall, 1990); "Leviathan in the Book of Job and Moby Dick" *Soundings* (1982). Mem: SBL. Rec: Softball, swimming, running. Addr: (o) Westminster College, Fulton, MO 65251 314-642-3361; (h) 5402 Dalcross Dr., Columbia, MO 65203 314-442-5501.

YOUNGBLOOD, Ronald F., b. Chicago, IL, August 10, 1931, s. of William & Ethel, m. Carolyn, chil: Glenn; Wendy Sue. Educ: Fuller Theol. Sem., BD 1955; Dropsie Coll., PhD 1961. Emp: Bethel Theol. Sem., 1961-78, 1982- Prof.; *JETS,* 1976- Ed.; Wheaton Coll. Grad. Sch., 1978-81 Acad. Dean & Prof.; Trinity Evang. Div. Sch., 1981-82 Prof. Spec: Archaeology, Hebrew Bible, Mesopotamian Studies, Semitic Languages, Texts and Epigraphy. Pub: *The Book of Genesis: An Introductory Comm.* (Baker, 1991); *The Genesis Debate* (Baker 1991); *Evangelicals and Inerrancy* (Thomas Nelson, 1984); *Exodus* (Moody, 1983); and others. Awd: General Electric Found. Grant 1959-61. Mem: NEAS; ETS. Rec: Swimming, spectator sports. Addr: (o) 6116 Arosa St., San Diego, CA 92115 619-582-8188.

YOUNGER, K. Lawson, Jr., b. Richmond, VA, November 29, 1953, s. of Kenneth & Doris (Hastings), m. Patti (Catchings), chil: Kenneth Lawson, III; William Andrew; Rebecca Rachel. Educ: Fla. Bible Coll., BA, Bibl Stud. 1976, ThB 1978; Dallas Theol. Sem., ThM 1982; Sheffield U., PhD, Semitics & OT Stud. 1988. Emp: LeTourneau U., 1988- Asst. Prof., Bibl. Stud. Spec: Anatolian Studies, Hebrew Bible, Mesopotamian Studies, Semitic Languages, Texts and Epigraphy, Egyptology. Pub: "Heads! Tails! or the Whole Coin?! Contextual Method & Intertextual Analysis: Judges 4 and 5" in *The Canon in Comparative Perspective: Scripture in Context IV,* co-ed. (Mellen, 1991); *Ancient Conquest Accounts: A Study of Ancient Near Eastern and Biblical History Writing* (Sheffield, 1990); "The Figurative Aspect and Contextual Method in the Evaluation of the Solomonic Empire (1 Kings 1-11)" in *The Bible in Three Dimensions* (Sheffield, 1990); "Panammuwa and Bar-Rakib: Two Structural Analyses" *JANES* 18 (1986); and others. Awd: Cambridge U., Tyndale Fellow. 1986-87. Mem: SBL 1986-; ASOR 1989-; AAR 1989-. Rec: Computers, chess, sports. Addr: (o) LeTourneau U., Heath-Hardwick Hall, Box 7001, Longview, TX 75607-7001 903-753-0231; (h) 1315 Regina, Longview, TX 75605 903-297-7557.

YOUNKER, Randall W., b. Auburn, CA, November 26, 1953, s. of Fred & Gwen (Sanders), m. April, chil: Rebecca; Michael; Elizabeth; Sarah. Educ: Pacific Union Coll., BA, Relig. 1975, MA 1977; U. of Ariz., MA, Near East. Arch. 1987.

Emp: Sacramento Adventist Acad., 1976-79 Instr.; Pacific Union Coll., 1979-84 Supr. Instr.; Andrews U., 1985 Instr., Anthrop. & Arch., 1986- Asst. Prof., OT & Bibl. Arch., Dir., Inst. of Arch. Excv: Madaba Plains Project, 1984 Ecologist & Zooarch., 1987 Field Supr., 1992 Co-dir.; Tell Jawa & Dreijat, 1989 Field Dir.; Tell Gezer, 1990 Assoc. Dir.; Tell Jalul, 1992 Dir. Spec: Archaeology, Hebrew Bible. Pub: Articles in *ABD* (Doubleday, 1992); *Madaba Plains Project 2: The 1987 Season at Tell el-'Umeiri and Vicinity and Subsequent Studies*, co-auth., co-ed. (Andrews U.P./Inst. of Arch., 1991); "Notes and News: Gezer, 1990," co-auth., *IEJ* 41/4 (1991); "A Preliminary Report of the 1990 Season at Tel Gezer: Excavations of the 'Outer Wall' and the 'Solomonic Gateway' (July 2 to August 10, 1990)" *AUSS* 29/1 (1991); "Madaba Plains Project: The 1989 Excavations at Tell el-'Umeiri and Vicinity," co-auth., *Ann. of the Dept. of Antiq. of Jordan* 25 (1991); *Madaba Plains Project 1: The 1984 Season at Tell el-'Umeiri and Vicinity*, co-auth., co-ed. (Andrews U.P., 1989); "Israel, Judah, and Ammon and the Motifs on the Baalis Seal" BA 48/3 (1985); and others. Mem: ASOR; Andrews Soc. for Relig. Stud; Adventist Theol. Soc. Rec: Travel, walking, biking, tennis. Addr: (o) Andrews U., Institute of Archaeology, Berrien Springs, MI 49102 616-471-3273.

YRIGOYEN, Charles, Jr., b. Philadelphia, PA, December 9, 1937, s. of Charles & Erma (Suters), m. Jean, chil: Debra; Charles. Educ: Lancaster Theol. Sem., BD 1962; East. Bapt. Theol. Sem., ThM 1964; Temple U., PhD 1973. Emp: 1958-68 Pastor; Albright Coll., 1968-82 Prof.; United Methodist Ch., Gen. Commn. on Archives & Hist., 1982- Gen. Sec.; Drew U., 1982- Adj. Prof.; Union Theol. Sem., 1982- Lect. Spec: New Testament. Pub: *Acts for Our Time: A Study of the Book of Acts* (Abingdon, 1992). Mem: Amer. Soc. of Ch. Hist. Addr: (o) PO Box 127, Madison, NJ 07940 201-822-2787; (h) 2 Hemlock Ln., Morristown, NJ 07960 201-538-7434.

YURCO, Frank J., b. New York, NY, July 31, 1944, s. of Ludwig & Della (Risavy), m. Dianne Margaret, chil: Edward Alexander; Miriam Ingrid. Educ: N.Y. U., BA, Class., Greek, Latin 1967; U. of Chicago, MA 1986, PhD, Egyptology. Emp: U. of Chicago, 1974-1977 Epigrapher, Oriental Inst. Epigraphic Survey, 1977- Tchr.; Field Mus. of Natural Hist., 1977- Tchr.; 1986- Egyptology Cons., 1992- Egypt Tour Guide; Indianapolis Children's Mus., 1989-92 Egyptology Cons. Spec: Egyptology. Pub: "The Shabaha-Shebitku Coregency and the Supposed Second Campaign of Sennacherib Against Judah: A Critical Assessment" *JBL* 110/1 (1991); "3,200-Year-Old Picture of Israelites Found in Egypt" *BAR* 16/5 (1990); "Were the Ancient Egyptians Black or White?" *BAR* 15/5 (1989); "Merenptah's Canaanite Campaign" *Jour. of the Amer. Res. Ctr. in Egypt* 23 (1986); *The Battle Reliefs of King Sety I*, Reliefs & Inscriptions at Karnak vol. 4, co-auth. (U. of Chicago Oriental Inst., 1986); *Temple of Khonsu* vol. 2, co-auth. (U. of Chicago Oriental

Inst., 1981); "Amenmesse: Six Statues at Karnak" *Metropolitan Mus. Jour.* 14 (1980); "Sennacherib's Third Campaign and the Coregency of Shabaka and Shebitku" *Serapis* 6 (1980); and others. Awd: Phi Beta Kappa 1967; Woodrow Wilson Fellow. 1967-68. Mem: Egypt Exploration Soc. 1971-; Intl. Assn. of Egyptologists 1976-; Amer. Res. Ctr. in Egypt 1974-. Rec: Photography, speed-walking, ch. choir. Addr: (o) Field Museum of Natural History, Roosevelt Rd. at Lake Shore Dr., Chicago, IL 60605 312-684-0439; (h) 5712 S Drexel Ave., Chicago, IL 60637-1420.

ZELLER, Dieter, b. Freiburg, Germany, June 24, 1939, s. of Wilhelm & Elisabeth (Mussler), m. Maria (Huebner). Educ: Pont. Bibl. Inst., Rome, LBS 1967; U. of Freiburg, DTh 1972, Habil. 1976. Emp: U. of Freiburg, 1973-78 Asst.; Theol. Fac. at Lucerne, Switzerland, 1980-82 Prof.; U. of Mainz, 1982- Prof. Spec: New Testament. Pub: *Charis bei Philon und Paulus* (KBW, 1990); *Der Brief an die Roemer* (Pustet, 1985); *Kommentar zur Logienquelle* (KBW, 1984); "Theologie der Mission bei Paulus" in *Mission im Neuen Testament* (1982); "Wunder und Bekenntnis" *BZ* (1981); *Die weisheitlichen Mahnsprueche bei den Synoptikern* (Echter, 1977); "Prophetisches Wissen um die Zukunft in synoptischen Jesusworten" *Theol. und Phil.* (1977); and others. Awd: U. of Heidelberg, Hon. Prof. 1989. Mem: SNTS; Deutsche Vereinigung fuer Religionsgeschichte. Rec: Sports, painting, piano. Addr: (o) Schillerweg 4, D-65346 Eltville 2, Germany; (h) Johannes Gutenberg-U., 55099 Mainz, Germany 06131-395-220.

ZERTAL, Adam, b. Hadera, Israel, December 3, 1936, s. of Moshe & Sarah, m. Judith, chil: Amotz; Imry; Rotem; Naboth. Educ: Tel Aviv U., BA 1977, MA 1980, PhD 1987. Emp: U. of Haifa, 1982- Lect. Excv: Lachish, 1976-81 Area Supr.; Narbata Excvn., 1980- Dir.; Mt. Ebal, 1982-85 Dir.; Manasseh hill country, Survey Dir. Spec: Archaeology. Pub: *The Syncline of Shechem, The Survey of the Hill Country of Manasseh* vol. 1 (U. of Haifa, 1992); "An Early Iron Age I Cultic Site on Mt. Ebal: Excavation Seasons 1982-1987, Preliminary Report" *Tel Aviv* 13-14 (1986-87); "Has Joshua's Altar Been Found on Mt. Ebal?" *BAR* 11/1 (1985); *Arubboth, Hepher and the Third Solominic District* (Hakibbutz Hameuchad, 1984); and others. Addr: (o) Haifa U., Dept. of Archaeology, Mt. Carmel, Haifa 31999, Israel 04-240-234.

ZEVIT, Ziony, b. February 13, 1942. Educ: Haim Greenberg Hebrew Tchr. Coll., Jerusalem, Cert. of Grad. 1963; U. of South. Calif., BA, Relig. 1964; U. of Calif., Berkeley, MA, Near East. Lang. 1967, PhD, Near East. Stud. 1973. Emp: Hebrew U., Israel, 1972-74 Lect., 1980-82 Vis. Assoc. Prof., Bible; U. of Judaism, Los Angeles, 1974- Prof., Bibl. Lit. & NW Semitic Lang.; Calif. State U., Northridge, 1983-85 Adj. Prof., Relig. Stud.; U. of South. Calif., 1988-89 Adj. Prof., Relig. Stud.; Claremont Grad. Sch., 1992 Adj. Prof., N Semitic Lang. Spec: Archaeology, Hebrew Bible,

Semitic Languages, Texts and Epigraphy. Awd: Zion Found., Fellow. in Bibl. Arch. 1968; Charles Brown Found., Fellow. 1980; NEH, Fellow. 1981; ASOR, Fellow. 1986; Hebrew Union Coll., Nelson Glueck Sch. of Bibl. Arch., Avaram Biran Fellow of Bibl. Arch. 1987. Mem: AOS; ASOR; AJS; SBL; WUJS. Addr: (o) U. of Judaism, 15600 Mulholland Dr., Los Angeles, CA 90077 310-476-9777; (h) 1913 Crest, Los Angeles, CA 90034.

ZIAS, Joseph E., b. Detroit, MI, February 27, 1941, s. of Joseph & Kathryn, chil: Shira; Eytan. Educ: Wayne State U., BA 1968, MA 1971. Emp: Israel Dept. of Antiq. and Mus., 1972- Cur. Spec: Archaeology. Pub: "Serial Craniectomies for Intercranial Infection from the Fourth Millenium BC" *Intl. Journ. of Osteoarchaeology* (1992); "Death and Disease in Ancient Israel" *BA* (1991); "Lust and Leprosy: Confusion or Correlation?" *BASOR* (1989); "How the Ancients De-loused Themselves," co-auth., *BAR* 15/6 (1989); "Ancient Dentistry in the Eastern Mediterranean: A Brief Review" *IEJ* (1986); "The Crucified Man from Givat Ha Mivtar: A Reappraisal" *IEJ* (1985); and others. Mem: Israel Anthrop. Assn. Rec: Long-distance running. Addr: (o) Israel Antiqities Authority, PO Box 586, Jerusalem, Israel.

ZIMANSKY, Paul E., b. Iowa City, IA, July 25, 1946, s. of Curt & Margaret (Lacy), m. Elizabeth (Stone). Educ: Johns Hopkins U., BA 1968; U. of Chicago, PhD 1980. Emp: NE Ill. U., 1973 Lect.; U. of Calif., Berkeley, 1979-80 Lect.; State U. of N.Y., Stony Brook, 1980-83 Adj. Asst. Prof.; U. of Aleppo, 1981-82 Fulbright Lect.; Boston U., 1983-90 Asst. Prof., 1990- Assoc. Prof. Excv: Bastam, 1975, 1977, 1978 Area Supr.; Nippur, 1973, 1975 Area Supr.; 'Ain Dara, 1982-84 Co-dir., Amer. Contingent; Tell Hamide, 1987 Co-dir.; Tell Abu Duwari, 1987-88, 1990 Co-dir. Spec: Archaeology, Anatolian Studies, Mesopotamian Studies. Pub: "Uncertain Geography and Sargon's 8th Campaign" *JNES* (1990); *Ecology and Empire: The Structure of the Urartian State* (Oriental Inst., 1985); "Bones and Bullae: An Enigma From Bastam, Iran" *Arch.* (1979); "The University of Iowa Cuneiform Texts" *JCS* (1979); "Texts and Fragments: Two Boghazkoy Fragments in Iowa City" *JCS* (1979). Awd: Woodrow Wilson Fellow 1968; Natl. Geog. Grants 1983, 1984, 1990, 1991. Mem: AIA; AOS. Addr: (o) Boston U., Dept. of Archaeology, 675 Commonwealth Ave., Boston, MA 02215 617-353-3415; (h) 12 Houghton Blvd., Stony Brook, NY 11790 516-751-3824.

ZIMMERMANN, Frank, b. New York, NY, April 17, 1907, s. of Samuel & Mollie (Moore), m. Betty, chil: David Baruch (dec.); Judy (Axelrod). Educ: CCNY, BA 1929; Dropsie Coll., PhD 1935; Jewish Theol. Sem., DHL, Rabbinical Ord. 1936. Emp: *JBL*, 1954-57 Assoc. in Coun.; Dropsie Coll., 1959-68 Prof., Bibl. Lit. Spec: Hebrew

Bible, New Testament, Semitic Languages, Texts and Epigraphy, Apocrypha and Post-biblical Studies. Pub: "The Language, the Date, and the Portrayal of the Messiah in IV Ezra" *Hebrew Stud.* (1985); *The Aramaic Origins of the Four Gospels* (Ktav, 1979); *Biblical Books Translated from the Aramaic* (Ktav, 1975); *The Inner World of Qohelet* (Ktav, 1973); "Folk Etymology of Biblical Names" in VTSup (1966); "The Book of Wisdom: Language and Character" *Jewish Quar. Rev.* (1966); *Book of Tobit, Text and Commentary* (Harper, 1959); "The Aramaic Provenance of Qohelet" *Jewish Quar. Rev.* (1945); and others. Mem: Amer. Assn. of U. Profs. 1966-92; SBL 1938-92. Rec: Reading, research, writing. Addr: (o) 112-20 72 Drive, Forest Hills, New York, NY 11375.

ZIPOR, Moshe A., m. Adina, chil: Hanna; Vered; Assaf; Gad; Iddo. Educ: Bar-Ilan U., PhD 1979. Emp: Bar-Ilan U., 1968- Sr. Lect., Dept. of Bible. Pub: "An Additional Expanded Edition of the Commentary of Rashi to Ruth, and Segments of Ruth Zuta in a Different Version" *Sidra* 9 (1993); "Notes sur les chapitres XIX-XXI du Levitique dans la Bible d'Alexandrie" *ETL* 57 (1991); "The 'Eighteen Tiqqune Sopherim': The Birth and Transformations of the Tradition" in *Proceedings of the 10th World Congress of Jewish Studies* (1990); "On the Transformation of the Al Tikre-Type Derashot" *Sinai* 100 (1987); "Restrictions on Marriage for the Priests" *Biblica* 68 (1987); and others. Awd: Hebrew U. Bibl. Project, Res. Fellow; Computer Assisted Tools for Septuagint Stud. Project, Res. Fellow. Mem: IOSCS; WUJS. Addr: (o) Bar-Ilan U., Dept. of Bible, Ramat-Gan, Israel; (h) 41 Yaakov St., Rehovot 76 262, Israel 08-475735.

ZOHAR, Mattanyah, Educ: Hebrew U., PhD, Arch. Emp: Hebrew U., Jerusalem, Inst. of Arch. Excv: Golan; Tel Yarmut; City of David. Spec: Archaeology. Pub: "Unlocking the Mystery of Rogem Hiri" *BAR* 19/4 (1993); "Megalithic Cemeteries in the Levant" in *Pastoralism in the Levant: Archaeological Materials in Anthropological Perspective*, Mon. in World Arch. 10 (Prehistory, 1992); and others. Addr: (o) Hebrew U., Institute of Archaeology, Mt. Scopus, Jerusalem, Israel.

ZORN, Walter D., b. Donaldsonville, GA, January 2, 1943, s. of Walter & Alice, m. Carolyn Ann, chil: Angela; Scott. Educ: Atlanta Christian Coll., BA 1965; Lincoln Christian Sem., MDiv 1969; Mich. State U., PhD 1983. Emp: 1965-70 Min.; Catlin Ch. of Christ, 1970-75 Dir. of Christian Educ.; Great Lakes Christian Coll., 1976-88 Prof.; Lincoln Christian Coll., 1988-93 Acad. Dean, 1993- Prof. Spec: Hebrew Bible, New Testament. Pub: Articles in *ISBE, New Theological Dict. of the Old Testament.* Mem: SBL 1981-. Rec: Jogging, softball. Addr: (o) Lincoln Christian College, 100 Campus View Dr., Lincoln, IL 62656 217-732-3168; (h) 400 Maywood Dr., Lincoln, IL 62656 217-735-2379.

ZUCKERMAN, Bruce, Educ: Princeton U., BA 1969; Yale U., PhD 1980. Emp: *Maarav*, 1978- Sr. Ed., Publ.; U. of South. Calif., 1981- Assoc. Prof., Dir. of Arch. Res. Collection, 1983- Dir. of W Semitic Res. Project; Hebrew Union Coll., Los Angeles, 1989 Vis. Prof.; Claremont Grad. Sch., 1990-91 Adj. Assoc. Prof. Spec: Semitic Languages, Texts and Epigraphy. Pub: *Job the Silent: A Study in Historical Counterpoint* (Oxford U.P., 1991); "The Date of 11Q Targum Job: A Paleographic Consideration of Its Vorlage" *JSP* (1987); "'A Kid in Milk': New Photographs of *KTU* 1.23, Line 14," co-auth., *HUCA* 57 (1986); "On Rereading the 'Kid in Milk' Inscription" *BR* 1/3 (1985); "For Your Sake, A Case Study in Aramaic Semantics" *JANES* 15 (1983); "Two Examples of Editorial Modification in 11QtgJob" in *Biblical and Near Eastern Studies, Essays in Honor of William Sanford LaSor* (1975); and others. Awd: U. of South. Calif., Grants 1984, 1985; Mitchell Dahood Memorial Prize 1986. Mem: SBL; ASOR; Anc. Bibl. Manuscript Ctr., Bd. of Dir. 1986-; Cyprus Amer. Arch. Res. Inst., Trustee 1991-. Addr: (o) U. of Southern California, School of Religion, 328 Taper Hall of Humanities, University Park, Los Angeles, CA 90089 213-740-0271; (h) 12 Empty Saddle Rd., Rolling Hills Estates, CA 90274 310-541-4573.

ZUGIBE, Frederick T., b. Garnerville, NY, May 28, 1928, s. of Benjamin & Anna (Zarich), m. Catherine F., chil: Frederick; Thomas; Cathryn; Theresa; Mary Eileen; Matthew; Kevin. Educ: St. Francis Coll., Brooklyn, BS 1951; U. of Chicago, MS 1959, PhD 1960; W. Va. U. Sch. of Medicine, MD 1968. Emp: U.S. Veterans Admin., Dir., Cardiovascular Res.; Columbia U. Coll. of Physicians & Surgeons, Adj. Assoc. Prof. of Pathology; County of Rockland, N.Y., Chief Medical Exam. Spec: Archaeology, New Testament. Pub: "The Man of the Shroud Was Washed" *Sindon* 1 (1989); *The Cross and the Shroud: A Medical Inquiry into the Crucifixion* (Paragon House, 1988); "Two Questions About Crucifixion" *BR* 5/2 (1984); "Death by Crucifixion" *Canadian Soc. Forensic Sci. Jour.* 17 (1983); *The Cross and the Shroud: A Medical Examiner Investigates the Crucifixion* (Angelus, 1982); and others. Rec: Computer technology, botany, gardening, gourmet cooking. Addr: (o) County of Rockland, Office of Chief Medical Examiner, Robert Yeagher Medical Complex, Pomona, NY 10970; (h) One Angelus Dr., Garnerville, NY 10923 914-354-1333.

ZUURMOND, Rochus, b. Voorburg, The Netherlands, December 5, 1930, s. of Jacob & Barendina (de Lange), m. Ruth S. (Farmer), chil: Jacob; Paul; Barend; Maria; Cornelis; Arie; Nico. Educ: Leyden U., Ch. Dip. 1962; Amsterdam U., PhD 1981; Utrecht U., ThD 1988. Emp: Reformed Ch. of The Netherlands, 1962 Min.; Technical U. of Delft, 1966 Chaplain; U. of Amsterdam, 1981 Assoc. Prof., Intertestamental Stud., 1991 Sr. Prof., Bibl. Stud.; Amsterdamse Cahiers voor Exegese en Bijbelse Theologie, 1981 Co-ed. Spec: Hebrew Bible, New Testament, Semitic

Languages, Texts and Epigraphy, Apocrypha and Post-biblical Studies. Pub: *De Dagen van Noach* (Ten Have, 1991); "The Flood According to Enoch in Early Christian Literature" in *SBL 1991 Seminar Papers* (Scholars, 1991); "Asshur in Jubilees 13.17?" *JSP* 4 (1989); *Novum Testamentum Aethiopice: General Introduction/The Gospel of Mark*, Aethiopistische Forschungen 27 (Steiner, 1989); "The Pentateuch Quotations of Aphrahat" in *Tussen Nijl en Herengracht* (Amsterdam: Fac. of Theol., 1988); *God noch Gebod* (Ten Have, 1984); "Sodom: de geschiedenis van een vooroordeel" in Amsterdamse Cahiers voor Exegese en Bijbelse Theol. 5 (1984); and others. Mem: SBL 1976-; SOTS 1981-. Rec: Textual criticism of the Hebrew and the Greek Bible, travel. Addr: (o) Delenus Institute, Oude Turfmarkt 147, 1012 GC Amsterdam, Netherlands 31-20-5252026; (h) Kanaalweg 11, 2628 EC Delft, Netherlands 3115135138.

Specialization Index

ARCHAEOLOGY

Valerie A. ABRAHAMSEN
David T. ADAMO
Stephen J. ADLER
Ralph H. ALEXANDER
Robert W. ALLISON
Pierre J. AMIET
Ruth AMIRAN
Emmanuel ANATI
Roger W. ANDERSON, Jr.
Diane APOSTOLOS-CAPPADONA
Gary P. ARBINO
Gleason L. ARCHER, Jr.
Carl E. ARMERDING
Michal ARTZY
Dewey F. ATKINSON
Gideon Y. AVNI
J. Arthur BAIRD
Charalambos BAKIRTZIS
Dan BARAG
Gabriel BARKAY
Kenneth L. BARKER
J. Edward BARRETT
John R. BARTLETT
George F. BASS
Richard A. BATEY
Todd S. BEALL
Dewey M. BEEGLE
V. Gilbert BEERS
Itzhaq BEIT-ARIEH
Meir BEN-DOV
Amnon BEN-TOR
Boyce M. BENNETT
Klaus BIEBERSTEIN
Piotr A. BIENKOWSKI
Neal BIERLING
Manfred F. K. W. BIETAK
John J. BIMSON
Avraham BIRAN
Edward P. BLAIR
Joseph BLENKINSOPP
Hanswulf BLOEDHORN
Robert G. BOLING
Elie BOROWSKI
Oded BOROWSKI
A. Wendell BOWES
Robert T. BOYD
Thomas V. BRISCO
Oscar S. BROOKS
Magen BROSHI

Daniel C. BROWNING, Jr.
Robert J. BULL
John M. BULLARD
Reuben G. BULLARD
Shlomo BUNIMOVITZ
Edward F. CAMPBELL
Glenn A. CARNAGEY, Sr.
Jeffrey R. CHADWICK
Debra A. CHASE
Marilyn J. CHIAT
Jerzy CHMIEL
Duane L. CHRISTENSEN
Douglas R. CLARK
Rudolph COHEN
Dan P. COLE
R. Dennis COLE
Oral E. COLLINS
Michael D. COOGAN
Robert A. COUGHENOUR
Frank Moore CROSS, Jr.
John D. CURRID
Adrian H. W. CURTIS
Frederick W. DANKER
Claudine M. DAUPHIN
Maxwell J. DAVIDSON
Graham I. DAVIES
John J. DAVIS
John A. DEARMAN
Aaron DEMSKY
Robert C. DENTAN
David A. DENYER
William G. DEVER
Ralph W. DOERMANN
William R. DOMERIS
David A. DORSEY
Moshe DOTHAN
Trude DOTHAN
Christos G. DOUMAS
Sally S. DUNHAM
J. Kenneth EAKINS
Gershon EDELSTEIN
Douglas R. EDWARDS
Carl S. EHRLICH
Robert H. EISENMAN
Josette ELAYI
J. Harold ELLENS
James R. ENGLE
Hanan ESHEL
William R. FARMER
Paul W. FERRIS, Jr.
Jack FINEGAN

Israel FINKELSTEIN
Moshe L. FISCHER
James W. FLEMING
Gideon FOERSTER
Samuel J. FOX
Gordon W. FRANZ
William H. C. FREND
Ernest S. FRERICHS
Steven J. FRIESEN
Volkmar O. FRITZ
Richard N. FRYE
William J. FULCO
Michael J. FULLER
Neathery B. FULLER
Paul L. GARBER
Moshe GARSIEL
Marie-Henriette GATES
Lawrence T. GERATY
Hillel GEVA
Shimon GIBSON
Seymour GITIN
Barry M. GITTLEN
James E. GOEHRING
Rivka GONEN
Edward W. GOODRICK
Stephen C. GORANSON
David F. GRAF
Samuel GREENGUS
Zvi GREENHUT
C. Wilfred GRIGGS
Dennis E. GROH
Joseph GUTMANN
Rachel HACHLILI
Judith M. HADLEY
J. Gordon HARRIS
Robert Laird HARRIS
Gerhard F. HASEL
Christian E. HAUER, Jr.
Charles W. HEDRICK
Holland L. HENDRIX
Robert C. HENRICKSON
Larry G. HERR
Ze'ev HERZOG
Brian C. HESSE
Ruth HESTRIN
Yizhar HIRSCHFELD
Kenneth G. HOGLUND
Robert L. HOHLFELDER
John S. HOLLADAY, Jr.
David C. HOPKINS
Leslie J. HOPPE

Siegfried H. HORN
Estella B. HORNING
Fred L. HORTON, Jr.
Stanley M. HORTON
Harry B. HUNT, Jr.
Patrick N. HUNT
A. Vanlier HUNTER
Frowald G. HUTTENMEISTER
Robert D. IBACH, Jr.
David ILAN
Samuel IWRY
Paul F. JACOBS
Ruth JACOBY
David W. JAMIESON-DRAKE
Albert J. JAMME
Clayton N. JEFFORD
Ferrell JENKINS
Richard N. JONES
Martha S. JOUKOWSKY
Walter C. KAISER, Jr.
Arvid S. KAPELRUD
Zdzislaw KAPERA
Vassos KARAGEORGHIS
Asher S. KAUFMAN
Howard Clark KEE
Othmar KEEL
George L. KELM
Aharon KEMPINSKI
Charles A. KENNEDY
Rami G. KHOURI
Ann E. KILLEBREW
S T KIMBROUGH, Jr.
Philip J. KING
Mordechai E. KISLEV
Kenneth A. KITCHEN
Naohiro KIYOSHIGE
Amos KLONER
Moshe KOCHAVI
Helmut KOESTER
Nikos KOKKINOS
Roy D. KOTANSKY
Frank L. KOUCKY
Alf T. KRAABEL
Edgar M. KRENTZ
Max B. KUECHLER
Oystein S. LA BIANCA
Peter LAMPE
George M. LANDES
Ernest-Marie LAPERROUSAZ
John C. H. LAUGHLIN
John I. LAWLOR
Gary L. LEASE
MaryJoan W. LEITH
André LEMAIRE
Niels P. LEMCHE
Lee I. A. LEVINE
Thomas E. LEVY
Arthur H. LEWIS
Jack P. LEWIS
Harold A. LIEBOWITZ
George H. LIVINGSTON
Thomas R. W. LONGSTAFF
Maurice S. LUKER, Jr.
John M. LUNDQUIST
Melvin K. LYONS
Leslie S. B. MACCOULL
Burton MACDONALD
Aren M. MAEIR
Izchak MAGEN
Menahem MAGEN
Jodi MAGNESS
David C. MALTSBERGER
Zvi 'Uri MA'OZ
William H. MARE
John MARSH
Ernest L. MARTIN
M. Pierce MATHENEY, Jr.
Philip MAYERSON
Amihai MAZAR
Benjamin MAZAR

Eilat MAZAR
P. Kyle MCCARTER, Jr.
Glenn W. MCCOY
Neil J. MCELENEY
Patrick E. MCGOVERN
Mary T. MCHATTEN
Robert K. MCIVER
Margaret M. MCKENNA
Larry E. MCKINNEY
John R. MCRAY
Stanislaw MEDALA
George E. MENDENHALL
Paul David MERLING
Ze'ev MESHEL
Yaakov MESHORER
Marvin W. MEYER
Carol L. MEYERS
Eric M. MEYERS
Alan Ralph MILLARD
Charles H. MILLER
J. Maxwell MILLER
Carey A. MOORE
P. R. S. MOOREY
James C. MOYER
James D. MUHLY
Kenneth V. MULL
Lukas M. MUNTINGH
Nadav NA'AMAN
Nira NAVEH
Avraham NEGEV
Ehud NETZER
Eugenia L. NITOWSKI
Robert NORTH
Kevin G. O'CONNELL
Eliezer D. OREN
Tallay ORNAN
Asher OVADIAH
David I. OWEN
H. Van Dyke PARUNAK
Joseph PATRICH
Birger A. PEARSON
Yehuda PELEG
Letizia PITIGLIANI
Virgil B. PIXNER
Daniel T. POTTS
Gary Davis PRATICO
James D. PURVIS
Avner RABAN
Anson F. RAINEY
Carl G. RASMUSSEN
Walter E. RAST
Paul J. RAY, Jr.
John REA
Donald B. REDFORD
Ronny REICH
Song N. RHEE
Kathleen M. RITMEYER
Leendert P. RITMEYER
C. Gilbert ROMERO
Arlene M. ROSEN
Steven A. ROSEN
Myriam ROSEN-AYALON
Beno ROTHENBERG
Ernest W. SAUNDERS
Torgny SAVE-SODERBERGH
Marilyn M. SCHAUB
R. Thomas SCHAUB
Denise SCHMANDT-BESSERAT
Harvey SCHNEIDER
Keith N. SCHOVILLE
Samuel J. SCHULTZ
Benedikt H. SCHWANK
Glenn M. SCHWARTZ
B. Elmo SCOGGIN
J. Julius SCOTT, Jr.
Joe D. SEGER
Hershel SHANKS
Thomas A. SHAVER
William H. SHEA
Malcolm W. SHELTON

Eli SHENHAV
Neil Asher SILBERMAN
Lawrence A. SINCLAIR
Suzanne F. SINGER
Elmer B. SMICK
Dennis E. SMITH
Philip E. L. SMITH
Robert H. SMITH
Graydon F. SNYDER
John R. SPENCER
Lawrence E. STAGER
Ephraim STERN
William H. STIEBING, Jr.
Robert R. STIEGLITZ
J. Björnar STORFJELL
James F. STRANGE
Yoshihide SUZUKI
James L. SWAUGER
Danny SYON
Lynn W. TATUM
J. Glen TAYLOR
Howard Merle TEEPLE
Henry O. THOMPSON
John A. THOMPSON
Stefan TIMM
Diane I. TREACY-COLE
John C. TREVER
Yoram TSAFRIR
Kathryn W. TUBB
George A. TURNER
Vassilios E. TZAFERIS
David USSISHKIN
Gerrit VAN DER KOOIJ
John VAN SETERS
Robert Lindley VANN
E. Jerry VARDAMAN
Kenneth L. VINE
Shelley WACHSMANN
Bruce K. WALTKE
Paula C. WAPNISH
Ewa C. WASILEWSKA
R. Bryan WIDBIN
David J. WIEAND
Jay G. WILLIAMS
John F. WILSON
Donald H. WIMMER
John D. WINELAND
Willard W. WINTER
Donald J. WISEMAN
Rolland Emerson WOLFE
Samuel R. WOLFE
Bryant G. WOOD
Richard A. WOOD
John E. WORRELL
T. John WRIGHT
Stephen V. WYRICK
Edwin M. YAMAUCHI
Ze'ev YEIVIN
Joseph YELLIN
John Y. H. YIEH
Ronald F. YOUNGBLOOD
Randall W. YOUNKER
Adam ZERTAL
Ziony ZEVIT
Joseph E. ZIAS
Paul E. ZIMANSKY
Mattanyah ZOHAR
Frederick T. ZUGIBE

HEBREW BIBLE

Martin G. ABEGG, Jr.
David T. ADAMO
Douglas G. ADAMS
William J. ADAMS, Jr.
Anneli P. M. AEJMELAEUS
Shmuel AHITUV
Robert L. ALDEN
Ralph H. ALEXANDER

Leslie C. ALLEN
Robert W. ALLISON
José ALONSO-DIAZ
Bernhard W. ANDERSON
Gary A. ANDERSON
George W. ANDERSON
Roger W. ANDERSON, Jr.
Maurice E. ANDREW
Gonzalo ARANDA PEREZ
Gary P. ARBINO
Gleason L. ARCHER, Jr.
Joseph R. ARMENTI
Carl E. ARMERDING
Bill T. ARNOLD
Timothy R. ASHLEY
Dewey F. ATKINSON
Walter E. AUFRECHT
Joseph M. AUNEAU
Hector I. AVALOS
D. Waylon BAILEY
Wilma Ann BAILEY
J. Arthur BAIRD
David W. BAKER
Samuel E. BALENTINE
Klaus BALTZER
Barry L. BANDSTRA
Robert J. BANKS
Kenneth L. BARKER
Hans M. BARSTAD
John R. BARTLETT
John BARTON
Bernard F. BATTO
Joseph M. BAUMGARTEN
Karel BAYER
Todd S. BEALL
Robert R. BECK
Dewey M. BEEGLE
Christopher T. BEGG
Barry J. BEITZEL
William H. BELLINGER, Jr.
Ehud BEN ZVI
Don C. BENJAMIN, Jr.
Dianne BERGANT
Kare BERGE
Robert D. BERGEN
Adele BERLIN
Bryan E. BEYER
Mark E. BIDDLE
Klaus BIEBERSTEIN
Neal BIERLING
John J. BIMSON
Avraham BIRAN
Bruce C. BIRCH
Phyllis A. BIRD
Matthew BLACK
Peter BLAESER
Edward P. BLAIR
Adrien Janis BLEDSTEIN
Joseph BLENKINSOPP
Daniel I. BLOCK
Lawrence E. BOADT
Walter R. BODINE
Robert G. BOLING
Oded BOROWSKI
A. Wendell BOWES
Paula J. BOWES
Steven J. BRAMS
S. Daniel BRESLAUER
Marc Z. BRETTLER
John BRIGHT
Louis A. BRIGHTON
Gershon A. BRIN
Thomas V. BRISCO
Thomas L. BRODIE
Harold BRODSKY
Leila L. BRONNER
George J. BROOKE
John P. BROWN
Harry M. BUCK
John M. BULLARD

Fred W. BURNETT
Martin J. BUSS
Clifford C. CAIN
Antony F. CAMPBELL
Edward F. CAMPBELL
David M. CARR
Robert P. CARROLL
Tony W. CARTLEDGE
Frank G. CARVER
Philip M. CASEY
Robert L. CATE
Henri CAZELLES
Anthony R. CERESKO
Jeffrey R. CHADWICK
Debra A. CHASE
Daniel CHAVEZ
Bruce D. CHILTON
Andrew M. J. CHIU
Jerzy CHMIEL
Duane L. CHRISTENSEN
Douglas R. CLARK
Ronald E. CLEMENTS
E. Ray CLENDENEN
David J. A. CLINES
George W. COATS
Mordechai COGAN
Chaim COHEN
Shaye J. D. COHEN
Robert L. COHN
R. Dennis COLE
John J. COLLINS
Oral E. COLLINS
Edgar W. CONRAD
Michael D. COOGAN
Robert B. COOTE
Michael R. COSBY
David W. COTTER
Robert A. COUGHENOUR
S. Peter COWE
Claude E. COX
Kenneth M. CRAIG, Jr.
James L. CRENSHAW
Jose S. CROATTO
Robert B. CROTTY
Alan D. CROWN
Adrian H. W. CURTIS
Stephanie M. DALLEY
Dwight R. DANIELS
Richard M. DAVIDSON
Graham I. DAVIES
John A. DAVIES
Philip R. DAVIES
Charles T. DAVIS
Ellen F. DAVIS
John J. DAVIS
John DAY
Peggy L. DAY
Simon J. DE VRIES
Jan DE WAARD
John A. DEARMAN
Walter W. G. DELLER
Stephen G. DEMPSTER
Aaron DEMSKY
Albert F. DEN EXTER BLOKLAND
Robert C. DENTAN
Michael P. DEROCHE
Alexander A. DI LELLA
Raymond B. DILLARD
Paul E. DION
Ralph W. DOERMANN
William R. DOMERIS
Louis O. DORN
David A. DORSEY
Jacques B. DOUKHAN
Israel DRAZIN
Michael W. DUGGAN
Patricia N. DUTCHER-WALLS
J. Kenneth EAKINS
James M. EFIRD
Carl S. EHRLICH

Barry L. EICHLER
Howard EILBERG-SCHWARTZ
Robert H. EISENMAN
Torleif ELGVIN
Mary Timothea ELLIOTT
Robert R. ELLIS
John C. ENDRES
James R. ENGLE
Donald M. ENGLERT
Svante Bernhard ERLING
Esther ESHEL
Lyle M. ESLINGER
Daniel J. ESTES
A. Joseph EVERSON
J. Cheryl EXUM
Kathleen A. FARMER
Steven E. FASSBERG
Natalio FERNANDEZ-MARCOS
Paul W. FERRIS, Jr.
Francis I. FESPERMAN
Weston W. FIELDS
Michael A. FISHBANE
Eugene J. FISHER
Henry J. FLANDERS, Jr.
Hubert L. FLESHER
Peter W. FLINT
Samuel D. FOHR
Georg FOHRER
Jan P. FOKKELMAN
Charles J. M. E. C. FONTINOY
A. Dean FORBES
Julia A. FOSTER
David M. FOUTS
Everett FOX
Michael V. FOX
Samuel J. FOX
Majella M. FRANZMANN
Daniel C. FREDERICKS
David Noel FREEDMAN
Ernest S. FRERICHS
Wendell W. FRERICHS
Terence E. FRETHEIM
Mark J. H. FRETZ
Richard Elliott FRIEDMAN
Volkmar O. FRITZ
Lawrence E. FRIZZELL
Stephen L. FUCHS
William J. FULCO
James H. GAILEY
Roy E. GANE
Paul L. GARBER
Zev GARBER
W. Randall GARR
Duane A. GARRETT
Moshe GARSIEL
Anthony GELSTON
Lawrence T. GERATY
Erhard S. GERSTENBERGER
George GIACUMAKIS, Jr.
Agustinus GIANTO
Ronald L. GIESE, Jr.
Maurice GILBERT
Yehoshua GITAY
Barry M. GITTLEN
Jerry A. GLADSON
Robert K. GNUSE
Jonathan A. GOLDSTEIN
Marian GOLEBIEWSKI
Charles GOODWIN
Stephen C. GORANSON
Isaac B. GOTTLIEB
Alfred GOTTSCHALK
Norman K. GOTTWALD
Donald E. GOWAN
Lester L. GRABBE
Douglas L. GRAGG
Arthur F. GRAUDIN
Ronald M. GREEN
Moshe GREENBERG
Samuel GREENGUS

Frederick E. GREENSPAHN
Leonard J. GREENSPOON
Edward GREENSTEIN
Pierre GRELOT
Kenneth R. R. GROS LOUIS
Walter GROSS
Daniel GROSSBERG
Mayer I. GRUBER
Michael D. GUINAN
David M. GUNN
Joseph GUTMANN
Klaus B. HAACKER
Herbert HAAG
Robert D. HAAK
Norman C. HABEL
Judith M. HADLEY
Hallvard HAGELIA
Suzanne HAIK-VANTOURA
Baruch HALPERN
E. John HAMLIN
Lowell K. HANDY
Paul D. HANSON
Menahem HARAN
Philip B. HARNER
Walter HARRELSON
Daniel J. HARRINGTON
J. Gordon HARRIS
Robert Laird HARRIS
John E. HARTLEY
David F. HARTZFELD
Gerhard F. HASEL
Christian E. HAUER, Jr.
Alan J. HAUSER
Roy E. HAYDEN
Christine E. HAYES
John H. HAYES
Boo HEFLIN
Timothy J. HEGG
George C. HEIDER
Michael HELTZER
Ronald S. HENDEL
Georg HENTSCHEL
Gary A. HERION
Richard S. HESS
John B. HIBBITTS
Sten L. HIDAL
Robert J. V. HIEBERT
Theodore HIEBERT
Trevor R. HOBBS
Harry A. HOFFNER, Jr.
Kenneth G. HOGLUND
William L. HOLLADAY
Fredrick C. HOLMGREN
Martin J. HOMAN
Joseph HOMERSKI
David C. HOPKINS
Leslie J. HOPPE
Malcolm J. A. HORSNELL
Stanley M. HORTON
Harold E. HOSCH
Benjamin J. HUBBARD
David A. HUBBARD
Robert L. HUBBARD
John R. HUDDLESTUN
F. B. HUEY, Jr.
Gordon P. HUGENBERGER
Harry B. HUNT, Jr.
A. Vanlier HUNTER
Victor B. HUROWITZ
Avi HURVITZ
Robert D. IBACH, Jr.
Rebecca G. S. IDESTROM
Karl-Johan ILLMAN
Stuart A. IRVINE
Tomoo ISHIDA
Samuel IWRY
Kent P. JACKSON
Paul F. JACOBS
David W. JAMIESON-DRAKE
Benedict F. JANECKO

Nathan R. JASTRAM
Allan K. JENKINS
Gregory C. JENKS
Joseph N. JENSEN
Knud O. JEPPESEN
Jacob Stephan JERVELL
Karen H. JOBES
Bo E. JOHNSON
R. Francis JOHNSON
Brian C. JONES
Bruce W. JONES
Gregory D. JORDAN
Yeong-Heum JYOO
Menahem Z. KADDARI
Walter C. KAISER, Jr.
Isaac KALIMI
Paul KALLUVEETIL
Arvid S. KAPELRUD
Asher S. KAUFMAN
Stephen A. KAUFMAN
Peter J. KEARNEY
Benjamin E. KEDAR-KOPFSTEIN
Othmar KEEL
Charles A. KENNEDY
Dan G. KENT
Gerald L. KEOWN
John KHANJIAN
Erich H. KIEHL
Isaac M. KIKAWADA
Ee Kon KIM
S T KIMBROUGH, Jr.
Hiroshi KIMURA
Philip J. KING
Mordechai E. KISLEV
Kenneth A. KITCHEN
Naohiro KIYOSHIGE
Natan KLAUS
Michael L. KLEIN
Ralph W. KLEIN
Douglas A. KNIGHT
George A. F. KNIGHT
Frederick W. KNOBLOCH
John R. KOHLENBERGER III
Michael F. KOLARCIK
John S. KSELMAN
Jeffrey K. KUAN
George KUFELDT
James L. KUGEL
J. Kenneth KUNTZ
Raymond KUNTZMANN
Antti J. LAATO
Leo LABERGE
Jan LACH
Andre LACOCQUE
Alice L. LAFFEY
James LAGRAND
George M. LANDES
John C. H. LAUGHLIN
Archie Chi Chung LEE
Jong Keun LEE
Martin W. LEESEBERG
Israel Otto LEHMAN
Manfred R. LEHMANN
MaryJoan W. LEITH
André LEMAIRE
Niels P. LEMCHE
Werner E. LEMKE
Adrian M. LESKE
Jon D. LEVENSON
Saul LEVIN
Amy-Jill LEVINE
Bernard M. LEVINSON
Arthur H. LEWIS
Jack P. LEWIS
Joe O. LEWIS
Theodore J. LEWIS
Stephen J. LIEBERMAN
Harold A. LIEBOWITZ
Betty Jane LILLIE
Timothy H. LIM

James W. LIMBURG
Edouard LIPINSKI
George H. LIVINGSTON
Norbert F. LOHFINK
Burke O. LONG
Robert E. LONGACRE
Francisco LOPEZ RIVERA
Alex T. LUC
Maurice S. LUKER, Jr.
Jerome A. LUND
Jack R. LUNDBOM
Johan LUST
Kenneth H. MAAHS
Burton MACDONALD
Jean MAGNE
John R. MAIER
Walter A. MAIER III
Abraham MALAMAT
Bruce V. MALCHOW
Hans-H. MALLAU
Sara R. S. MANDELL
Menahem MANSOOR
Yeshayahu MAORI
W. Eugene MARCH
David MARCUS
Claude F. MARIOTTINI
Herbert J. MARKS
Walter C. MARLOWE
Rick R. MARRS
John MARSH
Robert J. MARSHALL
Elmer A. MARTENS
Ernest R. MARTINEZ
Nils O. MARTOLA
Angel MARZAL
M. Pierce MATHENEY, Jr.
Victor H. MATTHEWS
Gordon H. MATTIES
Andrew D. MAYES
J. Clinton MCCANN, Jr.
P. Kyle MCCARTER, Jr.
Thomas E. MCCOMISKEY
James G. MCCONVILLE
Thomas P. MCCREESH
Thomas F. MCDANIEL
Neil J. MCELENEY
Sean E. MCEVENUE
Gerald E. MCGRAW
Mary T. MCHATTEN
Robert K. MCIVER
Heather A. MCKAY
Margaret M. MCKENNA
Steven L. MCKENZIE
Larry E. MCKINNEY
Mark D. MCLEAN
Phillip E. MCMILLION
Martin J. MCNAMARA
Warren L. MCWILLIAMS
Tirzah Yoreh MEACHAM
Samuel A. MEIER III
George E. MENDENHALL
Dan MERKUR
Paul David MERLING
Arthur L. MERRILL
Eugene H. MERRILL
Tryggve N. D. METTINGER
Carol L. MEYERS
G. Tom E. J. MILAZZO
Jacob MILGROM
J. T. MILIK
Alan Ralph MILLARD
Charles H. MILLER
J. Maxwell MILLER
James E. MILLER
John W. MILLER
Patrick D. MILLER
Pamela J. MILNE
Caetano MINETTE DE TILLESSE
Harvey MINKOFF
Christopher W. MITCHELL

Walter R. W. L. MOBERLY
David P. MOESSNER
Carey A. MOORE
Rick D. MOORE
Shelomo MORAG
Donn F. MORGAN
Nobuko MORIMURA
Paul G. MOSCA
James C. MOYER
Martin J. MULDER
Everett T. MULLEN, Jr.
Lukas M. MUNTINGH
Roland E. MURPHY
Donald F. MURRAY
Robert P. R. MURRAY
Nadav NA'AMAN
Peter J. NAYLOR
Gerhard-Wilhelm NEBE
Philip J. NEL
Richard D. NELSON
Jacob NEUSNER
Edward G. NEWING
Carol NEWSOM
George G. NICOL
Frederick A. NIEDNER
Maren NIEHOFF
Kirsten NIELSEN
Solomon A. NIGOSIAN
Scott K. NIKAIDO
Brian M. NOLAN
Robert NORTH
Gerard J. NORTON
Julia M. O'BRIEN
Peter W. OCHS
Kevin G. O'CONNELL
Robert H. O'CONNELL
Michael Patrick O'CONNOR
Margaret S. ODELL
Robert A. ODEN, Jr.
Graham S. OGDEN
John W. OLLEY
Dennis T. OLSON
Martin J. OOSTHUIZEN
Noel D. OSBORN
John N. OSWALT
Magnus Y. OTTOSSON
Benedikt OTZEN
Robert J. OWENS, Jr.
Mitchell C. PACWA
Samuel PAGAN
Randall J. PANNELL
Geoffrey H. PARKE-TAYLOR
Donald W. PARRY
H. Van Dyke PARUNAK
Dale A. PATRICK
Richard D. PATTERSON
Maarten J. PAUL
Shalom M. PAUL
J. Brian PECKHAM
Claude J. PEIFER
David PENCHANSKY
Hayim G. PERELMUTER
René PETER-CONTESSE
David L. PETERSEN
Anthony J. PETROTTA
Philip H. PFATTEICHER
Anthony C. J. PHILLIPS
Dana M. PIKE
Stephen F. PISANO
Wayne T. PITARD
George V. PIXLEY
W. Gunther PLAUT
Max E. POLLEY
Marvin H. POPE
Joshua R. PORTER
R. Ferdinand POSWICK
Gary Davis PRATICO
Gian-Luigi PRATO
Devadasan N. PREMNATH
Willem S. PRINSLOO

William H. PROPP
Iain W. PROVAN
Reinhard PUMMER
James D. PURVIS
Kandy M. QUEEN-SUTHERLAND
Paul R. RAABE
Yehuda T. RADDAY
Anson F. RAINEY
George W. RAMSEY
Ilona N. RASHKOW
Carl G. RASMUSSEN
Walter E. RAST
Susan RATTRAY
Paul J. RAY, Jr.
John REA
Paul L. REDDITT
John C. REEVES
Daniel G. REID
Stefan C. REIF
Gary A. RENDSBURG
Rolf RENDTORFF
Stephen D. RENN
E. John REVELL
R. Blair REYNOLDS
Song N. RHEE
Josep RIBERA-FLORIT
Gene RICE
Kent H. RICHARDS
Hans F. RICHTER
Stephen D. RICKS
Thomas E. RIDENHOUR
Alexander ROFE
John W. ROFFEY
Cleon L. ROGERS, Jr.
Max G. ROGERS
Robert G. ROGERS
Wayne G. ROLLINS
C. Gilbert ROMERO
Mark F. ROOKER
Eugene F. ROOP
Jonathan ROSENBAUM
Joel W. ROSENBERG
Roy A. ROSENBERG
James ROSS
Henry L. ROWOLD
Jean-Pierre M. RUIZ
Leona G. RUNNING
John E. RYBOLT
Leopold SABOURIN
Jonathan D. SAFREN
James L. SAGARIN
Katherine Doob SAKENFELD
James A. SANDERS
Judith E. SANDERSON
Nahum M. SARNA
Jack M. SASSON
Marilyn M. SCHAUB
Donald G. SCHLEY
John J. SCHMITT
Harvey SCHNEIDER
Keith N. SCHOVILLE
Paul L. SCHRIEBER
Eileen M. SCHULLER
Carl SCHULTZ
Baruch J. SCHWARTZ
B. Elmo SCOGGIN
Alan F. SEGAL
Joe D. SEGER
Stanislav SEGERT
Hans E. SEIDEL
August H. SEUBERT
Klaus D. SEYBOLD
Byron E. SHAFER
Donald B. SHARP
Judson R. SHAVER
William H. SHEA
Rodney H. SHEARER
Byron L. SHERWIN
Sandra R. SHIMOFF
Lou H. SILBERMAN

Moisés SILVA
Morris SILVER
Horacio SIMIAN-YOFRE
Lawrence A. SINCLAIR
Joel C. SLAYTON
Rudolf SMEND
Elmer B. SMICK
Clyde Curry SMITH
Daniel C. SNELL
Barbara W. SNYDER
Daud H. SOESILO
Seock-Tae SOHN
Rifat SONSINO
John R. SPENCER
Frank A. SPINA
Joe M. SPRINKLE
William P. STEEGER
Hartmut STEGEMANN
Andrew E. STEINMANN
David M. STERN
William H. STIEBING, Jr.
Robert R. STIEGLITZ
J. Björnar STORFJELL
Cullen I. K. STORY
Dennis C. STOUTENBURG
John STRUGNELL
Andrzej STRUS
Carroll STUHLMUELLER
Louis STULMAN
Raymond F. SURBURG
Yoshihide SUZUKI
Marvin A. SWEENEY
Dennis D. SYLVA
Roger J. B. SYREN
Miguel Angel TABET-BALADY
Shemaryahu TALMON
Marvin E. TATE
Lynn W. TATUM
Arch B. TAYLOR, Jr.
J. Glen TAYLOR
Marion A. TAYLOR
Savina J. TEUBAL
Paul THEOPHILUS
Henry O. THOMPSON
John A. THOMPSON
Yaakov THOMPSON
Thorir Kr. THORDARSON
Mark A. THRONTVEIT
Jeffrey H. TIGAY
Everett TILSON
Stefan TIMM
Philip N. TINDALL
Emanuel TOV
Julio C. TREBOLLE
John C. TREVER
Phyllis TRIBLE
Arie C. TROOST
L. Paul TRUDINGER
Meishi TSAI
Matitiahu TSEVAT
David Toshio TSUMURA
Steven S. TUELL
John H. TULLOCK
Eugene C. ULRICH
William J. URBROCK
Cornelis VAN DAM
Karel VAN DER TOORN
Christiana VAN HOUTEN
Raymond C. VAN LEEUWEN
Harry F. VAN ROOY
John VAN SETERS
Ellen J. VAN WOLDE
Robert P. VANDE KAPPELLE
James C. VANDERKAM
J. Robert VANNOY
Shmuel VARGON
Ronald A. VEENKER
Geza VERMES
Kenneth L. VINE
Pauline A. VIVIANO

Walter A. VOGELS
Nancy Jean VYHMEISTER
Howard N. WALLACE
Jerome T. WALSH
Bruce K. WALTKE
John H. WALTON
Roy Bowen WARD
David L. WASHBURN
James W. WATTS
John D. W. WATTS
Beat WEBER
Moshe WEINFELD
Earl A. WEIS
John W. WELCH
Gordon J. WENHAM
Herbert S. WENTZ
Raymond WESTBROOK
Claus WESTERMANN
John H. WHEELER
J. Benton WHITE
John Bradley WHITE
Leland J. WHITE
Marsha C. WHITE
Brady B. WHITEHEAD
William D. WHITT
R. Norman WHYBRAY
R. Bryan WIDBIN
Geo WIDENGREN
Walter R. WIFALL, Jr.
Aaron WILDAVSKY
John Keating WILES
Jay G. WILLIAMS
William C. WILLIAMS
Bruce E. WILLOUGHBY
John W. WILSON
Marvin R. WILSON
Robert R. WILSON
Donald H. WIMMER
Willard W. WINTER
Donald J. WISEMAN
Rolland Emerson WOLFE
Albert M. WOLTERS
Richard A. WOOD
John E. WORGUL
Addison G. WRIGHT
Benjamin G. WRIGHT
David P. WRIGHT
Robert B. WRIGHT
T. John WRIGHT
Stephen V. WYRICK
Tadanori YAMASHITA
Edwin M. YAMAUCHI
Gale A. YEE
Dwight Wayne YOUNG
Fred E. YOUNG
William A. YOUNG
Ronald F. YOUNGBLOOD
K. Lawson YOUNGER, Jr.
Randall W. YOUNKER
Ziony ZEVIT
Frank ZIMMERMANN
Walter D. ZORN
Rochus ZUURMOND

NEW TESTAMENT

James W. AAGESON
Valerie A. ABRAHAMSEN
James ACKERMAN
Andrew K. M. ADAM
Douglas G. ADAMS
James B. ADAMSON
Lars J. T. AEJMELAEUS
Rafael AGUIRRE
Larry J. ALDERINK
Patrick H. ALEXANDER
Dale C. ALLISON
Robert W. ALLISON
José ALONSO-DIAZ
John E. ALSUP

Thomas J. J. ALTIZER
Hugh ANDERSON
Janice Capel ANDERSON
Julian G. ANDERSON
Franz ANNEN
Diane APOSTOLOS-CAPPADONA
Sasagu ARAI
Gonzalo ARANDA PEREZ
Gleason L. ARCHER, Jr.
Eduardo F. ARENS
Harold W. ATTRIDGE
David E. AUNE
Roger D. AUS
Kenneth E. BAILEY
Robert E. BAILEY
J. Arthur BAIRD
William R. BAIRD
David L. BALCH
Horst BALZ
Robert J. BANKS
Joe Edward BARNHART
David L. BARR
C. Kingsley BARRETT
J. Edward BARRETT
S. Scott BARTCHY
Gerhard BARTH
Markus K. BARTH
John R. BARTLETT
Roman BARTNICKI
Stephen C. BARTON
Richard A. BATEY
Richard J. BAUCKHAM
David R. BAUER
Norbert BAUMERT
Karel BAYER
Alan J. BEAGLEY
George R. BEASLEY-MURRAY
Pier Franco BEATRICE
MaryAnn L. BEAVIS
Robert R. BECK
Francis J. BECKWITH
V. Gilbert BEERS
Per Jarle BEKKEN
Arthur J. BELLINZONI
Don C. BENJAMIN, Jr.
Stephen BENKO
Roland BERGMEIER
Ernest BEST
Hans D. BETZ
Otto W. BETZ
Johannes H. BEUTLER
Reimund BIERINGER
Neal BIERLING
Hermann F. BINDER
Claude M. E. BIOSMARD
J. Neville BIRDSALL
C. Clifton BLACK
David Alan BLACK
Matthew BLACK
Peter BLAESER
Edward P. BLAIR
James L. BLEVINS
Craig L. BLOMBERG
Gabriele BOCCACCINI
Darrell L. BOCK
Otto BOECHER
Plutarco BONILLA-ACOSTA
Thomas E. BOOMERSHINE
Gerald L. BORCHERT
Marcus J. BORG
Peder J. BORGEN
M. Eugene BORING
Irvin J. BOROWSKY
Frederick H. BORSCH
Edgar W. BOSS
Francois BOVON
Rudolf BRAENDLE
James A. BRASHLER
Robert G. BRATCHER
Robert L. BRAWLEY

H. Alan BREHM
Louis A. BRIGHTON
Thomas L. BRODIE
Ingo BROER
George J. BROOKE
Oscar S. BROOKS
Edwin C. BROOME, Jr.
Bernadette J. BROOTEN
Kent E. BROWER
Cheryl A. BROWN
Colin BROWN
John P. BROWN
Milton P. BROWN
Raymond E. BROWN
Schuyler BROWN
James V. BROWNSON
George W. BUCHANAN
Erwin BUCK
Harry M. BUCK
Thomas W. BUCKLEY
John M. BULLARD
Harold H. BULS
Gary M. BURGE
Delbert R. BURKETT
Fred W. BURNETT
Brendan J. BYRNE
P. Joseph CAHILL
Clifford C. CAIN
Terrance D. CALLAN
Ron CAMERON
David B. CAPES
Chrys C. CARAGOUNIS
Muriel M. CARDER
David M. CARR
George P. CARRAS
Warren C. CARTER
Frank G. CARVER
Anthony CASURELLA
David R. CATCHPOLE
Robert L. CATE
Thomas S. CAULLEY
Hans C. C. CAVALLIN
Jeffrey R. CHADWICK
J. Daryl CHARLES
James H. CHARLESWORTH
Daniel CHAVEZ
Bruce D. CHILTON
Jerzy CHMIEL
Settimio CIPRIANI
Gareth L. COCKERILL
Johannes Christiaan COETZEE
Gary D. COLLIER
Adela Y. COLLINS
Oral E. COLLINS
Raymond F. COLLINS
Hans J. B. COMBRINK
Francis D. CONNOLLY-WEINERT
Gail P. CORRINGTON
Bruno CORSANI
Michael R. COSBY
Charles H. COSGROVE
Edouard COTHENET
Claude COULOT
L. William COUNTRYMAN
John M. COURT
William L. CRAIG
Charles E. B. CRANFIELD
Robert B. CROTTY
Oscar CULLMANN
R. Alan CULPEPPER
John R. CUSTIS, Jr.
John V. DAHMS
William J. DALTON
Giuseppe DANIELI
Frederick W. DANKER
John A. DARR
John S. DART
Peter H. DAVIDS
Charles T. DAVIS
James A. DAVIS

James M. DAWSEY
Henk J. DE JONGE
Theo C. DE KRUIJF
Roy C. DE LAMOTTE
Pieter G. R. DE VILLIERS
Jan DE WAARD
Donald S. DEER
Agustin DEL AGUA
Jean DELORME
Willoughby H. DEMING
William D. DENNISON
John D. M. DERRETT
Charles C. DICKINSON III
William R. DOMERIS
Terence L. DONALDSON
Karl P. DONFRIED
Detlev DORMEYER
Loretta DORNISCH
William G. DOTY
Sharyn E. DOWD
B. Rod DOYLE
John W. DRANE
Richard H. DRUMMOND
Andries B. DU TOIT
Dennis C. DULING
Marcel DUMAIS
Demetrius R. DUMM
James W. DUNKLY
James D. G. DUNN
Walter M. DUNNETT
Kendell H. EASLEY
Kermit A. ECKLEBARGER
Elly H. ECONOMOU
Douglas R. EDWARDS
James R. EDWARDS
Richard A. EDWARDS
Sarah A. EDWARDS
James M. EFIRD
Robert H. EISENMAN
J. Harold ELLENS
J. Keith ELLIOTT
Mary Timothea ELLIOTT
E. Earle ELLIS
Troels ENGBERG-PEDERSEN
S. Ifor ENOCH
Eldon J. EPP
Richard J. ERICKSON
Lewis J. ERON
Bernardo ESTRADA
Craig A. EVANS
A. Joseph EVERSON
Rinaldo FABRIS
Mark R. FAIRCHILD
Terry C. FALLA
William R. FARMER
Hobert K. FARRELL
Stephen C. FARRIS
Gregory L. FAY
Gordon D. FEE
Helmut FELD
John C. FENTON
Wm. Everett FERGUSON
Francis I. FESPERMAN
Peter FIEDLER
David A. FIENSY
Jack FINEGAN
Benjamin FIORE
Eugene J. FISHER
Alger M. FITCH
John T. FITZGERALD, Jr.
Joseph A. FITZMYER
Henry J. FLANDERS, Jr.
James W. FLEMING
Hubert L. FLESHER
Camille L. A. G. FOCANT
J. Terence FORESTELL
Tord FORNBERG
Jarl E. FOSSUM
David M. FOUTS
David C. FOWLER

Robert M. FOWLER
Daniel J. FRAIKIN
Richard T. FRANCE
Hubert FRANKEMOELLE
David T. M. FRANKFURTER
Janusz FRANKOWSKI
Majella M. FRANZMANN
Paula FREDRIKSEN
Edwin D. FREED
Arthur J. FREEMAN
Steven J. FRIESEN
Lawrence E. FRIZZELL
Albert FUCHS
Reginald H. FULLER
Robert W. FUNK
Wolf-Peter Paul FUNK
Victor Paul FURNISH
Vittorio FUSCO
George A. GALITIS
Paul L. GARBER
Antonio GARCIA-MORENO
Paul GARNET
W. Ward GASQUE
Beverly R. GAVENTA
Olivette GENEST
Dautzenberg H. GERHARD
Birger GERHARDSSON
George GIACUMAKIS, Jr.
James M. GIBBS
John G. GIBBS
Florence M. GILLMAN
John L. GILLMAN
F. Wilbur GINGRICH
Mark E. GLASSWELL
W. Edward GLENNY
James E. GOEHRING
Paul W. GOOCH
Deirdre J. GOOD
Edward W. GOODRICK
Charles GOODWIN
Stephen C. GORANSON
Victor R. GORDON
Michel GOURGUES
David B. GOWLER
Douglas L. GRAGG
John D. GRASSMICK
Arthur F. GRAUDIN
Prospero GRECH
H. Benedict GREEN
Michael D. GREENE
Pierre GRELOT
C. Wilfred GRIGGS
Robert G. GROMACKI
Kenneth R. R. GROS LOUIS
Klaus B. HAACKER
Donald A. HAGNER
Roger L. HAHN
Robert G. HALL
Stuart G. HALL
M. Dennis HAMM
Karel HANHART
Philip B. HARNER
Daniel J. HARRINGTON
Roy A. HARRISVILLE III
Clayton K. HARROP
Patrick J. HARTIN
Lars O. HARTMAN
Van A. HARVEY
David J. HAWKIN
Paul Toshihiko HAYAMI
Richard B. HAYS
Charles W. HEDRICK
Timothy J. HEGG
Ronald E. HEINE
Susanne L. HEINE
Herman N. HENDRICKX
Holland L. HENDRIX
Carl F. H. HENRY
Jozef M. HERIBAN
William R. HERZOG II

Catherine HEZSER
John B. HIBBITTS
D. Edmond HIEBERT
Richard H. HIERS
Glenn O. HILBURN
Earle HILGERT
Charles E. HILL
Craig C. HILL
David HILL
Julian V. HILLS
Verlin O. HINSHAW
Toshio HIRUNUMA
Robert HODGSON, Jr.
Harold W. HOEHNER
Robert G. HOERBER
Paul HOFFMANN
Frayda D. HOFFNUNG
Otto Friedrich HOFIUS
Peter L. HOFRICHTER
Glenn S. HOLLAND
Harm W. HOLLANDER
J. Warren HOLLERAN
Charles L. HOLMAN
Bengt V. HOLMBERG
Michael W. HOLMES
Traugott HOLTZ
Morna D. HOOKER
Herlin H. HOOPS
Roy W. HOOVER
Rudolf HOPPE
Estella B. HORNING
Richard A. HORSLEY
Fred L. HORTON, Jr.
Stanley M. HORTON
James Leslie HOULDEN
George E. HOWARD
Tracy L. HOWARD
Benjamin J. HUBBARD
Frank W. HUGHES
John J. HUGHES
Paul A. HUGHES
William Edward HULL
Arland J. HULTGREN
Lawrence F. HUNDERSMARCK
Patrick N. HUNT
John C. HURD
Larry W. HURTADO
Pauli Taisto HUUHTANEN
Niels HYLDAHL
Bastiaan M. F. VAN IERSEL
Marie E. ISAACS
Lambert D. JACOBS
Arland D. JACOBSON
Augustyn B. JANKOWSKI
Clayton N. JEFFORD
Ferrell JENKINS
Gregory C. JENKS
Louis B. JENNINGS
Jacob Stephan JERVELL
L. Ann JERVIS
Robert JEWETT
Christie A. JOACHIM PILLAI
Karen H. JOBES
Alfred M. JOHNSON, Jr.
E. Elizabeth JOHNSON
Marshall D. JOHNSON
William G. JOHNSSON
George JOHNSTON
Robert M. JOHNSTON
Donald L. JONES
F. Stanley JONES
Giorgio JOSSA
Klaus K. M. JUNACK
Yeong-Heum JYOO
John I. KAMPEN
Robert J. KARRIS
Akinori KAWAMURA
Naymond H. KEATHLEY
Leander E. KECK
Howard Clark KEE

Craig S. KEENER
Frederic R. KELLOGG
Charles A. KENNEDY
Reggie M. KIDD
René J. J. KIEFFER
Erich H. KIEHL
Jarmo V. KIILUNEN
Mark C. KILEY
Donald M. KINDER
Walter KIRCHSCHLAGER
Oliver M. KIRKEBY
William KLASSEN
William W. KLEIN
Otto B. KNOCH
Nobuo KOBAYASHI
Dietrich-Alex G. KOCH
Jerome KODELL
Craig R. KOESTER
Helmut KOESTER
Nikos KOKKINOS
Judette Marie KOLASNY
Anitra Bingham KOLENKOW
Roy D. KOTANSKY
Judith L. KOVACS
Alf T. KRAABEL
Ross S. KRAEMER
Jacob KREMER
Edgar M. KRENTZ
Robert L. KRESS
Sakae KUBO
Max B. KUECHLER
Werner G. KUMMEL
Hans KUNG
Jan LACH
James LAGRAND
Peter LAMPE
Michael S. LATTKE
Eugene A. LAVERDIERE
Sophie S. LAWS
Fred D. LAYMAN
Bentley LAYTON
Donn A. LEACH
Alfred R. C. LEANEY
Dorothy A. LEE
Martin H. G. LEHMANN-
HABECK
André LEMAIRE
Xavier LEON-DUFOUR
Adrian M. LESKE
Theodore P. LETIS
David B. LEVENSON
Saul LEVIN
Amy-Jill LEVINE
John R. LEVISON
Arthur H. LEWIS
Jack P. LEWIS
Paul S. H. LIAO
Judith M. LIEU
Betty Jane LILLIE
Timothy H. LIM
Andrew T. LINCOLN
Millard C. LIND
Andreas LINDEMANN
Wilhelm C. LINSS
Henrik LJUNGMAN
William R. G. LOADER
Gebhard LOEHR
I-Jin LOH
Richard N. LONGENECKER
Thomas R. W. LONGSTAFF
Johannes A. LOUBSER
O. Evald LOVESTAM
William L. LUDLOW
Dieter H. LUEHRMANN
David J. LULL
Jack R. LUNDBOM
Edmondo F. LUPIERI
Gerard P. LUTTIKHUIZEN
George L. LYONS
Kenneth H. MAAHS

Dennis R. MACDONALD
Margaret Y. MACDONALD
Geddes MACGREGOR
R. Sheldon MACKENZIE
Peter W. MACKY
Jean MAGNE
J. Lee MAGNESS
John R. MAIER
Edward J. MALATESTA
Abraham J. MALHERBE
Elliott C. MALONEY
Linda M. MALONEY
Christopher S. MANN
William H. MARE
Jean-Claude MARGOT
Daniel L. MARGUERAT
Claude F. MARIOTTINI
Antti MARJANEN
Stanley B. MARROW
I. Howard MARSHALL
John W. MARTENS
Clarice J. MARTIN
Ernest L. MARTIN
Ralph P. MARTIN
Ernest R. MARTINEZ
Corrado MARUCCI
John P. MASON
Steve N. MASON
Kikup MATSUNAGA
Andrew J. MATTILL, Jr.
Ulrich W. MAUSER
Arthur H. MAYNARD
Pedrito U. MAYNARD-REID
John S. MBITI
Harvey K. MCARTHUR
Byron R. MCCANE
J. Clinton MCCANN, Jr.
Dan G. MCCARTNEY
Daniel L. MCCONAUGHY
Glenn W. MCCOY
Gerald W. MCCULLOH
John C. MCCULLOUGH
James I. H. MCDONALD
Lee M. MCDONALD
Neil J. MCELENEY
Lane C. MCGAUGHY
Gerald E. MCGRAW
Mary T. MCHATTEN
John F. MCHUGH
Robert K. MCIVER
Heather A. MCKAY
Margaret M. MCKENNA
Larry E. MCKINNEY
Edgar V. MCKNIGHT
Bradley H. MCLEAN
Ray MCMANAMAN
Martin J. MCNAMARA
John R. MCRAY
Warren L. MCWILLIAMS
David G. MEADE
David L. MEALAND
Stanislaw MEDALA
Wayne A. MEEKS
James J. MEGIVERN
John P. MEIER
Manfred O. MEITZEN
George F. MELICK, Jr.
Richard R. MELICK, Jr.
Maarten J. J. MENKEN
Calvin R. MERCER, Jr.
Helmut M. MERKLEIN
Bruce M. METZGER
Ben F. MEYER
Marvin W. MEYER
J. Ramsey MICHAELS
Stephen F. MILETIC
Donald G. MILLER
Eddie L. MILLER
John W. MILLER
Paul S. MINEAR

Caetano MINETTE DE TILLESSE
Paul A. MIRECKI
Alan C. MITCHELL
Aldo MODA
David P. MOESSNER
Ian A. MOIR
Francis J. MOLONEY
Hugh W. MONTEFIORE
Douglas J. MOO
Robert R. MOORE
Stephen D. MOORE
Robert C. MORGAN
William G. MORRICE
Leon L. MORRIS
William G. MOST
Stephen Charles MOTT
Charles F. D. MOULE
Robert L. MOWERY
Halvor MOXNES
James R. MUELLER
John J. MUELLER
Mogens MUELLER
Paul-Gerhard MUELLER
M. Robert MULHOLLAND, Jr.
Earl C. MULLER
Terence Y. MULLINS
Domingo MUNOZ LEON
Winsome MUNRO
Frederick J. MURPHY
Jerome J. MURPHY-O'CONNOR
Robert P. R. MURRAY
Matti MYLLYKOSKI
André MYRE
Takeshi NAGATA
Peter J. NAYLOR
Gerhard-Wilhelm NEBE
Gottfried NEBE
Jacob NEEDLEMAN
Avraham NEGEV
Kenneth V. NELLER
Peter K. NELSON
Edmund K. NEUFELD
Fritz NEUGEBAUER
Kenneth J. NEUMANN
Carey C. NEWMAN
Robert G. NEWMAN
Jerome H. NEYREY
George W. E. NICKELSBURG
Keith F. NICKLE
Kurt NIEDERWIMMER
Frederick A. NIEDNER
Helge K. NIELSEN
Eugenia L. NITOWSKY
Brian M. NOLAN
John L. NOLLAND
John G. NORDLING
Douglas E. OAKMAN
Margaret S. ODELL
Gerbern S. OEGEMA
Thomas H. OLBRICHT
Howard S. OLSON
Birger O. OLSSON
Roger L. OMANSON
John C. O'NEILL
Takashi ONUKI
Dom J. Bernard ORCHARD
Grant R. OSBORNE
Carroll D. OSBURN
Carolyn A. OSIEK
Robert F. O'TOOLE
Samuel PAGAN
Sydney H. T. PAGE
John PAINTER
Daniel L. PALS
Salvatore PANIMOLLE
George C. PAPADEMETRIOU
David C. PARKER
Pierson PARKER
H. Van Dyke PARUNAK
Federico PASTOR-RAMOS

Joseph PATHRAPANKAL
Bebe Rebecca PATTEN
Stephen J. PATTERSON
Jon PAULIEN
Philip B. PAYNE
Birger A. PEARSON
Claude J. PEIFER
James R. C. PERKIN
Pheme PERKINS
Mauro PESCE
Rudolf PESCH
Norman R. PETERSEN
William L. PETERSEN
Jacobus H. PETZER
Joseph N. PFAMMATTER
Philip H. PFATTEICHER
Victor C. PFITZNER
Lindsey P. PHERIGO
William E. PHIPPS
John J. PILCH
Antonio PINERO
Ronald A. PIPER
Virgil B. PIXNER
Eckhard PLUEMACHER
Petr POKORNY
Wiard U. POPKES
Stanley E. PORTER
R. Ferdinand POSWICK
Donald R. POTTS
Wilhelm PRATSCHER
W. Russell PREGEANT
Terrence PRENDERGAST
Emil A. C. PRETORIUS
James L. PRICE, Jr.
John W. PRYOR
Benno PRZYBYLSKI
Charles B. PUSKAS
Kevin B. QUAST
Michel QUESNEL
Rosemary RADER
Walter RADL
Heikki M. RAISANEN
Timothy J. RALSTON
Emilio RASCO
Mary T. RATTIGAN
Mitchell G. REDDISH
Jeffrey T. REED
Daniel G. REID
John K. S. REID
Harold E. REMUS
James L. RESSEGUIE
John P. REUMANN
David M. RHOADS
Erroll F. RHODES
Earl J. RICHARD
Peter RICHARDSON
John K. RICHES
Hans F. RICHTER
Wille H. J. RIEKKINEN
Mathias RISSI
Vernon K. ROBBINS
James M. ROBINSON
Stephen E. ROBINSON
Gérard G. R. ROCHAIS
Cleon L. ROGERS, Jr.
Robert G. ROGERS
Joachim W. A. ROHDE
Richard L. ROHRBAUGH
Philippe ROLLAND
Wayne G. ROLLINS
John T. ROOK
Roy A. ROSENBERG
Marie-Eloise ROSENBLATT
John M. ROSS
Jean-Pierre M. RUIZ
Leona G. RUNNING
Anthony J. SALDARINI
Marilyn J. SALMON
Alwyn P. SALOM
Karl-Gustav SANDELIN

E. P. SANDERS
Jack T. SANDERS
James A. SANDERS
D. Brent SANDY
Ernest W. SAUNDERS
Zdenek SAZAVA
David P. SCAER
Jane D. SCHABERG
J. Berndt SCHALLER
Gottfried SCHILLE
Jacques SCHLOSSER
Guenther SCHMAHL
Thomas K. SCHMELLER
Andreas SCHMIDT
Daryl D. SCHMIDT
Frederick W. SCHMIDT, Jr.
Richard J. SCHNECK
Bernardin V. SCHNEIDER
Delwin B. SCHNEIDER
Gerhard J. SCHNEIDER
Paul G. SCHNEIDER
Sandra M. SCHNEIDERS
Udo SCHNELLE
David M. SCHOLER
Luise SCHOTTROFF
Wolfgang SCHRAGE
Tim F. SCHRAMM
Christopher J. SCHRECK
Hans-Hartmut A. SCHROEDER
Heinz SCHUERMANN
Donald R. SCHULTZ
Elisabeth SCHUSSLER FIORENZA
Benedikt H. SCHWANK
Eduard R. SCHWEIZER
Bernard B. SCOTT
J. Julius SCOTT, Jr.
Alan F. SEGAL
Giuseppe SEGALLA
Stanislav SEGERT
Fernando F. SEGOVIA
Torrey SELAND
Donald J. SELBY
Philip H. SELLEW
Gerhard SELLIN
Donald P. SENIOR
August H. SEUBERT
Jean-Marie SEVRIN
Donald B. SHARP
Judson R. SHAVER
Thomas A. SHAVER
Steven M. SHEELEY
Tom R. SHEPHERD
Bruce E. SHIELDS
Kazuhito SHIMADA
Melvin H. SHOEMAKER
Willis A. SHOTWELL
Lou H. SILBERMAN
Moisés SILVA
Scott G. SINCLAIR
Marcos A. SIOTIS
Léas SIRARD
Thomas B. SLATER
Gerard S. SLOYAN
Dorothy I. SLY
Stephen S. SMALLEY
Clyde Curry SMITH
D. Moody SMITH
David W. SMITH
Dennis E. SMITH
Robert H. SMITH
Klyne R. SNODGRASS
Barbara W. SNYDER
Graydon F. SNYDER
George M. SOARES-PRABHU
Marta SORDI
Aida Besancon SPENCER
F. Scott SPENCER
Robert A. SPIVEY
John T. SQUIRES
Jeffrey L. STALEY

Dennis L. STAMPS
Christopher D. STANLEY
Graham N. STANTON
Hugo STAUDINGER
Hartmut STEGEMANN
Robert H. STEIN
Michael G. STEINHAUSER
Krister STENDAHL
William H. STEPHENS
Gregory E. STERLING
Gert J. STEYN
Cullen I. K. STORY
Dennis C. STOUTENBURG
Stanley K. STOWERS
Kenneth A. STRAND
James F. STRANGE
Georg STRECKER
Gerald B. STRICKLER
William D. STROKER
William J. STROUD
Thomas M. STROUSE
John STRUGNELL
Earl R. STUCKENBRUCK
Paul F. STUEHRENBERG
Geoffrey M. STYLER
M. Jack SUGGS
Alfred Wilhelm SUHL
David W. SUTER
Walter C. SUTTON
Jón SVEINBJORNSSON
Reuben J. SWANSON
John P. M. SWEET
James H. SWETNAM
Dennis D. SYLVA
Kari A. SYREENI
Jan SZLAGA
James D. TABOR
Jens W. TAEGER
Charles H. TALBERT
Anthony J. TAMBASCO
Robert C. TANNEHILL
Arch B. TAYLOR, Jr.
J. Justin TAYLOR
Myron Jackson TAYLOR
Walter F. TAYLOR, Jr.
Howard Merle TEEPLE
William R. TELFORD
Douglas A. TEMPLETON
Francis C. R. THEE
Gerd THEISSEN
Carsten P. THIEDE
Frank S. THIELMAN
Pamela L. THIMMES
Anthony C. THISELTON
John Christopher THOMAS
John A. THOMPSON
Leonard L. THOMPSON
Michael B. THOMPSON
Burton H. THROCKMORTON, Jr.
Lauri Tuomas THUREN
Bonnie Bowman THURSTON
Everett TILSON
Philip N. TINDALL
Thomas Herbert TOBIN
Iain R. TORRANCE
Joseph L. TRAFTON
Demetrius C. TRAKATELLIS
Diane I. TREACY-COLE
Jay C. TREAT
Paul R. TREBILCO
Warren C. TRENCHARD
John C. TREVER
Ramon TREVIJANO
Allison Albert TRITES
Etienne P. TROCME
Arie C. TROOST
L. Paul TRUDINGER
Jeffrey A. TRUMBOWER
Meishi TSAI
William P. TUCK

Christopher M. TUCKETT
George A. TURNER
John D. TURNER
James C. TURRO
Graham Hedley TWELFTREE
Joseph B. TYSON
Kazuhiko UCHIDA
Franz Georg UNTERGASSMAIR
Risto I. URO
Andries Gideon VAN AARDE
Pieter W. VAN DER HORST
Jan Willem VAN HENTEN
Sjef VAN TILBORG
Hermias C. VAN ZYL
Robert P. VANDE KAPPELLE
Gerald W. VANDER HOEK
Albert F. VANHOYE
Ugo A. V. VANNI
E. Jerry VARDAMAN
Antonio VARGAS-MACHUCA
Matthew VELLANICKAL
Geza VERMES
Donald J. VERSEPUT
Dan O. VIA
John J. VINCENT
Richard B. VINSON
Benedict T. VIVIANO
Werner VOGLER
Samuel VOLLENWEIDER
Urban C. VON WAHLDE
Johannes S. VOS
Francois VOUGA
Christos Sp. VOULGARIS
Nancy Jean VYHMEISTER
Herman C. WAETJEN
Günter E. A. WAGNER
Elaine Mary WAINWRIGHT
William O. WALKER, Jr.
Daniel B. WALLACE
Robert W. WALL
Jerome T. WALSH
Nikolaus WALTER
Joseph S. WANG
Henry J. WANSBROUGH
Richard F. WARD
Roy Bowen WARD
Virgil WARREN
Duane F. WATSON
JoAnn F. WATSON
Nigel M. WATSON
David W. WEAD
Randall C. WEBBER
Beat WEBER
Alexander J. M. WEDDERBURN
Hans WEDER
Peter A. M. WEIGANDT
Jeffrey A. D. WEIMA
Earl A. WEIS
Alfons WEISER
Herold D. WEISS
Wolfgang R. WEISS
John W. WELCH
David WENHAM
John W. WENHAM
J. Benton WHITE
John Bradley WHITE
John L. WHITE
Leland J. WHITE
Brady B. WHITEHEAD
Ronald E. WHITELY, Jr.
David J. WIEAND
David N. WIGTIL
Robert L. WILKEN
Wilhelm H. F. WILKENS
Michael J. WILKINS
David Salter WILLIAMS
Michael A. WILLIAMS
Ronald WILLIAMSON
J. Christian WILSON
John F. WILSON

John W. WILSON
Robert McL. WILSON
Vincent L. WIMBUSH
Donald H. WIMMER
Carlton L. WINBERY
R. Neal WINDHAM
John D. WINELAND
Walter P. WINK
Ben WITHERINGTON III
Charles E. WOLFE
Rolland Emerson WOLFE
Christian WOLFF
Michael WOLTER
Eric K. C. WONG
Addison G. WRIGHT
Benjamin G. WRIGHT
N. Thomas WRIGHT
Wilhelm H. WUELLNER
Edwin M. YAMAUCHI
Makoto YAMAUCHI
Norman A. YANCE
O. Larry YARBROUGH
Robert W. YARBROUGH
John Y. H. YIEH
Norman H. YOUNG
Charles YRIGOYEN, Jr.
Dieter ZELLER
Frank ZIMMERMANN
Walter D. ZORN
Frederick T. ZUGIBE
Rochus ZUURMOND

EGYPTOLOGY

Shmuel AHITUV
Gleason L. ARCHER, Jr.
Manfred F. K. W. BIETAK
A. Wendell BOWES
Thomas V. BRISCO
Schuyler BROWN
Henri CAZELLES
Michael V. FOX
Samuel J. FOX
David T. M. FRANKFURTER
William H. C. FREND
Michael J. FULLER
Wolf-Peter Paul FUNK
Hans GOEDICKE
James E. GOEHRING
C. Wilfred GRIGGS
Carleton T. HODGE
Kenneth G. HOGLUND
Susan T. HOLLIS
John R. HUDDLESTUN
Walter C. KAISER, Jr.
Othmar KEEL
Kenneth A. KITCHEN
Bentley LAYTON
Gary L. LEASE
Harold A. LIEBOWITZ
Burton MACDONALD
Aren M. MAEIR
Paul A. MIRECKI
Lukas M. MUNTINGH
Gottfried NEBE
Takashi ONUKI
Eliezer D. OREN
John N. OSWALT
Richard D. PATTERSON
Birger A. PEARSON
Paul-Hubert POIRIER
Anson F. RAINEY
Donald B. REDFORD
D. Brent SANDY
Torgny SAVE-SODERBERGH
Alan R. SCHULMAN
Byron E. SHAFER
Morris SILVER
Joel C. SLAYTON
Elmer B. SMICK

Anthony J. SPALINGER
John A. THOMPSON
Janet A. TIMBIE
Stefan TIMM
John L. WHITE
Dwight Wayne YOUNG
Fred E. YOUNG
K. Lawson YOUNGER, Jr.
Frank J. YURCO

ANATOLIAN STUDIES

Alfonso ARCHI
Karel BAYER
Gary M. BECKMAN
Henry J. FLANDERS, Jr.
William H. C. FREND
Edward W. GOODRICK
Roy E. HAYDEN
Harry A. HOFFNER, Jr.
Bo E. JOHNSON
Martha S. JOUKOWSKY
Paul KALLUVEETIL
Kenneth A. KITCHEN
Alf T. KRAABEL
James C. MOYER
Edgar C. POLOME
Jack M. SASSON
Itamar SINGER
Paul R. TREBILCO
Matitiahu TSEVAT
Robert Lindley VANN
E. Jerry VARDAMAN
Ewa C. WASILEWSKA
Jak YAKAR
K. Lawson YOUNGER, Jr.
Paul E. ZIMANSKY

MESOPOTAMIAN STUDIES

Pierre J. AMIET
Alfonso ARCHI
Carl E. ARMERDING
Bill T. ARNOLD
Hector I. AVALOS
Kenneth L. BARKER
Bernard F. BATTO
Gary M. BECKMAN
Adele BERLIN
Bryan E. BEYER
Mark E. BIDDLE
Erika S. BLEIBTREU
Elie BOROWSKI
A. Wendell BOWES
John A. BRINKMAN
Henri CAZELLES
Mordechai COGAN
Chaim COHEN
Stephanie M. DALLEY
Stephen G. DEMPSTER
Aaron DEMSKY
Raymond B. DILLARD
Sally S. DUNHAM
Barry L. EICHLER
J. Harold ELLENS
Robert S. FALKOWITZ
Gertrud FARBER
Walter FARBER
Samuel J. FOX
Tikva Simone FRYMER-KENSKY
Michael J. FULLER
Neathery B. FULLER
Maureen L. GALLERY
Marie-Henriette GATES
George GIACUMAKIS, Jr.
Jonathan A. GOLDSTEIN
Samuel GREENGUS
Edward GREENSTEIN
William W. HALLO
Rivkah HARRIS

Michael HELTZER
Robert C. HENRICKSON
Brian C. HESSE
Harry A. HOFFNER, Jr.
Victor B. HUROWITZ
Martha S. JOUKOWSKY
Walter C. KAISER, Jr.
Paul KALLUVEETIL
Arvid S. KAPELRUD
Stephen A. KAUFMAN
John KHANJIAN
Isaac M. KIKAWADA
George KUFELDT
Archie Chi Chung LEE
Jong Keun LEE
Niels P. LEMCHE
Stephen J. LIEBERMAN
John M. LUNDQUIST
Peter B. MACHINIST
John R. MAIER
Abraham MALAMAT
Sara R. S. MANDELL
Claude F. MARIOTTINI
Angel MARZAL
Victor H. MATTHEWS
Eugene H. MERRILL
Piotr MICHALOWSKI
Alan Ralph MILLARD
P. R. S. MOOREY
Lukas M. MUNTINGH
Nadav NA'AMAN
Richard C. NELSON
John N. OSWALT
David I. OWEN
Richard D. PATTERSON
Shalom M. PAUL
Anson F. RAINEY
Erica REINER
Song N. RHEE
Francesca R. ROCHBERG
C. Gilbert ROMERO
Ronald H. SACK
Jonathan D. SAFREN
Jack M. SASSON
Donald G. SCHLEY
Carl SCHULTZ
Glenn M. SCHWARTZ
B. Elmo SCOGGIN
Morris SILVER
Elmer B. SMICK
Clyde Curry SMITH
Philip E. L. SMITH
Daniel C. SNELL
Joe M. SPRINKLE
Savina J. TEUBAL
John A. THOMPSON
Stefan TIMM
Matitiahu TSEVAT
Steven S. TUELL
Karel VAN DER TOORN
Ronald A. VEENKER
John H. WALTON
John W. WELCH
Raymond WESTBROOK
Joan M. Goodnick WESTENHOLZ
Geo WIDENGREN
Donald J. WISEMAN
T. John WRIGHT
Dwight Wayne YOUNG
Gordon D. YOUNG
Ronald F. YOUNGBLOOD
K. Lawson YOUNGER, Jr.
Paul E. ZIMANSKY

**SEMITIC LANGUAGES,
TEXTS AND EPIGRAPHY**

Martin G. ABEGG, Jr.
William J. ADAMS, Jr.
Shmuel AHITUV

Ralph H. ALEXANDER
Gleason L. ARCHER, Jr.
Bill T. ARNOLD
Timothy R. ASHLEY
Walter E. AUFRECHT
Alan J. AVERY-PECK
David W. BAKER
Samuel E. BALENTINE
Barry L. BANDSTRA
Gabriel BARKAY
Kenneth L. BARKER
Bernard F. BATTO
Joseph M. BAUMGARTEN
Dewey M. BEEGLE
William H. BELLINGER, Jr.
Robert D. BERGEN
Bryan E. BEYER
Mark E. BIDDLE
Matthew BLACK
Peter BLAESER
Joseph BLENKINSOPP
Daniel I. BLOCK
Lawrence E. BOADT
Walter R. BODINE
Robert G. BOLING
A. Wendell BOWES
Leila L. BRONNER
George J. BROOKE
Bernadette J. BROOTEN
John P. BROWN
Erwin BUCK
Edward F. CAMPBELL
Robert P. CARROLL
Tony W. CARTLEDGE
Henri CAZELLES
James H. CHARLESWORTH
Debra A. CHASE
Daniel CHAVEZ
Bruce D. CHILTON
Chaim COHEN
R. Dennis COLE
Oral E. COLLINS
Michael D. COOGAN
Edward M. COOK
Robert B. COOTE
Jose S. CROATTO
Frank Moore CROSS, Jr.
Alan D. CROWN
Stephanie M. DALLEY
Kathryn P. DARR
Graham I. DAVIES
John A. DEARMAN
Gregorio DEL OLMO LETE
Stephen G. DEMPSTER
Aaron DEMSKY
Alexander A. DI LELLA
Raymond B. DILLARD
Paul E. DION
David A. DORSEY
Israel DRAZIN
J. Kenneth EAKINS
Carl S. EHRLICH
Josette ELAYI
Torleif ELGVIN
Robert R. ELLIS
Esther ESHEL
Hanan ESHEL
A. Joseph EVERSON
Steven E. FASSBERG
Weston W. FIELDS
Joseph A. FITZMYER
Peter W. FLINT
Charles J. M. E. C. FONTINOY
J. Terence FORESTELL
Julia A. FOSTER
Samuel J. FOX
Daniel C. FREDERICKS
Mark J. H. FRETZ
Richard Elliott FRIEDMAN
William J. FULCO

Isaiah M. GAFNI
James H. GAILEY
W. Randall GARR
Duane A. GARRETT
Anthony GELSTON
Lawrence T. GERATY
Agustinus GIANTO
Ronald L. GIESE, Jr.
Seymour GITIN
Jonathan A. GOLDSTEIN
Isaac B. GOTTLIEB
Lester L. GRABBE
David F. GRAF
Jonas GREENFIELD
Samuel GREENGUS
Frederick E. GREENSPAHN
Leonard J. GREENSPOON
Edward GREENSTEIN
Pierre GRELOT
Daniel GROSSBERG
Robert D. HAAK
Judith M. HADLEY
Baruch HALPERN
Paul D. HANSON
Daniel J. HARRINGTON
Robert Laird HARRIS
Tapani HARVIAINEN
Gerhard F. HASEL
Christine E. HAYES
Michael HELTZER
Larry G. HERR
Richard S. HESS
Ruth HESTRIN
Robert J. V. HIEBERT
Glenn O. HILBURN
Carleton T. HODGE
Harry A. HOFFNER, Jr.
William L. HOLLADAY
Malcolm J. A. HORSNELL
Fred L. HORTON, Jr.
Paul Y. HOSKISSON
David A. HUBBARD
Harry B. HUNT, Jr.
Patrick N. HUNT
Victor B. HUROWITZ
Avi HURVITZ
Frowald G. HUTTENMEISTER
Ephraim ISAAC
Samuel IWRY
Kent P. JACKSON
Albert J. JAMME
Peter JEFFERY
Joseph N. JENSEN
Bo E. JOHNSON
Richard JONES
Walter C. KAISER, Jr.
Isaac KALIMI
Paul KALLUVEETIL
Richard KALMIN
Arvid S. KAPELRUD
Stephen A. KAUFMAN
John KHANJIAN
Isaac M. KIKAWADA
Kenneth A. KITCHEN
Michael L. KLEIN
Ralph W. KLEIN
Douglas A. KNIGHT
George A. F. KNIGHT
Roy D. KOTANSKY
George KUFELDT
George M. LANDES
Michael S. LATTKE
Jong Keun LEE
Martin W. LEESEBERG
Israel Otto LEHMAN
André LEMAIRE
Saul LEVIN
Bernard M. LEVINSON
Arthur H. LEWIS
Theodore J. LEWIS

Stephen J. LIEBERMAN
Edouard LIPINSKI
George H. LIVINGSTON
Sara R. S. MANDELL
Menahem MANSOOR
David MARCUS
Rick R. MARRS
Angel MARZAL
M. Pierce MATHENEY, Jr.
P. Kyle MCCARTER, Jr.
Daniel L. MCCONAUGHY
Thomas F. MCDANIEL
Steven L. MCKENZIE
Mark D. MCLEAN
Martin J. MCNAMARA
Tirzah Yoreh MEACHAM
Samuel A. MEIER III
George E. MENDENHALL
Eugene H. MERRILL
Tryggve N. D. METTINGER
J. T. MILIK
Alan Ralph MILLARD
Patrick D. MILLER
Stuart S. MILLER
Harvey MINKOFF
Christopher W. MITCHELL
Shelomo MORAG
Paul G. MOSCA
Martin J. MULDER
Everett T. MULLEN, Jr.
Lukas M. MUNTINGH
Robert P. R. MURRAY
Peter J. NAYLOR
Gerhard-Wilhelm NEBE
Avraham NEGEV
Philip J. NEL
Solomon A. NIGOSIAN
Gerard J. NORTON
Julia M. O'BRIEN
Martinez José O'CALLAGHAN
Kevin G. O'CONNELL
Michael Patrick O'CONNOR
Benedikt OTZEN
David I. OWEN
Robert J. OWENS, Jr.
Randall J. PANNELL
Donald W. PARRY
H. Van Dyke PARUNAK
Richard D. PATTERSON
Shalom M. PAUL
J. Brian PECKHAM
Stephen J. PFANN
Dana M. PIKE
Wayne T. PITARD
Paul-Hubert POIRIER
Marvin H. POPE
Joshua R. PORTER
R. Ferdinand POSWICK
Gian-Luigi PRATO
Elisha QIMRON
Paul R. RAABE
Anson F. RAINEY
Susan RATTRAY
Stefan C. REIF
Gary A. RENDSBURG
E. John REVELL
Josep RIBERA-FLORIT
Gene RICE
Stephen D. RICKS
Louis W. ROBERTS
Francesca R. ROCHBERG
Jonathan ROSENBAUM
Kurt H. RUDOLPH
Leona G. RUNNING
Ronald H. SACK
James L. SAGARIN
James A. SANDERS
Jack M. SASSON
Donald G. SCHLEY
Harvey SCHNEIDER

Keith N. SCHOVILLE
Carl SCHULTZ
B. Elmo SCOGGIN
Joe D. SEGER
Stanislav SEGERT
Donald B. SHARP
William H. SHEA
Joel C. SLAYTON
Elmer B. SMICK
Clyde Curry SMITH
Joe M. SPRINKLE
Robert R. STIEGLITZ
John STRUGNELL
Marvin E. TATE
J. Glen TAYLOR
John A. THOMPSON
Stefan TIMM
Philip N. TINDALL
Iain R. TORRANCE
Paul R. TREBILCO
John C. TREVER
Matitiahu TSEVAT
David Toshio TSUMURA
Steven S. TUELL
John H. TULLOCK
Eugene C. ULRICH
Gerrit VAN DER KOOIJ
Karel VAN DER TOORN
Raymond C. VAN LEEUWEN
Harry F. VAN ROOY
John VAN SETERS
Ellen J. VAN WOLDE
James C. VANDERKAM
Shmuel VARGON
Bruce K. WALTKE
Paula C. WAPNISH
David L. WASHBURN
R. Bryan WIDBIN
Geo WIDENGREN
David J. WIEAND
Walter R. WIFALL, Jr.
Bruce E. WILLOUGHBY
Rolland Emerson WOLFE
Samuel R. WOLFE
Tadanori YAMASHITA
Edwin M. YAMAUCHI
Dwight Wayne YOUNG
Fred E. YOUNG
Ronald F. YOUNGBLOOD
K. Lawson YOUNGER, Jr.
Ziony ZEVIT
Frank ZIMMERMANN
Bruce ZUCKERMAN
Rochus ZUURMOND

APOCRYPHA AND
POST-BIBLICAL STUDIES

Martin G. ABEGG, Jr.
Robert W. ALLISON
José ALONSO-DIAZ
Hugh ANDERSON
Diane APOSTOLOS-CAPPADONA
Sasagu ARAI
Gonzalo ARANDA PEREZ
Joseph R. ARMENTI
Harold W. ATTRIDGE
Alan J. AVERY-PECK
Robert E. BAILEY
Robert J. BANKS
John R. BARTLETT
Bruce W. BARTON
Richard J. BAUCKHAM
Joseph M. BAUMGARTEN
Todd S. BEALL
Pier Franco BEATRICE
Arthur J. BELLINZONI
Roland BERGMEIER
Otto W. BETZ
J. Neville BIRDSALL

Matthew BLACK
Peter BLAESER
Gabriele BOCCACCINI
Peder J. BORGEN
Frederick H. BORSCH
Francois BOVON
Rudolf BRAENDLE
James A. BRASHLER
Louis A. BRIGHTON
Gershon A. BRIN
Leila L. BRONNER
George J. BROOKE
Bernadette J. BROOTEN
Cheryl A. BROWN
Milton P. BROWN
Erwin BUCK
Stanley M. BURGESS
Fred W. BURNETT
Brendan J. BYRNE
David M. CARR
George P. CARRAS
Robert P. CARROLL
Philip M. CASEY
Robert L. CATE
Hans C. C. CAVALLIN
James H. CHARLESWORTH
Daniel CHAVEZ
Michael L. CHERNICK
Marilyn J. CHIAT
Bruce D. CHILTON
Settimio CIPRIANI
Johannes Christiaan COETZEE
Adela Y. COLLINS
John J. COLLINS
Oral E. COLLINS
Raymond F. COLLINS
Gail P. CORRINGTON
Edouard COTHENET
Robert A. COUGHENOUR
L. William COUNTRYMAN
Alan D. CROWN
Oscar CULLMANN
Stephanie M. DALLEY
John S. DART
Maxwell J. DAVIDSON
Philip R. DAVIES
Roy C. DE LAMOTTE
Agustin DEL AGUA
Aaron DEMSKY
Robert C. DENTAN
Ferdinand DEXINGER
Alexander A. DI LELLA
Charles C. DICKINSON III
Devorah DIMANT
Israel DRAZIN
Dennis C. DULING
Walter M. DUNNETT
Kermit A. ECKLEBARGER
Howard EILBERG-SCHWARTZ
Robert H. EISENMAN
Torleif ELGVIN
J. Harold ELLENS
John C. ENDRES
S. Ifor ENOCH
Lewis J. ERON
Esther ESHEL
Craig A. EVANS
William R. FARMER
Helmut FELD
Wm. Everett FERGUSON
David A. FIENSY
Michael A. FISHBANE
Joseph A. FITZMYER
James W. FLEMING
Hubert L. FLESHER
Paul V. M. FLESHER
Peter W. FLINT
Jarl E. FOSSUM
David C. FOWLER
David T. M. FRANKFURTER

Majella M. FRANZMANN
Edwin D. FREED
Arthur J. FREEMAN
Wendell W. FRERICHS
Lawrence E. FRIZZELL
Albert FUCHS
Robert W. FUNK
Wolf-Peter Paul FUNK
Isaiah M. GAFNI
George GIACUMAKIS, Jr
Martin J. GILBERT
Maurice GILBERT
Edward A. GOLDMAN
Jonathan A. GOLDSTEIN
Deirdre J. GOOD
Charles GOODWIN
Stephen C. GORANSON
Donald E. GOWAN
Lester L. GRABBE
Henry A. GREEN
Leonard J. GREENSPOON
Pierre GRELOT
Dennis E. GROH
Klaus B. HAACKER
Donald A. HAGNER
Robert G. HALL
Stuart G. HALL
Daniel J. HARRINGTON
Patrick J. HARTIN
Lars O. HARTMAN
Gohei HATA
Christian E. HAUER, Jr.
Robert C. HAYWARD
Timothy J. HEGG
Ronald E. HEINE
Susanne L. HEINE
Michael HELTZER
John B. HIBBITTS
Sten L. HIDAL
Glenn O. HILBURN
Earle HILGERT
Charles E. HILL
Julian V. HILLS
Robert HODGSON, Jr.
Peter L. HOFRICHTER
Barbara A. HOLDREGE
Harm W. HOLLANDER
Martin J. HOMAN
Fred L. HORTON, Jr.
George E. HOWARD
Patrick N. HUNT
Larry W. HURTADO
Morris A. INCH
Samuel IWRY
Peter JEFFERY
Gregory C. JENKS
Jacob Stephan JERVELL
Alfred M. JOHNSON, Jr.
Marshall D. JOHNSON
Robert M. JOHNSTON
F. Stanley JONES
Richard N. JONES
Richard KALMIN
John I. KAMPEN
Zdzislaw KAPERA
Asher S. KAUFMAN
Stephen A. KAUFMAN
Howard Clark KEE
Charles A. KENNEDY
Mordechai E. KISLEV
William KLASSEN
Otto B. KNOCH
Helmut KOESTER
Michael F. KOLARCIK
Anitra Bingham KOLENKOW
Roy D. KOTANSKY
David C. KRAEMER
Ross S. KRAEMER
Robert A. KRAFT
Max B. KUECHLER

Werner G. KUMMEL
André LACOCQUE
James LAGRAND
Peter LAMPE
Bernhard LANG
Ernest-Marie LAPERROUSAZ
Michael S. LATTKE
Bentley LAYTON
Alfred R. C. LEANEY
Manfred R. LEHMANN
David B. LEVENSON
Amy-Jill LEVINE
Lee I. A. LEVINE
John R. LEVISON
Anfir LIBACKYJ
Judith M. LIEU
Betty Jane LILLIE
Timothy H. LIM
Edmondo F. LUPIERI
Gerard F. LUTTIKHUIZEN
Dennis R. MACDONALD
Margaret Y. MACDONALD
Geddes MACGREGOR
R. Sheldon MACKENZIE
Sara R. S. MANDELL
Claude F. MARIOTTINI
Antti MARJANEN
John W. MARTENS
Nils O. MARTOLA
Steve N. MASON
Lee M. MCDONALD
Neil J. MCELENEY
Heather A. MCKAY
Margaret M. MCKENNA
Ray MCMANAMAN
Martin J. MCNAMARA
Kathleen E. MCVEY
Tirzah Yoreh MEACHAM
Stanislaw MEDALA
James J. MEGIVERN
Jacques-Edouard MENARD
Alan MENDELSON
Dan MERKUR
Bruce M. METZGER
Marvin W. MEYER
J. Ramsey MICHAELS
G. Tom E. J. MILAZZO
James E. MILLER
Stuart S. MILLER
Paul A. MIRECKI
Ian A. MOIR
Carey A. MOORE
William G. MOST
James R. MUELLER
Earl C. MULLER
Terence Y. MULLINS
Domingo MUNOZ LEON
Frederick J. MURPHY
Robert P. R. MURRAY
Senzo NAGAKUBO
Gerhard-Wilhelm NEBE
Jacob NEEDLEMAN
Kenneth V. NELLER
Carey C. NEWMAN
George W. E. NICKELSBURG
Eugenia L. NITOWSKI
Gerard J. NORTON
Peter W. OCHS
Gerbern S. OEGEMA
John C. O'NEILL
Takashi ONUKI
Carolyn A. OSIEK
John N. OSWALT
Benedikt OTZEN
Samuel PAGAN
Elaine PAGELS
Louis PAINCHAUD
John PAINTER
Stephen J. PATTERSON
Birger A. PEARSON

Mauro PESCE
William L. PETERSEN
Lindsey P. PHERIGO
Antonio PINERO
Ronald A. PIPER
Virgil B. PIXNER
Eckhard PLUEMACHER
Paul-Hubert POIRIER
R. Ferdinand POSWICK
Gian-Luigi PRATO
Wilhelm PRATSCHER
Reinhard PUMMER
James D. PURVIS
Rosemary RADER
Heikki M. RAISANEN
Mitchell G. REDDISH
Paul L. REDDITT
John C. REEVES
Stefan C. REIF
Peter RICHARDSON
Vernon K. ROBBINS
Louis W. ROBERTS
Stephen E. ROBINSON
Gérard G. R. ROCHAIS
Cleon L. ROGERS, Jr.
John T. ROOK
John M. ROSS
Kurt H. RUDOLPH
David T. RUNIA
Anthony J. SALDARINI
Marilyn J. SALMON
Karl-Gustav SANDELIN
E. P. SANDERS
James A. SANDERS
D. Brent SANDY
Richard S. SARASON
Ernest W. SAUNDERS
Torgny SAVE-SODERBERGH
J. Berndt SCHALLER
David M. SCHOLER
Wolfgang SCHRAGE
Eileen M. SCHULLER
Carl SCHULTZ
Donald R. SCHULTZ
Madeleine M. SCOPELLO
J. Julius SCOTT, Jr.
Alan F. SEGAL
Stanislav SEGERT
Hans E. SEIDEL
Philip H. SELLEW
Jean-Marie SEVRIN
Donald B. SHARP
Fitzhugh Lewis SHAW
Byron L. SHERWIN
Sandra R. SHIMOFF
Joseph SIEVERS
Lou H. SILBERMAN
Moisés SILVA
Thomas B. SLATER
Gerard S. SLOYAN
Clyde Curry SMITH
Robert A. SPIVEY
Dennis L. STAMPS
Hugo STAUDINGER
Michael E. STONE
Dennis C. STOUTENBURG
Stanley K. STOWERS
Kenneth A. STRAND
William D. STROKER
William J. STROUD
John STRUGNELL
Raymond F. SURBURG
David W. SUTER
Marvin A. SWEENEY
Roger J. B. SYREN
Shemaryahu TALMON
J. Justin TAYLOR
Francis C. R. THEE
John A. THOMPSON
Maureen A. TILLEY

Janet A. TIMBIE
Thomas Herbert TOBIN
Iain R. TORRANCE
Joseph L. TRAFTON
Demetrius C. TRAKATELLIS
Jay C. TREAT
Paul R. TREBILCO
Warren C. TRENCHARD
Leo TREPP
John C. TREVER
Ramon TREVIJANO
Antonia TRIPOLITIS
Arie C. TROOST
L. Paul TRUDINGER
John D. TURNER
Graham Hedley TWELFTREE
Eugene C. ULRICH
Pieter W. VAN DER HORST
Jan Willem VAN HENTEN
Harry F. VAN ROOY
Gerald W. VANDER HOEK
James C. VANDERKAM
Geza VERMES
Burton L. VISOTZKY
Benedict T. VIVIANO
Samuel VOLLENWEIDER
Francois VOUGA
Ben Zion WACHOLDER
Ernest WALLWORK
Nikolaus WALTER
Peter A. M. WEIGANDT
John W. WELCH
J. Benton WHITE
John Bradley WHITE
Geo WIDENGREN
David N. WIGTIL
Michael J. WILKINS
David Salter WILLIAMS
Michael A. WILLIAMS
J. Christian WILSON
John W. WILSON
Robert McL. WILSON
David S. WINSTON
Benjamin G. WRIGHT
Robert B. WRIGHT
Makoto YAMAUCHI
Robert W. YARBROUGH
Dwight Wayne YOUNG
Frank ZIMMERMANN
Rochus ZUURMOND

Geographical Index

Theodore A. PERRY
Marvin H. POPE
Jonathan ROSENBAUM
Neil Asher SILBERMAN
Paul F. STUEHRENBERG
Richard F. WARD
Addison G. WRIGHT

DELAWARE

Robert Laird HARRIS

DISTRICT OF COLUMBIA

Diane APOSTOLOS-CAPPADONA
Dewey M. BEEGLE
Christopher T. BEGG
Bruce C. BIRCH
George W. BUCHANAN
J. Daryl CHARLES
Alexander A. DI LELLA
Cain H. FELDER
Eugene J. FISHER
Joseph A. FITZMYER
Robert C. HENRICKSON
David C. HOPKINS
Albert J. JAMME
Joseph N. JENSEN
Peter J. KEARNEY
Leslie S. B. MACCOULL
Thomas P. MCCREESH
Neil J. MCELENEY
John P. MEIER
Alan C. MITCHELL
Roland E. MURPHY
Gene RICE
Hershel SHANKS
Suzanne F. SINGER
Anthony J. TAMBASCO
Michael E. WILLETT

FLORIDA

Andrew K. M. ADAM
Julian G. ANDERSON
John T. FITZGERALD, Jr.
David F. GRAF
Henry A. GREEN
Richard H. HIERS
Ferrell JENKINS
Reggie M. KIDD
Manfred R. LEHMANN
David B. LEVENSON
Sara R. S. MANDELL
G. Tom E. J. MILAZZO
James R. MUELLER
Jacob NEUSNER
Howard S. OLSON
Samuel PAGAN
Daniel L. PALS
Kandy M. QUEEN-SUTHERLAND
Mitchell G. REDDISH
Paul G. SCHNEIDER
Christopher J. SCHRECK
Samuel J. SCHULTZ
James F. STRANGE
Marvin A. SWEENEY
Maureen A. TILLEY

GEORGIA

Oded BOROWSKI
Martin J. BUSS
Roy C. DE LAMOTTE
William D. DENNISON
James H. GAILEY
Paul L. GARBER
Jerry A. GLADSON
David M. GUNN
John H. HAYES

George E. HOWARD
Brian C. JONES
Theodore J. LEWIS
David J. LULL
Gerald E. MCGRAW
J. Maxwell MILLER
David P. MOESSNER
Carol NEWSOM
Vernon K. ROBBINS
Steven M. SHEELEY
Thomas B. SLATER
Joe M. SPRINKLE
Walter C. SUTTON
David Salter WILLIAMS

IDAHO

Janice Capel ANDERSON
A. Wendell BOWES
George L. LYONS

ILLINOIS

Roger W. ANDERSON, Jr.
Gleason L. ARCHER, Jr.
David E. AUNE
V. Gilbert BEERS
Barry J. BEITZEL
Dianne BERGANT
Hans D. BETZ
Phyllis A. BIRD
Adrien Janis BLEDSTEIN
Robert G. BOLING
Edgar W. BOSS
Robert L. BRAWLEY
John A. BRINKMAN
Gary M. BURGE
Edward F. CAMPBELL
Dan P. COLE
Adela Y. COLLINS
John J. COLLINS
Charles H. COSGROVE
Albert F. DEN EXTER BLOKLAND
Gertrud FARBER
Walter FARBER
Michael A. FISHBANE
Paul V. M. FLESHER
Norman GOLB
Dennis E. GROH
Robert D. HAAK
Lowell K. HANDY
Rivkah HARRIS
Earle HILGERT
Harry A. HOFFNER, Jr.
Fredrick C. HOLMGREN
Leslie J. HOPPE
Estella B. HORNING
Morris A. INCH
Nathan R. JASTRAM
Robert JEWETT
Walter C. KAISER, Jr.
Ralph W. KLEIN
Edgar M. KRENTZ
André LACOCQUE
James LAGRAND
John R. LEVISON
Wilhelm C. LINSS
Jack R. LUNDBOM
Claude F. MARIOTTINI
Robert J. MARSHALL
Angel MARZAL
Thomas E. MCCOMISKEY
Daniel L. MCCONAUGHY
Gerald W. MCCULLOH
Ray MCMANAMAN
John R. MCRAY
Douglas J. MOO
Robert L. MOWERY
Kenneth V. MULL
John G. NORDLING

Grant R. OSBORNE
Carolyn A. OSIEK
Mitchell C. PACWA
Claude J. PEIFER
Hayim G. PERELMUTER
Wayne T. PITARD
Erica REINER
David M. RHOADS
Eugene F. ROOP
James L. SAGARIN
David M. SCHOLER
J. Julius SCOTT, Jr.
Donald P. SENIOR
Byron L. SHERWIN
Klyne R. SNODGRASS
Graydon F. SNYDER
Christopher D. STANLEY
Carroll STUHLMUELLER
Howard Merle TEEPLE
Thomas Herbert TOBIN
Willem A. VAN-GEMEREN
Pauline A. VIVIANO
Urban C. VON WAHLDE
John H. WALTON
Earl A. WEIS
John L. WHITE
David J. WIEAND
R. Neal WINDHAM
Samuel R. WOLFE
Dwight Wayne YOUNG
Frank J. YURCO
Walter D. ZORN

INDIANA

Martin G. ABEGG, Jr.
James ACKERMAN
Harold W. ATTRIDGE
Bernard F. BATTO
Joseph BLENKINSOPP
Harold H. BULS
Fred W. BURNETT
Clifford C. CAIN
John J. DAVIS
Mark R. FAIRCHILD
Kenneth R. R. GROS LOUIS
Carleton T. HODGE
Clayton N. JEFFORD
George KUFELDT
Bernard M. LEVINSON
Millard C. LIND
Walter A. MAIER III
Herbert J. MARKS
Everett T. MULLEN, Jr.
Jerome H. NEYREY
Frederick A. NIEDNER
Roger L. OMANSON
Walter E. RAST
Francesca R. ROCHBERG
David P. SCAER
Gregory E. STERLING
Raymond F. SURBURG
Eugene C. ULRICH
James C. VANDERKAM
Herold D. WEISS
John Bradley WHITE
Gordon D. YOUNG

IOWA

Robert R. BECK
Richard H. DRUMMOND
Gregory L. FAY
Jonathan A. GOLDSTEIN
Charles E. HILL
Alf T. KRAABEL
J. Kenneth KUNTZ
George W. E. NICKELSBURG
Dale A. PATRICK

KANSAS

Dale C. ALLISON
S. Daniel BRESLAUER
Thomas S. CAULLEY
Victor R. GORDON
Verlin O. HINSHAW
Paul A. MIRECKI
Stephen D. MOORE
Virgil WARREN
Fred E. YOUNG

KENTUCKY

David R. BAUER
George R. BEASLEY-MURRAY
James L. BLEVINS
Gerald L. BORCHERT
Sharyn E. DOWD
Gerald L. KEOWN
Fred D. LAYMAN
Joe O. LEWIS
George H. LIVINGSTON
W. Eugene MARCH
Robert R. MOORE
M. Robert MULHOLLAND, Jr.
Carey C. NEWMAN
John N. OSWALT
Paul L. REDDITT
Marvin E. TATE
Arch B. TAYLOR, Jr.
Joseph L. TRAFTON
William P. TUCK
George A. TURNER
Ronald A. VEENKER
Joseph S. WANG
John D. W. WATTS
Randall C. WEBBER
Richard A. WOOD

LOUISIANA

Alan J. AVERY-PECK
D. Waylon BAILEY
R. Dennis COLE
Robert K. GNUSE
Stuart A. IRVINE
Earl J. RICHARD
William H. STIEBING, Jr.
Carlton L. WINBERY

MAINE

Robert W. ALLISON
Burke O. LONG
Thomas R. W. LONGSTAFF
Mathias RISSI
Ernest W. SAUNDERS
Burton H. THROCKMORTON, Jr.

MARYLAND

Joseph M. BAUMGARTEN
Todd S. BEALL
Adele BERLIN
Lawrence E. BOADT
Paula J. BOWES
James A. BRASHLER
Harold BRODSKY
Israel DRAZIN
Michael W. DUGGAN
Barry M. GITTLEN
Hans GOEDICKE
Susan HANDELMAN
A. Vanlier HUNTER
Samuel IWRY
Louis B. JENNINGS
William G. JOHNSSON
Christopher S. MANN
P. Kyle MCCARTER, Jr.

Donald G. MILLER
John J. PILCH
Glenn M. SCHWARTZ
William H. SHEA
Sandra R. SHIMOFF
Janet A. TIMBIE
Robert Lindley VANN
Raymond WESTBROOK
David N. WIGTIL
Charles E. WOLFE

MASSACHUSETTS

Valerie A. ABRAHAMSEN
Patrick H. ALEXANDER
Francois BOVON
Marc Z. BRETTLER
Bernadette J. BROOTEN
Thomas W. BUCKLEY
Oral E. COLLINS
Michael D. COOGAN
Frank Moore CROSS, Jr.
John A. DARR
Katheryn P. DARR
Karl P. DONFRIED
James W. DUNKLY
J. Cheryl EXUM
Hubert L. FLESHER
Everett FOX
Samuel J. FOX
Paula FREDRIKSEN
Richard N. FRYE
Paul D. HANSON
Daniel J. HARRINGTON
Theodore HIEBERT
William L. HOLLADAY
Richard A. HORSLEY
Gordon P. HUGENBERGER
Peter JEFFERY
Isaac KALIMI
Philip J. KING
Helmut KOESTER
John S. KSELMAN
James L. KUGEL
Alice L. LAFFEY
MaryJoan W. LEITH
Jon D. LEVENSON
Melvin K. LYONS
Peter B. MACHINIST
Jodi MAGNESS
Stanley B. MARROW
Harvey K. MCARTHUR
Stephen Charles MOTT
Frederick J. MURPHY
George C. PAPADEMETRIOU
Simon B. PARKER
Pheme PERKINS
Norman R. PETERSEN
Gary Davis PRATICO
W. Russell PREGEANT
James D. PURVIS
R. Blair REYNOLDS
Wayne G. ROLLINS
Joel W. ROSENBERG
Anthony J. SALDARINI
Nahum M. SARNA
R. Joseph SCHORK
Elisabeth SCHUSSLER FIORENZA
Elmer B. SMICK
Rifat SONSINO
Aida Besancon SPENCER
Lawrence E. STAGER
Krister STENDAHL
John STRUGNELL
Samuel TERRIEN
Demetrius C. TRAKATELLIS
Marsha C. WHITE
Robert A. WILD
Marvin R. WILSON
John E. WORRELL

David P. WRIGHT
Tadanori YAMASHITA
Paul E. ZIMANSKY

MICHIGAN

Barry L. BANDSTRA
Astrid B. BECK
Neal BIERLING
Gabriele BOCCACCINI
James V. BROWNSON
Robert A. COUGHENOUR
Richard M. DAVIDSON
Jacques B. DOUKHAN
Elly H. ECONOMOU
J. Harold ELLENS
Jarl E. FOSSUM
Joseph GUTMANN
Gerhard F. HASEL
John R. HUDDLESTUN
Robert M. JOHNSTON
Oliver M. KIRKEBY
Oystein S. LA BIANCA
George E. MENDENHALL
Paul David MERLING
Piotr MICHALOWSKI
H. Van Dyke PARUNAK
Jon PAULIEN
Leona G. RUNNING
Jane D. SCHABERG
J. Björnar STORFJELL
Kenneth A. STRAND
Christiana VAN HOUTEN
Raymond C. VAN LEEUWEN
Gerald W. VANDER HOEK
Nancy Jean VYHMEISTER
Jeffrey A. D. WEIMA
Bruce E. WILLOUGHBY
Randall W. YOUNKER

MINNESOTA

James W. AAGESON
Larry J. ALDERINK
Robert E. BAILEY
Daniel I. BLOCK
Marilyn J. CHIAT
Robert D. CULVER
Walter M. DUNNETT
Svante Bernhard ERLING
Wendell W. FRERICHS
Terence E. FRETHEIM
John G. GIBBS
W. Edward GLENNY
Roy A. HARRISVILLE III
Michael W. HOLMES
Arland J. HULTGREN
Arland D. JACOBSON
Marshall D. JOHNSON
Arthur H. LEWIS
James W. LIMBURG
Arthur L. MERRILL
Winsome MUNRO
Peter K. NELSON
Richard C. NELSON
Louis E. NEWMAN
Michael Patrick O'CONNOR
David PENCHANSKY
Charles B. PUSKAS
Rosemary RADER
Carl G. RASMUSSEN
Marilyn J. SALMON
Philip H. SELLEW
David W. SMITH
Robert H. STEIN
Mark A. THRONTVEIT
Ronald E. WHITELY, Jr.
Gale A. YEE

MISSISSIPPI

Daniel C. BROWNING, Jr.
Gareth L. COCKERILL
John D. CURRID
Daniel C. FREDERICKS
Paul F. JACOBS
Joe D. SEGER
E. Jerry VARDAMAN

MISSOURI

Robert D. BERGEN
Louis A. BRIGHTON
Stanley M. BURGESS
Warren C. CARTER
Frederick W. DANKER
Steven J. FRIESEN
Michael J. FULLER
Neathery B. FULLER
Arthur F. GRAUDIN
Christian E. HAUER, Jr.
Charles W. HEDRICK
Robert HODGSON, Jr.
Robert G. HOERBER
Stanley M. HORTON
Erich H. KIEHL
William H. MARE
M. Pierce MATHENEY, Jr.
Victor H. MATTHEWS
J. Clinton MCCANN, Jr.
Larry E. MCKINNEY
Mark D. MCLEAN
J. Ramsey MICHAELS
Christopher W. MITCHELL
James C. MOYER
John J. MUELLER
Stephen J. PATTERSON
Lindsey P. PHERIGO
Paul R. RAABE
John E. RYBOLT
Paul L. SCHRIEBER
Robert W. YARBROUGH
William A. YOUNG

MONTANA

John J. HUGHES

NEBRASKA

M. Dennis HAMM
George C. HEIDER
John D. TURNER
James W. WATTS

NEVADA

Francis J. BECKWITH

NEW HAMPSHIRE

David W. COTTER
Ronald M. GREEN
Donald J. SELBY
John Y. H. YIEH

NEW JERSEY

Robert J. BULL
James H. CHARLESWORTH
Lewis J. ERON
Gordon W. FRANZ
Lawrence E. FRIZZELL
Beverly R. GAVENTA
Christine E. HAYES
Ephraim ISAAC
E. Elizabeth JOHNSON
S T KIMBROUGH, Jr.
Robert L. KRESS
Robert S. MACLENNAN

Ulrich W. MAUSER
Kathleen E. MCVEY
George F. MELICK, Jr.
Bruce M. METZGER
Patrick D. MILLER
Peter W. OCHS
Dennis T. OLSON
Elaine PAGELS
Mary T. RATTIGAN
Katharine Doob SAKENFELD
Robert R. STIEGLITZ
Cullen I. K. STORY
William D. STROKER
Yaakov THOMPSON
Antonia TRIPOLITIS
James C. TURRO
Donald H. WIMMER
Charles YRIGOYEN, Jr.

NEW MEXICO

Glenn W. MCCOY

NEW YORK

Thomas J. J. ALTIZER
Arthur J. BELLINZONI
Boyce M. BENNETT
Steven J. BRAMS
Raymond E. BROWN
Michael L. CHERNICK
Bruce D. CHILTON
Francis D. CONNOLLY-WEINERT
S. Peter COWE
Robert C. DENTAN
David A. DENYER
Louis O. DORN
Samuel H. DRESNER
Dennis C. DULING
Mary Timothea ELLIOTT
Louis H. FELDMAN
Benjamin FIORE
Deirdre J. GOOD
Cyrus GORDON
Norman K. GOTTWALD
Edward GREENSTEIN
Daniel GROSSBERG
David F. HARTZFELD
Holland L. HENDRIX
Gary A. HERION
William R. HERZOG II
Lawrence F. HUNDERSMARCK
Richard KALMIN
Brigitte A. A. KERN-ULMER
Mark C. KILEY
Craig R. KOESTER
David C. KRAEMER
George M. LANDES
Eugene A. LAVERDIERE
Werner E. LEMKE
Saul LEVIN
Anfir LIBACKYJ
John M. LUNDQUIST
John R. MAIER
David MARCUS
Clarice J. MARTIN
Philip MAYERSON
David G. MEADE
Harvey MINKOFF
Kevin G. O'CONNELL
David I. OWEN
Letizia PITIGLIANI
Devadasan N. PREMNATH
Ilona N. RASHKOW
Gary A. RENDSBURG
Erroll F. RHODES
Louis W. ROBERTS
Roy A. ROSENBERG
Jean-Pierre M. RUIZ
Lawrence H. SCHIFFMAN

Alan R. SCHULMAN
Carl SCHULTZ
Alan F. SEGAL
Byron E. SHAFER
Morris SILVER
Robert D. SPENDER
Paul THEOPHILUS
Phyllis TRIBLE
Burton L. VISOTZKY
Ernest WALLWORK
Jerome T. WALSH
Leland J. WHITE
R. Bryan WIDBIN
Walter R. WIFALL, Jr.
Jay G. WILLIAMS
Vincent L. WIMBUSH
Walter P. WINK
Frank ZIMMERMANN
Frederick T. ZUGIBE

NORTH CAROLINA

Hector I. AVALOS
Samuel E. BALENTINE
Robert G. BRATCHER
Delbert R. BURKETT
Tony W. CARTLEDGE
Kenneth M. CRAIG, Jr.
James L. CRENSHAW
Charles T. DAVIS
James M. EFIRD
Stephen C. GORANSON
David B. GOWLER
Michael D. GREENE
Alan J. HAUSER
Richard B. HAYS
Kenneth G. HOGLUND
Fred L. HORTON, Jr.
David W. JAMIESON-DRAKE
Alfred M. JOHNSON, Jr.
Craig S. KEENER
Byron R. MCCANE
James J. MEGIVERN
Calvin R. MERCER, Jr.
Carol L. MEYERS
Eric M. MEYERS
Julia M. O'BRIEN
Max E. POLLEY
James L. PRICE, Jr.
Max G. ROGERS
Ronald H. SACK
E. P. SANDERS
Jack M. SASSON
B. Elmo SCOGGIN
D. Moody SMITH
F. Scott SPENCER
James D. TABOR
Charles H. TALBERT
John VAN SETERS
Dan O. VIA
William D. WHITT
John Keating WILES
J. Christian WILSON

OHIO

Bill T. ARNOLD
J. Arthur BAIRD
David W. BAKER
David L. BARR
J. Edward BARRETT
Thomas E. BOOMERSHINE
Reuben G. BULLARD
Terrance D. CALLAN
David M. CARR
Edward M. COOK
Simon J. DE VRIES
Ralph W. DOERMANN
Patricia N. DUTCHER-WALLS
Eldon J. EPP

Daniel J. ESTES
Kathleen A. FARMER
David A. FIENSY
Julia A. FOSTER
Robert M. FOWLER
Edwin D. FREED
Edward A. GOLDMAN
Alfred GOTTSCHALK
Samuel GREENGUS
Robert G. GROMACKI
E. John HAMLIN
Philip B. HARNER
Martin J. HOMAN
Herlin H. HOOPS
John I. KAMPEN
Stephen A. KAUFMAN
Frank L. KOUCKY
Israel Otto LEHMAN
Betty Jane LILLIE
William L. LUDLOW
Jerome A. LUND
Samuel A. MEIER III
James L. RESSEGUIE
Richard S. SARASON
Robert H. SMITH
John R. SPENCER
Andrew E. STEINMANN
Louis STULMAN
Robert C. TANNEHILL
Walter F. TAYLOR, Jr.
Pamela L. THIMMES
Everett TILSON
Matitiahu TSEVAT
Ben Zion WACHOLDER
Roy Bowen WARD
Duane F. WATSON
JoAnn F. WATSON
John D. WINELAND
Willard W. WINTER
Ben WITHERINGTON III
Edwin M. YAMAUCHI

OKLAHOMA

Robert L. CATE
Roger L. HAHN
Roy E. HAYDEN
Warren L. MCWILLIAMS
Bernard B. SCOTT
Malcolm W. SHELTON
Dennis E. SMITH
Daniel C. SNELL

OREGON

Marcus J. BORG
Anthony CASURELLA
Michael R. COSBY
Willoughby H. DEMING
Edward W. GOODRICK
Donald M. KINDER
John R. KOHLENBERGER III
Ernest L. MARTIN
Lane C. MCGAUGHY
Mary T. MCHATTEN
Song N. RHEE
Richard L. ROHRBAUGH
Jack T. SANDERS
Jeffrey L. STALEY

PENNSYLVANIA

Joseph R. ARMENTI
Wilma Ann BAILEY
Irvin J. BOROWSKY
Robert T. BOYD
Harry M. BUCK
Robert L. COHN
John R. CUSTIS, Jr.
Raymond B. DILLARD

David A. DORSEY
Demetrius R. DUMM
Barry L. EICHLER
Donald M. ENGLERT
Samuel D. FOHR
Arthur J. FREEMAN
Tikva Simone FRYMER-KENSKY
W. Ward GASQUE
F. Wilbur GINGRICH
Donald E. GOWAN
Judith M. HADLEY
Baruch HALPERN
Glenn S. HOLLAND
Frank W. HUGHES
Benedict F. JANECKO
Karen H. JOBES
Howard Clark KEE
Frederick W. KNOBLOCH
Ross S. KRAEMER
Robert A. KRAFT
John I. LAWLOR
Amy-Jill LEVINE
Stephen J. LIEBERMAN
Kenneth H. MAAHS
Peter W. MACKY
Elliott C. MALONEY
Dan G. MCCARTNEY
Thomas F. MCDANIEL
Patrick E. MCGOVERN
Margaret M. MCKENNA
Carey A. MOORE
James D. MUHLY
Terence Y. MULLINS
Richard D. NELSON
Keith F. NICKLE
William L. PETERSEN
Philip H. PFATTEICHER
John P. REUMANN
Marilyn M. SCHAUB
R. Thomas SCHAUB
Frederick W. SCHMIDT, Jr.
Donald R. SCHULTZ
Rodney H. SHEARER
Moisés SILVA
Gerard S. SLOYAN
Barbara W. SNYDER
David M. STERN
James L. SWAUGER
Henry O. THOMPSON
Jeffrey H. TIGAY
Jay C. TREAT
Robert P. VANDE KAPPELLE
J. Robert VANNOY
Sidnie A. WHITE
Bryant G. WOOD
John E. WORGUL
Benjamin G. WRIGHT
Robert B. WRIGHT

RHODE ISLAND

Shaye J. D. COHEN
Ernest S. FRERICHS
Martha S. JOUKOWSKY
Stanley K. STOWERS

SOUTH CAROLINA

Bryan E. BEYER
John M. BULLARD
Paul W. FERRIS, Jr.
Francis I. FESPERMAN
David T. M. FRANKFURTER
Leonard J. GREENSPOON
Craig C. HILL
Louis I. HODGES
R. Francis JOHNSON
Donald L. JONES
Alex T. LUC
Edgar V. MCKNIGHT

Margaret S. ODELL
George W. RAMSEY
John C. REEVES
Thomas E. RIDENHOUR
Steven S. TUELL

TENNESSEE

Richard A. BATEY
Mark E. BIDDLE
Milton P. BROWN
E. Ray CLENDENEN
Gail P. CORRINGTON
Kendell H. EASLEY
David M. FOUTS
Stephen L. FUCHS
Walter HARRELSON
Gregory D. JORDAN
Douglas A. KNIGHT
Jack P. LEWIS
J. Lee MAGNESS
Steven L. MCKENZIE
Phillip E. MCMILLION
Rick D. MOORE
Robert J. OWENS, Jr.
Anthony J. PETROTTA
Fernando F. SEGOVIA
Bruce E. SHIELDS
Scott G. SINCLAIR
William H. STEPHENS
Earl R. STUCKENBRUCK
John Christopher THOMAS
John H. TULLOCK
David W. WEAD
Herbert S. WENTZ
Brady B. WHITEHEAD

TEXAS

John E. ALSUP
Dewey F. ATKINSON
William R. BAIRD
David L. BALCH
Kenneth L. BARKER
Joe Edward BARNHART
George F. BASS
William H. BELLINGER, Jr.
Don C. BENJAMIN, Jr.
C. Clifton BLACK
Darrell L. BOCK
Walter R. BODINE
M. Eugene BORING
H. Alan BREHM
Thomas V. BRISCO
David B. CAPES
George W. COATS
R. Alan CULPEPPER
John A. DEARMAN
Charles C. DICKINSON III
E. Earle ELLIS
Robert R. ELLIS
William R. FARMER
Hobert K. FARRELL
Wm. Everett FERGUSON
Henry J. FLANDERS, Jr.
Victor Paul FURNISH
John D. GRASSMICK
Boo HEFLIN
Ronald S. HENDEL
Glenn O. HILBURN
Harold W. HOEHNER
Tracy L. HOWARD
F. B. HUEY, Jr.
Paul A. HUGHES
Harry B. HUNT, Jr.
Robert D. IBACH, Jr.
Naymond H. KEATHLEY
George L. KELM
Dan G. KENT
Harold A. LIEBOWITZ

Robert E. LONGACRE
David C. MALTSBERGER
Richard R. MELICK, Jr.
Eugene H. MERRILL
Charles H. MILLER
Carroll D. OSBURN
Randall J. PANNELL
Edgar C. POLOME
Donald R. POTTS
Timothy J. RALSTON
Mark F. ROOKER
Denise SCHMANDT-BESSERAT
Daryl D. SCHMIDT
Thomas A. SHAVER
M. Jack SUGGS
Lynn W. TATUM
Joseph B. TYSON
Shelley WACHSMANN
William O. WALKER, Jr.
Daniel B. WALLACE
K. Lawson YOUNGER, Jr.

UTAH

William J. ADAMS, Jr.
C. Wilfred GRIGGS
Paul Y. HOSKISSON
Kent P. JACKSON
Richard N. JONES
Eugenia L. NITOWSKI
Donald W. PARRY
Dana M. PIKE
Stephen D. RICKS
Stephen E. ROBINSON
Ewa C. WASILEWSKA
John W. WELCH

VERMONT

Bernhard W. ANDERSON
Luther H. MARTIN, Jr.
Jeffrey A. TRUMBOWER
O. Larry YARBROUGH

VIRGINIA

Gary A. ANDERSON
John BRIGHT
Edwin C.BROOME, Jr.
Debra A. CHASE
Donald S. DEER
James R. ENGLE
Mark J. H. FRETZ
Reginald H. FULLER
Ronald L. GIESE, Jr.
James E. GOEHRING
Robert G. HALL
Carl F. H. HENRY
Charles L. HOLMAN
Frederic R. KELLOGG
Charles A. KENNEDY
Judith L. KOVACS
John C. H. LAUGHLIN
Maurice S. LUKER, Jr.
John P. MASON
Stephen F. MILETIC
William G. MOST
Richard D. PATTERSON
Robert G. ROGERS
James ROSS
D. Brent SANDY
Robert A. SPIVEY
Richard B. VINSON
Robert L. WILKEN
Rolland Emerson WOLFE
Norman A. YANCE

WASHINGTON

Edward P. BLAIR

Glenn A. CARNAGEY, Sr.
George P. CARRAS
Kenneth E. CHRISTOPHERSON
Douglas R. CLARK
James A. DAVIS
Douglas R. EDWARDS
Richard J. ERICKSON
David C. FOWLER
Timothy J. HEGG
Roy W. HOOVER
Pedrito U. MAYNARD-REID
Douglas E. OAKMAN
Philip B. PAYNE
Daniel G. REID
Judith E. SANDERSON
Donald B. SHARP
Frank A. SPINA
David W. SUTER
Francis C. R. THEE
Robert W. WALL
Michael A. WILLIAMS

WEST VIRGINIA

Manfred O. MEITZEN
Robert G. NEWMAN
William E. PHIPPS
Bonnie Bowman THURSTON

WISCONSIN

Karel BAYER
Loretta DORNISCH
Richard A. EDWARDS
Michael V. FOX
Julian V. HILLS
Harold E. HOSCH
Judette Marie KOLASNY
Bruce V. MALCHOW
Menahem MANSOOR
James E. MILLER
Earl C. MULLER
John J. SCHMITT
Keith N. SCHOVILLE
Lawrence A. SINCLAIR
Clyde Curry SMITH
Thomas M. STROUSE
Dennis D. SYLVA
Leonard L. THOMPSON
William J. URBROCK

WYOMING

David L. WASHBURN

ARGENTINA

Jose S. CROATTO

AUSTRALIA

Brendan J. BYRNE
Antony F. CAMPBELL
Edgar W. CONRAD
Robert B. CROTTY
Alan D. CROWN
William J. DALTON
Maxwell J. DAVIDSON
John A. DAVIES
B. Rod DOYLE
Terry C. FALLA
Majella M. FRANZMANN
Norman C. HABEL
Gregory C. JENKS
Michael S. LATTKE
Dorothy A. LEE
William R. G. LOADER
Robert K. MCIVER
Francis J. MOLONEY
Leon L. MORRIS

Edward G. NEWING
Graham S. OGDEN
John PAINTER
Victor C. PFITZNER
Daniel T. POTTS
John W. PRYOR
Stephen D. RENN
John W. ROFFEY
Alwyn P. SALOM
John T. SQUIRES
Graham Hedley TWELFTREE
Elaine Mary WAINWRIGHT
Howard N. WALLACE
Nigel M. WATSON
John W. WILSON
T. John WRIGHT
Norman H. YOUNG

AUSTRIA

Ralph H. ALEXANDER
Carl E. ARMERDING
Manfred F. K. W. BIETAK
Erika S. BLEIBTREU
Ferdinand DEXINGER
Albert FUCHS
Douglas L. GRAGG
Peter L. HOFRICHTER
Jacob KREMER
Kurt NIEDERWIMMER
Wilhelm PRATSCHER

BELGIUM

Reimund BIERINGER
Raymond F. COLLINS
William L. CRAIG
Albert-Marie DENIS
Camille L. A. G. FOCANT
Charles J. M. E. C. FONTINOY
Maurice GILBERT
Edouard LIPINSKI
Johan LUST
R. Ferdinand POSWICK
Jean-Marie SEVRIN

BRAZIL

Tom R. SHEPHERD
Caetano MINETTE DE TILLESSE

CANADA

Timothy R. ASHLEY
Walter E. AUFRECHT
MaryAnn L. BEAVIS
Ehud BEN ZVI
Schuyler BROWN
Erwin BUCK
P. Joseph CAHILL
Muriel M. CARDER
Ernest George CLARKE
Claude E. COX
John V. DAHMS
Peter H. DAVIDS
Peggy L. DAY
Walter W. G. DELLER
Stephen G. DEMPSTER
Michael P. DEROCHE
Paul E. DION
Terence L. DONALDSON
Marcel DUMAIS
Lyle M. ESLINGER
Craig A. EVANS
Stephen C. FARRIS
Gordon D. FEE
J. Terence FORESTELL
Daniel J. FRAIKIN
Wolf-Peter Paul FUNK
Paul GARNET

Duane A. GARRETT
Olivette GENEST
Paul W. GOOCH
Michel GOURGUES
David J. HAWKIN
Larry G. HERR
John B. HIBBITTS
Robert J. V. HIEBERT
Trevor R. HOBBS
John S. HOLLADAY, Jr.
Malcolm J. A. HORSNELL
John C. HURD
Larry W. HURTADO
L. Ann JERVIS
Christie A. JOACHIM PILLAI
George JOHNSTON
William KLASSEN
Michael F. KOLARCIK
Leo LABERGE
Martin W. LEESEBERG
Adrian M. LESKE
Richard N. LONGENECKER
Burton MACDONALD
Margaret Y. MACDONALD
R. Sheldon MACKENZIE
John W. MARTENS
Steve N. MASON
Gordon H. MATTIES
Bradley H. MCLEAN
Sean E. MCEVENUE
Tirzah Yoreh MEACHAM
Alan MENDELSON
Dan MERKUR
Ben F. MEYER
John W. MILLER
Pamela J. MILNE
Paul G. MOSCA
André MYRE
Edmund K. NEUFELD
Kenneth J. NEUMANN
Solomon A. NIGOSIAN
Sydney H. T. PAGE
Louis PAINCHAUD
Geoffrey H. PARKE-TAYLOR
J. Brian PECKHAM
James R. C. PERKIN
Albert PIETERSMA
W. Gunther PLAUT
Paul-Hubert POIRIER
Stanley E. PORTER
Terrence PRENDERGAST
Benno PRZYBYLSKI
Reinhard PUMMER
Kevin B. QUAST
Donald B. REDFORD
Harold E. REMUS
E. John REVELL
Peter RICHARDSON
Gérard G. R. ROCHAIS
John T. ROOK
Leopold SABOURIN
Eileen M. SCHULLER
Léas SIRARD
Dorothy I. SLY
Philip E. L. SMITH
Michael G. STEINHAUSER
Dennis C. STOUTENBURG
J. Glen TAYLOR
Marion A. TAYLOR
Warren C. TRENCHARD
Allison Albert TRITES
L. Paul TRUDINGER
Cornelis VAN DAM
Walter A. VOGELS
Bruce K. WALTKE
Albert M. WOLTERS

COSTA RICA

Plutarco BONILLA-ACOSTA

CYPRUS

Kenneth E. BAILEY
Vassos KARAGEORGHIS

CZECH REPUBLIC

Petr POKORNY
Zdenek SAZAVA

DENMARK

Troels ENGBERG-PEDERSEN
Niels HYLDAHL
Knud O. JEPPESEN
Niels P. LEMCHE
Mogens MUELLER
Helge K. NIELSEN
Kirsten NIELSEN
Benedikt OTZEN

ENGLAND

C. Kingsley BARRETT
John BARTON
Stephen C. BARTON
Piotr A. BIENKOWSKI
John J. BIMSON
J. Neville BIRDSALL
George J. BROOKE
Kent E. BROWER
Philip M. CASEY
David R. CATCHPOLE
Ronald E. CLEMENTS
David J. A. CLINES
John M. COURT
Charles E. B. CRANFIELD
Adrian H. W. CURTIS
Stephanie M. DALLEY
Graham I. DAVIES
Philip R. DAVIES
John DAY
John D. M. DERRETT
James D. G. DUNN
J. Keith ELLIOTT
John C. FENTON
Richard T. FRANCE
William H. C. FREND
Anthony GELSTON
James M. GIBBS
Shimon GIBSON
Martin J. GILBERT
Mark E. GLASSWELL
Lester L. GRABBE
H. Benedict GREEN
Robert C. HAYWARD
Catherine HEZSER
David HILL
Morna D. HOOKER
James Leslie HOULDEN
Rebecca G. S. IDESTROM
Marie E. ISAACS
Kenneth A. KITCHEN
Nikos KOKKINOS
Sophie S. LAWS
Donn A. LEACH
Alfred R. C. LEANEY
Judith M. LIEU
Timothy H. LIM
Andrew T. LINCOLN
John MARSH
Ralph P. MARTIN
James G. MCCONVILLE
John F. MCHUGH
Heather A. MCKAY
Alan Ralph MILLARD
Walter R. W. L. MOBERLY
Hugh W. MONTEFIORE
P. R. S. MOOREY
Robert C. MORGAN

William G. MORRICE
Charles F. D. MOULE
Donald F. MURRAY
Robert P. R. MURRAY
John L. NOLLAND
Dom J. Bernard ORCHARD
David C. PARKER
Anthony C. J. PHILLIPS
Joshua R. PORTER
Stefan C. REIF
Kathleen M. RITMEYER
Leendert P. RITMEYER
John M. ROSS
Stephen S. SMALLEY
Dennis L. STAMPS
Graham N. STANTON
Geoffrey M. STYLER
John P. M. SWEET
William R. TELFORD
Anthony C. THISELTON
Michael B. THOMPSON
Philip N. TINDALL
Diane I. TREACY-COLE
Jonathan TUBB
Kathryn W. TUBB
Christopher M. TUCKETT
Geza VERMES
John J. VINCENT
Henry J. WANSBROUGH
Alexander J. M. WEDDERBURN
David WENHAM
Gordon J. WENHAM
John W. WENHAM
R. Norman WHYBRAY
John WILKINSON
Ronald WILLIAMSON
Donald J. WISEMAN
N. Thomas WRIGHT

FINLAND

Lars J. T. AEJMELAEUS
Tapani HARVIAINEN
Pauli Taisto HUUHTANEN
Karl-Johan ILLMAN
Jarmo V. KIILUNEN
Antti J. LAATO
Antti MARJANEN
Nils O. MARTOLA
Matti MYLLYKOSKI
Heikki M. RAISANEN
Wille H. J. RIEKKINEN
Karl-Gustav SANDELIN
Kari A. SYREENI
Roger J. B. SYREN
Lauri Tuomas THUREN
Risto I. URO

FRANCE

Pierre J. AMIET
Joseph M. AUNEAU
Henri CAZELLES
Edouard COTHENET
Claude COULOT
Claudine M. DAUPHIN
Jan DE WAARD
Jean DELORME
Josette ELAYI
Pierre GRELOT
Suzanne HAIK-VANTOURA
Raymond KUNTZMANN
Ernest-Marie LAPERROUSAZ
André LEMAIRE
Xavier LEON-DUFOUR
Jean MAGNE
J. T. MILIK
Michel QUESNEL
Philippe ROLLAND
Jacques SCHLOSSER

Madeleine M. SCOPELLO
Etienne P. TROCME

GERMANY

Anneli P. M. AEJMELAEUS
Roger D. AUS
Klaus BALTZER
Horst BALZ
Gerhard BARTH
Norbert BAUMERT
Roland BERGMEIER
Otto W. BETZ
Johannes H. BEUTLER
Peter BLAESER
Hanswulf BLOEDHORN
Otto BOECHER
Ingo BROER
Detlev DORMEYER
Carl S. EHRLICH
Helmut FELD
Peter FIEDLER
Hubert FRANKEMOELLE
Volkmar O. FRITZ
Dieter GEORGI
Dautzenberg H. GERHARD
Erhard S. GERSTENBERGER
Walter GROSS
Klaus B. HAACKER
Ronald E. HEINE
Georg HENTSCHEL
Paul HOFFMANN
Otto Friedrich HOFIUS
Traugott HOLTZ
Rudolf HOPPE
Frowald G. HUTTENMEISTER
Klaus K. M. JUNACK
Otto B. KNOCH
Dietrich-Alex G. KOCH
Roy D. KOTANSKY
Werner G. KUMMEL
Hans KUNG
Peter LAMPE
Bernhard LANG
Andreas LINDEMANN
Gebhard LOEHR
Norbert F. LOHFINK
Dieter H. LUEHRMANN
Jacques-Edouard MENARD
Helmut M. MERKLEIN
Paul-Gerhard MUELLER
Gerhard-Wilhelm NEBE
Gottfried NEBE
Fritz NEUGEBAUER
Gerbern S. OEGEMA
Rudolf PESCH
Eckhard PLUEMACHER
Wiard U. POPKES
Walter RADL
Rolf RENDTORFF
Hans F. RICHTER
Cleon L. ROGERS, Jr.
Joachim W. A. ROHDE
Kurt H. RUDOLPH
J. Berndt SCHALLER
Gottfried SCHILLE
Guenther SCHMAHL
Thomas K. SCHMELLER
Andreas SCHMIDT
Gerhard J. SCHNEIDER
Udo SCHNELLE
Luise SCHOTTROFF
Wolfgang SCHRAGE
Tim F. SCHRAMM
Hans-Hartmut A. SCHROEDER
Heinz SCHUERMANN
Benedikt H. SCHWANK
Hans E. SEIDEL
Gerhard SELLIN
Rudolf SMEND

Hugo STAUDINGER
Hartmut STEGEMANN
Georg STRECKER
Alfred Wilhelm SUHL
Jens W. TAEGER
Gerd THEISSEN
Carsten P. THIEDE
Stefan TIMM
Donald J. VERSEPUT
Werner VOGLER
Francois VOUGA
Nikolaus WALTER
Peter A. M. WEIGANDT
Alfons WEISER
Wolfgang R. WEISS
Claus WESTERMANN
Wilhelm H. F. WILKENS
Christian WOLFF
Michael WOLTER
Dieter ZELLER

GREECE

Charalambos BAKIRTZIS
Christos G. DOUMAS
George A. GALITIS
Marcos A. SIOTIS
Christos Sp. VOULGARIS

HONG KONG

Andrew M. J. CHIU
Archie Chi Chung LEE
Henry L. ROWOLD
Eric K. C. WONG

ICELAND

Jón SVEINBJORNSSON
Thorir Kr. THORDARSON

INDIA

Anthony R. CERESKO
Paul KÁLLUVEETIL
Joseph PATHRAPANKAL
George M. SOARES-PRABHU
Matthew VELLANICKAL

INDONESIA

Daud H. SOESILO

IRELAND

John R. BARTLETT
Andrew D. MAYES
Martin J. MCNAMARA
Brian M. NOLAN
Gerard J. NORTON

ISRAEL

Stephen J. ADLER
Shmuel AHITUV
Ruth AMIRAN
Michal ARTZY
Yosef AVIRAM
Gideon Y. AVNI
Dan BAHAT
Dan BARAG
Gabriel BARKAY
Pirhiya BECK
Itzhaq BEIT-ARIEH
Meir BEN-DOV
Amnon BEN-TOR
Claude M. E. BIOSMARD
Avraham BIRAN
Elie BOROWSKI
Gershon A. BRIN

Magen BROSHI
Shlomo BUNIMOVITZ
Jeffrey R. CHADWICK
Mordechai COGAN
Chaim COHEN
Rudolph COHEN
Hannah M. COTTON-PALTIEL
Avinoam DANIN
Aaron DEMSKY
Devorah DIMANT
Moshe DOTHAN
Trude DOTHAN
Gershon EDELSTEIN
Avi EITAN
Esther ESHEL
Hanan ESHEL
Steven E. FASSBERG
Weston W. FIELDS
Israel FINKELSTEIN
Moshe L. FISCHER
James W. FLEMING
Gideon FOERSTER
Georg FOHRER
Isaiah M. GAFNI
Moshe GARSIEL
Hillel GEVA
Seymour GITIN
Rivka GONEN
Isaac B. GOTTLIEB
Moshe GREENBERG
Jonas GREENFIELD
Zvi GREENHUT
Mayer I. GRUBER
Rachel HACHLILI
Menahem HARAN
Michael HELTZER
Ze'ev HERZOG
Ruth HESTRIN
Yizhar HIRSCHFELD
Victor B. HUROWITZ
Avi HURVITZ
David ILAN
Ruth JACOBY
Menahem Z. KADDARI
Asher S. KAUFMAN
Benjamin E. KEDAR-KOPFSTEIN
Aharon KEMPINSKI
Ann E. KILLEBREW
Mordechai E. KISLEV
Natan KLAUS
Michael L. KLEIN
Amos KLONER
Moshe KOCHAVI
Lee I. A. LEVINE
Zvi 'Uri MA'OZ
Aren M. MAEIR
Izchak MAGEN
Menahem MAGEN
Abraham MALAMAT
Yeshayahu MAORI
Baruch MARGALIT
Amihai MAZAR
Benjamin MAZAR
Eilat MAZAR
Ze'ev MESHEL
Yaakov MESHORER
Shelomo MORAG
Jerome J. MURPHY-O'CONNOR
Nadav NA'AMAN
Nira NAVEH
Avraham NEGEV
Ehud NETZER
Maren NIEHOFF
Eliezer D. OREN
Tallay ORNAN
Asher OVADIAH
Joseph PATRICH
Shalom M. PAUL
Yehuda PELEG
Stephen J. PFANN

Virgil B. PIXNER
Bezalel PORTEN
Jonathan J. PRICE
Elisha QIMRON
Avner RABAN
Yehuda T. RADDAY
Anson F. RAINEY
Ronny REICH
Alexander ROFE
Arlene M. ROSEN
Steven A. ROSEN
Myriam ROSEN-AYALON
Beno ROTHENBERG
Jonathan D. SAFREN
Harvey SCHNEIDER
Baruch J. SCHWARTZ
Eli SHENHAV
Itamar SINGER
Ephraim STERN
Michael E. STONE
Varda SUSSMAN
Danny SYON
Shemaryahu TALMON
J. Justin TAYLOR
Emanuel TOV
Yoram TSAFRIR
Vassilios E. TZAFERIS
David USSISHKIN
Shmuel VARGON
Benedict T. VIVIANO
Moshe WEINFELD
Joan M. Goodnick WESTENHOLZ
Samuel R. WOLFE
Jak YAKAR
Ze'ev YEIVIN
Joseph YELLIN
Adam ZERTAL
Joseph E. ZIAS
Moshe A. ZIPOR
Mattanyah ZOHAR

ITALY

Emmanuel ANATI
Alfonso ARCHI
Pier Franco BEATRICE
Settimio CIPRIANI
Bruno CORSANI
Giuseppe DANIELI
Angelico Salvatore DI MARCO
Bernardo ESTRADA
Rinaldo FABRIS
Vittorio FUSCO
Agustinus GIANTO
Prospero GRECH
Jozef M. HERIBAN
Giorgio JOSSA
Robert J. KARRIS
Edmondo F. LUPIERI
Ernest R. MARTINEZ
Corrado MARUCCI
Aldo MODA
Robert NORTH
Robert F. O'TOOLE
Salvatore PANIMOLLE
Mauro PESCE
Stephen F. PISANO
Gian-Luigi PRATO
Emilio RASCO
Giuseppe SEGALLA
Joseph SIEVERS
Horacio SIMIAN-YOFRE
Marta SORDI
Andrzej STRUS
James H. SWETNAM
Miguel Angel TABET-BALADY
Albert F. VANHOYE
Ugo A. V. VANNI

JAPAN

Sasagu ARAI
Gohei HATA
Paul Toshihiko HAYAMI
Toshio HIRUNUMA
Tomoo ISHIDA
Akinori KAWAMURA
Hiroshi KIMURA
Naohiro KIYOSHIGE
Nobuo KOBAYASHI
Kikup MATSUNAGA
Nobuko MORIMURA
Senzo NAGAKUBO
Takeshi NAGATA
Takashi ONUKI
Bernardin V. SCHNEIDER
Kazuhito SHIMADA
Yoshihide SUZUKI
David Toshio TSUMURA
Kazuhiko UCHIDA
Makoto YAMAUCHI

JORDAN

Rami G. KHOURI

KOREA

Charles GOODWIN
Yeong-Heum JYOO
Ee Kon KIM
Seock-Tae SOHN

MEXICO

Francisco LOPEZ RIVERA

NETHERLANDS

Henk J. DE JONGE
Theo C. DE KRUIJF
Jan P. FOKKELMAN
Karel HANHART
Harm W. HOLLANDER
Bastiaan M. F. VAN IERSEL
Gerard P. LUTTIKHUIZEN
Walter C. MARLOWE
Maarten J. J. MENKEN
Martin J. MULDER
Maarten J. PAUL
David T. RUNIA
Arie C. TROOST
Pieter W. VAN DER HORST
Gerrit VAN DER KOOIJ
Karel VAN DER TOORN
Jan Willem VAN HENTEN
Sjef VAN TILBORG
Ellen J. VAN WOLDE
Johannes S. VOS
Rochus ZUURMOND

NEW GUINEA

Norman A. MUNDHENK

NEW ZEALAND

Maurice E. ANDREW
George A. F. KNIGHT
Anthony J. SPALINGER
Paul R. TREBILCO

NICARAGUA

George V. PIXLEY
August H. SEUBERT

NIGERIA

David T. ADAMO

NORTHERN IRELAND

John C. MCCULLOUGH

NORWAY

Hans M. BARSTAD
Per Jarle BEKKEN
Kare BERGE
Peder J. BORGEN
Torleif ELGVIN
Hallvard HAGELIA
Jacob Stephan JERVELL
Arvid S. KAPELRUD
Halvor MOXNES
Torrey SELAND

PERU

Eduardo F. ARENS

PHILIPPINES

Herman N. HENDRICKX
Noel D. OSBORN

POLAND

Roman BARTNICKI
Jerzy CHMIEL
Janusz FRANKOWSKI
Marian GOLEBIEWSKI
Joseph HOMERSKI
Augustyn B. JANKOWSKI
Zdzislaw KAPERA
Jan LACH
Stanislaw MEDALA
Jan SZLAGA

ROMANIA

Hermann F. BINDER

SCOTLAND

George W. ANDERSON
Hugh ANDERSON
Richard J. BAUCKHAM
Ernest BEST
Matthew BLACK
Robert P. CARROLL
John W. DRANE
Stuart G. HALL
Richard S. HESS
Theodore P. LETIS
I. Howard MARSHALL
James I. H. MCDONALD
David L. MEALAND
Ian A. MOIR
George G. NICOL
John C. O'NEILL
Ronald A. PIPER
Iain W. PROVAN
John K. S. REID
John K. RICHES
Douglas A. TEMPLETON
Iain R. TORRANCE
Robert McL. WILSON

SOUTH AFRICA

Thomas L. BRODIE
Johannes Christiaan COETZEE
Hans J. B. COMBRINK

Pieter G. R. DE VILLIERS
William R. DOMERIS
Andries B. DU TOIT
Yehoshua GITAY
Zefira GITAY
Patrick J. HARTIN
Lambert D. JACOBS
Johannes A. LOUBSER
Lukas M. MUNTINGH
Philip J. NEL
Martin J. OOSTHUIZEN
Jacobus H. PETZER
Emil A. C. PRETORIUS
Willem S. PRINSLOO
Gert J. STEYN
Andries Gideon VAN AARDE
Harry F. VAN ROOY
Hermias C. VAN ZYL

SOUTH KOREA

Jong Keun LEE

SPAIN

Rafael AGUIRRE
José ALONSO-DIAZ
Gonzalo ARANDA PEREZ
Agustin DEL AGUA
Gregorio DEL OLMO LETE
Natalio FERNANDEZ-MARCOS
Antonio GARCIA-MORENO
Domingo MUNOZ LEON
Martinez José O'CALLAGHAN
Federico PASTOR-RAMOS
Antonio PINERO
Josep RIBERA-FLORIT
Julio C. TREBOLLE
Ramon TREVIJANO
Antonio VARGAS-MACHUCA

SWEDEN

Chrys C. CARAGOUNIS
Hans C. C. CAVALLIN
Tord FORNBERG
Birger GERHARDSSON
Lars O. HARTMAN
Sten L. HIDAL
Bengt V. HOLMBERG
Bo E. JOHNSON
René J. J. KIEFFER
Henrik LJUNGMAN
O. Evald LOVESTAM
Tryggve N. D. METTINGER
Birger O. OLSSON
Magnus Y. OTTOSSON
Torgny SAVE-SODERBERGH
Geo WIDENGREN

SWITZERLAND

Franz ANNEN
Markus K. BARTH
Klaus BIEBERSTEIN
Rudolf BRAENDLE
Oscar CULLMANN
Robert S. FALKOWITZ
Herbert HAAG
Susanne L. HEINE
Othmar KEEL
Walter KIRCHSCHLAGER
Max B. KUECHLER
Hans-H. MALLAU
Jean-Claude MARGOT
Daniel L. MARGUERAT
John S. MBITI
René PETER-CONTESSE
Joseph N. PFAMMATTER
Eduard R. SCHWEIZER

Klaus D. SEYBOLD
Samuel VOLLENWEIDER
Günter E. A. WAGNER
Beat WEBER
Hans WEDER

TAIWAN

Alan J. BEAGLEY
Paul S. H. LIAO
I-Jin LOH

TURKEY

Marie-Henriette GATES

UGANDA

Paul J. RAY, Jr.

WALES

S. Ifor ENOCH
Allan K. JENKINS
Peter J. NAYLOR

ZIMBABWE

Martin H. G. LEHMANN-
HABECK